Phil Edmonston

LEMON-AID

2008-09

SUVs, VANS, and TRUCKS

Copyright © 2008 Les Editions Edmonston

Published in Canada by Fitzhenry and Whiteside Limited,
195 Allstate Parkway, Markham, Ontario L3R 4T8

www.fitzhenry.ca   godwit@fitzhenry.ca

1 3 5 7 9 10 8 6 4 2

A cataloguing record for this publication is available from Library and Archives Canada.

Fitzhenry & Whiteside acknowledges with thanks the Canada Council for the Arts, and the
Ontario Arts Council for their support of our publishing program. We acknowledge the financial
support of the Government of Canada through the Book Publishing Industry Development
Program (BPIDP) for our publishing activities.

Printed in Canada by Webcom
Packaged by Colborne Communications, Toronto
Publications manager: Greg Ioannou
Project co-ordinator: Andrea Douglas
Layout and production: Jack Steiner, Cheryl Hawley
Editing: Jenny Govier, Andrea Battiston, Andrea Douglas,
Greg Ioannou, Natalie Jano
Illustrations: Rachel Rosen
Design: Ingrid Paulson

CONTENTS

KEY DOCUMENTS

Lemon-Aid is a feisty owner's manual that has no equal anywhere. We don't want you stuck with a lemon, or to wind up paying for repairs that are the automaker's fault and are covered by secret "goodwill" warranties. That's why we are the only book that includes many hard-to-find, confidential, and little-known documents that automakers don't want you to see.

In short, we know you can't win what you can't prove.

The following charts, documents, and service bulletins are included in this index so that you can stand your ground and be treated fairly. Photocopy and circulate whichever document will prove helpful in your dealings with automakers, dealers, service managers, insurance companies, or government agencies. Remember, most of the hundreds of summarized service bulletins outline repairs or replacements that should be done for free.

Part Three
LIARS AND LAWYERS

Part Four
VEHICLE RATINGS: THE BEST AND THE WORST

Sport-Utility Vehicles

SHOCK AND AWE

Canadian Dollar: We're Getting Hosed

Retail prices in Canada have responded to the loonie's moonshot with all the speed and alacrity of a three-toed sloth on a hot summer's day. Canada's dollar has surged 50 percent against the greenback in the past five years, producing plenty of pain for the country's exporters, yet it has created very little joy for the average consumer. Instead of cutting prices, Canadian companies have reported record profits....

DOUGLAS PORTER, CFA, DEPUTY CHIEF ECONOMIST
BMO NESBITT BURNS
"THE PRICE IS WRONG," *ECONOMIC RESEARCH FOCUS,* JUNE 15, 2007

Cross-Border Savings

I just bought a Subaru Outback in Burlington, Vermont, this past weekend. I estimate that I saved approx $11K (after taxes) in comparison to the price that I was being quoted at a Montreal dealer. I take possession of the vehicle at the end of the month, and my understanding is that the process is quite easy to get the car fully registered provincially and federally. Financing was also much lower in the States....

Yes, I am shocked and angry that Canadian retailers are ripping off Canadians with prices that are almost 20 percent higher than what the same product costs in the States. Mr. Porter, cited above, is no wild-eyed NDPer. To the contrary, he is a methodical, conservative financial analyst working for one of Canada's most respected financial institutions. Nevertheless, he minces no words in blasting Canadian retailers (except Crocs Shoes and McDonald's) for putting greed ahead of fairness, and he concludes that Canadians must take direct action to roll back prices:

Canadian consumers are far from reaping the full rewards of the massive run-up in their currency in the past five years. This is keeping inflation higher than it otherwise should be, contributing to the upward pressure on interest rates. If Bob Barker was still on the job, he would likely say, "Canadian retail prices, come on down!" and Canadian consumers should too.

Interestingly, Porter acknowledges that Canadian retailers are getting generous rebates and other sales incentives to lower prices in Canada on a per-transaction basis. He suggests that smart shoppers should aggressively bargain down the suggested retail prices of everything from books to Buicks (*Lemon-Aid* has always suggested a 10 to 15 percent reduced price for new vehicles; about double that reduction from warehouse retailers like Costco or Sam's Club for my *Lemon-Aid*

COMPARISON SHOPPING: NO COMPARISON

PRODUCT	CANADIAN PRICE (CDN$)	CDN PRICE (U.S.$)*	U.S. PRICE (U.S.$)	GAP (%)
Economist Magazine	7.50	6.60	5.99	10
Business Week	6.99	6.15	4.99	23
Sports Illustrated	4.99	4.39	3.99	10
Harry Potter Book	45.00	39.60	34.99	13
New York Times	1.40	1.23	1.00	23
CD	18.95	16.68	15.95	5
Birthday Card (Sample of 5)	4.25	3.74	3.13	20
Honda Accord	26,500	23,320	20,475	14
Chrysler 300	31,265	27,513	24,995	10
Big Mac	3.63	3.19	3.22	−1
Tim Hortons Coffee	1.35	1.19	1.29	−8
BlackBerry 8100	499	439	399	10
Canon Rebel Camera	829	730	699	4
Ethan Allen Rug	859	756	559	35
Crocs Shoes	34.99	30.79	29.99	3
			Average	**11.4**

*Converted at 88¢, average exchange rate of 18 months ending June 2007.

This BMO Nesbitt Burns chart was created when the loonie was worth 94 cents; at the time of writing, it is almost at par with the American dollar.

guides). Drivers looking for lower fuel prices in the 10 percent range would do well to use *www.gasbuddy.com*, which can help you benefit from the traditional ten-cents-per-litre spread between gas stations in most regions.

The Chinese Connection

Canadian consumers should be wary of 2009 model imports from China using American brand names. All the major automakers are making deals to put their labels on made-in-China imports, which sell for a quarter less than the competition, or about $10,000 (CDN).

Indeed, most of us would normally applaud the arrival in North America of cheaper, fuel-efficient vehicles from China. However, consumer advocates and auto safety researchers dread the arrival of these imports. They've seen the country's latest products and are appalled by the poor quality and lack of safety features evident in Chinese imports.

Why are China-built vehicles junk?

Because the Chinese government's policies encourage producers to make a quick buck, even if this endangers public safety. If quality lags, prices can be cut. Because the state owns most automakers or supports them through free government loans, it can hire or fire management out of political expediency rather than according to managerial performance. As a result, many senior auto executives are cadres on the government payroll. They think that if they improve quality, their results will lag, which may stall their careers. Instead, the Chinese automakers' objective seems to be to flood the market with cheap, poor-quality knock-offs, then improve their products once market share has been gained. Hyundai tried this strategy with its early Pony, Stellar, and Excel models, and the resulting consumer backlash almost drove the company out of North America. So far, Chinese automakers don't appear to have learned much from Hyundai's experience.

Presently, J.D. Power and Associates says that China-built vehicles have about twice as many defects as Detroit-built models do. As for crashworthiness, the latest crash tests carried out by European authorities have given the 2007 Brilliance BS6 one star out of five.

Is it any surprise that a country whose low safety standards would allow Mattel to sell lead-tainted toys would produce a car that offers no crash protection?

But lagging quality control is not only the Chinese automakers' problem. Toyota's quality-control decline has been particularly evident over the past decade. The main areas affected: emissions controls, automatic transmission failures, drivetrain vibration and rumbling, delayed shifting, and structural integrity.

Awesome Changes

High fuel prices will make it less costly to own a large new or used minivan, SUV, or pickup this year. No, that's not a misprint. Large vehicles are getting dumped by their owners, and automakers are cutting prices by tens of thousands of dollars on their new

Prices on large 2008–09 SUVs, trucks, and minivans will dip so low this year that the vehicles will look almost like they're being given away.

products, more than compensating for higher fuel consumption. Furthermore, Chrysler's new owners, Cerberus, want immediate profits, so they've priced Chrysler's entire 2008 lineup thousands of dollars below what the 2007s fetched—firing the opening salvo in what will likely become a brutal rebate battle over 2009 models.

Why *Lemon-Aid*?

In these days of political scams and corporate skulduggery, *Lemon-Aid* stands out as an honest guide that can't be bought or intimidated. Since we don't accept ads, we're free to tell the truth, as we've been doing for over 36 years. Sure, we're a pain in the backsides of automakers and dealers alike, but the facts we unearth save you big bucks in buying and servicing costs.

And we don't play favourites, as Honda and Nissan will confirm: Three decades ago, their $5-million lawsuits against *Lemon-Aid* were unsuccessful: Honda didn't appreciate us calling its early models "biodegradable rust-buckets," and Nissan went ballistic after we called its 240Z sportster a "kamikaze car" due to its faulty brakes. Even venerable Toyota has been on the receiving end of our activism when we said the company's Access pricing scheme amounted to price-fixing; warned that many Toyota and Lexus engines had sludge problems and that the 2004 revised Sienna and Camry were seriously glitch-prone; and called for an engineering fix for dangerous engine/transmission hesitation when accelerating.

And, believe it or not, all of the above-mentioned firms have used many of *Lemon-Aid*'s laments to improve their product lineups and better serve their customers.

Potholes along the *Lemon-Aid* Road

In researching this year's guide, I have uncovered many confidential service bulletins that list a number of unbelievable mechanical and body problems, and some failures that border on the bizarre. Below are 15 of the most unusual factory goofs affecting SUVs, trucks, and minivans. I've listed the models and years involved at the end of this Introduction. Additional information can be gleaned from the specific model ratings in Part Four.

1. You will find large rustholes in these Detroit-made minivans' roofs and gasket leaks in the engines.
2. These Detroit-built minivans have disintegrating automatic transmissions, paint that turns chalky white, and ice-locked rear drum brakes.
3. These minivans' power-sliding doors won't open when they should, or open when they shouldn't.
4. These Asian minivans' power-sliding doors reportedly snare passengers.
5. *Duck!* This Asian minivan's rear power liftgate may suddenly fall and knock you out.
6. One Asian minivan's run-flat tires wear out early, are hard to service, and cost $100 more per tire than regular tires; another's run-flats may catch on fire.
7. *Hurry up and wait!* This Asian automaker's minivans, SUVs, and trucks suddenly accelerate and then stall.
8. These Asian minivans and SUVs constantly pull sharply to the right when accelerating.
9. *Barf!* These Asian minivans, SUVs, and trucks stink like rotten eggs.

10. This Detroit Big Three SUV will suddenly lose all transmission power, and in cold weather, it may leak engine oil.
11. Top-of-the-line Detroit SUVs and pickups won't shift properly due to water contamination of the transmission fluid.
12. The aluminum body panels on these Detroit SUVs and trucks quickly corrode, causing the paint to bubble or blister.
13. *Kapow!* This American-built SUV has a glass tailgate that spontaneously explodes.
14. *Yikes!* This Asian SUV's electronic stability control causes brake lock-up or makes the vehicle suddenly swerve to the side. As a bonus, water pours in from behind the glove box.
15. *Ptooey!* Be careful with sharp turns and tune-ups; these American-made pickups and SUVs spit out sparkplugs and eat coil springs and idler arms.

It's fair to say that the *Lemon-Aid* series has also enraged some automakers with its tough-customer buying tips (singling out Ford's Explorer as a "roll me over in the clover" SUV), pro-consumer jurisprudence (like DaimlerChrysler Canada's Supreme Court drubbing over its fire-prone Ram), and realistic new and used car, truck, SUV, minivan, and van ratings.

But *Lemon-Aid SUVs, Vans, and Trucks 2008/2009* is different from the other books in the series: It's a comprehensive consumer guide that rates both new and used SUVs, vans, and trucks sold during the past three decades. It includes more data than ever before on 1998–2009 models and makes that information easily accessible and fun to read. It has more content to help you decide whether you should buy, sell, or hold your present vehicle; determine which makes are luxury lemons; and find vehicles that are fuel-efficient and reliable. It also gives you tips to get your money back when things go wrong.

We give you reliability information early. To this end, we have expanded our regional field reports to expose "secret" warranties and sales and service scams, to list "real" prices, and to publicize little-known pro-consumer court decisions rendered from the small claims court level all the way to the Supreme Court of Canada.

Of course, all of this data means *Lemon-Aid* has grown to over 600 pages, with more current information such as

- How to write dealer/automaker complaint letters that work
- How to get dealer bids by fax or email (including sample letters)
- How to use the dealer markup to trim your offer for each model
- Which fuel economy ratings are simply lies
- Which safety features may be unsafe or unnecessary
- Which 2008 models may be better buys than 2009s
- Why this is not the time to buy a diesel model
- Which optional features are wastes of money
- What's every vehicle's secret legal guarantee, even if sold "as is"
- How to find and use "secret" warranties that are yours for the asking

There are plenty of safe, reliable, fuel-efficient, and reasonably priced new and used vehicles available on the Canadian market. *Lemon-Aid* simply makes them easier to find and cheaper to maintain.

Phil Edmonston
June 2008

Answers to "Potholes along the Lemon-Aid Road": (1) GM front-drive minivans; (2) Chrysler minivans; (3) all American and Asian minivans; (4) Honda Odyssey, Nissan Quest, and Toyota Sienna; (5) Toyota Sienna; (6) Honda Odyssey and Toyota Sienna; (7) most of the Toyota and Lexus lineup; (8) Honda CR-V and Toyota Sienna and RAV4; (9) most of the Toyota and Lexus lineup, but the bad smell is almost as common among Detroit Big Three automakers; (10) Saturn Vue; (11) GM Tahoe, Yukon, Suburban, Avalanche, Silverado, and Sierra; (12) Ford F-series truck and Explorer and Expedition SUV; (13) Ford Explorer; (14) Hyundai Tucson; and (15) Ford Explorer and Expedition SUVs, and Ranger and F-Series trucks.

Part One

A BUYER'S MARKET

Screw Canada! Says Chrysler

Chrysler is offering lifetime warranties on the powertrains of its new cars and trucks in the U.S. but the auto giant won't offer the same coverage to motorists in Canada.

A DaimlerChrysler Canada Inc. spokesperson said yesterday the company has a different marketing strategy in Canada and won't change its coverage of five years or 100,000 kilometres on engines, transmissions and drive systems.

Wheels.ca
JULY 27, 2007

Aside from Chrysler's short-changing of Canadians with its warranty, in almost 40 years of writing *Lemon-Aid* I have never seen a more opportune time to buy a new or used vehicle. Sure, automakers and dealers are reluctant to lower their suggested retail prices to reflect the loonie's soaring value, but wider dealer profit margins and more-generous sales incentives are making up for much of the difference. Additionally, Chrysler's purchase by equity investor Cerberus means the automaker needs cash fast, prompting it to announce that the 2009 models will sell for less than the 2008s. This "fire sale" strategy could trigger a brutal price war with dirt-cheap new-car financing, longer warranties, and optional equipment included as standard fare.

There's more good news. New and used SUVs, trucks, and vans in particular will cost thousands of dollars less this year as dealers attempt to lure buyers panicked by $1.35-a-litre gas prices. Weak housing starts have also hurt demand for full-sized pickups, as many are bought by construction workers. Used model prices are crumbling, with the Asian lineup and diesel-equipped SUVs and trucks selling for 20 percent less than their price last year. Furthermore, many of these vehicles offer more standard safety features like electronic stability control, a proven lifesaver.

Why a New SUV, Truck, or Van?

Even though you'll save much more money buying used (see Part Two), buying new isn't a bad idea if you can put off your purchase until the late winter or early spring of 2009 to get the most discounts, keep your new vehicle eight to 10 years to amortize depreciation, and resist the lure of recently re-engineered diesel powerplants and problematic hybrids. Although you'll likely spend more than you expect for a new truck, sport-utility, or van, you won't lose much money through depreciation, unless you go for the largest models—and even they will be carrying price tags already cut by about 25–30 percent.

Downsized

Canadians are reacting to high fuel costs by downsizing their purchases. In fact, auto industry consultant Dennis DesRosiers points out that most of the bestselling cars and trucks are compacts or subcompacts. He feels the smaller, entry-level SUVs and trucks are cannibalizing the larger versions of the same vehicles:

> Well over half the market is now entry-level vehicles. Large sport utilities now represent only 1 percent of the market, although luxury sport utilities have grown to about 3 percent of the market. Still, together the least fuel-efficient vehicles only account for about 4 percent of the market. To put this in perspective, in the U.S. they still account for about 15 percent of the market.

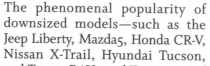

In 2006, Hyundai's "Recommended" Tucson (L) outsold the larger Santa Fe (R). If fuel prices continue to rise, Hyundai's largest SUV, the just-launched Veracruz (at right), may not survive.

The phenomenal popularity of downsized models—such as the Jeep Liberty, Mazda5, Honda CR-V, Nissan X-Trail, Hyundai Tucson, and Toyota RAV4 and Tacoma—is due to a number of factors. They can do almost everything that their big brothers are capable of doing; they are safer, more practical, more fuel-efficient, and more reliable than larger versions; and rebates or discounts more than compensate for increased fuel, insurance, and financing costs. Plus, depreciation is practically non-existent—good news for purchasers of new models. Patient used-vehicle buyers, however, can get a substantial depreciation payoff by getting a 4- or 5-year-old model that hasn't changed much over the years.

SUVs, trucks, and vans can be easily converted to suit anyone's needs or tastes. Most owners also feel safer driving them, especially since they now offer many standard safety features, such as multiple airbags, electronic stability control, and adjustable pedals. And improved crashworthiness, larger passenger- and cargo-carrying capacities, extra weight, all-wheel-drive (AWD) capability, and better-than-average forward and rear visibility further enhance driver confidence.

The cheaper, hard-riding, truck-based SUVs, vans, and AWD-equipped models will generally use more fuel than vehicles set on an extended car platform; however, they are said to offer better side-impact protection and are more durable and easier to repair. Still, if you want to save fuel, maximize on-road performance, and have a comfortable ride, you should consider a small model built on a car platform and equipped with a 4-cylinder engine, and exclude the AWD option.

2008–09 Prices: How Low Will They Go?

Approximately 1.3 million Canadians buy a new car or truck in a given year, excluding fleet sales, and at the moment consumers are truly in the driver's seat. It's been a particularly dismal sales year for Detroit automakers, with full-sized SUV, truck, and van sales slowing to a crawl as inventory piles up on dealers' lots.

Automakers increased prices on the 2008s by a moderate 2 percent on their more popular entry-level models, while poor-sellers, leftovers, and gas hogs were discounted $3,000–$5,000. Large Detroit-made vehicles in the $30,000–$40,000 bracket, however, were discounted by more than 20 percent through hard bargaining because their suggested retail price doesn't ordinarily reflect the Canadian dollar's higher value. ("You deal, or I buy across the border.")

In fact, Toronto-based DesRosiers automotive consultants say a typical new vehicle will likely cost 17 percent more in Canada than in the United States because many automakers have not adjusted their 2008 and 2009 model prices to reflect the Canadian dollar's new-found strength.

Although DesRosiers says the difference represents only $5,842 (CDN) for a typical vehicle, a comparison of American and Canadian retail prices for high-end vehicles shows clearly that Canadians may pay thousands of dollars more than DesRosiers' estimate. No wonder dealers can drop prices by almost $10,000 on some high-end models and still make a killing.

Don't overpay for a crossover model. Detroit's latest marketing ploy is to sell feature-laden tall-wagon versions of existing models as "crossovers"—vehicles that are built off of a car platform and combine the attributes of more than one vehicle category. For example, the PT Cruiser is classified as a truck for emissions purposes, but it's actually a wagon model of the Dodge Neon.

As smaller SUVs, trucks, and vans gain added features usually seen in cars, many crossovers are morphing into vans sans the long hood (think of the Mazda5 or the long-gone Nissan Axxess) rather than becoming a brand new category of vehicle. Usually, crossovers provide a more comfortable ride, better handling, and higher fuel economy than the truck-based versions they replace.

Focus on Real Costs (And Don't Go Alone)

There are over 19 million vehicles on Canada's roads, and about 2,100 dealerships (a drop from 3,500 operations a few years ago) wanting to sell you a new one—at almost $32,000 for the average vehicle and lots more for fully equipped sport-utilities, trucks, and vans. This means that you have to figure out a realistic budget for a vehicle that suits your needs, spending no more than 20 percent of your take-home pay on auto payments. So, if you're bringing home $2,000 a month in paycheques, no more than $400 of it should go toward car payments.

According to the Canadian Automobile Association's (CAA) December 2006 survey, a 2007 Chevrolet Cobalt LTZ driven 18,000 kilometres will cost the owner $2,250 in variable operating costs and an additional $7,081 in fixed ownership costs, for a total cost of $9,331. A 2007 Chrysler Caravan driven similarly will cost $2,709 and $9,030, respectively, for a total cost of $11,739, or almost $2,500 more (see the complete 2007 "Driving Costs" study at *www.caasco.com/automotive/DrivingCosts.pdf*).

Is a 2007 Chrysler Caravan worth an extra $2,500 over a 2007 Chevrolet Cobalt LTZ during the first year of ownership?

Keep in mind that it's practically impossible to buy a bare-bones SUV, truck, or van, because automakers cram them with costly, non-essential performance and convenience features in order to maximize their profits. Nevertheless, you can pass on money-wasting gadgets like electronic navigation and sophisticated entertainment systems with little impact on safety or convenience.

Before paying big bucks, you should know what your real needs are and how much you can afford to spend. Don't confuse *needs* with *style*, or *trendy* with *essential*. Visiting the showroom with your spouse or a level-headed relative or friend will help you steer a course through all the non-essential options you'll be offered.

Automakers market sport-utilities and pickups to appeal to the macho crowd (just look at the ads) by emphasizing luxury, power, adventure, and ruggedness. This is quite a marketing coup when you consider that *Popular Mechanics* estimates that 95 percent of all sport-utilities are driven on paved roads 95 percent of the time— that is, they aren't purchased for off-road use—and that *Consumer Reports* doesn't consider sport-utilities all that rugged or dependable anyway.

Consider All the Choices

Determine how much money you can spend and then decide which vehicles in that price range interest you. Have several models in mind so that the overpriced ones won't tempt you. As your benchmarks, use the ratings, alternative models, and estimated purchase cost and residual value figures shown in Part Four of this guide. Remember, logic and prudence are the first casualties of showroom hype, so carefully consider your actual requirements and how much you can budget to meet them before comparing models and prices at a dealership. Write down your first, second, and third choices relative to each model and list the equipment offered. Browse automakers' websites and *www.carcostcanada.com* for manufacturers' suggested retail prices (MSRP), pre-delivery and freight fees, package discounts, promotions, and the most popular options.

Look for special low prices that may apply only to Internet-generated referrals, or $500–$1,000 rebates given to recent school graduates. Be leery of these graduate rebates, however. Sometimes they're used as bait to sell overpriced vehicles to new drivers.

Once you get a good idea of the price variations, use your fax machine or computer to make offers and get the dealers bidding against each other (see pages 94–96). Then, to be assured of getting a sales agent's complete attention, call the lowest-bidding dealership and ask for an appointment. Take along the downloaded info from the automaker's website to avoid arguments.

Cheaper, Identical Models

Sure, sometimes a cheaper twin will fill the bill. Twins are those nameplates made by different auto manufacturers, or different divisions of the same company, that are virtually identical in body design and mechanical components. Examples are GM's Escalade, Tahoe, and Yukon SUVs; Ford's Escape and Mazda's Tribute pickups; and Chrysler's Caravan and Voyager minivans.

This premise often works in reverse, as well: You frequently get less when you pay more. For example, a perfectly acceptable 2003 Dodge Grand Caravan that originally listed for $29,300 is now worth about $10,000. An upscale 2003 Chrysler Town & Country that performs similarly to the Grand Caravan, with just a few additional gizmos, first sold for $42,700 and is now worth about $14,000. Where once $13,400 separated the two minivans, the price difference is now only $4,000—and you can expect the gap to close to almost nil over the next few years. Did the little extras really justify the Town & Country's higher price? Obviously, the marketplace thinks not.

American manufacturers are a wily bunch. While beating their chests and shouting about the need to "Buy American!" they have joined Asian automakers in co-ventures where they know they can't compete on their own. This has resulted in models with parentage that is impossible to nail down but that incorporate a high degree of quality control. Suzuki built a fairly reliable Chevrolet Tracker 4×4 (formerly known as the Geo) in Ontario, and Ford and Mazda churn out identical Rangers and B-Series pickups in the United States, though for some strange reason the Mazda Tribute has posted better quality ratings than the equivalent Ford Escape.

Sometimes choosing a higher trim line that packages many options as standard features will cost you less when you take all the standard features into account. It's hard to compare these bundled prices with the manufacturer's base price and added options, though. All of the separate prices are inflated and must be negotiated downward individually, while fully equipped vehicles don't allow for options to be deleted or priced separately. Furthermore, many of the bundled options are superfluous, and you probably wouldn't have chosen them to begin with.

There are other ways to reduce the selling price. Minivans, for example, often come in two versions: a base commercial, or cargo, version and a more luxurious model for private use. The commercial version doesn't have as many gadgets, but it's more likely to be in stock and will probably cost much less. And if you're planning to convert it, there's a wide choice of independent customizers that will likely do a better—and less expensive—job than the dealer. Of course, you will want a written guarantee from the dealer or customizer, or sometimes both, that no changes will invalidate the manufacturer's warranty. Also, look on the lot for a low-mileage (less than 5,000 km) current-year demonstrator that is carried over unchanged as a 2009 version. You will get an end-of-model-year rebate, a lower price for the extra mileage, and sundry other sales incentives that apply. Remember, if the vehicle has been registered to another company or individual, it is *not* a demo and should be considered used and be discounted accordingly (by at least 25 percent). You will also want to carry out a CarProof search and have a complete printout of the vehicle's service history.

Canadian car buyers are shopping across the border and saving tons of dough—like $25,000 on one car! A 2008 Porsche Cayenne Turbo SUV bought in the States costs $93,700 (U.S.), or the equivalent of approximately $99,000 (CDN) at the time of writing. The same model bought in Canada costs about $124,300 (CDN).

Cross-Border Shopping

Can you save money by shopping for a new vehicle in the States? The answer is a resounding *yes* if you count the increasing number of Canadian cross-border-shopping "nomads" who are saving thousands of dollars by buying new and used vehicles in the States. The number of cars and trucks Canadians bought in the United States last year represent about 2.9 percent of the 3.9 million new and used vehicles sold in all of Canada last year.

Usually when the loonie gains strength over the American greenback, as it has been over the past five years, Canadians buy about 100,000 vehicles south of the border. In the past year, however, thanks to Canada's bustling economy and bargain-savvy consumers, the cross-border trade has gone wild, with 160,000 vehicles sold to Canadian residents in 2006, according to the North American Automobile Trade Association (NAATA).

Superior Auto Sales Inc., a Lake Erie car dealership located just south of Buffalo, isn't complaining. Canadian bargain hunters are welcome at this dealership and hundreds more scattered along the border. In business for more than 50 years, Superior finds new and used cars and trucks in the United States and delivers them to penny-pinching Canadian customers.

Cross-border dealers have never had it so good. The Canadian sticker price for the average new vehicle is $5,842 (or 17 percent) higher in Canada than in the United States, according to DesRosiers Automotive Consultants Inc. Superior says the average Canadian buyer pockets 10 percent of the vehicle's price by shopping cross-border. For example, a Honda Accord costs about $2,500 less, all sundry items considered.

Buyers who import a vehicle pay GST and a government registration fee, in addition to an extra duty of 6.1 percent if the automobile was made outside North America. They also have to get the car inspected to meet emissions and safety standards. Most auto brokers will do it all. Superior sells about a car a day to Canadian dealers and private buyers who call the company's office for a specific vehicle. Once found in the States, that car, truck, or SUV is delivered to the customer's door in Canada, with all paperwork and regulatory testing done.

General Motors, Chrysler Canada, and most other automakers have tried to stamp out this cross-border trade by threatening to deny warranty coverage to Canadian buyers and warning American dealers they could lose their franchises if caught selling to Canadians. However, little action has been taken because the Free Trade Agreement between the two countries permits car-buying on either side, and automakers fear pro-consumer judges would laugh them out of court.

Cross-Border Bargains Tip Sheet

First, let's look again at the typical savings one can realize with some of the more popular vehicles sold in June 2007 when the Canadian dollar was worth only 90 cents to the American dollar—not 99 cents, as has been the case this past summer.

How about a new Acura MDX for $11,000 (CDN) less?

U.S. AND CANADIAN PRICES: UGH! WHAT A FEELING!

	PRICE IN U.S.	CDN. EXCHANGE	PRICE IN CDN.
Acura MDX	$37,740	$41,933	$ 53,030
Chevrolet Corvette	$44,490*	$49,433	$ 67,805*
Ford Freestyle AWD/SEL	$28,030	$31,144	$ 39,099
Mazda6 Sportwagon GT	$27,720	$30,800	$ 34,570
Porsche 911 Carrera	$71,300*	$79,222	$104,300*
Subaru Impreza Sedan WRX	$25,620	$28,466	$ 36,990
Toyota Prius	$22,305	$24,783	$ 32,520
Volvo XC70 AWD	$37,305	$41,450	$ 49,010

*Does not include freight and PDI.

Cross-border shopping can also net you cars that aren't normally available in Canada, like the Toyota Scion, or old Japanese roadsters with the steering wheel on the right side.

No, buying a vehicle in the States doesn't require a lot of paperwork, secret meetings, or money left for pick-up on restaurant chairs. Actually, the Canadian government has streamlined its procedures following the North American Free Trade Agreement (NAFTA) to help individuals and businesses buy vehicles across the Canada–U.S. border with a minimum of bureaucratic hassle and expense.

- Contact Canada's Registrar of Imported Vehicles (*www.riv.ca*). Ottawa uses this private contractor to give you step-by-step help so that importing a new or used vehicle is about as easy as registering your car.
- Read through Transport Canada's list of admissible U.S. vehicles, found on the website above.
- Check safety regulations: Vehicles older than 15 model years have a few minor restrictions, and newer ones have to meet Canadian safety standards. These may differ from the U.S. standards as to bumper strength, seat belt anchorage (GM's door-mounted belts are unacceptable), and labelling. On older models, adding a pair of daytime running lamps and metric stickers for the instrument panel should be sufficient.
- Have your vehicle inspected for compliance within 45 days of entry to Canada.
- Use a vehicle-history-search service such as CarProof to check the title of the vehicle you're considering for true ownership, salvage status, collision repairs, flood damage, or odometer rollbacks.

The costs of importing a vehicle are quite reasonable:

- Bring cash or make a wire transfer through a bank or credit union.
- Ask to be exempted from paying the state sales tax by securing an in-transit permit.

- Pay the $195 RIV fee, the GST on the Canadian exchange value of what you paid for the vehicle (if you appear to be fibbing, border agents can assess a higher value), and excise tax of $100 on the air conditioner.
- Note that models that fail to meet NAFTA content rules or are assembled outside North America will be charged an extra 6.1 percent duty. Big polluters weighing more than 2,007 kg are subject to another excise tax.
- Remember, you will have to pass a safety inspection and pay sales tax when you buy your licence plates.

The North American Automobile Trade Association (NAATA) is a not-for-profit association of vehicle dealers that import and export vehicles across international borders. Its mandate is to facilitate the purchase and sale of cross-border vehicles. NAATA will help buyers find reputable Canadian dealers that source American vehicles, American dealers that source Canadian vehicles, European dealers buying from North American exporters, and service providers in this market.

NAATA's website (*www.naata.org*) contains a free comprehensive database of brokers and frequently asked questions that make the cross-border process a breeze. Some of the brokers listed are

- Atlantic Auto Exporters Inc.
- Atlantic Auto Performance Ltd.
- Auto Enterprises Inc.
- Auto Sales Unlimited
- Circle T Inc.
- Cross Border Trading
- Foch Leasing
- North Pacific International Trading Limited
- Superior Auto Sales
- Terra2 Imports Inc.
- The Car Company of Canada
- United CAMC Autos International Inc.

AmeriCarr (*www.auto-broker-magic.com/Canada_Import.html*) has a website that goes through the buying process for Canadians who are on vacation in the States and would like to use their newly purchased vehicle for part of their U.S. sojourn. The site also lists where independent warranties can be purchased.

Be Wary of Leases

Why Leasing May Cost More

There are many reasons why leasing is a bad idea. It's often touted as an alternative to make high-cost vehicles more affordable, but for most people, it's really more expensive than buying outright. Lessees usually pay the full MSRP on a vehicle loaded with costly options, plus hidden fees and interest charges that wouldn't be included if the vehicle were purchased instead of leased. Researchers have found that some fully loaded entry-level cars *leased* with high interest rates and deceptive "special fees" could cost more than some luxury models would cost to *buy*. A useful website that takes the mystery out of leasing is at *www.federalreserve.gov/pubs/leasing* (Keys to Vehicle Leasing), run by the U.S. Federal Reserve Board. It goes into incredible detail, comparing leasing versus buying, and has a handy dictionary of the terms you're most likely to encounter.

Decoding Leasing Ads

Take a close look at the small print found in most leasing ads. Pay particular attention to words relating to the model year, condition of the vehicle (demonstration or used), equipment, warranty, interest rate, buy-back amount, down payment, security payment, monthly payment, transportation and preparation charges, administration fees ("acquisition" and "disposal" fees), insurance premiums, number of free kilometres, and excess kilometre charges.

Pros and Cons?

Leasing in Canada makes up almost 35 percent of all motor vehicle sales transactions because of rising interest rates and prices. This has led to 40-month leases being stretched to 60 months (Hyundai, Kia, and Toyota) and a proliferation of entry-level models that are now being leased, in addition to the traditional "luxe" toys. Nevertheless, insiders say that almost 95 percent of all vehicles costing $60,000 or more are leased.

Experts agree: If you must lease, keep your costs to a minimum by leasing for the shortest time possible, by assuming the unexpired portion of an existing lease (see "Leasebusters" later in this section), and by making sure that the lease is close-ended (meaning that you walk away from the vehicle when the lease period ends)—an option used by 75 percent of lessees, according to CAA.

Leasing does have a few advantages, though. First, it saves some of your capital, which you can invest to get a return greater than the leasing interest charges. Second, if you are taking a chance on a new model that hasn't been proven, you know that yours can be dumped at the dealer when the lease expires. But that raises more questions: What are you doing choosing such a risky venture in the first place? Will you have the patience to wait in the service bay while your luxury lemon is being repaired for the umpteenth time? Finally, do you want to be saddled with a 4-year contract where the dealer is the judge and jury as to whether you go carless or not?

 Instead of leasing, consider purchasing used. Look for a 3- to 5-year-old off-lease vehicle with 60,000–100,000 km on the clock and some of the original warranty left. Such a vehicle will be just as reliable but less than half the cost of one bought new or leased. Parts will be easier to find, independent servicing should be a breeze, insurance premiums will come down from the stratosphere, and your financial risk will be lessened considerably if you end up with a lemon.

On both new and used purchases, be wary of unjustified hidden costs, like a $495 "administrative" or "disposal" fee, an "acquisition" charge, or boosted transport and freight costs that can collectively add several thousand dollars to the retail price. Also, look at the lease transfer fee charged by the leasing company or dealer or both. This can vary considerably. For example, Ford Credit, GMAC Financial Services, and BMW Financial Services may charge $175, $450, and $1,500, respectively. Ford and BMW dealers may also impose a transfer fee.

Breaking a Lease

Not an easy thing to do, and you may wind up paying $3,000 to $8,000 in cancellation fees.

The last thing you want to do is stop your payments: The dealer can easily sue you for the remaining money owed, and you will have to pay the legal fees for both sides. You won't be able to prove the vehicle was defective or unreliable because it would have been seized after the lease payments stopped. So, there you are without your evidence, and on the receiving end of a costly lawsuit.

Lawyers advise three ways of breaking a lease. First, you can ask for free Canadian Motor Vehicle Arbitration Plan (CAMVAP) arbitration (see page 180). A second recourse, if there's a huge debt remaining, is to send a lawyer's letter cancelling the contract by putting the leasing agency and automaker on notice that the vehicle is unacceptable. This should lead to some negotiation. If this fails, inspect the vehicle, have it legally tendered back to the dealer, and then sue for what you owe plus inconvenience and assorted sundry expenses. You can use the small claims court on your own if the amount in litigation is less than the court's claim limit.

The third way is to legally transfer the lease using a firm like Leasebusters (*www. leasebusters.com*).

Leasebusters

Leasebusters is a Canadian company, affiliated with Car Cost Canada, that puts you in touch with people willing to take over your lease. Before listing your vehicle, the company will evaluate your present lease obligations online and free of charge to determine if a lease transfer is a wise idea.

Leasebusters has been in business since 1990 and says about 80 percent of the leased vehicles they offer are transferred within 60 days. For $295 plus GST, Leasebusters provides a how-to-exit-a-car-lease guide, a large display ad, and an aggressive advertising campaign to shop your lease around.

Here is how the process works through Leasebusters: All lease transfers are credit-approved legal transfers sanctioned by the lessor. Typically, the original selling dealership must participate in the transfer because they are the selling agent for the lessor and, in many cases, own the leasing agency. The order of operations for the person accepting the lease is as follows:

- Go see the vehicle (inspect, test-drive, and discuss the vehicle with the original lessee).
- Make a deal-in-principal with the original lessee (including who pays for transfer fees, inspections, security deposits, cash incentives, and/or down payments). The deal is subject to credit approval.
- Complete a credit application and submit it to the original selling dealership.
- Wait for a credit decision after the dealership submits the deal to the lessor.
- Coordinate a delivery and signing date with the dealership and the original lessee upon receipt of credit approval.
- Pay the fee that will be charged for the transfer by either or both the dealer and the lessor.

Assuming an existing lease from another driver has many advantages and a few pitfalls. First, you get a vehicle that may be depreciated by almost 40 percent of its original value, and you don't have to pay for freight, pre-delivery inspection (PDI), air tax, gas tax, etc.—increasing your savings even more. And of course, you reduce PST and GST and get the balance of all factory warranties. Second, you can have a short-term fling with an exotic vehicle without risking a long-term commitment. This is especially advantageous when leasing imports and "luxe" toys, where servicing and performance aren't up to the advertised hype.

On the downside, you may be asked to assume the obligation to pay for a lease that was a bad deal in the first place. However, if you can get the previous lessee to put additional money up front as compensation, the deal may be acceptable. Furthermore, servicing by the dealer will likely be obligatory in order to maintain the warranty, which will add to overall maintenance costs.

The leasing agency or dealer may claim extra money when the lease expires, because the vehicle might miss some original equipment or show "unreasonable" wear and tear (dings, paint problems, and excessive tire wear are the most common reasons for extra charges). Prevent this from happening by having the vehicle inspected prior to the lease takeover. Remember, some leasing companies will hold the original lessee liable for the lease until the end of the term; once a buyer is approved to take over the lease, the next lessee will be added on to the original contract, making the current lessee like a co-signer on the lease.

Deciding to Buy

Know Your Driving Needs

Our driving needs are influenced by where we live, our lifestyles, and our ages. In the city, a small wagon or hatchback is more practical and less expensive to drive than a minivan. However, if you're going to be doing a lot of highway driving, transporting small groups of people (especially kids), or loading up on accessories, a small minivan like the Mazda5 or a compact SUV such as a front-drive 4-cylinder-equipped Hyundai Tucson could be a better choice for price, comfort, and reliability.

Don't let the recent surge in fuel prices stampede you into buying a vehicle unsuitable to your driving needs. Most families who travel less than 20,000 km per year can get along fine with a vehicle powered by a 4-cylinder engine. However, these small engines usually come with bare-bones models, where fuel economy trumps high-speed merging into traffic and driving comfort isn't important. Try a model with a small engine (not necessarily the smallest one) that offers economy, performance, and a comfortable ride and interior.

Conversely, driving more than 20,000 km a year in high-speed traffic with extra passengers or cargo means a larger vehicle and engine is required (preferably a 6-cylinder). This will provide more reserve power for better performance and handling and will better accommodate the energy drain from additional safety, comfort, and convenience accessories.

If you must have a larger engine but wish to protect the environment and your wallet, take advantage of the many bargains available on used SUVs and trucks with large engines. You score in three ways:

1. You'll save thousands of dollars, which will buy more fuel than you would ever conserve with an econobox.
2. You're recycling what's out there and not adding to the car population.
3. You'll save energy and resources because there will be one less vehicle built.

Be especially wary of the towing-capability claims bandied about by automakers. They routinely exaggerate towing capability and seldom mention the need for expensive optional equipment or that the maximum safe towing speed may be only 72 km/h (45 mph), as is the case with some Japanese minivans and trucks. Chrysler, for example, bought back many 1997–99 Ram pickups because they would tow only 900 kg (2,000 lb.), not the 2,700 kg (6,000 lb.) advertised. GM pickups and vans have been the objects of similar complaints.

Finally, remember that crew cab pickups sacrifice some utility with a shorter bed but provide a much roomier interior—essential for carrying rear passengers in greater comfort, or for keeping some cargo out of the weather.

Are you choosing a comfortable, safe vehicle?

The advantages of many sport-utilities, pickups, and vans quickly pale in direct proportion to your tolerance for nuisances such as these: a harsh ride, a high step-up, a cold interior, lots of buffeting from wind and passing trucks, excessive interior noise when driving with the roof hatch or windows open, and rear visibility that's blocked by the spare tire hanging on the rear tailgate.

 Take the following simple tests to see if the vehicle's interior is user-friendly: Can you sit a foot away from the steering wheel and still reach the accelerator and brake pedals? Can you reach the sound system and AC controls without straining or taking your eyes off the road? Are the controls just as easy to operate by feel as by sight? When you look out the windshield and use the rear- and side-view mirrors, do you detect any serious blind spots? Are you sure that optional mirrors will give you an unobstructed view? What about dash glare on the front windshield? Does the seat feel comfortable enough for long trips, and do rear-seat passengers have to be contortionists to enter or exit? Is there a head restraint to protect you from hitting the rear windshield in a collision? And, finally, do all rear seating positions have head restraints?

To answer these questions, you need to drive the vehicle over a period of time to test how well your driving needs are met by your choice—without having some impatient sales agent yapping in your ear. And speaking of your ears, be sure to carry out a "howling" and "harmonic vibration" test by driving between 50 and 120 km/h with one or more windows lowered or with the sunroof open. This test often produces a painful noise described as a howl or roar, which is associated especially with SUVs and trucks.

Do you have the required driving skills?

Maybe not. You will have to drive more conservatively than you would in a car when you're behind the wheel of an SUV, truck, or van to avoid rolling over or losing control. Front-drive braking (especially with anti-lock brakes) is quite different from braking with a rear-drive. Rear-drive minivans handle like trucks, and full-sized vans tend to scrub the right rear tire during sharp right-hand turns until you get the hang of making wider turns. Limited rear visibility is another problem with larger sport-utilities and vans, forcing drivers to carefully survey side and rear traffic before changing lanes or merging. Also, be wary of mirrors. Side-view mirrors are notorious for showing vehicles to be much farther away than they actually are. In fact, they often show a 3-metre distance when there is only a 1-metre separation. You will have to trust your centre-mounted rear-view mirror more.

Which safety features are unsafe?

Some safety innovations, like anti-lock brakes and adaptive cruise control, don't deliver the safety payoffs promised by automakers and may create additional dangers. Yet there are more effective safety features that do quite well. Many vehicles offer superior front, side, and offset crash protection; high resistance to rollovers; head-protecting side and de-powered airbags; electronic stability control; adjustable brake and accelerator pedals; standard integrated child safety seats; seat belt pretensioners; innovative head restraints; and sophisticated communication systems.

Size Doesn't Always Matter

Statistics show that if two vehicles with the same National Highway Traffic Safety Administration (NHTSA) full-frontal rating crash into each other head-on, but one vehicle weighs twice as much as the other, the occupants of the lighter vehicle (909 kg/2,000 lb.) are eight times more likely to be killed than the occupants of the heavier one (1,818 kg/4,000 lb.). However, vehicle weight offers no safety advantage or disadvantage in single-vehicle crashes.

In March 2005, the Insurance Institute for Highway Safety (IIHS), a Washington-based safety research group, published a status report titled "The Risk of Dying in One Vehicle Versus Another" (*www.hwysafety.org*). The IIHS study concluded that the death rate in some larger vehicles was two to three times higher than in others—a contradiction of what the safety establishment has said for decades about large size enhancing safety.

In a two-vehicle crash with a smaller car, occupants of SUVs and trucks are more likely to be killed than are the people in the car, according to the IIHS report, which is based on a 2002–03 study of U.S. highway traffic fatalities involving vehicles made from 1999 through 2002.

In the two-vehicle crashes studied, 7 percent of the people in the cars were killed versus 10 percent of the people in the SUVs and trucks. Some reasons given for

---

IIHS SAFETY REPORT RESULTS

LOWEST DRIVER DEATH RATES	HIGHEST DRIVER DEATH RATES
Mercedes E-Class	Chevrolet Blazer (two door)
Toyota 4Runner	Mitsubishi Mirage
Volkswagen Passat	Pontiac Firebird
Lexus RX 300	Kia Rio
Toyota RAV4	Kia Sportage 4X2 (four door)
Honda Odyssey	Chevrolet Blazer (four door)
Mercury Villager	Ford Explorer (two door)
Mercedes S-Class	Chevrolet Camaro
Nissan Pathfinder	Mazda B Series
Cadillac DeVille	Chevrolet Tracker
Nissan Quest	Chevrolet S10
Toyota Camry Solara	Chevrolet Cavalier (two door)
Cadillac Eldorado	Kia Sportage 4X4 (four door)

the higher death rate are that SUV and truck drivers are more aggressive and push the vehicles beyond their rollover tolerances, seat belts aren't used often enough, and these vehicles are often overloaded with cargo and passengers.

More Safety Considerations

There are no more cheap or easy safety solutions; most of the low-hanging fruit has been picked. Except for increasing roof and side crashworthiness, changing driver behaviour (increased seat belt use and more severe DUI enforcement), and requiring young people up to the age of 14 (up from 12) to sit in the rear seat, there aren't any more feasible safety innovations.

According to NHTSA, 59 percent of the vehicle occupants who died in 2002 weren't wearing seat belts, and 42 percent of the highway deaths occurred in alcohol-related crashes. Although figures show a dramatic reduction in fatalities and injuries over the past three decades, safety experts agree that more built-in safety features will henceforth pay small dividends.

NHTSA says 76 percent of the almost 7 million annual crashes on North American highways are caused by driver error. This means safety programs that concentrate primarily upon motor vehicle standards won't be as effective as measures that target the driver, like graduated licence privileges and stricter licence requirements and law enforcement.

Incidentally, police studies have shown an important side benefit to arresting traffic scofflaws: They often net dangerous career criminals and seriously impaired drivers before they harm others. Apparently, sociopaths and substance abusers don't care which laws they break.

Active Safety

Advocates of active safety stress that accidents are caused by the proverbial "nut behind the wheel" and believe that safe driving is best taught through schools or private driving courses. Active safety components are generally those mechanical systems—such as anti-lock brake systems (ABS), high-performance tires, and traction control—that may help to avoid accidents if the driver is skillful and mature.

The theory of active safety has several drawbacks. First, drivers who are under the influence of alcohol or drugs cause about 40 percent of all fatal accidents. All the high-performance options and specialized driving courses in the world will not provide much protection from impaired drivers who draw a bead on your vehicle. And because active safety components get a lot of use—you're likely to need anti-lock brakes 99 times more often than you'll need an airbag—they have to be well designed and well maintained to remain effective. Finally, consider that independent studies show that safe driving taught to young drivers doesn't necessarily reduce the number of driving-related deaths and injuries (*Lancet*, July 2001; 1978 DeKalb County, Georgia, study):

In 1980, the U.S. Department of Transportation conducted a study designed to prove the value of driver education in the nation's high schools. It's commonly referred to as the DeKalb Study, from the county in Georgia where the research took place. The DeKalb Study compared the accident records of 9,000 teens that had taken driver education in the county's high schools with 9,000 teens that had no formal driver training. The final results showed no significant difference between the two groups. In other words, DeKalb County, Georgia, paid a large amount of money for absolutely no value.

Passive Safety

Passive safety assumes that you will be involved in life-threatening situations and should be warned in time to avoid a collision, or automatically protected from collision forces when they occur. Daytime running lights, a centre-mounted third brake light, and head-protecting airbags are three passive safety features that have paid off handsomely in reducing injuries and saving lives. Stability-control features have potential, but their long-term effectiveness is still unproven.

Passive safety features also assume that some accidents aren't avoidable and that, when an accident occurs, the vehicle should provide as much protection as possible to the driver, the vehicle's other occupants, and other people who may be struck by the vehicle—without depending on the driver's reactions. Passive safety components that have consistently proven to reduce vehicular deaths and injuries are seat belts, electronic stability control, and vehicle structures that enhance crashworthiness by absorbing or deflecting crash forces away from the vehicle's occupants.

All the above factors have led researchers to the conclusion that *what* you drive can kill you because of poor crashworthiness. Large SUVs and trucks usually show very low death-rate figures, while models with the highest rates are mostly small cars and small- to mid-sized SUVs. For example, the two-door, front-drive 1999–2002 Chevrolet Blazer has had three times the driver death rate of any passenger vehicle on the road in both single- and multiple-vehicle accidents, according to IIHS.

Rollovers

When you buy a pickup, van, or SUV, you should be concerned about the vehicle rolling over when cornering or changing lanes. Although rollovers represent only 3 percent of crashes (out of 10,000 annual U.S. road accidents), they cause one-third of all traffic deaths. And these crashes aren't with other vehicles. Most rollover deaths occur in single-vehicle accidents, representing nearly 40 percent of the fatal accidents that involved SUVs. While additional passengers make low-riding sedans more stable, additional passengers make high-riding SUVs more unstable, says Consumers Union, publisher of *Consumer Reports* magazine.

Ford's Explorer Sport Trac 4×2 posted the single worst rating for rollover propensity among all 2004 vehicles analyzed—including cars, vans, and SUVs. Its two-star rating indicated a nearly 35 percent chance of tipping over. In NHTSA's August

2004 rankings of one to five stars, the Explorer Sport Trac 4×4, the Explorer four-door 4×2, and the Mountaineer four-door 4×2 were in the bottom six of the SUV class, which as a group posted the lowest three-star scores.

These results give a black eye to Ford and add credibility to Firestone's claims that previous Explorer rollover accident deaths and injuries were caused by the Explorer's design rather than by faulty tires. Bridgestone/Firestone raised the design argument at hearings in 2001 where the tiremaker disclosed that independent tests showed conclusively that the Explorer would roll over when equipped with competitors' tires. Ford claimed the tests were rigged.

When asked to comment upon the poor NHTSA crash protection scores, Ford spokesperson Kristen Kinley dropped the "rigged" excuse and gave the following lame statement:

> While we believe the NHTSA rating system has some value, we don't believe it's a good indicator of how a vehicle performs in the real world.

For the first time, NHTSA's 2004 results included dynamic tests that simulate real-world performance instead of the previously used mathematical formula. This has led to striking differences in results. For example, Saturn's Vue SUV received three stars in the earlier test. However, when two models were tested dynamically, the rear wheels collapsed. GM voluntarily recalled all 2002–04 models. Fortunately, other vehicles that are based on the Vue platform, like the Chevrolet Equinox, have posted excellent crashworthiness scores. All of the latest results can be found in Part Four, or at *www.safercar.gov.*

Crashworthiness

A vehicle with a high crash protection rating is a lifesaver. In fact, crashworthiness is the one safety improvement over the past 30 years that everyone agrees has paid off handsomely without presenting any additional risks to drivers or passengers. By surrounding occupants in a protective cocoon and deflecting crash forces away from the interior, auto engineers have successfully created safer vehicles without increasing size or cost. And purchasing a vehicle with the idea that you'll be involved in an accident at some point is not unreasonable. According to IIHS, the average car will likely have two accidents before ending up as scrap, and it's twice as likely to be in a severe front-impact crash as a side-impact crash.

Side Impacts and Seat Design: A Few Surprises

Although side-impact collisions occur less frequently than frontal collisions, they often happen to seniors turning at intersections. Without full-torso side curtain airbags, an occupant's head will bounce off the side window or pillar, which is only about 7.5 cm away from the occupant sitting on the side that's been struck. Furthermore, there are no bumpers or designed-in "crumple zones" on the sides of vehicles to help absorb and deflect the energy of the impact.

This means that full-torso side airbags are needed to protect you from collision forces generated by side impacts. For example, among five 2005 mid-sized sedans tested by IIHS, two entry-level cars, the Audi A4 with standard side airbags and the Chevrolet Malibu equipped with optional side airbags, earned Good ratings. They also scored the "best pick" designation in side-impact crash tests conducted by the same organization.

Interestingly, Volvo's much-vaunted safety reputation took a major hit: Its S60 earned only an Acceptable rating. The Nissan Maxima and Suzuki Verona got Marginal scores.

Better head-restraint and seatback design will also have a large impact upon reducing neck and back injuries caused by rear-end collisions. In North America, these kinds of injuries account for 2 million insurance claims each year, costing at least $8.5 billion (U.S.). Such injuries aren't usually life-threatening, but they can be painful and debilitating.

The key to reducing whiplash injury risk is to keep the head and torso moving together. This means the head restraint has to be high enough to be near the back of the head. Then the seat structure must be designed to work with the head restraint to support an occupant's neck and head, as the vehicle is pushed forward and the head is thrown back.

In the IIHS 2007 tests, SUVs improved their ratings on a greater scale than trucks and minivans. The seat/head-restraint combinations in 17 of 59 SUV models were rated Good, five were Acceptable, 14 were Marginal, and 23 were rated Poor. In 2006 only six of 44 SUV models earned a Good rating.

In minivans, seat/head restraints in three models were rated Good, two were Acceptable, one was Marginal, and five were rated Poor. In pickups, one was rated Good, five were Acceptable, five were Marginal, and six were rated Poor. Analysts explain that the poor minivan showing is a result of carried-over designs, while SUV innovations are flourishing.

In the latest tests, seat/head restraints in the Mitsubishi Outlander improved to Good from the previous design, which was rated Acceptable. Those in the Acura MDX, Honda CR-V, Honda Element, Hyundai Santa Fe, and Kia Sorento improved from their previous ratings of Poor to Good. Those in the Honda Pilot and Mercedes M class improved from Marginal to Good. The seat/head restraints in the Toyota Tundra pickup improved to Good from Acceptable.

Surprisingly, some manufacturers have introduced new models with subpar seat designs. The ones in the BMW X5, Dodge Nitro, and Suzuki XL7 were rated Poor. Those in the new Mazda CX-7 and CX-9 were rated Marginal.

IIHS also found seven head restraint/seat designs that were so poorly designed, they couldn't be positioned to protect tall people and therefore were not worth

IIHS studies show that tall Ford Ranger occupants are among those most likely to be injured in a rear-ender.

testing. Among these lowest-rated seats are those in the Cadillac SRX SUV, Nissan Quest minivan, and Ford Ranger pickup.

The Insurance Corporation of British Columbia (ICBC) mostly confirms the IIHS conclusions in its own study results announced in April 2007:

Our studies show that vehicles with well-designed head restraints can reduce injuries in rear-impact crashes by 24–44 per cent. However, only 40 per cent of current car models provide adequate protection from neck injury or whiplash. Seat/head restraint designs in 22 cars are rated good, but 59 other cars are rated marginal or poor.

The best-rated 2007 vehicles include all Volvos, Audi A4, and A6, Ford Five Hundred/Mercury Montego, Nissan Sentra and Versa, Saab 9-3, and Subaru Impreza and Legacy Outback.

Seven designs earned better ratings compared with tests in 2004. Seat/head restraints improved from poor to good in the 2007 Audi A4, Honda Civic, Hyundai Sonata, Kia Optima, and Nissan Sentra. Seat/head restraints improved from acceptable to good in the 2007 Mercedes E Class, and Subaru Legacy/Outback.

Seat/head restraints ratings for the Chrysler 300, Kia Amanti and Nissan Altima went from acceptable to poor compared with tested 2004 models.

Flying Seats and Seatbacks

Seat anchorages have to conform to government load regulations, but the regulations are so minimal that seats can easily collapse or tear loose from their anchorages, leaving drivers and passengers vulnerable in accidents. NHTSA's complaint database is replete with instances where occupants report severe injuries caused by collapsing seatbacks that have injured front-seat occupants or crushed children in safety seats placed in the rear seat.

Driver and passenger seatbacks frequently collapse in rear-end collisions. In one Illinois Appeal Court decision (*Carillo v. Ford*, Cook County Circuit Court), a $14.5-million jury verdict was levied against Ford after a driver's 1991 Explorer seatback failed, leaving the driver paralyzed from the chest down.

Experts testified that the seatback design was unreasonably dangerous in high-speed rear-impact collisions. Ford's experts countered that the "yielding seats" were reasonably safe and met the NHTSA safety standard for seatback strength established in 1971, based on a 1963 recommendation by the Society of Automotive Engineers. This standard requires a seat to withstand 90–136 kg (200–300 lb.) of force. However, in a typical rear-impact crash, seats are subjected to four or five times that much force, according to Kenneth Saczalski, an engineering consultant who specializes in seat design. The Appeal Court rejected Ford's plea.

Other elements may affect crashworthiness, like a vehicle's size and heft. Nevertheless, smart engineering can make small models just as safe as large ones. And a large vehicle will likely roll over more easily. Therefore, look for something that gives you the best protection from frontal, frontal offset, and side collisions while keeping rollover potential to a minimum. There are plenty of good choices available that offer optimum crash safety at prices far less than those sold by manufacturers that beat their chests over their concern for crashworthiness (hear that, Volvo?).

IIHS Minivan Top Safety Picks: Cheap and Safe Choices

The South Korean 2009 Hyundai Entourage and Kia Sedona ($29,995 and $29,495) nosed out the Honda Odyssey and Toyota Sienna ($33,300 and $31,200) for occupant crash protection. And they're almost $4,000 cheaper.

The Hyundai Entourage.

The Kia Sedona.

This year, the Insurance Institute for Highway Safety shocked much of the North American motoring press by giving its "Top Safety Pick" designation (vehicles that excel in front, side, and rear-impact occupant protection) to a bevy of low-cost minivans, entirely ignoring the perennial Japanese favourites, Honda and Toyota.

IIHS' "Top Safety Pick" award is a good starting point for independent crashworthiness information, but be very wary of the crash-rating hoopla touted by automakers. There isn't any one vehicle that can claim a prize for being the safest. Vehicles that do well in NHTSA side and front crash tests may not do very well in IIHS offset crash tests, or may have poorly designed head restraints that would increase the severity of neck injuries. Or a vehicle may have a high number of

DYNAMICALLY TESTED SEAT/HEAD RESTRAINTS

MINIVANS Make/model	Seat type tested	OVERALL RATING	DYNAMIC RATING	GEOMETRY OF SEAT/HEAD RESTRAINT
BUICK TERRAZA CHEVROLET UPLANDER SATURN RELAY 2005–07 models	ALL SEATS	P	P	A
CHRYSLER TOWN & COUNTRY DODGE CARAVAN 2004–07 models	SEATS WITH LUMBAR	A	A	A
CHRYSLER TOWN & COUNTRY DODGE CARAVAN 2004–07 models	SEATS WITHOUT LUMBAR	P	P	A
FORD FREESTAR 2005–07 models	SEATS WITH ADJUSTABLE HEAD RESTRAINTS	G	G	G
FORD FREESTAR 2004–07 models	SEATS WITH FIXED HEAD RESTRAINTS	G	G	G
HONDA ODYSSEY 2005–07 models	ALL SEATS	M	M	A
HYUNDAI ENTOURAGE 2007 models KIA SEDONA 2006–07 models	ALL SEATS (ACTIVE HEAD RESTRAINTS)	G	G	G
TOYOTA SIENNA 2005–07 models	SEATS WITH LUMBAR	P	P	A

G	GOOD
A	ACCEPTABLE
M	MARGINAL
P	POOR

Source: IIHS Press Release, July 3, 2007.

airbag failures. Before making a final decision on the vehicle you want, look up its crashworthiness and overall safety profile in Part Four.

 NHTSA and IIHS are two reputable Washington-based agencies that monitor how vehicle design affects crash safety. Crash information from these two groups doesn't always correspond because, while IIHS's results incorporate all kinds of accidents, including offset crashes and bumper damage sustained from low-speed collisions, NHTSA's figures relate only to 56 km/h (35 mph) frontal collisions and some side collisions. The frontal tests are equivalent to two vehicles of equal weight hitting each other head-on while travelling at 56 km/h, or to a car slamming into a parked car at 114 km/h (70 mph). Bear in mind that a vehicle providing good injury protection may also cost more to repair because its structure, not the occupant, absorbs most of the collision force. That's why safer vehicles don't always have lower insurance rates.

Cars versus Trucks (When Size Does Matter)

Occupants of large vehicles have fewer severe injury claims than do occupants of small vehicles. This was proven conclusively in a 1996 NHTSA study that showed collisions between light trucks or vans and small cars resulted in an 81 percent higher fatality rate for the occupants of the small cars than for the occupants of the light trucks or vans. Interestingly, NHTSA's study contradicts the 2002–03 IIHS study mentioned earlier, which shows a higher level of fatalities and injuries for SUV and truck drivers. Apparently, the IIHS considered factors beyond crash-worthiness (such as driver attitude, single-vehicle crashes, and rollovers) and concluded that a larger size may be detrimental to safety.

Vehicle weight offers the most protection in two-vehicle crashes. In a head-on crash, for example, the heavier vehicle drives the lighter one backward, which decreases force inside the heavy vehicle and increases force in the lighter one. All heavy vehicles, even poorly designed ones, offer this advantage in two-vehicle collisions. However, they may not offer good protection in single-vehicle crashes.

Crash test figures show that SUVs, vans, and trucks also offer more protection to adult occupants than do passenger cars in most crashes because their higher set-up allows them to ride over other vehicles (Ford's 2002 4×4 Explorer lowered its bumper height to prevent this hazard). Conversely, because of their high centre of gravity, easily overloaded tires, and unforgiving suspensions, these vehicles have a disproportionate number of single-vehicle rollovers, which are far deadlier than frontal or side collisions. In the case of the early Ford Explorer, Bridgestone/Firestone CEO John Lampe testified in August 2001 that 42 of 43 rollovers involving Ford Explorers in Venezuela were on competitor's tires—shifting the rollover blame to the Explorer's design and crashworthiness.

IIHS figures show that for every 450 kg (1,000 lb.) added to a vehicle's mass, the risk of injury to an unrestrained driver is lowered by 34 percent and the risk of injury to a restrained driver is lowered by 25 percent. GM's series of two-car crash tests carried out a decade ago dramatically confirm this fact. Its engineers concluded that if two cars collide and one weighs half as much as the other, the driver in the lighter car is 10 times more likely to be killed than the driver in the heavier one. This held true no matter how many stars the smaller car was awarded in government crash tests.

There doesn't have to be a trade-off between crash safety and fuel economy. Vehicles can be built lighter to use less fuel and can also be designed to protect occupants as well as or better than heavier vehicles. Robert Hall, professor emeritus of operations management at Indiana University, says automakers simply have to take their cue from how race cars are built:

> In the last 40 years, auto racing speeds have increased, yet deaths have decreased significantly while the weights of the vehicles have gone down progressively. Why? Crushable fronts that absorb impact, "tubs" that shelter drivers after the entire car has disintegrated, a relocation of the front axle and, yes, crash bags. In this case, lighter is markedly safer.

Interestingly, a vehicle's size or past crashworthiness rating doesn't always guarantee that you won't be injured. For example, a 2004 Honda Civic earned five stars for front collision protection and four stars in side-impact tests. However, four years earlier, the 2000 Civic garnered only four stars in frontal crashes and two stars in side-impact crashes. GM's 2004 Extended Cab Silverado pickup earned four stars for the driver and three for the passenger in similar frontal crash tests.

Unsafe Designs

Although it sounds hard to believe, automakers *will* deliberately manufacture a vehicle that will kill or maim simply because, in the long run, it costs less to stonewall complaints and pay off victims than to make a safer vehicle. I learned this lesson after listening to the court testimony of GM engineers—who deliberately placed fire-prone "sidesaddle" gas tanks in millions of pickups to save $3 per vehicle—and after reading the court transcripts of *Grimshaw v. Ford* (fire-prone Pintos). Reporter Anthony Prince wrote the following assessment of Ford's indifference in an article titled "Lessons of the Ford/Firestone scandal: Profit motive turns consumers into road kill," *People's Tribune* (Online Edition); Vol. 26, No. 11, November 2000:

> Rejecting safety designs costing between only $1.80 and $15.30 per Pinto, Ford had calculated the damages it would likely pay in wrongful death and injury cases and pocketed the difference. In a cold and calculating "costs/benefits" analysis, Ford projected that the Pinto would probably cause 180 burn deaths, 180 serious burn injuries, 2,100 burned vehicles each year. Also, Ford estimated civil suits of $200,000 per death, $67,000 per injury, $700 per vehicle for a grand total of $49.5 million. The costs for installing safety features would cost approximately $137 million per year. As a result, the Pinto became a moving target, its unguarded fuel tank subject to rupture by exposed differential bolts shoved into it by rear-end collisions at speeds of as little as 21 miles per hour [34 km/h]. Spewing gasoline into the passenger compartment, the car and its passengers became engulfed in a raging inferno.

And here are more recent examples of corporate greed triumphing over public safety: Pre-1997 airbag designs that maim or kill women, children, and seniors; anti-lock brake systems that don't brake (a major problem with some GM minivans, trucks, and sport-utilities and Chrysler minivans and sport-utilities); flimsy front seats and seatbacks; the absence of rear head restraints; and fire-prone GM pickup fuel tanks and Ford truck, van, and SUV cruise-control deactivation switches. Three other examples of hazardous engineering designs that put profit ahead of safety are rear pickup seats that injure children; failure-prone Chrysler, Ford, and GM minivan sliding doors; and automatic transmissions that suddenly shift into Neutral, allow the vehicle to roll away when parked on an incline, or break down in traffic.

Children in the rear jump seats of compact extended-cab pickup trucks run a higher risk of becoming injured in an accident than children riding in other vehicles, because they are more likely to hit something in the confined space, according to a University of Pennsylvania School of Medicine study published in the April 2002 *Journal of the American Medical Association*:

Children in rear side-facing, fold-down or jump seats of compact pickup trucks are at substantially increased risk of injury compared with children in the rear seats of other vehicles. This increase in risk appears to be caused at least in part by contact with the interior of the vehicle at impact.

Flaming Fords

Over 16 million Fords may have a defective cruise-control deactivation switch that can cause the vehicle to catch fire—even when the engine is shut off and the key is taken from the ignition. Over 559 spontaneous fires have been reported to NHTSA (almost half involving vehicles never recalled), and one wrongful death lawsuit has been filed.

The $20 switch was used from 1992–2007 to shut off the cruise control when the brakes are applied. The switch, also known as a "brake pressure switch," is attached to the brake master cylinder and cruise control. Electrical current passes through the switch continuously, causing ignition even if the vehicle is shut down.

Ford has recalled millions of vehicles to replace the switch (1992 and 1993 Crown Victoria, Grand Marquis, and Lincoln Town Car; 2000 F-150 pickup, Expedition, and Navigator; and 2001 F-Series SuperCrew). In its recall notice, Ford cautioned owners that the "switch may overheat, smoke or burn which could result in an underhood fire.... This condition may occur either when the vehicle is parked or when it is being operated, even if the speed control is not in use."

> ### CRUISE-CONTROL FIRE DANGER
>
> The following signs could indicate that you have a problem with your cruise-control switch: The cruise control is not working properly; brake fluid is leaking around the switch; fuses are blown near the switch; or the fuse for the speed control cannot be opened.
>
> Until the above-named vehicles have been recalled or declared safe, owners would be wise to consider the following steps:
> * Do not park your vehicle in an enclosed garage; many incidents involve homes destroyed when the fire ignited while the vehicle was parked in a garage.
> * Disconnect the switch (Ford dealers will do this free of charge for owners of vehicles with recalled switches that are waiting for replacement parts).
> * Replace the old switch with a 2004 improved version.
> * If the vehicle has caught fire, do not tow it to the dealer. Instead, ask your insurance provider to hire an accident reconstruction expert who can prove if Ford is at fault.

Why would Ford use the same fire-prone switch through the 2007 model year? Its own internal documents show that the same switch is used on 16 million cars, SUVs, trucks, minivans, and vans.

In August 2007, Ford recalled another 3.6 million passenger cars, trucks, sport-utility vehicles, and vans to replace fire-prone cruise control switches recalled earlier on about a million older models.

Ford's latest recall covers more than a dozen vehicle models built from 1992–2007: 1998–2002 Ford Ranger, 1992–97 Lincoln Town Car, 1992–97 Ford Crown Victoria, 1992–97 Mercury Grand Marquis, 1993–98 Lincoln Mark VIII, 1993–95 Taurus SHO, and 1999–2001 Ford Explorer and Mercury Mountaineer.

Also covered are the 2001–02 Ford Explorer Sport, 2001–02 Ford Explorer Sport Trac, 1992–93 E-Series vans from E-150 to E-350, 1997–2002 E-Series vans from E-150 to E-350, 1993 Ford F-Series pickups, 1993 Ford Bronco, 1994 Mercury Capri, 2003–04 Ford F-150 Lightning, and 1995–2002 Ford F53 motor homes.

Safety Features That Kill

In the late '60s, Washington forced automakers to include essential safety features like collapsing steering columns and safety windshields in their cars but exempted trucks and vans and, later, SUVs and minivans. As the years passed, the number of mandatory safety features increased to include seat belts, airbags, and crashworthy construction, and fewer vehicles were exempted. These improvements met with public approval until quite recently, when reports of deaths and injuries caused by anti-lock brake systems (ABS) and airbag failures showed that defective components and poor engineering negated the potential life-saving benefits associated with these devices.

For example, one out of every five ongoing NHTSA defect investigations concerns inadvertent airbag deployment, failure of the airbag to deploy, or injuries suffered when the bag did go off. In fact, airbags are the agency's single largest cause of current investigations, exceeding even the full range of brake problems, which runs second.

Transport Canada allows car owners to have a mechanic disengage airbags for several reasons: needing to sit closer than 25 cm from the steering wheel, needing to put children in the front seat, or having adult passengers with medical conditions that may intensify airbag injuries. Motorists are required by regulation to submit the forms, but Transport Canada does not verify the accuracy of the information. People can have the work done without waiting for a response from the government, and the department does not track people who disconnect their bags without going through the official route.

Anti-Lock Brake Systems (ABS)

I am not a fan of ABS brakes. They are often ineffective, failure-prone, and expensive to service.

Essentially, ABS prevents a vehicle's wheels from locking when the brakes are applied in an emergency situation, thus reducing skidding and the loss of directional control. When braking on wet or dry roads, your stopping distance will be about the same as with conventional braking systems. But in gravel, slush, or snow, your stopping distance will be greater.

The most important feature of ABS is that it preserves steering control. As you brake in an emergency, ABS will release the brakes if it senses wheel lock-up. Braking distances will lengthen accordingly, but at least you'll have some steering control. However, if you start sliding on glare ice, don't expect ABS to help you out very much. The laws of physics (no friction, no stopping!) still apply on ABS-equipped vehicles. You can decrease the stopping distance, however, by removing your all-season tires and installing four snow tires that are of the same make and size.

Transport Canada studies show ABS effectiveness is highly overrated. IIHS—an American insurance research group that collects and analyzes insurance-claims data—says that cars with ABS brakes are actually more likely to be in crashes where no other car is involved but a passenger is killed. Other insurance-claim statistics show that ABS brakes aren't producing the overall safety benefits that were predicted by the government and automakers. One IIHS study found that a passenger has a 45 percent greater chance of dying in a single-vehicle crash in a car with anti-lock brakes than in the same car with traditional brakes. On wet pavement, where ABS supposedly excels, that figure rises to a 65 percent greater chance of being killed. In multi-vehicle crashes, ABS-equipped vehicles have a passenger death rate 6 percent higher than vehicles not equipped with ABS.

The high cost of ABS maintenance is one disadvantage that few safety advocates mention, but consider the following: Original parts can cost five times more than regular braking components, and many dealers prefer to replace the entire ABS unit rather than troubleshoot a very complex system.

Keep in mind that anti-lock brakes are notoriously unreliable on all makes and models. They often fail completely, resulting in no braking whatsoever, or they may extend stopping distances by 30 percent. This phenomenon is amply documented throughout NHTSA's complaint database.

Airbag Dangers: Unsafe at Any Speed?

First, the good news. It is estimated that airbags have reduced head-on crash fatalities by up to 30 percent and moderate-to-severe injuries by 25–29 percent. Injury claims at hospitals resulting from traffic crashes have dropped 24 percent as a result of airbag use.

Now for the bad news. To begin with, no airbag is safe, although some model years are safer than others. Pre-1997 airbags explode too forcefully and can seriously injure or kill small-statured or older occupants. Later de-powered "smart" devices are less hazardous, but they're not that smart. Many systems will disable the airbag even though a normal-sized adult occupies the passenger seat, as may be the case with Nissan's Quest minivan and Titan pickup, Hyundai's Elantra, and Jaguar, Jeep, Lexus, and Toyota models.

Inadvertent airbag deployment

Airbags frequently go off for no apparent reason, usually because of faulty sensors. Causes of sudden deployment include passing over a bump in the road, slamming the car door, having wet carpets, or, in some Chrysler minivans, simply putting the key into the ignition.

This happens more often than you might imagine, judging by the frequent recalls and thousands of complaints recorded on NHTSA's website at *www-odi.nhtsa.dot. gov/cars/problems/complain*. Incidentally, dealers and manufacturers routinely ask owners to pay for the interior damage caused by exploding airbags, denying claims by alleging that airbags don't go off without a collision. They usually pay the claim if the insured has proof the airbag went off for no reason.

> On June 17, 2004, after dropping my son off for baseball practice in Toronto, I decided to run a couple of errands. Upon returning to the ball field, I put my 1998 Dodge Grand Caravan in park and turned off the ignition. Immediately thereafter, my air bag deployed. I was struck on the left side of my face and neck and my left ear received some trauma. The BANG from the air bag deploying was so loud that people from 3 surrounding ball fields heard the blast.

•

> Our airbags on our 2003 Volkswagen Jetta TDI deployed for no reason on a smooth surface [on] July 3, 2004. We were denied warranty [coverage] because the Calgary Volkswagen field technician found two small dents on the bottom of the car. We met another Volkswagen Jetta TDI driver who experienced basically the same as us on July 1, 2004, and was also denied warranty. An employee at the dealership stated that another customer had an airbag deploy on a Jetta one month earlier, causing $5,600 in damage.... The deployment of our airbag tore open the ceiling along the passenger side of the car, ruptured the seat, damaged the panel beside the passenger seat, and immobilized the front passenger seatbelt.... These airbags, instead of bringing safety, are more of a danger. If we had been aware of this or the way Volkswagen would respond to this problem, we never would have bought from them.

Airbags, except for full-powered, pre-1997 systems, shouldn't be disabled; their benefits generally outweigh their shortcomings. If you feel vulnerable, you'll want to choose a vehicle with adjustable brake and accelerator pedals or an adjustable seat that can travel backward far enough to keep you at a safe distance (over 25 cm, or 1 ft.) from the front airbag's explosive force. You can assure children's safety by getting a vehicle with an airbag shut-off switch, or by having the children sit in the rear middle-seat position, away from front seatbacks that frequently collapse in rear-enders.

Nevertheless, airbags are still dangerous, even when they work properly. In fender-benders, for example, where no one would have been hurt if the airbag hadn't deployed, early, full-power airbag systems can kill women, seniors, and children—or leave occupants horribly scarred or deaf.

If you are hit from the rear and thrown within 25 cm of the steering wheel as the airbag deploys, you risk severe head, neck, or chest trauma, or even death. If you are making a turn with your arms crossing in front of the steering wheel, you are out of position and risk fractures to both arms. If you drive with your thumbs extended a bit into the steering hub area, as I often do, you risk losing both thumbs when the housing cover explodes.

Sometimes, just being female is enough to get you killed.

Two startling Transport Canada studies were uncovered in October 1999 as part of a CBC TV *Marketplace* investigation into airbag safety. The consumer TV show unearthed government-financed research that showed airbags reduce the risk of injury by only 2 percent for adults who wear seat belts. Even more incredible, the studies confirm that airbags actually *increase* the risk of injury to women by 9 percent and the risk of death for children by 21 percent, but they decrease the risk of injury to men by 11 percent. Any guesses whom the test dummy resembled?

The research was conducted in 1996 and 1998 on early, full-powered airbags. Fearing the public disclosure of the findings, it took Transport Canada four months to release the studies to *Marketplace*. American government officials have refused to comment on the Canadian research, despite the fact that it contradicts the basic premise of airbag use—that they are safe at any speed, regardless of gender.

In fact, the danger to women is so great that an earlier 1996 Transport Canada and George Washington University study of 445 drivers and passengers drew these frightening conclusions:

DANGER OF AIRBAGS TO WOMEN

While the initial findings of this study confirm that belted drivers are afforded added protection against head and facial injury in moderate to severe frontal collisions, the findings also suggest that these benefits are being negated by a high incidence of bag-induced injury. The incidence of bag-induced injury was greatest among female drivers. Furthermore, the intervention of the airbag can be expected to introduce a variety of new injury mechanisms such as facial injuries from "bag slap," upper extremity fractures, either directly from the deploying airbag module or from arm flailing, and thermal burns to the face and arms.

Side airbags—good and bad

In crashes with another passenger vehicle, 51 percent of driver deaths in contemporary model year cars during 2000–01 occurred in side impacts, up from 31 percent in 1980–81.

Side airbags and side curtains are included in most SUVs, vans, and pickups as standard or optional equipment. The airbag deploys from the ceiling, the seat, or the door and is designed to protect drivers and passengers in rollovers and side-impact crashes, which are estimated to account for almost one-third of vehicle deaths. Studies show that torso-protecting side airbags reduce deaths by 26 percent. The fatality rate drops by 37 percent when head protection is included. Serious crash injuries are reduced by 45 percent with the head-protection feature, versus only 10 percent when the torso-protecting side airbag is employed.

Because side airbags aren't required by federal regulation in the States or in Canada, neither government has developed any tests to measure their safety for children and smaller adults. IIHS hopes its test results will goad government regulators and automakers into standardizing side airbag design and increasing their effectiveness and safety.

In the meantime, keep in mind that preliminary safety studies show some early side airbag designs may be deadly to children or to any occupant sitting too close to the airbag, resting his or her head on the side pillar, or holding onto the roof-mounted assist handle. Research carried out in 1998 by safety researchers (Anil Khadikar, Biodynamics Engineering, Inc., and Lonney Pauls, Springwater Micro Data Systems, "Assessment of Injury Protection Performance of Side Impact Airbags") shows that there are four hazards that vehicle occupants should consider:

1. Airbags can inadvertently fire (due to a short circuit or faulty hardware or software).
2. Airbags can fire unnecessarily (sometimes the opposite side airbag will fire, or the airbag may deploy when a low-speed side-swipe wouldn't have endangered occupant safety).
3. Small children (a three-year-old, for example) restrained in booster seats can be seriously injured with early airbag designs.
4. Out-of-position restrained occupants can be seriously injured.

The researchers conclude with the following observation: "Even properly restrained vehicle occupants can have their upper or lower extremities in harm's way in the path of an exploding [side] airbag."

More recent studies of 2004–05 vehicles equipped with side airbags have determined that only 3 percent of "out-of-position" children would be injured (*www-nrd. nhtsa.dot.gov/pdf/nrd-01/esv/esv20/07-0213-O.pdf*).

The Khadikar–Pauls study and dozens of other scientific papers confirm that small and tall restrained drivers face death or severe injury from frontal and side airbag deployments for one simple reason—they are outside of the norm of the 5′8″, 180-pound male test dummy.

These studies also debunk the safety merits of ABS brakes, so it's no surprise they go unheralded by Transport Canada and other government and private safety groups. With a bit of patience, however, you can find these studies and the results of other research—such as what percentage of airbag deployments cause eye injuries, the effectiveness of electronic stability devices, and the need for laminated glass in side windows to prevent occupants' partial ejection—at *www.nhtsa.dot.gov* or *www-nrd.nhtsa.dot.gov/departments/nrd-01/esv/esv.html* (Enhanced Safety of Vehicles (ESV) Home Page).

In the meantime, don't forget NHTSA's side airbag warning issued on October 14, 1999:

> Side impact airbags can provide significant supplemental safety benefits to adults in side impact crashes. However, children who are seated in close proximity to a side airbag may be at risk of serious or fatal injury, especially if the child's head, neck, or chest is in close proximity to the airbag at the time of deployment.

 Protect yourself and your passengers

Additionally, you should take the following steps to reduce the danger from airbag deployment:

- Don't buy a vehicle with side airbags unless it offers head protection and you are confident that all occupants will remain properly positioned and out of harm's way. This is another reason why children should sit in the middle of the back seat.
- Make sure that seat belts are buckled and that all head restraints are properly adjusted (to about ear level).
- Make sure the head restraints are rated good by IIHS (check Part Four). Remember, expensive vehicles can have inadequate restraints.
- Insist that passengers who are frail or short, or who have recently had surgery, sit in the back.
- Make sure that the driver's seat can be adjusted for height and has tracks with sufficient rearward travel to allow short drivers to remain a safe distance (25 cm) away from the bag's deployment.
- If you are short-statured, consider buying aftermarket pedal extensions from auto parts retailers, or buying optional adjustable accelerator and brake pedals to keep you at a safe distance from a deploying airbag.
- Buy a vehicle that uses sensors to detect the presence of an electronically tagged child safety seat in the passenger seat and disables the airbag for that seat.

Top 20 Safety Defects

The U.S. federal government's online safety complaints database contains well over 100,000 entries going back to vehicles made in the late '70s. Although the database was originally intended to record only incidents of component failures that relate to safety, you will find every problem imaginable dutifully recorded by clerks working for NHTSA.

A perusal of the listed complaints shows that some safety-related failures occur more frequently than others and often affect one manufacturer more than another. Here is a summary of some of the more commonly reported failures, in order of frequency:

1. Airbags not deploying when they should, or deploying when they shouldn't
2. ABS total brake failure; wheel lock-up
3. Tire-tread separation
4. Electrical or fuel-system fire
5. Sudden acceleration
6. Sudden stalling
7. Sudden electrical failure
8. Transmission failing to engage or suddenly disengaging
9. Transmission jumping from Park to Reverse or Neutral; vehicle rolling away when parked
10. Steering or suspension failure
11. Seat belt failure
12. Collapsing seatback
13. Defective sliding door, door locks, and latches
14. Poor headlight illumination
15. Dash reflecting onto windshield
16. Hood flying up
17. Wheel falling away
18. Steering wheel lifting off
19. Transmission lever pulling out
20. Exploding windshield

Senior Safety

Canadian seniors are driving full throttle. They are living longer, keeping their driver's licences, and buying more cars. The National Advisory Council on Aging (NACA) says in its 2006 report that life expectancy at age 65 has continued to increase over the past five years. On average, a 65-year-old man can expect to live an additional 17.4 years, and a 65-year-old woman an additional 20.8 years. These figures place Canada among the OECD countries with the highest life expectancy at age 65.

Not surprisingly, Statistics Canada's 2006 census showed a spectacular increase in the number of seniors living in Canada:

> The fastest growing age group between 2001 and 2006 consisted of individuals aged 55 to 64 who are nearing retirement. The census counted nearly 3.7 million in this age group, an increase of 28.1% from 2001. This rate of growth was more than five times the national average of 5.4%.

According to the Canada Safety Council, half of Canadians aged 65 and older living in private households drive motor vehicles—though drivers over 80 years old are the fastest-growing segment of the driving population. This group of aging drivers are generally safer drivers, in that only one-third are as likely as drivers aged 15 to 24 to cause auto accidents, says the Rand Corporation research institute. By contrast, people aged 15 to 24 accounted for 13 percent of licensed drivers but caused 43 percent of all accidents

The bulk of senior driving usually involves short trips (11–17 km per day, on average) for medical appointments and visits to family, friends, and shopping malls. And more of that driving is done by women, concludes the NACA in its 2006 report:

> Access to transportation gives seniors greater independence, better access to services and improved opportunities for social interaction. In 2003, 67% of seniors had their driver's license (86% of men and 52% of women), a 2 percentage point increase from 2000. Between 2000 and 2003, the percentage of senior women having a driver's license increased by 2 percentage points.

> The percentage of senior households with a vehicle increased significantly between 1999 and 2003. The increase was highest for senior women living alone, from 41% to 50% and for couples, from 84% to 92%. In 2003, 72% of senior men living alone owned a vehicle (vs. 70% in 1999). This suggests that the new generation of seniors, especially women, are enjoying greater mobility than before.

Safe, Reliable Choices

Older drivers, like most of us, want cars that are reliable, relatively inexpensive, and fuel-efficient. Additionally, they require vehicles that compensate for some of the physical challenges associated with aging and that provide protection for accidents more common to mature drivers (full-torso airbags for side-impact protection and electronic stability control to counter unexpected steering corrections, for example). Furthermore, as drivers get older, they find that the very act of getting into a car (sitting down while moving sideways without bumping their heads or twisting their necks) demands considerable acrobatic skill.

OLD FAVOURITES

New vehicles with the highest percentage of buyers over 70, first four months of 2006 (American data).

1. Mercury Grand Marquis	55.4%
2. Lincoln Town Car	52.4%
3. Buick Lucerne	48.6%
4. Cadillac DTS	46.6%
5. Buick LaCrosse	46.5%
6. Ford Crown Victoria	35.4%
7. Mercury Monterey	30.9%
8. Mercury Montego	28.0%
9. Lincoln Zephyr	25.8%
10. Lexus LS	24.2%

Vans, small SUVs set upon car platforms, and Cadillac SUVs such as the Escalade generally meet the above requirements and remain quite popular with senior drivers who have limited mobility. Nevertheless, seniors are sometimes reluctant to change their buying habits, so traditional full-sized cars still dominate the seniors' market, though more frugal and reliable Japanese luxury compacts are coming on strong.

Access and Comfort

Drivers with arthritic hands may have to insert a pencil into their key ring to twist the key in the ignition. Make sure that your ignition lock doesn't require that much effort. Power locks and windows are a must, especially if the vehicle will be operated with hand controls. However, make sure the window switch cannot be activated by a child standing on the armrest and hanging out the window. A remote keyless entry will allow entry without having to twist a key in the door lock. A vehicle equipped with a buttonless shifter will be less difficult to activate for arthritis sufferers and for drivers with limited upper-body mobility. Cruise control can be helpful for those with lower-body mobility challenges.

Forget minivans and large trucks unless you invest in a step-up, choose one with an easily reached inside grip handle, and don't mind bumping the left-side steering column stalk with your right knee each time you slide into the driver's seat.

Drivers with limited mobility or those who are recovering from hip surgery give kudos to the Buick LeSabre, the Cadillac Escalade, and the GM Venture/Montana minivans; Toyota's Echo, Matrix, and Avalon; and small SUVs like the Honda CR-V, the Hyundai Tucson and Santa Fe, or the Toyota RAV4.

Incidentally, General Motors' minivans offer a Sit-N-Lift option, which is a motorized, rotating lift-and-lower rear passenger seat that's accessed through the middle door and can be taken out when not needed.

Seeing, Driving, and Surviving

The driver's seat should be mounted high enough to give a commanding view of the road (with slower reaction times, seniors need earlier warnings). Driver's seats must offer enough rearward travel to attenuate the force of an exploding airbag, which can be particularly hazardous to older or small-statured occupants, children, or anyone recovering from surgery. Adjustable gas and brake pedals are a must for short-legged drivers.

And, while we're discussing airbags, remember that, prior to 1997, most airbags were full-force, making it especially important that you put at least 25 cm between your upper torso and the front airbag. As full-powered airbags deploy, they expand with an explosive force that is greatest in the first 8 cm of travel. Sit within this zone, and you are likely to be killed or seriously injured from the explosion. Tests have shown that short drivers tend to sit about 24 cm from the steering wheel (measured from the chest), in comparison to an average-sized male, who sits at a distance of about 39 cm. Moreover, pre-impact braking may throw you even closer to the airbag prior to its deployment, which certainly isn't a confidence-builder, is it?

Transport Canada recommends that adults sit more than 25 cm away from the airbag housing and that children sit in the rear of the vehicle. Also, since most intersection collisions involving mature drivers occur when drivers are making a turn into oncoming traffic, head-protecting side airbags are a must.

Look for handles near the door frame that can be gripped for support when entering or leaving the vehicle, bright dashboard gauges that can be seen in sunlight, and instruments with large-sized controls.

Remote-controlled mirrors are a must, along with adjustable, unobtrusive head restraints and a non-reflective front windshield (many drivers put a cloth on the dash top to cut the distraction). Make sure brake and accelerator pedals aren't mounted too close together.

As far as safety features are concerned, a superior crashworthiness rating is essential, as well as torso- and head-protecting side airbags. The extra head protection can make a critical difference in side impacts. For example, Toyota's 2004 RAV4 with $680 head-protecting side airbags earned a "best pick" designation from IIHS. When tested without the head protection, it received a "Poor" rating in the side test.

Although vehicles equipped with electronic stability control work well keeping a vehicle stable during sudden steering corrections, anti-lock brakes don't fully deliver the safety they promise. Their proper operation (no tapping on the brakes) runs counter to everything you have been taught, they aren't that reliable, and maintenance costs can be horrendous. Look for headlights that give you a comfortable view at night, as well as easily seen and heard dash-mounted turn

A SAFE CAR FOR SENIORS

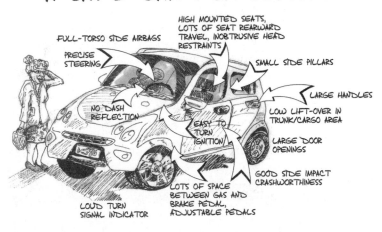

FULL-TORSO SIDE AIRBAGS

HIGH MOUNTED SEATS, LOTS OF SEAT REARWARD TRAVEL, INOBTRUSIVE HEAD RESTRAINTS

PRECISE STEERING

SMALL SIDE PILLARS

LARGE HANDLES

NO DASH REFLECTION

LOW LIFT-OVER IN TRUNK/CARGO AREA

EASY TO TURN IGNITION

LARGE DOOR OPENINGS

GOOD SIDE IMPACT CRASHWORTHINESS

LOUD TURN SIGNAL INDICATOR

LOTS OF SPACE BETWEEN GAS AND BRAKE PEDAL, ADJUSTABLE PEDALS signal indicators. Ensure that the vehicle's knobs and switches are large and easy to identify. An easily accessed, full-sized spare tire and user-friendly lug wrench and jack stand are also important.

Senior Trip Tips

Before you begin a—perhaps oxymoronic—driving vacation, make sure that the vehicle is properly serviced, that baggage and occupants don't exceed a safe limit, and that visibility is unobstructed. Above all, don't treat the trip as an endurance marathon. Plan your route with rest stops scheduled every two hours or 200 km (empty tennis ball canisters are excellent for bladder emergencies), don't drive at night (even with glasses, your night vision can be poor) or during weekends (lots of impaired or aggressive drivers), and if you fall behind schedule, call ahead to say you'll be a bit late.

Sooner or later, you'll find that everyone on the highway is going much faster than you are. Although the speed limit says 100 km/h, most drivers will speed by at 120 km/h. It will also seem as if every vehicle in your rear-view mirror is a huge commercial truck hugging your rear bumper. All the more reason to stay in the middle lane and to let the speeders pass you by. Why not simply stay all the way to the right, you ask? Because there are too many exits that cut off the right lane and too many merging cars entering the highway. Your slow speed will likely cause them to speed up and then cut you off as they dart from the far-right lane to the middle lane.

Other Buying Considerations

When "New" Isn't New

There's no guarantee that what you buy is really new. The odometer may have been disconnected, or the vehicle could have been involved in an accident; both of these are common occurrences.

Even if the vehicle hasn't been used, it may have been left outdoors for a considerable length of time, causing the deterioration of rubber components, premature body and chassis rusting, or severe rusting of internal mechanical parts (leading to brake malfunction, fuel line contamination, hard starting, and stalling).

 You can check a vehicle's age by looking at the date-of-manufacture plate usually found on the driver-side door pillar. If the date of manufacture reads "7/07" your vehicle was probably one of the last 2007 models made before the September changeover to the 2008s. Redesigned vehicles or those new to the market are exceptions to this rule. They may arrive at dealerships in early spring or mid-summer, but they're considered to be next year's models. They also depreciate more quickly, owing to their earlier launching, but this difference narrows over time.

Sometimes, a vehicle can be too new and end up costing you more in maintenance because redesign glitches haven't yet been worked out. As Honda's North American manufacturing chief, Koki Hirashima, so ably put it, carryover models generally have fewer problems than vehicles that have been significantly reworked or just introduced to the market. Newly redesigned vehicles get quality scores that are, on average, 2 percent worse than vehicles that have been around for a while, says J.D. Power and Associates. Some surprising poor performers are the 2002 Jaguar X-Type, 2002 Nissan Altima, 2002 Toyota Avalon and Camry, and 2001 Honda Civic. More recently, the 2004 Nissan Quest and Titan and the Toyota Sienna failed to live up to expectations.

Because they're the first off the assembly line for a model year, most vehicles assembled between September and February are called "first series" cars. "Second series" vehicles, made between March and August, incorporate more assembly-line fixes and are better built than the earlier models, which may depend on ineffective "field fixes" to mask problems until their warranties expire. Both vehicles will initially sell for the same price, but the post-February one will be a far better buy because it benefits from more assembly-line upgrades and rebates. This is an important fact to remember if you are considering the purchase of a reworked 2007 GM Silverado or Sierra pickup, for example.

There's also the very real possibility that the new vehicle you've just purchased was damaged while being shipped to the dealer and was later fixed in the service bay during the pre-delivery inspection. It's estimated that this happens to about 10 percent of all new vehicles. Although there's no specific Canadian legislation allowing buyers of vehicles damaged in transit to cancel their contracts, B.C. legislation says that dealers must disclose damages of $2,000 or more. In a more general sense, Canadian common-law jurisprudence *does* allow for cancellation or compensation whenever the delivered product differs markedly from what the buyer expected to receive. Ontario's revised *Consumer Protection Act* is particularly hard-nosed in prohibiting this kind of misrepresentation.

Fuel Economy Fantasies

The hidden expense of poor gas mileage is one of the top complaints among owners of new cars and minivans. Drivers say gas mileage is seldom as high as it's hyped to be; in fact, it's likely to be 10–20 percent *less* than advertised. (Fuel efficiency, measured in mpg, is the opposite of metric fuel consumption, measured in L/100 km. In other words, you want gas mileage to be high and consumption to be low.) *Consumer Reports* magazine estimates that 90 percent of vehicles sold don't get the gas mileage advertised, and their reporters target hybrids built by Honda and Toyota as the worst offenders.

This is not a new phenomenon. Environment Canada's independent research confirms that 2003–04 models were much less fuel efficient than vehicles built 15 years ago. At that time, cars and trucks averaged 10.5 L/100 km (22 mpg); now that figure is estimated by independent analysis to be 11.2 L/100 km (21 mpg),

Oh, Canada!

once all of the gas-guzzling SUVs and pickups are factored into the study. Even more astounding, a Ford Model T got 7.8–11.5 L/100 km (20–30 mpg) nearly a century ago. Today, the average Ford gets 12.5 L/100 km (19 mpg).

Oh, we wanted so badly to believe in the 1.2 L/100 km (200 mpg) Pogue carburetor invented in 1953 by Charles Nelson Pogue, a Montreal automotive engineer. As his 15 minutes of fame approached the 14-minute mark, Pogue recanted, saying that he had never claimed that his carburetor would get 200 miles per gallon, "or even half of that," declaring all such numbers were "violently distorted by newspapermen and magazine writers."

And who can forget '70s icon Liz Carmichael, a 6-foot, 200-pound transsexual born Jerry Dean Michael, who formed the Twentieth Century Motor Car Corporation in 1974 and announced she would soon launch a two-seater, three-wheeled car called the Dale that was to be powered by a 2-cylinder engine, get 3.4 L/100 km (70 mpg), and sell for under $2,000. Two other cars were to follow: the $2,450 Revelle that would give 4.7 L/100 km (50 mpg) and an eight-seater station wagon called the Vanagon (a name VW later picked up), for the same amount, that would deliver 5.9 L/100 km (40 mpg). Dealers bought franchises, but no cars were delivered, and Carmichael was hauled off to jail.

From the brochure:

The eyes of the world are on the amazing new Dale. A masterpiece in automotive design and engineering. A whole new standard of performance, economy, and safety available in no other car on the road today....

There are no wires in the Dale. No chance of electrical malfunctions. The car is operated electronically through a printed circuit dashboard. All accessories (radio, heater and air conditioner) are simply plugged in....

Safety? You can't drive a safer car. The body and frame are constructed of rocket structural resin...stronger than steel or aluminium pound for pound. Will absorb 4 times the impact of a Cadillac, without serious damage.... Sledge-hammer force won't dent or shatter the body. It's super solid and minor scratches won't show because the surface pigment is the same colour as the structural material underneath.

Like the Pogue carburetor, the Dale three-wheelers were mostly fuelled by hype.

Now, after we've had our hopes dashed by Pogue and Carmichael, Transport Canada hoodwinks us with gas mileage figures that are impossible to achieve, even after the United States government revises its figures downward by over 20 percent.

Gas mileage claims on individual models trumpeted by the manufacturers or Transport Canada have never been very reliable: They can be lower than "real-life" mileage by 40–45 percent for city driving and about 20–23 percent lower overall, says *Consumer Reports*. Additionally, the Union of Concerned Scientists levels some harsh criticism at government-sanctioned fuel consumption figures (*www. ucsusa.org/clean_vehicles/fuel_economy/fixing-the-epas-fuel-economy-tests.html*).

A serious flaw in the testing procedures is that automakers submit their own test results to the American government after running the vehicles under optimum conditions, and Transport Canada then publishes these self-serving cooked figures as gospel truth. In fact, one Ford bulletin warns dealers,

> Very few people will drive in a way that is identical to the EPA[-sanctioned] tests.... These [fuel economy] numbers are the result of test procedures that were originally developed to test emissions, not fuel economy.

Stephen Akehurst, a senior manager at Natural Resources Canada, which tests vehicles and publishes the annual *Fuel Consumption Guide*, admits that his lab tests vehicles under ideal conditions. He says that actual driving may burn about 25 percent more fuel than what the government tests show. Too bad we never see this fact hyped in the automakers' fuel economy ads.

Some examples: One of the biggest gas-guzzlers tested, the Lincoln Aviator, burned 44 percent more than the *Fuel Consumption Guide*'s estimate. A Nissan Quest burned twice as much fuel as was advertised in the *Guide*. Only the Hyundai Elantra did well. It burned a full litre less than predicted by the guys in the white lab coats. It's not surprising, therefore, that J.D. Power and Associates' 2003 quality survey showed that poor gas mileage was one of the top complaints among owners of 2003 model cars and trucks.

The U.S. Environmental Protection Agency says it will share new fuel economy figures, based upon revised tests, with Transport Canada in late 2007. These tests will give more accurate fuel economy ratings and, according to *Detroit News* columnist John McCormick ("The threat of realistic fuel economy numbers," February 1, 2006), are likely to cut truck and hybrid ratings dramatically:

> It's expected that fuel economy figures will drop by between five and 20 percent, perhaps more, depending on the testing cycle [to be adopted in 2007].... This issue is particularly pertinent to two vehicle types on the market today: full-size sport utilities/pick-ups and hybrids. It's a given that large SUVs are relatively heavy on fuel versus cars, but when the new EPA tests are conducted, full size SUVs are going to end up with composite mpg numbers in the low rather than the mid to high teens. For

the really heavy metal, trucks with extra large V8 or V10 engines, the mpg numbers may plunge into the single digits.

 "Miracle" Fuels

The lure of cheap, "clean" fuel has never been stronger, and the misrepresentations as to the advantages of different fuels have never been greater. Take a look at the following list of flavour-of-the-month alternate fuels that have been proposed by politicians and businesses, and consider that, except for diesel (an alleged carcinogen), *not a single other alternate fuel is economically viable.*

Ethanol and flex-fuel vehicles (FFVs)

The trendy fuel of the month for automakers, oil companies, and politicians who have their heads stuck up their tailpipes. All three groups recite the mantra that increased ethanol use will cut fuel costs, make us less dependent upon foreign oil sources (goodbye, Big Oil; hello, Big Corn), and create a cleaner environment. Unfortunately, this is simply not true—it's reminiscent of the misguided embrace of the 1997 Kyoto Accord by governments who promised they would be effective in cutting emissions that lead to global warming. Ironically, research now shows signatories to the Accord produce more emissions than non-signatories.

FFVs are all the rage with the Detroit Big Three and Nissan, and they're being promoted over hybrids and diesel engines because the switchover is less costly for them. Millions of their vehicles already on the market can run on a mixture of 85 percent ethanol and 15 percent gasoline (called E85). Oil companies have no problem with ethanol, either, since they can continue to charge high gasoline prices—governments won't pony up with the billions of dollars needed to construct new ethanol pipelines (at an estimated cost of $1.6 million per kilometre for 322,000 km) and to convert filling stations that would provide real competition for gas-selling stations ($240,000 for a new tank and pump). At the moment, most E85 FFVs are powered by gasoline because ethanol retailers can't be found (only 608 out of 168,987 filling stations sell ethanol in the States, and there are only a couple in Canada that do).

Brazil, a huge ethanol producer since the late '70s, doesn't need a pipeline, because most of its sugar cane fields are located where they can be distilled and the resulting ethanol marketed—thereby forgoing expensive transportation costs. In North America, most of the corn and other ethanol-producing crops are found in the U.S. Midwest and central and western Canada, far away from major population areas.

Indeed, ethanol is smokeless, burns cleaner, and (theoretically) leads to less engine maintenance. Plus, you can drink it (diluted, or with a chaser).

But will the increased use of ethanol make North America much less dependent upon gasoline? No way, not if you do the math: About 4 billion gallons of ethanol

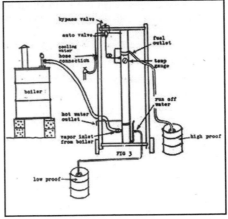

This photo, courtesy of Dogwood Energy, was taken in April 1933 and shows a Lincoln, Nebraska, gas station selling ethanol fuel. According to Dogwood, grain alcohol (ethanol) is a renewable fuel, and it's pretty much pollution free, since the by-products of combustion are only water and CO_2.

Dogwood Energy, of Tullahoma, Tennessee, sells recipes for 190-proof grain alcohol (ethanol) on its website, *www.dogwoodenergy.com*. For $1,600, you can buy a still like this one and legally brew up to 9.8 L (2.6 gallons) of ethanol in two and a half days at a cost of about 65 cents (U.S.) per gallon. For the average car, that's about a tank full of ethanol every two weeks. Home brewers are expected not to drink the stuff (Scout's honour).

is produced annually in the States, but they burn an average of 140 billion gallons of gasoline each year.

Ethanol filling stations are practically non-existent, the fuel costs almost as much as gasoline in some places (unless you distill it yourself), gas mileage *drops* by up to 30 percent when ethanol is used, and the product is highly corrosive, with a particular fondness for plastic and rubber components.

Hybrids

You'd be misguided to plunk down about $30,000 for a hybrid vehicle in the hope of saving gas—or the environment.

Hybrids are a pie-in-the-sky alternative fuel systems that use expensive and complex electronic and mechanical components to achieve the same fuel economy that a bare-bones Honda Civic or Toyota Yaris can achieve at half the initial purchase price—and without polluting the environment with exotic toxic metals leeched from used battery packs. The Union of Concerned Scientists weighs in:

> The idea that hybrids will save their owners money is gradually being replaced by a realization that the payback period of these more expensive vehicles is to be measured in years. Furthermore the launch of more performance-oriented hybrids has confused environmentalists who thought the hybrid concept was purely aimed at saving fuel. But even more alarming to hybrid fans will be the impact of real world EPA mpg

testing, especially on the city driving cycle. Because hybrids currently have such impressively high fuel economy numbers, their percentage drop will appear all the more dramatic.

Want the real-world hybrid fuel economy and cost-of-ownership numbers?

Consumer Reports tested six pairs of vehicles, with each pair including a conventional vehicle and the equivalent hybrid model, and published the astounding results in its April 2006 edition. *CR* found that in each category of car, truck, and SUV, the extra cost for the hybrid version was unacceptably higher than the same vehicle equipped with a conventional propulsion system.

Other disadvantages of hybrids are their mechanical and electronic complexities, dependence upon specialized dealers for basic servicing, high depreciation rates and insurance costs, overblown fuel-efficiency numbers (owners report getting 40 percent less than promised), and $6,000 to $8,000 costs to replace their battery packs.

ESTIMATED COSTS FOR 2006 GASOLINE-FUELLED VEHICLES VS. HYBRIDS

Over a 5-year period, the smallest estimated U.S.-dollar operating cost difference was between the two Honda Civics ($3,700), followed by Toyota's Corolla and Prius ($5,250). The biggest gap between two similar models was registered by the gasoline-powered Toyota Highlander SUV and its hybrid version ($13,300 U.S.), with the Lexus RX330 and RX400h posting a $13,100 higher cost for the hybrid version. The first two figures are the manufacturers' suggested retail prices.

	GASOLINE	HYBRID	HIGHER OPERATING COST
Ford Escape SUV	$22,818	$29,140	$8,350
Honda Accord EX	$25,862	$31,540	$10,250
Honda Civic	$18,444	$22,400	$3,750
Lexus RX330/RX400h	$37,960	$46,755	$13,100
Toyota Highlander	$32,650	$39,835	$13,300
Toyota Corolla/Prius	$16,607	$22,305	$5,250

Source: *Consumer Reports*, April 2006.

Hybrid reliability has been problematic as well. For example, Honda's first hybrid, the Insight, was dropped in 2007, and Honda's Hybrid Accord was cancelled the following year. Owners of both models are expected to face long servicing waits, high maintenance costs, and plummeting depreciation values. One 2001 Insight owner wrote *Lemon-Aid* about the following problems:

- Honda Insight hybrid MSRP: $26,000. The total cost of warranty, repair, recalls, and diagnosis as of Nov. 7, 2005 is approx. $14,119.94, which is 54.3% of the MSRP. Out of pocket expense approx. $5,000.
- Random complete loss of the Integrated Motor Assist engine (battery power) which I believe has put my life at risk.

- Honda's consistent inability to properly diagnose my Honda hybrid's problems without a "Check Engine Light"; this has [led] to even MORE damage.
- Three catalytic converters within 155,000 km. Because of the complexity of this Honda hybrid there aren't any other options then to purchase the parts through Honda, at approximately $2,000. How can Honda allow the need for replacement every 60,000 km?
- Long waiting periods for almost every part I have ever needed for my Honda hybrid, which in turn has caused weeks, if not months of vehicle downtime and approx. 367 days of open work orders/unresolved problems, 6 months of loss of use due to the IMA failure, 6 months of inconsistent/unreliable use due to IMA periodic failure, approx 4–5 months of loss of use due to other failures/matters.
- At 150,000 km I have a lifetime mpg of only 42.3 mpg [5.6 L/100 km], a large contrast from Honda's initially advertised 68 mpg [3.5 L/100 km].
- Strange, electric noises randomly coming from the IMA battery compartment.
- Water damaged $300+ speakers, carpet rot and interior rust probably due to a chronic drivers side window leak that they can't seem to permanently fix.
- Transmission failure, ABS brake system failure, and AC failure.

In June 2006, Ford announced that it would not launch more hybrid models to join its popular Escape Hybrid, despite a previous promise made a year earlier that its goal was for most of its production to change to hybrids. Instead, the company pledged to add ethanol flex-fuel vehicles to its model lineup—in a sense, a promise to stand pat.

Diesel

Of all the alternate fuels tested by independent researchers, diesel comes closest to the estimated fuel economy figures. It's also widely available and neither requires a steep learning curve in the service bay nor exotic replacement parts. Additionally, unlike hybrids, diesel-equipped vehicles are reasonably priced and hold their value quite well. Unfortunately, all this will change this year as diesel fuel formulation is modified and the fuel delivery systems are radically revamped to reduce emissions. Already Chrysler has thrown in the towel, dropping its best-selling diesel-equipped Jeep Liberty in late 2006, although the Cherokee will soldier on with the Mercedes-sourced 3.0L diesel.

As with the changeover to unleaded gasoline two decades ago, owners of diesel-equipped vehicles can expect horrendously expensive maintenance costs, considerable repair downtime, and worsening of the diesel's poor reliability trend, which was seen over the past decade with Ford's Powerstroke and General Motors' Duramax.

There's also the pricing and availability of diesel fuel to consider. Diesel already costs almost as much as regular gasoline, and Michael Tusiani, a senior fellow at Columbia University's Center for Energy, Marine Transportation and Public Policy says shortages of diesel fuel are imminent. In a research paper published in the *Washington Post* on August 8, 2005 titled, "Diesel Won't Solve Our Gasoline Woes," Tusiani issued the following warning:

Automakers are eager to sell you a diesel-powered vehicle. One of their responses to the rising price of gasoline has been to tell American motorists they can keep their large, powerful vehicles and at the same time save on fuel by buying a car or truck that burns diesel instead of gasoline.... Diesel-fueled vehicles do afford somewhat better mileage and may not require as much maintenance as gasoline-burners. But now and for years to come, the U.S. refining industry simply cannot produce enough diesel fuel to accommodate a significant increase in the number of vehicles that burn it.... Diesel oil prices in Europe are soaring as demand pushes past the amount refiners can make.

2004 FORD F-250 4×4 SUPER DUTY 6.0L V8 POWERSTROKE DIESEL SERVICE BULLETINS

NUMBER	DATE	TITLE
07-1-4	01/22/2007	Cooling System—Cooling Fan Inoperative
06-26-5	01/08/2007	Body—Running Board Corrosion
06-25-14	12/11/2006	Engine—Coking Deposit Diagnostics
06-23-2	12/06/2006	Diesel Engine—Low Power/Exhaust Smoke/Possible DTC's
06-23-4	12/06/2006	Drivetrain—Drive-Away Shudder/Vibration
06-24-6	11/15/2006	Engine Controls—P006A or P132B/Lacks Power
06-22-15	11/13/2006	A/C, Cooling System—Heater Core Leaks
06-22-3	11/13/2006	Diesel Fuel System—White Smoke/Low Power/Hard Start
06-22-12	11/13/2006	Engine Controls—WIF Lamp ON/Flickering
06-21-19	10/30/2006	A/C—Heater Core Electrolysis/Leakage
06-21-2	10/30/2006	Cooling System—Coolant Venting From Reservoir Cap
06-19-14	10/02/2006	Starting System—No Crank Condition
06-17-12	09/04/2006	A/C—Poor Cooling Performance
06-17-7	09/04/2006	Lighting—Addition of Bulbs to Turn/Hazard Flashers
06-15-5	08/07/2006	Body—Power Sliding Back Window Sticking/Binding
06-13-3	07/10/2006	Diesel Fuel System—Smoke/Low Power/Bucking/Jerking
06-8-5	05/01/2006	Cruise Control—Diagnostic Updates
06-7-1	04/17/2006	Vehicle—Tow Capability/Service Kit Requirements
06-6-1	04/03/2006	Lighting—Trailer Tow Lighting Diagnostic Tips
06-4-9	03/06/2006	A/C—Compressor Leaking/Inoperative
05-26-24	12/31/2005	Tires/Wheels—Excessive Run-Out Vibration
05-22-3	11/14/2005	Diesel Engine—Oil Leaks at CAC Connection/Low Power
05-21-5	10/31/2005	Diesel Engine—Buck/Surge on Light Acceleration
05-21-9	10/31/2005	Diesel Engine—Turbocharger Whine/Whistle
05-20-3	10/17/2005	Diesel Engine—Engine Oil Pan Corrosion
05-20-1	10/17/2005	Battery—Cable Terminal Bolt Corrosion
05-19-12	10/03/2005	Diesel Engine—Turbo Induced Exhaust Moan/Drone
05-19-14	10/03/2005	Diesel Engine—Hard Start/Runs Rough
05-17-16	09/05/2005	Engine Controls—Harsh A/T Shifts/DTC's Set/White Smoke
05-17-4	09/05/2005	Diesel Engine—Vacuum Pump Inop/Runs Continuously
05-16-11	08/22/2005	Restraints—Seat Belts Slow to Retract
05-16-6	08/22/2005	Diesel Engine—Misfire/Low Power/Hard Start When Cold

NUMBER	DATE	TITLE
04B24S3	08/18/2005	Campaign—5R110 A/T Reverse Planet Replacement
05B29S3	08/17/2005	Campaign—Diesel Charge Air Cooler Duct Replacement
05-13-9	07/11/2005	Diesel Engine—Exhaust Smell in Cab
05-13-16	07/11/2005	Diesel Engine—FEAD Belt Frayed/Shredded
05-13-5	07/11/2005	Diesel Engine—Boost or Oil Leak at Air Charge Cooler
05-11-5	06/13/2005	Engine Controls—Low Power/Surge/Rough Idle/Smoke
NHTSA05V270000	06/07/2005	Fuel System—Upgrade for Possible Stalling
05-6-4	04/04/2005	Instruments—False Parking Aid Warnings
05-5-7	03/21/2005	Charging System—Low Battery Voltage Using Snow Plow
05-3-10	02/21/2005	Restraints—Seat Belt Stop Button Service
05-3-6	02/21/2005	Drivetrain—Transfer Case Jumps Out Of 4L or 4H
04-25-16	12/27/2004	A/T Controls—MIL ON/DTC's Set After A/T R & R
04-24-3	12/13/2004	Steering—Leather Coming Loose From Steering Wheel
04-23-6	11/29/2004	Suspension—Vehicle Leans/Sags To One Side
04-23-9	11/29/2004	Body—Water Leaks From Roof Flange Area
04-23-8	11/29/2004	Steering—Moan/Grunt Noise Mainly on Left Turns
04-20-9	10/18/2004	Diesel Engine—Oil Leak/Low Power/Low Boost Performance
04-18-5	09/20/2004	4×4 System—Front Hubs Won't Lock/Disengage
04-18-6	09/20/2004	Diesel Fuel System—No Start/Misfire Condition
04-17-4	09/06/2004	Engine Controls—MIL ON/Lean DTC Service Tips
04-17-13	09/06/2004	Diesel Engine—Hard or No Start Condition
04-16-8	08/23/2004	Diesel Engine—Vacuum Pump Inoperative/Runs Constantly
04-15-10	08/09/2004	Instruments—Overhead Trip Computer DTE Inaccurate
04-14-12	07/26/2004	Diesel Engine—Accessory Drive Belt Squeal/Squawk
04-13-8	06/12/2004	Engine Controls—Low RPM, Buck/Jerk/Miss/Stumble
04-9-3	05/11/2004	Diesel Engine—Driveability/Oil Fuel Dilution
04-9-4	05/11/2004	Diesel Engine—Turbo Induced Exhaust Drone/Moan
04-9-2	05/11/2004	Diesel Fuel System—Water In Fuel Lamp ON
03B11	01/01/2004	Campaign—Roof Panel Appearance
03-23-2	11/24/2003	Body—Exterior Mirror Glass/Motor Service Tips
03-20-10	10/13/2003	Diesel Fuel System—Injector Combustion Seal Service
03-20-12	10/13/2003	Engine Controls—Diesel Engine Driveability Concerns

Ford's 6.0L Powerstroke diesel engine is often called the "Power Joke" by owners due to its poor reliability. The service bulletins listed above clearly confirm that Ford diesel defects have been disproportionately present since 2003. The changeover to a new diesel system and fuel will likely make these trucks even less reliable.

Fuel economy misrepresentation

So, if you can't make a gas-saving product that pours into your fuel tank or attaches to the fuel or air lines, you have to use that old standby and, well, lie. Hell, if auto-makers and government fuel efficiency advocates can do it, then why not dealers?

Fuel economy misrepresentation is actionable, and there is Canadian jurisprudence that allows for a contract's cancellation if the gas-mileage figures are false.

Most people, however, simply keep the car they bought and live with the fact that they were fooled.

There are a few new-car choices you can make that will lower fuel consumption. First off, choose a smaller version of the vehicle style you are interested in buying. Second, choose a manual transmission or an automatic with a fuel-saving Fifth gear. Third, an engine with a cylinder deactivation feature or variable valve timing will increase fuel economy by 8 and 3 percent, respectively.

FUEL ECONOMY CONVERSION TABLE

L/100 KM	MPG	L/100 KM	MPG	L/100 KM	MPG
5.0	56	7.4	38	12.5	23
5.2	54	7.6	37	13.0	22
5.4	52	7.8	36	13.5	21
5.6	50	8.0	35	14.0	20
5.8	48	8.5	33	15.0	19
6.0	47	9.0	31	15.0	18
6.2	46	9.5	30	17.0	17
6.4	44	10.0	28	18.0	16
6.7	43	10.5	27	19.0	15
6.8	42	11.0	26	20.0	14
7.0	40	11.5	25	21.0	13
7.2	39	12.0	24	23.0	12

Although good fuel economy is important, it's hardly worth a harsh ride, excessive highway noise, side-wind buffeting, anemic acceleration, and a cramped interior. If you make your choice based entirely on fuel economy, you may end up with much worse gas mileage than advertised and a vehicle that's underpowered for your needs.

If you never quite got the hang of metric fuel economy measurements, use the fuel conversion table at left to establish how many miles to a gallon of gas your vehicle provides.

Excessive Maintenance Fees

Maintenance inspections and parts costs represent hidden expenses that are usually exaggerated by dealers and automakers to increase their profits on vehicles that rarely require fixing or that are sold in insufficient numbers to support a service bay. Both Mazda and Honda owners suspect this to be the case, and a CBC TV *Marketplace* survey confirms the accusations against Mazda dealers.

In an investigative report shown on February 18, 2003, *Marketplace* surveyed 12 Mazda dealers across the country to determine how much they charged for a "regularly scheduled maintenance inspection," as listed in the owner's manual of a 2001 Mazda MPV with 48,000 km (*www.cbc.ca/consumers/market/files/cars/mazda_warranty*). Even with different labour rates, Mazda says the check-up should not cost more than about $280 anywhere in Canada. Here are the prices they were quoted:

- $400 (Montreal)
- $546 (Burlington)
- $225 (Toronto)
- $300 (Toronto)
- $271 (Winnipeg)
- $700 (Winnipeg)
- $253 (Calgary)
- $340 (Calgary)
- $450 (Calgary)
- $350 (Vancouver)
- $500 (Vancouver)
- $525 (Vancouver)

The first quote for service in Winnipeg was $700. A service technician told *Marketplace*'s producer that the price varied between $400 and $500 and warned that the work was needed to maintain the warranty. However, a check of the owner's manual showed no connection between the service and keeping the warranty in place. Gregory Young, director of Corporate Public Relations for Mazda Canada, said, "There's nothing in the owner's manual that says if you don't have this work done in its entirety at a prescribed time that automatically your warranty is void."

A popular service scam that's making the rounds is the false "recall notice" used by car dealers to attract customers to their service bays. The trick works like this: The dealer mails a flyer designed to look like a recall notice issued by the automaker to car owners, when no recall was ever issued. The telephone number printed on the flyer is the contact number for a service appointment. Once your car is held captive, they'll try to sell you unnecessary maintenance and repairs.

The rip-off letter might look like the one at right.

Alan Gelman, a well-known Toronto garage owner and host of CFRB radio's *Car Talk*, warns drivers,

> There are actually two maintenance schedules handed out by car companies and dealers. The dealer inspection sheets often call for far more extensive and expensive routine maintenance checks than what's listed in the owner's manual. Most of those checks are padding; smart owners will stick with the essential checks listed in the manual and have them done by cheaper, independent garages.

 Getting routine work done at independent facilities will cost about one-third to one-half the price usually charged by dealers. Just be sure to follow the automaker's suggested schedule so no warranty claim can be tied to botched servicing. Additionally, a $25 ALLDATA service bulletin subscription (see Appendix II) will keep you current as to your vehicle's factory defects, required check-ups, and recalls; tell you what's covered by little-known "goodwill" warranties; and save you valuable time and money when troubleshooting common problems (I just *hate* it when mechanics say they had to replace all of the good parts to get to that one defective component).

High Fender-Bender Repair Costs

Ownership cost is also impacted considerably by the cost of accident repairs following low-speed, "fender-bender" collisions. Once again, as with the dynamic crashworthiness tests carried out by both the government-run NHTSA and privately-funded IIHS, we find cheaper vehicles doing as well or better than more

Dear Customer,

We believe your vehicle qualifies for a free service campaign/recall. Please call our appointment hotline at 1-(866) 495-4444 to schedule your appointment to get your free service...

Plus a *FREE 28 Point Safety Inspection* on your vehicle.

Thank you,

Milton Watts
Program Director

expensive makes, according to Insurance Institute for Highway Safety crash tests completed August 2007.

To assess and compare bumper performance, IIHS conducts a series of four low-speed tests—full front and rear impact into a barrier designed to mimic the front or back bumper of another vehicle, plus front and rear corner impacts. The full-width impacts are conducted at 9.7 km/h (6 mph), while the more demanding corner impacts are run at 4.8 km/h (3 mph).

BUMPER PERFORMANCE IN LOW-SPEED CRASH TESTS: VEHICLE REPAIR COSTS

	FRONT FULL	FRONT CORNER	REAR FULL	REAR CORNER	TOTAL DAMAGE
Saab 9-3	$1,476	$1,076	$1,722	$ 969	$ 5,243
Audi A4	$ 976	$2,038	$ 918	$1,899	$ 5,831
Lincoln MKZ	$1,001	$1,966	$2,330	$ 669	$ 5,966
BMW 3 Series	$3,658	$1,256	$ 989	$ 778	$ 6,681
Acura TSX	$1,693	$1,274	$3,430	$1,157	$ 7,554
Volvo S60	$4,517	$ 543	$2,142	$1,022	$ 8,224
Lexus IS	$4,695	$2,223	$1,922	$ 737	$ 9,577
Lexus ES	$3,921	$2,093	$3,709	$1,101	$10,824
Mercedes C-Class	$5,486	$ 963	$3,728	$ 877	$11,054
Acura TL	$4,985	$1,244	$3,814	$1,156	$11,199
Infiniti G35	$5,223	$3,544	$4,035	$1,181	$13,983

Source: IIHS News Release, August 2, 2007.

These repair costs are even more astounding if you consider that soccer players are running at an average speed of over 7 km/h when they collide (*www.brianmac.co.uk/football/nutrition.htm*).

More Information Sources

The government lies to us about fuel economy and airbag dangers. Automakers lie to us about the reliability and "real" prices of their products. Car dealers routinely charge us for services covered by "goodwill" extended warranties and put pricing information in such small print in newspapers that no one can read it. And many car journalists lie to us when they say that they're unbiased, aren't intimidated by their editors and automaker reps, and can't be, ahem…bribed.

Most investigative stories done on the auto industry in Canada (such as exposés on secret car warranties, dangerous airbags, and car company shenanigans) are written by business columnists, freelancers, or "action line" troubleshooters rather than by reporters on the auto beat. This is because most car journalists are regularly beaten into submission by myopic editors and greedy publishers who don't give them the time or the encouragement to do hard-hitting investigative exposés. In fact, it's quite impressive that we do have a small cadre of reporters who won't be cowed. Links to some of the best Canadian and American websites on these subjects can be found at *www.lemonaidcars.com* or in this book's Appendix II. Here are some examples:

- The non-profit Automobile Protection Association (*www.apa.ca*) is a consumer-protection website. The group specializes in exposing unsafe and unreliable cars and trucks. Presently, it is in the middle of a campaign to get Ford Canada to recall 1997–2004 F-Series trucks with defective tie-rod ends that may suddenly throw the truck out of control. After almost two years of APA pressure, Ford's only response has been to send a service letter reminding owners to inspect or repair their trucks—at the owners' expense, of course.
- *Straight-six.com* is an independent, Ottawa-based car enthusiast website that offers a unique and entertaining voice to the dedicated car zealot. The editorial content, mostly written by publisher John LeBlanc, who also writes regularly for the *Ottawa Citizen*, focuses on topics right through the automotive enthusiast spectrum, from automaker marketing strategies to product and business trends. Readers of *straight-six.com* get unbiased, BS- and PR-free reviews and commentary on automotive issues related to the love of driving cars. LeBlanc is at his best when he gives no-nonsense reviews of high-performance vehicles and proves that dollar power doesn't always convert to performance power.
- Toronto-based Kurt Binnie's *OnTheHoist.com* is a well-written site replete with auto information from consumer advocacy and car enthusiast perspectives (not an easy balance). Binnie buttresses information files and frequent blog entries with URLs from around the world that run the gamut from the well known to the obscure. He is particularly effective as a price analyst who tracks down auto companies' suggested retail prices, customer and dealer rebates, and sales incentives and discount programs and then compares them on both sides of the border. His website is an essential free tool for effective price haggling.
- The Canadian Driver website (*www.canadiandriver.com*) offers a cornucopia of Canadian car critics who are relatively independent of industry influence.

Canada also has a number of media personalities who are not afraid to take on the auto industry and follow good stories, no matter where they lead. Here are some of my favourites:

- Jeremy Cato and Michael Vaughan, two of Canada's best-known business journalists, host *Car Business*, shown Friday, Saturday, and Sunday on Report on Business Television (ROBTv). This duo epitomizes the best combination of auto journalism and business reporting by asking the tough questions automakers hate to answer and poking fun at auto industry suits who take themselves too seriously.
- Mohamed Bouchama, president of Car Help Canada, shakes up the auto industry by rating new and used cars, providing legal advice, and teaching consumers the art of complaining on *AutoShop* every Sunday on Toronto's CityPulse24.
- The *Vancouver Sun*'s Linda Bates does an outstanding job as editor of the Auto section. She has years of experience and always asks the right questions.

- There's also the *Toronto Star*'s Ellen Roseman, one of Canada's foremost consumer advocates and business columnists. Many of her stories are inspired by personal experience or misdeeds reported by *Star* readers.
- Maryanna Lewyckyj is another crusading consumer advocate and journalist. She has been a *Toronto Sun* business and consumer columnist, and is more car-savvy than most automaker PR stuffed shirts. For example, Chrysler press honchos once had the Toronto motoring press fawning over their announcement that they were extending low-interest financing throughout Canada as a service to buyers everywhere. When Lewyckyj took a close look at the numbers, she came away unimpressed, and effectively challenged Chrysler's pro-consumer pretensions.
- Phil Bailey is a Lachine, Quebec, garage owner with over four decades of experience with European, Japanese, and American cars. In his insightful comments on the car industry, he's as skillful with his pen as he is with a wrench, and he's got the everyday garage experience that make him and Toronto CFRB broadcaster Alan Gelman unimpeachable auto industry critics. Bailey was particularly prophetic when he said this about hybrids in 2003, four years before *Consumer Reports* confirmed his findings (*www.baileycar.com/baileyblog. html*):

> Everybody in the hybrid market is losing money. The current units, which are very complex, cost about $5,000 more than a normal IC engine. The buyer is paying about a $3,000 premium, which means the manufacturer is upside down for about $2,000. That, plus the fact that fuel economy gains are less than people think, what with winter when the heater and defroster are used and summer when the AC is in operation. Yes, there is a small improvement in city mpg, but it's negligible on the open road. Couple that with the still undetermined cost of maintenance of the Rube Goldberg power units and the unknown life cycle of the battery packs, and the economic advantages become hazy at best. A great deal depends on the future price of gasoline or if the government radically increases fuel mileage standards. But as it stands now, the average customer is going to stay with a conventional automobile because the mpg cost factor makes obvious economic sense. The price of fuel and lower cost technology will govern the market, and the role hybrids will play remains doubtful at best.

These reporters and consumer advocates are the exception, not the rule. Even the most ardent reporters frequently have to jump through hoops to get their stories out, simply because their editors or station managers have bought into many of the fraudulent practices so common to the auto industry. Haranguing staff for more "balance" is the pretext du jour for squelching hard-hitting stories that implicate dealers and automakers. News editors don't want truth; they want copy and comfort, ignoring the auto industry scams threaded throughout their own advertisers' ads and commercials.

Want proof? Try to decipher the fine print in the *Globe and Mail*'s or *Toronto Star*'s new car sales or leasing ads, or better yet, tell me what the fine print scrolled at breakneck speed on television commercials really says. Where is the investigative reporter who will take on management over this trickery?

And the car dealers are even bigger hypocrites. For example, dealers selling used cars from residences, posing as private parties ("curbsiders"), are periodically exposed by dealer associations and crusading auto journalists. Yet these scam sellers are allowed to place dozens of ads weekly in the classified sections of local newspapers, and the papers' muckraking reporters ne ver take on these crooks. The trickery is obvious since the same phone numbers and billing addresses appear week after week. Ad order-takers know who these crooks are. News editors know they are promoting these scammers. Why isn't there an exposé by reporters working for these papers? Why don't they publish the fact that it's mostly new-vehicle dealers who supply curbsiders with their cars? That's what I'd call balanced reporting.

My conclusion: Although car columnists claim that their integrity is not for sale, there's no doubt that it can be rented. Travel junkets and public relations and advertising contracts all sweeten the pot for these pseudo-journalists.

Two of my favourite auto journalists, Dan Neil, automotive writer for the *Los Angeles Times*, and Robert Farago, a long-time columnist, auto critic, and creator of *The Truth About Cars*, a British-based website, have both been punished for writing the truth.

Neil's paper was hit with a $10-million (U.S.) loss after General Motors and its dealers pulled their ads in response to his sharp criticism of GM for a series of poor management decisions that lead to the flop of its 2005 G6 model:

> GM is a morass of a business case, but one thing seems clear enough, and Lutz's mistake was to state the obvious and then recant: The company's multiplicity of divisions and models is turning into a circular firing squad...someone's head ought to roll, and the most likely candidate would be the luminous white noggin of Lutz...[the G6] is not an awful car. It's entirely adequate. But plainly, adequate is not nearly enough.
>
> *LOS ANGELES TIMES,* APRIL 6, 2005

The *Times* stood by Neil, a Pulitzer Prize–winning automobile columnist. GM's ads eventually returned after a hiatus of several months.

Farago didn't fare as well. In late August 2005, he was canned and stayed canned. His column was permanently axed, without explanation, by the uber-liberal *San*

Francisco Chronicle after his criticism of Subaru's Tribeca, an SUV-wannabe that never will be:

> And here's the thing: I believe the media in general, and newspapers in particular, have an obligation to tell the truth about cars. You know all those puff pieces that fill up the odd blank spot in every single automotive section in this great country of ours?... And that's why so many car enthusiasts have turned to the web. Other than Dan Neil at the *Los Angeles Times,* there are no print journalists ready, willing and able to directly challenge the auto manufacturers' influence with the plain, unvarnished truth (including the writers found in the happy clappy buff books). Car lovers yearn for the truth about cars. Sites like *www.jalopnik.com* are dedicated to providing it. And that's why the mainstream press' cozy little Boys' Club is doomed.

Steer Clear of the "Car of the Year"

Once you've established a budget and selected some vehicles that interest you, the next step is to ascertain which ones have high safety and reliability ratings. Be wary of the ratings announced by car journalist groups, magazines, and enthusiast websites; their supposedly independent tests are a lot of baloney (see Part Four, "Vehicle Ratings: The Best and the Worst").

In 1994, North American car journalists awarded the first annual North American Car of the Year at the Detroit Auto Show. They picked the Mercedes C-Class—an entry-level compact noted for its mediocre reliability and poor performance. The Dodge Ram garnered the top truck award, while the Chevrolet S-10/GMC Sonoma and Land Rover Defender 90 (another sales and quality loser) were chosen as top contenders.

A year later, top honours went to the Chrysler Cirrus, Ford Contour, and Oldsmobile Aurora. Chevrolet's Blazer was named Truck of the Year, along with finalists Ford Explorer and Windstar.

All of these vehicles, except for the Explorer and Ram, are now extinct.

You want proof of how misleading the magazine ratings can be? Take *Car and Driver* as an example. It rated the Ford Focus as a "Best Buy" during its first three model years, while government and consumer groups decried the car's dozen or so recall campaigns and the huge number of owner safety and reliability complaints. *Consumer Reports* made the same mistake with the 2006 Focus and then recanted the following day.

Getting Reliable Info

Funny, as soon as people hear that you're shopping for a new vehicle, they all want to tell you what to buy. After a while, you'll get so many conflicting opinions that it'll seem as if any choice you make will be the wrong one. Before making your decision, remember that you should invest a couple of months in researching costs and models. The following sources provide a variety of useful information that will help you to ferret out which vehicle best suits your needs and budget.

There are hundreds of organizations and magazines that rate cars for everything from their overall reliability and frequency of repairs (J.D. Power and *Consumer Reports*) to their crashworthiness and appeal to owners (NHTSA, IIHS, and Strategic Vision's Total Quality Index, or TQI). These ratings don't always match. For instance, BMW's Mini ranked only 25th out of 28 brands in J.D. Power's Initial Quality Survey (IQS). But the popular import ranked second out of 30 brands included in the TQI. Quite a difference, I'd say.

Auto shows

Auto shows are held from January through March throughout Canada, starting in Montreal and ending in Vancouver. Although you can't buy or drive a car at the show, you can easily compare prices and the interior/exterior styling of different vehicles. In fact, show officials estimate that about 20 percent of auto show visitors are actively seeking info for an upcoming new-car purchase. Interestingly, while the shows are open, dealer traffic nosedives, making for much more generous deals in showrooms. Business usually picks up following the show.

Online services

Anyone with access to the Internet can now obtain useful information relating to the auto industry in a matter of minutes at little or no cost. This is accomplished in two ways: subscribing to an online service, like America Online (AOL), that offers consumer forums and easy Internet access; or going directly to the Internet through a low-cost Canadian Internet service provider (ISP) and using a search engine like Google to help you find thousands of useful sites. An extensive listing of informative and helpful sites can be found in Appendix II; however, I've listed a few of my favourite sites below. Many of them are a bit offbeat and highly critical of the auto industry:

American Car Fans
www.worldcarfans.com/country.cfm/country/acf

Autoblog
www.autoblog.com

Autoextremist
www.autoextremist.com

Automobile Magazine
www.automobilemag.com

AutoMuse
www.vehicleinfo.com/AutoMuse

AutoSpies
www.autospies.com

AutoWeek
www.autoweek.com

AutoWonder
www.autowonder.com

Cars! Cars! Cars!
www.carscarscars.blogs.com

Car Connection
www.thecarconnection.com

Car Design News
www.cardesignnews.com

Jalopnik
www.jalopnik.com

Shopping on the Internet

The key word here is "shopping," because *Consumer Reports* magazine has found that barely 2 percent of Internet surfers actually buy a new or used car online. Yet over 80 percent of buyers admit to using the Internet to get prices and specifications before visiting the dealership. Apparently, few buyers want to purchase a new or used vehicle without seeing what's offered and knowing that all the money paid will be accounted for.

New-vehicle shopping through automaker and independent websites is a quick and easy way to compare prices and model specifications, but you will have to be careful. Many so-called independent sites are merely fronts for dealers and automakers, tailoring their information to steer you into their showroom or convince you to buy a certain brand of car. One of the best independent Canadian sites that lists and explains discounted prices is *OnTheHoist.com*.

Shoppers now have access to information they once were routinely denied or had trouble finding, such as dealer price markups and incentive programs, the book value for trade-ins, and considerable safety data. Canadian shoppers can get invoice prices and specs by contacting the Automobile Protection Association (APA) by phone or fax, or by visiting *CarCostCanada.com*.

Other advantages to online shopping are as follows: Some dealers offer a lower price to online shoppers; the entire transaction, including financing, can be done on the Internet; and buyers don't have to haggle—they merely post their best offer electronically to a number of dealers in their area code (for more convenient servicing of the vehicle) and then await counteroffers. But here are three caveats: (1) You will have to go to a dealer to finalize the contract and be preyed upon by the financing and insurance (F&I) sales agents; (2) as far as bargains are concerned, *Consumer Reports* says its test shoppers obtained lower prices more frequently by visiting the dealer showroom and concluding the sale there; and (3) only one-third of online dealers respond to customer queries.

Auto Quality Rankings

There are two major surveyors of automobile quality: J.D. Power and Associates and Consumers Union, an American non-profit consumer organization that publishes *Consumer Reports*.

J.D. Power and Associates

Each year, J.D. Power and Associates publishes the results of two important surveys measuring vehicle quality (Vehicle Dependability Study, or VDS) and owners' customer service satisfaction (Customer Service Satisfaction Index Study, or CSI).

Interestingly, these two polls often contradict each other. For example, the Dependability Study places Saturn near the bottom of the list; however, Saturn has placed sixth from the top in the Service Index. This leads one to conclude that the car isn't very reliable, but service comes with a smile!

J.D. Power does have influence in the auto industry. Its criticism of Nissan's 2004 Quest minivan had that company's engineers working overtime fixing or replacing faulty sliding doors, power window switches, interior reading lights, second-row seat levers, and airbag sensors after the group's 2004 Initial Quality Study rated the Quest last among minivans in consumer perceptions of quality during the first 100 days of ownership. Nissan's Titan full-sized pickup and Armada full-sized SUV also placed last in their segments for other problems. All three models continue to sell poorly because of their poor-quality image and ongoing mechanical and body deficiencies.

Consumer Reports

Consumer groups and non-profit auto associations like the Automobile Protection Association (see Appendix II) are your best bets for the most unbiased auto ratings for Canadians. They're not perfect, though, so it's a good idea to consult both groups and look for ratings that match.

Consumer Reports (*CR*) is an American publication that once had a tenuous affiliation with the Consumers' Association of Canada. Its ratings, extrapolated from Consumers Union's annual U.S. member survey, don't quite mirror the Canadian experience. Components that are particularly vulnerable to our harsh climate usually don't perform as well as the *CR* reliability ratings indicate, and poor servicing caused by a weak dealer body in Canada can make some service-dependent vehicles a nightmare to own here, whereas the American experience may be less problematic.

Based on just over one million responses from subscribers to *Consumer Reports* and *ConsumerReports.org*, *CR*'s annual auto reliability findings are impressively comprehensive, though they may not always be correct. Statisticians agree that *CR*'s sampling method leaves some room for error, but, with a few notable exceptions, the ratings are fair, conservative, and consistent guidelines for buying a reliable vehicle.

One of my only criticisms is that many Asian models, like Toyota's and Honda's, are not as harshly scrutinized as their American counterparts, yet service bulletins and extended "goodwill" warranties have shown for years that they also have serious engine, transmission, brake, and electrical problems. *Consumer Reports* confirmed this anomaly in its April 2006 edition, where it pointed out that Asian vehicle quality improvement had "slowed" since 2002. Too bad the organization didn't consult the auto companies' own service bulletins four years earlier, as *Lemon-Aid* did when we downrated a slew of formerly sacrosanct Japanese models, like the Honda Odyssey, Nissan Quest, and Toyota Sienna minivans.

Older vehicles (pre-1998) are excluded from *CR*'s detailed ratings, just as statistics show that owners are keeping their vehicles for a decade or longer. Also, many of the ratings about the frequency of repairs of certain components aren't specific enough. For example, instead of just mentioning problems with the engine or the fuel or electrical system, ratings should be specific about which components are likely to fail. Is it the engine intake manifold and fuel pumps that are failure-prone, or is it the injectors that clog up, or is it the battery that suddenly dies?

Lemon-Aid *or* Consumer Reports*?*

I have a lot of respect for *Consumer Reports,* having been an elected member of its board almost 30 years ago. Readers will note that *CR* and *Lemon-Aid* ratings often agree; however, when they differ it is usually due to *Lemon-Aid*'s greater reliance upon NHTSA safety complaints, service bulletin admissions of defects, and owner complaints received through the Internet (rather than from *CR*'s subscriber base, which may simply attract owners singing from the same hymnal).

When and Where to Buy New Vehicles

When to Buy

A good time to buy a new sport-utility, van, or truck that hasn't been redesigned is between January and March, when you get the first series of rebates and dealer incentives and production quality begins to improve. Try not to buy when there's strike action—it will be especially tough to get a bargain, because there's less product to sell and dealers have to make as much profit as possible on each vehicle remaining in their diminishing stock. Furthermore, work stoppages increase the chances that on-the-line defects will go uncorrected and the vehicle will be delivered, as is, to product-starved dealers.

Instead, lie low for a while and then return in the summer and early fall, when you can double-dip from additional automakers' dealer incentives and aggressive price-cutting, which can mean getting thousands of dollars in additional savings. Remember, too, that vehicles made between March and August offer the most factory upgrades based on field complaints from those unfortunate fleet managers and rental car agencies who bought the vehicles when they first came out.

Allow yourself at least two weeks to finalize a deal if you're not trading in your vehicle, and longer if you sell your vehicle privately. Visit the showroom at the end of the month, just before closing, when the salesperson will want to make that one last sale to meet their month's quota. If sales have been terrible, the sales manager may be willing to do some extra negotiating in order to boost sales-staff morale.

Where to Buy

If all you care about is a low price, then shopping in auto-factory towns will get you the cheapest vehicles, as assembly-line workers "flip" their heavily discounted cars. Large towns have more of a selection and a variety of payment plans that will likely suit your budget. On the downside, servicing is likely to be hit or miss because of the transient nature of the customers and mechanics. And you can forget about individual service.

Good dealers aren't always the ones with the lowest prices, though. Buying from someone who you know gives honest and reliable service is just as important as getting a good price. Check a dealer's honesty and reliability by talking with motorists who drive vehicles purchased from that dealer (identified by the nameplate on the trunk). If these customers have been treated fairly, they'll be glad to recommend their dealer. You can also ascertain the quality of new-vehicle preparation and servicing by renting one of the dealer's minivans or pickups for a weekend, or by getting your trade-in serviced.

How can you tell which dealers are the most honest and competent? Well, judging from the thousands of reports I receive each year, dealerships in small suburban and rural communities are fairer than big-city dealers because they're more vulnerable to negative word-of-mouth advertising and to poor sales—when their vehicles aren't selling, good service takes up the slack.

Dealers selling more than one manufacturer's product line present special problems. Overhead can be quite high, and the cancellation of a dual dealership by an automaker in favour of an exclusive franchise elsewhere is an ever-present threat. Parts availability may also be a problem because a dealer with two separate vehicle lines must split the inventory and may, therefore, have an inadequate supply on hand.

The quality of new-vehicle service is directly linked to the number and competence of dealerships within the network. If the network is weak, parts are likely to be unavailable, repair costs can go through the roof, and the skill level of the mechanics may be questionable. Among foreign manufacturers, Asian automakers, except for Mitsubishi and Kia, have the best overall dealer representation across Canada.

Chrysler has the weakest dealership network among Detroit-based automakers in Canada after going through three owners in ten years. This instability has panicked dealer owners who are reluctant to stay in business or invest in the parts and service training needed to satisfy customers. Adding to their insecurity is a warning from the automaker's new owners that the dealer body will soon be trimmed by 20 percent.

BMW and Porsche still lead the European automakers in sales profits despite a downturn in 2008 sales. Sure, their cars are highly dealer-dependent for parts and service, and they tend to be pricier than Japanese and American components, but their popularity continues to grow. Servicing by other European automakers in Canada is still woefully inadequate, with VW's lack of a Canadian customer-assistance office making a bad situation even worse.

Despite the above drawbacks, you can always get better treatment by patronizing dealerships that are accredited by auto clubs such as CAA or consumer groups like APA or Car Help Canada. Auto club accreditation is no ironclad guarantee of courteous, honest, or competent business practices; however, if you're insulted, cheated, or given bad service by one of their recommended garages (look for the accreditation symbol in their phone book ads or on their shop windows), the accrediting club is one more place to take your complaint and apply additional mediation pressure. And as you'll see in "Key Court Decisions" in Part Three, plaintiffs have won substantial refunds by pleading that the auto club is legally responsible for the actions of the garage it recommends.

Automobile Brokers and Vehicle-Buying Services

Brokers are independent agents who act as intermediaries to find the new or used vehicle you want at a price below what you'd normally pay. They have their Rolodex of contacts, speak the sales lingo, know all of the angles and scams, and can generally cut through the bull to find a fair price—usually within days. Their services may cost a few hundred dollars, but you may save a few thousand. Additionally, you save the stress and hassle associated with the dealership experience, which for many people is like a trip to the dentist.

Brokers get new vehicles through dealers, while used vehicles may come from dealers, auctions, private sellers, and leasing companies. The broker's job is to find a vehicle that meets a client's expressed needs and then to negotiate its purchase (or lease) on behalf of that client. The majority of brokers tend to deal exclusively in new vehicles, with a small percentage dealing in both new and used vehicles. Ancillary services vary among brokers and may include such things as comparative vehicle analysis and price research.

The cost of hiring a broker can be charged either as a flat fee of a few hundred dollars or as a percentage of the value of the vehicle (usually 1–2 percent). The flat fee is usually best because it encourages the broker to keep the selling price low. Reputable brokers are not beholden to any particular dealership or make, and they'll disclose their flat fee up front or tell you the percentage amount they'll charge on a specific vehicle.

 Finding the right broker

Good brokers are hard to find, particularly in western Canada. Buyers who are looking for a broker should first ask friends and acquaintances if they could recommend one. Word-of-mouth referrals are often the best because people won't refer others to a service with which they were dissatisfied. Your local credit union or the regional CAA office is a good place to get a broker referral. For instance, Toronto's Alterna Savings (formerly Metro Credit Union) recommends a car-buying service called Dealfinder (see the following section); if you take out an Alterna Savings vehicle loan, they'll refund your Dealfinder fee.

Dealfinder

For most buyers, going into a dealer showroom to negotiate a fair price is intimidating and confusing. Numbers are thrown at you, promises are made and broken, and after getting the "lowest price possible," you realize your neighbour paid a couple thousand dollars less for the same vehicle.

No wonder smart consumers are turning away from the "showroom shakedown" and letting professional buyers, like Ottawa-based Dealfinder Inc. (*www.dealfinder. ca*), separate the steak from the sizzle and real prices from "come-ons." In fact, simply by dealing with the dealership directly, Dealfinder can automatically save you the $200+ sales agent's commission, before negotiations even begin.

For a $159 flat fee, Dealfinder acts as a price consultant after you have chosen the vehicle you want. The agency then shops dealers for the new car or truck of your choice in any geographic area you indicate. It gets no kickbacks from retailers or manufacturers, and if you can negotiate and document a lower price than Dealfinder, the fee will be refunded. What's more, you're under no obligation to buy the vehicle they recommend, since there is absolutely no collusion between Dealfinder and any manufacturer or dealership.

Dealfinder is a small operation that has been run by Bob Prest for over 15 years. He knows the ins and outs of automobile price negotiation and has an impressive list of clients, including some of Canada's better-known credit unions. His reputation is spread by word-of-mouth recommendations and the occasional media report. He can be reached by phone at 1-800-331-2044, or by email at *dealfinder@magma.ca*.

Finding a Reliable, Cheap Vehicle

Detroit Quality?

Today, Detroit's Big Three quality control is still way below average when compared with Japanese and South Korean automakers. Where the gap is particularly noticeable is in engine, automatic transmission, airbag, and anti-lock brake reliability as well as in fit and finish.

Do this simple test: Next time you're stuck in traffic, look closely at how the trunk and body panels are out of alignment on most Chrysler, Ford, and GM models. Notice the different-sized gaps on each side of the trunk lid and around the light assembly. Finally, ask yourself, "Who let these vehicles leave the factory uncorrected?"

Don't get the impression that Chrysler, Ford, and GM can't make reasonably good vehicles. Chrysler's Sebring and PT Cruiser, Ford's Mustang, and GM's full-sized rear-drive vans are fairly reliable, but the Asian competition still makes better products.

GM's Tahoe (L), Yukon, and Escalade are good-quality SUVs, but its front-drive minivans, like the decontinued Chevy Venture (R), are a disaster.

Ford's best vehicles are the Crown Victoria, the Mustang, and the Econoline full-sized van—all rear drives that have changed little over the past three decades.

General Motors is more of a mixed bag. Its full-sized vans and SUVs, small cars, and joint ventures with Daewoo and Toyota have all performed well, but its trucks and newly released mid-sized family cars are mediocre at best—and its minivans are poison.

Most studies done by consumer groups and private firms show that, in spite of improvements attempted over the past two decades, vehicles made by Chrysler, Ford, and (to a lesser extent) GM still don't measure up to Japanese and some South Korean products, such as Hyundai, in terms of quality and technology. This is particularly evident in SUVs and minivans, where Honda, Nissan, and Toyota have long retained the highest reliability and dependability ratings, despite a handful of recent missteps with powertrain quality.

Whether you buy domestic or imported, overall vehicle safety and corrosion resistance have improved among all automakers during the past three decades. On the other hand, repairs are outrageously expensive and complicated. Owners of cars and minivans made by GM, Ford, and Chrysler still report serious powertrain deficiencies, often within the vehicle's first year in service. These defects include electrical system failures caused by faulty computer modules; malfunctioning ABS systems, brake rotor warpage, and early pad wearout; failure-prone air conditioning and automatic transmissions; and defective suspensions, steering, paint, engine head gaskets, intake manifolds, and diesel fuel injectors and pumps.

Asian Automakers

Don't buy the myth that parts for imports are overpriced or hard to find. It's actually easier to find parts for Japanese vehicles than for domestic ones because of the large number of units produced, the presence of hundreds of independent suppliers, the ease with which relatively simple parts can be interchanged among different models, and the large reservoir of used parts stocked by junkyards.

Sadly, customer relations is the Japanese automakers' Achilles heel. Dealers are spoiled rotten by decades of easy sales and have developed a "take it or leave it" showroom attitude, often accompanied by a woeful ignorance of their own model lineup. This was once a frequent complaint of Honda and Toyota shoppers, though recent APA undercover surveys show a big improvement among Toyota dealers.

Where it has gotten worse is in the service bay, where periodic maintenance visits and warranty claims are like sessions with the Sopranos. Well-known factory-related defects (Honda and Toyota engine and tranny problems, for example) are eventually corrected under extended warranties, but you always have the feeling you owe the "family."

There's no problem with discourteous or ill-informed South Korean automakers. Instead, poor quality has been their bugaboo (remember the Hyundai Pony, Stellar, and Excel?). Yet, like Honda's and Toyota's recoveries following their own start-up quality glitches, Hyundai and its Kia division have made considerable progress in bringing quality up to Toyota and Honda's level. Furthermore, comprehensive base warranties protect owners from most of the more expensive breakdowns that may occur.

Both South Korean companies now have an extensive, more-refined product lineup that's priced thousands of dollars less than the Japanese competition. True, Hyundais and Kias lose their value quickly, but this doesn't mean much to entry-level buyers who keep their cars longer than most, thereby easily amortizing the higher depreciation rate.

European Models

Lemon-Aid doesn't recommend any new or used European SUVs or minivans; there are way too many with serious and expensive quality and servicing problems. We all know the European automakers have fallen all over themselves trying to get larger pieces of the lucrative SUV and minivan markets—such is the pull of sky-high profits (a Lincoln Navigator may garner $15,000). But they haven't given us the same high-quality vehicles offered by many Asian automakers. Heck, even the Germans have abandoned their own products. For example, a 2002 J.D. Power survey of 15,000 German luxury car owners found that German drivers are happiest at the wheel of a Lexus, a Toyota spin-off. This survey included compact and luxury cars as well as off-roaders. Toyota won first place on quality, reliability, and owner satisfaction, while Nissan's Maxima headed the luxury class standings.

Money-losing Land Rover, now owned by Tata motors, an Indian conglomerate, is still struggling since it moved into the North American market with its overpriced, quality-challenged, and under-serviced SUVs. But Land Rover of North America shrugs off its quality problems, and Tata isn't likely to improve things much while it struggles with its own poor-quality woes. For many years, Land Rovers got a free ride from fawning car columnists on this side of the Atlantic (although British press criticism had been merciless about the vehicles' terrible quality control and marginal sales figures). A 2003 study of 34,000 car owners with vehicles up to eight years old published by Britain's Consumers' Association found that less than half of British owners would recommend a British-made Rover or Vauxhall to a friend. The most highly rated cars in the study were the Japanese Subaru, Isuzu, and Lexus: Over 85 percent of British drivers would recommend them.

Here's another surprise: Although it builds some classy vehicles loaded with high-tech gear, Mercedes-Benz's SUV quality control isn't equal to the company's pretensions. After stumbling badly when it first launched its rushed-to-production, American-made ML320 for the 1998 model year, the automaker has sent out many urgent service bulletins that seek to correct a surprisingly large number of production deficiencies.

Volkswagen's quality is just as bad as Mercedes', and its sales have been equally dismal. True, VW has always been early on the scene with great concepts, but they have also always been accompanied by poor execution and a weak servicing network. With its failure-prone and under-serviced EuroVan and Camper, the company hasn't been a serious minivan player since the late '60s, and VW's few sport-utility and pickup variants have been resounding duds. Even the company's forays into the luxury cruiser market have been met with underwhelming enthusiasm or outright derision.

With European models, your service options are limited, and customer-relations staffers can be particularly insensitive and arrogant. You can count on lots of aggravation and expense because of the unacceptably slow distribution of parts and their high markup. Because these companies have a quasi-monopoly on replacement parts, you can turn to few independent suppliers for help. And auto wreckers, the last-chance repository for inexpensive car parts, are unlikely to carry European parts for vehicles that are more than three years old or were manufactured in small numbers.

These vehicles also age badly. The weakest areas remain the drivetrains, electronic control modules, electrical and fuel systems, brakes, accessories (sound system, AC, etc.), and body components.

Warranties

Most automakers offer bumper-to-bumper warranties, good for at least the first 3 years/60,000 km, and powertrain coverage for 5 years/100,000 km. It's also becoming an industry standard for car companies to pay for roadside assistance, a loaner car, or hotel accommodations if your vehicle breaks down while you're away from home and it's still under warranty. *Lemon-Aid* readers report few problems with these ancillary warranty benefits.

There's a big difference between warranty promise and warranty performance, however, because dealers and automakers have so much wiggle room to deny claims. For example, they can blame a part failure on abusive driving or poor maintenance, or simply call it normal wear and tear. When this happens, the majority of owners angrily walk away vowing never to use that dealer or buy that make again. Less than 10 percent of valid claims are taken to arbitration or small claims court.

Part Three has all the answers to the above lame excuses. There, you will find plenty of court decisions and sample claim letters that will make automakers and their dealers think twice about rejecting your claim.

Don't buy more warranty than you need

If you pick a vehicle rated Recommended by *Lemon-Aid*, you don't need additional bumper-to-bumper protection and you can pocket the money an extra warranty would cost. However, you could get a good price on a vehicle known for some engine or transmission problems with past models. In that case, you may want a $1,000 extended powertrain warranty. If you are picking up an SUV or truck that has a sorry repair history, you will likely need a full $2,000 comprehensive warranty. But first, ask yourself this question: "Why am I buying a vehicle so poorly made that I need to spend several thousand dollars to protect myself until the warranty company gets tired of seeing my face?"

Don't pay for repairs covered by "secret" warranties

Automobile manufacturers are reluctant to publicize their secret warranty programs, because they feel that such publicity would weaken consumer confidence in their products and increase their legal liability. The closest they come to an admission is to send out a "goodwill policy," "special policy," or "product update" service bulletin for dealers' eyes only. These bulletins admit liability and propose free repairs for defects that include faulty paint and engine and transmission failures on Chrysler, Ford, and GM vehicles (see Part Three).

If you're refused compensation, keep in mind that secret warranty extensions are, first and foremost, an admission of manufacturing negligence. You can usually find them in technical service bulletins (TSBs) that are sent daily to dealers by automakers. Your bottom-line position should be to accept a pro rata adjustment from the manufacturer, whereby you share one-third of the repair costs with the dealer and automaker. If polite negotiations fail, challenge the refusal in court on the grounds that you should not be penalized for failing to make a reimbursement claim under a secret warranty that you never even knew existed!

Trim Insurance Costs

Insurance premiums can average between $900 and $2,000 per year, depending on the type of vehicle you own, your personal statistics and driving habits, and whether you can obtain coverage under your family policy. Small SUVs and pickups are charged huge insurance premiums because they are considered to be high risks.

There are some general rules to follow when looking for insurance savings. For example, vehicles older than five years don't necessarily need collision coverage, and you may not need loss-of-use coverage or a rental car. Here are some other factors that should be considered:

- When you phone for quotes, make sure you have your serial number in hand. Many factors—such as the make of the car, the number of doors, the inclusion of a sports package, and the insurer's experience with the car—can affect the quote. And be honest, or you'll find your claim denied, the policy cancelled, or your premium cost boosted.
- Where you live and work also determine how much you pay. Auto insurance rates are 25–40 percent lower in London, Ontario, than in downtown Toronto, for example, because there are fewer cars in London and fewer kilometres to drive to work. Similar disparities are found in B.C. and Alberta.
- A driver-training course can save you thousands of premium dollars. For example, a policy on a '98 Honda Civic for a schooled driver under 25 years old may be $3,000 less than the regular premium price.
- You may be able to include your home or apartment insurance as part of a premium package that's eligible for additional discounts.

InsuranceHotline.com, based in Ontario but with quotes for other provinces, says that it pays to shop around for cheap auto insurance rates. In February 2003, the group discovered that the same insurance policy could vary in cost by a whopping 400 percent. For example, a 41-year-old married female driving a 2002 Honda Accord and a 41-year-old married male driving a 1998 Dodge Caravan, both with unblemished driving records, should pay no more than $1,880, but some companies surveyed asked as much as $7,515.

InsuranceHotline.com tells consumers which companies have the lowest car insurance rates. The service can be accessed only through the Internet, and a very reasonable fee is charged.

Other Money-Saving Ideas

Appreciating Depreciation

Depreciation is the biggest—and most often ignored—expense that you encounter when you trade in your vehicle, or when an accident forces you to buy another vehicle before the depreciated loss can be amortized. Most new cars depreciate a whopping 30–45 percent during the first two years of ownership. Fortunately, some average-sized minivans, vans, trucks, and sport-utilities don't lose that much of their value before their fourth year of use. The best way to use depreciation rates to your advantage is to choose a vehicle listed as being both reliable and economical to own and then keep it for five to 10 years. Generally, by choosing a lower-depreciating vehicle—such as one that keeps at least half its value over three years—you are storing up equity that will give you a bigger down payment and fewer loan costs with your next purchase.

More Dirt on Diesels

The only reasons to buy a diesel-equipped vehicle are for its potential to deliver outstanding fuel economy and for its much lower maintenance and repair costs when compared with similar-sized vehicles powered by gasoline engines. Unfortunately, independent data suggest that both claims by automakers may be false.

Let's examine the fuel-savings issue first. In theory, when compared with gasoline powerplants, diesel engines are up to 30 percent more efficient in a light vehicle and up to 70 percent cheaper to run in a heavy-duty towing and hauling truck or SUV. They become more efficient as the engine load increases, whereas gasoline engines become less so. This is the main reason diesels are best used where the driving cycle includes a lot of city driving—slow speeds, heavy loads, frequent stops, and long idling times. At full throttle, both engines are essentially equal from a fuel-efficiency standpoint. The gasoline engine, however, leaves the diesel in the dust when it comes to high-speed performance.

On the downside, fleet administrators and owners report that diesel fuel economy in real driving situations is much less than what's advertised—a complaint also voiced by owners of hybrids. Many owners say that their diesel-run rigs get about 30 percent less than what the manufacturer promised.

Also undercutting fuel savings claims is the fact that in some regions, the increased cost of diesel fuel—because of high taxes and oil company greed, some say—makes it more expensive than regular fuel.

The diesel engine's reputation for superior reliability may have been true in the past, but no longer. This fact is easily confirmed if you cross-reference owner complaints with confidential automaker service bulletins and independent industry polling results put out by J.D. Power and others, a task done for you in Part Four's pickup trucks section.

Many owners of diesel-equipped vehicles are frustrated by chronic breakdowns, excessive repair costs, and poor road performance. It's practically axiomatic that bad injectors have plagued Dodge Cummins, Ford Power Stroke, and GM Duramax engines.

Defective injectors were often replaced in the past at the owner's expense and at a cost of thousands of dollars. Now, GM and Ford are

> ### J.D. POWER AND ASSOCIATES' TAKE ON DIESEL ENGINES
>
> J.D. Power and Associates' 2004 Vehicle Dependability Study concludes that the most fuel-efficient vehicles—diesels and gas-electric hybrids—have more engine problems than similar gasoline-powered vehicles. The discrepancies can be dramatic.
>
> - Owners of 2001 Toyota and Honda hybrids reported twice as many engine problems as owners of gas-engine Toyotas and Hondas.
> - Owners of Volkswagen diesels reported up to twice as many engine problems as owners of VWs burning gas. Walter McManus, executive director of forecasting at J.D. Power, says diesel engine problems "are more surprising" because it's an older technology.
> - Ford and Chevrolet diesel pickups were worse than similar gas models, while Dodge and GMC trucks were better overall.

using special programs to cover the replacement cost long after the base warranty has expired. Chrysler has been more recalcitrant in making payouts, apparently because fewer vehicles may be involved and costs can be quite high (defective lift pumps and injectors are the main culprits affecting Cummins diesels).

And here are even more diesel-equipped-vehicle disadvantages: They use enough performance-robbing, poorly performing, and unreliable special components to fill a hardware store in order to meet emissions regulations that will get more stringent now that cleaner fuel has been introduced in North America. This new fuel requires major changes to the engine and additional expensive emissions hardware, as well as mechanics who know what they are doing when servicing these modified engines (an iffy proposition at best). Owners of diesel-equipped models made before 2007 also have to contend with some engine clatter, a smelly exhaust, high nitrous oxide emissions (a cause of acid rain), and excessive particulates (soot) that aggravate respiratory maladies.

Performance Should Be Tested

Take the phrase "carlike handling" with a large grain of salt. Since many rear-drive models are built on a modified truck chassis and use steering and suspension components from their truck divisions, they tend to handle more like trucks than cars, in spite of automakers' claims to the contrary. Also, what you see isn't necessarily what you get when you buy or lease a new sport-utility, van, or pickup, because these vehicles seldom come with enough standard features to fully exploit their versatility. Additional options are usually a prerequisite to making them safe and comfortable to drive. Consequently, the term "multipurpose" is a misnomer unless you are prepared to spend extra dollars to outfit your sport-utility, van, or pickup. Even fully equipped, these vehicles don't always provide the performance touted by automakers. And bear in mind that off-roading requires suspension, engine, and drivetrain packages as well as other components, such as off-road tires and a skid plate, that seldom come as standard equipment. Also be wary of ABS brakes when going off-road, as they can degrade handling considerably.

Front-drives handle better than rear-drives, but the size and weight of multipurpose vehicles still require a whole new set of driving skills when cornering at moderate speeds or when parking or turning. Sport-utilities and pickups are more likely to roll over than passenger cars, and it sometimes takes only a moment's inattention.

Four-Wheel/All-Wheel Drive Not for Everyone

An old mechanic friend of mine once told me, "Four-wheel drive will only get you stuck deeper, farther from home. If the weather is too bad to drive a car safely, stay home."

Four-wheel drive (4×4) directs engine power through a transfer case to all four wheels, which pull and push the vehicle forward, giving you twice as much traction. On most models, when four-wheel drive isn't engaged, the vehicle reverts to rear-drive. The large transfer-case housing makes the vehicle sit higher, giving you additional ground clearance.

Keep in mind that extended driving over dry pavement with 4×4 engaged will cause the driveline to bind and will result in serious damage. Some buyers are turning, instead, to rear-drive pickups equipped with winches and large, deep-lugged rear tires.

Many 4×4 customers have been turned off by the typically rough and noisy drive-line; a tendency for the vehicle to tip over when cornering at moderate speeds (a Ford Bronco and Isuzu Rodeo specialty); vague, trucklike handling; high repair costs; and poor fuel economy. No wonder car-based SUVs like the Toyota RAV4, Honda CR-V, and Hyundai Tucson are so popular: Buyers want versatility without sacrificing fuel economy, comfort, or handling.

All-wheel drive (AWD) is essentially four-wheel drive that's engaged *all* the time, a feature first popularized by Subaru. It never needs to be de-activated when running over dry pavement and doesn't require the heavy transfer case that cuts fuel economy (although some sport-utilities and pickups do use a special transfer case). AWD-equipped vehicles aren't recommended for off-roading because of their lower ground clearance and fragile driveline parts, which aren't as rugged as 4×4 components.

Rust Protection Scams

Vehicles are much less rust-prone than they were several decades ago, thanks to more durable body panels and better designs. When rusting occurs now, it's usually caused by either a poor paint job or the use of new metal panels that create galvanic corrosion or promote early paint peeling—two causes that are excluded from most rustproofing warranties. So put your $300 elsewhere and remember that the best rustproofing protection is to park the vehicle in a dry, unheated garage or under an outside carport and then wash it every few weeks. Never bring it in and out of a heated garage during the winter months, since it is most prone to rust when temperatures are just a bit above freezing; keep it especially clean and dry during that time. If you live in an area where roads are heavily salted in winter, or in a coastal region, have your vehicle's undercoating sprayed annually.

Whether you are rustproofing the entire car or just undercoating key areas, make sure to include the rocker panels (make a small mark inside the door panels on the plastic hole plugs to make sure that they were removed and that the inside was actually sprayed), the rear hatch's bottom edge, the tailgate, and the wheelwells. It's also a smart idea to stay at the garage while the work is being done to see that the overspray is cleaned up and all areas have been sufficiently covered.

Undercoating, which costs less than $100, will usually do as good a job as rust-proofing. It will protect vital suspension and chassis components, make the vehicle ride more quietly, and allow you to ask a higher price at trade-in time. The only downside, which can be checked by asking for references, is that the undercoating may give off an unpleasant odour for months, and it may drip, soiling your driveway.

Surviving the Options Jungle

The best options for your buck are a 5-speed automatic transmission, electronic stability control (for vehicles with a history of poor rollover scores), an anti-theft immobilizer, air conditioning, a premium sound system, and higher-quality tires—features that may bring back one-third to half their value. Rustproofing makes cars easier to sell in some provinces that have salted roads in the winter, but paint protection and seat sealants are wastes of money. Most option packages can be cut by 20 percent. Extended warranties are overpriced by about 75 percent. And what will happen when the warranty runs out?

Dealers make more than three times as much profit selling options as they do selling most cars (50 percent profit versus 15 percent profit). No wonder their eyes light up when you start perusing their options list. If you must have some options, compare prices with independent retailers and buy where the price is lowest and the warranty is the most comprehensive. Buy as few options as possible from the dealer—you'll get faster service, more comprehensive guarantees, and lower prices from independent suppliers. Remember, extravagantly equipped vehicles hurt your pocketbook in three ways: They drive up maintenance costs, they often consume extra fuel, and they cost more to begin with and return only a fraction of what they cost when the car is resold.

A heavy-duty battery and suspension and, perhaps, an upgraded sound system will generally suffice for American-made vehicles. Most imports already come well equipped. An engine block heater with a timer—said by the CAA to be favoured by 39 percent of new-car shoppers—isn't a bad idea either. It's an inexpensive investment that ensures winter starting and reduces fuel consumption by allowing you to start out with a semi-warm engine.

When ordering parts, remember that purchases from American outlets can be slapped with a small customs duty if the part isn't made in the United States; you'll pay the inevitable GST levied on the part's cost and customs duty. Finally, your freight carrier may charge a $15–$20 brokerage fee for representing you at the border.

Smart Options

The problem with options is that you often can't refuse them. Dealers sell very few bare-bones cars, SUVs, trucks, or vans, and they option-pack each vehicle with features that can't be removed. You'll be forced to dicker over the total cost of what you are offered, whether you need the extras or not. So it's not a case of "Yes or no?" but more a decision of "Is it necessary, and at what cost?"

Adjustable Pedals and Extensions

This device moves the brake and accelerator pedals forward or backward about 10 cm (4 inches) to accommodate short-statured drivers and protect them from airbag-induced injuries.

If the manufacturer of your vehicle doesn't offer optional power-adjustable pedals, there are several companies selling inexpensive pedal extensions by mail order through the Internet, such as Drive-Master (*www.drive-master.com*). If you live in Toronto or London, Ontario, check out Kino Mobility (*www.kinomobility.com*).

Adjustable Steering Wheel

This option allows easier access to the driver's seat and permits a more comfortable driving position. It's particularly useful if more than one person will drive the vehicle.

Air Conditioning

AC systems are far more reliable than they were a decade ago, and they have a lifespan of five to seven years. Sure, replacement and repair costs can hit $1,000, but that's very little when amortized over an 8- to 10-year period. AC also makes your car easier to resell.

Does AC waste or conserve fuel when a vehicle is driven at highway speeds? Interestingly, *MythBusters*, a popular Discovery TV program, concluded that, although their computer models indicated that using air conditioning with the windows up saved the most fuel, actual road tests showed that having the windows down and the AC turned off was the more fuel-efficient method of keeping the vehicle cool. However, Edmunds, a popular automotive information website, conducted their own fuel-efficiency tests and concluded that there wasn't that much difference between open or closed windows, as they point out at *www. edmunds.com/advice/fueleconomy/articles/106842/article.html*:

> While the A/C compressor does pull power from the engine wasting some gas, the effect appears to be fairly minimal in modern cars. And putting the windows down tends to increase drag on most cars, canceling out any measurable gain from turning the A/C off. But...[it] depends on the model you're driving. When we opened the sunroof in our SUV, the mileage did decrease even with the A/C off. Still, in our experience, it's not worth the argument because you won't save a lot of gas either way. So just do what's comfortable.

AC provides extra comfort, reduces wind noise (from not having to roll down the windows), and improves window defogging. Buy a factory-installed unit. You'll get a longer warranty and reduce the chance that other mechanical components will be damaged during installation.

Anti-Theft Systems

You'd be a fool not to buy an anti-theft system, including a lockable fuel cap, for your much-coveted sport-utility, van, or pickup. Auto break-ins and thefts cost Canadians more than $400 million annually; there's a one-in-130 chance that your vehicle will be stolen, and only a 60 percent chance that you'll ever get it back. In fact, older pickups are particularly easy pickings for thieves. Chevrolet and GMC trucks are at the top of the list, say Calgary police, mainly because most Chrysler keys will open GM truck doors and the steering column locks are easily bypassed. Chrysler minivans are also theft-prone because of their rudimentary door lock assemblies. Car security specialist Dan Friesen told The Canadian Press in July 2001 that he's not surprised pickups are so popular: "Most of these trucks are so easy to break into, it's a joke. I tell some people they shouldn't even lock their doors because it will save them money in the end."

Since amateurs are responsible for stealing most vehicles, the best theft deterrent is a visible device that complicates the job while immobilizing the vehicle and sounding an alarm. For less than $150, you can install both a steering-wheel lock and a hidden remote-controlled ignition disabler. Satellite tracking systems like GM's OnStar feature are also very effective. Remember, new vehicles bought in the States must be equipped with a special alarm if the vehicle is imported into Canada ($300).

Airbag theft protection

In Canada, about 8,000 to 10,000 airbags are stolen annually, many by organized theft rings that are active along the 401 corridor in the Greater Toronto Area, especially in cities like Markham and Scarborough. Thieves can steal a few dozen airbags in one night and then sell them to body shops for $150 to $200 each. The repairers then install them as original equipment or rebuilt or salvaged units for $1,500 to $2,000.

The best protection from airbag theft is a $50 (U.S.) (shipping and handling included) device called The Shield. It attaches onto The Club, a steering-wheel locking device, and can be ordered through the Internet from sites such as eBay Motors (*www.motors.ebay.com*).

Auxiliary Lighting

Essential only for serious off-roaders, extra lighting improves safety and makes night driving less tiring. In the city, it's a pain in the butt to other drivers, who are constantly blinded by the lights' intensity and high placement.

Battery (Heavy-Duty)

The best battery for northern climates is the optional heavy-duty type offered by many manufacturers for about $80. It's a worthwhile purchase, especially for vehicles equipped with lots of electric options. Most standard batteries last only two winters; heavy-duty batteries give you an extra year or two for about 20 percent more than the price of a standard battery. A good rule of thumb is to buy the freshest and largest reserve capacity (RC) battery that will physically fit into the engine compartment. You will also want it to have a cold cranking amp (CCA) rating that meets or exceeds the car's original equipment manufacturer's (OEM) cranking amp guidelines for your climate. Make sure you retest the battery after deep discharges or jump-starts.

Bed Protectors (Pickups)

Selling for $100–$200, these protectors range from simple mats to deluxe moulded polyethylene liners. They guard against rusting in the panel joints and bolt areas by preventing water accumulation, and they protect the cargo bed walls and tailgate from scratches and dents. These benefits help to keep resale value high.

Central Locking Control

Costing around $200, this option is most useful for families with small children, car-poolers, or drivers of pickups, minivans, and vans who can't easily slide across the seat to lock the other doors.

Child Safety Seat (Integrated)

Integrated safety seats are designed to accommodate any child more than one year old or weighing over 9 kg (20 lb.). Since the seat is permanently integrated into the seatback, it takes the fuss out of installing and removing the safety seat and then finding somewhere to store it. When not in use, it quickly folds away out of sight, becoming part of the seatback. Two other safety benefits are these: You know the seat has been properly installed, and your child gets used to having a "special" seat in the back, where it's usually safest to sit.

Electronic Stability Control (ESC)

The latest IIHS studies conclude that as many as 10,000 fatal crashes could be prevented if all vehicles were equipped with ESC. Its June 2006 report concluded that stability control is second only to seat belts in saving lives because it reduces the risk of fatal single-vehicle rollovers by 80 percent and the chance of having other kinds of fatal collisions by 43 percent.

A $500–$1,000 option or standard feature that's offered on over half of this year's new models (a $1,500 option when bundled), ESC helps prevent the loss of control in a turn, on slippery roads, or when you must make a sudden steering correction. The system applies the brakes to individual wheels or cuts back the engine power when sensors find the vehicle is beginning to spin or skid. It's particularly useful in maintaining stability with SUVs, but is less useful with passenger coupes and sedans.

Although Honda has put ESC into all its SUVs and Chrysler plans to equip all its sport-utilities with the feature, there presently is no federal standard governing the performance of these systems. This is worrisome, considering that not all electronic stability control systems work as they should. In tests carried out by *Consumer Reports* on 2003 models, the stability-control system used in the Mitsubishi Montero was rated "unacceptable," BMW's X5 3.0i system provided poor emergency handling, and Acura's MDX and Subaru's Outback VDC stability systems left much to be desired.

Electric Winch

Ideal for hauling logs, boats, rocks, and stumps, and for getting you out of rough terrain. Serious off-roaders will find that an electric winch that can pull 675–1,350 kg (1,500–3,000 lb.) is a worthwhile $200–$350 investment.

Emergency Bladder Assistant (Tennis Ball Canister)

A tennis ball canister is a $4 device that's ideal for seniors or anyone needing to "go" in a hurry. The contents can be used for tennis, and the canister can be carried between the front seats or stored in the console without attracting attention.

Engines

Choose the most powerful 6- or 8-cylinder engine available if you're going to be doing a lot of highway driving, if you plan to carry a full passenger load and luggage on a regular basis, or if you intend to load up the vehicle with convenience features like air conditioning. Keep in mind that multipurpose vehicles with larger engines are easier to resell and retain their value the longest. For example, Honda's '96 Odyssey minivan was a sales dud in spite of its bulletproof reliability, mainly because buyers didn't want a minivan with an underpowered 4-cylinder powerplant. Some people buy underpowered vehicles in the mistaken belief that increased fuel economy is a good trade-off for decreased engine performance. It isn't. That's why there's so much interest in peppy 4-cylinders hooked to 5-speed transmissions, or larger engines with a "cylinder deactivation" feature.

In fact, cylinder deactivation is one feature that appears more promising than most other fuel-saving add-ons. For example, *AutoWeek* magazine found the overweight Jeep Commander equipped with a Multiple Displacement System still managed a respectable 13.8 L/100 km (17 mpg) on the highway in tests published in its March 2006 edition.

Honda employs a similar method, which cuts fuel consumption by 20 percent on the 2005 and later Odyssey and the 2006 and 2007 Accord Hybrid. It runs on all six cylinders when accelerating and three cylinders when cruising. So far, there have been neither reliability nor performance complaints concerning this feature.

Engine and Transmission Cooling System (Heavy-Duty)

This relatively inexpensive option can extend the life of your transmission and engine by preventing overheating when heavy towing is required.

Extended Warranties

A waste of $1,500–$2,000 for vehicles rated Recommended in *Lemon-Aid* or for vehicles sold by automakers that have written "goodwill" warranties covering engine and transmission failures (Ford and GM). If you can get a great price for a vehicle rated Average or Above Average but you want protection from costly repair bills, patronize garages that offer lifetime warranties on parts listed in this guide as failure-prone, such as powertrains, exhaust systems, and brakes.

Buy an extended warranty only as a last resort, and make sure you know what it covers and for how long. Start with a $1,000 powertrain warranty if other mechanical components have a good reputation. Incidentally, auto industry insiders say the average markup on these warranties varies from 50 to 65 percent, which seems almost reasonable when you consider that appliance warranties are marked up from 40 to 80 percent.

Gas Tank (Extra Capacity)

If full-sized vans weren't such gas hogs, larger gas tanks wouldn't be necessary. Nevertheless, owners will appreciate the extra cruising range that a larger tank provides. Expect to spend about $250.

Keyless Entry (Remote)

This safety and convenience option saves you from fiddling with the key in a dark parking lot, or taking off a glove in cold weather to unlock or lock the vehicle. Try to get a keyless entry system combined with anti-theft measures such as an ignition kill switch or some other disabler. Incidentally, many automakers no longer make vehicles with an outside key lock on the passenger side.

Paint Colour

Choosing a popular colour can make your vehicle easier to sell at a good price. DesRosiers automotive consultants say that blue is the preferred colour overall, but green and silver are also popular with Canadians. Manheim auctioneers say that green-coloured vehicles brought in 97.9 percent of the average auction price, while silver ones sold at a premium 105.5 percent. Remember that certain paint colours require particular care:

Black (and other dark colours): These paints are most susceptible to sun damage because of their heavy absorption of ultraviolet rays.

Pearl-toned colours: These paints are the most difficult to work with. If the paint needs to be retouched, it must be matched to look right from both the front- and side-angle views.

Red: This paint also shows sun damage, so keep your car in a garage or shady spot whenever possible.

White: Although grime looks terrible on a white car, white is the easiest colour to care for.

Power-Assisted Doors, Mirrors, Windows, and Seats

Merely a convenience feature with cars, power-assisted windows and doors are a necessity with minivans—crawling across the front seat a few times to roll up the passenger-side window or to lock the doors will quickly convince you of their value. Power mirrors and power seats with memory are convenient on vehicles that have a number of drivers. Automatic window and seat controls currently have few reliability problems, and they're fairly inexpensive to install, troubleshoot, and repair. As a safety precaution, make sure the window control has to be lifted. This will ensure no child is strangled from pressing against the switch. Power-sliding doors found on minivans are even more of a danger. They are failure-prone on all makes and shouldn't be purchased by families with children.

Roll Bars

Roll bars protect sport-utility occupants from rollovers. This is an essential safety item because these vehicles have a nasty habit of overturning without warning. A good roll bar and cage kit sells for about $350.

Running Boards

Throughout this guide, I recommend that you buy optional running boards. Far from returning you to '50s styling, running boards are practically essential for climbing into most full-sized vans, sport-utilities, and pickups. They can be purchased from independent suppliers for $65–$200, which is much less than the $250–$700 charged by the automakers.

Side Airbags

A worthwhile feature if you are the right size and properly seated, side airbags are presently overpriced and aren't very effective unless both the head and upper torso are protected. Side airbags are often featured as a $700 add-on to the sticker price, but you would be wise to bargain aggressively.

Skid Plates

A steel skid plate protects a sport-utility or pickup from rocks and other obstacles when off-roading. It should be at least a quarter-inch thick and cover the rear differential and oil pan. Some sport-utilities and pickups have a low-slung front gear housing that is easily damaged and pushes large amounts of mud and debris up into the front end, raising it to the point that front-end traction is lost.

Stow 'n Go Seating

Pioneered by Chrysler in its minivans, Stow 'n Go seating allows the second- and third-row seats to be folded into, not onto, the floor. Folding the seats is a one-handed operation, and the head restraints don't need to be removed. Pop the spring-loaded seats back up, and there's an in-floor storage bin under each seat. There's one caveat: These seats sacrifice comfort for versatility. But check them out anyway.

Suspension (Heavy-Duty)

Always a good idea, this inexpensive option pays for itself. It provides better handling, makes the ride more comfortable (though a bit on the firm side), and extends shock life for an extra year or two.

Tires

There are three rules to remember when purchasing tires. First, neither brand nor price is a reliable gauge of performance, quality, or durability. Second, choosing a tire recommended by the automaker may not be in your best interest, since traction and long tread life are often sacrificed for a softer ride and maximum EPA mileage ratings. And third, don't buy any new tire that's older than two years, since the rubber compound may have deteriorated because of poor handling and improper storage (if they've been stored near electrical motors). You can check the date of manufacture on the side wall of the tire.

Two types of tires are generally available: all-season and performance. "Touring" is just a fancier name for all-season tires. All-season radial tires cost from $90 to $150 per tire. They're a compromise, since according to Transport Canada, they won't get you through winter with the same margin of safety as snow tires will, and they don't provide the same durability on dry surfaces as regular summer tires.

In areas with low to moderate snowfall, however, these tires are adequate as long as they're not pushed beyond their limits.

Mud or snow tires provide the best traction on snowy surfaces, but traction on wet roads is actually decreased. Treadwear is also accelerated by the use of softer rubber compounds. Beware of using wide tires for winter driving; 70-series or wider give poor traction and tend to float over snow.

Spare tires

Be wary of space-saver spare tires. They often can't match the promised mileage, and they seriously degrade steering control. Furthermore, they are usually stored in spaces inside the trunk that won't hold a normal-sized tire. The location of the stored spare can also have safety implications. Watch out for spares stowed under the chassis or mounted on the rear hatch on some sport-utilities. Frequently, the attaching cables and bolts rust out or freeze, so the spare falls off or becomes next to impossible to use when you need it.

Self-sealing and run-flat tires

Today there are two technologies available to help maintain vehicle mobility when a tire is punctured: self-sealing and self-supporting/run-flat tires.

Self-sealing: Ideal if you drive long distances. Punctures from nails, bolts, or screws up to 4.8 mm ($3/_{16}$) of an inch in diameter are fixed instantly and permanently with a sealant. A low air-pressure warning system isn't required. Expert testers say a punctured self-sealing tire can maintain air pressure for up to 200 km—even in freezing conditions. The Uniroyal Tiger Paw NailGard ($85–$140, depending on the size) is the overall winner in a side-by-side test conducted by The Tire Rack (*www.tirerack.com*).

Self-supporting/run-flat: Priced from $175 to $350 per tire, 25–50 percent more than the price of comparable premium tires, Goodyear's Extended Mobility Tire (EMT) run-flat tires were first offered as an option on the 1994 Chevrolet Corvette and then became standard on the 1997 model. These tires reinforce the side wall so it can carry the weight of the car for 90 km, or about an hour's driving time, even after all air pressure has been lost. You won't feel the tire go flat; you must depend upon a $250–$300 optional tire-pressure monitor to warn you before the side wall collapses and you begin riding on your rim. Also, not all vehicles can adapt to run-flat tires; you may need to upgrade your rims. Experts say run-flats will give your car a harder ride, and you'll likely notice more interior tire and road noise. The car might also track differently. The 2004 Sienna's standard Dunlop run-flat tires have a terrible reputation for premature wear. At 25,000 km, one owner complained that her Sienna needed a new set at $200 each. You can expect a backlog of over a month to get a replacement, and Toyota doesn't include any type of spare. Goodyear EMT and Pirelli PZero tires have been on the market for some time now, and they seem to perform adequately. Don't make a final choice before talking with an auto manufacturer rep about what's recommended and how your warranty will be affected.

Which tires are best?

There is no independent Canadian agency that evaluates tire performance and durability. However, U.S.-based NHTSA rates treadwear, traction, and resistance to sustained high temperatures, etches the ratings onto the side walls of all tires sold in the States and Canada, and regularly posts its findings on the Internet (*www.nhtsa.dot.gov*). The treadwear grade is fixed at a base 100 points, and the tire's wear rate is measured after the tire is driven through a course that approximates most driving conditions. A tire rated 300 will last three times as long as one rated 100, for example.

I've come up with the following tire ratings after researching government tests and comments from consumers and industry insiders. Remember, some of the brand names may be changed from year to year for marketing reasons. Simply ask any tire specialist for the updated name of tires that are listed in this section. On the Internet, check out *www.tirerack.com/tires/surveyresults/index.jsp*.

Dunlop D65 Touring and SP20 AS: Treadwear rated 520. These tires are the bargain of the group. They provide excellent wet and dry cornering and good steering response.

Goodrich Control TA M65: Treadwear rated 360. This tire excels at snowbelt performance.

Goodyear Aquatred #3: Treadwear rated 340. This tire is a bit noisy, and its higher rolling resistance cuts fuel economy. Still, it's an exceptional performer on wet roads, and it works especially well on front-drive cars where the weight is carried over the front tires. Average performance on dry pavement.

Goodyear Regatta #2: Treadwear rated 460. This tire does everything well, including keeping tire noise to a minimum.

Michelin MX4: Treadwear rated 320. This tire gives a smoother ride and a sharper steering response than the Goodyear Aquatred. The MX1 is also an excellent winter performer.

Pirelli P300 and P400: Treadwear rated 460 and 420, respectively. These are two of the best all-around, all-season tires.

Yokohama TC320: Treadwear rated 300. This is a Goodyear Aquatred knock-off that performs almost as well for half the price.

Other good tire choices are as follows: Dayton Timberline A/T, General XP, Goodrich Touring T/A HR4, Goodyear Eagle LS, Kelly Navigator Platinum TE,

Pirelli P3000, and Scorpion A/T. And here are some good winter tires: Futura Euro-Metric, Goodyear Ultra Grip Ice, Michelin Arctic Alpin, and Pirelli Winter Ice Assimmetrico.

The following tires aren't recommended: Bridgestone Potenza RE 92; Continental truck tires; Cooper Lifeline Classic II; all Firestone makes; Goodrich Advantage; General Hydro 2000 and Ameri G4S; Goodyear Eagle GA, Wrangler, and WeatherHandler; Michelin XGT H4, XW4, and MXV4 Green X; Pirelli P4000 Super Touring (not to be confused with the recommended P400); and Toyo 800 Plus.

Trailer-Towing Equipment

Just because you need a vehicle with towing capability doesn't mean that you have to spend big bucks buying more power than you really need or tacking on a lot of fuel-wasting accessories. The first things you should determine before choosing a towing option are whether you need a pickup or a small van to do the job and whether your tires will handle the extra burden. For most towing needs (up to 900 kg/2,000 lb.), a passenger car, small pickup, or minivan will work just as well as a full-sized pickup or van (and will cost much less). If you're pulling a trailer that weighs more than 900 kg, most passenger cars won't handle the load unless they've been specially outfitted according to the automaker's specifications. Pulling a heavier trailer (up to 1,800 kg/4,000 lb.) will likely require a compact passenger van. You may, however, have to keep your speed at 72.4 km/h (45 mph) or less, as Toyota suggests with the 2004 Sienna.

Automakers reserve the right to change limits whenever they feel like it, so make any sales promise an integral part of your contract (see info on false advertising in Part Three, "Key Court Decisions"). A good rule of thumb is to reduce the promised tow rating by 20 percent. In assessing towing weight, factor in the cargo, passengers, and equipment of both the trailer and the tow vehicle. Keep in mind that five people with luggage add about 450 kg (1,000 lb.) to the load, and a full 227-litre (50-gallon) water tank adds another 225 kg (500 lb.). The manufacturer's gross vehicle weight rating (GVWR) takes into account the anticipated average cargo and supplies that your vehicle is likely to carry.

Automatic transmissions are fine for towing trailers, although there's a slight fuel penalty. Manual transmissions tend to have greater clutch wear caused by towing than do automatic transmissions. Both transmission choices are equally acceptable. Remember, the best compromise is to shift the automatic manually for maximum performance going uphill and to maintain control while not overheating the brakes when descending mountains.

Unibody vehicles (those without a separate frame) can handle most trailering jobs as long as their limits aren't exceeded. Front-drives aren't the best choice for pulling heavy loads in excess of 900 kg, since they lose some steering control and traction because of all the weight concentrated in the rear.

Whatever vehicle you choose, keep in mind that the trailer hitch is crucial. It must have a tongue capacity of at least 10 percent of the trailer's weight; otherwise, it may be unsafe to use. Hitches are chosen according to the type of tow vehicle and, to a lesser extent, the weight of the load.

Most hitches are factory-installed, even though independents can install them more cheaply. Expect to pay about $200 for a simple boat hitch and a minimum of $600 for a fifth-wheel version.

Equalizer bars and extra cooling systems for the radiator, transmission, engine oil, and steering are a prerequisite for towing anything heavier than 900 kg. Heavy-duty springs and brakes are a big help, too. Separate brakes for the trailer may be necessary to increase your vehicle's maximum towing capacity.

Transmission: Automatic, Manual, and CVT

Despite its many advantages, the manual transmission is an endangered species in North America, where manuals equip only 12 percent of all new vehicles (mostly econocars, sports cars, and budget trucks). European buyers opt for a manual transmission almost 90 percent of the time.

A transmission with four or more forward speeds is usually more fuel efficient than one with three forward speeds (hardly seen anymore), and manual transmissions are usually more efficient than automatics, although this isn't always the case.

Shoppers who want a Dodge truck with the highly recommended Cummins diesel engine but don't want to be stuck with Chrysler's infamous automatic transmission

---

GM SPECIAL POLICY ADJUSTMENT—EXTENDED TRANSMISSION WARRANTY COVERAGE FOR VARIABLE TRANSMISSION WITH INTELLIGENCE (VTI) TRANSMISSION

BULLETIN NO.: 04020   DATE: APRIL 21, 2004

2002–04 VUE Vehicles
Equipped with VTi (M75 and M16)
2003–04 ION Quad Coupe Vehicles
Equipped with VTi (M75)

CONDITION: Saturn has determined that 2002–04 VUE and 2003–04 ION Quad Coupe vehicles equipped with the VTi transmission may experience certain transmission concerns that might affect customer satisfaction, and may require repair or replacement.

SPECIAL POLICY ADJUSTMENT: This special policy bulletin has been issued to extend the warranty on the VTi transmission assembly for a period of 5 years or 75,000 miles (120,000 km), whichever occurs first, from the date the vehicle was originally placed in service, regardless of ownership. The repairs will be made at no charge to the customer.

GM has put an optional Fiat-built CVT in its Saturn Ion and Vue since 2002 and has had to extend the warranty to deal with chronic drivetrain failures.

breakdowns should opt for the 6-speed transmission. Don't invest in the continuously variable transmission (CVT) used by Ford, GM, or Chrysler. GM is ditching theirs, and Ford's is just going into its fourth-year production. Sure, CVTs improve fuel economy by about 10 percent through the use of pulleys connected by a steel belt or chain to drive the wheels. But the system is relatively new in North America, where automakers like GM haven't quite worked the bugs out. CVT transmissions have been used for decades in the rest of the world by companies like Audi, Honda, and Nissan, with few problems.

Options for Seniors

Self-Installed Devices

Advancing age brings about physical changes that can cause the loss of mobility, vision, and strength, making driving difficult and even painful. The following inexpensive devices make driving safer and more pleasant:

Swivel seat cushion

Get in and out of a car without performing acrobatics, especially if you suffer from limited mobility or hip pain. This padded seat is 38 cm in diameter and turns 360 degrees. Price: $24.99 (U.S.); Tel: 1-888-940-0605; Website: *www.dynamic-living.com.*

Handybar car aid

This support handle helps you exit a vehicle safely. An innovative bar inserts into the U-shaped striker plate on the door frame. It can be used on both the driver- and passenger-side doors, and supports up to 159 kg (350 lb). Price: $34.99 (U.S.); Tel: 1-888-940-0605; Website: *www.dynamic-living.com.*

Sun Zapper glare shield

Hooks to your existing visor and includes a sliding shield to block out extra-bright glare spots. Price: $19.95 (U.S.); Tel: 1-800-953-0814; Website: *www.autosportcatalog.com.*

Panoramic rear-view mirror

A clip-on, 33 cm–wide, panoramic rear-view mirror that reduces blind spots. Useful for those with limited neck mobility. Price: $19.95 (U.S.); Tel: 1-888-484-9560; Website: *www.autobarn.com.*

Stick-on side safety mirror

This self-adhesive safety mirror (similar to a convex mirror) eliminates most blind spots in your side-view mirrors. Price: $2.99 (U.S.); Tel: 1-888-484-9560; Website: *www.autobarn.com.*

Easy Reach seat belt handle

For occupants with shoulder pain or limited mobility, this inexpensive seat belt extension offers an additional 15 cm to grab on to, without pain or difficulty. Price: $9.99 (U.S.); Tel: 1-888-940-0605; Website: *www.dynamic-living.com*.

Sheepskin seat belt cover

This soft covering protects the neck and shoulder from rubbing and chafing. Price: $14.95 (U.S.); Tel: 1-800-953-0814; Website: *www.autosportcatalog.com*.

Seat belt strap adjuster

This device will keep the seat belt shoulder strap off your neck, and positions it between your neck and shoulder. Price: $4.99 (U.S.) for two adjusters; Tel: 1-888-484-9560; Website: *www.autobarn.com*.

Tush-Cush

This seat cushion reduces back pressure and raises the upper body for a better view. Price: $39.95 (U.S.); Tel: 1-800-953-0814; Website: *www.autosportcatalog.com*.

Easy-to-grasp key holder

For drivers with limited hand mobility or arthritis, this little tool gives you more leverage for turning the ignition key. It holds two keys and folds up for easy carrying. Price: $7.99 (U.S.); Tel: 1-888-940-0605; Website: *www.dynamic-living.com*.

Custom Features

Many custom features that can help older drivers living with mobility loss can be added by dealers to new and older model cars, vans, trucks, and SUVs. For more information, ask a driver rehabilitation specialist at *www.aota.org/olderdriver* or 1-888-232-1184 to assess your needs and make the right recommendations.

Power turnout seat

This electric-powered seat (a manual seat is available) will rotate 90 degrees to help occupants enter or exit a vehicle. Price: $2,200+ (U.S.), including installation; Website: *www.bruno.com*.

Turny Orbit seat

This electric-powered seat rotates up to 90 degrees, lifts occupants in and out of the vehicle, and lowers them to the ground. It's useful for the severely disabled and can be installed in vans, SUVs, and pickups. Price: $6,700+ (U.S.), including installation; Website: *www.bruno.com*.

Curb-Sider VSL 6000 lift

This electric-powered lift will hoist wheelchairs and scooters up to 181 kg (400 lb.) into hatchback cars, minivans, SUVs, full-sized vans, and pickups. Price: $3,100+ (U.S.), including installation; Website: *www.bruno.com*.

VSL-900 Scooter-Lift II vehicle lift

A cheaper electric-powered lift used only on minivans, the VSL will hoist wheel-chairs, power chairs, and scooters up to 102 kg (225 lb). Price: $3,200+ (U.S.), including installation; Website: *www.bruno.com*.

Although I'm not a fan of leather seats, they do make it easier for seniors to slide in and out of any vehicle. They're not recommended for transporting your pets, though: The ease of cleaning drool, barf, and other "gifts" is far outweighed by leather's high cost, vulnerability to paws and teeth, tendency to hold animal smells, and slipperiness, making it difficult for a harnessed animal to gain traction.

Buckle Pup

The American Kennel Club says that 52 percent of dog owners choose their vehicle according to how safely and conveniently it will transport their animal. These owners know that a 27 kg (60 lb.) animal weighs about 1,225 kg (2,700 lb.) on impact in a collision at 56 km/h (35 mph).

The ideal animal transporter will prevent your pet from becoming a deadly projectile in the event of a collision. This means there should be a roomy cargo hold that will accommodate a protective cage, safety-approved tethers, fold-down seats, and easy access. Where possible, *Lemon-Aid* notes in its ratings which vehicles are recommended by independent sources as being the best for carrying animals.

DogCars.com is a website run by animal lovers who test-drive vehicles for pet-friendliness and ask questions like, How well does a car hold dogs and their gear? How easy it is to get crates into the back or otherwise restrain a dog for safety? Can they get air in the back? Do the seats fold flat? Is the interior easy to clean? And is the vehicle economical to own and operate?

Its highest-rated vehicles: Dodge Grand Caravan and Nitro; Jeep Compass; Honda CR-V, Element, Odyssey, and Fit Sport (for smaller animals); Hyundai Entourage; Kia Sedona; Nissan Xterra; Range Rover Sport; Subaru Forester; Suzuki Forenza Wagon; Toyota RAV4; and Volvo XC90. Volvo is singled out for being particularly pet-minded with its net partitions; Kevlar restraints and fold-down metal safety gates; pet-friendly cargo holds; removable ventilation panels; optional cargo-area cage structure, which can be purchased as an accessory and installed in its XC-70 wagon or XC-90 SUV; and aftermarket mats that protect the vehicle's interior from hair, slobber, urine, and other unwanted pet "by-products."

Among the above-mentioned vehicles, only the Chrysler Nitro, Jeep Compass, and Range Rover Sport models are unfavourably rated by *Lemon-Aid* for reliability and performance.

Safety Tips for Fido and Felix

When driving, always protect your animal companion with a pet safety belt or car seat. Most are more effective than a crate and cost less. Apart from the obvious danger of injury, there have been reports of unrestrained dogs that have been strangled by automatic car windows or decapitated in low-speed collisions, have attacked rescuers, or have become dazed and run into traffic after an accident. Some things to remember about transporting your pet:

- Securing an animal with a regular seat belt is a bad idea because an animal's anatomy precludes a safe and comfortable fit. Instead, buy a harness made just for dogs or cats. Choose a one-piece harness with wide, padded straps that can be attached to your car's seat belt or some other sturdy anchor point. Note that seat belts can be awkward or uncomfortable for tall, skinny dogs.
- Car seats keep small pets secure while allowing them to see what's going on. Most pet car seats are made for animals up to 11–14 kg (25–30 lb.).
- Whether you restrain your pet with a seat belt or a car seat, it's safest in the middle of the back seat. Front and side airbags deploy at 225 km/h (140 mph) and, as with small children, airbags can be lethal for pets. Also, because of the short distance between the animal's nose and the windshield, the chances of your pet hitting the windshield are very good.
- If your dog or cat rides in a crate, secure it with a tie-down or run a seat belt through the handle on top. This keeps it from being tossed around in the event of an accident. Keep in mind, though, that neither dogs nor passengers are safe when you carry an animal in a crate. A crash test done by Allianz Insurance

The Roadie, by Ruff Rider (*www.ruffrider.com*), is one of the strongest, most convenient harnesses on the market. It's been independently tested to human seat belt standard, and sells for $25 (U.S.).

The Pet Voyage Car Seat, for animals weighing up to 8 kg (18 lb.), has a five-star rating from *DogCars.com* and costs $21 (U.S.).

Company in Germany showed debris flying freely in the test car after the seat-belt-secured dog crate exploded on impact. The pet test dummy hit the inside of the crate with such extreme force that the crate opened and the dummy flew out of the car.

Ultimately, a safety harness (either alone or as part of a car seat) prevents a pet from flying through the air and possibly hitting its head on the side of a crate during a collision. It also allows the animal to see out the window. That said, a crate does protect your pet from flying objects in some accidents, prevents the animal from flying about in low-speed collisions, keeps pet droppings in an easy-to-clean area, and has a calming effect on most pets.

Unnecessary Options

Anti-Lock Brakes (ABS)

ABS is a safety feature that's fine in theory but impractical under actual driving conditions. The system maintains directional stability by preventing the wheels from locking up. This will *not* reduce the stopping distance, however. In practice, ABS makes drivers overconfident. Many still pump the brakes and render them ineffective. Total brake failure is common, and repairs are frequent, complicated, and expensive to perform.

All-Wheel Drive (AWD)

Mark Bilek, editorial director of Consumer Guide's automotive section (*auto. consumerguide.com/index.cfm*), is a critic of AWD. He says AWD systems generally encourage drivers to go faster than they should in adverse conditions, which creates trouble stopping in emergencies. Automakers use AWD as "a marketing ploy to make more money," Bilek contends.

Cruise Control

Automakers provide this $250–$300 option, which is mainly a convenience feature, for motorists who use their vehicles for long periods of high-speed driving. The constant rate of speed saves some fuel and lessens driver fatigue during long trips. Still, the system is particularly failure-prone and expensive to repair, can lead to driver inattention, and can make the vehicle hard to control on icy roadways. Malfunctioning cruise-control units are also one of the major causes of sudden acceleration incidents. At other times, cruise control can be very distracting, especially to inexperienced drivers who are unaccustomed to sudden speed fluctuations.

Adaptive cruise control is the latest evolution of this feature. It senses a vehicle ahead of you and then automatically downshifts, brakes, or cuts your vehicle's speed. Unfortunately, this commonly occurs when passing another car or when a car passes you, and it can make for a harrowing experience. Mercedes was the first out with the feature in 2000, followed by BMW in 2002. The 2006 BMW 5 Series sold it for $2,500, Cadillac's DTS cost $1,200 more with the device, and the 2008 Toyota Avalon XLS tacks on $700 for the option.

Electronic Instrument Readout

If you've ever had trouble reading a digital watch face or resetting your VCR, you'll get more of the same from this electronic gizmo. Gauges are presented in a series of moving digital patterns that are confusing, distracting, and unreadable in direct sunlight. A trip computer and vehicle monitor that determine fuel use and how many kilometres until the tank is empty, indicate average speed, and signal component failures often accompany the electronic instrument readout system. Figures are frequently incorrect or slow to catch up.

Foglights

A pain in the eyes for other drivers, foglights aren't necessary for most drivers who have well-aimed original-equipment headlights on their vehicles.

Gas-Saving Gadgets and Fuel Additives

The accessory market has been flooded with hundreds of atomizers, magnets, and additives that purport to make vehicles less fuel-thirsty. However, tests on over 100 gadgets and fuel or crankcase additives carried out by the U.S. Environmental Protection Agency have found that only a handful produce an increase in fuel economy, and the increase is tiny. These gadgets include cylinder deactivation systems, warning devices that tell the driver to ease up on the throttle or shift to a more fuel-frugal gear, hardware that reduces the engine power needed for belt-driven accessories, and spoilers that channel airflow under the car. The use of any of these products is a quick way to lose warranty coverage and fail provincial emissions tests.

GPS Navigation Systems (Portable)

This $1,500–$2,000 navigation aid links a GPS satellite unit to the vehicle's cellular phone and electronics. For a monthly fee, the unit connects drivers to live operators who will help them with driving directions, give repair or emergency assistance, or relay messages. If the airbag deploys or the car is stolen, satellite-transmitted signals are automatically sent from the vehicle to operators who will notify the proper authorities of the vehicle's location.

Many of the systems' functions can be performed by a cellular telephone, and the navigation screens may be obtrusive, distracting, washed out in sunlight, and hard to calibrate. A portable GPS unit, such as the $300 (U.S.) Garmin Street Pilot c330 or the $250 (U.S.) Magellan Roadmate 2000, is easier to use and more reasonably priced.

High-Intensity Headlights

These headlights are much brighter than standard headlights, and they cast a blue hue. Granted, they provide additional illumination of the roadway, but they are also annoying to oncoming drivers, who will flash their lights at you, thinking your high beams are on. These lights are easily stolen and expensive to replace.

ID Etching

This $150–$200 option is a scam. The government doesn't require it, and thieves and joyriders aren't deterred by the etchings. If you want to etch your windows for your own peace of mind, several private companies will sell you a $15–$30 kit that does an excellent job (try *www.autoetch.net*), or you can wait for your municipality or local police agency to conduct one of their periodic free VIN ID etching sessions in your area.

Paint and Fabric Protectors

Selling for $200–$300, these "sealants" add nothing to a vehicle's resale value. Although paint lustre may be temporarily heightened, this treatment is less effective and more costly than regular waxing, and it may also invalidate the manufacturer's guarantee at a time when the automaker will look for any pretext to deny your paint claim.

Auto fabric protection products are nothing more than variations of Scotchgard, which can be bought in aerosol cans for a few dollars—a much better deal than the $50–$75 charged by dealers.

Power-Assisted Minivan Sliding Doors

Not a good idea if you have children. These doors have a high failure rate, opening or closing for no apparent reason and injuring occupants caught between the door and post.

Reverse-Warning System

Selling for about $500 as part of an option package, this safety feature warns the driver of any objects in the rear when backing up. Although a sound idea in theory, in practice the device often fails to go off or sounds an alarm for no reason. Drivers eventually either disconnect or ignore it.

Rollover Detection System

This feature makes use of sensors to determine if the vehicle has leaned beyond a safe angle. If so, the side airbags are automatically deployed and then remain inflated to make sure occupants aren't injured or ejected in a rollover accident.

This is a totally new system that has not been proven. It could have disastrous consequences if the sensor malfunctions, as has been the case with front- and side-airbag sensors over the past decade.

Rooftop Carrier

Although this inexpensive option provides additional baggage space and may allow you to meet all your driving needs with a smaller vehicle, a loaded roof rack can increase fuel consumption by as much as 5 percent. An empty rack cuts fuel economy by about 1 percent.

Rustproofing

Rustproofing is no longer necessary since automakers have extended their own rust warranties. In fact, you have a greater chance of seeing your rustproofer go belly up than having your untreated vehicle ravaged by premature rusting. Even if the rustproofer stays in business, you're likely to get a song and dance about why the warranty won't cover so-called internal rusting, or why repairs will be delayed until the sheet metal is actually rusted through.

Be wary of electronic rustproofing. Selling for $425 to $665, these electrical devices claim to inhibit vehicle corrosion by sending out a pulse current to the grounded body panels, protecting areas that conventional rust-inhibiting products can't reach. There is much debate as to whether these devices are worth the cost, or if they work at all.

If you live in an area where roads are heavily salted in winter or in a coastal region, have your vehicle washed every few weeks and undercoated annually, paying particular attention to rocker panels (door bottoms) and wheelwells. Also, don't use a heated garage in winter; Canadian studies show that a heated garage will accelerate the damage caused by corrosion.

Sunroof

Unless you live in a temperate region, the advantages of a sunroof are far outweighed by the disadvantages. You're not going to get better ventilation than a good AC system would provide, and a sunroof may grace your environment with painful booming wind noises, rattles, water leaks, and road dust accumulation. A sunroof increases gas consumption, reduces night vision because overhead highway lights shine through the roof opening, and can lose you several inches of headroom.

Tinted Glass

On the one hand, tinting jeopardizes your safety by reducing your night vision. On the other hand, it does keep the interior cool in hot weather, reduce glare, and hide the car's contents from prying eyes. Factory applications are worth the extra cost, since cheaper aftermarket products (costing about $100) distort visibility and peel away after a few years. Some tinting done in the United States can run afoul of provincial highway codes that require more transparency.

Cutting the Price

Bidding by Fax or Email

Dealers are more receptive to non-traditional forms of selling since the advent of Internet-generated leads and negotiations. The process is quite easy: Simply fax or email an invitation for bids to area dealerships, asking them to give their bottom-line price for a specific make and model. Be clear that all final bids must be sent within a week. When all the bids are received, the lowest bid is sent to the other dealers to give them a chance to beat that price. After a week of bidding, the lowest price gets your business.

Dozens of *Lemon-Aid* readers have told me how this approach has cut thousands of dollars from the advertised price and saved them from the degrading showroom song-and-dance routine between the buyer, sales agent, and sales manager ("he said, she said, the sales manager said").

A *Lemon-Aid* reader sent in the following suggestions for buying by fax:

> First, I'd like to thank you for writing the *Lemon-Aid* series of books, which I have used extensively in the fax-tendering purchase of my '99 Accord and '02 Elantra. I have written evidence from dealers that I saved a bare minimum of $700 on the Accord (but probably more) and a whopping $900 on the Elantra through the use of fax-tendering, over and above any deals possible through Internet-tendering and/or showroom bargaining.
>
> Based on my experience, I would suggest that in reference to the fax-tendering process, future *Lemon-Aid* editions emphasize:
>
> - Casting a wide geographical net, as long as you're willing to pick the car up there. I faxed up to 50 dealerships, which helped tremendously in increasing the number of serious bidders. One car was bought locally in Ottawa, the other in Mississauga.
> - Unless you don't care much about what car you end up with...be very specific about what you want. If you are looking at just one or two cars, which I recommend, specify trim level and all extended warranties and dealer-installed options in the fax letter. Otherwise, you'll end up with quotes comparing apples and oranges, and you won't get the best deal on options negotiated later. Also, specify that quotes should be signed—this helps out with errors in quoting.
> - Dealerships are sloppy—there is a 25–30 percent error rate in quotes. Search for errors and get corrections, and confirm any of the quotes in serious contention over the phone.

- Phone to personally thank anyone who submits a quote for their time. Salespeople can't help themselves, they'll ask how they ranked, and often want to then beat the best quote you've got. This is much more productive than faxing back the most competitive quote (I know, I've tried that too).

Another reader, in British Columbia, was successful with this approach:

> I purchased your 2005 edition *SUVs, Vans, and Trucks* earlier this year from Chapters. Thanks for all the information that helped me decide to purchase a new Honda Odyssey EX-L for a super price from a good dealer. After completing my research (and vacillating for a few weeks) I ended up issuing a faxed "request for quotation" (RFQ) from several dealerships. I can tell you that some of them were not happy and tried to tell me that Honda Canada was clamping down on this activity. In the end, one dealership did not respond and one "closer" salesperson called to attempt to get me in their dealership so he could "assess my needs." I told him that my needs were spelled out very specifically in my request but he refused to give me a price. In the end, I received five quotations by phone, fax, and email. I purchased my van in Chilliwack for about $2,200 off list. It turned out that the salesperson just started selling cars two months ago and was very appreciative of my business. The whole deal was completed in half an hour. I was in full control but treated every respondent fairly. I did not play dealers off one another and went with the lowest first offer.

On the following page is the fax bid request he sent to the dealers.

Figuring a Fair Price

What's the Dealer's Cut?

Most new-car salespeople are reluctant to give out information on the amount of profit figured into the cost of each new car, but a few years ago, *Automotive News* gave American dealer markups based on MSRP. I've reduced the percentages a bit to reflect what Canadian dealers now receive, and I've included negotiable freight, dealer pre-delivery inspection (PDI), and administrative fees—all of which you should bargain down.

DEALER MARKUP

DEALER MARKUP (AMERICAN VEHICLES)	DEALER MARKUP (JAPANESE VEHICLES)
Base minivans: 20+ percent	Base minivans: 24+ percent
High-end minivans: 22+ percent	High-end minivans: 15+ percent
Base pickups: 20+ percent	Base pickups: 15+ percent
High-end pickups: 23+ percent	High-end pickups: 17+ percent
Vans and sport-utility vehicles: 22+ percent	Sport-utility vehicles: 14+ percent
Fully equipped, top-of-the-line vans and SUVs: 24+ percent	Fully equipped, top-of-the-line vans and SUVs: 17+ percent

---

SAMPLE FAX BID REQUEST

WITHOUT PREJUDICE

Date: _____

Dear Sir or Madam,

I will be purchasing a new 2008 Toyota Sienna or a new 2008 Honda Odyssey and am issuing a request for quotation to several dealerships. I am willing to travel to complete a deal.

The quoted price is to *include* my requested options as well as any applicable pre-delivery inspection, administration, documentation, freight, and delivery fees. I understand that tire tax, air conditioning tax, battery tax, and provincial and federal sales tax are extra and are not required on your quotation. The dealer may sell off the lot or order the vehicle.

Please complete the attached form and either fax or email it back to me before the deadline of *5:00pm, August 14, 2008*. All respondents will be contacted after the deadline to confirm their bid. The winning bidder will then be contacted soon after to complete the transaction.

I will accept an alternate price quotation for a demonstration model with similar options, but this is not a mandatory requirement.

Please direct any questions via email to me at _____ and I will respond promptly. Alternately you may call me at my office at _____.

Sincerely,
Joe Buyer

South Korean prices are the most flexible, while Japanese and European vehicle prices are much firmer. In addition to the dealer's markup, some vehicles may also have a 3 percent carryover allowance paid out in a dealer incentive program. Finance contracts may also tack on a 3 percent dealer commission.

Can You Get a Fair Price?

Yes, but you'll have to keep your wits about you and time your purchase well into the model year—usually in late winter or spring.

New-car negotiations aren't wrestling matches where you have to pin the sales agent's shoulders to the mat to win. If you feel that the overall price is fair, don't jeopardize the deal by refusing to budge. For example, if you've brought the contract price 10 percent or more below the MSRP and the dealer sticks you with a $200 "administrative fee" at the last moment, let it pass. You've saved money and the sales agent has saved face.

Of course, someone will always be around to tell you how he or she could have bought the vehicle for much less. Let that pass, too.

 To come up with a fair price, subtract one-half of the dealer markup from the MSRP and then trade the carryover and holdback allowance for a reduced delivery and transportation fee. Compute the options separately, and sell your trade-in privately. Buyers can more easily knock $2,000–$3,000 off a $20,000 base price if they choose a vehicle in stock, resist unnecessary options, and wait until January or February when sales are stagnant.

Beware of Financing and Insurance Traps

Once you and the dealer have settled on the vehicle's price, you aren't out of the woods yet. You'll be handed over to a financing and insurance (F&I) specialist, whose main goal is to convince you to buy additional financing, loan insurance, paint and seatcover protectors, rustproofing, and extended warranties. These items will be presented on a computer screen as costing only "a little bit more each month."

Compare the dealer's insurance and financing charges with those from an independent agency that may offer better rates and better service. Often the dealer gets a kickback for selling insurance and financing, and guess who pays for it? Additionally, remember that if the financing rate looks too good to be true, you're probably paying too much for the vehicle. The F&I closer's hard-sell approach will take all your willpower and patience to resist, but when he or she gives up, your trials are over.

Add-on charges are the dealer's last chance to stick it to you before the contract is signed. Dealer pre-delivery inspection (PDI) and transportation charges, "documentation" fees, and extra handling costs are ways that the dealer gets extra profits for nothing. Dealer preparation is often a once-over-lightly affair, with a car seldom getting more than a wash job and a couple of dollars' worth of gas in the tank. It's paid for by the factory in most cases, and when it's not, it should cost no more than 2 percent of the car's selling price. Reasonable transportation charges are acceptable, although dealers who claim that the manufacturer requires the payment often inflate them.

"No Haggle" Pricing Means "Price-Fixing"

All dealers bargain. They hang out the "No dickering; one price only!" sign simply as a means to discourage customers from asking for a better deal. Like parking lots and restaurants that claim they won't be responsible for lost or stolen property, they're bluffing. Still, you'd be surprised by how many people believe that if it's posted, it's non-negotiable.

In June 2004, Toyota Canada abandoned its Access no-haggle price strategy sales system after settling out of court over a price-fixing probe undertaken by the federal Competition Bureau. Toyota has also been the target of class action lawsuits in Quebec and British Columbia.

Price Guidelines

When negotiating the price of a new vehicle, remember there are several price guidelines and dealers use the one that will make them the most profit on each transaction. Two of the more common prices quoted are the MSRP (what the automaker advertises as a fair price) and the dealer's invoice cost (which is supposed to indicate how much the dealer paid for the vehicle). Both price indicators leave considerable room for the dealer's profit margin, along with some extra padding in the form of inflated transportation and preparation charges. If you are presented with both figures, go with the MSRP, since it can be verified by calling the manufacturer. Any dealer can print up an invoice and swear to its veracity. If you want an invoice price from an independent source, contact Car Cost Canada at *carcostcanada.com* or 1-866-453-6995.

Buyers who live in rural areas and in western Canada are often faced with grossly inflated auto prices compared to those charged in major metropolitan areas. A good way to get a more competitive price without buying out of province is to buy a couple of out-of-town newspapers (the Saturday *Toronto Star* "Wheels" section is especially helpful) and demand that your dealer bring the selling price, preparation charges, and transportation fees into line with the prices advertised.

Another tactic is to take a copy of a local competitor's car ad to a competing dealer selling the same brand and ask for a better price. Chances are they've already lost a few sales due to the ad and will work a little harder to match the deal; if not, they're almost certain to reveal the tricks in the competitor's promotion to make the sale.

Dealer Incentives and Customer Rebates

Automobile incentives have been around ever since Henry Ford offered $40–$60 rebates on the Model T in 1914. However, rebates were first used as a sales incentive in Canada and the States during Super Bowl Sunday in 1975, just after Detroit automakers raised prices 10 percent and lost sales because of what would later be called "sticker shock." Backpedalling furiously to regain sales, automakers cut some prices immediately and added cash rebates of a few hundred dollars as an additional inducement. Sports broadcaster Joe Garagiola became the Chrysler rebate pitchman with his unforgettable tag line: "Buy a car. Get a check."

Sales incentives haven't changed much in the past 30 years. When vehicles are first introduced in the fall, they're generally overpriced; early in the new year, they'll sell for about 30 percent less. In the summer, many models will sell for almost half their original retail price through a combination of dealer sales incentives (manufacturer-to-dealer), cash rebates (manufacturer-to-customer), zero percent interest financing (manufacturer-to-finance company-to-customer), and discounted prices (dealer-to-customer).

The enormity of these discounts came to light a few years back when Detroit's Big Three engaged in cut-throat discounting in late winter and then followed up with even more generous "employee discounts for all" during the summer.

In most cases, the manufacturer's rebate is straightforward and mailed directly to the buyer from the automaker. There are other rebate programs that require a financial investment on the dealer's part, however, and these shared programs tempt dealers to offset losses by inflating the selling price or pocketing the manufacturer's rebate. Therefore, when the dealer participates in the rebate program, demand that the rebate be deducted from the MSRP and not from some inflated invoice price concocted by the dealer.

Sometimes automakers will suddenly decide that a rebate no longer applies to a specific model, even though their ads continue to include it. When this happens, take all brochures and advertisements showing your eligibility for the rebate plan to provincial consumer protection officials. They can use false advertising statutes to force automakers to give rebates to every purchaser who was unjustly denied one.

If you are buying a heavily discounted vehicle, be wary of "option packaging" by dealers who push unwanted protection packages (rustproofing, paint sealants, and upholstery finishes) or who levy excessive charges for preparation, filing fees, loan guarantee insurance, and credit life insurance.

Rebates and Quality

Forget the old adage "you get what you pay for." Many reliable, top-performing vehicles come with rebates—they just aren't as generous as what you'll find with more mediocre choices. For example, rarely will Toyota and Honda offer more than $1,000 rebates, whereas Chrysler, Ford, and GM routinely hand out $3,000 discounts and other sales incentives. To come out ahead, you have to first choose a few quality vehicles rated Recommended by *Lemon-Aid* and then shop for sales incentives.

Customer and dealer incentives are frequently given out to stimulate sales of year-old models that are unpopular, scheduled to be redesigned, or headed for the axe. By choosing carefully which rebated model you buy, it's easy to realize important savings with little risk. For example, GM's $3,000–$5,000 incentives are good deals when applied to its reasonably reliable large SUVs and rear-drive vans, but they're not worth it when applied to the company's glitch-prone front-drive minivans. Similar rebates applied to Ford's F-series pickups and Freestar minivan aren't sufficient to offset the greater risk of factory-related defects afflicting these failure-prone models. Chrysler rebates can be a good deal when applied to minivans but not advisable as a reason to buy the company's less reliable SUVs.

Inflated or Deflated Prices

Generally, vehicles are priced according to what the market will bear and then are discounted a few months later as the competition heats up (Chrysler, Ford, and GM minivans are prime examples). A vehicle's stylishness, scarcity, or general popularity can inflate its value considerably. For example, Chrysler's four-door Jeep Wrangler has a prevailing market value higher than its suggested selling price, mainly because it's in a hot market niche and in short supply. Once sales slow down later in the new year, these vehicles usually sell at the normally discounted rate. VW's New Beetle and Chrysler's PT Cruiser are two other examples that come to mind. With vehicles that have an inflated value, wait two years for their popularity to subside or purchase the previous year's version. If your choice has a deflated market value (like overly maligned South Korean models), find out why it's so unpopular and then decide if the savings are worth it. Vehicles that don't sell because of their weird styling are no problem, but vehicles with a history of poor quality control can cost big bucks.

 ## Leftovers

In the fall, at the beginning of each new model year, most dealers still have a few of last year's vehicles left. Some are new, and some are demonstrators with a few thousand kilometres on them. The factory gives the dealer a 3–5 percent rebate on late-season vehicles, and dealers will often pass on some of these savings to clients. But are these leftovers really bargains?

They might be, if you can amortize the first year's depreciation by keeping the vehicle for eight years. But if you're the kind of driver who trades every two or three years, you're likely to come out a loser by buying an end-of-the-season vehicle. The simple reason is that as far as trade-ins are concerned, a leftover is a used vehicle that has depreciated at least 20 percent. The savings the dealer gives you may not equal that first year's depreciation (a cost you'll incur without getting any of the first year's driving benefits). If the dealer's discounted price matches or exceeds the 20 percent depreciation, then you're getting a pretty good deal. But if the next year's model is only a bit more expensive, has been substantially improved, or is covered by a more extensive and comprehensive warranty, it could represent a better buy than a cheaper leftover.

Ask the dealer for all work orders relating to the vehicle, including the PDI checklist, and make sure that the odometer readings follow in sequential order. Remember as well that most demonstrators should have less than 5,000 km on the ticker and that the original warranty has been reduced from the day the vehicle was first put on the road. Have the dealer extend the warranty or lower the price accordingly—about $100 for each month of warranty that has expired. If the vehicle's file shows that it was registered to a leasing agency or any other third party, you're definitely buying a used vehicle disguised as a demo. You should walk away from the sale—you're dealing with a crook.

Cash versus Financing

Let's clear up one myth right away: Dealers won't treat you better if you pay cash, although many buyers think so (34 percent of Canadian new- and used-car buyers pay cash, says Chris Travell, vice-president of the Automotive Research Group of Maritz Research). Actually, barely 8 percent of *new*-car buyers pay cash. They want you to buy a fully loaded vehicle and finance the whole deal. Paying cash is not advantageous to the dealer, since kickbacks on finance contracts represent an important part of the F&I division's profits.

Those buyers may be making a big mistake. Financial planners say it can be smarter to borrow the money to purchase a new vehicle even if you can afford to pay cash, because if you use the vehicle for business, a portion of the interest may be tax-deductible. The cash that you free up can then be used to repay debts that aren't tax-deductible (mortgages or credit card debts, for example).

Rebates versus Low or Zero Percent Financing

If you are buying an expensive vehicle—like a luxury car or an SUV—and going for longer financing, the low-rate financing will be a better deal than the rebate. A zero percent loan will save you $80 per $1,000 financed over 24 months, or $120 per $1,000 financed over 36 months, compared with 7.5 percent financing. If you were financing a $30,000 car for two years, you'd multiply $80 × 30 and save about $2,400.

Low-financing programs have the following disadvantages:

* Buyers must have exceptionally good credit.
* Shorter financing periods mean higher payments.
* Cash rebates are excluded.
* Only fully equipped or slow-selling models are eligible.
* Buyers pay full retail price.

To get the best price, first negotiate the price of the vehicle without disclosing whether you are paying cash or financing the purchase (say you haven't yet decided). Once you have a fair price, you can then take advantage of the financing.

Getting a Loan

To borrow, you must be at least 18 years old (age of majority), have a steady income, prove that you have discretionary income sufficient to make the loan payments, and either be willing to guarantee the loan with additional collateral or have your parent or spouse as a co-signer.

Before applying for a loan, you should have established a good credit rating via a paid-off credit card and have a small savings account with your local bank, credit union, or trust company. Prepare a budget listing your assets and obligations. This will quickly show whether you can afford a car. Next, pre-arrange your loan with a phone call. This will protect you from much of the smoke-and-mirrors showroom shenanigans.

Incidentally, if you do get in over your head and require credit counselling, contact Credit Counselling Service (CCS), a non-profit organization located in many of Canada's major cities (*www.creditcanada.com*).

Hidden Loan Costs

Don't trust anyone. The APA's undercover shoppers have found that most deceptive deals involve major banking institutions rather than automaker-owned companies.

In your quest for an auto loan, remember that the Internet offers help for people who need a loan and want quick approval but don't want to face a banker. The Bank of Montreal (*www.bmo.com*) was the first Canadian bank to allow vehicle buyers to post a loan application on its website. Other banks, such as the Royal Bank (*www.rbc.com*), offer a similar service. Loans are available to any web surfer, including those who aren't current BMO or RBC customers.

 Be sure to call various financial institutions to find out the following:

- The annual percentage rate on the amount you want to borrow and the rate for the duration of your repayment period
- The minimum down payment that the institution requires
- Whether taxes and licence fees are considered part of the overall cost and, thus, are covered by part of the loan
- Whether lower rates are available for different loan periods, or for a larger down payment
- Whether discounts are available to depositors and, if so, how long you must be a depositor before qualifying

When comparing loans, consider the annual rate and calculate the total cost of the loan offer; that is, how much you'll pay above and beyond the total price of the vehicle.

Dealers can finance your purchase at interest rates that are competitive with the banks' because of the rebates they get from the manufacturers and some lending institutions. Some dealers, though, mislead their customers into thinking they can borrow money at as much as five percentage points below the prime rate. Actually, they're jacking up the retail price to more than make up for the lower interest charges. Sometimes, instead of boosting the price, dealers reduce the amount they pay for the trade-in. In either case, the savings are illusory.

When dealing with banks, keep in mind that the traditional 36-month loan has now been stretched to 48 or 60 months. Longer payment terms make each month's payment more affordable, but over the long run, they increase the cost of the loan considerably. Therefore, take as short a term as possible.

Be wary of lending institutions that charge a "processing" or "document" fee ranging from $25 to $100. Sometimes consumers will be charged an extra 1–2 percent of the loan up front in order to cover servicing. This is similar to lending institutions adding "points" to mortgages, except that with auto loans, it's totally unjustified. In fact, dealers in the States are the object of several state lawsuits and class actions for inflating loan charges.

Some banks will cut the interest rate if you're a member of an automobile owners' association or if loan payments are automatically deducted from your chequing account. This latter proposal may be costly, however, if the account charges exceed the interest-rate savings.

Most finance companies affiliated with automakers offer no-interest or low-interest loans many points below the prime rate. These loans are usually announced early in the new year or in the summer. Read the loan contract carefully because the low rate may be applicable only to hard-to-sell models or vehicles equipped with expensive options. And, the low rate may not cover the entire loan period. If vehicles recommended in this book are covered by low-interest loans, however, then the automaker-affiliated finance companies become a useful alternative to regular banking institutions.

Loan Protection

Credit insurance guarantees that the vehicle loan will be paid if the borrower becomes disabled or dies. There are three basic types of insurance that can be written into an installment contract: credit life, accident and health, and comprehensive. Most bank and credit union loans are already covered by some kind of loan insurance, but dealers sell the protection separately at an extra cost to the borrower. For this service, the dealer gets a hefty 20 percent commission. The additional cost to the purchaser can be significant. The federal 5 percent GST is applied to loan insurance, but PST may be exempted in some provinces.

Collecting on these types of policies isn't easy. There's no payment if your illness is caused by some condition that existed prior to your taking out the insurance. Nor will the policy cover situations like strikes, layoffs, or being fired. Generally, credit insurance is unnecessary if you're in good health, you have no dependants, and your job is secure.

Personal loans from financial institutions now offer lots of flexibility. Most offer financing (with a small down payment), fixed or variable interest rates, a choice of loan terms, and no penalties for prepayment. Precise conditions depend on your personal credit rating. Finally, credit unions can also underwrite new vehicle loans that combine a flexible payment schedule with low rates.

Leasing contracts are less flexible: There's a penalty for any prepayment, and rates aren't necessarily competitive.

Financing Scams

Financing was turned down

This scam usually begins after you have purchased the car and left your trade-in with the dealer. A few days later, you are told that your loan was rejected and that you now must put down a larger down payment and accept a higher monthly payment. Of course, your trade-in has already been sold.

Protect yourself from this rip-off by getting a signed agreement that stipulates the financing has been approved and that monthly payments can't be readjusted. Don't give up your trade-in until that agreement has been reached.

Dealer offers to pay off your existing lease or loan

The dealer will. And then the dealer will add what was paid to your new loan at a much higher interest rate. Early termination of your lease will also likely expose you to substantial penalty costs. How likely are you to be cheated when buying a new car? APA staffers posing as buyers visited 42 dealerships in four Canadian cities in early 2002. Almost half the dealers they visited (45 percent) flunked their test, and (hold onto your cowboy hats) auto buyers in western Canada were especially vulnerable to dishonest dealers.

In Vancouver and Edmonton, dealer ads either left out important information or vehicles in the ads weren't available or were selling at higher prices. Fees for paperwork and vehicle preparation were frequently excessive, with Chrysler dealerships in Vancouver and Toronto charging the most ($299–$632). In some cases, the dealers may have double-billed the buyer. In Toronto, pre-delivery charges of $343 and $89 were levied on top of Chrysler's $955 PDI/transport fee.

Chrysler and Ford dealerships performed the worst overall, Toyota and General Motors performed best, and Mazda and Hyundai dealers were mediocre (they charged extra for items other automakers include in the base price). APA found that Toyota dealers demonstrated a superior level of product knowledge, covered all the bases more consistently, and applied the least pressure to make a sale. But Toyota dealers in the regions with Access-fixed selling prices appeared to charge substantially more.

Negotiating the Contract

The Devil's in the Details

Watch what you sign, since any document that requires your signature is a contract. Don't sign anything unless all the details are clear to you and all the blanks have been filled in. Don't accept any verbal promises that you're merely putting the vehicle on hold. And when you are presented with a contract, remember it doesn't have to include all the clauses found in the dealer's pre-printed form. You and the sales representative can agree to strike some clauses and add others.

When the sales agent asks for a deposit, make sure that it's listed on the contract as a deposit and try to keep it as small as possible (a couple hundred dollars at the most). If you decide to back out of the deal on a vehicle taken from stock, let the seller have the deposit as an incentive to cancel the contract (believe me, it's cheaper than a lawyer and probably equal to the dealer's commission).

Scrutinize all references to the exact model (there is a heck of an upgrade from base to LX or Limited), prices, and delivery dates. Delivery can sometimes be delayed three to five months, and you'll have to pay all price increases announced during the interim (1–2 percent) unless you specify a delivery date in the contract that protects the price.

Make sure that the contract indicates that your new vehicle will be delivered to you with a full tank of gas. Once this was the buyer's responsibility, but now, with drivers spending over $30,000 for the average new vehicle, dealers usually throw in the tank of gas.

Clauses You Should Change

You can put things on a more equal footing by negotiating the inclusion of as many clauses as possible from the sample additional contract clauses found on page 106. To do this, write in a "Remarks" section on your contract and then add "See attached clauses, which form part of this agreement." Attach a photocopy of the "Additional Contract Clauses" page and then persuade the sales agent to initial as many of the clauses as possible. Although some clauses may be rejected, the inclusion of just a couple of them can have important legal ramifications later on if you want a full or partial refund.

"We Can't Do That"

Don't take the dealer's word that "we're not allowed to do that"—heard most often in reference to your reducing the PDI or transportation fee. Some dealers have been telling *Lemon-Aid* readers that they are "obligated" by the automaker to charge a set fee and could lose their franchise if they charge less. This is pure hogwash. No dealer has ever had their franchise licence revoked for cutting prices.

ADDITIONAL CONTRACT CLAUSES

1. **Original contract:** This is the ONLY contract; i.e., it cannot be changed, retyped, or rewritten, without the specific agreement of both parties.

2. **Financing:** This agreement is subject to the purchaser obtaining financing at _____% or less within _____ days of the date below.

3. **"In-service" date and mileage:** To be based on the closing day, not the day the contract was executed and will be submitted to the automaker for warranty and all other purposes. The dealership will have this date corrected by the automaker if it should become necessary.

4. **Delivery:** The vehicle is to be delivered by _____, failing which the contract is cancelled and the deposit will be refunded.

5. **Cancellation:**
   (a) The purchaser retains the right to cancel this agreement without penalty at any time before delivery of the vehicle by sending a notice in writing to the vendor.
   (b) Following delivery of the vehicle, the purchaser shall have two days to return the vehicle and cancel the agreement in writing, without penalty. After two days and before thirty-one days, the purchaser shall pay the dealer $25 a day as compensation for depreciation on the returned vehicle.
   (c) Cancellation of contract can be refused where the vehicle has been subjected to abuse, negligence or unauthorized modifications after delivery.
   (d) The purchaser is responsible for accident damage and traffic violations while in possession of the said vehicle.

6. **Protected price:** The vendor agrees not to alter the price of the new vehicle, the cost of preparation or the cost of shipping.

7. **Trade-in:** The vendor agrees that the value attributed to the vehicle offered in trade shall not be reduced, unless it has been significantly modified or has suffered from unreasonable and accelerated deterioration since the signing of the agreement.

8. **Courtesy car:**
   (a) In the event the new vehicle is not delivered on the agreed-upon date, the vendor agrees to supply the purchaser with a courtesy car at no cost. If no courtesy vehicle is available, the vendor agrees to reimburse the purchaser the cost of renting a vehicle.
   (b) If the vehicle is off the road for more than five days for warranty repairs, the purchaser is entitled to a free courtesy vehicle for the duration of the repair period. If no courtesy vehicle is available, the vendor agrees to reimburse the purchaser the cost of renting a vehicle of equivalent or lesser value.

9. **Work orders:** The purchaser will receive duly completed copies of all work orders pertaining to the vehicle, including warranty repairs and the pre-delivery inspection (PDI).

10. **Dealer stickers:** The vendor will not affix any dealer advertising, in any form, on the vehicle.

11. **Fuel:** Vehicle will be delivered with a free full tank of gas.

12. **Excess mileage:** New vehicle will not be acceptable and the contract will be void if the odometer has more than 50 km at delivery/closing.

13. **Tires:** Original equipment Firestone, Bridgestone, or Goodyear tires are not acceptable.

_____   _____   _____
Date   Vendor's Signature   Buyer's Signature

Furthermore, the automakers clearly state that they don't set a bottom price, since doing so would violate Canada's *Competition Act*—that's why you always see them putting disclaimers in their ads saying the dealer can charge less.

The Pre-Delivery Inspection (PDI)

The best way to ensure that the PDI (written as PDE in some regions) will be done is to write in the sales contract that you'll be given a copy of the completed PDI sheet when the vehicle is delivered to you. Then, with the PDI sheet in hand, verify some of the items that were to be checked. If any items appear to have been missed, refuse delivery of the vehicle. Once you get home, check out the vehicle more thoroughly and send a registered letter to the dealer if you discover any incomplete items from the PDI.

Selling Your Trade-In

When Is the Right Time?

It doesn't take a genius to figure out that the longer one keeps a vehicle, the less it costs to own—up to a point. The Hertz Corporation has estimated that a small car equipped with standard options, driven 16,000 km (10,000 mi.), and traded each year costs approximately 6 cents/km more to run than a comparable compact traded after five years. A small car kept for 10 years and driven 16,000 km per year would cost 6.75 cents/km less than a similar vehicle kept for five years and a whopping 12.75 cents/km less than a comparable vehicle traded in each year. That would amount to savings of $20,380 over a 10-year period.

If you're happy with your vehicle's styling and convenience features and it's safe and dependable, there is no reason to get rid of it. But when the cost of repairs becomes equal to or greater than the cost of payments for a new car, then you need to consider trading it in. Shortly after your vehicle's fifth birthday (or whenever you start to think about trading it in), ask a mechanic to look at it to give you some idea of what repairs, replacement parts, and maintenance work it will need in the coming year. Find out if dealer service bulletins show that it will need extensive repairs in the near future (see Appendix II for information on how to order bulletins from ALLDATA). If it's going to require expensive repairs, you should trade the vehicle right away; if expensive work isn't necessary, you may want to keep it. Auto owner associations provide a good yardstick. They estimate that the annual cost of repairs and preventive maintenance for the average vehicle ranges from $700 to $800. If your vehicle is five years old and you haven't spent anywhere near $3,500 in maintenance, it would pay to invest in your old vehicle and continue using it for another few years.

Consider whether your vehicle can still be serviced easily. If it's no longer on the market, the parts supply is likely to dry up and independent mechanics will be reluctant to repair it.

Don't trade for fuel economy alone. Most fuel-efficient vehicles, such as front-drives, offset the savings through higher repair costs. Also, the more fuel-efficient vehicles may not be as comfortable to drive because of their excessive engine noise, lightweight construction, stiff suspension, and torque steering.

Reassess your needs. Has your family grown to the point that you need a new vehicle? Are you driving less? Are you taking fewer long trips? Let your truck or van show its age and pocket the savings if its deteriorating condition doesn't pose a safety hazard and isn't too embarrassing. If you're in sales and are constantly on the road, it makes sense to trade every few years—in that case, the vehicle's appearance and reliability become a prime consideration, particularly since the increased depreciation costs are mostly tax deductible.

Getting the Most for Your Trade-In

Customers who are on guard against paying too much for a new vehicle often sell their trade-ins for too little. Before agreeing to any trade-in amount, check out Part Four to find the selling price for your vehicle.

Now that you've nailed down your trade-in's approximate value, here are some tips on selling it with a minimum of stress:

- Never sign a new vehicle sales contract unless your trade-in has been sold—you could end up with two vehicles.
- Negotiate the price from *retail* (dealer price) down to *wholesale* (private sales).
- If you haven't sold your trade-in after two weekends, you might be trying to sell it at the wrong time of year or have it priced too high.

Private Sales

If you must sell your vehicle and want to make the most out of the deal, consider selling it yourself and putting the profits toward your next purchase. You'll likely come out hundreds of dollars ahead—buyers will pay more for your vehicle because they won't have to pay the 6 percent GST on a private sale. The most important thing to remember is that there's a large market for used vehicles in good condition in the $4,000–$5,000 range. Although most people prefer buying from individuals rather than from used car lots, they may still be afraid that the vehicle is a lemon. By using the following suggestions, you should be able to sell your vehicle quite easily:

1. Know its value. Study dealers' newspaper ads and compare them with the prices listed in this book. Undercut the dealer price by $300–$800 and be ready to bargain down another 10 percent for a serious buyer. Remember, prices can fluctuate wildly depending on which models are trendy, so watch the want ads carefully.
2. Enlist the aid of the salesperson who's selling you your new car. Offer her a few hundred dollars if she finds you a buyer. The fact that one sale hinges

on the other, along with the prospect of making two commissions, may work wonders.

3. Post notices on bulletin boards at your office or local supermarkets and place a "For Sale" sign in the window of the vehicle itself. Place a newspaper ad only as a last resort.

4. Don't give your address right away to a potential buyer responding to your ad. Instead, ask for the telephone number where you may call that person back.

5. Be wary of selling to friends or family members. Anything short of perfection and you'll be eating Christmas dinner alone.

6. Don't touch the odometer. You may get a few hundred dollars more—and a criminal record.

7. Paint the vehicle. Some specialty shops charge only $300 and give a guarantee that's transferable to subsequent owners.

8. Make minor repairs. This includes a minor tune-up and patching up the exhaust. Again, if any repair warranty is transferable, use it as a selling point.

9. Clean the vehicle. Go to a reconditioning firm or spend the weekend scrubbing the interior and exterior. First impressions are important. Clean the chrome, polish the body, and peel off old bumper stickers. Remove butts from the ashtrays and clean out the glove compartment. Make sure all tools and spare parts have been taken out of the trunk. Don't remove the radio or speakers—the gaping holes will lower the vehicle's worth much more than the cost of radio or speakers. Replace missing or broken dash knobs and window cranks.

10. Change the tires. Recaps are good buys.

11. Let the buyer examine the vehicle. Insist that it be inspected at an independent garage, and then accompany the prospective buyer to the garage. This gives you protection if the buyer claims you misrepresented the vehicle.

12. Don't mislead the buyer. If the vehicle was in an accident, or some financing is still to be paid, admit it. Any misleading statements may be used later against you in court. It's also advisable to have someone witness the actual transaction in case of a future dispute.

Many owners sell their old cars to dealers because they want a deal that won't come back to haunt them.

13. Keep important documents handy. Show prospective buyers the sales contract, repair orders, owner's manual, and all other documents that show how the vehicle has been maintained. Authenticate your claims about fuel consumption.
14. Write an effective ad, if you need to use one.

Selling to Dealers

Selling to a dealer means that you're likely to get 20 percent less than if you sold your vehicle privately, unless the dealer agrees to participate in an accommodation sale. Most sellers will gladly pay some penalty to the dealer, however, for the peace of mind that comes with knowing that the eventual buyer won't lay a claim against them. This assumes that the dealer hasn't been cheated by the seller—if the vehicle is stolen, isn't paid for, has had its odometer spun back (or forward to a lower setting), or is seriously defective, the buyer or dealer can sue the original owner for fraud. Sell to a dealer who sells the same make. He or she will give you more because it's easier to sell your trade-in to customers who are interested only in that make of vehicle.

Drawing Up the Contract

The province of Alberta has prepared a useful bill of sale applicable throughout Canada that can be accessed at *governmentservices.gov.ab.ca/pdf/registries/reg3126. pdf.* Your bill of sale should identify the vehicle (including the serial number) and include its price, whether a warranty applies, and the nature of the examination made by the buyer. The buyer may ask you to put in a lower price than what was actually paid in order to reduce the sales tax. If you agree to this, don't be surprised when a Revenue Canada agent comes to your door. Although the purchaser is ultimately the responsible party, you're an accomplice in defrauding the government. Furthermore, if you turn to the courts for redress, your own conduct may be put on trial.

Summary: Buy Safe and Buy Smart

Purchasing a used vehicle and keeping it for at least five years saves you the most money. It takes about eight years to realize similar depreciation savings when buying new. Giving the biggest down payment you can afford, using zero percent financing programs, and piling up as many kilometres and years as possible on your trade-in are the best ways to save money with new vehicles. Remember that safety is another consideration that depends largely on the type of vehicle you choose.

Here's a list of safety features to look for:

1. High NHTSA and IIHS crashworthiness ratings for front, offset, and side collisions as well as low rollover potential; pay particular attention to the side rating if you are a senior driver
2. Electronic stability control (ESC)
3. Good-quality tires; be wary of "all-season" tires and Bridgestone/Firestone makes
4. Three-point belts with belt pretensioners and adjustable shoulder belt anchorages
5. Integrated child safety seats and seat anchors, safety door locks, and override window controls
6. Side airbags with head protection; a knee cushion for front occupants; unobtrusive, effective head restraints; and pedal extenders
7. A front driver's seat with plenty of rearward travel, a height adjustment, good all-around visibility, and a dash that doesn't reflect onto the windshield
8. An ergonomic interior with an efficient heating and ventilation system
9. Headlights that are adequate for night driving and don't blind oncoming traffic
10. Dash gauges that don't wash out in sunlight or produce windshield glare
11. Adjustable head restraints for all seating positions
12. Delaminated side-window glass
13. An easily accessed sound system and climate controls
14. Navigation systems that don't require a degree from MIT to calibrate
15. Manual sliding doors in vans (if children are transported)

And here's a list of tips for savvy vehicle buyers:

1. Buy the vehicle you need and can afford, not the one someone else wants you to buy or one loaded with options that you'll probably never use. Take your time. Price comparisons and test-drives may take a month, but you'll get a better vehicle and price in the long run.
2. Buy in winter or later in the new year to double-dip from dealer incentives and customer rebate or low-cost financing programs.
3. Sell your trade-in privately.
4. Arrange financing before buying your vehicle.
5. Test-drive your choice by renting it overnight or for several days.
6. Buy through the Internet or by fax, or use an auto broker if you're not confident in your own bargaining skills, you lack the time to haggle, or you want to avoid the "showroom shakedown."
7. Ask for at least a 10 percent discount off the MSRP, and cut PDI and freight charges by at least 50 percent. Insist on a specific delivery date written in the contract, as well as a protected price in case there's a price increase between the time the contract is signed and when the vehicle is delivered. Also ask for a free tank of gas.
8. Order a minimum of options and seek a 20–30 percent discount on the entire option list. Try not to let the total option cost exceed 15 percent of the vehicle's MSRP.

9. Avoid leasing. If you must lease, choose the shortest time possible, drive down the MSRP, and refuse to pay an "acquisition" or "disposal" fee.

10. Japanese vehicles made in North America, co-ventures with American automakers, and re-badged imports often cost less than imports and are just as reliable. However, some Asian and European imports may not be as reliable as you might imagine—early Kia Sportage and Mercedes' M-Class sport-utilities, for example. Get extra warranty protection from the automaker if you're buying a model that has a poorer-than-average repair history. Use auto club references to get honest, competent repairs at a reasonable price.

Part Two

BUYING USED:
BARGAINS AND PITFALLS

Airbag Fraud

[Air bags] have replaced stereo units as the No. 1 automotive theft target in Canada. Aside from the damage to cars and the cost of replacing air bags—together up to $4,000 each theft—there are serious risks involved for those who buy black-market units to replace those deployed in collisions because the delicate units may no longer function.

On one November night alone, a gang pillaged a Scarborough car dealership, wreaking $180,000 damage and stealing air bags from 45 cars.

With new air bags costing between $750 and $1,500, stolen air bags are selling like hot cakes on the street.

"You can get 20 or 30 in a night and at $100 to $150 each, that's $2,000 to $4,500," said Detective Sam Cosentino of the Toronto Organized Crime Enforcement Unit.

IAN HARVEY
TORONTO STAR, DECEMBER 17, 2005

Toronto automotive consultant Dennis DesRosiers estimates that a quarter of the light trucks operating in Canada will still be on the road after 20 years of use. Furthermore, despite the fact that the federal Goods and Services Tax (GST) favours private sales, dealers have become a major force in used-car sales in Canada: 15 years ago, dealers sold about a third of all used cars; now they sell 44 percent. Conversely, in 1993, half of used cars were sold privately by their owners; that portion has been reduced to 38 percent today.

And we are putting more mileage on vehicles before we replace them. The used-fleet mileage has almost doubled in the past 30 years. Back in the 1970s, the average car racked up 160,000 km before it was dropped off at the junkyard. In the 1990s, the average car reached 240,000 km before being "recycled." Now, new models are expected to see 300,000 km before they're discarded, and they aren't necessarily discarded because they've become unreliable.

In fact, one CAA ownership survey revealed that less than 10 percent of owners of cars five years or younger, and only 22 percent of owners of vehicles six to 10 years old, got rid of them because of reliability problems or high maintenance costs: 43 percent sold because the lease expired, 30 percent of owners said they just wanted a change, and 21 percent said the vehicle no longer met their requirements.

A Good Time to Buy Small and Used

Because new vehicles are selling for much less this year, used prices are tumbling, making this a great time to buy a used SUV, truck, or van. Fortunately, you won't find as much late-'70s to early-'90s junk out there as there once was. Modern vehicles are safer and loaded with extra convenience and performance features that first appeared a decade ago.

But dealers aren't giving anything away. Popular 2-year-old SUVs, trucks, and minivans are selling for two-thirds of their original price, and they aren't likely to depreciate by much more than half their original price over five years. Better bargains can be found with small minivans, like the Mazda5, and downsized SUVs, like the Hyundai Tucson and the Ford/Mazda Escape/Tribute. South Koreans are shaking up the minivan market with cheap, high-quality vans like the Entourage and Sedona, which are loaded with standard safety, performance, and convenience features that aren't found, or that cost extra, on competitors' vehicles. Rather than getting a used Jeep Grand Cherokee, Ford Expedition, or GM Suburban, SUV buyers are opting for 2-year-old Hyundais and Kias (older South Korean models aren't as reliable or as well equipped) or less-expensive off-lease vehicles like the Honda CR-V, Jeep Wrangler, Subaru Forester, and Toyota RAV4. Customers looking for trucks are attracted to smaller pickups like the Ford Ranger, Mazda B-series, Nissan Frontier, and Toyota Tacoma.

This trend plays right into most buyers' budgets because Canadians aren't large-car lovers. We are "small-minded" when choosing what we drive. Small SUVs, like the Subaru Forester, Honda CR-V, and Toyota RAV4, make up almost half of our market, but only a quarter of the sales south of the border. As far as minivans go, we believe that less is more and favour small imports over Detroit's truck-based rear-drives. Heck, we even go for the toy-like Mercedes-Benz Smart car.

Will Detroit Survive?

No. Greed, maladministration, dishonesty in giving warranty refunds, and a penchant for selling the deal rather than the product are the nails driven into the Detroit Big Three's coffins. That hasn't changed, and isn't likely to.

American automakers lost the knack for making quality machines over three decades ago. Suppliers of high-quality components were often rewarded with increased demands for price cuts and constantly changing parts specifications during production. Quality dropped, and owner loyalty shifted to Asian automakers. This has created a huge pool of used Chrysler, Ford, and GM products on the Canadian market that are dirt cheap but unsafe, unreliable, and expensive to troubleshoot and repair.

Chrysler

Chrysler has been the transmission-failure champion since 1991; before that, it was only a contender. The company continues to make a lot of low-quality vehicles, and its transferable 7-year/100,000 km warranty gives only buyers of 2002–04 models the protection they need when faced with Chrysler's traditional engine, transmission, and steering/suspension failures. Furthermore, there is no guarantee that the old warranty will be honoured by Chrysler's new owners. Nevertheless, the company's 2007–08 American-only lifetime powertrain warranty and ball joint Special Extended Warranty, applicable to the Dakota and Durango, are useful tools when arguing for repair refunds for all other models and years.

Ford

Used Fords are an even greater risk to your life and pocketbook than new models. Defects run the gamut, from collapsing tie-rod ends on 1997–2004 pickups to coil-spring breakage that sends 1995–98 Windstars careening out of control. And if your Ford SUV or pickup doesn't roll over after losing its tire tread, its windows may explode, or the truck may suddenly accelerate when driven or burn up when parked overnight, as these reports from the National Highway Transit Safety Authority database show (*www-odi.nhtsa.dot.gov/cars/problems/complaints*):

> My 2004 Explorer was parked in a driveway with its rear window towards [the] garage door. The back window of the car along with a piece of the actual door exploded off. The piece of the door flew up into the air and came crashing back down onto the car. There was glass everywhere. Had anyone been facing the car it could have caused some serious bodily injury. Or had the car been in motion anyone inside the car could have been hurt or anyone driving behind could have been hurt.

> •

> While driving my 2004 Explorer, it suddenly started accelerating uncontrollably. Driver applied the brakes and the pedal went to the floor. Vehicle continued to accelerate excessively. While making a right turn driver hit the curb and flipped four times landing upside down in a ditch. Driver and passenger sustained injuries, and were transported by an ambulance to a hospital. Vehicle was towed and totaled by the insurance company.

Ever since the fire-prone Pinto became known as Ford's "you light up my life" compact, the company has had a history of manufacturing vehicles that spontaneously ignite. Vehicles manufactured between 1992 and 2004 have been the most affected, resulting in six recalls—affecting 10.5 million cars, trucks, and SUVs—to fix a cruise-control switch that may overheat. The fires are particularly lethal because they can ignite even when the vehicle is shut down and parked for the night, as the following owner complaint confirms:

My 2002 Ford F150 burst into flames in my carport while I was sleeping. My daughter came home and woke me just in time to get out of the house before the entire house burned. I received the recall notice just a few days after the fire. The fire was witnessed to start in my truck. The truck was so severely burned that several investigators reported this was typical of what they were experiencing with Ford fires although Ford's investigators reported the cruise switch was properly functioning according to an X-ray of the part. How the part could be found is a mystery since the truck was so damaged. Ford is not taking responsibility for anything. We lost everything we owned.

The latest recall covers 16 brands of cars, sport-utility vehicles, and trucks from model years 1992 to 2004, including the following: Ford Ranger, Ford Crown Victoria, Mercury Grand Marquis, Lincoln Town Car, Lincoln Mark VIII, Ford Taurus SHO, Mercury Capri, Ford Explorer, Mercury Mountaineer, Ford Explorer Sport and Explorer Sport Trac, Ford E-Series vans from E-150 to E-350 plus the E-450, Ford Bronco, Ford F-150 Lightning, some models of F-Series trucks, and Ford F53 Motor Home chassis.

General Motors

GM also has its share of lemons, as Sierra and Silverado truck owners will confirm. Major engine, transmission, suspension, and brake problems returned with a vengeance when GM redesigned its truck line in 1998 and its SUVs a bit later on. GM's poor quality now rivals Ford's for diesel engine (Duramax), fuel-injector, and tranny failures. Plus, its front-drive minivans have carried "biodegradable" intake manifold gaskets from 1996 through 2005. The trucks were redesigned again for 2007, and already owners are reporting serious powertrain and brake problems, including one report that the drive shaft suddenly dropped out of its housing while the truck was underway.

But let's not just pick on Ford, GM, and Chrysler. European automakers make their share of lemons as well. J.D. Power and Associates has ranked Mercedes' quality as much worse than average. If, however, you've been a steady reader of *Lemon-Aid* over the past 35 years, you have known of Mercedes' poor quality for almost a decade—and you probably have saved money buying a Toyota Highlander or Lexus 350 instead.

Keep in mind that there's absolutely no correlation between safe and dependable transportation and the amount of money a vehicle costs. In fact, almost the opposite conclusion can be reached: Cheap, simple vehicles—originally retailing for about $20,000—that have been on the market for a few years are far better buys than most vehicles costing two or three times as much. Again, J.D. Power confirms this fact.

 Nevertheless, you can reduce your risk of buying a lemon by getting a used vehicle rated "Recommended" in this guide, and one that has some of the original warranty still in effect. This protects you from some of the costly defects that are bound to crop up shortly after your purchase. The warranty allows you to make one final inspection before it expires, and requires both the dealer and the

2005 and Prior GM Light Duty Truck Models

2003–05 HUMMER H2

Supercede: This bulletin is being revised to add model years. Please discard Corporate Bulletin Number 99-04-20-022B (Section 04–Driveline/Axle).

Important: The condition described in this bulletin should not be confused with the following previous bulletins:

Info—Discontinue Flushing and Replacing Transfer Case Fluid Due to Bump/Clunk Concern (Corporate Bulletin Number 99-04-21-004A or newer).

Clunk, Bump or Squawk when Vehicle Comes to Complete Stop or Accelerating from Complete Stop (Replace Rear Drive Shaft Nickel-Plated Slip Yoke) (Corporate Bulletin Number 01-04-17-004B or newer).

Some owners of light duty trucks equipped with automatic transmissions may comment that the vehicle exhibits a clunk noise when shifting between Park and Drive, Park and Reverse, or Drive and Reverse. Similarly, owners of vehicles equipped with automatic or manual transmissions may comment that the vehicle exhibits a clunk noise while driving when the accelerator is quickly depressed and then released.

Whenever there are two or more gears interacting with one another, there must be a certain amount of clearance between those gears in order for the gears to operate properly. This clearance or freeplay (also known as lash) can translate into a clunk noise whenever the gear is loaded and unloaded quickly, or whenever the direction of rotation is reversed. The more gears you have in a system, the more freeplay the total system will have.

The clunk noise that owners sometimes hear may be the result of a buildup of freeplay (lash) between the components in the driveline.

For example, the potential for a driveline clunk would be greater in a 4-wheel drive or all-wheel drive vehicle than in a 2-wheel drive vehicle. This is because in addition to the freeplay from the rear axle gears, the universal joints, and the transmission (common to both vehicles), the 4-wheel drive transfer case gears (and their associated clearances) add additional freeplay to the driveline.

In service, dealers are discouraged from attempting to repair driveline clunk conditions for the following reasons:

Comments of driveline clunk are almost never the result of one individual component with excessive lash, but rather the result of the added freeplay (or lash) present in all of the driveline components. Because all of the components in the driveline have a certain amount of lash by design, changing driveline components may not result in satisfactory lash reduction.

While some owners may find the clunk objectionable, this will not adversely affect durability or performance.

GM ENGINE OIL OR COOLANT LEAK

BULLETIN NO.: 03-06-01-010A

DATE: APRIL 2003

ENGINE OIL OR COOLANT LEAK (INSTALL NEW INTAKE MANIFOLD GASKET)

2000–03 Buick Century

2002–03 Buick Rendezvous

1996 Chevrolet Lumina APV

1997–2003 Chevrolet Venture

1999–2001 Chevrolet Lumina

1999–2003 Chevrolet Malibu, Monte Carlo

2000–03 Chevrolet Impala

1996–2003 Oldsmobile Silhouette

1999 Oldsmobile Cutlass

1999–2003 Oldsmobile Alero

1996–99 Pontiac Trans Sport

1999–2003 Pontiac Grand Am

2000–03 Pontiac Grand Prix, Montana

2001–03 Pontiac Aztek with 3.1L or 3.4L V6 engine
  (VINs J, E - RPOs LGB, LA1)

Condition: Some owners may comment on an apparent oil or coolant leak. Additionally, the comments may range from spots on the driveway to having to add fluids.

Cause: Intake manifold may be leaking allowing coolant, oil or both to leak from the engine.

Correction: Install a new-design intake manifold gasket. The material used in the gasket has been changed in order to improve the sealing qualities of the gasket. When replacing the gasket, the intake manifold bolts must also be replaced and torqued to a revised specification. The new bolts will come with a pre-applied threadlocker on them.

GM Canada will pay for this repair under a proposed class acton settlement.

automaker to compensate you for all warrantable defects found at that time, even if they are fixed after the warranty ends.

Why Canadians Buy Used

We *are* different. We are frugal, unpretentious, and faithful. We don't have short love affairs—with cars or trucks, that is. We are very reluctant to trade in a vehicle or to abandon a model that suits our needs. In fact, over half of the vehicles on Canada's roads are nine years old or more, says Toronto-based industry analyst Dennis DesRosiers. We are also more conservative than Americans in our vehicle choices. We still love minivans, while Americans embrace SUVs; we buy down-sized sport-utilities, while Americans go for humongous Hummers; and because of our higher fuel costs, we still support economy cars.

Cheaper Prices and No Transport or "Administration" Fees

New- and used-vehicle prices have crumbled over the past year, but they're still too high—Dennis DesRosiers pegs the cost of an average new vehicle at over $31,200. Insurance is another wallet buster, costing about $2,500 a year for young drivers. And once you add financing costs, maintenance, taxes, and a host of other expenses, CAA calculates the yearly outlay for a medium-sized car at over $8,252, or 36.7 cents/km; trucks or SUVs may run you about 10 cents/km more. For a comprehensive, though depressing, comparative analysis (cars versus trucks, minivans, SUVs, etc.) of all the costs involved over a 1- to 10-year period, access Alberta's consumer information website at *www.agric.gov.ab.ca/app24/costcalculators/vehicle/getvechimpls.jsp.*

Used vehicles aren't sold with $900–$1,600 transport fees or $495 "administration" charges, either. And you can legally avoid paying sales tax when you buy privately. That's right: You'll pay at least 10 percent less than the dealer's price and you may avoid the 5 percent federal Goods and Services Tax (GST) that applies in some provinces to dealer sales only.

Slower Depreciation

If someone were to ask you to invest in stocks or bonds guaranteed to be worth about one-half of their initial purchase value after three or four years, you'd probably head for the door. But you're falling into exactly this trap when you buy a new SUV, truck, or van. You will feel the depreciation bite less than passenger-car owners do, but in any new vehicle purchase, the trend is toward less value.

Now, shoppers buying a new vehicle will argue that the warranty and status far outweigh any inconvenience and that the initial cost will be amortized after a few years. The Ontario buyer in this example thus forks over $33,906 and then drives away in a brand new sport-utility vehicle:

COST OF A NEW VEHICLE (BOUGHT IN CANADA)

2008 FORD ESCAPE XLT (3.0L V6 4✕4)

MSRP	$28,899
Freight/PDI	$ 1,250
Federal GST (5 percent)	$ 1,507
Ontario PST (8 percent)	$ 2,412
Total price	**$34,068**

Even before considering how much the buyer could save by purchasing a used vehicle, first take a look at the cross-border savings on the same new Escape XLT. Not only is the American MSRP $5,414 less than the Canadian price, but the GST and PST levies are also less, and freight/PDI charges are less than half of what Ford of Canada charges:

COST OF A NEW VEHICLE (BOUGHT IN THE U.S.)

2008 FORD ESCAPE XLT (3.0L V6 4✕4)

MRSP*	$23,485
Freight/PDI (included)	$ 665
Rebate (included)	$ 1,000
Federal GST (5 percent)	$ 1,174
Ontario PST (8 percent)	$ 1,879
RIV fee	$ 205
Total price	**$26,743**

*MSRP is calculated assuming the U.S. and Canadian dollar are at par.

A motorist buying that same model in Canada when it is three years old will save about $17,870 off the Canadian new-vehicle price. Here's how the savings would apply to the Ontario buyer:

COST OF A USED VEHICLE (BOUGHT IN CANADA)

2005 FORD ESCAPE XLT (3.0L V6 4✕4)

Value (as of November, 2007)	$15,000
No GST (if sold privately)	—
Ontario PST (8 percent)	$ 1,200
Total price	$16,200

In this example, the used Ford Escape buyer gets a *Lemon-Aid*-recommended set of wheels that likely has some unexpired warranty coverage left, saves $13,899 on the selling price, cuts another $2,719 in federal and provincial taxes, and avoids paying the $1,250 freight charge that's added to the selling price of a new vehicle. Furthermore, the depreciation hit will be only a few thousand dollars in each of the ensuing years. And we haven't even gone into the interest savings from the $17,870.

The 2005 Escape XLT's Canadian used price is less than half of what the new, 2008 model costs in Canada and about $4,000 more than what it would sell for in the States. Therefore, the Canadian cross-border buyer saves money in the initial purchase and then makes extra cash in the resale in Canada after three years. Furthermore, the American price in this example is calculated at parity with the American greenback. Actually, the American MSRP could be reduced another 7–10 percent, considering the Canadian dollar's $1.07–$1.10 fluctuation at the time of writing.

Can you think of a better deal than this?

"Secret Warranty" Repair Refunds

Almost all automakers use secret "goodwill" warranties to cover factory-related defects long after the original warranty has expired. This creates a huge fleet of used vehicles eligible for free repairs.

We're not talking about a few months' extension. In fact, some free repairs—like those related to GM diesel engines—are authorized up to 13 years under these secret "goodwill" programs. Still, most of these warranty extensions hover around the 5- to 7-year mark and seldom cover vehicles whose mileage exceeds 160,000 km (100,000 mi.). This benchmark includes engine and transmission defects affecting Detroit's Big Three, Honda, Hyundai, Lexus, and Toyota. Ford's 1995–98 Windstars carry a little-known 10-year warranty extension covering front coil-spring breakage and offering free tire replacement if a tire is punctured (see NHTSA campaign on page 121).

Knowing which free repairs apply to your car will cut maintenance costs dramatically.

Incidentally, automakers and dealers claim that secret warranties don't exist, since all warranties are published in service bulletins. Although this is technically correct, have you ever tried to get a copy of a service bulletin? Or, if you did manage to get a copy, has the dealer or automaker told you the benefits are applicable only in the States?

NHTSA CAMPAIGN ID NUMBER: 011007000

DEFECT SUMMARY: This is not a safety defect in accordance with the safety act. However, it is deemed a safety improvement campaign by the agency. Vehicle description: 1995–98 Ford Windstar Minivans. The front coil springs could potentially fracture due to corrosion.
CONSEQUENCE SUMMARY: Some tires have deflated due to contact with a broken spring.
CORRECTIVE SUMMARY: Ford is extending the warranty for front coil spring replacement to a total of 10 years of service from the warranty start date, with unlimited mileage. This coverage is automatically transferred to subsequent owners at no charge. If either front coil spring fractures during the coverage period noted above, the dealer will replace both springs at no charge to the owner.

---

20 secret warranties that will save you big bucks

One of *Lemon-Aid*'s most popular features is its annual round-up of hundreds of secret warranties authorizing free major repairs for SUVs, trucks, and vans. While most are detailed in Part Four under their respective eligible models and years, on the following pages are 20 recent programs that represent thousands of dollars in free repairs, whether you bought your vehicle new or used. Manufacturers can't weasel out of their obligations by claiming that they never wrote such a bulletin.

Service bulletins are great guides for warranty inspections, and they're useful in helping you decide when it's best to trade in your car. They're written by automakers in "mechanic-speak" because service managers relate better to them that way.

If your vehicle is out of warranty and you can't get a "goodwill" warranty extension, show these bulletins to less-expensive, independent garage mechanics so they can quickly find the trouble and order the most recent *upgraded* part, ensuring that you aren't just replacing one defective component with another.

Because these bulletins are sent out by U.S. automakers, Canadian service managers and automakers may deny, at first, that they even exist. (Are you listening, Chrysler and Ford?) However, when they're shown a copy, they usually find the appropriate Canadian part number or bulletin in their files. The problem and its solution don't change from one side of the border to the other. Imagine American and Canadian tourists being towed across the border because each country's technical service bulletins were different! Mechanical fixes do differ in cases where a bulletin is for California only, or relates to a safety or emissions component used only in the States. But these instances are rare.

The best way to get bulletin-related repairs carried out is to visit the dealer's service bay and attach the specific ALLDATA-supplied service bulletin covering your vehicle's problems to a work order.

Free summaries of automotive recalls and technical service bulletins listed by year, make, model, and engine can be found at the ALLDATA (*www.alldatadiy.com*) and NHTSA (*www.safercar.gov*) websites. Like the NHTSA summaries, ALLDATA's summaries are so short and cryptic that they're of limited use. So pay the $24.95 (U.S.) subscription fee and download the complete contents of all the bulletins applicable to your vehicle from ALLDATA.

CHRYSLER UPPER BALL JOINT EXTENDED WARRANTY

BULLETIN NO.: 02-010-04

DATE: DECEMBER 16, 2004

OVERVIEW: This bulletin involves inspecting and if necessary replacing the upper ball joints.

NOTE: The upper ball joint warranty period has been extended to 10 years or 100,000 miles [170,000 km]. Refer to Warranty Bulletin D-04-34 for complete details.

2000–03 (AN) Dakota 4X2

2000–03 (DN) Durango 4X2

NOTE: This bulletin applies only to the above vehicles built through December 31, 2002.

CHRYSLER UPPER BODY SEAM SEAL WATER LEAK

BULLETIN NO.: 23-002-05

DATE: JANUARY 14, 2005

OVERVIEW: This bulletin involves repairing a crack/split in the upper body seam sealer at the "B" or "C" pillar.

2003–05 (RS) Town & Country/Caravan/Voyager

SYMPTOM/CONDITION: Customer may describe a visible crack/split and/or a water leak in the upper body seam sealer at the "B" or "C" pillar.

DIAGNOSIS: If the customer's description matches the Symptom/Condition, perform the Repair Procedure.

CHRYSLER SHUDDER WHILE BRAKING

BULLETIN NO.: 05-002-06

DATE: MAY 10, 2006

OVERVIEW: This bulletin involves replacing the rear brake shoes and, if necessary, the axle shafts and refacing the front brake rotors.

2005–06 (ND) Dakota

NOTE: **This bulletin applies to vehicles built on or before January 31, 2006 (MDH 0131XX).**

SYMPTOM/CONDITION: A vibration or shudder in the brake pedal when the brakes are applied at highway speeds.

CHRYSLER A/C—WATER LEAKS UNDER PASSENGER SIDE CARPET

BULLETIN NO.: 24-001-06 REV A   DATE: NOVEMBER 10, 2006

HVAC DRAIN WATER (AC CONDENSATE) LEAKS UNDER PASSENGER SIDE CARPET

OVERVIEW: This bulletin involves installing a HVAC drain tube O-ring.

2001–06 Town & Country/Caravan/Voyager and 2004–06 Pacifica

SYMPTOM/CONDITION: The customer may describe a wet front passenger floor or floor carpet. This condition may be due to water (A/C condensate) from the HVAC assembly drain tube.

DIAGNOSIS: Verify the passenger side front floor or carpet is wet. Check the source of the water leak. As A/C condensate leaves the HVAC drain tube, it may run back along the outside of the drain tube, past the seal, and under the passenger side front floor carpet.

FORD SPRING TOWER FLANGE CRACKING

BULLETIN NO.: 05-22-16   DATE: NOVEMBER 14, 2005

SPRING TOWER WELD REPAIR AND REPLACEMENT PROCEDURE

1997–2006 E-350 and E-450

Some higher-mileage E-350 and E-450 cutaway vans may exhibit cracks in the left or right spring tower flange.

ACTION: Certain front spring tower cracks can be repaired effectively by welding a reinforcement plate at the crack following the Service Procedure in this TSB. If the crack does not meet the criteria for this reinforcement plate repair, the spring tower should be replaced.

FORD FRONT END SHUDDER/VIBRATION WHEN BRAKING

BULLETIN NO.: 05-5-2   DATE: NOVEMBER 18, 2004

VEHICLES BUILT BEFORE 11/18/2004

FORD: 2004–05 F-150

ISSUE: Some 2004–05 F-150 vehicles built before 11/18/2004 may exhibit a shudder/vibration from the front brakes when braking.

ACTION: Replace the front rotors. On vehicles built prior to 8/20/2003 also replace the rack and pinion.

FORD TRUCK INTERMITTENT NOISE, 4X4 INOPERATIVE

BULLETIN NO.: TSB 06-8-15   DATE: MAY 1, 2006

2004–06 F-150 and 2006 Mark LT

Some 2004–06 F-150 and 2006 Mark LT 4X4 vehicles built before 4/24/2006 may exhibit a noise in 2 wheel drive from the front Integrated Wheel Ends (IWE) and/or the 4X4 system being inoperative. The IWE solenoid may have ingested water and passed it to the IWE system causing water contamination in the vacuum portion of the system. A shorted IWE solenoid can set the codes C1979 and C1980. If either code is present, the 4WDH light will be inoperative.

Ford will replace the faulty solenoid under warranty or through an extended "goodwill" powertrain warranty. Parts and labour would normally cost $150.

GM NEW DESIGN WINDSHIELD/DOOR GLASS

BULLETIN NO.: 04-08-48-002B

DATE: APRIL 27, 2006

AVAILABILITY OF NEW DESIGN WINDSHIELD AND FRONT DOOR GLASS

2004–06 Buick Rainier; 2005–06 Chevrolet TrailBlazer, TrailBlazer EXT;
2005 GMC Envoy XUV; 2005–06 GMC Envoy, Envoy XL; and 2005–06 Saab 9-7X

CONDITION: Due to the difference in processing, along with the difference in the curvature of the glass, the optics of the glass may appear wavy on a cross-car view from the outside of the vehicle. This is a normal condition and the windshield glass should not be replaced for this condition. The view through the glass from the driver's position is clear and not affected.

IMPORTANT: Replace the windshield ONLY if there is a wavy condition or any type of distortion as seen from the driver's seating position that is within the wipe zone on the windshield.

GM's solution for front windshields and door windows that distort visibility is to replace them only if the driver's view is seriously affected. Idiotic, but true.

GM PREMATURE ALUMINUM PANEL HOOD CORROSION/BLISTERING (REFINISH)

BULLETIN NO.: 01-08-51-004D

DATE: JUNE 05, 2006

2000–03 Buick LeSabre; 2002–06 Buick Rendezvous; 2000–05 Cadillac DeVille; 2003–06 Cadillac CTS; 2004–06 Cadillac SRX; 2005–06 Cadillac STS; 2006 Cadillac DTS; 1997–2002 Chevrolet Trans Sport (Export Only), Venture; 1997–2002 Oldsmobile Silhouette; 2001–03 Oldsmobile Aurora; 1997–98 Pontiac Trans Sport; 1999–2002 Pontiac Montana; 2002–03 Pontiac Bonneville

CONDITION: Some vehicles may have the appearance of blistering or bubbling paint on the top of the hood or under the hood edges and hem flanges.

GM TRANNY DEBRIS

BULLETIN NO.: 02-07-30-013E

DATE: MAY 20, 2005

INCORRECT TRANSMISSION SHIFTS, POOR ENGINE PERFORMANCE, HARSH 1–2 UPSHIFTS, SLIPS 1ST AND REVERSE, TORQUE CONVERTER CLUTCH (TCC) STUCK OFF/ON

2001–05 GM Passenger Cars with 4T65-E Automatic Transmission

2001–05 Buick Rendezvous

2005 Buick Terraza

2001–04 Chevrolet Venture

2005 Chevrolet Uplander

2001–04 Oldsmobile Silhouette

2001–05 Pontiac Aztek, Montana

2005 Saturn Relay

with 4T65-E Transmission (RPOs M15, MN3, MN7, M76)

GM TRANSMISSION DELAYED ENGAGEMENT, COLD HESITATION, MALFUNCTION INDICATOR LAMP (MIL) ILLUMINATED

BULLETIN NO.: 03-07-30-011C   DATE: APRIL 4, 2005

REPLACE TORQUE CONVERTER RELIEF SPRING, TRANSMISSION FLUID ILLUMINATOR AND LUBE REGULATOR SPRING IN FRONT SUPPORT

2001–03 Chevrolet Silverado 2500/3500 Series

2001–03 GMC Sierra 2500/3200 Series

with Allison® 1000 Series Automatic Transmission (RPO M74)

CONDITION: Some customers may comment that the transmission has a delayed engagement, cold hesitation or may illuminate the MIL on the first start-up after sitting for a period of time.

CAUSE: Torque converter bleed down over an extended period of non-usage, usually over a week, may cause this condition.

GM ENGINE—REAR CRANKSHAFT MAIN SEAL OIL LEAKS

BULLETIN NO.: 05-06-01-019D   DATE: MAY 12, 2006

ENGINE OIL LEAK AT CRANKSHAFT REAR MAIN OIL SEAL (INSTALL REVISED CRANKSHAFT REAR MAIN OIL SEAL USING REVISED REAR MAIN SEAL INSTALLER)

1986–2007 GM Cars and Light Duty Trucks with 2.8L, 3.1L, 3.4L, 3.5L, 3.9L 60 V6 Engine

This bulletin is being revised to add the 2007 model year, additional RPOs and updated part number information for Canada only.

GM SPECIAL POLICY ADJUSTMENT—
ELECTRONIC DIESEL FUEL INJECTION PUMP FAILURE—REPAIR/REPLACE

BULLETIN NO.: 00064F   DATE: SEPTEMBER 2004

1994–2002 Chevrolet and GMC C/K, G and P model trucks; and 1997–98 B7 school bus chassis, equipped with a 6.5L diesel engine

CONDITION: Some customers of 1994–2002 Chevrolet and GMC C/K, G, and P model trucks; and 1997–98 B7 school bus chassis, equipped with a 6.5 liter diesel engine (RPO L49—VIN Code P; RPO L56—VIN Code S; or RPO L55 —VIN Code F), may experience a failure of the electronic diesel fuel injection pump.

SPECIAL POLICY ADJUSTMENT: This special policy covers the condition described above for a period of eleven (11) years or 120,000 miles (193,000 km), whichever occurs first, from the date the vehicle was originally placed in service, regardless of ownership. Damage from poor quality or incorrect grade diesel fuel, and gasoline or water contamination, is not covered under the terms of the 6.5L diesel warranty or this Special Policy.

This special policy applies ONLY to electronic diesel-fuel injection pump repairs and/or replacement as a result of **injection pump failure**. The pump repair or replacement will be made at **no charge** to the owner. Fuel quality may cause driveability problems such as hesitation, lack of power, stall, no start, etc. For best results, use Number 2-D diesel fuel year-round (above and below freezing conditions) as oil companies blend Number 2-D fuel to address climate differences.

HONDA EGR VALVE CONTAMINATION OR EGR PORT CLOGGING MAY CAUSE ENGINE HESITATION/SURGE

BULLETIN NO.: 05-026

DATE: JULY 20, 2005

1999–2002 Odyssey; 2003 Pilot

BACKGROUND: In some 1999–2003 Odysseys and 2003 Pilots, the EGR system may become contaminated or clogged. If this happens, the vehicle may hesitate or surge during light acceleration, and the MIL (malfunction indicator lamp) may come on with DTC P0401 (EGR insufficient flow) or P1491 (EGR valve insufficient lift). Because of these possible problems, affected vehicles now have a warranty extension that covers EGR port clogging and/or EGR valve sticking.

Here are the details of the extended coverage:

- On 1999–01 Odysseys thru VIN 2HKRL18..1H586575, EGR port clogging and EGR valve sticking is covered for 8 years or 80,000 miles [130,000 km], whichever occurs first.
- On 2001 Odysseys after VIN 2HKRL18..1H586575, all 2002 Odysseys, 2003 Odysseys within the affected VIN ranges, and 2003 Pilots within the affected VIN range, EGR valve sticking is covered for 8 years or 80,000 miles [130,000 km], whichever occurs first.

HONDA HARD START/POOR PERFORMANCE

BULLETIN NO.: 03-038

DATE: NOVEMBER 5, 2004

1999–01 CR-V

SYMPTOM: The engine idles roughly, is hard to start, performs poorly, or has the MIL on with DTC P0301, P0302, P0303, P0304 (cylinder misfire), or P0172 (fuel system too rich). NOTE: The exhaust valves and seats may be damaged (burnt or cracked) to further indicate that the cylinder head has a problem.

PROBABLE CAUSE: One or more exhaust valves have receded into the cylinder head.

CORRECTIVE ACTION: Inspect the valve clearance and, if necessary, replace the cylinder head.

FAILED PART: P/N 12100-P75-010, H/C 5604970

DEFECT CODE: 00503

OUT OF WARRANTY: Any repair performed after warranty expiration may be eligible for goodwill consideration by the District Parts and Service Manager or your Zone Office. You must request consideration, and get a decision, before starting work.

HONDA VEHICLE DOES NOT MOVE IN DRIVE; MIL COMES ON OR D INDICATOR BLINKS WITH A/T DTC P0730

BULLETIN NO.: 04-036

DATE: JANUARY 7, 2005

2001–04 Civic 2-door with A/T

2001–04 Civic 4-door DX, EX, LX with A/T

SYMPTOM: The vehicle does not move when you select Drive. The MIL comes on ('01–03 models) or the **D** indicator blinks ('04 models) with A/T DTC P0730 (shift control system) set.

PROBABLE CAUSE: Excessive wear in the 2nd clutch.

CORRECTIVE ACTION: Replace the A/T. Use the Honda Interface Module (HIM) to update the PCM software ('01–03 models only).

Mazda North American Operations

June 2005

2000-2003 MPV Rear Heater Pipe & Hose Assembly Warranty Extension Program SSP 65

Dear Mazda Owner:

Mazda Motor Corporation has decided to conduct a Special Service Program to extend the warranty coverage on the rear heater pipe and hose assembly on certain 2000-2003 MPV vehicles. The warranty for the rear heater pipe and hose assembly will be extended to 7 years from warranty start date, with no mileage limitation.

On certain 2000-2003 model year MPV vehicles currently or previously registered in 23 "Salt Belt" states, the accumulation of road salt may cause rust and corrosion to the rear heater pipe and hose assembly. If the rust and/or corrosion is severe, there is a possibility of an engine coolant leakage.

If your vehicle is functioning normally, there is no need to contact your dealer. We suggest keeping this letter with the vehicle's warranty information for future reference.

If your MPV is leaking engine coolant from the rear of the vehicle, please make an appointment with your Mazda dealer. If the leak is from the rear heater pipe and hose assembly, your dealer will replace the affected parts **free of charge**. The repair should take approximately one-half day to complete. However, it may take longer depending on parts availability and the service workload at your Mazda dealership.

TOYOTA INCREASED STEERING EFFORT IN HIGH ROAD SALT AREAS

BULLETIN NO.: ST001-07   DATE: JANUARY 19, 2007

INTERMEDIATE SHAFT IN HIGH ROAD SALT AREAS

2004–06 Sienna

In areas where road salt is used during winter months, some customers may experience a slight increase in steering effort, which may gradually become more noticeable over time. The steering intermediate shaft has been modified to help address this condition.

This repair is covered under the Toyota Comprehensive Warranty. This warranty is in effect for 36 months or 36,000 miles [58,000 km], whichever occurs first, from the vehicle's in-service date.

*Warranty application is limited to correction of a problem based upon a customer's specific complaint.

TOYOTA POWER REAR DOOR SHUDDER/ WATER LEAKS

BULLETIN NO.: B0003-04   DATE: MARCH 9, 2004

BACK DOOR STAY LEAK & COLD WEATHER SHUDDER IMPROVEMENT

2004–06 Sienna

The back door stays have been redesigned to improve the operating effort of the rear hatch, provide improved resistance to seal damage, and prevent leakage. The improvement will also address the power back door shudder that can occur when operating during cold weather conditions.

TOYOTA NO START IN EXTREME COLD

BULLETIN NO.: EG032-06   DATE: MAY 9, 2006

NO START IN SUB-FREEZING AMBIENT AIR TEMPERATURES

2004–05 Sienna

Some customers may experience a "no start" condition and/or M.I.L. "ON" with DTCs P0300, P0171, and P0174 after the vehicle has cold soaked in sub-freezing ambient air temperatures. To correct this condition, a new fuel pump sub-tank assembly is now available. Follow the repair procedure to replace the fuel pump sub-tank assembly.

Better and Cheaper Parts Availability

Used parts can have a surprisingly long lifespan. Generally, a new gasoline-powered car or minivan can be expected to run with few problems for at least 200,000–300,000 km (125,000–150,000 mi.) in its lifetime; a diesel-powered vehicle can easily double those figures. Some repairs will crop up at regular intervals, and, along with preventive maintenance, your yearly running costs should average about $800. Buttressing the argument that vehicles get cheaper to operate the longer you keep them, the U.S. Department of Transportation points out that the average vehicle requires one or more major repairs after every five years of use. Once these repairs are done, however, the vehicle can be run relatively trouble-free for another five years or more, as long as the environment isn't too hostile. In fact, the farther west you go in Canada, the longer owners keep their vehicles—an average of 10 years or more in some provinces.

Time is on your side in other ways, too. Three years after a model is launched, the replacement-parts market usually catches up to consumer demand. Dealers stock larger inventories, and parts wholesalers and independent parts manufacturers expand their outputs.

Used replacement parts are unquestionably easier to come by after this point. You can bargain with local garages, carefully search auto wreckers' yards, or look on the Internet. A reconditioned or used part usually costs one-third to one-half the price of a new part. There's generally no difference in the quality of reconditioned mechanical components, and they're often guaranteed for as long as, or longer than, new ones. In fact, some savvy shoppers use the information in Part Four of this guide to see which parts have a short life and then buy those parts from retailers who give lifetime warranties on their brakes, exhaust systems, tires, batteries, etc.

Buying from discount outlets or independent garages or ordering through mail-order houses can save you big bucks (30–35 percent) on the cost of new parts, and another 15 percent on labour, when compared with dealers' charges. Costco is another good source for savings realized through independent retailers. It sells competitively priced replacement tires and sometimes offers free rotation, balancing, and other inspections during the life of the tire.

Body parts are a different story. Although car-company repair parts cost 60 percent more than certified generic aftermarket parts, buyers would be wise to buy only original equipment manufacturer (OEM) parts supplied by automakers in order to get body panels that fit well, protect better in collisions, and have maximum rust resistance, says *Consumer Reports* in its February 1999 study. Insurance appraisers often substitute cheaper, lower-quality aftermarket body parts in collision repairs, but *Consumer Reports* found that 71 percent of policyholders who requested OEM parts got them with little or no hassle. *CR* suggests that consumers complain to their provincial Superintendent of Insurance if OEM parts aren't provided. Ontario car owners filed a class action lawsuit against that province's major insurers, alleging that making repairs with non-OEM parts is an unsafe practice and that it violates insureds' rights.

Liberty Mutual settled the lawsuit out of court, and other insurers have become less insistent that consumers accept knock-off parts.

The U.S. Supreme Court has ruled that insurers must replace damaged parts with original equipment parts sold by the auto manufacturer (*Avery v. State Farm*; 1999; *www.state.il.us/court/Opinions/AppellateCourt/2001/5thDistrict/April/Html/5990830. htm*), and an Ontario class action seeking similar relief was settled on January 31, 2006 in *Albert Hague and Terrance O'Brien v. Liberty Mutual Insurance Company* (Ontario Superior Court, Case No. 01-CV-204787CP; June 14, 2004).

The Ontario class action settlement isn't just for Liberty Mutual policyholders. *Lemon-Aid* readers throughout Canada may use the settlement as a bargaining chip with any insurer to get OEM parts put in their vehicles or to get a refund of the cost difference for non-OEM parts already installed, going back to 1990 (see *www. deloitte.com/dtt/cda/doc/content/Liberty%20Notice%20of%20Approval.pdf*).

European and Japanese parts

With some European models, you can count on a lot of aggravation and expense due to the high markup and unacceptably slow distribution of parts. Because European automakers have a quasi-monopoly on replacement parts, there are few independent suppliers you can turn to for help. And junkyards, the last-chance repository for inexpensive car parts, are unlikely to carry foreign parts for vehicles that are more than three years old or are manufactured in small numbers.

Finding parts for Japanese and domestic cars and vans is no problem because of the large number of vehicles produced, the presence of hundreds of independent suppliers, the ease with which relatively simple parts can be interchanged from one model to another, and the large reservoir of used parts stocked by junkyards.

Insurance Costs Less

The price you pay for insurance can vary significantly, not only between insurance companies but also within the same company over time. But one thing does remain constant: Insurance for used vehicles is a lot cheaper than new-car coverage, and through careful comparison shopping, insurance premium payouts can be substantially reduced.

Although the cost of insurance premiums for used cars is often one-third to one-half the cost of the premiums you would pay for a new vehicle, using the Internet to find the lowest auto insurance quote and accepting a large deductible are critical to keeping premiums low.

Beware of "captive" brokers

The Consumers' Association of Canada's (CAC) national study on auto insurance rates released July 19, 2005, found that consumers in Ontario paid 45 percent more for their auto insurance than B.C. drivers. The average auto insurance rate in Ontario was $2,383, while it was only $1,324 in B.C.

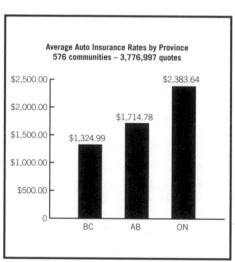

The extraordinarily high rates were charged throughout Ontario in cities such as Thunder Bay, Sault St. Marie, Sudbury, Windsor, Guelph, London, Kingston, and Ottawa. The CAC blamed the high costs on Ontario insurance brokers who, it says, may be fronts for a handful of affiliated insurers offering non-competitive rates.

Investigators say a pattern that drives up prices has emerged among so-called independent brokers. With almost 100 auto insurance companies operating in Ontario, a typical broker may sell policies from one or two insurance companies only. "Many of these brokerage firms have financial ties to insurance companies, which limits real consumer choice," said Bruce Cran, president of the Ottawa-based association.

 ### Use InsuranceHotline.com

One effective agency that tracks the lowest premiums is *InsuranceHotline.com*. It has created a watchdog service to alert drivers to the changes in their insurance rates and to keep their rates low. For $20 per year, the agency will automatically rerun members' profiles to ensure that they always know which insurer has the lowest rate from its database of 30 insurance companies (representing over 80 percent of the written premiums in Canada). There is no telephone access for the service; all comparisons are done online.

Surprisingly, some of the vehicles with the poorest reliability, durability, and fuel economy ratings—like General Motors' Hummer—have good insurance rates. Additionally, if you are ticketed or have one accident, your premiums can almost quadruple. When rates for a 2006 Hummer and a 2006 Honda Civic were calculated, the Civic driver saved only $49 compared to the Hummer premium. But add a police ticket and accident to the equation, and the Civic owner could pay over $2,500 more (see the chart below).

INSURANCE PREMIUMS COMPARISON

MODEL	NO CLAIMS		ONE TICKET & ONE ACCIDENT	
	LOW	HIGH	LOW	HIGH
Hummer	$1,651	$3,138	$2,812	$8,769
Honda Civic	$1,602	$3,125	$2,812	$11,271

A spreadsheet of the different insurance rates applicable to many 2006 models can be found at www.insurancehotline.com/2006_rate_comparison.html.

And here are some other *InsuranceHotline.com* findings:

- Family cars priced under $35,000 can cost more to insure than those that are over $35,000.
- SUVs priced under $35,000 don't always cost more to insure than family cars or small luxury models.
- Luxury cars mean luxury premiums, costing on average about $500 more annually to insure than family cars, SUVs, muscle cars, or hybrids.
- Hybrids' fuel savings can be wiped out by higher-cost insurance premiums that rival what one would pay to insure muscle cars.

Defects Can't Hide

You can easily avoid any nasty surprises by having your choice checked out by an independent mechanic (for $85–$100) before paying for a used vehicle. This examination before purchase protects you against any hidden defects the vehicle may have. It's also a tremendous negotiating tool, since you can use the cost of any needed repairs to bargain down the purchase price.

It's easier to get permission to have the vehicle inspected if you promise to give the seller a copy of the inspection report should you decide not to buy it. If you still can't get permission to have the vehicle inspected elsewhere, walk away from the deal, no matter how tempting the selling price. The seller is obviously trying to put something over on you. Ignore the standard excuses that the vehicle isn't insured, that the registration tags have expired, or that the vehicle has a dead battery.

You Know the Vehicle's History

Smart customers will want answers to the following questions before signing a contract: What did it first sell for, and what is its present insured value? Who serviced it? Has it had accident repairs? Are parts easily available? How much of the original warranty and/or repair warranties are left? Does the vehicle have a history of costly performance-related defects? What free repairs are available through "goodwill" warranty extensions? (See "Secret Warranties/Internal Bulletins/Service Tips" in Part Four.)

Cheap and Easy Lawsuits

In most courtrooms, lawyers win, regardless of whether you win or lose. And, after several years of being on tenterhooks, even if you do succeed, the award will likely be much less than what you lost and not worth the emotional highs and lows you endured.

But, by being just a bit creative and using the small claims courts, you'll discover there are many federal and provincial consumer protection laws that go far beyond whatever protection may be offered by the standard new-vehicle warranty. Furthermore, buyers of used vehicles don't usually have to conform to any arbitrary rules or service guidelines to get this protection.

Let's say you do get stuck with a vehicle that's unreliable, has undisclosed accident damage, or doesn't perform as promised. Most small claims courts have a jurisdiction limit of $3,000–$10,000, which should cover the cost of repairs or compensate you if the vehicle is taken back. Alberta, B.C., and Ontario now have a $25,000 ceiling—more than enough for most car purchases. That way, any dispute between buyer and seller can be settled within a few months, without lawyers or excessive court costs. Furthermore, you're not likely to face a battery of lawyers standing in for the automaker and dealer in front of a stern-faced judge. You may not even have to face a judge at all, since many cases are settled through court-imposed mediators at a pretrial meeting, usually scheduled a month or two after filing.

When and Where to Buy Used Vehicles

When to Buy

In the fall, dealer stocks of good-quality trade-ins and off-lease returns are at their highest level and private sellers are moderately active. Prices are higher, but a greater choice of vehicles is available. In winter, prices decline substantially and dealers and private sellers are generally easier to bargain with because buyers are scarce and weather conditions don't help them to present their wares in the best light. In spring and summer, prices go up a bit as private sellers become more active and increased new-car rebates bring in more trade-ins.

Private Sellers

Private sellers are your best source for cheap and reliable used vehicles, because you're on an equal bargaining level with vendors who aren't trying to profit from your inexperience. A good private-sale price would be about 5 percent *more* than the rock-bottom wholesale price, or approximately 20 percent *less* than the retail price advertised by local dealers. You can find estimated wholesale and retail prices in Part Four.

Remember, no seller, be it a dealer or private party, expects to get his or her asking price. As with price reductions on home listings, a 10–20 percent reduction on the advertised price is common with private sellers. Dealers usually won't cut more than 10 percent off their advertised price.

Repossessed Vehicles

Repossessed pickups and SUVs are quite common among contractors and other small businesses that have gone bankrupt. You can usually find them at auctions, but sometimes finance companies or banks sell them as well. Canadian courts have held that financial institutions are legally responsible for defects found in what they sell, so don't be at all surprised by the disclosure paperwork shoved under your nose. Also, as with rental-car company transactions, these companies' deep pockets and abhorrence of bad publicity means you'll likely get your money back if you make a bad buy. The biggest problem with repossessed vans, sport-utilities, and pickups, in particular, is that they were likely abused or neglected by their financially troubled owners. Although you rarely get to test-drive or closely examine these vehicles, a local dealer may be able to produce a vehicle maintenance history by running the VIN through its manufacturer's database.

Rental and Leased Vehicles

Next to buying privately, the second-best choice for getting a good used vehicle is a rental company or leasing agency. Budget, Hertz, Avis, and National sell vehicles that have one to two years of service and approximately 80,000–100,000 km at cut-rate prices. These rental companies will gladly provide a vehicle's complete history and allow an independent inspection by a qualified mechanic of the buyer's choice, and they'll arrange for competitive financing.

Rental vehicles are generally well maintained, sell for a few thousand dollars more than privately sold vehicles, and come with strong money-back guarantees. Rental car companies also usually settle purchasers' complaints without much hassle so as not to tarnish their image with rental customers.

Rental agencies tend to keep their stock of cars on the outskirts of town near the airport, and they advertise in the local papers. Sales are held year-round as inventory is replenished. Late summer and early fall is usually the peak time to get the best choice, because the new rentals arrive during that period.

Vehicles that have just come off a 3- or 5-year lease are much more competitively priced, generally have less mileage, and are usually as well maintained as rental vehicles. You're also likely to get a better price if you buy directly from the lessee rather than going through the dealership or an independent agency, but remember, you won't have the dealer's leverage to extract post-warranty "goodwill" repairs from the automaker.

New-Car Dealers

New-car dealers aren't bad places to pick up a good used SUV, truck, or van, although prices are 15–20 percent higher than those for vehicles sold privately. Dealers are insured against selling stolen vehicles or vehicles with financing or other liens owing. They also usually allow prospective buyers to have the vehicle inspected by an independent garage, offer a much wider choice of models than do private sellers, and have their own repair facilities to do warranty work. Additionally, if there's a possibility of getting post-warranty "goodwill" compensation from the manufacturer, your dealer can provide additional leverage, particularly if the dealership is a franchisee for the model you have purchased. Finally, if things do go terribly wrong, dealers have deeper pockets than most private sellers, and there's a better chance of getting a refund through the courts because judges hold professional sellers more accountable for what they sell.

"Certified" Vehicles

Almost all automakers provide "certified" used vehicles that have been refurbished by the dealer according to the manufacturer's guidelines. Sometimes, an auto association will certify a vehicle that has been inspected and has had the designated defects corrected. In Alberta, the Alberta Motor Association (AMA) will perform a vehicle inspection at a dealer's request. On each occasion, the AMA gives a written report to the dealer that identifies potential and actual problems, required repairs, and serious defects.

Automaker-certified vehicles guarantee the vehicle's mechanical fitness and provide a warranty according to the age of the vehicle. But these vehicles don't come cheap, mainly because manufacturers force their dealers to bring them up to better-than-average condition before certifying them. Choosing an older certified model can reduce the higher price, or the price can be amortized by keeping the vehicle longer.

Leasing a Used Car

With the exception of using *Leasebusters.com*, which offers extra protection, leasing a used car is a lousy idea. It's generally costlier than an outright purchase, and for most people, the pitfalls far outweigh any advantages. If you must lease, do so for the shortest time possible and make sure the lease is close-ended (meaning that you walk away from the vehicle when the lease period ends). Also, make sure there's a maximum allowance of at least 25,000 km per year and that the charge per excess kilometre is no higher than 8–10 cents.

Used-Car Dealers

Used-car dealers usually sell their vehicles for a bit less than what new-car dealers charge. However, their vehicles may be worth a lot less because they don't get the first pick of top-quality trade-ins. Many independent urban dealerships are marginal operations that can't invest much money in reconditioning their vehicles, which are often collected from auctions and new-car dealers reluctant to sell the vehicles to their own customers. And used-car dealers don't always have the repair facilities to honour what warranties they do provide. Often, their credit terms are easier (but more expensive) than those offered by franchised new-car dealers.

That said, used-car dealers operating in small towns are an entirely different breed. These small, often family-run businesses recondition and resell cars and trucks that usually come from within their communities. Routine servicing is usually done in-house, and more complicated repairs are subcontracted out to specialized garages nearby. On one hand, these small outlets survive by word-of-mouth advertising and wouldn't last long if they didn't deal fairly with local townsfolk. On the other hand, their prices will likely be higher than elsewhere due to the better quality of their used vehicles and the cost of reconditioning and repairing what they sell under warranty.

Auctions

First of all, make sure any auction is legitimate. Many are fronts for used-car lots where sleazy dealers put fake ads in complicit newspapers, pretending to hold auctions that are no more than weekend selling sprees.

Furthermore, you'll need lots of patience, smarts, and luck to pick up anything worthwhile. Government auctions—places where the mythical $50 Jeeps are sold—are fun to attend but highly overrated as places to find bargains. Look at the odds stacked against you: It's impossible to determine the condition of the vehicles put up for bid; prices can go way out of control; and auction employees, professional sellers, and their relatives and friends usually pick over the good stuff long before you ever see it.

To attend commercial auctions is to swim with the piranhas. These auctions are frequented by "ringers," who bid up the prices, and by professional dealers, who pick up cheap, worn-out vehicles unloaded by new-car dealers and independents. There are no guarantees, cash is required, and the vehicles' quality is apt to be as low as their prices. Remember, too, that auction purchases are subject to provincial and federal sales taxes, the auction's sales commission (3–5 percent), and, in some cases, an administrative fee of $25–$50.

If you are interested in shopping at an auto auction, remember that certain days are reserved for dealers only, so call ahead. You'll find the vehicles locked in a compound, but you should have ample opportunity to inspect them and, sometimes, to take a short drive around the property before the auction begins.

Internet

The Internet is the worst place to buy a used car. You don't know the seller, and you know even less about the car. It's easy for an individual to sell a car they don't own, and even easier to create a virtual dealership—with photos of a huge inventory and a modern showroom—when the operation is really run by one guy working out of his basement.

Rating systems are unreliable, too. Ratings from "happy customers" may be nothing but ploys—fictitious posts planted by the seller to give out five-star ratings and create the appearance of an honest and reliable company.

If you must use the Internet, get the seller's full name and a copy of their driver's licence, plus lots of references. Then go see the vehicle, take a road test, and have a mechanic verify whether the car is roadworthy and able to pass a safety inspection.

Although you are taking a bigger risk buying out of province or getting a car from the States, there are a few precautions you can take to protect yourself. First, compare shipping fees with a Canadian automobile transporter like Hansen's (*www.lhf.com/ebay/index.php*). Second, put your money into an escrow account until the vehicle is delivered in satisfactory condition.

 If the car is located in the United States, print out the tips found on eBay's website at *cars.ebay.ca/ebaymotors/explained/checklist/howtobuyUS.html*. eBay takes you through each step in detail, and will tell you if the car is admissible in Canada and what modifications are likely required. If the car will need modification, check with a mechanic for an estimate. And you'll need to get a recall clearance letter from the dealer or automaker to pass the federal inspection. Additional information can be obtained at *www.riv.ca* or by calling the Registrar of Imported Vehicles (RIV) at 1-888-848-8240.

Canada car sales websites

- *AMVOQ.com*—Quebec used car classifieds
- *AutoHunter.ca*—Alberta used car classifieds

- *Autonet.ca*—New and used cars and trucks, new car dealers, new car prices, and reviews
- *AutoTrader.ca*—Used car classifieds from all across Canada
- *BuySell.com*—Classifieds from all across Canada
- *cars.eBay.ca*—The Canadian branch of the premiere site for used cars located anywhere in the world
- *Samarins.com/dealers/index.html*—Toronto and GTA new- and used-car dealers
- *Samarins.com/links.html*—A valuable compendium of other helpful links for Canadians
- *UsedCarsOntario.com*—Classifieds for major cities in Ontario, with links and articles

U.S. car sales websites

- *AutoTrader.com*—New- and used-cars classifieds
- *Cars.com*—Ditto, except it features an "Advanced Search" option
- *CarsDirect.com*—One of the largest car-buying sites on the Internet
- *motors.eBay.com*—Similar to the Canadian site
- *Edmunds.com*—Lots of price quotes and articles
- *TheBigLot.com*—Another large car-buying site

Promises and Precautions

As a buyer, you should get a printed sales agreement, even if it's just handwritten, that includes a clause stating that the vehicle has no outstanding traffic violations or liens against it. It doesn't make a great deal of difference whether the car will be purchased "as is" or certified under provincial regulation. A vehicle sold as "safety certified" can still turn into a lemon or be dangerous to drive. The certification process can be sabotaged if a minimal number of components are checked, the mechanic is incompetent, or the instruments are poorly calibrated. "Certified" is not the same as having a warranty to protect you from engine seizure or transmission failure. It means only that the vehicle has met minimum safety standards on the day tested.

Make sure the vehicle is lien-free and has not been damaged in a flood or written off after an accident. Flood damage can be hard to see, but it impairs ABS, power steering, and airbag functioning (making deployment 10 times slower).

Canada has become a haven for rebuilt U.S. wrecks. Write-offs are also shipped from provinces where there are stringent disclosure regulations to provinces where there are lax rules or no rules at all.

If you suspect your vehicle is a rebuilt wreck from the States, or was once a taxi, there's a useful Canadian search agency called CarProof that can quickly give you a complete history of any vehicle within a day.

CarProof (www.carproof.com)

Operating out of London, Ontario, CarProof's services cost $34.95, $49.95, or $59.95, plus GST, per report. For your $35-plus (depending on which package you choose), you can get the following:

- **Section 1:** Vehicle identification number (VIN) decode and complete vehicle description.
- **Section 2:** Report summary, which highlights the data found in the complete report.
- **Section 3:** Cross-Canada current vehicle registration update, which includes vehicle warning tags applied by any provincial or territorial Department or Ministry of Transportation, such as *Normal, Salvage, Rebuilt, Non-repairable,* and *Stolen.* This section includes registration-effective dates and odometer data, if available.
- **Section 4:** Cross-Canada lien search, which reports any enforceable lien registered against the VIN in all 13 provinces and territories.
- **Section 5:** United States and Canadian vehicle history details. CarProof provides these details through a live connection to Experian Automotive. This section includes all data that would be provided in Experian's AutoCheck report, plus other insurance and registration history provided by CarProof's other data suppliers.
- **Section 6:** New import/export section. Data in this section is already accessed by CarProof and comes from Transport Canada's Registrar of Imported Vehicles (RIV) as well as from the U.S. Department of Transportation. This section reports whether a vehicle has been legally imported into either country as a used vehicle.
- **Section 7:** Odometer history. Reports any odometer records found in Canada or the United States in chronological order.
- **Section 8:** Third-party history. Includes information about aftermarket anti-theft system installations, independent inspections, and other maintenance records.
- **Section 9:** Canadian insurance history. This section provides insurance coverage information and insurance claims history from the private insurance industry all across Canada.

Information requests can be completed overnight online. Contact the company through its website, or if you prefer to talk, call 519-675-1415.

In most provinces, you can do a lien and registration search yourself, but it's hardly worth the effort, considering the low cost and comprehensive nature of the CarProof service.

If a lien does exist, you should contact the creditor(s) listed to find out whether any debts have been paid. If a debt is outstanding, you should arrange with the vendor to pay the creditor the outstanding balance or agree that you can put the purchase price in a trust account to pay the lender. If the debt is larger than the purchase price of the car, it's up to you to decide whether you wish to complete the deal. If the seller agrees to clear the title personally, make sure that you receive a written relinquishment of title from the creditor before transferring any money to the seller. Make sure the title doesn't show an "R" for "restored," since this indicates that the vehicle was written off as a total loss and may not have been properly repaired.

Even if all documents are in order, ask the seller to show you the vehicle's original sales contract and a few repair bills in order to ascertain how well it was maintained. The bills will show you if the odometer was turned back and will also indicate which repairs are still guaranteed. If none of these can be found, run (don't walk!) away. If the contract shows that the car was financed, verify that the loan was paid. If you're still not sure that the vehicle is free of liens, ask your bank or credit union manager to check for you. If no clear answer is forthcoming, look for something else.

Paying the Right Price

Even though prices have become considerably more moderate with large and mid-sized models, get ready for sticker shock when first quoted a price for a small minivan, SUV, or pickup. These vehicles hold their value well because they're more fuel-frugal and owners are reluctant to part with them. Be suspicious of any vehicle that carries a price much lower than you've found elsewhere: It may not be lien-free, the odometer could be rolled back, or it may have been abused through hard off-roading or lack of care. Some bargains can be real, though. For example, it's quite likely that used Jeeps and Chrysler minivans will be more reasonably priced than other makes this year due to dealer "fire sale" prices on new models.

If you don't want to pay too much when buying used, you've got four alternatives:

- Buy an older vehicle. Choose one that's five years old or more and has a good reliability and durability record. Buy extra protection with an extended warranty. The money you save from the extra years' depreciation and lower insurance premiums will more than make up for the extra warranty cost.
- Look for off-lease vehicles sold privately by owners who want more than what their dealer is offering. If you can't find what you're looking for in the local classified ads, put in your own ad asking for lessees to contact you if they aren't satisfied with their dealer's offer.
- Buy a vehicle that's depreciated more than average simply because of its bland styling, unpopular colour (dark blue, white, and champagne are out; silver is in), lack of high-performance features, or discontinuation.
- Buy a cheaper twin or re-badged model, like a fully loaded Camry instead of a Lexus ES, a Toyota Matrix in lieu of a Pontiac Vibe, or a Plymouth Voyager instead of a Dodge Caravan.

 **Price Guides**

The best way to determine the price range for a particular model is to read the *Lemon-Aid* values found in Part Four. From there, you may wish to get a free second opinion by accessing Vehicle Market Research International's (VMR) Canadian Used Car Prices at *www.vmrcanada.com*. It is one of the few free sources listing wholesale and retail values for used cars in Canada. The site even includes a handy calculator that adjusts a vehicle's value according to model, mileage, and options.

Black Book and *Red Book* price guides, found in most libraries, banks, and credit unions, can also be helpful. But accessing their information for free on the Internet takes a little "insider" knowledge. To access the Canadian *Black Book* values, simply type the following URL into your web browser: *www.canadianblackbook.com/prv/auth.cfm?token=AB04DC39ZKL01*.

If you want to use the *Canadian Red Book Vehicle Valuation Guide*, which seems more attuned to Quebec and Ontario sales, you can order single copies of their used car and light truck wholesale and retail price guide for $16.95 at *www.canadianredbook.com* (an annual subscription costs $95 plus PST).

You may also go to *Auto Trader* magazine's website at *www.autotrader.ca* to see what price other Canadians are asking for your vehicle.

Don't be surprised to find that many national price guides have an eastern Ontario and Quebec price bias. They often list unrealistically low prices compared with what you'll actually see in the eastern and western provinces and in rural areas, where good used cars are often sold for outrageously high prices or simply passed down through the family for an average of eight to 10 years. Other price guides may list prices that are much higher than those found in your region. Consequently, use whichever price guide lists the highest value when selling your trade-in or negotiating a write-off value with an insurer. When buying, use the guide with the lowest values as your bargaining tool.

Financing Choices

You shouldn't spend more than 30 percent of your annual gross income on the purchase of a new or used vehicle. By keeping the initial cost low, there is less risk to you, and you may be able to pay mostly in cash. This can be an effective bargaining tool to use with private sellers, but dealers are less impressed by cash sales because they lose their kickback from the finance companies.

Credit Unions

A credit union is the best place to borrow money for a used car at competitive interest rates and with easy repayment terms. You'll have to join the credit union before the loan is approved. You'll also probably have to come up with a larger down payment relative to what other lending institutions require.

Banks

Banks are less leery of financing used cars than they once were, and they generally charge rates that are competitive with what dealers offer. The loan officer will be impressed by a prepared budget and sound references, particularly if you seek out a loan before choosing a vehicle. If you haven't got a loan yet, it won't hurt to buy from a local dealer, since banks like to encourage businesses in their area.

PRICING ON A $15,000 CAR LOAN

LENDER	INTEREST RATE (%)		
	36 months	48 months	60 months
Bank of Montreal	8.75	8.75	8.75
Bank of Nova Scotia	7.75	7.90	8.65
Caisse Desjardin	9.98	9.98	9.98
CIBC	7.25	7.50	7.75
Comtech Credit Union	5.00	5.00	5.00
First Ontario Credit Union	8.25	8.25	8.25
Laurentian Bank	8.00	8.00	8.00
National Bank	8.75	9.00	9.30
Ontario Civil Service Credit Union	5.90	5.90	5.90
Pace Savings & Credit Union	6.00	6.00	6.00
Royal Bank	8.35	8.40	8.45
So-Use Credit Union	6.75	6.75	6.75
Steinbach Credit Union	5.25	5.25	5.25
TD Canada Trust	9.00	9.00	9.00
Virtual One Credit Untion	N/A	N/A	6.49

Dealers

Dealer financing isn't the rip-off it once was, but still be watchful for all the expensive little extras the dealer may try to pencil into the contract, because, believe it or not, dealers make far more profit on used-car sales than on new-car deals. Don't write them off for financing, though—they can finance your purchase at rates that compete with those of banks and finance companies, because they agree to take back the vehicle if the creditor defaults on the loan (Mitsubishi is adrift in red ink because of its sub-prime loans to dead-beat drivers). Some dealers mislead their customers into thinking they can get financing at rates far below the prime rate. Actually, the dealer jacks up the base price of the vehicle to compensate for the lower interest charges.

Dealer Scams

Most dealer sales scams are so obvious, they're laughable. But like the Nigerian "lost fortune" email scams, enough stupid people get sucked in to make these dealer deceptions profitable.

One of the more common tricks is to not identify the previous owner because the vehicle was used commercially, was problem-prone, or was written off as a total loss after an accident. It's also not uncommon to discover that the mileage has been turned back, particularly if the vehicle was part of a company's fleet. Your best defence? Demand the name of the vehicle's previous owner and then run a VIN check through CarProof as a prerequisite to purchasing it.

It would be impossible to list all the dishonest tricks employed in used-vehicle sales. As soon as the public is alerted to one scheme, crooked sellers use other, more-elaborate frauds. Nevertheless, under industry-financed provincial compensation funds, buyers can get substantial refunds if defrauded by a dealer.

The following sections outline some of the more common fraudulent practices you're likely to encounter.

 ## Lying to Save Sales Tax

Here's where your own greed will do you in. In a tactic used almost exclusively by small, independent dealers and some private sellers, the buyer is told that he or she can pay less sales tax by listing a lower selling price on the contract. But what if the vehicle turns out to be a lemon, or the sales agent has falsified the model year or mileage? The hapless buyer is offered a refund on the fictitious purchase price indicated on the contract. If the buyer wanted to take the dealer to court, it's quite unlikely that he or she would get any more than the contract price. Moreover, both the buyer and dealer could be prosecuted for making a false declaration to avoid paying sales tax.

Phony Private Sales ("Curbsiders")

Many used-car buyers prefer to shop private ads in order to get the best price. Crooked dealers know this and get in on the action by posing as private sellers. Called "curbsiders," these scammers lure unsuspecting buyers through lower prices, cheat the federal government out of the GST, and routinely violate provincial registration and consumer protection regulations. Bob Beattie, executive director of the Used Car Dealers Association of Ontario, *www.ucda.org*, says his organization has found that about 20 percent of so-called private sellers in Ontario are actually curbsiders. Dealers in large cities like Toronto, Calgary, and Vancouver believe curbsiders sell half of the cars advertised in the local papers. This scam is easy to detect if the seller can't produce the original sales contract or show repair bills made out over a long period of time in his or her own name. You can usually identify a car dealer in the want ads section of the newspaper—just check to see if the same telephone number is repeated in many different ads. Sometimes you can trip up a curbsider by requesting information on the phone, without identifying the specific vehicle. If the seller asks you which car you are considering, you know you're dealing with a dealer.

Legitimate car dealers claim to deplore the dishonesty of curbsider crooks, yet they are their chief suppliers. Dealership sales managers, auto auction employees, and newspaper classified ad sellers all know the names, addresses, and phone numbers of these thieves but don't act on the information. Newspapers want the ad dollars, auctions want the action, and dealers want someplace they can unload their wrecked, rust-cankered, and odometer-tricked junkers with impunity. Talk about hypocrisy, eh?

Curbsiders are particularly active in western Canada, importing vehicles from other provinces where they were sold by dealers, wreckers, insurance companies, and junkyards (after having been written off as total losses). They then place private classified ads in B.C. and Alberta papers, sell their stock, and then import more. Writes one Vancouver *Lemon-Aid* reader frustrated by the complicity of the provincial government and local papers in this rip-off:

> The story is the lack of sensitivity by the newspapers who turn a blind eye and let consumers get ripped off.... The newspapers are making money, ICBC [Insurance Corporation of British Columbia] is making money, the cops acknowledge wide-scale dumping on the West Coast.... Governments have no willpower to take on organized fraud.

Buyers taken in by these scam artists should sue both the seller and the newspaper that carried the original classified ad in small claims court. When just a few cases are won in court and other media play up the story, the practice will cease.

"Free-Exchange" Privilege

Dealers get a lot of sales mileage out of this deceptive offer. The dealer offers to exchange any defective vehicle for any other vehicle in stock. What really happens, though, is that the dealer won't have anything else selling for the same price and so will demand a cash bonus for the exchange—or you may get the dubious privilege of exchanging one lemon for another.

"Money-Back" Guarantee

Once again, the purchaser feels safe in buying a used car with this kind of guarantee. After all, what could be more honest than a money-back guarantee? Dealers using this technique often charge exorbitant handling charges, rental fees, or mechanical repair costs to the customer who's bought one of these vehicles and then returned it.

"50/50" Guarantee

This can be a trap.

Essentially, the dealer will pay half of the repair costs over a limited period of time. It's a fair offer if an independent garage does the repairs. If not, the dealer can always inflate the repair costs to double their actual worth and then write up a bill for that amount (a scam sometimes used in "goodwill" settlements). The buyer winds up paying the full price of repairs that would probably have been much cheaper at an independent garage. The best kind of used-vehicle warranty is 100 percent with full coverage for a fixed term, even if that term is relatively short.

"As Is" and "No Warranty"

Neither phrase means much.

Remember, every vehicle carries a provincial legal warranty protecting you from misrepresentation and the premature failure of key mechanical or body components. Nevertheless, sellers often write "as is" or "no warranty" in the contract in the hope of dissuading buyers from pressing legitimate claims.

Generally, a vehicle with "as is" written in the contract or bill of sale usually means that you're aware of mechanical defects, you're prepared to accept the responsibility for any damage or injuries caused by the vehicle, and you're agreeing to pay all repair costs. However, the courts have held that the "as is" clause is not a free pass to cheat buyers and must be interpreted in light of the seller's true intent. Was there an attempt to deceive the buyer by including this clause? Did the buyer really know what the "as is" clause could do to his or her future legal rights? It's also been held that the courts may consider oral representations ("parole evidence") as an expressed warranty, even though they were never written into the formal contract. So, if a seller makes claims as to the fine quality of the used vehicle, these claims can be used as evidence. Courts generally ignore "as is" clauses when the vehicle has been intentionally misrepresented, when the dealer is the seller, or when the defects are so serious that the seller is presumed to have known of their existence. Private sellers are usually given more latitude than dealers or their agents.

Odometer Fraud

Who says crime doesn't pay? It most certainly does if you turn back odometers for a living in Canada.

Carfax (*www.carfax.com*) estimates that each year close to 90,000 vehicles with tampered odometers reach the Canadian marketplace—at a cost to Canadians of more than $3.56 million. This is about double the incidents one would expect based on a 2002 U.S. National Highway Traffic Safety Administration study that pegs odometer fraud at 450,000 vehicles annually. NHTSA estimates that half of the cars with reset odometers are relatively new high-mileage rental cars or fleet vehicles.

Obviously, gangs of odometer scammers ply their trade in Canada because it seems as if no one cares what they do, and the average resale value of a doctored car can be boosted by thousands of dollars, or 10 cents profit for each mile erased from the odometer. Moreover, electronic digital odometers make tampering child's play for anyone with a laptop computer, or anyone who has sufficient skill to simply replace the dashboard's instrument panel.

Think: When was the last time you heard of a dealership being charged with odometer fraud? Probably a long time ago, if at all. And what is the punishment for those dealers convicted of defrauding buyers? Not jail time or loss of their franchises. More than likely, it'll be just a small fine.

The RCMP hate odometer-tampering complaints because rolling back a vehicle's odometer is a common crime that's hard to prove and gobbles up law enforcement employees' hours. In theory, these fraud artists face $100,000 fines and two years in jail under the *Federal Weights and Measures Act,* the Canadian *Criminal Code,* and provincial consumer-protection statutes. However, in practice, few odometer-tampering cases make it to court because the intent to defraud is so difficult to prove against mechanics who claim they only fixed the odometer, a practice allowed under Canadian federal and provincial laws.

Misrepresentation

Used vehicles can be misrepresented in a variety of ways. A used airport commuter minivan may be represented as having been operated by a Sunday school class. A mechanically defective pickup that's been rebuilt after several major accidents may have plastic filler in the body panels to muffle the rattles or hide the rust damage, heavy oil in the motor to stifle the clanks, and cheap retread tires to eliminate the thumps. Your best protection against these dirty tricks is to have the vehicle's quality completely verified by an independent mechanic before completing the sale. Of course, you can still cancel the sale if you learn of the misrepresentation only after taking the vehicle home, but your chances of doing so successfully dwindle as time passes.

> I'm finding it difficult finding a reasonably priced used car in the Toronto area. Many of the ads for private sales here turn out to be dealers or mechanics selling cars pretending to be private persons. Also, the prices are ridiculously inflated. Your books are a great read and have made me at least slow down and ask questions. For example, I almost got caught in a lease the other day and pulled out at the last minute. All this advertising had me believe there would be zero down, zero delivery, etc. until I found out there would be a $350 lease acquisition fee and a $250 admin. fee and all kinds

of other charges, some legitimate such as licensing. However, my zero down turned into a whopping $1,200! I'm just now getting into your leasing section.

Private Scams

A lot of space in this guide has been used to describe how used-car dealers and scam artists cheat uninformed buyers. Of course, private individuals can be dishonest, too. In either case, protect yourself at the outset by keeping your deposit small and by getting as much information as possible about the vehicle you're considering. Then, after a test drive, you may sign a written agreement to purchase the vehicle and give a deposit of sufficient value to cover the seller's advertising costs, subject to cancellation if the automobile fails its inspection. After you've taken these precautions, watch out for the following private sellers' tricks.

Vehicles That Are Stolen or Have Finance Owing

Many used vehicles are sold privately without free title because the original auto loan was never repaid. You can prevent being cheated by asking for proof of purchase and payment from a private seller. Be especially wary of any individual who offers to sell a used vehicle for an incredibly low price. Check the sales contract to determine who granted the original loan, and call the lender to see if it's been repaid. Place a call to the provincial or territorial Department or Ministry of Transportation to ascertain whether the car is registered in the seller's name. Find out if a finance company is named as beneficiary on the auto insurance policy. Finally, contact the original dealer to determine whether there are any outstanding claims.

In Ontario, all private sellers must purchase a Used Vehicle Information Package at one of 300 provincial Driver and Vehicle Licence Issuing Offices, or online at *www.mto.gov.on.ca/english/dandv/vehicle/used.htm*. This package, which costs $20, contains the vehicle's registration history in Ontario; the vehicle's lien information (i.e., if there are any liens registered on the vehicle); the fair market value on which the minimum tax payable will apply; and other information such as consumer tips, vehicle safety standards inspection guidelines, retail sales tax information, and forms for bills of sale.

In other provinces, buyers do not have easy access to this information. Generally, you have to contact the provincial office that registers property and pay a small fee for a computer printout that may or may not be accurate. You'll be asked for the current owner's name and the car's VIN, which is usually found on the driver's side of the dashboard.

There are two high-tech ways to get the goods on a dishonest seller. First, have a dealer of that particular model run a "vehicle history" check through the automaker's online network. This will tell you who the previous owners and dealers were, what warranty and recall repairs were carried out, and what other free repair programs may still apply. Second, you can use CarProof (*www.carproof. com*) to carry out a background check.

Wrong Registration

Make sure the seller's vehicle has been properly registered with provincial transport authorities; if it isn't, it may be stolen, or you could be dealing with a curbsider.

If you are selling a vehicle, protect yourself from legal liability by ensuring the registration has been transferred to the buyer. Normally, once you take off the plates and give the buyer a bill of sale, you're no longer the registered owner. Nonetheless, it's a good idea to go down to the registry office to make sure the title has changed. As long as you're still listed as the owner of record, you could be sued for damages arising from an accident.   .

Selling Your Vehicle

Usually you will get the best price by selling to a private buyer. Expect a dealer to give you only about half as much, though you may get a bit more if the dealer sells the same make of vehicle.

Selling privately carries its own burdens, however: several hundred dollars to make the vehicle presentable; another $100 or so for ads; prospects calling you at all times of the day and night (even after the car has been sold); and "tire kickers" who aren't serious buyers.

Worst of all, private buyers can hassle you for a complete refund of the purchase price or for money they spent on repairs to fix defects they say you failed to disclose. Remember, they have your home address and telephone number, and nothing stops them from filing a small claims court lawsuit.

Phew. Now that you're petrified by all that can go wrong, keep the following in mind: Most private buyers don't mind signing a receipt that says the vehicle was sold "as is," and they accept the fact that the vehicle may have some flaws. Furthermore, Canadian courts, while tough on dealers (who are *presumed* to know which defects exist), seldom rule against private sellers, unless it's obvious there was an attempt to deceive the buyer. That's why it's a smart idea to indicate on your "as is" receipt that the buyer was offered a chance to have the vehicle inspected by a third party prior to the purchase.

Incidentally, this third-party inspection gets you a free $75–$100 check-up, separates the serious buyers from the shoppers, and allows you to reduce the selling price as partial compensation for expected repairs.

Car Heaven?

Some vehicles are in such poor shape that they can't be re-sold. For them, there's always Car Heaven.

Operating as a non-profit group, Car Heaven was founded by the Clean Air Foundation, an organization working specifically on air quality issues in Canada. The Car Heaven Program encourages Canadians to get their old, high-polluting cars off the road sooner than they might do otherwise by giving each donor a free tow (valued at $200) and a minimum $50 or $60 charitable tax receipt. Additional incentives include bicycles, transit passes, or a $1,000 coupon toward the purchase or lease of a new GM vehicle. Incentives vary depending on the condition of your vehicle and the province in which you live. Details are available on the Car Heaven website (*www.carheaven.ca*).

Donated cars are picked up and processed by local members of the Automotive Retailers Association of British Columbia (ARA) in B.C., the Automotive Recyclers of Manitoba (ARM) in Manitoba, the Ontario Automotive Recyclers Association (OARA) in Ontario, L'Association des Recycleurs de Pièces d'Autos et de Camions (ARPAC) in Quebec, and the Automotive Recyclers Association of Atlantic Canada (ARAAC) in the Atlantic provinces. Their members are committed to the environmentally friendly processing of cars and their parts—including oil, fluids, and tires. Any reusable parts that don't produce emissions are removed and prepared for resale, but none of the vehicles donated to the program are allowed back out on the street to continue polluting. So far, Car Heaven has raised over $2 million for affiliated charities.

Car Heaven covers large cities but cannot handle requests in some small communities, or may require that vehicles be dropped off.

Summary: Saving Money and Keeping Safe

You can get a reliable used SUV, truck, or van at a reasonable price—it just takes some patience and homework. Prevent potential headaches by becoming thoroughly familiar with your legal rights as outlined in Part Three and by buying a vehicle that's rated Recommended in Part Four. The following is a summary of the steps to take to keep your level of risk to a minimum:

1. Keep your present vehicle at least eight to 10 years. Don't get panicked over high fuel costs—depreciation is a greater threat to your pocketbook.
2. Sell to a dealer if the reduction in GST and PST on your next purchase is greater than the potential profit of selling privately.

3. Sell privately if you can get at least 15 percent more than what the dealer offers.
4. Buy from a private party, a rental car outlet, or a dealer (in that order).
5. Use an auto broker to save time and money, but pay a set fee, not a commission.
6. Buy a *Lemon-Aid*-recommended 3- to 5-year-old vehicle with some original warranty left that can be transferred.
7. Carefully inspect front-drive vehicles that have reached their fifth year. Pay particular attention to the engine intake manifold and head gasket, CV joints, steering box, and brakes. Make sure that the spare tire and tire jack haven't been removed.
8. Buy a full-sized, rear-drive delivery van and then add the convenience features that you would like (seats, sound system, etc.) instead of opting for a more-expensive, smaller, less-powerful minivan.
9. Don't buy an extended warranty for a particular model year unless it's recommended in *Lemon-Aid*.
10. Have repairs done by independent garages that offer lifetime warranties.
11. Install used or reconditioned fenders and powertrain parts, demand that original parts be used for accident repairs that are covered by an insurance claim, and install brake and exhaust system parts that are covered by a lifetime warranty.
12. Keep all the previous owners' repair bills to facilitate warranty claims and to let mechanics know what's already been replaced or repaired.
13. Upon delivery, adjust mirrors to reduce blind spots and adjust head restraints to prevent your head from snapping back in the event of a collision. On airbag-equipped vehicles, move the seat backward more than half of its travel distance and then sit at least 25 cm (1 ft.) away from the airbag housing.
14. Ensure that the side airbags include head protection.
15. Make sure that both the dealer and automaker have your name in their computers as the new owner of record. Ask for a copy of your vehicle's history, which should be stored in the same computer. Get a $25 Internet download or data disc of all your vehicle's service bulletins from ALLDATA (see Appendix II). This will keep you current regarding the latest secret warranties, recalls, and troubleshooting tips for correcting factory screw-ups.

Part Three

LIARS AND LAWYERS

Iran's Lemon Law

Iranian President Mahmoud Ahmadinejad…under a decree has notified the Law of Protection of Car Users for implementation. The law was passed by the Iranian Parliament on 13 June 2007.

According to the Law, the guarantee period cannot be less than one year from the time of delivery of the car to the user or a performance equal to 30,000 kilometers (or whichever expires first). The warranty period for provision of spare parts and technical services shall be ten years from the date of actual delivery.

The law stipulates that, "During the guarantee period the supplier is obliged to remove all defects from the car at his own expense and compensate all damages inflicted upon the user and third parties resulting from the defects that are not covered by the related insurance."

The legislation…also foresees that a new car (or its price upon agreement) must be reimbursed to the owner if sensitive defects are not removed after repair, or the car has become unusable for more than thirty days due to repairs.

Presstv.com, AUGUST 3, 2007

Can you believe it? Car buyers in Iran have more protection than Canadians. Particularly, that provision giving manufacturers only 30 days to fix or replace the vehicle. If such a statute were in force in Canada, automakers would have to improve their products and servicing, or shut down.

Take General Motors, for example. "GM" doesn't stand for "*Generous* Motors." The company lies, obfuscates, and distorts, and seldom admits to its mistakes, such as minivans with sliding doors that open on their own or break your arm when closing, diesel engines that self-destruct, vans with rust holes in their roofs, and Corvettes with roofs that fly off on the highway.

But Chrysler and Ford don't level with their customers, either. This is the case whether it's Chrysler's automatic transmissions that disintegrate; Dodge's trucks and SUVs that wander all over the road when their ball joints fail; or Ford's Explorers and pickups that suddenly run amok when their brakes fail or tie-rods break, or that suddenly stop when their 4.6L, 5.4L, or V10 engines spit out their spark plugs. No wonder owners feel as if they need exorcists, not mechanics. The NHTSA complaint on the following page is from the owner of a 2000 Ford F-150:

Two weeks ago while traveling on a two lane highway with the cruise control set at 55 mph [89 km/h], I blew the #4 plug right out of the cylinder head. Dealer quoted a price of $3,668 plus tax to fix the engine. This is ludicrous! I am expected to pay this much money for a Ford design issue! I can get another engine for slightly more than that! Heck, I can get a decent commuter car for that much money! In researching this issue, I have found that this is a somewhat common problem with Ford's Triton engines. I also found an alternative method of fixing the engine, which only cost me $350, of which $300 was in the cost of the tools. I cannot believe that Ford will not admit to this engineering design problem and assist those of us who have loyally supported them for years. I guess if people are not dying, it is just seen as an easy way to overcharge people and make extra money via their service departments!

As unbelievable as it seems, these defects aren't that rare. If you've bought an unsafe or unreliable vehicle, whether new or used, and the automaker stonewalls your complaint, this part of the book is for you. My intention is to help you make a successful claim—without fear and loathing, becoming frazzled, or going to court. But if going to court is your only recourse, here is 40 years' worth of information on strategies, tactics, negotiation tools, and jurisprudence to help you hang tough and either get an out-of-court settlement or win your case without spending a fortune on lawyers and research.

TOP 35 U.S.-BASED WARRANTY PROVIDERS: IMPROVEMENT IN CLAIMS RATES, FIRST HALF 2007 VS. FIRST HALF 2006 (IN $ MILLIONS AND PERCENT)

COMPANY	CLAIMS PAID 1/2 2007	CLAIMS PAID 1/2 2006	LATEST CLAIMS RATE	VS. YEAR AGO
Goodrich Corp.	$18	$33	0.5%	−52%
Nortel Networks Corp.	$79	$140	1.8%	−42%
Delphi Corp.	$53	$85	0.4%	−36%
Eastman Kodak Co.	$20	$46	1.1%	−27%
Deere & Co.	$206	$255	1.6%	−26%

COMPANY	CLAIMS PAID 1/2 2007	CLAIMS PAID 1/2 2006	LATEST CLAIMS RATE	VS. YEAR AGO
American Standard	$58	$69	1.1%	−26%
IBM Corp.	$327	$386	3.2%	−18%
Western Digital Corp.		$29	1.0%	−18%
Applied Materials Inc.	$87	$94	1.7%	−18%
EMC Corp.	$63	$59	1.4%	−17%
AGCO Corp.	$58	$57	1.8%	−15%
General Electric Co.		$333	1.0%	−15%
Eaton Corp.		$42	0.7%	−14%
Agilent Technologies	$28	$34	1.3%	−13%
Exide Technologies		$27	1.7%	−10%
Hewlett-Packard Co.	$1,208	$1,197	2.9%	−10%
Ford Motor Co.	**$1,949**	**$2,060**	**2.5%**	**−10%**
Boeing Co.	$108	$102	0.7%	−7.8%
Daher Corp.	$46	$43	0.9%	−7.1%
Cummins Inc.	$150	$144	2.4%	−6.7%
Terex Corp.	$47	$44	1.1%	−5.8%
Sun Microsystems		$174	4.3%	−5.8%
Cisco Systems Inc.	$240	$187	1.6%	−5.1%
Jarden Corp.	$60	$59	4.5%	−3.6%
Apple Inc.	$153	$138	1.7%	−3.1%
Ingersoll-Rand	$36	$50	0.9%	−1.7%
Masco Corp.	$28	$30	0.6%	−1.1%
Navistar International			2.4%	
Dell Inc.		$898	4.0%	
Pulte Homes Inc.	$51	$82	1.3%	+0.8%
General Motors Corp.	**$2,240**	**$2,193**	**2.5%**	**+1.8%**
Palm Inc.	$42	$37	5.0%	+1.9%
Novellus Systems Inc.	$40	$41	5.1%	+4.6%
Brunswick Corp.	$56	$54	2.3%	+6.5%
Motorola Inc.		$446	2.1%	+6.9%

Source: Warranty Week from SEC data.

WarrantyWeek.com says Chrysler and Ford will likely cut warranty costs, making it tempting to deny warranty claims altogether.

The Road to a Refund

You don't have to depend upon the written warranty terms in order to get a refund.

Vehicles usually turn out to be bad buys for two reasons: Either they were misrepresented or they are afflicted with defects that make them unreliable or dangerous to drive. Misrepresentation is relatively easy to prove; you simply have to show that the vehicle doesn't conform to the oral or written sales representations made before or during the time of purchase. These representations include sales brochures and newspaper, radio, and television ads.

Private sales can easily be cancelled if the mileage has been turned back, if accident damage hasn't been disclosed, or if the seller is really a dealer in disguise. Even descriptive phrases like "well maintained," "driven by a woman" (is this supposed to be a positive or negative feature?), or "excellent condition" can get a seller in trouble if it's not 100 percent true.

Defects are usually confirmed after purchase by an independent garage examination that shows the deficiencies are premature, are factory-related and not maintenance-related, or were hidden at the time of purchase. However, more and more buyers are using information services like CarProof to bolster their demand for a refund:

> A couple of weeks ago we at CarProof received a decision that came out from the Motor Dealer Council in B.C. (now called the Vehicle Safety Authority (similar to OMVIC in Ontario)) regarding a woman we helped to get her money back on a 2005 Honda Odyssey minivan.
>
> This lady is a police officer who purchased the van for her family and became concerned when the [head restraint] didn't work and the dealer (Scott Gillies, owner of SRG Auto in Victoria, B.C.) wouldn't assist. She reached the previous owner in California by searching on the navigation unit which still had their name and phone number listed. After talking to the previous owner she came to find out that the vehicle was in a head-on collision and the family dog was killed in the van as a result of the accident. The family was so distraught that they sold the van at auction for $10,000 less than what they owed on it. The buyer, Scott Gillies of SRG Auto, imported the vehicle and sold it to a woman in B.C. as "Normal" and when she returned it, sold it again as "Normal" to our customer, notwithstanding the fact that it had major damage to it which was disclosed at the auction as the vehicle was run as red light and the invoice had "FRAME DAMMAGE" [sic] stamped on it when Gillies bought the vehicle at the auction in California. He then had the audacity to resell it to someone else in Calgary (a father of 4 young children).
>
> Gillies tried to hide behind a Carfax report that did not disclose any damage on the vehicle. He even went as far as saying to our customer that he had never heard of CarProof and they were likely some phony Internet company. When we investigated, we determined he had in fact run a CarProof report on this vehicle four days before telling our customer that he had never heard of the CarProof report, so he was well aware of the damage and the report.... I have updated our report for this vehicle: *reports.carproof.net/view_report.aspx?id=CD1791A32DA9* (there are no names or addresses) and have run a new Carfax report for this vehicle. Carfax still indicates that there is no damage to the vehicle.
>
> HOLDEN J. RHODES, VICE-PRESIDENT & CORPORATE COUNSEL
> *CarProof.com*

Nipping That Lemon in the Bud

It's really not that hard to get a refund if you take it one step at a time. Vehicle defects are covered by two warranties: the *expressed* warranty, which has a fixed time limit, and the *implied* (or legal) warranty, which is entirely up to a judge's discretion.

Expressed warranties

The expressed warranty given by the seller is often full of empty promises, and it allows the dealer and manufacturer to act as judge and jury when deciding whether a vehicle was misrepresented or is afflicted with defects they'll pay to correct. Rarely does it provide a money-back guarantee.

Some of the more familiar lame excuses used in denying expressed warranty claims are "You abused the car," "It was poorly maintained," "It's normal wear and tear," "It's rusting from the outside, not the inside," and "It passed the safety inspection." Ironically, the expressed warranty sometimes says that there is no warranty at all, or that the vehicle is sold "as is." And, when the warranty's clauses (or lack of) don't deter claimants, some dealers simply say that a verbal warranty or representation as to the vehicle's attributes is unenforceable. Fortunately, courts routinely throw out these exclusions by upholding three legal concepts:

- Vehicles must be fit for the purpose for which they were purchased.
- Vehicles must be of merchantable quality when sold.
- Verbal promises or representations carry the strength of written warranties, and buyers and their relatives *can* testify as to what they were told.

Watch fuel economy claims

Canadian courts are cracking down on lying dealers and deceptive sales practices, and the misrepresenting of fuel economy figures is squarely in the judiciary's sights. Ontario's recently amended *Consumer Protection Act* (*www.e-laws.gov.on.ca/ html/statutes/english/elaws_statutes_02c30_e.htm*), for example, lets vehicle buyers cancel a contract within one year of entering into an agreement if a dealer made a false, misleading, deceptive, or unconscionable representation. This includes using exaggeration, innuendo, or ambiguity as to a material fact, or failing to state a material fact if such use or failure deceives or tends to deceive consumers.

This law means that new- or used-car dealers cannot make the excuse that they were fooled about the condition or performance of a vehicle, or that they were simply providing data supplied by the manufacturer. The law clearly states that both parties are jointly liable and that dealers are *presumed* to know the history, quality, and true performance of what they are selling.

Details like fuel economy can lead to a contract's cancellation, if the dealer gives a higher-than-actual figure. In *Sidney v. 1011067 Ontario Inc. (c.o.b. Southside Motors)*, a precedent-setting case that was filed before Ontario's *Consumer Protection Act* was toughened, the buyer was awarded $11,424.51 plus prejudgment interest because of a false representation made by the defendant regarding fuel efficiency. The plaintiff claimed that the defendant advised him the vehicle had a fuel efficiency of 800–900 km per tank of fuel when, in fact, the maximum efficiency was only 500 km per tank.

This consumer victory is particularly important as fuel prices soar and everyone from automakers to sellers of ineffective gas-saving gadgets make outlandishly false fuel economy claims.

Not surprisingly, sellers try to use the expressed warranty to reject claims, while smart plaintiffs ignore the expressed warranty and argue for a refund under the implied warranty instead.

Implied warranties

The implied warranty ("of fitness") is your ace in the hole. As clearly stated in the unreported Saskatchewan decision *Maureen Frank v. General Motors of Canada Limited* (found exclusively in *Lemon-Aid* on page 188)—in which the judge declared that paint discoloration and peeling shouldn't occur within 11 years of the purchase of a vehicle—the implied warranty is an important legal principle. It's solidly supported by a large body of federal and provincial laws, regulations, and jurisprudence, and it protects you primarily from hidden dealer- or factory-related defects. But the concept also includes misrepresentation and a host of other scams.

This warranty also holds dealers to a higher standard of conduct than private sellers because, unlike private sellers, dealers are presumed to be aware of the defects present in the vehicles they sell. That way, they can't just pass the ball to the automaker or to the previous owner and then walk away from the dispute.

Provincial laws say a vehicle must be built to last for a reasonable period of time or else its purchase price may be refunded.

Dealers are also expected to disclose defects that have been repaired. For instance, in British Columbia, provincial law (the *Motor Dealer Act*) says that a dealer must disclose damages that cost more than $2,000 to fix. This is a good law to cite in other jurisdictions.

In spite of all your precautions, there's still a 10 percent chance you'll buy a lemon, says Runzheimer International. It confirms that one out of every 10 vehicles produced by the Detroit Big Three is likely to be a lemon (a figure also used by GM Vice President Bob Lutz when he was a Chrysler executive). And owners of engine- and transmission-challenged Chrysler Caravans and Ford Windstars, GM vans with peeling paint and rust holes in the roof, and failure-prone Silverados and Sierras would probably put that figure much higher.

Why the implied warranty is so effective

- It establishes the concept of reasonable durability (see "How Long Should a Part or Repair Last?", following), meaning that parts are expected to last for a reasonable period of time, as stated in jurisprudence, judged by independent mechanics, or expressed in extended warranties given by the automaker in the past (7–10 years/160,000 km for engines and transmissions).
- It covers the entire vehicle and can be applied for whatever period of time the judge decides.
- It can order that the vehicle be taken back or that a major repair cost be refunded.
- It can help plaintiffs claim compensation for supplementary transportation, inconvenience, mental distress, missed work, screwed-up vacations, insurance paid while the vehicle was in the repair shop, repairs done by other mechanics, and exemplary, or punitive, damages in cases where the seller was a real weasel.
- It is frequently used by small claims court judges to give refunds to plaintiffs "in equity" (out of fairness) rather than through a strict interpretation of contract law.

How Long Should a Part or Repair Last?

How do you know when a part or service hasn't lasted as long as it should, or whether you should seek a full or partial refund? Sure, you have a gut feeling based on the use of the vehicle, how you maintained it, and the extent of work that was carried out. But you'll need more than emotion to win compensation from garages and automakers.

You can definitely get a refund if a repair or part lasts beyond its guarantee but not as long as is generally expected. But you'll have to show what the auto industry considers to be "reasonable durability." Automakers, mechanics, and the courts all have their own benchmarks as to what's a reasonable period of time or amount of mileage that one should expect a part or adjustment to last. Consequently, I've prepared the "Reasonable Part Durability" table to show what most automakers consider to be reasonable durability, as expressed by their original and "goodwill" warranties.

Many of these guidelines were extrapolated from Chrysler's and Ford's payouts to thousands of dissatisfied customers over the past decade, in addition to Chrysler's original 7-year powertrain warranty (applicable from 1991 to 1995 and reapplied from 2001 to 2004). Other sources of information for this table include Ford and GM transmission warranties, outlined in their secret warranties; Ford, GM, and Toyota engine "goodwill" programs, laid out in their internal service bulletins; and court judgments where judges have given their own guidelines as to what constitutes reasonable durability.

REASONABLE PART DURABILITY

ACCESSORIES

Air conditioner	7 years
Cruise control	5 years/100,000 km
Power doors, windows	5 years
Radio	5 years

BODY

Paint (peeling)	7–11 years
Rust (perforations)	7–11 years
Rust (surface)	5 years
Water/wind/air leaks	5 years

BRAKE SYSTEM

Brake drum	120,000 km
Brake drum linings	35,000 km
Brake rotor	60,000 km
Brake calipers/pads	30,000 km
Master cylinder	100,000 km
Wheel cylinder	80,000 km

ENGINE AND DRIVETRAIN

CV joint	6 years/160,000 km
Differential	7 years/160,000 km
Engine (diesel)	15 years/350,000 km
Engine (gas)	7 years/160,000 km
Radiator	4 years/80,000 km
Transfer case	7 years/160,000 km
Transmission (auto.)	7 years/160,000 km
Transmission (man.)	10 years/250,000 km
Transmission oil cooler	5 years/100,000 km

EXHAUST SYSTEM

Catalytic converter	8–10 years/100,000 km or more
Muffler	2 years/40,000 km
Tailpipe	3 years/60,000 km

IGNITION SYSTEM

Cable set	60,000 km
Electronic module	5 years/80,000 km
Retiming	20,000 km
Spark plugs	20,000 km
Tune-up	20,000 km

SAFETY COMPONENTS

Airbags	life of vehicle
ABS brakes	7 years/160,000 km
ABS computer	10 years/160,000 km
Seat belts	life of vehicle

STEERING AND SUSPENSION

Alignment	1 year/20,000 km
Ball joints	10 years/160,000 km
Coil springs	10 years/160,000 km
Power steering	5 years/80,000 km
Shock absorber	2 years/40,000 km
Struts	5 years/80,000 km
Tires (radial)	5 years/80,000 km
Wheel bearing	3 years/60,000 km

VISIBILITY

Halogen/fog lights	3 years
Sealed beam	2 years
Windshield wiper motor	5 years

Safety features—with the exception of anti-lock brake systems (ABS)—generally have a lifetime warranty. Chrysler's 10-year "free-service" program, part of its 1993–99 ABS recall, can serve as a handy benchmark as to how long one can expect these components to last on more-recent models.

Airbags are a different matter. Those that are deployed in an accident—and the personal injuries and interior damage their deployment will likely have caused—

Download data from a "black box" data recorder to prove that your airbag, brake, or accelerator malfunctioned, regardless of whether an accident ensued. This gets around the excuse that "there was nothing wrong."

are covered by your accident insurance policy. However, if there is a sudden deployment for no apparent reason, the automaker and the dealer should be held jointly responsible for all injuries and damage caused by the airbag. You can prove their liability by downloading the data from your vehicle's data recorder. This will likely lead to a more generous settlement from the two parties and will prevent your insurance premiums from being jacked up.

Use the manufacturer's emissions warranty as your primary guideline for the expected durability of high-tech electronic and mechanical pollution-control components such as powertrain control modules (PCMs) and catalytic converters. Look first at your owner's manual for an indication of which parts on your vehicle are covered. If you come up with few details, ask the auto manufacturer for a list of the specific components covered by the emissions warranty. As a last resort, sue for the parts and labour costs in small claims court and then let the dealer and automaker sort it out. Usually, these claims result in a three-party split of the costs.

Getting Action

Before we go any further, let's get one thing straight: A telephone call usually won't get you much action from a corporation. Automakers and their dealers want to make money, not give it back. You must send a registered letter or an email to create a paper trail and to get attention. What's more, that correspondence must contain the threat that you will use the implied warranty against the defendant and cite powerful jurisprudence to win your small claims court action in the same region where that business operates.

On pages 178–179 are two sample complaint letters that give you much of what you'll need to invoke the implied warranty, in order to get a refund for a bad vehicle or for ineffective repairs.

Legal "Secrets" That Work for You

Send a claim letter to both the seller and the automaker and let them work out together how much they will give you back. Make sure your letter is sent to the automaker's legal affairs department (usually in Ontario) where policy is made, not to where it's simply carried out.

Unfair sales contracts can be cancelled, but sales contracts aren't supposed to be fair. Lawyers spend countless hours making sure their corporate clients are well protected with ironclad standard-form contracts. Judges look upon these agreements, called "contracts of adhesion," with a great deal of skepticism. They know these loan documents, insurance contracts, and automobile leases grant consumers little or no bargaining power. So when a dispute arises over terms or language, provincial consumer protection statutes require that judges interpret these contracts in the way most favourable to the consumer. Simply put, ignorance can be a good defence.

Hearsay can be admitted if you introduce it in the right way. It's essential that printed evidence and/or witnesses (relatives are included) be available to confirm that a false representation actually occurred, that a part is failure-prone, or that a part's replacement is covered by a secret warranty or internal service bulletin alert. If you can't find an independent expert, introduce this evidence through the automaker reps and dealership service personnel, who have to be at the trial anyway. They know all about the service bulletins and extended warranty programs cited in *Lemon-Aid*, and they'll probably contradict each other—particularly if they are excluded from the courtroom prior to testifying. Incidentally, you may wish to have the court clerk send a subpoena requiring the deposition of the documents you intend to cite, all warranty extensions relevant to your problem, and other lawsuits filed against the company for similar failures. This will make the fur fly in Oshawa, Oakville, and Windsor, and it will likely lead to an out-of-court settlement. Sometimes, the service manager or company representative will make key admissions if questioned closely by you, a court mediator, or the trial judge. Here are some questions to ask: Is this a common problem? Do you recognize this service bulletin? Is there a case-by-case "goodwill" plan covering this repair?

Automakers often blame owners for having pushed their vehicles beyond their limits. Therefore, when you seek to set aside the contract or to get repair work reimbursed, it's essential that you get an independent mechanic—or your co-workers, friends, or neighbours—to prove the vehicle was well maintained and driven prudently.

When asking for a refund, keep in mind the "reasonable diligence" rule that requires that a suit be filed within a reasonable time after a vehicle's purchase, which usually means less than a year. Because many symptoms of factory-related deficiencies take years to appear, the courts have ruled that the reasonable diligence clock starts ticking only after the defect is confirmed to be manufacturer- or dealer-related. This allows you to make a claim up to seven years after the vehicle was originally put into service, regardless of whether it was bought new or used. If there have been negotiations with the dealer or the automaker, or if either the dealer or the automaker has been promising to correct the defects for some time or has carried out repeated unsuccessful repairs, the deadline for filing the lawsuit can be extended.

Yes, you can claim for hotel and travel costs or for compensation for general inconvenience. Fortunately, when legal action is threatened—usually through small claims court—automakers quickly up their out-of-court offer to include most of the owner's expenses, because they know the courts will be far more generous. For example, a British Columbia court decision gave $2,257 for hotel and travel costs to a motorist fed up with his lemon Cadillac, and then the judge capped it off with a $5,000 award for "inconvenience and loss of enjoyment of their luxury vehicle" (*Wharton v. Tom Harris Chevrolet Oldsmobile Cadillac Ltd. and General Motors of Canada Limited*; B.C. Supreme Court, Vancouver, 1999; Docket C982104). In the *Sharman v. Ford* case (see the Windstar section in Part Four), the judge gave the plaintiff $7,500 for "mental distress" caused by the fear that his children would fall out of his 2000 Windstar equipped with a faulty sliding door.

As of March 19, 2005, the Supreme Court confirmed that car owners can ask for punitive, or exemplary, damages when a seller's or automaker's conduct has been so outrageously bad that the court wants to protect society by awarding a sum of money large enough to dissuade others from engaging in similar immoral, unethical conduct. I call this the "weasel-whacker" law. In *Prebushewski v. Dodge City Auto (1985) Ltd. and Chrysler Canada Ltd.* (2001 SKQB 537; Q.B. No. 1215), the plaintiff got $25,000 in a judgment handed down December 6, 2001, in Saskatoon. The Supreme Court upheld the judgment on March 9, 2005. The award followed testimony from Chrysler's expert witness that the company was aware of many cases where daytime running lights shorted and caused 1996 Ram pickups to catch fire. The plaintiff's truck had burned to the ground. Chrysler had refused the owner's claim, saying it had fulfilled its expressed warranty obligations, in spite of its knowledge that fires were commonplace. The plaintiff sued on the grounds that there was an implied warranty that the vehicle would be safe. Justice Rothery gave this stinging rebuke in his judgment against Chrysler and its dealer:

> Not only did Chrysler know about the problems of the defective daytime running light modules, it did not advise the plaintiff of this. It simply chose to ignore the plaintiff's requests for compensation and told her to seek recovery from her insurance company. Chrysler had replaced thousands of these modules since 1988. But it had also made a business decision to neither advise its customers of the problem nor to recall the vehicles to replace the modules. While the cost would have been about $250 to replace each module, there were at least one million customers. Chrysler was not prepared to spend $250 million, even though it knew what the defective module might do.

> Counsel for the defendants argues that this matter had to be resolved by litigation because the plaintiff and the defendants simply had a difference of opinion on whether the plaintiff should be compensated by the defendants. Had the defendants some dispute as to the cause of the fire, that may have been sufficient to prove that they had not willfully violated this part of the [*Consumer Protection Act*]. They did not. They knew about the defective daytime running light module. They did nothing to replace the burned truck for the plaintiff. They offered the plaintiff no compensation for her loss. Counsel's position that the definition of the return of the purchase price is an arguable point is not sufficient to negate the defendants' violation of this part of the *Act*. I find the violation of the defendants to be willful. Thus, I find that exemplary damages are appropriate on the facts of this case.

In this case, the quantum ought to be sufficiently high as to correct the defendants' behaviour. In particular, Chrysler's corporate policy to place profits ahead of the potential danger to its customers' safety and personal property must be punished. And when such corporate policy includes a refusal to comply with the provisions of the *Act* and a refusal to provide any relief to the plaintiff, I find an award of $25,000 for exemplary damages to be appropriate. I therefore order Chrysler and Dodge City to pay: Damages in the sum of $41,969.83; Exemplary damages in the sum of $25,000; Party and party costs.

Warranty Rights

The manufacturer's or dealer's warranty is a written legal promise that a vehicle will be reasonably reliable, subject to certain conditions. Regardless of the number of subsequent owners, this promise remains in force as long as the warranty's original time and kilometre limits haven't expired. Tires aren't usually covered by car manufacturers' warranties; instead, they're covered on a pro-rated basis by the tiremaker. This isn't such a good deal, because the manufacturer is making a profit by charging you the full list price. If you were to buy the same replacement tire from a discount store, you'd likely pay less without the pro-rated rebate.

But consumers have gained additional rights following Bridgestone/Firestone's massive recall of its defective ATX II and Wilderness tires in 2001. Because of the confusion and chaos surrounding Firestone's handling of the recall, Ford's 575 Canadian dealers stepped into the breach and replaced the tires with any equivalent tires that they had in stock, no questions asked. This is an important precedent that tears down the traditional wall separating tire manufacturers from automakers in product liability claims. In essence, whoever sells the product can now be held liable for damages. In the future, Canadian consumers will have an easier time holding the dealer, the automaker, and the tire manufacturer liable, not only for recalled products but also for any defect that affects the safety or reasonable durability of that product.

This is particularly true now that the Supreme Court of Canada (*Winnipeg Condominium v. Bird Construction* [1995] 1 S.C.R. 85) has ruled that defendants are liable for negligence for any designs that result in a risk to the public's safety or health. The Supreme Court reversed a long-standing policy and provided the public with a new course of action that had not existed before in Canada.

Other Warranties

In the U.S., safety restraints such as airbags and seat belts have warranty coverage extended for the lifetime of a vehicle, following an informal agreement made between automakers and NHTSA. In Canada, however, many automakers try to dodge this responsibility, alleging that they are separate entities, their vehicles are different, and no U.S. agreement or service bulletin binds them. That distinction is both disingenuous and dishonest, and wouldn't likely hold up in small claims court—probably the reason why most automakers relent when threatened with legal action.

Aftermarket products and services—such as gas-saving gadgets, rustproofing, and paint protectors—can render the manufacturer's warranty invalid, so make sure you're in the clear before purchasing any optional equipment or services from an independent supplier.

How fairly a warranty is applied is more important than how long it remains in effect. Once you know the normal wear rate for a mechanical component or body part, you can demand proportional compensation when you get less than normal durability—no matter what the original warranty says. Some dealers tell customers that they need to have original-equipment parts installed in order to maintain their warranties. A variation on this theme requires that selling dealers do routine servicing—including tune-ups and oil changes (with a certain brand of oil)—or the warranty is invalidated. Nothing could be further from the truth. Canadian law stipulates that whoever issues a warranty cannot make that warranty conditional on the use of any specific brand of motor oil, oil filter, or any other component unless that component is provided to the customer free of charge.

Sometimes dealers will do all sorts of minor repairs that don't correct a problem and then, after the warranty runs out, they'll tell you that your vehicle needs major repairs. You can avoid this nasty surprise by repeatedly bringing your vehicle to the dealership before the warranty ends. During each visit, insist that the written work order includes the specific nature of the problem, as you see it, and states that this is the second, third, or fourth time the same problem has been brought to the dealer's attention. Write all of this down yourself, if need be. This paper trail allows you to show a pattern of non-performance by the dealer during the warranty period, and it establishes that the problem is both serious and chronic. When the warranty expires, you will have the legal right to demand that it be extended on those items that consistently appear on your work orders. *Lowe v. Fairview Chrysler* (see page 204) is an excellent judgment that reinforces this important principle. In another lawsuit, *François Chong v. Marine Drive Imported Cars Ltd. and Honda Canada Inc.* (see page 204), a Honda owner forced Honda to fix his engine six times—until they got it right.

A retired GM service manager gave me another effective tactic to use when you're not sure that a dealer's warranty "repairs" will actually correct the problem for a reasonable period of time after the warranty expires. Here's what he says you should do:

> When you pick up the vehicle after the warranty repair has been done, hand the service manager a note to be put in your file that says you appreciate the warranty repair, however, you intend to return and ask for further warranty coverage if the problem reappears before a reasonable amount of time has elapsed—even if the original warranty has expired. A copy of the same note should be sent to the automaker.... Keep your copy of the note in the glove compartment as cheap insurance against paying for a repair that wasn't fixed correctly the first time.

Extra-Cost Warranties

The manufacturer, the dealer, or an independent third party may sell supplementary warranties that provide extended coverage, and this coverage is automatically transferred when a vehicle is sold. They cost between $1,500 and $2,000 and should be purchased only if the vehicle you're buying is off its original warranty, if it has a reputation for being unreliable or expensive to service (see Part Four), or if you're reluctant to use the small claims courts when factory-related trouble arises. Don't let the dealer pressure you into deciding right away.

Generally, you can purchase an extended warranty at any time during the period in which the manufacturer's warranty is in effect or, in some cases, shortly after buying the vehicle from a used-car dealer. An automaker's supplementary warranty is the best choice, but it will likely cost about a third more than warranties sold by independents. In some parts of the country, notably British Columbia, dealers have a quasi-monopoly on selling warranties, with little competition from the independents.

Dealers love to sell you extended warranties, whether you need them or not, because up to 60 percent of the warranty's cost represents dealer markup. Out of the remaining 40 percent comes the sponsor's administration costs and profit margin, calculated at another 15 percent. What's left to pay for repairs is a minuscule 25 percent of the original amount. The only reason that automakers and independent warranty companies haven't been busted for operating this Ponzi scheme is that only half of the vehicle buyers who purchase extended service contracts actually use them.

It's often difficult to collect on supplementary warranties because independent companies frequently go out of business or limit the warranty's coverage through subsequent mailings. Provincial laws cover both situations. If the bankrupt warranty company's insurance policy won't cover your claim, take the dealer to small claims court and ask for the repair costs and a refund of the original warranty payment. Your argument for holding the dealer responsible is a simple one: By accepting a commission to act as an agent of the defunct company, the dealer also took on the obligations of that company. As for limiting the coverage after you have already bought the warranty policy, this is illegal and allows you to sue both the dealer and the warranty company for a refund of both the warranty and the repair costs.

Emissions-Control Warranties

These little-publicized warranties can save you big bucks if major engine or exhaust components fail prematurely. They come with all new vehicles and cover major components of the emissions-control system for up to 8 years/130,000 km, no matter how many times the vehicle is sold. Unfortunately, although owner's manuals vaguely mention the emissions warranty, most don't specify which parts are covered. The U.S. Environmental Protection Agency has intervened on several occasions, with hefty fines against Chrysler and Ford, and ruled that all major motor and fuel-system components are covered. These components include fuel metering, ignition spark advance, restart, evaporative emissions, positive crank-case ventilation (PVC), engine electronics (computer modules), and catalytic converter systems, as well as parts like hoses, clamps, brackets, pipes, gaskets, belts, seals, and connectors. Canada, however, has no governmentally defined list, so it's up to each manufacturer and the small claims courts to decide which emissions-control components are covered.

Many of the confidential technical service bulletins listed in Part Four show parts failures that are covered under the emissions warranty (stinky exhausts caused by defective catalytic converters, for example), even though motorists are routinely charged for their replacement. The Ford bulletin below, applicable to the 2002–05 Taurus and Sable, shows that the automaker will pay for fuel gauge repairs under the emissions warranty. Applying the same principles to other automakers' fuel gauges, such as GM's front-drive minivans, should be a breeze.

FORD FUEL GAUGE DOES NOT READ FULL AFTER FILLING TANK

BULLETIN NO.: 04-14-14   **DATE: MAY 2002**

Ford Taurus, Sable

ISSUE: Some 2002–05 Taurus/Sable vehicles may exhibit a fuel gauge which indicates the tank is only 7/8 full after filling the fuel tank. This may be due to the calibration of the fuel level indication unit.

ACTION: To service, remove the fuel delivery module and replace the fuel level indication unit. DO NOT REPLACE THE ENTIRE FUEL DELIVERY MODULE FOR THIS CONDITION.

WARRANTY STATUS: Eligible under provisions of new vehicle limited warranty coverage and **emissions warranty coverage**.

Operation	Description	Time
041414A	Replace Fuel Gauge tank unit (includes time to remove tank, drain and refill)	1.3hrs

GM fuel gauges are also failure-prone and fall under the same emissions warranty, which is much longer than the base warranty.

Make sure to get your emissions system checked out thoroughly by a dealer or an independent garage before the emissions warranty expires or before having the vehicle inspected by provincial emissions inspectors. In addition to ensuring that you'll pass provincial tests, this precaution could save you up to $1,000 if your catalytic converter and other emissions components are faulty.

Psst! A Secret Warranty Update

Few vehicle owners know that secret warranties exist. Automakers issue technical service bulletins (TSBs) to dealers or the first owners of record. Consequently, motorists who find out about these policies tend to be the original owners who haven't moved or leased their vehicles. But the other group of motorists who get compensated for repairs are the ones who read *Lemon-Aid* each year, staple TSBs to their work orders, and yell the loudest.

Remember, second owners and repairs done by independent garages are included in these secret warranty programs. Large, costly repairs such as blown engines, burned transmissions, and peeling paint are often covered. Even mundane little repairs—which can still cost you a hundred bucks or more—are frequently included in these programs.

If you have a TSB but you're still refused compensation, keep in mind that secret warranties are an admission of manufacturing negligence. Try to work out a compromise by asking for a pro rata adjustment from your vehicle's manufacturer. If polite negotiations fail, challenge the refusal in court on the grounds that you shouldn't be penalized for failing to make a reimbursement claim under a secret warranty that you never knew existed!

Read on to check out a few examples of secret warranties that can save you thousands of dollars. (More extensive listings are found in Part Four's model ratings.)

Acura/Honda

1999–2003 Acura CL and TL; 1999–2003 Honda Accord, Prelude, and Odyssey

Problem: Defective automatic transmission and torque converter. **Warranty coverage:** This "goodwill" warranty extension was confirmed in the August 4, 2003, edition of *Automotive News*. Honda will fix or replace the transmission free of charge up to 7 years/160,000 km (100,000 mi.), regardless of whether you bought your vehicle new or used. The company will also reimburse owners who already paid for the repair.

2001–04 MDX

Problem: Defective front hydraulic engine mount may cause excessive vibration at idle and harsh shifting. **Warranty coverage:** This "goodwill" warranty extension will be applied up to eight years, without any mileage limitations.

Audi, Chrysler, Mercedes-Benz, Saab, Toyota, and VW

1997–2004 Audi A4; 1999–2002 Chrysler models equipped with a 2.7L V6; 1998–2002 Mercedes-Benz; 1998–2003 Saab 9-3 and 9-5; 1997–2002 Toyota and Lexus vehicles with 2.2L 4-cylinder or 3.0L V6 engines; 1997–2004 VW Passat

Problem: Engine sludge. **Warranty coverage:** Varies; usually 7–10 years/160,000 km. Automakers can't automatically deny this free repair if you don't have proof of all of your oil changes, unless they can show that the sludge was caused by a missed oil change (which, according to independent mechanics, is impossible to prove). Remember, the warranty has been extended to fix a factory-related problem that occurs *despite* regular oil changes. That's why it's the automaker's responsibility.

Service bulletins, press releases, and dealer memos are all admissions of responsibility. From there, the legal doctrine of "the balance of probabilities" applies. To wit, a missed oil change *may* cause engine sludge, but a factory defect *definitely* causes engine sludge. Therefore, it's more probable that the defect caused the sludge.

Once the sludge condition is diagnosed, the dealer and automobile manufacturer are jointly liable for all corrective repairs, plus additional damages for your inconvenience, loss of use (or the cost of a loaner vehicle), and the cost to replace the oil. The automaker's owner notification letter may not have gone out to Canadian owners, because it isn't required by any Canadian recall or statute. If a letter goes out, it's usually sent only to the first owners of record.

Some automakers say owners should use an expensive special oil to prevent engine sludge. This after-sale stipulation is illegal, and it can also provide owners with a reason to ask for damages, or even a refund, because it wasn't disclosed at the time of sale. All of the letter restrictions and decisions made by the dealer and the manufacturer can be easily appealed in small claims court, where the sludge letter is powerful proof of the automaker's negligence.

Chrysler

1998–2003 Dodge Durango and Dakota

Problem: Worn, rusted, and broken upper ball joints may cause steering loss, or the wheel may fall off. Over 1,000 complaints have been recorded by NHTSA. **Warranty coverage:** Chrysler has recalled the 2000–03 models and will replace defective ball joints for free up to 10 years/160,000 km. This warranty extension creates an excellent benchmark for all owners stuck with prematurely worn-out ball joints.

All Grand Cherokees

Problem: AC evaporator failure or malfunction. **Warranty coverage:** 7 years/ 115,000 km (71,500 mi.). Although originally applicable only to 1993–97 models, this "goodwill" extension sets a standard for what Chrysler considers the normal durability of its ACs:

ADDENDUM TO BASIC WARRANTY

The following applies to 1993 through 1997 New Yorker, LHS, Concorde, Intrepid, Vision and Grand Cherokee vehicles equipped with factory-installed air conditioning:

The Basic Warranty coverage for the air conditioner evaporator has been extended to 7 years or 115,000 kilometres, whichever occurs first, from the vehicle's warranty start date.

This extended coverage applies to all owners of the vehicle. All of the other warranty terms apply to this extension.

1997–2005 Jeep

Problem: Water leaks from the AC onto the passenger-side carpet. **Warranty coverage:** Jeep will install an HVAC drain tube free of charge up to 7 years/160,000 km on a case-by-case basis.

Chrysler, Ford, General Motors, and Asian Automakers

All years, all models

Problem: Faulty automatic transmissions that self-destruct, shift erratically, gear down to "limp mode," are slow to shift in or out of Reverse, or are noisy. **Warranty coverage:** If you have the assistance of your dealer's service manager, expect an offer of 50–75 percent (about $2,500). File the case in small claims court, and a full refund will be offered up to 7 years/160,000 km. Acura, Honda, Hyundai, Lexus, and Toyota coverage varies between seven and eight years.

> I've just been told that I need my fourth transmission on my '96 Town & Country minivan with 132,000 miles [212,000 km] on it. I've driven many cars well past that mileage with only *one* transmission. The dealer asked Chrysler, who said they would not help me. My appeals to Chrysler's customer service department yielded me the same result…. Chrysler split some of the costs with me on the previous rebuilt replacements.

CHRYSLER TRANSMISSION DELAYED ENGAGEMENT

BULLETIN NO.: 21-004-05   DATE: JANUARY 22, 2005

OVERVIEW: This bulletin involves replacing the front pump assembly in the transmission and checking the Transmission Control Module (TCM) for the latest software revision level.

2004 (CS) Pacifica
2002– 2004 (JR) Sebring Convertible/Sebring Sedan/Stratus Sedan
2003 (KJ) Liberty
2003 (KJ) Cherokee (International Markets)
2002 2004 (LH) 300M/Concorde/Intrepid
2002 2003 (PL) Neon
2002 2003 (PT) PT Cruiser
2002 2003 (RG) Chrysler Voyager (International Markets)
2002 2003 (RS) Town & Country/Caravan/Voyager
2003 (TJ) Wrangler

All years, all models

Problem: Premature wearout of brake pads, calipers, and rotors. Produces excessive vibration, noise, and pulling to one side when braking. **Warranty coverage:** *Calipers and pads:* "Goodwill" settlements confirm that brake calipers and pads that fail to last 2 years/40,000 km will be replaced for 50 percent of the repair cost; components not lasting 1 year/20,000 km will be replaced for free. *Rotors:* If they last less than 3 years/60,000 km, they'll be replaced at half the price; replacement is free up to 2 years/40,000 km.

All years, all models

Problem: A nauseating rotten-egg smell permeates the interior. **Warranty coverage:** At first, owners are told they need a tune-up. And then they're told to change the fuel and wait a few months for the problem to correct itself. When this tactic fails, likely the catalytic converter will be replaced and the power control module recalibrated. Toyota has been particularly hard hit by this stink.

Chrysler, Ford, General Motors, Honda, Mazda, and Toyota

All years, all models

Problem: Faulty paint jobs that cause paint to turn white and peel off of horizontal panels. **Warranty coverage:** Automakers will offer a free paint job or partial compensation up to six years, with no mileage limitations. Thereafter, most manufacturers offer 50–75 percent refunds on the small claims courthouse steps.

In *Frank v. GM*, the Saskatchewan small claims court set a 15-year benchmark for paint finishes, and three other Canadian small claims judgments have extended the benchmark to seven years, second owners, and pickups.

> I wanted to let you and your readers know that the information you publish about Ford's paint failure problem is invaluable. Having read through your "how-to guide" on addressing this issue, I filed suit against Ford for the "latent" paint defect. The day prior to our court date, I received a settlement offer by phone for 75 percent of what I was initially asking for.
>
> This settlement was for a 9-year-old car. I truly believe that Ford hedges a bet that most people won't go to the extent of filing a lawsuit because they are intimidated or simply stop progress after they receive a firm no from Ford.
>
> M.D.

Chrysler, Ford, General Motors, and Hyundai

1994–2005 engine head gasket and intake manifold failures; 1998–99 Hyundai Accent

Problem: At around 60,000–100,000 km, the engine may overheat, lose power, and burn extra fuel or, possibly, self-destruct. Under the best of circumstances, the repair will take a day and cost about $800–$1,000. **Warranty coverage:** If you have the assistance of your dealer's service manager, expect a full refund up to 7 years/160,000 km, although initial offers will hover at about 50 percent of the costs. Ford Windstars and GM minivans are particularly afflicted with this defect; if you threaten small claims court action, cite the *Dufour* or *Reid* Windstar judgments (see pages 195–196).

No matter which automaker you're dealing with, filing your claim in small claims court always sweetens the company's settlement offer. Furthermore, you likely won't have to step inside a courtroom to get your refund, since most small claims court filings are settled at the pretrial mediation stage.

Engine claims are now entering a second phase where the original free repair needs to be repaired again. Car owners are told they had one kick at the can and that's it, but, once again, small claims court judges don't always see it that way. Courts have held that the company's first repair was an admission that the product

Ford's settlement offer was approved, and Canadian owners are also covered by the warranty extension applicable to the above-cited vehicles.

GM owners have been systematically refused engine repair refunds, despite evidence—like this intake manifold internal service bulletin—that shows the factory screwed up in the design and choice of materials. No wonder GM is on the receiving end of a $1.2-billion class action lawsuit in Canada for the intake manifold gasket problem (*www.autoblog.com/2006/04/26/gm-slapped-with-gasket-class-action-lawsuit-in-canada-claims-co*). Settlement talks are ongoing.

was faulty; therefore, its correction must either last a reasonable period of time or be redone.

Ford

1992–2004 Aerostar, Focus, Sable, Taurus, and Windstar

Problem: Defective front coil springs may suddenly break, puncturing the front tire and leading to the loss of steering control. **Warranty coverage:** Under a "Safety Improvement Campaign" negotiated with NHTSA, Ford will replace *broken* coil springs at no charge up to 10 years/unlimited mileage. The company initially said that it wouldn't replace the springs at all—if you survived to submit a claim, that is—but it relented when threatened with a lawsuit. Also, 1997–98 models that are registered in either the rust-belt states or Canada have been recalled for the installation of a protective shield (called a "spring catcher bracket" in the Canadian recall) to prevent a broken spring from shredding the front tire.

1996–2004 F-Series trucks, Windstar vans, and SUVs

Problem: Sudden steering loss because of the premature wear and separation of the steering tie-rod ends. **Warranty coverage:** Presently, Ford is advising owners to have their vehicles inspected regularly. If pressed, the dealer will replace the component for free up to 5 years/100,000 km (62,000 mi). Filing a claim in small claims court will likely result in a partial refund.

1999–2001 F-150 and Super Duty F-Series pickups, Econoline, Expedition, and Lincoln Navigator

Problem: Faulty engine head gaskets cause oil or coolant leakage, resulting in the loss of power, excessive fuel consumption, engine overheating, or complete engine destruction. **Warranty coverage:** Ford will repair or replace affected engines. Insiders say that the automaker is spending up to $4,500 (U.S.) to replace the engine and $800 to replace the cylinder heads and head gasket. Ford says that the faulty engines usually fail within the warranty period (according to the April 1, 2002, issue of *Automotive News*), but independent warranty data suggests they may begin to leak at any time.

1997–2001 F-150 and F-250 LD F-Series pickups, Econoline, Expedition, and Lincoln Navigator

Problem: Extensive door bottom and tailgate rusting; cracked outer door panel. **Warranty coverage:** Ford will repair or replace the door or body panels for free up to six years. Small claims courts have ruled automakers may be liable for body defects up to 11 years.

2003–05 Excursion; 2003–06 Super Duty F-Series pickups; 2004–06 E-Series vans

Problem: 6.0L diesel engine lacks power, bucks/jerks, produces excessive smoke, and is hard to start or won't start. **Warranty coverage:** Ford will replace the diesel injectors for free up to seven years.

2004–06 F-150 pickups

Problem: Shudder and vibration when accelerating due to a misaligned rear axle pinion. **Warranty coverage:** Ford will install a shim kit for free up to six years.

General Motors

1999–2004 trucks equipped with 3.1L, 3.4L, 4.3L, 4.6L (Northstar), 4.8L, 5.3L, 5.7L (LS1), 6.0L, or 8.1L engines

Problem: Engine-damaging piston slap, engine knock, excessive oil consumption, and engine failure (see *www.pistonslap.com*):

> Excessive "piston slap" occurs because an automobile manufacturer (GM) designs and/or manufactures a defective engine in which the clearance between the piston and cylinder bore is too great. Essentially, the piston moves sideways and "slaps" or "knocks" hard against the cylinder bore and causes damage to the engine pistons and cylinders, excessive smoke emissions, excessive oil consumption, carbon buildup on piston heads, decreased mileage, and a loud and obnoxious "slapping" or "knocking" noise, all of which diminishes vehicle resale value.

Warranty coverage: GM will cover this defect for up to 5 years/100,000 km, but only on a case-by-case basis with considerable service-manager jawboning. The U.S.-based *Kelley Blue Book* confirms that "a knocking engine could lower the value of a vehicle by $4,000 to $6,000 at trade-in."

1994–2000 trucks equipped with a 6.5L diesel engine

Problem: Fuel-injection pump failure. **Warranty coverage:** Up to 11 years (TSB #00064C; September 2002).

1997–2003 Venture, TranSport/Montana, and Silhouette

Problem: Hood corrosion/blistering. **Warranty coverage:** GM will replace, repair, or repaint the roof for free up to 6 years/100,000 km.

Honda

1997–99 CR-V

Problem: Harsh-shifting automatic transmission and torque converter. **Warranty coverage:** Honda will fix or replace the transmission free of charge up to 7 years/160,000 km under a "goodwill" program, whether you bought your vehicle new or used (TSB #00-012; June 26, 2001).

1998–2003 Accord, Odyssey, and Pilot models equipped with 6-cylinder engines

Problem: Defective aluminum engine block. **Warranty coverage:** Honda will repair or replace the engine under a "goodwill" program.

1999–2003 Odyssey; 2003 Pilot

Problem: Engine hesitation or surge. **Warranty coverage:** Honda will replace the EGR valve or clean the EGR port free of charge up to 8 years/128,000 km (80,000 mi.) under a "goodwill" program, whether you bought your vehicle new or used (TSB #05-026; July 20, 2005).

Mazda

2002–03 MPV

Problem: A faulty fan control module may cause fan failure or battery drain. **Warranty coverage:** Free replacement of the fan control module.

Toyota

1997–2002 Toyota and Lexus vehicles with 2.2L 4-cylinder or 3.0L V6 engines

Problem: Sludge buildup may require you to get a rebuilt engine. **Warranty coverage:** Toyota will repair or replace the engine at no charge up to 8 years/160,000 km, whether you bought your vehicle new or used. Toyota has said that owners will not be forced to show oil change receipts. But some dealers, apparently, haven't gotten the message:

> The service manager quietly told me that there was a "flaw" in the engine but would not elaborate. When I asked if there was a flaw why wouldn't Toyota warranty it, I was told, "Because you can't prove you did the oil change, there is no use taking it to Toyota."
>
> In May 2002 we received the letter mentioned in your article, and we took our 1998 Sienna into the dealer (after spending three weeks talking to them and producing all the oil change records except the missing one). The engine could not be rebuilt—it had to be replaced. The cost was $5,017.22, finally covered by this goodwill warranty.
>
> T.C., TORONTO

Recall Repairs

Vehicles are recalled for one of two reasons: They may be unsafe, or they don't conform to federal pollution control regulations. Whatever the reason, recalls are a great way to get free repairs—if you know which ones apply to your vehicle and you have the patience of Job.

Auto recalls are on the rise in Canada, despite automakers' claims that build quality has improved. Transport Canada says that auto recalls rose 44 percent to 3.77 million vehicles in 2004 (approximately one in six vehicles on the road). Safety experts like NHTSA's Rae Tyson ascribe this rise in recall numbers to the generic components used in many different models:

Manufacturers are sharing drive-train components and platforms among several different models, so when you do a recall now, it will affect a lot more vehicles.

In North America, over a half-billion unsafe vehicles have been recalled by automakers for the free correction of safety-related defects since American recall legislation was passed in 1966 (a weaker Canadian law was enacted in 1971). During that time, about 28 percent of the recalled vehicles never made it back to the dealership for repairs, because owners were never informed, didn't consider the defect to be that hazardous, or just gave up waiting for corrective parts.

 If you've moved or bought a used vehicle, it's smart to pay a visit to your local dealer. Give the dealer your address to get a "report card" on which recalls, free service campaigns, and warranties apply to your vehicle. Simply give the service advisor the vehicle identification number (VIN)—found on your insurance card or on the dash, just below the windshield on the driver's side—and have the number run through the automaker's computer system. Ask for a computer printout of the vehicle's history (or have it faxed to you, if you're so equipped) and make sure you're listed in the automaker's computer as the new owner. This process ensures that you'll receive notices of warranty extensions and emissions- and safety-related recalls.

Regional Recalls

Don't let any dealer refuse you recall repairs because of where you live. In order to cut recall costs, many automakers try to limit a recall to vehicles in a certain designated region. This practice doesn't make sense. Cars are mobile; therefore, an unsafe, rust-cankered steering unit can be found anywhere—not just in certain rust-belt provinces or American states.

No matter where you live or drive, don't expect to be welcomed with open arms when your vehicle develops a safety- or emissions-related problem that's not yet part of a recall campaign. Automakers and dealers generally take a restrictive view of what constitutes a safety or emissions defect, and they frequently charge for repairs that should be free under federal safety or emissions legislation. To counter this tendency, look at the following list of typical defects that are clearly safety-related. If you experience similar problems, insist that the automaker fix them at no expense to yourself, including the cost of a car rental:

- Airbag malfunctions
- Corrosion affecting the safe operation of the vehicle
- Disconnected or stuck accelerators
- Electrical shorts
- Faulty windshield wipers
- Fuel leaks
- Problems with original axles, drive shafts, seats, seat recliners, or defrosters
- Seat belt problems
- Stalling or sudden acceleration

- Sudden steering or brake loss
- Suspension failures
- Trailer coupling failures

In the U.S., recall campaigns compel automakers to pay the entire cost of fixing a vehicle's safety-related defect for any vehicle purchased up to eight years before the recall's announcement. Forcing automakers to extend a campaign for a reasonable period beyond eight years is usually a slam dunk in small claims court. Recalls may be voluntary or ordered by the U.S. Department of Transportation. Canadian regulations have an added twist: Transport Canada can order automakers only to notify owners that their vehicles may be unsafe; it can't force them to correct the problem. Fortunately, most U.S.-ordered recalls are carried out in Canada, and when Transport Canada makes a defect determination on its own, automakers generally comply by sending owner notification letters.

Voluntary recall campaigns, frequently called "Special Service" or "Safety Improvement Campaigns," are real problems, though: The government doesn't monitor the notification of owners; dealers and automakers routinely deny that a recall even exists, thereby dissuading most claimants; and the company's so-called fix, not authorized by any governing body, may not correct the hazard at all. Also, the voluntary recall may leave out many of the affected models, or it may unreasonably exclude certain owners.

Safety Defect Information

If you wish to report a safety defect or want to find recall info, you may access Transport Canada's website at *www.tc.gc.ca/roadsafety/recalls/search_e.asp*. You can get recall information in French or English, as well as general information on topics such as road safety or how to import a vehicle into Canada. Web surfers can now access the recall database for 1970–2008 model year vehicles, but—unlike on NHTSA's website—owner complaints aren't listed, defect investigations aren't disclosed, voluntary warranty extensions (secret warranties) aren't shown, and service bulletin summaries aren't provided. You can also contact Transport Canada directly to get additional information (Tel: 613-990-2309; TTY: 1-888-675-6863; Fax: 613-954-4731/613-998-8620; Email: *webfeedback@tc.gc.ca*).

If you aren't happy with Ottawa's treatment of your recall inquiry, try NHTSA. Its website is more complete than Transport Canada's (NHTSA's database is updated daily and covers vehicles built since 1952). You can search the database for your vehicle or tires at *www.nhtsa.dot.gov/cars/problems* (Tel: 1-888-327-4236; TTY: 1-800-424-9153). You'll get immediate access to four essential database categories applicable to your vehicle and model year: the latest recalls, current and closed safety investigations, defects reported by other owners, and a brief summary of TSBs.

"Black Box" Data Recorders

Event data recorders (EDRs) the size of a VCR tape have been hidden under the seat or in the centre consoles of about 30 million airbag-equipped Ford and GM vehicles since the early '90s. Presently, about 90 percent of new cars have the devices.

To find out if your car or truck carries an EDR, go to *www.harristechnical.com/downloads/cdrlist.pdf*.

These devices operate in a fashion similar to the flight data recorders used in airplanes. Recorded data varies, but it usually includes a vehicle's speed, the force of the impact, accelerator and braking performance, the time and speed of airbag deployment, and seat belt use prior to impact. A new NHTSA rule requires that the data be recorded from the instant a crash starts until half a second after it ends (to a maximum of 10 seconds).

Ford and GM have systematically hidden their collected data from U.S. and Canadian vehicle safety researchers who investigate thousands of complaints relating to anti-lock brakes that don't brake and to airbags that don't deploy when they should or do deploy when they shouldn't. This refusal to voluntarily share data with customers and researchers is unfortunate, because the recorders collect critical information that could lead to better-functioning safety devices.

To assist accident investigators in reconstructing crashes, NHTSA will soon require that crash data compiled by EDRs is accessible by common diagnostic tools and stored in a standard format. The rule takes effect on September 1, 2008, and will likely apply to some 2008 models and to all 2009s sold in the United States and Canada.

In the meantime, the Vetronix Corporation sells a $2,500 (U.S.) portable download device that accesses the data and stores it on any PC. Litigants can also subpoena the info through an automaker's dealer if the data is needed in court to dispute criminal charges, oppose an insurer's decision as to fault, or hold an automaker responsible for a safety device's failure.

Safety Benefits

Enthusiastically promoted by government and law enforcement agencies around the world, these data recorders have actually had a positive effect on accident prevention: A 1992 study by the European Union, cited by the Canada Safety Council, found that EDRs reduced the collision rate by 28 percent and costs by 40 percent in police fleets where drivers knew they were being monitored.

The recorders are also sending guilty people to jail, helping accident victims reap huge court awards, and prompting automaker recalls of unsafe vehicles. For example, in July 2002, New Brunswick prosecutors sent a dangerous driver to jail for two years based on his car's EDR data (see *R. v. Daley*; 2003 NBQB 20; Docket(s): S/CR/7/02; *www.canlii.org/nb/cas/nbqb/2002/2003nbqb20.html*). And GM was forced to recall more than 850,000 Cavaliers and Sunfires when its own data recorders showed that the cars' airbags often deployed inadvertently. Incidentally, California is the only jurisdiction where EDR data cannot be downloaded unless the car owner agrees or a court order is issued.

Traffic accident reconstructionists Harris Technical Services have prepared a chronological list of dozens of Canadian and American court cases related to automotive EDRs. It's available at *www.harristechnical.com/cdr5.htm*.

Three Steps to a Settlement

Step 1: Informal Negotiations

If your vehicle was misrepresented, has major defects, or wasn't properly repaired under warranty, the first thing you should do is give the seller (both the dealer and automaker) a written summary of the outstanding problems by registered mail or fax. Stipulate a time period in which the dealer and/or automaker will need to either correct the problems or refund your money. Keep a copy for yourself, along with all your repair records. Be sure to check all of the sales and warranty documents you were given to see if they conform to provincial laws. Any errors, omissions, or violations can be used to get a settlement from the dealer in lieu of making a formal complaint.

Most vehicle owners won't take the steps outlined above. Instead, they'll try to settle things informally with a phone call. This tactic rarely works: Private sellers won't want to talk with you, and customer service agents (who recite policies but don't make them) will tell you the vehicle's warranty doesn't apply. This brush-off usually convinces 90 percent of complainers to drop their claims after some angry venting.

Nevertheless, don't take no for an answer. Contact someone higher up who has the authority to bend policies to satisfy your request. Speak in a calm, polite manner, and try to avoid polarizing the issue. Talk about co-operating to solve the problem. Let a compromise emerge—don't come in with a hardline set of demands.

An independent estimate of the vehicle's defects and the cost of repairing them is essential if you want to convince the seller that you're serious in your claim and that you stand a good chance of winning your case in court. Come prepared to use your estimate to challenge the dealer who agrees to pay half the repair costs and then tries to jack up the price 100 percent so that you wind up paying the whole shot.

Don't insist on getting the settlement offer in writing, but do make sure that you're accompanied by a friend or relative who can confirm the offer in court if it isn't honoured. Be prepared to act upon the offer without delay so that if the seller or automaker withdraws it, they won't be able to blame your hesitancy.

Dealer and service manager help

Service managers have more power than you may realize. They make the first determination of what work is covered under warranty or through post-warranty "goodwill" programs, and they're directly responsible to the dealer and manufacturer for their decisions. (Dealers hate manufacturer audits that force them to pay back questionable warranty decisions.) Service managers are paid to save the dealer and automaker money while mollifying irate clients—an almost impossible balancing act. Nevertheless, when a service manager agrees to extend warranty coverage, it's because you've raised solid issues that neither the dealer nor the automaker can ignore. All the more reason to present your argument in a confident, forthright manner with your vehicle's service history and *Lemon-Aid*'s "Reasonable Part Durability" chart (see page 157) on hand.

Also, bring as many technical service bulletins and owner complaint printouts as you can find from websites like NHTSA's. It's not important that they apply directly to your problem; they establish parameters for giving out after-warranty assistance, or "goodwill." Don't use your salesperson as a runner, because the sales staff are generally quite distant from the service staff and usually have less pull than you do.

If the service manager can't or won't set things right, your next step is to convene a mini-summit with the service manager, the dealer principal, and the automaker's rep. By getting the automaker involved, you run less risk of having the dealer fob you off on the manufacturer, and you can often get an agreement where the seller and automaker pay two-thirds of the repair costs.

Step 2: Sending a Registered Letter, Fax, or Email

The pen is mightier...

If you haven't sent a written claim letter, fax, or email, you haven't really complained—or at least that's the auto industry's mindset. Send the seller and manufacturer a polite registered letter or fax that asks for compensation for repairs that have been done or need to be done, insurance costs during the vehicle's repair, towing charges, supplementary transportation costs like taxis and rented cars, and damages for your inconvenience (see the samples following). If a private seller misrepresented the vehicle, there's no reason to implicate the manufacturer.

Specify five days (but allow 10 days) for either party to respond. If no satisfactory offer is made or your claim is ignored, file suit in small claims court. Make the manufacturer a party to the lawsuit, especially if an emissions warranty, a secret warranty extension, a safety recall campaign, or extensive chassis rusting is involved.

USED VEHICLE COMPLAINT LETTER/FAX/EMAIL

WITHOUT PREJUDICE

Date: _____

Name: _____

Please be advised that I am dissatisfied with my used vehicle, a [state model], for the following reasons:

1. _____
2. _____
3. _____
4. _____
5. _____

In compliance with the provincial consumer protection laws and the "implied warranty" set down by the Supreme Court of Canada in *Donoghue v. Stevenson*, *Wharton v. GM*, and *Sharman v. Ford Canada*, I hereby request that these defects be repaired without charge. This vehicle has not been reasonably durable and is, therefore, not as represented to me.

Should you fail to repair these defects in a satisfactory manner and within a reasonable period of time, I shall get an estimate of the repairs from an independent source and claim them in court, without further delay. I also reserve my right to claim up to $1 million for punitive damages, pursuant to the Supreme Court of Canada's February 22, 2002, ruling in *Whiten v. Pilot*.

I have dealt with your company because of its honesty, competence, and sincere regard for its clients. I am sure that my case is the exception and not the rule.

A positive response within the next five (5) days would be appreciated.

Sincerely,

Sincere[signed with telephone number, fax number, or email address]

NEW VEHICLE COMPLAINT LETTER/FAX/EMAIL

WITHOUT PREJUDICE

Date: _____

Name and address of dealer: _____

Name and address of manufacturer: _____

Please be advised that I am not satisfied with my _____ [indicate year, make, model, and serial number of vehicle]. The vehicle was purchased on [indicate date] and currently indicates _____ km on the odometer. The vehicle presently exhibits the following defects:

      1. Premature rusting
      2. Paint peeling/discoloration
      3. Water leaks
      4. Other defects [explain]

[List previous attempts to repair the vehicle. Attach a copy of a report from an independent garage, showing the estimated cost of repairs and confirming the manufacturer's responsibility.]

I hereby request that you correct these defects free of charge under the terms of the implied warranty provisions of provincial consumer protection statutes as applied in *Kravitz v. General Motors* (1979), I.S.C.R., and *Chabot v. Ford* (1983), 39 O.R. (2d).

If you do not correct the defects noted above to my satisfaction and within a reasonable length of time, I will be obliged to ask an independent garage to _____ [choose (a) estimate or (b) carry out] the repairs and claim the amount of $_____ [state the cost, if possible] by way of the courts without further notice or delay.

I have dealt with your company because of its competence and honesty. I close in the hope of hearing from you within five (5) days of receiving this letter, failing which I will exercise the alternatives available to me. Please govern yourself accordingly.

Sincerely,

[signed with telephone number, fax number, or email address]

Step 3: Mediation and Arbitration

If the formality of a courtroom puts you off, or you're not sure that your claim is all that solid and don't want to pay the legal costs to find out, consider using mediation or arbitration offered by these groups: the Better Business Bureau (BBB), the Automobile Protection Association (APA), the Canadian Automobile Association (CAA), small claims court (mediation is often a prerequisite to going to trial), provincial and territorial government-run consumer mediation services, and the Canadian Motor Vehicle Arbitration Plan (CAMVAP).

Consumer complained that her 2007 Toyota Camry with 8,441 km pulls to the left and after it was test driven three times, no fault was found. The Manufacturer's Representative testified that although the Consumer presented United States veering concerns from *Lemon-Aid* and the Internet, that this was American-based which did not relate to the same alignment specifications as in Canada. There was also no Technical Service Bulletins on the matter in Canada.

The independent expert found that "Leaving the vehicle in this condition will be a source of constant aggravation and monitoring on the highway, as the vehicle has a great tendency to drift into the oncoming traffic lane."

I concur with the Consumer that a buy-back of her vehicle is justified with a reduction for use. The Manufacturer shall buy back the vehicle at a price of $25,542.34.

WEILER AND TOYOTA CANADA
CAMVAP CLAIM #251506
JUNE 11, 2007

CAMVAP (*www.camvap.ca*) is the best known and most efficient organization offering free arbitration in Canada, rendering decisions after only a few months of deliberation. CAMVAP can be reached at 1-800-207-0685, and arbitration documents can be obtained from the following automakers:

AUTOMAKER CONTACT INFORMATION

Chrysler Canada, Inc.	1-800-465-2001	Kia Canada, Inc.	1-877-542-2886
	1-800-387-9983 (Quebec)	Land Rover Group Canada, Inc.	1-800-346-3493
		Mazda Canada, Inc.	1-800-263-4680
Ford Motor Company of Canada, Ltd.	1-800-565-3673	Mercedes-Benz Canada, Inc.	1-800-387-0100
General Motors of Canada, Ltd.	1-800-263-3777 (English)	Nissan Canada, Inc.	1-800-387-0122
		Porsche Cars Canada, Ltd.	1-800-545-8039
	1-800-263-7854 (French)	Subaru Canada, Inc.	1-800-894-4212
	1-800-263-3830 (TTY)	Suzuki Canada, Inc.	905-889-2677 ext 2254
		Toyota Canada, Inc.	1-888-869-6828 (Toyota)
Honda Canada, Inc.	1-888-946-6329 (Honda)		1-800-265-3987 (Lexus)
	1-888-922-8729 (Acura)	Volkswagen Canada, Inc.	1-800-822-8987 (Volkswagen)
Hyundai Auto Canada	1-800-461-8242 (English)		1-800-822-2834 (Audi)
	1-800-461-5695 (French)	Volvo Cars Canada, Ltd.	1-800-663-8255
Jaguar Canada, Inc.	1-800-668-6257		

Getting Outside Help

Don't let poor preparation scuttle your case. Ask government or independent consumer protection agencies to evaluate how well prepared you are before going to your first hearing. Also, use the Internet and media sources to ferret out additional facts and to gather support (*www.lemonaidcars.com* is a good place to start).

Auto Industry Groups

Ontario consumers may file an online claim with the Ontario Motor Vehicle Industry Council (OMVIC) at *https://ewconsumers.omvic.on.ca/complaint/complaint.asp*. Sure, OMVIC is the dealer's self-defence lobby—made up of 9,000 registered dealers and 20,000 registered salespeople—but it has the following mandate:

> To maintain a fair, safe and informed marketplace in Ontario by protecting the rights of consumers, enhancing industry professionalism and ensuring fair, honest and open competition for registered motor vehicle dealers.

The way your complaint is handled will test the veracity of the above-stated goals.

Alberta has a similar self-regulating auto industry group, the Alberta Motor Vehicle Industry Council (AMVIC). You can visit their website at *www.amvic.org/main.htm*. During 2006, 1,573 consumer files were opened with AMVIC and 1,591 were closed. Their investigators laid 150 charges under the *Fair Trading Act* and the Canadian *Criminal Code*. Court fines and restitution payments totalled $22,100. Also, AMVIC obtained $3,682,146 by mediation in restitution for victims of unfair trade practices.

Classified Ads and Television Exposés

Put an ad in the local paper describing your plight, and ask for information from people who may have experienced a problem similar to your own. This approach alerts others to the potential problem, helps build a base for a class action or a group meeting with the automaker, and puts pressure on the local dealer and manufacturer to settle with you. Sometimes the paper's news desk will assign someone to cover your story after your ad is published, or you may gain attention by setting up a website.

Television producers and their researchers need articulate consumers with issues that are easily filmed and understood. If you want media coverage, you must summarize your complaint and have visual aids that will hold the viewer's interest (viewers should be able to understand the issues with the sound turned off). Paint delamination? Show your peeling car. Bought a lemon vehicle? Show your repair bills. Holding a demonstration? Make it a "lemon" parade: Target one of the largest dealers, give your group a nifty name, and then drive past the dealership in vehicles decorated with "lemon" signs.

In a five part special investigative series, CTV's Chris Olsen investigates how CarProof is different than Carfax in Canada. The series also features a specific case in Victoria, B.C. where CarProof saved a consumer from buying a badly damaged vehicle that was advertised as having "no accidents" by the selling dealer and Carfax. The series reveals that this dealer actually tried to sell the same vehicle to 3 different consumers without disclosing the previous accident history.

CTV EVENING NEWS, "OLSEN ON YOUR SIDE" JANUARY 9–15, 2007

BELL GLOBEMEDIA TRANSCRIPT

The dealer in the above exposé, SRG Enterprises (Scott Gillies), temporarily lost his dealer licence and paid over $13,000 in fees after refunding the purchase price to several clients (*www.carproof.com/downloads/article34.pdf*).

Federal and Provincial Consumer Affairs

The wind left the sails of the consumer movement over two decades ago, leaving consumer agencies understaffed and unsupported by the government. This has created a passive mindset among many staffers who are tired of getting their heads kicked in by businesses, deadwood bosses, and budget cutters. They find it much easier to blame consumers for not being educated enough to make sound buying decisions, instead of "educating" businesses through the strict enforcement of our federal and provincial laws.

Consumer affairs offices can still help with investigation, mediation, and some litigation. Strong and effective consumer protection legislation has been left standing in most of the provinces, and resourceful consumers can use these laws in conjunction with media coverage to prod provincial consumer affairs offices into action. Furthermore, provincial bureaucrats aren't as well shielded from criticism as their federal counterparts. A call to your MPP or MLA, or to their executive assistants, can often get things rolling.

Federal consumer protection is a government-created PR myth. Don't expect the staffers in the reorganized Competition Bureau (formerly the Office of Consumer Affairs) to be very helpful—they've been de-fanged and de-gummed through budget cuts and a succession of ineffective ministers. Although the beefed-up *Competition Act* has some bite in regard to misleading advertising and a number of other illegal business practices, the federal government has been more reactive than proactive in applying the law.

Nevertheless, you can lodge a formal complaint with the Competition Bureau if you encounter misleading advertising, odometer tampering, or price-fixing. Use the Online Complaint/Enquiry Form found at *www.competitionbureau.gc.ca*. An online complaint sent through this form made Toyota cease its Access price-fixing practices and pay out almost $2 million as a settlement fee.

Invest in Protest

You can have fun and put additional pressure on a seller or garage by putting a lemon sign on your car and parking it in front of the dealer or garage, by creating a lemon website, or by forming a self-help group like the Chrysler Lemon Owners Group (CLOG) or the Ford Lemon Owners Group (FLOG). After forming your group, you can have the occasional parade of creatively decorated cars visit area dealerships as the local media are convened. Just remember to keep your remarks pithy and factual, don't interfere with traffic or customers, and remain peaceful.

One other piece of advice from this consumer advocate with 40 years of experience and hundreds of pickets and mass demonstrations under his belt: Keep a sense of humour and never break off negotiations.

Finally, don't be scared off by threats that it's illegal to criticize a product or company. Unions, environmentalists, and consumer groups do it regularly (it's called "informational picketing"), and the Supreme Court of Canada in *R. v. Guinard* reaffirmed this right in February 2002. In that judgment, an insurance policyholder posted a sign on his barn claiming the Commerce Insurance Company was unfairly refusing his claim. The municipality of Saint-Hyacinthe, Quebec, told him to take the sign down. He refused, maintaining that he had the right to state his opinion. The Supreme Court agreed. This judgment means that consumer protests, signs, and websites that criticize the actions of corporations cannot be banned simply because they say unpleasant things.

Typical Problems and Solutions

Sudden Acceleration, Chronic Stalling, and ABS and Airbag Failures

Incidents of sudden acceleration or chronic stalling are quite common. However, they are very difficult to diagnose, and individual cases can be treated very differently by federal safety agencies. Sudden acceleration is considered to be a safety-related problem—stalling isn't. Never mind that a vehicle's sudden loss of power on a busy highway puts everyone's lives at risk (as is the case with 2001–03 VW and Audi ignition coil failures). The same problem exists with engine and transmission powertrain failures, which are only occasionally considered to be safety-related. ABS and airbag failures are universally considered to be life-threatening defects. If your vehicle manifests any of these conditions, here's what you need to do:

1. Get independent witnesses to confirm that the problem exists. Your primary tools include an independent mechanic's verification, passenger accounts, downloaded data from your vehicle's data recorder, and lots of Internet browsing using *www.lemonaidcars.com* and a search engine such as Google. Notify the dealer or manufacturer by fax, email, or registered letter that you consider the problem to be a factory-induced, safety-related defect. Make sure you address your correspondence to the manufacturer's product

liability or legal affairs department. At the dealership's service bay, make sure that every work order clearly states the problem as well as the number of previous attempts to fix it. (You should end up with a few complaint letters and a handful of work orders confirming that this is an ongoing deficiency.) If the dealer won't give you a copy of the work order because the work is a warranty claim, ask for a copy of the order number "in case your estate wishes to file a claim, pursuant to an accident." (This will get the service manager's attention.) Leaving a paper trail is crucial for any claim you may have later on, because it shows your concern and persistence, and it clearly indicates that the dealer and manufacturer have had ample time to correct the defect.

2. Note on the work order that you expect the problem to be diagnosed and corrected under the emissions warranty or a "goodwill" program. It also wouldn't hurt to add the phrase on the work order or in your claim letters that "any deaths, injuries, or damage caused by the defect will be the dealer's and manufacturer's responsibility" since the work order (or letter, fax, or email) constitutes you putting them on "formal notice."

3. If the dealer does the necessary repairs at little or no cost to you, send a follow-up confirmation that you appreciate the "goodwill." Also, emphasize that you'll be back if the problem reappears—even if the warranty has expired—because the repair renews your warranty rights applicable to that defect. In other words, the warranty clock is set back to its original position. Understand that you won't likely get a copy of the repair bill, because dealers don't like to admit that there was a serious defect present and don't feel that they owe you a copy of the work order if the repair was done *gratis*. You can, however, subpoena the complete vehicle file from the dealer and manufacturer (this costs about $50) if the case goes to small claims or a higher court. This request has produced many out-of-court settlements when the internal documents show extensive work was carried out to correct the problem.

4. If the problem persists, send a letter, fax, or email to the dealer and manufacturer saying so, look for ALLDATA service bulletins to confirm that your vehicle's defects are factory-related, and report the failure by calling Transport Canada or NHTSA or by logging on to NHTSA's website. Also, call the Ralph Nader–founded Center for Auto Safety (Tel: 202-328-7700) in Washington, D.C., to get a lawyer referral and an information sheet covering the problem.

5. Now come two crucial questions: Repair the defect now or later? Use the dealer or an independent? Generally, it's smart to use an independent garage if you know the dealer isn't pushing for free corrective repairs from the manufacturer, if weeks or months have passed without any resolution of your claim, if the dealer keeps repeating that it's a maintenance item, and if you know an independent mechanic who will give you a detailed work order showing the defect is factory-related and not caused by poor maintenance. Don't mention that a court case may ensue, since this will scare the dickens out of your only independent witness. An added bonus is that the repair charges will be about half of what a dealer would demand. Incidentally, if the automaker later denies warranty "goodwill" because you used an independent repairer, use the argument that the defect's safety implications required emergency repairs, carried out by whoever could see you first.

6. Dashboard-mounted warning lights usually come on prior to airbags suddenly deploying, ABS brakes failing, or engine glitches causing the vehicle to stall out. (Sudden acceleration usually occurs without warning.) Automakers consider these lights to be critical safety warnings and generally advise drivers to *immediately* have the vehicle serviced to correct the problem when any of the warning lights come on (advice that can be found in the owner's manual). This fact bolsters the argument that your life was threatened, emergency repairs were required, and your request for another vehicle or a complete refund isn't out of line.

7. Sudden acceleration can have multiple causes, isn't easy to duplicate, and is often blamed on the driver mistaking the accelerator for the brakes or failing to perform proper maintenance. Yet NHTSA data shows that with the 1992–2000 Explorer, for example, a faulty cruise-control or PCV valve and poorly mounted pedals are the most likely causes of the Explorer's sudden acceleration. So how do you satisfy the burden of proof showing that the problem exists and it's the automaker's responsibility? Use the legal doctrine called "the balance of probabilities" by eliminating all of the possible dodges the dealer or manufacturer may employ. Show that proper maintenance has been carried out, you're a safe driver, and the incident occurs frequently and without warning.

8. If any of the above defects causes an accident, or if the airbag fails to deploy or you're injured by its deployment, ask your insurance company to have the vehicle towed to a neutral location and clearly state that neither the dealer nor the automaker should touch the vehicle until your insurance company and Transport Canada have completed their investigation. Also, get as many witnesses as possible and immediately go to the hospital for a check-up, even if you're feeling okay. You may be injured and not know it because the adrenalin coursing through your veins is masking your injuries. A hospital exam will easily confirm that your injuries are accident-related, which is essential evidence for court or for future settlement negotiations.

9. Peruse NHTSA's online accident and service bulletin database to find reports of other accidents caused by the same failure, bulletins that indicate part upgrades, current defect investigations, and reported failures that have resulted in recalls or closed investigations.

10. Don't let your insurance company bully you. Refuse to let them settle the case if you're sure the accident was caused by a mechanical failure. Even if an engineering analysis fails to directly implicate the manufacturer or dealer, you can always plead the aforementioned balance of probabilities. If the insurance company settles, your insurance premiums will soar and the manufacturer will get away with the perfect crime.

Tires

Tire companies are far easier to deal with than automobile manufacturers because, under the legal doctrine of *res ipsa loquitur* ("the thing speaks for itself," meaning, in negligence cases, that liability is shown by failure), tires aren't supposed to fail.

And when they do, smart claimants can use the *Robson v. General Motors* B.C. class action judgment to make the American corporation a co-defendant in their lawsuit. They can also refer to the Supreme Court of Canada judgment *Winnipeg Condominium No. 36 v. Bird Construction Co. Ltd.* (1995; 1 S.C.R.85), which ruled that defendants are liable in negligence for any designs that result in a public safety or health risk. This 10-year-old decision reversed a long-standing policy and provided the public with a new cause of action that had not existed before in Canada.

No wonder tire and auto companies routinely avoid liability by imputing blame to someone or something else, like punctures, impact damage, overloading, over-inflating, or under-inflating.

If your tires wear out prematurely or fail, review the guidelines found in the previous section, and consider taking the following additional steps:

1. Access NHTSA on the Internet (see Appendix II) for current data about which tires are failure-prone and which companies are under investigation, conducting recalls, or carrying out "silent" recalls.
2. Keep the tire. If the tiremaker says an analysis must be done, permit only a portion of the tire to be taken away.
3. Plead the balance of probabilities, using friends and family to refute the tire company's contention that you caused the failure.
4. Ask for damages that are adequate to replace all the tires on your vehicle, including mounting costs.
5. Include in your damage claim any repairs needed to fix the body damage caused by the tire's failure.

Paint and Body Defects

The following settlement advice applies mainly to paint defects, but you can use these tips for any other vehicle defect that you believe is the automaker's or dealer's responsibility. If you're not sure whether the problem is a factory-related deficiency or a maintenance fault, have it checked out by an independent garage or get a technical service bulletin summary for your vehicle. The summary may include specific bulletins relating to diagnosis and correction, as well as information about ordering the upgraded parts needed to fix your problem.

Four good examples of favourable paint judgments are *Shields v. General Motors of Canada, Bentley v. Dave Wheaton Pontiac Buick GMC Ltd. and General Motors of Canada, Maureen Frank v. General Motors of Canada Limited*, and the most recent, *Dunlop v. Ford of Canada*.

In *Dunlop v. Ford of Canada* (January 5, 2005; No. 58475/04; Ontario Superior Court of Justice, Richmond Hill Small Claims Court; Deputy Judge M.J. Winer), the owner of a 1996 Lincoln Town Car, purchased used in 1999 for $27,000, was awarded $4,091.64. Judge Winer cited the *Shields* decision (below) and gave the following reasons for finding Ford of Canada liable:

> Evidence was given by the Plaintiff's witness, Terry Bonar, an experienced paint auto technician. He gave evidence that the [paint] delamination may be both a manufacturing defect and can be caused or [sped] up by atmospheric conditions. He also says that [the paint on] a car like this should last ten to 15 years, [or even for] the life of the vehicle....

> It is my view that the presence of ultraviolet light is an environmental condition to which the vehicle is subject. If it cannot withstand this environmental condition, it is defective.

DON'T BE SILLY. THAT'S CAUSED BY BIRD DROPPINGS!

INADEQUATE PRIMER CAUSED MY PAINT TO PEEL!

Paint delamination is a common defect that automakers often blame on everything from bird droppings to ultraviolet light—or they simply say the warranty has expired. The courts haven't been very receptive to these kinds of excuses.

In *Shields v. General Motors of Canada* (July 24, 1997; No. 1398/96; Ontario Court, General Division, Oshawa Small Claims Court; Robert Zochodne, Deputy Judge), the owner of a 1991 Pontiac Grand Prix had purchased the vehicle used with over 100,000 km on its odometer. Beginning in 1995, the paint began to bubble and flake, and it eventually peeled off. Deputy Judge Zochodne awarded the plaintiff $1,205.72 and struck down every one of GM's arguments that the peeling paint was caused by acid rain, UV rays, or some other environmental factor. Here are some other important aspects of this 12-page judgment that GM didn't appeal:

1. The judge admitted many of the technical service bulletins referred to in *Lemon-Aid* as proof of GM's negligence.
2. Although the vehicle had 156,000 km on its odometer when the case went to court, GM still offered to pay 50 percent of the paint repairs if the plaintiff dropped his suit.
3. The judge ruled that the failure to protect the paint from the damaging effects of UV rays is akin to engineering a car that won't start in cold weather. In essence, vehicles must be built to withstand the rigours of the environment.
4. Here's an interesting twist: The original warranty covered defects that were present at the time it was in effect. The judge, taking statements found in the GM technical service bulletins, ruled that the UV problem was factory-related, existed during the warranty period, and, therefore, represented a latent defect that appeared once the warranty expired.
5. The subsequent purchaser was not prevented from making the warranty claim, even though the warranty had long since expired from both time and mileage standpoints and he was the second owner.

The small claims judgment in *Bentley v. Dave Wheaton Pontiac Buick GMC Ltd. and General Motors of Canada* (December 1, 1998; Victoria Registry No. 24779; British Columbia Small Claims Court; Judge Higinbotham) builds upon Ontario's *Shields v. General Motors of Canada* decision and cites other jurisprudence as to how long paint should last on a car. If you're wondering why Ford and Chrysler haven't been hit by similar judgments, remember that they usually settle out of court.

From *Maureen Frank v. General Motors of Canada Limited* (October 17, 2001; No. SC#12 (2001); Saskatchewan Provincial Court, Saskatoon, Saskatchewan; Provincial Court Judge H.G. Dirauf):

> On June 23, 1997, the Plaintiff bought a 1996 Chevrolet Corsica from a General Motors dealership. At the time, the odometer showed 33,172 km. The vehicle still had some factory warranty. The car had been a lease car and had no previous accidents.
>
> During June of 2000, the Plaintiff noticed that some of the paint was peeling off from the car and she took it to a General Motors dealership in Saskatoon and to the General Motors dealership in North Battleford where she purchased the car. While there were some discussions with the GM dealership about the peeling paint, nothing came of it and the Plaintiff now brings this action claiming the cost of a new paint job.
>
> During 1999, the Plaintiff was involved in a minor collision causing damage to the left rear door. This damage was repaired. During this repair some scratches to the left front door previously done by vandals were also repaired.
>
> The Plaintiff's witness, Frank Nemeth, is a qualified auto body repairman with some 26 years of experience. He testified that the peeling paint was a factory defect and that it was necessary to completely strip the car and repaint it. He diagnosed the cause of the peeling paint as a separation of the primer surface or colour coat from the electrocoat primer. In his opinion no primer surfacer was applied at all. He testified that once the peeling starts, it will continue. He has seen this problem on General Motors vehicles. The defect is called delamination.
>
> Mr. Nemeth stated that a paint job should last at least 10 years. In my opinion, most people in Saskatchewan grow up with cars and are familiar with cars. I think it is common knowledge that the original paint on cars normally lasts in excess of 15 years and that rust becomes a problem before the paint fails. In any event, paint peeling off, as it did on the Plaintiff's vehicle, is not common. I find that the paint on a new car put on by the factory should last at least 15 years.
>
> It is clear from the evidence of Frank Nemeth (independent body shop manager) that the delamination is a factory defect. His evidence was not seriously challenged. I find that the factory paint should not suffer a delamination defect for at least 15 years and that this factory defect breached the warranty that the paint was of acceptable quality and was durable for a reasonable period of time.
>
> There will be judgment for the Plaintiff in the amount of $3,412.38 plus costs of $81.29.

Some of the important aspects of the *Frank* judgment are:

Chrysler blamed bird excrement and the sun for its paint problems.

1. The judge accepted that the automaker was responsible, even though the car had been bought used. The subsequent purchaser wasn't prevented from making the warranty claim, even though the warranty had long since expired, from both time and mileage standpoints, and she was the second owner.
2. The judge stressed that the provincial warranty can kick in when the automaker's warranty has expired or isn't applied.
3. By awarding full compensation to the plaintiff, the judge didn't feel that there was a significant "betterment" or improvement added to the car that would warrant reducing the amount of the award.
4. The judge decided that the paint delamination was a factory defect.
5. The judge also concluded that without this factory defect, a paint job should last up to 15 years.
6. GM offered to pay $700 of the paint repairs if the plaintiff dropped the suit; the judge awarded five times that amount.
7. Maureen Frank won this case despite having to confront GM lawyer Ken Ready, who had considerable experience arguing other paint cases for GM and Chrysler.

Other paint and rust cases

Martin v. Honda Canada Inc. (March 17, 1986; Ontario Small Claims Court, Scarborough; Judge Sigurdson): The original owner of a 1981 Honda Civic sought compensation for the premature "bubbling, pitting, [and] cracking of the paint and rusting of the Civic after five years of ownership." Judge Sigurdson agreed with the owner and ordered Honda to pay the owner $1,163.95.

Thauberger v. Simon Fraser Sales and Mazda Motors (3 B.C.L.R., 193): This Mazda owner sued for damages caused by the premature rusting of his 1977 Mazda GLC. The court awarded him $1,000. Thauberger had also previously sued General Motors for a prematurely rusted Blazer truck and was awarded $1,000 in the same court. Both judges ruled that the defects couldn't be excluded from the automaker's expressed warranty or from the implied warranty granted by British Columbia's *Sale of Goods Act.*

Whittaker v. Ford Motor Company (1979) (24 O.R. (2d), 344): A new Ford developed serious corrosion problems despite having been rustproofed by the dealer. The court ruled that the dealer, not Ford, was liable for the damage for having sold the rustproofing product at the time of purchase. This is an important judgment to use when a rustproofer or paint protector goes out of business or refuses to pay a claim, because the decision holds the dealer jointly responsible.

See also:

- *Danson v. Chateau Ford (1976) C.P.* (Quebec Small Claims Court; No. 32-00001898-757; Judge Lande)
- *Doyle v. Vital Automotive Systems* (May 16, 1977; Ontario Small Claims Court, Toronto; Judge Turner)
- *Lacroix v. Ford* (April 1980; Ontario Small Claims Court, Toronto; Judge Tierney)
- *Marinovich v. Riverside Chrysler* (April 1, 1987; District Court of Ontario; No. 1030/85; Judge Stortini)

Using the Courts

Sue Now or Later?

If the seller you've been negotiating with agrees to make things right, give him or her a deadline to complete the repairs and then have an independent garage check them over. If no offer is made within 10 working days, file suit in court. Make the manufacturer a party to the lawsuit only if the original, unexpired warranty is still in place; if your claim falls under the emissions warranty, a TSB, a secret warranty extension, or a safety recall campaign; or if there is extensive chassis rusting caused by poor engineering.

Sue Whom?

Usually the automaker and seller can be held responsible, if you are alleging that the vehicle is defective due to a factory-related problem. If the vehicle was misrepresented in national advertising, both parties can, again, be held liable. However, if the vehicle was misrepresented solely by the dealer, the automaker should not be made a party to the lawsuit, except to back up your claim as a witness.

Remember, you must identify the defendant correctly, which may require some help from the court clerk (look for other recent lawsuits naming the same party). Crooks often change their company's name to escape liability; for example, it would be impossible to sue Joe's Garage (1999) if your contract is with Joe's Garage, Inc. (1984).

Sue Where?

Most claims can be handled without a lawyer in small claims court, especially now that the court's jurisdiction varies between $10,000 and $25,000. Still, it's up to you to decide what remedy to pursue; that is, whether you want a partial refund or a cancellation of the sale. To determine the refund amount, add the estimated cost of repairing the existing mechanical defects to the cost of prior repairs. Don't exaggerate your losses or claim for repairs that are considered to be routine maintenance. A suit for the cancellation of a sale involves practical problems. The court requires that the vehicle be "tendered," or taken back, to the seller at the time the lawsuit is filed. This leaves you without transportation for as long as the case continues, unless you purchase another vehicle in the interim. If you lose the case, you must then take back the old vehicle and pay the accumulated storage fees. You could go from having no vehicle to having two—one of which is a clunker!

Generally, if the cost of repairs or the sales contract amount falls within the small claims court limit (discussed later), file the case there to keep your costs to a minimum and to get a speedy hearing. Small claims court judgments aren't easily appealed, lawyers aren't necessary, filing fees are minimal (about $125), and cases are usually heard within a few months. In fact, your suit is almost always best argued in the provincial small claims court to keep costs and frustrations down and to get a quick resolution within a few months.

> Mr. Edmonston, I emailed you earlier in the year seeking help on my small claims case against Ford. I'm happy to report that I won my case and received a $1,900 settlement cheque from Ford in the mail yesterday! As you may recall I have a 1991 Explorer that has a significant paint peel problem.
>
> I followed all the steps recommended by your website—ultimately I ended up in small claims court. Ford had indicated in court documents that they were going to send a representative to the hearing, but nobody showed. The judge made a quick ruling in my favour and I was out the door. I didn't even get a chance to show the load of material I had brought to make my case.
>
> MARK G.

Here's another reason not to be greedy: If you claim more than the small claims court limit, you'll have to go to a higher court—where costs quickly add up, lawyers routinely demand 30 percent of your winnings or settlement, and delays of a few years or more are commonplace.

Small Claims Courts

Crooked automakers scurry away from small claims courts like cockroaches from bug spray, not because the courts can issue million-dollar judgments or force litigants to spend millions in legal fees (they can't), but because dealers and manufacturers don't want the bad publicity arising from the filings and eventual judgments. Other disincentives are that small claims courts can award sizeable sums to plaintiffs not represented by lawyers, and they make jurisprudence that other judges on the same bench are likely to follow.

For example, in *Dawe v. Courtesy Chrysler* (July 30, 2004; Dartmouth Nova Scotia Small Claims Court; SCCH #206825;), Judge Patrick L. Casey, Q.C., rendered an impressive 21-page decision citing key automobile product liability cases from the past 80 years, including *Donoghue, Kravitz,* and *Davis.* The court awarded $5,037 to the owner of a new 2001 Cummins-engine-equipped Ram pickup with the following problems: It wandered all over the road; lost power, or jerked and bucked; shifted erratically; lost braking ability; bottomed out when passing over bumps; allowed water to leak into the cab; produced a burnt-wire and oil smell in the interior as the lights would dim; and produced a rear-end whine and wind noise around the doors and under the dash. Dawe had sold the vehicle and reduced his claim to meet the small claims threshold. Anyone with engine, transmission, and suspension problems or water leaking into the interior will find this judgment particularly useful.

Interestingly, "small claims" is quickly becoming a misnomer, now that Alberta and British Columbia allow claims of up to $25,000 and most other provinces permit $10,000 filings.

There are small claims courts in most counties of every province, and you can make a claim in the county where the problem happened or where the defendant lives and conducts business. Simply go to the small claims court office and ask for a claim form (instructions on how to fill it out accompany the form).

At this point, it wouldn't hurt to hire a lawyer or a paralegal for a brief walk-through of small claims procedures to ensure that you've prepared your case properly and that you know what objections will likely be raised by the other side. If, instead, you'd like a lawyer to do all the work for you, there are a number of law firms around the country that specialize in small claims litigation. "Small claims" doesn't mean "small legal fees," however. In Toronto, some law offices charge a flat fee of $1,000 for a basic small claims lawsuit and trial.

Remember that you're entitled to bring to court any evidence relevant to your case, including written documents such as a bill of sale or receipt, contract, or letter. If your car has developed severe rust problems, bring a photograph (signed and dated by the photographer) to court. You may also have witnesses testify in court. It's important to discuss a witness's testimony prior to the court date. If a witness can't attend the court date, he or she can write a report and sign it for representation in court. This situation usually applies to an expert witness, such as an independent mechanic who has evaluated your car's problems.

If you lose your case in spite of all your preparation and research, some small claims court statutes allow cases to be retried, at a nominal cost, in exceptional circumstances. If a new witness has come forward, additional evidence has been discovered, or key documents (that were previously not available) have become accessible, apply for a retrial. In Ontario, this little-known provision is Rule 18.4 (1).B.

Alan MacDonald, a *Lemon-Aid* reader who won his case in small claims court, gives the following tips on beating Ford over a faulty automatic transmission:

I want to thank you for the advice you provided in my dealings with the Ford Motor Company of Canada Limited and Highbury Ford Sales Limited regarding my 1994 Ford Taurus wagon and the problems with the automatic transmission (Taurus and Windstar transmissions are identical). I also wish to apologize for not sending you a copy of this judgment earlier...(*MacDonald v. Highbury Ford Sales Limited,* Ontario Superior Court of Justice in the Small Claims Court London, June 6, 2000, Court File #0001/00, Judge J.D. Searle).

In 1999, after only 105,000 km, the automatic transmission went. I took the car to Highbury Ford to have it repaired. We paid $2,070 to have the transmission fixed, but protested and felt the transmission failed prematurely. We contacted Ford, but to no avail: Their reply was we were out of warranty, period. The transmission was so poorly repaired (and we went back to Highbury Ford several times) that we had to go to Mr. Transmission to have the transmission fixed again nine months later at a further $1,906.02.

It is at that point that I contacted you, and I was surprised, and somewhat speechless (which you noticed) when you personally called me to provide advice and encouragement. I am very grateful for your call. My observations with going through small claims court involved the following: I filed in January of 2000, the trial took place on June 1 and the judgment was issued June 6.

At pretrial, a representative of Ford (Ann Sroda) and a representative from Highbury Ford were present. I came with one binder for each of the defendants, the court and one for myself (each binder was about 3 inches thick—containing your reports on Ford Taurus automatic transmissions, ALLDATA Service Bulletins, Taurus Transmissions Victims (Bradley website), Center for Auto Safety (website), Read This Before Buying a Taurus (website), and the Ford Vent Page (website).

The representative from Ford asked a lot of questions (I think she was trying to find out if I had read the contents of the information I was relying on). The Ford representative then offered a 50 percent settlement based on the initial transmission work done at Highbury Ford. The release allowed me to still sue Highbury Ford with regards to the necessity of going to Mr. Transmission because of the faulty repair done by the dealer. Highbury Ford displayed no interest in settling the case, and so I had to go to court.

For court, I prepared by issuing a summons to the manager at Mr. Transmission, who did the second transmission repair, as an expert witness. I was advised that unless you produce an expert witness you won't win in a car repair case in small claims court. Next, I went to the law school library in London and received a great deal of assistance in researching cases pertinent to car repairs. I was told that judgments in your home province (in my case Ontario) were binding on the court; that cases outside of the home province could be considered, but not binding on the judge.

The cases I used for trial involved *Pelleray v. Heritage Ford Sales Ltd.*, Ontario Small Claims Court (Scarborough) SC7688/91 March 22, 1993; *Phillips et al. v. Ford Motor Co. of Canada Ltd. et al*, Ontario Reports 1970, 15th January 1970; *Gregorio v. Intrans-Corp.*, Ontario Court of Appeal, May 19, 1994; *Collier v. MacMaster's Auto Sales*, New Brunswick Court of Queen's Bench, April 26, 1991; *Sigurdson v. Hillcrest Service & Acklands* (1977), Saskatchewan Queen's Bench; *White v. Sweetland*, Newfoundland District Court, Judicial Centre of Gander, November 8, 1978; *Raiches Steel Works v. J. Clark & Son*, New Brunswick Supreme Court, March 7, 1977; *Mudge v. Corner Brook Garage Ltd.*, Newfoundland Supreme Court, July 17, 1975; *Sylvain v. Carroseries d'Automobiles Guy Inc.* (1981), C.P. 333, Judge Page; [and] *Gagnon v. Ford Motor Company of Canada, Limited et Marineau Automobile Co. Ltée.* (1974), C.S. 422–423.

In court, I had prepared the case, as indicated above, [and] had my expert witness and two other witnesses who had driven the vehicle (my wife and my 18-year-old son). As you can see by the judgment, we won our case and I was awarded $1,756.52, including pre-judgment interest and costs.

Key Court Decisions

The following Canadian and U.S. lawsuits and judgments cover typical problems that are likely to arise. Use them as leverage when negotiating a settlement or as a reference should your claim go to trial. Legal principles applying to Canadian and American law are similar; however, Quebec court decisions may be based on legal principles that don't apply outside that province. You can find a comprehensive listing of Canadian decisions from small claims courts all the way to the Supreme Court of Canada at *www.canlii.org* (Canadian Legal Information Institute).

Additional court judgments can be found in the legal reference section of your city's main public library or at a nearby university law library. Ask the librarian for help in choosing the legal phrases that best describe your claim.

LexisNexis (*www.lexisnexis.com*) and FindLaw (*www.findlaw.com*) are two useful Internet sites for legal research. Their main drawback, though, is that you may need to subscribe or use a lawyer's subscription to access jurisprudence and other areas of the sites. However, there *is* a free online summary of class actions filed in Canada at *classactionsincanada.blogspot.com*. It's run by Ward Branch, one of the legal counsels in the $1.2-billion class action filed against General Motors for defective engine intake manifold gaskets.

An excellent reference book that will give you plenty of tips on filing, pleading, and collecting your judgment is Judge Marvin Zuker's *Ontario Small Claims Court Practice 2008* (Carswell, 2008). Judge Zuker's book is easily understood by non-lawyers and uses court decisions from across Canada to help you plead your case successfully in almost any Canadian court.

Product Liability

Almost three decades ago, the Supreme Court of Canada, in *General Motors Products of Canada Ltd. v. Kravitz* (1979; 1 S.C.R. 790), clearly affirmed that automakers and their dealers are jointly liable for the replacement or repair of a vehicle if independent testimony shows that it is afflicted with factory-related defects that compromise its safety or performance. The existence of secret warranty extensions or technical service bulletins also helps prove that the vehicle's problems are the automaker's responsibility. For example, in *Lowe v. Fairview Chrysler* (see page 204), technical service bulletins were instrumental in showing an Ontario small claims court judge that Chrysler had a history of automatic transmission failures dating back to 1989.

In addition to replacing or repairing the vehicle, an automaker can also be held responsible for any personal damages arising from the defect. This means that lost wages, supplementary transportation costs, and damages for personal inconvenience can be awarded. However, in the States, product liability damage awards often exceed millions of dollars, while Canadian courts are far less generous.

Implied Warranty (Reasonable Durability)

The implied warranty is that powerful "other" warranty they never tell you about. It applies during and after the expiration of the manufacturer's or dealer's expressed or written warranty and requires that a part or repair will last a "reasonable" period of time. What is considered reasonable depends in large part on benchmarks used in the industry, the price of the vehicle, and how it was driven and maintained. Look at the "Reasonable Part Durability" chart on page 157 for some guidelines as to what you should expect.

Judges usually apply the implied, or legal, warranty when the manufacturer's expressed warranty has expired and the vehicle's manufacturing defects remain uncorrected. For example, in *Kravitz,* the court said that the seller's warranty of quality was an accessory to the property and was transferred with it on successive sales. Accordingly, subsequent buyers could invoke the contractual warranty of quality against the manufacturer, even though they didn't contract directly with it. This precedent is now codified in articles 1434, 1442, and 1730 of Quebec's *Civil Code.*

In the following decisions, the implied warranty forced Ford to pay for its Windstars' chronic engine failures.

Dufour v. Ford Canada Ltd. (April 10, 2001; Quebec Small Claims Court, Hull; No. 550-32-008335-009; Justice P. Chevalier): Ford was forced to reimburse the cost of engine head gasket repairs carried out on a 1996 Windstar's 3.8L engine—a vehicle not covered by the automaker's Owner Notification Program, which cut off assistance after the '95 model year.

Schaffler v. Ford Motor Company Limited and Embrun Ford Sales Ltd. (July 22, 2003; Ontario Superior Court of Justice, L'Orignal Small Claims Court; Court File No. 59-2003; Justice Gerald Langlois): The plaintiff bought a used 1995 Windstar in 1998. Its engine head gasket was repaired for free three years later, under Ford's 7-year extended warranty. In 2002 at 109,600 km, the head gasket failed again, seriously damaging the engine. Ford refused a second repair. Justice Langlois ruled that Ford's warranty extension bulletin listed signs and symptoms of the covered defect that were identical to the problems written on the second work order ("persistent and/or chronic engine overheating; heavy white smoke evident from the exhaust tailpipe; flashing 'low coolant' instrument panel light, even after coolant refill; and constant loss of engine coolant"). Judge Langlois concluded that "the problem was brought to the attention of the dealer well within the warranty period; the dealer was negligent." The plaintiff was awarded $4,941 plus 5 percent interest. This figure includes $1,070 for two months' car rental fees.

John R. Reid and Laurie M. McCall v. Ford Motor Company of Canada (July 11, 2003; Superior Court of Justice, Ottawa Small Claims Court; Claim No. #02-SC-077344; Justice Tiernay): A 1996 Windstar, bought used in 1997, experienced an engine head gasket failure in October 2001 at 159,000 km. Judge Tiernay awarded the plaintiffs $4,145 for the following reasons:

> A Technical Service Bulletin dated June 28, 1999, was circulated to Ford dealers. It dealt specifically with "undetermined loss of coolant" and "engine oil contaminated with coolant" in the 1996–98 Windstar and five other models of Ford vehicles. I conclude that Ford owed a duty of care to the Plaintiff to equip this vehicle with a cylinder head gasket of sufficient sturdiness and durability that would function trouble-free for at least seven years, given normal driving and proper maintenance conditions. I find that Ford is answerable in damages for the consequences of its negligence.

New-Vehicle Defects

Bagnell's Cleaners v. Eastern Automobile Ltd. (1991; 111 N.S.R. (2nd), No. 51, 303 A.P.R., No. 51 (T.D.)): This Nova Scotia company found that the new van it purchased had serious engine, transmission, and radiator defects. The court held that there was a fundamental breach of the implied warranty and that an exclusionary clause could not protect the seller.

Burridge v. City Motors (Nfld) Ltd. (10 Nfld. & P.E.I.R.; No. 451): This Newfoundland resident complained repeatedly of his new car's defects during the warranty period and stated that he hadn't used his car for 204 days after spending almost $1,500 for repairs. The judge awarded all repair costs and cancelled the sale:

> Where the defects are so numerous that taken *en masse* they destroy the whole workable character of the thing sold, this amounts to a fundamental breach and total breach of the contract, so as to disentitle the Defendant from taking advantage of it.

Davis v. Chrysler Canada Ltd. (1977; 26 N.S.R. (2nd), No. 410 (T.D.)): The owner of a new $28,000 diesel truck found that a faulty steering assembly prevented him from carrying on his business. The court ordered that the sale be cancelled and that $10,000 in monthly payments be reimbursed.

Fox v. Wilson Motors and GM (February 9, 1989; Court of Queen's Bench, New Brunswick; No. F/C/308/87): A trucker's new tractor-trailer had repeated engine malfunctions. He was awarded damages for loss of income, excessive fuel consumption, and telephone charges under the provincial *Sale of Goods Act.*

Gibbons v. Trapp Motors Ltd. (1970; 9 D.L.R. (3rd), No. 742 (B.C.S.C.)): The court ordered the dealer to take back a new car that had numerous defects and required 32 hours' worth of repairs.

Johnson v. Northway Chevrolet Oldsmobile (1993; 108 Sask. R., No. 138 (Q.B.)): The court ordered the dealer to take back a new car that had been brought in for repairs on 14 different occasions. Two years after purchasing the vehicle, the buyer initiated a lawsuit for the purchase price of the car and for general damages. General damages were awarded.

Julien v. GM of Canada (1991; 116 N.B.R. (2nd), No. 80): The plaintiff's new diesel truck produced excessive engine noise. The plaintiff was awarded the $5,000 cost of repairing the engine through an independent dealer.

Lightburn v. Belmont Sales Ltd., et al. (1969; 6 D.L.R. (3rd), No. 692): The court held that the defendant was required to provide the plaintiff with a vehicle that was in working order capable of giving sustained reliable performance. The plaintiff's vehicle had been returned for repairs 17 times over the first eight months of ownership. The frequency of these repairs was held to be in breach of the condition to provide a vehicle in working order, and a fundamental breach of contract.

Magna Management Ltd. v. Volkswagen Canada Inc. (May 27, 1988; Vancouver (B.C.C.A.); No. CA006037): This precedent-setting judgment allowed the plaintiff to keep his new $48,325 VW while awarding him $37,101—three years after the car was purchased. The problems had to do with poor engine performance.

Maughan v. Silver's Garage Ltd. (Nova Scotia Supreme Court; 6 B.L.R., No. 303, N.S.C. (2nd), No. 278): The plaintiff leased a defective backhoe. The manufacturer had to reimburse the plaintiff's losses because the warranty wasn't honoured. The court rejected the manufacturer's contention that the contract's exclusion clause protected the company from lawsuits for damages resulting from a latent defect.

Murphy v. Penney Motors Ltd. (1979; 23 Nfld. & P.E.I.R.; No. 152, 61 A.P.R., No. 152 (Nfld. T.D.)): This Newfoundland trucker found that his vehicle's engine problems took his new trailer off the road for 129 days during a seven-month period. The judge awarded all repair costs, as well as compensation for business losses, and cancelled the sale.

Murray v. Sperry Rand Corp. (Ontario Supreme Court; 5 B.L.R., No. 284): The seller, dealer, and manufacturer were all held liable for breach of warranty when a forage harvester didn't perform as advertised in the sales brochure or as promised by the sales agent. The plaintiff was given his money back and reimbursed for his economic loss, based on the amount his harvesting usually earned. The court held that the advertising claims acted as a warranty.

Oliver v. Courtesy Chrysler (1983) Ltd. (1992; 11 B.C.A.C., No. 169): Over a 3-year period, a new car showed symptoms of numerous defects that the dealer attempted to fix, to no avail. The plaintiff put the car in storage and sued the dealer for the purchase price. The court ruled that the car wasn't roadworthy and that the plaintiff couldn't be blamed for putting it in storage rather than selling it and purchasing another vehicle. The purchase price was refunded, minus $1,500 for each year the plaintiff used the car.

Olshaski Farms Ltd. v. Skene Farm Equipment Ltd. (January 9, 1987; Alberta Court of Queen's Bench; 49 Alta. L.R. (2nd), No. 249): The plaintiff's Massey-Ferguson combine caught fire after the manufacturer had sent two notices to dealers informing them of a defect that could cause a fire. The judge ruled under the *Sale of Goods Act* that the balance of probabilities indicated that the manufacturing defect caused the fire, even though there was no direct evidence proving that the defect existed.

Western Pacific Tank Lines Ltd. v. Brentwood Dodge (June 2, 1975; B.C.S.C., No. 30945-74; Judge Meredith): The court awarded the plaintiff $8,600 and cancelled the sale of a new Chrysler New Yorker with badly adjusted doors, water leaks into the interior, and electrical short circuits.

Used-Vehicle Defects

Fissel v. Ideal Auto Sales Ltd. (1991; 91 Sask. R. 266): Shortly after the vehicle was purchased, its motor seized. The dealer refused to replace it, even though the car was returned on several occasions. The court ruled that the dealer had breached the statutory warranties in sections 11(4) and 11(7) of the provincial *Consumer Products Warranties Act*. The purchasers were entitled to cancel the sale and recover the full purchase price.

Friskin v. Chevrolet Oldsmobile (72 D.L.R. (3d), 289): A Manitoba used-car buyer asked that his contract be cancelled because of a chronic stalling problem. The garage owner did his best to correct the problem, but despite his good intentions, the Manitoba *Consumer Protection Act* allowed for the cancellation of the sale.

Graves v. C&R Motors Ltd. (April 8, 1980; British Columbia County Court; Judge Skipp): The plaintiff bought a used car on the condition that certain deficiencies be remedied, but they never were. The buyer was promised a refund, but it never arrived. He brought suit, claiming that the dealer's deceptive activities violated the provincial *Trade Practices Act*. The court agreed, concluding that a deceptive act that occurs before, during, or after the transaction can lead to the cancellation of the contract.

Hachey v. Galbraith Equipment Company (1991; 33 M.V.R. (2d) 242): The plaintiff bought a used truck from a dealer for hauling gravel. Shortly thereafter, the truck's steering failed. The plaintiff's suit was successful because expert testimony showed that the truck wasn't roadworthy. The dealer was found liable for damages for being in breach of the implied condition of fitness for the purpose for which the truck was purchased, as set out in section 15(a) of the New Brunswick *Sale of Goods Act*.

Henzel v. Brussels Motors (1973; 1 O.R., 339 (C.C.)): The dealer sold this used car while brandishing a copy of the mechanical fitness certificate as proof that the car was in good shape. The plaintiff was awarded his money back because the court held the certificate to be a warranty that was breached by the car's subsequent problems, caused by defects.

Johnston v. Bodasing Corporation Limited (February 23, 1983; Ontario County Court (Bruce); No. 15/11/83; Judge McKay): The plaintiff bought a used 1979 Buick Riviera for $8,500 that was represented as being "reliable." Two weeks after the car's purchase, its motor self-destructed. Judge McKay awarded the plaintiff $2,318 as compensation to fix the Riviera's defects.

One interesting aspect of this particular decision is that the trial judge found the *Sale of Goods Act* applied in this case, notwithstanding the fact that the vendor used a standard contract that said there were no warranties or representations. The judge also accepted the decision in *Kendal v. Lillico* (1969; 2 Appeal Cases, 31), which indicates that the *Sale of Goods Act* covers not only defects that the seller ought to have detected but also latent defects that even his utmost skill and judgment couldn't have spotted. This places a very heavy onus on the vendor, and it should prove useful in similar actions in other common-law provinces with laws similar to Ontario's *Sale of Goods Act*.

Kelly v. Mack Canada (53 D.L.R. (4th), 476): The plaintiff bought two trucks from Mack Sales. The first, a used White Freightliner tractor and trailer, was purchased for $29,742. It cost him over $12,000 in repairs during the first five months, and another $9,000 was estimated for future engine repairs. Mack Sales convinced Kelly to trade in the old truck for a new Mack truck. Kelly did this, but, shortly thereafter, the new truck had similar problems. He sued for the return of all his money, arguing that the two transactions were really one.

The Ontario Court of Appeal agreed and awarded Kelly a complete refund. It stated, "There was such a congeries of defects that there had been a breach of the implied conditions set out in the *Sale of Goods Act*."

Although Mack Sales argued that the contract contained a clause excluding any implied warranties, the court determined that the breach was of such a magnitude that the dealer couldn't rely on that clause. The dealer then argued that because the client used the trucks, the depreciation of both should be taken into account in reducing the award. This contention was refused on the grounds that the plaintiff never had the product he bargained for and that in no way did he profit from the transaction. The court also awarded Kelly compensation for loss of income while the trucks were being repaired as well as the interest on all of the money tied up in both transactions from the time of purchase until the final judgment.

Morrison v. Hillside Motors (1973) Ltd. (1981; 35 Nfld. & P.E.I.R. 361): A used car advertised to be in "A-1" condition and carrying a 50/50 warranty developed a number of problems. The court decided that the purchaser should be partially compensated because of the ad's claim. In deciding how much compensation to award, the presiding judge considered the warranty's wording, the amount paid for the vehicle, the model year of the vehicle, its average life, the type of defect that occurred, and how long the purchaser had use of the vehicle before its defects became evident. Although this judgment was rendered in Newfoundland, judges throughout Canada have since used a similar approach for more than a decade.

Neilson v. Maclin Motors (71 D.L.R. (3d), 744): The plaintiff bought a used truck on the strength of the seller's assurances that the motor had been rebuilt and that it had 210 hp. The engine failed. The judge awarded damages and cancelled the contract because the motor hadn't been rebuilt, it didn't have 210 hp, and its transmission was defective.

Parent v. Le Grand Trianon and Ford Credit (1982; C.P., 194; Judge Bertrand Gagnon): After paying $3,300 for a used 1974 LTD, the plaintiff sued the Ford dealer 19 months later for his money back because the car was prematurely rusted out. The dealer replied that rust was normal, there was no warranty, and the claim was too late. The court held that the garage was still responsible. The plaintiff was awarded $1,500 for the cost of rust repairs.

"As is" clauses

Since 1907, Canadian courts have ruled that a seller can't exclude the implied warranty as to fitness by including such phrases as "there are no other warranties or guarantees, promises, or agreements than those contained herein." See *Sawyer-Massey Co. v. Thibault* (1907; 5 W.L.R. 241).

Adams v. J&D's Used Cars Ltd. (1983; 26 Sask. R. 40 (Q.B.)): Shortly after the vehicle's purchase, its engine and transmission failed. The court ruled that the inclusion of "as is" in the sales contract had no legal effect and, therefore, the dealer had breached the implied warranty set out in Saskatchewan's *Consumer Products Warranties Act*. The sale was cancelled, and all monies were refunded.

Leasing

Ford Motor Credit v. Bothwell (December 3, 1979; Ontario County Court (Middlesex); No. 9226-T; Judge Macnab): The defendant leased a 1977 Ford truck that had frequent engine problems, characterized by stalling and hard starting. After complaining for one year and driving 35,000 km, the defendant cancelled the lease. Ford Credit sued for the money owing on the lease. Judge Macnab upheld the cancellation of the lease and ordered Ford Credit to repay 70 percent of the amount the plaintiff had paid during the leasing period. Ford Credit was also ordered to refund the repair costs, even though the corporation claimed that it should not be held responsible for Ford's failure to honour its warranty.

Schryvers v. Richport Ford Sales (May 18, 1993; B.C.S.C., No. C917060; Justice Tysoe): The court awarded $17,578.47, plus costs, to a couple who paid thousands of dollars more in unfair and hidden leasing charges than if they had simply purchased their Ford Explorer and Escort. The court found that this price difference constituted a deceptive, unconscionable act or practice, in contravention of the *Trade Practices Act,* R.S.B.C. 1979, c. 406.

Judge Tysoe concluded that the total of the general damages awarded to the Schryvers for both vehicles would be $11,578.47. He then proceeded to give the following reasons for awarding an additional $6,000 in punitive damages:

> Little wonder Richport Ford had a contest for the salesperson who could persuade the most customers to acquire their vehicles by way of a lease transaction. I consider the actions of Richport Ford to be sufficiently flagrant and high handed to warrant an award of punitive damages.
>
> There must be a disincentive to suppliers in respect of intentionally deceptive trade practices. If no punitive damages are awarded for intentional violations of the legislation, suppliers will continue to conduct their businesses in a manner that involves deceptive trade practices because they will have nothing to lose. In this case I believe that the appropriate amount of punitive damages is the extra profit Richport Ford endeavoured to make as a result of its deceptive acts. I therefore award punitive damages against Richport Ford in the amount of $6,000.

Salvador v. Setay Motors/Queenstown Chev-Olds (Hamilton Small Claims Court; Case No.1621/95): The plaintiff was awarded $2,000 plus costs from Queenstown Leasing. The court found that the company should have tried harder to sell the leased vehicle, and at a higher price, when the "open lease" expired.

Western Tractor v. Dyck (7 D.L.R. (3rd), No. 535): The plaintiff specifically required a vehicle for work purposes, and the vehicle was no longer able to maintain the required performance one year following the purchase.

See also:

- *Barber v. Inland Truck Sales* (11 D.L.R. (3rd), No. 469)
- *Canadian-Dominion Leasing v. Suburban Super Drug Ltd.* (1966; 56 D.L.R. (2nd), No. 43)

- *Neilson v. Atlantic Rentals Ltd.* (1974; 8 N.B.R. (2d), No. 594)
- *Volvo Canada v. Fox* (December 13, 1979; New Brunswick Court of Queen's Bench; No. 1698/77/C; Judge Stevenson)

Return of security deposit

Dealers routinely keep much of a lease customer's security deposit when the lease expires. However, this action can always be challenged. In the following claim, settled out of court, Ontario lawyer Harvey Goldstein (*www.loop.on.ca/goldstein*) forced GMAC Financial Services and a GM dealer to refund his $525 security deposit:

1. The Plaintiff Claims:

   (A) Return of his security deposit of $525.00; and a finding that no amount is owing to the Defendants;

   (B) Alternatively, damages in the above amount;

   (C) Prejudgment interest on $525.00 at the rate of 2% per month (24% per annum) from June 22, 2005, to the date of this Claim, and thereafter on the date of payment or Judgment at the rate of 4% per annum, pursuant to Section 128 of the Courts of Justice Act, R.S.O. (1990) as amended;

   (D) Post-judgment interest at the post-judgment rate of interest, pursuant to Section 129 of the Courts of Justice Act, R. S. O. (1990) as amended;

   (E) His costs of this action;

   (F) Punitive damages in an amount to be determined; and

   (G) Such further and other relief as this Honorable Court deems just and proper....

• • •

4. On or about June 10, 2005 the Plaintiff advised the Defendant North York Chevrolet Oldsmobile Ltd that he wanted it to inspect the said vehicle for chargeable damage prior to its return or that he be present when it was inspected after its return to the said Defendant.

5. The said Defendant advised that it had no control over the inspection process and that the Defendant GMAC Leaseco Limited would inspect the vehicle only after the lease expired, the vehicle was returned to the dealer and the Plaintiff was not present.

6. The Plaintiff sent an email on June 10, 2005 to the Defendant GMAC Leaseco Limited asking it for an inspection prior to the vehicle being returned.

7. The said Defendant did not respond to the request.

8. The Plaintiff called and spoke with a representative of the said Defendant on June 17, and wrote her a letter sent by fax the same day, again asking that an inspection be scheduled in his presence. The said Defendant did not respond to the letter.

9. On June 23, 2005, the Plaintiff again called the said Defendant. He was told that it had no record of the vehicle being returned to the dealership.

10. Shortly thereafter, the Plaintiff called the Defendant North York Chevrolet Oldsmobile Ltd to enquire as to the status of his security deposit. The said Defendant advised that it had no record of the vehicle being returned to it.

11. Not having heard from either Defendant, the Plaintiff called the Defendant GMAC Leaseco Limited on July 15, 2005. He was advised that he owed the said Defendant $550.00, less the amount of the security deposit held by it. He was further advised that details of its claim to that amount could be found on the said Defendant's website. He was told that it did not inspect the said vehicle until July 7, 2005, 15 days after it was left in the dealership's service bay. He was told that the vehicle was at an auction and that he could not inspect the alleged damages for which the Defendants claimed compensation. He was advised that no adjustment would be made to their claim even though the vehicle was returned with 20,000.00 kilometers less than allowed by the lease agreement. Further, he was told that the alleged damages to the vehicle were not repaired prior to sending it to auction.

12. The Plaintiff denies that the vehicle required repairs claimed by the Defendants and puts them to the strict proof thereof.

13. The Plaintiff further claims that the process by which the Defendants seek to claim compensation from him is unfair, open to abuse and contrary to the principles of natural justice. The Defendants pay the fee of the alleged independent inspectors and deny the Plaintiff the opportunity to dispute the charges in any meaningful fashion. Further, its delay in inspecting the vehicle for 15 days leaves open the question of when, if ever, the damages occurred.

Repairs

Faulty diagnosis

Davies v. Alberta Motor Association (August 13, 1991; Alberta Provincial Court, Civil Division; No. P9090106097; Judge Moore): The plaintiff had a used 1985 Nissan Pulsar NX checked out by the AMA's Vehicle Inspection Service prior to buying it. The car passed with flying colours. A month later, the clutch was replaced, and numerous electrical problems ensued. At that time, another garage discovered that the car had been involved in a major accident, had a bent frame and a leaking radiator, and was unsafe to drive. The court awarded the plaintiff $1,578.40 plus three years of interest. The judge held that the AMA set itself out as an expert and should have spotted the car's defects. The AMA's defence—that it wasn't responsible for errors—was thrown out. The court held that a disclaimer clause couldn't protect the association from a fundamental breach of contract.

Insurance repairs

Don't let a repairer put used or off-brand parts in your car. In *Avery v. State Farm*, the U.S. Supreme Court ruled that insurers must replace damaged parts with original equipment manufacturer (OEM) parts (1999; *www.state.il.us/court/Opinions/AppellateCourt/2001/5thDistrict/April/Html/5990830.htm*). An Ontario class action lawsuit seeking similar relief was settled on January 31, 2006, in *Albert Hague and Terrance O'Brien v. Liberty Mutual Insurance Company* (Ontario Superior Court; Case No. 01-CV-204787CP; June 14, 2004).

 ## Secret Warranty Extensions

It's common practice for manufacturers to secretly extend their warranties to cover components with a high failure rate. Customers who complain vigorously get extended warranty compensation in the form of "goodwill" adjustments.

In *François Chong v. Marine Drive Imported Cars Ltd. and Honda Canada Inc.* (May 17, 1994; British Columbia Provincial Small Claims Court; No. 92-06760; Judge C.L. Bagnall), Mr. Chong was the first owner of a 1983 Honda Accord with 134,000 km on the odometer. He had six engine camshafts replaced—four under Honda "goodwill" programs, one where he paid part of the repairs, and one via this small claims court judgment.

In his ruling, Judge Bagnall agreed with Chong and ordered Honda and the dealer to each pay half of the $835.81 repair bill for the following reasons:

> The defendants assert that the warranty, which was part of the contract for purchase of the car, encompassed the entirety of their obligation to the claimant, and that it expired in February 1985. The replacements of the camshaft after that date were paid for wholly or in part by Honda as a "goodwill gesture." The time has come for these gestures to cease, according to the witness for Honda. As well, he pointed out to me that the most recent replacement of the camshaft was paid for by Honda and that, therefore, the work would not be covered by Honda's usual warranty of 12 months from date of repair. Mr. Wall, who testified for Honda, told me there was no question that this situation with Mr. Chong's engine was an unusual state of affairs. He said that a camshaft properly maintained can last anywhere from 24,000 to 500,000 km. He could not offer any suggestion as to why the car keeps having this problem.

> The claimant has convinced me that the problems he is having with rapid breakdown of camshafts in his car is due to a defect, which was present in the engine at the time that he purchased the car. The problem first arose during the warranty period and in my view has never been properly identified nor repaired.

Automatic transmission failures (Chrysler)

Lowe v. Fairview Chrysler-Dodge Limited and Chrysler Canada Limited (May 14, 1996; Ontario Court, General Division, Burlington Small Claims Court; No. 1224/95):

The judgment, in the plaintiff's favour, raised important legal principles relative to Chrysler:

- Technical dealer service bulletins are admissible in court to prove that a problem exists and that certain parts should be checked out.
- If a problem is reported prior to a warranty's expiration, warranty coverage for the problematic component(s) is automatically carried over after the warranty ends.
- It's not up to the car owner to tell the dealer or automaker what the specific problem is.
- Repairs carried out by an independent garage can be refunded if the dealer or automaker unfairly refuses to apply the warranty.
- The dealer or automaker cannot dispute the cost of the independent repair if they fail to cross-examine the independent repairer.
- Auto owners can ask for and win compensation for their inconvenience, which amounted to $150 in this judgment.

Court awards quickly add up. Although the plaintiff was given $1,985.94, with the addition of court costs and prejudgment interest, plus costs of inconvenience fixed at $150, the final award amounted to $2,266.04.

False Advertising

Truck misrepresentation

Goldie v. Golden Ears Motors (1980) Ltd. (June 27, 2000; British Columbia Small Claims Court; Port Coquitlam; Case No. CO8287; Justice Warren): In a well-written eight-page judgment, the court awarded the plaintiff $5,000 for engine repairs on a 1990 Ford F-150 pickup in addition to $236 in court costs. The dealer was found to have misrepresented the mileage and sold a used vehicle that didn't meet Section 8.01 of the provincial motor vehicle regulations (it had unsafe tires plus a defective exhaust and headlights).

In rejecting the seller's defence that he disclosed all information "to the best of his knowledge and belief," as stipulated in the sales contract, Justice Warren stated:

> The words "to the best of your knowledge and belief" do not allow someone to be willfully blind to defects or to provide incorrect information. I find as a fact that the business made no effort to fulfill its duty to comply with the requirements of this form.... The defendant has been reckless in its actions. More likely, it has actively deceived the claimant into entering into this contract. I find the conduct of the defendant has been reprehensible throughout the dealings with the claimant.

This judgment closes a loophole that sellers have used to justify their misrepresentation, and it allows for the cancellation of the sale and the awarding of damages if the vehicle doesn't meet highway safety regulations.

MacDonald v. Equilease Co. Ltd. (January 18, 1979; Ontario Supreme Court; Judge O'Driscoll): The plaintiff leased a truck that was represented as having an axle stronger than it really was. The court awarded the plaintiff damages for repairs and set aside the lease.

Seich v. Festival Ford Sales Ltd. (1978; 6 Alta. L.R. (2nd), No. 262): The plaintiff bought a used truck from the defendant after being assured that it had a new motor and transmission. It didn't, so the court awarded the plaintiff $6,400.

Used car sold as new (demonstrator)

Bilodeau v. Sud Auto (Quebec Court of Appeal; No. 09-000751-73; Judge Tremblay): This appeals court cancelled the contract and held that a car can't be sold as new or as a demonstrator if it has ever been rented, leased, sold, or titled to anyone other than the dealer.

Rourke v. Gilmore (January 16, 1928; published in *Ontario Weekly Notes*, Vol. XXXIII, p. 292): Before discovering that his "new" car was really used, the plaintiff drove it for over a year. For this reason, the contract couldn't be cancelled. However, the appeals court instead awarded damages for $500, which was quite a sum in 1928!

Vehicle not as ordered

Whether you're buying new or used, the seller can't misrepresent the vehicle. Anything that varies from what one would commonly expect, or from the seller's representation, must be disclosed prior to signing the contract. Typical scenarios are odometer turnbacks, accident damage, used or leased cars sold as new, new vehicles that are the wrong colour or the wrong model year, or vehicles that lack promised options or standard features.

Chenel v. Bel Automobile (1981) Inc. (August 27, 1976; Quebec Superior Court; Judge Desmeules): The plaintiff didn't receive his new Ford truck equipped with Jacob brakes, essential for transporting sand in hilly regions. The court awarded the plaintiff $27,000, representing the purchase price of the vehicle less the money he earned while using the truck.

Lasky v. Royal City Chrysler Plymouth (February 18, 1987; Ontario High Court of Justice; 59 O.R. (2nd), No. 323): The plaintiff bought a 4-cylinder 1983 Dodge 600 that was represented by the salesman as being a 6-cylinder model. After putting 40,000 km on the vehicle over a 22-month period, the buyer was given her money back, without interest, under the provincial *Business Practices Act*.

False fuel economy claims

Sidney v. 1011067 Ontario Inc. (c.o.b. *Southside Motors*): This is a precedent-setting case that awarded a used-car buyer $11,424.51 plus prejudgment interest because of a false representation made by the defendant regarding fuel efficiency. This judgment puts new-car dealers and automakers on notice that the courts will strictly interpret their gas mileage claims. And, because hardly anyone comes within 10 percent of the fuel efficiency that they claim, we'll likely see more lawsuits of this nature in the future.

Punitive Damages

Punitive damages (also known as exemplary damages) allow the plaintiff to get compensation that exceeds his or her losses as a deterrent to those who carry out dishonest or negligent practices. These kinds of judgments, common in the U.S., sometimes reach hundreds of millions of dollars. Canadian courts, however, seldom award substantial punitive damages.

Nevertheless, there have been a few relatively recent cases where the Supreme Court has shocked the business establishment by levying huge exemplary damage awards. One such case was the *Whiten v. Pilot Insurance Co.* decision rendered in 2002. In this case, the plaintiff's home caught fire and burned to the ground, destroying all of the home's contents and killing three pet cats. Pilot Insurance made a single $5,000 payment for living expenses and covered the family's rent for a couple of months, and then they cut off the rent payments without forewarning the family. The insurance claim went to trial, based on the respondent's allegation that the family had torched their own home, even though the local fire chief, the respondent's own expert investigator, and its initial expert all said there was no evidence whatsoever of arson. The original trial jury awarded the plaintiff compensatory damages and $1 million in punitive damages. Pilot Insurance fought this decision at the Court of Appeal, where the punitive damages award was reduced to $100,000. The case was then taken all the way to the Supreme Court, where the trial jury's unprecedented award of $1 million was restored:

> The jury's award of punitive damages, though high, was within rational limits. The respondent insurer's conduct towards the appellant was exceptionally reprehensible. It forced her to put at risk her only remaining asset (the $345,000 insurance claim) plus $320,000 in costs that she did not have. The denial of the claim was designed to force her to make an unfair settlement for less than she was entitled to. The conduct was planned and deliberate and continued for over two years, while the financial situation of the appellant grew increasingly desperate. The jury evidently believed that the respondent knew from the outset that its arson defence was contrived and unsustainable. Insurance contracts are sold by the insurance industry and purchased by members of the public for peace of mind. The more devastating the loss, the more the insured may be at the financial mercy of the insurer, and the more difficult it may be to challenge a wrongful refusal to pay the claim.

Punitive damages are rarely awarded in Canadian courts against automakers. When they are given out, it's usually for sums less than $100,000. In *Prebushewski v. Dodge City Auto (1985) Ltd. and Chrysler Canada Ltd.*, the plaintiff got $25,000 in a judgment handed down in 2001 and confirmed by the Supreme Court in 2005 (see "Getting Action," earlier in Part Three). The court basically said aggrieved car owners may sue for much more than the depreciated value of what they bought under provincial consumer protection statutes. The Supreme Court reaffirmed the power of the lower courts to assess an additional financial penalty to punish automakers who treat their customers unfairly and to ensure they don't repeat the offense.

Vlchek v. Koshel (1988; 44 C.C.L.T. 314, B.C.S.C., No. B842974): The plaintiff was seriously injured when she was thrown from a Honda all-terrain cycle on which she had been riding as a passenger. The court allowed for punitive damages because the manufacturer was well aware of the injuries likely to be caused by the cycle. Specifically, the court ruled that there is no firm and inflexible principle of law stipulating that punitive or exemplary damages must be denied unless the defendant's acts are specifically directed against the plaintiff. The court may apply punitive damages "where the defendant's conduct has been indiscriminate of focus, but reckless or malicious in its character. Intent to injure the plaintiff need not be present, so long as intent to do the injurious act can be shown."

See also:

- *Granek v. Reiter* (Ontario Court, General Division; No. 35/741)
- *Morrison v. Sharp* (Ontario Court, General Division; No. 43/548)
- *Schryvers v. Richport Ford Sales* (May 18, 1993; B.C.S.C., No. C917060; Judge Tysoe)
- *Varleg v. Angeloni* (B.C.S.C., No. 41/301)

Provincial business practices acts cover false, misleading, or deceptive representations and allow for punitive damages should the unfair practice toward the consumer amount to an unconscionable representation (see *Canadian Encyclopedic Digest (C.E.D.)*, 3rd Edition, s. 76, pp. 140–45). And here are some specific cases to keep in mind:

- Exemplary damages are justified where compensatory damages are insufficient to deter and punish. See *Walker et al. v. CFTO Ltd. et al.* (1978; 59 O.R. (2nd), No. 104; Ontario C.A.).
- Exemplary damages can be awarded in cases where the defendant's conduct was "cavalier." See *Ronald Elwyn Lister Ltd. et al. v. Dayton Tire Canada Ltd.* (1985; 52 O.R. (2nd), No. 89; Ontario C.A.).
- The primary purpose of exemplary damages is to prevent the defendant and all others from doing similar wrongs. See *Fleming v. Spracklin* (1921).
- Disregard of the public's interest, lack of preventive measures, and a callous attitude all merit exemplary damages. See *Coughlin v. Kuntz* (1989; 2 C.C.L.T. (2nd); B.C.C.A.).
- Punitive damages can be awarded for mental distress. See *Ribeiro v. Canadian Imperial Bank of Commerce* (1992; Ontario Reports 13 (3rd)) and *Brown v. Waterloo Regional Board of Commissioners of Police* (1992; 37 O.R. (2nd)).

In the States, punitive damage awards have been particularly generous. Do you remember the Alabama fellow who won a multi-million dollar award because his new BMW had been repainted before he bought it and the seller didn't tell him so? The case was *BMW of North America, Inc. v. Gore* (517 U.S. 559, 116 S. Ct. 1589; 1996). In this case, the U.S. Supreme Court cut the damages award and established standards for jury awards of punitive damages. Nevertheless, million-dollar awards are still quite common.

An Oregon dealer, for example, learned that a $1-million punitive damages award wasn't excessive under *Gore* or Oregon law. The Oregon Supreme Court determined that the standard it set forth in *Oberg v. Honda Motor Company* (888 P.2d 8; 1996), on remand from the Supreme Court, survived the Supreme Court's subsequent ruling in *Gore*. The court held that the jury's $1-million punitive damages award—87 times larger than the plaintiff's compensatory damages in *Parrott v. Carr Chevrolet, Inc.* (2001 Ore. LEXIS 1; January 11, 2001)—wasn't excessive. In that case, Mark Parrott sued Carr Chevrolet, Inc., over a used 1983 Chevrolet Suburban under Oregon's *Unlawful Trade Practices Act*. The jury awarded Parrott $11,496 in compensatory damages and $1 million in punitive damages because the dealer failed to disclose collision damage to a new-car buyer.

Class Action Settlements

In October 2006, B.C.'s Supreme Court approved a $1.5-million class action settlement from Ford of Canada for a defect in its Thick Film Ignition (TFI)/engine computer module. The settlement is related to these class actions and involves more than a dozen different models built from 1983 to 1995. It principally covers B.C. and Ontario residents; however, claims from other provinces and territories will be accepted by Ford on a case-by-case basis.

According to the plaintiffs, the TFI module is an integral part of the solid state ignition system used by Ford in most of its vehicles. It regulates the current that creates the ignition spark, and was mounted on the distributor above the engine block, where it could be damaged by overheating.

Ford has agreed to pay up to $325 each to those who replaced the module or need the part replaced. See *www.tfisettlementsupplemental.com* for information about the U.S. settlement. Information about the Ontario and B.C. settlements can be found at *www.classproceedings.ca/present%20cases%20ford.htm* or by contacting Stevensons LLP at *cstevenson@stevensonlaw.net* or 416-599-7900.

TFI module class actions were filed and settled in the following cases: *Howard v. Ford Motor Company* (U.S.); *Barbara Reid v. Ford Motor Company* (B.C.); and *Royal Fine Cars, Reuben Covello, and Justin Lauria v. Ford Motor Company* (Ontario).

Part Four

VEHICLE RATINGS:
THE BEST AND THE WORST

Wipe Away the Swan Fat

Over the years I've been wined and dined by car firms at the Burj Al Arab in Dubai, the Carlton in Cannes, the Regent in Hong Kong, the Fairmont in San Francisco, the George V in Paris, the Arts in Barcelona, the Hyatt in Beaver Creek, the Phoenician in Phoenix, the Byblos in St Tropez...there's no point going on because the list is endless.

Once, Alfa Romeo took me to the Cipriani in Venice. It actually had a press launch for a car in a city with no roads.

It was great but I spent so much time flying round the world, wiping swan fat from round my chops with the silken underpants of Vietnamese virgins, that in my first year of motoring journalism I earned £2,100.

JEREMY CLARKSON
BBC TV TOP GEAR

The Jeep has gone from a rudimentary all-terrain war wagon to a four-door "chick magnet" that handles terrain no tougher than Toronto's Yonge Street.

A GM Toaster?

Look, let's face it: I don't like cars, SUVs, trucks, or vans. They are a necessary evil and are one of the main reasons why the poor stay poor, corporate ethics have moved from the absolute to the relative, and air pollution is worse than ever.

Sure, it's hard to resist the lure of the open road, but we forget that the "open road" has been closed for years. Now, automobiles are mostly costly, inefficient appliances. Although some do their job efficiently over the years, the social and economic costs inherent with auto ownership are becoming more than we can afford. And, like appliances, the more time saved, the more time wasted in their care and feeding. We get more done, but then find we have more to do.

No, it's not about high fuel costs, highway safety, and pollution alone. There is also an awesome psychological burden associated with auto ownership that few people consider when buying their first car or truck.

First, you become anti-social. You see other drivers as morons with driving skills far inferior to your own, or as predators who seek to cut you off or steal your parking spot at the first opportunity. The surrounding environment becomes abstract as the landscape whizzes by. Concentration is focused on the radio, now called the "sound system," and the cell phone, as there's always one more call to be made. Then there's all the paper work, bills to pay, and maintenance to schedule and argue about. And don't forget the hours lost each day commuting to work, school, and social events.

Perhaps it does seem odd that we discuss the dark side of car ownership in an auto guide. But, what better place? Furthermore, by following the many smart buying tips outlined in the first three chapters, costs and frustration can be contained. In fact, my enthusiasm for used vehicles is driven by a realization that the simplest way to stay above the fray is to recycle the vehicles that have already been built.

Auto Show Penguins

There's an interesting and entertaining phenomenon that occurs every time I attend the annual auto shows in Montreal, Toronto, and Vancouver. As I walk by each automaker's kiosk, which front dozens of beautifully spiffed new cars and trucks, the manufacturers' reps follow me cautiously, almost in lock-step fashion. Decked out in similarly styled suits and walking in unison, they play out a scene reminiscent of the movie *March of the Penguins*, except no one lays an egg (at least, not literally).

All car journalists (an oxymoron?) know it's tough rating new and used vehicles without selling out to the car industry. This fact has been repeatedly confirmed by some of the best writers and broadcasters who are critical of automobile manufacturers. Indeed, the road to auto harlotry is so subtle, few people can resist compromising their integrity. The smooth-talking car pimps are always there to say how much the company admires your work, and how much better it would be with more *balance*.

Then they invite you on their trips to Japan and Europe, where they give you hats, jackets, specially prepared vehicles, and interviews with the top brass. They even sponsor annual awards to make sure their coterie of friendly scribes spout the party line.

You feel like nobility; they see you as a pesky prostitute.

Keeping Ratings Honest and Fair

Lemon-Aid has managed to be both honest and fairly accurate (okay, I did mistakenly recommend the Dodge Aspen and Ford Windstar years ago) for more than 36 years by following these simple rules:

Good rating systems will downgrade models when customer complaints and service bulletins confirm performance and reliability failings, as seen with the 2004–08 Nissan Quest (powertrain failures and lousy fit and finish).

212

- Ratings should be used primarily as a comparative database where the low-ranked or recommended models reappear in different driving tests and owner surveys. The best rating approach is to combine a driving test with an owner survey about past models (only *Consumer Reports* does this).
- The responses must come from a large owner pool (over a million responses from *Consumer Reports* subscribers). Anecdotal responses should then be cross-referenced, updated, and given depth and specificity through NHTSA's safety-complaint prism.

Responses must again be cross-referenced through automaker internal service bulletins to determine the extent of the defect over a specific model and model year range, and to alert owners to problems that are likely to occur.

J.D. Power 2007 Initial Quality Study—Van

Company	Overall Quality	Overall Quality – Mechanical	Powertrain Quality – Mechanical	Body & Interior Quality – Mechanical	Features & Accessories Quality – Mechanical
Chevrolet Express Award Recipient	●●●●●	●●●●○	●●●●●	●●●●○	●●●○○
Buick Terraza	●●○○○	●●○○○	●●○○○	●●○○○	●●○○○
Chevrolet Uplander	●●○○○	●●○○○	●●○○○	●●○○○	●●●○○
Chrysler Town & Country	●●●○○	●●●○○	●●●○○	●●●○○	●●●○○
Dodge Caravan	●●●○○	●●●○○	●●○○○	●●●○○	●●●●○
Ford E-Series	●●●●○	●●●○○	●●●○○	●●●●○	●●○○○
Ford Freestar	●●●○○	●●●○○	●●●○○	●●●○○	●●●○○
Honda Odyssey	●●●○○	●●●●○	●●●●●	●●●○○	●●●●○
Hyundai Entourage	●●○○○	●●○○○	●●○○○	●●○○○	●●○○○
Kia Sedona	●●●●○	●●●●●	●●●●●	●●●●●	●●●●●
Nissan Quest	●●●○○	●●○○○	●●●○○	●●○○○	●●○○○
Toyota Sienna	●●●●○	●●●●●	●●●●●	●●●●●	●●●●○

Scoring Legend

●●●●● Among the best   ●●●●○ Better than most   ●●●○○ About average   ●●○○○ The rest

Consumer Reports and J.D. Power and Associates agree: Detroit's Big Three make mediocre minivans.

- Rankings should be predicated upon important characteristics measured over a significant period of time, unlike "Car of the Year" beauty contests, owner-perceived value, or J.D. Power surveys that consider only problems experienced after three months of ownership (Power's three-year survey results are more relevant).
- Ratings must come from unimpeachable sources. There should be no conflicts of interest such as advertising or consultant ties, or self-serving tests done under ideal conditions.
- Beware of self-generated fuel-economy ratings used by automakers in complicity with the federal government. *Automotive News* found that Honda and Toyota hybrids get 20 percent less "real world" gas mileage than advertised because hybrids require a particular style of driving to be fuel efficient, short trips penalize the efficiency of hybrids more than regular cars, air conditioning penalizes hybrids more, and colder climates increase fuel consumption. *Consumer Reports* found a 40 percent shortfall.
- Tested cars must be bought rather than borrowed, and serviced rather than pampered as part of a journalists' fleet lent out for ranking purposes. Automakers must not be members of the ranking body. Also, all automakers need to be judged equally. At one time, Toyota did not accept weekend car journalist "roundup" tests as valid; the company refused to lend its vehicles to the events, so it was penalized. Toyota now participates enthusiastically…sigh.

Key Factors

A good sport-utility, van, or pickup *must* be reasonably priced, crashworthy, easy to handle, and durable (lasting 10–15 years). And don't believe for one moment that the more you spend, the better the vehicle. For example, the Honda Pilot and Toyota Highlander are two great performers that rival luxury SUVs costing over $10,000 more, like the Acura MDX, BMW X5, Infiniti FX35, or Lexus RX330. The extra money only buys you more features of dubious value and newer, unproven technology, like "adaptive" cruise control and electronic tire sensors.

A good choice should cost no more than about $850 a year to maintain, and should provide you with a 40–50 percent resale value after five years of use. Parts and servicing costs shouldn't be excessive, as CBC TV *Marketplace* found to be the case with some Mazda dealers, and dealer servicing must be easily accessible, unlike Land Rover, Mercedes, and Kia.

Fuel economy

Fuel economy isn't all that important when you're buying used, since all of your other savings should easily compensate you for the extra fuel costs. We don't recommend new or used electric and gasoline engine hybrids, which are found in some SUVs and trucks, because their fuel economy can be 40 percent worse than the automakers report, their long-term reliability is unknown, the cost of replacing their battery is $7,000, their retail prices are incredibly high, and their potential resale value is no better than that of similar vehicles equipped with conventional engines. For example, a 2001 Prius that originally sold for $29,990 is now valued at a disappointing $9,500 (and we're only a year away from the expiration of that $7,000 battery pack warranty).

And forget about hybrids saving the planet. All of those exotic metals used to power your "green machine" and soothe your conscience will end up in a mound in some Third World country. There, children will pick through the toxic waste and then put what is recoverable into buckets for pennies a day, while the remaining toxic metal leaches into the soil and water table. Instead of a hybrid, go for a small conventional vehicle, like a downsized Mazda5 minivan, a Jeep Wrangler or Liberty, or a Hyundai Tucson.

Depreciation

The costliest component of auto ownership, depreciation *is* an important consideration. Vehicles that hold their value well after four years may not be bargains now, but they will still have considerable equity in them should you have to sell because of a cash emergency. And, yes, models that depreciate slowly are usually seen as dependable vehicles that hold up better than others over the long run.

Due to high fuel prices, real-world resale values are much lower than average for some makes like Chrysler Ram trucks, General Motors' minivans and full-sized pickups, Mercedes-Benz, Infiniti, and Nissan. Chrysler's new owners are selling most models with huge discounts, Mercedes has lost ground to more reliable and better-performing BMW and Lexus models, while GM's overall poor quality control has given most Asian automakers the trade-in advantage. Resale values for Mazda and Nissan have been eroded because of massive new-car rebates and dealer sales incentives used to discount unreasonably high suggested retail prices. Infiniti resale values have declined primarily because the company has propped up a declining leasing market through unrealistically high buy-back offers. And buyers see Infinitis as overpriced to begin with.

Road (and off-road) performance

Off-roading requires sufficient low-range power (torque) and lots of ground clearance, which can make a vehicle more likely to tip. The suspension has to be adequate to take the punishment of off-roading challenges. ABS can be hazardous when used off-road, since you can't lock the brakes to build up a vehicle-decelerating wedge of earth in front of the wheels. Consequently, when the ABS sensors kick in to prevent wheel lock-up, it seems like you have no brakes at all. This is especially evident when descending a hill, where the driver is forced to shift into low gear and reduce speed to a crawl. Stability control is another feature that may promise much more than it delivers on some models (early BMWs, for example).

Lemon-Aid Ratings

Lemon-Aid uses mostly owner feedback and confidential service bulletins to rate vehicles. We don't try to curry any automaker's favour. Our guides are ad-free and don't depend on free "loaner" vehicles. We don't play favourites, even with car companies who traditionally turn out some of the better-made vehicles, like Honda, Mazda, Nissan, and Toyota. For almost a decade, we have chastised and down-rated these companies for their sliding-door, automatic transmission, and engine glitches—problems now covered by generous extended warranties. Additionally, *Lemon-Aid*'s 2002 price-fixing complaint against Toyota led to the company's $2-million settlement with Ottawa a year later. In 2006, we filed a similar complaint against Honda.

Customer comments alone do not make a scientific sampling, and that's why we use them in conjunction with other sources of information. Owner complaints, combined with inside information found in service bulletins, are a good starting point to cut through the automakers' hyperbole and get a glimpse of reality.

This guide emphasizes those important new features that add to a vehicle's safety, reliability, road performance, and comfort, and points out those changes that are merely gadgets and styling revisions. Also noted are important changes to be made in the future, including the ending of model lines. In addition to the "Recommended" or "Not Recommended" rating (the current year's rating is reflected in the number of stars beside the vehicle's name), *Lemon-Aid* summarizes each vehicle's strong and weak points.

What the Ratings Mean

Recommended

This rating indicates a best buy, and is almost exclusively the domain of Asian automakers. Interestingly, some vehicles that are identical but marketed and serviced by different automakers, like the Ford Ranger and Mazda B-series pickups, may have different ratings. This occurs because servicing and after-warranty assistance may be better within one dealer network than another.

Recommended vehicles usually combine a high level of crashworthiness with good road performance, few safety-related complaints, decent reliability, and better-than-average resale value. Servicing is readily available and parts are inexpensive and easy to find.

Above Average

Vehicles in this class are pretty good choices. They aren't perfect, but they're often more reasonably priced than the competition. Most vehicles in this category have quality construction, good durability, and plenty of safety features as standard equipment. On the downside, they may have expensive parts and servicing, too many safety-related complaints, or only satisfactory warranty performance—one or all of which may have disqualified them from the Recommended category.

Average

Vehicles in this group have some deficiencies or flaws that make them a second choice. In many cases, certain components are prone to premature wear or breakdown, or some other aspect of long-term ownership is problematic. An Average rating can also be attributed to factors such as substandard assembly quality, lack of a solid long-term reliability record, a number of safety-related complaints, or some flaw in the parts and service network.

Below Average

This rating category denotes an unreliable vehicle that may have also had a poor safety record. Improvements may have been made to enhance durability or safety. An extended warranty is advised.

Not Recommended

Chances of having major breakdowns or safety-related failures are omnipresent. Inadequate road performance and poor dealer service, among other factors, can make owning one of these vehicles a traumatic and expensive experience.

Vehicles that have not been on the road long enough to assess, or that are sold in such small numbers that owner feedback is insufficient, are either Not Recommended or left unrated.

Model Features and Model History

These sections outline the vehicle's specifications and the differences between model years. The "Model History" section provides information on the evolution of the vehicle, including redesigns and modifications.

Technical data

Note that towing capacities differ depending on the kind of powertrain/suspension package or towing package you buy. There's a difference between how a vehicle is rated for cargo capacity or payload and how heavy a boat or trailer it can pull.

In the ratings, cargo capacity is measured with the vehicle's rear seat up and is expressed in cubic feet. With the rear seat folded or removed, cargo capacity becomes much larger. The Gross Vehicle Weight Rating (GVWR) is the vehicle's own weight plus the weight of the maximum load it is rated to carry. Subtracting the curb weight from the GVWR reveals the vehicle's maximum payload capacity.

Cost analysis

Each vehicle's Manufacturer's Suggested Retail Price (MSRP) is given a percentage markup in *Lemon-Aid*. Bargain the markup down by half or more; other charges, such as PDI and transportation, can be reduced by at least 50 percent. The new-car discount war initiated by Chrysler's new owners for the 2007 and 2008 models means the negotiated price for these vehicles will be much lower than the original MSRP. Lower-cost new vehicles soften the resale prices of used makes as well.

 ## Quality and Reliability

Lemon-Aid bases its quality and reliability evaluations on owner comments, confidential technical service bulletins (TSBs), and government reports from NHTSA safety complaint files, among other sources. We also draw on the knowledge and expertise of professionals working in the automotive marketplace, including mechanics and fleet owners.

As you read through the quality and reliability ratings (safety is more of a mixed bag), you'll quickly discover that most Japanese automakers are far ahead of Chrysler, Ford, GM, and European manufacturers in maintaining a high level of quality control in their vehicles. Although GM quality control has improved a bit as of late, you wouldn't believe it after looking over GM owner complaints recorded by NHTSA at *www.nhtsa.dot.gov/cars/problems/complain*.

The following legend is used to show a vehicle's relative degree of overall reliability; the numbers lighten as the rating becomes more positive:

1	**2**	**3**	**4**	**5**
Unacceptable	Below Average	Average	Above Average	Excellent

Warranty performance

I'm more impressed by performance than promise. A manufacturer's warranty is a legal commitment that the product it sells will perform in the normal and customary manner for which it is designed. It's an important factor in *Lemon-Aid*'s ratings: A warranty is judged by how fairly it's applied, not by what it promises.

For example, Ford and General Motors are stricter in their warranty and extended warranty payouts than Chrysler or the Asian automakers. Europeans are the worst, often demonstrating a scornful arrogance when customers question the quality or reliability of their products. The fact that Volkswagen Canada operates mostly out of the States adds another layer of indifference to the equation in Canada—as seen in its recent warranty-extension debacle over ignition coil failures and its reluctant admission that VW engines were afflicted with oil sludging.

Chrysler's pullback from its 7-year/115,000 km powertrain warranty to 5 years/100,000 km—while offering a lifetime powertrain warranty in the States—is as worrisome as it is unfair. In the past, the company's automatic transmission and engine failures have clustered around the five-year mark, often forcing owners with shorter warranties to pay up to $3,000 to fix what are essentially factory defects.

Smart shoppers have noted this shift to less warranty coverage and are paying a premium of a few hundred dollars for 2003 and 2004 models carrying the longer powertrain warranty. Similar powertrain warranties sold by independent agencies often cost between $1,500 and $2,000. Vehicles with less warranty coverage are worth less, says Charlie Vogelheim, executive editor of the *Kelley Blue Book:*

> I will say that a vehicle under warranty is worth more than a vehicle that's not. That's a known fact. And we always see a marked drop in vehicle value once it falls out of warranty, either by calendar or by miles.

Besides protecting owners from costly powertrain repairs, manufacturers' warranties are particularly important in covering expensive computer hardware and software defects. Considering that the typical passenger car has 70 or more tiny, powerful computers onboard that control safety devices and the engine, transmission, fuel delivery, and emissions systems, failures will likely occur more frequently as these electronic systems become more sophisticated.

European automakers like Mercedes, BMW, and VW admit that they have been hit hard by electronic glitches related to computer malfunctions, and IBM estimates that automakers generally spend $2 billion to $3 billion a year fixing software problems.

 ## Safety Summary

Some of the main features weighed in the safety ratings are a model's crashworthiness and insurance claims experience (as assessed by NHTSA and various insurers' groups, including the Highway Loss Data Institute and IIHS), the availability of standard safety features, and front and rearward visibility. Also listed here are a summary of safety-related complaints that will astound and worry you. Many of the quotes in this section are taken from NHTSA's complaints database.

Front and side crash protection figures are taken from NHTSA's New Car Assessment Program. Vehicles are crashed into a fixed barrier, head-on, at 56 km/h (35 mph). NHTSA uses star rankings to express the likelihood of the belted occupants being seriously injured. The higher the number of stars, the greater the protection. NHTSA's side crash test represents an intersection-type collision with a 1,368 kg (3,015 lb.) barrier moving at 62 km/h (38.5 mph) into a standing vehicle.

IIHS rates head restraint, frontal offset, and side crash protection as "Good," "Acceptable," "Marginal," or "Poor." In the Institute's 64 km/h (40 mph) offset test, 40 percent of the total width of each vehicle strikes a barrier on the driver's side. The barrier's deformable face is made of aluminum honeycomb, which makes the forces in the test similar to those involved in a frontal offset crash between two vehicles of the same weight, each going just less than 64 km/h.

The 50 km/h (31 mph) side-impact test performed by IIHS is carried out at a slower speed than the NHTSA test, but uses a barrier with a front end shaped to simulate the typical front end of a pickup or SUV. The Institute also includes the degree of head injury in its ratings.

Secret Warranties/Internal Bulletins/Service Tips

A *Lemon-Aid* exclusive, confidential technical service bulletins (TSBs) are listed for each rated model so that readers have ammunition to get free repairs.

Some vehicles have more TSBs than others, but this doesn't necessarily mean they're lemons. It may be that the listed problems affect only a small number of vehicles or are minor and easily corrected. TSBs should also be used to verify that a problem was correctly diagnosed, the correct upgraded replacement part was used, and the billed labour time was fair.

Costs

Here we list the manufacturer's suggested retail price (MSRP) in Canada for standard models at press time, that price's negotiability—"firm," "negotiable," or "soft" (very negotiable)—and the range of the dealer's markup, including freight and other added fees.

Cross-border parity

The difference between the Canadian and American suggested retail price for any given new model indicates by how much the dealer is inflating the Canadian list price and freight fees. It's this difference you much hack away. To bolster your argument that the vehicle is way overpriced, print out a copy of the American MSRP, which you can find on all U.S. automaker websites by typing the automaker's name and adding ".com"; for Canadian MSRPs, simply add ".ca". Or type "GM U.S." or "GM Canada," for instance, in a search engine such as Google.

SPORT-UTILITY VEHICLES

Mercedes Hits a Pothole

Spend $25,000 on a car that doesn't run the way you expect it to, and you get pretty angry. Spend $50,000 or $100,000, and you get really angry. Just listen to the anguished howls of Mercedes-Benz owners on websites like *troublebenz.com, lemonmb.com,* and *www.mercedesproblems.com* as they vent about the latest mishap to afflict their Benzes. Depending on the model, the complaints range from faulty key fobs and leaky sunroofs to balky electronics that leave drivers and their passengers stranded. Regardless of the severity, a single sentiment runs through the gripes: This shouldn't be happening to a Mercedes.

ALEX TAYLOR III
FORTUNE
OCTOBER 13, 2003

Large SUVs—Low Prices

Although insurance premiums have moderated, high fuel costs and interest rates continue to savage full- and mid-sized SUV sales, forcing Detroit's Big Three to drop negotiated prices by up to tens of thousands of dollars (for example, Dodge Rams selling at $12,000 below list price), and causing the market to shift to downsized and crossover models. Independent industry sources believe lower "real" prices will continue well into the new year due to deep discounting led by Chrysler, an oversupply of gas hogs, and shoppers' demands for sweeter rebates and other sales incentives.

Large SUVs, like the Ford Expedition and Excursion, and the GM Suburban, Yukon, and Tahoe, are selling for a song—3-year-old vehicles are worth less than 50 percent of their original MSRP. Beside depreciation and steep gas prices, SUV shoppers are put off by high insurance costs and the increasingly complex mechanical and electronic systems associated with these Goliaths, which compromise both their safety and reliability.

For the past few years, dealers have responded with $5,000–$10,000 discounts on leftover models, while used prices spiralled downward to match the incentives. But some behemoths like the Ford Excursion and Hummer H1 couldn't even be given away and, therefore, were discontinued. Now, the Ford Expedition, Lincoln Navigator and Aviator, and Mercedes M series are at the top of the hit list—even though Mercedes-Benz is in denial that its sport-utility models are in peril. In fact, no SUV larger than Honda's CR-V or Toyota's RAV4 has a secure future.

Small sport wagons—like the Ford Escape, Honda CR-V, Hyundai Tucson, Mazda Tribute, and Toyota RAV4—are doing well this year because they offer more reasonable prices, better fuel economy, and easier handling than the larger SUVs. Shoppers have simply downsized their choices rather than switching to another kind of vehicle. Instead of scintillating 0–100 km/h performance, buyers are looking for fuel economy bragging rights and innovative convenience and safety features.

And don't forget the fastest growing segment of SUVs: "crossover" car-based sport-utilities, and tall wagons that take on SUV attributes and blend cargo-carrying versatility with carlike comfort and handling. Prime examples of

Ford's small Escape SUV (above) and the identical Mazda Tribute are two successful Detroit models that perform well, are fairly reliable, and aren't usually overpriced.

these fusions are the Chrysler Pacifica, Honda Pilot, Mitsubishi Outlander, Nissan Xterra, Pontiac Vibe, Subaru Forester, and Toyota Matrix.

Car- or Truck-Based?

SUV buyers must decide whether they would rather have the ruggedness and increased towing capability of a truck-based SUV or the ride comfort, more predictable handling, and increased crashworthiness of a car-based version or a crossover. For example, the failure-prone though stylish Chrysler Pacifica is much closer to being a station wagon than what many of us think of as an SUV. It has one of the best highway rides of any SUV, plus exceptional handling, and one of the lowest rollover risks among SUVs tested. Furthermore, its fuel economy is almost equal to that of a minivan or large sedan. Is it any wonder that sales of truck-based SUVs have been flat for six years, while sales of many car-based and crossover vehicles have grown steadily?

Don't assume that all truck-based models have similar towing capabilities. The Chevy Tahoe/GMC Yukon and Ford Expedition can tow more than 4 tons. Chevrolet's TrailBlazer has more than double the torque of the Buick Rendezvous, whose towing capacity can max out at 1,600 kg (3,500 lb.) with the optional towing package; the standard towing limit could be just 1 ton.

The United States military made its contribution to the SUV craze with its Jeep lineup (now a division of Chrysler LLC) and the Hummer (now marketed by General Motors). Imagine, what was designed for use as a military vehicle during World War II has now become the toy of baby-boomer G.I. Joes who miss the irony of a German company (Daimler-Benz), once part of Hitler's war machine, selling Jeeps to Americans:

> [Daimler-Benz] avidly supported Nazism and in return received arms contracts and tax breaks that enabled it to become one of the world's leading industrial concerns.

(Between 1932 and 1940 production grew by 830 percent.) During the war the company used thousands of slaves and forced laborers including Jews, foreigners, and POWs.

www.straightdope.com/classics/a5_078.html

Now, a final word for that 5 percent of us who do enjoy off-roading. Listing "adventure" as the top reason for choosing SUVs, buyers stress that they expect outstanding off-road performance combined with good handling, a comfortable ride, good traction, and high ground clearance.

Don't be a sucker. You want lots of off-road comfort? Stick to Montreal's Beaver Lake's parking lot or Vancouver's Stanley Park.

A soft suspension and precision handling are inversely proportional to true off-road capability, though some automakers are providing vehicles that offer a good compromise. Bear in mind that real off-roading takes place at about 15 km/h and can be a kidney-pounding, white-knuckle experience (kind of like driving early MGs, Triumphs, and Ladas).

Hatchback and Wagon Alternatives

Hatchbacks and wagons can be good alternatives to SUVs if you don't need to accommodate more than five passengers or carry very much cargo. Some pros and cons you may wish to consider are outlined in the chart "Wagons versus SUVs."

Part- or Full-Time 4x4?

There are two types of 4×4 vehicles: part-time and full-time. Part-time 4×4 should be engaged when roads are wet, muddy, or snow-covered. The four wheels are locked together to turn at the same speed. On dry pavement, driving in 4×4 mode may strain the drivetrain and damage the driveline components (check the owner's manual).

Full-time 4×4 (also called "all-wheel drive," or AWD) is a more sophisticated system that permits driving on any surface, all the time. A centre differential lets all four wheels turn at different speeds. If front or rear wheels lose traction, sensors send more power to those wheels. Most buyers prefer the convenience of all-wheel drive, and most automakers are moving in that direction.

Keep in mind that while a 4×4 drivetrain will help you keep traction on muddy, snowy roads, it does little to aid cornering ability and is practically useless in improving braking.

222

PART FOUR • SPORT-UTILITY VEHICLES

WAGONS VERSUS SUVS

WAGON ADVANTAGES

- Reasonable pricing
- Low rollover risk
- Good handling, braking
- Many advanced safety features
- Good fuel economy
- Low step-in height

WAGON DISADVANTAGES

- Lower view of the road in front
- Less passenger, cargo room
- Difficult to access small third-row seats; limited seating flexibility
- Low towing capability
- Limited off-roading, even with AWD

SUV ADVANTAGES

- Competitive prices and slow depreciation on smaller models
- Good front visibility and predictable driving in winter and on rough terrain
- Seat five to nine passengers with lots of seating flexibility
- Lots of cargo room and easy loading and unloading
- 907–2,270 kg towing capability
- Truck frame good for heavy-duty off-roading
- Car-based models are relatively fuel-efficient and easy to handle when compared to minivans and trucks
- Versatile performance
- Post-1997 models have safety features similar to those found in cars
- Impressive crashworthiness scores for car-based models

SUV DISADVANTAGES

- Overpriced, fuel-thirsty, with high insurance premiums
- Accessories, such as running boards, roll bars, and sophisticated anti-theft systems, are expensive but essential
- Inferior handling, rough riding, moderate to very high rollover risk
- Increased risk of injury to children
- Inferior braking
- Truck frames may be deadly to small cars in multi-vehicle crashes, and in crashes with other trucks
- Awkward to enter and exit, difficult to access third row seats, smaller rear doors, and high step-in height
- Lower crashworthiness scores for truck-based models
- Good off-road performers are poorly suited for highway or city use, and vice versa

Safety

One of the main reasons buyers choose sport-utility vehicles is for the safety advantages they offer. The large windshield and high seating give you a commanding, reassuring view of the road ahead, though your rear vision may be obstructed by side pillars, rear head restraints, or the spare tire hanging off the back end. As we react more slowly with age, this increased forward visibility comes in handy (a few extra seconds of warning can make a big difference). Improvements have also been made with three-point seat belts in the front and rear, seat belt pretensioners, optional adjustable brake and accelerator pedals, four-wheel anti-lock brakes, electronic stability control, a high centre brake light, adjustable head restraints on all seatbacks, side head-protecting airbags, side-door beams, and reinforced roofs to protect occupants in rollovers.

Most large SUVs will protect you fairly well in a frontal collision—while creaming whoever hits you. But rollovers are an ever-present safety risk, particularly with early production models that were made through the mid-1990s (we're talking Suzuki, Isuzu, and Ford Bronco) and that poster child for rollovers, Ford's 1992–2004 Explorer. SUVs with electronic stability control reduce this hazard.

Reliability and Quality

In the last two decades, many domestic and imported SUVs were rushed to market with serious quality and performance deficiencies. Mercedes' 1997–2005 M-Class luxury sport-utilities, for example, are nowhere near as reliable as the SUVs produced by Asian automakers.

Chrysler and Ford have a long way to go to close the quality gap. Dodge's Durango has a barely acceptable reliability score. Chrysler's Jeep Cherokee and Grand Cherokee have been afflicted with serious powertrain, AC, brake, and body defects, and the Jeep Commander is just as bad. And don't forget the Ford Explorer, the most popular SUV ever produced. It has a terrible reputation for poor quality control and reliability, plus it shows signs of a plethora of safety-related factory mistakes, highlighted by sudden, unintended acceleration, rollovers (a problem first raised with the previous Bronco series), and under-hood fires.

GM's post-2000 SUVs are the best of Detroit's worst. Their relatively recent redesigns have improved overall safety and performance, but reliability is still the pits, with serious engine, transmission, and fit-and-finish defects. After three to five years of use (about when the warranty ends), buyers would be wise to get an extended warranty or dump these vehicles.

SPORT-UTILITY RATINGS

RECOMMENDED

Chrysler Jeep TJ Wrangler
   (2003–08)
Honda CR-V (2002–08)
Honda Pilot (2006–08)

Hyundai Santa Fe (2007–08)
Hyundai Veracruz (2007–08)
Toyota Sequoia (2005–08)

ABOVE AVERAGE

Acura MDX (2007–08)
Ford Escape/Mazda Tribute,
   Escape Hybrid (2005–08)
Honda CR-V (1997–2001)
Honda Element (2003–08)
Honda Pilot (2003–05)
Hyundai Santa Fe (2001–06)
Hyundai Tucson (2007–08)
Infiniti FX35, FX45 (2003–08)

Lexus RX 300, RX 330, RX 350
   (1999–2003)
Nissan Armada (2008)
Nissan Pathfinder (2006–08)
Nissan Xterra (2005–08)
Nissan X-Trail (2005–07)
Subaru Forester (2006–08)
Toyota 4Runner (2003–08)
Toyota Highlander (2001–08)

Infiniti QX4, QX56 (2006–08; 1997–2003)
Kia Sorento (2008)
Kia Sportage (2005–08)
Lexus GX 470, LX 470 (1998–2008)

Toyota Highlander Hybrid (2006–08)
Toyota RAV4 (1997–2008)
Toyota Sequoia (2001–04)

AVERAGE

Acura MDX (2001–06)
BMW X3 (2004–08)
BMW X5 (2007–08)
Chrysler Jeep Cherokee, Grand
    Cherokee (2002–08)
Chrysler Jeep Liberty, Nitro (2006–08)
Chrysler Jeep TJ, YJ Wrangler
    (1987–2002)
Ford Escape/Mazda Tribute (2002–04)
General Motors Envoy, Rainier,
    TrailBlazer (2002–08)
General Motors Escalade, ESV, EXT,
    Denali (1995–2008)
General Motors Suburban, Tahoe,
    Yukon, Yukon XL (2002–08)
General Motors Tahoe, Yukon Hybrids
    (2008)
General Motors/Suzuki Tracker/Sidekick, Vitara,
    Grand Vitara, XL-7 (1994–2008)

Hyundai Tucson (2006)
Infiniti QX56 (2005)
Kia Sorento (2005–07)
Lexus RX 300, RX 330, RX 350
    (2004–08)
Mitsubishi Endeavor (2004–08)
Mitsubishi Montero (2004–06)
Mitsubishi Outlander (2004–08)
Nissan Armada (2007)
Nissan Murano (2005–07)
Nissan Pathfinder (1990–2005)
Nissan Xterra (2003–04)
Subaru Forester (1994–2005)
Subaru Impreza (1997–2008)
Subaru WRX (2008)
Toyota 4Runner (1986–2002)

BELOW AVERAGE

BMW X5 (2000–06)
Chrysler Jeep Liberty (2002–05)
Ford Aviator, Explorer, Mountaineer,
    Sport, Sport Trac (2003–08)
Ford Escape/Mazda Tribute (2001)
General Motors Aztek,
    Rendezvous (2001–07)
General Motors Suburban,Tahoe,
    Yukon, Yukon XL (1995–2001)
Hyundai Tucson (2005)
Infiniti QX56 (2004)

Kia Sorento (2003–04)
Kia Sportage (2000–02)
Mitsubishi Montero (2003)
Mitsubishi Outlander (2003)
Nissan Armada (2005–06)
Nissan Murano (2003–04)
Nissan Pathfinder (1987–89)
Nissan Xterra (2000–02)
Saab 9-7X (2005–08)
Subaru Tribeca (2006–08)
Subaru WRX (2002–07)

NOT RECOMMENDED

Audi allroad Quattro (2001–05)
Audi Q7 (2007–08)
Chrysler Durango, Aspen (1998–2008)
Chrysler Jeep Cherokee, Grand
    Cherokee (1985–2001)
Chrysler Jeep Commander (2006–08)
Chrysler Jeep Compass, Patriot (2007–08)

Ford Excursion (2000–05)
Ford Expedition, Navigator (1997–2008)
General Motors Blazer, Envoy,
    Jimmy (1995–2005)
General Motors Equinox, Torrent (2005–08)
General Motors Suburban, Tahoe,
    Yukon, Yukon XL (1985–94)

Chrysler Pacifica (2004–08)
Ford Aviator, Explorer, Mountaineer,
    Sport, Sport Trac (1991–2002)
Ford Edge, Lincoln MKX (2007–08)

Lexus RX 400h (2006–08)
Nissan Armada (2004)
Saturn Vue (2002–08)

Small Sport-Utilities

From Tool-Hauling to Latte-Sipping

Forget about compact sport-utilities as puny, unreliable, and unsafe SUV wannabes, like the AMC Eagle or Russian-built Lada Nivea. There are actually more than two dozen compact-sized SUVs on the market, with base retail prices ranging from just over $16,995 for a two-wheel drive Jeep Patriot Sport with a 4-cylinder engine and a manual transmission to $51,000 for a fully equipped, all-wheel-drive BMW X3 powered by a 3.0L 6-cylinder engine.

Compact SUVs can be light on the wallet but still stylish.

Don't underestimate small sport-utility vehicles because of their size. They may be compact—with seating, generally, for only four or five people. But all have an addictive high seating position, modern styling, and loads of safety and convenience features and are available in all- or four-wheel drive, and many are suitable for off-road terrain.

Two (actually, three, if you count the U.S.-sold Mercury Mariner Hybrid, twin to the Escape) gasoline-electric hybrids are found in this segment: the Ford Escape Hybrid and the Saturn Vue Green Line. Saturn's less complex hybrid system isn't as fuel-efficient as the Escape and Mariner hybrids'.

Chrysler's Jeep Compass SUV was introduced as a 2007 model. Selling for $17,995, the Compass is the first front-drive Jeep with a fully independent suspension. It's intended to appeal to women and drivers who rarely go off-road.

Targeting young urban professionals, Acura's RDX SUV is the company's first compact SUV, and is powered by a turbocharged 4-cylinder capable of producing a V6-like 240 hp.

Why Small SUVs Are Better Buys

Let's begin with price. Your $10,000 to $17,000 investment (depending on whether you buy new or used) will burn up less money through the first three years of depreciation.

Fuel savings are considerable. Shoppers can find many models in this segment with 4-cylinder engines, which burn much less fuel (figure 15 to 30 percent less) than bigger SUVs with larger engines. And, due to the carlike performance of many small SUVs, the 4-cylinder engine provides plenty of power for most driving needs when hooked to a front-drive powertrain. A 4×4 model should be considered only if you plan to do serious off-roading. Then, you will need a 6-cylinder engine and a bigger fuel budget.

Smaller SUVs also have more-nimble handling than bigger SUVs because automakers are shifting from truck to car platforms. For instance, the turning circle of a Jeep Wrangler is 34.9 feet, less than the Toyota Camry's. Compare that to the 43-foot turning circle of a full-sized GM Suburban SUV, which can make U-turns and some parking manoeuvres only if you are skillful and have plenty of patience.

4- and 6-cylinder power

The cheapest compact SUVs come with 4-cylinder engines, but there are many models with 6-cylinder optional powerplants. For example, the Saturn Vue and Mazda Tribute offer both 4- and 6-cylinder engines. The Vue's 250-hp 3.5-L V6 is a better engine that's built by Honda. Some compact SUVs, like the Nissan Xterra, are offered only with 6-cylinder engines. After the 4-cylinder was dropped in the 2005 model year, the Xterra's engine changed over to a 265-hp 4.0-L V6.

Loaded with features

Automakers tend to load as many safety, performance, and convenience features as they can into the small SUV segment in order to keep a high profit margin and compete with Asian automakers.

Some small SUVs with nifty features are the easy-to-load Honda Element, which has no side door pillar and a clamshell tailgate; the easily accessed Toyota RAV4 and Mitsubishi Outlander, which provide three rows of seats; and the Nissan Xterra, which has a step integrated into the side of the rear bumper for handling cargo on the roof rails.

Safety

Compact SUVs are no longer the underpowered, rollover-prone mini-trucks that first appeared in force about three decades ago. They are now larger, more crashworthy, and far more stable due to the increased distance between the two front or two rear wheels and the proliferation of electronic stability control (ESC).

Additionally, even entry-level models like the Hyundai Tucson and Kia Sportage come with standard anti-lock brakes, traction control, stability control, and six standard airbags, including front seat–mounted side airbags and side curtain airbags for both front and rear seats.

Electronic stability control has been phased in as a standard feature over the past three years because poor stability is a well-researched trait of all compact SUVs, light trucks, minivans, and 15-passenger vans. In fact, there have been numerous rollover lawsuits against almost all brands and model years of SUVs, including these:

Acura MDX 4×4

Chrysler Jeep CJ

Chrysler Jeep Liberty

Chrysler Jeep Wrangler

Ford Bronco II

Ford Escape

Ford Explorer

Ford Freestyle

General Motors Escalade and ESV

General Motors Suburban

General Motors Tahoe

General Motors Yukon and Yukon XL

Geo Tracker

Honda CR-V

Hyundai Santa Fe

Isuzu Rodeo

Isuzu Trooper

Mitsubishi Montero

Nissan Pathfinder

Suzuki Samurai

Suzuki Sidekick

Toyota 4Runner

Toyota RAV4

Pet Transport: Mixed Reviews

Ideal for combining good fuel economy with sufficient cargo space for side-by-side pet crates, downsized SUVs and their crossover spin-offs usually do their pet-transportation job well. When they do come up short, it's usually because the rear hatch is hard to lift, or the hatch is rounded, reducing useable interior room. Wheelwells can be particularly troublesome on some of the more rounded interiors of many small- and mid-sized SUVs. For example, dog crates often require a specially built platform over the wheelwells, which then makes them sit too high to fit properly. Bottom line: Boxy is best.

Other common shortcomings: The rear interior doesn't deal well with animal "by-products" (staining, cleaning, and residual smell), there aren't enough tie-downs, and the rear seats don't easily fold down to make a flat floor. Nevertheless, small SUVs and crossovers handle more like cars than trucks, and show great promise as dogmobiles, with the best of them (like the Chrysler Nitro) combining the desired attributes of cars, wagons, and SUVs.

Small Disadvantages

Forget towing anything heavy. The towing limit for a V8-powered GM Tahoe or Yukon is about 8,200 pounds—enough for a large trailer or boat—while the much smaller, 4-cylinder-engine-equipped Honda CR-V (there is no 6-cylinder) has a towing capacity of just 1,500 pounds. Maximum payload is also greater in the bigger sport-utilities.

Small SUVs have less storage space than their bigger brothers. However, innovative styling and convenience features allow sufficient room for a small family and pets. Room behind the front seats for cargo is generally in the range of 72.0 cubic feet or so in compact SUVs; the Hummer H2, a large sport-utility, has 86.6 cubic feet of room.

While small SUVs are typically more fuel-thrifty than large sport-utilities, they don't get nearly as much gas mileage as compact sedans. For example, the highway/ city fuel economy rating for Toyota's RAV4 compact sport utility, equipped with a 4-cylinder engine and AWD, is 7.8/10.1 L/100 km (36/28 mpg). But a Toyota Corolla compact sedan, also equipped with a 4-cylinder engine and with an automatic transmission, will burn far less fuel: 5.6/7.8 L/100 km (50/36 mpg).

Chrysler

JEEP COMPASS, PATRIOT ★

bad buy

The Chrysler Jeep Compass.

RATING: Not Recommended (2007–08) due to their short time on the market, limited customer and service-bulletin feedback, and rumours that Chrysler may drop these models in the near future due to poor sales. Although this rating may seem harsh, it follows Jeep's history of putting out glitch-ridden first-year vehicles that are a nightmare to own. Both the Cherokee and Liberty, for example, needed almost three years to work out many of their factory-related defects and to convince dealers to stock up on parts. The Patriot is essentially a Compass with a different suspension and styled more along the lines of the Liberty.

As much as the Commander is the wrong SUV launched at the wrong time, the Compass and Patriot may be two crossover SUVs that are right on target, at least on paper. Jeep's first front-drive-based SUVs, these two vehicles are designed to capitalize on the public's shift to compact sport-utilities. The first fruit of a trium- virate venture with Mitsubishi and Hyundai, they combine the packaging and functionality of an SUV with the performance, handling, fuel economy, and price of a small pickup, thus rivaling established models like the Toyota RAV4, Honda CR-V, and Ford Escape. Other competitors are the Honda Element, Hyundai Tucson, Kia Sportage, Mazda Tribute, Mitsubishi Outlander, Nissan Xterra and X-Trail, Pontiac Torrent, and Toyota FJ Cruiser.

Both vehicles use the Dodge Caliber platform and are about 13 cm (5 in.) longer and 360 kg (800 lb.) heavier than the Liberty. A fuel-efficient and quiet-running 172-hp 2.4L 4-cylinder engine may be hooked to a 5-speed manual transaxle or an optional continuously variable transaxle (CVT) that is said to improve fuel economy by 5 percent. The CVT itself has an AutoStick option that allows for the manual control of a simulated 6-speed. Although CVT transaxles have been used in Japanese vehicles for many years without any reliability problems, American models, notably Saturn's Vue, have had serious problems with their CVT. Furthermore, Jeep drivetrains are notoriously unreliable—another reason why buyers should steer clear of a Compass or Patriot.

An optional full-time 4×4 system enhances overall driving performance and includes a number of standard features like Brake Traction Control, Electronic Stability Program (ESP), Brake Assist, Electronic Roll Mitigation (ERM), and anti- lock brakes. Off-roaders will also appreciate the 20 cm (8 in.) of ground clearance. Additional standard features include side curtain airbags, a fold-flat vinyl load floor, an AM/FM CD radio with an auxiliary audio input jack, cloth seats, tilt steering wheel, dome and cargo lights, floor mats, and a centre console sliding armrest.

The Compass and the larger Commander are slated to be retired at the end of the 2008 model year. Poor sales, high fuel prices, and a fear the Compass will canni- balize other Jeep model sales have led to Chrysler LLC dropping both models.

Compass—a carlike Jeep

The Compass is an exceptional pet hauler. The Stow 'N Go seats fold easily and completely flat. There are lots of well-placed cargo tie-downs, the large cargo area is fully functional, and rubber matting makes clean-up a breeze.

The manufacturer's suggested retail price (MSRP) for a 2007 Compass was $17,995 (not including a $1,050 freight and PDI fee). It's now worth $11,0000. The MSRP

The Patriot has the rugged Jeep styling the Compass lacks, but extra-cost off-road capability may be a tough sell.

for 4×4 models was $19,995 (now $13,500). 2008–09 prices are identical. Smart shoppers can cut prices by asking the dealer to match American Jeep prices listed on the Internet (*www.jeep.com*) (Compass Sport 4×2: $17,375; 4×4: $19,125).

Patriot—a "Jeeplike" Compass

The Patriot takes the Compass up a couple of notches in styling and performance capability. It has more of the Jeep's traditional rugged look and, unlike the Compass, can be made into a Trail Rated off-roader with the Freedom Drive II off-road package that offers full skid plates and automatic four-wheel drive with a locking low-range gear for no-worry off-roading. The package also includes 17-inch all-terrain outline white letter (OWL) tires and aluminum wheels, a full-sized spare tire, an air-filtration system, tow hooks, fog lamps, and a seat-height adjuster—all for an estimated price that varies from $14,745 to $20,545 (U.S.: $16,375–$22,845). In Canada, a used 2007 is worth $11,000.

Family ties

When you buy the car, you marry the family, and the three members of this auto alliance—Chrysler, Mitsubishi, and Hyundai—have their share of dysfunctional elements. For example, in the '80s when Chrysler teamed up with Mitsubishi to produce several generations of Colts, they made compact cars with a good reputation for quality control, and Mitsubishi began riding the crest of a surge in fuel-frugal car sales.

Then all hell broke loose.

From the late 1990s through 2004, seven top Mitsubishi executives in Japan were arrested and charged with covering up safety recalls and falsifying defect reports, including a failure that killed a driver. Then the press found evidence that the company regularly made payoffs to Yakuza crime bosses for protection from union leaders and disgruntled stockholders. Reacting to the scandals and mounting losses, the parent company in 2005 forced the resignation of Mitsubishi's president, chairman, and vice chairman. DaimlerChrysler's Mercedes masters in Germany were horrified, and they soon began cutting their ties with Mitsubishi.

Not soon enough, though. Shortly thereafter, the company was hit by lawsuits alleging a pattern of systematic sexual harassment of women at Mitsubishi's Illinois assembly plant. Although these suits were settled, Chrysler ran for cover and sold off its 37 percent interest in the company. Interestingly, now it has come to light that Mercedes-Benz, Hitler's favourite employer of slave labour, has its own hands full fending off allegations of sexual harassment, illegal payoffs, maladministration, and poor quality control.

In the 2006 edition of J.D. Power and Associates Initial Quality Study, Mitsubishi placed 23rd out of 37 brands ranked, and the Eclipse is the company's only bestseller; Hyundai has a full plate pulling its Kia subsidiary sales out of the mud and launching delayed new products; and Chrysler LLC is stuck with a huge inventory of large trucks and SUVs that nobody wants (don't even mention Dodge's B-Van replacement, the $44,490 Mercedes/Dodge Sprinter).

JEEP LIBERTY, NITRO ★★★

The 2007 Jeep Nitro.

RATING: Average (2006–08); Below Average (2002–05). This heavier, more versatile successor to the Cherokee had many reliability and quality problems clustered around its first three model years. More recent models have had fewer deficiencies reported, but they haven't been on the road that long, nor do they have the all-important lifetime powertrain warranty that covers the Jeep's automatic transmission failures in the States. **Strong points:** A 7-year powertrain warranty on the 2002–04 models, good towing capability for a V6, very comfortable ride, generous interior volume despite the narrow interior, well-appointed, and a nice array of standard and optional safety features. A tight turning circle, low-range gearing, load-levelling shocks, and a front skid plate enhance off-road performance. Electronic stability control is a proven standard feature. U.S. prices are not much lower than the Canadian MSRPs. **Weak points:** Liberty's pre-2006 base engine is an underpowered 150-hp Cirrus-sourced 4-cylinder. The 160-hp 2.8L turbo-diesel gets only three extra miles per gallon over the V6 and was dropped for 2007. Selec-Trac 4×4 is not as user-friendly as rivals' AWD; there's excessive swaying, rocking, and jiggling on uneven roads; the steering is less responsive than that of the RAV4; and independent front suspension can limit off-roading prowess. The Liberty has compromised rear-seat comfort; rear visibility that's blocked by a spare tire; a driver's seat that is positioned closer to the door than usual and could use additional lumbar and lateral support; a high step-in and narrow door openings; a bulging heater box that protrudes into the cabin area; no folding centre rear armrest; 4×4 gear whine (a Jeep trademark for years) and excessive engine clatter, turbo whistle, and tire and wind noise; cheap-looking plastic interior trim; and surprisingly poor fuel economy. **New for 2008:** A larger Liberty has been redesigned along the lines of the Nitro, complete with a new Sky Slider retractable canvas roof; a $28,545 (U.S.: $27,145) high-performance SRT Nitro arrived in early 2008.

MODEL HISTORY: Introduced as a 2002 model, the Liberty is a four-door that's longer, wider, taller, and generally roomier than the Cherokee it replaced; it has less cargo space and ground clearance, however. It also weighs a lot more than its predecessor, eating into its fuel economy figures. **2002**—The second-series model was given larger, stronger brake rotors and drums than the Cherokee (brake problems remain a constant complaint) and a new ABS with electronic brake force distribution. **2003**—Standard four-wheel disc brakes. **2006**—A 160-hp 2.8L 4-cylinder diesel engine debuted on the 2006 models and then was dropped for the 2007 model year. **2007**—The Nitro, a Liberty-derived Dodge sport-utility, entered the marketplace in late 2006 as a 2007 model. A restyled exterior uses flat surfaces, crisp lines, and a downsized version of the macho crosshair grille to set this spin-off apart from its Liberty brother. Nitro's interior space feels a bit larger than the Liberty's, and its "Load and Slide" textured vinyl cargo floor slides for easy loading and unloading.

Marketed as a mid-sized alternative to the Durango SUV, the Nitro has a 210-hp 3.7L single overhead cam (SOHC) V6 coupled to a full-time 4×4 and a 4-speed automatic.

2008 LIBERTY TECHNICAL DATA

POWERTRAIN (FRONT-DRIVE/4×4)
Engine: 3.7L V6 (210 hp); Transmissions: 6-speed man. • 4-speed auto.
DIMENSION/CAPACITY
Passengers: 2/3; Wheelbase: 106.1 in.; H: 70.1/L: 176.9/W: 72.4 in.; Headroom F/R: 6.0/7.0 in.; Legroom F/R: 40.8/38.8 in.; Cargo volume: 64.2 cu. ft.; Fuel tank: 78L/regular; Tow limit (V6): 5,000 lb.; Load capacity: 1,150 lb.; GVWR: 5,350 lb. (av.); Turning circle: 37.0 ft.; Ground clearance: 6.5 in.; Weight: 4,222 lb.

COST ANALYSIS: *Liberty:* Priced at $24,195/$24,295 (U.S.: $21,340/$26,990) (Sport/ Limited), the 2008 Liberty is overpriced by about 20 percent. Stay away from the little 4-banger—the same failure-prone beastie used on the Cirrus (complete with biodegradable head gaskets). The little engine is completely overwhelmed by the Liberty's extra weight, although it does manage to eke out a 900 kg (2,000 lb.) tow rating. If you choose the torquier turbodiesel, fuel economy will benefit, but acceleration is still sluggish and long-term reliability is unknown. The V6 is the best choice. It's fairly powerful, with plenty of low-end grunt, and can tow up to 2,265 kg (5,000 lb.) when equipped with the optional towing package. *Nitro:* As with the Liberty, this year's Nitro base price varies considerably: $19,595–$28,545 ($20,580–$28,805 in the States) depending on the model or equipment chosen. Its prices can be easily bargained down by 20 percent. **Best alternatives:** A new Honda CR-V, Hyundai Tucson, Nissan Xterra, or Toyota RAV4. The 2001 Jeep Cherokee isn't a bad choice, either. **Rebates:** Look for $3,000 rebates or low-financing deals on both vehicles. **Delivery/PDI:** $1,050. **Warranty:** Bumper-to-bumper 3 years/60,000 km; powertrain 5 years/100,000 km; rust perforation 5 years/160,000 km. **Supplementary warranty:** A powertrain warranty is a wise buy. **Options:** Get the V6 engine, 4-speed automatic transmission, and Selec-Trac full-time 4×4. Larger 16-inch tires are a performance plus. Here are two worthwhile, though overpriced, option packages worth considering: a trailer towing package ($480), which includes an engine oil cooler, Class 3 trailer hitch, and 7-pin wiring harness; and a convenience package ($2,485), which includes air conditioning, CD changer, roof rack, deluxe steel wheels, full-sized spare tire, power front windows with one-touch-down feature, and a tilt steering wheel. The extra cost can be easily amortized after five years of use and won't be felt at all if the car is bought in the States. **Depreciation:** Slower than average. **Insurance cost:** Average. **Parts supply/cost:** Expect high parts costs and month-long waits until the parts supply line gets filled. **Annual maintenance cost:** Average, thanks to the 7-year extended powertrain warranty. **Highway/city fuel economy:** *4-cyl.:* 9.4/11.8 L/100 km; *2.8L turbodiesel:* 8.0/10.5 L/100 km; *V6:* 10.7/12.4 L/100 km.

QUALITY/RELIABILITY: Average. **Owner complaints:** Some powertrain, suspension, electrical, and brake problems seen during the car's first few years on the market have been addressed; later models are much more reliable. **Warranty performance:** Warranty performance is about average; no owner feedback as to how well owners' claims are handled by Chrysler's new management, except that the lifetime powertrain warranty offered in the States isn't offered to Canadians.

ROAD PERFORMANCE: Acceleration/torque: Plenty of power with the V6, although it could use more high-end grunt for highway cruising. Diesel engine acceleration is adequate, though some owners note a bit of clatter and turbo whine. **Transmission:** Quite versatile over a variety of roads. For ordinary day-to-day driving on dry roads, 4×2 is fine; on wet or snow-covered roads, full-time 4×4 enhances stability and traction; for gravel and dirt roads, part-time 4×4 provides more traction; and for steep, slippery inclines, 4×4 Low gives you lots of engine braking and pulling power. **Steering:** Fairly accurate and predictable, though less so with the diesel-equipped version. **Routine handling:** A firm, jittery ride. The low ground clearance limits the Liberty's off-road capability. **Braking:** Works quite well. Off-roaders will appreciate that the ABS is defeated when the transfer case is placed in Low and that it has been redesigned to limit false activation on bumpy surfaces.

 SAFETY SUMMARY: Airbags: Front. **ABS:** Optional; disc/drum. **Safety belt pre-tensioners:** Front. **Traction control:** Yes. **Head restraints F/R:** ★★. **Visibility F/R:** ★★★★★/★★★. **Pet transport:** *Liberty:* ★★★; *Nitro:* ★★★★★. The tall, square back provides plenty of easily accessed cargo space for side-by-side crates, which can be secured by six cargo tie-downs. Back strain can be avoided with the rolling rear Load 'N Go platform, which can support 400 lbs. of food and accessories and gently slide them into the storage bay.

SAFETY COMPLAINTS: Government probes have logged over 100 safety complaints on the 2002–05 models. This is an astounding figure, given that the Liberty was Mercedes' first chance to show it could produce a top-quality vehicle in co-operation with Chrysler.

All years: Many complaints of electrical fires, faulty airbags, no brakes, sudden acceleration, chronic stalling, transmission failures, excessive on-road vibration, and recall snafus, with owners not being notified, parts not being available, and the correction not fixing the problem. **2002**—Fire ignites on right side of vehicle. • Vehicle tips over quite easily; in two incidents, from a side impact and from the wheel/axle suddenly collapsing. • Transmission may slip from Park to Reverse. • Side airbags deploy while driving. • Low suspension allows underside to be easily damaged, making off-roading unsafe. • Part of steering wheel falls off while driving. • Front seats propel forward when braking. **2003**—Vehicle suddenly shuts down because of chronic fuel-pump failures. • Front ball joint/strut mount failures. **2004**—Airbag-induced injuries:

> While driving at 25 mph [40 km/h], the driver-side airbag deployed for no logical reason. The consumer lost control of the vehicle and collided with an embankment. The vehicle never ran over anything or hit anything before the mishap. The consumer suffered a sprained wrist, a concussion and trauma to his back. The consumer also reported that before the airbag deployed, electrical currents from the steering wheel were shocking whoever drove the vehicle.

• Fuel smell in cabin, followed by a fire. • Hood latch failure. • Goodyear Wrangler tire tread separation. **2005**—Sudden acceleration caused by a defective accelerator pedal pressure sensor. • Chronic stalling. • Airbags fail to deploy during a severe collision. • Excessive steering-wheel play; vehicle tends to wander all over the highway, forcing driver to constantly make steering corrections. • Plastic fuel tank and its mounting increase the possibility of fuel leakage from minor impacts. • Premature wearout of the lower front ball joints. • Airbag Off light comes on when an adult sits in the passenger seat:

> Airbag Off light comes on with adult in passenger seat. [The light] seems to go off only over 110 lb [50 kg]. Many adult passengers around 100 lb, and thus do not have safety of system on. Been to dealer three times. They say nothing can be done.

• Tire jack bends under the weight of the vehicle. • Gas sloshes out of a full tank. **2006**—Severe toe lacerations caused by the AC blower fan falling out of its dash housing. • Frequent brake failures. **2006–07**—Parts needed to complete recall repairs are often unavailable. **2007**—Upper ball joint suspension failures. • Excessive shaking when underway. • Brake pedal goes to the floor without effect.

Secret Warranties/Internal Bulletins/Service Tips

2002—Remedy for skunk-like odour. • Front engine-compartment harness may have an intermittent loose ground. • Loss of crankshaft position sensor signal. • Troubleshooting 45RFE transmission solenoids. • Radiator oil cooler contamination. • Longer-than-normal crank time prior to start. • Reduced power-steering assist when steering wheel is turned quickly. • Excessive wind buffeting. • Software improvement for unlatching flip-up glass. • Flickering panel lights or display. • Difficulty refuelling. • Exhaust rattle caused by flange bolt springs. • Front-end creaking noise. • Wind whistle from Mopar brush guard or front air deflector. • AC drain water leaks under passenger-side carpet are caused by a factory mistake, says TSB #24-012-01. **2003**—An erratically shifting automatic transmission may require a re-calibrated powertrain control module (PCM) or transmission control module (TCM). • Harsh-shifting countermeasures. • Scored 3.7L engine crankshaft. • Insufficient body sealer in cowl area. **2003–04**—Liftgate glass lifts up. • AC won't cool or heat properly. • Harsh downshifts. • Excessive brake noise (see bulletin). **2004**—Slow gear engagement after a cold start requires reprogramming of the PCM. **2005**—Faulty connection may cause automatic tranny to "limp" home. • Remedy for diesel hard starts. **2005–06**—Improved hill-climbing capability in Reverse. • Ring marks on glass. • Manual 6-speed won't stay in gear.

BRAKE MOANING
BULLETIN NO.: 05-001-04   DATE: JANUARY 13, 2004

REAR DISC BRAKE MOAN

This bulletin involves the replacement of the rear disc brake pads and rotors.

2003–04 Liberty (Domestic Market)

The customer may experience a rear brake moan-like sound during light or no brake application pressure. This condition is more likely to occur when the brakes are cool (first use) and ambient temperatures are below 50°F [10°C]. The moan-like sound may be intermittent.

JEEP LIBERTY PROFILE

	2002	2003	2004	2005	2006	2007
Cost Price ($) (soft)						
Liberty Sport (22%)	22,800	24,490	25,695	27,360	29,815	29,815
Liberty Limited (23%)	28,680	29,790	30,675	33,420	33,550	33,560
Used Values ($)						
Liberty Sport ▲	8,500	12,000	13,500	15, 000	17,000	20,000
Liberty Sport ▼	7,000	10,500	12,000	14,000	15,500	18,000
Liberty Limited ▲	10,000	13,500	15,500	17,500	21,000	24,000
Liberty Limited ▼	8,000	12,000	14,000	16,000	19,500	22,500
Reliability	2	3	3	3	3	3
Crash Safety (F)	5	5	5	5	5	5
Side	5	5	5	5	5	5
Offset	2	2	2	2	2	2
Rollover	2	3	3	3	3	3

JEEP TJ WRANGLER

★★★★★

best buy

2008 TJ WRANGLER TECHNICAL DATA

POWERTRAIN (4×4)

Engine: 3.8L V6. (205 hp); Transmissions: 6-speed man. • 4-speed auto.

DIMENSION/CAPACITY

Passengers: 2/2, 2/3; Wheelbase: 116.0 in.; H: 71.0/L: 173.0/W: 74.0 in.; Headroom F/R: 5.5/5.0; Legroom F/R: 41.0/28.0 in.; Cargo volume: 34.5 cu. ft. with the four-door; Fuel tank: 72L/regular; Tow limit: 3,500 lb.; Load capacity: 850 lb.; GVWR: 4,602 lb.; Turning circle: 36.0 ft./43.0 ft. with the four-door; Ground clearance: 8.0 in.; Weight: 4,105 lb.

RATING: Recommended (2003–08); Average (1987–2002). A direct descendant of the original Jeep—the 1941 Willys MB—this should be the first choice for all off-roaders. It's primitive, capable, and fun to drive. Plus, the Wrangler's not a bad looker for Saturday night cruising along Yonge or Burrard streets, and short commutes with the 4-speed automatic are a breeze (2003 and later models). Here are your best choices: Get an improved, second-series 2007 model for both on- and off-roading capabilities, or get a 2003–06 version equipped with the 4-speed automatic tranny, for acceptable highway performance while burning less fuel. **Strong points:** The 2007 model added more standard features and handles much better than earlier versions. Entry-level models are reasonably priced, depreciate slowly, are attractively styled, and have comfortable front seating. Also, controls and displays are nicely laid out, though controls on older models aren't as user-friendly. Low-speed handling is fairly competent, making the Wrangler a versatile off-roader. For concerned parents: The Wrangler also has good frontal, offset, and rollover crashworthiness ratings. **Weak points:** Pre-2007 base models are bereft of many standard features; rough and noisy ride; vague, imprecise steering; mediocre braking; cramped rear seating; little storage space; the canvas top is a chore to open; plastic windows don't stay clean for long; high step-in; chronic powertrain and body shortcomings; poor fuel economy; and many reports of engine- and steering-column-related fires. **New for 2008:** Nothing significant; this popular small SUV will be coasting on its 2007 model improvements and four-door popularity until the revamped 2009 models arrive.

MODEL HISTORY: 1999—Upgraded rotary climate controls and a larger standard fuel tank. **2000**—Sport and Sahara got a more refined, quieter 6-cylinder powerplant along with an upgraded 5-speed manual shifter. **2003**—An optional 4-speed automatic is introduced. SE models use the Liberty's 147-hp 2.4L 4-cylinder engine, and the X, Sport, Sahara, and Rubicon versions now carry a 190-hp 4.0L inline-six powerplant. **2004**—Unlimited gets a wheelbase that's 25 cm (10 in.) longer than other Wranglers and 38 cm (15 in.) longer overall, adding 5 cm (2 in.) of rear leg-room and more cargo volume. A tilt steering wheel is standard. **2005**—A 6-speed manual transmission replaced the 5-speed. **2007**—A new 205-hp 3.8L V6 with 15 more horses than the 4.0L V6; electronic stability control (ESP); electronic roll mitigation; dual-stage airbags, seat-mounted side airbags, and an occupant classification system (OCS); increased ground clearance; larger wheels and tires; enhanced Dana solid front and rear axles; Command-Trac and Rock-Trac transfer cases; new electric axle lockers; and a revamped front sway bar. Additionally, you get a stiffer frame, a 5 cm (2 in.) longer wheelbase, a 9 cm (3.5 in.) wider track, lower suspension spring rates, better brakes, and a retuned suspension. The larger interior gives more hip, shoulder, and leg room. The three-piece modular hardtop is also new along with this year's Unlimited version.

COST ANALYSIS: Priced at $17,995–$30,595 (U.S.: $19,680–$28,240), the Wrangler is the smallest and least expensive (we're talking bare-bones here) Jeep you can find. It and the Liberty are the only Jeeps likely to survive through the 2009 model year. Interestingly, Chrysler just cut its Canadian prices to bring them more in line with its American MSRPs. Hardly worth the bother shopping in the States, except for the lifetime powertrain warranty and lower freight charges. The Unlimited's extended wheelbase adds to rear-seat comfort, and the 6-speed manual gearbox improves fuel economy and performance. The 2003–04 versions, with their longer powertrain warranty and base engine and automatic transmission improvements, should be better buys than earlier versions, but they don't offer the handling and performance refinements found with the post-2006 models. **Best alternatives:** Other comparable sport-utilities worth a look are the GM Tracker (V6), Suzuki Sidekick, Honda CR-V or Element, Hyundai Tucson, Subaru Forester, and Toyota RAV4. But remember, none of these other models can follow the Wrangler off-road. **Rebates:** These cars usually sell for their full list price and come fully loaded. Buying a model stateside will net you a savings of only about $2,000. **Delivery/ PDI:** $1,300. **Warranty:** Bumper-to-bumper 3 years/60,000 km; powertrain 5 years/100,000 km; rust perforation 5 years/160,000 km. **Supplementary warranty:** An extended powertrain warranty is strongly recommended if the car is bought in Canada; only American cars get the free lifetime powertrain warranty on 2007–08 models. **Options:** For serious off-roading, opt for the 6-cylinder engine and 5-speed manual transmission. Keep an eye out for the optional suspension system, which includes larger shock absorbers and heavy-duty springs. An aftermarket anti-theft system is also a plus. Ditch the Firestone tires. **Depreciation:** Much slower than average. **Insurance cost:** Above average. **Parts supply/cost:** Above-average supply. **Annual maintenance cost:** Higher than average without the 7-year warranty. A spotty service record at Jeep dealerships inflates maintenance costs, so you'll want to frequent independent service agencies after the warranty expires. **Highway/city fuel economy:** The 6-speed manual and 3.8 L V6 engine give you slightly better fuel economy than the old 4.0L 6-cylinder, but it's still unimpressive. *2.4L 4-cyl. and auto.: 12.1/15.7 L/100 km; 4.0L 6-cyl. and man.: 11.6/15.4 L/100 km; 6-cyl. and auto.: 11.7/16.8 L/100 km.*

 QUALITY/RELIABILITY: Average. Factory-related defects have always plagued these vehicles, but not as much as before. Premature front brake wear is a frequent complaint:

> While driving at 55–60 mph [88–97 km/h] and applying the brakes, my 2006 Jeep Wrangler shakes like it is going to fall apart. It has less than 12,000 miles [19,000 km] on it and this is the second pair of rotors within a short period of time, around 3 months. Now I'm told by the service department that it's my driving style, that I should down shift to make it easier on the brakes...I already do down shift. The repair was taken care of free of charge because of the short period of time between the rotor changes. [But] the next time I will have to pay for it!!... I'm not going to be pushed over and told it's the way I drive, when it's apparent that there is something else causing the problem. Funny, I don't need brake pads but the rotors keep $%&in' up...a defect or what? Excuse my language but I'm a 43 year old woman that doesn't want to be jerked around by [my] service dept. and told it's my driving style!

Owners say that the 5-speed and 6-speed manual transmissions don't shift smoothly. The 6-speed grinds when going into Reverse, or it pops out of Reverse. The 5-speed constantly grinds when shifting or when in Neutral and the clutch is depressed; the shifter won't come out of or go into gear; it, too, may suddenly pop out of gear; it sticks in Second gear when hot, or when accelerating in First or Second; and the Fifth gear suddenly disengages. Watch out for transfer-case malfunctions, engine overheating, engine and transfer-case oil leaks, worn-out suspension (ball joints, especially) and steering components, and ignition-component malfunctions.

Owners report that the Wrangler's off-road prowess is compromised by poor original-equipment tires and thin body panels:

> Suffers from cheap quality, paper-thin, sheet metal front fenders that bend from rocks thrown from the worthless Goodyear Wrangler street-treaded, pebble-throwing tires.... My Jeep has 8,400 easy-driven miles [13,500 km], but now has dented fenders with cracked paint finish and paint flaking!

Body welds and seams are susceptible to premature rusting, and there have been frequent complaints about peeling paint and water leaks. The worst leaks occur at the bottom of the windshield frame. An easy way to check for this is to examine the underside of the frame to see if there's excessive rust. This has consistently been a problem area for Jeeps; hence all of the ads for aftermarket windshield frames. Watch for corroded windshield bracket bolts. The good news is that you can replace the windshield frame and all of the seals relatively cheaply. AC condensers are also failure-prone. **Warranty performance:** Average.

 ROAD PERFORMANCE: Acceleration/torque: Off-road capability is impressive with the 4-cylinder engine, thanks to gobs of low-end torque when it's shifted into low range. Smooth, above-average acceleration and torque with the 6-cylinder engine, as well (0–100 km/h: 10.5 sec.). The 2.4L 4-cylinder engine is noisy and lacks the power for serious hauling; it's especially sluggish when hooked to the automatic transmission. **Transmission:** The 3-speed automatic shifts harshly and saps power from the engine. Hold out for a 4-speed automatic or the 6-speed manual, but test-drive the manual tranny to make sure it shifts as it should. **Steering:** Clumsy; vehicle tends to wander on the highway, especially on pre-2007s. **Routine handling:** The ride is harsh and bouncy on all but the smoothest roads, and there's considerable body roll when cornering. Handling is mediocre on the highway but outstanding off-road. P225/75R tires cause the vehicle to wander. Doesn't take curves very well, owing to the short wheelbase and high centre of gravity. Good ground clearance and stiff suspension for off-roading. **Braking:** Unacceptably long braking distance (100–0 km/h: 47 m), with or without ABS.

 SAFETY SUMMARY: Insurance industry figures show a much higher-than-average number of accident injury claims, aggravated by a high incidence of sudden rollovers when drivers exceed the Jeep's very low tolerance for sporty driving. In fact, Jeeps, along with the Ford Bronco and Suzuki Samurai, have always been among the SUVs most frequently cited in rollover deaths. There are lots of recall campaigns to check out. There have also been reports of front seat belts that fail to retract and that interfere with the door latch, as well as seat belts that failed to restrain occupants in a collision. **Airbags:** Front airbags are standard; side airbags are available on later models. Many complaints that the airbags fail to deploy or are late deploying, or that the Airbag warning light stays on. **ABS:** Standard with the electronic stability control package; four-wheel disc brakes. Upgraded a few years ago, but brakes continue to be problematic. **Head restraints F/R:** 1999–2006: ★; 2007: ★★. **Visibility F/R:** ★★★★★/★. **Pet transport:** ★.

SAFETY COMPLAINTS: All years: Owners report chronic engine stalling when accelerating or decelerating, clutch master and slave cylinder leaks, premature brake wear, and brake failure. There have been several incidents of sudden brake loss where the pedal went all the way to the floor with no braking effect (corrected by replacing the master cylinder). Other brake complaints include a seal leak in the power-brake booster that might cause a brake failure; the brake drum not keeping its shape; the vehicle pulling to left when braking; the rear brakes suddenly locking up while driving in the rain and approaching a stop sign; and the vehicle going into open throttle position when the brakes are applied. There have also been many instances where drivers mistook the accelerator for the brake because the pedals are so close together. There have been many complaints of airbag failures, fuel-tank leaks, fuel-pump failures, and malfunctioning fuel gauges. **1999**—Exhaust manifold leaks. • Vehicle rolls back when in gear. **1999–2005**—Manual and automatic transmission failures. **2000**—Under-hood fires. • Right rear wheel separates from vehicle. • Vehicle goes into Reverse after being shifted into Drive. **2001**—Many engine-related steering-column fires. • Sudden, unintended acceleration in Reverse gear. • Rear brakes often fail to engage. • Sudden steering lock-up. • Camshaft sensor binding and breaking, causing vehicle to stall. • Broken rear axle seal. • Manual tranny pops out of Third gear and grinds as the clutch is let out. • Premature wearout of the rear brake pads. • Faulty catalytic converter. **2002**—Manual transmission shifts poorly between Fourth and Fifth gear. • Defective dash cluster. • Intermittent stalling and rough running. • Vehicle accelerates when foot is taken off the gas pedal. **2003**—Driveshaft falls out while driving. • Vehicle slips into Neutral from Drive. • Sudden axle and steering failure. • Seat belts unlatch too easily. • Seat is angled to the left. **2004**—Sudden stalling caused by defective crankshaft position sensor. • Engine and transmission oil leak. • Front left axle seal leak. • Gas-line leaks cause fumes to enter the cabin. • Seized front brakes. • Front brakes vibrate violently when applied. • Cracked driver-seat frame. • Seat belt doesn't retract. • Cloth top comes off while vehicle is underway (in one incident, driver had to hold it down with his hand). • Window pops open. **2005**—Sudden acceleration:

> I was sitting at a stop sign with my foot resting on the brake. I was not pressing the pedal actively, but the brakes were applied. The Jeep surged forward. My foot was nowhere near the gas pedal, yet the Jeep revved and moved about a foot. I pressed hard on the brake and it stopped, but took a second to rev back down.

www.rubiconownersforum.com

• Defective steering stabilizer responsible for steering shudder. • Partial loss of control when passing over bumps or railroad tracks. • Carpet causes accelerator pedal to stick. • Carbon monoxide leakage into cabin. • Seat belt gets caught in door. **2006**—A noxious odour permeates the interior. • Faulty 6-speed manual transmission:

The clutch rod comes out of the floor board and attaches to the clutch pedal with a clip/attachment that bolts into the clutch pedal. The problem here is, as part of their new design, the clip or attachment piece can break very easily and disable your Jeep.

• Excessive front shimmy. • Faulty instrument cluster. • Windshield cracks. **2007**—ABS brakes may suddenly lock up while underway. • Faulty T-tops:

2007 Jeep Wrangler Sahara may have a faulty T-top clasp. Owner states T-top flew off into on-coming traffic when driving.

2008—Chronic stalling, similar to the complaints that led to the previous model year's recall. • Vehicle loses its directional stability after passing over the smallest bumps. • Faulty 6-speed manual transmission may pop out of gear:

It makes noise, and vibrates horribly going over rough roads! The shifter slams back and forth making contact with the metal undercarriage. The dealer says they know of this problem but Chrysler currently has no fix and that it can even pop out of gear over rough terrain—terrible design!

Secret Warranties/Internal Bulletins/Service Tips

1999—Measures to reduce disc brake rotor pulsation, transfer-case shifter and universal-joint noise, and tailgate rattles or knocks; diagnostic tips for plugging water leaks. **1999–2000**—Interior roof sagging and water accumulation can be corrected through the installation of foam blocks. **1999–2001**—Tips for correcting windshield/cowl water leaks. **1999–2002**—Water leaks under the passenger-side carpet. **1999–2004**—A rough idle may require the installation of a fuel-injector insulator sleeve. **1999–2005**—Tips on repairing a leak in the engine rear main oil seal. **1999–2006**—Tips on plugging door leaks. • AC may produce a musty odour. **2001–05**—If the vehicle tends to drift, install upgraded ball joints and get Jeep to pay half the cost up to five years of use (see next page). **2003**—Delayed or temporary loss of transmission engagement and harsh 4–3 downshift (NHTSA TSB #2100503, June 20, 2003). • Manual transmission may have defective Third gear weld. • 4.0L engine crankshaft burr. • Faulty fuel-injector wiring connections. **2003–04**—Automatic transmission leaks (see next page). **2003–06**—Drivebelt noise countermeasures. **2005**—Manual 6-speed won't stay in gear. **2006–07**—Excessive vehicle shimmy after passing over small bumps in the road. • Manual transmission clutch squealing. • Windshield crack diagnosis (whether it's due to a foreign object or is factory-related). **2007**—Electronic stability control may suddenly activate when taking a curve. • Automatic transmission shift shudder, or clutch squealing. • Wind noise from the A-pillar area. • Hardtop water leaks. • Tips on silencing an oil-canning, thumping, or popping sound emanating from the front passenger area. • Soft top slaps against speaker bar. • Radio cuts out intermittently. • Inoperative door handles (Unlimited). • Door weatherseal won't stay in place. • Exterior light lens fogging.

LEAD OR DRIFT TO EITHER SIDE OF ROAD

BULLETIN NO.: 02-006-04   DATE: AUGUST 20, 2004

SPECIAL OFFSET BALL JOINT ALLOWS ADJUSTMENT TO CASTER AND CAMBER ANGLES

This bulletin involves the replacement of one or both front upper ball joints when front end alignment specifications can not be obtained using normal alignment practices.

2001–05 Wrangler

2001–04 Grand Cherokee

2001 Cherokee

SYMPTOM/CONDITION: The customer may experience a slight lead or drift to either side of the road. This condition may occur when there is no driver input to the steering system, or when the driver must maintain a constant input to the steering system in order to maintain a straight ahead direction of the vehicle.

AUTOMATIC TRANSMISSION FLUID LEAK

BULLETIN NO.: 21-003-04   DATE: MARCH 9, 2004

FLUID SEEPAGE FROM AREA OF REAR OUTPUT SHAFT RETAINER

OVERVIEW: This bulletin involves the replacement of the NV-241 transfer case rear output shaft retainer/extension housing and related seals.

2003–04 (TJ) Wrangler

JEEP TJ WRANGLER PROFILE

	1999	2000	2001	2002	2003	2004	2005	2006	2007
Cost Price ($) (firm)									
TJ, SE (20%)	19,205	19,445	20,355	21,000	21,340	21,995	22,910	23,230	19,995
Sahara (22%)	25,305	26,020	29,285	28,120	28,715	29,950	—	—	26,450
TJ Rubicon (25%)	—	—	—	—	29,425	30,420	31,790	32,210	28,150
Unl. Rubicon (25%)	—	—	—	—	—	—	33,250	33,160	29,895
Used Values ($)									
TJ, SE ▲	4,500	5,500	6,500	8,000	9,500	11,500	13,500	15,000	15,500
TJ, SE ▼	4,000	5,000	6,000	7,000	8,500	10,500	12,500	13,500	14,000
Sahara ▲	6,000	7,000	8,000	9,500	12,500	14,500	—	—	20,500
Sahara ▼	5,500	6,500	7,500	8,500	11,500	13,000	—	—	19,000
TJ Rubicon ▲	—	—	—	—	13,000	15,500	16,500	18,500	21,500
TJ Rubicon ▼	—	—	—	—	12,000	14,500	15,500	17,500	20,000
Unl. Rubicon ▲	—	—	—	—	—	—	17,000	19,000	22,000
Unl. Rubicon ▼	—	—	—	—	—	—	16,000	18,160	20,500

Reliability	3	3	3	4	4	4	4	4	4
Crash Safety (F)	4	4	4	4	4	4	4	4	5
IIHS Side	2	2	2	2	2	2	2	2	—
Offset	3	3	3	3	3	3	3	3	—
Rollover	—	—	3	3	3	—	4	4	4

Note: The 2008 models earned crashworthiness scores similar to the 2007 versions.

Ford/Mazda

ESCAPE/TRIBUTE, ESCAPE HYBRID ★★★★

Ford's Escape SUV.

RATING: *Escape/Tribute:* Above Average (2005–08); Average (2002–04); Below Average (2001). One of the most improved vehicles in Ford's lineup, but its highway performance cannot match its rivals'. *Escape Hybrid:* Above Average (2005–08). Improvements on 2005 model year vehicles correct the quality, power, and performance deficiencies of previous models. Up to the 2003 model year, the Escape/Tribute promised a lot but delivered a low-quality SUV that would frequently stall or suddenly accelerate at any time. Interestingly, Mazda dealers generate fewer servicing complaints. **Strong points:** *2005 and later models:* A smoother driveline; a more powerful base engine; a quieter, more comfortable cabin; soothing blue dash lights; less V6 engine noise and vibration; more standard equipment; and lots of standard safety features. *Pre-2005 models:* Quick 6-cylinder acceleration; good manoeuvrability; plenty of passenger space and cargo room; well laid-out and easy-to-read instruments and controls; good visibility; easy-to-fold rear seatbacks; and rear liftgate's flip-up glass gives quick access to cargo. **Weak points:** No passenger assist handles. Head restraints have to be removed to fold the seats, and there is no place to store the restraints. Front seats on 2006 and earlier models may cause some lower back pain. Trailer towing package doesn't include a transmission cooler or a trailer brake wiring harness. AdvanceTrac vehicle stability control won't be available on the Escape Hybrid until 2009. *2005 and later models:* Mediocre road performance highlighted by a sluggish, old-tech 4-speed automatic gearbox; poor braking due to the 2008's return to rear drum brakes; and disappointing fuel economy. Plastic cover on gauges reflects too much sunlight in the bottom left and right corners. Early 2008 version only rated "Acceptable" for frontal impact protection and rollover resistance by IIHS, but later version regains a better four-star rating. 2005–07 models still merit only a three-star rollover rating. *Pre-2005 models:* Poorly equipped and underpowered, with unimpressive snow traction; historically poor-quality Ford-designed engines and transmissions. There's a sluggish 4-cylinder and a V6 that needs more high-end grunt for long upgrades; no low-speed transfer case; excessive engine and road noise; and a significant number of safety- and performance-related complaints clustered around the 2001 first-year lineup. Bumps can be jolting, and entry and exit are compromised by a high step-in. **New for 2008:** A new body and interior, an electrically assisted power-steering system, revised suspension spring rates, and a stiffer anti-sway bar.

MODEL HISTORY: Launched as 2001 models, both the Escape and Tribute combine a carlike ride and handling—thanks to an independent rear suspension and front MacPherson struts—with the ability to drive in the snow and carry up to five passengers and their luggage. Neither vehicle is an upsized car or a downsized truck—they're four-doors that sip fuel, look like sport-utilities, and drive like sedans. **2005**—Foremost, you get a quieter engine and 26 more horses with the 2.3L Duratec 4-banger, which raises towing capability from 454 kg (1,000 lb.) to 680 kg (1,500 lb.). The V6 engine has one less horse (200 hp), but uses upgraded engine mounts and computers to smooth out the idle and improve throttle response. Safety is also enhanced with dual-stage airbags, head restraints and three-point safety belts for all seats, side curtain airbags, "smart" seat sensors that can prevent airbag deployment if a child or small adult is seated, and larger diameter four-wheel disc and anti-lock brakes. The Escape and Tribute's front

> ## 2008 ESCAPE/TRIBUTE TECHNICAL DATA
>
> **POWERTRAIN (FRONT-DRIVE/4×4)**
> Engines: 2.3L 4-cyl. (140 hp) • Hybrid (155 hp) • 3.0L V6 (200 hp);
> Transmissions: 5-speed man. • 4-speed auto. • CVT Hybrid
> **DIMENSION/CAPACITY**
> Passengers: 2/3; Wheelbase: 103.0 in.; H: 70.0/L: 175.0/W: 72.0 in.; Headroom F/R: 4.5/5.0 in.; Legroom F/R: 40.5/28.0 in.; Cargo volume: 29.3 cu. ft.; Fuel tank: 62L/regular; Tow limit: 3,500 lb.; Load capacity: 900 lb.; GVWR: 4,120–4,520 lb.; Turning circle: 40.0 ft.; Ground clearance: 8.0 in.; Weight: 3,580 lb.

structure has been reinforced to better protect occupants in offset frontal crashes. Other enhancements include an improved 4×4 system that is fully automatic (it no longer needs to be switched on); front shocks that are larger in diameter; a new stabilizer system; a floor-mounted shifter; new headlights, foglights, grille, and front and rear ends; different gauges; upgraded seat cushions; more storage space; additional sound-absorbing materials (though it still lets in excessive wind noise); and alloy wheels. *Escape Hybrid:* This gasoline-electric hybrid is equipped with a 2.3L 4-cylinder engine, a 65-kilowatt electric motor, and a 28-kilowatt generator. It has off-road and towing capability, plus acceleration comparable to the 200-hp Escape V6 engine.

COST ANALYSIS: The cheapest, best used buy? The 2005 model 4×2 version for the upgraded quality control, additional equipment, and about $11,000 off the original $23,000 sales price. 2008–09 prices vary between $23,999 and $28,899. Stateside, you will pay $19,140 to $24,415. A Hybrid will cost $31,499 (U.S.: $26,640) for the base model and an additional $2,000 for the 4×4 variant. There is an almost 20 percent dealer profit cushion figured into the base prices; most hybrid models are selling close to list. **Best alternatives:** Roughly the size of a Ford Focus sedan, the base Escape XLS 4×2 targets the low-priced, compact sport-utility market presently dominated by the Honda CR-V, Jeep Wrangler, Mitsubishi Outlander, Nissan Xterra, Pontiac Vibe, and Toyota RAV4 and Matrix. **Rebates:** These compact SUVs are hot, so expect only modest discounting and low financing rates. **Delivery/PDI:** $1,250. **Warranty:** Bumper-to-bumper 3 years/60,000 km; powertrain 5 years/100,000 km; rust perforation 5 years/unlimited km. *Hybrid:* Essentially the same, except for an 8 year/160,000 km electrical components warranty. **Supplementary warranty:** Yes, at least for the powertrain. **Options:** AWD, if you really need it; 1,588 kg (3,500 lb.) towing package; sunroof reduces headroom considerably. Convenient snap-in pet barrier and mountain-bike hauler from Ford Outfitters. **Depreciation:** Quite slow. **Insurance cost:** Average for a small SUV. **Parts supply/cost:** Few complaints so far. Generic powertrain parts aren't hard to find, though electronics can be expensive and hard to troubleshoot. Long delays for parts needed for recall campaigns. **Annual maintenance cost:** Average to less than average. Ford's quality control is baby-stepping to higher levels. **Highway/city fuel economy:** *2.3L 4-cyl.:* 7.3/9.7 L/100 km; *2.3L Hybrid:* 7.0/6.6 L/100 km (remember, hybrids are more economical in the city); *3.0L V6:* 9.9/13.3 L/100 km. Notwithstanding the above fuel economy estimates, owners often report their Escape and Tribute burn much more fuel than estimated.

 QUALITY/RELIABILITY: Ford and Mazda have a poor record for quality control during the first few years their vehicles are on the market (think Focus and MPV). **Owner complaints:** Vehicle was out of service 36 days while dealer looked for cause of raw fuel smell entering cabin; chronic stalling and hard starts; engine oil leaks (engine crankshaft out of spec); transmission refuses to go into gear; automatic transmission won't upshift at 85 km/h; loses Reverse gear; automatic transmission gearshift handle gets stuck halfway down when changing gears because of a design flaw; transmission fluid leaks; excessive front brake dust turns wheels black; frequent short circuits; rear defogger won't shut off; Alternator light comes on intermittently; cruise control turns itself off; faulty side windows; ice forming on front wheels causes excessive vibrations; lots of squeaks, rattles, and wind noise; poor fit and finish; the internal support beam on the rear passenger door contracts and pulls the door panel inward, causing a dimpling effect in six separate areas; tires make a humming noise; engine hesitates when AC is engaged; AC makes a loud, cyclic sound; mildew odour from AC and vents; can't remove key from ignition. **Warranty performance:** Average. Ford's large number of secret warranty programs are a giant step backward from its Owner Notification Programs (ONPs), which notified all owners.

 ROAD PERFORMANCE: Acceleration/torque: Good performance with the 2005–08 models, but the 4-cylinder engines are overwhelmed by the Escape's heft. The V6 performs well, though it's a bit rough and could use some more power for passing and merging. **Transmission:** Smooth and quiet shifting. The automatic transmission lever blocks access to controls for the rear defogger, parking lights, and radio; transmission levers are often knocked inadvertently into Neutral when adjusting the radio. Dial-up 4×4 engagement is a pain on 2004 and earlier versions. **Steering:** Above average. **Routine handling:** Surprisingly good for an SUV. Easy to manoeuvre in tight places, and corners very well at high speeds, with only a bit of body lean. Taut four-wheel independent suspension may be too firm for some, but it enhances handling considerably. **Braking:** Brakes perform very well, with little fading after successive stops; there's some nosedive, however.

 SAFETY SUMMARY: Five three-point seat belts and five height-adjustable head restraints. **Airbags:** Front and side. Owners have reported that airbags may go off without warning, may fail to deploy in a collision, or are disabled when an adult sits in the front passenger seat. **ABS:** Optional/standard; disc/drum. **Electronic stability control:** Standard. **Safety belt pretensioners:** Front. **Head restraints F/R:** 2001: ★; 2002–04: ★★★★★/★★★. **Visibility F/R:** ★★★★★. **Pet transport:** ★★. The cargo space is tall but too narrow for side-by-side crates for animals of any significant size, and the rear seats are awkward to configure. True, the seats do fold flat, but only after you pull out the bottom cushions and remove the headrests.

SAFETY COMPLAINTS: 2001–04—Chronic stalling, sudden unintended acceleration (gas pedal sticking), airbag and brake malfunctions, windshield wiper failure, headliner sagging, and frequent transmission replacements are major problems. *Escape, Tribute:* **2001**—Fuel vapours enter passenger compartment via ventilation ducts (to fix, tighten bolts on the left-side intake manifold). • Fuel leakage around fuel injectors. • Fuel line clip fails, causing loss of power, and fuel sprays onto hot engine. • Vehicle rolls over while driving 25–40 km/h. • CV joints and front axle fall off vehicle. • Clutch cable often comes off when driving. • Automatic transmission pops out of Drive into Neutral while underway. • Sudden, unintended acceleration when shifting into Reverse or First gear. • When going downhill, vehicle often suddenly loses all electrical power and shuts down on the highway with loss of steering and brake assist (faulty EGR valve suspected as the cause of the problem). • Chronic electrical problems. • Left rear wheel suddenly locks up, pulling vehicle into traffic. • Vehicle pulls randomly to the right or left when steering wheel is let go. • Steering is too tight. • Sometimes steering tugs a bit to one side and then freezes, brakes won't work, and Check Engine light comes on (engine still running). • Part of power-steering system falls out of car when put into Park. • Rear seats don't lock properly. • Car seatback collapses in collision. • Left rear seat belt frequently jams. **2002**—Stuck accelerator pedal; engine surging. • Vehicle pulls to the left when cruising on the highway. • Gas tank filler pipe allows fuel to spill out when refuelling. **2002–04**—Cruise control won't deactivate. • Rear window explodes. • Nauseating mildew smell from AC. **2003**— Fire ignites due to faulty fuel injectors. • Throttle cable jams. • Poor starting. • Rainwater leaks at the driver window pillar area, shorting out the electrical system. **2004**—Headlights go on and off. **2005**—More than 115 complaints recorded. • Sudden engine surge when backing up, when turning, and while parking. • Accelerator sticks when gas pedal is depressed; throttle body replaced five times. • Faulty transmission pump shaft causes vehicle to jump out of gear and not shift. • Excessive steering play. • Constant pulling to the left when underway. • Vehicle nosedives when stopping, due to poorly calibrated suspension. • Excessive vibration. • Passenger door latch failure causes door to fly open. • Airbag disables when normal-weight passenger occupies the front seat. • Sunroof explodes. • Foglights afflicted with stress cracks. **2006**—Driver's window suddenly shatters. • Brakes fail. • Radio switches on by itself, draining the battery. **2006–07**— Liftgate fails:

> I was knocked out and pinned by the rear hatch door of our 2006 Ford Escape. I opened the rear hatch and leaned in to remove some items from rear of the Ford Escape and the hatch came slamming down, hitting me in the back of the head and rendering me unconscious (I am not sure as to how long). I came to face-first inside the Ford Escape with the door pinning me down and my feet hanging out the rear.

2007—Fire ignites in the trunk area. • In one incident, driver-side airbag and seat belt failed in a head-on collision. • Passenger-side airbag is disabled even though a small adult occupies the seat. • All four wheels suddenly lock up while the vehicle is underway. • Gas smell permeates the interior. • Excessive Continental tire vibration. *Hybrid:* **2005**—Sudden shutdown while underway, allegedly due to a defective water pump. • Shifter gets stuck in Park. **2005–06**—Loss of power:

> As fleet manager, I have experienced engine failure on all three 2006 Ford Escape Hybrid vehicles. During each failure, the main engine shuts down and the vehicle goes to straight electrical power, which could cause a wreck in situations where a rapid drop in speed could cause an accident. The failure has happened on all three hybrids at about 15,000 miles [24,000 km] and now again at 36,000 miles [58,000 km]. The dealership replaces the water pump that supplies coolant to the electric motor after each failure. I feel that this situation should be reported due to the fact that I researched *Edmunds.com* and this problem is well documented in their CarSpace automotive [forums]. Ford needs to re-engineer this system.

2005–07—Loss of brakes and steering. **2006**—Fuel tank slow to fill; frequent pump shut-offs.

Secret Warranties/Internal Bulletins/Service Tips

All years: Engine hydromount insulator and rear drive shaft replacement. • No forward transmission engagement (yes, the forward clutch piston, the cause of so many Windstar and Taurus/Sable failures, once again rears its ugly head). • Rear axle pinion seal leak. • Driveline grinding and clicking. • Possible leak in the transmission converter housing near the cooler line. • Intermittent loss of First and Second gears. • Manual transmission gear shifter buzz or rattle in Third or Fourth gear is being investigated by Ford technicians. • Possible causes for a lit malfunction indicator light (MIL). • EGR valve failures. • Fuel-pump whine heard through speakers (a Ford problem since 1990). • Vehicles with 3.0L engines may show a false "low coolant" condition. • ABS light may stay lit. • AC temperature-control knob may be hard to turn or adjust. **2001–02**—Harsh, delayed upshifts • Defective door latches. • Power-steering leaks. **2001–03**—Steering squeaking noise. • 3.0L engine stalling remedy:

ENGINE CONTROLS/EMISSIONS—IDLE DIP/INTERMITTENT STALL

BULLETIN NO.: 02-23-1   DATE: NOVEMBER 25, 2002

2001–03 ESCAPE

ISSUE: Some vehicles equipped with the 3.0L Duratec engine may exhibit an intermittent engine quit and restart condition. This is usually a one-time event during closed throttle deceleration with no Diagnostic Trouble Codes (DTCs) and no Malfunction Indicator Lamp (MIL). Due to the intermittent nature of the condition and the multiple potential causes of the condition, the complete bulletin checklist, and all appropriate part replacements should be performed regardless of whether the condition can be duplicated by the technician. Otherwise, customers may experience the intermittent condition and be forced to return to the dealership. If the vehicle is no longer eligible for warranty coverage, discuss this service with the customer before performing.

2001–04—Engine misfire troubleshooting tips. • Correction for a sagging rear headliner. **2001–05**—Diagnostic and repair tips for an unstable idle, transmission shuddering, and steering pull and drifting. • Poor shifting in cold weather; install a Cooler Bypass Kit. • Slow-to-retract seat belts. • Instrument panel vents hard to adjust. **2001–06**—3.0L engine ticking noise. • Driveline whine. • **2001–07**—Heater core leakage. **2002**—Coolant, oil leakage from engine cylinder head area. • Defective Duratec engines. • Brake squealing. • Wheels make a clicking sound. **2003**—Automatic transmission shudder and whine. • Powertrain throttle body service replacement. • Front wheel bearing noise. • Rear shock leak and noise. **2003–04**—False activation of Parking Assist ("Stop, there's something behind you! Just kidding."). You know what's most worrisome? Ford says this device may be operating as it should. **2003–06**—Inoperative AC; compressor leakage. **2003–08**—Remedy for excessive wheel/tire vibration. **2005**—Engine overheating. • Troubleshooting engine hesitation, miss. • An engine oil leak from the oil dipstick or front/rear crankshaft seals can be fixed by installing a Heated PCV Kit. • Rear brake noise. **2005–06**—Hard starts may require a recalibrated PCM; the half-hour labour charge is covered by the emissions warranty, says TSB #05-26-1. • Excessive steering vibration likely caused by faulty Continental tires, which will be replaced under an extended warranty. **2005–08**—Engine stalling when vehicle is put in gear, likely caused by excessive torque converter wear.

ESCAPE/TRIBUTE, ESCAPE HYBRID PROFILE

	2001	2002	2003	2004	2005	2006	2007
Cost Price ($) (negotiable)							
XLS 4×2 (18%)	22,895	21,510	21,595	21,895	22,795	23,000	23,000
XLS 4×4 (18%)	24,795	24,190	30,300	27,825	28,125	28,399	28,399
Tribute 4×2 (17%)	22,150	22,415	22,790	22,790	24,495	24,595	23,295
Tribute 4×4 (17%)	24,800	25,065	25,575	25,445	27,295	27,395	26,990
Hybrid 4×2 (20%)	—	—	—	—	33,195	33,599	33,600
Hybrid 4×4 (20%)	—	—	—	—	35,925	36,399	36,399
Used Values ($)							
XLS 4×2 ▲	6,000	7,000	8,500	10,000	12,000	14,000	16,500
XLS 4×2 ▼	5,500	6,000	7,500	9,000	10,500	12,500	15,000
XLS 4×4 ▲	7,500	9,000	10,500	12,500	14,500	17,000	19,000
XLS 4×4 ▼	6,500	8,000	9,500	11,000	13,000	15,500	18,000
Tribute 4×2 ▲	7,000	8,500	10,000	11,500	15,000	16,500	16,000
Tribute 4×2 ▼	6,500	7,500	9,000	10,500	13,500	15,000	15,000
Tribute 4×4 ▲	7,500	9,500	10,500	13,000	15,000	18,000	18,500
Tribute 4×4 ▼	6,500	8,500	9,500	11,500	13,500	17,000	17,500
Hybrid 4×2 ▲	—	—	—	—	18,000	22,000	25,500
Hybrid 4×2 ▼	—	—	—	—	16,500	20,500	24,000
Hybrid 4×4 ▲	—	—	—	—	20,000	24,500	28,000
Hybrid 4×4 ▼	—	—	—	—	19,000	23,000	26,500
Reliability	2	2	2	2	2	3	4
Crash Safety (F)	5	5	5	5	4	4	4
Side	5	5	5	5	5	5	5
Offset	2	2	2	2	3	3	3
Rollover	3	3	3	—	3	3	3

Note: The 2008 first-series models earned only a three-star rating for frontal impact driver protection. Subsequent models returned to a four-star rating.

General Motors

EQUINOX, TORRENT ★

RATING: Not Recommended (2005–08). The Equinox is an international parts bin: It's designed in the United States, engineered and built in Canada, powered by a Chinese engine, and loaded with parts from Japan, Mexico, and the Philippines. Usually, vehicles with so many outsourced parts are found on the bottom rung of the quality/reliability ladder, and Equinox seems to prove the rule. *Torrent:* Introduced as a 2006 model, Pontiac's Torrent is only slightly better built than its Equinox brother. Equipped with a bit firmer suspension, fresh styling, and a slightly higher price ($27,575 before rebates and discounting), Torrent will be dropped by Pontiac within the next two years. **Strong points:** Well-equipped and reasonably priced, this is one of the largest, most powerful compact SUVs available. 2007 models were the first to adopt the highly recommended electronic stability control. Other pluses are its versatile drivetrain, carlike unibody frame, and fully independent suspension that smoothes out the ride. A unique rear seat slides forwards and backwards to accommodate long-legged passengers, and an adjustable shelf behind the rear seats can be used as a picnic table. Received a five-star rating for front and side occupant crash protection and a four-star rating for rollover prevention. **Weak points:** Uses an unproven Chinese-bred V6 instead of the more reliable and peppy Honda 3.5L V6 found in the 2004 Saturn Vue. Mediocre handling; suspension bottoms out noisily when passing over bumps; no low-range gearing for off-roading; rear drum brakes instead of better-performing discs; wide turning circle makes for tough handling in tight areas; power-window controls are found on the centre console instead of on the doors; seats could use more side support and may be too firm for some; no third-row seat available; rear hatch doesn't have separately opening glass; rear suspension housings intrude into rear cargo space; and the Equinox uses many of the Saturn Vue's quality-challenged mechanical components, making for uncertain long-term reliability. Owners also report that the interiors of early models sometimes literally stink—giving off an odour that's part dead animal and part propane. **New for 2008:** Carried over unchanged until the Equinox revamp, scheduled for 2010, when the Torrent will be dropped.

MODEL HISTORY: A replacement for GM's Suzuki-*cum*-Chevrolet Tracker, the five-passenger Equinox distinguishes itself from the rest of the SUV pack by offering standard V6 power, a 5-speed automatic transmission, and a comfortable ride. Although it uses many of the Vue's underpinnings (without the

---

2008 TECHNICAL DATA

POWERTRAIN (4×2/4×4)
Engine: 3.4L V6 (185 hp); Transmission: 5-speed auto. OD

DIMENSION/CAPACITY (4D)
Passengers: 2/3; Wheelbase: 113.0 in.; H: 69.0/L: 189.0/W: 71.0 in.; Headroom F/R: 4.0/5.0 in.; Legroom F/R: 41.0/32.0 in.; Cargo volume: 36.5 cu. ft.; Fuel tank: 75L/regular; Tow limit: 3,500 lb.; Load capacity: 1,115 lb.; GVWR: 5,070 lb.; Turning circle: 44.0 ft.; Ground clearance: 6.5 in.; Weight: 3,845 lb.

plastic body panels), it has a longer wheelbase and a wider body. Third-year 2007 models got revised suspension and steering systems, a restyled interior, and additional standard safety features like ABS and traction control. Optional side curtain airbags now come with sensors for rollover deployment. Equinox's instrument panel, radio, and climate controls were also redesigned.

COST ANALYSIS: The 2008 Equinox LS front-drive costs $28,870 in Canada and $23,355 (U.S.) in the States; Torrent is $27, 575 in Canada and $23,835 (U.S.) in the States. In Canada, a 2007 Equinox LS front-drive is now worth $14,500; the LT front-drive, $16,000; the LS AWD, $17,000; and the LT AWD, $19,000. The same 2005 models would cost you $9,000–$10,000, $9,500–$10,500, $11,000–$12,000, and $12,000–$12,500, respectively. Buyers would be wise to get a 2008–09 version for the improvements and to distance themselves as far as possible from the multitude of defects that afflict the 2005 through 2007 models. **Best alternatives:** Honda CR-V, Hyundai Santa Fe, Mazda Tribute, Nissan X-Trail, Subaru Forester, and Toyota RAV4. **Rebates:** $3,000–$5,000 on the 2008s, and about half as much on the 2009s in early 2009. Low-financing programs will be applicable to both model years. **Delivery/PDI:** $1,100. **Warranty:** Bumper-to-bumper 3 years/60,000 km; powertrain 5 years/100,000 km; rust perforation 5 years/unlimited km. **Supplementary warranty:** A bumper-to-bumper warranty is essential. **Options:** Nothing worth buying. **Depreciation:** Faster than average. **Insurance cost:** Average. **Parts supply/cost:** Body parts are often back-ordered; mechanical and electronic components are easily found. All parts will be a bit pricey until independent suppliers are out in force. **Annual maintenance cost:** Predicted to be higher than average, inasmuch as these vehicles are somewhat dealer-dependent. **Highway/city fuel economy:** 8.6/12.7 L/100 km.

QUALITY/RELIABILITY: Although these are identical vehicles, *Consumer Reports* gives the Equinox a "Below Average" mark for both reliability and owner satisfaction, while the Torrent gets a "Recommended" rating, with reliability scored as "Above Average" and owner satisfaction as "Below Average." Puzzling. **Likely failures:** Engines and engine head gaskets; DEX-COOL apparently corroding the engine and cooling system—one owner says the engine coolant smells like rotten meat:

> Bad odor coming from vents. DEX-COOL is corroding cooling system and engine. 17,000 miles [27,000 km] have had it in 3 times for entire coolant system flush...still is unbearable. Be aware, this is not an isolated case. After extended drive (greater than 30 minutes) results [are] light-headedness, headache, or watery burning eyes. It leaves a film of antifreeze vapor on the windshield, on the inside. GM does not consider this vehicle inoperable. Go figure. GM has done little to satisfy our needs, they pay for new hoses and flush—which obviously doesn't work. 900 dollars a pop, for the same result.

Other problem areas are as follows: automatic transmission; AC condenser; rear-drive clutch unit; electrical system; front struts; fit and finish (water leaks, noise, and loose moulding); early wearout of the front brake calipers and rotors; wheel cover clicking, ticking; instrument panel rattle, squeak; liftgate creaks on rough roads; and fuel economy is far worse than what is advertised.

SAFETY COMPLAINTS: 2005—Airbags fail to deploy in a collision. • Sudden stalling when accelerating. • Car shuts down when going down a steep incline. • Accelerator pedal sticks. • When turning into a parking space or backing up, vehicle suddenly accelerates:

> While backing out from the car port, vehicle accelerated in reverse. Vehicle went down an incline and was totalled. Consumer stated the dealer told him that transmission had an adaptive learning transmission.

• Engine fumes enter the cabin, causing headaches and dizziness:

> I had about 300 miles [480 km] on the car and it started smelling of a propane odor/dead animals. Took it to dealer and they flushed the coolant system but the odor returned. Then the car overheated due to the coolant system. They put a new thermostat and flushed once again. Still a bad odor, the car leaks water and it runs hot. I have had the car in the shop three times and they still cannot fix the odor.

• Transmission fails to shift into Fourth gear. • Brake failure. • Defective suspension struts. • The design of the coil-spring mount leaves a razor-sharp edge on the strut. • Erratic steering produces too-sharp steering corrections. • Repeated windshield cracks. • When driving with the rear windows down, car produces a flat-tire sound. • Faulty window regulators. • No assist handles. • Driver's head restraint tilts too far forward. • Cupholder blocks the emergency brake. • Standing water in the tire well. • Dome light fills with water after vehicle passes through a car wash. • Tailgate collapses if the left strut gives out. **2006**—Chronic stalling. • Loses power when driven in the rain. • Original-equipment jack may collapse. • Faulty electrical system may cause doors to lock by themselves, make the automatic transmission default to "limp" mode, and deactivate the engine control module. • Rear seat belts ratchet tighter than they should. • Instrument cluster gauges go out on their own. • Ignition switch grinding. • Water leaks through the side passenger door, causing extensive corrosion of the wires leading to the computer module. **2007**—Engine front main seal leaks. • Vehicle will not move forward in Drive. • Vehicle easily hydroplanes in rainy weather. • Passenger-side front airbag is disabled when a passenger occupies the seat. • Power-steering failures.

Secret Warranties/Internal Bulletins/Service Tips

All models/years: Clogged engine fuel injectors. • Front-end rattles and noise when passing over bumps. • Inoperative, grinding power-assisted driver's seat. **2005**—Automatic transmission hesitation, flare; harsh cold shifts. • No Reverse, Second, or Fourth gears. • Harsh 1–2 upshift. • Transmission growl, moan, and shudder at low speeds. • Steering groan, hiss, or grinding when turning. • Inadequate AC cooling. • Liftgate strut bracket deformation. • Parasitic battery drain. • Vehicle glass distortion. • Chrome wheel pitting and dust accumulation. •

Popping noise on bumps. • Front- and rear-end rattle. • Troubleshooting wind noise. • Loose, missing plastic wheel-nut covers. • Spoiler not properly fastened on rear hatch. • Door handle sticks out, won't latch. • Tips on eliminating interior odours. **2007**—Airbag light fails to illuminate when the front passenger seat is occupied.

General Motors/Suzuki

TRACKER/SIDEKICK, VITARA, GRAND VITARA, XL-7 ★★★

RATING: Average (1994–2008). Although *Consumer Reports* once designated the XL-7 a "Recommended" buy, *Lemon-Aid* believes this rating was way too high considering the vehicle's failings, particularly the absence of side-impact protection on pre-2006 models. Yes, Suzuki has a reputation for building affordable, durable, quality small cars, but only its most recent SUVs provide real 4×4 performance, important safety features, and an acceptable level of quality control. The players in this market segment are the Honda Pilot; Hyundai Tucson, Veracruz, and Santa Fe; Jeep Liberty; Kia Sorento; Lexus Highlander; Nissan Murano, Xterra, and X-Trail; and Toyota 4Runner. **Strong points:** *Vitara and Grand Vitara 2006 and later models:* A much different vehicle that's less trucklike on the road, thanks to the fully independent suspension and new unibody construction, which also gives rear-seat passengers more room—at the expense of cargo space. A competent, though unimpressive, 2.7L V6 and permanent four-wheel drive offer low-range gearing and a locking differential. Side/head-protection airbags and stability control are standard. On earlier model years, the Grand Vitara is the better performer, with its minimal body lean when cornering and good emergency handling and braking. Lots of front and rear passenger space, but having three passengers in the rear remains a tight squeeze. **Weak points:** *2005 and earlier Vitara and Grand Vitara models:* The 4-cylinder and V6 engines are weak, rough-running, and not very fuel-thrifty; part-time 4×4 isn't suitable for dry pavement; stiff riding; sluggish automatic transmission; frequent downshifting with the base Vitara; skimpy interior appointments; the heater is slow to warm the interior on sub-freezing days and employs a noisy fan; the AC struggles to keep the Vitara cool; the accelerator is placed too far left; seats feel cheap, are inadequately padded, and lack thigh support; seatbacks lack shoulder and lower back support; driver's seat may not adjust for height, making it hard for short drivers to get a clear view; spare tire further restricts rear

2008 GRAND VITARA TECHNICAL DATA

POWERTRAIN (REAR-DRIVE/4×4, AWD)
Engines: 2.7L V6 (185 hp) • 3.6L V6 (252 hp); Transmissions: 5-speed man. • 3-speed auto. • 5-speed auto.

DIMENSION/CAPACITY
Passengers: 2/3/2; Wheelbase: 104.0 in.; H: 67.0/L: 176.0/W: 71.0 in.; Headroom F/R: 5.0/3.5 in.; Legroom F/R: 41.5/28.0 in.; Cargo volume: 25.0 cu. ft.; Fuel tank: 66L/regular; Tow limit: 3,000 lb.; Load capacity: 905 lb.; GVWR: 4,630 lb.; Turning circle: 38.0 ft.; Ground clearance: 7.0 in.; Weight: 3,650 lb.

visibility; and lots of axle whine and road, wind, and engine noise invade the cabin. Below-average reliability. *XL-7:* The 2007–08 versions have been redesigned in a similar fashion to the 2006 Grand Vitara and the Chevrolet Equinox. The XL-7 still seats 7 passengers, uses a standard 3.6L V6, and rides and handles much better than the Equinox. Earlier models fall short in many areas: Four-wheel drive usable only on dry pavement; so-so fuel economy; a stiff and jerky ride; a wide turning circle; excessive body lean when cornering; little steering feedback; mushy braking that doesn't inspire confidence; lots of engine, road, and tire noise; cheap-looking interior materials; high fuel consumption; rapid depreciation; and inadequate occupant crash protection and poor quality, as highlighted in *Consumer Reports'* owner surveys and crash test results, as well as bulletins gathered by *Lemon-Aid*. The narrow cabin provides only average legroom, seat cushions don't provide enough leg support, and third-row headrests obstruct rearward visibility. **New for 2008:** *Grand Vitara:* Nothing significant. The 2009 model will be lightly restyled; the following year, a hybrid version comes on board. *XL-7:* Carried over unchanged; living on borrowed time.

MODEL HISTORY: Introduced as a GM/Suzuki co-venture in 1989, these fuel-frugal vehicles have been quite successful as entry-level 4×4s for city dwellers who want off-roading allure. They will provide some off-road thrills (if they're not pushed too hard), but they're more show than go.

The Tracker and Sidekick, available as two-door convertibles and four-door wagons, come with a standard 1.6L 4-cylinder powerplant. The 1997 Sport version, sold only by Suzuki, carries a 1.8L 4-cylinder with dual overhead camshafts, rated at 120 hp. The GM Tracker and Vitara are built in Ontario and use similar designs and components.

All of these cars have been quite primitive in construction and performance; however, their overall reliability is more than reasonable, considering their low retail prices.

Vitara

The Vitara is longer, wider, taller, and handles much better than the Sidekick it replaced. It's essentially an entry-level version of the Grand Vitara and carries a smaller 127-hp 2.0L 4-cylinder engine and less standard equipment. Nevertheless, it projects a more solid appearance, has a more refined interior, and exhibits less noise and vibration than its primitive predecessor. It was dropped for the 2005 model year.

Grand Vitara

The 2006 and 2007 models underwent a major redesign that enhances safety, performance, and interior comfort. However, reliability and quality control on the newest models has nosedived. The top-of-the-line 2005 and earlier Grand Vitara is wider, longer, and taller than its predecessor, the Sidekick Sport, plus it gives a more supple ride. It comes with an adequate, though not very powerful, 24-valve 165-hp 2.5L V6 powerplant, shared with GM's Tracker. Other standard features include a full-sized spare tire and four-wheel ABS on any Plus model. Peppy in the lower gears (good for off-roading), the engine quickly loses steam in the higher gear ranges (a drawback to highway cruising). It has competent road holding and handling, though the handling isn't as carlike as the Honda CR-V's or Toyota RAV4's.

Inside, there's plenty of headroom, armroom, and legroom, but the interior is somewhat narrow. The rear seats and seatbacks fold flat, adding to cargo capacity, and there are plenty of small trays, bins, and compartments to store things.

Tracker/Vitara/Grand Vitara: **1999–2000**—The four-door carried a standard 120-hp 2.0L 4-cylinder 16-valve engine, shift-on-the-fly 4×4, rack-and-pinion steering, and revised interior and exterior styling. **2002**—Standard air conditioning, AM/FM CD stereo, and child-seat tethers. The base 1.6L engine was dropped in favour of the more powerful 127-hp 2.0L version. The Tracker also got the Suzuki V6 it had been lusting for, since many buyers found the 4-banger inadequate. **2003**—An upgraded dash and centre console. **2004**—Tracker's last model year. *Grand Vitara:* **2000**—First year on the market. **2002**—V6 engine gets 10 more horses. **2003**—Given a new dash, aluminum wheels, smaller rear head restraints, and interior upgrades. **2006**—Totally redesigned with help from GM's Torrent/Equinox platform and parts bin.

XL-7

Through the 2006 model year, this mid-sized SUV is basically a larger Grand Vitara wagon, built on a truck-type platform, with a side-hinged rear cargo door and seating for five with a split folding second-row seat, or for seven with an available split folding third-row seat. A 185-hp V6 with a 5-speed automatic transmission is the only powertrain. XL-7 offers rear-wheel drive or four-wheel drive that shouldn't be left engaged on dry pavement, but has low-range gearing. ABS is standard.

Towing capacity is 1,360 kg (3,000 lb.). City driving is no problem, but the car lacks adequate power for worry-free highway passing and merging, especially when carrying more than two adults. You often have to run the car full out and endure considerable engine noise and tire drone.

The harsh, bouncy suspension is annoying, and cornering under speed results in excessive noseplow, tire scrub, and body lean. The car doesn't track well when encountering crosswinds, which easily blow it off course. Steering feedback is minimal, and braking is only adequate despite the ABS.

The narrow cabin gives barely adequate leg, hip, and shoulder room. Narrow rear seats are somewhat hard. Head restraints have been given a five-star top rating for occupant protection, although rear head restraints cut visibility considerably. Figuring out how to fold the second-row seat takes an engineering degree.

XL-7: **2002**—The V6 engine gained 13 horses, and a user-friendly rear child-seat anchor system was installed. The Standard model adopted five-passenger seating, losing its third-row seat. Other versions kept the seven-passenger seating. Standard and Plus 4×4 models came with ABS, and 4×4 versions used heated door mirrors. **2003**—Five-passenger seating was standard, with a third-row seat optional, including rear air conditioning. **2004**—A mild facelift, new model names, and a new 5-speed automatic transmission. **2005**—A tire-pressure monitor was added to the 2005 model. **2006**—Fewer models and added standard features. The fuel-efficient 5-speed manual was dropped. Neither front side airbags nor side curtain airbags are offered. **2007**—Redesigned and set on the Equinox/Torrent platform used on the Grand Vitara. The wimpy 185-hp V6 was replaced with a 250-hp variant.

COST ANALYSIS: The revamped 2006 Grand Vitara and 2007 XL-7 ($31,000) are the best buys for overall performance. A 2003 Tracker 4×4 convertible is one of the best micro-convertible buys around. **Best alternatives:** For serious off-roading, look to a 2004 or later Jeep Wrangler or Liberty. For pretend off-roading, consider the Honda CR-V, Hyundai Tucson or Santa Fe, Subaru Forester, and Toyota RAV4, or, if you really want to splurge, look at a Toyota Highlander. **Rebates:** $3,500–$4,000 on the 2008s and 2009s; low-interest financing plans worth about $3,000. **Delivery/PDI:** $995. **Warranty:** *Suzuki:* Bumper-to-bumper 3 years/80,000 km; rust perforation 5 years/unlimited km. *GM:* Bumper-to-bumper 3 years/60,000 km; rust perforation 6 years/160,000 km. **Supplementary warranty:** An extended warranty is a good idea for the redesigned 2006–08 models; previous versions can do without. **Options:** Stick with the manual tranny; an automatic will sap too much power and eat into fuel economy. **Depreciation:** Average; faster than average with 2005 and earlier models. **Insurance cost:** Average. **Annual maintenance cost:** Average repair costs; easily repaired at independent garages and Chevrolet or Suzuki dealerships. **Parts supply/cost:** Good supply. Parts are usually reasonably priced. **Highway/city fuel economy:** *2.0L:* 8.4/10.3 L/100 km; *V6:* 10.2/12.6 L/100 km. Fuel consumption (regular fuel) has been about 25 percent more than what government-inspired figures show.

QUALITY/RELIABILITY: Suzuki's models haven't been plagued by the large number of owner complaints and service bulletin admissions of poor quality that we've seen with some Nissans and Kias and with most of Detroit's offerings. Still, prudent buyers will opt for a second-series 2006 Grand Vitara or 2007 XL-7 to dodge any first-year quality glitches that may be present. Although this hasn't been a problem with Suzuki's previous revamped models, the Equinox platform and other components have had a large number of quality problems during the past few years, and these are likely to carry over to the Grand Vitara and XL-7. Conversely, quality control on 2005 and earlier models is about average. Defects haven't led to a lot of shop downtime or rendered these cars unreliable, and repairs are usually quite simple and relatively easy to perform. **Owner-reported problems:** Most owners' complaints target poor handling caused by underperforming brakes, steering, and suspension components. There are also a number of gripes related to excessive vibrations and road and engine noise. Other failure-prone components are the serpentine belt, electrical system, catalytic converter, and muffler/exhaust system. Some owners report early transmission failures. Poor body fit and finish allows water and wind to enter the cabin. **Warranty performance:** Average. Although warranty performance and dealer servicing are unimpressive, these vehicles aren't very dealer-dependent, so it doesn't matter a great deal.

 SAFETY SUMMARY: These lightweights are very vulnerable to side-wind buffeting. **ABS:** Optional 4W. Later models have standard rear ABS; disc/drum. **Head restraints F/R:** *Tracker 2d 1997:* ★; *1999:* ★★★; *2001:* ★★★★★/★★★; *2002–03:* ★★★; *Tracker 4d 2001:* ★★★★★/★★★; *2002–03:* ★★★★★; *Grand Vitara 1999–2002:* ★★★; *2003–05:* ★; *2006:* ★★; *XL-7 2003–04:* ★★★★★; *2005–06:* ★. **Visibility F/R:** ★★★/★★. **Pet transport:** ★★★.

SAFETY COMPLAINTS: All models/years: Sudden, unintended acceleration. • Airbags fail to deploy. • Brake failures. • Lots of road wander. • Premature tire wearout and poor tire and wheel design compromise handling. • Excessive road vibration. *Sidekick/Tracker:* **2000**—Rear side-window air vents allow exhaust fumes to enter cabin. • Steering linkage suddenly fails when turning. • Continuously low brake-fluid level causes failure of front and rear calipers. • Brake and accelerator pedals are too close together. • Loose plastic inner fender damaged by tire. • Inadequate peripheral visibility. • Headlights don't adequately light up the road. • Hard to stay in lane when driving with the top off. • Automatic light sensor is designed to turn on the lights when it gets dark; however, it seldom works properly. **2001**—Drive shaft failure. • In one incident, driver tapped brakes to disengage cruise control, brakes locked up, and vehicle went out of control. • Extended braking stopping distance. *Vitara, Grand Vitara:* **1999**—Excessive vibration at 100 km/h. • Electrical shorts (a common Suzuki failing). • Excessive brake fade. • Stalling and surging (stuck accelerator). • Defective motor mounts. **2000**—Vehicle pulls right when accelerating and vibrates excessively. **2001**—Blown oil line drips oil on hot exhaust and can cause a fire. • Vehicle is tippy when cornering. **2002**—Brakes grind when stopping. **2003**—Vehicle flipped over, and airbags didn't deploy. **2004**—Accelerator stuck after recall fix for sudden acceleration. • Vehicle suddenly lost power and hit a tree; airbags didn't deploy. *Grand Vitara:* **2002**—Brake and gas pedal are set too close together. • Fuel-filler door falls off. • Passenger seat belt frequently locks up and doesn't retract fully. **2003**—Rear seat belt shreds in half. **2005**—Don't leave vehicle while engine is idling: Doors often self-lock. **2006**—Driveshaft and axle failures. • Chronic rear brake problems. • Interior lights and electrical system function erratically. **2007**—Hard starting. *XL-7:* **2002**—Door armrest caught on fire due to a defective fuse nearby. • Shredded rear seat belt. • Many complaints of bad Bridgestone original-equipment tires. **2003**—Accelerator pedal sticks. • Automatic transmission slippage. **2004**—Premature failure of the passenger-side seat airbag sensor. **2005**—Windshield rake (slant) makes it almost impossible to have a clear view of the road.

Secret Warranties/Internal Bulletins/Service Tips

All models/years: 4×4 may not fully engage, or it may pop out of gear. • Get rid of an annoying engine ticking noise by purging the air from the valve lifters. *Tracker:* **1999–2003**—Troubleshooting automatic transmission slipping. • Engine ticking. • Serpentine belt frays or squeals. • Brake pulsation, vibration. *Tracker, Vitara:* **1999–2000**—On vehicles equipped with a 2.0L engine and manual transmission, the engine may not start or may idle poorly in cold temperatures until it warms up because of a faulty ECM/PCM program. Reprogram the PCM under the emissions warranty (TSB #TS06-01-03099).• Manual transmission gears that clash when shifting may require a new synchronizer spring kit. • If the transmission won't upshift after downshifting with cruise control engaged, chances are the cruise-control module is at fault. • An inoperative or malfunctioning (blows warm air) AC may simply require a new O-ring. **1999–2002**—Windows bind and tip forward. **1999–2003**—Oil level reads low. **2001**—Excessive driveline vibration. • Serpentine belt frays. • Instrument panel squeaks and rattles. • Heating, ventilation system may not work properly. • Key sticks in the ignition. **2002**—Air or AC leak out of dash vents when fan isn't on. **2003**—Oil seepage from left front of engine. *Grand Vitara, XL-7:* **1999–2002**—Engine rattling can be silenced by adjusting the timing-chain tensioner, says TSB #TS07 04213R. **1999–2003**—Engine oil leaks (see bulletin).

OIL LEAKS FROM LEFT FRONT OF ENGINE
BULLETIN NO.: TS 06 02244R2 WS

GRAND VITARA/XL-7

1999–2003 models

CONDITION: Engine oil leaking down left front of engine.

CORRECTION: If the condition appears to be only light (weepage/seepage) it may be due to dirt accumulating on engine protective coating applied during manufacturing. This condition can be corrected by cleaning the affected area.

If the condition is oil leaking down left front of engine, remove the timing cover and thoroughly clean the sealing surfaces of the cover block and cylinder head of any oil, old sealer, and dirt. Replace the front crankshaft seal and reseal; paying particular attention to the areas noted in this bulletin.

TRACKER/SIDEKICK, VITARA, GRAND VITARA, XL-7 PROFILE

	1999	2000	2001	2002	2003	2004	2005	2006	2007
Cost Price ($) (negotiable)									
Tracker 4×4	19,400	19,710	21,395	21,395	21,500	25,605	—	—	—
Vitara	20,795	18,695	18,695	18,695	20,295	21,995	—	—	—
Grand Vitara (19%)	23,495	23,995	24,495	23,995	23,995	24,995	25,595	24,495	25,495
Vitara XL-7 (17%)	—	—	28,995	26,495	26,995	27,495	29,495	29,495	30,995
Used Values ($)									
Tracker 4×4 ▲	3,000	3,500	4,000	4,500	6,000	8,000	—	—	—
Tracker 4×4 ▼	2,500	3,000	3,500	4,000	5,000	7,000	—	—	—
Vitara ▲	2,500	3,000	4,500	5,500	6,500	8,000	—	—	—
Vitara ▼	2,000	2,500	3,500	4,500	6,000	6,500	—	—	—

Grand Vitara ▲	3,500	4,000	5,000	5,500	8,000	9,000	11,500	13,500	16,000
Grand Vitara ▼	3,000	3,500	4,500	5,000	7,000	8,000	10,000	12,000	14,500
Vitara XL-7 ▲	—	—	5,500	7,000	8,500	10,000	13,000	17,000	20,000
Vitara XL-7 ▼	—	—	5,000	5,500	7,500	9,000	11,500	15,000	18.000

Reliability

Sidekick, Tracker	4	4	4	4	4	5	—	—	—
Vitara, Grand Vitara	4	4	4	4	4	5	5	—	—
Vitara XL-7	—	—	4	4	4	4	4	4	4

Crash Safety (F)

Sidekick, Tracker 2d	—	—	4	4	4	4	—	—	—
Vitara	—	—	4	4	4	4	—	—	—
Grand Vitara	—	—	4	4	4	4	4	4	4
Side (Vitara)	—	—	4	4	4	4	—	—	—
Grand Vitara	—	—	—	5	5	5	5	5	5
Tracker	—	—	4	4	4	4	—	—	—
Offset (all)	3	3	3	3	3	3	3	—	—
Vitara XL-7	—	—	5	5	5	5	5	5	—
Rollover (Tracker)	—	—	3	3	3	—	—	—	—
Vitara	—	—	3	3	3	—	—	—	—
Grand Vitara	—	—	3	3	3	—	—	4	4

Honda

CR-V ★★★★★

best buy

RATING: Recommended (2002–08); Above Average (1997–2001). **Strong points:** The small power boost and improved chassis added in 2002 give additional interior room (interior volume has grown by 8 percent) and provide improved functionality. Lots of standard features; impressive steering and handling, particularly around town; easy front entry and exit; top-quality fit and finish; comfortable seating with lots of passenger room; innovative use of storage space; easily storable flip-folding seats; plastic cargo floor panel *cum* picnic table; outstanding NHTSA front crashworthiness scores; fair fuel economy; and superior reliability. **Weak points:** Acceleration is somewhat compromised on vehicles equipped with an automatic transmission, though the 2005 4-beater rivals many V6 competitors; no low-range gearing for off-roading; a long history of severe steering pull to the right when accelerating ("torque steer"); jittery ride on less-than-perfect roadways; excessive engine and road noise; 2005 redesign reduces front legroom slightly; rear cargo door opens to the street, rather than the curb; not suitable for true off-roading; and 1999–2001 models may be tippy in a side impact, according to NHTSA crash results. "Marginal" IIHS offset crash rating on earlier models, and head restraints scored poorly. Unlike the Toyota RAV4, there's no third-row seat. Fuel economy is nowhere near Honda's or Transport Canada's figures. **New for 2008:** Fresh from a 2007 redesign, the 2008 and 2009 models return unchanged. A 4-cylinder diesel engine will be added for the 2010 model year.

2008 CR-V TECHNICAL DATA

POWERTRAIN (FRONT-DRIVE/4×4)
Engine: 2.4L 4-cyl. (166 hp);
Transmission: 5-speed auto.
DIMENSION/CAPACITY
Passengers: 2/3; Wheelbase: 103.1 in.;
H: 66.1/L: 177.9/W: 71.6 in.; Headroom
F/R: 4.0/4.0 in.; Legroom F/R: 41.0/29.5
in.; Cargo volume: 25.5 cu. ft.; Fuel
tank: 58L/regular; Tow limit: 1,500 lb.;
Load capacity: 850 lb.; GVWR: 4,165 lb.;
Turning circle: 37.0 ft.; Ground clearance:
6.5 in.; Weight: 3,505 lb.

MODEL HISTORY: The 2002–05 versions don't look that different from their predecessors, though they are a bit longer, wider, and higher. The interior, however, underwent a major change, with more space for both passengers and cargo, and more user-friendly features and controls.

The CR-V's Civic-based platform incorporates a four-wheel independent suspension that shortens the nose and frees up more rear cargo room. Steering components have also been modified. The base 160-hp 2.4L I-VTEC 4-cylinder engine is offered with either a 5-speed manual or a 4-speed automatic transmission (through the 2004 models).

The CR-V is offered in three trim levels, all offering full-time 4×4. Combining sport-utility styling with minivan versatility, this SUV is essentially a restyled Civic with 4×4 capability added. Since its '97 launch, the car changed little until the revamped 2002 came out. **1999**—Picked up 20 more horses and an Overdrive On-Off switch. **2001**—Standard-issue ABS and user-friendly child-seat tether anchors added to the EX and SE. **2002**—Restyled and given more power, interior room, and features, like a side-hinged tailgate and new interior panels. **2004**—A front-passenger power door lock switch. **2005**—Standard side curtain airbags, skid control, and ABS; an upgraded 5-speed automatic transmission; and minor styling changes. **2007**—A new platform borrowed from the Civic, and a restyled interior and exterior that includes a new swing-up tailgate and a hiding spot underneath the cargo floor for the spare tire. These changes make the car wider and shorter than the previous year's model and enhance ride and handling, especially in turns. Cargo is also easier to load and unload; however, the spare tire is more difficult to access with a full load.

COST ANALYSIS: 2009 prices are expected to match the 2008s ($28,000), since the verhicles are simply carryovers of the reworked 2007 version. In the States, the car costs $25,500. Don't expect much discounting or price-haggling—buyers downsizing in the wake of higher fuel prices are keeping prices high. **Best alternatives:** An upgraded second-series 2002, or 2007 model, if you can find one. Take solace in knowing that, even if you pay too much, you can drive this bantam 4×4 until you outgrow it and then trade it in for almost as much as you paid originally. Good second choices are the Hyundai Tucson or Santa Fe, Subaru Forester, and Toyota RAV4. **Rebates:** Mostly low-financing programs. **Delivery/ PDI:** $1,455. **Warranty:** Bumper-to-bumper 3 years/60,000 km; powertrain 5 years/100,000 km; rust perforation 5 years/unlimited km. **Supplementary warranty:** Honda's impressive quality control makes an extended warranty unnecessary. **Options:** Make sure a moonroof doesn't reduce your headroom to an uncomfortable degree. Be wary of the cruise control—it's quirky, and when it's engaged, you may find that the car won't hold its speed over hilly terrain. One other bit of advice: Because of their design, CR-Vs tend to sandblast the paint off the side-door bottoms. Invest in a pair of $25 mudflaps. Also, steer clear of the original-equipment Bridgestone and Firestone tires. Owners report poor performance on wet roads and premature failures. Try Michelin, Yokohama, or Pirelli, instead. **Depreciation:** Much slower than average. **Insurance cost:** Average. **Parts supply/cost:** Parts are easily found and reasonably priced (they come mostly from the Civic parts bin). **Annual maintenance cost:** Well below average; easily repaired at independent garages. **Highway/city fuel economy:** Estimated to be 8.9/10.9 L/100 km.

QUALITY/RELIABILITY: Traditionally beyond reproach, but quality has slipped a bit lately. **Owner-reported problems:** Harsh shifting on the 1997–99 models, and high-rev shifting, slipping, pulsing, and surging on the 2000 version. The 1999–2001 CR-Vs also have a history of engine failures caused by defective cylinder heads (see "Secret Warranties/Internal Bulletins/Service Tips"). Other reported problems include minor body trim defects, premature front brake wear and vibrations, drive shaft popping noises, accessories that malfunction (particularly the sound system and AC), and electrical glitches. **Warranty performance:** Like most other automakers, Honda frequently extends its warranty through "goodwill" policies that cover generic factory-related defects. The company denies this is the case, but, interestingly enough, almost all of its service bulletins include a paragraph stating that post-warranty goodwill compensation will be considered if requested by the dealer. Be wary, though. Sometimes owners are asked to show maintenance receipts as a prerequisite for "goodwill" repairs. Stand your ground, as did this American *Lemon-Aid* reader:

> My 2001 Honda CR-V started to run rough and stall. The engine light came on [at] 79,000 miles [127,000 km]. The codes retrieved were P0300, P0302, P0302, P0304. These are misfire codes. A repairman stated that Honda has a well known

defect in their 1999–2001 Honda CR-V [in] which valves cause internal damage to their engine, and it should be under "GOODWILL" warranty. The dealer said it would not fix it unless I have proof of "Honda Dealer" Maintenance, which I don't have....

I refused and dealer later offered to do the repair for $500.

ROAD PERFORMANCE: Acceleration/torque: The 2005's more powerful, upgraded engine is faster when accelerating from a standing start and is less prone to hunting for the right gear when pressed. Manual transmissions need to downshift less frequently, as well. Generally, though, the CR-V is slow to accelerate when loaded—add passengers and an automatic transmission, and you're likely to get passed by bicycling seniors. Nevertheless, the engine's increased low-end torque adds 227 kg (500 lb.) to the towing rating (680 kg/1,500 lb.). **Transmission:** The 5-speed manual is precise, with short throws and easy shifting, while the automatic is quick and smooth. The full-time 4×4 disengages under braking, allowing the ABS to engage. **Steering:** Many reports of severe "torque steer," where vehicle pulls hard to the right when accelerating. Variable-assisted steering, however, is nimble and accurate, and it provides just the right boost for highway and city driving. On the downside, the 2002 modifications have reduced road feel. **Routine handling:** The CR-V isn't tippy, and handles remarkably well. Excellent ride over smooth surfaces. The car's small size doesn't handle road imperfections well, making for a bumpy, jittery ride. Forget about off-roading: There's no locking feature for the centre differential and no low-range 4×4 capability. **Emergency handling:** Very good, partly because of the four-wheel independent suspension and precise steering. Little body lean when cornering under power. **Braking:** Better than average, with good directional control and little fading after repeated applications.

SAFETY SUMMARY: When compared with Toyota, Honda has had fewer safety-related defects reported to NHTSA. One recurring complaint, though, is that large occupants can't use the original-equipment seat belts. Note also that the CR-V flipped over in 1999 side-impact tests carried out by NHTSA. **Airbags:** There's a concern that the steering-wheel design is on an angle, which could result in an injury if the airbag deploys at an angle. There have been reports of airbags failing to deploy or deploying inadvertently. In one incident, the vehicle was going about 25 km/h when the driver's airbag suddenly exploded. The vehicle went off the road, flipped over, and injured the driver. **ABS:** Standard; disc/disc. **Seat belt pretensioners:** Standard. **Head restraints F/R:** *1997:* ★★★; *1998:* ★★; *2001:* ★★★/★★; *2002–03:* ★★★★★. *2005–06:* ★; *2007:* ★★★★★. **Visibility F/R:** ★★★★★. **Pet transport:** ★★★. Although the rear seats easily fold down flat, side-by-side crates will fit only in an "L" formation: one facing the back door, and the other facing the rear side.

SAFETY COMPLAINTS: All years: Sudden acceleration. • Chronic stalling. • ABS lock-up. • Bridgestone tire blowouts. **1999**—Engine cylinder failure causes excessive vibration and stalling. • Automatic transmission slams into First gear. • Hatch window blows out while driving. **2000**—Bumper assembly catches fire. • Vehicle rolled over; A-pillar collapsed and killed driver. • Automatic transmission takes an inordinate amount of time to go into First gear and doesn't hold car when stopped in traffic on an incline. • Unacceptable slippage, poor traction of Bridgestone tires on wet pavement. • Excessive shimmying and front suspension vibration when accelerating. • Chronic steering-wheel vibrations. **2001**—Short drivers find airbags point toward their faces. • Rear wheel lock-up while turning caused head-on collision (clutch failure suspected). • Driver's seatback collapsed in rear-ender. • Seat belt tightens uncomfortably. **2002**—Loud popping noise when braking and changing direction (replacing the brake pads doesn't fix the problem). • Vehicle hesitates when accelerating, or surges and then stalls. • Dim driver-side headlight. **2002–03**—Hood suddenly flies open while cruising. **2003**—Driver-side and rear centre seat belts unbuckled when car was rear-ended. • Steering wheel doesn't return to normal position after making a turn. **2003–07**—Airbags fail to deploy. **2004**—Wheel freezes while making a turn. • Stress fractures in windshield. • Wheel lug bolt breaks off. • Removable picnic table caused serious head injuries in a rollover accident. • Gas spews out of filler tube when refuelling. • Water can enter the fuel tank from gas-cap vent. • Door lock doesn't function with key as indicated in the owner's manual. • No seat belt extender available. **2004–05**—Many reports of engine fires after oil has been changed. **2004–06**—Gas pedal sticks. **2005**—Airbags deploy for no reason:

> Airbags deployed (both front and side) while driving through a mall parking lot. The obstruction of view caused the vehicle to run into a light pole. The driver sustained a broken arm, fractured cheek, dislocated nose and jaw, and 8 stitches in her lip.

• Failure of the CV joint protective boot. • Windshield is easily chipped. **2005–06**—Dozens of complaints that the vehicle pulls sharply to the right when accelerating:

> Purchased 2005 Honda CR-V for teenaged daughter in December 2004. Her mother drove the car for the first time on March 5, 2005, and was unfamiliar with the severe torque steer present in the vehicle. After making a right turn onto a major highway under hard acceleration, the steering wheel slipped from my wife's hands and the car struck the curb on the right side of the road. This blew both tires on the right side. At my own expense, I had all four tires replaced and a four-wheel alignment done at an independent dealer. Torque steer is still very prevalent.

2006—Vehicle won't hold its alignment settings. • Excessive tire wear. • Seat belt fails to retract. **2007**—Poor acceleration, followed by surging. • Sudden stalling while underway:

> My wife was driving her new CR-V with our newborn infant on the highway at 8pm. Without any warning the car died and the dashboard went black. She was in the middle lane and almost got rear-ended by a semi trying to get to the right shoulder. She tried starting it and it caught after a few tries. What kind of crap vehicle is Honda putting out? This is our first Honda and it will be the last. There is no way my wife and baby will get in that death mobile again.

• Vehicle is unstable when passing over a grooved highway. • Automatic transmission failures. • Defective engine oil seal. • Visibility impaired by windshield lamination. • Frequent AC failures blamed on road debris, but poor quality is suspected. • Hard starts. • False alerts displayed by the tire pressure warning system.

Secret Warranties/Internal Bulletins/Service Tips

All years: Keep in mind that Honda service bulletins almost always mention that "goodwill" extended warranties may be applied to any malfunction. **1999**—Harsh shifting caused by faulty solenoid; subject to free "goodwill" repair. • Front suspension clunking can be corrected by replacing the upper-arm flange bolts. • Cargo-cover end-caps come off. **1999–2001**—Differential noise. • Engine cylinder head failures causing poor engine performance covered by a secret warranty:

HARD START/POOR PERFORMANCE/MIL ON/MISFIRE DTC

BULLETIN NO.: 03-038   **DATE: NOVEMBER 5, 2004**

1999–2001 CR-V – ALL

SYMPTOM: The engine idles roughly, is hard to start, performs poorly, or has the MIL on with DTC P0301, P0302, P0303, P0304 (cylinder misfire), or P0172 (fuel system too rich).

PROBABLE CAUSE: One or more exhaust valves have receded into the cylinder head.

CORRECTIVE ACTION: Inspect the valve clearance and, if necessary, replace the cylinder head.

WARRANTY CLAIM INFORMATION: In warranty: The normal warranty applies.
Failed Part: P/N 12100-P75-010
              H/C 5604970
Defect Code: 00503
Symptom Code: 03203

OP#	DESCRIPTION	FRT
110345	Check/adjust valve clearance only	0.8
110163	Check valve clearance, and replace cylinder head with new assembly	6.9

Out of warranty: Any repair performed after warranty expiration may be eligible for goodwill consideration by the District Parts and Service Manager or your Zone Office. You must request consideration, and get a decision, before starting work.

INSPECTION PROCEDURE

1. Remove the cylinder head cover, and check the valve clearance on all exhaust valves.
   - If any of the valve clearances are below 0.09 mm, go to step 2.
   - If any of the valve clearances are between 0.09 and 0.16 mm, adjust the valves to specification (0.16 to 0.20 mm) Return the vehicle to the customer.
   - If the clearances are within specification, disregard this bulletin and look for other possible causes (ignition, fuel injection, etc.).
2. Ask the customer if the valves were adjusted shortly before the problem occurred.
   - If the valves were recently adjusted, readjust the valves to specification.
   - If the valves were not adjusted, proceed to REPAIR PROCEDURE.

REPAIR PROCEDURE: Replace the cylinder head: The exhaust valves and seats may be damaged (burnt or cracked) to further indicate that the cylinder head has a problem.

1999–2007—Vehicle pulls/drifts to one side. 2000—Information regarding shudder or vibration upon hard acceleration. • The remedy for differential moan during turns. • Malfunctioning Low Fuel light. 2001—Rear differential noise. • Water leaks into the interior. 2002—Rattling from the passenger grab handle area and above the doors. 2002–03—A front brake clicking noise is caused by faulty lower retaining clips on the front brake pad that may be replaced for free under a "goodwill" program. • Engine stumbles or stalls after a stop. • Vehicle pulls to the right:

VEHICLE DRIFTS TO THE RIGHT

BULLETIN NO.: 03-004   DATE: JANUARY 21, 2003

2002–03 CR-V 4WD WITH A/T

SYMPTOM: The vehicle drifts or pulls to the right while driving at highway speeds.

CORRECTIVE ACTION: Realign the damper spring on the upper spring seat.

OUT OF WARRANTY: Any repair performed after warranty expiration may be eligible for goodwill consideration by the District Parts and Service Manager or your Zone Office. You must request consideration, and get a decision, before starting work.

• Misaligned door glass. 2002–04—Troubleshooting a rear brake grinding noise. • Correcting harsh or noisy automatic transmission downshifts when slowing down. 2002–05—Remedy for a rattle, grind, or growl coming from the A-pillar of the front-right side of the vehicle when turning left. • Troubleshooting rear seat belt retractor rattles/squeaks. 2003—Coolant in the oil pan. 2007—Low Tire Pressure light stays on.

CR-V PROFILE

	1999	2000	2001	2002	2003	2004	2005	2006	2007
Cost Price ($) (firm)									
LX (20%)	26,000	26,000	26,300	26,900	27,300	27,200	28,200	29,300	27,700
Used Values ($)									
LX ▲	6,000	7,000	8,500	11,000	13,000	15,000	17,000	19,500	21,000
LX ▼	5,000	6,000	7,500	9,500	12,000	14,000	15,500	18,000	19,000
Reliability	4	5	5	5	5	5	5	5	5
Crash Safety (F)	4	4	4	5	5	5	5	5	5
Side	5	5	5	5	5	5	5	5	5
IIHS Side	—	—	—	2	2	2	5	5	5
Offset	2	2	2	5	5	5	5	5	5
Rollover	—	—	3	3	3	—	4	4	4

All ratings on a numbered scale where 5 is good and 1 is bad. See page 217 for a more detailed description.

RATING: Above Average (2003–08). Honda launched this oddly styled SUV as a youth magnet, but has only succeeded in giving soccer moms and baby boomers a minivan alternative. **Strong points:** It's almost the same size as a CR-V, with a better package, and it costs thousands of dollars less. Other notable features include a limited, though adequate, powertrain; a roomy, versatile interior; an unusually large cargo door opening; a low liftover; a sliding roof partition that allows it to carry bulky items like kayaks, fishing poles, and surfboards; interior tie-down hooks that easily handle dog crates; and a dash that allows for Internet access. Slow depreciation and excellent quality control round out the Element's assets. **Weak points:** No 6-cylinder option; engine is noisy when pushed; mediocre passing performance; doesn't corner very well; unusual driving position; gauges are sometimes difficult to see; the front windshield is more vertical than most and seems far away from the driver; lacks a third seat in rear; side windows don't roll down; poor stereo sound; some high-speed wind noise; side crashworthiness rated "Poor" by IIHS; 20 cm (8 in.) shorter than the Civic coupe; looks a bit like the 2003 Hummer H2. **New for 2008:** Nothing important; Element will return unchanged for 2009.

MODEL HISTORY: A CR-V clone based on the Civic platform, the tall, square-looking Element is a crossover sport wagon SUV launched in early 2003 and priced in the $25,000–$30,000 range. Aimed at the youth market with its rugged exterior styling, buyers get the versatility of an SUV, the cargo-hauling capability of a pickup, and the interior access of a minivan. **2007**—A slight restyling (new headlights and grille); seat-integrated front safety belts, allowing for much easier rear passenger access; a 5-speed automatic transmission; and standard side curtain airbags and Vehicle Stability Assist. An all-new sporty variation, the Element SC, debuted with a sport-tuned suspension and "Street Custom" styling.

2008 ELEMENT TECHNICAL DATA

POWERTRAIN (FRONT-DRIVE/4×4)
Engine: 2.4L 4-cyl. (166 hp);
Transmissions: 5-speed man. • 5-speed auto.

DIMENSION/CAPACITY
Passengers: 2/2; Wheelbase: 101.4 in.; H: 70.4/L: 169.2/W: 71.5 in.; Headroom F/R: 4.5/4.0 in.; Legroom F/R: 40.0/30.0 in.; Cargo volume: 25.1 cu. ft.; Fuel tank: 60L/regular; Tow limit: 1,500 lb.; Load capacity: 675 lb.; GVWR: 4,450 lb.; Turning circle: 34.9 ft.; Ground clearance: 6.9 in.; Weight: 3,380 lb.

Campers are well served by front- and second-row seats that fold flat for sleeping. The second-row seats can be folded away to the side, or removed to make more room for sports equipment and other toys.

Powered by a 166-hp 2.4L 4-cylinder engine coupled with a 5-speed automatic transmission or a 5-speed manual, the Element's powertrain and light weight make it a good all-around performer. Nonetheless, the lack of a V6 engine compromises its sporty pretensions.

COST ANALYSIS: Smart buyers will opt for the more refined 2007 version ($21,500) over the 2006. The 2007 vehicle's additional features are well worth their higher cost as used vehicles. Nevertheless, the 2008 models are excellent buys. They sell for $25,290, only $90 more than what the 2007 models cost new. 2009 Elements are expected to carry a $500 premium. **Best alternatives:** The Honda CR-V, Hyundai Santa Fe GLS, Nissan X-Trail or Xterra, Subaru Forester, and Toyota Highlander AWD. **Rebates:** Few rebates because of the limited production. **Delivery/PDI:** $1,455. **Warranty:** Bumper-to-bumper 3 years/60,000 km; powertrain 5 years/100,000 km; rust perforation 5 years/unlimited km. **Supplementary warranty:** A waste of money. **Options:** Nothing that's necessary. **Depreciation:** Much slower than average. **Insurance cost:** Average. **Parts supply/cost:** Average. **Annual maintenance cost:** Less than average. **Highway/city fuel economy:** 8.5/11.1 L/100 km.

QUALITY/RELIABILITY: Likely failures: Windshield cracks plus minor fit and finish, electrical system, AC, and sound system glitches.

SAFETY SUMMARY: The driver's and front passenger's shoulder belts are attached to the rear doors. This means front occupants must unbuckle their seat belts before the rear passengers can open the rear doors (assuming the front doors are open). This problem has been corrected on the 2007 model. Windshield pillars are quite thick, and they occasionally obscure vision when turning. **Airbags:** Front and side. **ABS:** Optional; disc/disc. **Safety belt pretensioners:** Front. **Head restraints F/R:** 2003–06: ★; 2007: ★★★★★. **Visibility F/R:** ★★★/★. **Pet transport:** ★★★★★. The ideal dogmobile. Plenty of room for side-by-side crates, well-positioned cargo tie-downs, and concave rear doors that provide additional room.

SAFETY COMPLAINTS: 2003—Extensive low-speed collision damage. • Loose rear torsion bar nut. **2003–05**—Many complaints related to windshield cracking (covered by a "goodwill" policy on a case-by-case basis). **2004**—Fire occurs in driver-side door. • Loose driver's seat rocks back and forth. **2004–07**—Airbags deploy for no reason. **2005**—You cannot open the back door unless the front door is opened first. • Airbags fail to deploy. **2006**—Sunlight washes out dashboard gauges. **2007**—Following deployment of airbags, driver lost hearing ability. • Poor braking; apparently, only the front brakes operate effectively. • Spare tire lug nuts tend to loosen and shear off over time. • Chipped windshield, similar to problem with previous model years, targeted in a class action.

Secret Warranties/Internal Bulletins/Service Tips

2003—Windshield cracks in the lower corners because of an uneven flange surface (TSB #03-028; issued May 6, 2003). • Driver's seat rocks back and forth. • Troubleshooting ABS problems. **2003–04**—Correcting harsh or noisy automatic transmission downshifts when slowing down. • What to do when the tailgate rattles, Hatch Open indicator is on, and interior light is lit. **2003–05**—Noisy front seatback. **2005**—Axle seal leaks.

	2003	2004	2005	2006	2007
Cost Price ($) (firm)					
Base (20%)	23,900	23,900	24,000	24,200	25,200
Used Values ($)					
Base ▲	9,500	11,500	14,000	16,000	19,000
Base ▼	8,500	10,000	12,500	14,500	18,000
Reliability	5	5	5	5	5
Crash Safety (F)	5	5	5	5	5
Side	5	5	5	5	5
IIHS Side	1	1	1	1	—
Offset	5	5	5	5	5
Rollover	3	—	—	—	3

Hyundai

TUCSON ★★★★

RATING: Above Average (2007–08); Average (2006); Below Average (2005). With this Kia Sportage twin, you get a lot of features for your money, but a competent 4-cylinder engine isn't one of them. **Strong points:** Fairly cheap; well-equipped with standard side airbags and stability control; NHTSA five-star front and side crashworthiness ratings; excellent braking; very comfortable ride; roomy interior; and good fit and finish. **Weak points:** Underpowered and "undergeared"; bland interior; mediocre handling; sluggish steering; limited rear visibility; numerous first-year factory-related deficiencies; noisy suspension; poor fuel economy; and IIHS gives it an "Average" for offset and side crash protection, and head restraints are rated "Poor" for occupant protection. **New for 2008:** Nothing significant, until the 2010 model's redesign.

MODEL HISTORY: Hyundai's second and smallest sport-utility is built on a strengthened and stretched Elantra platform powered by the Elantra's engine and offering the addition of four-wheel drive. The interior looks fairly low-tech and uses cheap-looking plastics everywhere. The optional 2.7L V6 is harnessed to a manumatic 4-speed automatic transmission, a setup that leads to excessive gear-hunting, imprecise

2008 TUCSON TECHNICAL DATA

POWERTRAIN (FRONT-DRIVE/4×4)
Engines: 2.0L 4-cyl. (140 hp) • 2.7L V6 (173 hp); Transmissions: 5-speed man. • 4-speed manumatic
DIMENSION/CAPACITY
Passengers: 2/3; Wheelbase: 103.5 in.; H: 66.1/L: 170.3/W: 70.7 in.; Headroom F/R: 5.0/4.0 in.; Legroom F/R: 41.0/29.0 in.; Cargo volume: 22.7 cu. ft.; Fuel tank: 58L/regular; Tow limit: 2,000 lb.; Load capacity: 860 lb.; GVWR: 4,431 lb.; Turning circle: 39.0 ft.; Ground clearance: 7.0 in.; Weight: 3,240 lb.

automatic-to-manual shifting, and compromised fuel economy. What's really needed is a conventional 5-speed, or for the Santa Fe's 242-hp 3.3L V6 to handle the Tucson's heft.

While we're on the subject of weight, the Tucson is heavier than either the Honda CR-V or Toyota RAV4, so true handling enthusiasts will want to throw their lot in with the RAV4 or Ford/Mazda Escape/Tribute to get their performance thrills.

COST ANALYSIS: The base 2008 models are reasonably priced; however, AWD and V6-equipped versions are much pricier: $21,195/$28,796/$28,796/$30,996 (GL/ GL AWD/GL V6/GL AWD V6). Stateside: $17,420 and $22,970 for the GL series; $22,240 and $24,770 for the 4×4 and AWD Limited. 2009 prices should remain the same. Since there are no real improvements on the 2008 and 2009 models, buy a used 2007 version ($16,000); there are plenty available. Don't buy a first-year 2005 unless it has been thoroughly checked over, is incredibly cheap, and has much of the original warranty left. Also, try to find an improved second-series version that was built after March 2005. Prices for used 2005s are fairly firm and are as follows: *Front-drive GL:* $10,000–$11,000; *Front-drive GL V6:* $11,000–$12,000; *4×4 GL V6:* $13,000–$14,000; *4×4 GLS V6:* $14,000–$15,000. **Best alternatives:** Ford Escape, Honda CR-V, Jeep Liberty, and Toyota RAV4. **Rebates:** $2,500. **Delivery/PDI:** $1,545. **Warranty:** Bumper-to-bumper 5 years/100,000 km; powertrain 5 years/100,000 km; rust perforation 5 years/ unlimited km. **Supplementary warranty:** Not necessary. **Options:** The V6 engine is a must-have to compensate for the 4-banger's lack of passing power. **Depreciation:** Average. **Insurance cost:** Average. **Parts supply/cost:** Easily found and reasonably priced. **Annual maintenance cost:** Rather high for the first-year 2005s; predicted to be lower than average for the 2006–09 models. **Highway/city fuel economy:** *2.0L 4-cyl.:* 7.9/10.6 L/100 km; *V6:* 8.4/11.9 L/100 km.

QUALITY/RELIABILITY: Although the 2005 first-series models were somewhat glitch-ridden, overall quality control is quite good. **Owner-reported problems:** Failures related to the cruise control, automatic transmission, manual transmission shift-lever cable assembly, and stability-control module. Poor fit and finish; water pours in from behind the glove box:

> Upon removing the glove box and pulling out the cabin filter, I noticed the water coming down through the AC system...similar complaint filed on service bulletins. Car was parked on a 10 degree angle nose end down. Water leak through and near electrical components and near passenger side airbag.

Warranty performance: Better than average, but service is a big disappointment. **Likely failures:** The automatic transmission, electronics, cruise control, stability-control system, and ABS brakes.

SAFETY SUMMARY: Airbags: Standard front, side, and side curtain. **ABS:** Standard; disc/disc. **Safety belt pretensioners:** Front. **Traction control:** Standard. **Head restraints F/R:** *2006:* ★. **Visibility F/R:** Good overall. **Pet transport:** ★★★★. Crates are easy to load, there is plenty of room for side-by-side placement, and air easily circulates to the rear cargo area.

SAFETY COMPLAINTS: All years: Airbags fail to deploy. **2005**—A faulty Electronic Stability Program (ESP) module can cause the vehicle to stall and the ABS to suddenly engage, and can result in the vehicle going out of control. This has happened to vehicles that have been recalled and "fixed" for the problem and to cars that aren't included in the recall:

> There is a recall on this vehicle by Hyundai however due to the VIN number this car is not included. The problem is there is an ESP (stability control) which activates one of the wheels and causes the vehicle to swerve in the direction of the braking. In this case, the vehicle locked up and the consumer nearly lost control while driving about 40 mph [64 km/h] and the right front wheel and brake locked up.

• Manual and automatic transmissions suddenly fail to go into gear. • Power steering fails while passing through small pools of water on the road. **2005–06**— The passenger-side airbag is disabled even though an adult occupies the seat. **2007**—Head restraints cause neck stiffness and headaches. • Rear window explodes for no reason.

Secret Warranties/Internal Bulletins/Service Tips

2005—No movement in Drive or Reverse. • Fluid may leak from the area around the automatic transmission torque converter or between the transaxle and the transfer case. • Correcting harsh gear engagement. • Tips on silencing a rattling sunroof. **2006–07**—Troubleshooting complaints relative to a cloudy paint condition.

THE HYUNDAI/KIA NAME GAME

The following vehicles are twins with only minor variations. The Kia Rondo doesn't count because it's a clone of the Optima wagon—a derivate of the Hyundai Sonata.

Accent = Rio
Azera = Amanti/XG300/350
Elantra = Spectra
Entourage = Sedona
Santa Fe = Sorento
Sonata = Optima
Tucson = Sportage
Veracruz = Mesa

Kia

SORENTO ★★★★

RATING: Above Average (2008); Average (2005–07); Below Average (2003–04). Kia has a history of poor quality control in a model's early years, then bailing out when the model doesn't sell. The Sorento has, apparently, escaped that fate. On the other hand, Kia Canada loves to price gouge and then cut prices substantially in mid-winter—a sure-fire way to tick off buyers who paid the higher prices. **Strong points:** Engines are good performers that have been road-proven on Hyundai's Santa Fe mid-sized SUV and Entourage minivan. In fact, the cheaper 3.3L-equipped model with its smaller wheels actually seems to be the best performer over regular roads. A roomy interior and lots of standard performance and safety features. Four-wheel drive, low-range gearing, and good ground clearance make the Sorento a capable off-road performer. Top-notch construction and high-quality materials. **Weak points:** *2007 and earlier models:* So-so acceleration, mediocre handling and braking, a jolting ride over uneven terrain, poor fuel economy, cheap-looking seat upholstery, and a tacky plastic dash. *2008:* New models are outrageously overpriced in Canada by almost $8,000. Plus, the much-vaunted 10-year warranty applied stateside is cut to only five years in Canada. **New for 2008:** A competent, entry-level 3.3L engine. The next redesign is scheduled for 2010, when Sorento will get new standard features to improve handling and safety. At that time, its body-on-frame construction will be switched to the unibody platform used by Hyundai's Santa Fe. Remember what we said about Kia price-gouging in Canada? This year, we have a choice of two engines to replace the outgoing 3.5L V6. Buyers can choose between the $32,495 LX 4×4 with a 3.3L V6 and 242 hp, or the $38,995 LX Luxury with a more powerful 3.8L V6 that produces 262 hp. $38,995? Indeed. That same LX Luxury model sells for $26,195 (U.S.) just across the border. Oh, don't forget the freight charges of $700 in the States versus $1,495 in Canada. Are you starting to get ANGRY?

2008 SORENTO TECHNICAL DATA

POWERTRAIN (4×4)
Engine: 3.3L V6 (242 hp) • 3.8L V6 (262 hp); Transmission: 5-speed manumatic.

DIMENSION/CAPACITY
Passengers: 2/3; Wheelbase: 107.0 in.; H: 71.0/L: 179.8/W: 74.6 in.; Headroom F/R: 3.0/3.5 in.; Legroom F/R: 40.0/27.5 in.; Cargo volume: 30.5 cu. ft.; Fuel tank: 80L/regular; Tow limit: 5,000 lb.; Load capacity: 1,145 lb.; GVWR: 5,467 lb.; Turning circle: 39.0 ft.; Ground clearance: 7.0 in.; Weight: 4,500 lb.

Mesa

In the meantime, Kia will bring out the 2009 Mesa, a full-sized 7-seater SUV, slated to be a bit smaller than Hyundai's full-sized Veracruz. Set on a stretched Sorento platform, the Mesa will share mostly Sorento and Veracruz parts, including the same 262-hp 3.8L V6 mated to a 6-speed automatic transmission for the North American market, and a 250-hp V6 diesel for local use. An independent suspension and Hyundai's more potent 300-plus-hp 4.7L V8 may also be offered; however, higher fuel prices are likely to torpedo that possibility. Furthermore, you will have to be patient: The Mesa won't be sold in Canada until early 2009.

MODEL HISTORY: This SUV crossover carries passenger-car genes in a compact SUV body. Although the "torque on demand" 4×4 system is better suited to navigating slippery surfaces than cavorting off-road, the Sorento's full- and part-time low range gearing gives it a decided off-road advantage over many competing models. Other off-road assets are a wide track, fully independent suspension, high ground clearance, and short front and rear overhangs.

2004—A 5-speed manual transmission. **2005**—Addition of an upgraded 5-speed automatic transmission. **2007**—A fuel-thrifty and more powerful 3.8L V6 with 36 percent more horsepower, standard stability control, and ABS brakes. This allows for a 5,000 lb. towing capacity in both two- and four-wheel drive modes. Other refinements are redesigned front headlights, a reworked grille, new bumpers, and restyled tail lights. Interior improvements include a redesigned instrument panel and classier-looking interior garnishings.

COST ANALYSIS: Kia dealers are hungry—on both sides of the Canadian border. However, sales have been particularly bad in the States, so shop the U.S. border states to get the best bargains—like $24,195 (plus $600 freight) for a 2008-09 LX 4×4 that would cost $32,495 in Canada. Plus, at press time, Kia dealers stateside were eager to get Canadian customers. A used $24,000 2007 will give you the best price and performance/safety upgrades. Don't touch anything earlier than the 2005 model with its upgraded automatic tranny and better quality workmanship. Throw in a 10-year warranty for good measure. **Best alternatives:** The Honda CR-V or Pilot, Hyundai Tucson or Santa Fe, Nissan Murano, and Toyota Highlander are all good choices. **Rebates:** Look for $3,000 rebates or zero percent financing programs. **Delivery/PDI:** $1,495 (for a Kia?). **Warranty:** Bumper-to-bumper 5 years/100,000 km; powertrain 5 years/100,000 km; rust perforation 5 years/100,000 km. **Supplementary warranty:** Always a smart idea with Kia, though, judging by the Sportage evolution, the 2005 and later products are apparently better made. **Options:** Forget the Sport Package: It's more show than go. **Depreciation:** Higher than average. **Insurance cost:** Higher than average. **Parts supply/cost:** Average; reasonably priced. **Annual maintenance cost:** Average. **Highway/city fuel economy:** *3.5L:* 10.9/14.9 L/100 km; *3.3L:* 9.2/14.0 L/100 km; *3.8L:* 9.8/14.0 L/100 km.

QUALITY/RELIABILITY: Average, and getting better; poor dealer servicing is now the source of most complaints. **Owner-reported problems:** Many owners of 2003–06 Sorentos report crankshaft/accessory pulley and vibration damper bolt failures, causing the loss of power-steering capability:

> This problem affects 2003 to 2006 Kia Sorento V6 engines. Many owners have had multi failures of this bolt, the updated bolts fail too. Kia is trying to hide this serious problem and has no intention of a real fix. [Owners] are afraid to drive our Kia Sorentos.

Constant engine ticking; automatic transmission slips out of gear, surges, and shudders; prematurely worn-out brake rotors and calipers; excessive drive shaft and brake pedal vibration; fuel and electrical system malfunctions (chronic starting problems, clock not working, lights and gauges inoperative); and radiator hoses blow within a year. **Warranty performance:** Average. **Likely failures:** Airbag sensors, automatic transmission, fuel and electrical systems, accessories, and brakes.

 SAFETY SUMMARY: Thick roof pillars cut visibility, but the large side mirrors compensate somewhat. The 2006–07 models earned a five-star crashworthiness rating for side passenger protection; 2006s also scored well for frontal crash protection (four stars) and were given three stars for rollover prevention. **Airbags:** Standard front, side, and side curtain airbags. **ABS:** Optional 4W; disc/disc. **Head restraints F/R:** 2003–06: ★. **Visibility F/R:** ★★★. **Pet transport:** ★★. The Sorento's streamlined design sabotages the usefulness of its cargo area. For example, dog crates require a specially built platform over the wheelwells, which restricts their height. The seats fold flat, but not effortlessly. You have to pull off the headrests, lift the seat bottoms forward, and then fold the seatbacks into place. On the other hand, the rear hatch has a flip-up top glass that augments ventilation.

SAFETY COMPLAINTS: 2003—Defective front axle (gear oil leakage). • Drive shaft installed upside down. • Harmonic balancer's main bolt shears off, causing severe vibration. • Front axle causes tire to wear faster on the inside. **2003–04**—Many complaints of hard starts and no-starts, thought to be related to the fuel pump. • Automatic transmission grinds and then breaks down. • Excessive on-road vibration despite having drive shaft replaced. **2003–05**—Sudden acceleration blamed on faulty engine intake manifold. • Power-steering failures. **2003–06**—Airbags fail to deploy. **2004**—Hesitation upon acceleration. • Steering assembly fails, spewing fluid onto the engine. • Delayed gear shifts. • When in 4×4, it feels as if the emergency brake is on. • Rear differential bearing failure. • Brakes engaged for no reason. • Speedometer reads fast. **2005**—Sudden loss of power. • Electrical shorts cause light failures and hard starts. • Key cannot be removed from the ignition. • Gas spurts out when refuelling. **2005–06**—Low beam headlights overheat and burn out prematurely:

> I have had the headlights replaced twice. They both went out within a day of each other. The first time, I had to pay $129.00 U.S. and the car was less than a year old. The second time, they replaced it under warranty. This is serious. A lot of Kia owners are complaining, but Kia says nothing is wrong.

2005–07—Many reports of quirky airbag sensors that deactivate airbag as if underweight occupant was seated; occupants are advised not to lean on the door or to sit too far forward, or they may disable the system:

The manager I spoke with said this was a "known problem" with the 2006 and 2007 Sorento but that the company could not "reproduce a hard error." The service manager went on to tell me that there are sensors in the seat cushion and seatback and that a passenger has to sit in the seat in a particular way in order for contact to be made properly.

2006—Shifter handle pops out of its housing. • Brakes lock up when stopping. • Gas gauge reads empty after a fill-up. • Tail lights burn out prematurely.

Secret Warranties/Internal Bulletins/Service Tips

2003—Enhanced power-steering feel. • Hood anti-corrosion treatment. • Rattling heard from the jack compartment. • Service campaign to inspect and re-position the driver's seat-belt-buckle wire harness. **2004**—Engine misfiring or white smoke signal an engine cylinder head leak. • Hesitation on cold starts. **2005**—Free correction of malfunctioning front airbag sensors. • Free wheel guard installation to prevent snow and ice clogging the evaporative air filter. **2005–06**—Free correction for delayed shifting:

TRANSMISSION SHIFT HESITATION	
BULLETIN NO.: KT2006120701	DATE: DECEMBER 7, 2006

SORENTO TRANSMISSION SHIFT HESITATION (TRANS/DRIVE–017)
This service bulletin provides information related to replacing the vehicle speed sensor wire with a shielded cable. The shielded cable to be replaced is routed from the vehicle speed sensor to the TCM. Some 2005–06 MY Sorentos equipped with a 5-speed automatic transmission (A5SR1) may exhibit a vehicle hesitation and shift shock resulting from an engine rpm drop during the 1–2 and/or 2–3 upshift at approximately 4000 rpm. When this event occurs the TCM engages Engine Torque Reduction (ETR) Mode due to abnormal electrical noise created from the internal vehicle speed sensor located in the transmission assembly.

2007—Kia will install a trim pad kit, free of charge, to eliminate front seat belt rattling.

SORENTO PROFILE

	2003	2004	2005	2006	2007
Cost Price ($) (negotiable)					
LX (27%)	29,795	29,845	29,995	29,995	—
EX (27%)	33,795	34,545	34,995	33,725	—
Luxury (27%)	35,795	36,745	37,595	37,795	38,995

Used Values ($)

LX ▲	9,000	11,000	14,000	17,000	—
LX ▼	8,000	10,000	13,000	16,000	—
EX ▲	7,500	9,000	11,000	17,500	—
EX ▼	6,000	8,000	9,500	16,500	—
Luxury ▲	6,500	11,500	14,000	16,500	23,000
Luxury ▼	5,000	10,000	13,000	15,000	21,000

Reliability	2	3	4	4	4
Crash Safety (F)	4	4	4	4	5
Side	5	5	5	5	5
Offset	3	3	3	3	—
Rollover	3	—	—	3	3

Note: Look for 10–15 percent discounts with the $32,495 2008 Sorento LX. The $6,500 difference between the entry-level LX and the Luxury model narrows considerably over time. Crashworthiness: The 2008 version posted similar crashworthiness ratings as the 2007, and the carried over 2009s will likely be just as safe. Rollover resistance was rated at four stars on the 2007 and 2008 4×4 Sorentos and also isn't likely to change before the scheduled 2010 model redesign.

SPORTAGE ★★★★

RATING: Above Average (2005–08); Below Average (2000–02). On the one hand, the 2005–08 Sportage is a Hyundai Tucson twin that's a better-than-average choice and fairly dependable, thanks to the Hyundai DNA transplant. On the other hand, the 2000–02 model is an entirely different SUV that lacks refinement, is a poor highway performer, and has one of the worst quality-control records in its class.

2008 SPORTAGE TECHNICAL DATA

POWERTRAIN (4×4)
Engines: 2.0L 4-cyl. (140 hp) • 2.7L V6 (173 hp); Transmissions: 5-speed man. • 4-speed auto.

DIMENSION/CAPACITY
Passengers: 2/3; Wheelbase: 104.0 in.; H: 66.0/L: 170.0/W: 71.0 in.; Headroom F/R: 5.0/4.0 in.; Legroom F/R: 41.0/29.0 in.; Cargo volume: 31.0 cu. ft.; Fuel tank: 58L/regular; Tow limit: 2,000 lb.; Load capacity: 860 lb.; GVWR: 4,519 lb.; Turning circle: 38.0 ft.; Ground clearance: 7.0 in.; Weight: 3,750 lb.

There were no 2003 or 2004 models. **Strong points:** The 2005 and later models are reasonably priced and subject to deep discounting. Pre-2005s are dirt cheap, reflecting their poor reputation. **Weak points:** The 2005–08 model engines need more power, there's an excess of engine and road noise invading the cabin, and overall handling is only acceptable. Pre-2005 models, though, are worse. They are slow, hard-riding, clumsy, and unstable. These older versions have posted unimpressive crashworthiness scores and face an uncertain future with a limited dealership network. As if that's not enough, there are other deficiencies, including brake failures accompanied by the premature wearout of the brake rotors and calipers, a constantly shifting automatic transmission, a part-time 4×4 that's not suited for dry pavement use, uneven interior ventilation, a noisy engine and fan, obstructed rear visibility with the raised convertible top, and tight rear seating. **New for 2008:** Nothing important; the 2005 model incorporated the last major redesign. However, Kia does plan to launch a 2009 crossover hatchback 4×4 wagon called the Soul, which will sell in the $16,000–$18,000 range.

MODEL HISTORY: *Pre-2005:* The early Sportage is a rudimentary compact sport-utility that's an unimpressive performer and full of expensive-to-repair powertrain and body "surprises." It's offered as a five-passenger, four-door wagon, or as a four-passenger, two-door convertible. The only engine available is an anemic 130-hp 2.0L 4-cylinder attached to either a rear-drive or 4×4 system.

The 2005–08 Sportages are much better-performing vehicles with loads of safety and performance features, which make them the only ones worth consideration. They use the Hyundai Tucson's carlike platform, along with Hyundai's 4- or 6-cylinder engines and front-drive or all-wheel drive. Entry-level LXs come with a 140-hp 4-cylinder and a 5-speed manual or 4-speed automatic transmission. LX V6s and EXs offer a gutsier 173-hp V6 that's hobbled a bit by the automatic tranny (the only choice available). Optional AWD lacks low-range gearing and uses a dashboard switch that locks in a 50/50 front/rear torque split. Standard safety features include anti-lock four-wheel disc brakes, traction control, an anti-skid system, front side airbags, and head-protecting side curtain airbags.

COST ANALYSIS: Selling for $21,695, the entry-level 2008–09 Sportage LX isn't all that different from the redesigned $9,000 2005 model, making the cheaper earlier versions worth considering. The same Sportage LX sells for about $17,000 (U.S.) across the border. **Best alternatives:** Consider Honda's CR-V, Hyundai's Tucson or Santa Fe, and Toyota's RAV4. Nissan's Xterra and Toyota's Highlander are good second choices. **Rebates:** $3,000. **Supplementary warranty:** Not needed for 2005–08 models, but essential for earlier versions. **Depreciation:** A bit slower than average on recent models; quite fast with early versions. **Insurance cost:** Higher than average. **Annual maintenance cost:** High for early models; average for the 2005 and later versions. **Parts supply/cost:** Parts aren't easily found, but they are reasonably priced. **Highway/city fuel economy:** *Pre-2005:* 10.3/11.9 L/100 km with an automatic transmission; *2005–06 4-cyl:* 7.9/10.6 L/100 km; *2005–08 V6:* 8.4/11.9 L/100 km.

QUALITY/RELIABILITY: Best with current models. The J.D. Power and Associates Initial Quality Study placed Kia either at or near dead last in its annual surveys from 1993–2003, forcing the company's American CEO to admit that "up until 1999, the company wasn't focused on quality." Shortly thereafter the 2006 Sportage was given a "Better than Average" quality rating, and the company has continued to receive accolades for its quality control. **Owner-reported problems:** *2000–02:* Fuel and electrical system malfunctions; transmission glitches; AC water leaks; premature catalytic converter, brake pad, and rotor replacement; and poor body fit and finish (rattles, paint peeling, doors often ajar, and wind noise from all doors). *2005–07:* Premature brake wear; rear-end squeaking related to the axle spindle. Fuel tank is easily "over-filled"—it must then be removed and repaired for about $300. The rear windshield wiper arm is regularly torn off by car washes, and the wiper motor has a short lifespan:

The rear wiper arm of the Kia Sportage is made of weak plastic and cannot withstand going through a car wash. The first car wash it went through ripped off the wiper blade and cover over the installation nut. The second car wash then broke the arm.

Warranty performance: Average.

SAFETY SUMMARY: Airbags: Kia includes a unique knee-level airbag to protect the lower extremities. **ABS:** Optional 4W; disc/drum. **Head restraints F/R:** *1999:* ★★★; *2001–02:* ★★; *2005–07:* ★. **Visibility F/R:** ★★★★★/★. **Pet transport:** ★★.

SAFETY COMPLAINTS: All years: Fuel filler leaks gas. • Fumes enter passenger compartment when driving. • Defective front hub assembly won't let driver shift into 4×4 on the fly. • During highway driving, vehicle vibrates excessively. • Vehicle veers from right to left because of faulty suspension. • When driving, 4×4 comes on and off on its own, leading to vehicle almost going off the road. • Brake lights won't turn off • Sudden failure of the turn signals and flashers. • Seat belts tighten uncomfortably on their own. • Gears grind as they shift into Third or Fourth. • Excessive shaking when braking. • Airbags fail to deploy in several collisions. • Airbag and ABS lights stay on. • Driver-side shoulder belt doesn't work. • Water leaks through the door frame. **2001**—Chronic stalling. • Complete brake failure. • Low-speed rear-ender causes seatback to collapse. • Vehicle pulls to one side upon acceleration, or it rocks side to side when turning. • Dash indicators fail from blown fuse. • Fuel tank hard to refuel. **2001–02**—Very loose steering. • Check Engine light is constantly lit. • Doors won't latch unless pulled up when closing. **2002**—Fire ignites from oil dripping onto the exhaust manifold. • Gasoline leaks from the vehicle. • Panel lights go out intermittently. • Steering locks up or has excessive play. • Prematurely worn brake rotors and calipers. • Rear seats move backward or forward when accelerating or braking. • Driver's door suddenly swings open or freezes shut. • Windows lock up. • Plastic fan blades break off and strike the radiator. • Water seeping into the hub assembly wears out wheel hubs. **2005**—Electronic stability system causes braking at the wrong time and pulls car in the direction of the braking wheel (see bulletin reference in "Secret Warranties/ Internal Bulletins/Service Tips," following). • Recall repairs take over a month to perform. **2006**—Fire in the engine compartment. • Sudden, unintended acceleration. • Fuel tank leakage caused by premature corrosion.

Secret Warranties/Internal Bulletins/Service Tips

2001–02—Free catalytic converter replacement under emissions campaign #022. • Front windows won't close at freeway speeds. • Airbag warning light stays lit. • Cooling-fan blade cracking. **2005–06**—Reprogramming campaign to improve the functioning of the electronic stability system detailed in TSB #056, published November 2005.

SPORTAGE PROFILE

	2000	2001	2002	2005	2006	2007
Cost Price ($) (negotiable)						
Sportage (20%)	20,995	20,995	22,095	19,995	20,665	21,695
Used Values ($)						
Sportage ▲	2,500	4,000	5,000	9,500	12,000	14,000
Sportage ▼	2,000	3,000	3,500	8,000	10,500	12,500
Reliability	1	1	1	3	3	3
Crash Safety (F)	—	—	—	5	5	5
Side	—	—	—	5	5	5
Offset	2	2	2	3	3	3
IIHS Side	—	—	—	3	3	3
Rollover	—	—	—	—	—	3

Note: The 2007–08 4×4 models earned a four-star rating for rollover resistance. Also, the 2005–07 jump in the reliability rating is due primarily to the use of more Hyundai-sourced parts.

Mitsubishi

OUTLANDER ★★★

RATING: Average (2004–08); Below Average (2003). Mitsubishi finally gave the 2007 Outlander much-needed powertrain and handling enhancements to catch up to the competition. Still, it's too little, too late. **Strong points:** Outlander owners say that their "real-world" gas mileage is fairly close to government-supplied figures. *2006 and earlier models:* The redesign producing 20 more horses and a quieter cabin for 2004 was a good start, but more power is needed and steering/suspension geometry isn't sufficiently refined. Stable handling. Longer than most SUVs in the compact class, so there's plenty of cargo room. An ideal pet hauler with lots of useable cargo space, thanks to the squarish interior styling and rear seats that easily flip forward. The rear door lifts effortlessly, and the bottom of the rear gate flips down so dogs can jump in. Prices are heavily discounted, and depreciation is fairly dramatic. The front-drive 2008 Outlander LS sells for $24,998, plus $1,595 for freight/PDI in Canada. In the States, the 2008 LS sells for $22,185 (U.S.), plus a $650 freight/PDI fee (less a cash-back rebate). **Weak points:** Throttle lag:

2008 OUTLANDER TECHNICAL DATA

POWERTRAIN (PERMANENT AWD)
Engine: 3.0L V6 (220 hp); Transmission: 6-speed auto.
DIMENSION/CAPACITY
Passengers: 2/3/2; Wheelbase: 105.0 in.; H: 66.1/L: 182.7/W: 70.9 in.; Headroom F/R: 4.5/3.0 in.; Legroom F/R: 41.0/30.0 in.; Cargo volume: 33.5 cu. ft.; Fuel tank: 59L/regular; Tow limit: 3,500 lb.; Load capacity: 1,155 lb.; GVWR: 4,431 lb.; Turning circle: 38.0 ft.; Ground clearance: 7.5 in.; Weight: 3,925 lb.

> My 2007 Outlander had the throttle lag [that has been] discussed in several forums.
> I printed off the two service bulletins and took them into the dealership. They fixed
> everything and the vehicle runs MUCH more smoothly.

Excessive wind noise includes mirror noise that sounds like two parts vibrating, and poor sealing of the side windows. *2006 and earlier models:* Weak, noisy engine; fuel-thirsty; automatic transmission constantly downshifts; not suitable for off-roading; steering is way too light; and there's too much body lean. Other minuses are the dash displays that aren't readable during daylight hours, narrow body, excessive road noise, weak dealer network, and "Poor" IIHS-rated side crashworthiness. **Best alternatives:** Honda CR-V, Hyundai Tucson, and Toyota RAV4. **New for 2008:** Nothing significant, following last year's extensive makeover. A more powerful, gas-sipping 4-cylinder engine is planned for the 2009 model year, along with a $1,000 price increase.

MODEL HISTORY: This compact SUV was originally a spin-off of Mitsubishi's Lancer, which explains its carlike handling and ride. Unfortunately, the Lancer's 140-hp 2.4L 4-banger is no match for the larger and heavier Outlander, even with its transmission set in manual mode. On top of that, the lack of low-range gearing compromises its off-road capability. Smart buyers will opt for a used 2004 version with its 20 extra horses and other improvements. The early Outlanders seat five comfortably, though tall occupants may wish for a bit more legroom. All models also offer good all-around visibility and are easy to enter and exit. **2005**—A manual transmission, upgraded airbags, four-wheel disc brakes, updated styling, and new Limited features. **2007**—A new platform that accommodates seven seats and a 220-hp 3.0L V6 hooked to a 6-speed automatic transmission. This setup provides 60 more horses than the previous year's puny 4-beater. Also new are standard stability and traction control, a lower centre of gravity, side and side curtain airbags, a lowered cargo floor, and a tailgate extension flap/seat capable of supporting up to 180 kg (400 lb.).

 QUALITY/RELIABILITY: Likely failures: Running it in 4×4 eliminates front-drive torque steer, which can be a problem with a V6. Brake pads and rotors are noisy, produce excessive steering vibration, and wear out quickly. Other problems are tranny leaks; electrical shorts; suspension clunks, especially when turning; excessive wheel-bearing and wind noise; erratic lights and radio volume; and fit and finish deficiencies:

> The vehicle was inspected by a dealer who determined the water leak originated from
> the front driver side door water barrier trim. The dealer resealed the water barrier trim
> along the left front driver side door. Afterwards, the problem persisted.

SAFETY COMPLAINTS: 2005—Faulty body welds in the driver-side A-pillar. **2007**—Airbags fail to deploy. • Brakes lock up and vehicle stalls when the brakes are applied. • False alerts of low tire air pressure when weather turns cold. • When AC cycles on, headlights and dash lights dim and blower slows down.

Secret Warranties/Internal Bulletins/Service Tips

2003–05—Shift flare when going from Second to Third gear.

OUTLANDER PROFILE

	2003	2004	2005	2006	2007
Cost Price ($) (firm)					
Outlander LS	26,757	24,458	23,348	23,998	25,498
Outlander AWD	28,697	27,078	26,018	26,668	32,998
Used Values ($)					
Outlander LS ▲	6,500	8,000	9,500	12,500	17,000
Outlander LS ▼	6,000	7,000	8,000	10,500	15,000
Outlander AWD ▲	8,000	9,500	11,000	14,500	18,500
Outlander AWD ▼	7,000	8,500	10,000	13,500	17,500
Reliability	3	3	3	3	3
Crash Safety (F)	4	4	—	—	—
Side	5	5	—	—	—
IIHS Side	1	1	1	—	—
Offset	5	5	5	5	5
Rollover	3	—	—	—	—

Note: IIHS rates 2007 model head restraints as "Marginal;" 2003–06 model head restraints are rated "Marginal" to "Acceptable," depending whether they are perforated or not.

Nissan

XTERRA ★★★★

RATING: Above Average (2005–08); Average (2003–04); Below Average (2000–02). **Strong points:** Reasonably priced, a competent off-roader and highway cruiser (with the 4.0L V6), smooth-shifting automatic transmission, good braking, interior space for five adults, well laid-out instruments and controls, elevated rear seats, and good handling and ride. Engine and transmission skid plates and a short front overhang enhance its off-road prowess. Depreciation is quite slow, and first-year quality-control problems are minimal. **Weak points:** The underpowered 4-cylinder and early V6 engines are most suitable for off-road use where torque is more important than speed, but they could still use a few more horses. The super-charged V6 doesn't impress, and requires premium fuel. All engines are noisy and fuel-thirsty; however, the latest 4.0L V6 is the most competent performer. The part-time 4×4's low-range gearing could be lower, steering is a bit over-assisted for highway driving, the ride is a bit stiff, and the pre-2002 knee-banging handbrake is an irritant. Early-model dash gauges are hard to read, and small rear-door openings complicate entry and exit. To get more cargo space with 2004 and earlier

2008 XTERRA TECHNICAL DATA

POWERTRAIN (REAR-DRIVE/4×4)

Engine: 4.0L V6 (261 hp); Transmissions:
6-speed man. • 5-speed auto.

DIMENSION/CAPACITY

Passengers: 2/3; Wheelbase: 106.3 in.;
H: 74.9/L: 178.7/W: 72.8 in.; Headroom
F/R: 4.0/4.0 in.; Legroom F/R: 41.0/28.0
in.; Cargo volume: 45.5 cu. ft.; Fuel
tank: 80L/regular; Tow limit: 5,000 lb.;
Load capacity: 920 lb.; GVWR: 5,200 lb.;
Turning circle: 37.7 ft.; Ground clearance:
9.5 in.; Weight: 4,258 lb.

versions, you must first remove the flimsy blocks of foam that were passed off as the rear-seat cushions. Seats are hard and lack thigh support. There's insufficient rearward seat travel for tall drivers. Some engine, wind, and road noise. **New for 2008:** Nothing important; a major redesign is scheduled for 2009.

MODEL HISTORY: Essentially a $34,598 (plus a $1,400 freight/PDI fee) Frontier and Pathfinder spin-off, the 2008 Xterra is a four-door, five-passenger sport-utility vehicle that's longer and wider than the Jeep Cherokee. Its fully loaded top price is a few loonies less than what one would pay for an unadorned Pathfinder. The 2004 and earlier models came with a base 2.4L 4-cylinder (XE version) or an optional 3.3L V6 or supercharged variant. Top-line models offer rear-drive or 4×4; however, the 4×4 isn't to be used on dry pavement. **2001**— Minor revisions. **2002**—An optional supercharged V6 and limited slip differential. **2003**—An additional 10 horses, optional head-protecting side curtain airbags, an anti-skid system, 16-inch alloy wheels, optional tire pressure monitoring, side step rails, 90 more watts for the entertainment system, a new driver-seat height and lumbar support adjuster, and dual 12-volt power outlets. **2005**—Redesigned as a smaller version of Nissan's Titan and Frontier pickups, the 2005 Xterra now uses the Pathfinder's platform, but with a solid rear axle instead of the independent one used by Pathfinders. The 4-banger is replaced by a more powerful V6 coupled to new transmissions that equip the 350Z. In addition to being wider and taller, the wheelbase has been stretched a couple of inches, enhancing ride comfort and interior room, most of which is given to rear-seat passengers. Seats are more practical and comfortable; there's a newly available fold-down front passenger seat (great for skis); the instrument panel has been revised; and the radio and climate controls in the centre console have been made more user-friendly. The roof rack has a latching lid, ground clearance is higher, and the Off-Road model now uses high-performance gas shocks.

COST ANALYSIS: Wait for the upgraded 2009; prices won't change much. A 2005 sells for $14,500 and is also a good buy. It's practically identical to the new versions that will cost a whopping $36,000, once freight fees are added. Stateside, the same entry-level 2008 S model would cost $22,880 plus $660 freight (U.S.), making the Xterra quite an enticing buy south of the border, where smart shoppers can save up to $13,000 (U.S.). **Best alternatives:** Other vehicles worth considering are the Honda CR-V, Hyundai Tucson or Santa Fe, and Toyota RAV4 or Highlander. **Rebates:** $3,500 rebates, and zero percent financing. **Delivery/PDI:** $1,400 (sometimes included in the MSRP). **Warranty:** Bumper-to-bumper 3 years/60,000 km; powertrain 5 years/100,000 km; rust perforation 5 years/ unlimited km. **Supplementary warranty:** Not necessary. **Options:** Stability control is a worthwhile option for the 2005 and later models. Stay away from the dealer-ordered Firestone/Bridgestone tires. **Depreciation:** Very slow. **Insurance cost:** Above average. **Annual maintenance cost:** Less than average. **Parts supply/cost:** Good supply of relatively inexpensive parts. **Highway/city fuel economy:** *2.4L:* 9.2/12.6 L/100 km with a manual transmission; *3.3L:* 11.4/14.2 L/100 km with a manual transmission, 11.1/14.8 L/100 km with an automatic; *3.3L and 4×4:* 11.9/14.5 L/100 km with a manual tranny, 11.7/15.6 L/100 km with an automatic; *4.0L:* 10.1/13.5 L/100 km with a manual, 10.2/14.6 L/100 km with an automatic. Be careful with this last estimate: "Real-world" owner reports say fuel consumption on vehicles equipped with an automatic gearbox is actually 15–20 percent higher than the government/industry figures.

QUALITY/RELIABILITY: Owner-reported problems: Complaints of transmission failures (front and rear differentials are easily damaged); oil, transmission fluid, and coolant leaks; cooling system problems; assorted squeaks and rattles; steering clunk or rattle; front bumper rattling; AC idler pulley whine and compressor continuing to run when defogger is switched off; engine chirping or tapping noise following a cold start; electrical short circuits; erratic speedometer performance; excessive fuel consumption; paint chipping and blisters; and the premature rusting of the front-wheel spindles. AC shuts down and won't operate; engine drivebelt fails frequently and squeals constantly; Check Engine light comes on because of a faulty fuel tank, canister, or valve assembly; Airbag warning light stays lit; the grille stains from windshield wiper fluid; and rainwater leaks into the interior:

> Water enters the vehicle when parked on an uphill incline. The water enters through the air vents under the cowling and drops onto the blower motor under the passenger side dashboard. The water then exits the blower motor through an electrical connector and onto the front passenger carpet. Nissan has offered no remedy for the problem.

Warranty performance: Below average.

ROAD PERFORMANCE: Acceleration/torque: Sluggish 4-cylinder performance, though the non-supercharged V6 is an adequate performer. Supercharged version is peppier, but no more so than larger V6 engines offered by the competition. **Transmission:** Smooth and quiet shifting with the automatic gearbox. **Steering:** Competent steering that's a bit vague on-centre. **Routine handling:** Corners well, with minimal body lean; however, the Xterra's truck platform doesn't react well to sudden steering corrections. **Emergency handling:** Acceptable, though the steering feels too loose at higher speeds. **Braking:** Quite good; some fading after successive stops.

SAFETY SUMMARY: Airbags: Optional and standard side airbags. Reports of airbags failing to deploy. **ABS:** Standard 4W; disc/drum. **Safety belt pretensioners:** Standard. **Traction control:** Standard. **Head restraints F/R:** *2000:* ★★★/★★; *2001:* ★★★★; *2002–03:* ★★★/★★; *2005–08:* ★. **Visibility F/R:** ★★★★★. **Maximum load capacity:** *Pre-2005:* 885 lb.; *2005 and later:* 920 lb. **Pet transport:** ★★★★★. An excellent off-road pet crate hauler, thanks to high road clearance and tall and squared-off styling. Rubber cargo mats prevent muck accumulation and make the vehicle easy to clean.

SAFETY COMPLAINTS: All years: Sudden acceleration. • Front and side airbags may deploy inadvertently, or not deploy when needed. • Passenger-side airbag may be disabled even though a regular-sized passenger occupies the seat:

> Passenger air bag will not go on when my wife who weighs 110 lbs. [50 kg] sits in the passenger seat. We tried to get the air bag to go on [in] a couple of the same vehicles. None worked.

• Vehicle pulls sharply when braking. **2000**—In one incident, vehicle was parked with engine running and suddenly took off. • On one vehicle, three of the six wheel studs failed, and five of the six on another. • Rear end suddenly goes out of control. • Stalling at full throttle. • Driver's seat belt doesn't buckle. • ABS light comes on for no reason. **2001**—Fuel splashes out of filler tube when refuelling. • Right rear wheel and axle fly off vehicle. • Centre seat belt won't adequately accommodate a child safety seat. • Windshield wipers stop intermittently. • Dash lights are way too dim. **2002**—Sudden loss of power, and stalling. • Vehicle wanders all over the road. • When keyless remote entry is activated, airbag deploys. • Axle-bearing inner seal failure. **2003**—Vehicle suddenly goes out of control when brakes are lightly applied. • General Grabber tire blowout. • Complete brake loss. • Driver-side upper ball joint collapses, leading to loss of steering. • Brake and gas pedals are mounted too close together. **2004**—Engine fire caused by a faulty fuel-line clamp. • Side mirrors show distorted images. • Fuses ignite. • Cruise control causes engine to surge. • Wobbly gear; takes forever to get out of 4×4. • Dash lights and gauges operate erratically. **2005**—Rear differential failures:

> At 24,000 miles [38,600 km] the rear differential had to be replaced. It took over 6 weeks to get the part. Again at 42,000 [67,600 km] it needs to be replaced for the same problem.

• Recall campaign corrective parts are slow to arrive (trailer hitch). **2006**—The vehicle frame hits the axle when passing over small dips in the road. • Vehicle surges forward when brakes are applied. • Sudden steering failure. • Steering is degraded as vehicle reaches 100 km/h. • Fuel gauge gives false readings. • Dash lights come on or go off for no reason. **2007**—Steering may suddenly lock up. • Off-road jarring may cause the side curtain airbags to deploy for no reason:

> I was driving through plain mud on a plain dirt ground and without any impact, nor any bad driving, the curtain airbags from both sides deployed and injured me. For those interested in reviewing the video, the link is *www.youtube.com/watch?v=Gw6HUoQ2gvl.*

Secret Warranties/Internal Bulletins/Service Tips

All years: Cracked right-hand exhaust manifold. **1999–2004**—Coolant problems may be caused by a defective radiator cap. **2000**—If the MIL comes on, it may be because of poor grounding between the intake manifold and the engine cylinder head. • Idle fluctuation can be eliminated by updating the electronic control module (ECM) program. • Tips on troubleshooting Xterra squeaks and rattles. **2000–02**—Troubleshooting a noisy transfer case and hard shifting. • Bearing noise. • Coolant leak from intake manifold water outlet. **2001**—Idle fluctuation when coasting to a stop with the clutch depressed. • Roof paint damage at lower edge of roof-rack air dam. • Paint chipping at the rear of the hood or top of the fender area. • Water may have entered the distributor assembly. • V6 engines may experience a rough idle or engine vibration at idle. **2001–02**—Goodwill warranty will replace faulty window regulators free of charge. **2001–04**—Headlight fogging. **2002**—Engine knocking noise. • Coolant leak from intake manifold water outlet. • Steering pull during braking. • Airbag warning light continually flashes. • Malfunctioning engine MIL. • Bearing noise from transfer case area. • Oil leak from the front transfer-case oil seal. **2002–04**—Cold engine rattle or clatter. **2003**—ABS light stays lit. • All lights shut down. • AC won't turn off. **2004**—Tips on silencing engine clatter when starting up in cold weather. • Remedies for brake shudder. • Special campaign to tighten the differential's left front flange-fixing bolt to prevent oil leakage or excessive noise. **2005**—Free body control module sub-harness to improve electrical connection for trailering. **2005–06**—No-start in cold weather (replace the IPDM module). • Rear leaf spring squeaks. • Right front seatback rattles and moves sideways. **2005–07**—Remedy for engine chirping or squeaking.

XTERRA PROFILE

	2000	2001	2002	2003	2004	2005	2006	2007
Cost Price ($) (negotiable)								
Xterra (12%)	29,998	28,498	29,498	29,798	29,798	32,700	33,748	33,848
Used Prices ($)								
Xterra ▲	6,500	8,000	9,500	11,000	12,000	14,500	17,500	20,000
Xterra ▼	5,500	6,500	8,000	9,500	11,000	12,500	16,000	18,000
Reliability	4	5	5	5	5	5	5	5
Crash Safety (F)	4	4	4	4	4	4	4	4
Side	4	4	4	4	5	5	5	5
IIHS Side	—	—	—	—	—	5	5	5
Offset	3	3	3	3	3	5	5	5
Rollover	—	2	2	2	—	—	3	3

Note: The 2008 models rate similarly to the 2007s. IIHS's 2005–08 side-impact protection rating drops to three stars on vehicles lacking side airbags.

RATING: Above Average (2005–07). The X-Trail was dropped for 2008. Nissan's X-Trail isn't very high-tech, and it's not as refined as the Honda and Toyota competition. The small, five-passenger SUV has been on sale in the rest of the world (excluding the United States) since the end of 2000, which means that Nissan's engineers have had ample time to work out the early production bugs (a problem still afflicting recent Altimas, Maximas, Quests, and Titans). **Strong points:** Few first-year reliability problems, and competitively priced. The 4-cylinder engine is quiet and smooth. A huge, easy-to-operate sunroof makes the cabin seem more spacious than it is, and there's very little wind buffeting with the sunroof open. Good outward visibility due mainly to the high seating. You will find the ride a bit stiff but comfortable. The 8.1/10.8 L/100km (highway/city) fuel consumption rating is fairly realistic. There isn't any IIHS or NHTSA crashworthiness data available because the X-Trail isn't sold in the States; however, European, Japanese, and Australian crash testers have given the 2001 and later X-Trails a four-star rating for occupant protection in offset collisions (see *users.tpg.com.au/mpaine/ncaplist.html*). **Weak points:** A little sluggish at 80–110 km/h (expect a 0–100 km/h time of just over 10 seconds), and the automatic tranny is hesitant to downshift. Vague steering. Some jarring when going over bumps, potholes, and cracks. Problematic rear-seat access. Some tire noise as well as squeaks and rattles from the hatch, dash, and pedals. Head restraints are positioned too far back and seem to be bargain-basement prototypes—you can feel the seatback flex when you put your head on it. The power-window switch isn't very accessible on the 2006 models. **New for 2008:** Replaced by the 2008 Rogue (see Appendix I), the 2007 X-Trail Bonavista was the X-Trail's last model sold in Canada, although it is still sold throughout Asia, Europe, and Latin America. A 2009 X-Trail diesel may arrive at the end of 2008.

2007 X-TRAIL TECHNICAL DATA

POWERTRAIN (REAR-DRIVE/4×4)
Engine: 2.5L 4-cyl. (165 hp); Transmissions: 5-speed manual. • 4-speed auto.
DIMENSION/CAPACITY
Passengers: 2/3; Wheelbase: 103.3 in.; H: 65.9/L: 175.4/W: 69.5 in.; Headroom F/R: 3.0/3.0 in.; Legroom F/R: 40.0/26.0 in.; Cargo volume: 29.2 cu. ft.; Fuel tank: 60L/regular; Tow limit: 2,000 lb.; Load capacity: 800 lb.; GVWR: 2,913–2,958 lb.; Turning circle: 34.8 ft.; Ground clearance: 7.8 in.; Weight: 3,121 lb.

MODEL HISTORY: The X-Trail was launched in Canada as a 2005 model and is based on the Nissan C (compact) car platform used by the Sentra. Equipped with a fully independent suspension and all-wheel drive, 2007s started at $30,998. Resale values are also fairly high. Used 2007s are worth $22,000–23,000. A second-series 2005 front-drive now fetches $11,500–$12,500. Similarly, a 2005 AWD variant that once sold for $27,200 is now worth $13,500–$14,500. A 5-speed manual is available, but only on the all-wheel-drive versions. X-Trail competes in the small SUV niche that includes the Honda CR-V, Ford Escape, Mazda Tribute, Jeep Liberty, Subaru Forester, Toyota RAV4, Hyundai Santa Fe, Mitsubishi Outlander, Saturn VUE, Suzuki Vitara/Grand Vitara, and Chevrolet Tracker and Equinox.

The X-Trail is powered by a peppy 165-hp 2.5L 4-cylinder Sentra/Altima engine that'll give the small Honda and Toyota SUVs a run for their money. Both the 5-speed manual and 4-speed automatic transmissions work effortlessly, making this a fun car to drive if you have a bias toward cruising rather than off-roading. A fully independent suspension, responsive steering, and exceptionally well-performing four-wheel vented disc brakes with ABS enhance handling. A Snow-Mode switch, standard on all front-drive models, is particularly useful in that it retards engine power to provide extra traction in slippery conditions.

The X-Trail's unusually tall and boxy styling takes a little bit of getting used to, but it does provide a surprisingly large amount of interior room for dog crates, many cleverly located storage compartments, plenty of legroom and headroom, a low step-in height, and a nice view of the road (though the extra-wide rear D-pillars obstruct the view somewhat).

Saturn

VUE ★

RATING: Not Recommended (2002–08). You couldn't buy a worse SUV, and that includes the Ford Explorer and defunct Lada Niva. Honda gave a new heart to this dying patient with its 3.5L V6, while GM cut if off at the knees with its failure-prone CVT transmission. Will its re-engineered, restyled 2008 model cure the VUE's ills? Not likely, with the first year's production using a United Nations of parts suppliers. Nevertheless, the 2008 has some potential, judging by the high-quality marks Opel has received in Europe as of late. **Strong points:** Honda's 3.5L V6 and 5-speed automatic transmission work well in the Odyssey and Pilot and do just as well with the lighter VUE. Some other pluses: Dent-resistant plastic side body panels (up to the 2007 model year); head-protecting side curtain airbags; average handling and a comfortable ride; easily accessible, clearly marked instruments and controls; low step-in height and trunk liftover; and an adequate, versatile interior that includes a split-folding seat to accommodate long objects. **Weak points:** Mediocre acceleration with the base 2.2L engine; the GM-bred 3.0L V6 had a history of factory-induced glitches that compromise performance and overall powertrain reliability; CVT automatic transmission is not very durable and is hard to service; AWD is slow to engage; not a serious off-roader (no low-range gearing, for example); there's excessive torque steer (twisting) when

2008 VUE TECHNICAL DATA

POWERTRAIN (FRONT-DRIVE/4×4)
Engines: 2.4L 4-cyl. (169 hp) • 2.4L hybrid (169 hp) • 3.5L V6 (215 hp) • 3.6L V6 (250 hp); Transmissions: 5-speed man. • 4-speed auto. • 6-speed auto. • CVT

DIMENSION/CAPACITY
Passengers: 2/3; Wheelbase: 106.6 in.; H: 66.5/L: 181.3/W: 71.5 in.; Headroom F/R: 6.0/6.0 in.; Legroom F/R: 43.1/32.4 in.; Cargo volume: 36.5 cu. ft.; Fuel tank: 63L/regular; Tow limit: 1,500 lb. (3,500 lb. with the V6); Load capacity: 1,175 lb.; GVWR: 4,598–4,839 lb.; Turning circle: 42.0 ft.; Ground clearance: 6.5 in.; Weight: 3,740 lb.

accelerating, and excessive body roll and rocking in turns; there's lots of noseplow when stopping; the vague steering is too light at low speeds, requiring drivers to constantly make corrections (corrected on the 2008 model); there's excessive engine noise when accelerating, and lots of road noise; the driver's visor is too low; the seats aren't as comfortable as those offered by competitors; the liftgate doesn't have separate opening glass; there are no ceiling-mounted grab handles for easy entry and exit; the second-row seats are firmer and not as comfortable as the front seats; the rear seats are too low; the interior and plastic trim look cheap; the vehicle is rated "Poor" in the IIHS side-impact crash test, and almost rolled over in NHTSA tests; and quality control is below average. Leak-prone hybrid batteries.

New for 2008: Re-engineered and more sleekly styled, the new VUE is based on the Opel Antera and reworked by GM's North American, European, and Korean divisions. It carries three powertrains shared among four models. The XE with front-drive and the Green Line use a 169-hp 2.4L 4-cylinder mated to a 4-speed automatic. Both models also have a 5-speed manual option. The all-wheel-drive version gets a 215-hp 3.5L V6 engine. The XR and Red Line models now come with a 250-hp 3.6L V6 with variable valve timing. A 6-speed automatic transmission is the norm for all V6 equipped models. Handling is enhanced by an independent suspension and anti-roll bars, and noise has been reduced through the addition of more effective soundproofing materials. Note that the dent-resistant plastic panels that were once a Saturn hallmark have been replaced by steel body panels. Safety equipment includes standard anti-lock brakes, side-impact airbags for the front seats, side curtain airbags, active front head restraints, and an electronic stability system. Also standard is GM's rollover-mitigation system, which brakes the outside wheels and deploys the side curtain airbags if a rollover seems imminent.

MODEL HISTORY: The part-time 4×4 VUE is a conventionally styled, compact SUV that targets competitors in the Ford Escape, Honda CR-V, and Toyota RAV4 class. Until its 2008 model revamp, the VUE's performance and quality shortcomings put it in the rear of the SUV pack. GM's insistence that Saturn models are somehow better than the competition—because Saturn is a "different" car company that cares about its customers—rings hollow with legions of owners stuck with problem-plagued VUE powertrains. *VUE Green Line hybrid:* Launched as a 2007 model, the $28,795 Green Line sold for about $500 more than the V6-equipped VUE and almost $5,000 less than the Recommended Ford Escape hybrid. It is not as fuel-efficient as the smaller Honda Civic and Toyota Prius hybrids and, unlike the Japanese competition, doesn't hold its value as well (the 2007 is now worth about $23,000, or almost $6,000 less than a year ago). Acceleration is adequate, but the 4-speed transmission is a bit jerky when changing gears. There have been very few owner complaints; however, electrical problems are often mentioned:

> Our new 2007 Saturn VUE Green Line hybrid SUV had a Check Engine and Battery light at 2,334 mileage [3,800 km]. We luckily were in town and parked the car in our driveway, [and had it towed] to the dealership for repair. This could have resulted in failure of the vehicle in traffic or on an interstate, with catastrophic consequences. Saturn had a tech doc# 1978388 and TSB# 07-06-03-004 as noted on our service

receipt. It is very disturbing that they knew the problem existed with these vehicles and did not perform [an] engine harness jumper replacement and reprogram before the new vehicle was sold. I would refer the NHTSA to the Edmund[s] Townhall Forum at the web address below...which also list[s] incidences of the Saturn VUE Green Line stopping in traffic due to the same problem (*townhall-talk.edmunds.com/webx/. f0d7fdb*). I believe this is a potentially life-threatening safety problem that needs to be addressed.

2003—Expanded powertrain combination. **2004**—Honda's 250-hp V6 engine replaces the unreliable GM-bred powerplant. It delivers lots of power on regular fuel and offers a high degree of reliability and durability. A new Red Line "high-performance" version sits 2.5 cm (1 in.) lower, uses a tighter suspension, offers better-performing 18-inch wheels, and sports a racier appearance. Horsepower remains the same, no matter what the salesperson says. **2005**—Red Line enhanced high-performance handling and cosmetic improvements. A slight body makeover with changes to the hood, grille, and headlights, as well as an updated interior, radio, centre stack, and door trim. **2007**—A 170-hp gas-electric hybrid model came on board.

COST ANALYSIS: Unless you want to take a chance on GM's 2008 hybrid for $30,790, or $24,795 in the States (I suggest buying a used Ford Escape hybrid instead), get a used, $12,500 2004 VUE with a conventional Honda engine. A 2008 entry-level VUE sells new for $26,990 (CDN) plus $1,200 freight/PDI. That same VUE sold across the border would cost about $21,450 (U.S.). **Best alternatives:** Ford Escape, Honda CR-V or Element, Hyundai Tucson or Santa Fe, Jeep TJ or Liberty, Mazda Tribute, Nissan Xterra or X-Trail, Subaru Forester, and Toyota Highlander or RAV4. **Rebates:** $3,000 rebates to clear out the 2008s. **Delivery/PDI:** $1,200. **Warranty:** Bumper-to-bumper 3 years/60,000 km; powertrain 5 years/100,000 km; rust perforation 5 years/unlimited km. **Supplementary warranty:** Absolutely. **Options:** I recommend the Honda-sourced V6 engine and traction control along with side curtain airbags. The 2007–08 hybrid option is Not Recommended until more reliability/safety data is available. Replace historically poor-performing Firestone and Bridgestone original-equipment tires with Michelins. **Depreciation:** Faster than average. **Insurance cost:** Average. **Parts supply/ cost:** Parts can be costly; hybrid parts and servicing costs are expected to be particularly high. **Annual maintenance cost:** Higher than average. **Highway/ city fuel economy:** 2.2L: 8.1/11.0 L/100 km; 3.5L V6: 7.8/11.9 L/100 km; *Hybrid:* 8.8/6.7 L/100 km. Hybrids typically burn much more fuel than advertised.

QUALITY/RELIABILITY: Below average—with unreliable powertrain, brake, electrical system, and body components—plus there's a mountain of service bulletins that cast doubt on the VUE's long-term dependability. Honda engines in later models are fairly dependable. Hybrid engines often stall out due to a well-known electrical problem. **Owner-reported problems:** Engine knocking and stalling, automatic transmission and suspension failures, hard downshifts, steering-column thumping, frequent brake caliper and rotor replacement, and premature failure of Bridgestone tires. Horn is hard to operate, the key sticks in the ignition switch, there's a plethora of electrical malfunctions, anti-lock brakes hammer excessively, the driver's seatback is easily broken, the cupholder is so low as to be useless, water collects in the roof rack pin wells, and there are excessive wind, rattling, and brake noises. **Warranty performance:** When you first buy the car new, dealers will welcome you with open arms. But after the warranty expires, you'll get arm gestures of a different sort! Let's just say that after-warranty assistance is parsimonious, at best.

 SAFETY SUMMARY: Vehicle has a reputation for being tippy at highway speeds, a fault corrected with the 2008 VUE:

> 2005 Saturn VUE feels like it is going to tip over when taking sharp turns. This is particularly noticeable when driving at high rates of speed but within the posted speed limits such as leaving the interstate freeways onto adjoining on ramps/off ramps which tend to have various curves in the road. The car feels scary when this happens and requires a complete reduction of speed by the driver with all other nearby cars and SUVs passing by with no visible similar handling problem.

Airbags: Optional side airbags. Numerous reports of airbags failing to deploy. **ABS:** Optional; standard. Front disc/rear drum. There have been many complaints of ABS failures and the premature wearout of brake components. **Head restraints F/R: ★★. Visibility F/R: ★★★★. Pet transport: ★★★★.**

SAFETY COMPLAINTS: All years: Loss of steering, transmission failure, airbag malfunction, chronic stalling and surging, and horn is hard to activate. **2002**—Transmission fluid lines are vulnerable to road debris. **2002–03**—Airbags fail to deploy. • Reduced Power light comes on, and vehicle shuts down. • Torque steer jerks car to the right when accelerating. **2003**—Transmission breakdown (variable drive unit). • Vehicle slides backward when stopped on a hill. • Inside door latches can't open the door. • Incorrect speedometer readings. • Electrical short circuit in the signal/headlight control stalk. • Headlight and daytime driving lights burn out prematurely, and vehicle stalls when it rains. **2004**—Side airbags fail to deploy. • Rear suspension collapses. • Cruise control won't disengage. • Recall repairs related to the Rear Drive Module cause excessive front-wheel spin and torque steer when accelerating. • Manual transmission failure. • When the brakes are applied, the automatic transmission shifts to Neutral. • Vehicle continues to roll even though brakes are applied. • Chronic electrical shorts. • Corrosion from bolt holes in roof-rail mounting. • Rear window shatters when side door is closed. **2005**—Airbags fail to deploy, or deploy without inflating. • Vehicle rolls backward when in Drive. • CVT transmission slippage:

> If the car is cold, the computer will prevent the transmission from being engaged, to avoid transmission damage. They also said that the slipping in the transmission was "normal operation" for the CVT transmission. Well, I did not have this issue happen when I test drove the car, and for approximately 5 months after. I do not have the problem for a week or so after an oil change. I feel that there is a blatant performance problem with the CVT (continuous variable transmission). Continuous implies that the

transmission varies "continuously." I can assure you, if my car had done this while I was test driving it, I never would have bought the car. It is a safety hazard, and makes me extremely anxious when I am driving, as there is no way to anticipate when it will happen. Saturn has repeatedly stated that this "slipping" is normal. I have found several web sites on the web with people complaining of this exact problem.

Also, see GM's March 2006 "What, me worry?" service bulletin in "Secret Warranties/Internal Bulletins/Service Tips." **2006**—Vehicle suddenly shuts down and won't restart due to a defective fuel pump. **2007**—More reports of hybrid stalling, followed by a no-start condition, caused by an electrical short. • Seatback and tire failures (Bridgestone).

Secret Warranties/Internal Bulletins/Service Tips

2001–06—Diagnosis for trannies stuck in Second or Third gear, harsh upshifts, and an upshift/downshift clunk. **2001–07**—No-starts can be traced to either stripped battery threads or a faulty battery bolt. **2002**—Engine flare during 2–3 upshifts. • Timing-belt coolant contamination. • Rattle or tapping noise from steering-column shroud area. • Creaking noise may come from left or right rear of vehicle while driving. • Troubleshooting a defective MIL. • Rear-seat cushion cover is baggy or loose along the bottom edge. • Horn design makes it difficult to activate at night. • AC and lower condenser are exposed to road debris. **2002–03**—No-starts, stalling, a rough-running engine, and a poor idle may all be caused by a stuck engine intake manifold pressure-relief valve. • A history of faulty valve seals and poor cold-weather engine performance:

BLUE SMOKE AT START-UP	
BULLETIN NO.: 04-06-01-010	DATE: APRIL 2004

(Inspect Valve Stem Seal Color and Perform Service Procedure)
2000–04 Saturn L-Series
2002–03 Saturn VUE with 3.0L V6
This condition may be caused by leaking valve seals (on engines with brown seal color) or excessive clearance between valve stem and valve guide.

OIL LEAKS IN SUB-FREEZING TEMPS.	
BULLETIN NO.: 04-06-01-001	DATE: JANUARY 2004

OIL LEAKS FROM ENGINE AFTER SUB-FREEZING TEMPERATURES
(Remove Ice/Water from Positive Crankcase Ventilation (PCV) Hose and Re-route Hose)
2002–03 Saturn VUE Vehicles
with 3.0L V6 Engine

• Powertrain vibration when AC is activated. • A moan/growl noise and vibration from rear of vehicle can be corrected by replacing the rear-drive module's limited slip clutch drum. • Torque converter shudder, vibration. • Shudder, vibration in Reverse. • Transaxle whine. • Starter stays engaged after start-up. • Electrical accessories fail intermittently. • Fluid leak caused by loose VTI transaxle-converter housing bolts. • Transmission won't go into gear (see bulletin). • Noisy upper steering column. • Incorrect speedometer and fuel gauge readings. • Insufficient AC cooling and heating. • Instrument panel condensation. • Fluid drips onto driver's floormat. • Engine compartment whistling and chirping. • Front-end

NO SHIFT/NO GEAR ENGAGEMENT

BULLETIN NO.: 03-07-30-023 **DATE: NOVEMBER 2003**

VEHICLE DOES NOT SHIFT OR MOVE AFTER RUNNING FOR A PERIOD OF TIME AND/OR CHECK ENGINE LIGHT IS ON AND DTC P0741 IS SET

(Replace Torque Converter, Valve Body, Clean Out Transaxle and Install New Flex Plate Bolts and Washers)
2002–03 Saturn VUE

squeaking. • Buzzing, grinding, and growling from rear of vehicle when fuel pump is activated. • Clunk, pop, or click when accelerating or decelerating. • Upgraded liftgate latching system. **2002–04**—Free replacement of the rear lateral link assembly, a suspension component that may fail during hard cornering. A one-day rental ($35 U.S.) is authorized. **2002–05**—Free tranny case cover assembly and filter if transmission won't shift into Drive or Reverse. **2002–06**—Front-end rattle. • Front-seat squeaking. • Excessive windshield wind noise. **2002–07**—Automatic transmission vent fluid leakage. • Poor acceleration, excessive fuel consumption, and a generally rough-running engine may all be attributable to clogged fuel injectors, says TSB #03-06-04-030D, issued May 3, 2007. • Free replacement of the instrument panel cluster if the lenses are broken, cracked, scratched, or cloudy. **2003–05**—Automatic transmission grind or rattle when starting up requires the replacement of the case cover assembly, torque converter, and filter. **2003–06**—Excessive A-pillar wind noise. **2003–07**—Manual transmission grinds when passing from Third to Fourth gear. • Sticking ignition lock cylinder. **2004**—Special warranty policy adjustment for the CVT transmission. • Hard starts. • Moan, growl, and vibration when turning. • Steering rattle. • Suspension pop, clunk noise. • AC hissing. • Exhaust system rattle or buzz. • Drone noise between 80 and 120 km/h. • Outside rear-view mirror cracking. **2004–05**—Remedy for an inoperative cruise control. **2004–06**—Incredibly, GM says delayed CVT transmission shifts are "normal" (see bulletin on following page). **2006–07**—Poor radio performance. • Hem flange sealer is *gratis* for corrosion protection, as well as free body panel replacement and repaint for stone damage from road debris kicked up by the tires:

FREE PAINT DAMAGE REPLACEMENT/REPAINT

BULLETIN NO.: 06-08-51-004 **DATE: OCTOBER 24, 2006**

Paint damage on lower rear rocker panel extensions (replace existing panels, paint and apply film to replacement parts).

2007—Reversed instrument panel wiring could compromise side airbag deployment.

TRANSAXLE SHIFT LAG AND/OR HESITATION DURING WARM-UP FOLLOWING INITIAL START-UP— NORMAL CHARACTERISTIC, NO SERVICE NECESSARY

2004–06 Saturn VUE with 5AT 5-Speed Automatic Transaxle

The 5AT transaxle (RPO MJ7/MJ8) is a 5-speed, electronically controlled, automatic transaxle featuring transaxle shift calibration that adjusts and assures consistent shift feel. However, transaxle shift feel adaptation on the 5AT automatic transaxle does not initiate until after the first series of shifts are completed, after a cold soak (i.e. when the vehicle parked for extended periods of time). The Saturn VUE SAT automatic transaxle shift calibration is designed to provide optimum shift feel during normal driving, and more specifically, during normal operating temperatures (transaxle fluid temperatures of 65–110°C [150–230°F]).

This method of providing consistent shift feel is to ensure the best possible shift feel during the ideal operating temperatures. Because of this programming, some customers may experience shift performance that is described as firm or a sensation of a slight up shift lag when comparing the shift feel after warm up to pre-warm up operating modes.

During initial pre-warm up periods, customers may experience a lag/delay during 1–2, 2–3 upshift after accelerating from a stop, or during acceleration during a rolling stop. The delayed 1–2/2–3 upshift can occur between the speeds of 32–48 km/h (20–30 mph), during the initial warm up period. As the transaxle fluid warms, the transaxle control module (TCM) calibration is optimized to refine shift feel for smoothness and responsiveness during the normal range of temperatures experienced.

The shift feel characteristics experienced by customers is considered a normal characteristic. There is no need to attempt a repair for cold shift performance.

VUE PROFILE

	2002	2003	2004	2005	2006	2007
Cost Price ($) (negotiable)						
Base Vue (21%)	21,565	21,980	22,745	23,095	22,995	23,300
Green Line (15%)	—	—	—	—	—	28,795
4×4 (22%)	26,055	27,595	26,390	26,595	29,795	30,725
Used Values ($)						
Base Vue ▲	5,500	6,500	7,500	9,000	12,000	15,000
Base Vue ▼	4,500	5,500	6,500	7,500	10,500	14,000
Green Line ▲	—	—	—	—	—	19,000
Green Line ▼	—	—	—	—	—	17,000
4×4 ▲	6,500	8,500	9,500	11,500	17,000	20,000
4×4 ▼	5,000	7,000	8,500	10,000	15,500	19,000
Reliability	2	2	2	2	2	2
Crash Safety (F)	5	5	5	5	5	5
Side	5	5	5	5	5	5
IIHS Side	1	1	1	1	1	1
Offset	5	5	5	5	5	5
Rollover	3	3	3	3	3	3

Subaru

BAJA

See Appendix I.

FORESTER, IMPREZA, TRIBECA, WRX  ★★★★/★★★/★★/★★★

2008 FORESTER TECHNICAL DATA

POWERTRAIN (AWD)
Engines: 2.5L 4-cyl. (173 hp) • 2.5L turbo (230 hp); Transmissions: 5-speed man. • 4-speed auto.

DIMENSION/CAPACITY
Passengers: 2/3; Wheelbase: 99.0 in.; H: 65.0/L: 176.6/W: 68.1 in.; Headroom F/R: 5.5/5.0; Legroom F/R: 41.5/27.0 in.; Cargo volume: 32.0 cu. ft.; Fuel tank: 60L/regular, premium; Tow limit: 2,400 lb.; Load capacity: 900 lb.; GVWR: 4,120 lb.; Turning circle: 38.0 ft.; Ground clearance: 7.0 in.; Weight: 3,185 lb.

2008 IMPREZA TECHNICAL DATA

POWERTRAIN (AWD)
Engines: 2.5L 4-cyl. (173 hp) • 2.0L turbo (227 hp) • 2.5L turbo (230 hp) • 2.5L turbo (300 hp); Transmissions: 5-speed man. • 6-speed man. • 4-speed auto.

DIMENSION/CAPACITY
Passengers: 2/3; Wheelbase: 99.0 in.; H: 57.0/L: 174.0/ W: 69.0 in.; Headroom F/R: 4.5/1.5 in.; Legroom F/R: 41.0/26.0 in.; Cargo volume: 11.0 cu. ft.; Fuel tank: 60L/regular, premium; Tow limit: 2,000 lb.; Load capacity: 830 lb.; GVWR: 4,120 lb.; Turning circle: 39.0 ft.; Ground clearance: 5.0 in.; Weight: 3,165 lb.

RATING: *Forester:* Above Average (2006–08); Average (1994–2005). *Impreza:* Average (1997–2008). *Tribeca:* Below Average (2006–08). Living on borrowed time, the Tribeca (originally the B9 Tribeca) is overweight and overpriced, and it's outclassed by the competition. *WRX:* Average (2008); Below Average (2002–07). Earlier WRX models have been downgraded mainly because of their tricky handling and reliability issues (powertrain, brake, and steering). Except for the Forester, Subaru's model lineup is mostly the bland leading the bland. There's nothing remarkable about Subaru except for its early use of AWD for its entire lineup as a desperate move to stave off bankruptcy in the mid-1990s. Incidentally, the company isn't in great financial shape right now. Quality control has declined markedly over the past five years, and customer service has suffered equally. Smart shoppers will choose a cheaper Asian SUV until Subaru lowers its prices and raises performance and quality-control levels. The 2006 Forester improvements were a good start. **Strong points:** Some long-awaited performance and size improvements. A refined AWD drivetrain; a powerful WRX engine, and good acceleration with the base 2.5L; competent handling, without any torque steer; impressive crashworthiness; well-appointed base models; and a nice control layout. **Weak points:** Generally stiff-riding, and the Outback Sport doesn't ride as comfortably or handle as well as other Imprezas. Problematic entry and exit; the coupe's narrow rear window and large rear pillars hinder rear visibility; wagon has limited cargo volume; heater is insufficient, and air distribution is inadequate; comfort is compromised by the WRX's short wheelbase, suspension, and 16-inch tires; front- and rear-seat legroom may be insufficient for tall drivers;

small doors and entryways restrict rear access; the WRX requires premium fuel; and there's a surprisingly large number of safety-related complaints that include complete brake loss, chronic surging, and stalling. **New for 2008:** *Forester:* Nothing significant; the Forester will be redesigned for its 2009 model year and should be shunned during its first six months. *Impreza, WRX:* This year's Impreza and WRX are restyled; the sedans are almost five inches longer and two inches wider than their predecessors, and five-door versions are two inches shorter than the 2007 models. The WRX STI sits on a stiffer chassis and is available only as a five-door. The 2.5L turbocharged and intercooled engine gets 12 additional horses that increase total horsepower to 305; the all-wheel-drive system has three automatic performance settings and six manual differential-locking settings. A new double-wishbone rear suspension and Brembo performance brakes with larger rotors round out this year's changes. *Tribeca:* Greeted by dismal sales during its first two years on the market, the Tribeca has been slightly restyled and gets an upgraded 3.6L 6-cylinder engine that runs on regular fuel. The premium-fuelled 3.0L powerplant has been ditched along with the B9 moniker, which no one ever understood, anyhow. A tweaked suspension smoothes out the ride.

MODEL HISTORY: The full-time 4×4 Impreza is essentially a shorter Legacy with additional convenience features. It comes as a four-door sedan, a wagon, and an Outback Sport Wagon, all powered by a 165-hp 2.5L flat-four engine. The rally-inspired WRX models have a more powerful 227-hp 2.0L turbocharged engine, lots of standard performance features, a sport suspension, an aluminum hood with a functional scoop, and higher-quality instruments, controls, trim, and seats. The 2003 Impreza and WRX were carried over unchanged.

Another Subaru spin-off, the Forester is a cross between a tall wagon and a sport-utility. Based on the shorter Impreza, the Forester adds eight horses to the Legacy Outback's 2.5L 165-hp engine and couples it to a 5-speed manual transmission or an optional 4-speed automatic. Its road manners are more subdued, and its engine provides more power and torque for off-roading than most vehicles its size.

All models: 1999—Stronger engines, more torque, and upgraded transmissions. **2002**—The 2.2L 4-cylinder was dropped, along with Subaru's pretensions for making affordable entry-level cars. Totally redesigned models include the 2.5 TS Sport Wagon, 2.5 RS sedan, Outback Sport Wagon, WRX sporty sedan, and Sport Wagon. There is no longer a two-door version available. *Impreza:* **2004**—New front end with larger headlights and a restyled interior and exterior. **2006**—Given better-performing brakes and a freshened interior. *Forester:* **1999**—A quieter, torquier engine; a smoother-shifting transmission; and a more solid body. **2000**—Standard cruise control (L) and limited slip differential (S). **2003**—Improved interior materials, an upgraded suspension, and enhanced handling and ride quality. You'll also find larger tires and fenders as well as revised head restraints and side-impact airbags. **2004**—A turbocharged 210-hp 2.5L 4-banger, and a racier appearance. **2006**—More power, and a slightly restyled interior and exterior. The 2006 turbocharged XT adds 20 hp via a redesigned engine intake manifold (this could be troublesome in the future); other models get eight more horses, for a total of 173. A retuned suspension enhances ride smoothness and handling response, and there's improved braking feel on all models. Ground clearance has been slightly increased, an alarm system is now standard, and the 5-speed manual transmission isn't available with L.L. Bean models. *WRX:* **2003**— An AWD car for the high-performance crowd, the WRX is a goofy-looking, squat little wagon/SUV with a large rear end and a 227-hp 2.0L 4-cylinder engine mated to a high-boost turbocharger. **2004**—A 300-hp engine. **2006**—The 2.5L gets 20 extra horses (230). **2007**—The spec.B adds standard stability control and a Torsen rear differential, while the WRX STI adopts a 6-speed manual transmission.

Tribeca

Sized between the Forester and Legacy Outback, Subaru's $42,000 Tribeca is the automaker's first crossover SUV. Its on- and off-road performance is similar to that of a slightly bigger Legacy—impressive body control, a comfortable and supple ride (even with standard 18-inch wheels), and an adequate steering response that's muted by the car's heft.

2008 TRIBECA TECHNICAL DATA

POWERTRAIN (AWD)

Engine: 3.6L 6-cyl. (256 hp);
Transmission: 5-speed auto.

DIMENSION/CAPACITY

Passengers: 2/3, 2/3/2; Wheelbase: 108.2/189.8 in.; H: 66.4/W: 189.8/L:73.9 in.; Headroom F/R1/R2: 4.5/3.5/1.0 in.; Legroom F/R: 42.3/34.3 in.; Cargo volume: 37.5 cu. ft.; Fuel tank: 64L/ premium; Tow limit: 3,500 lb.; Load capacity: 900 lb.; GVWR: 5,700 lb.; Turning circle: 41.0 ft.; Ground clearance: 7.5 in.; Weight: 4,155 lb.

Cramped second- and third-row seating, excess weight, an unrealistically high list price, and atrocious fuel economy are the Tribeca's most serious drawbacks. Although its swoopy styling gives it an aerodynamic appearance, the car's 13.3 L/100 km (17.7 mpg) highway fuel consumption rating combined with its small gas tank means you'll quickly get to know your gas station attendants on a first-name basis.

Furthermore, the car lags in many other areas. For example, take its power-to-weight ratio: Tribeca has to haul 8.8 kg (19.4 lb.) per lb.-ft. of torque, while most of the competitors only need to pull around 7–8 kg (16–17 lb.). Even Nissan's fuel-thirsty Murano betters the Tribeca in the power-to-weight category. Also, the Tribeca has the smallest amount of rear legroom and the shortest combined front/rear legroom in a field where most automakers offer much more. Plus, it has one of the smallest cargo capacities and the smallest third-row cargo capacity.

Other minuses include spongy braking and excessive tire noise when cruising; the steering wheel blocks the view of the fuel and temperature gauges; the view rearward is obscured by thick rear pillars; and the small, hard-to-access third-row seats are for kids only, offering no legroom if the second-row seats are pushed rearward.

With the B9 Tribeca, Subaru undoubtedly did a pretty nice job of moving up in scale and class, but it has seriously misjudged the car's limited market potential. It screams "big SUV" at a time when buyers are downsizing their choices because of high fuel costs and inflated price tags for large Asian SUVs. Moreover, it will be an uphill battle to move the traditionally conservative, "function-over-form" Subaru commuter upscale. Despite its non-conformist looks and smooth boxer-six engine, I'm betting Subaru owners will walk away feeling betrayed.

COST ANALYSIS: Unlike some automakers, Subaru doesn't object that strongly to its American dealers selling to Canadian residents, and tries to keep sales in Canada by cutting prices. A 2009 Forester 2.5X costs $25,795—or $1,200 *less* than the 2008 version—in Canada; the same vehicle sold in the States retails for $21,195 (U.S.). Stay away from the Tribeca unless you buy a 2007 or later version. This means that first-series 2006 model glitches have been remedied. And for a savings of at least $10,000, get your 2009 Tribeca in the States, where it sells for $29,995 (U.S.) (five-passenger) or $30,995 (U.S.) (7-passenger). The 2008 base Impreza WRX starts at $32,995 in Canada and $24,350 (U.S.) in the States—also a sizeable savings. Both models are better choices than the less-refined 2005. Just remember to budget an extra $1,500 for an extended powertrain warranty to protect you from premature and repeated clutch failures. Cheaper 2002 redesigned Imprezas or an upgraded 2003 Forester are also good second choices. WRX versions are expensive Imprezas that equal the sporty performance of the Audi A4 and BMW 3 Series—cars costing $10,000 more. But can you handle the brake failures and quirky handling? **Best alternatives:** Excellent alternatives are the Toyota Matrix/Pontiac Vibe front-drive or AWD models. If you really don't need a 4×4, and most people don't, here are some front-drives worth considering: Honda Civic, Hyundai Elantra, Mazda3, and Toyota Corolla. Other alternatives are the Honda Pilot EX AWD and the Lexus RX 330 four-door AWD. **Rebates:** Subaru is so cash hungry, its MSRP has actually drifted lower over the years and $4,000 rebates and discounts are the norm. **Delivery/PDI:** $1,495. **Warranty:** Bumper-to-bumper 3 years/60,000 km; powertrain 5 years/100,000 km; rust perforation 5 years/unlimited km. **Supplementary warranty:** Not needed. **Options:** Larger tires smooth out the ride. **Depreciation:** Very slow for the Forester; average for the Impreza; and incredibly rapid with the Tribeca and WRX. **Insurance cost:** Higher than average. **Parts supply/cost:** Parts aren't easy to find, can be costly, and lead to delayed recall repairs. **Annual maintenance cost:** Higher than average. Mediocre, expensive servicing is hard to overcome because independent garages can't service key AWD components. **Highway/city fuel economy:** *2.5L:* 7.2/10.3 L/100 km; *WRX 2.0L turbo:* 8.0/11.8 L/100 km; *2.5L turbo:* 9.1/13.4 L/100 km.

 QUALITY/RELIABILITY: Poor sales are negatively affecting the quality of servicing and warranty work. Mediocre quality control. Subaru reps sometimes cop too much of an attitude when faced with serious safety-related complaints:

> While attempting to slow my 2003 WRX for a corner on a well groomed, dry gravel road, the ABS system of the car initiated a mode that would not allow the car's brakes to function at all. During the episode (which has been and can be re-created) pedal pressure and pedal height was maintained as during normal braking operations. The

brakes would not work despite the fact that I was standing with both feet on the brake pedal. I am in the process of disconnecting my ABS. Subaru North America claims that I'm nuts.

There's a history of premature powertrain, fuel system, and brake failures and some body panel and trim fit and finish deficiencies. Servicing quality is spotty. **Owner-reported problems:** Poor engine idling, cooling; frequent cold-weather stalling; manual transmission malfunctions (mostly clutch chatter and shudder); rear wheel bearing failures; alloy wheels cause excessive vibration; suspension clunks; premature exhaust system rust-out and early brake wear; minor electrical short circuits; catalytic converter failures; doors don't latch properly; water leaks and condensation problems from the top of the windshield or sunroof; windshield scratches too easily; and paint peeling. **Warranty performance:** Has declined markedly during the past couple of years (especially in relation to brake and clutch complaints).

SAFETY SUMMARY: Huge fold-away side mirrors. Front shoulder belts can be uncomfortable, and rear seat belts may be hard to buckle up. **Airbags:** Numerous reports of airbags failing to deploy; also reports of airbags injuring passengers or deploying but not inflating. **ABS:** Standard. There have been many complaints of ABS failures and the premature wearout of brake components. **Head restraints F/R:** *Forester 1999:* ★★/★; *2001–02:* ★★★/★★; *2003:* ★★★★★; *2006–08:* ★★★★★; *Impreza 2001:* ★★; *2002–03:* ★★★; *2005–08:* ★★★★★; *Impreza WRX 2004–07:* ★★; *Tribeca 2006–08:* ★★★★★. **Visibility F/R:** *Coupe:* ★★★★★/★★. **Pet transport:** ★★★. *Forester 2007:* The rear seats easily fold flat. It's tall enough to take a single large crate, but as with most smaller SUVs and wagons, the side-by-side crates won't fit. Optional rubber cargo mats are worth the extra cost. Tribeca's cargo space is insufficient for most pets.

SAFETY COMPLAINTS: *Impreza:* **All years:** Sudden acceleration, stalling, transmission failures, steering loss, airbag malfunctions, brake and engine lights continually on, and front seats move fore and aft. **1999**—Engine failure caused by a cracked #2 piston. • When accelerating or decelerating, vehicle will jerk because of excessive play in the front axle. • Front bumper skirt catches on parking blocks; the bumper twists and rips off. • Total loss of braking capability. • The centre rear seat belt's poor design prohibits the installation of many child safety seats. **2000**—A mountain of complaints relative to the loss of braking and premature wearout of key brake components. **2001**—ABS overreacts when braking over an irregular surface. • Rear wheel bearings fail repeatedly. **2002**—Chronic brake failures. • Brake rotors are frequently scored after only a few kilometres. • Many reports of blown transmissions. • First gear is hard to engage. **2003**—Sudden, unintended acceleration; brake pedal won't respond. • Very poor braking when passing over rough surfaces:

On my 2003 Subaru Impreza Outback Sport, the anti-lock brakes are dangerous. If you hit a bump while braking, it will trigger the ABS—and result in an almost complete loss of braking ability. I notice a bulletin is listed for the WRX only, but this is a major problem in my car as well.

• Seat belt ratchets tighten and refuse to unlock. • Windshield chips easily.
2004—Vehicle won't go into gear. • Complete loss of brakes. • Car wanders all
over the road because of defective suspension struts. **2004–05**—Windshield is
easily cracked. • Raw fuel smell in the cabin. **2004–06**—Airbags fail to deploy.
2005—Chronic rear strut failure. • Side window shatters spontaneously. **2006**—
Manual transmission's pitch rod mount is easily broken. • Bridgestone tire failures.
2007—More manual transmission failures. • Vehicle surges and bucks uncontrollably. • When shifting from Fifth to Fourth gear, the gears become stuck or shift
into Reverse. • Premature failure of Bridgestone tires. *Forester:* **2000**—Driver
burned from airbag deployment. • Sudden loss of transmission fluid. • Driver's
seatback may suddenly recline because seat belt gets tangled up in the recliner
lever. • Fuel-filler cap design is too complicated for gas station attendants to put
on properly, which causes the Check Engine light to come on. Driver, therefore,
has to pay dealer to reset the Check Engine light. **2000–01**—Frequent wheel
bearing failures. **2001**—Brake and accelerator pedals are too close together. • In a
collision, airbags failed to deploy and seat belt didn't restrain occupant. • In a
similar incident, shoulder belt allowed driver's head to hit the windshield. •
Headlights don't illuminate the edge of the road and are either too bright on High
or too dim on Low. • In one incident, alarm system self-activated, trapping a baby
inside the car until fire rescue arrived. **2002**—Dangerous delay and then surging
when accelerating forward or in Reverse. • Surging at highway speeds and stalling
at lower rpm. • Transmission failure; gears lock in Park intermittently. •
Intermittent backfire when shifting the manual transmission. • Open wheel design
allows snow and debris to pack in the area and throw wheel out of balance, creating dangerous vibrations. • High hood allows water onto the engine. (Note: The
preceding comments apply to the Forester but can be relevant to Impreza owners
too.) **2003**—When backing vehicle into a parking space, the hill-holder feature
activates, forcing the driver to use excessive throttle in Reverse. • Brake pedal goes
to floor without braking. • Heater, defroster failure. • Five doors but only one key-
hole makes for difficult access when the keyless entry fails. **2004**—Airbags fail to
deploy. • One vehicle caught fire due to an oil leak. • Stuck accelerator. • Loss of
power. • No-starts in cold weather. • Premature wheel bearing failures. • Airbag
warning light is frequently lit for no reason. • Speedometer cannot be read in sunlight. • Vehicle generates excessive static shock. • Fuel door release button falls
off. **2005**—Vehicle is not as crashworthy as claimed:

> The symmetrical all-wheel-drive system of my 2005 Subaru [Forester] XT failed, the
> vehicle fishtailed and drifted, resulting in a rollover and severe bodily injury. The
> vehicle was so flimsy, it was disgusting. Every door and window opening collapsed, glass
> flew everywhere. The ceiling collapsed on the passengers' head. This is a death car.

2006—Side airbag fails to deploy. • Smoldering fire near the gearshift lever:

> There was a smell of burning plastic inside the vehicle. The interior dome light also
> did not illuminate upon opening the door. Upon opening the passenger door, the
> contact noticed that the floor of the front passenger side appeared to have been
> charred. The contact also noticed that the plastic around the manual gearshift had

melted and re-solidified. The fabric of both the driver and passenger seats appeared charred as well.

• Hard starting; engine surging:

> Car began to experience unexpected engine rpm increases immediately after a "cold start." When car is first started, engine rpms are at around 1500. Put car into Reverse and backed out of parking space. When the clutch is depressed, engine rpms shoot up to 3000+. Then, after putting car in 1st gear, and releasing clutch, engine rpms drop to about 1500 but slowly increase to around 2500–3000 rpm and vehicle speed increases without foot even being on the accelerator. Problem usually clears up after driving a few minutes.

• Sudden, unintended acceleration accompanied by loss of brakes. • Frequent coil pack failures. • Hesitation when accelerating. • Cruise control performs erratically. • Seatback collapses from a low-speed rear-ender. • Yellow Airbag warning light is a distraction. • Low beam headlights provide inadequate illumination. • Yokohama original-equipment tires fail prematurely. **2007**—Passenger-side airbag is disabled even though a normal-sized adult is seated. • Engine surges when driving downhill:

> The engine surges when driving down hill (not under load) and you are giving just enough throttle to keep up speed. It causes the car to have a jerking back and forth motion.

WRX: **2001**—Brake rotors are easily grooved, degrading braking ability. **2002**—First gear is hard to engage. **2002–03**—Windshield cracking. • Chronic ABS failures. • Fuel smell in the cabin caused by fuel pooling in the engine manifold recess. **2003**—Increased braking distance when brakes are applied on an uneven surface. **2004**—Defective Bridgestone tires. • Failure-prone, clunking struts will not rebound, causing the rear end to sag and degrading handling. **2005**—Tricky handling is still a problem. **2006**—Motor mount failures. • Brembo brakes are poor performers in the rain. • High-intensity discharge (HID) headlights provide inadequate illumination due to their low mounting. • Front windshield is easily cracked:

> I am finding many complaints and similar cracks in other WRXs. I feel as if the windshields on a WRX are either weak or need to be thicker.

Secret Warranties/Internal Bulletins/Service Tips

All years: Bulletins relate to the automatic transmission popping out of gear. • At least three bulletins deal with manual transmission malfunctions. • Diagnostic and repair tips are offered on transfer clutch binding and/or bucking on turns. • Troubleshooting tips on a sticking anti-lock brake relay are offered. This problem is characterized by a lit ABS warning light or the ABS motor continuing to run and buzz when the ignition is turned off. • A rotten-egg smell could be caused by a defective catalytic converter. It will be replaced, after a bit of arguing, free of charge up to five years under the emissions warranty. **1999**—A broken air intake chamber box will cause stalling during start-up and the Check Engine light to remain lit. **1999–2002**—Sliding seat belt latch. **2000**—Growling noises from the engine area. • Automatic Transmission light flashing. • Low brake pedal adjustment procedure. **2000–01**—Front oxygen air/fuel sensor cracking. **2001–03**—Premature brake pad wear. **2002–03**—Insufficient AC cooling. **2003**—Defective 4EAT transmission parking pawl rod. • Clutch pedal sticking. *Impreza:* **2002–07**—Excessive vibration from the front door speakers. *Impreza, Forester:* **2006**—Correction for a hesitation when accelerating. *WRX:* **2004–05**—Tips on silencing a noisy rear differential.

FORESTER, IMPREZA, TRIBECA, WRX PROFILE

	1999	2000	2001	2002	2003	2004	2005	2006	2007
Cost Price ($) (negotiable)									
Forester (24%)	26,695	26,895	28,395	28,395	27,995	27,995	27,995	27,995	26,995
Impreza sedan (22%)	21,995	21,995	22,196	21,995	22,995	22,995	22,995	23,495	22,695
Tribeca (20%)	—	—	—	—	—	—	—	41,995	41,995
WRX (26%)	—	—	—	34,995	34,995	35,495	35,495	35,495	35,495
Used Values ($)									
Forester ▲	4,500	5,500	7,000	9,000	11,000	12,000	16,000	18,000	20,000
Forester ▼	3,500	5,000	6,000	7,500	9,000	10,000	14,000	17,500	18,000
Impreza sedan ▲	3,500	5,000	6,000	7,500	9,000	10,000	13,000	15,000	17,000
Impreza sedan ▼	3,000	4,500	5,000	6,000	7,000	8,000	11,000	13,000	15,000
Tribeca ▲	—	—	—	—	—	—	—	22,000	24,000
Tribeca ▼	—	—	—	—	—	—	—	20,000	22,500
WRX ▲	—	—	—	9,500	11,000	13,000	16,000	21,000	24,000
WRX ▼	—	—	—	8,000	9,000	11,000	14,000	19,000	22,000
Reliability	3	3	3	4	4	4	4	4	4
Crash Safety (F)									
Forester	4	4	4	4	5	5	5	5	5
Impreza	—	—	—	4	4	—	—	4	4
Tribeca	—	—	—	—	—	—	—	5	5
Side (Forester)	—	—	5	5	5	5	5	5	5
Impreza	—	—	—	4	4	—	—	4	4
Tribeca	—	—	—	4	4	—	—	5	5
IIHS Side	—	—	—	—	5	5	5	5	5
Offset (Forester)	5	5	5	5	5	5	5	5	5
Impreza	—	—	—	—	5	5	5	5	5
Rollover (Forester)	—	—	3	3	3	4	4	4	4
Impreza	—	—	—	4	4	—	—	4	4
Tribeca	—	—	—	—	—	—	—	4	4

Note: The 2008 crash ratings are similar to last year's scores.

Toyota

FJ CRUISER

Going into its second model year, the FJ Cruiser is evaluated in summary form in Appendix I.

RAV4 ★★★★

RATING: Above Average (1997–2008) This small SUV is an impressive performer that carries a remarkable array of standard features suitable for limited off-road tasks. But there is a serious downside: The car's faulty powertrain and erratically functioning cruise control can put your life in danger. **Strong points:** *All model years:* The peppy 6-cylinder engine provides excellent acceleration while sipping fuel; it gets about the same fuel economy as the 4-cylinder-equipped competition putting out 100 fewer horses. Full-time 4×4; adequate 4-cylinder acceleration, good handling, and smooth riding (the four-door model has a handling advantage over the two-door version); all passengers have more than enough headroom and legroom; the four-door has more cargo space than most passenger cars, but the two-door version reduces that cargo capacity by half; the split rear bench seat folds for extra cargo space; easy access and a low liftover; the four-door is nicely equipped, while the two-door is spartan, though adequate; and an incredibly high resale value. *2006–08 models:* A V6 and a small horsepower boost for the 4-cylinder engine; additional cabin space allows for more cargo room and optional seven-passenger seating. The 2007s and 2008s carry standard side curtain airbags (formerly a $750 option). **Weak points:** *2005 and earlier models:* Serious throttle delay and engine surging, and excessive road and engine noise. Automatic gearbox and 4×4 reduces engine performance (front-drive is faster); rearward visibility is seriously compromised by the RAV4's convertible top, high headrests, and spare-tire placement. *2006–08 models:* V6 throttle is super-sensitive and tough to modulate, leading to jerky acceleration and rough low-speed shifts; speed control constantly shifts in and out of gear; tall drivers will find the cockpit cramped; wide rear roof pillars obstruct rearward view; second-row seats give insufficient legroom; third-row seats hard to access. No manual transmission available, cheap-looking glove box lid and headliner, and no separately opening hatch glass. **New for 2008:** Nothing important. A major redesign is scheduled for 2010.

MODEL HISTORY: Selling for $27,400 ($22,235 in the States), the RAV4 is a cross between a small car and an off-road wagon with a tall roof, and it marks Toyota's entry into the mini-sport-utility market. RAV4 stands for "recreational active vehicle with four-wheel drive." It has attractive lines, a high profile, and two drivetrains: permanent 4×4 or front-drive (which doesn't include low-range gearing but has a locking centre differential).

The RAV4 is based on the Camry platform and features a four-wheel independent suspension and unibody construction; the 2005 and earlier models ride and handle like a stiffly sprung, small-wheelbase car. Like Honda's CR-V, it's an upsized car that has been made more rugged with the addition of AWD, larger wheels, more ground clearance, and a boxy body. Following the car's 2006 redesign, two engines are now offered: a 166-hp 4-cylinder and a 269-hp V6—RAV4's first V6. Both engines come only with an automatic transmission. ABS and traction/anti-skid control are standard. Front-drive RAV4s have a limited slip differential. Hill ascent/descent control is standard on V6 models and on seven-passenger 4-cylinder models. Sport models have a sport suspension. RAV4s have a side-hinged rear gate that makes for difficult curbside loading. The second-row seat is a split folding bench that moves fore and aft and has a reclining seatback. The optional third-row seat folds into the floorwell.

Although RAV4s have been around for a few years, you won't find many bargains on the used-car market. The 1999 and 2000 models aren't much different from their predecessors except for a minor face-lift, the addition of a two-door softtop, and a full-sized spare tire. The two-door convertible was dropped from the 2000 models. **2001**—Completely redesigned, growing in size and getting a more powerful engine, an upgraded suspension, a more rigid body, and new, aggressive styling. **2004**—Given the Camry's 2.4L engine, rear disc brakes, vehicle skid control, a revised suspension and steering, a tire pressure monitor, and optional side curtain airbags. **2006**—A major redesign gives the 2006 new styling, a longer

2008 RAV4 TECHNICAL DATA

POWERTRAIN (FRONT-DRIVE/4×4)
Engines: 2.4L 4-cyl. (166 hp) • 3.5L V6 (269 hp); Transmissions: 4-speed auto. • 5-speed auto.

DIMENSION/CAPACITY
Passengers: 2/3, 2/3/2; Wheelbase: 104.7 in.; H: 66.3/L: 181.1/W: 68.0 in.; Headroom F/R: 6.5/4.0 in.; Legroom F/R: 41.5/29.0 in.; Cargo volume: 38.5 cu. ft.; Fuel tank: 60L/regular; Tow limit: 1,500–3,500 lb.; Load capacity: 825 lb. (1,144 lb. on manual-shift front-drive models); GVWR: 4,535–4,865 lb.; Turning circle: 37.0 ft.; Ground clearance: 7.0 in.; Weight: 3,444 lb.

wheelbase, additional length, more width, a more powerful engine, and third-row seating to carry a total of seven passengers. **2007**—Standard front seat-mounted side airbags and roll-sensing front and rear head/side curtain airbags.

COST ANALYSIS: Toyota has barely raised prices on the 2008 models in Canada, but the base RAV4 is still overpriced by $5,000 compared to the U.S. MSRP. The base 2008–09 RAV4 starts at $27,400, while the Limited sells for $33,295. Base V6 models go for $31,900; the Sport starts at $32,730; and the Limited V6 goes for $35,745. Buying the same models in the States can save you lots of dough: The $24,400 base model, for example, costs $21,885 (U.S.)—a savings of more than $5,000. **Best alternatives:** Ford Escape, Honda CR-V, Hyundai Tucson or Santa Fe, and Mazda Tribute. Other choices worth looking at are the Nissan Xterra or X-Trail, Subaru Forester, and Toyota Highlander. **Rebates:** Look for 10–15 percent discounts throughout 2008. **Delivery/PDI:** $1,390. **Warranty:** Bumper-to-bumper 3 years/60,000 km; powertrain 5 years/100,000 km; rust perforation 5 years/unlimited km. **Supplementary warranty:** An extended warranty isn't needed. **Options:** Don't buy the V6 unless you are a power freak or carry heavy cargo; the 4-banger has plenty of power for most driving chores. Take a test-drive and see. **Depreciation:** Slow. **Insurance cost:** Above average. **Parts supply/cost:** Parts are moderately priced and fairly easy to find from independent suppliers. **Annual maintenance cost:** Below average, owing to the proven reliability of Camry and Corolla components used in the RAV4. **Highway/city fuel economy:** 8.1/10.7 L/100 km. *2006 and later models:* 7.8/10.1 L/100 km; V6 is estimated to be 7.7/11.1 L/100 km.

QUALITY/RELIABILITY: Quality control has declined over the past five years. **Owner-reported problems:** Many reports of frequent stalling or hesitation when accelerating. Faulty speed control causes the transmission to shift constantly in a jerky manner, causing the engine to race:

> When using the cruise control (with the automatic transmission) the vehicle will shift rapidly between 2nd and 3rd gears when climbing small inclines and even sometimes on flat ground. This action starts when the transmission downshifts to maintain current speed. This was first noted when the vehicle had just over 8,000 miles [12,900 km]. It now has over 17,000 [27,400 km] and the problem still exists. It has been into the dealership twice for repairs. The first time I was told there was no problem. The second time I was told it was a computer problem and could not be repaired at this time. I was advised by the servicing dealer that in order to make a repair Toyota would have to create a computer program for the technicians to install. After talking with Toyota I have been told this is not a problem but a "characteristic" of the vehicle and no efforts were being made for any type of repair. This condition makes for an unstable and dangerous driving condition when the cruise is utilized because you do not know how the vehicle will react during the drive. Currently I am aware of 12 case numbers that have been created with the Toyota customer support center addressing this situation. Some of these cases even involve 2006 models.

Brake noise, and throttle body whine between 2700 and 3000 rpm. Suspension clunks when making slow-speed turns. Owners note that the brakes screech, squeal, or grind even after the pads have been replaced. Other noises: dash and cowl rattling (worse in low temperatures), rear suspension creaking when accelerating from a stop, and windshield cowling rattles (particularly in cold weather). To a lesser degree, owners tell of rear-view mirror and windshield cowling vibrations as well as minor electrical shorts. The AC and heating display is nearly impossible to read in daylight. **Warranty performance:** Average.

ROAD PERFORMANCE: Acceleration/torque: Brisk acceleration with the manual gearbox (found only on pre-2007 models), with an acceptable amount of low-end torque—this makes the RAV4 a competent performer for most daily chores, while giving it the power for traversing hilly terrain and doing some light off-roading. **Transmission:** When working properly, the automatic transmission is smooth-shifting and particularly well suited for off-roading when mated to the AWD. With the 5-speed manual transmission, the 4×4 mode can be engaged by a push of a button on the dashboard. With the 4-speed automatic transmission, the standard centre differential is controlled by a hydraulic multi-plate clutch. Large 16-inch wheels provide stability. The high ground clearance, wide track, short overhangs, and four-wheel independent suspension make it more suitable for off-roading than some other "light" sport-utilities lacking these features. The automatic transmission, however, performs erratically, especially when coupled to the speed control. **Steering:** Power steering is now much more precise than with the pre-2004 versions. **Routine handling:** Good. Minimal body lean, a smooth ride, and less trucklike handling. **Emergency handling:** Despite the vehicle's high centre of gravity, its handling feels sure and responsive. **Braking:** Good.

SAFETY SUMMARY: Airbags: Dual front; optional side. **ABS:** Optional; disc/disc. **Safety belt pretensioners:** Standard. **Traction control:** Optional. **Head restraints F/R:** *1999:* ★★★; *2001–02:* ★★★★★; *2003–08:* ★★. **Visibility F/R:** ★★★★★/★. **Pet transport:** ★★★★★. Two dog crates will fit side-by-side between the wheelwells with the second seat folded down. With the crates pushed away from the hatch, there's still a lot of storage space and easy access to the under-floorboard storage compartment.

SAFETY COMPLAINTS: 1999—Fire ignites in the engine compartment (electrical wires) and fuse box (insulation). • Spot welds break away from frame, causing trailer hitch to separate. • Alternator short causes sudden loss of power. • Uneven pavement causes the vehicle to flip over. • Cruise control causes a power loss when it engages. • When driver applies the brakes gently, cruise control doesn't disengage; instead, it kicks in harshly when vehicle speeds up. • Fuel tank is easily punctured by rocks thrown up by the front wheels. • Premature failure of the rear shocks. • Frequent brake pad replacement. **2000**—Windshield is easily chipped. • Sudden tire blowout. **2001**—In one incident, airbag deployed when key was inserted into the ignition. • Sudden, unintended acceleration. • Vehicle suddenly accelerates when applying ABS brakes. • Vehicle pulls to one side when accelerating; alignment and tires eliminated as cause. • Intermittent hesitation when accelerating or making a slow turn. • Rear brake problems. • Brakes squeal or grind when braking. • Rear window suddenly shatters. • Excessive mirror vibration. • Front brake groan noise. **2002**—Fuel throttle linkage failure causes abnormally high engine revs, sudden acceleration. • Excessive noise and vibration when driving with rear window lowered halfway. • Brake pedal is too small. **2002–03**—Airbags fail to deploy. **2002–04**—Fire ignites in the engine compartment. **2003**—Bridgestone tire failure. **2004**—Rear-door window shatters for no reason while vehicle is underway. • Sudden acceleration in Reverse accompanied by brake failure. • Stuck accelerator. **2005**—Engine rust protection (Cosmoline) heats up and emits a sickening odour into the cabin. • Fuel-hose leakage. • Sun visor is no longer padded. **2006**—Passenger-side airbag shuts off even though an adult occupies the seat. • More complaints of engine hesitation and surging when accelerating or when coming to a stop:

> My 2006 Toyota RAV4 has a non-responsive throttle. On many occasions, when you give it gas it does nothing, then it takes off like a rocket. I have nearly been in accidents because I pull out from a stop and the throttle is unresponsive while traffic is bearing down on me.

2007—Sudden loss of steering. • Faulty cruise control and engine hesitation when accelerating (a common Toyota problem over the past decade):

> Hesitation when trying to press gas pedal usually from a stop. This could cause an accident when I believe I have enough time to get out on main highway from side street and the SUV won't go. Took to dealer, who said [this is] normal. Cruise does not work properly on inclines. It will jerk back and forth until cruise turned off...called Toyota call center. They said this vehicle was not meant to use cruise on inclines (what a joke).

• Yokohama tire tread disintegrates after only two months of use.

Secret Warranties/Internal Bulletins/Service Tips

All years: Remedy for front brake clicking found in TSB #BR004-00. • Loose, poorly fitted trim panels. **1999–2000**—Delayed upshift to Overdrive with cruise control engaged. **1999–2002**—The MIL stays lit because of a damaged fuel-tank vent. **2001**—Windshield creak noise. • Diagnosing noises in passenger-side dash and the A- and C-pillar areas. • Headlight retainer tab broken. • Improvement to the rear wiper washer nozzle. • Exhaust fumes enter into the interior. • Roof rack rattle or buzz. **2001–02**—Troubleshooting rear brake squeal. • Back door rattles. • Noise from top of instrument panel. **2001–03**—Cowl noise troubleshooting tips. **2001–04**—Fix for a squealing accessory drivebelt and a rattling belt tensioner. **2001–05**—Key sticks in the ignition lock. **2002**—Service campaign to inspect or repair the cruise-control switch. • Wind whistle from front edge of hood. • Steering wheel may be off-centre. • Speedometer fluctuations. **2002–06**—Correction for vehicles that pull to the right when accelerating. **2003–07**—Windshield ticking noise considered a factory-related problem (TSB

#NV009-06, published September 18, 2006). **2004–05**—Tire Pressure warning light may come on for no reason. **2004–06**—Sulfur exhaust countermeasures. **2004–07**—Front-seat squeaking. **2006**—Engine timing cover oil leaks. **2006–07**—Automatic transmission shift lever doesn't move smoothly. • Water leaks onto the passenger floorboard. • Whining noise at low speed/idle. • Fuel pump droning noise and vibration at highway speeds:

4×4 SYSTEM—DRONING NOISE AT 60 MPH [97 KM/H]

BULLETIN NO.: TC006-07 **DATE: APRIL 24, 2007**

2006–07 RAV4

Some 2006–07 model year 4×4 RAV4 vehicles equipped with a 2GR-FE engine may exhibit an intermit-tent drone noise and vibration at highway speeds, peaking at approximately 60 mph [97 km/h]. A new 4×4 computer assembly has been made available to address this concern.

• Front door locks may be inoperative in cold weather. **2007**—Paint stains on horizontal surfaces.

RAV4 PROFILE

	1999	2000	2001	2002	2003	2004	2005	2006	2007
Cost Price ($) (firm)									
4×2	22,150	—	—	—	—	—	—	—	—
4×4 (22%)	22,500	24,185	23,260	24,420	24,485	24,485	24,585	28,700	29,300
Used Values ($)									
4×2 ▲	6,000	—	—	—	—	—	—	—	—
4×2 ▼	5,500	—	—	—	—	—	—	—	—
4×4 ▲	5,000	6,500	8,000	9,500	11,000	12,500	15,500	19,500	22,000
4×4 ▼	4,500	6,000	7,000	8,000	9,500	11,000	13,500	17,500	20,500
Reliability	5	4	4	4	4	3	3	3	3
Crash Safety (F)	4	4	4	4	4	4	4	5	5
Side	5	5	—	5	5	5	5	5	5
IIHS Side	—	—	1	1	1	5	5	5	5
Offset	2	2	3	3	3	3	5	5	5
Rollover	—	—	—	3	3	3	—	4	4

Note: The 2001–05 models earned five stars from IIHS only if they were equipped with side airbags; vehicles without side airbags were given only one star. Overall, the 2008 model crash ratings are quite similar to last year's scores.

Mid-Sized Sport-Utilities

Fuel-Thirsty Bruisers

Mid-sized sport-utility vehicles are the second-most popular class of SUVs, following those in the small SUV category. Ample cargo space and towing capabilities make these sport-utilities a highly versatile class of vehicle. However, excessive fuel consumption and mediocre handling are two other characteristics that have to be considered.

Although prices are fairly high, varying from the mid-$30,000s to over $60,000, these vehicles provide much of the comfort and utility of luxury SUVs for about $10,000 less. Furthermore, the recent spike in fuel prices has forced automakers to offer Canadians substantial rebates and discounts that can cut the suggested retail price by a whopping 20 percent. Vehicles bought in the States are routinely sold for about two-thirds of the Canadian price—a $20,000 savings in some cases.

A major trend with mid-sized versions is that more models are coming with third-row seats, increasing carrying capacity from five to seven or eight people. Ford's Edge is one of the few vehicles missing this feature. Keep in mind, though, that third-row seats in SUVs are typically tight and hard to access (except for the well-designed one in the Saturn Outlook). Unless you enjoy riding with your chin resting on your knees, leave the third-row seats for kids.

Lemon-Aid's top-rated mid-sized SUVs, the Toyota Highlander and Honda Pilot, are due to be replaced soon. A second-generation Highlander arrived this year, with a hybrid version due in the fall of 2008. The 2009 Pilot came out in the spring of 2008. Ford also launched two new SUVs in 2008: the Ford Taurus X (formerly the Freestyle) and the Ford Flex.

The Saturn Outlook, a corporate twin of GM's Acadia and Enclave, is the "best American SUV we've tested, and ranks among the top vehicles in our mid-sized and large SUV ratings," says *Consumer Reports* magazine.

The Saturn Outlook.

Acura

MDX ★★★★

RATING: Above Average (2007–08); Average (2001–06). Last year's improved model has made a world of difference to the car's road performance and comfort. Still, why spend $52,300 for a warmed-over Odyssey when you can do better with the cheaper and larger Honda Pilot? Sure, it has 50 less horses, but odds are you won't feel it. **Strong points:** Drives and rides like a car; good acceleration with plenty of low-end grunt; well-appointed, roomy interior with a standard third-row seat; and a gas-saving engine cylinder deactivation system. 2007 and later models have successfully tackled most of the following negatives found with 2006 and earlier models. **Weak points:** No low-speed transfer case; transmission failures on early models; stability control on 2001–03 models doesn't deliver promised performance; rivals have better designs. Lots of road, drivetrain, and exhaust system noise, and lots of wind noise (many owners complain of poor body construction) and rear suspension clunk (covered by a service bulletin). On early models, imprecise steering has insufficient feedback; third-row seat is adequate for small adults or children only; earlier models have a tacky-looking interior with lots of plastic garnishing; climate controls are difficult to access and indicator lights wash out in sunlight; and navigation system isn't user-friendly. Problematic fit and finish; limited seatback adjustment and thigh support; lacks a "smart key" system; mediocre braking performance. High MSRP and freight/PDI charges are way out of line, no-haggle policy borders on price-fixing, real-world fuel economy is mediocre, and premium fuel is required. Steering wheel can't be adjusted for reach,

2008 MDX TECHNICAL DATA

POWERTRAIN (REAR-DRIVE)
Engine: 3.7L V6 (300 hp); Transmission: 5-speed auto.

DIMENSION/CAPACITY
Passengers: 2/3/2; Wheelbase: 108.3 in.; H: 68.2/L: 190.7/W: 78.5 in.; Headroom F/R: 4.0/4.0 in.; Legroom F/R: 41.0/30.0 in.; Cargo volume: 42.0 cu. ft.; Fuel tank: 72.7L/premium; Tow limit: 5,000 lb.; Load capacity: 1,160 lb.; GVWR: 5,732 lb.; Turning circle: 40.0 ft.; Ground clearance: 5.0 in.; Weight: 4,541 lb.

forcing small drivers to sit perilously close to the airbag housing. **New for 2008:** Nothing much, except that the auto-dim rearview mirror is now a standard feature; a V6 diesel will be offered for the 2010 model year.

MODEL HISTORY: Introduced as a 2001 model, the MDX initially carried a 212-hp 6-cylinder engine. It seats seven and is longer than the rival five-seat BMW X5 and Lexus RX 300. Its second- and third-row bench seats conveniently fold flat with the load floor (the last row is suitable for small children only). **2002**—Some noise-reduction measures. **2003**—More power, a new transmission, and a standard anti-skid system; a Honda clone called the Pilot is introduced. **2004**—Updated styling, a tire-pressure monitor, and head-protecting side curtain airbags. **2005**—A larger fuel tank, an improved hands-free cell phone link, and a standard CD changer. **2007**—Redesigned with a lower and wider stance, a more powerful engine, and fuel-saving cylinder deactivation. The standard 3.7L V6 is the most powerful Acura engine available, producing 300 hp—a gain of 47 hp over the 2006 model's 3.5L V6.

COST ANALYSIS: The 2007's extra horsepower is a critical improvement. It's a better-performing, higher-quality vehicle than the previous year's model. The $52,300 2008–09 versions are carried over mostly unchanged. A 2008 MDX sells for $40,195 (U.S.) in the States—a savings of almost $13,000. Interestingly, in October 2007, Radio-Canada sent a crew to film one Quebecer's MDX purchase just across the border. After the SUV was driven back to Canada and the segment shown on TV, Honda sent a memo to its American dealers telling them they could not sell to Canadian residents. Many dealers ignored the edict. **Best alternatives:** You want comparable performance for about $12,000 less? Try a Honda Pilot (the MDX's cheaper cousin) for its additional passenger/cargo hauling capability, or a Nissan Xterra or Toyota Highlander. The Volvo XC90 and ML320/350/500 have very good cargo room with all the rows down, but they have neither comparable cargo room behind the second row nor a comparable level of quality control and dealer servicing. Furthermore, Ford's announcement that it may sell Volvo could make its future in North America even shakier. **Rebates:** Look for $5,000+ rebates on the 2008 models this year and a similar amount in the late fall, applicable to the early 2009 models. **Delivery/PDI:** $1,855 (outrageously high). **Warranty:** Bumper-to-bumper 3 years/60,000 km; powertrain 5 years/100,000 km; rust perforation 5 years/unlimited km. **Supplementary warranty:** Not needed. **Options:** Vehicle comes fully loaded, except for the non-essential navigation system, rear backup camera, and DVD player. Replace the stock Goodyear tires with Michelins or their equivalent (see *www.tirerack.com* owner reports) for a better, quieter ride. Change only the radio speakers for improved audio quality. The roof crossrails aren't adjustable and are a bit wider than those on other SUVs, making it difficult to get roof cargo carriers that will fit. Make sure the navigation system DVD is a recent issue from Alpine; it is sent out every September. **Depreciation:** Lower than average. **Insurance cost:** Much higher than average. **Parts supply/cost:** Parts are reasonably priced and easily found in the Odyssey/Honda generic parts bin. **Annual maintenance cost:** Less than average. **Highway/city fuel**

economy: 10.4/13.9 L/100 km, but many owners say their fuel consumption is much higher. Cylinder deactivation is a definite plus.

QUALITY/RELIABILITY: Reliability shouldn't be a problem, unless you actually believe this vehicle can go off-road. If so, make sure you get an extended warranty and find a friendly garage. Buying the latest model will save you some of the first-year re-engineering glitches commonly found with most reworked makes. **Owner complaints:** 2007 models have registered only a few complaints concerning premature brake wear, minor electrical shorts, AC compressor failures, and some fit and finish concerns. Owners of earlier models note automatic transmission and front spring failures, alloy wheel cracks, a rotten-egg exhaust smell, engine hesitation around 60 km/h, an exhaust droning noise when underway, a metallic clanging and rumbling heard at 2000 rpm, squeaks and rattles (dash, door lock, and tailpipe), brake-caliper clicking and clunking, gas tank sloshing, wind noise, and a high-speed harmonic drone. The repair of the recalled transmission is not effective, the moonroof leaks water, auto AC mode is slow to cool the car in stop-and-go driving, AM radio reception is poor, the Bose radio may have too much bass, the driver's seatback doesn't go vertical enough for some, seats have insufficient thigh and back support, and seat memory settings are gradually lost. **Warranty performance:** Average.

ROAD PERFORMANCE: Acceleration/torque: Smooth, quiet, and sustained acceleration; one of the best among V6 competitors (0–100 km/h: 8.7 seconds). The 2003 model got a power boost of 20 extra horses. **Transmission:** Flawless shifting with the only transaxle available, the 5-speed automatic. **Steering:** Vague, with insufficient feedback. **Routine handling:** A bit cumbersome, particularly when cornering, as body lean becomes more evident. This unsteady behaviour becomes worse as the speed increases or if the steering correction is more severe. Say Consumers Union testers: "The MDX does not inspire confidence in emergency handling, even with its new stability control." Firm suspension also jostles occupants when passing over uneven pavement (the Lexus RX 300/330 and Toyota Sequoia handle this better). The lack of a low-speed transfer case limits this SUV's off-roading prowess. **Braking:** Unimpressive; brakes are difficult to modulate until you adapt to their sensitivity with a lighter foot.

SAFETY SUMMARY: Airbags: Front and side. **ABS:** Standard; disc/disc. **Head restraints F/R:** 2001–02: ★★★; 2003–04: ★★★★. **Visibility F/R:** ★★★★. **Pet transport:** ★★★★.

SAFETY COMPLAINTS: 2001—Chronic stalling on the highway. • Seat belts won't hold a child booster seat securely. **2001–03**—Many automatic transmission breakdowns: Automatic transmission suddenly downshifts, causing loss of control; front wheels suddenly lock up because of transmission failure. • Airbag fails to deploy. **2002**—Transmission can be shifted from Park to Reverse without key in ignition. • Cell phones or laptops in the cabin can disable the airbag feature:

Consumer stated whenever an electric device like a cell phone or laptop computer was used, the airbags deactivated until the device was turned off. Consumer felt as though he didn't have any control over the airbag system. The dealer stated a cell phone or laptop could not be on or near the seats.

• Seat belts tighten progressively once buckled. **2002–03**—Sudden acceleration. **2003**—Front spring breakage. • Navigation system gives incorrect information. • Seat belt crosses at driver's neck. • Front seat belt locks up. **2004**—In one incident, tire slipped off the rim and vehicle went out of control despite stability-control feature. • Vehicle continues in Reverse after it is shifted into Drive. • Passenger injured by deployment of side airbag:

During a collision the passenger fell to the side window and airbags deployed, resulting in head injuries. Passenger was transported by ambulance to the hospital.

2005—Child put seat belt around her neck and was almost strangled because the mechanism would not release. • Chronic stalling and hard starts. • Airbag malfunction warning light constantly illuminated. • A multiplicity of electrical malfunctions affecting simple controls and powertrain performance. • Fuel sloshing in the fuel tank creates a banging sound when coming to a stop. **2006**—Sudden, unintended acceleration is caused by a stuck accelerator pedal. • Vehicle stability assist (VSA) feature suddenly engages for no reason, causing an unexpected loss of power. • Excessive steering-wheel shake. • Blue-white halogen lights are glaringly bright. • Windshield cracks:

Windshield has a 20 inch (hook shape) edge crack from passenger side starting from the first two inches of the perimeter. Probably caused by "residual stress" and "induced stress" due to installation or design flow. Both are manufacturer defects.

2007—Horn failure.

Secret Warranties/Internal Bulletins/Service Tips

2001—Throttle bracket buzzes or rattles. • Clunking when braking or accelerating, thought to be caused by front lower control arm. • Noisy power-steering pump. • Supplementary restraint system (SRS) unit internal failure. • Product update/secret warranty relative to the seat belt harness. • Second-row seat may not fold down or recline. • Water dripping from the outside mirror. • Loose rear wiper arm. • Loose or detached seatback panel covered by a TSB. **2001–02**—V6 engine oil leaks. • Missing speed-sensor plug. • Brief hesitation when accelerating. • Cranks, but won't start. • Loose driver's seat. • Thumping from sloshing fuel. • Under-hood buzzing or rattling. • Booming noise from rear of vehicle at 90–100 km/h. • Squeaking noise from the middle roof area and the moonroof. • Broken seat belt tongue-stopper button. **2001–03**—Faulty remote audio controls. • Dash or front strut creaking or ticking. **2001–04**—Clunking brakes. • Buzzing from the front blower motor. **2001–06**—Noise and judder from the rear when turning. • Driver's seat won't move sufficiently. **2001–07**—Repair tips to correct steering/

suspension drifting/pulling while vehicle is underway. **2002–03**—Remedy for front damper noise. **2003**—Sunroof water leaks will be fixed for free under TSB #03-018, issued June 2003. **2004**—Correction for an exhaust system drone. • Subwoofer rattling noise. **2004–05**—Free tire valve cap replacement. **2005–06**—Engine runs roughly, stalls. **2006**—Suspension pops or clunks when turning. **2007**—Battery drain from misaligned, defective power door lock switch. • Front suspension buzz or rattle (replace the right-front damper spring). • Steering wheel clicking when turning.

MDX PROFILE

	2001	2002	2003	2004	2005	2006	2007
Cost Price ($) (soft)							
MDX (25%)	47,000	48,000	49,000	50,300	50,800	51,600	52,500
Used Values ($)							
MDX ▲	13,500	15,000	18,000	22,000	27,000	33,000	39,000
MDX ▼	12,000	13,500	16,500	20,000	25,000	31,000	37,000
Reliability	4	4	5	5	5	5	5
Crash Safety (F)	—	5	4	5	5	5	5
Side	—	5	5	5	5	5	5
Offset	5	5	5	5	5	5	5
IIHS Side	—	—	—	—	—	—	5
Rollover	—	4	4	—	4	4	4

Audi

Q7/ALLROAD QUATTRO ★/★

RATING: Not Recommended (2007–08). Earlier AWD models, called the allroad Quattro, were beset by many factory-related deficiencies and poor servicing; they are also Not Recommended (2001–05). The Q7 is severely underpowered and overpriced, and its third-row back seat could have been made by Mattel. Get a Saturn Outlook or a GM Acadia or Enclave, instead.

If you intend to buy a 2008 Q7 in Canada, better speak to your bank manager first. You'll likely have to secure a sizeable loan to pay the $57,800 for the cheapest 3.6L Premium version, or $75,100 for the top-of-the-line 4.2L Premium model. Of course, these figures fly out the window once you cross the border into the States, where the Q7 is sold at more reasonable prices: $42,500 (U.S.) for the base Q7 3.6L model, and $58,600 (U.S.) for the 4.2L Premium version. Depreciation is moderate for the Q7: A used 2007 3.6L sold in Canada is now worth $39,000–$41,000; the 4.2L Premium costs $61,000–$63,000. The allroad Quattro versions

2008 Q7 TECHNICAL DATA

POWERTRAIN (AWD)

Engines: 3.6L V6 (280 hp) • 4.2L V8 (350 hp); Transmission: 6-speed manumatic

DIMENSION/CAPACITY

Passengers: 2/3/2; Wheelbase: 118.0 in.; H: 68.0/L: 200.0/W: 78.0 in.; Headroom F/R: 4.0/3.0/1.0 in.; Legroom F/R: 42.0/29.0/24.5 in.; Cargo volume: 37.0 cu. ft.; Fuel tank: 100L/premium; Tow limit: 6,615 lb.; Load capacity: 1,325 lb.; GVWR: N/A; Turning circle: 40.0 ft.; Ground clearance: 8.0 in.; Weight: 5,464 lb.

sold from 2001 through 2005 have depreciated at an astounding rate: A 2001 is barely worth a third of its original $60,000 MSRP.

Strong points: All Q7s come with an impressive array of premium features and a sharp-looking interior, making them a top choice for those who desire a seven-passenger luxury crossover SUV and don't mind throwing $25,000 down the drain. That's the difference in price between the Q7 and the far more practical and fuel-efficient GM Saturn Outlook (see Appendix I). Nevertheless, Q7s come fully loaded with performance-oriented handling, high-tech luxury and safety features, first-class interior design, and superior fit and finish. **Weak points:** Keep in mind that several cheaper competitors cost far less, get better fuel economy, are quicker, and are more practical for transporting kids. **New for 2008:** When compared with last year's model, the 2008's ride is much smoother, handling's not as stiff, and the brakes are less grabby, making them much easier to modulate. A diesel engine comes online in late 2008, and a hybrid powerplant is being considered for the 2009 or 2010 model.

NHTSA crash tests give the 2007–08 models five stars for frontal and side occupant crash protection and four stars for rollover resistance.

Owner complaints have been few, even though *Consumer Reports* has traditionally given Audi a truckload of black "Unacceptable" marks for reliability. Only six complaints have been received so far on the 2007 model. They include: Children can easily lock themselves in the car after pressing the back seat Lock button inadvertently; children can easily trap and crush a finger in the rear passenger window; the second- and third-row head restraints prevent the safe installation of a child safety seat; the engine oil pump fails; and the fuel supply is shut off if the brake and accelerator pedal are both pushed down.

Internal service bulletins address the following quality issues: hesitation upon acceleration; a cracking noise coming from the Panorama roof; a ticking noise from behind the dash panel or the centre console; troubleshooting squealing brakes on all 2003–07 models; radio speaker popping sound and loss of audio level; condensation inside of exterior lights; paint spotting or discoloration; wind noise from the door mirror; erratic sunroof operation; windshield wipers streak or smear; can't remove key when shift lever is in Park; and Xenon headlights fail.

BMW

RATING: Average (2004–08). BMW downsizes and disappoints, although the 6-cylinder engine enhances overall performance. **Strong points:** High seating gives a good view of the road, and it has a full complement of high-tech safety features. The 3.0L engine, optional until the 2007 model year, provides an impressive power range and towing capability for a compact SUV. A new X3 costs $16,700 less than an X5 ($61,900). **Weak points:** The 2.5L engine is underpowered, and overall highway performance isn't up to the 3 Series standard. Lacks many standard features found on other $45,000 compact SUVs, has bland styling, and cargo-carrying capacity can't touch the Honda CR-V or Ford Escape. The ride is hard and choppy; long shifter throws; slower and less precise steering than the competition. It's heavier and about 15 percent less fuel efficient than a Lexus RX, service bulletins show serious engine and automatic transmission failures on early models, and there's an excessively high freight and preparation charge. It doesn't project the same quality cachet as other BMWs. **New for 2008:** Carried over virtually unchanged; the 2010 model will be completely redesigned.

MODEL HISTORY: Introduced as a 2004 model, the X3 dropped the 2.5L sedan in 2006 and kept the 3.0L wagon. The first major redesign targeted the 2007 version. Some of the changes incorporated a major facelift, including front and rear styling, a cabin upgrade, and a standard twin-cam 3.0L inline 6-cylinder engine that produces 260 hp—an increase of 35 hp over the previous 3.0L. A 6-speed manual became a standard feature, and the new 6-speed Steptronic automatic transmission was offered as a no-charge option.

2008 X3 TECHNICAL DATA

POWERTRAIN (AWD)
Engines: 3.0L 6-cyl. (215 hp) • 3.0Lsi 6-cyl. (260 hp); Transmissions: 6-speed man. • 6-speed Steptronic auto.

DIMENSION/CAPACITY
Passengers: 2/3; Wheelbase: 110.0 in.; H: 65.9/L: 180.0/W: 73.0 in.; Headroom F/R: 4.0/3.0 in.; Legroom F/R: 42.0/27.5 in.; Cargo volume: 33.0 cu. ft.; Fuel tank: 67L/premium; Tow limit: 3,500 lb.; Load capacity: 1,005 lb.; GVWR: 4,993 lb.; Turning circle: 39.0 ft.; Ground clearance: 7.5 in.; Weight: 4,065 lb.

COST ANALYSIS: Look, you've got two ways to get this BMW on the cheap. First, you can buy a used 2007 for about $34,000, or $11,000 less than what it sold new. Or you could buy a 2008 in the States for $38,000 (U.S.) and save about $7,000 from the Canadian price of $45,200. It is also possible to save more than $10,000 by purchasing a used BMW in the States, but then you might miss out on the 2007's important upgrades. Be wary of production glitches on the first-series 2004 X3. Also, stay away from the 2.5L powerplant, and hold out for the 3.0L instead. **Best alternatives:** The Honda CR-V or Pilot, Infiniti FX35, Lexus RX series, and Nissan Murano. **Rebates:** Look for $2,000 rebates on leftover 2008s in early 2009; 2009 prices likely won't be discounted. **Delivery/PDI:** $1,995. **Warranty:**

Bumper-to-bumper 4 years/80,000 km; rust perforation 12 years/unlimited km. **Supplementary warranty:** A good idea with the 2004 model. **Options:** High-intensity headlights may be too bright. Sport package low-profile tires will bounce you around on rough pavement, and the run-flat tires degrade handling and are unreliable, way overpriced, and not very durable. **Depreciation:** Slower than average. **Insurance cost:** Higher than average. **Parts supply/cost:** Average. **Annual maintenance cost:** Higher-than-average repair costs with the first-year 2004s; average for later years. Cheaper independent garages won't touch these vehicles, adding to their servicing costs. **Highway/city fuel economy:** *2.5L 6-cyl.:* 8.9/13.6 L/100 km; *3.0L 6-cyl.:* 8.8/13.8 L/100 km.

QUALITY/RELIABILITY: 2004 models appear to have serious quality and reliability problems, judging by BMW's internal service bulletins. Although subsequent models have fewer complaints, delayed acceleration is a frequent refrain—all the more ironic with a company that touts the highway performance of its vehicles. **Warranty performance:** Better than average.

ROAD PERFORMANCE: Acceleration/torque: BMW's smallest SUV offers a wimpy, torque-challenged 184-hp 2.5L and a better-performing 3.0L inline-six. **Transmission:** Power is handled smoothly in 3 Series fashion via a 6-speed manual and permanent all-wheel-drive system. **Steering:** Very responsive and precise. **Routine handling:** Very good, but the ride is a bit bumpy, making for constant steering corrections. Emergency handling is compromised by the X3's stiff suspension. **Braking:** Excellent.

SAFETY SUMMARY: Airbags: Standard. **ABS:** Standard; disc/disc. **Safety belt pretensioners:** Front. **Traction control:** Yes. **Head restraints F/R:** ★★★. **Visibility F/R:** ★★★★/★★★. **Pet transport:** ★★★★.

SAFETY COMPLAINTS: 2004—A faulty Steptronic system causes the vehicle to suddenly surge forward. • In one incident, vehicle suddenly accelerated and crashed through the garage wall. • Automatic transmission won't go into Drive after vehicle is parked overnight; can be shifted without first stepping on the brakes. • Multiple electronic problems (dash gauges, AC, and ignition system). • High-intensity headlights are too bright. • Vehicle doesn't come with a Door Ajar warning light or buzzer. • Original-equipment tires leak air. **2005**—Sudden acceleration. • The passenger-side airbag is often disabled because of a sensor failure. • One driver's heated seat burned through the seatcover and singed his butt. **2007**—Dangerously delayed acceleration when shifting from First to Second gear (also a common failing among Toyotas):

> [The] BMW X3 is extremely dangerous to drive [because] it will not accelerate slowly. It hesitates in acceleration from a stop, on hills, on corners and then takes off very rapidly. The dealership in Seattle has worked on it three times and reports that they cannot fix it; they are aware of it but no fix is available. BMW in Fife refused to even try to fix it because it cannot be repaired. Someone is going to get killed because of this defect.

Secret Warranties/Internal Bulletins/Service Tips

2004—Radio reception problems. • Delayed cold engagement of automatic transmission. • Engine head bolt threads pull out of block. • Engine cylinder head leaks. **2004–05**—Noise emanating from the door frame area. **2004–07**—Troubleshooting hard/no-starts. • Plugging Panorama roof leaks. • Fix for an inoperative or rattling centre dash vent. • Silencing squeaking, creaking doors. • Blower motor malfunctions. • Inoperative side-mirror heaters. **2005**—Engine runs poorly due to faulty ignition coil. • Trunk lid won't latch. • Engine drivebelt tensioner noise. • Windshield whistling. • Panorama roof gurgles. • The AC produces a strong musty smell. **2007**—Service bulletin (SI B 24 08 07, Automatic Transmission, May 2007) details how to troubleshoot delayed acceleration when shifting from First to Second gear.

X3 PROFILE

	2004	2005	2006	2007
Cost Price ($) (soft)				
X3 2.5i	44,600	44,800	44,800	—
X3 3.0i (25%)	49,800	49,900	50,100	45,200
X3 3.0si (25%)	—	—	—	50,800
Used Values ($)				
X3 2.5i ▲	19,000	24,000	29,000	—
X3 2.5i ▼	17,000	22,000	27,000	—
X3 3.0i ▲	22,000	27,000	33,000	35,000
X3 3.0i ▼	20,000	25,000	31,000	33,000
X3 3.0si ▲	—	—	—	46,000
X3 3.0si ▼	—	—	—	44,000
Reliability	3	4	4	4
Crash Safety (F)	5	4	5	5
Side	5	5	5	5
Offset	5	5	5	5
IIHS Side	—	—	—	5
Rollover	—	4	4	4

X5 ★★★

RATING: Average (2007–08); Below Average (2000–06). This SUV is way overrated by car journalists who enjoy the BMW cachet on BMW's dime, because they get everything for free, including fuel. Sure, the X5 has lots of power and convenience features, but its high-speed performance isn't all that impressive. Quality control up to the 2006 models has been far below average, particularly when it comes to electronic hardware and program software (Mercedes and VW are also feeling the byte bite). **Strong points:** Rapid acceleration with plenty of torque in all gear ranges; nimble low-speed handling; good braking; first-class interior; a

2008 X5 TECHNICAL DATA

POWERTRAIN (AWD)
Engines: 3.0L 6-cyl. (260 hp) • 4.8L V8 (350 hp); Transmission: 6-speed auto.

DIMENSION/CAPACITY
Passengers: 2/3/2; Wheelbase: 116.0 in.; H: 70.0/L: 191.0/W: 76.0 in.; Headroom F/R: 3.5/3.0 in.; Legroom F/R: 40.5/26.5 in.; Cargo volume: 36.0 cu. ft.; Fuel tank: 93L/premium; Tow limit: 6,000 lb.; Load capacity: 1,350 lb.; GVWR: 5,860 lb.; Turning circle: 42.0 ft.; Ground clearance: 7.0 in.; Weight: 5,025 lb.

wide array of standard safety, performance, and convenience features; and a "Good" crashworthiness rating from IIHS. **Weak points:** High-speed handling is seriously compromised by this wagon's choppy, unstable ride and excessive weight; loading is made difficult by the high liftover; an unusually small interior makes for limited rear-seat and cargo space (the small X3 and most competitors are roomier); rapid depreciation; and it's a real gas-guzzler. No low-range gearing for off-roading; lots of engine noise; complicated iDrive driver-interaction controls and transmission shifter; tall step-up and narrow doorways; and an unusually large number of safety-related recalls and owner complaints (confidential BMW service bulletins show manufacturing mistakes are the source of most problems). **New for 2008:** Nothing significant; however, the 2009 models will be slightly restyled and priced more competitively.

MODEL HISTORY: 2001—A V8-powered X5 4.4i and 6-cylinder 3.0i edition debuted in Canada after a year in the States. **2002**—A high-performance 4.6is model gave BMW a high-performance counterpunch against Mercedes-Benz's ML500/ML55 AMG. **2004**—New front-end styling, AWD system, and V8 engine; a high-performance model was added mid-year; and a standard 6-speed transmission was added. **2007**—Longer, wider, and taller, with an optional third-row seat.

COST ANALYSIS: This $61,900 sport wagon isn't worth its high price, and don't expect to recover the excess cost through a higher-than-average resale value—BMW resale values are dropping fast. In the States, the same car will cost you $45,900 (U.S.). The freight charge across the border is about one-third ($775) what is in Canada. Unless you want the fuel-thirsty 4.8L V8 ($73,500 in Canada; $54,500 in the U.S.), stick with the 3.0L 6-cylinder. Be wary of the smaller V6 engine coupled with a manual transmission on earlier models—clutch action is rough and hard to modulate. **Best alternatives:** When it comes to off-roading, the X5 is blown away by the prowess of the Toyota Land Cruiser or Lexus RX 300 series and other less-expensive SUVs. Even Land Rover's Range Rover outperforms the X5 in off-road driving, although it would be hell to repair. Think seriously of getting a BMW 5 Series wagon for storage capability and performance. Forget Nissan's FX35 if you want a comfortable ride and lots of storage capacity. **Rebates:** Look for $5,000 rebates on leftover 2008s in early 2009; 2009s will get $3,000 rebates in the late fall of 2008. **Delivery/PDI:** $1,995. **Warranty:** Bumper-to-bumper 4 years/80,000 km; rust perforation 12 years/unlimited km. **Supplementary warranty:** A good idea. **Options:** Rear-obstacle warning system and 5-speed automatic transmission with manual shift capability are worthwhile investments. Sport package low-profile tires will bounce you around on rough pavement, and the run-flat tires degrade handling and are unreliable, way overpriced, and not very durable. **Depreciation:** Faster than average. **Insurance cost:** Much higher than average. **Parts supply/cost:** Average. **Annual maintenance cost:**

Predict higher-than-average repair costs, if owner complaints already recorded and dealership servicing costs for passenger cars are any indication. Cheaper independent garages won't touch these vehicles, adding to their servicing costs. **Highway/city fuel economy:** *6-cyl.: 10.6/15.6 L/100 km; V8: 11.9/16.4 L/100 km.*

QUALITY/RELIABILITY: Overall reliability has been quite poor, judging by owner complaints on the Internet (*www.roadfly.com*, among others) and by BMW's internal service bulletins. Aside from the X5's many recall campaigns, owners report a number of safety-related defects that are indicative of poor quality control. Many of the owner complaints go to the heart of the X5's reliability, as well as its overall safety. **Warranty performance:** Average. It would be comforting to see the company expend as much energy eliminating defects at the factory level.

ROAD PERFORMANCE: Acceleration/torque: Both the 6-cylinder and V8 provide acceptable acceleration. **Transmission:** Shifting is acceptable, but takes some getting used to. **Steering:** Impressive steering is very responsive and accurate, though a bit heavy when parking. Power-adjustable steering wheel keeps small-statured drivers away from the airbag housing. **Routine handling:** Acceptable. Emergency handling, however, is quite poor. The ride is choppy, requiring constant steering corrections. The car doesn't inspire handling confidence when pushed; it seems ready to tip over, despite its stability-control feature. **Braking:** Excellent, with no fading after successive stops.

SAFETY SUMMARY: 2001–03 models have received a "Best Pick" offset crash rating from IIHS. Before you purchase this vehicle, make sure the headlight illumination is adequate. On some model years, the gas and brake pedals are poorly designed; anyone with a size 12 or larger shoe can inadvertently hit the wrong pedal. **Airbags:** Standard. There have been reports that airbags on the 2000 models didn't deploy during head-on collisions. **ABS:** Standard; disc/disc. **Safety belt pretensioners:** Front. **Traction control:** Yes. **Head restraints F/R:** ★★★. **Visibility F/R:** ★★★★/★. **Pet transport:** ★★★★.

SAFETY COMPLAINTS: 2000—Vehicle suddenly leaps forward or stalls. • Airbags fail to deploy. • Engine runs rough and warning light is constantly lit. • In one incident, door latch would not release; driver had to crawl out through the window. • Rear doors open while vehicle is underway. • Hooking mechanism fails to hold up shade and flies across vehicle. • Poorly designed brake pedals won't accommodate large feet. **2000–03**—Headlight illumination is blinding. • Windshield shatters for no reason. **2001**—ABS light remains lit. • Fuel leakage into the passenger's compartment from the fuel-pump seal. • Inadvertent deployment of front airbags. • Chronic stalling problem with 3.0L engines. • Parked vehicle rolls away because of emergency brake failure. • Transmission loses First, Second, and Fifth gears because of faulty electronic chip. • Transmission often spontaneously shifts into Neutral. • Bent suspension control arm causes prematurely worn-out tires. • Front door design can injure an occupant's head. • Front door locks occupants inside vehicle. • Seat heater burns leather and occupant's butt. **2001–02**—Sudden brake failure. • Faulty electronic side-view mirrors. **2002**—Rear blind spot contributed to fatal accident. • While underway, driver-side door suddenly opens. • Floor mat may cause throttle to stick. • Airbag light stays lit. • Power windows won't stay up. • Wipers come on for no reason. • Fragile bumpers. **2002–03**—Frequent major electrical system failures. **2003**—Headlights may suddenly cut out while driving. **2004**—Engine suddenly surges, causing unintended acceleration. • Despite recall fix for stalling, vehicle continues to stall. • Chronic electrical system shutdowns. • Transmission shuts down while engine is running. **2006**—Engine surging while vehicle stopped. • Transmission failures.

Secret Warranties/Internal Bulletins/Service Tips

All years: Troubleshooting tips for a Check Engine light that's constantly lit. • Intermittent electrical faults related to circuits in the upper rear hatch. • Rough running, black smoke, and starter may stay engaged. • Troubleshooting AC musty odours. • Squealing, groaning, or grinding noise when turning the steering wheel. • Outer door releases fail to operate in freezing weather. • Service action to replace the passenger-side mirror. **2000**—Fuel-tank vent-line fitting weld may be faulty, allowing gas fumes to enter the passenger compartment; dealer will re-weld it under a "product update campaign" (read: secret warranty) as per TSB #16-5200. • Incorrect fuel gauge readings. • Faulty windshield wiper blades. • Generator whine on AM band. **2000–01**—Poor starting, no-starts, and erratic shifting. **2000–07**—Steering column will not adjust at all, or sometimes sticks. • Broken sunroof wind deflector. **2002**—Campaign to troubleshoot faulty Check Engine light. • Loose air intake boot. • Defective rear hatch switch. • Inoperative AC blower. • Brake pedal rattling. • Correcting steering squealing, grinding, or groaning. **2002–03**—Hard shift or no-shift condition (automatic transmission). **2004**—Engine head bolt threads pull out of block. • Defective engine cylinder head. • Hydraulic belt tensioner installation. • Campaign to troubleshoot Low Oil Level warning. • Cold weather may damage the engine valve cover. • Harsh downshifts. • Delayed cold engagement of automatic transmission. • Difficulty coding navigation system; erratic performance. • Replace alternator belt tensioner to silence annoying noise. • Poor radio reception. • Defective keyless entry. • Telematic inspection/replacement campaign. • Campaign to troubleshoot electrical failure of rear hatch latch. • Headlight condensation. • Transmission suddenly self-destructs. **2004–05**—Compass loses calibration. **2004–06**—Vehicle may not start, the gear indicator display may not work, or a transmission fail-safe light may come on. **2007**—Horn self-activates. • Inoperative tail light and turn signals.

X5 PROFILE

	2000	2001	2002	2003	2004	2005	2006	2007
Cost Price ($) (soft)								
X5 (23%)	—	56,960	56,900	57,800	58,500	58,800	59,400	61,900
X5 4.4i (25%)	—	—	68,900	69,800	71,400	69,800	72,100	—
X5 4.6is	—	—	93,900	94,500	—	—	—	—
X5 4.8is (30%)	—	—	—	—	96,500	96,500	98,100	73,500

Used Values ($)

X5 ▲	—	16,000	18,000	21,000	26,000	30,000	38,000	47,000
X5 ▼	—	14,500	16,000	19,000	24,000	28,000	36,000	45,000
X5 4.4i ▲	—	—	21,000	25,000	30,000	36,000	46,000	—
X5 4.4i ▼	—	—	19,000	23,000	28,000	34,000	44,000	—
X5 4.6is ▲	—	—	22,000	28,000	—	—	—	—
X5 4.6is ▼	—	—	20,000	26,000	—	—	—	—
X5 4.8is ▲	—	—	—	—	33,000	43,000	58,000	55,000
X5 4.8is ▼	—	—	—	—	31,000	41,000	55,000	53,000
Reliability	4	4	4	4	3	3	3	4
Crash Safety (F)	—	—	—	5	5	5	5	—
Side	—	—	—	4	4	4	4	—
Offset	—	5	5	5	5	5	5	5
Rollover	—	—	—	3	—	3	—	—

Note: The 2008 models' crashworthiness scores are identical to the 2007 ratings. Head restraint protection was rated "Poor" though 2007; however, the 2008 models were rated "Excellent." Also, the difference in price between a new 4.6L and 4.8L model narrows to about half that amount on the 2004 through 2006 used versions.

Chrysler

DURANGO, ASPEN ★

bad buy

RATING: Not Recommended (1998–2008). **Strong points:** Incredible price cuts on the 2008–09s. Powerful V8 engines provide brisk acceleration with plenty of low-end torque for trailering heavy loads; lots of passenger and cargo room; a seven-year powertrain warranty on the 2002–04 models; and a comfortable ride. **Weak points:** Both the Durango and Aspen will be axed in late 2009. 2005–07 models dropped the seven-year powertrain warranty, and the 2008s don't have the standard lifetime powertrain warranty given by dealers across the border. Poor acceleration with the V6; excessive fuel consumption because of the Durango's heft, especially with the more powerful engines; chronic Hemi engine stalling; unacceptable emergency handling; unsteady road manners; sudden jerks when passing over bumps; harsh abrupt downshifts; obstructed rear visibility; and difficult rear entry and exit. The climate-control system won't blow air on the floor and your face at the same time (on early models); the drivetrain's durability is problematic; ball joints are practically biodegradable (also a Dakota failing); and a painfully loud pounding noise is heard while cruising with the rear windows down. **New for 2008:** Nothing significant. Both vehicles will be sold as hybrids for the 2009 model year. Equipped with a 325-hp 5.7L V8, the vehicles will run on electric power to about 40 km/h (25 mph), when the gasoline engine takes over. Fuel savings are estimated to increase by about 25 percent.

2008 TECHNICAL DATA

POWERTRAIN (FRONT-DRIVE/4×4)

Engines: 3.7L V6 (210 hp) • 4.7L V8
(235 hp) • 5.7L Hemi V8 (330 hp);
Transmissions: 4-speed auto. • 5-speed
auto.

DIMENSION/CAPACITY

Passengers: 3/3/2; Wheelbase: 119.2 in.;
H: 74.3/L: 201.0/W: 76.0 in.; Headroom
F/R1/R2: 3.5/3.5/3.5 in.; Legroom F/R1/
R2: 41.0/27.5/28.0 in.; Cargo volume:
44.5 cu. ft.; Fuel tank: 102L/regular; Tow
limit: 8,700 lb.; Load capacity: 1,260 lb.;
GVWR: 6,600 lb.; Turning circle: 43.0
ft.; Ground clearance: 6.0 in.; Weight:
5,335 lb.

MODEL HISTORY: Essentially a re-badged Dakota pickup, the Durango is larger than the Jeep Grand Cherokee but shorter than the Ford Expedition. It underwent a redesign in 2004, when it got heavier and more complex. Interestingly, the Durango's 5.7L Hemi V8 has a 3,950 kg (8,700 lb.) towing capacity, giving this mid-sized truck as much hauling power as some costlier full-sized sport-utilities. A few 1998–2005 models carry the then-standard V6, but most Durangos have been ordered with the more robust 4.7L, 5.2L, 5.7L Hemi, and optional 5.9L V8 engines. **1999**—Added rear-wheel drive, a rear power outlet, steering-wheel-mounted radio controls, and heated mirrors. **2000**—The standard V6 was replaced by the 4.7L V8, suspension was upgraded, and a sporty R/T package was introduced. **2001**—A standard electronic transfer case, interior upgrades, 15-inch wheels, and a tilt steering column. The 5.2L V8 was dropped. **2003**—An upgraded 5-speed automatic transmission; standard four-wheel disc brakes. **2004**—Reworked, with a larger chassis, more power, an improved ride and handling, additional interior luxury features, and a slightly restyled front end. This SUV also gains almost 180 kg (400 lb.). The Durango is now offered with rear-wheel drive and two all-wheel-drive systems, one with low-range gearing. **2005**—Addition of a new optional navigation system. Three engines are available: a new 3.7L V6, a 4.7L V8, and a newly optional 5.7L Hemi V8 with almost 100 more horses than the largest previous engine. **2006**—The Hemi V8 comes with a fuel-saving cylinder deactivation feature called MDS (Multi-Displacement System), borrowed from Chrysler's Hemi-powered car lines. **2007**—The 4.7L V8 engine allows drivers the choice of using ethanol, gasoline, or any mixture of the two. The exterior was restyled, and second-row bucket seats were added. Aspen joins the ranks as an "elegant" Durango.

COST ANALYSIS: A new Durango SLT 4×4 sells for $33,545 in Canada; across the border, you can get it for $33,810 (U.S.), so stay in Canada. Buy a second-series 2004 or later model for more savings. The 2006's cylinder deactivation feature has so far not generated any reports of malfunctions, so it's not as risky a buy as first thought. This year's exterior restyling is no big deal. **Best alternatives:** Check out the Honda Pilot, Nissan Xterra, and Toyota Highlander. **Options:** Get the 4.7L V8 or 5.2L V8 engine. Although the Hemi option pays for itself at resale time, the engine is still relatively unproven and has elicited serious reliability and performance complaints over the past several years. An anti-theft system is a must-have. **Rebates:** $5,000+ rebates likely by the end of 2008. **Delivery/PDI:** $1,300. **Depreciation:** Fairly rapid; slower if equipped with the Hemi engine. **Insurance cost:** Above average. **Parts supply/cost:** Parts have been moderately priced and plentiful because of the availability of competitively priced parts from the Dakota parts bin, but this will change if Chrysler drops the Dakota after 2009 (see

Chrysler/Mitsubishi Dakota/Raider). Expensive brake and drivetrain servicing. **Annual maintenance cost:** Average. **Warranty:** Bumper-to-bumper 3 years/60,000 km; powertrain 5 years/100,000 km; rust perforation 5 years/160,000 km. **Supplementary warranty:** An extended warranty is a must. **Highway/city fuel economy:** *3.7L V6:* 11.0/15.9 L/100 km; *4.7L V8:* 12.0/17.4 L/100 km; *5.7L Hemi V8:* 12.1/18.0 L/100 km; *5.9L V8:* 13.2/18.9 L/100 km.

QUALITY/RELIABILITY: Quality control has declined markedly. Body components and trim items still seem to be blue-light specials. For additional owner comments, go to *www-odi.nhtsa.dot.gov/cars/problems/complain*. **Owner-reported problems:** Chronic stalling (Hemi engine); engine crankshaft, drive shaft, differential, motor mount, ball joint (covered by a 10-year extended warranty), and wheel bearing failures; chronic drivetrain whines and howls; electrical system and brake defects (spongy brakes, warped rotors); seat controls need to be continually reset; Airbag warning light is constantly lit; airbag shuts off; AC failures, or air not cold enough; rear air vents work only part-time; dash rattles; and premature differential bearing failures. **Warranty performance:** Average. **Likely failures:** Automatic transmission, steering, ball joints, and control arms:

> 2003 Dodge Durango upper ball joint failed on interstate at 65 mph [105 km/h]. Right front wheel and assembly separated from vehicle, causing single-car accident. Skidded into guard rail. Damage estimated at $10,000 plus.

Other problem spots are brake rotors and pads; centre wheel caps, which may fly off; AC compressor and evaporator; and water leaks.

ROAD PERFORMANCE: Acceleration/torque: Although the V6 may look like a bargain, it's not powerful enough for a vehicle this large. The 4.7L V8 is the best compromise for most driving chores. If you intend to tow a trailer or carry a full load of passengers, move up to the huskier 5.7L. **Transmission:** Automatic transmission downshifts can be abrupt at times. The floor-mounted transfer-case lever can be a stretch for some drivers. **Routine handling:** 2004 models provide easier handling and a more pleasant ride. Some body lean and front-end plowing in fast turns. **Emergency handling:** Acceptable. Not as ponderous as most vehicles this size. Cornering is well controlled and handling is more crisp and predictable on the 2004 version. **Steering:** Good, most of the time. Very responsive, with lots of road feedback. **Braking:** Mediocre (100–0 km/h: 43 m with the 4.7L V8).

SAFETY SUMMARY: Side-view mirror is too large to see around and blocks view when making turns. Owners report long waits for recall repairs that in some cases don't improve performance, notably the recall to fix the ABS. **Airbags:** Reports of airbags failing to deploy. **ABS:** Standard; on rear wheels only. **Head restraints F/R:** *1999–2003:* ★; *2004:* ★★★★. **Visibility F/R:** ★:

> I have a 2005 Dodge Durango. The way the vehicle is engineered there are serious blind spots. This is observed when the driver looks to his [or her] right. The passenger side "B" pillar is in their direct view. The way the front cockpit is designed you can't

see overhead street lights while stopped or approaching a stop bar. There are also blind spots to the passenger side and rear and driver's side rear.

Pet transport: ★★★★.

SAFETY COMPLAINTS: All models/years: Sudden acceleration and frequent stalling. • Vehicle wanders all over the road. • Transmission/differential breakdowns. • Collapsing ball joints (warranty extended). • Loss of brakes. • Electrical fires. • Violent shaking. **1999**—Horn failure. • Power windows go down by themselves and won't go back up. • Brakes slow down but don't completely stop vehicle when in Reverse on an incline. • Rear liftgate support rod breaks. **1999–2001**—Vehicle can be put into gear without pressing the brake pedal; in one incident, child accidentally moved shift lever out of Park, causing vehicle to roll into lake; in another, child placed transmission into Drive and vehicle took off. **2000**—Accelerator tends to stick. • Loss of all electrical power. • Defective brake retainer spring causes loss of braking ability and cracks the rim. • In one incident, the steering wheel locked up while driving and had to be jerked free; dealer suggested that the clock spring broke. • Steering wheel falls off. • Seat belt fails to release when release button is fully depressed. **2001**—Left front wheel flies off vehicle. • Suspension causes vehicle to go out of control over uneven roads. • Steering will suddenly pull to the left or right. • Surging when cruise control is engaged. • Middle fold-down rear seat doesn't lock properly; in one case, it hit the driver in the head when brakes were applied, causing a concussion. • Second-row seat leaves a sharp edge exposed when it's tumbled forward for rear access. • Cracked fuel tank. **2002**—Vehicle slips into gear without keys in the ignition. • Passenger-side window suddenly shatters. • Exhaust fumes come in through back door. **2003**—Early engine failure caused by oil system defect. • Faulty ABS pump results in extended stopping distance. • Erratically performing cruise control. • Door locks and unlocks for no reason. **2004**—Instrument-cluster fire. • Misfiring caused by water getting into the spark plug area. • Complete loss of steering. • Polymer bumper cracks in cold weather. • Rear wiper falls off. • Unsafe speed control on Hemi-equipped models causes engine to race when going downhill. • Rear-view mirror creates a serious blind spot. **2005**—270 safety complaints already logged by NHTSA; half that number would be normal. • Vehicle shakes violently when driven with rear windows down. • Tie rod snaps:

> When I got out and walked around to the driver's side, I saw my left front tire laying flat parallel with the ground, pinned partially under the vehicle. All of the components of the tire (the brakes, suspension, brake line, etc.) were still attached to the tire. Where the upper ball joint should have been, there was a large crack in the metal, and the tie rod was snapped. There was damage to the front left side of the vehicle due to the impact with the pillar.

• Fuel spurts out when refuelling (covered by a recall). • Sudden acceleration caused by the accelerator sticking. • Tons of complaints relative to chronic stalling when going uphill, decelerating, or shifting into Reverse from a cold start:

I have a 2005 Hemi Durango Limited with 3,300 miles [5,300 km] on it. Since new, the vehicle has occasionally died when making low speed turns. The dealer has informed me that the PCM flash provided by Dodge has not corrected the problem and they are still working on a fix. Overall the vehicle has stalled five times. I have also filed a similar complaint for my '05 Ram 2500 with the Hemi engine.

• Sudden steering loss:

My firm represents several passengers and the personal representatives of the estates of two decedent[s] who were killed when a 2005 Dodge Durango lost steering control on the Florida Turnpike. The vehicle is a rental vehicle from Dollar [Rent A] Car. It may be a case where the bolts in the steering were missing.

2006—What a difference a year makes: Only 56 safety-related complaints registered by NHTSA. • Airbags inadvertently deploy. • Chronic stalling continues to plague the Durango. • Vehicle won't start. • Steering wheel locks, or jerks to one side when turning. • ABS activates prematurely. **2007**—Faulty wheel sensor causes traction control to activate at the wrong time. • When in Reverse, transmission jumps into Neutral. • Driver has to steer to the left to stay in a straight line. • Passenger front window goes down on its own. • Fuel spews out of the filler pipe when fuelling. • Spare tire not the same size or type as others. This caused serious problems with light trucks, so Dodge switched to same-size spares for trucks. The automaker should do the same with the Durango spares.

Secret Warranties/Internal Bulletins/Service Tips

All models/years: Internal service bulletins cover the following problems: Engine knocking, stalling, poor performance; vehicle bucking during wide-open throttle operation; and transmission and suspension defects. **1999**—Engine overheating. • Hard starts and stalling. • Poor AC performance. • Front-end squeaking or creaking. • Brake grinding or growling. **1999–2003**—Upper and lower ball joints, control arm, and bushing failures. Chrysler has extended the warranty to 10 years/160,000 km (100,000 mi.) on the 2000–03 Durangos and Dakotas. On other model years, Chrysler sometimes offers a 50 percent replacement refund, which doesn't help much when applied to the full retail charge. Stand your ground and ask that the 10-year extension be applied (see CanadianDriver, "Chrysler recalls 600,000 Dodge Durangos, Dakotas," *www.canadiandriver.com/news/041213-2.htm*). **2000**—The central timer module can be short-circuited by electromagnetic interference from airports, military installations, power fields, etc. When this happens, many of the vehicle's electrical systems will go haywire. Ask Chrysler to install a revised module. • Harsh upshifts or downshifts can be smoothed out by reprogramming the PCM or TCM. • A front axle noise on acceleration may be fixed by replacing the right-side front axle bearing. • Driveline noise, vibration. **2000–01**—If the MIL comes on, indicating a TCC/OD solenoid performance problem, consider replacing the transmission pressure-boost valve cover plate. **2000–04**—AC water leak into passenger area. **2001**—Constant velocity joint-boot integrity (the joint boot wears out quickly). • Troubleshooting Transmission warning lights. • Silencing a noisy suspension. • Steering column pop or snap. **2002–03**—An erratically shifting automatic transmission may require a re-calibrated PCM or TCM. • Automatic transmission may overheat. • A "customer satisfaction program" will fix the automatic transmission's torque converter for free. • Brake pads will be replaced for free to cure excessive vibration (TSB #05-007-03). • Water leak at the B-post seam and roof. **2004**—AC/heater fluttering. • Suspension squawk or screech. • Campaign to correct left-front door flange rusting. • Exhaust system drone. **2004–05**—Tips for eliminating a steering snapping or ticking sound. • Troubleshooting a malfunctioning AC. • Installation of improved brakes to reduce vibration and shudder. **2005**—Idle vibration and body resonance. • Wind noise at top of rear door. • AC hissing. **2005–06**—Ring marks on glass. **2007**—Automatic transmission may default to Neutral. • Torque converter shudder. • AC sends warm air out from the vents. • Side door wind noise.

DURANGO PROFILE

	1999	2000	2001	2002	2003	2004	2005	2006	2007
Cost Price ($) (negotiable)									
4×2	36,705	37,750	—	—	—	—	—	—	—
4×4 (26%)	38,070	39,115	38,410	38,060	38,765	41,975	42,750	43,320	42,540
Used Values ($)									
4×2 ▲	5,000	6,500	—	—	—	—	—	—	—
4×2 ▼	4,500	5,500	—	—	—	—	—	—	—
4×4 ▲	3,500	4,000	5,000	7,000	8,000	11,000	14,000	18,000	23,000
4×4 ▼	3,000	3,500	4,500	5,500	6,500	10,000	12,000	16,000	21,000
Reliability	2	2	2	2	2	2	2	3	4
Crash Safety (F)	2	2	4	4	4	5	5	5	5
Side	—	—	—	—	—	—	5	—	—
Offset	3	3	3	3	3	—	—	—	—
Rollover	—	—	3	3	3	3	3	3	3

JEEP CHEROKEE, GRAND CHEROKEE ★★★

RATING: Average (2002–08); Not Recommended (1985–2001). Oh, how the mighty have fallen. Jeep's Cherokee and Grand Cherokee were perennial bestsellers a decade ago when the Japanese and South Korean competition was practically non-existent. Now, they are also-ran SUVs that have no future due to their mediocre performance and poor quality control. As with the Wrangler, the Cherokee's forte is its superior off-roading capability (it was replaced in 2002 by the Liberty). For highway cruising, off-roading, or city use, the Grand Cherokee is the better choice of the two. **Strong points:** 2008 and 2009 prices are much lower. Powerful V8 and plenty of cargo space (Grand Cherokee); easy handling; a comfortable ride; and a smooth-shifting transmission—when it's not in the shop for repairs. Good fuel economy and smooth, integrated drivetrain performance with the 6-cylinder.

A comprehensive 7-year powertrain warranty on 2002–04 versions. **Weak points:** Abrupt throttle tip-in; restricted rear visibility; high fuel consumption with the Grand Cherokee; an unreliable powertrain and fuel system; cheap, rattle-prone interior trim; low door openings make for difficult entry and exit; uncomfortable rear seating; an unusually high number of safety-related complaints; and severe rusting around fenders, wheelwells, doors, and door handles. *Cherokee:* The high step-up and narrow rear doors make entry and exit difficult. Back-seat access is also problematic. **New for 2008:** Lightly restyled this year with a new interior, front and rear styling, high intensity headlights, and larger wheel sizes. The new 4.7L V8 gives 30 percent more power but drives down fuel economy.

MODEL HISTORY: Cherokee and its early partner, the Wagoneer, were the first four-door Jeeps designed under the tutelage of American Motors (boy, do I miss the straight-talking Bill Pickett, AMC Canada's former prez). Intended to be downsized and upgraded replacements for the old full-sized wagons, they were an instant success. They kept AMC afloat until the Chrysler buyout.

2008 GRAND CHEROKEE TECHNICAL DATA

POWERTRAIN (REAR-DRIVE/4×4)

Engines: 3.7L V6 (210 hp) • 3.0L 6-cyl. diesel (215 hp) • 4.7L V8 (235 hp) • 5.7L V8 (330 hp) • SRT8 6.1L V8 (420 hp); Transmissions: 5-speed auto./man. • 5-speed man.

DIMENSION/CAPACITY

Passengers: 2/3; Wheelbase: 109.5. in.; H: 67.7/L: 186.6/W: 73.3 in.; Headroom F/R: N/A; Legroom F/R: 41.7/35.5 in.; Cargo volume: 34.5 cu. ft.; Fuel tank: 78L/regular; Tow limit: 3,500–6,500 lb.; Load capacity: 1,050–1,100 lb.; GVWR: 4,889–6,200 lb.; Turning circle: 37.4 ft.; Ground clearance: 7.0 in.; Weight: 4,441 lb.

Transmission choices over the past two decades include 4- or 5-speed manuals and 3- or 4-speed automatics. The 3-speed automatic is the most reliable; the manuals have heavy clutches and notchy shifting. The smaller engines are jokes in such large vehicles, most of which are available with optional, larger engines. These Jeeps wander at highway speeds (now a Dodge truck/SUV problem; see *Dawe v. Courtesy Chrysler* in Part Three), and the numb power steering doesn't help. They aren't a pleasure to manoeuvre or park around town. Interiors are spacious— although the spare tire reduces interior space—and will easily and comfortably accommodate five people on long rides.

Early Cherokees have very poor repair histories. Buyers should be especially wary of the 4-cylinder engine; premature brake wear; the electrical system; the fuel system; and the failure-prone, expensive-to-repair 4×4 system. The 1995–2001 Cherokees provide smoother, more integrated drivetrain performance (later models offered full-time AWD) and give better fuel economy. However, interior room is still limited, standard features are few, rear visibility is restricted, and brakes remain troublesome. These later models are apparently less failure-prone, although long-term reliability remains questionable.

Grand Cherokee

Although early Grand Cherokees are just as failure-prone as other early Jeeps, they are easier to handle, give a more comfortable ride, and are equipped with an optional 5.9L V8. Yet you'll still find limited rear seating, a difficult entry and exit, high fuel consumption, failure-prone engines and transmissions, and poor-quality fit and finish. **1999**—Grand Cherokee is longer, wider, roomier, and generally more refined. A new optional 235-hp 4.7L V8 replaced the base 4.0L 6-cylinder, used since the early '60s in American Motors' Ramblers. A Dana-built Quadra-Trac transmission was added, and a restyled exterior gave this upscale Cherokee a more modern look. Brakes and steering components were upgraded as well. **2003–04**—Improved steering and brake feel; additional storage space. These models still suffer from poor quality control, which afflicts the engine, transmission, brakes, AC, and body fit and finish. **2005**—A major redesign softened the Grand Cherokee's road manners, and a re-engineered suspension improved the ride via three 4×4 systems and a longer and wider platform. The new models offered three engines, including a new 325-hp 5.7L Hemi V8 with fuel-saving cylinder deactivation. **2006**—Introduction of the Grand Cherokee SRT8, Jeep's first high-performance SUV. Powered by a 420-hp 6.1L Hemi that will reportedly go 0–100 km/h in under 5 seconds, beating the Porsche Cayenne Turbo and BMW X5. Other nice features: a lighter-weight four-wheel drive system, a modified suspension, upgraded brakes and exhaust, and a fresh-air induction system that allows for a fording depth of up to 48 cm (19 in). **2007**—Standard curtain airbags, stability control, and a Mercedes-sourced 3.0L turbo diesel engine.

COST ANALYSIS: Selling new for $31,595/$46,795 (Laredo/Overland 5.7L), both Grand Cherokee models cost almost as much in the States ($31,185/$44,135) but they have lower actual transaction prices (a $3,000 cash allowance) due to Chrysler's desperate need for cash and the imploding American economy. The cheapest bargain would be a 2005 model bought either in the States or in Canada. Stay away from the new, totally redesigned diesel powerplant, however. Its Mercedes roots guarantee a fair amount of start-up glitches. Plus, it will have to handle reformulated fuel from 2007 on. Wait on the 2008–09 upgraded diesels. **Best alternatives:** *Cherokee:* When compared with the 2002 Liberty, a used 2001 (its last model year) Cherokee offers more base power, sells for thousands less, and is much more reliable. *Grand Cherokee:* The 2003 and 2004 Grand Cherokee returned heavily discounted with some important upgrades, like a longer warranty, that make it a better choice than earlier models. Other 4×4s worth a look are the Honda CR-V, Hyundai Tucson or Santa Fe, Nissan Xterra or X-Trail, and Toyota RAV4 or 4Runner. **Rebates:** Prices will be cut by several thousand dollars to keep up with GM's deep discounting. Also, look for $2,000–$3,500 rebates. **Delivery/ PDI:** $1,300. **Warranty:** Bumper-to-bumper 3 years/60,000 km; powertrain 5 years/100,000 km; rust perforation 5 years/160,000 km. **Supplementary warranty:** A good idea for the powertrain of any model not covered for 7 years. **Options:** Get an anti-theft system, or kiss your vehicle goodbye. Choose your tires carefully. Off-road rubber with an aggressive tread isn't conducive to comfortable highway driving. *Grand Cherokee:* Get the 4.7L V8 for the best overall performance; the Hemi 5.7L doesn't give the fuel economy promised. **Depreciation:** Average. **Insurance cost:** Average for the Cherokee, but higher than average for the Grand Cherokee. **Parts supply/cost:** Moderately priced parts that are usually easily found. Owners report waits of several months for recall campaign parts. **Annual maintenance cost:** Higher than average without the 7-year warranty. The drivetrain is particularly expensive to repair. **Highway/ city fuel economy:** *Cherokee: 2.5L 4-cyl. and auto.: 10.0/13.4 L/100 km; 4.0L 6-cyl. and auto.: 10.2/15.0 L/100 km; 4.0L 6-cyl. and 4×4: 10.4/14.9 L/100 km. Grand Cherokee: 3.7L V6 and auto.: 10.3/14.2 L/100 km; 4.0L 6-cyl. and auto: 10.4/ 14.7 L/100 km; 4.0L 6-cyl. and 4×4: 10.4/14.9 L/100 km; 4.7L V8 and 4×4: 11.1/16.3 L/100 km; 5.7L Hemi V8: 11.2/16.5 L/100 km.*

QUALITY/RELIABILITY: Although not as badly built as the Ford Explorer, quality control is quite poor. Transmission, torque converter, brake, and fuel-system problems continue to dog Chrysler—and its customers. An inadequate base warranty and a spotty service record at Jeep dealerships compound a poor overall reliability record for the Cherokee. Long-term reliability doesn't look good for the Grand Cherokee either, despite its recent makeover. AWD components are expensive to maintain after the fourth year of use. The transfer cases and axles are unreliable, noisy, and prone to early wearout.

Another quality problem is the binding of the wheels in the Quadra-Trac system when the outer wheel can't rotate faster than the inner wheel during a turn, causing excessive noise and premature wear. Electrical system, power windows, and body deficiencies continue to plague these redesigned models, and everything points toward these vehicles being hazardous, underperforming, and costly to maintain as they age. **Owner-reported problems:** *Cherokee:* Knocking connecting rods on 6-cylinder engines. Selec-Trac 4×4 often requires expensive servicing after a few years of use or high mileage. Transmission bangs or clunks when shifting; steering fails; Engine and ABS warning lights stay on; frequent and expensive brake repairs because of warped rotors and cracked shoes; and excessive vibration and pulling when brakes are applied. The electrical system shorts, power windows fail, and rear wipers won't work. Premature shock absorber and tie-rod wearout results in uneven tire wear. Alloy wheels can fuse to the drums. AC leaks and failures, and engine and transfer-case oil leaks. *Grand Cherokee:* Engine is difficult to start, and diesel engine on 2007 models stalls. Crankshaft seal leaks, cylinder misfires, wobbly crank pulley and damper, chronic automatic transmission failures, rear-end whine on acceleration, excessive steering wander and noisy operation (honking), and premature wearout of original-equipment tires and ball joints. Excessive vibration at cruising speed may be caused by defective drive shafts or Goodyear Fortera HL tires that are out of round. Electrical and fuel-system glitches, poorly performing and expensive-to-maintain brakes, subpar body hardware and paint, and premature failure of the catalytic converter. Premature rusting of the undercarriage, steering spindle, brake lines, and exhaust. Plus, it's hard to secure loads to the roof rack. **Warranty performance:** Very tight-fisted in handling warranty claims.

ROAD PERFORMANCE: Acceleration/torque: *Cherokee:* The 6-cylinder engine provides a smooth and powerful performance with brisk acceleration (0–100 km/h: 9 sec.). The 2.5L 4-cylinder engine is noisy and lacks the power for serious hauling, and it is especially sluggish when hooked to the automatic transmission. *Grand*

Cherokee: Plenty of power with the inline 6-cylinder and V8 engines. The V8s accelerate to 100 km/h about as fast as the Ford Explorer. Excellent engines for off-roading, and the Hemi 5.7L provides impressive all-around performance—when it's not stalling out. **Transmission:** *Cherokee:* Smooth-shifting automatic, but it's the 5-speed manual gearbox that gives the best performance. *Grand Cherokee:* Usually shifts smoothly in all gear ranges (if working properly). Occasional abrupt throttle response can cause jerky shifting. **Steering:** *Cherokee:* Precise, with good road feedback. Many reports that the steering will suddenly veer to the right at highway speeds. *Grand Cherokee:* Fairly good, as a result of the 2000's enhancements. Suspension geometry requires constant steering corrections to keep vehicle on the highway. **Routine handling:** *Cherokee:* Average at moderate speeds. The ride is harsh and bouncy when the going gets rough. Doesn't take curves graciously, and likes to wander on the highway. *Grand Cherokee:* Ride comfort is augmented by a three-link rear axle. Handling is precise, with improved high-speed cornering stability. The Quadra-Trac system has a "Vari-Lok" feature that provides a mechanical lock in the low-range position for extra traction. Many complaints that the vehicle tends to wander all over the road. **Emergency handling:** *Cherokee:* Average. Good ground clearance and stiff suspension for off-roading. *Grand Cherokee:* Good. Cornering is well controlled, and handling is predictable and precise. Little body roll. **Braking:** *Cherokee:* Average (100–0 km/h: 41 m). *Grand Cherokee:* Very good (100–0 km/h: 40 m with the V8). Some plowing in hard stops. Braking upgrades have followed years of criticism related to sudden brake failure, poor braking performance, and the premature wearout of expensive major brake components.

SAFETY SUMMARY: Seat adjuster bar may increase severity of injury to lower legs in a collision. Location of fuel tank makes it fire-prone. In *Rolf v. Winger* (Jackson County, Missouri; October 2001), lawyers obtained a $5.7-million verdict in a wrongful death case in which a driver was killed when his Jeep Cherokee was rear-ended by a drunk driver. The collision caused the gas tank on the Cherokee to explode on impact. Confidential settlements were reached before trial with DaimlerChrysler and the pub where the drunk driver became intoxicated. (The case was tried against the remaining defendants, including the drunk driver's employer.) There are also many complaints that the low beam headlights give insufficient illumination. Be wary of tow figures given out by salespeople. They are often wrong; in particular, salespeople often don't divulge the lower rating for manual transmissions. **Airbags:** *Grand Cherokee:* Side airbags are standard. There have been many reports of airbags not deploying when they should or deploying when they shouldn't. **ABS:** 4W optional on Cherokee; standard on Grand Cherokee. ABS failures characterized by pedal going to the floor with no braking action and extended stopping distances. **Traction control:** Optional on Grand Cherokee. **Head restraints F/R:** *Cherokee: 1999:* ★★/★; *2001:* ★. *Grand Cherokee: 1999:* ★; *2001:* ★; *2002–04:* ★★/★; *2005–08:* ★★/★. **Visibility F/R:** *Cherokee:* ★★★★★/★; *Grand Cherokee:* ★★★★★/★★. **Pet transport:** ★★★/★★★★.

SAFETY COMPLAINTS: All models/years: Under-hood fires; one fire in the under-hood area believed to be caused by the headlight switch shorting out. • Ignition switch and steering column overheat. • Fuel leakage from the gas tank. • Transfer-case grinding, fluid leakage, and failure; leakage causes fire to ignite in exhaust system area. • Engine-mount bolts shear off, causing the engine to fall down. • Easy to mistake accelerator for brake pedal. • Brake rotors corrode, crack, and warp. • Brake rotor failure causes extended stopping distance and vibration when braking. • Frequent replacement of the master cylinder and proportioning valve. • Sudden, unintended acceleration, especially in vehicles equipped with a 4.7L engine:

> Local carwash employee entered into my 2005 Jeep Grand Cherokee. When ignition was turned on, the vehicle redlined and accelerated off of conveyor. Employee hit the brakes with no response. It collided with another vehicle and went through a towel cabinet and a brick wall. Four employees and myself were nearly killed. I took the driver out of the vehicle and while no one was in it, it was still trying to drive through the wall on its own (nothing was touching the accelerator).

• Frequent automatic transmission and differential failures. • Automatic transmission jumps from Park to Reverse. • Transmission allows vehicle to roll away even though it's in Park. • Power-steering bracket shears off, causing steering loss. • Complete electrical failure and sudden stalling. • Airbag, ABS, and Check Engine lights come on for no reason (Check Engine light often comes on due to a loose gas cap, defective #5 spark plug, or ignition coil). • Erratically functioning interior and exterior lights. • Headlights dim when the AC engages. • Frequent AC malfunctions. • Water leaks from dash and doors; water leakage through improperly welded seam near dash causes chronic electrical shorts. • Doors fall off because of defective hinges. 2000—Right rear door latch catches on fire while underway. • Leaking gas comes out of hoses (which appear to be dry-rotted) between gas tank filler and fuel tank. • Fuel leakage from tailpipe causes fumes to enter passenger compartment; in one case, dealer replaced fuel injectors and PCM. • Sudden stalling with loss of brakes and steering. • Premature transmission failure. • Rear axle misalignment causes vehicle to sway to the side of the road. • Steering lock-up while driving in a parking lot. • Plastic fuel tank is located too close to the rear bumper. • Tailgate glass shatters for no reason. 2001—Suspension, steering, and driveline fall off vehicle. • Cam sensor failures cause vehicle to lose all power. • Seat belt abrades from catching on door latch. • Horn is hard to access. • Incorrect speedometer readings. 2001–02—Airbag fails to deploy during collision. 2001–04—Brake goes to the floor without any braking effect. 2002—Waits of several months for recalled parts. • Check Engine light comes on, and vehicle suddenly stalls in traffic • 2003—Rear axle mounting bolt snaps. • Rear end sways left and right while driving. • Dashboard reflects onto windshield at night. • Driver seat unstable. 2004—Faulty ECM causes chronic stalling. • Imprecise steering. • Sunroof explodes while driving. • Power outlet wiring can easily overheat under a 20-amp load. 2005—Hemi engine loss of power; sudden acceleration. • Chronic stalling. • Shift lever stuck in Park. • Automatic transmission self-destructs just after transmission seal recall fix. Owners state the powertrain recall doesn't fix the problem. • Differential seal leaks fluid, grinds. • Windows won't open in cold weather if water seeps through the housing. • Seat belts are too short. • Sudden loss of power-steering fluid results in loss of steering ability. • Head restraint tilts driver's head too far forward. • Heated seats may burn occupant:

> I am a paraplegic and was a passenger in a 2005 Grand Cherokee with heated seats. It was a cool day and I turned on the seats. The heated seats burned both cheeks of my butt. I am confined to a bed until the burns heal.

• Tire jack won't lift vehicle high enough to change a tire. **2005–06**—Driver's knee can hit the ignition switch, shutting off vehicle. **2006**—It is easy to catch one's foot under the brake pedal. • Steering-wheel lockup. • Driver and passenger doors are not designed to stay open; they return with excessive force and smash ankles. • Horn is hard to activate. • Tilting head restraints prevent the use of some forward-facing child safety seats. • Running lights are blinding. **2006–07**—Chronic loss of power when accelerating:

> On many occasions my car has stalled out while I am driving. When this happens my power steering goes out and my wheels lock up. It mainly happens when I am going at a slow speed...but on 2 different occasions it has happened on the interstate at 110 [km/h].

2007—Excessive driveline vibration.

Secret Warranties/Internal Bulletins/Service Tips

All models: 1999–2000—Harsh upshifts or downshifts may require the reprogramming of the TCM or PCM under the emissions warranty, says TSB #21-09-00, published September 15, 2000. • Jeep's bulletins for these two model years address front axle whines or moans, rear-end whines at speeds greater than 65 km/h, long cranking times to start, steering-gear honking on turns, slow-to-retract seat belts, an intermittent bump felt when stopping, front-seat binding or sticking, brake roughness or pedal pulsation when brakes are applied, and cold air leaking into the passenger footwell. • A worn-out O-ring (quad ring) in the fuel-module assembly may be the cause of long cranking before starts. **1999–2001**—A front axle whine may require extensive repairs to correct, says TSB #03-001-01 Rev A. **1999–2003**—Paint delamination, peeling, or fading. • Many anecdotal reports of Chrysler paying for brake caliper and rotor replacement after the warranty has expired. **1999–2004**—Rough-running engine (see bulletin). • Front-door wind noise. • Suspension noise. **2001**—Harsh upshifts; a clunk or shudder noticed when accelerating. • Exhaust boom when idling. • Honking noise when turning. • Troubleshooting geartrain sound that enters into the passenger compartment. • Remedy for climate-control setting that may be too warm or too cool. **2001–02**—Vehicle runs rough or exhibits a bucking or hesitation. • Excessive vibration and brake-pedal pulsation. **2001–03**—Steering-wheel pop or tick noise. **2002**—4.7L engine crankshaft problems. • Brake roughness; front-brake pulsation. • Premature fuel-nozzle shutoff when fuelling. • Faulty seat cushion heater. • Inadvertent

---

HOT START MISFIRE, ROUGH IDLE

BULLETIN NO.: 18-031-03   DATE: SEP. 5, 2003

4.0L ROUGH ENGINE IDLE AFTER RESTART FOLLOWING A HOT SOAK

This bulletin involves the installation of a fuel injector insulator sleeve.
2000–04 (TJ) Wrangler
1999–2004 (WJ) Grand Cherokee
2000–01 (XJ) Jeep Cherokee

---

activation of panic alarm. **2002–03**—Shift/speed control improvements. • Transmission may operate only in Second gear. **2002–04**—Engine idle gets progressively rougher as the engine warms up. **2003**—Crankshaft burr. • Erratically shifting automatic transmission may require a re-calibrated PCM or TCM. • Automatic transmission may overheat. • A "customer satisfaction program" will fix the automatic transmission's torque converter for free. • Power-steering moan or whine. **2003–04**—Liftgate glass lifts up in wet conditions. **2004**—Rough cold engine operation. **2005**—Faulty connection may cause automatic tranny to "limp" home. • Remedy for diesel hard starts. • Water leaks at front pillar. • AC compressor growl. • Power-steering whine. • Roof rack wind turbulence. • Tailgate secondary seal may be loose, misaligned, or wrinkled. • Improved AC settings. **2005–06**—Improved temperature-control settings. • Troubleshooting tips to correct a rear suspension squeak. • Tips on removing windshield ring marks. **2006**—Loose, binding front-door window. **2007**—AC doesn't distribute cold air.

JEEP CHEROKEE, GRAND CHEROKEE PROFILE

	1999	2000	2001	2002	2003	2004	2005	2006	2007
Cost Price ($) (soft)									
Base 4×2	22,460	22,460	—	—	—	—	—	—	—
Cherokee 4×4	24,680	24,680	28,550	—	—	—	—	—	—
Gr. Cherokee (25%)	36,295	38,860	—	—	—	—	—	—	—
Gr. Cherokee 4×4 (25%)	36,295	38,860	39,790	39,005	39,225	39,775	38,990	39,470	40,285
Used Values ($)									
Base 4×2 ▲	3,000	3,500	—	—	—	—	—	—	—
Base 4×2 ▼	2,500	3,000	—	—	—	—	—	—	—
Cherokee 4×4 ▲	3,500	4,000	5,500	—	—	—	—	—	—
Cherokee 4×4 ▼	3,000	3,500	4,000	—	—	—	—	—	—
Gr. Cherokee ▲	4,000	4,500	—	—	—	—	—	—	—
Gr. Cherokee ▼	3,500	4,000	—	—	—	—	—	—	—
Gr. Cherokee 4×4 ▲	4,500	5,000	7,000	8,000	10,500	13,000	15,000	18,000	23,000
Gr. Cherokee 4×4 ▼	4,000	4,500	5,500	6,500	8,500	11,000	13,000	16,000	21,000
Reliability	3	3	3	3	4	4	4	3	3
Crash Safety (F)	3	3	3	—	—	—	—	—	—
Grand Cherokee	3	3	3	3	3	3	5	5	5
Side	3	3	3	—	—	—	—	—	—
Grand Cherokee	4	4	4	4	4	4	5	5	5
IIHS Side									
Grand Cherokee	—	—	—	—	—	—	2	2	2
Offset	2	2	2	—	—	—	—	—	—
Grand Cherokee	2	2	2	2	2	2	5	5	5
Rollover	—	—	2	2	2	—	4	3	3

Note: The 2008 models posted crashworthiness scores similar to the 2007s.

JEEP COMMANDER

bad buy

★

RATING: Not Recommended (2006–08). This huge SUV makes no sense whatso-ever, even with its 2008 $10,000 price cut, and 2009 is likely to be this behemoth's last model year. Commander is essentially a $32,295–$43,395, five- and seven-pas-senger, supersized Grand Cherokee with undersized tires (until this year). You get the same Grand Cherokee platform and off-road capability with similar overall highway performance and reliability. However, powertrain (transmission), brake, and fit and finish (rain leaks through the side rails, above the dashboard) glitches are worrisome, and the dropping of Jeep's 7-year powertrain warranty and change of ownership will likely mean long-term maintenance costs will surge. Buyers have the choice of a rather lacklustre 3.7L V6, a more suitable 4.7L V8, or a 5.7L Hemi V8, and of three full-time 4×4 systems. The V6 comes with a 5-speed automatic transmission, while a multi-speed auto-matic is used with both V8s. Two models are available with two- or four-wheel drive and a towing capacity of 1,590 kg (3,500 lb.).

Styling is rather bland, squarish, and utilitarian, yet for a vehicle so large it has a surprisingly small interior that is just average for pet and cargo transport. The three passenger-seat rows provide raised "theatre" seating, and the second and third rows fold flat. Some major design miscues include a minuscule third row that's too small for most adults, fake-looking riveted fender flares, three sunroofs, four driver-side air vents, and a huge rear overhang. Two important safety features found on the Commander are electronic stability control and

2008 COMMANDER TECHNICAL DATA

POWERTRAIN (REAR-DRIVE/4×4)

Engines: 3.7L V6 (210 hp) • 4.7L V8 (305 hp) • 5.7L V8 (330 hp); Transmissions: 5-speed auto./man. • 5-speed auto.

DIMENSION/CAPACITY

Passengers: 2/3/2; Wheelbase: 109.5. in.; H: 71.9/L: 188.5/W: 74.8 in.; Headroom F/R1/R2: 4.5/5.0/0.1 in.; Legroom F/R1/R2: 42.0/26.5/24.5 in.; Cargo volume: 34.5 cu. ft.; Fuel tank: 77.6L/regular; Tow limit: 3,500–7,200 lb.; Load capacity: 1,230–1,620 lb.; GVWR: 4,889–6,200 lb.; Turning circle: 37.0 ft.; Ground clearance: 9.9 in.; Weight: 4,441 lb.

electronic roll mitigation, a system that selectively deploys side curtain airbags as directed by sensors whenever a rollover appears imminent. Incidentally, although the 2006–08 Commander's front crashworthiness ratings have been excellent, NHTSA tests have concluded it has an average tendency to roll over—in spite of the standard stability control.

Jeep is selling this gas-guzzler while most shoppers are downsizing their SUV choices in reaction to higher fuel prices and insurance premiums. This means smart buyers will wait at least until the end of 2009 to get a cheaper, better quality Commander. Expect the Commander to carry a profit margin of at least 25 percent of its MSRP, which will help pay for the estimated $10,000 in rebates and discounts that should be available throughout 2008 and 2009. In Canada, the Sport sells for $32,295; the top-of-the-line Limited costs $43,395. These same models sell in the States for $26,610 (U.S.) and $36,120 (U.S.), respectively. A new 2006 Commander (its first year) that sold for $40,000 is now worth only a bit more than $19,000. **New for 2008:** A more powerful 4.7L V8, a new five- and seven-passenger Sport R model, and more off-road drivetrain options.

SAFETY COMPLAINTS: All years: Poor wet weather performance:

> The Jeep Commander, on a wet highway, is a major problem for anyone behind. Reason: Horrible design results in more spray and mist kicked up than an eighteen wheeler. This horribly designed, unaerodynamic pile of junk is a major menace that turns a wet highway into a moving cloud and [it] will be the cause of major pile-ups.

2006—Sudden, unintended acceleration, or total loss of power:

> I have purchased a 2006 Jeep Commander. It has 6,000 miles [9,660 km] on it. At 4,200 miles [6,760 km] it started stalling for no apparent reason. It has done it in stop and go traffic and has done it when I was traveling at 35 mph [56 km/h]. Other Jeep Commander owners are experiencing the same problem. See Jeep Commander thread at *Edmunds.com.*

• Engine self-destructs. • Headrests can't be removed, making it impossible to secure a child booster seat:

> The Commander headrests seem to be fixed in place. They just seem to move forward when you flip the seat down to access the third row. To make matters worse, they are fixed in a slightly forward position, which forces the booster seat to pitch forward. I can correct that slightly by reclining the seat back, but, in the Commander, the second row seat only slightly reclines. In any case, the booster can't be installed properly or safely, according to the manual.

• Tire jack bends under weight of the vehicle. • Windshield is easily cracked by small pebbles. **2007**—Airbags and seat belt pre-tensioner may fail to deploy in a collision. • Chronic stalling when accelerating or turning may be related to poor ignition design:

It is my belief that the placement and design of the ignition may be to blame for this and other stalls (which are now under NHTSA investigation). It appears that if you hit your knee on the key while it is in the ignition you can easily turn the truck off while it is in operation.

 ecret Warranties/Internal Bulletins/Service Tips

2006—Improved temperature-control settings. • Troubleshooting tips to correct a rear suspension squeak. • Loose, binding front-door window. • Interior water leaks and excessive wind noise. **2007**—Poor AC distribution of cold air.

bad buy **PACIFICA** ★

RATING: Not Recommended. (2004–08). This car shouldn't be bought at all, but if you're feeling lucky yet also want to keep your risks to a minimum, buy an AWD Pacifica in the States for about $10,000 less than in Canada (AWD versions keep their value better). Forget the hype: This is neither a performance nor an off-road vehicle; it's more like your dad's luxury station wagon—or a mini-minivan with four swing-out doors. **Strong points:** A comfortable ride and quiet interior; lots of front- and middle-row seating space and storage areas; easily accessible seat controls; a cargo floor that's low enough for easy loading and unloading; excellent front and side crashworthiness scores, and three-point seat belts for all six seats; impressive ventilation system; and a 7-year powertrain warranty on 2004 models. Low resale values for smart used-car shoppers. **Weak points:** Scheduled to get the axe in late 2008, this move will guarantee parts shortages, poor and expensive servicing, and a low resale value. The 2007's 4.0L is a gas hog; abrupt transmission shifts remain a problem through the 2007 model year; and second-row seats accommodate only two occupants, making it necessary for whoever picks the shortest straw to sit in the cramped third-row seat, bereft of a seatback head restraint. Other problems are restricted rear visibility, and unproven body and mechanicals. **New for 2008:** Nothing good. Pacifica will cease production in late 2008 and possibly return as a redesigned 2011 model with more car attributes for better highway performance.

MODEL HISTORY: Pacifica is an SUV, minivan, and station wagon all rolled into one. It's a big, tall vehicle that appears much lower and longer than it really is. Second- and third-row seats fold flat, and those in the third row split 50/50. Built in Windsor, Ontario, on the same production line as Chrysler's minivans, Chrysler calls it a "sports tourer" and cringes every time it's referred to as a "mini-minivan." It's actually

2008 PACIFICA TECHNICAL DATA

POWERTRAIN (FRONT-DRIVE/AWD)
Engines: 3.8L V6 (253 hp) • 4.0L V6 (255 hp); Transmissions: 4-speed auto. • 6-speed auto.
DIMENSION/CAPACITY
Passengers: 2/2/2; Wheelbase: 116.3 in.; H: 68.3/L: 198.5/W: 79.3 in.; Headroom F/R1/R2: 5.5/5.0/0.0 in. (that's right, zilch); Legroom F/R1/R2: 38.0/31.0/22.5 in.; Cargo volume: 35.5 cu. ft.; Fuel tank: 87L/regular; Tow limit: 2,600–3,500 lb.; Load capacity: 897 lb.; GVWR: 6,600 lb.; Turning circle: 39.8 ft.; Ground clearance: 4.8 in.; Weight: 4,556 lb.

wider and heavier than the Chrysler Town & Country minivan, and almost as long.

Pacifica's V6 uses both a front-drive and all-wheel-drive powertrain (an on-demand 4×4 system, transferring power to the rear wheels when the front wheels lose traction). The original 4-speed automatic transmission included an AutoStick manual-shift feature. Handling and ride are enhanced through a strut-type suspension in the front and a multi-link independent suspension in the rear, featuring automatic load levelling.

Safety features include standard four-wheel disc brakes with ABS, a tire-pressure monitoring system, three-row head curtain airbags, adjustable pedals, and driver-side inflatable knee bolsters.

2007—A 4.0L SOHC aluminum V6 engine mated to an all-new 6-speed transmission replaced the old 3.8L V6 and added 53 horses. All-row side curtain airbags, electronic stability control, electronic throttle control (ETC), and traction control were added, as well as an available ParkView rear backup camera.

COST ANALYSIS: In Canada, the base front-drive Touring sells for $32,795; across the border, you can get it for almost $7,000 less, or $25,976 (U.S.) (plus $730 freight). An AWD Limited costs $33,034 in the States, while Canadian dealers charge $38,795, or almost $6,000 more (plus $1,300 freight). With just a few options, the Pacifica's Canadian price tag can hit $40,000—the price for an option-loaded AWD Town & Country, or his-and-hers entry-level Caravans. **Best alternatives:** Try the Honda Pilot, Lexus RX series, Nissan Murano, or Toyota Highlander. **Options:** The most expensive and non-essential options include a $1,200 video system and a navigation system with a small screen located in the instrument cluster (bright sunlight washes out the navigation map). Traction control is not available for all-wheel-drive Pacificas, but it comes standard on front-drive models. **Rebates:** 2008 models will get huge rebates of $5,000+ by the summer of 2008. Another $2,000 will be added in early 2009. **Delivery/PDI:** $1,300. **Depreciation:** Faster than average. **Insurance cost:** Fairly costly. **Parts supply/cost:** Parts aren't easily found and are relatively expensive. **Annual maintenance cost:** Predicted to be costlier than average. **Warranty:** Bumper-to-bumper 3 years/60,000 km; powertrain 5 years/100,000 km; rust perforation 5 years/160,000 km. **Supplementary warranty:** An extended warranty would be a wise buy until long-term reliability has been established. **Highway/city fuel economy:** 8.7/13.4 L/100 km. Owners say fuel consumption is much more than advertised because of the vehicle's heft and rather high drag coefficient.

QUALITY/RELIABILITY: Quality control has been fair, though powertrain performance continues to be problematic (for example, many owners report a clanging noise when shifting from Park to Reverse). Other recurring deficiencies that aren't safety-related are a constant popping and clicking caused by a defective power transfer unit, frequent stalling when turning, an inoperative climate control screen, and driver-side water leaks. **Warranty performance:** Predicted to be average.

ROAD PERFORMANCE: Acceleration/torque: The new V6 performs reasonably well but may not be powerful enough for a vehicle this heavy. Earlier engines are annoyingly loud when climbing long grades or passing at high speeds. **Transmission:** Some gear-hunting and occasional abrupt shifts. The 4-speed automatic also kicks down for long periods when the vehicle is fully loaded or going uphill. The tranny performs much less erratically than the transmissions used in the vehicle's first two years of production. **Routine handling:** Fairly nimble. **Emergency handling:** Feels top-heavy; some body lean in hard cornering. Fairly wide turning circle. **Steering:** Not much steering feel; road feedback is limited. **Braking:** Large four-wheel disc brakes perform quite well with little fade, even under heavy use.

SAFETY SUMMARY: NHTSA-rated five-star occupant protection in front and side collisions. Rear visibility is seriously compromised by the car's high beltline and the thick rear side pillars. Backing up and changing lanes can be scary. **Airbags:** Front and side curtain. **ABS:** Standard; on all four wheels. **Visibility F/R:** ★★★:

> The first incident occurred backing up in my bank parking lot...bam! Where did that pole come from? Cost: $850. My deductible: $500. The second occurrence happened in my driveway. Again, backing up. This time, the coast was clear before I got into the car. Next thing I heard as I was looking back was a crunch. Between $5K and $8K damage to the other vehicle. Oh, I wasn't going any more than 5 mph [8 km/h]! Thing is, even after the accident, I still didn't see the car when I looked back to see what the ?#$@ happened!

Pet transport: ★★★★.

SAFETY COMPLAINTS: All years: Many reports that the glass roof explodes. **2004—** About 264 safety-related complaints registered by NHTSA up to July 2006. • Chronic stalling continues despite recall fix. • Drivers often inadvertently hit the ignition key with their knee, shutting off the vehicle while underway. • Transmission shifts abruptly, slips, or flares, especially when the AC is enabled. • Transmission sticks in Drive. • In one incident, the rear control arm fractured, and inner tie-rods had to be replaced:

> It was found via NY state inspection at about 27,000 miles [43,450 km] that the right front tie rod end was worn to the point of near failure, which would have the potential to cause the front right wheel to fall off.

• Many reports of ignition switch failures. • Incorrect fuel gauge readings ($750 (U.S.) to replace the fuel tank). • Gas tank is easily punctured. • Sharp door edge cuts an exiting occupant's leg. • Headlights won't work (not part of recall). **2004–05**—Lower front bumper falls off. **2005**—Almost 300 safety incidents registered (double what is average), many of them recounting hair-raising "adventures" caused by the Pacifica suddenly stalling in traffic or on the highway (also confirmed by *www.edmunds.com*):

> I have owned a 2005 Chrysler Pacifica for seven months. Over that period, I have documented a total [of] 6 stalling events. The common trigger seems to be

deceleration while turning or slightly turning either left or right. The speeds during the stalling events have twice occurred at highway speeds and four times while decelerating from speeds of 30–45 [48–72 km/h] to near 0. On one occasion, while at 45–50 mph [72–80 km/h] and changing lanes to the right, the vehicle stalled, affecting the steerability, and the car ran off the road, striking a hard object that caused the front tire to blow out and [the] destruction of the front rim and bending [of] the rear rim…the dealer failed to notify us of the 2004 recall for the same type of stalling event.

• Sudden acceleration. • Side airbags fail to deploy on impact. • Automatic transmission failure. • Excessive shimmying and steering-wheel vibrations, despite having replaced both lower control arms. • Extreme shaking when braking. • Headlights go on and off on their own. **2005–07**—Faulty ABS wheel brake sensors cause ABS warning light to stay lit. • **2006**—Only 54 complaints, which is much lower than average. • Stalling when turning. • In one incident, the automatic transmission jumped from Park to Reverse while a passenger was unloading cargo. • Backup sensor failure. • Backup lights do not provide sufficient illumination. • Severe brake pulsation and vehicle vibration when braking. • Vehicle pulls to the right when accelerating. • Airbag warning lights are constantly lit. **2007**—Steering failure; three reports of leaking steering fluid catching fire. • Sudden acceleration into Overdrive from 30 km/h. • Sudden acceleration accompanied by brake loss. • Transmission and torque converter failure. • Side-door window shatters on impact, sending dangerous glass shards into the interior, but airbags fail to deploy.

Secret Warranties/Internal Bulletins/Service Tips

2004—An erratically shifting automatic transmission may require a re-calibrated PCM or TCM. • Rattling front splash shield. • Interior materials may give off an offensive odour. **2004–05**—Remedy for a rough-running engine or idle fluctuation. • Inoperative power seats or adjustable pedals. • Inoperative steering-wheel tilt mechanism. • Correction for a popping, clicking sound. • Front strut squeaking, squawking. • Tips on silencing a front/rear rattle. • Replacing the front suspension lower control arms may eliminate a suspension clunk or rattle. • Dip, sag in centre of instrument panel. • Troubleshooting water leaks into the passenger compartment or leaks found on the front floor. • Seat belts may stink:

FRONT SEAT BELTS EMIT FOUL ODORS

BULLETIN NO.: 23-026-04 REV. A   DATE: JULY 30, 2004

OVERVIEW: This bulletin involves replacing the seat belt assembly and removing the foam material behind the seat belt retractor.

MODELS: 2004–05 Pacifica

SYMPTOM/CONDITION: The vehicle operator may describe a foul odor from the front seat belt(s). The odor does not originate from the seat belt but from the foam to plastic cup material interaction. Under warm ambient temperatures, the foam gives off an odor which permeates the plastic cup behind the seat belt retractor, into the seat belt itself. Replacing only the seat belt assembly will not correct the condition.

2004–06—Hard starts; no-starts. 2004–07—Loose upper appliqué above the driver-side front door. • Tips on eliminating AC musty odours. 2005—Front-door glass sticks or binds. 2005–06—Headliner gap at front-door weather stripping. • Circular marks on the glass. 2005–07—Moonroof makes a popping, thumping sound when moving to the Vent position. 2006–07—Windshield cracks are a common problem and will be repaired under warranty, but only if Chrysler is threatened with small claims action. Above all, don't accept the dealer's contention that it's an insurance claim and not a warranty or "goodwill" item. 2007—Engine clunk, harsh transmission engagement with the 4.0L engine. • Torque converter shudder with the 3.8L engine. • Brake buzzing and clicking. • Moisture on the carpet means that the plenum cowl ends should be resealed.

PACIFICA PROFILE

	2004	2005	2006	2007
Cost Price ($) (soft)				
Base (23%)	39,995	36,065	37,495	34,440
Used Values ($)				
Base ▲	11,500	13,500	15,500	19,000
Base ▼	10,000	12,000	13,500	17,000
Reliability	4	4	4	4
Crash Safety (F)	5	5	5	5
Side	5	5	5	5
Offset	5	5	5	5
Rollover	4	4	4	4

Note: The 2008 models posted identical crashworthiness and rollover results.

Ford

AVIATOR, EXPLORER, MOUNTAINEER, SPORT, SPORT TRAC ★★

RATING: Below Average (2003–08); Not Recommended (1991–2002). The upgraded 2002–04 Explorers were a big improvement from a performance point of view, but quality remained low until the next redesign of the 2005 version. We have been misled in the past when Explorers literally fell apart after accumulating some mileage. They are particularly prone to rolling over through the 2001 model year (and up until the 2004 Sport Trac). The Lincoln Aviator is essentially a baby Navigator spun off from the Explorer 4×4. Mountaineers are 1997-Mercury spin-offs with chrome and standard luxury features. Not quite a pickup truck, not quite an SUV, the Sport Trac takes elements from both to create a vehicle able to transport five passengers and carry tall objects in the small rear bed. Remember the Ford Ranchero? **Strong points:** Well appointed, with many standard safety features; a good 4.6L V8 powertrain matchup that gives you much-needed power without too severe a fuel penalty (when compared with the thirsty V6); stable and forgiving handling when performing routine and emergency manoeuvres; steering is accurate and smooth; comfortable ride; permanent, full-time 4×4; versatile seven-passenger seating; attractively styled. The redesigned model has larger doors for easy entry and exit and a lower step-up. Lots of cargo space—more than the Chevrolet Blazer or Jeep Cherokee. Impressive crashworthiness scores and insurance injury claim data, except for head restraint performance. All trucks, SUVs, and crossovers are now covered by a longer base warranty. **Weak points:** The 5- and 6-year base warranties are still inadequate when dealing with chronic factory defects. There's a cluster of safety-related defects around 2002 because of the Explorer's redesign that model year. Unacceptable off-road performance: slow, noisy acceleration with the base powerplant; hard riding over rocky terrain at slow speeds; and slow steering response. Excessive road noise and fuel consumption with the V6 engine (11.5/16.8 L/100 km, or 14.0/20.5 mpg). Power driver-seat and seat-heater controls are hard to access; short drivers may have trouble reaching the pedals because of the driver-seat cushion; interior takes a while to warm up on very cold days; fuel-filler door is inconveniently located on the passenger side; step bars (remember when they were called running boards?) are too narrow to be useful; and the 2007 Sport Trac's door handles aren't very user-friendly, making it difficult to close the doors. **New for 2008:** Nothing important this year. Explorer is slated to become a crossover when the body-on-frame truck platform is replaced by a Volvo-sourced, carlike unibody frame for the 2011 model year. However, if Explorer and Sport Trac sales continue to spiral downward, both models will be dropped after the 2010 model year.

MODEL HISTORY: The Explorer was introduced in 1991 as a compact sport-utility that combined the solidity of a truck with carlike handling. Despite its Firestone and quality woes, it remains the top-selling sport-utility in North America. It's available with two or four doors and in 4×2 or 4×4 modes. The V6 engine can be hooked to a 5-speed manual with Overdrive or a 5-speed automatic with Overdrive. The Control-Trac 4×4 system is controlled by a dial on the instrument panel and has three modes. Unlike a traditional 4×4 system, Control-Trac can be left in 4×4 all the time. 4×4 High is a constant 50/50 front/rear split, and it should be used only on loose or slippery road surfaces. 4×4 Low is a low-range gear for climbing steep hills or for travelling on very poor roads. The vehicle must be stopped and the transmission put into Neutral to engage or disengage the low range.

Explorers have generous cargo space, large doors, and lots of rear headroom and legroom. The 4.0L V6 engine does a respectable job of pulling the Explorer's hefty

---

2008 EXPLORER TECHNICAL DATA

POWERTRAIN (REAR-DRIVE/4×4)
Engines: 4.0L V6 (210 hp) • 4.6L V8 (292 hp); Transmissions: 5-speed auto. • 6-speed auto.

DIMENSION/CAPACITY
Passengers: 2/3; 2/3/2; Wheelbase: 113.7 in.; H: 72.8/L: 193.4/W: 73.7 in.; Headroom F/R1/R2: 2.5/4.0/0.5 in.; Legroom F/R1/R2: 40.5/28.0/27.0 in.; Cargo volume: 48.0 cu. ft.; Fuel tank: 79L/regular; Tow limit: 7,130 lb.; Load capacity: 1,510 lb.; GVWR: 6,020 lb.; Turning circle: 18.4 ft.; Ground clearance: 7.0 in.; Weight: 4,632 lb.

weight, but passing power is underwhelming. **1999**—An improved braking system, a 5-hp boost for the 210-hp 4.0L V6, optional side airbags, a sonar sensing system that warns drivers of objects behind the vehicle when backing up, a slight revamping of the exterior, and the addition of a new four-door XLS series. **2000**—Debut of the Explorer Sport Trac as a 2001 model. **2001**—Explorer Sport arrives. Automatic transmission becomes standard, and a 210-hp V6 replaces the standard 160-hp V6. **2003**—Sport Trac gets four-wheel disc brakes and an optional side curtain airbag system. Side airbags have been dropped on the Sport model. **2004**—The two-door Explorer Sport is dropped, leaving only the pickup/SUV combo. **2006**—A more powerful V8 engine, a quieter V6, upgraded frame, and updated front, rear, and interior styling. **2007**—Ford boosts its warranty coverage to 5 years/100,000 km on trucks, SUVs, and crossovers, and to 6 years/110,000 km on Lincoln products. *Aviator:* Transformed into more of a sport wagon, Aviator gets a smaller, sleeker profile and two rows of adjustable seating surrounded by a restyled interior. It uses the same platform as the Ford Fusion, Mercury Milan, and Lincoln Zephyr. Power is provided by a 245-hp 3.5L V6 coupled to a 6-speed automatic transmission, harnessed to either a front-drive or all-wheel-drive configuration. *Explorer:* More accessible inside door handles and a longer warranty. *Sport Trac:* After a year's hiatus, this redesigned half-SUV, half-truck Explorer spin-off is longer, wider, and taller than its previous iteration. Other improvements: more safety features, like Roll Stability Control; an independent rear suspension; and a choice of either a 4.0L V6 or 4.6L V8 engine. (Incidentally, previous Sport Tracs were exclusively V6-powered.) Available in rear drive or four-wheel drive, 6-cylinder versions use a 5-speed automatic transmission, while the V8 is mated to a 6-speed automatic.

The 1995–2001 models are acceptable performers (when they aren't rolling over), although they still have some traditional quirks. For example, the 160-hp 4.0L V6 is slow to accelerate and even slower when hauling a full passenger load. It's noisy and not as refined as the new V6—or the old V8, for that matter. The 210-hp 4.0L V6, on the other hand, is a smoother-running engine that gives better fuel economy, but much less than one would expect. Expect impressive acceleration with the V8 engine. Though smoother than the Jeep Grand Cherokee's 5.2L, it's not quicker, and, again, you will pay a huge fuel penalty.

The 2002–05 models have a split personality: The Sport and Sport Trac were carried over unchanged, which means they remain tippy and unreliable, while the four-door 4×4 was substantially reworked for 2002, taking on additional safety features and becoming more powerful, roomy, and carlike in its comfort and handling. Its "smart" airbags deploy at different speeds, depending on the severity of the crash and whether occupants are wearing seat belts. Buyers also get a more powerful standard 4.0L V6 engine and, for the first time, an optional 4.6L V8. Although it's 3.0 cm (1.2 in.) shorter than the 2001, width and wheelbase have increased by 4.8 and 5.3 cm (1.9 and 2.1 in.), respectively. The cargo area behind the second-row seat is 7 percent bigger, and the new optional third-row seating makes the Explorer a seven-seater. Suspension, steering, and drivetrain improvements also reduce the chances of rollovers, but the risk is still serious.

The 2006–08 models come with additional V8 power and revised interior and exterior styling. V8 acceleration is better than average, although the 6-speed transmission isn't as smooth as the competition's. Fuel economy is quite poor as well. Although handling is trucklike, ride quality is quite good. Ford's standard AdvanceTrac anti-skid system and Roll Stability Control help prevent two of the major problems that have plagued these SUVs in the past. There is also plenty of passenger and cargo room, and road noise is kept to a minimum.

The interior redesign has some glaring deficiencies, like the continuing problem of excessive dash glare onto the windshield. Owners complain that the radio controls are hard to reach; climate controls are mounted too low, with buttons that are hard to calibrate; the gearshift mechanism blocks access to the climate controls; the turn-signal control is mounted at an awkward angle; rear climate controls are set into the ceiling; and armrests block access to the door handles. Exterior styling is more attractive, but entry and exit are complicated by the high step-in, and access to the third-row seat is for only the most limber. Although the second- and third-row seats fold nearly flat into the floor, they leave gaps that can swallow small items. Opening and closing the rear hatch requires more strength than some may have.

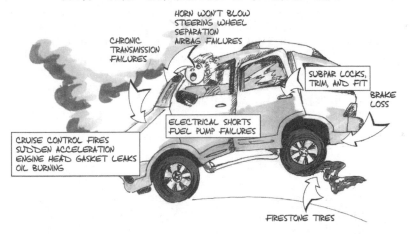

WHY THE EXPLORER IS A BAD SUV

HORN WON'T BLOW
STEERING WHEEL
SEPARATION
AIRBAG FAILURES

CHRONIC
TRANSMISSION
FAILURES

SUBPAR LOCKS,
TRIM, AND FIT

BRAKE
LOSS

ELECTRICAL SHORTS
FUEL PUMP FAILURES

CRUISE CONTROL FIRES
SUDDEN ACCELERATION
ENGINE HEAD GASKET LEAKS
OIL BURNING

FIRESTONE TIRES

COST ANALYSIS: The 2006–08 models are much improved but way overpriced, making a new or used model bought across the border your best bet. (Top choice: a used 2006 or 2007; drive it for two years and then sell it in Canada for more than you paid.) In the States, prices are $15,000 to $20,000 cheaper. In Canada, a 2008 Explorer costs $41,399–$49,299 and the Sport Trac is $32,099. Still, the standard stability control and extra features are important additions that are worth a few extra loonies. This extra cost can be shaved, however, by waiting for prices to fall drastically once competition heats up in the first quarter of 2009 as Ford attempts to crawl out from under a huge inventory of unsold Explorers (sales are down about 40 percent). It's also interesting to note that a new Sport Trac 4×2 is about $8,000 cheaper than the Explorer 4×4, but after a few years, it's actually worth almost as much as the Explorer. An Aviator costs about $20,000 more than an Explorer 4×4, but the difference is narrowed by $12,000 after a year's depreciation. **Best alternatives:** Some competitors worth checking out are the Nissan Pathfinder Xterra or X-Trail, Hyundai Santa Fe or second-series Veracruz, and Toyota 4Runner, Sequoia, or Highlander. Forget about the luxury European SUVs: BMWs and Mercedes' M-Class have worse quality control records and much heftier sticker prices, plus both are returning this year with major redesigns, which means there's a greater chance of things going wrong (mostly fuel-delivery and electrical systems and electronics) and mechanics will be on the downside of the learning curve. **Rebates:** Look for zero percent financing and $4,000+ rebates on the 2008–09 models. **Delivery/PDI:** $1,250. **Warranty:** Bumper-to-bumper 5–6 years/60,000–110,000 km; rust perforation 5 years/unlimited km. **Supplementary warranty:** A toss-up on the 2007s; essential on earlier models. **Options:** Stay away from the gas-guzzling V8; it exacts too great a penalty for the 292 horses it delivers. Shorter drivers will want the power-adjustable brakes and accelerator pedals. Stay away from Bridgestone, Goodyear Wrangler, and Continental tires. Michelin Cross Terrain tires are an excellent alternative. The $700 side curtain airbags add head protection for those in the first two rows, but their safety is questionable. The power running boards aren't very useful due to their narrow design. The Reverse Sensing System, which sounds an audible warning when backing up too close to another vehicle or obstacle, has been glitch-prone—learn to turn your head. **Depreciation:** Higher than average. **Insurance cost:** Unusually high. **Annual maintenance cost:** Average during the warranty period. Driveline, fuel system, brake, suspension/steering, and electrical defects cause maintenance costs to rise after the third year of ownership. **Parts supply/cost:** Parts are expensive but easily found. **Highway/city fuel economy:** *4.0L V6 and auto.:* 11.5/16.8 L/100 km; *4.6L V8 and 4×4:* 12.5/17.8 L/100 km.

QUALITY/RELIABILITY: Reliability record is dismal, particularly with the V6 and V8 engines. Ford factory workers and Explorer owners say that the older, 239-hp 4.6L V8 engine has a propensity for blowing head gaskets and overheating big time. Furthermore, according to these sources, cars and trucks equipped with 4.6L and 5.4L V8 engines are burning oil because of engine blocks that were improperly cast, causing the #2 cylinder bore to fail. The PCMs on early 2002 Explorers were allegedly programmed with corrupted software. Some Explorers have been repaired up to five times to correct driveline defects.

> Ford just replaced the differential on my 2002 4×2 Explorer. I took it in with gear howling and clunking. When I tried to get more specifics about what happened and why, I was stonewalled by "It was worn out." The SUV is one year old, [with] 16,000 miles [25,600 km], [and] used like a family car. As I was leaving, the service writer quietly confided she didn't know what happened but I was the fourth such replacement this week. This is not a large dealership so the repair ratio sounds really bad.

Owner-reported problems: Although there have been many quality and performance improvements since 2006, a perusal of owner comments indicates that these SUVs will likely continue to have serious factory-related defects in the future. Topping the list will be automatic transmission failures, fuel-system glitches, air conditioning system malfunctions, premature brake wear and noise, and brake failures. Ford cannot continue to tell suppliers to give them more for less. Instead, they are getting less for less. **Warranty performance:** Much worse than average. The company's staff is overwhelmed by complaints from owners who are poorly served by an inadequate base warranty.

1998–2007 defects

Explorers have higher failure rates than their Sport Trac spin-off. Whether this is because of better quality control or the shorter time the Sport Trac has been on the market has yet to be decided. The same phenomenon can be seen with post-2005 quality; there are fewer complaints and service bulletin fixes for factory-related defects. Components with a high failure history include the engine, cooling, fuel, and electrical systems; automatic transmission; brakes; AC; suspension; and body hardware. Here are some specific problem areas: AC remains on a high setting; Airbag Service light stays on for no reason; transmission lacks power on acceleration; faulty speed sensor; excessive drivetrain vibration throughout vehicle; automatic transmission fluid leakage at the radiator; premature fuel-pump failure; steering binding; and engine knocking. One owner replaced the engine at 15,000 km, but the new engine made the same knocking noise, which the dealer now describes as being normal. Other problem areas: Defective 4×4 electronic module; roof shakes and an ear-piercing sound occurs when rear windows are lowered while cruising; overwhelming rotten-egg, sulphur, fuel, and oil-burning smells; and a rusted-out fuel-filler pipe that leaks and allows dirt to contaminate fuel in the gas tank:

> I thought your readers should be made aware of a problem we experienced on a 1999 Ford Explorer Sport.
>
> The fuel-filler pipe rusted out at the top of the inlet pipe right behind the inlet area. The area is subjected to road splash and the rust out point is not visible from beneath the car. The local mechanics could not find the cause of the problem and the vehicle was eventually towed to a dealer where the problem was finally figured out. The total bill was $2,500 because the cause was so obscure. Ford would not pay for the rust out, [which] caused damages, water and dirt in fuel lines, new fuel pump, etc.

> •

> I had a serious problem with my 2001 Explorer as described and found on the bottom of page 232 and top of page 233 of your book [*Lemon-Aid SUVs, Vans, and Trucks 2006*]. My costs to date exceed $6,000. Two dealerships failed to diagnose the problem. *www.cartalk.com* led me to solving the problem myself, after dealerships and

Ford tried to explain my vehicle is out of warranty. I had a lawyer write Ford, giving them 21 days before I proceed to Division Court. Your book helped me in establishing [that] a secret warranty [exists] between Ford and Utilimaster Corporation. In Sept. 2002, Utilimaster issued a confidential bulletin #03101937: "Fuel Pump and Fuel Neck Retrofit Replacement" for Ford and Utilimaster employees. It says: "In USPS Flex fuel vehicles built in the years 1999–2001, the fuel pump may corrode from the use of ethanol fuel"! I have checked Ford bulletins, recalls, Transport Canada, ALLDATA, etc. Service managers are not aware of the problem and seem surprised when I show them the actual parts with Ford part numbers stamped on them. A Ford representative called to tell me they won't do anything, and that their quality control department has not reported a problem.

The premature rusting of the fuel filler neck could have caused a fire. I have had 4 fuel pumps burn out prematurely due to lack of pressure in the system. Interesting is that muffler exhaust and tail pipe original equipment are still intact. Even if the secret warranty is not effective, there is an implied warranty. The dealer says he won't or can't do anything, so I am suing the dealer and Ford for $10,000.00 (the maximum in Ontario's Division Court).

Owners also complain about the flimsy front bumper; cracked moulding under the rear light; sticking rear door handle; door handles that are easily broken; ice and slush entering the door panels, causing the doors to freeze shut; water leaks into the interior; running-board cracks and paint peeling; and a broken power driver's seat:

I bought a 2002 Ford Explorer last April (2004) with an extended mechanical warranty for 5 years. The original full warranty [had] run out. Last week, the driver's electric seat got stuck in my driving position and we were not able to move the seat forward or backwards. We took the car into our local Ford Dealership where they told us that a metal cable had snapped. Unfortunately, they stated they are not able to simply replace the cable but instead have to replace the Power Tracking System. This system costs $662 plus labor and tax. I think this is absolutely outrageous but I have been unable to find a wreckers' yard with the equivalent part, and have been told we are not able to swap the passenger (manual) seat with the electric driver seat. To top this off, the new power-tracking system has a warranty which only lasts 1 year, so we are very concerned that this may happen every year and we have to pay $1,000/year for a seat. The dealership stated that our warranty will not cover this and so we have had to order this part from the dealer as we need the car to commute.

 ROAD PERFORMANCE: Acceleration/torque: The overhead cam 210-hp V6 is an adequate all-around performer that puts the rougher 2001 base V6 to shame. The better-made, 292-hp V8 engine, however, provides a more versatile power supply—at a substantial premium. The engine is smoother—though not quicker—than the Jeep Grand Cherokee's 4.7L V8, but you'll pay a stiff fuel penalty. With the standard Class 2 towing package on models equipped with the V6 or V8 engines, towing capacity is 1,600 kg (3,500 lb.). Explorers carrying a V6 engine may tow between 1,588–2,268 kg (3,500–5,000 lb.); a V8 engine increases towing capability 1,588–

3,234 kg (3,500–7,130 lb.). V6-equipped Sport Tracs will tow 2,386 kg (5,260 lb.); V8-equipped Sport Tracs max out at 3,175 kg (7,000 lb.). **Transmission:** Rough-shifting often leads to complete failure after the third year or 100,000 km. Automatic transmission low-speed driveline vibration and occasional jerky shifting when changing from Second to Third under light acceleration. **Routine handling:** Handles like a large sedan and rides better as the load is increased. The V8 handles better because the engine is positioned lower and farther back in the frame, improving steering responsiveness, reducing wallowing, and making the Explorer less nose-heavy. Models not equipped with an independent suspension roll excessively in turns. With a light load, the ride gets choppy on bumpy roads; off-road, the suspension frequently bottoms out. Owners report vehicle has a propensity for hydroplaning on wet roads. Inadequate ground clearance and excessive front and rear overhangs preclude serious off-roading. **Emergency handling:** Good on dry highways. The tendency to fishtail when cornering under speed or on hard acceleration has been reduced with the new independent rear suspension. **Steering:** Precise and predictable. Some steering-column noise. **Braking:** Very good (100–0 km/h: 41 m).

 SAFETY SUMMARY: Now, a question everyone's asking: Is the Explorer more dangerous than other vehicles if it has a blowout? Absolutely. Just look at NHTSA's 2004 rollover ratings: Sport Trac (virtually unchanged post-Firestone) got an "Unacceptable" two-star ranking, while the re-engineered Explorer (with steering and suspension upgrades) scored three stars. In August 2004, a Fort Meyers, Florida, jury rendered a $2-million negligence judgment against Ford after seeing internal documents that showed that the company was aware of a stability problem with Explorers manufactured through the 2001 model year.

Ford's PR mantra is that Explorer owners are being killed and injured only because of faulty Firestone tires, while Firestone maintains that the Explorer's faulty design sends the vehicle out of control. Firestone's finger pointing has been buttressed by the *Washington Post*'s October 9, 2000, analysis of 27,000 fatal and non-fatal sport-utility accidents from 1997 to 1999. The study's conclusions:

> The Explorer has a higher rate of tire-related accidents than other sport-utility vehicles—even when equipped with Goodyear tires; the Explorer was 53 percent more likely than other compact SUVs to roll over when an equipment failure such as faulty brakes, bald tires, or blowouts caused an accident; in 187 fatal blown-tire accidents, the Explorer rolled over 95 percent of the time, compared with 83 percent for other SUVs.

Before we close the file on Ford's Firestone fiasco, keep in mind that safety investigators have recently seen a surge in Firestone blowout rollovers due to Firestone spare tires. Apparently, the spares were never replaced during the last recall. Watch out!

Many owners report excessive engine knocking and premature engine replacement in vehicles that have yet to reach 10,000 km. When the Explorer stalls, brakes and steering are lost, the Check Engine light comes on, and the driver has to wait a few minutes before the vehicle can be restarted. Automatic transmission malfunctions and failures are still quite common with low-mileage Explorers. Poor braking or no brakes are a frequent complaint. Other safety-related complaints include fires erupting in the rear of the vehicle and within the rear-view mirror wiring harness; no seat belt for the rear middle seat; seat belts failing to retract, or detaching from the wall anchor; the power steering locking up or leaking fluid; the wheel separating when backing up; front-brake rotor warping; the emergency brake not stopping the vehicle; tail lights filling with water when it rains; and cracks in the liftgate glass appliqué. **Airbags:** Side airbags may not be present. Many reports of airbags failing to deploy or deploying for no reason. **ABS:** Standard for all wheels; disc/disc. **Safety belt pretensioners:** Standard. **Traction control:** Standard. **Head restraints F/R:** *1997–2001: ★; 2002: ★★/★; 2003: ★★★/★★; 2004–08: ★.* **Visibility F/R:** *2003–05: ★★★; 2006: ★.* **Pet transport: ★★★★★.** The versatile cargo area has seats that fold in all sorts of ways to accommodate double crates and pet gear. Well-placed anchors secure cargo for added safety, and a split rear door with a flip-up glass panel keeps the area well-ventilated.

SAFETY COMPLAINTS: All models/years: Brake fluid could leak through the cruise control's deactivation switch into the system's electrical components, leading to corrosion, a buildup of electrical current, overheating, and fire. Apparently, fires caused by the cruise-control deactivation switch go back as far as 1994, with Ford's recall of the 1998 model Explorer. In September 2005, Ford recalled 3.8 million pickups and SUVs from the 1994–2002 model years, including the top-selling F-150 pickup, because of concerns over engine fires. Then, after announcing another massive recall in August 2006, NHTSA closed a nearly 2-year-long investigation into the switch fires. The agency had received 1,472 complaints connected to the problem, including 65 reports of fires. • Vehicle lacks stability on the highway; it tends to bounce around and veer off to one side or the other, and it's excessively prone to hydroplaning on wet roadways. • Because it has no rear leaf springs, the Explorer becomes even more unsteady when engaged for towing. • Sudden acceleration or stalling, often related to erratic cruise-control operation. • Sticking accelerator pedal and throttle linkage. • Engine overheating. • After driving the vehicle through water, engine dies when water is sucked into it because the air intake is located on bottom of vehicle. • Fuel, water pump, and ignition module failures. • Transmission slips in forward gears, Overdrive light comes on, and vehicle loses power. • Overdrive failures. • Repeated transmission failures caused by defective planetary gear. • Repeated transfer-case failures. • Excessive drive shaft vibration. • Brake master cylinder and fluid-line failures. • Emergency parking brake won't stay engaged. • Brake pedal sticks. • Repeated brake failures. • Brake lock-up. • Power-steering pump fluid leakage. • Steering lock-up. • Front-end suspension failure. • Faulty rear liftgate support assembly allows hatch to fall. • Horn pad failure. • Seat belts fail to retract. • Rear seat belts are hard to unbuckle. • Driver-seat frame breaks. • Door handles break easily. • Power-door lock and antenna failures. • Electric door locks disengage while driving. • Steering wheel comes off steering column because of missing bolt. • Power-steering failure. • Gas gauge failure. • Under-dash wiring short causes a fire to ignite. • Fire erupts in the centre console. • Overheated ignition electronic control unit catches fire. • Engine fire. • Engine failure. • Power-seat switch failure. • Aluminum wheels cause tires to go flat. • Spare tire is too small. • Speed-control failure. • Rear-view mirror sits too low; obstructs forward vision. • Fuel spews out of fuel-filler tube, no matter how slowly it is filled. • In one incident, anti-sway bar pulled loose from the suspension when the vehicle was pulling into a parking lot. • Axle bearing assembly failure. **2000**—Firestone tire failures are paramount, with new allegations that the wheel rims aren't symmetrically round, making for difficult tire mounting. A number of tires have failed that weren't in the Firestone recall. **2001**—Rear-view mirror sparks a fire in the dash wiring. • Fires continue to be a problem:

> While [the driver was] attempting to back up a 2001 Explorer, [the vehicle] caught fire without warning. The driver was pronounced dead at the scene.

> •

> Vehicle was parked in the garage for an hour when all of a sudden it caught on fire along with consumer's home. Results showed that there was a short with the cruise control switch under the hood.

• Exhaust fumes invade the passenger compartment. • While driving, gas line explodes. • Driver-side window shatters while cruising at 100 km/h. • Reports of windshield suddenly shattering. • Water puddles or sudden turns cause vehicle to roll onto its side. • In one incident, 4×4 suddenly kicked in while driving at 110 km/h, causing transmission to downshift and vehicle to suddenly accelerate. • Wheel fell off one vehicle when backing out of the driveway. • Lug nuts loosen while driving. • Sudden steering loss. • Front-suspension lower ball joint failure at 50,000 km. • Rear suspension unsafe for towing a boat. • Premature brake rotor replacement. • Excessive rear-end sag, and rear axle jumps when load is placed in the cargo area. • Bolt that attaches the seat belt for the integrated child safety seat comes apart. • Broken seat-track weld. • Front and rear shoulder belts ride up on occupants' necks and slip off small-statured people. • Sudden loss of all electrical power. • Windshield wiper failure; wipers are activated when you hit a bump or use the turn signal, or may stop suddenly in rainy weather. • Inadequate defrosting. • Brake lights don't work during gentle braking. • Overheated CD player melts CD. • Key is hard to turn in the ignition. • Goodrich tire-tread separation. **2001–02**— Gearshift sticks in Park; vehicle can roll backward even though transmission is engaged in Drive or Park. **2002**—Over 300 safety-related complaints, similar to other model years. • Tail light fire. • Hydraulic liftgate cylinder arm often comes off. • Window explodes and blows out the rear door:

> Four hours after new 2002 Explorer was picked up from the dealer, glass tailgate exploded on being closed gently. Rear window shattered with such force that metal components of the door were badly bent and scratched. Glass was scattered over a radius of 20 feet [6 metres], including into the back seats and onto the roof. My right leg was cut in three places.... The entire door was replaced by the dealer. Unless recalled, this apparently common defect will result in serious injury.

Ford has a "Safety Improvement Program," NHTSA #01I010000, which will fix the defect for free. It is not a recall. • Three out of five wheel lug nuts were sheared off. • Head restraints sit too low; could snap one's neck in a rear-end collision. • Smoky rear-view mirror. • Message Center dash light is too dim. • Headlights suddenly fail. **2002–03**—Airbags fail to deploy. **2003**—Same old complaint patterns relating mainly to the engine, transmission, brakes, and electrical system. • Sudden, unintended acceleration in Drive as well as in Reverse gear. • Driver's airbag deploys when key is put into the ignition. • Fire ignites in the engine compartment's front right side. • ABS brakes perform poorly. • Many complaints that the rear lift glass shatters for no reason, despite recall fix; right-side window has a history of shattering as well. • Liftgate window frequently pops open. • Defective engine, transmission, drive shaft, and steering clock spring. • Faulty sensor module causes the ignition, seats, and other electrical features to fail. **2004**—Sudden acceleration when parking. • No-start, stalling. • Running board breaks when stepped upon. • Steering wheel sticks when turning; power steering suddenly disengages. **2005**—Both front airbags deploy for no reason. • Constant stalling • Automatic transmission malfunctions; long shift delay. • Leaking axle seals. • It's easy to confuse the accelerator and brake pedals. • Tailgate latch won't hold. • Multiple electrical shorts cause Explorers to play out a scene from *Close Encounters of the Ford Kind:*

> While driving at no specific speed all the windows went up and down, the driver seat moved forward and backward, the radio came on and went off, and the air conditioner came on and went off. Also, while attempting to apply brake pressure the brakes vibrated and a clunking noise was heard from the rear of the vehicle. The dealership inspected the vehicle and unknown repairs were made; however the repairs did not remedy the problem.

2006—Frequent reports of excessive dash glare onto the front windshield. • Rear seat headrests block rear and side visibility and cannot be moved up or down. • Many transmission failures, including surging and slamming into gear, and the gearshift lever fails to engage. • Side rear axle spindle failure. • Rear seat belt buckle loosens without warning. • Driver's memory seat feature won't keep its memory. **2006–07**—Intermittent throttle hesitation and then surging when foot is taken off the accelerator when turning or stopping. **2007**—Electrical malfunctions caused by faulty computer modules. • Light fuses blow constantly. • Severe wear of brake rotors. • Instrument panel cannot be seen during the day.

Secret Warranties/Internal Bulletins/Service Tips

All models/years: Press Ford for "goodwill" warranty coverage if your AC fails within 5 years/80,000 km. **1999**—Service the air blend door if AC doesn't cool the interior. • Automatic transmission slipping, delayed shifting, or no engagement may be solved by a new EPC solenoid and bracket. **1999–2000**—Transmission fluid may leak between the radiator transmission oil cooler and the transmission oil cooler fitting because of insufficient thread sealer on the transmission oil cooler fitting; install O-ring #W705181-S onto the oil cooler fitting. • A buzzing or grinding noise heard during a shift from Second to Third gear with a manual transmission usually signals the need to replace the 3–4 synchronizer assembly. **1999–2001**—Hesitation on acceleration or when turning may be caused by cavitation in fuel pump; install a revised fuel pump and sender assembly, says TSB #00-20-1. • 4×4 front axle squealing or whistling countermeasures. **1999–2002**—Troubleshooting a constantly lit MIL. • Automatic transmission defects:

NO 2ND, 3RD GEAR/NO ENGINE BRAKING

BULLETIN NO.: 03-22-10   DATE: NOVEMBER 10, 2003

1995–2001 EXPLORER, 1995–2002 RANGER, 1996–97 AEROSTAR, 2000–02 EXPLORER SPORT, 2001–02 EXPLORER SPORT TRAC, 1997–2001 MOUNTAINEER

ISSUE: Some vehicles may exhibit the following shift and engagement conditions:
- No 2nd Gear
- No 3rd Gear
- No Engine Braking In Manual 1st.

ACTION: The main control valve body separator plate may need to be updated to the latest level.

1999–2005—Paint delamination, peeling, or fading. • A buzzing or rattling noise coming from underneath the vehicle indicates the need to secure the heat shield. **2000–05**—Ford has a special kit to correct seat belts that are slow to retract. • Paint blistering caused by contaminated coating is a "smoking gun" bulletin for owners wanting their vehicle repainted at Ford's expense:

ALUMINUM CORROSION SERVICE TIP

BULLETIN NO.: 04-25-1   DATE: DECEMBER 27, 2004

ALUMINUM CORROSION—SERVICE TIP

2000–04 Crown Victoria, Taurus, Expedition, F-150, and Ranger; 2000–05 Explorer; 2000–04 LS, Town Car, Navigator; 2000–04 Grand Marquis, Sable; and 2000–05 Mountaineer.

ISSUE: Some vehicles may exhibit a bubbling or blistering under the paint on aluminum body parts. This is due to iron contamination of the aluminum panel.

ACTION: This TSB provides service tips and procedures, outlining methods to properly prepare and protect aluminum body parts from cross contamination.

BACKGROUND: Ford's Scientific Research Laboratory has performed a number of tests on vehicle body parts returned for corrosion related concerns. Testing has revealed that the aluminum corrosion was caused by iron particles working their way into the aluminum body part, prior to it being painted.

2002–04—4.6L engine ticking; replace the cylinder head and cam assembly with part #4L3Z-6049-AA (RH) or #4L3Z-6049-BA (LH). • Inoperative rear power windows. **2002–05**—Rear AC moan, buzz, groan. • Driveline vibration, boom. • Rear axle noise, binding, or vibration. • Noisy axle hub bearings. • Rear half-shaft axle leaks. • Ford will fix vehicles that are hard to shift from Drive to Park. • AC hooting upon light acceleration. • Back glass hard to close. **2002–06**—Fuel gauge drops to Empty or is slow to reset after a refuel. **2002–07**—Damaged liftgate glass appliqué.

2003—Incorrectly installed gear-driven camshaft-position sensor synchronizer assemblies can cause engine surge, loss of power, and a lit MIL. • Front axle leaks fluid from the vent tube. • Rear driveline click, creak, or pop. • Squeaking accelerator pedal. 2003–05—Inoperative AC; compressor leakage. 2004–05—Hard starts are likely caused by a miscalibrated PCM. • Delayed, harsh shifts or delayed acceleration. • Cracked leather seat cushions. 2006–07—Improved driveability measures will be covered by the base warranty (fix for delayed acceleration, hard starts, stalling and engine surging—all problems that have remained unresolved for over a decade). • Whistling AC blower motor. • AC noise behind dash when in vent mode; lack of airflow to the floor. • Wheel clearcoat peeling, cracking.

AVIATOR, EXPLORER, SPORT TRAC PROFILE

	1999	2000	2001	2002	2003	2004	2005	2006	2007
Cost Price ($) (very soft)									
Explorer 4×2 (25%)	28,995	—	—	—	—	—	—	—	—
Explorer 4×4 (26%)	30,095	29,995	35,400	37,700	37,795	39,140	39,140	39,999	40,499
Sport Trac (26%)	—	—	27,050	28,440	30,840	31,155	31,295	—	30,599
Aviator (30%)	—	—	—	—	58,950	59,240	59,895	—	—
Used Values ($)									
Explorer 4×2 ▲	3,000	—	—	—	—	—	—	—	—
Explorer 4×2 ▼	2,500	—	—	—	—	—	—	—	—
Explorer 4×4 ▲	3,500	4,000	4,500	5,500	7,500	11,000	13,000	17,500	22,000
Explorer 4×4 ▼	3,000	3,500	4,000	4,500	6,000	8,500	11,500	16,000	20,000
Sport Trac ▲	—	—	5,000	6,500	8,000	10,000	11,000	—	18,000
Sport Trac ▼	—	—	4,000	5,500	7,000	8,000	9,500	—	16,000
Aviator ▲	—	—	—	—	12,500	16,000	18,000	—	—
Aviator ▼	—	—	—	—	10,500	14,500	16,000	—	—
Reliability	2	2	2	1	1	1	3	3	3
Crash Safety (F)	4	4	4	4	4	4	4	5	5
Side	5	5	5	5	5	5	5	5	5
Offset	3	3	3	5	5	5	5	5	5
Rollover	—	—	2	3	3	3	3	3	3
Sport Trac	—	—	—	—	2	2	2	—	3

Note: Mercury Mountaineers aren't sold in Canada. The almost $10,000 difference in price between an Explorer and Sport Trac narrows to about $1,000 after a few years. Also, keep in mind that the prices of new Explorers have changed little since 2002; Sport Tracs, since 2003. In fact, the price of a new 2007 Sport Trac is about $700 less than the 2005's MSRP. The 2007 and 2008 model crashworthiness scores are identical.

FREESTYLE, TAURUS X

Because it has been on the market barely three years, the Freestyle's (renamed the Taurus X) owner and service bulletin feedback is too limited for a full evaluation. A summary rating can be found in Appendix I.

Ford/Lincoln

EDGE, MKX ★

RATING: Not Recommended (2007–08). Launched as a 2007 model, the 2008 $34,349 ($25,735 in the States) Ford Edge is a car-based SUV that uses the Mazda6 platform and shares many components with the Lincoln MKX, its luxury big brother ($43,299 in Canada; $35,840 in the States). A used 2007 MKX sells for about $29,500 in Canada. Depreciation is fairly rapid and new prices are relatively soft because sales have been slow. Customers and reviewers have slammed the car for its lack of third-row seating, unrefined powertrain, and unimpressive fit and finish.

Owners of the 2007 version complain of the transmission shuddering and banging into gear; driver-side airbags inadvertently deploying; false low tire-pressure alerts; electrical malfunctions; and blinding glare from the dash reflecting upon the front windshield:

> This vehicle has such a glare that you only have about 50% visibility. You can see the full dash, [including] all the vents and other items on the dash. I [contacted] my local dealer to which they acted as if "Wow, this is the first we have heard about this." They [advised] that they did not have an answer. So, I contacted Ford customer relations. I went through the problem with the person on the other end of the phone. He acted surprised and said they had not heard of a problem like this, but, get this, he had a ready remedy. He suggested that I go and buy a mat to cover the dash. I asked him if he would want to do that to a new vehicle that was just purchased. I suggested to him that he needs to get his engineers and persons in authority to read all of the blogs on Ford windshields. I told him that I found complaints where the customers had contacted Ford about a major glare, that dated back to 2005 on the Explorers. Somebody needs to get the auto manufacturers to take action.

2008 EDGE TECHNICAL DATA

POWERTRAIN (4×2/4×4)
Engine: 3.5L V6 (265 hp); Transmission: 6-speed auto.

DIMENSION/CAPACITY
Passengers: 2/3; Wheelbase: 111.0 in.; H: 67/L: 186/W: 76 in.; Headroom F/R: 2.5/2.0 in.; Legroom F/R: 41.0/31.0 in.; Cargo volume: 36.0 cu. ft.; Fuel tank: 79L/regular; Tow limit: 3,500 lb.; Load capacity: 910 lb.; GVWR: N/A; Turning circle: 39.0 ft.; Ground clearance: 7.0 in.; Weight: 4,540 lb.

Other complaints: doors seal poorly, gasoline spews out of the filler pipe, the vehicle rolls backward when stopped on an incline, the AC leaks, and the headlight lever is not intuitive.

The Edge comes in three styles: SE, SEL, and Limited, all featuring a 265-hp V6 coupled to a 6-speed automatic transmission. It is loaded with standard safety features, including electronic stability control, and has garnered a five-star crash test rating for front and side impacts and four stars for rollover resistance from NHTSA. IIHS has given the car a Top Safety Pick designation due to its "Good" offset/side-impact crashworthiness and head restraint protection. Optional features include a power liftgate, panoramic sunroof, and a reverse sensing system that warns drivers of an object behind the vehicle.

Neither human- nor pet-friendly

Few people will be able to single-handedly lift the tailgate of the Ford Edge. You grab the handle from underneath to unlatch it, then press up and out to lift the tailgate. But the latch is in the middle of the door, which is wider at the bottom than at the top, so most of the weight is below the handle. Interior cargo space is also severely restricted by round edges and by the downward slope of the car's rear end.

General Motors

AZTEK, RENDEZVOUS ★★

RATING: Below Average (2001–07). More luxury minivans than sporty SUVs, neither vehicle is any match for the Asian competition. **Strong points:** Quiet, comfortable ride; two of the more affordable seven-passenger SUVs; tight steering; lots of passenger and storage room; low step-in and large doors; use regular fuel; and are bargain-priced, either new or used. **Weak points:** The 3.4L V6 lacks the kick of GM's new inline-six; the interior materials don't say "Buick luxury"; one-piece tailgate. Very expensive for what little you get. If you want four-wheel discs, for example, you have to get the higher-end AWD version, or if you want the better-suited 242-hp 3.6L V6, you have to opt for the more expensive versions and stick with 2006 or earlier models. The rear hatch is often coated with road grime that can't be removed because there's no rear wiper. Over-the-shoulder visibility is hampered by the thick side roof pillars, and front body corners are hard to see. Large doors could be a problem when parking in tight spaces. Poor acceleration, and mediocre handling and road holding. Low ground clearance and no low-range gearing make off-roading a no-no. The Rendezvous' additional seating isn't that comfortable; plus, to access the more-than-ample storage areas, you have to remove the seats. Imprecise steering has insufficient feedback. Marginal head restraint and offset crash scores; excessive road, tire, and engine noise; mediocre fuel economy; and spotty quality control highlighted by hard starts, chronic stalling, and engine intake manifold failures afflicting all model years. **New for 2008:** Introduction of the Buick Enclave, a better-made crossover that replaces the Rainier, Rendezvous, and Terraza.

2007 RENDEZVOUS TECHNICAL DATA

POWERTRAIN (FRONT-DRIVE/4×4)
Engine: 3.5L V6 (196 hp); Transmission: 4-speed auto.

DIMENSION/CAPACITY
Passengers: 2/3/2; Wheelbase: 112.0 in.; H: 69.0/L: 187.0/W: 74.0 in.; Headroom F/R1/R2: 4.5/6.0/1.0 in.; Legroom F/R1/R2: 40.0/29.5/24.0 in.; Cargo volume: 45.0 cu. ft.; Fuel tank: 70L/regular; Tow limit: 3,500 lb.; Load capacity: 1,215 lb.; GVWR: 4,986–5,218 lb.; Turning circle: 40.0 ft.; Ground clearance: 6.0 in.; Weight: 3,900 lb.

MODEL HISTORY: Essentially minivan/SUV crossovers, the Aztek and Rendezvous are practically identical except for the Rendezvous' 4-inch-longer wheelbase that accommodates third-row seating. Both have been sales flops, despite the Rendezvous' designation by *Consumer Reports* as a "Recommended" buy—an opinion *Lemon-Aid* doesn't share.

The Aztek is built on a shorter Montana minivan platform, while the Rendezvous' larger wheelbase allows for more, but not as comfortable, seating. The Aztek is especially roomy, with more cargo room than a Ford Explorer, and is capable of carrying a bicycle upright. The Rendezvous also excels in storage capacity once you remove the seats. These vehicles are also full of innovative features, like a centre console that doubles as a portable cooler, and three special packages for biking, camping, and hiking. The Aztek's stiff suspension makes for an uncomfortable ride, though, and is likely to cause more severe rattling as the vehicle ages. The Rendezvous provides a more forgiving, gentler ride. Driving performance is minivan-boring, though, with considerable under-steer, sluggish steering, and mediocre handling. It takes almost 11 seconds to reach 100 km/h.

The Rendezvous comes with standard ABS and four-wheel disc brakes, two features not found on the base Aztek. Second-row seating is provided by a three-person split bench or twin-bucket seats. The optional two-passenger third-row seat folds flush with the floor. **2002**—A revised front end and a spoiler added to the Aztek. **2003**—A rear-seat DVD player, upgraded wheels, and a tire-inflation monitoring system. **2004**—An all-new, plush AWD Rendezvous Ultra equipped with a 242-hp 3.6L V6. **2005**—The Aztek's last model year. **2006**—The 3.6L V6 is dropped. **2007**—Rendezvous loses its optional 242-hp 3.6L V6 engine and available all-wheel drive in its last model year.

COST ANALYSIS: Prices have fallen dramatically since GM announced that the Rendezvous, Rainier, and Terraza would not be coming back for the 2008 model year. Although the 2007 Rendezvous is listed at about $28,855/$39,305 for the CX and CXL Plus, respectively, both vehicles can be bought for thousands of dollars less in Canada and almost $10,000 less in the States. **Best alternatives:** If you can downsize a bit to save fuel and insurance costs, consider the Honda CR-V, Hyundai Santa Fe or a second-series 2007 Veracruz, and Toyota's RAV4. **Rebates:** These mid-sized SUVs attract hefty $8,000+ rebates and zero percent financing as GM seeks to unload its bloated large- and mid-sized-SUV inventory. **Delivery/PDI:** $1,220. **Warranty:** Bumper-to-bumper 3 years/60,000 km; powertrain 5 years/100,000 km; rust perforation 5 years/unlimited km. **Supplementary warranty:** Yes, powertrain coverage is a must-have. **Options:** AWD, if you really need it. Stay away from the distracting and not-always-accurate rear obstacle detection feature, as well as the head-up instrument display. **Depreciation:** Faster than average, now that GM has dropped the Rendezvous. **Insurance cost:** Higher than average. **Parts supply/cost:** Few complaints so far. These SUVs use generic Montana parts that are found everywhere and are usually reasonably priced. **Annual maintenance cost:** Expected to be just a bit higher than average once the warranty expires. **Highway/city fuel economy:** 8.3/12.6 L/100 km.

QUALITY/RELIABILITY: Owner complaints: Engine, front wheel bearing, steering column, and AC failures are commonplace. Other frequently reported deficiencies: excessive vibration or pulling, possibly caused by a faulty drive shaft or tie-rod ends; transmission grinding; a growling noise when sitting in Park on a hill or slope with the engine running and the parking brake not applied; shock absorber rattling; instrument panel may be warped rearward of the defroster outlet; water may enter the passenger compartment near the H-back module; water soaks the front carpet; and heavy condensation in the tail lights. **Warranty performance:** Fair.

 SAFETY SUMMARY: Airbags: Front and side. **ABS:** Standard; disc/drum. **Safety belt pretensioners:** Yes. **Traction control:** Optional. **Head restraints F/R:** *2001–02 Aztek:* ★★; *2003 Aztek:* ★★★/★★; *2004 Aztek:* ★★★★★/★★★; *2002–03 Rendezvous:* ★★★/★★; *2004–07 Rendezvous:* ★★. **Visibility F/R:** *Aztek:* ★★★/★; *Rendezvous:* ★. Exterior rear-view mirrors cause a huge blind spot. **Pet transport:** ★★★.

SAFETY COMPLAINTS: All models/years: Airbags fail to deploy in a collision. • Delayed automatic transmission shifts, slippage, extended shifts, or flaring during cold operation. • Fill hose enters gas tank at a very vulnerable location. • Faulty sending unit causes inaccurate fuel gauge readings. • Rear spoiler obstructs vision. • Horn is hard to blow. **2001**—Numerous reports of rollover accidents where occupants were ejected. • Vehicle fire caused by shorted wiring harness. • Steering tie-rod/drive bar fails, sending vehicle out of control. • Rear brake failure. • Excessive vibration while driving. • GM says windshield distortion could be caused by car washes. • Rear liftgate will not release the secondary latch position when opened automatically. • Wiper blades hit each other. *Aztek:* **2001**—Chronic stalling. • Dealer says front wheels cannot be realigned without bending the frame. • Faulty rear door security-lock lever. **2002**—Engine surges when braking. • Brakes work intermittently. **2003**—ABS control unit failure. • Vehicle's rear end skips about when passing over highway bumps. *Rendezvous:* **2002**—Chronic differential leak. • Vehicle won't stay in gear while stopped on an incline. • Car stalls when changing gears. • Sudden loss of all electrical power. • Loss of steering when right axle spindle gear breaks. • Wind blows door back, breaking hinge. **2003**— Engine, transmission, and brake failures. • Electrical shorts; blown fuses. **2004**—Gas tank neck snaps off. • Chronic stalling. • Radio and horn self-activate. • Unable to open windows and rear doors. • Middle seat belt securing baby seat suddenly unlatches. **2005**—Sudden, unintended acceleration. • Chronic stalling, possibly related to the ignition relay recall on the 2004 model. • Instrument panel cannot be read under certain daylight conditions. • ABS and AWD lights are often lit. **2006**—Total loss of steering control. • Airbag sensor inadvertently disables the passenger-side airbag. • Turn signals operate erratically. • Windshields crack, or have a distorted view. **2007**—Dash gauges cannot be seen if driver is wearing sunglasses. • Back window shatters for no reason. • Window in rear door is too high; mirror doesn't give an adequate view rearward. • Outside mirrors block view:

The side mirrors (outside) of the Rendezvous are so huge that they completely block out pedestrians, cars, and even semi-truck size vehicles when making turns.

Secret Warranties/Internal Bulletins/Service Tips

All models/years: Harsh transmission shifts while Check Engine light is on. • Poor engine and transmission performance. • Rear axle seal leaks. • Hard start, no-start, stalling, and fuel gauge fluctuation. • Muffler heat shield rattle. **2001**— No forward, delayed forward, or the automatic transmission may lock in Reverse. **2001–02**—Customer Satisfaction Program (secret warranty) regarding the brake booster power piston, valve springs replacement, and dead battery replacements. • Grinding noise, or failure of 4-speed automatic transmission to engage when shifting into Drive or Reverse. **2001–03**—Faulty intake manifold may cause coolant/oil loss (TSB #03-06-01-010A). • Defective AC, compressor. • Exhaust rattle, buzz. • Radio speaker static. **2001–05**—No Reverse, Second, or Fourth gears (Bulletin #00-07-30-022B says to replace the reaction sun shell with a more durable, heat-treated part). **2001–06**—Hard start, stalling, inoperative gauges, and lit warning lights can all be traced to water leaking onto the C305 connector, says TSB #01-08-45-005D. **2002**—Hard shifting, shuddering with automatic transmission (TSB #02-07-30-039B). **2002–03**—Engine exhaust manifold defect correction:

INTAKE MANIFOLD OIL/COOLANT LEAK	
BULLETIN NO.: 03-06-01-010B	DATE: OCTOBER 24, 2003

ENGINE OIL OR COOLANT LEAK (INSTALL NEW INTAKE MANIFOLD GASKET)

2000–03 Buick Century	1996–2003 Oldsmobile Silhouette
2002–03 Buick Rendezvous	1999 Oldsmobile Cutlass
1996 Chevrolet Lumina APV	1999–2003 Oldsmobile Alero
1997–2003 Chevrolet Venture	1996–99 Pontiac Trans Sport
1999–2001 Chevrolet Lumina	1999–2003 Pontiac Grand Am, Montana
1999–2003 Chevrolet Malibu, Monte Carlo	2000–03 Pontiac Grand Prix
2000–03 Chevrolet Impala	2001–03 Pontiac Aztek with 3.1L or 3.4L V-6 Engine.

CONDITION: Some owners may comment on an apparent oil or coolant leak. Additionally, the comments may range from spots on the driveway to having to add fluids.

CORRECTION: Install a new design intake manifold gasket. The material used in the gasket has been changed in order to improve the sealing qualities of the gasket. When replacing the gasket, the intake manifold bolts must also be replaced and torqued to a revised specification. The new bolts will come with a pre-applied threadlocker on them.

2002–04—Tips on silencing an engine boom or drone noise (install a revised torque tube mount). **2003**—Long, hard starts; rough idle; clogged fuel injectors. *Rendezvous:* **2002**—Wet carpet in the passenger footwell produces a foul odour. • Water enters passenger compartment at the area of the H-back module. **2002– 06**—Noisy steering can be silenced by replacing the inner tie-rod boot, says TSB #06-02-32-005. **2002–07**—Eliminate 1–2 shift shudder by replacing the second clutch assembly. **2005–07**—Silencing front suspension noise.

	2001	2002	2003	2004	2005	2006	2007
Cost Price ($) (very negotiable)							
Aztek	29,255	29,255	29,500	28,180	28,655	—	—
GT 4×4	36,185	36,185	36,985	34,060	35,895	—	—
Rendezvous (23%)	—	30,995	31,545	32,440	32,750	28,610	28,855
Rendezvous 4×4 (25%)	—	34,995	35,595	36,415	36,940	32,020	—
Used Values ($)							
Aztek ▲	3,500	4,500	5,500	7,500	9,500	—	—
Aztek ▼	3,000	4,000	4,500	5,500	7,500	—	—
GT 4×4 ▲	4,500	5,500	7,000	11,000	13,500	—	—
GT 4×4 ▼	3,500	4,500	5,500	9,500	12,000	—	—
Rendezvous ▲	—	6,500	7,500	8,500	10,000	13,000	17,000
Rendezvous ▼	—	5,000	6,000	7,000	8,500	11,000	15,000
Rendezvous 4×4 ▲	—	7,500	8,500	10,000	11,500	—	—
Rendezvous 4×4 ▼	—	6,500	7,000	8,000	9,500	—	—
Reliability	2	3	3	3	3	3	3
Crash Safety (F) (4×4)	3	3	3	3	3	3	3
Side (Aztek)	5	5	5	5	—	—	—
Rendezvous	—	3	3	—	5	5	5
Offset (Aztek)	2	2	2	2	2	—	—
Rendezvous	—	3	3	3	3	3	3
Rollover	3	3	3	—	—	—	—

BLAZER, ENVOY, JIMMY ★

bad buy

RATING: Not Recommended (1995–2005). These are three of the worst SUVs you could possibly buy. Blazer and Jimmy are identical, and both were dropped after the 2005 model year. **Strong points:** Reasonably well appointed; comfortable ride; nice handling; low noise levels. Full-time AutoTrac 4×4 shifts on the fly and can be used on dry pavement. Comfortable seating, and sufficient headroom and legroom for all but the last row of passengers. Plenty of cargo space, and expanding the cargo room by folding the rear seat is a snap. **Weak points:** Blazer embodies a decade's worth of safety-related problems, poor quality, and mediocre performance. Drivers have had to contend with a gas-guzzling engine that quickly runs out of steam; poor emergency handling; a hard, jiggly ride; and GM's subpar fit and finish. The thick centre and rear roof pillars and the tinted rear windows compromise rear visibility; rear interior access is restricted; and the short, hard rear seats can make for a harsh ride.

MODEL HISTORY: These are identical two-door and four-door mid-sized sport-utility vehicles, incorporating 4×2 and 4×4 drive and based on the GM S-series pickup platform. Part-time 4×4 (InstaTrac) is standard with all models, while the optional

All ratings on a numbered scale where 5 is good and 1 is bad. See page 217 for a more detailed description.

AutoTrac system delivers full rear-drive power until road conditions require it to automatically readjust the power ratio to other wheels. The only available engine is a 4.3L V6, rated at 190 hp and hooked to a 4-speed automatic transmission with Overdrive. Only two-door models come with a 5-speed manual gearbox.

The compact Blazer and Jimmy were first launched in 1983 as spin-offs of the full-sized GM Blazer and Jimmy—1970 SUV offshoots of GM's full-sized trucks. Although the Blazer and Jimmy are identical, separate GM divisions market them. The Envoy, a Jimmy clone with some styling twists and more standard features, was launched in 1998, dropped for the 2001 model year, and then revived as a totally different 2002 model. However, the Jimmy and Blazer continued to soldier on as cheaper alternatives to Chevrolet's larger, more powerful TrailBlazer and the resurrected GMC Envoy.

1999—An upgraded 4L60-E automatic transmission and optional AutoTrac transfer case that automatically engages 4×4 when needed. **2000**—Some engine, exhaust system, manual transmission, and ABS enhancements, but horsepower remains the same. Vehicles equipped with the ZR2 package were given an upgraded axle ratio to improve shifting and acceleration. Watch the payload rating, though; some vehicles were sold with incorrect payload ratings. **2003**—A new fuel injection system, and some trim changes. A mid-year cost-cutting change replaced the front-drive's disc brakes with drums. **2005**—Four-door models are relegated to fleets.

COST ANALYSIS: These are cheap SUVs to buy used from phased-out fleet sales, but what savings you get up front will be quickly eaten up in accelerated depreciation and high maintenance payouts. **Best alternatives:** Check out the Hyundai Tucson, Nissan Xterra or X-Trail, and Toyota Highlander, Sequoia, or 4Runner. **Warranty:** Bumper-to-bumper 3 years/60,000 km; rust perforation 6 years/160,000 km. **Supplementary warranty:** An extended warranty is a good idea. **Options:** Rear window defroster, remote keyless entry, power door locks, engine block heater, and an upgraded sound system are worth considering. Have a transmission oil cooler installed. Get a sophisticated anti-theft system, or you'll keep your Blazer for only a few days. **Depreciation:** Quite rapid. **Insurance cost:** Average. **Annual maintenance cost:** Higher than average. **Parts supply/cost:** Parts are inexpensive from independent suppliers and widely available. **Highway/city fuel economy:** High fuel consumption in city driving. V6 4×2: 10.4/14.4 L/100 km; V6 4×4: 12.2/17.8 L/100 km.

QUALITY/RELIABILITY: Below average. **Owner-reported problems:** Fuel injection glitches; noisy and roughly shifting transmissions; electrical system shorts, causing blown fuses and brake light, hazard light, and turn signal failures; excessive engine knocking; and front suspension noise. Excessive steering-wheel play makes the vehicle wander all over the road, and makes it difficult to control at times. Body assembly and paint application have been below standard. **Warranty performance:** Below average. Don't get your hopes up if you're beyond the warranty period. GM is tight-fisted in allocating after-warranty compensation, especially on vehicles that are no longer sold.

SAFETY SUMMARY: These vehicles have registered an extraordinarily large number of accident injury claims. IIHS collected data on traffic accidents involving passenger vehicles and small-sized trucks from 2000–03 on U.S. highways and calculated the death rates of drivers for each vehicle. In March 2005, it released its report, which concluded that Blazer drivers are at the highest risk of death. About 308 Blazer drivers per 1 million would die if their cars were involved in accidents; the average death rate for all vehicles was 87 per 1 million.

Airbags: Standard side. Reports of airbags failing to deploy. **ABS:** Standard 4W; disc/disc. **Head restraints F/R:** *2001–04 Blazer:* ★★★; *2001 Jimmy 2d:* ★★★★★; *1999–2001 Jimmy 4d:* ★★★/★. **Visibility F/R:** ★★★★/★. **Pet transport:** ★★.

SAFETY COMPLAINTS: All models: 1999–2000—Wiring-harness fires, and other non-specific under-hood fires. • Plastic fuel tank is easily punctured. • Accelerator pedal sticks. • Cruise control stays engaged when brakes are applied. • Chronic stalling when decelerating (likely fuel-pump failure). • Premature automatic transmission failure; leaks, delayed and harsh shifting are the first signs of eventual breakdown. • Transfer case gets stuck in 4×4 High and Low. • Jumps out of First gear when accelerating. • Right wheel comes off because of a missing cotter pin that locks the spindle in place. • Spare-tire cable breaks, allowing tire to fly off. • Defective locking nut on the steering shaft allows the steering wheel to come off in the driver's hands. • Inner tie-rod and ball joint failure. • ABS light remains lit for no apparent reason. • Brake pedal goes to floor with little braking effect. • On bumpy and rough surfaces, brake pedal goes soft and then stiffens. • When applying brakes while going downhill, vehicle fishtails out of control. • A weak spring causes the driver and passenger seats to slide back and forth. • Bad switch causes sudden headlight failure. • Windshield wipers work poorly. • Exhaust fumes invade cabin. • Seat belt retractor fails to restrain driver in a collision. • Horn goes off by itself. • In cold weather, driver-side window shatter as passenger door is closed. • Liftgate may suddenly fall because of collapsing support struts. • Interior and exterior light failures. **1999–2001**—Brake pedal hits floor without activating brakes. *Blazer, Jimmy:* **2001**—Power-steering hose falls off. • Malfunctioning brake lights said to be covered by a "silent" recall. • Theft-deterrent alarm goes off for no reason. • Faulty rear hatch actuator. • Vehicle accelerates when foot is taken off the accelerator. **2001–03**—Airbags fail to deploy. **2002**—Extreme buffeting when driving with rear window open. • 4×4 suddenly engages, locking up wheels. • 4×4 fails to engage. • Faulty electronic mirror memory. • Seat belt continually retracts while worn. • Faulty camshaft position sensor. • Fuel tank leak; fuel line falls off. **2002–03**—Incorrect fuel gauge readings. **2002–04**—Sudden, unintended acceleration. **2003**—Manual and automatic transmission fall into Neutral when driving. • Fuel splashes outside of tank when refuelling. • Unacceptably long braking distance. **2004**—Loss of steering control when passing over bumpy roads. • Excessive rusting of the brake rotors and ABS module failure. • Water leaks into the B-pillar, soaking the seat belt webbing. • Spare tire is mounted in the rear, where it blocks almost all rear visibility.

Secret Warranties/Internal Bulletins/Service Tips

All models/years: No Reverse, Second, or Fourth gear (replace the reaction sun shell with more robust heat-treated parts, says TSB #00-07-30-022B; November 18, 2004). • Hood hinge rattling. **1999–2000**—Before spending big bucks for engine head gasket repairs or the replacement of costly emissions components to fix a hot-running engine or stop coolant loss, first replace the radiator cap and polish the radiator filler neck. • GM's infamous driveline clunk has been carried over in another "don't worry about it" bulletin sent to dealers. **1999–2001**—TSB #01-07-30-038B indicates transmission malfunctions likely caused by debris plugging the bleed orifice of the 2–3 shift solenoid. • A faulty ignition switch may cause the transmission to stick in Third gear. **1999–2002**—Paint delamination, peeling, or fading. **1999–2004**—Inaccurate fuel gauge readings. **2000–03**—Hard-to-close doors. *Blazer, Jimmy:* **2001**—Harsh shift remedies. • Premature wearout of automatic transmission and clutch components. • Automatic transmission 2–4 band or 3–4 clutch damage. • Transmission sticks in Third gear, MIL stays lit, and instrument cluster is inoperative. • Transmission slips when placed in 4×4. • No-starts, hard starts, and stalling while Security light flashes. • Rear roof corrosion or perforation. **2001–02**—Poor engine performance and erratic shifting. • Service Engine light comes on, and transmission feels like it has slipped into Neutral. **2001–05**—Tips on correcting a harsh 1–2 upshift. **2002**—Diagnostic tips for loss of Third or Fourth gear. • Wet carpet and mildew odour in the front passenger-seat area. **2003–05**—Lack of power in high ambient temperatures. **2004**—Transmission fluid leak, inoperative gears, no movement, case cracked or broken at 2–4 servo (repair transmission and install new retaining ring).

BLAZER, ENVOY, JIMMY PROFILE

	1999	2000	2001	2002	2003	2004	2005
Cost Price ($) (negotiable)							
Blazer/Jimmy 4×2	26,899	28,305	—	—	—	—	—
Blazer/Jimmy 4×4 (25%)	28,750	31,005	32,085	28,770	29,270	29,350	26,045
Envoy	45,185	45,185	—	—	—	—	—
Used Values ($)							
Blazer/Jimmy 4×2 ▲	3,000	3,500	—	—	—	—	—
Blazer/Jimmy 4×2 ▼	2,500	3,000	—	—	—	—	—
Blazer/Jimmy 4×4 ▲	3,000	3,500	4,000	5,000	6,500	8,000	9,500
Blazer/Jimmy 4×4 ▼	2,500	3,000	3,500	4,000	5,500	6,500	8,000
Envoy ▲	3,000	3,500	—	—	—	—	—
Envoy ▼	2,500	3,000	—	—	—	—	—
Reliability	2	2	2	2	2	3	3
Crash Safety (F) (Blazer 4d)	3	3	3	3	3	3	3
Side	5	5	5	5	5	5	5
Offset	1	1	1	1	1	1	—
Rollover	—	—	1	1	1	—	—

CADILLAC SRX

Going into its fifth model year, the Cadillac SRX is evaluated in summary form in Appendix I.

ENVOY, RAINIER, TRAILBLAZER / (SAAB) 9-7X ★★★/★★

RATING: Average (2002–08). *Saab:* Below Average (2005–08). Offering five- and seven-passenger seating, these mid-sized sport-utilities are bigger, wider, and roomier than the Blazer/Jimmy they replace. The TrailBlazer is the least luxurious; Buick's Rainier, the newest and cushiest; and the 9-7X is a Saab facsimile that offers little that is new or innovative, and is the least popular of the group. **Strong points:** Good acceleration in all gear ranges; high tow rating; AutoTrac 4×4 can be left engaged on dry pavement and has low-range gearing for off-road use; comfortable ride; easy city manoeuvring, thanks to the relatively tight turning radius; less tippy than competitors, with a higher centre of gravity; plenty of headroom and legroom, plus ample cargo space; rear seating for three adults; and supportive seats. *Saab:* The 9-7X Saab is identical to its Chevy and GMC counterparts except for a stiffer, more performance-oriented suspension; precise, responsive steering; better brakes; and a unique dashboard design. The ride is smoother, lower, and more refined than that of an Envoy, Blazer, Rainier, or TrailBlazer. The V8 engine is responsive and powerful; however, the car's all-wheel-drive system lacks a low range, compromising the 9-7X's off-road performance. **Weak points:** Subpar crashworthiness through 2008; trucklike handling (vague steering and excessive body lean in turns) without the standard stability-control feature found on post-2005 models; excessive vibration and droning with the 6-cylinder engine; white-knuckle braking because of numb and spongy brakes; tacky-looking interior; excessive wind noise; awkward loading because of the rear hatch's high sill;

2008 ENVOY TECHNICAL DATA

POWERTRAIN (REAR-DRIVE/4×4)
Engines: 4.2L V6 (291 hp) • 5.3L V8 (300 hp); Transmission: 4-speed auto.
DIMENSION/CAPACITY
Passengers: 2/3; Wheelbase: 113.0 in.; H: 71.9/L: 191.6/W: 74.7 in.; Headroom F/R: 2.5/3.5; Legroom F/R: 40.0/25.5 in.; Cargo volume: 39.0 cu. ft.; Fuel tank: 71L/regular; Tow limit: 5,200 lb.; Load capacity: 1,146–1,209 lb.; GVWR: 5,550–6,001 lb.; Turning circle: 36.4 ft.; Ground clearance: 8.0 in.; Weight: 4,404 lb.

2008 TRAILBLAZER TECHNICAL DATA

POWERTRAIN (REAR-DRIVE/4×4)
Engines: 4.2L 6-cyl. (285 hp) • 6.0L V8 (390 hp); Transmission: 4-speed auto.
DIMENSION/CAPACITY (7-PASSENGER)
Passengers: 2/3/2; Wheelbase: 129.0 in.; H: 63.5/L: 208.0/W: 75.0 in.; Headroom F/R1/R2: 5.5/4.5/3.0 in.; Legroom F/R1/R2: 42.0/27.5/27.5 in.; Cargo volume: 42.0 cu. ft.; Fuel tank: 95L/regular; Tow limit: 6,400 lb.; Load capacity: 1,360 lb.; GVWR: 5,550 lb.; Turning circle: 36.4 ft.; Ground clearance: 6.5 in.; Weight: 4,442 lb.

and awful real-world fuel economy. Sudden stops lead to severe nosedive and steering instability; ground clearance 3.0 to 3.3 cm (1.2 or 1.3 in.) lower than the competition compromises off-road prowess; front seats lack lateral support; climate controls are hard to adjust by feel; and rear visibility is blocked by head restraints and rear pillars. *Saab:* Poor gas mileage, despite GM's active fuel management (a cylinder-deactivation feature); mediocre braking; a limited and demoralized dealership network; and rapid depreciation. Priced higher than GM's own already overpriced alternatives. It's likely to be axed within the next year or so, a move that will further drive down resale values and add to servicing woes. **New for 2008:** Nothing. The Rainier's last model year was 2007, and the TrailBlazer was dropped earlier this year. Envoy will barely last through the 2008 model year.

MODEL HISTORY: With the debut of these four-door, five-passenger wagons, GM repositioned the TrailBlazer as a small, entry-level SUV. Each of these models is larger than the model it replaces, although they all share the same styling details, rear-drive and 4×4 platforms, and mechanical components. **2003**—Seven-passenger stretched version. **2004**—TrailBlazer returns unchanged. Arrival of the Envoy XUV, an SUV with a number of pickup features. It's basically an XL Envoy with a sliding rear roof and a small pickup bed. **2005**—The Buick Rainier gets more power and an upgraded interior and tires. **2006**—A standard vehicle stability and anti-skid system, an Active Fuel Management feature that selectively deactivates four of the V8's cylinders for fuel-saving cruising, and a freshened exterior. Optional side airbags have been upgraded to deploy during rollovers. **2007**—TrailBlazer ditched its extended-length seven-passenger models. This is the Rainier's last model year.

Rainier

Talk about GM's misjudging the market. Selling for about $48,810 new and $23,000 used, Buick's mid-sized, five-passenger 2007 Rainier went into its third year just as buyers were switching to smaller SUVs in the $30,000 range. Look for heavy discounting and rapid depreciation now that the model has been discontinued.

Saab 9-7X

GM has ruined the Saab cachet by making its latest models a parts bin for a hodge-podge of components used in GM's quality-challenged cars and trucks, and by assembling these creations in the States. Saab, for its part, continues to drain GM's resources with vehicles nobody wants, a marketing strategy that's bizarre at best ("Born from jets"?), and a dealership body that fled for the hills years ago. This is the second Saab dud neither assembled in Sweden nor sold in Europe (the 9-2X AWD sports compact was the first). It's also the only Saab that doesn't offer a manual transmission. GM figured that a European SUV that's serviced by an atrophied dealer body and not even built or sold in Europe was just the ticket to goose American sales, proving that automakers can exhibit just as much arrogance as federal felon Lord Conrad Black. Really, who wants to buy a discontinued TrailBlazer from Saab? In fact, a TrailBlazer SS is thousands of dollars cheaper and offers 100 more horses. On top of that, the 9-7X's name is a major turn-off for buyers who are used to names that depict something, and aren't just a jumble of letters and numbers for the "wink, wink; nudge, nudge" car *cognoscenti*.

True, this GM truck–wagon with European styling and performance provides handling that is more driver-oriented through steering, suspension, and brake system enhancements. The 9-7X is Saab's first-ever SUV, and hefty discounts and rebates can easily cut the high retail price by $7,000 to $10,000. Although this is a TrailBlazer clone, there are a few Saab features that have been retained, like the centre console ignition switch and the distinctive air vents and cockpit. It has a wheelbase of 2.87 m (113 in.), is 4.91 m (193 in.) long, and can carry up to 1.16 cu. m (41 cu. ft.) of luggage in the trunk with the seats up. There's a standard 60/40 split rear seat, and a trailer hitch receiver and cover. The V8 model is estimated to have a maximum towing capacity of 2,950 kg (6,500 lb.). Two engines are available: a 275-hp 4.2L inline-six and a 300-hp 5.3L V8. Both engines are teamed with a 4-speed automatic transmission, standard all-wheel drive, and a limited slip differential. Due to abysmally poor sales, it's doubtful this Saab spin-off will last through the 2008 model year. And, when it is taken off the market, its resale value will fall even faster and servicing will become a search-and-beg affair. **Best alternative:** The Acura TSX.

COST ANALYSIS: All of these vehicles are way overpriced and are selling only with huge discounts and highly depreciated resale values. For example, the 2008 TrailBlazer's entry-level LT model sells for $39,695, or about $5,700 more than last year's model, but its price is so soft this year that $8,000 discounts are commonplace. The 2007 models originally sold for $34,000–$40,915 (LT base/4×4), and used models are worth about $14,000–$20,000 less—and those prices are still falling. The 2006 models are practically identical and are cheaper still. Be wary of the even cheaper 2005s—they lack the all-important standard stability control package, an essential safety feature for this class of vehicle. In the States, these cars are cheaper still, new or used. New, you will pay about $27,720 (U.S.) for an entry-level 2008 LT; the 4×4 goes for $29,820 (U.S.). **Best alternatives:** The Lexus RX 300/350 and Toyota Highlander or 4Runner. **Rebates:** Look for $8,000+ rebates/sales incentives and low financing rates. **Delivery/PDI:** $1,220. **Warranty:** Bumper-to-bumper 3 years/60,000 km; powertrain 3 years/60,000 km; rust perforation 6 years/160,000 km. **Supplementary warranty:** A wise buy. **Options:** Air suspension makes for a less jolting ride, but it degrades handling. Dual exhausts will give you 30 extra horses, and skid plates are essential to counteract undercarriage damage from excessive suspension dive. **Depreciation:** Faster than a speeding bullet. **Insurance cost:** Higher than average. **Parts supply/cost:** Most parts seem to be reasonably priced and easy to find. **Annual maintenance cost:** Higher than average once these models go off warranty. **Highway/city fuel economy:** 11.2/16.0 L/100 km.

QUALITY/RELIABILITY: Likely failures: Automatic transmission and transmission forward sprag; transfer case; broken sway bar; cooling fan motor; brake rotors (excessive rusting and scoring), linings, and ABS module; electrical (shorts); alternator (often on back order); and fuel systems (leaks). Fit and finish deficiencies include water leakage at the driver-side B-pillar (seat belt will be wet), water leakage into the rear passenger compartment if vehicle is parked on an incline, excessive wind noise and front axle whistling, along with constant clicks and rattles. Noisy power-steering pump. Usually, GM will fix the problem or pay compensation after a small claims lawsuit is filed, as was the case with this Albertan Rainier owner:

> Phil, SUCCESS! I sued GM in small claims as per your recommendation. They waited 2-and-a-half months (until 1 week before the court appearance) and asked if they could have a field engineer look at the Rainier. The field engineer (truly a good guy) took the vehicle for 3 days, ultimately duplicated the concern, identified it as a problem with the transfer case, changed the case oil and solved the problem—21 hours before the court date. Interestingly—I had surmised to both dealerships and to GM's regional service manager that exact theory.

> As this was just a pre-trial conference, the judge advised me my case was at best shaky (I had sued for cost of inconvenience—which is not covered in the warranty—and for the cost to buy out the remainder of my lease). As the problem was resolved, the judge told me I would have at best a big uphill fight. As I only got a resolution because of the filing of the suit, I asked GM to at least cover the costs of the court filing and to make an offer if they were interested in keeping me as a customer. I was offered $1,000—which I accepted.

> So—to recap—cost to solve actual problem—under $100. GM's legal fees—several thousand for sure plus all the "darts" they threw at the problem (A/C upgrades, sway bars, trailing arms, bushings, slip-yolk services, and six rental vehicles).

> Ultimately, my goal was to have the problem fixed, which they did, and I came out $800 bucks ahead after the cost of the court fee. Thanks for your assistance.

> TIM

SAFETY SUMMARY: Airbags: Front. **ABS:** Standard; disc/disc. **Traction control:** Optional; stability control is a standard feature on 2006 and later models. **Head restraints F/R:** *2002:* ★★; *2003–08:* ★. **Visibility F/R:** ★★★★★/★★. **Pet transport:** ★★★.

SAFETY COMPLAINTS: *Saab:* No safety complaints registered. *Envoy, Rainier, TrailBlazer:* **2002**—Detached fuel lines. • Airbag fails to deploy. • Transfer-case and 4×4 failures. • Stalling caused by oil seeping onto the camshaft position sensor wiring harness. • Loss of steering; loose steering. • Sudden tie-rod failure. • Horn doesn't blow. • Faulty brake light switch. • Wind blows lightweight hood open. • Front passenger window suddenly shatters. • Side-view mirrors change position at random. • Dash lights and gauges go blank. • Seat belt locks up too easily; has no slack. **2003**—Transfer-case failure. • Brake failure. • Wiper motor works erratically. • Rear window shatters for no reason. • Seat belts pin occupants against the seat. • Jack handle is too short to safely change the tire. **2004**—Engine surging. • Temporary loss of steering control when passing over bumpy terrain. • Tie-rod steering-arm adjusting sleeve may rust out prematurely. • Loose plastic running board cuts driver's leg. • Security and dome lights remain lit. **2005**—Seat belt doesn't restrain driver sufficiently in a collision. • Voltage fluctuates, causing lights to go dim (a common problem mentioned in GM bulletins). • Windshields can distort view (see "Secret Warranties/Internal Bulletins/Service Tips."):

> The windshield in my 2005 Chevrolet TrailBlazer was defective from the factory. It had such bad ripples in the glass that it made me feel as if I were looking through a pair of bifocals. After a couple of trips back to the dealer I finally convinced them to replace it! The new one is better but still has flaws in it. I've been looking at other TrailBlazers now and see the same defect in many other vehicles.

2006—Chronic stalling. • Floor mat may jam accelerator. • Transmission goes into Neutral when shift lever is in Drive. • Horn doesn't always work; may be on backorder. • Erratic fuel gauge readings:

> Filled my vehicle up with gas and my gas gauge reads low fuel. Poor equipment is the cause. This happened on a new SUV and they should fix them. The cost is over $500.00 dollars.

Envoy: **2006**—Passenger-side airbag is disabled if a small adult is seated. • High beam headlights project light straight up. **2007**—Fire ignited in the door wiring. • Vehicle rolled forward with gearshift lever in Park.

Secret Warranties/Internal Bulletins/Service Tips

All models: 1999–2004—TSB #01-07-30-038B indicates transmission malfunctions likely caused by debris plugging the bleed orifice of the 2–3 shift solenoid. **2002**—Cracking of the 4.2L-engine cylinder bore liner will be repaired under a Special Policy (Bulletin #03019; June 2003) up to 7 years/160,000 km (100,000 miles). • Service Engine light comes on, and transmission feels like it has slipped into Neutral. • Delayed transmission shift, harsh shift, and shudder. • Transfer case may be poorly calibrated, causing erratic operation. • Poor engine performance and transmission slips. • Diagnostic tips for loss of Third or Fourth gear. • Surging in First gear. • Campaign (secret warranty) to replace the left and right front lower control-arm brackets. • Excessive noise from the fan and side mirror. • Service Engine or Service 4×4 light stays on. • Loss of electrical power to dash. • Front axle seal high-pitched noise emanating from the front of vehicle. • Roof rack howling. • Heater may not warm driver's feet. **2002–03**—Rear axle whine. • Drivetrain shudder or binding. • Faulty ignition switch may cause transmission to stick in Third gear. • Front-drive axle noise. • AC blows warm air.

• Inoperative AC. • Steering column noise remedies. • Adjust striker on hard-to-close doors. • Front carpet gets wet because of poor weather stripping. **2002–04**—Liftgate unlatches on bumpy roads. • Scratched side-window glass. • Front hood rattles. • Jammed seat belt retractor. • Inoperative 4×4/AWD (see bulletin). **2002–07**—Key sticks in ignition lock cylinder. • Hard-to-close doors may simply need a readjustment of the door striker.**2003**—Transmission slippage. **2003–04**—GM will replace the fuel-tank fill-up pipe and lower hose under "goodwill" to prevent "spit back" when refuelling. **2003–05**—An inoperative AC blower may need a new blower motor

AWD/4WD SYSTEM INOPERATIVE
BULLETIN NO.: 02-04-21-006D   DATE: MARCH 24, 2004

INOPERATIVE 4WD/AWD LAMPS, INOPERATIVE 4WD/AWD SYSTEM (REPROGRAM TRANSFER CASE CONTROL MODULE)

2004 Buick Rainier, 2002–04 Chevrolet TrailBlazer, TrailBlazer EXT, 2003–04 Chevrolet Avalanche, Silverado, Suburban, Tahoe, 2002–04 GMC Envoy, Envoy XL, 2003–04 GMC Sierra, Yukon, Yukon XL, 2004 GMC Envoy XUV, 2002–04 Oldsmobile Bravada

control module. • Steering moan, groan, shudder, or vibration when turning may be caused by a defective steering gear. **2004**—Harsh transmission shifts. **2004–05**—Front-end oil leaks. **2004–06**—GM's solution for front windshields and door windows that distort visibility is to replace them only if the driver's view is seriously affected. Idiotic, but true (see bulletin on page 124). **2004–07**—Paint chipping on the car's side panels, wheelwells, etc., will be fixed free of charge under a 5-year secret warranty (see bulletin). After that time, repair costs will be shared. Not a great deal, but a beginning, and a small claims court judge can change the above terms at will.

PAINT CHIPPING BY WHEEL OPENINGS
BULLETIN NO.: 03-08-111-002F   DATE: APRIL 30, 2007

PAINT CHIPPING BEHIND FRONT WHEELS/FRONT OF REAR WHEELS, DAMAGED LOWER DOOR/ CLADDING AND ROCKER PANELS (REPAINT DAMAGED AREA, INSTALL ASSIST STEP)
2004–07 Buick Rainier, 2002–06 Chevrolet TrailBlazer EXT, 2002–07 Chevrolet TrailBlazer, 2006–07 Chevrolet TrailBlazer SS, 2002–06 GMC Envoy XL, 2002–07 GMC Envoy, 2004–05 GMC Envoy XUV, 2002–04 Oldsmobile Bravada, 2005–07 Saab 9-7X.
ATTENTION: Implementation of this Service Bulletin requires case-by-case review and approval by your District Service Manager (DVM) (U.S.) or District Service Manager (DSM) (Canada) PRIOR to the performance of any repairs.
CONDITION: Some customers may comment that the paint is chipped just behind the front wheels as well as just in front of the rear wheels. Some customers may also comment about damage to the lower door/cladding and rocker panels.
CAUSE: The rocker and lower door areas may be damaged by road debris thrown up by the tires at highway speeds.
CORRECTION: It may be necessary to perform the following repair in order to meet customer expectations and gain their product satisfaction.
In Canada, the 2007 GM Approved Refinish Materials booklet is also available on the GM infoNET under the Service and Body tab. For all of the above vehicles except TrailBlazer SS, install the assist step. For the TrailBlazer SS, install a Protector Kit. Instructions are included in the kit.

2005–07—Poor engine performance due to clogged fuel injectors. • Rear crankshaft oil leaks with 6-cylinder engine. • AC blower motor may be inoperative or cannot be shut off in cold weather; it should be replaced. • Headliner sag (reattach with adhesive sticks). 2007—Rear-end bump, thump felt when braking. • GM recognizes that sluggish acceleration or hard starts can be a factory-related problem and may be caused by a fractured fuel sender port. The company has set up a special program to replace the faulty part free of charge (TSB #07005, February 16, 2007).

ENVOY, RAINIER, SAAB 9-7X, TRAILBLAZER PROFILE

	2002	2003	2004	2005	2006	2007
Cost Price ($) (negotiable)						
Envoy 4×2 (25%)	37,995	37,195	41,475	39,390	32,320	32,655
Envoy AWD (25%)	37,995	37,195	41,820	42,715	41,505	39,960
Envoy XUV (26%)	—	—	41,895	42,830	33,615	—
Envoy XUV AWD (28%)	—	—	31,025	46,150	42,800	—
Rainier AWD (30%)	—	—	49,245	49,645	49,350	48,810
Saab 9-7X (30%)	—	—	—	—	50,900	48,900
TrailBlazer 4×2 (25%)	34,600	37,500	39,705	38,670	31,820	32,065
TrailBlazer AWD (29%)	37,455	—	40,120	41,945	40,955	39,410
Used Values ($)						
Envoy 4×2 ▲	10,500	12,500	13,000	13,500	16,000	21,000
Envoy 4×2 ▼	9,000	11,500	12,000	12,000	14,500	19,000
Envoy AWD ▲	11,000	12,500	14,500	17,500	20,000	24,000
Envoy AWD ▼	10,000	11,000	13,000	16,500	18,000	22,000
Envoy XUV ▲	—	—	13,500	15,000	19,500	—
Envoy XUV ▼	—	—	12,500	13,500	18,000	—
Envoy XUV AWD ▲	—	—	16,500	17,500	22,500	—
Envoy XUV AWD ▼	—	—	15,000	16,000	21,000	—
Rainier AWD ▲	—	—	15,000	17,000	20,000	25,000
Rainier AWD ▼	—	—	14,000	16,000	19,000	23,000
Saab 9-7X ▲	—	—	—	—	26,000	32,000
Saab 9-7X ▼	—	—	—	—	25,000	31,000
TrailBlazer 4×2 ▲	7,000	8,000	9,000	11,000	13,000	17,000
TrailBlazer 4×2 ▼	6,000	7,000	8,000	10,000	12,000	16,000
TrailBlazer AWD ▲	9,500	—	14,000	16,000	17,000	20,000
TrailBlazer AWD ▼	8,500	—	12,500	14,500	16,000	19,000
Reliability	2	2	2	2	2	2
Crash Safety (F)	3	3	3	3	3	3
TrailBlazer EXT	—	—	—	—	4	—
Envoy XT	—	—	—	—	4	—
Envoy XUV	—	—	3	—	—	—
Side	5	5	5	5	5	5
IIHS Side	—	—	—	2	2	2

All ratings on a numbered scale where 5 is good and 1 is bad. See page 217 for a more detailed description.

Offset	2	2	2	3	3	3
Envoy	2	2	2	3	3	3
Saab 9-7X	—	—	—	3	3	3
Rollover	3	3	3	3	3	3
Saab 9-7X	—	—	—	—	—	4

Note: The 2008 model crashworthiness ratings are identical to the previous year's models.

General Motors/Hummer

H2, H3

Both the H3 and larger H2 Hummer are relatively new on the market and are rated in Appendix I.

Honda

PILOT ★★★★★

best buy

RATING: Recommended (2006–08); Above Average (2003–05). The only mistake you can make buying a Pilot is paying too much for it. Think of the Pilot as a large, upscale minivan with all-wheel drive—a cheaper alternative to the Acura MDX. **Strong points:** Roomier and more powerful than most of the mid-sized competition; good acceleration with the AWD V6 powertrain; can tow a small trailer or boat; drives and rides like a nicely balanced luxury car where comfort, performance, and handling are optimized; has seating for eight with three-point seat belts for all; impressive crashworthiness and three-row side curtain airbags; has a reasonably equipped, versatile, and roomy interior with lots of cargo space; and the second- and third-row seats fold flat. **Weak points:** Front headrests are mounted too far back, causing neck pain and strain; lacks low-range gearing for off-road use; transmission shifts a bit slowly when accelerating at 100 km/h; steering is a bit heavy during parking manoeuvres; high-speed corrections are somewhat slow because of the tires' high side walls; a fair amount of body lean is present when cornering, and front-end noseplow occurs in high-speed turns and sudden stops; the steering wheel can be a long reach for some drivers; fuel consumption is high; rear hatch door doesn't have a convenient, separate rear liftglass;

2008 PILOT TECHNICAL DATA

POWERTRAIN (FRONT-DRIVE/4×4)
Engine: 3.5L V6 (244 hp); Transmission: 5-speed auto./man.
DIMENSION/CAPACITY
Passengers: 2/3/3; Wheelbase: 107.0 in.; H: 70.6/L: 188.0/W: 78.0 in.; Headroom F/R1/R2: 7.5/6.0/2.5 in.; Legroom F/R1/R2: 41.0/29.0/24.5 in.; Cargo volume: 42.5 cu. ft.; Fuel tank: 77L/regular; Tow limit: 3,500 lb.; Load capacity: 1,320 lb.; GVWR: 5,954 lb.; Turning circle: 40.0 ft.; Ground clearance: 5.0 in.; Weight: 4,535 lb.

entry and exit are made difficult by the Pilot's trucklike height; rear legroom is at a premium; the third-row seat is best suited for small kids because access is hampered by a narrow passageway and the limited forward travel of the second-row seats; visibility is hindered by thick front roof pillars; and road noise intrudes into the cabin. **New for 2008:** Nothing significant; a redesign is scheduled for the 2009 model year. Look for bold new styling, similar to the CR-V, and a more powerful V6. A diesel V6 will power the 2010 model.

MODEL HISTORY: Introduced as a 2003 model, the Pilot borrows the basic design of its chassis and powertrain from the MDX. The Pilot differs from its more expensive brother with more conservative styling, a softer suspension, larger wheels, and a shorter body that's slightly wider and taller than the Acura, and seats eight passengers versus the MDX's seven. The Odyssey-sourced 240-hp V6 engine coupled to a full-time all-wheel-drive unit enhances overall performance. Four-wheel independent suspension ensures fairly good handling and a comfortable ride. The Pilot is built in Alliston, Ontario, along with the Honda Odyssey, Honda Civic, Acura 1.7EL, and Acura MDX. **2005**—15 more horses, a standard anti-skid system with the EX-L, a tire-pressure monitor, a larger fuel tank, and a slight restyling. **2007**—Slightly restyled.

COST ANALYSIS: With 2008 models selling in Canada for $36,820/$46,690 (LX/EX-L), go for the equivalent 2007 model if you can get it for about $25,000. Better yet, do your shopping across the border where the same cars cost at least $10,000 less. The entry-level front-drive version is priced at $36,820 in Canada, but $27,595 (U.S.) in the States. **Best alternatives:** Infiniti QX4, Lexus RX 300/350, and Toyota Highlander AWD or Sequoia. **Rebates:** Look for $3,000 rebates in the late fall. **Delivery/PDI:** $1,540. **Warranty:** Bumper-to-bumper 3 years/60,000 km; powertrain 5 years/100,000 km; rust perforation 5 years/unlimited km. **Supplementary warranty:** Not needed. **Options:** Nothing that's necessary. **Depreciation:** Slower than average, but soaring fuel prices and Detroit discounting will likely speed up depreciation a bit by year's end. **Insurance cost:** Has been higher than average. **Parts supply/cost:** Parts have been moderately priced and easily found in the MDX/Odyssey generic parts bin. **Annual maintenance cost:** Much less than average. **Highway/city fuel economy:** 9.7/14.1 L/100 km.

QUALITY/RELIABILITY: Likely failures: Quite a few first-year glitches were reported to government safety agencies, but things seem to have settled down with the latest models. Still, watch out for engine oil leaks, transmission fluid leaks, excessive steering vibration, electrical problems (low or no alternator output), body glitches (body, grill, and bumper discoloration and corrosion), an inoperable horn, intolerable cabin wind noise, and an annoying thunking noise from the gas tank. Owners report that oil seeps through the engine block, requiring the block's replacement.

SAFETY SUMMARY: Airbags: Front and side. **ABS:** Standard; disc/disc. **Safety belt pretensioners:** Front. **Head restraints F/R:** 2003–05: ★ (cloth seats); 2003–05: ★★ (leather seats); 2006–08: ★★★★★ (LX seats). **Visibility F/R:** ★★★★/★★★★★. **Pet transport:** ★★★★★.

SAFETY COMPLAINTS: 2003—Small road imperfections make the Pilot suddenly veer left or right. • In one incident, vehicle rolled over after driver made a small steering correction. • Airbags fail to deploy. • Engine oil leakage caused by damaged timing belt and valves. • Intermittent hard starts. • ABS lock-up. • Power-steering pulley breakage. • Head restraints are too low for tall occupants. • Shoulder straps cut across neck. • Intolerable noise and turbulence is produced when cruising with the windows open. • Weak headlights. **2004**—Automatic transmission suddenly downshifts on its own. • Transmission recall parts aren't available. • Hard starting because of poor electrical connection. • Alarm goes off whenever car is started. • Airbag constantly disables itself. • Weak low beam headlights. • Plastic fuel tank is easily punctured. • Interior cabin light flickers on and off, door locks cease to function, and window won't go down. • Passenger window shatters after a drop in temperature. • Severe wind buffeting when driving with the rear windows down. • Sunroofs are failure-prone; they leak and create wind and vibration noise. **2004–07**—Frequent complaints of excessive steering vibration (check *www.hondapilot.org/forums*) that is *not* corrected by re-balancing or changing the tires. Don't waste your money. **2005**—Airbag deployment causes severe burns to the driver's hands. • Loss of braking ability caused by brake master cylinder failure. • Brakes suddenly lock up on one side, causing the vehicle to suddenly veer out of control. • Sudden loss of steering. • Vehicle starts on its own, even though it isn't equipped with a remote starter. • Non-adjustable, doughnut-style head restraints are literally a pain in the neck (see *www.edmunds.com*). • Middle second-row seat belt is mounted too far forward on the ceiling so that it passes the shoulder and sits near the neck and cheek. • Instrument panel data is hard to see in daylight. **2006**—Only 26 complaints logged by NHTSA. • Front airbags fail to deploy. • Excessive braking distance; fishtailing when accelerating:

> Knowing my 2003's stopping distance when ABS kicks in, I was flabbergasted that the new [2006 model] car didn't come close to stopping in time. I noticed one time since that the ABS system just doesn't compare to the 2003, and is extremely dangerous as a result. Another dangerous thing it has done twice is fishtail if I accelerate going into a turn or curve.

• Poorly designed backup lights are practically useless, and low beam headlights don't provide sufficient illumination, especially when going downhill. **2007**—Vehicle may not be capable of handling a tongue weight of 350 lb., as advertised by Honda. • Total differential failure. • Frequent tire blowouts. • Bridgestone Dueler tires may be prone to hydroplane. • Goodyear Integrity tires often go flat due to leaking. • AC condenser failure caused by road debris hitting the unprotected coil. The repair/replacement is covered by a secret "goodwill" warranty. • Severe high-frequency noise emanating from the side windows.

Secret Warranties/Internal Bulletin/Service Tips

2003—V6 engine oil leaks. • Noisy power-steering pump, front strut and damper, hood air deflector, dash, and fuel tank (fuel sloshes when accelerating or stopping). • Security system won't arm. • Steering vibration. • Power-window failure. •

HomeLink remote system can't be programmed. • Third-row seat won't fold, tilt, slide, or recline. • Right rear suspension clicking. **2003–04**—Noise and shudder when turning. • Rear brake clunk. **2003–05**—Hood air deflector cracks. **2003–06**—Noisy drivetrain cause and cure. **2003–07**—Pull, drift to one side. • Rear differential noise, judder on turns. **2005**—Tire valve stem cap replacement campaign. **2006–07**—Wet front floor below A-pillar.

PILOT PROFILE

	2003	2004	2005	2006	2007
Cost Price ($) (firm)					
Base LX (25%)	41,000	38,800	39,000	39,400	36,400
Used Values ($)					
Base LX ▲	15,000	16,000	18,000	23,000	25,000
Base LX ▼	13,500	15,000	17,000	22,000	24.000
Reliability	4	4	4	5	5
Crash Safety (F)	5	5	5	5	5
Side	5	5	5	5	5
Offset	5	5	5	5	5
IIHS Side	—	—	—	5	5
Rollover	4	4	4	4	4

Hyundai

SANTA FE ★★★★★

best buy

RATING: Recommended (2007–08); Above Average (2001–06). Santa Fe occupies the middle ground between the entry-level Tucson and the full-sized Veracruz. **Strong points:** Small turning circle; very comfortable ride; generous occupant space; practical, versatile interior; optional third-row seat; well appointed; competitively priced; and good build and finish quality. *2007 and 2008 models:* Ample power hooked to a smooth-shifting automatic transmission; more agile than previous versions; and standard stability control. **Weak points:** *2006 and earlier models:* Underpowered with the 4-cylinder; little V6 reserve power; engine struggles with too-tall second gearing; no low-range gearing; mediocre handling and braking (with rear drum brakes); limited headroom; head restraint protection is rated "Poor"; excessive engine noise; and thirsty around town. **New for 2008:** Nothing much; no changes are scheduled through the 2010 model year.

MODEL HISTORY: Hyundai's first sport-utility was seen as essentially a Sonata with SUV amenities. It's about the same size as the Honda CR-V or the Ford Escape, but it's a bit wider and its interior room is slightly larger than either of the aforementioned vehicles. Attractively styled, with a user-friendly cockpit, comfortable seating, and lots of storage area, the Santa Fe has appealed mostly to budget-minded buyers looking for SUV versatility.

Less appealing is the Santa Fe's highway performance. The car's heavy weight combined with the puny 4-cylinder engine hampers performance considerably. And the 185-hp V6 powerplant's additional 35 horses still don't give this SUV wannabe sufficient power to overcome its heft. All the more reason to save your loonies for the 2007 or 2008, equipped with a new 242-hp V6. On all models, handling is good, with responsive steering and a comfortable ride. The 4×4 system works efficiently too, without any harshness or undue noise. There isn't any low-range gear; instead, a limited slip rear differential does the job.

This mid-sized SUV, nevertheless, has lots of potential because of its many standard features, reasonable price, and comprehensive warranty. Furthermore, the powertrain shortcomings may not be very important if your driving requirements don't include a lot of high-speed commuting or trailering. **2003**—Front side airbags, an upgraded optional CD changer, and a garage door opener. **2005**—No more 4-cylinder engine. **2007**—Larger, with more power, features, and interior room. The base 2.7L engine got a 15-hp boost, while the new 3.3L V6 adds 30 more horses. ABS, traction/anti-skid control, and front side and side curtain airbags are now standard safety features.

COST ANALYSIS: Buy a 2008 base FWD GL model with the 185-hp 2.7L V6 and a 5-speed manual transmission for $25,995, almost the same price as the 2007 model. The 2008 AWD GL Premium with the 242-hp 3.3L V6 and a standard 5-speed automatic starts at $30,545 (a $500 increase over last year's price). A side-airbag-equipped 2003 Santa Fe V6 is also a good buy. As with most SUVs, you can

2008 SANTA FE TECHNICAL DATA

POWERTRAIN (FRONT-DRIVE/AWD)
Engines: 2.7L V6 (185 hp) • 3.3L V6 (242 hp); Transmissions: 5-speed man. • 4-speed auto. • 5-speed auto.

DIMENSION/CAPACITY
Passengers: 2/3, 2/3/2; Wheelbase: 106.3 in.; H: 68.0/L: 184.1/W: 74.0 in.; Headroom F/R: 3.0/4.5 in.; Legroom F/R: 41.0/27.5 in.; Cargo volume: 37.5 cu. ft.; Fuel tank: 72L/regular; Tow limit: 3,500 lb.; Load capacity: 1,120 lb.; GVWR: 5,240 lb.; Turning circle: 39.0 ft.; Ground clearance: 7.0 in.; Weight: 4,345 lb.

save almost $10,000 buying these Hyundais across the border. **Best alternatives:** Check out the Ford Escape, Honda CR-V or Element, Hyundai Tucson (2006–08), Jeep Liberty, Mazda Tribute, Nissan Xterra, Subaru Forester, and Toyota RAV4. **Rebates:** Look for $4,000 rebates throughout 2008 on the 2008 models, and half as much taken off the 2009s early in the new year. **Delivery/PDI:** $1,610. **Warranty:** Bumper-to-bumper 5 years/100,000 km; powertrain 5 years/ 100,000 km; rust perforation 5 years/unlimited km. **Supplementary warranty:** Not necessary. **Options:** The GL option is a must for the V6 engine. **Depreciation:** Slower than average. **Insurance cost:** Average. **Parts supply/ cost:** Santa Fe shares the compact Sonata platform, so parts should be easily found and reasonably priced. **Annual maintenance cost:** Lower than average. **Highway/city fuel economy:** The 2.7L is rated at 8.4/11.3 L/100 km, while the more powerful 3.3L can be expected to deliver 8.8/12.2 L/100 km.

QUALITY/RELIABILITY: Hyundai's quality control is a heck of a lot better than the Detroit Big Three's and practically as good as Honda's or Toyota's. **Owner-reported problems:** Remarkably few complaints reported so far, although there's been a smattering of engine and transmission problems mentioned. **Warranty performance:** Much better than average. **Likely failures:** The automatic transmission, electrical system, cruise control, catalytic converter, speedometer, alternator, and fit and finish (water leaks, door misalignment, and paint peeling under the hood). In rainy weather, air intake sucks water into the engine and shorts out the mass air sensor (MAS).

SAFETY SUMMARY: For some drivers, the rear-view mirror obstructs the right-side view. **Airbags:** Front, side, and side curtain. **ABS:** Standard or optional; disc/ drum; disc/disc on some recent models. **Safety belt pretensioners:** Front. **Traction control:** Optional and standard. **Head restraints F/R:** 2001–06: ★; 2007–08: ★★★★★. **Visibility F/R:** Vision is clear in the front and rear. **Pet transport:** ★★★.

SAFETY COMPLAINTS: All years: Engine hesitates and then surges, causing unintended acceleration. • Windshield cracking. • Alternator failures drain battery and cause instruments and gauges to malfunction. • Check Engine light is constantly lit, prompting dealers to replace the ECU module and gas tank float, but to no avail. **2001**—Fire ignites in the starter. • Airbags fail to deploy. • Steering wheel locks up while driving. • Sudden, unintended acceleration. • Chronic stalling and hesitation when accelerating. • Accelerator and pedal set too close together. • Power-steering belt shredded repeatedly. • Refuelling is difficult because gas pump shuts off prematurely. • Defective speedometers and alternators replaced under a secret "goodwill" warranty. **2002**—Coolant leak onto engine causes fire. • Premature failure of the transmission and engine. • Passenger window suddenly shatters. • Loose wheel lug bolts. **2003**—Engine camshaft and axle failures. • Steering wheel won't lock. **2004**—Vehicle will suddenly pull to the left while underway. • Complete brake failure; vehicle out of service for a month. • Sudden, unintended acceleration. • Airbag deploys for no reason. • Jerky automatic transmission engagement. **2005**—Only 51 complaints logged, one-third of the average

(150 annually) for 3-year-old models. • Sudden, unintended acceleration when the vehicle is put into Reverse. • Computer-assisted gas pedal on vehicles equipped with a 3.5L V6 causes a dangerous delay in acceleration, followed by a sudden surging:

> The optional 3.5 engine is equipped with a computer operated acceleration throttle engine. This new set up is very poorly designed, has a few second delay and then the car darts off fast, sometimes spinning all drive wheels on dry pavement. I bought a 4 wheel drive unit for our rain, snow covered roads in Oregon, however it's much [worse in these types] of conditions. I've almost rear ended the car ahead of me several times and also have to have one foot on brake pedal in heavy traffic or where I have to stop for people crossing the street.

• Traction control allows wheels to slip in the snow. • Vehicle bucks whenever cruise control is deactivated. • Side front airbag is often disabled when an adult passenger occupies the seat. **2005–06**—Airbags fail to deploy. **2006**—Very few safety-related complaints registered (13); 50 complaints per model year would be average. • Sudden acceleration and loss of brakes. • Engine surges when decelerating. • Brakes fail when coming to a stop. • ABS comes on unexpectedly. • Headlights shut off while driving. **2007**—Cruise control fails to disengage when brakes are applied. • Unpredictable automatic downshifts. • Many complaints that the Airbag Service light is constantly lit; passenger-side airbag is disabled when a normal-sized passenger is seated. • AC condenser is easily damaged from road debris. • Inside dome light illumination is barely adequate, and due to poor design, it doesn't turn on when the door is opened. • Headlights give inadequate illumination beyond 10 metres.

Secret Warranties/Internal Bulletins/Service Tips

All years: No movement in Drive or Reverse. • Paint may have a cloudy appearance. **2001**—A faulty automatic transaxle oil temperature sensor or solenoid may be the cause of poor shifting or no-shifts. • Troubleshooting a harsh gear engagement. • Fluid may leak from the area around the automatic transmission torque converter. • Harsh or delayed Park–Reverse or Park–Drive engagement. • Engine runs and idles roughly. • Inoperative or intermittent operation of the sport mode switch. • Noise from rear wheels. • Wind noise from front doors. • Poor AM radio reception. **2001–02**—Delayed, erratic, and harsh shifts. • Front suspension knocking. **2001–03**—Cruise control disengages on its own. • Automatic transmission erratic performance or whining. • Headlight dimming. **2003**—Cruise control doesn't downshift. • 2.7L V6 engine oxygen sensor upgrade. **2006–07**—3.3L engine misfire, hesitation (oxygen sensor). **2007**—Automatic transmission gear whine when cruising or upon deceleration. • Hard to shift in or out of Park.

SANTA FE PROFILE

	2001	2002	2003	2004	2005	2006	2007
Cost Price ($) (negotiable)							
GL (23%)	25,250	21,050	21,050	22,595	20,995	20,995	25,595
GLS (25%)	29,250	29,500	29,950	30,195	30,395	30,585	35,595
Used Values ($)							
GL ▲	7,000	7,000	8,000	9,000	11,000	14,000	17,500
GL ▼	5,000	5,500	6,000	7,000	9,500	12,500	15,500
GLS ▲	8,500	8,500	10,500	12,000	13,500	19,000	24,000
GLS ▼	6,000	7,000	9,000	10,500	11,500	17,000	22,500
Reliability	4	4	4	5	5	5	5
Crash Safety (F)	—	5	5	5	4	4	5
Side	—	5	5	5	5	5	5
IIHS Side	—	3	3	3	3	3	5
Offset	5	5	5	5	5	5	5
Rollover	—	3	3	—	3	3	4

Note: The 2002 base model price was cut because Hyundai GL reverted to front-drive from AWD. The price increase for the 2007s represents the additional power, a larger interior, and new standard features on these models.

VERACRUZ ★★★★★

RATING: Recommended (2007–08). Prices have moderated during the second year following the Veracruz's launch, mainly due to high fuel prices and a cooling of the market. **Strong points:** Much less expensive than the competition, which may have fewer standard features. Plenty of power; fair, but not agile, handling; and standard electronic stability control and side curtain airbags. Precise steering response and good braking. Fuel economy isn't bad for an SUV this large, and overall reliability is better than most of the competition. Few safety-related complaints have been reported, and front/side crashworthiness has scored the maximum five stars; rollover resistance is rated four stars. IIHS also gives the Veracruz its top crashworthiness rating for front, side, and rear collisions. **Weak points:** Some suspension noise. **New for 2008:** Nothing of importance. No changes are slated in the near future; however, the 2009 or 2010 model may be equipped with a diesel powerplant.

MODEL HISTORY: Not much history yet. Named after the Mexican state, this mid-sized SUV went on sale

2008 TECHNICAL DATA

POWERTRAIN (FRONT-DRIVE/AWD)
Engine: 3.8L V6 (260 hp); Transmission: 6-speed auto.

DIMENSION/CAPACITY
Passengers: 2/3/2; Wheelbase: 110.0 in.; H: 69.0/L: 191.0/W: 77.0 in.; Headroom F/R/R1: 3.0/4.0/1.0 in.; Legroom F/R/R1: 39.0/29.5/25.5 in.; Cargo volume: 41.5 cu. ft.; Fuel tank: 78L/regular; Tow limit: 3,500 lb.; Load capacity: 1,160 lb.; GVWR: 5,240 lb.; Turning circle: 41.0 ft.; Ground clearance: 7.0 in.; Weight: 4,610 lb.

in the second quarter of 2007. It competes with the Saturn Outlook and GMC Acadia, Honda Pilot, Nissan Murano, Subaru Tribeca, and Lexus RX 350. Power is provided by a 3.8L V6 coupled to a 6-speed automatic transmission. As with all Hyundai SUVs, side and side curtain airbags and electronic stability control/anti-skid capability are standard features. A fold-in-the-floor third-row seat that can seat two passengers increases the maximum passenger load to seven. It is larger than the Honda Pilot and has more cargo volume than the full-sized Mercedes-Benz GL (plus, it costs a lot less). Speaking of cost: The Veracruz is slotted in size and price a bit above the Santa Fe ($35,995–$46,295). In Canada, you will pay $29,000–$30,000 for a used 2007 that sold new for almost $40,000. A 2008 sells for about the same price. Yes, in the States you will pay much less. Try $26,900 (U.S.) for a new entry-level 2008 GLS front-drive, representing a huge savings before rebates, sales, incentives, and just plain old hard bargaining.

Infiniti

FX35, FX45 ★★★★

RATING: Above Average (2003–08). A luxury SUV and Nissan Murano clone for buyers secretly wanting a sports sedan. **Strong points:** The FX35 rivals BMW's X5 in its carlike handling. Excellent acceleration, steering response, and braking; good fuel economy; and much more reliable than most of the competition. Few safety-related complaints. **Weak points:** The AWD lacks low-range gearing and is not intended for off-roading. An uncomfortable, stiff, jerky ride when going over road imperfections. A wide turning circle complicates parking and in-town manoeuvring. Annoying tire noise and excessive exhaust roar. The sports sedan driving position isn't for everyone; its low driving position, sloping roof, and high door sills create a claustrophobic feeling. Sporty interior limits cargo space, and the narrow rear windshield impairs visibility. Power front seat and dash- and steering-mounted controls are confusing and not user-friendly. Child safety seat installation is even less user-friendly. Premium fuel is required. **New for 2008:** Nothing important; a redesigned 2009 model is scheduled.

MODEL HISTORY: Launched in 2003, this crossover model is a high-performance, five-passenger, four-door wagon spin-off of Infiniti's G35 sedan. The FX35 comes with a 3.5L V6 and rear-drive or all-wheel drive, while the FX45 has a 4.5L V8 and comes only with all-wheel drive. Every FX has ABS, anti-skid/traction control, front torso-protecting side airbags, head-protecting side curtain airbags, and xenon headlights. The FX45 uses an innovative Lane Departure

2008 FX35 TECHNICAL DATA

POWERTRAIN (REAR-DRIVE/AWD)
Engines: 3.5L V6 (275 hp) • 4.5L V8 (420 hp); Transmission: 5-speed auto.
DIMENSION/CAPACITY
Passengers: 2/3; Wheelbase: 112.0 in.; H: 65.0/L: 189.0/W: 77.0 in.; Headroom F/R: 4.5/4.0 in.; Legroom F/R: 42.5/29.0 in.; Cargo volume: 29.0 cu. ft.; Fuel tank: 90L/premium; Tow limit: 3,500 lb.; Load capacity: 950 lb.; GVWR: 5,624 lb.; Turning circle: 42.0 ft.; Ground clearance: 7.0 in.; Weight: 4,295 lb.

Warning system that alerts the driver when the vehicle has wandered outside of the designated traffic lane. The FX35 rides on 18-inch wheels; the FX45 offers a standard sport suspension with 20-inch wheels. 2006 models got exterior styling tweaks and a redesigned centre console. **2007**—A minor restyling.

COST ANALYSIS: Go for the 2008 FX35 AWD ($55,050) or FX45 AWD ($62,950). They are only about $150 more than the 2007 models were. Used, 2005s are worth about $26,000 and $29,000, respectively. For really big savings, though, shop south of the border, where the same new FX35 goes for $39,550 (U.S.) and an AWD FX45 sells for $50,100 (U.S.). Remember, Infiniti dealers are crying for new products and slashing prices on most of their inventory. If buying used, all the previous models are good buys except for the more glitch-ridden, first-year 2003s. **Best alternatives:** The FX beats BMW's X5 in almost every category. The Lexus RX 300 series, a second-series 2007 ES 350, and the Toyota Highlander are good alternatives from a reliability and performance perspective. **Rebates:** Price cuts of $3,000–$5,000 are quite likely in the late summer as Detroit's SUV discounting picks up speed. **Delivery/PDI:** $1,650. **Warranty:** Bumper-to-bumper 4 years/100,000 km; powertrain 6 years/100,000 km; rust perforation 7 years/unlimited km. **Supplementary warranty:** Not necessary. **Options:** The Touring and Sport packages don't give you much for your money. **Depreciation:** Although average, depreciation is much faster than one would think; 2003s often go for less than half their original cost. **Insurance cost:** Higher than average. **Parts supply/cost:** Average parts supply, but relatively costly electronic and body parts. **Annual maintenance cost:** Lower than average, so far, but most vehicles are still on warranty. **Highway/city fuel economy:** *V6:* 9.9/14.4 L/100 km; *V8:* 11.2/15.6 L/100 km. Owners report real-world fuel consumption is much higher, and sometimes double these figures.

QUALITY/RELIABILTY: Better than average. **Owner-reported problems:** Excessive oil consumption, transfer case failures, premature front and rear brake caliper and rotor wear and noise (chronic squeaking and groaning), and body trim defects. **Warranty performance:** Average; owners mention that problems are seldom fixed at the first servicing visit.

SAFETY SUMMARY: Child safety seats are hard to install because the lower anchor points aren't very accessible. **Airbags:** Side airbags are standard. Reports of airbags failing to deploy. **ABS:** Standard 4W; disc/disc. **Safety belt pretensioners:** Standard. **Head restraints F/R:** *2003–08:* ★★. **Traction control:** Standard. **Visibility F/R:** ★★★/★. **Pet transport:** ★★★.

SAFETY COMPLAINTS: All models: 2003—Many complaints that the driver's seat rocks back and forth, possibly increasing crash forces during a collision. • *FX35:* **2003**—Front axle and differential separation. • Sudden loss of steering control. • In one incident, passenger-side front seat belt would not release and had to be cut away. • When activating the turn blinker switch, the headlights are inadvertently turned off due to the close proximity of the headlight switch. **2004**—Child safety seats are difficult to install or remove. • Erratic cruise control operation doesn't maintain set speed. • Fuel gauge continues to give inaccurate readings, even with a new fuel sender. • Mud flaps on all four wheels cause ice buildup, hampering steering. • When door locks are forced open, windows roll down automatically. **2005**—Sudden, unintended acceleration. • Excessive window condensation. • AC condenser does not drain well, creating a petri-dish environment for harmful mould and bacteria. **2006**—Erratic performing cruise control sometimes "sees" cars that aren't there. **2007**—LED brake lights cause severe eye strain in drivers following the vehicle. *FX45:* **2003**—Sudden, unintended acceleration when stopping. • In one incident, drive shaft fell out from under the vehicle while it was on the highway. • Vehicle suddenly downshifts while underway on the highway. • The gearshift lever can be moved from Park without the key in the ignition or the brakes depressed. • Many complaints of the front windshield cracking (see *www. freshalloy.com*). **2004**—Bright brake and turning lights blind drivers in the rear. • Braking effectiveness and durability questioned. **2005**—Excessive heat in the driver-side footwell.

Secret Warranties/Internal Bulletins/Service Tips

All models: 2003–05—Tips on adjusting a too-high idle rpm. • Correcting excessive steering-column play. • Ways to fix driver seat rocking are outlined in TSB #ITB05-018A. • Kit available for inoperative door mirror. • A fuel tank that's difficult to refuel requires a new shutter valve. **2003–06**—Troubleshooting hard cold starts. **2003–07**—Cause and cure for brake shake and exterior light fogging. **2005**—Remedy for front brake noise.

FX35/FX45 PROFILE

	2003	2004	2005	2006	2007
Cost Price ($) (soft)					
FX35 (30%)	52,700	52,700	52,900	54,500	54,900
FX45 (30%)	60,200	60,200	60,500	61,100	62,800
Used Values ($)					
FX35 ▲	18,000	21,000	26,000	32,000	35,500
FX35 ▼	17,000	20,000	25,000	31,000	34,500
FX45 ▲	20,000	23,000	30,000	36,000	42,000
FX45 ▼	19,000	22,000	29,000	35,000	41,000
Reliability	4	4	5	5	5
Crash Safety (F)	—	—	5	5	5
Side	—	—	5	5	5
Offset	5	5	5	5	5
Rollover	—	—	4	4	4

Note: The 2008 models posted crashworthiness scores identical to earlier models.

RATING: Above Average (2006–08; 1997–2003); Average (2005); Below Average (2004). With its more powerful engine and better-than-average quality control, the QX4 is the better choice—too bad 2003 was its last model year. The QX56 is an Infiniti clone of the full-sized Pathfinder Armada SUV (with 10 extra horses), a spin-off of the Nissan Titan. Its 2004 model redesign hurt overall reliability and performance. **Strong points:** *QX4:* Reasonably priced, with a long list of standard features, and it depreciates slowly. Impressive acceleration on 2001 and later models; attractively styled, mostly posh interior; front seats are especially supportive; automatic 4×4; cargo bay has a low, wide opening; excellent front and side crashworthiness scores, and few safety- and quality-related complaints. *QX56:* A powerful base engine; towing capacity is almost double that of its competitors. Can carry up to eight passengers more comfortably than most luxury models. Impressively responsive handling, thanks to the independent, load-levelling suspension. **Weak points:** *QX4:* Feeble acceleration with earlier models; rear-wheel-only ABS; rear drum brakes; limited rear legroom and cargo space; no third-row seat; fake wood interior trim; interior door handles are too small; rear windows don't roll all the way down; small, narrow rear door openings; useless running boards; and it's a gas-guzzler. Average reliability. Low ground clearance and large bumpers limit off-road capabilities. Below-average offset crashworthiness and head restraint scores. *QX56:* Major braking defects and other serious quality deficiencies. It's way overpriced for what you get, it depreciates rather dramatically, and it's also a gas-guzzler. The QX56's cargo area is long and rather shallow, providing less maximum cargo capacity than an Escalade or Navigator. A stiff ride is accompanied by excessive engine noise. Too much interior plastic trim (doors and dash top). Rollover resistance is only average. **New for 2008:** A plusher interior and better sound system.

2008 QX56 TECHNICAL DATA

POWERTRAIN (4×4)
Engine: 5.6L V8 (320 hp); Transmission: 5-speed auto.

DIMENSION/CAPACITY
Passengers: 2/3/3; Wheelbase: 123.2 in.; H: 78.7/L: 206.9/W: 78.8 in.; Headroom F/R1/R2: N/A; Legroom F/R1/R2: 41.8/41.9/32.2 in.; Cargo volume: 20.0 cu. ft.; Fuel tank: 105L/premium; Tow limit: 8,900–9,000 lb.; Load capacity: 1,400–1,550 lb.; GVWR: 6,622 lb.; Turning circle: 41.0 ft.; Ground clearance: 10.6 in.; Weight: 5,631 lb.

MODEL HISTORY: In 1997, Nissan waved its magic wand and created another Infiniti out of what was once a Nissan—in this case, a Nissan Pathfinder. Don't be surprised—it had been done before with the Altima/G20 and Maxima/I30. What is surprising, though, is that people buy these high-priced clones simply because they carry the Infiniti moniker. **2001**—A larger 240-hp 3.5L V6 engine on the QX4; reworked instrument panel; improved power-window controls; xenon headlights (you'll love 'em, but your neighbours won't); minor exterior restyling; a new roof rack; and a redesigned grille. The previous model had only a 170-hp 3.3L V6 with lower torque. It barely provided adequate performance for the 1,810+ kg (4,000+ lb.) truck.

COST ANALYSIS: A 2008 QX56 goes for $79,600, but getting a used 2007 shaves off about $40,000 and leaves you some of the original warranty for extra protection. Cheaper used 2004–05 models are money traps: You'll pay big bucks to correct quality deficiencies, and lose money and time. A new QX56 bought in the States will cost you $52,250 (U.S.), or about $27,000 less than what it sells for in Canada. **Best alternatives:** Pre-2001 QX4 models changed little over the years, so look for the cheapest model available. If you want convenience upgrades and 40 extra horses with the V6, a 2001 model with a March 2001 or later build plate is the best choice (the build plate is usually found on the inside edge of the driver's door or door pillar). Credible alternatives would be the Cadillac Escalade, GMC Yukon or Denali, and Toyota Land Cruiser, in addition to the Lexus RX 300/330, Nissan Xterra, and Toyota Highlander. **Rebates:** Look for $5,000–$7,000 discounts or zero percent financing programs. **Delivery/PDI:** $1,798. **Warranty:** Bumper-to-bumper 4 years/100,000 km; powertrain 6 years/110,000 km; rust perforation 7 years/unlimited km. **Supplementary warranty:** Not needed. **Options:** A second-row bench seat to accommodate an eighth passenger. **Depreciation:** Faster than average. **Insurance cost:** Higher than average. **Parts supply/cost:** Good parts supply, but relatively costly. Body parts may be back-ordered. **Annual maintenance cost:** Lower than average, since most of these cars are still under warranty. **Highway/city fuel economy:** QX4: 11.8/15.8 L/100 km; QX56: 12.1/18.1 L/100 km.

QUALITY/RELIABILTY: Infiniti quality control is the pits on 2004 models. **Owner-reported problems:** Automatic transmission slippage; many complaints of premature front brake wear, vibration, and noise; minor electrical glitches; driver window won't roll up; body trim defects, door clicking or creaking, paint peeling, and windshield wiper fluid that discolours paint; liftgate and backup sensors beep for no reason; and headliner squeaks and rattles. **Warranty performance:** Average.

SAFETY SUMMARY: Airbags: Side airbags are standard. Reports of airbags failing to deploy. **ABS:** Standard 4W; disc/drum; disc/disc. **Safety belt pretensioners:** Standard. **Traction control:** Optional; standard. **Head restraints F/R:** *1999:* ★★; *2001–03:* ★★★★. **Visibility F/R:** ★★★★★. **Pet transport:** *QX56:* ★★★. The QX56 has the room and the tie-downs for pet-hauling; however, its plush interior won't forgive stains and odours.

SAFETY COMPLAINTS: All models/years: Hesitation, followed by sudden acceleration. • Airbags fail to deploy. **1999**—Sudden loss of steering control; steering lock-up. • Excessive drive shaft vibration. • Distorted front windshield. **2000**—Under-hood fire. **2001**—Stalling when going uphill. • Early automatic transmission replacement. • Complete brake failure. **2002**—Rear suspension bottoms out with four passengers in the car. • Inaudible turn signal indicator. **2003**—Severe rear brake pulsation. **2004**—Passenger's airbag turns off intermittently because of "light" weight (120 lb.). • Brakes continue to wear out early, and suspension system degrades steering control:

Infiniti QX56 has a brake system design flaw. Front brakes need replacement on average every 4,000–6,000 miles [6,400–9,700 km]. Brake rotors are too small, which causes rotor warpage. As a result, the steering wheel shutters back and forth when brakes are applied. There is no fix for this from Nissan. This brake design flaw also affects similar platforms, such as the Armada and the Titan. There also is a design flaw in the front end, which causes the steering wheel to shake violently when going over bumps at speeds in excess of 45 mph [70 km/h]. Hitting certain bumps in the road can cause the front end to go into resonance, thus shaking the steering wheel enough to lose control of vehicle.

• Sudden loss of cruise control cuts engine power. • Parked vehicle rolls downhill. • False backup alerts. **2005**—Suspension suddenly collapses. • Brakes overheat and wear out prematurely, causing severe shaking when braking. **2006**—Left rear axle bolts shear off.

Secret Warranties/Internal Bulletins/Service Tips

All models/years: Brake vibration, excessive vehicle shake, noise, and premature wear are covered in service bulletin #ITB00-024b, published August 30, 2004. • Brake noise, judder, and feel are treated in a more recent bulletin published April 24, 2007 (#ITB00-024d). **1999–2000**—Remedy for steering-wheel vibration and brake pedal pulsation. • Service tips to silence a rear hatch that squeaks or rattles. • Tips on troubleshooting hard starts at high elevations or low temperatures after vehicle has been parked for a few hours. **2001**—Automatic transmission flares on the 1–2 shift when accelerating from a hard stop and then backing off on the throttle. • Engine won't start, or intermittently fails to start. • Incorrect engine idle speed. • Steering fluid leak near the pump-hose fitting. **2001–02**—Transfer-case oil leak, clunk, or sticking in Low gear. • Steering-column noise. • Speaker static. • Navigation system freezes. **2002–03**—Roof rack whistle. **2002–05**—Adjusting a too-high idle speed. **2003–04**—Vibration/shudder may be related to low engine oil. **2004**—No-starts and transmission malfunctions. • No-start in extreme cold. • Engine knocking. • Inoperative cruise control. • Rear axle clicking. • Front brake shudder. • Inoperative second-row seat actuator. • AC humming. • Inoperative navigation system. • Cabin buffeting noise. **2004–05**—Vehicle won't start. • Poor cooling at idle. • TSB #BR04-004e gives many troubleshooting tips to correct brake shudder, pedal vibration, and vehicle shake. • Mushy brakes; long brake pedal travel. • Fluid leaks from automatic transmission air-cooler line. • Free body control module sub-harness to improve electrical connection for trailering. • Fuel gauge always reads full. • AC condenser fan rattles. • Door clicks and creaks. **2004–06**—AC wets front-passenger carpet. **2004–07**—Low power when accelerating. **2004–08**—Water on front floor after rain or wash. **2005**—Free replacement of the third-row seat belt buckle. **2007**—Overheating, or poor AC performance.

	1999	2000	2001	2002	2003	2004	2005	2006	2007
Cost Price ($) (very negotiable)									
QX4	45,700	45,500	48,000	48,000	48,800	—	—	—	—
QX56 (30%)	—	—	—	—	—	69,550	77,500	78,200	78,500
Used Values ($)									
QX4 ▲	6,000	7,000	8,000	9,500	11,000	—	—	—	—
QX4 ▼	5,500	6,500	7,500	8,000	10,000	—	—	—	—
QX56 ▲	—	—	—	—	—	23,000	28,000	35,000	40,000
QX56 ▼	—	—	—	—	—	21,000	26,000	33,000	37,000
Reliability	5	5	5	5	5	3	3	4	4
Crash Safety (F)	4	4	4	4	—	—	—	4	4
Side	5	5	5	5	5	—	—	—	—
Offset									
QX4	2	2	2	2	2	—	—	—	—
QX56	—	—	—	—	5	5	5	5	5
Rollover	—	—	3	3	3	—	—	3	3

Land Rover

Because of their limited production, Land Rover SUVs are included in Appendix I.

Lexus

GX 470, LX 470   ★★★★

RATING: Above Average (1998–2008). **Strong points:** Strong, smooth V8 engine performance; carlike handling; an adjustable suspension; hill-descent control; user-friendly instrumentation and controls; lots of passenger and cargo room; comfortable seating; pleasant ride; excellent fit and finish; and exceptional reliability. *LX470:* "Good" head-restraint crashworthiness score. **Weak points:** Acceleration is only fair, the brakes are overly sensitive, and the ride can be busy. Difficult middle-row entry and exit; antiquated rear-seat folding system (Honda's Pilot gets it right); cramped third-row seats; side-opening tailgate can be inconvenient; lots of tire and wind noise; and poor fuel economy. Owners report automatic transmission "thumping." Head restraints and roof pillars may obstruct rear vision. No front or side crashworthiness data. *2004–06 GX 470:* "Poor" head-restraint crashworthiness score. **New for 2008:** Nothing important. The GX 470 will be revamped in the fall of 2009, when a 6-speed automatic transmission will be added.

2008 GX 470 TECHNICAL DATA

POWERTRAIN (4×4)
Engine: 4.7L V8 (263 hp); Transmission: 5-speed auto.

DIMENSION/CAPACITY
Passengers: 2/3/3; Wheelbase: 109.8 in.; H: 74.6/L: 188.2/W: 74.0 in.; Headroom F/R1/R2: 4.0/6.0 in./N/A; Legroom F/R1/R2: 41.5/29.0/24.0 in.; Cargo volume: 43.7 cu. ft.; Fuel tank: 87L/premium; Tow limit: 6,500 lb.; Load capacity: 1,329 lb.; GVWR: 6,200 lb.; Turning circle: 41.0 ft.; Ground clearance: 7.5 in.; Weight: 4,825 lb.

GX 470

MODEL HISTORY: Having made its debut in early 2003, the GX 470 is a mid-sized, four-door luxury SUV that bridges the price and performance gap between the RX 300 series and the LX 470. With promised seating for eight adults (don't be too hopeful), this newer entry has a minivan's passenger-carrying capability without the minivan "mommy-mobile" cachet.

Set on a modified truck platform and lacking an independent rear suspension, the GX 470 doesn't have as comfortable a ride and isn't as manoeuvrable as its car-based brethren. Downhill Assist Control helps drivers maintain control on very steep descents (I still think independent rear suspension would be more useful). **2005**—Given 35 extra horses, a roll-detection sensor, a rear-view camera, and a tire-pressure monitor.

LX 470

MODEL HISTORY: Launched in early 1998, the 230-hp 4.7L V8-equipped LX 470 still has all of its Land Cruiser trappings and a few additional features that are all its own, including a 2,903 kg towing capacity, adaptive variable suspension, stability control, automatic height control, rear air conditioning, side running boards, and an in-dash CD changer. But the 470 comes only with an automatic transmission.

The V8 engine, based on that of the Lexus LS 400, provides lots of low- and mid-range torque, essential to propel the 470's extra heft to 100 km/h in less than 10 seconds. Off-roading is no problem, either, thanks to the transfer case's low-range gearing and a centre differential that locks in low range for better traction. These SUVs can seat up to eight passengers, though the third-row seat isn't suitable for anyone larger than a pre-teen. Other sport-utilities have more room but not as much off-road capability.

2000—Standard vehicle stability control, power sunroof, and illuminated running boards. **2002**—Navigation system becomes a standard feature. **2003**—Additional airbags, a small horsepower boost, a new gated shifter for the 5-speed automatic, improved steering and brakes, a voice-controlled navigation system, 18-inch wheels, rain-sensing windshield wipers, radio controls on the steering wheel, and a new grille, bumper, headlights, and lower rear hatch. **2004**—A rear-view camera is added. **2008**—A larger, more powerful, and fully loaded 2009 LX 570 arrives.

COST ANALYSIS: The 2008 GX 470 and LX 470 sells for $68,500 and $84,600, respectively ($46,815 and $73,800 (U.S.) in the States), and they aren't much different from the previous two model years. In the spring of 2008, though, a redesigned 2009 LX 570 will cost an additional $3,000 and arrive carrying a 381-hp 5.7L V8 engine housed in a bigger body and coupled to a 6-speed sequential auto-shifter, with full-time four-wheel drive, a limited slip differential, and an enhanced suspension. Fully loaded, the LX 570 will carry eight in comfort, tow 8,500 lbs., and pack 10 standard airbags. Earlier 470s have about 35 to 40 fewer horses and will see their prices soften due to higher fuel costs, a sour American economy, and competition cost-cutting. **Best alternatives:** Some credible Toyota alternatives are the 4Runner and Sequoia. **Rebates:** Expect $5,000–$10,000 discounts and attractive leasing programs to kick in by mid-2008. **Delivery/PDI:** $1,775. **Warranty:** Bumper-to-bumper 4 years/80,000 km; powertrain 6 years/110,000 km; rust perforation 6 years/unlimited km. **Supplementary warranty:** Not necessary. **Options:** None. **Depreciation:** Much slower than average. **Insurance cost:** Above average. **Annual maintenance cost:** Average. **Parts supply/cost:** Parts are often back ordered and can be costly. **Highway/ city fuel economy:** *2007–08 GX: 11.4/15.7 L/100 km; 2007–08 LX 470: 12.9/17.9 L/100 km.*

 SAFETY SUMMARY: Amazingly, these luxury toys have never been crash-tested by NHTSA. **Airbags:** Standard front, side, and side curtain airbags. Reports of airbags failing to deploy. **ABS:** Standard 4W; disc/disc. **Safety belt pretensioners:** Standard. **Traction control:** Standard. **Head restraints F/R:** *1999 LX 470:* ★★★; *2001–03 LX 470:* ★★★★; *2003–06 GX 470:* ★. **Visibility F/R:** ★★★★/★★. **Pet transport:** ★★★★.

SAFETY COMPLAINTS: *GX 470:* **2004**—Airbags fail to deploy. • Excessive drive shaft vibration. • Loose steering; vehicle wanders all over the road, requiring constant steering corrections. • Premature wearout of brake rotors and calipers. • Child safety seat cannot be installed to perform safely. **2005**—Power tailgate striker may trap fingers. **2006**—Seat belt locks up when vehicle isn't on level ground:

> My vehicle started sliding out toward the edge next to a rather long drop off. I stopped my vehicle to see the progress and select a route. The seat belt would not let me re-connect it. I had to drive the most dangerous part of the road without a seat belt.

2007—Excessive vibration degrades handling. *LX 470:* **1999**—Airbags fail to deploy. **2000**—Sudden, unintended acceleration. **2003**—Airbags fail to deploy. **2004**—Engine surges when the AC compressor is activated. • Gas tank will fill up only two-thirds of the way. **2005**—Excessive transmission/differential vibration. • Headlights come on even though vehicle has been parked for some time. **2006**— Vehicle suddenly accelerates when the brakes are applied.

Secret Warranties/Internal Bulletins/Service Tips

All models: 2003–04—Rear drive shaft clunk, thump. • Driveline vibration, groan. • AC cools the vehicle poorly. • A rotten-egg exhaust odour signals the need to install an upgraded catalytic converter. • Field fix for a difficult-to-open rear door. **2003–05**—No-start in cold weather. • Highway-speed steering flutter.

2003–07—Drive shaft clunk, thump noise. • Front door won't fully open; window malfunctions. • Windshield ticking noise. **2005**—Inaccurate fuel gauge. *LX 470:* **1999**—AC noise can be silenced by replacing the expansion valve. • Roof rack wind noises may be caused by improperly installed crossbars. **1999–2000**—If the AC fan continues to run after the ignition has been turned off, it's likely caused by a corroded relay. Lexus has a repair kit that will correct the problem. • To eliminate a transfer-case buzzing at moderate speeds, TSB #NV008-00 suggests installing an upgraded high-speed output gear and shift lever assembly. • The in-dash CD player and changer may work erratically. Lexus will replace it under warranty. **1999–2003**—Steering-column noise/roughness. **1999–2006**—Correction for a booming exhaust at idle. **2001–02**—Front brake vibration. • Continuous alarm chime noise. • Upgrade to reduce noise from telescopic steering wheel and enhance smoothness. **2001–06**—Ways to silence A-pillar wind noise. **2002**—Upgraded rear-view mirror. **2002–06**—A correction for steering that pulls vehicle to one side. **2003–07**—To improve corrosion resistance, new and improved front and rear height sensors and a rear height sensor sub-wiring harness have been developed. **2004–06**—Inconsistent ride height. **2004–07**—Doors won't lock.

GX 470, LX 470 PROFILE

	1999	2000	2001	2002	2003	2004	2005	2006	2007
Cost Price ($) (negotiable)									
GX 470 (30%)	—	—	—	—	—	66,800	67,700	68,400	68,150
LX 470 (30%)	83,265	83,265	90,100	90,600	98,200	99,950	100,400	101,400	101,400
Used Values ($)									
GX 470 ▲	—	—	—	—	—	28,000	36,000	42,000	45,000
GX 470 ▼	—	—	—	—	—	26,000	34,000	40,000	43,000
LX 470 ▲	14,000	15,000	18,000	20,000	26,000	33,000	40,000	50,000	63,000
LX 470 ▼	12,500	14,000	16,000	18,000	24,000	31,000	38,000	48,000	61,000
Reliability	5	5	5	5	5	5	5	5	5

RX 300, RX 330, RX 350/RX 400H ★★★/★

RATING: *RX 300, RX 330, RX 350:* Average (2004–08); Above Average (1999–2003). The rating has been lowered post-2003 because of Toyota's engine sludge problems, dangerous automatic transmission delayed shifts, complete loss of braking ability, sudden acceleration, and inadequate, theft-prone headlights. These vehicles are not suitable for serious off-roading. *RX 400h:* Not Recommended (2006–08). Ridiculously expensive and unproven, it's essentially a more fuel-frugal RX 330 with plenty of horsepower and full-time AWD. If you must go "green," get a cheaper used Toyota Highlander and keep one more new vehicle off the road. **Strong points:** *RX 300:* Strong powertrain performance; handles well; fully equipped; top-quality mechanical components and fit and finish; pleasant riding (better than the Acura MDX and Mercedes' M series); plenty of passenger room; very comfortable seating; lots of small storage areas; easy entry and exit; and slow depreciation. Reliability has been its strong suit over many years. *RX 330:* Quieter, longer, wider, slightly taller, a bit more powerful, and with a longer wheelbase than its predecessor. Comfortable rear seats are adjustable and are easily folded out of the way. Better interior ergonomics, and ride comfort doesn't deteriorate with a full load. Much better emergency handling than with the RX 300. Improved fuel economy; can take regular unleaded fuel. Predicted to be quite reliable. **Weak points:** *RX 300:* Pricey, and it's too big and heavy for sporty handling. No low-range gearing for off-roading, and traction control is optional. Thick roof pillars obstruct outward visibility. Head restraint crashworthiness for 2004–06 models rated "Poor" by IIHS. Instrument displays wash out in direct sunlight. Tilt steering wheel may not tilt sufficiently for some drivers. Expect some wind noise, squeaks, and rattles in addition to wind roar from the moonroof. Limited rear storage area, with a high liftover and excessive wind noise. Takes premium fuel. *RX 330:* Additional power is undermined by the added kilos. Dangerous shift delay when downshifting with the automatic transmission. There's considerable body lean when cornering, the suspension bottoms out easily, steering could be more sensitive, and there's excessive bouncing and body roll with original-equipment shocks. Front and rear seat cushions lack thigh support. Thick rear roof panels obstruct visibility. No third-row seating, and the sloping rear end cuts into cargo space. The power rear door is slow to open, and the moonroof takes up too much headroom. Reduced ground clearance. The optional navigation system screen washes out in sunlight. High freight charges would make Tony Soprano proud. Overpriced when compared to the Toyota Sienna or Highlander. *RX 400h:* Way overpriced, simply to avoid a few extra trips to the gas station. The long delivery wait means that you may be charged more a few months later, unless your contract price is "protected." Makes you a captive customer of Toyota/Lexus and limits where you can go for servicing. The $8,000 (U.S.) battery replacement cost may require a bank loan to pay off. Crashworthiness hasn't been tested yet. Unusually long time for the vehicle to start; slow and vague steering; and the instrument panel power gauge is too small. The 18-inch wheels and beefy P235/55R18 tires don't enhance fuel efficiency. **New for 2008:** Nothing significant. Next redesign is scheduled for the 2010 model, when the vehicle will use a slightly larger platform.

2008 RX 350 AND 2007 RX 400H TECHNICAL DATA

POWERTRAIN (AWD)
Engines: 3.5L V6 (230 hp) • 3.5L V6 (270 hp) • 3.3L V6 (208 hp) + Electric (68 hp); Transmissions: 5-speed auto. • 6-speed auto. • CVT

DIMENSION/CAPACITY (RX 350)
Passengers: 2/3; Wheelbase: 107.0 in.; H: 66.1/L: 186.2/W: 72.6 in.; Headroom F/R: 3.0/4.0 in.; Legroom F/R: 41.0/29.5 in.; Cargo volume: 34.5 cu. ft.; Fuel tank: 73L/regular; Tow limit: 3,500 lb.; Load capacity: 925 lb.; GVWR: 5,245–5,520 lb.; Turning circle: 40.0 ft.; Ground clearance: 7.1 in.; Weight: 4,065 lb.

DIMENSION/CAPACITY (RX 400H)
Passengers: 2/3; Wheelbase: 107.0 in.; H: 66.4/L: 187.2/W: 72.6 in.; Headroom F/R: 3.0/4.0 in.; Legroom F/R: 41.0/29.5 in.; Cargo volume: 34.5 cu. ft.; Fuel tank: 65L/regular; Tow limit: 3,500 lb.; Load capacity: 925 lb.; GVWR: 5,245–5,520 lb.; Turning circle: 37.4 ft.; Ground clearance: 7.1 in.; Weight: 4,365 lb.

MODEL HISTORY: The RX is a compact luxury sport-utility based partly on Toyota's passenger-car platform. It's a bit longer and wider than a Jeep Grand Cherokee, and it's sold as either a front-drive or permanent all-wheel drive. Available only with a 4-speed automatic transmission and a Camry/Lexus ES 300–derived, upgraded 220-hp V6, the RX 300 handles competently on the highway but isn't suitable for off-roading because of its lack of low-range gearing and its tall, four-door wagon body.

First launched in Canada as a 1999 model, the RX 300 was a pioneer crossover SUV that combined minivan versatility with the practicality of a 4×4 drivetrain, suitable for light tasks. And as practically the only game in town for its first several years on the market, many critics ignored this Lexus' many shortcomings and aging design. Now all that's changed, with Acura, Ford, Nissan, Hyundai, and Toyota raising the bar with their cutting-edge SUVs and, in Toyota's case, with a revamped Sienna minivan that offers the same features and performs just as well—for a lot less money.

RX 330 and 350

Introduced as a 2004 replacement for the RX 300, Lexus calls the RX 330 a "luxury utility vehicle." And yes, it does eclipse the old model with its many luxury features and extra-cost gadgets, extra interior room, and an upgraded powertrain. But, in many ways, competing minivans have more utility, more room inside, more seats, and even, as in the Toyota Sienna, four-wheel drive. All they lack is the RX 330's luxury cachet.

The RX 330 and 350 offer a good ride, a plush and innovative interior, great all-around visibility, plenty of power, all-wheel drive, and better-than-average quality and reliability. Not bad for a bestselling SUV cobbled together from ES 330, Camry, and Sienna parts. **2005**—Roll-sensing side curtain airbags, rain-sensing wipers, and an eight-way power passenger seat. **2007**—The RX 350 carries a 3.5L V6 that boosts horsepower from 223 to 270; a 6-speed automatic transmission is also new.

RX 400h

The RX 400h Lexus hybrid debuted as a 2006 model, joining other hybrid models like Toyota's Prius and Highlander, Honda's Insight and Civic, and Ford's Escape. Toyota hopes that by putting the hybrid system in a luxury Lexus, it will get back the high costs of hybrid technology—an impossible feat with a $30,000 Toyota Prius. In fact, industry insiders say Toyota loses thousands of dollars with each Prius sale.

In addition to the hybrid fuel system, your 12,000 extra loonies buy you a vehicle stability-control system, leather upholstery, power tilt/telescoping steering wheel, power moonroof, DVD navigation system with rear backup camera, six-disc CD changer, HID headlights with adaptive lighting, and 18-inch wheels.

The 230-hp 3.3L engine is detuned to just 208 horses; however, when coupled with the 68-hp electric motor, there's a net gain in horsepower. Like the Prius, it operates mainly by allowing the gasoline and electric motors to kick in when the engine load varies. For example, the electric motor is used when accelerating from a stop or in city traffic, while the gasoline engine is useful for highway cruising. If you floor the accelerator, both motors work in unison to give you the extra horsepower needed (posting 0–100 km/h acceleration scores of about 7 seconds). Nevertheless, Lexus hybrid technology isn't as refined as that of the Honda Accord hybrid, which shuts down half the engine's cylinders when carrying a light load to save even more gas.

Fortunately, there's no need to recharge the battery pack. That's done by the gasoline-engine generator. Toyota guarantees the battery for eight years. A new pack will cost about $8,000 (U.S.)—or a few thousand dollars more than what the vehicle will be worth.

Other reasons to be wary of a hybrid-equipped vehicle: Fuel economy is hyped by 15–40 percent; cold weather performance isn't as fuel-efficient; repairs and servicing are dealer-dependent; highway rescuers are wary of cutting through the high-voltage electrical system to save occupants; there's no long-term reliability data; the vehicles have a faster-than-average rate of depreciation; and you have to drive several hundred thousand kilometres to amortize the hybrid's start-up costs.

COST ANALYSIS: The 2008 RX 400h sells for $55,050, or about $3,500 more than the $51,500 AWD RX 350. In the States, the same models cost $41,280 (U.S.) and $37,400 (U.S.), respectively. Lexus hybrid sales are relatively soft, but with oil hitting over $125 a barrel, the market can quickly change. **Best alternatives:** *RX 330 and 350:* Consider buying a Toyota Highlander as a cheaper, more reliable, and more refined alternative. Any used RX 300 series is also a good buy. Other vehicles worth considering are the Nissan Murano and the Toyota 4Runner. **Rebates:** Not likely. **Delivery/PDI:** $1,775. **Warranty:** Bumper-to-bumper 4 years/80,000 km; powertrain 6 years/110,000 km; rust perforation 6 years/unlimited km. *RX 400h:* 96 months/160,000 km (applies to the battery control module, hybrid vehicle control module, hybrid vehicle battery, and the inverter/converter). **Supplementary warranty:** Not necessary for the RX 330; a prudent idea with the RX 400h. **Options:** The $7,000+ Premium and Ultra Premium Package bundled options are a waste of money. The moonroof has generated many complaints about excessive wind noise entering the cabin. **Depreciation:** Slower than normal, but not slow enough to pay for a new battery pack. **Insurance cost:** Above average. **Parts supply/cost:** Parts are taken from the Camry bin and are reasonably priced. **Annual maintenance cost:** Average. **Highway/city fuel economy:** *RX 300:* 9.7/13.0 L/100 km; *RX 330:* 9.0/12.8 L/100 km; *RX 400h:* 8.1/7.5 L/100 km. (Remember that hybrids save the most fuel in city use, where the electric motor proves its worth.)

 QUALITY/RELIABILITY: Good quality control for most years except 2004, where brake, transmission, and headlight failures reign. Hybrid quality and durability is still unproven. **Owner-reported problems:** The automatic transmission lurches between gears and lags in shifting at low speeds, making the car vulnerable to rear-enders. The fuel gauge gives inaccurate readings, and there have been some minor electrical shorts, prematurely worn brake calipers and warped rotors, excessive brake noise, and a variety of interior squeaks and rattles. Also, there are some body trim defects, and the instrument panel display may be too dim. *RX 400h:* The continuously variable transmission has had a checkered past, with early failures reported by other automakers (like Saturn); independent repairers are unable to service it. Sudden, unintended acceleration and engine surging make for risky winter driving. **Warranty performance:** Lousy on the 2004. Shame on Toyota/ Lexus for telling its RX 330 customers that it's "normal" to drive with a dangerously defective transmission:

> The automobile has a latent defect and is inherently dangerous. In November 2003, I attempted to back up in a crowded parking lot, and while in reverse, I pressed the accelerator—there was a lag and the vehicle then accelerated backward very rapidly, striking another vehicle. I assumed the fault was my own (since in moving my foot from the accelerator to the brake, my foot was caught under the brake because the pedals are close together, but that is another item) and after the vehicle was repaired (approximately $7,000 worth of damage) I resumed driving the vehicle. On June 29, 2004, again I was attempting to back up and again the vehicle was in reverse and again when I pressed on the accelerator, there was a lag and then again the vehicle accelerated rapidly backwards, striking a building. It is estimated that the damage to the vehicle is over $10,000, and I do not know what the cost of the damage to the building is. Interestingly, as well, in neither case did the airbags deploy. The second incident received some local press coverage, and on July 8, 2004, I received a call from a visitor to Massachusetts from Florida who had heard about the second incident.... [O]n July 1, 2004, that driver, while in a parking lot, had also had sudden rapid acceleration and had struck a building.... [She] also stated that she had heard of a third incident in Massachusetts of a Lexus RX 330 striking a building following sudden acceleration. The faulty transmission, coupled with the power and torque of the vehicle and the resulting sudden acceleration, is a serious defect; I will not drive the vehicle again. The response of the Lexus dealer when the incidents were reported to it was silence.

 SAFETY SUMMARY: Airbags: Standard front and head-protection side airbags; a driver's knee airbag. There have been reports of airbags failing to deploy. **ABS:** Standard; disc/disc. **Safety belt pretensioners:** Standard. **Traction control:** Standard. **Head restraints F/R:** *1999:* ★★★; *2001–03:* ★★★★★; *2004–08:* ★. **Visibility F/R:** ★★★★★/★★. **Pet transport:** ★★★★.

SAFETY COMPLAINTS: All models/years: Sudden, unintended acceleration. • Airbags fail to deploy. **1999**—Engine overheating and under-hood fires. • Car suddenly accelerates when shifted from Reverse to Drive. • In one incident, the right rear axle sheared in two, causing the wheel to fall off and the vehicle to roll over. **2000**—During hard acceleration from a standing start on dry pavement, the left front tire loses traction and spins free, causing vehicle to veer to the left. • A power distribution problem in the transfer case causes the wheels to lock up at 100 km/h. • Displays on the instrument panel are too dim. • If the wireless remote entry is used to lock the vehicle with an occupant inside, that person may be trapped inside if he or she doesn't exit the vehicle within 30 seconds. • When vehicle is travelling at 70–100 km/h, air entering through the open sunroof makes the whole vehicle shake and produces a horrendous noise. • Original-equipment tires aren't acceptable for off-roading. **2001**—Engine compartment burst into flames after one vehicle accelerated from a stop. • Transmission jumps from Park to Reverse. • Defective jack. **2002**—Vehicle rolls backward when stopped on a hill. • Sunroof doesn't offer pinch protection. • Cupholders are too shallow. **2003**—Major rear blind spot. **2004**—Most complaints concern transmission lag and lurch, accompanied by sudden acceleration. • Cruise control won't release. • Many complaints that brakes fail because of a faulty brake booster. • Side airbags fail to deploy. • Suspension defect causes car to pull into oncoming traffic. • Poor headlight illumination:

> The headlights on a 2004 RX 330 have cost me a lawsuit against dealer. Drove car second night, 3 miles [5 km], on country roads. I had motion sickness after that experience. Every time I hit a bump, the car lights would bounce, as if on a spring. The line from lights goes across center of windshield at eye level. The driver can't see beyond 20 ft [6 m]. When looking beyond 20 ft, you see total darkness. When passing a person on the side of the road you can only see them from the knees down. Very scary driving the RX 330 at night.

• Dash reflects onto the windshield. • Wipers don't clean effectively. • Suspension bottoms out with a 320 kg (700 lb.) load. • Rear hatch closes on driver's neck. • Rear window shatters for no reason. **2005**—Automatic transmission delay when downshifting or when accelerating. • Xenon headlights are often stolen. • Headlight low beam falls short. • White tail light lens reflects sunlight and can blind drivers following the vehicle. • Exhaust fumes are sucked into the cabin if the rear hatch is left ajar. **2006**—Extended stopping distance caused by brake fluid leaking from the brake booster, making the master cylinder inoperative. • Blue-tinted headlights blind oncoming drivers. **2007**—Vehicle suddenly accelerates as brakes are applied. • Backup lights are too dim. • Airbag light comes on for no reason. *RX 400h:* **2006**—Seat belts don't retract properly. • Erratic cruise-control operation. • Vehicle constantly pulls to the left. • Sudden brake loss. • Surging when brakes are applied. • Sudden, unintended acceleration and engine surging make for risky winter driving:

> The vehicle does not gear down while going down an icy road. There are no 1st, 2nd or 3rd gears. There is no way to stop the vehicle from hydroplaning. The dealership determined that this is the way the vehicle is designed to operate.

2007—Stuck accelerator. • Airbag light stays on.

Secret Warranties/Internal Bulletins/Service Tips

All models/years: Free engine sludge repairs. • Lexus blames rotten-egg exhaust smells on fuel, not on its vehicles. **1999**—If the MIL alert comes on, you may have to install an improved air/fuel ratio sensor under the emissions warranty. • A 2–3 shift shudder can be corrected by installing an upgraded transaxle valve body. • Tips on improving the driver-side door master switch. • To reduce noise and vibration at idle speeds, a dynamic damper has been added to the centre exhaust pipe. • There are dozens of bulletins that address the correction of various squeaks and rattles found throughout the vehicle. • Countermeasures are outlined to reduce wind-rushing noise from the moonroof wind deflector panel. **1999–2000**—Glove box rattling and front suspension noise. **1999–2001**—Measures to silence front brake squeal. **2000**—Low-speed drivetrain noise and vibration (TSB #SU007-02, dated November 22, 2002). • Outside mirror stress cracks. **2001–03**—Front seatback popping or clicking. • Inoperative mirror compass. **2002**—Drivetrain vibration. **2002–03**—Troubleshooting front brake vibration. **2002–06**—Diagnosis and repair of vehicles that pull excessively to one side. **2003**—Remedy for ABS noise. **2003–07**—Windshield ticking. **2004**—Free replacement of the exhaust manifold converter assemblies under "Special Service Campaign" #3LE to curb excessive exhaust noise. Lexus has a deal with Enterprise Rent-A-Car to pay $47 per day for a rental if the dealer has no loaner vehicles available. Additionally, owners will get a free full tank of gas, a free car wash up to $20, and a refund for repairs done at a "remote facility" (this probably means an independent garage). One replacement per car is authorized, and there are no ownership, time, or mileage restrictions. • A brake booster upgrade. • Front brake vibration remedy. • Coolant may leak from a crack in the base of the radiator. • Drone, vibration upon acceleration. • AC groaning, moaning; diminished blower speed. • Deceleration thump. • Front suspension creaking and knocking. • Hatch area creak or tick. • Glove box and instrument panel rattles. • Rear wiper upgrade. **2004–05**—No-start in cold weather. • Toyota/Lexus suggests a remedy for "poor shift quality" in an August 11, 2003, bulletin (#TC005-03). Owners say this didn't fix the lagging and lurching shifts. In May 2005, Toyota proposed another remedy and revised the earlier service bulletin, which kept its original bulletin number • Front-door window noise. • Free headlight theft-prevention kit. **2004–06**—Rear door–stay improvement. • Unacceptable power backdoor operation. **2004–07**—Transmission fluid or gear oil leaks from the transfer case vent. • Troubleshooting dash rattles. • Front seat squeak. **2005**—Upgraded front brake rotors should silence a high-pitched front brake squeal. • Tonneau cover latch rattle. **2007**—Engine timing cover oil leaks. • Engine squealing. • Loose shift lever. • Moonroof rattle.

	1999	2000	2001	2002	2003	2004	2005	2006	2007
Cost Price ($) (negotiable)									
RX (28%)	46,000	46,640	53,000	51,250	51,600	49,900	50,200	50,500	51,550
400h (26%)	—	—	—	—	—	—	—	62,200	62,250
Used Values ($)									
RX ▲	11,000	13,000	15,000	16,000	18,500	23,000	28,000	33,000	36,000
RX ▼	9,500	11,500	14,000	15,000	17,000	21,000	26,000	31,000	34,000
400h ▲	—	—	—	—	—	—	—	38,000	43,000
400h ▼	—	—	—	—	—	—	—	36,000	41,000
Reliability	5	5	5	5	5	2	3	3	3
Crash Safety (F)	—	—	4	4	4	5	5	—	—
Side	—	—	5	5	5	5	5	—	—
Offset	5	5	5	5	5	5	5	5	5
Rollover	—	—	3	3	3	—	—	—	—

Note: The 2008 RX 400h scored five stars for front and side crashworthiness. The 2008 RX series models posted similar crash protection scores to the previous year's models.

Mazda

CX-7, CX-9

These two crossover SUVs have only been on the market since the fall of 2006, so they are given a summary rating in Appendix I.

Mercedes-Benz

Mercedes' SUVs have limited owner and service bulletin feedback, so they are covered in Appendix I in a summary fashion.

Mitsubishi

ENDEAVOR

RATING: Average (2004–08). An unimpressive mid-sized SUV that was spun off the 2004 Galant sedan platform, giving the Endeavor carlike handling and a comfortable ride. **Strong points:** A strong 225-hp 3.8L V6; a liftgate with separate

2008 ENDEAVOR TECHNICAL DATA

POWERTRAIN (PERMANENT AWD)

Engine: 3.8L V6 (225 hp); Transmission: 4-speed manumatic

DIMENSION/CAPACITY

Passengers: 2/3; Wheelbase: 108.3 in.; H: 67.3/L: 190.2/W: 73.6 in.; Headroom F/R: 4.5/4.5 in.; Legroom: 41.5/30.0 in.; Cargo volume: 40.7 cu. ft.; Fuel tank: 81L/premium; Tow limit: 3,500 lb.; Load capacity: 970 lb.; GVWR: 5,250 lb.; Turning circle: 38.4 ft.; Ground clearance: 8.3 in.; Weight: 3,847 lb.

opening glass; "Good" IIHS offset crashworthiness scores; and an NHTSA five-star rating for front- and side-impact crashworthiness. **Weak points:** Fuel-thirsty; off-roading is compromised by the lack of low-range gearing; cornering produces excessive body lean; and head-restraint protection rated "Poor" by IIHS. Overpriced, and depreciation is much more rapid than usual. **Best alternatives:** GMC Acadia, Honda Pilot, Hyundai Santa Fe or Veracruz, Saturn Outlook, and Toyota Highlander or 4Runner. **New for 2008:** Standard stability and traction control; the rear glass no longer works independently from the tailgate; the tow package now includes a transmission and power-steering cooler; and the 4×4 versions have a larger radiator. Mitsubishi is on the ropes due to poor sales. The company has mistakenly put its development and marketing money into the redesigned Outlander, a larger, 7-passenger SUV that may be dropped in 2009 if fuel prices continue surging.

MODEL HISTORY: This mid-sized SUV carries five passengers and offers front-drive or all-wheel drive. Safety features include four-wheel disc brakes, a tire-pressure monitor, 17-inch alloy wheels, standard front and side curtain airbags (XLS and Limited), traction control, and ABS (optional on the front-drive LS). The base 2008 Endeavor SE front-drive sells for $35,998, and the AWD version goes for $39,298; however, dealer discounts of up to 20 percent are quite common. There is also the car's rapid depreciation to consider: A used 2004 that sold originally for $34,000 is now worth only $9,500, and a 2005 goes for between $11,500 and $12,500. This is good news if you buy used, but it's a bit distressing if you have to sell within the first five years. American prices are even more attractive, with the 2008 SE priced at only $29,399 (the AWD model costs $30,899). Interestingly, Mitsubishi Canada pokes us in the eye again with a $1,345 freight charge, double the $650 (U.S.) fee charged in the States.

QUALITY/RELIABILITY: Average. **Likely failures:** Automatic transmission (whine and flaring); brake pads and rotors; power windows, door locks, and plastic outside door handles; windshield wiper motor; heater core; AC (debris collects in the housing and blower motor); and radiator (it's easily punctured due to the large grille opening and the absence of a shield or deflector, and it costs about $700 to replace). Water leaks into the driver's footwell area due to a plugged AC hose. Front windshield may shatter, and liftgate glass may also shatter as the liftgate is closed.

Secret Warranties/Internal Bulletins/Service Tips

2004—Power seats operate poorly. • Troubleshooting tips for eliminating a body whistle produced when the vehicle is underway. **2004–05**—A spark knock, engine ping, and delayed shift may be caused by a miscalibrated PCM. •

Troubleshooting tips to reduce gear whine. • Shift delay and/or no Overdrive. • Shift flare when going from Second to Third gear. • Steering column noisy when turning. • Poor AC performance. • AC water leaks. • Plugged HVAC drain. • Torn seat side seam (cloth seats). • Body noise diagnosis and repair. • Water leaks into the rear of the vehicle. • Fuel tank is hard to fill.

ENDEAVOR PROFILE

	2004	2005	2006	2007
Cost Price ($) (negotiable)				
Base LS/SE (22%)	33,998	34,298	34,998	35,998
Used Values ($)				
Base LS/SE ▲	9,500	11,500	17,000	22,000
Base LS/SE ▼	9,000	12,500	16,000	21,000
Reliability	3	3	4	4
Crash Safety (F)	4	4	5	—
Side	5	5	5	—
Offset	3	3	5	—

MONTERO ★★★

RATING: Average (2004–06); Below Average (2003). There's nothing fundamentally wrong with Mitsubishi's cars (like the low-cost Colt compacts, the 1991–99 3000GT, and the Stealth sporty coupe), but the SUVs look much better than they drive. And charging $48,598 for a new Montero is close to committing a felony. The problem is the company itself: It's always one step away from bankruptcy; its officials are doing jail time for concealing defects and paying Yakuza mobsters to hush irate stockholders; and Chrysler, its former partner, treats it with benign neglect. Chrysler's abandoning will, undoubtedly, negatively impact warranty claims and servicing. Plus the dropping of the Montero for 2007 has driven down resale values appreciably and complicated servicing and parts availability. **Strong points:** Seats seven, and features lots of passenger and cargo room. The classy interior has well-designed seats; an attractive, user-friendly dash and cabin controls; and good fit and finish. There's also low-range gearing for off-roading; anti-skid and traction control, beginning with the 2003s; and ABS on four-wheel disc brakes. A good reliability record is another plus. *Montero Sport:* Overall performance is quite similar to the Montero, although the Sport's crashworthiness ratings are better. NHTSA gives frontal crashworthiness for the 2001–04 models

2006 MONTERO TECHNICAL DATA

POWERTRAIN (PERMANENT AWD)
Engine: 3.8L V6 (215 hp); Transmission: 5-speed manumatic
DIMENSION/CAPACITY
Passengers: 2/3/2; Wheelbase: 109.7 in.; H: 71.5/L: 190.2/W: 74.8 in.; Headroom: N/A; Legroom: N/A; Cargo volume: 39.8 cu. ft.; Fuel tank: 90L/premium; Tow limit: 3,500 lb.; Load capacity: 1,165 lb.; GVWR: 5,997 lb.; Turning circle: 37.4 ft.; Ground clearance: 8.6 in.; Weight: 4,718 lb.

four stars, and side protection for the 2002–04 models five stars. IIHS also rates the Sport "Good" in providing offset crash protection. **Weak points:** The V6 is adequate for highway use, but it requires a full throttle for passing and merging, hurting fuel economy. A tightly sprung chassis degrades handling and ride comfort. Lots of body lean in turns, and steering isn't as precise as the Japanese competition's. Problematic rear-seat access. IIHS says 2001–06 Monteros give only "Average" offset crash protection, and have head restraints that are "Average" as well. The Montero also has a propensity to roll over: *Consumer Reports* magazine found the 2001–03 models tend to roll over under hard cornering, a conclusion also reached by NHTSA in its two-star rollover rating given to the 2001–04 models. Rear head restraints block rearward vision and have been judged by the IIHS as giving "Poor" collision protection. Rapid depreciation—the top-of-the-line 2005 Limited sold for $48,748 new and is now worth less than $21,000. *Montero Sport:* Also overpriced and quick to lose resale value. For example, the entry-level 2003 Sport ES sold for $32,497; its resale price now varies between $8,000 and $9,000. It's more trucklike than the Montero, resulting in poor handling, an uncomfortable ride, considerable wind and engine noise, and excessive fuel consumption. Entry and exit are made difficult by the low roofline and high floor. The narrow rear bench seat is uncomfortable. Head restraints have been ranked "Below Average," and the 2004 and later models don't come with standard side airbags, though 2003 and earlier models did.

MODEL HISTORY: Going into its 12th year in the States, Mitsubishi's sales have been a roller coaster ride that may soon end in bankruptcy or new ownership. Montero drivers are the not-so-proud owners of an auto "orphan" that has been axed to pay for Mitsubishi's new model realignment, which highlights bigger vehicles when everyone else is downsizing to save fuel.

The base Montero uses a 215-hp 3.8L V6 coupled with a 5-speed manumatic transmission. The Sport employs a 197-hp variant and seats five passengers rather than seven. Montero also offers a third-row bench seat that folds flush with the cargo floor. Standard features include front side airbags; ActiveTrac 4×4, suitable for prolonged use on dry pavement; low-range gearing; ABS; anti-skid/traction control; rear air conditioning; and a power sunroof. **2004**—Standard front side airbags become optional. **2005**—17-inch wheels.

QUALITY/RELIABILITY: Likely failures: Owner complaints have targeted airbags (failure to deploy), tie-rods, loss of braking and premature brake wear (rotors and pads), Bridgestone tires, and electrical systems. Chronic stalling is also a common complaint. The 1999–2003 Sport models are noted for costly speedometer failures, covered in TSB #03-23-002.

Secret Warranties/Internal Bulletins/Service Tips

All years: Engine pinging diagnosis. **1999–2005**—Diagnosis and correction of body squeaks when turning. **2001–04**—Rear seat won't unlatch. **2004**—Shift delay and/or no Overdrive. **2005**—Engine valve lifter noise diagnosis.

MONTERO PROFILE

	2003	2004	2005	2006
Cost Price ($) (very soft)				
Montero Sport	32,497	—	—	—
Montero LTD	48,507	48,550	48,748	48,598
Used Values ($)				
Montero Sport ▲	9,000	—	—	—
Montero Sport ▼	8,000	—	—	—
Montero LTD ▲	12,000	16,000	20,500	27,000
Montero LTD ▼	11,000	15,000	19,500	26,000
Reliability	2	2	3	4
Crash Safety (F) (Sport)	4	4	—	—
Side (Sport)	5	5	—	—
Offset (Sport)	3	3	3	3
Rollover (Sport)	2	2	—	—

Note: There are no recent NHTSA crashworthiness ratings for the Montero. The last frontal crash test gave the 1997 model a three-star designation.

Nissan

MURANO ★★★

RATING: Average (2005–07); Below Average (2003–04). The Murano is essentially a tall Altima AWD with serious steering, alternator, and transmission problems afflicting its first two model years. Thereafter, the car's screeching brakes (especially in Reverse) are a sufficient turn-off. **Strong points:** Powerful, responsive engine; carlike handling; an easily accessed interior; and plenty of passenger and cargo room. **Weak points:** Some serious reliability and safety deficiencies up to the 2005 model year (like leaking fuel tanks). A stiff ride, poor rear visibility, and limited off-road use. Fit and finish may disappoint. **New for 2008:** Nothing. Nissan skipped the Murano's production for a year. A redesigned 2009 model has just arrived. It's unrated, until we see if its revamping affects reliability. With any luck, Nissan will have put a silencer on its screeching brakes.

MODEL HISTORY: This is a stylish five-passenger, mid-sized SUV crossover that's essentially a tall wagon with 4×4 capability. Built on the Altima sedan's platform, the 2009 Murano has 25 more horses and additional standard features and refinements that make it a much better buy at $37,648 ($26,330 the States) than the higher-priced, $39,098 2007 version. Restyled, sporting an upgraded interior, and equipped only with a more refined CVT hooked to a 265-hp 3.5L V6, the 2009 Murano combines performance with comfort. It features standard four-wheel disc

2009 MURANO TECHNICAL DATA

POWERTRAIN (PERMANENT AWD)
Engine: 3.5L V6 (265 hp); Transmission: CVT

DIMENSION/CAPACITY
Passengers: 2/3; Wheelbase: 111.2 in.; H: 66.9/L: 188.5/W: 74.1 in.; Headroom F/R: 3.5/5.0 in.; Legroom F/R: 40.0/29.0 in.; Cargo volume: 32.6 cu. ft.; Fuel tank: 82L/premium; Tow limit: 3,500 lb.; Load capacity: 1,055 lb.; GVWR: 4,918–5,051 lb.; Turning circle: 40.0 ft.; Ground clearance: 5.5 in.; Weight: 3,847 lb.

brakes with Brake Assist (BA) and Electronic Brakeforce Distribution (EBD).

With its 245 horses and CVT transmission, the Murano 2007 accelerates effortlessly, posting some of the fastest times in its class. The car rides comfortably with little jostling of passengers when passing over uneven terrain. The SE's sport-tuned suspension adds very little to ride quality.

On the downside, the 2007's CVT has been troublesome and takes some getting used to (it slips rather than shifts), and third-row seating isn't available. The body feels cheap, there's lots of wind buffeting with the windows or sunroof open, first-year models were plagued by a variety of squeaks and rattles, and the doors don't sound solid when closed. The optional navigation system is complicated to operate. Furthermore, despite the Murano's rugged looks, it can't handle serious off-roading, and its towing ability is quite limited at 1,587 kg (3,500 lb.) when equipped with a $750 tow package.

COST ANALYSIS: The front-drive 2009 Murano SL will sell for its full list price during the second half of 2008. Thereafter, look for rebates of $3,000–$5,000 kicking in during early 2009. American prices are cheaper by about $10,000 (hint, hint). **Best alternatives:** The EX35 for easier access and storage, or the 2009 FX35/45 sporty crossover twins. **Rebates:** $3,000–$5,000. **Delivery/PDI:** $1,395. **Warranty:** Bumper-to-bumper 3 years/60,000 km; powertrain 5 years/ 100,000 km; rust perforation 5 years/unlimited km. **Supplementary warranty:** Not needed. **Options:** Navigation system and Cold Package (heated seats and mirrors) add $3,000 to the price with little benefit. **Depreciation:** Slower than average. **Insurance cost:** Much higher than average. **Annual maintenance cost:** Average. **Parts supply/cost:** Parts aren't easily found and can be expensive. **Highway/city fuel economy:** 6.8/11.7 L/100 km.

QUALITY/RELIABILITY: Average quality, which is all the more surprising considering that the 2004–05 redesigned Altima, Armada, Maxima, Quest, and Titan versions have been plagued by unreliable components and poor fit and finish. **Owner-reported problems:** Poor fuel economy; sudden loss of power; faulty ECM, throttle body, engine oil seals, and AC amplifier; no current through PIN connectors; CVT transmission won't hold vehicle stopped on an incline; transmission and alternator failures; chronic ABS brake failures (actuator and sensor); premature brake wear and constant brake screech, squeaks, and squeals:

> When the vehicle is in reverse and brake pedal applied, there is a horrible screeching/ squealing noise that occurs. It is a very loud noise that can be heard from far away. This happens almost every time the car is in reverse. The problem does not occur when [the] vehicle is going forward. The brakes continue to work except for the noise.

There are also lots of interior squeaks and rattles, as well as frequent shock-absorber thunking. **Warranty performance:** Average, but problems don't get solved quickly and Nissan often stonewalls legitimate customer complaints.

SAFETY SUMMARY: Adjustable pedals. **Airbags:** Front, rear, and side. **ABS:** Standard 4W; disc. **Head restraints F/R:** *2003–05:* ★. *2006–07:* ★★. **Visibility F/R:** ★★★★★/★. **Pet transport:** ★★. The sloping rear hatch reduces usable cargo space to haul safely crated animals; however, the seats easily fold flat.

SAFETY COMPLAINTS: All years: Airbags fail to deploy. • Brake calipers and rotors wear out prematurely. **2003**—Sudden, unintended acceleration. • Early transmission failure. • Vehicle vibrates violently when driven with the rear windows down. • Front seat rocks, causing driver's seat belt to tighten progressively. • Suspension is hard and stiff; with a full load, the Murano tends to bounce around. • Doors randomly lock themselves. • Rear roof pillars block rear view. • Wipers clog easily, and can't be raised to wipe off accumulated snow and ice without opening the hood. • Ineffective defroster system. • False Open Door alert. **2003–04**—Complete loss of power steering; sometimes occurs when turning steering wheel rapidly. • Alternator failure causes stalling, loss of power, and no-starts; preceded by the illumination of the Brake and Battery warning lights (see *www.nissanmurano.org*):

> 2004 Nissan Murano SE AWD with only 1,901 miles [3,000 km] had the alternator
> fail today. The car completely lost power, leaving me unable to accelerate or use power
> steering or braking functions. Occurred on local city streets—had this occurred on the
> highway, travelling at highway speeds, it could have easily led to an accident.

• Early replacement of the CVT transmission and transfer case. **2004**—Shifts out of Park without the keys in the ignition. • Gas tank is vulnerable to puncture from road debris. • Loose, leaking power-steering line. • Low brake pedal causes foot to hit the accelerator pedal. • Wipers get bent out of shape. • Headlight switch moves too easily, so you can inadvertently turn off the lights. • Xenon headlights are easily stolen. **2005**—Gas tank leaks fuel and is vulnerable to damage from road debris:

> Noticed gas leaking on the parking lot. I proceeded to Jamestown, NY (50 miles
> [80.5 km]), to take the car to the closest Nissan dealer. Signature Nissan 716-
> 664-0175 discovered that something had gone through the gas tank and I would
> need to replace it. He showed me how the gas tank drops down and has a smooth
> unprotected surface facing forward where (whatever it was that hit the tank) went
> through the plastic surface.

• Cruise control cuts out, and vehicle suddenly slows down when ascending or descending hills. • Transmission often slips into "limp" mode. • Chronic throttle body failures cause stalling or loss of power. • Vehicle suddenly jumps to the right when passing over bumps. • Alternator failures continue despite a recall to correct the problem. • Child safety seats are difficult to install. • Distorted windshields. • Windshield washer spray nozzle doesn't adequately clean passenger-side windshield. **2006**—Gas tank is still vulnerable to puncture by road debris. • AC condenser is also vulnerable. • Automatic fuel pumps won't work with the Murano fuel tank (Nissan has a bulletin that tackles this problem):

> When filling up with gas, the pump stops generally after pumping only 0.5 gallons [1.9 litres] to 3 gallons [11.4 litres]. Often, I cannot fill it up anymore at that pump. Sometimes, I can start to fill it up at a slower rate and continue to get the rest of the gas in the tank. This has happened at 7 or 8 different stations in town, at numerous pumps—so it is not a case where 1 pump at a station is pumping too fast (as was used as the initial excuse). I have read in forums of this exact same problem.

• Front headlight burns out after only a year, and it costs $279 to replace each one. **2007**—Brake and gas pedals are mounted too close together. • Windshield wipers are often stuck when it snows, and ice forms in their housing. • When passing over small puddles, poor design allows water to be thrown up onto the front windshield. • Vehicle suddenly loses 90 percent of its power when accelerating from a stop.

Secret Warranties/Internal Bulletins/Service Tips

2002–03—Engine fails to start. • Automatic transmission clicking noise. • ABS or Airbag light may remain lit. • Doors lock and unlock intermittently, front window rolls down, and alarm sounds. • Centre console lid is hard to close. • Inoperative interior courtesy lamps. **2003–04**—Front brake vibration. • Defective sunroof. • Door glass ticking. **2003–06**—Hard starts, no-starts in cold weather may call for the replacement of the power distribution module (PDM). **2003–07**—Loss of power when accelerating. **2006–07**—Difficulty fuelling vehicle.

MURANO PROFILE

	2003	2004	2005	2006	2007
Cost Price ($) (negotiable)					
Murano (25%)	39,500	37,700	37,900	38,998	39,098
Used Values ($)					
Murano ▲	12,500	14,000	16,000	21,000	23,000
Murano ▼	11,500	13,000	15,000	20,000	22,000
Reliability	3	3	4	4	4
Crash Safety (F)	4	—	4	5	5
Side	5	5	5	5	5
Offset	—	5	5	5	5
Rollover	4	4	4	4	4

RATING: *Pathfinder:* Above Average (2006–08); Average (1990–2005); Below Average (1987–89). *Armada:* Above Average (2008); Average (2007); Below Average (2005–06); Not Recommended (2004). Performance wasn't the early Pathfinder's strong suit, and you still have to pay big bucks for the LE's more refined drivetrain and performance enhancements. **Strong points:** The powerful and smooth 4.0L V6 matches some V8s for impressive acceleration and reserve power while delivering good fuel economy and a 2,720 kg (6,000 lb.) towing capability. Standard stability control provides acceptable handling and a stiff ride. Little road or wind noise, and plenty of cargo room. The quiet interior is nicely finished with plenty of standard convenience and comfort features plus third-row seating. An attractive and user-friendly dashboard is at the head of the class in terms of clear instrumentation and easily accessed controls. SE and LE transmissions have low-range gearing on recent models. Very slow depreciation. **Weak points:** Handling can get scary at times, as the vehicle tends to wander over the highway and to twist violently when passing over bumps. Weak suspension, second- and third-row seats are cramped, side and head-protection airbags are optional, limited visibility to the rear, and it's a gas hog. *Pathfinder: 2004 and earlier models:* Lethargic engine, subpar emergency handling, and unimpressive braking. Part-time 4×4 isn't to be used on dry pavement. Vehicle can be hard to control when going over a bump. Difficult entry and exit because of a high step-up and doors that aren't wide enough to permit easy access. Rear has barely adequate leg space and restricted visibility; rear seats lack sufficient back support and aren't easily folded out of the way. Standard running boards on the LE are more decorative than practical. No third-row seating. A history of sudden, unintended acceleration. Poor fuel economy. *Armada:* Terrible safety and reliability history. **New for 2008:** *Pathfinder:* Restyled; loads of new optional features; addition of the Armada's V8. *Armada:* A restyled front and rear end.

MODEL HISTORY: Introduced in 1987, the Pathfinder has developed slowly over the years. Originally based on the Nissan pickup, it was seriously underpowered until 1990, when multipoint fuel injection was added to the 3.0L V6, which boosted horsepower from 153

2008 PATHFINDER TECHNICAL DATA

POWERTRAIN (REAR-DRIVE/AWD)

Engines: 4.0L V6 (270 hp) • 5.6L V8 (300 hp); Transmission: 5-speed auto. OD

DIMENSION/CAPACITY

Passengers: 2/3/2; Wheelbase: 112.2 in.; H: 73.3/L: 187.6/W: 72.8 in.; Headroom F/R: 2.5/3.5 in.; Legroom F/R: 42.4/34.2 in.; Cargo volume: 17.4 cu. ft.; Fuel tank: 80L/premium; Tow limit: 6,000–7,000 lb.; Load capacity: 1,188–1,686 lb.; GVWR: 5,050–5,300 lb.; Turning circle: 40.0 ft.; Ground clearance: 8.3 in.; Weight: 4,682 lb.

2008 ARMADA TECHNICAL DATA

POWERTRAIN (PERMANENT AWD)

Engine: 5.6L V8 (317 hp); Transmission: 5-speed auto.

DIMENSION/CAPACITY

Passengers: 2/3/3; Wheelbase: 123.0 in.; H: 69.0/L: 207.0/W: 79.0 in.; Headroom F/R1/R2: 6.0/5.0/0.5 in.; Legroom F/R1/R2: 41.5/33.5/27.0 in.; Cargo volume: 58.5 cu. ft.; Fuel tank: 106L/regular; Tow limit: 9,100 lb.; Load capacity: 1,459–1,728 lb.; GVWR: 6,800 lb.; Turning circle: 44.0 ft.; Ground clearance: 9.0 in.; Weight: 5,715 lb.

to 180. **1999**—A mid-year facelift. **2001**—Given a 3.5L V6 (240–250 hp). The QX4's on-demand All-Mode drivetrain given to the LE, making it okay for dry pavement, though the SE's system can't be used on dry pavement. Other new features are standard cruise control and a restyled interior. **2002**—A slight restyling, and larger wheels. **2003**—Traction control, front side/curtain airbags, and user-friendly child-seat anchors were offered for the first time. **2005**—Redesigned as a larger, more luxurious version of the Xterra, the 2005 Pathfinder was given a 270-hp 4.0L V6, independent double-wishbone front and rear suspensions, and a standard third-row seat for seven-passenger seating. A 5-speed automatic is the only transmission available.

Pathfinder

Handling isn't the Pathfinder's strong suit. There's lots of body roll in turns, and braking distance is unacceptably long. Some people will find the ride harsh, owing to the stiffer suspension and Nissan's adoption of a unibody frame instead of the separate body-on-frame construction used in most large sport-utilities. Some recent models have the spare tire mounted under the vehicle, where it's more vulnerable to premature corrosion and highway contaminants.

The 3.3L V6 delivers so-so acceleration, and it's noisy when pushed; a more refined and efficient 3.5L V6 replaced it in March 2000. It was then replaced by the much better performing 4.0L V6 in 2005.

Armada

A new Pathfinder Armada arrived in 2004 and then ditched the Pathfinder name for 2005. Built on the Nissan Titan pickup platform, it's a larger, meaner-looking SUV with more angular lines, a 317-hp 5.6L DOHC V8, and a 5-speed automatic that it shares with the Titan. Armada's long wheelbase gives it a longer interior with plenty of cargo room. The short front and rear overhangs add to the Armada's manoeuvrability. Interior amenities provide exceptional versatility, roominess, and flexibility—including standard fold-flat second- and third-row seats; the most second-row legroom in the full-sized, light-duty SUV class; and a full-length overhead console.

COST ANALYSIS: Used second-series 2005s (those built in mid-2005) look like the best deal for price and quality. The 2006–08 Pathfinders (S/SE/Off-Road/LE) are mostly carryovers and don't merit their higher prices; however, horsepower and reliability have improved somewhat, giving these later models a slightly better rating. The 2008 S, SE, and LE Pathfinders sell in Canada for $38,298, $42,998, and $49,298, respectively. Are you ready for a real shocker? Just across the border these same Pathfinders cost $26,300, $29,600, and $35,400. What about the Armada? In Canada, the Armada LE's MSRP is listed at $63,298. In the States, you will pay $36,130 (SE) and $43,980 (LE) for 2009 versions. Pathfinder/Armada freight charges are another scam; you will pay $1,400–$1,480 in Canada and only $745 (U.S.) in the States. **Best alternatives:** The Honda Pilot; Lexus RX 300/330;

Nissan Murano, X-Trail, or Xterra; and Toyota Highlander. **Rebates:** $7,000 rebates and zero percent financing guaranteed to be sweetened by late 2008. **Delivery/PDI:** $1,400–$1,480. **Depreciation:** Slower than average for the Pathfinder; Armada is faster than average. **Warranty:** Bumper-to-bumper 3 years/60,000 km; powertrain 5 years/100,000 km; rust perforation 5 years/ unlimited km. **Supplementary warranty:** Not needed. **Options:** Worthwhile options include electronic stability control, remote keyless entry, theft-deterrent system, rear window defroster and wiper, and air conditioning. Not recommended are fender flares (standard on the LE) and large tires that will make turning in tight corners more difficult. Don't take original-equipment Firestone or Bridgestone tires. **Insurance cost:** Higher than average. **Annual maintenance cost:** Average; easily repaired by independent garages. **Parts supply/cost:** Parts are widely available and of average cost. **Highway/city fuel economy:** *3.5L V6:* 11.1/14.2 L/100 km; *4.0L V6:* 10.4/15.5 L/100 km. Owners report they get far less fuel economy than government figures claim. The V8 is the worst offender.

 QUALITY/RELIABILITY: Powertrain components, electronics, and brakes are often troublesome. Paint and trim are acceptable, but body hardware quality has been below average for some time. The Pathfinder's overall reliability is average; Armada's is way below average, with even more complaints relating to poor-quality brakes. **Owner-reported problems:** The engine intake manifold, automatic transmission, electrical and cooling systems, brakes, and exhaust components are problematic. Owners also report underbody squeaks and vibration:

> My 2005 Nissan Pathfinder LE has a loud squeak/vibration coming from the under-body. Dealer (Ramsey Nissan—Ramsey, NJ) has confirmed that the source of the loud squeak/vibration is due to the change in design for the "fuel pump spring assembly." Apparently, the 2004 Pathfinder had a 2 spring design which was changed to a 1 spring design in 2005. Once the fuel tank becomes pressurized (car running for approximately 10 minutes), a loud, constant, and obtrusive squeak/vibration comes from underneath the car. To date, Nissan does not have a fix for this which is unacceptable since the vibration is coming from a critically sensitive area such as the fuel tank. This is an expensive vehicle that should not sound and feel like it is 10 years old.

Brakes can be extremely noisy, particularly when applied while the vehicle is in Reverse. Armada owners report excessive wind noise; roof, door, and dash rattles; a harmonic hum that occurs when the defroster is activated; and leaking sun-roofs. **Warranty performance:** Warranty service and customer relations are below average, particularly since Nissan sales have taken a nosedive during the past year.

 ROAD PERFORMANCE: Acceleration/torque: The 4.0L V6 transforms the Pathfinder into an impressively powerful SUV. Power is delivered smoothly with little engine noise. **Transmission:** Usually functions smoothly, but there are some reports of delayed downshifts when passing. Long-term durability may be a problem. LE's 4×4 is more useful and refined than the SE's system. **Steering:** A bit vague and over-assisted at times. Turning radius is larger than the competition's. **Routine handling:** Barely acceptable. The vehicle tends to wander and shake when passing over bumps—poor brakes, shocks, and steering are the chief culprits. Ride is a bit jarring. **Emergency handling:** Not good. Moderate body lean in turns. Armada handling is particularly poor. **Braking:** Average in controlled tests; bad in real-world practice.

 SAFETY SUMMARY: Airbags: Optional side and head-protecting side airbags become standard features in later model years. **ABS:** Standard 4W. **Safety belt pretensioners:** Standard. **Traction control:** Standard on recent models. **Head restraints F/R:** *1999:* ★★★/★★; *2001–03:* ★★/★. *2005–08:* ★★. **Visibility F/R:** ★★★★★/★. **Pet transport:** ★★★★★.

SAFETY COMPLAINTS: All models/years: Many reports of sudden, unintended acceleration after coming to a stop. • Airbag failures. • Sudden loss of steering control, lock-up. • ABS lock-up and failure. • Transmission failure. • Gas and brake pedals are set too close. **1999**—Electrical arcing beneath hood at right front fender, along wiring harness from ABS actuator to fuse block, caused wiring insulation to ignite in a vehicle while it was parked. • Complete engine and brake failure on a hill with no guardrail. • When in 4×4 High, 4×2 High won't engage. • Excessive vibration felt throughout vehicle while driving 70 km/h, and then a severe front-end shimmy kicks in around 100 km/h. • Premature tread wear, blowouts with Bridgestone tires. • Front driver-side strut, housing, and bearings self-destruct. **2000**—Excessive steering-wheel vibration (steering rack replaced). • ABS doesn't work properly on wet pavement. **2001**—Brake pedal takes too much effort to stop vehicle; extended stopping distances are the result. • All gauges and instruments fail intermittently. • Steering pull and excessive body vibration at 100 km/h. • Passenger-side window suddenly explodes. • Strut-tower bolt breaks. • Although rated to pull 2,250 kg (5,000 lb.), one vehicle flipped while pulling a 1,400 kg (3,100 lb.) trailer. **2002**—Stuck throttle. • Rear window falls out. **2003**—Excessive shaking when brakes are applied. **2004**—Pathfinder has 13 complaints logged in NHTSA's database; Armada has 124. • Multiple brake problems include early wearout of rotors and pads, rotor warpage, grinding, vibration, and master cylinder failures:

> Fourth time since April 2004: The 2004 Pathfinder [Armada]'s brakes deteriorate to the point of imminent failure. The steering wheel vibrates and shakes, the brake pedal travel increases, and brakes become unresponsive. Rotors have been cut, pads replaced, rotors replaced, caliper "kits" installed, pins replaced, grease applied, etc. The problem keeps returning. Many other annoyance type problems as well…rattles, navigation system failure, radio replaced, overhead console cracked, replaced window motors and switches, poor wheel alignment from factory.

> The Nissan Armada has been designed with a much inferior brake system [with regard to its size and weight]. They have cut costs by installing a Nissan Frontier brake system, which weighs about half the weight of a Nissan Armada. This has caused the brakes to give out every 5,000 miles [8,000 km] and also creates an unsafe

braking system. It also allows the vehicle to dive when braking, not giving a safe braking reaction time. The dealerships have constantly replaced my brakes (three times within 15,000 miles [24,000 km]) and did admit that Nissan has admitted to an inferior braking system.

2005—Rear hatch flies open while underway. • Entire electrical system shuts down during highway travel. *Pathfinder:* **2004**—Automatic roll-up windows can be dangerous to children. • Brake wiring harness interferes with foot travel from accelerator to brake pedal. **2005**—Rear suspension can barely support four passengers. • Excessive highway wander and violent shaking occurs when passing over a bump:

> 2005 Nissan Pathfinder becomes very unstable at highway speeds when hitting a bump. The vehicle rocks violently diagonally and sways out of the lane. It also bottoms out constantly since it was new with no load in it. Dealer has attempted a fix by reprogramming the vehicle dynamic control, this has not fixed the problem. This vehicle is extremely unsafe to drive at any speed above 40 mph [64 km/h]. Driver feels as if he has lost total control when hitting a bump. I followed my wife when she was driving the vehicle and it appears that the rear shocks are trying to overcompensate for every little bump as they are jumping up and down like crazy as the vehicle drives over bumps.

Armada: **2004**—Surging, stalling engine. • Centre seat shoulder strap won't unbuckle; in one collision it failed, tossing child and safety seat forward. • Third-row centre seat belt fails. • Airbag sensor shuts off airbags even if a 110-pound occupant is seated. • Low Tire Pressure warning light comes on in cold temperatures. • Stuck fuel gauge. • Window regulators break easily. **2005**—Brake failures continue unabated, apparently due to brakes that are undersized for this size of this vehicle. • Windshield glass distorts visibility. **2005–06**—Steering wheel feels loose and sloppy, jerks sharply to one side when passing over bumps; it may require a new steering column. **2006**—Excessive swaying from the rear of the vehicle. • Upper bearing in the steering column may fail, making it hard to turn the wheel. • Vehicle may roll when parked on an incline. • Defective fuel gauge gives inaccurate readings. • Driver's power seatback constantly inches forward; it is never in the same position when you return to the vehicle. • In order to refuel the vehicle, all locks must be unlocked. One owner had the vehicle's contents stolen. • Back of the passenger seat falls off. • Goodrich Radial Longtrail tire failures. **2007**—Sudden, unintended acceleration when shifted into Reverse. • Passenger-side airbag deploys for no reason.

Secret Warranties/Internal Bulletins/Service Tips

All models/years: Brake noise, vibration, and pulling to one side are diagnosed in a comprehensive bulletin #NTB00-033B, issued August 30, 2004. • Brake pedal slowly drops to the floor. • Vehicle wanders. **1999**—If the MIL comes on, it may be because of poor grounding between the intake manifold and the engine cylinder head. • TSB #96-032 addresses hard starting and no-starts.

FRONT BRAKE VIBRATION/ PULSATION/JUDDER

BULLETIN NO.: NTB03-091   DATE: OCTOBER 8, 2003

BRAKE JUDGER FROM FRONT BRAKES

2001–03 Pathfinder (R50)

While braking, a steering wheel shake, body vibration, or brake pedal pulsation (also known as "brake judder"), especially during high speed braking.

ACTIONS:

* Check front wheel bearing axial end play.
* "Turn" the front brake rotors using an On-Car Brake Lathe.
* Install the new front brake pads and hardware kit (see Parts Information).
* Burnish the brake pads.

1999–2002—Transfer-case noise or hard shifting. **1999–2004**—Engine overheating or coolant problems traced to a faulty radiator cap. **2000–02**—Rear suspension bottoms out. **2001**—Computer module may have incorrect idle setting. • Power-steering fluid leak near the pump hose fitting. **2001–02**—Transfer case stuck in 4×4 Low. • Troubleshooting navigation system malfunctions. • Steering-column noise when turning. **2001–03**—Front brake problems (see bulletin). **2001–04**—Headlight fogging. **2002–03**—Roof rack noise or poor appearance. **2002–05**—Idle speed too high. **2003**—ABS light stays lit. • Tire-pressure monitor stays lit. **2003–04**—Oil leak in transfer case. **2004**—Special campaign to tighten the differential's left front flange-fixing bolt to prevent oil leakage or excessive noise. **2005**—Defective power seat (driver-side). • Free body control module sub-harness. • AC clunk, thump noise. • Popping noise from rear of headliner. • Poor AM radio reception. • Engine and sunroof rattles. **2005–06**—Right front seatback rattles and moves sideways. • Tailgate rust near licence plate. **2005–07**—Engine chirping and squeaking. **2007**—Inoperative front passenger window. • Auto-up driver window malfunction. *Armada:* **2004**—No-starts in cold temperatures likely caused by a defective powertrain control module. • Remedies for brake vibration, etc., are found in bulletin #NTB04-066b, issued August 31, 2004. • Tips on silencing AC humming. • Rear axle clicks. • Countermeasures for a brake pedal that feels mushy or has too much travel. • Wind noise from rear side-door window. • Sunroof water leaks. • Cracked overhead DVD console. • Faulty cruise control. • Inoperative navigation system. • Booming noise when passing over rough roads. • Slow tire leak. **2004–05**—Free body control module sub-harness. **2004–07**—Reduced power when accelerating. **2007**—Engine overheating, or condenser fan is inoperative.

PATHFINDER, ARMADA PROFILE

	1999	2000	2001	2002	2003	2004	2005	2006	2007
Cost Price ($) (soft)									
Pathfinder 4×4 (27%)	33,500	33,500	34,700	34,700	34,700	34,200	36,500	37,698	37,798
Armada (30%)	—	—	—	—	—	53,500	53,500	54,298	61,798
Used Values ($)									
Pathfinder ▲	5,000	6,000	7,000	8,000	10,000	12,000	14,000	19,000	20,000
Pathfinder ▼	4,500	5,500	6,000	7,000	8,500	11,000	13,000	17,500	18,500
Armada ▲	—	—	—	—	—	18,000	21,000	24,000	28,000
Armada ▼	—	—	—	—	—	17,000	19,500	23,000	27,000

Reliability									
Pathfinder	3	3	3	3	3	3	3	4	4
Armada	—	—	—	—	—	1	2	3	3
Crash Safety (F)	4	4	4	—	—	4	4	4	4
Side	5	5	5	5	5	5	5	5	5
IIHS Side	—	—	—	—	—	—	5	5	5
Offset	2	2	2	2	2	2	5	5	5
Rollover (2×4)	2	2	2	2	—	—	3	3	3
4×4	—	—	3	3	3	—	3	3	3

Note: IIHS side impact ratings fell to "Below Average" on 2005–08 Pathfinders not equipped with side curtain airbags. Safety ratings for all 2008 models are identical to the 2007s.

Toyota

4RUNNER ★★★★

RATING: Above Average (2003–08); Average (1986–2002). Beefed up considerably for the 2003 model year, with the exception of a few first-year glitches, the newer version is an on- and off-road winner. Previous models had been yuppified so much that their off-roading capability was seriously compromised. **Strong points:** Part-time 4×4 system allows the driver to shift on the fly and can be used on dry pavement. The instrument panel features easy-to-read gauges and user-friendly controls. Plenty of legroom and headroom. Three can sit in the back as long as the road isn't rough. Seats are generally quite comfortable, though the rear seat feels too low; rear passengers especially may feel cramped. Good off-road performance, high ground clearance, top-quality mechanical components and body construction, legendary reliability, and incredibly slow depreciation. **Weak points:** This SUV often stinks—the exhaust smells like rotten eggs. The vehicle vibrates excessively and assaults the ears when driven with a rear window or sunroof open. It's much less practical than the Highlander on-road; it's underpowered, especially when compared with Nissan's Pathfinder; it has no manual gearbox for a safer and more thrilling off-roading experience; it's hard-riding; its steering is somewhat numb; it has a cramped interior and a serious lack of headroom with the sunroof option; entry and exit are difficult because of the narrow doors and steep step-in height; the ventilation controls aren't easy to access; and it's a gas guzzler. The optional differential lock has been discontinued, a serious blow to hardcore off-roaders. **New for 2008:** Side curtain airbags, whiplash-protection active front head restraints, and a cut-off

2008 4RUNNER TECHNICAL DATA

POWERTRAIN (REAR-DRIVE/4×4)
Engines: 4.0L V6 (236 hp) • 4.7L V8 (260 hp); Transmission: 5-speed auto.
DIMENSION/CAPACITY
Passengers: 2/3, 2/3/2; Wheelbase: 110.0 in.; H: 68.5/L: 189.0/W: 75.2 in.; Headroom F/R: 3.0/4.5 in.; Legroom F/R: 41.0/29.0 in.; Cargo volume: 42.2 cu. ft.; Fuel tank: 87L/regular/regular; Tow limit: 5,000–7,300 lb.; Load capacity: 1,185–1,500 lb.; GVWR: 5,250 lb.; Turning circle: 40.0 ft.; Ground clearance: 9.1 in.; Weight: 4,345 lb.

device for the stability control system. A much-needed redesign is planned for the 2009 models.

MODEL HISTORY: One of the most rugged compact sport-utilities on the market, 1996–2002 4Runners are powered by a 3.4L V6—the same engine that powers Tacoma 4×4 pickups.

What can you expect after paying top dollar for a new or used 4Runner? Excellent off-road performance, better-than-average reliability, and incredibly slow depreciation. What you overspend in buying one, you'll likely recoup when you sell. Still, be wary of early 4Runner "bargains"—they're hard-riding, have mediocre highway handling, use biodegradable head gaskets up to 1997, and guzzle fuel. Whatever you do, don't try to save money by purchasing an underpowered, 4-cylinder-equipped version. Also ditch the Bridgestone, Firestone, or Goodyear tires (have them replaced with Michelin or Pirelli tires).

If the most recently redesigned 2003 and later models are too rich for your blood, consider a cheaper 1996–2001 version that underwent a previous revamping. They are lower, wider, and longer; have much more passenger room; are easier to enter and exit; use dual airbags and four-wheel ABS; and offer a user-friendly one-piece tailgate. Both the 4- and 6-cylinder engines were upgraded, and a fully independent suspension was added along with rack-and-pinion steering. Channel your savings into a model equipped with the more versatile 6-cylinder engine.

Handling wasn't the 4Runner's strong suit until the redesigned 1996 models came along. The slow steering response and excessive body roll on previous models didn't exactly inspire confidence. Although a bit harsh, the ride is relatively civilized for a truck-based sport-utility, but you should expect lots of cabin vibration. Despite the stronger V6, the 4Runner is no tire-burner. Transmission engagement isn't smooth or very precise, either, and the absence, until 1998, of full-time 4×4 in such a pricey vehicle is disappointing.

Interiors are acceptably appointed and finished, though one would expect a bit more luxury and some additional features, considering the 4Runner's cost. The body on pre-1996 4Runners is also fairly narrow, and rear-seat passengers especially may feel cramped. Entry and exit are also difficult for many who find the step-in height too steep when compared to the Ford Explorer or GM Blazer and Jimmy.

1999—Both the grille and bumper were restyled, along with the addition of a new 4×4 system that allows for full-time 4×4 as well as two-high, four-high, and four-low modes. Inside amenities include a new cupholder and centre console, along with an overhead console that houses a garage door opener. **2001**—Base models were killed, leaving only the Limited and SR5 versions, with all 4Runners coming with an automatic transmission. **2003**—Completely redesigned: It's larger than the outgoing model and features more powerful V6 and V8 engines borrowed from the Tundra pickup.

COST ANALYSIS: A 2008 SR5 V6 starts at $38,560—a reduction of $2,020 from its earlier MSRP—the Limited V6 sells for $47,925, and the Limited V8 goes for $50,565. The huge difference between Canadian and American prices is surprising. In the States, the 4Runner's prices begin at $28,015. Off-roaders will want a second-series 2004 for the enhanced 4×4 capability and additional torque. Be wary of used models equipped with the 4-cylinder engine, because it's suitable only for the lighter rear-drive versions. **Best alternatives:** Also look at the Lexus LX 470 or RX 300/330 and Toyota Sequoia. The Jeep Grand Cherokee is more agile but nowhere near as reliable. **Rebates:** $3,000, along with zero percent financing. **Delivery/PDI:** $1,390. **Warranty:** Bumper-to-bumper 3 years/60,000 km; powertrain 5 years/100,000 km; rust perforation 5 years/unlimited km. **Supplementary warranty:** Don't waste your money. **Options:** A good anti-theft system. **Depreciation:** A very slow rate of depreciation beats out most vehicles in its class. **Insurance cost:** Average. **Annual maintenance cost:** Average. **Parts supply/cost:** Good, owing to a strong dealer network. Expensive parts, though. **Highway/city fuel economy:** V6: 10.7/13.7 L/100 km; V8: 11.5/15.5 L/100 km.

QUALITY/RELIABILITY: Better than average, but why the heck can't Toyota clean up its stinking exhaust after almost seven years? And how can they ignore the overpowering noise and vibration produced when their SUVs and pickups are driven with an open window? **Owner-reported problems:** Frequent owner complaints of stalling under all driving conditions, rear differential oil leaks, electrical shorts, premature brake wear, brake buzzing, and loss of brake pressure when going over a bump. Owners also report excessive driver-seat and seat-track creaking/ticking (covered by a TSB), driver-seat rattling, a foul-smelling exhaust, harmonic vibrations, and engine ticking. Windshield light distortion creates double vision, and accessories and trim items don't hold up. **Warranty performance:** Average.

SAFETY SUMMARY: Handling is steady at low speeds, but the rear end can swing out unexpectedly on slippery surfaces, or when cornering at high speeds. All versions have built-in roll bars and a removable roof. **Airbags:** There have been reports of airbags failing to deploy. **ABS:** Standard; some later models may have optional four-wheel ABS. **Safety belt pretensioners:** Standard. **Head restraints F/R:** *1999:* ★★/★; *2001–02:* ★★/★; *2003–08:* ★. **Visibility F/R:** ★★★★★. **Pet transport:** ★★★.

SAFETY COMPLAINTS: All years: Sudden acceleration. • Intermittent stalling, especially when braking or decelerating. • Fuel, ammonia, or rotten-egg exhaust smell leaks into the cabin:

> The exhaust smell from the truck has a horrific and sickening smell. I have not been driving the vehicle due to this issue. It has made me sick to my stomach at times and my wife and kids cannot stand the continuous smell either. I am very upset with this and would like a refund of my purchase price. Toyota sent out a TSB regarding the smell, saying it was the gasoline (poor) that people use. Wrong! I use Amoco and Texaco only.

• Brake failures. • Warped front rotors. • Tire side wall blowouts. • Excessive engine/drivetrain vibration and harmonic humming, felt initially through the gas pedal between 1400 and 2000 rpm (worst in Fifth gear). • Painful noise produced when vehicle is driven with the rear window down or the sunroof opened. **1999**—Fuel line leak sprays gasoline all over the engine. **1999–2000**—Incorrect fuel gauge readings: Low Fuel warning light comes on way too early; gas gauge reads empty when the tank is half full. **2000**—In one incident, a wheel came off and the vehicle rolled over. • Driver's door-mounted rear-view mirror is warped. **2001**—When applying brakes, driver has to turn foot sideways. • Emergency braking causes vehicle to slide or skid. **2003**—Shifter pops out of Fourth gear while underway. • Insufficient heating, defrosting. • Faulty Dunlop Grand Trek tire. • Wheel caps fly off. **2004**—Sudden, unintended acceleration when braking. • Instrument panel is washed out in daylight. • Tire-pressure sensors malfunction. **2004–05**—Excessive steering-wheel and gas pedal vibration at highway speeds. • Loose driver's seat moves and rattles. **2005**—Shifter can be knocked from Drive into Reverse. • Vehicle pulls sharply to the right at cruising speed. • No brakes, believed to be caused by a malfunctioning brake master cylinder. • Driver-side rear window suddenly shatters. **2005–07**—Engine surging, especially when the AC compressor kicks on. • **2006**—Airbags fail to deploy. • Passenger overcome by carbon monoxide inhalation in one vehicle required CPR. • Vehicle suddenly loses power. • In one incident, rear liftgate closed on its own, injuring owner's hand. • Bridgestone and Michelin tire failures. • Right front wheel stud separates. **2007**—Brake and accelerator pedals mounted too close together. • Excessive steering-wheel shimmy.

Secret Warranties/Internal Bulletins/Service Tips

All years: Loose, poorly fitting trim panels. **1999–2000**—An inaccurate fuel gauge may require a new fuel sender. **1999–2001**—Power windows activate on their own. **2000**—On vehicles equipped with a supercharger, a squeaking or rattling noise coming from the idler pulley is likely caused by an out-of-tolerance idler pulley shaft. **2002–06**—Tips on troubleshooting and fixing vehicles that pull to the right when accelerating. **2003**—Sunroof and headliner rattles. • Front-seat squeaks covered by TSB #00403, issued April 2003. • Free replacement of the fuel pulsation damper. **2003–04**—Replace deformed, warped windshield mouldings with a free, new service part to correct the condition (TSB #BO005-04). • Moonroof rattle correction. **2003–05**—No-start in cold temperatures. **2003–07**—AC blower motor ice buildup. • Second-row seatback noise. • Windshield ticking. • Moonroof malfunctions. **2004**—Free replacement of the engine crankshaft pulley and seal until May 31, 2007. Program has expired, but can be extended through the small claims court. **2004–07**—Front seat squeak noise. **2005**—Free installation of an upgraded catalytic converter to curtail a rotten-egg exhaust smell. **2006–07**—Navigation system shows vehicle in the wrong location. **2007**—Paint staining.

4RUNNER PROFILE

	1999	2000	2001	2002	2003	2004	2005	2006	2007
Cost Price ($) (firm)									
4Runner 4×4 (24%)	30,800	30,800	36,670	36,250	39,100	39,220	39,620	39,960	39,970
Used Values ($)									
4Runner 4×4 ▲	7,500	9,000	11,000	12,000	14,000	16,000	20,000	23,000	25,000
4Runner 4×4 ▼	7,000	8,000	9,500	11,000	12,500	14,500	18,000	21,000	24,000
Reliability	4	4	5	5	4	5	5	5	5
Crash Safety (F)	4	4	4	4	4	4	4	4	4
Side	5	5	5	5	5	5	5	5	5
IIHS Side	—	—	—	—	—	—	—	5	5
Offset	3	3	3	3	5	5	5	5	5
Rollover	—	—	2	2	3	3	3	3	3

HIGHLANDER ★★★★/★★★★

RATING: Above Average (2001–08). *Hybrid:* Above Average (2006–08). **Strong points:** Good acceleration with the V6; impressive manoeuvrability; comfortable but firm ride; well equipped; plenty of passenger space and cargo room; well laid-out and easy-to-read instruments and controls; little engine or road noise; offset crashworthiness and head restraint protection rated "Good" by IIHS; reasonably priced; slow depreciation; base engine uses regular fuel; high-quality components and fit and finish. *Hybrid:* More powerful than the gasoline-powered version, a bit less fuel-thirsty, and fairly reliable during its first year on the market. **Weak points:** The 4-cylinder engine is adequate but has little reserve power; audio and climate system graphics aren't intuitive; high step-in; unbelievably high freight and PDI charges; poor fuel economy; and no low-speed transfer case. *Hybrid:* Way overpriced; over-hyped fuel economy; its stiff suspension makes it cumbersome around tight turns; the AC condenser is easily damaged by road debris; not designed for off-roading. **New for 2008:** Completely redesigned, this mid-size SUV gets a new V6 engine and gains almost four inches in length and three inches in width. Standard on all non-hybrid AWD models is a Downhill Assist Control, which helps regulate speed on downhill slopes. All hybrids gain an EV mode that allows the driver to engage a full-electric drive mode for a short time. There is also a new driver-initiated Econ mode that massages the throttle for optimum fuel economy.

2008 HIGHLANDER TECHNICAL DATA

POWERTRAIN (FRONT-DRIVE/AWD)
Engine: 3.5L V6 (270 hp); Transmission: 5-speed auto.

DIMENSION/CAPACITY
Passengers: 2/3, 2/3/2; Wheelbase: 110.0 in.; H: 69.3/L: 188.0/W: 75.2 in.; Headroom F/R1/R2: 4.0/4.0/1.5 in.; Legroom F/R1/R2: 41.0/29.5/23.0 in.; Cargo volume: 38.0 cu. ft.; Fuel tank: 72.5L/regular/premium; Tow limit: 5,000 lb.; Load capacity: 1,679–1,822 lb.; GVWR: 4,985 lb.; Turning circle: 38.7 ft.; Ground clearance: 8.1 in.; Weight: 4,178 lb.

2008 HIGHLANDER HYBRID TECHNICAL DATA

POWERTRAIN (4×4)
Engine: 3.3L V6 (270 hp); Transmission: CVT

DIMENSION/CAPACITY
Passengers: 2/3; Wheelbase: 110.0 in.; H: 69.3/L: 185.4/W: 75.2 in.; Headroom F/R: 40.0/39.8 in.; Legroom F/R: 40.7/36.4 in.; Cargo volume: 10.5 cu. ft.; Fuel tank: 65L/premium; Tow limit: 3,500 lb.; Load capacity: 1,200 lb.; GVWR: 5,675 lb.; Turning circle: 39.0 ft.; Ground clearance: 7.0 in.; Weight: 4,500 lb.

MODEL HISTORY: The Highlander is a Camry-based sport-utility that's similar to the Lexus RX 300 Series, though roomier and cheaper. It comes with either a 4-cylinder engine or optional V6 mated to a 4- or 5-speed automatic. A vulnerable undercarriage and the absence of a transfer case for low-range gearing compromises serious off-road performance.

Although not as powerful as the Sequoia, the Highlander runs quietly and comfortably accommodates five passengers, though it claims to carry seven. With its responsive handling, user-friendly controls, full-time 4×4, smooth powertrain, and folding third-row seat (for kids only), this is the ideal SUV for folks who want to step up from a 2005 or earlier RAV4 but don't want to shell out about $20,000 more for an RX.

2004—A 5-hp boost for the 4-banger, and a new 3.3L V6, used by the 2004 Sienna and Lexus RX 330. **2007**—Standard side and side curtain airbags.

Highlander Hybrid

Priced at $41,075 for the five-passenger base model, Toyota's 2008 Highlander Hybrid costs about $2,000 less than last year's model, which sold for about the same price as the 2006s. Apparently, sales have been disappointing because buyers are reluctant to pay a higher price for debatable fuel savings. Its combined 270-hp rating is identical to the 2008's V6 gasoline-powered model that sells for $36,900. Most people wouldn't mind spending the extra money if the hybrid delivered the 8.3 L/100 km highway and 7.7 L/100 km city fuel economy ratings touted by Toyota. It doesn't. Owners complain they barely get 11.7 L/100 km (20 mpg), and independent journalists have pegged the real fuel consumption at an average of 10.2 L/100 km (23 mpg). They estimate that it would take about four years for a buyer to break even with the Highlander Hybrid and about five years with the Lexus RX 400h.

COST ANALYSIS: A 2008 base Highlander costs $27,300 (U.S.) in the States—almost $10,000 (U.S.) less than the Canadian list price. A hybrid bought in the States for $33,700 (U.S.), versus a $41,075 Canadian price, will save buyers about $8,000, not counting discounts, rebates, and half the $1,400 Canadian freight fees. A used 2004 model offers the most quality and standard features at the lowest price. The 2005–07 models aren't sufficiently depreciated and are relatively underpowered when compared with the 2008 upgraded Highlander. **Best alternatives:** Other good buys are the Honda CR-V, Hyundai Tucson or Santa Fe, Subaru Forester, and Toyota RAV4. If you really want to go green, consider buying a 2006 Jeep Liberty diesel. **Rebates:** Not likely; these cars are way too popular. **Delivery/PDI:** $1,390. **Warranty:** Bumper-to-bumper 3 years/60,000 km; powertrain

5 years/100,000 km; rust perforation 5 years/unlimited km. **Supplementary warranty:** Not necessary. **Options:** The V6 is essential for passing and merging with traffic; the sunroof, however, eats up valuable headroom. **Depreciation:** Below average. Hybrids lose their value just as quickly as conventional versions. **Insurance cost:** Higher than average. **Parts supply/cost:** Generic parts also used by the RX series are easy to find and moderately priced. **Annual maintenance cost:** Much lower than average; however, if you choose the hybrid, get ready to pay $4,000–$7,000 for a battery pack after the warranty expires. **Highway/city fuel economy:** *2.4L:* 7.9/10.6 L/100 km; *3.3L:* 9.0/12.7 L/100 km; *Hybrid:* 8.3/7.7 L/100 km. Remember, hybrids save the most fuel in city traffic.

QUALITY/RELIABILITY: Owner-reported problems: Excessive vibrations; poor acceleration; hard gear shifts; erratic speedometer; AC and door-lock glitches; a musty interior odour; paint peeling or chipping; and faulty automatic transmission and computer control unit. A painful pulsating pressure felt in the ears is caused by wind noise when the vehicle is driven with the rear windows down. **Warranty performance:** Better than average. Toyota has confirmed that it has let quality slip, admitting that 2007 models were delayed due to quality control deficiencies.

SAFETY SUMMARY: Cupholders are positioned too close to the gearshift lever, making it easy to inadvertently bump the lever into Neutral when reaching for a drink (the Lexus RX 300 has the same problem). **Airbags:** Front; optional/standard side. **ABS:** Standard; disc/disc. **Safety belt pretensioners:** Front. **Traction control:** Optional limited slip differential. **Head restraints F/R:** 2004–07: ★★. 2008: ★★★★★. **Visibility F/R:** ★★★★★. **Pet transport:** ★★★.

SAFETY COMPLAINTS: All years: Pedal goes to the floor without braking when brakes are applied. • If the back window is open while underway, the vehicle vibrates wildly and creates a vacuum that's painful to the ears; rolling down the front window or opening the moonroof eliminates the problem:

> Extreme air pressure when driving above 35 mph [56 km/h] and either rear window is open. It feels [like] riding in an airplane.

2001—Airbags fail to deploy. • Automatic transmission failure. • Transmission bangs into gear. • Speedometer is unreadable with sunglasses and tinted windows. • Plastic fuel-tank shield is ineffective. • Centre cupholders are poorly designed; when you remove a drink, it's easy to knock the gearshift lever, taking vehicle out of gear. **2002**—ABS failure. • The top of the dash panel reflects sunlight, blinding the driver. **2003**—Brake and gas pedal are mounted too close to each other. • Brakes provide inadequate stopping power. • Brake failures, overheating, defective master cylinder. • Inoperative door locks. **2004**—Side airbags failed to deploy when one car was T-boned. • Faulty stability control system. • Brake fluid cylinder-pin failure. • The jack is inadequate, particularly with 16-inch wheels. • Daytime running lights blind oncoming drivers (the 2004 Sienna has the same problem). •

Doors lock themselves following a collision. • Toyo tires wear out prematurely. **2004–05**—Transmission takes a few seconds to respond to the throttle:

> While traveling approximately 30 mph [48 km/h] (or cruising speed), attempted to pass another vehicle. The accelerator was pressed to the floor and the vehicle refused to accelerate for a period of approximately 2 seconds. Acceleration resumed after this period. Contacted Toyota. Toyota said this is a normal phenomenon in their drive-by-wire systems.

2004–06—Steering wheel suddenly locks up because of a faulty steering sensor. **2004–07**—Sudden, unintended acceleration. **2005**—In one incident, vehicle rolled over three times but airbags didn't deploy. • In another incident, the seat belt failed to restrain the driver when the vehicle was rear-ended. • Sudden stalling. • Gas pedal sticks. • Wheel studs are easily broken. • Vehicle shudders excessively if driven on the highway with the side window down. **2005–06**—Hesitation followed by surging when accelerating:

> The car hesitated about 2 seconds after I pressed the gas pedal, then lurched forward, spinning the drive wheels. The length of delay or hesitation in response to accelerator input is frequently there, but is somewhat unpredictable, making stop-and-go traffic performance dangerous. Poor performance of the cruise control function is probably related to this defect. Dealer states that there are no service bulletins for this problem, in spite of the fact that Toyota has acknowledged this problem and promised to fix it since December 2004.

2005–07—Impossible to read instrument cluster while wearing sunglasses or in direct sunlight. **2006**—Airbags fail to deploy. • Sudden acceleration in Reverse. • Hybrid steering stiffens up; one owner had to pay $5,000 for a new transaxle assembly. • Hybrid stalling. • Hybrid brake failure. • Goodyear Integrity tire-tread separation • Stinky exhaust. • Key fob may not work due to radio interference. **2007**—Uncontrolled transmission surging when car unexpectedly gears down. • Slow, intermittent battery drain caused one hybrid battery to fail five times. • Hybrid inverter failures. • When hybrid batteries are charging, a noxious gas invades the cabin:

> On several occasions we have had to roll the windows down or stop and exit the vehicle to allow the fumes to clear. The local dealer says that there is nothing wrong with the vehicle, and that there is nothing they can do about our complaints.

Secret Warranties/Internal Bulletins/Service Tips

All years: Poorly fitted trim panels. • Sulfur smell (Toyota will change the catalytic converter). **2001**—"Goodwill" extended warranty to correct engine oil sludge problem. • Check Engine light troubleshooting. • Wind noise at the A-pillar. **2001–03**—Drive axle squeak. **2001–04**—Hood protector wind-noise countermeasures. **2001–05**—Engine fuel-injector ticking. **2002**—Excessive brake noise and increased pedal stroke when applying brakes. • Malfunctioning MIL. • Moonroof moulding creak. • Squeak and rattle remedies. • Reducing front seat-back noise. **2002–06**—Diagnosing and correcting vehicle's tendency to pull to the right when accelerating. **2003–07**—Windshield ticking. **2004**—Install improved catalytic converter to clean up smelly exhaust (TSB #EG009-04). **2004–05**—No-start in cold temperatures. **2004–07**—Front seat squeaks. **2006–07**—Hybrid rocks back and forth at highway speed.

HIGHLANDER PROFILE

	2001	2002	2003	2004	2005	2006	2007
Cost Price ($) (firm)							
Highlander FWD (18%)	33,000	31,990	32,330	32,900	32,900	—	—
Highlander AWD (19%)	36,100	36,190	34,530	36,900	36,900	37,855	38,470
Hybrid (23%)	—	—	—	—	—	44,205	44,850
Used Values ($)							
Highlander FWD ▲	8,000	10,500	12,000	12,000	15,000	—	—
Highlander FWD ▼	7,000	9,000	11,000	10,500	14,000	—	—
Highlander AWD ▲	10,000	12,000	13,500	14,500	18,000	22,000	25,000
Highlander AWD ▼	8,500	10,500	12,000	13,000	17,000	20,000	23,000
Hybrid ▲	—	—	—	—	—	26,000	30,000
Hybrid ▼	—	—	—	—	—	24,000	28,000
Reliability	4	4	4	4	4	4	4
Crash Safety (F)	—	4	4	5	5	5	5
Side	—	4	5	5	5	5	5
Offset	5	5	5	5	5	5	5
Rollover	—	3	3	—	4	4	4

Note: The 2008 crashworthiness ratings are identical to the 2007 ratings. Side protection on the 2008 models is rated "Good" by IIHS; however, head restraint protection was rated "Marginal" on 2004–07 vehicles equipped with tilt-style head restraints and adjustable lumbar seats.

Volvo

XC90

Owner and service bulletin feedback on the XC90 is too limited for a full evaluation because it has been on the market barely three years. A summary rating can be found in Appendix I.

Large Sport-Utilities

Talk about an endangered species. Large SUVs will soon be a dim memory thanks mostly to their high fuel costs, poor quality, and mediocre highway performance. Sure, automakers are telling us they will keep producing these vehicles for a few more years, but don't bank on it. In fact, sales are so bad that dealers are scrambling to move the piled-up inventory of 2008 models with up to $10,000 in rebates and sales incentives as well as reduced prices.

But lower prices won't save these giant gas-guzzlers. Granted, some buyers want maximum space to carry eight to nine people and all their gear, plus enough towing capability for a small boat or trailer, but they are finding these advantages with smaller SUVs. They are downsizing their choices and embracing mid-sized and small, crossover SUVs—like the Ford Edge or GM Acadia, Enclave, and Outlook—that provide lots of interior room along with carlike performance.

Large SUVs are available with rear-drive or four-wheel drive. The full-time 4×4 systems allow drivers to set a switch on the dashboard to direct power to all four wheels in any condition; part-time systems should be engaged only on wet or snowy pavement. Most have three-row, eight-passenger seating, and some automakers offer nine-passenger seating.

Domestic brands continue to dominate sales in this class. Of the largest SUVs available for 2008–09, GM's Tahoe, Yukon, and Escalade are three of the best known, and are in the crosshairs of new entries like the Hyundai Veracruz, which offers fully loaded models that are more reliable than the competition for $10,000 less. And don't forget the restyled Nissan Armada (see "Mid-Sized Sport-Utilities"). Its interior has been revised, and it can run on both gasoline and E85 ethanol fuel.

Truck-based large SUVs are best used for hauling passengers and cargo, towing large trailers and boats, and off-roading, thanks to their powerful drivetrains and flat-folding second- and third-row seats. With all seats folded or removed, large SUVs offer at least 95 cubic feet of cargo space. The highest-rated models in this class can tow in excess of 10,000 lb. via a special tow/haul mode for the automatic

The Ford Expedition's third-row seat is among the roomiest and most comfortable you'll find.

GM's Tahoe and Yukon are the first ever gas-electric hybrid SUVs of this size. Sales are dismal.

The Toyota Sequoia's optional 381-hp 5.7L V8 engine is the most powerful among large SUVs.

transmission. It automatically adjusts the transmission's gearing to compensate for towing, and uses a load-levelling suspension to balance the extra weight.

But large SUVs have three serious drawbacks: They generally handle poorly, burn excessive amounts of fuel, and carry sky-high sticker prices that are later slashed. Recent Asian makes have tackled the poor handling, and GM is using cylinder deactivation and hybrid technology on some of its large SUVs to help increase fuel economy. Cylinder deactivation shuts off half of the engine's cylinders under cruising and light throttle conditions, increasing gas mileage up to 7 percent, and has been used by Honda and other importers without a problem. The GM system's reliability is untested, however, and if GM's first disappointing foray into this technology with its '80s Cadillacs is considered, buyers would be wise to wait for the second-year models.

The 2008 Chevrolet Tahoe Hybrid, 2008 GMC Yukon Hybrid, and 2009 Cadillac Escalade Hybrid feature GM's Two Mode technology that works much like the Ford Escape Hybrid and Toyota Prius. The 332-hp Tahoe and Yukon use a 6.0L 332-hp V8 gasoline engine with an electric motor, which can run exclusively on the electric motor at low speeds and then switch to the traditional gas engine when needed.

These hybrids come with a number of drawbacks, however. They are more expensive to buy and maintain than non-hybrids, mechanics are not yet familiar with their design, and fuel consumption estimates are highly unrealistic. Although hybrid gas consumption may stretch from 12–17 L/100 km in the city, very little fuel is saved on the highway, where most large trucks travel.

Ford

EXCURSION ★

RATING: Not Recommended (2000–05). Recipe for building an Excursion: Take an F-350, replace the bed with three rows of seats, ditch the tailgate, and buy a gas station. This unreliable, gas-guzzling Godzilla SUV was doomed from the start. **Strong points:** Well appointed, powerful 6.8L V10 gas engine, standard stability control, good optional powertrain match for highway cruising or city commuting, automatic 4×4, versatile interior, good passenger room, comfortable seating, and a low floor for easy access and loading. **Weak points:** Slow acceleration with the base 5.4L and 6.0L diesel powerplants, unacceptable off-road performance, excessive engine noise, mediocre handling, obstructed rear visibility, poor head-restraint protection, no crashworthiness data, and non-existent fuel economy. Government safety investigators have recorded an unusually high number of safety-related complaints. Owners also report that the suspension cannot handle the towing weight recommended by Ford.

2005 EXCURSION TECHNICAL DATA

POWERTRAIN (4×4)

Engines: 5.4L V8 (255 hp) • 6.0L turbodiesel V8 (325 hp) • 6.8L V10 (310 hp); Transmissions: 4-speed auto. • 5-speed auto.

DIMENSION/CAPACITY

Passengers: 3/3/2; Wheelbase: 137.0 in.; H: 80.0/L: 226.0/W: 80.0 in.; Headroom F/R1/R2: 6.5/6.0/4.0 in.; Legroom F/R1/R2: 41.5/31.0/28.5 in.; Cargo volume: 48.0 cu. ft.; Fuel tank: 167L/regular; Tow limit: 7,600–11,000 lb.; Load capacity: 1,630 lb.; GVWR: 8,600–9,200 lb.; Turning circle: 50.4 ft.; Ground clearance: 8.5 in.; Weight: 6,680–7,770 lb.

MODEL HISTORY: Gone but not forgotten, the Excursion is a restyled version of Ford's three-quarter-ton Super Duty pickup, equipped with a standard 255-hp 5.4L V8 engine on its 4×2s, and a choice of a 310-hp 6.8L V10 or a 325-hp 6.0L turbodiesel V8 powerplant on the 4×4 versions. A dash-mounted switch permits shifting on the fly; however, unlike the GM competition, Ford's 4×4 system can't be used on dry pavement.

First launched in 1999 to compete against GM's full-sized Chevrolet Suburban SUV, the 2001 Excursion got a beefed-up 250-hp 7.3L diesel powerplant and additional entertainment and convenience features. Since then, it has returned each model year relatively unchanged. Its last model year was 2005.

COST ANALYSIS: Poor quality mixed with unreliable drivetrain components make these problem-prone behemoths no bargain, despite their bargain prices. **Best alternatives:** The redesigned Suburban is a wiser choice because of its better quality, handling, and performance refinements. GM's Tahoe, Yukon, Acadia, Enclave, or Outlook are all much better choices. **Warranty:** Bumper-to-bumper 3 years/60,000 km; rust perforation 5 years/unlimited km. **Supplementary warranty:** An extended warranty is essential. **Options:** Nothing worth the extra money, unless you absolutely need running boards. Stay away from Firestone and Bridgestone tires. **Depreciation:** Much faster than average—a 2000 Excursion 4×4 that sold for $47,695 new is now worth about...$8,500! **Insurance cost:** Goes in the other direction—sky-high premiums. **Annual maintenance cost:** Average during the warranty period; fairly costly once the warranty expires. **Parts supply/cost:** Parts are moderately priced and easily found, since they all come from Ford's truck parts bin. **Highway/city fuel economy:** *5.4L V8:* 12.1/16.7 L/100 km; *6.8L V10:* 13.0/20.0 L/100 km.

QUALITY/RELIABILITY: Amazingly bad for a vehicle this expensive. Next time someone suggests that "you get what you pay for" in vehicle quality, show them the service bulletin references for luxury SUVs like the Excursion, Expedition/Navigator, BMW X5, and Mercedes SUV series. **Owner-reported problems:** Steering instability and poor handling; drive shaft, differential, motor mount, and wheel bearing failures; chronic drivetrain whine and howl; electrical system problems; poor braking, high brake maintenance costs (chronic rotor warpage) and excessive brake noise; and assorted clunks, rattles, and wind noise. Excessive vibration at cruising speed (not tire-related); vehicle bounces all over the road and nosedives as front shocks bottom out; hard to control the vehicle when towing a trailer. **Warranty performance:** Below average. Now that the Excursion has been dropped, Ford is concentrating on the servicing of smaller SUVs and trucks it plans to keep around awhile.

SAFETY SUMMARY: No head restraints or shoulder belts on centre rear seats. Vehicle has yet to be crash-tested by NHTSA. **Airbags:** Side airbags are optional. Front and side airbags have failed to deploy in collisions. **ABS:** Standard; disc/disc. **Head restraints F/R: ★. Visibility F/R: ★★★★★/★★. Pet transport: ★★★★★.**

SAFETY COMPLAINTS: 2000—A plethora of Firestone tire failures (check that spare!). • Cracked fuel tank leaks gasoline. • Passenger-side Airbag warning light stays lit because of a short circuit in the system. • Transmission fluid leaks onto drive shaft, causing a fire. • Transmission pops out of gear while vehicle is parked (a common Ford failure seen over the past three decades). • Sudden breakage of the right front tie-rod end. • Turbocharger malfunctions cause oil leaks and stalling. • Drive shaft falls out because of loose bolts. • Complete brake failure when slowing down. • Brakes pulsate violently. • Poor steering and handling compromise safety. • Poorly designed suspension causes vehicle to move laterally on dry pavement. • Severe shaking and vibrating while driving over 90 km/h. • Excessively sharp seat tracks injure passengers. • Jack won't align with suspension pins and may suddenly fail. • If you close the rear tri-doors in the wrong order, the rear window glass may explode. **2001**—Tie-rod end falls off, resulting in complete steering loss. • Frequent failure of the transmission gasket seal and main central valve. • Failed wheel bearings can't be serviced. • Grease leaks onto brake rotors. • Rear-end instability when passing over uneven terrain. • Cruise control surges when set at 110 km/h. • Chronic brake rotor warpage. • Driver-side seat belts unlatch. **2001–02**—Spark plug pops out of the engine head:

> The 3rd spark plug on the [right-hand] side of the engine blew out and took the cylinder head threads with it. $3,000 to repair. The Ford inspector refused to admit fault on Ford's part, yet the service manager at the dealership told me that the plug blowout was no fault of mine.

2002—No airbag deployment. • Sudden acceleration. • Chronic stalling. • Rough roads cause sudden loss of steering control. • Steering binds. • Vehicle shakes excessively when rear windows are open while underway. • Loose seat belt bolt pulls out. **2002–04**—Under-hood fires. **2003**—Vehicle (gas and diesel) suddenly shuts down. • Diesel fuel leaks from the fuel filter onto the engine:

> Faulty fuel injectors in the 6.0L diesel engine resulting in excessive amounts of diesel fuel to enter the oil crankcase. Oil level in crankcase is diluted with fuel to the extent of being measured on the dipstick by several inches and flash point of oil reduced to half of the flash point of the oil.

• Total automatic transmission failure. • Early ball joint replacement. • Hatchback window shatters for no reason. • High-intensity headlights blind other drivers. • Seat belts fail to lock. • Overheated power-window switch. **2004**—Engine surges and stalls while cruising. • Cruise control goes on and off when descending a hill. • Early transmission replacement. • Vehicle frequently goes out of alignment. • ABS brake failure. • Premature brake rotor wearout. • Firestone side wall blowout saga continues. • Limited spring travel causes suspension to bottom out easily. •

Passenger window suddenly explodes. • Exhaust fumes enter the cabin. **2005**—Automatic transmission slips and jerks into gear. • Faulty electrical unit. • Windows won't roll down. • Locks don't work. • Radio malfunctions. • Suspension won't support the extra weight of a trailer that's much lighter than the recommended maximum towing weight. • Frame is easily bent. • Brake lines leak fluid.

Secret Warranties/Internal Bulletins/Service Tips

All years: Front brake caliper rattling. **2000**—Engine knocking. • Because of low fuel pressure, diesel engine may produce a loud knocking or cackle noise. • The Reverse Park Aid may sound a false alarm if contaminated by debris in the system. **2000–03**—Rough idle or hesitation when accelerating is covered in TSB #03-9-11. **2000–04**—Front hubs won't lock or disengage. • Repair tips for diesel engine vacuum pumps that won't run, or that run continuously. • The 4×4 system may be compromised, and climate control may default to defrost. **2000–05**—AC heater core leakage. • Seat belts are slow to retract. • Brake pedal kick-back and grabbing. **2001**—No-starts, stalling with the 7.3L engine. • Engine stalls when vehicle is shifted into Reverse. • Ford admits investigating cam sensor failures (which lead to loss of power, engine shutdown, and no-starts). • Sudden loss of Second gear; vehicle won't move. • Delayed shifts. • Turbo hooting. • Sway bar clunks and pops. • Front shaft seal leaks. • Water-pump shaft seal leaks. • A buck or jerk may be felt with cruise control engaged. • Higher-than-normal steering effort required at low speeds. • Incorrect oil pressure readings. **2002**—Heater core leaks. • Ignition switch lock cylinder is faulty. • Engine cylinder heads leak oil or coolant. • Oil contamination in the cooling system. • Vehicle pulls to one side when braking. • Popping noise from the floorboard area. • Increased low-speed steering effort required. • Hard starts; battery won't charge. **2003**—Special Customer Satisfaction Program to enhance cold-weather engine performance (reduces rough idle). • Special Customer Satisfaction Program #03B05 to replace ICP sensor. • Exhaust noise and loss of power. • Remedy for faulty adjustable pedals. • Correction for starter failures. **2003–04**—Steering grunt, moan on left-hand turns. **2003–05**—Inoperative AC; compressor leakage. *Diesel engines:* **2003–04**—Diesel fuel in the oil may cause the engine to run rough or lose power. • Troubleshooting tips for water in diesel fuel and a warning light that won't shut off. • Diesel engine misfiring or no-starts may be caused by a defective fuel-injection control module (TSB #04-18-06). TSB #04-17-13 says diesel hard starts or no-starts can also be traced to a faulty glow-plug control module. • Excessive accessory drivebelt squeal or squawk with diesel engine; turbo-induced moan, groan. • Overall poor diesel engine performance requires a revised computer module calibration (TSB #03-20-12) and the following countermeasures (see bulletins on following page). **2003–05**—Additional diagnostic and repair tips for 6.0L diesel-equipped models that misfire, lose power, buck and jerk, produce excessive smoke, are hard to start, or won't start (injector failure is the prime suspect, but the TSB delves into other causes as well). • Erratic shifts and engagement shudder at cruising speed. **2004**—6.0L diesel low-power and oil-leak diagnostic tips. • Diesel engine may buck, jerk, or stumble after deceleration down long grade with the cruise control engaged. • Turbo-induced diesel engine exhaust moan, drone.

DIESEL ENGINE—DRIVEABILITY/OIL FUEL DILUTION

BULLETIN NO.: 04-9-3   DATE: MAY 11, 2004

DRIVEABILITY—RUNS ROUGH, LOW POWER
2003–04 EXCURSION, F SUPER DUTY
2004 ECONOLINE
ISSUE: Some vehicles equipped with the 6.0L diesel engine may exhibit engine oil diluted with fuel (OIL LEVEL MAY APPEAR OVER FULL), runs rough and/or a low power condition.

DIESEL ENGINE—TURBO-INDUCED EXHAUST DRONE/MOAN

BULLETIN NO.: 04-9-4   DATE: MAY 11, 2004

TURBO-INDUCED EXHAUST MOAN/DRONE—VIBRATION—6.0L
2003–04 EXCURSION, F SUPER DUTY
ACTION: To service, neutralize the exhaust system. It may also be necessary to install a revised turbocharger pedestal mounting bracket if it is not already installed. Refer to the following Service Procedure.

2004–05—Lack of AC cooling. **2005**—Steering fluid leaks. • Rust stains on bumper. • Chronic stalling.

EXCURSION PROFILE

	2000	2001	2002	2003	2004	2005
Cost Price ($) (very negotiable)						
4×2 XLT	46,219	42,481	45,925	46,940	48,945	51,510
4×4 XLT	47,695	47,245	56,460	56,880	52,905	54,370
Used Values ($)						
4×2 XLT ▲	6,000	8,000	10,000	12,000	14,500	17,000
4×2 XLT ▼	5,000	6,000	8,000	10,000	12,500	15,000
4×4 XLT ▲	7,500	9,500	12,000	15,000	16,500	19,000
4×4 XLT ▼	6,500	7,500	9,500	13,000	15,000	17,500
Reliability	2	2	2	2	2	3

EXPEDITION, NAVIGATOR   ★

bad buy

RATING: Not Recommended (1997–2008). The Lincoln Navigator is a re-badged Expedition, selling for a $25,000 premium and saddled with tons of chrome and plastic cladding, along with a sad history of powertrain and fit and finish glitches identical to the Expedition's. **Strong points:** Torquier engines are suitable for heavy hauling; excellent ride and visibility; lots of passenger room; and a luxury, carlike interior. Will seat nine in a pinch. The EL version replaces the Excursion, with a wheelbase longer by a foot. **Weak points:** Hard to park or drive in the city; rough, sluggish 5.4L V8 performance; lethargic steering; ride is a bit busy at low speeds; limited rear-seat access and cargo space; slow to heat or cool; entry is hampered by a high step-in and lack of a grab handle on the driver's side; poor fuel economy; and poor quality control that gets worse after the 2003 model redesign. **New for 2008:** Nothing significant. Ford says it will revamp the Expedition for the 2010 model year; insiders say it will get the axe.

2008 TECHNICAL DATA

POWERTRAIN (4×4)
Engine: 5.4L V8 (300 hp); Transmission: 6-speed auto.

DIMENSION/CAPACITY
Passengers: 2/3/3; Wheelbase: 119.0 in.; H: 76.7/L: 206.5/W: 91.8 in.; Headroom F/R1/R2: 2.5/4.0/3.5 in.; Legroom F/R1/R2: 40.5/29.5/28.0 in.; Cargo volume: 86.0 cu. ft.; Fuel tank: 106L/regular; Tow limit: 9,200 lb.; Load capacity: 1,400 lb.; GVWR: 8,000 lb.; Turning circle: 42.0 ft.; Ground clearance: 7.0 in.; Weight: 5,578 lb.

MODEL HISTORY: Based on the F-150 pickup and offered only as a four-door, the Expedition and Navigator handle serious trailer-towing with more comfort than a pickup or a van. They have nine-passenger potential if you use the optional third-row bench seat. The full-time 4×4 is taken from the Explorer, along with four-wheel ABS disc brakes. On one hand, both the 4.6L and 5.4L V8s are peppy, even though they can't match the torque and fuel economy of the Tahoe's diesel engines. On the other hand, both V8 engines experience a similar delay when accelerating, as do the Tahoe and Yukon. Keep in mind that these vehicles have many serious safety-related problems, reported repeatedly to NHTSA. Ditch the Firestone tires; many tires that weren't on the recall list have been defective.

1999—A small power boost, an upgraded Command-Trac 4×4 system that provides 4×4 when needed, and optional power-adjustable gas and brake pedals. **2000**—Standard power-adjusted foot pedals, a rear sonar backing-up alert system, a revised centre console, and optional side airbags. **2003**—An independent rear suspension, stiffer chassis, increased towing capability of 4,035 kg (8,900 lb.), improved braking and stability, and a third-row, foldable seat. Third-row passengers gain lots of legroom but lose some shoulder room. The 4.6L V8 gets a bit more horsepower. Navigators are given exceptionally large seats and tweaks to reduce vibrations and noise. Optional power-deployed running boards that pop out when the door is opened and a remote-controlled aluminum liftgate are also added. **2004**—Wider availability of 2003's new features. **2007**—Independent rear suspension provides a much better ride than previous versions. There's also a stiffer chassis and a new interior with third-row seats that fold flat. Seat-mounted side airbags, three-row curtain airbags, and electronic stability control with rollover protection.

COST ANALYSIS: Keep in mind that prices are unrealistic and can be easily cut by $8,000–$12,000, so haggle aggressively, with the knowledge that Expedition and Navigator sales are in free fall and not likely to recover. Your best bet is to go for a used 2007 Expedition with its safety and ride upgrades. It offers a quieter, smoother ride and more creature comforts for only $22,000–$24,000. The 2008 models cost a lot more money but offer nothing new. Expect to spend $46,499/$57,699 (XLT/Limited) for that new-car smell. Buying a 2008 Expedition in the States saves you $15,000–$20,000. A new Navigator will set you back $73,299 in Canada, or $48,745 in the States. A 2005 Navigator sells in Canada for $24,000—about one-third of its original price. **Best alternatives:** GM's large SUVs, like the Tahoe and Yukon (with an extended warranty), are far more nimble, reliable, and fuel-efficient, and their prices are way down. The Expedition EL is designed to compete against the Chevrolet Suburban. Toyota's Highlander and 4Runner are also worth a look. If they won't do, consider a Nissan Pathfinder or the Lexus LX 450 or 470. **Rebates:**

Look for $8,000+ rebates on the 2008 models and $5,000 on the 2009s early in the year. 2008 Navigators are already discounted about $12,000. New Lincolns aren't worth the extra $25,000 you pay; after 10 years, a Navigator sells for only $1,500 more than the Expedition. **Delivery/PDI:** $1,250. **Warranty:** Bumper-to-bumper 5–6 years/60,000–110,000 km; rust perforation 5 years/unlimited km. **Supplementary warranty:** An extended powertrain warranty is a good idea. **Options:** Stay away from any Firestone or Continental tires. Both the 16- and 17-inch Firestone tires have a history of sudden tread separation, while Continental tires simply lose chunks of tread. Bridgestone tires should be boycotted as well. Be wary of the moonroof option—many complaints of water leaks and wind noise have been reported. Consider the 5.4L powerplant with its sturdier transmission (the E4OD instead of the 4R70W), 20 additional horses, and extra torque. Other recommended options are running boards and adjustable accelerator and brake pedals. **Depreciation:** Much faster than average (sales are down almost 40 percent). **Insurance cost:** Higher than average. **Parts supply/cost:** Body parts are often back-ordered, but moderately priced mechanical parts are easily found either in the Explorer or F-Series bins. **Annual maintenance cost:** Costlier than average. **Highway/city fuel economy:** *4.6L V8: 12.2/17.6 L/100 km; 4.6L V8 and 4×4: 13.4/19.1 L/100 km; 5.4L V8: 12.1/16.6 L/100 km.*

QUALITY/RELIABILITY: Overall quality control and reliability are way below average, and only got worse with the 2003 revamped model. There's also a disturbingly high rate of safety-related complaints that suggest a "What, me worry?" attitude among Ford engineers. After all, how much engineering prowess does it take to prevent wheels from falling off or the rear hatch from falling on someone's head, or to plug water leaks from the back glass? Continental General and Firestone tires have a history of tread retention problems (that's my polite way of saying that they could be crap). **Owner-reported problems:** Inadequate troubleshooting of sudden acceleration or stalling; 4.6L engine piston-slap noise with cold starts; rough idling caused by a faulty throttle cable; excessive steering play requiring constant correction; chronic electrical shorts for all model years, affecting everything from gauges and lights to engine and transmission performance; transmission failures; excessive rear differential noise; engine oil leaks lead to engine replacement within first year of ownership; defective fuel-pump sensors; poor braking, high brake maintenance costs (chronic rotor warpage and brake dust everywhere), and excessive brake noise; automatic-adjusting side mirrors constantly readjust themselves to the wrong setting; and assorted clunks, rattles, and wind noise. The 2005 models are just as unreliable, as this owner reports:

> If you remove your foot from the brake the vehicle will roll out of control. The transmission will shift at odd times as you are driving. Rear passenger dome light flickers when you turn it on with the switch in the back. Driver door does not latch unless it is shut hard. In addition to the above the following new defects have been found: Turn signals will sometimes not work at all. When making a sharp turn the rear end will slip. You can feel it not holding the road. Outside fumes are sucked into the vehicle. Any smell or exhaust from this or other vehicles is pulled inside. The leather on the front seats has turned black.

Warranty performance: Mediocre.

ROAD PERFORMANCE: Acceleration/torque: 0–100 km/h: 9.9 seconds (about a second slower than the Tahoe) with the 2000's base engine; expect much better acceleration with the 2001 model's additional horses. **Transmission:** Well-spaced gearing shifts imperceptibly, without any gear hunting when traversing hilly terrain. **Steering:** Overly sensitive at lower speeds. **Routine handling:** Smooth, comfortable ride that's above average for a sport-utility. The variable-assist steering is fairly precise at lower speeds and gives adequate feedback from the road. Leaving the Expedition in AWD improves handling considerably. Parking is more like docking. **Emergency handling:** Above average. The Expedition's tight chassis and supple suspension keep the vehicle on track, without the wallowing and nose-diving evident in many other sport-utilities in its class. **Braking:** Adequate, but not impressive (100–0 km/h: 45 m).

SAFETY SUMMARY: An Ontario law firm (*www.willbarristers.com*) has filed a class action petition against Ford for defective door latches on 1997–2000 model year Expeditions, Navigators, and F-Series trucks. It will cost about $994 per four-door vehicle to replace the door latches, which have opened in side-impact crashes and rollover accidents. Many class actions have been filed in the States over this defect, and Ford has settled one lawsuit out of court. There have also been many cases where the wheel lug nuts sheared and the wheel flew off (it was later recalled). But the kicker is that even the spare tire is dangerous. Several reports have stated that the spare-tire cable broke while turning a corner, causing the spare tire to fly away. Also, an inaccurate fuel gauge indicates one-quarter tank full when you are actually out of gas. Many incidents have been reported of unintended, sudden acceleration, which has been blamed on a variety of causes. Horn design makes it difficult to activate in an emergency. Some complaints of insufficient low-beam illumination and an annoying dashboard reflection onto the front windshield. **Airbags:** Side airbags are optional. There have been reports of airbags failing to deploy and the Airbag warning light staying on for no reason. **ABS:** 4W is standard; disc/disc. ABS failure or lock-up often caused by faulty sensor or ABS module. **Traction control:** Optional. **Head restraints F/R:** 2003–04: ★★★★★/★★★. **Visibility F/R:** ★★★★★. **Pet transport:** ★★★★★.

SAFETY COMPLAINTS: All models/years: Fire ignites while vehicle is parked. • Cruise control fails to disengage when brakes are applied. • Chronic engine head gasket failures and oil leaks; Check Engine light comes on as coolant leaks onto plugs and #3 and #4 coil packs. • Too much steering play. • Excessive front-end wandering. • Tie-rod end and torsion bar failures. • Excessive suspension vibration. • Transmission failures. • Slips while in gear. • Rear axle failure. • Seat belt failures. • Plastic running board is slippery. • Rear hatch latch cylinders fail, allowing hatch to fall on driver's head. • Inoperative power windows. • Windows shatter for no reason. • Defective gas cap causes Check Engine light to come on and makes for poor driveability. • Gas and brake pedal are too close. **1999**—Vehicle explodes during refuelling. • Pitman arm suddenly detaches from the steering gear. • In one incident, rear door hinge cut off child's finger as door was opened. • Vehicle starts on its own without the key in the ignition. • Rear brake caliper seizure scores rotor, costs $1,000 to repair. • Rear-view mirror backing peels off. • Cracked hood welds. **2000**—Sudden loss of engine power when accelerating, especially when fuel tank is less than one-quarter full. • Suspension and steering combination makes the vehicle wander all over the road. • Over-sensitive steering also makes vehicle hard to control; one report that it almost tipped over. • Three bolts that hold the steering gearbox come apart. • In some cases, the steering assist may cut on and off. • Plastic fuel tank is quite vulnerable to leakage from road debris punctures. • Jack failures. • Driver-side seat belt clip won't go into buckle—apparently a common problem. **2001**—Stalling; unable to restart. • Can shift vehicle into Neutral without touching brake pedal. • Vehicle surges forward, despite brakes being applied. • Brake pedal falls to the floor when brakes are applied. • Adjustable gas pedal will sometimes get stuck under floor mat. • Vibration, moan at highway speeds. • Door lock is easily thwarted. • Driver-side seat belt unlatches. • Wheel lug nuts won't stay tight; wheel flies off vehicle. • Passengers sickened by white powder coming out of air vents. • Vehicle stalls and won't start when on an incline with one-quarter tank of fuel left. **2001–02**—Sudden, unintended acceleration when brakes are applied. **2002**—Airbags fail to deploy. • Vehicle fishtails out of control. • Steering-wheel lock-up. **2003**—Fires ignite from the seat-heating system because of a loose gas line and an overheated fuse. • Early failure of powertrain components:

> The driver-side tie-rod has broken twice. Both times [were] without warning. The dealer has fixed it once and now it is back to the dealer for the second time for same problem. The manufacturer took information from the consumer, but she has not heard back from them. Passenger-side rear window does not go down [when master switch is activated]. Door Ajar light does not go off. Left front ball joint separated, then vehicle hit sign. Lower control arm broken, upper ball joint bad, spindle broken, sway bar link broken, CV boot torn, and axle pulled out of front differential. Tie-rod end on left side broken and vacuum hub cracked on spindle and tire and rim damaged. Also fender liner ripped out. Spindle, upper control arm, lower control arm, CV boot replaced. Clip for axle vacuum hub and wheel and tire, removed front differential to reinstall, axle and clip replaced wheel and tire and performed alignment. Damage to hood when knuckle split.

• Drive shaft and tie-rod break while vehicle is underway. • Vehicle jumps from Park to Reverse. • Gas leaks from the filler cap area. • Continental tire blowouts. • Brake failures and premature rotor, caliper wearout. **2003–06**—Sudden, unintended acceleration:

> The vehicle transmission was in the Park position while waiting on a slow train. When engaging the transmission into the Drive position, after the train had passed, the vehicle uncontrollably fully accelerated on its own. To avoid a serious collision with oncoming traffic, the driver turned the vehicle onto the railroad tracks where it came to a stop after damaging two wheels and high centering on the tracks. This is a very dangerous vehicle.

•

Vehicle was being driven in a parking lot. We stopped to allow a car to pull out of the parking space. The brake was released to allow the car to slowly roll into the parking space when it suddenly accelerated. My wife plowed [on] the brakes as the vehicle came close to running over pedestrians walking by. Dealer checked and found nothing wrong. This is one of two incidents in a 3 month period. This vehicle is a major catastrophe waiting to happen, please beware of the danger.

2004—Steering wheel sticks when turning. • Still excessive brake wear and brake dust everywhere (a TSB confirms this problem). • Faulty tire-pressure monitor. • Throttle sticks, especially when the cruise control is engaged. • Total brake loss. • Serious Continental tire defects continue. **2005**—Automatic transmission slips from Park into Reverse while idling. • Transmission won't shift. **2005–06**—Airbags fail to deploy. **2006**—Sudden power loss. • Broken tie-rod assembly. • False Low Tire Pressure alert. • Horn hard to activate. • Long stopping distance. **2007**—Transmission slippage, shifts roughly, and sticks in high gear. • Repeated rear axle failures. • Transmission will not hold vehicle when it is stopped on a hill. • Gauges aren't illuminated sufficiently for daytime viewing. • Liftgate rear window shatters for no reason.

Secret Warranties/Internal Bulletins/Service Tips

All models/years: Free fuel gauge/sender replacement under ONP #97B17, Supplement 1 (a secret warranty). • Front engine-cover oil leaks. • No-starts in cold weather. **1999**—Vibration or shimmy above 70 km/h may require an upgraded drive shaft. • Diagnostic tips for correcting a front differential moaning, whining, or buzzing in the speakers and a whistling noise when driving with the AC off. • An exhaust system crack or break between the muffler and tailpipe may require a new drive shaft, muffler, and tailpipe assembly. **1999–2000**—A hesitation upon acceleration or while turning may be caused by fuel-pump cavitation because of fuel sloshing away from the filter sock in the fuel-tank reservoir. Ford TSB #00-20-1 says a new fuel pump should be installed if other possible causes have been eliminated. • Install a clutch pack kit under warranty to silence rear axle chattering (on vehicles with a limited slip rear axle) when turning or cornering, says TSB #00-8-4. **1999–2001**—Under a little-known extended warranty, Ford will repair or replace 5.4L engines with faulty head gaskets on the 1999–2001 F-150 and Super Duty F-Series pickups, Econoline, Expedition, and Lincoln Navigator. **1999–2002**—Throttle sticks in very cold weather. **2000**—A new side intake manifold gasket will correct a coolant leak from the passenger-side intake manifold. **2000–05**—Correction for seat belts that are slow to retract. **2001**—No-starts, stalling with the 7.3L engine. • Engine stalls when vehicle is shifted into Reverse. • A buck or jerk may be felt with cruise control engaged. • Turbo hooting. • Ford admits investigating cam sensor failures (which lead to loss of power, engine shutdown, and no-starts). • Sudden loss of Second gear; vehicle won't move. • Delayed shifts. • Sway bar clunk and popping. • Front shaft seal leakage. • Water-pump shaft seal leakage. • Higher-than-normal steering effort required. • Incorrect oil pressure readings. **2002**—Engine cylinder head leaks. • 5.4L engine power loss. • Engine vibration at idle, and droning noise when accelerating. • Lack of fuel pressure. • Driveline vibration at 100 km/h. • Loose axle bearing; axle-tube seal leakage. • Excessive braking required when decelerating. • Front suspension noise. • Heater core leaks. • Faulty ignition-switch lock cylinder. • Air leak in air suspension. • Excessive wind noise. **2003**—Frequent no-starts. • Front axle groan, hum, or vibration. • Powertrain fluid leaks from the rear half-shaft seal. • Transmission fluid leaks at the transmission oil cooler. • Rear axle whine. • Electrical shorts may cause gauge, alarm, radio/DVD, and door lock failures. • Power-steering leaks, noise, vibration. **2003–04**—Intermittent loss of cooling. • Excessive brake dust on wheels. **2003–05**—Rear axle seal leak (see bulletin). **2003–06**—Preventing electrical battery drain. **2003–07**—Scratched front door window. • Inoperative rear wiper. **2003–08**—Excessive wheel vibration. **2004–06**—Tips for correcting front brake vibration or shudder. **2005**—Remedy for engine knocking or ticking when warmed up. • Inoperative seat heaters. **2005–06**—Rough idle (4×2 only). • Hesitation or lack of power when shifting. **2007**—No crank or start. • Downshift hesitation. • 2–3 shift flare. • Harsh shifts. • Wind noise from doors. • Instruments, message centre switches malfunction.

REAR AXLE SEAL LEAKS
BULLETIN NO.: 04-10-5   DATE: MAY 25, 2004

AXLE SEAL LEAKS

2003–04 EXPEDITION, NAVIGATOR

ISSUE: Some vehicles may exhibit fluid leaks from the rear halfshaft axle seal. This may occur when the halfshaft spline comes in contact with the inner diameter of the axle seal. The leak may be more pronounced in cold weather.

ACTION: To service order and install Axle Seal Kit 3L1Z-4A109-BA. Review the revised instruction sheet and obtain the required tools before beginning any repairs. Also refer to the following installation service tips.

EXPEDITION, NAVIGATOR PROFILE

	1999	2000	2001	2002	2003	2004	2005	2006	2007
Cost Price ($) (very negotiable)									
Expedition 4×2	37,495	—	—	—	—	—	—	—	—
Expedition 4×4 (30%)	40,595	41,195	40,855	41,255	43,270	46,800	48,245	45,199	46,799
Navigator (30%)	63,765	68,690	66,425	66,425	69,995	72,625	73,195	75,899	73,299
Used Values ($)									
Expedition 4×2 ▲	6,000	—	—	—	—	—	—	—	—
Expedition 4×2 ▼	5,000	—	—	—	—	—	—	—	—
Expedition 4×4 ▲	5,000	6,000	8,500	9,500	11,000	12,000	14,000	19,000	24,000
Expedition 4×4 ▼	4,500	5,500	7,500	8,000	9,500	11,000	13,000	17,500	22,500
Navigator ▲	8,500	10,000	11,500	13,000	15,000	18,000	24,000	29,000	36,000
Navigator ▼	8,000	9,500	10,500	12,000	14,000	16,000	22,000	27,000	34,000
Reliability	3	3	3	2	1	1	1	1	1
Crash Safety (F)	4	4	5	5	5	5	5	5	5
Rollover	—	—	2	2	—	—	—	3	3

Note: A used 4×2 Navigator is worth about $2,000 less than a 4×4. Newer, more complicated versions have proven to be less reliable than early models. The 2008 models have crashworthiness ratings similar to the 2007s.

General Motors

ESCALADE, ESV, EXT, DENALI/SUBURBAN, TAHOE, YUKON, XL/TAHOE, YUKON HYBRIDS ★★★/★★★/★★★

RATING: *Escalade, ESV, EXT, Denali:* Average (2001–08); Average with an extended warranty (1995–2000). *Suburban, Tahoe, Yukon:* Average (2002–08); Below Average (1995–2001); Not Recommended (1985–94). *Tahoe, Yukon Hybrids:* Average (2008). Brawny, large SUVs for buyers who lack imagination, the GMC Yukon and Denali and the Cadillac Escalade share the basic Tahoe/Suburban design but differ in styling, options, and price. Although these models are some of GM's best-performing large SUVs, they can't match the Japanese competition in overall reliability and quality control. Plus, over $45,455 (Tahoe 4×2) for the cheapest model in this series is way too much. Used models, at about half that price, perhaps. New? You've gotta be kidding—or a former CEO of Nortel. **Strong points:** A good variety of competent engines that are great for trailering; standard stability control; a fuel-saving cylinder-deactivation feature; lavishly appointed; a good array of instruments and controls; a large and comfortable cabin that adds passenger and cargo space with the redesigned 2007s; high ground clearance; a rattle-resistant body; and slow depreciation. The Suburban and Yukon XL are the largest heavy-hitters of this group, and they actually acquit themselves quite well, with reasonably predictable handling and more than enough power for most driving needs. **Weak points:** Incredibly expensive, and loses value quickly. The 4-speed automatic transmission wastes fuel and hinders powertrain performance. *2006 and earlier models:* A high step-up takes some acrobatics, the wide turning circle complicates parking, and braking is barely acceptable; bizarre electrical short-circuits; biodegradable fuel pumps; premature brake wear; excessive suspension and steering vibrations; vague steering; a suspension that provides a too-compliant, wandering ride; and excessive road and engine noise. Reports that the airbags fail to deploy in a collision; Escalade models have been particularly failure-prone. **New for 2008:** Nothing significant, except for the introduction of a hybrid Tahoe/Yukon; a Cadillac Escalade Hybrid will debut for the 2009 model year. Both hybrids are said by GM to cut fuel consumption by 25 percent (take that with a huge grain of salt), thanks to a lower chassis for better aerodynamics, and provide enough torque to tow heavy loads.

Dan Neil, Pulitzer Prize–winning car columnist for the *Los Angeles Times*, is not impressed by GM's Tahoe/Yukon Hybrids:

2008 TECHNICAL DATA

POWERTRAIN (4×2/4×4)
Engines: 4.8L V8 (295 hp) • 5.3L V8 (325 hp) • 6.0L V8 (332 hp) (Hybrids) • 6.0L V8 (364 hp) • 6.2L V8 (380 hp) • 8.1L V8 (325 hp); Transmissions: 4-speed auto. • 6-speed auto. (Denali)

DIMENSION/CAPACITY (TAHOE/ SUBURBAN)
Passengers: 3/3/3; Wheelbase: 116.0–130.0 in.; H: 76.9/L: 202.0–222.0/W: 79.0 in.; Headroom F/R1/R2: 5.0/4.5/ 1.0 in.; Legroom F/R1/R2: 40.5/29.5/ 28.5 in.; Cargo volume: 65.0–75.0 cu. ft.; Fuel tank: 98L/regular; Tow limit: 8,200 lb.; Load capacity: 1,835 lb.; GVWR: 7,300 lb.; Turning circle: 39.0 ft.; Ground clearance: 9.0 in.; Weight: 5,265 lb.

For now, we have this paradox, a fantastically fuel-efficient vehicle that's still a gas hog. A hybrid that's simultaneously good (promise) and bad (reality). Matters can only get more muddled when the Hybrid Hummer comes rolling out.

Other improvements this year: standard side curtain airbags, an improved split bench seat in LS models, and a Remote Start system. Further changes will be minimal until the scheduled redesign and restyling of the 2012 models.

MODEL HISTORY: Although GM's recently redesigned pickups are piling up in dealer inventories, these expensive, full-sized, four-door rear-drives and 4×4s haven't lost much of their popularity over the last few years in spite of their large size, excessive fuel consumption, so-so reliability, and atrocious fit and finish. Except for a wimpy base 275-hp V8 powerplant (not available on newer models), the full array of engines is capable of hauling almost any load, towing a trailer, or carrying up to nine passengers.

The GMC Yukon 4×4 (and its twin, the Tahoe) came on the scene in 1992 when GMC gave the Jimmy name to its smaller sport-utility wagon line and re-badged the big one as the Tahoe/Yukon. During the 1995 model year, Blazers became Tahoes and a four-door version with standard driver-side airbags was added.

1999—Luxury trappings are added to the Yukon, which is then designated the Denali. **2000**—Wider and taller vehicles, the Tahoe and Yukon adopt a new V8 engine, front side airbags, and a seating capacity that grows from six to nine passengers. The familiar two-door version is dropped. **2001**—New engine cylinder heads. The 6.0L V8 gains 20 hp. A 340-hp 8.1L V8 for the Suburban 2500. **2002**—More standard features, such as AC, power windows, power front seats, heated power mirrors, and rear climate controls. **2003**—New entertainment options, an anti-skid system, four-wheel steering, and adjustable pedals. **2006**—No more Quadrastar; Yukons get a 5.3L V8 that uses gasoline and ethanol. Standard stability control. **2007**—More power (the 5.3L V8 comes with 320 hp versus 295), new styling, a larger interior, and additional features like improved second-row seats, a revised navigation system, a power liftgate, and a rear obstacle detection feature. Overall, buyers will find these models provide more agile handling, much better steering and braking responses, and a more comfortable and controlled ride.

Pre-2000 models are set on GM's C/K truck platform and have been available with a variety of V8s over the years. The best choice, though, is the 5.7L gas engine mated to an electronic 4-speed automatic. This matchup provides gobs of torque at low rpm, making these part-time 4×4s great for towing, stump pulling, or mountain climbing.

Except for the Denali's 6-speed automatic, transmission alternatives are limited to your choice of 4-speeds: the manual or the automatic. Standard-equipment hubs must be locked manually before shifting into 4×4 on early models. The diesel provides a good compromise between power and economy, although it has been plagued by malfunctions for decades and has never been the equal of the Cummins. Overall reliability is only average, and declining.

Suburban, Yukon XL

Although it's classed as a full-sized SUV, the Suburban is really a combination of a station wagon, a van, and a pickup. It can carry nine passengers, tow just about anything, and go anywhere with optional 4×4.

These vehicles didn't change much until the launch of the 2000 models. Chevrolet restyled the Suburban by setting it on the Silverado/Tahoe/Yukon platform and using generic parts from the same parts bin. With the changeover, GMC's Suburban name was swapped for the Yukon XL, while the Chevrolet division soldiered on, keepi ng the Suburban name alive.

Both the Suburban and Yukon XL are GM's largest sport-utilities: 37.3 cm (14.7 in.) longer than the Ford Expedition but 18.8 cm (7.4 in.) shorter than the Excursion. Handling improves considerably, but fuel economy remains atrocious. Improvements include a wider and taller body; new 5.3L and 6.0L V8 engines that replace the 5.7L and 7.4L engines, and a turbocharged diesel V8; an automatic transmission with tow/haul mode for smoother shifting; standard front side airbags; and four-wheel disc brakes. Rear leaf springs have been replaced by rear coil springs.

2001—Suburban gets an upgraded 6.0L V8 in addition to a totally new 340-hp 8.1L V8. The upscale Yukon Denali (the Cadillac Escalade's big brother) moves to GM's new full-sized platform. Until the changeover, when it became the Yukon XL, the Suburban was a Hummer in civilian garb, and like the Hummer, it's far less sturdy than it looks. **2005**—The StabiliTrak anti-skid system becomes standard for all Tahoe and 1500 models, and swing-out rear cargo doors are gone. **2006**—An Active Fuel Management cylinder shutoff system saves gas while cruising.

Cadillac Escalade

This is GM's pop culture party wagon, favoured by celebrities and "Do what I say, not what I do" politicos. Cadillac's first truck, the 1999 Escalade 4×4, was nothing more than a warmed-over GMC Yukon Denali covered with ugly, poorly designed side cladding in an effort to disguise its parentage. The redesigned 2002 Escalade got many improvements, including an EXT version (a Suburban/Avalanche clone with additional luxury features), a 6.0L V8, and a more refined AWD system. **2003**—A longer ESV and Escalade EXT, an all-dressed version of the Chevrolet Avalanche SUV/pickup truck. Other changes include standard power-adjustable gas and brake pedals and second-row bucket seats for the wagons. **2004**—A tire-pressure monitor, trailering package, and satellite radio are added. A new Platinum Edition offers a standard navigation system and 20-inch wheels. **2005**—An improved cooling system and upgraded interior trim and gauges. **2006**—Standard electronic stability control.

COST ANALYSIS: Unless you want to risk buying an untested 2008 Hybrid during its first year on the market (not advisable), buy a relatively identical used 2007 front-drive, gasoline-powered Tahoe for $25,000. A 2008 sells for about $45,455, but generous GM will give buyers a $7,500 rebate for cash transactions. Costs vary considerably depending on the model and powertrain configuration. For example, your cheapest 2008 model Tahoe 4×4 costs $49,255, and an entry-level Escalade EXT sells for $72,175. A 2008 Tahoe Hybrid costs $66,125—lots of dough to save a little gas. The 2008 base Yukons and Suburbans bought in Canada are no bargains, either, selling for $43,455 and $48,455, respectively. Now let's look at your savings if you buy in the States: 2008 Tahoe LS ($39,815); Tahoe LTZ ($46,540); Tahoe Hybrid ($50,490); Yukon front-drive ($36,245); Yukon XL ($36,245); Yukon Denali ($47,385); Yukon XL Denali ($53,075); Yukon Hybrid front-drive ($50,755); Yukon Hybrid AWD ($53,755); Cadillac Escalade ($56,890); Escalade ESV ($59,390); Escalade EXT ($58,465); Suburban LS front-drive ($38,985); and the Suburban LS AWD ($41,830). For this kind of money, Lexus and Toyota seem mighty attractive. **Best alternatives:** Choose a used 2007 model for the interior and performance upgrades. If you're looking for a cheaper used Tahoe or Yukon 4×4, opt for the 2005 versions that sell for about $17,000. Try to find a Suburban with the 7.4L V8 engine—the 5.7L is barely adequate for this behemoth. Don't become mesmerized by a luxury nameplate on a practically identical model. For example, a new 2000 Cadillac Escalade originally retailed for about $30,000 more than a Suburban, but there's only a few thousand dollars separating the two vehicles' resale values today. When looking for other choices, remember that few other similar-class vehicles equal the Suburban for sheer size. Alternatively, a full-sized van or extended minivan might be a better choice if off-road capability isn't a priority. If size isn't your primary concern, look to other, more reliable SUVs that are less costly to operate. **Rebates:** $10,000 rebates and zero percent financing should continue well into 2009. **Delivery/PDI:** $1,250. **Warranty:** Bumper-to-bumper 3 years/60,000 km; rust perforation 6 years/160,000 km. **Supplementary warranty:** An extended warranty is a good idea but not critical. **Options:** You won't find many bare-bones models, because dealers want the extra profit gained from selling these SUVs fully loaded. The transmission oil cooler, rear window defogger, engine block heater, and upgraded sound system are all worthy add-ons. Consider buying running boards ($300) if you plan to carry people who will have difficulty stepping up into the vehicle. Don't accept less-reliable Firestone or Bridgestone tires. **Depreciation:** Mind-spinning as fuel costs rise. Beware of paying a premium for the nameplate. **Insurance cost:** Insurance industry statistics indicate that these full-sized vehicles have a substantially lower-than-average number of accident injury claims, but the cost of insurance is way above average. Surprised? **Annual maintenance cost:** Higher than average. The early Suburban's many mechanical and body deficiencies boost its upkeep costs. One saving grace, however, is that it can be serviced practically anywhere. Escalade's redesign will probably result in higher maintenance costs once the warranty expires. **Parts supply/cost:** Good supply, and inexpensive. There have been long waits for transfer-case replacements. Competition from independent suppliers keeps prices down. **Highway/city fuel economy:** *Tahoe and Yukon 4.8L, with or without 4×4: 12.7/16.9 L/100 km; Tahoe, Suburban, Yukon, Yukon Denali, and Yukon XL 5.3L 4×4: 12.6/17.1 L/100 km; 6.0L: 12.5/17.3 L/100 km.*

QUALITY/RELIABILITY: The best of the Detroit Big Three…ho-hum. Overall reliability had improved up to the 2007 redesign—then it nosedived. **Owner-reported problems:** Lots of driveability complaints relating to excessive wander and vibration, hesitation when accelerating, transmission failures, wheel bearings wearing out after only a year's use, and incredibly loud, squeaking brakes. Other complaints pertain to the premature replacement of brake rotors, AC squealing, and electrical, fuel, and exhaust system malfunctions. Body assembly and paint application is below standard. **Warranty performance:** Average.

SAFETY SUMMARY: The vehicle will wander, requiring constant steering correction, particularly when buffeted by crosswinds. Airbags frequently fail to deploy, causing severe trauma. The early Suburbans are too large for safe off-road use—no surprise for most people. Braking is terrible—one of the worst in the sport-utility class (100–0 km/h: 50 m). Although standard four-wheel ABS first appeared on 1992 models, it has been failure-prone and not very effective. NHTSA reports 1,755 complaints, 604 accidents, and 142 injuries related to ABS failures on 1992–98 versions. In spite of the above findings, injury claim rates reported by insurance companies have been judged to be much better than average. Perhaps the drivers are more reliable than the brakes. **Airbags:** Standard side airbags (Escalade). **ABS:** Standard four-wheel; disc/disc. **Traction control:** Optional. **Head restraints F/R:** ★. **Visibility F/R:** ★★★★★. **Pet transport:** ★★★★★.

SAFETY COMPLAINTS: All models/years: Sudden, unintended acceleration. • Engine head gasket and exhaust manifold, transmission, steering, ABS brake and brake drum, tire, door lock, and airbag failures. • Vehicle wanders, vibrates excessively, and jerks to one side when braking. • Seat belt tightens progressively; in one incident, a child had to be cut free from a locked-up seat belt. • Gas tank leaks fuel. • Fuel pumps often need replacing. • Gas fumes permeate the interior. • Rear liftgate window explodes. • Chronic electrical failures. **2003–07**—Airbags fail to deploy in rollovers or in high-speed frontal collisions, and OnStar fails to activate:

> Involved in a horrific auto accident with another vehicle. Hit in front passenger and front part of vehicle (by radiator area) at high speed. (45–55 mph [72–88 km/h] with no skid marks). Unbelievably, none of our four airbags deployed. We and hundreds of our friends are in total disbelief when [we] see the condition [our] vehicle was left in. We were injured, but by [the] grace of God, injuries were not life threatening.

Tahoe, Yukon, Suburban, Yukon XL: **1999–2000**—Driver's seat rocks back and forth while accelerating and decelerating. • *Tahoe, Yukon:* **2000**—Steering breaks loose and causes complete loss of steering control. • Tie-rod falls off, causing serious steering difficulties. • Windshield wipers don't stay in contact with the windshield. • Factory roof rack comes off vehicle while hauling a lightweight object. • Passenger windows don't operate properly. • Mirror is mounted in such a way that it blocks visibility. **2000–04**—Steering-wheel clunk. **2001**—Erratic shifting, slipping, jerking, and clunking. • Sudden stalling. • Catalytic converter glows red. • Stones lodge between the brake calipers and wheel rims. • Finger can be cut from lowering head restraint. **2002**—Loose steering feels unstable, causes vehicle to wander. • Faulty transmission; delayed shifts. **2003**—Faulty steering linkage. • Vehicle can be shifted out of Park without pressing the brake pedal. • Rear passenger doors don't lock properly. •High beam light is too bright. **2005**— Overheated fuel-pump wiring. • Wheels intermittently lock up while driving. • Transmission slips from Drive to Neutral. • Goodyear P265/70R25 M&S on-/off-road tires are easily punctured by stones getting into the tread. **2006**—Driver's seatback suddenly collapses. • Tread of Goodyear Eagle LS tire splits. **2007**— Automatic transmission failure. • Transmission slips when accelerating after morning start-up. • Brake rotors quickly become deeply grooved. • Auto Start feature doesn't work properly:

> The heater fan does not run when I automatically start the vehicle with my remote starter/key fob. What good is it to start your vehicle to warm it up if the fan doesn't start up to defrost your windshield? The GM remote starte[r] was installed and programmed by the dealer after purchase. When it was checked, the fan ran and then didn't. I [can get] it to run only if I am 3 ft. [1 m] away and start the vehicle (or am sitting in it). Too funny; I guess at that point I may as well use the key.

• Incorrect speedometer. • Instrument panel cannot be read during the day. • Faulty wheel bearings. • Heated seats don't work. • Wipers start on their own (defective wiper module). • Car locks itself:

> The electric rear liftgate opens while driving 50 mph [80 km/h]. The failure also occurs while the vehicle is parked. The liftgate opens just enough so that all of the doors continuously lock and unlock and the interior lights illuminate.

• Premature tire wear ("feathering"):

> At 2,000 miles [3,200 km], I noticed my tires in front feathering…. Chevrolet refused to replace them, and dealership said to rotate…now, they want me to put the rear tires on front, to only do the same thing…. I have over 6,000 miles [9,700 km], and already need new tires on front as they were horrible and getting very choppy.

• Driver-side door handles don't always work. *Suburban, Yukon XL:* **1999–2000**— Emergency brake fails, allowing vehicle to roll downhill. • Battery acid runs down the negative cable and causes the brake line to rupture. • Loss of rear braking caused by leakage of brake cylinder fluid. • Fuel leakage from fuel injector and regulator. • All lights (including headlights) go off intermittently. • Driver-side door handle breaks. • Rear power windows often fail in the up or down position. • Window may shatter for no reason. • Rear left shoulder belts don't stay connected. • Unable to secure child safety seat into the middle position because of seat belt's location. • Driver's seat catches fire. • Lug nuts fail, and rear wheel flies off. • Cracked trailer hitch. • Spare-tire jack won't hold vehicle. **2001**—Total electrical shutdown. • Simultaneous failure of steering and brakes. **2002**—Headlights are aimed too high. • Dash lights reflect into mirror. • Dashboard lights are too bright. • Gas tank hard to refuel, causes premature shutoff. **2003**—Vehicle lunges forward when stopped. • Sudden brake loss. • Premature tie-rod wearout. • Steering shaft failure and differential leaking. • Steering clanking silenced by packing grease around the steering shaft. • Exhaust produces explosive noises. • Vehicle registers no gas when the tank is full. • Excessive shoulder belt tension. • Cab reverberation causes ear pain (not a problem with later models). **2004**—Vehicle fails to accelerate when merging into traffic. • Sharp pull to the right when accelerating, and then vehicle snaps to the left when foot is taken off the accelerator. • Excessive on-road vibration at 110 km/h; vehicle becomes very unstable. • When key is in the ignition Accessory position, one can shift out of Park without first applying the brake:

> When key is in the ACCESSORY position, vehicle can be put into gear without the brake being applied. A 3-year-old child died after shifting into gear a parked 1997 Chevy Tahoe.

• Defroster doesn't clear entire windshield and stops working intermittently. • When using the turn signal, the flashers are activated. • All memory presets for seats, mirrors, pedals, etc., are lost when vehicle is restarted or once it is underway; driver's seat moves forward unexpectedly. • Child safety seat latch is not secure. • When accelerating from a stop, transmission jumps into gear after a long delay. • Complete transmission replacement followed by chronic electrical system failures:

> The entire electric system failed in April, when radio, and other electric functions failed. Also, the Low PSI light did not illuminate when the tire went flat. This happened after the repair of electric system. Transmission failed, and had to be replaced. There were several bulletins regarding the stability control and electric systems, but dealer denied any problem with the stability control.

• While driving, tailgate window falls inward. • Inoperative emergency brake. • Static electricity shock when exiting vehicle. *Yukon, Yukon XL:* **2005**—Excessive exhaust popping, cracking, gurgling noise. *Yukon:* **2005**—Instrument panel gives bizarre readings or simply goes out when vehicle is started. • Chronic stalling. • One Denali steering pump failed a few days after purchase. • Headlight fuse burns out constantly. • Spare-tire security device doesn't work as described in manual. *Suburban:* **2005**—Vehicle rolls backward when parked on a hill. • Sudden brake loss. • OnStar frequently fails to work. • Firestone Wilderness tires lose air. *Yukon XL:* **2005**—Frequent no-starts. • Transmission shifts harshly when put into Reverse, or is slow to engage Drive. • Stability Trac fails to activate. • Driver's seat moves on its own; inoperative seat memory. • Satellite radio loses frequency. • Rear heater inoperative. • Excessive steering vibration. *Escalade:* **2005**—On EXT models, the horn often fails to sound if used infrequently. **2006–07**—LED tail lights are annoyingly distracting. **2007**—Inadvertent side airbag deployment. • Hesitation when accelerating. • Retractable steps don't work.

Secret Warranties/Internal Bulletins/Service Tips

All models: 2000–04—Remedies for inoperative power windows. **2000–06**—If the steering column makes a clunking noise, it may signal the need to change the upper intermediate steering-shaft assembly. **2001**—Fuel-tank leakage. • Harsh shifts. • 2–4 band or 3–4 clutch damage. • Rear heater puts out insufficient heat. • Carpet may be wet or have a musty odour. **2004–06**—Automatic transmission shudder due to water intrusion:

SHUDDER/WATER IN TRANSMISSION	
BULLETIN NO.: 05-07-30-017B	DATE: FEBRUARY 17, 2006

AUTOMATIC TRANSMISSION/TORQUE CONVERTER CLUTCH (TCC) SHUDDER, WATER IN TRANSMISSION (REPAIR TRANSMISSION AND SEAL COWL AREA)

2004–06 Cadillac Escalade; 2004–06 Chevrolet Avalanche, Silverado, Suburban, Tahoe; 2004–06 GMC Sierra, and Yukon models with 4L60-E (RPO M30), 4L65-E (RPO M32) or 4L70-E (RPO M70) automatic transmissions.

CONDITION: Some customers may comment on a shudder condition at approximately 64–80 km/h (40–50 mph) when the TCC engages.

CAUSE: This condition may be caused by water in the automatic transmission fluid (ATF). Water may enter the transmission by dripping from the cowl area onto the handle of the transmission fluid level indicator.

Tahoe, Yukon, Suburban, Yukon XL: **1999**—Upgraded rear brake shoes will eliminate brake lead and pull and reduce front brake wear. • Engine bearing knocking on vehicles equipped with a 5.0L or 5.7L V8 may be silenced by using a special GM countermeasure kit to service the crankshaft and select-fit undersized connecting rod bearings. • If the front wheels slip while in 4×4, consider replacing the transfer-case clutch plates and front-drive axle lubricant. **1999–2000**—If only all of the Suburban's problems were this easy to solve: A transfer-case bump or clunk on acceleration is usually caused by a slip-stick condition between the rear propeller shaft-slip yoke and the transfer-case output shaft. It can be eliminated by using a new transfer-case fluid that contains a better friction modifier, says TSB #99-04-21-004. *Tahoe, Yukon, Escalade:* **1999–2000**—Engine may misfire, water may mix with fuel, or the Service Engine light may come on if water has entered through the EVAP canister. Correct the problem by installing a new EVAP canister vent solenoid. **1999–2004**—Transmission failure caused by debris in the 2–3 shift solenoid bleed orifice. **2000–03**—Excessive engine noise (see following page). **2003–04**—Inoperative AWD. • Noisy, inoperative power windows. • Faulty heated seats. **2004–06**—Instrument panel ticking. **2004–07**—Poor AC performance. *Tahoe, Yukon:* **1999**—Hard starts on vehicles equipped with a 6.5L diesel engine may signal the need to replace the shutoff solenoid. • A steering-column squeak noise may be silenced by replacing the steering-wheel SIR module coil assembly. **1999–2000**—No-starts, hard starts, backfires, or an unusual grinding sound when starting can be eliminated by replacing the crankshaft position sensor. • GM, at no charge, will repaint the outside rear-view mirror housing if it turns a chalky, dull colour. • Stalling or surging following a stop may be corrected by re-calibrating the PCM settings. **1999–2002**—Paint

ENGINE KNOCK OR LIFTER NOISE (REPLACE O-RING)

2001–02 Chevrolet Camaro

2001–03 Chevrolet Corvette

2001–02 Pontiac Firebird

2002–03 Cadillac Escalade, Escalade EXT

2000–03 Chevrolet Suburban, Tahoe

2001–03 Chevrolet Silverado

2002–03 Chevrolet Avalanche

2000–03 GMC Yukon, Yukon XL

2001–03 GMC Sierra

with 4.8L, 5.3L, 5.7L or 6.0L V8 Engine (VINs V, T, Z, G, S, N, U – RPOs LR4, LM7, L59, LS1, LS6, LQ9, LQ4)

CONDITION: Some customers may comment on an engine tick noise. The distinguishing characteristic of this condition is that it likely will have been present since new, and is typically noticed within the first 161–322 km (100–200 mi.). The noise may often be diagnosed as a collapsed lifter. Additionally, the noise may be present at cold start and appear to diminish and then return as the engine warms to operating temperature. This noise is different from other noises that may begin to occur at 3,219–4,828 km (2,000–3,000 mi.).

delamination, peeling, or fading. **1999–2005**—No Reverse, Second, or Fourth gear may be caused by a defective reaction sun gear. *Suburban, Yukon XL:* **1999**—If you can't engage the 4×4 mode, it may be necessary to replace the transfer-case actuator/shift detent plunger. • AC blows hot air because of faulty inlet actuator. **1999–2000**—Increased accelerator pedal effort can be fixed by replacing the throttle body. • Silence front-door rattling by replacing the door window regulator bolts. **2000–05**—Tips on silencing a differential whine are found in TSB #03-04-17-001E. **2002–03**—Second-row footwell carpet may be wet with dirty water. GM will seal the rear wheelhouse under warranty (Bulletin #03-08-57-001; May 2003). **2002–04**—Suspension clunk, slap. GM will replace the spring insert and insulator for free (see Silverado "Secret Warranties/Internal Bulletins/Service Tips"). **2002–05**—Outside mirrors may fold in at highway speeds. **2002–06**—Discoloured cargo covers or body cladding (seen as a chalky colour) will be corrected under a secret warranty. **2003**—Harsh automatic transmission 1–2 shifting, slipping caused by a faulty pressure control solenoid (Bulletin #03-07-30-020; May 2003). **2003–05**—Inoperative AC blower motor should be replaced (hmmm...sounds like a defect to me). • Tires go flat slowly because of defective grommet. • Faulty AC and audio (replace RSA module). • Front suspension rattle, squeak. *Escalade:* **2006–07**—A Low Oil level indicator light or a visible oil leak may signal the need to reseal the oil pressure sensor. **2007**—Liftgate malfunctions. • Wind noise from the rear liftgate area. • Inoperative power-assisted running boards. • Steering gear fluid leaks. • Water leak guide. • Silencing buzz, rattles from the instrument panel. • High-pitched whistle heard while driving. • Driver seat squeak or creak. • Squeak, itching noise heard from the upper door area (replace the roof drip weatherstrip). • Rear suspension rubbing, clunking noise. • Inoperative keyless entry feature. • Front bumper paint peeling. **2007–08**—Great effort to close hood. • Buzz, rattle heard from the front fender area when accelerating.

ESCALADE, SUBURBAN, TAHOE, YUKON PROFILE

	1999	2000	2001	2002	2003	2004	2005	2006	2007
Cost Price ($) (negotiable)									
Escalade (30%)	63,055	63,805	63,805	72,700	74,970	70,675	71,405	71,805	72,175
Suburban (29%)	34,620	34,620	37,905	45,875	46,670	46,680	49,820	47,000	46,935
Tahoe, Yukon (30%)	31,555	33,305	31,715	42,680	42,530	44,105	45,615	42,795	45,455
4×4 (30%)	34,555	36,715	35,010	46,895	50,385	42,530	48,870	47,785	47,175
Yukon XL (30%)	—	34,620	35,760	46,895	47,290	44,720	50,415	47,665	47,595
Used Values ($)									
Escalade ▲	10,000	11,500	13,500	15,500	19,500	22,000	25,000	32,000	44,000
Escalade ▼	9,000	10,500	12,500	14,000	18,500	20,000	23,000	30,000	42,000
Suburban ▲	6,000	7,500	8,500	12,000	13,000	15,000	17,500	23,500	29,000
Suburban ▼	5,000	7,000	8,000	11,000	12,000	13,500	16,000	22,000	27,000
Tahoe, Yukon ▲	5,500	7,000	8,000	9,500	11,000	12,500	14,000	19,000	25,000
Tahoe, Yukon ▼	4,500	6,500	7,500	8,500	10,000	11,500	13,000	17,500	23,000
4×4 ▲	6,500	7,500	8,500	9,500	11,000	15,000	17,000	22,000	28,000
4×4 ▼	6,000	7,000	8,000	9,000	10,500	13,500	15,000	20,000	27,000
Yukon XL ▲	—	8,500	10,000	11,500	15,500	19,000	17,500	19,000	29,000
Yukon XL ▼	—	8,000	9,500	10,500	14,000	18,000	16,000	18,000	27,000
Reliability									
Tahoe, Yukon	3	3	3	3	3	3	3	4	2
Suburban, Yukon XL	3	3	3	3	3	3	3	4	2
Crash Safety (F)									
Suburban, Yukon XL	4	—	4	4	4	4	4	4	5
Denali 4d	—	4	—	—	—	—	—	—	—
Tahoe/Yukon	4	4	3	3	4	4	4	4	5
Escalade	4	4	—	3	4	4	4	4	5
Rollover (Escalade)	—	—	—	3	3	—	3	3	3

Note: The 2008 Tahoe Hybrid's crashworthiness scores are identical to the gasoline-powered 2007 Tahoe. All of the 2008 models posted crashworthiness ratings identical to the 2007s.

General Motors/Saturn

OUTLOOK

The Outlook's first model year was 2007; it is rated in Appendix I.

Toyota

SEQUOIA ★★★★★

RATING: Recommended (2005–08); Above Average (2001–04). A refined, well-equipped, and fairly reliable SUV that was way overpriced at $65,000 (2007) and is now much cheaper. **Strong points:** Price cuts on 2008s and 2009s. Potent V8 performance, though the earlier V8 was a decent performer. Plenty of torque and low-end grunt; acceptable big-truck manoeuvrability; comfortable ride; lots of passenger space and cargo room; well appointed, with a nice array of easy-to-understand-and-access instruments and controls; tailgate window that fully powers down; a smoother ride and roomier, more ergonomic, and plusher interior than with the 2007 model; much more third-row seatroom, aided by a sliding second-row seat; high-quality mechanical components and body construction; back door on 2008 takes less effort to close; and the vehicle runs on regular fuel. **Weak points:** High-priced; Sequoia's heft compromises acceleration needed for passing and merging up through the 2007 models; chronic engine and transmission hesitation/surging from 2001; large turning radius (shortened on the 2008); right rear-quarter vision is obstructed by the second-row head restraint; tough to parallel park; step-in may be difficult for some; rear-seat access a bit awkward prior to the 2008's wide doors; vehicle shakes when driven with the rear window open; clock is hard to see; high freight and PDI charges; and poor fuel economy. **New for 2008:** The restyled Sequoia is moved to the Tundra large pickup truck platform and gets more power with an available

2008 SEQUOIA TECHNICAL DATA

POWERTRAIN (4×4)
Engines: 4.7L V8 (276 hp) • 5.7L V8 (381 hp); Transmissions: 5-speed auto. • 6-speed auto.

DIMENSION/CAPACITY
Passengers: 2/3/3; Wheelbase: 122.0 in.; H: 74.6/L: 205.1/W: 79.8 in.; Headroom F/R1/R2: 5.0/4.0/3.0 in.; Legroom F/R1/R2: 41.0/32.0/26.0 in.; Cargo volume: 73.6 cu. ft.; Fuel tank: 100L/regular; Tow limit: 7,800–10,000 lb.; Load capacity: 1,250 lb.; GVWR: 7,000–7,300 lb.; Turning circle: 39.0 ft.; Ground clearance: 9.9 in.; Weight: 5,680/5,920 lb.; 5.7L: 5,730/5,030 lb.

381-hp 5.7L V8 engine. It's actually bigger than a Chevrolet Tahoe and about equal in size to a Ford Expedition.

MODEL HISTORY: A bit narrower than the domestic competition, the Sequoia nevertheless offers eight-passenger, third-row seating and generous interior dimensions. A high ground clearance allows for some off-roading; however, the rear suspension has been modified to prioritize comfortable cruising. Safety features include Vehicle Stability Control, standard four-wheel disc brakes with ABS, side curtain airbags, and three-way seat belts for all passenger positions.

2003—A rear load-levelling suspension, a centre differential lock button, Brake Assist, a seven-pin towing connect, and larger wheels and tires. **2005**—A more powerful engine (42 more horses); a new 5-speed, electronically controlled automatic transmission (ECT) with lock-up torque converter; an Overdrive cancel switch and cooler; and a tire-pressure monitoring system.

COST ANALYSIS: In Canada, a 2008 Sequoia sells for $44,675, or $13,535 less than the first-series 2008 version. In the States, the same Sequoia lists for $34,150 (U.S.). C'mon Toyota, you can do much better than that. In Canada, an upgraded 2005 is an excellent buy at $28,000. **Best alternatives:** Ford's reworked and less tippy 2002 or later Explorer 4×4 or Expedition/Excursion are bargains even when their poor reliability is taken into account. **Rebates:** $3,500 rebates plus other discounts and zero percent financing. **Delivery/PDI:** $1,390. **Warranty:** Bumper-to-bumper 3 years/60,000 km; powertrain 5 years/100,000 km; rust perforation 5 years/unlimited km. **Supplementary warranty:** Not needed. **Options:** Nothing worth the extra money. **Depreciation:** Unusually rapid for a Toyota. **Insurance cost:** Higher than average. **Parts supply/cost:** Tundra-sourced parts aren't expensive and are easily found. **Annual maintenance cost:** Much lower than average. **Highway/city fuel economy:** 12.1/15.7 L/100 km.

QUALITY/RELIABILITY: Better than average. **Owner-reported problems:** Premature brake wear and vibration; excessive engine noise; rotten-egg exhaust smell (Toyota service bulletins recommend replacing the catalytic converter under warranty); pungent ammonia smell. **Warranty performance:** Better than average.

ROAD PERFORMANCE: Acceleration/torque: Acceleration is quick, smooth, and quiet. **Transmission:** Flawless performance. The Multi-Mode 4×4 features shift-on-the-fly from rear-drive to four-wheel drive. Multi-Mode's Automatic Disconnecting Differential (ADD) provides part-time 4×4 but adds the capability of running in 4×4 mode on dry pavement, similar to a full-time 4×4 system. **Steering:** Precise and responsive; less trucklike than the Tahoe or Expedition. **Routine handling:** Pleasant ride quality and handling except in tight spots and twisty roads, where the 2007 and earlier Sequoias' size and large turning radius compromise handling. Nevertheless, the standard Torsen limited-slip centre differential improves traction on challenging terrain. Very effective Vehicle Stability Control, and an automatic anti-skid system that regulates the throttle and selectively applies the brakes to individual wheels to correct under-steer or over-steer.

Braking: Braking is exceptional when the system isn't breaking down (see "Safety Complaints").

 SAFETY SUMMARY: Airbags: Front, and side curtain. **ABS:** Standard; disc/disc. **Safety belt pretensioners:** Front. **Traction control:** Yes. **Visibility F/R:** ★★★★★/★★. **Pet transport:** ★★★★★.

SAFETY COMPLAINTS: All years: Inconsistent braking; Brake light constantly lit. • If the back window is opened while underway, the vehicle vibrates wildly and creates a vacuum that's painful to the ears. Rolling down the front window or opening the moonroof eliminates the problem. • Loose or poorly fitted trim panels. **2001**—Airbags fail to deploy. • Sudden stalling. • Chronic hesitation when accelerating. • Windshield is easily cracked by road debris. • Passengers slip on running board's "non-slip" strip. **2001–02**—Excessive vibration when braking. **2001–03**—Anti-skid system activates when it isn't needed. **2002**—Vehicle will suddenly drift across the highway. • Faulty automatic stability control system. • Defective drive shaft. **2003**—Transmission may slip from Park to Drive or from Park to Reverse. • Vehicle surges from a stop or when accelerating out of a turn. • Engine drops to idle for about 6–10 seconds when completing a turn. • Rear-view mirror is too small. • Noxious gas fumes enter the cabin. • Door latch failure allows door to open when turning. **2004**—Separation of passenger-side front wheel. • Excessive vibration; vehicle doesn't track well. **2005**—Excessive idle speed. • When vehicle is first started, engine surging causes rear wheels to spin, and the vehicle slides sideways, out of control. • Transmission hesitates and then jerks forward. • When going down an incline with foot off the gas pedal, vehicle won't coast for the first 5 or 6 seconds. • Sudden stalling during highway travel. • Brakes suddenly give out. **2006**—Sudden acceleration when parking. • Surging when stopped or when using the cruise control. • Excessive shimmy with Dunlop Grandtrek tires. • When coming to a stop, it feels like the vehicle has been rear-ended. • Wheel lug nuts fracture. • Radiator leak causes engine overheating. **2007**—Rear doors close unexpectedly on passengers. • Steering-wheel lock traps the ignition key, causes no-starts. • Exhaust fumes are toxic:

> The fumes have caused my friends to become ill with nausea, headaches, and sleepiness. The fumes have caused me to become very sleepy when traveling, and my friends say my thinking is off in the last couple of months.

Secret Warranties/Internal Bulletins/Service Tips

2001—Inoperative High Beam indicator light. • Foglight moisture. • Front seat cover damage. **2001–02**—Hard starts or no-starts. • Vibrating front brakes can be corrected by installing improved front brake caliper assemblies. • Upgraded back-door pull strap. **2001–03**—AC compressor durability improvement (see following page). **2001–04**—If the AC doesn't sufficiently cool the cabin, TSB #AC004-04 says that the water control valve is the likely culprit. • Faulty oil pressure gauge. **2002–06**—Diagnosing and correcting vehicles that pull to one side. **2003–07**—

POOR AC COMPRESSOR DURABILITY

BULLETIN NO.: AC001-04   **DATE: FEBRUARY 11, 2004**

2001–03 Sequoia

To improve the durability and integrity of repairs on 2001–03 model year Sequoia vehicles with rear AC, a new suction tube and in-line filter system is now available. Please follow the procedures in this bulletin if the compressor is being replaced because of a noise concern and/or has seized.

Windshield ticking. **2004–05**—AC blower motor noise. **2004–07**—Front seat squeak. **2005**—No-start in cold temperatures. • An upgraded catalytic converter has been developed to reduce sulfur dioxide exhaust odour. **2006–07**—Driveline vibration at 100 km/h.

SEQUOIA PROFILE

	2001	2002	2003	2004	2005	2006	2007
Cost Price ($) (firm)							
SR-5 (25%)	45,400	45,670	48,100	53,650	59,530	58,210	—
Limited (25%)	57,900	58,205	52,150	63,500	65,855	66,100	65,100
Used Values ($)							
SR-5 ▲	13,000	15,000	16,500	19,500	28,000	31,000	—
SR-5 ▼	11,500	14,000	15,500	18,000	26,000	29,000	—
Limited ▲	14,000	16,000	18,500	22,000	29,000	35,000	40,000
Limited ▼	13,000	14,500	17,000	20,000	27,000	33,000	38,000
Reliability	5	5	5	5	5	5	5
Crash Safety (F)	—	4	5	5	—	—	—
Rollover	—	3	3	—	—	—	—

Note: The 2001 Limited sold for $22,500 more than the SR-5; today, there is barely $1,000 difference. The Limited's depreciation is brutal.

MINIVANS AND VANS

In Praise of Older...Vans

Would KISS fans have remained so loyal in the 1970s, if underage followers couldn't drink Pabst Blue Ribbon and take bong hits in the privacy of a vehicle that was big enough for its own drapes? Would the punk rock movement of the 1980s and grunge movement of the '90s have existed if Mike Ness and Kurt Cobain were forced to rent U-Hauls to tote their gear? Would anyone have blown all that time following the Grateful Dead, if they had to search for the next miracle with their bongos and granola crammed in the trunk of a Ford Taurus?

Too many customers have submitted to the siren song of the minivan, which peaked in sales with 1.37 million units in 2000. It's a baffling figure, considering all minivans are impossible to have sex in and smell like spoiled apple juice.

PETER HARTLAUB
SAN FRANCISCO CHRONICLE
OCTOBER 14, 2005

Two Choices

Like sport-utilities, minivans fall into two categories: upsized cars and downsized trucks. The upsized cars are people-movers. They're mostly front-drives, they handle like cars, and they get much better fuel economy than truck-based rear-drives. The Honda Odyssey, Toyota Sienna, and Hyundai Entourage/Kia Sedona are the best examples of this kind of minivan, with Chrysler's Caravan-sourced lineup running fourth.

GM's Astro and Safari and Ford's Aerostar are primitive minivans based on a downsized truck platform. They are dirt cheap, particularly now that they are no longer manufactured. Using rear-drive, 6-cylinder engines and heavier mechanical components, these minivans handle both cargo and passengers. On the negative side, their fuel economy is no match for the front-drives, and highway handling is ponderous at best. Nevertheless, most rear-drive GM and Ford minivans are also somewhat more reliable and less costly to maintain than the front-drive Chrysler Caravan, Ford Windstar/Freestar, or GM's other products (Montana, Montana SV6, Relay, Silhouette, Terraza, Trans Sport, Venture, and Uplander). This is due mainly to their use of sturdy mechanicals that are easily diagnosed and repaired by independent mechanics everywhere. As AWDs, though, all of these Detroit minivans, whether front- or rear-drive, will keep you in the repair bay for weeks fixing powertrain defects that can easily cost up to $3,000 to repair.

NEW CARAVAN
$7000 Cash Back
or 0% Interest

2005 GRAND CARAVAN
7 pass, full pwr. group tri-zone A/C, loaded. Was $34,005
OUR PRICE $18,888*

Detroit automakers combat their poor quality reputations by cutting prices instead of improving their products.

Nevertheless, rear-drive vans are better suited for towing trailers in the 1,600–2,950 kg (3,500–6,500 lb.) range. Most automakers say their front-drive minivans can pull up to 1,600 kg with an optional towing package (often costing almost $1,000 extra), but don't you believe it. Owners report white-knuckle driving and premature powertrain failures caused by the extra load. It just stands to reason that front-drives equipped with engines and transmissions that blow out at 60,000–100,000 km under normal driving conditions are going to meet their demise much earlier under a full load.

Quality—Asians Best, Chrysler Next

Quality control has always been a more serious problem with minivans than vans, trucks, or SUVs because owners want a vehicle that provides both transportation and housing in a relatively small, "garageable" vehicle. This design makes minivans more complex and difficult to service. Plus, supplier cost-cutting and the addition of many new convenience, performance, and safety features have resulted in a steep decline in minivan reliability among the Detroit Big Three.

"Flower power" early VW minivans were noted for their Frigidaire interiors and motor-scooter performance.

Even VW, with the market all to itself in the '60s, couldn't build a minivan that was both reliable and an adequate highway performer. Despite a temporary hippie cult following, VW minivans quickly became known for constant breakdowns, glacial acceleration, and a inadequate heating system only raging teenage hormones could tolerate. To this day, the VW Eurovan is more of a curiosity than a credible transporter. VW's Chrysler-sourced 2009 minivan is much better built, but if you're thinking about getting one, wait a year for quality to improve.

Chrysler

Chrysler learned from VW's production and marketing mistakes and launched its own minivans in 1984. The vehicles were seen as fairly reliable and efficient

people-haulers and were an immediate success. Since they were backed by Chrysler's 7-year bumper-to-bumper warranty, much of the sting was taken out of repair costs. Since then, these minivans have dominated the market despite their shorter warranty and disintegrating automatic transmissions, brakes, air conditioners, and suspension strut towers. In fact, it's amazing how little Chrysler's defect patterns have changed during the past two decades.

From 1987 through 2007, Chrysler marketed two minivans: a standard version and the longer Grand models, which include the top-of-the-line Town & Country. Following this year's redesign, only the Grands are left, equipped with a 3.3L flexible-fuel V6 and an optional 4.0L six. The larger engine is coupled to a fairly responsive 6-speed automatic transmission, while the 3.3L uses a problematic, less-efficient 4-speed automatic.

Chrysler's revamped 2008–09 minivans pile on convenience features and house them in a much larger interior. The question remains, will Chrysler's new owners keep the minivan, or will they sell it off piecemeal along with the Jeep division to recoup their estimated $1.6-billion loss for 2007?

Chrysler minivans have always been noted more for their safety and convenience features than for their on-road performance. Buyers get state-of-the-art ergonomics, power liftgates, lots of entertainment goodies, swivel seats, hidden storage and seat compartments, and a user-friendly instrument panel. Fuel economy is on par with competing SUVs.

5- and 6-year-old full-sized rear-drive Chrysler vans are hidden bargains that are still relatively easy to find, a breeze to service, and versatile enough to satisfy retirees, campers, and small businesses.

The company's once-comprehensive warranty has changed dramatically over the years, however. It was the industry's longest and most complete powertrain warranty available, but since 2007 that's no longer the case. Chrysler Canada (through its new Cerberus owners) has replaced its 7-year powertrain warranty (resurrected from 2002 through 2004) with a 5-year guarantee, while extending a lifetime warranty to buyers in the States.

When it comes to full-sized rear-drive vans, Chrysler can't be beaten, but once again, the company's new owners couldn't leave well enough alone. For the 2004 model year, Daimler-Benz replaced the Dodge Tradesman and Ram B-series vans with the Sprinter, a $40,000 diesel-powered, 5-cylinder Mercedes van that was previously sold and serviced by Freightliner. Not surprisingly, the Sprinter has been a marketing disaster due to its heft, mediocre fuel economy (yes, despite being diesel-powered), problematic servicing, and rapid depreciation.

Ford

Ford's minivans have gone from bad to worse to gone. Its first minivan, the 1985–97 Aerostar, was fairly dependable, although it did have some tranny, brake, and coil spring problems. Collapsing coil springs may cause tire blowouts on all model years, although 1988–90 models are covered by a regional recall. Other model years fall under a "goodwill" program, as this *Lemon-Aid* reader reports:

> On vacation in Washington, our 1995 Aerostar blew a tire that was worn right through from the left rear coil spring (broken in two places). The right rear coil spring is broken, as well. I showed Dams Ford in Surrey, B.C., the broken spring and they have "graciously" offered to replace the tire or repair the right side at no cost to us.

Ford's quality decline continued with the Mercury Villager, a co-venture that also produced the Nissan Quest. The Villager/Quest duo lasted through the 2000 model year. Quest continued on its own with minimal changes to its 2001 through 2003 models. When the 2004 Quest was totally redesigned, it was so glitch-prone and poorly designed that Nissan dedicated over 200 engineers to the task of correcting factory-related defects and tweaking the looks.

Then Ford brought out the 1995 Windstar—one of the lowest quality, most dangerous minivans ever built. Renamed the Freestar in 2004, its failure-prone powertrain, suspension (broken coil springs), electrical, fuel, and braking systems can put both your wallet and your life at risk. Freestar and its U.S. Mercury Monterey stablemate got the axe in 2007. Both minivans have been poor sellers since their 2003 debut. In their place, Ford plans to introduce a 2009 Five Hundred/Mercury Montego crossover variant with boxy styling and a lower and wider stance.

Ford has compounded the Windstar/Freestar's failings by copping a hard-nosed attitude toward customers with complaints and by refusing warranty coverage for what are clearly factory-induced defects. Fortunately, there's been a flood of Canadian small claims court decisions that have come to Ford owners' aid when Ford wouldn't. These Canadian courts say Ford and its dealers must pay for engine and transmission repairs, even if the original warranty has expired (see Part Three).

Okay, I know GM has a secret warranty to plug roof holes free of charge, but why have holes in the first place?

General Motors

The second-best of a bad lot, GM's minivans are the most disappointing of all—not because of poor quality, but because of missed opportunities and shattered consumer expectations. Despite frequent redesigns and billions of dollars thrown at a series of 5-year plans, almost all of its minivans (except for the little-changed, discontinued, rear-drive Astro and Safari) are poor performers. Take, for example, GM's latest quartet of front-drive minivans: the Buick Terraza, Chevy Uplander, Saturn Relay, and Pontiac SV6. These identical models are slightly restyled versions of the decade-old Venture and Montana—spin-offs of GM's equally disappointing front-drive cars—known for their high maintenance costs, poor handling, lack of power, and fit and finish that's characterized by rust holes in the roof and blistering, peeling paint.

One would think that models that have been around for as long as these have would have quality built into them incrementally.

Think again. Each time General Motors tackles a generic defect—like failure-prone engine intake manifolds (part of GM's secret class action settlement talks), blown-out automatic transmissions, and defective brake and fuel systems—the problems get worse, and GM's market share continues to plummet. Realizing that it cannot survive by building minivans that few people buy, GM plans to ditch all of its minivans after 2008 in favour of large, crossover-style wagons.

Asian automakers

Asian competitors don't build perfect machines either, as a quick perusal of NHTSA-registered safety complaints, service bulletins, and online complaint forums will quickly confirm. Asian companies, looking to keep costs down, have also been bedeviled by chronic engine and automatic transmission failures, sliding door malfunctions, catastrophic tire blowouts, and electrical malfunctions.

There is one big difference, though—Asian companies usually admit to their mistakes. The Big Three cover them up.

Some words of warning about Hyundai, Kia, Nissan, and Toyota: Kia's entire model lineup has been seriously failure-prone through the 2004 model year. Hyundai turned its attention to improving Kia quality with redesigned 2005 models that addressed most of the vehicles' shortcomings. Hyundai's Entourage has had an almost problem-free 2007 model launch, and the 2008–09 models can only get better, though they aren't expected to be reworked until 2010. At the moment, new Hyundai and Kia minivans represent the best minivan choice from a price/quality perspective.

Nissan and Toyota have had the opposite problem. They made fairly dependable vehicles, including minivans, for over three decades. However, when the companies redesigned the 2004 Nissan Quest and Toyota Sienna minivans and Nissan launched the Titan and Armada trucks, reliability plummeted with these models. Even four years after the redesigns, overall quality is still nowhere near the pre-2004 levels. Toyota Tacoma and Tundra pickups have been especially failure-prone.

European automakers

Finally we come back to where we started—Volkswagen. Its Vanagon (1979) and Eurovan/Camper (1993) have never been taken seriously since they came to North America in 1950 as a Transporter cargo van and a nine-seat, 21-window Microbus. A reputation for poor overall quality, puny engines, and insufficient parts and servicing support continues to drive buyers away.

Getting More for Less

Most minivans are overpriced for what are essentially upgraded cars or downsized trucks, and motorists needing vehicles with large cargo- and passenger-carrying capacities should consider Chrysler, Ford, or GM full-sized vans, even if it means sacrificing some fuel economy. You just can't beat their excellent forward vision and easy-to-customize interiors. Furthermore, parts are easily found and competitively priced because of the large number of independent suppliers.

Please remember that the following minivan ratings may differ somewhat from those in *Lemon-Aid Used Cars and Minivans 2007–08* because they use more current data and an additional author review of the ratings. Some minivans that are no longer built or are new on the market, like the Ford Aerostar and Mazda5, are given mini-ratings in Appendix I.

Full-Sized Vans

The North American full-sized van is a venerable institution. Contractors, electricians, and plumbers have turned these vans into portable toolboxes. Campers have customized full-sized vans to travel the country in comfort with a canoe on top and a trailer in tow. And retirees are cruising our nation's highways with large vans chock full of every safety and convenience feature imaginable, turning their vehicles into mobile condos. Large family? Hockey mom? No problem—an extended van can seat up to 15. Whatever the need, the full-sized van can accommodate it—if you can afford the gas.

Cheaper than an RV

Sure, they may not be sleek, fuel efficient, or sexy, plus their styling is likely decades old and their popularity has certainly waned, but large vans are relatively cheap, versatile carriers that have more grunt than front-drives and are much more reliable too. Okay, they *are* fuel-thirsty. But I'll bet that'll be the last thought on your mind when you pass more fuel-efficient front-drive minivans stuck on the side of the road with cooked engines or burned-out transmissions. There are also some safety reasons for choosing a large van, including superb forward visibility and plenty of room to sit away from the airbag housing. SUVs and other vehicles are also less likely to run up over the van's frame and crash into the passenger compartment.

Handling, though, is definitely not carlike, regardless of any hype to the contrary. Expensive suspension modifications may be needed to produce a reasonable ride and manoeuvrability. Rear visibility is also problematic. Vans are susceptible to crosswinds, they wander at highway speeds, and they demand greater driving skills simply to corner safely and to park in the city. They are also not cheap, and in base form, all you get is a steel box on four wheels.

The 15-passenger van: A death trap on wheels?

15-passenger vans like the 1997 Ford Econoline that went out of control and killed seven basketball players and one teacher on January 13, 2008, near Bathurst, New Brunswick, are "death trap[s] on wheels," says The Safety Forum, a Washington,

D.C.–based consumer consulting group. In fact, NHTSA issued four consumer safety advisories about 15-passenger vans between 2000 and 2005, more than for any other vehicle type. They are considered so unsafe that the United States government has banned schools from purchasing them.

And Transport Canada sits back and smugly says, "We are studying the issue."

In 1971, the full-sized Dodge Ram Wagon passenger van, one of the oldest 15-passenger vans, came on the market. Since then, 15-passenger vans have been responsible for thousands of deaths and injuries. NHTSA says the vans are prone to fishtailing and are difficult to bring back under control, particularly at high speeds and especially when they are heavily loaded.

According to NHTSA, 1,003 people died in 15-passenger van crashes between 1990 and 2001, which included 316 rollovers. The National Transportation Safety Board (NTSB) has found that 15-passenger vans are involved in a greater number of single-vehicle accidents resulting in rollover crashes than any other passenger vehicle.

There are approximately 1.5 million 15-passenger vans registered in North America, used by schools, churches, daycare centres, retirement homes, and hotels. They were initially sold almost four decades ago as cargo vans, but automakers have left them relatively unchanged except for GM's introduction of electronic stability control on 2003 models and Ford's phase-in of the same feature on its 2006 versions.

In October 2004, IIHS released a study saying stability control systems could save up to 7,000 lives each year if they were standard equipment on all vehicles. Developed in the mid-1990s, this safety feature uses an electronic module that compares steering input with the van's actual steering arc and then, if necessary, makes quick, individual brake applications to enhance control and keep the vehicle on track. Brake pressure is automatically applied to each wheel individually when the module senses wheel slippage, understeer (plowing), or oversteer (fishtailing). If needed, engine torque may be adjusted to help the driver regain directional control.

Without stability control, the likelihood of a rollover during a sudden turn or when travelling over slippery roads increases significantly when five or more people are in the van. The van fishtails first, and, because it is top-heavy and overloaded in the rear, it then rolls over. This usually results in severe injuries and many casualties.

There are no federal regulations in Canada prohibiting the use of these vehicles by schools. A few provinces, such as Nova Scotia, ban their use in schools, but most provinces, including New Brunswick, allow them.

Transport Canada has treated 15-passenger van safety with benign neglect, despite being warned by the Canadian Standards Association in the summer of 2007 that the vans are killers. It still has no restrictions on the importation or sale of 15-passenger vans in this country.

What van owners should do

Stability and handling in turns can be improved with the addition of dual wheels to the back end of the van. For the manufacturers, this would cost $300 to $400 (U.S.) per vehicle to retrofit used vans, and about $135 (U.S.) per vehicle to equip new vans.

If your 15-passenger van is not equipped with stability control, stop using it. For group transportation, use a small school bus or rent a 2004–08 stability-control-equipped Ford or GM van (expect to pay about $100 a day) instead. If you still need to use your van while you look for other options, do the following to lower the risk of an accident:

- Check your model's NHTSA crashworthiness and rollover ratings (*www.safercar. gov/Index2.cfm*). Ford's 2006–08 models got two stars out of five for rollover resistance, while GM's 2004–08 models got a three-star rating. Also look for good frontal- and side-impact occupant-protection scores.
- Remove the rear seat to reduce weight behind the rear axle.
- Before and after every trip, conduct a full safety inspection. Check the tires, as tire blowouts are a major cause of rollovers.

- Use winter-rated tires in the winter, not poor-performing all-season tires.
- Keep a fire extinguisher, first aid kit, and cell phone in the van any time you travel.
- Make sure all drivers have a commercial driver's licence.
- To reduce the risk of rollover, allow only nine people (including the driver) to ride in the vehicle.
- Do not transport anything on the roof or tow anything behind the van.
- Make sure all occupants wear their seat belts at all times.

Incidentally, Ford paid $37.5 million in a 2004 Kentucky van crash case after a Scott County jury found the automaker's 15-passenger van to be responsible for three deaths.

Quality considerations

Ford, GM, and Chrysler have substantially redesigned their full-sized vans within the past few years to improve both the handling and the ride, and to add important safety features like stability control, ABS, and additional airbags. Following this redesign, GM has led the Detroit pack with better-handling and smoother-riding models than those available from Ford or Chrysler.

Because Chrysler has been moving considerably upscale with the Mercedes-bred rear-drive Dodge Sprinter, Ford and GM should do quite well. GM has hedged its bets, however, by shoehorning the Duramax 6600 diesel engine into its large vans. This switchover should make the vans less fuel-thirsty and more attractive to frugal buyers. However, overall dependability is expected to drop and servicing costs are expected to increase substantially due to the Duramax's poor past performance combined with the government-mandated reformulation of diesel fuel planned for early next year (see "More Dirt on Diesels," page 71).

Chrysler's full-sized, American-built rear-drive vans are more reliable than its front-drive minivans. On one hand, this isn't saying much when you consider the expensive repair bills generated by blown transmissions and collapsed ball joints. On the other hand, the problems are well known and easily fixed.

Ford's Econoline joins GM in the rear of the pack from a warranty performance standpoint. Both companies are sticking with 5-year guarantees, even though they are in serious need of a 7-year powertrain warranty to restore confidence in their lineups. Ford's 2008 Econoline has been re-engineered and restyled.

The quality of GM's full-sized vans hasn't improved much over the years (though it isn't as bad as the company's front-drive minivans), and it's about equal to what Ford and Chrysler offer (besides the Dodge Sprinter). Some of the more common problems shared by all three automakers are engine and drivetrain breakdowns, brake failures, premature brake and suspension/steering wearout, AC failures, electrical and computer module glitches, and both manual- and power-sliding-door defects.

The reason there's such similarity in defect trends among Asian and Detroit van builders is that they all get their key components from a small band of suppliers. And as they cut supplier profits, quality goes down the drain. Hence, as Toyota and Honda become more tightfisted in their supplier payouts, they also see a corresponding quality decline, evidenced by engine and transmission defects and sliding-door failures.

The important difference lies in how each automaker responds to these quality problems. Chrysler brought back its 7-year base powertrain warranty in 2001 and then dropped it again on 2005 models. Toyota and Honda set up publicly disclosed 7- and 8-year "goodwill" extended warranties after owners blasted the companies for blaming engine and transmission defects on "poor maintenance." Ford and GM hide their faults, paying repair costs on a case-by-case basis, depending on how much the customer yells. By the time they finally admit there is a factory-related problem and extend their corresponding warranties retroactively, public confidence has already been shattered.

Full-sized van advantages
- Lots of reasonably priced converted used models are available.
- Gasoline and diesel versions are easy to find.
- They are easy to repair, with excellent parts availability at reasonable prices.
- There's a huge network of independent converters.
- They are versatile people- and cargo-haulers.
- They can easily be converted to carry physically challenged occupants.
- You get a commanding view of the road.
- Front and side crash protection is excellent.
- Collision repair costs are much lower than average.

Full-sized van disadvantages
- They are quintessential gas hogs.
- Depreciated prices are still higher than what many people can afford.
- Homeowners' associations may prohibit vans parked outdoors.
- Base models require costly options for comfortable performance.
- Inadequate standard suspension may need expensive modifications.
- Base engines provide little power.
- Base models feature uncomfortable seats.
- Expensive interior upgrades are necessary.
- Standard-issue tires perform poorly. (Try replacing them with Michelin or Yokohama.)
- Handling at highway speeds and in winter conditions is poor.
- The engine is difficult to access.
- Excessive road and tire noise resonates in the cabin.
- Large interior requires an extra AC and defroster.
- Washing and waxing can be an all-day affair.
- Clunky transmission noise amplified by "echo chamber" styling.

- Sliding side doors usually rust out at the bottom and top runners; body panels rust out at the left and right upper-front welds, just above the windshield; and water pours off the roof into the power-window housing or onto front-seat passengers when they exit. (Add extra waterproofing to the window motor assembly, or expect to replace the motors every few years.)

Safety-related problems

- Inadequate acceleration
- Unforgiving, risky handling
- Trucklike manoeuvrability
- Uneven braking and loss of directional stability
- High-speed instability
- Poor rearward visibility
- Poor heating, defrosting, and ventilation systems
- Poor frontal crash protection (improved with airbag technology)
- Hazardous sliding doors
- Driveability affected by lateral winds

Full-sized van tips

- Car washes spray directly into door-panel window channels, playing havoc with the electrically operated windows and requiring at least $400 per door to correct.
- Side mirrors are extremely hazardous, as objects are much closer than they appear. Smart owners soon learn to rely on the rear-view mirror instead, pulling back into traffic only when they can see a full profile of the following car.
- Built-in ice coolers are of minimal value. They're hard to clean and don't hold much.
- Heavy doors frequently need oiling and adjusting.
- Large front windshields tend to leak water through the top moulding, and the surrounding metal panels rust out early. Roof leaks are legion and are best plugged by adding a "hi-top" roof.
- It's a good idea to buy a light-coloured van. Dirt won't show as much, they're cooler in the summer (reflecting rather than absorbing the sun's rays), and the colour is easier to match when repainting. Make sure the light-coloured dash doesn't reflect onto the front windshield in the daytime and gauges don't reflect at night.

Conversion Vans

A conversion van feels good and is cheaper than dirt these days. With dual captain's chairs (large plush seats with arm supports), lots of power accessories, a TV, a sofa/bed, and window shades…hey, it meets all our fantasies (or at least mine).

GM has one-half of a dying conversion van market, Ford has about one-third, and Dodge has the rest. Generating from $3,500 to $5,500 in profits, these new vans are coming under fire from more fuel-efficient SUVs and minivans. GM bought most of the conversion van companies in 2004 following a dismal decade of poor conversion sales. Since 1988, conversions have declined by more than 90 percent. In fact, during the first half of 2004, consumers bought only about 15,000 conversion vans, compared with 204,000 units sold in 1988. 2008 sales have also declined dramatically.

MINIVAN AND VAN RATINGS

RECOMMENDED
Honda Odyssey (2007–08)

Hyundai Entourage (2007–08)

ABOVE AVERAGE
Ford Econoline Cargo Van,
    Club Wagon (2008)
Honda Odyssey (2003–05)

Kia Sedona (2006–08)
Toyota Sienna (2005–08)

AVERAGE
Chrysler Caravan, Voyager,
    Grand Caravan, Grand Voyager,
    Town & Country (2002–08)
Chrysler Ram Van, Ram Wagon
    (1980–2003)
Ford Econoline Cargo Van,
    Club Wagon (2004–07)
Ford Villager/Nissan Quest
    (1997–2002)

General Motors Astro, Safari
    (1996–2005)
General Motors Express,
    Savana (1996–2008)
Honda Odyssey (1996–2002; 2006)
Kia Sedona (2002–05)
Nissan Quest (2008)
Toyota Sienna (1998–2004)

BELOW AVERAGE
Chrysler Caravan, Voyager,
    Grand Caravan, Grand Voyager,
    Town & Country (1998–2001)
Ford Econoline Cargo Van,
    Club Wagon (1980–2003)

Ford Freestar (2004–07)
Ford Villager/Nissan Quest (1995–96)
General Motors Astro, Safari (1985–95)
Mazda MPV (1989–2006)
Nissan Quest (2004–07)

NOT RECOMMENDED
Chrysler Caravan, Voyager,
    Grand Caravan, Grand Voyager,
    Town & Country (1984–97)
Chrysler Sprinter (2004–08)
Ford Villager/Nissan Quest (1993–94)

Ford Windstar (1995–2003)
General Motors Montana, Montana SV6,
    Relay, Silhouette, Terraza, Trans Sport,
    Uplander, Venture (1990–2008)

Chrysler

CARAVAN, VOYAGER, GRAND CARAVAN, GRAND VOYAGER, TOWN & COUNTRY ★ ★ ★

RATING: Average (2002–08); Below Average (1998–2001); Not Recommended (1984–97). These minivans are for skinflint buyers willing to sacrifice some quality and refinement for a vehicle made in Canada and a low negotiated price (remember, the manufacturers' suggested retail price is just that—a *suggestion*). Nevertheless, everybody knows Chrysler, Ford, and GM minivans are at the bottom of the heap as far as quality and dependability are concerned. Chrysler, however, has had the best warranty for engines and transmissions, and only its transmissions are seriously defective. Ford and GM have serious transmission *and* engine problems. The Chrysler 2002–04 lineup with some of the original powertrain warranty remaining is your best choice. If the warranty has expired or was never offered, ask the dealer to throw it into the deal. **Strong points:** *2008 models:* Competitive pricing likely to be reduced further as Chrysler's new Cerberus owners scramble for money. Quiet cabin, better highway manners, nicely restyled exterior, more entertainment options. Swivel seating and table give this minivan an RV allure. *2007 and earlier models:* Not as risky a buy because less money is in play. Discounting can easily take $5,000 off of the suggested list prices, and rapid depreciation brings down ownership costs considerably on used models. Engines are fairly reliable; braking is excellent; there are lots of innovative convenience features, including a driver-side sliding door; instruments and controls are user-friendly; and there's plenty of interior room. **Weak points:** *2008 models:* No more cheapo base Caravan model. Chrysler U.S. gives lifetime powertrain warranties to buyers; Chrysler Canada shoppers get no extension. Plus, Chrysler warranty funds are shrinking, and dealers are near panic as unwanted 2007 passenger cars, trucks, and SUVs pile up on backlots. The minivan segment, along with its Jeep brand, will be the first sold to other automakers if the American economy continues to sour. Dealers will then run for the hills, warranties will be worthless, and service costs will spike. Ponderous handling is worse than other top minivans. Stow 'n Go seats store better than they seat. *2007 and earlier models:* Neither as feature-laden nor as refined as the Japanese and South Korean competition. The 7-year powertrain warranty isn't available on most models, and the chintzy base warranty is inadequate to deal with automatic transmission, ABS, and body defects. Resale value plummets because of discounting on new minivans. Poor acceleration with the coarse 4-cylinder engine, and the 3.8L V6 is a loud gas

2008 GRAND CARAVAN TECHNICAL DATA

POWERTRAIN (FRONT-DRIVE)
Engines: 3.3L V6 (175 hp) • 3.8L V6 (197 hp) • 4.0L V6 (251 hp); Transmissions: 4-speed auto. • 6-speed auto.

DIMENSION/CAPACITY
Passengers: 2/2/3; Wheelbase: 201.0 in.; H: 68.9/L: 202.5/W: 76.9 in.; Headroom F/R1/R2: 4.5/3.5/2.5 in.; Legroom F/R1/R2: 38.5/31.0/26.5 in.; Cargo volume: 32.3 cu. ft.; Fuel tank: 76L/regular; Tow limit: 1,000–3,800 lb.; Load capacity: 1,185 lb.; GVWR: 5,800 lb.; Turning circle: 38.0 ft.; Ground clearance: 5.1 in.; Weight: 4,321 lb.

hog that's not as smooth or polished as the Honda or Toyota competition. Both the 3- and 4-speed automatic transmissions perform poorly in different ways, but the 3-speed (dropped after the 2003 model year) is decidedly the worse of the two. Mediocre handling with the extended versions; inadequate headlight illumination; skimpy storage compartments. Get used to a cacophony of rattles, squeals, moans, and groans caused by the vehicle's poor construction and subpar components. Side airbags are optional, and crashworthiness has declined. **New for 2008:** Nicely restyled and repowered with an optional 4.0L V6 and 6-speed automatic transmission. Other new or improved features include optional Swivel 'n Go seats, a power fold-flat third-row seat, more standard safety equipment, and new entertainment gadgets. You also get a roomier interior with more storage space behind the third row of seats, a smoother ride, and a quieter cabin.

MODEL HISTORY: These versatile minivans provide acceptable highway performance and offer a wide array of safety features like traction and stability control, anti-lock brakes with brake assist, three rows of side curtain airbags, childproof locks, and optional seatback-integrated child safety seats. The Town & Country, a luxury version of the Caravan, comes equipped with a 4.0L V6 and oodles of luxury features.

For over 25 years, Chrysler's minivans have dominated the new- and used-minivan market, though sales have fallen during the past decade as a result of more competition and better product quality from Japanese and South Korean automakers. Nevertheless, Chrysler minivans offer pleasing styling and lots of convenience features at used prices that can be very attractive. They can carry up to seven passengers in relative comfort, and they ride and handle better than most truck-based minivans. The shorter-wheelbase minivans also offer better rear visibility and good ride quality, and they're more nimble and easier to park than truck-based minivans and larger front-drive versions. Cargo-hauling capability is more than adequate. Caravans also give you excellent braking, lots of innovative convenience features, user-friendly instruments and controls, a driver-side sliding door, and plenty of interior room. Depreciation, though, is much faster than with pickups, SUVs, and Japanese minivans.

Owner complaints and service bulletins show that these vehicles continue to have automatic transmission, electrical system, brake, suspension, and body deficiencies similar to previous versions produced before the Mercedes-Benz buyout in 1998. The following *Lemon-Aid* reader's email is rather typical:

> My 2003 Dodge Caravan is a piece of garbage. My new Caravan had a recall for a part in the transmission. It's noisy, rough running, and it doesn't get the 21–27 mpg [8.7–11.2 L/100 km] as advertised. 12 mpg [19.6 L/100 km] is more realistic.

Over the years, these minivans have posed serious safety risks because of their chronic electronic, mechanical, and body component failures. Owners report bizarre behaviour in their minivans, like seat belts that may strangle children, defective heated seats that will burn your butt, airbags that deploy when the ignition is turned on, transmissions that jump out of gear, and sudden stalling and electrical short circuits when within radar range of airports or military installations.

Although Cerberus, Chrysler's new owners, say quality on the 2008 models is much improved, don't bet on it. Astoundingly, 2007 and earlier minivans have continued to exhibit an array of serious mechanical deficiencies that belie Chrysler's so-called commitment to quality improvement. And this was when the company was owned by "deep pockets" German quality icon Mercedes-Benz. Some of the more serious and most common problems include steering-column glitches and the premature wearout of the following parts: the engine tensioner pulley, automatic transmission speed sensors, engine head gaskets, motor mounts, starter motors, front brake discs and pads (the brake pad material crumbles in your hands), front rotors and rear drums, brake master cylinders, suspension components, exhaust system components, ball joints, wheel bearings, water pumps, fuel pumps and pump wiring harnesses, radiators, heater cores, and AC units. Fuel injectors on all engines have been troublesome; the differential pin breaks through the automatic transmission casing; sliding doors malfunction; engine supports may be missing or not connected; tie-rods may suddenly break; oil pans may crack; and the power-steering pump frequently leaks. Factory-installed Goodyear tires often fail prematurely at 40,000–65,000 km.

Despite the foregoing, Chrysler's V6 engines have been far more dependable than similar engines equipping Ford and GM minivans. That said, there still have been some reports of hard starts, stalling, serpentine belt failures, engine oil sludging and head gasket failures, and power-steering pump hose blowouts (causing loss of power steering).

Automatic transmissions: Chrysler's Achilles' heel

Chrysler's A604, 41TE, and 42LE automatic transmissions, phased in throughout the company's 1991 product lineup, are a reliability nightmare that can have serious safety consequences (see "Safety Complaints" below). Imagine having to count to three in traffic before Drive or Reverse engages, limping home in Second gear at 50 km/h, or suddenly losing all forward motion. Catastrophic transmission failures are commonplace because of poor engineering, as the following reader discovered:

> My '99 Grand Voyager had a complete differential failure at 104,000 km. The retaining pin sheared off, which allowed the main differential pin to work its way out and smash the casing and torque converter.

> In our case this is what happened. The gear bit, the pin spun, shearing the retaining pin off. With the centrifugal force the main pin worked its way out of the housing and smashed a 2″× 4″ [4 × 10 cm] hole through the bell housing and nearly punctured the torque converter. In my opinion this is a design flaw that should have been corrected

10 years ago. From my research I have determined that the transaxle identification number matches the original A604 transaxle. I was shocked that they would still use these in 1999.

Fit and finish has worsened over the past two decades. Body hardware and interior trim are fragile and tend to break, warp, or fall off (door handles are an example). The premature rust-out of key suspension and steering components is a major safety and performance concern. Paint delamination often turns these solid-coloured minivans into two-tone models with chalky white stripes on the hood and roof. Chrysler knows about this problem and often tries to get claimants to pay half the cost of repainting (about $1,500 on a $3,000 job) but will eventually agree to pay the total cost if the owner stands fast or threatens small claims court action.

And as the minivan takes on its albino appearance, you can listen to a self-contained orchestra of clicks, clunks, rattles, squeaks, and squeals as you drive. Giving new meaning to the phrase "surround sound," this noise usually emanates from the brakes, poorly anchored bench seats, suspension and steering assemblies, and misaligned body panels.

2000—A new AWD Sport model (it was a sales flop). **2001**—A small horsepower boost for the V6s, front side airbags, adjustable pedals, upgraded headlights, and a power-operated rear liftgate. **2002**—Fuel-tank assembly redesigned to prevent post-collision fuel leakage. A tire air pressure monitor and a DVD entertainment system were added. **2003**—AutoStick transmission dropped; standard power liftgate on the Grand EX and ES models. **2005**—Side curtain airbags (optional in Canada) and second- and third-row seats that fold flush with the floor; AWD dropped.

COST ANALYSIS: A 2008 Grand Caravan (the cheaper base Caravan got the axe) sells for $20,295 (the cargo van costs $1,000 more); a Town & Country sells for $28,995. In the States, you will pay $20,970 (U.S.) for a Grand Caravan SE and $23,190 (U.S.) for the Town & Country. If you want to save mega bucks, consider a much cheaper 2006 that has some of its original warranty left. **Best alternatives:** The 2005–08 Honda Odyssey should be your first choice, but earlier versions will do quite nicely. Toyota's 2004 Sienna should be avoided; however, 2005–08 and 2003 or earlier models are acceptable alternatives. GM and Ford front-drive minivans aren't acceptable because of their failure-prone powertrains, electrical short circuits, subpar bodywork, and brake, suspension, and steering problems. GM's Astro or Safari and Ford's Aerostar are cheap rear-drive minivans that are no longer made, but they are easily found and not particularly troublesome. Full-sized Ford, GM, and Chrysler rear-drive cargo vans, though, are more affordable and practical buys if you intend to haul a full passenger load, do some regular heavy hauling, are physically challenged, use lots of accessories, or take frequent motoring excursions. Don't splurge on a new luxury Chrysler minivan: The upscale Town & Country costs thousands of dollars more than a base Caravan and quickly loses its value after a few years. **Options:** As you increase body length, you lose manoeuvrability.

Don't even consider the 4-cylinder engine on used models—it has no place in a minivan, especially when hooked to the inadequate 3-speed automatic transmission. It lacks an Overdrive and will shift back and forth as speed varies, and it's slower and noisier than the other choices. This year's new 4.0L V6 adds some much-needed horsepower, and the 6-speed automatic transmission delivers that power more smoothly and economically, but the jury is still out on its long-term reliability and servicing. The 3.3L V6 is a better choice for most city-driving situations, but don't hesitate to get the 3.8L if you're planning lots of highway travel or carrying four or more passengers. Since its introduction, the 3.8L has been relatively trouble-free, and it's more economical on the highway than the 3.3L, which strains to maintain speed. None of the three engines listed above are as fuel-frugal, smooth-running, or quiet as what's offered by Honda or Toyota. As with all minivan manufacturers, sliding side doors have been trouble since they were first introduced. Child safety seats integrated into the rear seatbacks are convenient and reasonably priced, but Chrysler's versions have had a history of tightening up excessively or not tightening enough, allowing the child to slip out. Try the seat with your child before buying it. Power-adjustable pedals are an important upgrade, especially for short drivers. Other important features to consider are the optional defroster, power mirrors, power door locks, and power driver's seat (if you're shorter than 5′9″ or expect to have different drivers using the minivan). You may wish to pass on the tinted windshields; they seriously reduce visibility. Town & Country buyers should pass on the optional all-wheel drive coupled with four-wheel disc brakes (instead of the standard rear drums). Although the disc brakes have been improved, Chrysler's large number of ABS failures is worrisome. Ditch the failure-prone Goodyear original-equipment tires, and remember that a night drive is a prerequisite to check out headlight illumination, called inadequate by many. **Rebates:** $2,500–$3,000 rebates; 15 percent discounts and zero percent financing on the 2008 leftovers. **Delivery/ PDI:** $1,350. **Warranty:** Bumper-to-bumper 3 years/60,000 km; rust perforation 5 years/100,000 km. **Supplementary warranty:** An extended powertrain warranty is a must-have. If you're buying the warranty separately, bargain it down to about $700. Forget the bumper-to-bumper extended warranty—it's simply too expensive. **Depreciation:** Average; faster than average with the Town & Country. **Insurance cost:** Higher than average. **Parts supply/cost:** Easy-to-find, reasonably priced parts. **Annual maintenance cost:** Repair costs are average during the warranty period. **Highway/city fuel economy:** *Caravan:* 9.0/13.0 L/100 km; *Grand Caravan AWD:* 10.0/14.0 L/100 km; *Town & Country:* 9.0/14.0 L/100 km; *Town & Country AWD:* 10.0/15.0 L/100 km.

QUALITY/RELIABILITY: Below average. **Owner-reported problems:** These minivans are a hoot (and a howl, moan, squeal, chirp, and thunk) as they age. Powertrain failures are increasingly found to be caused by defective or poorly calibrated computer modules rather than by the hardware deficiencies of two decades ago. Owner complaints focus on electrical glitches, erratic AC performance (compressor clutch burnout), rapid brake wear, and the accumulation of brake dust.

The following parts wear out quickly and are expensive to repair or replace: cooling system, clutches, front suspension components, wheel bearings, AC, and body parts (such as the trim, weather stripping that becomes loose and falls off, and plastic pieces that rattle and break easily):

> The entire light cover panel fell off of my 2005 Dodge Caravan while driving on the interstate. It was glued on, and the heat melted the glue. There are no screws holding this onto the car. I have met two other people with the same problem in the last two weeks.

A word about brakes: The front brakes need constant attention, if not to replace the prematurely worn or rusted pads or calipers, then to silence the excessive squeaks. Early wearout and warping of the front brake rotors within two years or 30,000 km is common and has serious safety implications. **Warranty performance:** Below average through the 2006 model year; 2007–08 models much improved.

 SAFETY SUMMARY: Chrysler downplays the implications of its minivan safety defects, whether in the case of ABS failures or sudden transmission breakdowns. Seat belts are another recurring problem. They may become unhooked from the floor anchor, their buckles jam or suddenly release, and the child safety seat harness easily pulls out or over-retracts, trapping children. **Airbags:** Three-row side curtain airbags were optional on 2005–07 models; 2008–09 models include them as a standard feature. NHTSA has recorded numerous complaints of airbags failing to deploy in an accident or deploying unexpectedly, such as when passing over a bump in the road or simply starting the vehicle. **ABS:** Optional/standard. **Traction control:** Standard. **Head restraints F/R:** *Caravan:* ★; *Grand Caravan 1999:* ★★/★; *2001–03:* ★★★★/★★★; *2004–07 without adjustable lumbar support:* ★; *with adjustable support:* ★★★; *Voyager 2001–03:* ★★/★; *Town & Country 1999:* ★; *2001–03:* ★★★/★★/★; *2004– 07 without adjustable lumbar support:* ★; *with adjustable support:* ★★★. **Visibility F/R:** ★★★/★★★★★. **Maximum load capacity:** *2001 Grand Caravan Sport:* 1,150 lb. **Pet transport:** ★★★★★.

SAFETY COMPLAINTS: All models/years: Sudden, unintended acceleration; owners report that cruise-control units often malfunction, accelerating or decelerating the vehicle without any warning. • Airbag malfunctions. • Get used to the term "clock spring." It's an expensive little component that controls some parts within the steering wheel and, when defective, can make the Airbag warning light come on or cause the airbag, cruise control, or horn to fail. It has been a pain in the butt for Chrysler minivan owners since the 1996 model year. Chrysler has extended its warranty for 1996–2000 model year minivans in two separate recalls and has replaced the clock spring at no charge. Apparently, the automaker has found that the part fails because it was wound too tightly or has short-circuited from corrosion. • Defective engine head gaskets, rocker arm gaskets, and engine mounts. • Engine sag, hesitation, stumble, hard starts, or stalling. • No steering, or steering lock-up. • Carbon monoxide comes through air vents. • Brakes wear out prematurely or fail completely. • Transmission fails, suddenly drops into low gear, won't go into Reverse, delays engagement, or jumps out of gear when running or parked. • One can move automatic transmission shift lever without applying brakes. • Several incidents where ignition was turned and then vehicle went into Reverse at full throttle, although transmission was set in Park. • ABS failure. • Front suspension strut towers rust and then crack at the weld seams; jig-positioning hole wasn't sealed at the factory. • Brakes activate by themselves while underway. • Prematurely warped rotors and worn-out pads cause excessive vibrations when stopping. • Seatbacks fall backward. • Rear windows fall out or shatter. • Power window and door lock failures. • Sliding door often opens while vehicle is underway, or jams, trapping occupants. • Weak headlights. • Horn often doesn't work. • Several incidents where side windows exploded for no apparent reason. **1999**—Instrument panel fire. • Sudden tie-rod breakage, causing loss of vehicle control. • Chronic steering pump and rack failures. • Poor braking performance; brake pedal can be depressed to the floor with little or no effect. • Rusted-through front brake rotors and rear brake drums. **2000**—Gas tank ruptures. • Engine camshaft fails. • Although the owner's manual says the vehicle should have a transmission/brake interlock, the feature may be lacking. • Cruise control malfunctions. **2000–01**—Sudden loss of engine power accompanied by fuel leakage from the engine compartment. • Emergency parking brake may not release because of premature corrosion. • Right front brake locks up while driving, causing the vehicle to suddenly turn 90 degrees to the right; same phenomenon when braking. • Transmission shift lever blocks the driver's right knee when braking. • Fifth-wheel assembly falls off while the vehicle is underway. • Instruments are recessed too deep into the dash, making it hard to read the fuel gauge and speedometer, especially at night. **2001–02**—Engine camshafts may have an improperly machined oil groove. • Snow and water ingestion into rear brake drum. • Inaccurate fuel-tank gauge drops one-quarter to one-half while driving. **2002**—Airbags deploy for no reason. • Airbag warning light comes on randomly. • Headlights go on and off on their own. **2002–03**—Seat belts unlatch themselves. **2003**—Exposed electrical wires under the front seats. • Excessive steering vibration. • Missing suspension bolt causes the right side to collapse. • Wiper blades stick together. **2004**—Seat belts don't latch properly. **2004–05**—Chronic stalling caused by defective fuel-pump module. **2005**—Stuck accelerator and loss of brakes. • Van loses all power and steering while on the road. • Cold rain freezes the rear brake drum solid. • Chemical used in the preparation of the vehicle (Hexane) causes allergy flare-ups and respiratory distress for some. **2006**—Improperly torqued power-steering hose comes loose and sprays steering fluid throughout the engine compartment. • Turn signals function erratically, and headlights flicker and dim. **2007**—Front passenger-side wheel falls off. • Transmission slips into limp mode; many other transmission failures:

> I am an engineer on automatic transmission systems. The purpose of the complaint is to provide NHTSA and the manufacturer with one more example of an issue that seems to be common with this particular transmission/vehicle. The Dodge dealer has not been contacted and the vehicle has not been serviced. The vehicle exhibits an

extremely harsh 2–1 downshift. It also exhibits a mildly harsh 1–2 upshift. I suspect solenoid and/or valve body debris is present causing delayed/harsh shifts. There is also a moderate amount of torque converter lock-up clutch slippage in Third gear. The vehicle remains in Third gear until approximately 40 mph [64 km/h]. During Third gear torque converter lock-up mode, engine speed fluctuations are visible on the tachometer. The engine speed changes are audible as well.

•

I found the transmission was defective the day I drove off the lot. Took back to dealership and was told transmission was bad and Chrysler was aware of it but had no fix for it. Was told it would be okay to drive and a fix would take place in 60 to 90 days…. Took vehicle to dealership and was told that the fix was not there. Said it would be most any day. I've waited 102 days and I think it's long enough. [They] keep saying that the government is holding it up. They say they have to change the settings in the computer and when they do this it changes emissions on the vehicle and EPA [U.S. Environmental Protection Agency] has to okay this. Transmission has a hard shifting down and a hard shift taking off.

• Shredded power-steering belt causes complete loss of steering. • Ruptured front brake hose. • Rusty brake shoes and rotors make brakes less effective. • Accidentally bumping the ignition with your knee can suddenly shut down the vehicle. • Faulty Firestone/Bridgestone tires. • Sudden steering loss:

Control was lost and vehicle came to a stop in the highway center median. After removing steering column boot, the Chrysler technician found that the steering shaft was not properly installed at the factory. The roll pin was not installed in the right area of the shaft.

Town & Country: **2007**—Excessive stopping distance. • Electronic tailgate won't open or close. • Instrument panel light surging.

Secret Warranties/Internal Bulletins/Service Tips

All years: If pressed, Chrysler will replace the AC evaporator for free for up to seven years. Other AC component costs are negotiable. **1999**—A serpentine belt that slips off the idler pulley requires an upgraded bracket. • Upgraded engine head gasket. • Oil seepage from the cam-position sensor. • Front brakes continue to wear out quickly on front-drive minivans. Owners report that Chrysler will pay half the cost of brake repairs for up to 2 years/40,000 km. • Silence a chronic squeaking noise coming from underneath the vehicle by installing a new strut pivot bearing. **1999–2000**—Strut tower corrosion is a common structural defect. Chrysler has come up with a fix that will be partially compensated through a "goodwill" policy applied on a case-by-case basis. This defect is definitely caused by poor design and should have been targeted by a recall campaign. Stand your ground, and threaten to use the small claims court to get a full refund for the repair if Chrysler doesn't accept its responsibility for the correction of the problem. • Cruise control that won't hold the vehicle's speed when going uphill may have a faulty check valve. • Countermeasures detailed to correct a steering-column click or rattle. • Airbag warning light stays lit. • If the ignition key can't be turned or removed, TSB #23-23-00 proposes four possible corrections. • Troubleshooting AC compressor failure:

AC COMPRESSOR—LOCKS UP AT LOW MILEAGE
BULLETIN NO.: 24-15-99   **DATE: JULY 9, 1999**

OVERVIEW: This bulletin involves determining the extent of AC compressor lock-up and either working the compressor loose or replacing it.

1998– **2000** (NS) Town & Country/Caravan/Voyager

1998– **2000** (GS) Chrysler Voyager (International Market)

1998– **2000** (PL) Neon

SYMPTOM/CONDITION: The AC compressor may lock up, causing the drive belt to slip in the AC clutch pulley, producing a squealing noise at initial start-up.

• Measures to prevent the right side sliding-door trim panel from hitting the quarter panel when the door is opened. • Delayed shifts. **1999–2001**—AWD models *must* be equipped with identical tires, otherwise the power transfer unit may self-destruct. • A suspension squawk or knock probably means the sway-bar link needs replacing under Chrysler's "goodwill" policy (5 years/100,000 km). • Rear brake noise. **1999–2002**—Paint delamination, peeling, or fading. • A rotten-egg odour coming from the exhaust may be the result of a malfunctioning catalytic converter, probably covered under the emissions warranty. **1999–2006**—Rusted, frozen rear brake drums:

REAR DRUM WATER/SNOW INGESTION/FREEZING
BULLETIN NO.: 05-002-04   **DATE: FEBRUARY 17, 2004**

SNOW/WATER INGESTION INTO REAR BRAKE DRUM

This bulletin involves installing a revised rear drum brake support (backing) plate and possible replacement of the rear brake shoes and drums.

2001–06 Town & Country/Voyager/Caravan

1996–2000 Town & Country/Caravan/Voyager

1996–2000 Chrysler Voyager (International Markets)

SYMPTOM/CONDITION: While driving through deep or blowing snow/water, the snow/water may enter the rear brake drums causing rust to develop on the rear brake drum and shoe friction surfaces. This condition can lead to temporary freezing of the rear brake linings to the drums. This symptom is experienced after the vehicle has been parked in below freezing temperatures long enough for the snow/water to freeze inside of the rear brake drums. When the parking brake has been applied the symptom is more likely to occur.

• Roof panel is wavy or has depressions. **2000–01**—Poor starting. • AC compressor failure, loss of engine power when switching on the AC, serpentine belt chirping, and spark knock can all be traced to a miscalibrated PCM. • No heat on front right side because of a defective blend air door. • AC compressor squeal. • Rear bench seat rattle or groan. • Hood hinge rattle. • Inoperative overhead reading lamp and rear wiper. • Noisy roof rack and power-sliding door. **2001–02**—Engine surging at highway speeds. • Engine knocking. • Engine sag and hesitation caused by a faulty throttle position sensor (TPS). • Engine mount grinding or clicking. • Steering-wheel shudder; steering-column popping or ticking. • Poor rear AC performance. • Wind or water leaks at the rear quarter window. • High-pitched, belt-like squeal at high engine rpm. • Sliding door reverses direction. • Incorrect fuel gauge indicator. • Loose tail light. • Flickering digital display. • Install a new seal on a hard-to-remove fuel cap; this free repair applies to the entire 2002 vehicle lineup. **2001–03**—Rear brake rubbing sound. • Oil filter leaks with 3.3L and 3.8L engines (confirmed in TSB # 09-001-03):

> On February 25, 2003, my 2002 Grand Caravan lost almost all of its engine oil, which resulted in engine failure. At no time did the vehicle's warning sensors indicate any problem with the engine. The failure was the result of a leak in the filter gasket of the FE292 Mopar oil filter. Documentation from the oil filter manufacturer indicates that the oil filter gasket overhangs the inside diameter of the adapter head.

2001–06—AC water condensate under the passenger-side carpet can be eliminated by installing an HVAC drain tube O-ring, says TSB #24-001-06, published February 23, 2006. • Troubleshooting a musty interior odour emanating from the AC. **2002**—Transmission slips in First or Reverse gear. • Power-steering fluid leakage. • Rear side vent window explodes while driving. • Noisy engine and transmission. **2002–03**—Power-sliding door malfunctions. **2002–07**—Malfunctioning power liftgate. **2003**—Steering column pops, ticks, or creaks. • Troubleshooting water leaks. • Three bulletins relating to automatic transmission malfunctions: delayed gear engagement; harsh 4–3 downshift; and excessive vibration and transfer gear whine. **2004**—Rough idle, hesitation, and hard starts. • Accessory drivebelt chirping. • Front suspension rattling. **2004–05**—Warm engine rough idle. • Transmission ticking. • Electrical locks inoperative; liftgate triggers the alarm. **2005**—Steering moan. • Third-row front seat leg won't retract. **2005–06**—Whistle sound from rear quarter glass area. • Steering wheel rattles. • AC condenser road debris damage can be avoided by installing a condenser guard supplied by Chrysler (under warranty, of course). **2005–07**—Buzz, rattle from the quarter panel speaker area.

CARAVAN, VOYAGER, GRAND CARAVAN, GRAND VOYAGER, TOWN & COUNTRY PROFILE

	1999	2000	2001	2002	2003	2004	2005	2006	2007
Cost Price ($) (very negotiable)									
Caravan (25%)	24,230	24,970	24,885	25,430	25,430	27,620	28,330	28,880	27,445
Grand Caravan (26%)	25,890	26,665	29,505	28,875	29,295	30,190	30,865	31,500	29,305
Town & Country (27%)	41,260	41,815	41,150	40,815	42,705	44,095	44,595	44,750	42,255

Used Values ($)

Caravan ▲	3,000	3,500	4,000	4,500	6,000	7,000	9,000	10,500	13,000
Caravan ▼	2,500	3,000	3,500	4,000	4,500	5,500	7,500	9,500	11,500
Grand Caravan ▲	3,500	4,000	4,500	5,500	6,500	7,500	10,000	12,000	15,000
Grand Caravan ▼	3,000	3,500	4,000	4,500	6,000	6,000	8,500	10,500	13,000
Town & Country ▲	3,500	4,000	5,000	6,500	9,500	13,000	15,500	19,500	24,000
Town & Country ▼	3,000	3,500	4,000	5,500	8,500	11,500	14,500	18,000	23,000

Reliability	2	2	2	3	3	3	3	3	3
Grand Caravan, T&C	2	2	2	2	3	3	3	3	3
Crash Safety (F)									
Caravan	—	4	4	4	4	4	4	5	5
Grand Caravan	4	4	4	4	4	4	4	5	5
Town & Country	—	—	—	—	4	4	5	5	5
Town & Country LX	4	4	4	4	4	4	—	—	—
Side									
Caravan	5	5	4	4	4	4	4	4	4
Grand Caravan	5	5	4	5	5	5	5	5	5
Town & Country LX	5	5	—	—	—	—	—	4	4
IIHS Side									
Grand Caravan	—	—	—	—	—	—	—	3	3
Town & Country LX	—	—	—	—	—	—	—	2	2
Offset									
Grand Caravan	2	2	1	3	3	3	3	3	3
Town & Country	2	2	1	3	3	3	3	3	3
Rollover									
Caravan	—	—	3	3	3	—	—	4	4
Grand Caravan	—	—	3	3	3	—	4	4	4
Town & Country	—	—	3	3	3	—	4	4	4

Note: Voyager and Grand Voyager prices and ratings are almost identical to the Caravan and Grand Caravan. The Town & Country's rapid depreciation makes it almost as cheap as a Grand Caravan up to the 2000 models, despite a $15,000 premium when new. Also, the cargo versions (Caravan/Grand Caravan) are $4,000 cheaper than the base passenger models.

RAM VAN, RAM WAGON, SPRINTER ★

bad buy

RATING: *Sprinter:* Not Recommended (2004–08); *Ram Van, Ram Wagon:* Average (1980–2003). Fuel economy and cargo capacity trump performance, and dealer support is questionable. **Strong points:** *Sprinter:* Fuel-efficient diesel engine, and lots of passenger and cargo space. *Ram:* Powerful engines, lots of passenger and cargo space, airbag cut-off switch, and quiet running. **Weak points:** *Sprinter:* For starters, try a $1,990 freight charge. Also, it's overweight, underpowered, and hard to service, and it loses its value quickly. *Ram:* The technology is old, it's sparsely equipped, manoeuvring is ponderous, fuel consumption is excessive, and rear-wheel ABS has a history of failures.

All ratings on a numbered scale where 5 is good and 1 is bad. See page 217 for a more detailed description.

MODEL HISTORY: The B-series ("Tradesman") van is one of the oldest van designs around. The full-sized van shares the same strengths and weaknesses as all of Chrysler's rear-drive trucks. Chrysler says they are used commercially 97 percent of the time, mostly as small school buses, car-rental shuttles at airports, and delivery vehicles. The Ram Van is the commercial truck; the Ram Wagon is the people-hauler. Base 1500s are about the size of a short GM Astro van. Both versions aren't hard to find and are generally reasonably priced. Its last model year was 2003, when it was replaced by the 2004 Sprinter.

It's hard to get excited about the basic Chrysler van. Its seats are uncomfortable, and the lack of interior trimmings makes it essentially a shipping container on wheels. The sturdy 175-hp 3.9L V6 engine first appeared in the Dakota truck series and is adequate for most uses, but one of the optional V8s would be a better all-around choice, without much more of a fuel penalty. If you do get a used van with the V6, keep in mind that multi-point fuel injection, added in 1992 on both the V6 and V8 power-plants, makes for smoother engine performance (and more expensive troubleshooting).

Putting all of its cash into minivans, Chrysler didn't make any major improvements to these rear-drive trucks-disguised-as-vans until the spring of 1993; even then, the changes weren't all that dramatic. Five years later, Chrysler redesigned the 1998 version by restyling the interior and exterior, de-powering the airbags, adding a passenger-side airbag, and providing more front legroom and footroom. The 1999 models returned unchanged except for a larger fuel tank on vehicles equipped with 5.2L and 5.9L natural gas V8 engines. After that, these vans were carried over without any major changes.

Dodge Sprinter

The $48,490 Sprinter ($38,935 in the States) passenger van is actually an old rear-drive Mercedes-Benz model that's been tooting around Europe and foreign markets since 1995. Freightliner first sold it in the States as a 2001 commercial hauler. Since 2004, DaimlerChrysler and Freightliner dealers throughout Canada and the United States have sold Sprinter as a passenger/cargo van.

Early Sprinters offered a large load capacity and a fuel-sipping, 154-hp Mercedes-Benz 5-cylinder turbodiesel engine hooked to a 5-speed automatic transmission. Three wheelbase models were available through the 2007 model year: 118-inch, 140-inch, and 158-inch. The 2008 models have a much larger wheelbase. Cargo volume on the 2500 Regular model varies from 9.0 cubic metres (318 cubic feet) with the standard roof to 10.5 cubic metres (371 cubic feet) with the optional high

---

2008 SPRINTER TECHNICAL DATA

POWERTRAIN (REAR-DRIVE)
Engines: 3.0L V6 turbodiesel (154 hp) • 3.5L V6 (254 hp); Transmission: 5-speed auto.

DIMENSION/CAPACITY
Passengers: 12; Wheelbase: 144.3–170.3 in.; H: 96.3/L: 232.5/W: 79.7 in.; Headroom: N/A; Legroom: 37.9/33.0 in.; Cargo volume: 112–473 cu. ft.; Fuel tank: 98L/regular; Tow limit: 5,000 lb.; Load capacity: 2,937 lb.; GVWR: 8,550–9,990 lb.; Turning circle: 45.2 ft.; Ground clearance: 7.4 in.; Weight: 5,608 lb.

roof. Total cargo capacity is 17,000 litres (4,491 gallons), and GVWR is between 3,878 kg (8,550 lb.) and 4,531 kg (9,990 lb.). The 2008 models add seating for 12, instead of 10, an emergency exit window, and an optional power-sliding side door.

In its favour, the Sprinter offers impressive refinement, many body configurations, slightly better diesel fuel economy than other vans, and class-leading passenger and cargo capacity. On the minus side, it's much more expensive than the competition; it's overweight and underpowered for everyday tasks; it's not easily repaired (yes, there is a right way, a wrong way, and a German way); it lacks a V8 for towing, hauling, and high-speed cruising; and it has never been crash-tested by NHTSA.

In summary, it's a loser.

COST ANALYSIS: Look for an off-lease 2003 traditional Chrysler van selling for about one-third of its original retail price. Wait for the improved 2007 Sprinter to sell for about what the 2004–06 models originally cost. **Best alternatives:** Ford and GM full-sized vans are good choices. **Rebates:** Expect zero percent financing, rebates, and dealer incentives for the Sprinter. **Delivery/PDI:** $1,990. Yikes! **Warranty:** 3 years/60,000 km; powertrain 5 years/100,000 km; rust perforation 5 years/160,000 km. **Supplementary warranty:** Yes, on the powertrain, if it has expired. There is insufficient owner feedback regarding the Sprinter's long-term reliability. **Options:** None. The Sprinter comes well equipped. **Depreciation:** Faster than average with the Sprinter and the B-series wagon and van. **Insurance cost:** Above average; higher than average with the Sprinter. **Annual maintenance cost:** Higher than average with the Sprinter. Maintenance is a breeze on the traditional B-series vans, as is the case with most rear-drives. However, ABS, transmission, or AC repairs can easily wipe out your maintenance savings. **Parts supply/cost:** *Ram:* Good supply. Parts are a little less expensive than the competition's. *Sprinter:* Rare and costly. **Highway/city fuel economy:** *Ram 1500 van 3.9L with 3-speed automatic: 12.7/15.4 L/100 km; Ram 1500 van 5.2L V8 with 3-speed automatic: 15.2/18.2 L/100 km; 5.2 V8 with 4-speed automatic: 12.4/17.8 L/100km.*

QUALITY/RELIABILITY: *Sprinter:* Quirky and highly dealer-dependent for parts and servicing. The electronics, fuel system, and brakes are common trouble spots. *Ram:* Competent servicing by dealers or independent garages is easy to find, and troubleshooting most problems is easy. Quality control is below average, however, and each redesign seems to carry over the same problem components. Sloppy assembly and poor-quality parts, in addition to fragile hardware, make the bodies rattletraps and allow for lots of air and water leaks. Paint peeling and delamination isn't as bad as on Ford and GM vans, but rusting is a problem. Be sure to inspect a potential purchase for premature rust, especially around the front suspension attachment points, doors, and exhaust/catalytic converter (stainless-steel exhaust systems excepted). **Owner-reported problems:** *Sprinter:* Premature wearout or warping of the brake rotors. The lack of a tailpipe allows diesel soot to enter the cabin. *Ram:* Owners complain of AC, electrical system, fuel system, brake, and transmission failures. Paint delamination is also a common gripe, which Chrysler will often remedy for free up to six years of ownership. Owners also cite excessive brake pulsation (caused by premature front disc wear around 40,000 km). Corroded parking brake cables may also cause the brakes to seize. **Warranty performance:** Average.

SAFETY SUMMARY: Complaints about airbags, brakes, door locks, seat belt failures, and chronic stalling when turning are quite common throughout the last decade of the B-series' production. **Airbags:** No side airbags. Severe injuries have been caused by airbag deployment. There have been reports of airbags that deployed when the key was put into the ignition, and of airbags that did not deploy. **ABS:** Two-wheel ABS is standard. **Visibility F/R:** ★★★/★★. Some owners report annoying dash reflection onto the front windshield (corrected by placing a dark drop sheet on the dash). **Pet transport:** ★★★★★.

SAFETY COMPLAINTS: *Ram:* **1999**—Several wire harness fires under the dash. • Passenger-side wheel locks up and shears off. • Tire studs frequently shear off. • Cracked trailer hitch. • Cruise control self-activates. • Vehicle pulls unexpectedly to one side when braking. • Brakes lock up with light pressure. **1999–2000**—Many complaints of excessive wandering over the highway. **2000**—When brakes are applied, pedal goes to the floor, extending stopping distance. • Transmission seal leaks continuously because of previous drive shaft failures. • Transmission pops out of gear while pulling a load uphill. **2001**—Faulty latch can cause seat-back to collapse. • Vehicle can be put in gear without depressing brake pedal. **2002**—Not enough seat belts for the number of passengers that can be seated. *Sprinter:* **2005**—Chronic stalling while underway (disconnected fuel hose). • Transmission torque converter failures (see *autos.groups.yahoo.com/group/sprintervan*). • Tire valve stem failure. • Michelin tire failure. • Tires constantly lose air. • Electrical short circuit causes excessive battery drain. • Driver-side mirror doesn't adjust enough to see cars behind the vehicle. **2007**—Vehicle shuts down while underway. • Defective fuel gauge.

Secret Warranties/Internal Bulletins/Service Tips

1999—TSB #23-43-90 gives lots of tips on locating water leaks through the dual cargo doors. • If the MIL comes on, you may have to reprogram the JTEC power-train control module. • A knocking noise in the front suspension signals the need to install an upgraded stabilizer bar. • Measures to eliminate wind noise at the upper A-pillar area. **1999–2000**—Paint delamination, peeling, or fading. • Noisy rear leaf springs can be silenced by replacing the spring tip liners and installing new spring clinch clip isolators. • If the side or rear doors open beyond their normal travel, replace the check arm pin and bumper. • In cases where the sliding door won't open or close, consider installing a revised sliding-door rear latch assembly and latch rods and modifying the rear latch opening. **1999–2001**—Hard starts, no-starts, and stalling may be caused by a malfunctioning central timer module. **2000**—Excessive engine knock upon acceleration may be silenced by reprogramming the PCM. • Harsh transmission engagement can be fixed by replacing the transmission valve-body upper-housing separator plate and the valve-body check ball. You may also need to reprogram the JTEC PCM. **2000–01**—If the MIL comes on with a TCC/OD alert, consider replacing the transmission-pressure boost-valve cover plate. • A likely cause of sudden, widespread electrical failures may be a locked-up central timer module. • If the engine won't start or crank, you may have a blown starter relay; install a starter solenoid and circuit fuse. **2000–03**—Doors lock and unlock on their own. **2001**—Radiators may leak between the filler neck and the cap. **2002**—Indicated 9.25-axle vehicle speed may be inaccurate. **2004–05**—Lack of power can be corrected by replacing the intake air temperature sensor. • Tips for fixing a chattering automatic transmission that is slow to engage.

RAM VAN, RAM WAGON, SPRINTER PROFILE

	1999	2000	2001	2002	2003	2004	2005	2006	2007
Cost Price ($) (very negotiable)									
Ram Van	25,120	25,695	26,250	26,008	26,100	—	—	—	—
Ram Wagon	28,845	29,080	29,720	31,000	31,300	—	—	—	—
Sprinter (22%)	—	—	—	—	—	40,290	40,290	39,525	43,620
Used Values ($)									
Ram Van ▲	2,500	3,000	3,500	4,500	6,000	—	—	—	—
Ram Van ▼	2,000	2,500	3,000	3,500	4,500	—	—	—	—
Ram Wagon ▲	4,000	5,000	6,000	8,000	11,000	—	—	—	—
Ram Wagon ▼	3,500	4,500	5,000	7,000	9,500	—	—	—	—
Sprinter ▲	—	—	—	—	—	14,500	17,500	22,500	28,000
Sprinter ▼	—	—	—	—	—	13,000	16,000	20,500	26,500
Reliability	2	2	2	2	2	2	3	3	3
Crash Safety (F)	—	—	4	4	4	—	—	—	—
Rollover	—	—	3	3	3	—	—	—	—

Ford

WINDSTAR, FREESTAR ★★

RATING: *Freestar:* Below Average (2004–07). Freestar is a warmed over Windstar, with its own serious quality control problems; 2007 was its last model year. *Windstar:* Not Recommended (1995–2003). Infamous for atrocious quality control, stonewalled complaints, and life-threatening defects, 2003 was the minivan's last model year. Windstars have similar transmission, brake, and AC failures to their Chrysler and GM competition, and their engines aren't very reliable. Unfortunately, Ford doesn't protect its owners with a 7-year powertrain warranty as Chrysler does, hence the lower rating for the Ford vehicles. **Strong points:** *Freestar:* The 4.2L V6 engine, new cabin appointments, optional side curtain airbags, easier rear access, flat-folding third-row seats, and larger four-wheel disc brakes. *Windstar:* Comfortable and well-appointed interior; comfortable ride; good instrument/controls layout; plenty of passenger space; lots of small storage spaces in addition to the large amount of space for larger items; a low floor that improves cargo handling; and a five-star crashworthiness rating. **Weak points:** *Windstar:* Mediocre handling and restricted side and rear visibility. Driver's seat isn't comfortable for big, tall drivers, who complain of the lack of legroom, seat contouring, and lower back support. An abundance of clunks, rattles, and wind and road noise. These minivans have major failures that include faulty engines, transmissions, brakes, electrical systems, and suspension components. Sure, the Windstar combines an impressive five-star safety rating, plenty of raw power, an exceptional ride, and impressive cargo capacity. But self-destructing automatic transmissions, defective engine head gaskets and bearings, and "Do I feel lucky?" brakes and front coil springs can quickly transform your dream minivan into a nightmare. And, as a counterpoint to Ford's well-earned Windstar crashworthiness boasting, take a look at the summary of safety-related complaints recorded by the U.S. Department of Transportation: sudden acceleration, stalling, loss of steering, windows exploding, wheels falling off, horn failures, coil spring breakage that blows the front tire, sliding doors that open and close on their own, and vehicles rolling away while parked.

MODEL HISTORY: Ford can call it the Windstar or the Freestar; the fact remains, car shoppers want no part of it. In 2003, it competed as the Windstar and posted 70,404 sales in the first half of the year. In 2004, it was reincarnated under the Freestar name. Sales fell off by about 22 percent and have never recovered.

Freestar does feature upgrades in safety, interior design, steering, ride, and performance, but it still lags far behind the Japanese competition for performance and dependability. An optional "safety canopy" side curtain airbag system offers protection in side-impact collisions and rollovers for all three rows of seating. There's also better access to the third-row seat, which folds flat into the floor. Entry-level LX models came with a 193-hp 3.9L V6, based on the Windstar's 3.8L engine. Up-level SE and top-line Limited models got a new 201-hp 4.2L V6, also derived from the 3.8L.

1999—A bit more interior space; the third-row bench gets built-in rollers; improved steering and brakes (compromised by rear drums, though); ABS; an anti-theft system; new side panels; a new liftgate; larger headlights and tail lights; and a revised instrument panel. **2001**—No more 3.0L V6; an upgraded automatic transmission; a low-tire-pressure warning system; "smart" airbags; new airbag sensors; and a slight restyling. **2002**—Dual sliding doors. **2003**—Freestar debuts

---

2007 FREESTAR TECHNICAL DATA

POWERTRAIN (FRONT-DRIVE)
Engines: 3.9L V6 (193 hp) • 4.2L V6 (201 hp); Transmission: 4-speed auto.

DIMENSION/CAPACITY
Passengers: 2/2/3; Wheelbase: 120.8 in.; H: 68.8/L: 201.0/W: 76.4 in.; Headroom F/R1/R2: 5.5/6.0/5.0 in.; Legroom F/R1/R2: 40.0/29.0/27.5 in.; Cargo volume: 61.5 in.; Fuel tank: 75–94L/regular; Tow limit: 2,000–3,500 lb.; Load capacity: 1,315 lb.; GWVR: 5,880 lb.; Turning circle: 40.0 ft.; Ground clearance: 6.5 in.; Weight: 4,295 lb.

as a 2004 model; in the States, Mercury sells an upscale Freestar called Monterey to replace that brand's defunct Nissan-based Villager.

Engine and transmission failures

Engine and transmission failures are commonplace. The 3.0L engine is overwhelmed by the Windstar's heft and struggles to keep up, but opting for the 3.8L V6 may get you into worse trouble. Even when it's running properly, the 3.8L knocks loudly when under load and pings at other times. Far more serious is the high failure rate of 3.8L engine head gaskets shortly after the 60,000 km mark. Ford's 7-year/160,000 km Owner Notification Program only covers '95s, so owners are asked to pay $1,000–$3,000 for an engine repair, depending on how much the engine has overheated. Transmission repairs seldom cost less than $3,000.

Early warning signs are few and benign. The engine may lose some power or overheat, or the transmission pauses before downshifting or shifts roughly into a higher gear. Owners may also hear a transmission whining or groaning sound accompanied by driveline vibrations. There is no other prior warning before the transmission breaks down completely and the minivan comes to a sudden, banging, clanging halt:

> Phil, I just want to thank you for saving us at least $1,500. The transmission in our '98 Windstar went bang with only 47,300 miles [75,700 km]. After reading about Ford's goodwill adjustment, we were told by our local Ford dealer that owner participation would be $495. We received a new rebuilt Ford unit installed. Believe it or not, I am a fairly good mechanic myself and this came with no warning! We even serviced the transmission at 42,000 miles [67,200 km] and found no debris or evidence of a problem.

Ford admits automatic transmission glitches may afflict its 2001 Taurus, Sable, Windstar, and Continental. In a March 2001 Special Service Instruction (SSI) #01T01, Ford authorized its dealers to replace all defective transaxles listed in its TSB, which describes the defect in the following manner:

> The driver may initially experience a transaxle "slip" or "Neutral" condition during a 2–3 shift event. Extended driving may result in loss of Third gear function and ultimately loss of Second gear function. The driver will still be able to operate the vehicle, but at a reduced level of performance.

Ford's memo states that owners weren't to be notified of the potential problem (they obviously didn't count on *Lemon-Aid* getting a copy of their memo).

Brakes are another Windstar worry. They aren't reliable, and calipers, rotors, and the master cylinder often need replacing. Other frequent Windstar problems concern no-starts and chronic stalling, believed to be caused by a faulty fuel pump or PCM; electrical system power-steering failures; hard steering at slow speeds; excessive steering-wheel vibration; sudden tire-tread separation and premature tread wear; advanced coil spring corrosion, leading to spring collapse and the puncturing of the front tire (only 1997–98 models were recalled); rear shock failures at 110 km/h; left-side axle breakage while underway; exploding rear windshields; power-sliding door malfunctions; and failure-prone digital speedometers that are horrendously expensive to replace. There have also been many complaints concerning faulty computer modules, engine oil leaks, AC failures, and early replacement of engine camshafts, tie-rods, and brake rotors and calipers.

Getting compensation

Since 1997, I've lobbied Ford to stop playing *Let's Make a Deal* with its customers and to set up a formal 7-year/160,000 km engine and transmission warranty similar to its 3.8L engine's extended warranty and emission warranty guidelines (see bulletin on page 477). I warned the company that its failure to protect owners would result in huge sales losses as word spread that Ford's vehicles were lemons.

In the ensuing three years, under the capable leadership of Bobbie Gaunt, President of Ford Canada, hundreds of engine and transmissions claims were amiably settled using my suggested benchmark. But it didn't last. Ford U.S. got wind of it and squashed the Canadian initiative. Interestingly, the three top Ford Canada executives who pleaded the Canadian case have since left the company. And Jac Nasser, the Ford U.S. CEO who rejected additional protection for owners, was fired shortly thereafter when he tried a similar move with Firestone claimants. No, Nasser isn't one of my favourite auto executives.

And as I predicted, Ford sales have plummeted, small claims court judgments are pummelling the company, and owners are vowing to never again buy any Ford product.

> Hi Phil: I just wanted to let you know that I did have to go to small claims court to nudge Ford into action. In pretrial settlement proceedings, the Ford representative at first gave me an offer of $980 for my troubles. I countered with the actual cost of $2,190 to replace my '96 Windstar's transmission. He did not like that idea, and we went back into the court setting. After instruction from the judge, I began to copy my 200+ pages (for the judge as evidence) of documentation for why this is a recurring problem with Ford transmissions (thank you, by the way, for all the great info).
>
> I think it made him a little scared, so I asked if he would settle for $1,600 (a middle ground of our original proposals) to which he accepted. My transmission costs were $2,190, so I basically paid about $600 for a new transmission (*not* a Ford replacement, either).
>
> Anyway, I figured a guaranteed $1,600 was better than not knowing what would happen in court. Thanks for your help!

Ford's denial of owners' claims has been blasted in small claims court judgments across Canada during the past few years. Judges have ruled that engines and transmissions (as well as power-sliding doors) must be reasonably durable long after the warranty expires, whether the vehicle was bought new or used, even if it was repaired by an independent mechanic or had the same problem repaired earlier for free. (See the *Dufour, Schaffler,* and *Reid* engine judgments in Part Three.)

Automatic transmission lawsuits have also been quite successful. They are often settled out of court because Ford frequently offers 50–75 percent refunds if the lawsuit is dropped. See pages 193–194 for *Lemon-Aid* reader Alan MacDonald's tips on successfully beating Ford.

Dangerous doors

The courts have slammed Ford for allowing dangerously defective sliding doors to go uncorrected year after year. Here are some rather typical scenarios reported by owners and concerned parents: A sliding door slammed shut on a child's head while the vehicle was parked on an incline; a driver's finger was broken while closing a manual sliding door; passengers are often pinned by the closing door; the door reopens as it is closing; the door often pops open while the vehicle is underway; and the door's handle is too close to the door jamb, a hazard that has been reported by NHTSA since 1999:

> I am writing about our 2003 Ford Windstar. Our passenger automatic sliding door frequently pops open after it appears to have latched shut. It has opened by itself on three occasions while the van was in Drive. Recently my three-year-old daughter almost fell out of the van headfirst onto concrete because the door popped back open as soon as it "latched" shut. The van has been in to repair this problem seven times without success. We first started having problems with both doors within the first two weeks of purchase. The times the door has popped back open are way too numerous to count.

> •

> The 2003 Windstar automatic sliding door opens by itself—no command; door will not power open; door lock assembly freezes. The door has opened itself while the vehicle is in motion—very scary and dangerous for my children. This is a problem Ford has known about but has not been proactive about fixing (see Ford TSB article 03-6-8).

Mental distress (door failures)

In *Sharman v. Formula Ford Sales Limited, Ford Credit Limited, and Ford Motor Company of Canada Limited* (Ontario Superior Court of Justice; No. 17419/02SR, 2003/10/07), Justice Shepard awarded the owner of a 2000 Windstar $7,500 for mental distress, resulting from the breach of the implied warranty of fitness, plus $7,207 for breach of contract and breach of warranty. The problem: The Windstar's sliding door wasn't secure and leaked air and water even after many attempts to repair it. Interestingly, the judge cited the *Wharton* decision (see page 160), among other decisions, as support for his award for mental distress:

> The plaintiff and his family have had three years of aggravation, inconvenience, worry, and concern about their safety and that of their children. Generally speaking, our contract law did not allow for compensation for what may be mental distress, but that may be changing. I am indebted to counsel for providing me with the decision of the British Columbia Court of Appeal in *Wharton v. Tom Harris Chevrolet Oldsmobile Cadillac Ltd.*, [2002] B.C.J. No. 233, 2002 BCCA 78. This decision was recently followed in *T'avra v. Victoria Ford Alliance Ltd.*, [2003] B, CJ No. 1957.
>
> In *Wharton*, the purchaser of a Cadillac Eldorado claimed damages against the dealer because the car's sound system emitted an annoying buzzing noise and the purchaser had to return the car to the dealer for repair numerous times over two-and-a-half years. The trial court awarded damages of $2,257.17 for breach of warranty with respect to the sound system, and $5,000 in non-pecuniary damages for loss of enjoyment of their luxury vehicle and for inconvenience, for a total award of $7,257.17....
>
> In the *Wharton* case, the respondent contracted for a "luxury" vehicle for pleasure use. It included a sound system that the appellant's service manager described as "high end." The respondent's husband described the purchase of the car in this way: "[W]e bought a luxury car that was supposed to give us a luxury ride and be a quiet vehicle, and we had nothing but difficulty with it from the very day it was delivered with this problem that nobody seemed to be able to fix.... So basically we had a luxury product that gave us no luxury for the whole time that we had it."
>
> It is clear that an important object of the contract was to obtain a vehicle that was luxurious and a pleasure to operate. Furthermore, the buzzing noise was the cause of physical, in the sense of sensory, discomfort to the respondent and her husband. The trial judge found it inhibited listening to the sound system and was irritating in normal conversation. The respondent and her husband also bore the physical inconvenience of taking the vehicle to the appellant on numerous occasions for repairs....
>
> In my view, a defect in manufacture that goes to the safety of the vehicle deserves a modest increase. I would assess the plaintiff's damage for mental distress resulting from the breach of the implied warranty of fitness at $7,500.
>
> Judgment to issue in favour of the plaintiff against the defendants, except Ford Credit, on a joint and several basis for $14,707, plus interest and costs.

COST ANALYSIS: Buyers should steer clear of both the Windstar and Freestar; however, if you have your heart set on a Freestar, get a 2007 used model for less than $13,500 and haggle for a free powertrain warranty. **Best alternatives:** The Honda Odyssey and pre-2004 Toyota Sienna are recommended alternatives. Other, more reliable used minivans you may wish to consider are late-model Ford or GM rear-drives and the pre-2004 Quest. **Rebates:** $4,000 rebates, $2,500 discounts, and zero percent financing on 2007 Freestars. **Delivery/PDI:** $1,200.

Depreciation: Much faster than average. **Warranty:** Bumper-to-bumper 3 years/60,000 km; rust perforation 5 years/unlimited km. **Supplementary warranty:** An extended bumper-to-bumper warranty is a good idea. **Options:** Dual-integrated child safety seats for the middle bench seat and adjustable pedals are worthwhile options. Power-sliding side doors are an overpriced convenience feature and are failure-prone. The Parking Assist beeper's false warnings will drive you crazy. **Insurance cost:** Above average. **Parts supply/cost:** Reasonably priced parts are easy to find, mainly because of the entry of independent suppliers. Digital speedometers are often defective and can cost almost $1,000 to repair. **Annual maintenance cost:** Average while under warranty; outrageously higher than average thereafter, primarily because of powertrain breakdowns either not covered by warranty or insufficiently covered by parsimonious "goodwill" gestures. **Highway/city fuel economy:** *Windstar:* 9.5/13.3 L/100 km.

 QUALITY/RELIABILITY: Worst quality control among all minivans, including the much-maligned Kia. "Goodwill" payouts, where owners pay over one-third of the cost, have been used as a substitute for better quality control. **Owner-reported problems:** Engine, transmission, suspension (coil springs), and power-sliding door malfunctions lead the list of factory-related problems, but there have also been many complaints concerning computer modules, engine oil leaks, the timing cover gasket leaking coolant, early engine camshaft replacement, AC failures, premature brake rotor and caliper wear, and excessive brake noise. Poor body seam sealing causes excessive interior wind noise and allows water to leak into the cabin. Owners also report a smattering of paint delamination complaints and a windshield glare from the dash. **Warranty performance:** Incredibly bad. Customer reps read a script that says there's no more warranty protection and that requested repairs are the owner's responsibility. This is particularly sad because Ford had been improving customer service progressively over the past couple of years. Now, owners are once again complaining that Ford is unusually tight-fisted and duplicitous in giving out refunds for the correction of factory-related deficiencies.

 SAFETY SUMMARY: The 2006 models earned a "Good" rating from IIHS for protecting occupants in frontal offset collisions. Head-restraint protection on vehicles with curtain head restraints was designated "Average," but the rating was "Poor" on models without side airbags. Base models may not have head restraints for all seats. The digital dash can be confusing. Optional adjustable pedals help protect drivers from airbag injuries. Be careful, though—some drivers have found that they are set too close together and say they often feel loose. Other nice safety features are a Sliding-Door warning light and airbags that adjust their deployment speed according to occupant weight. **Airbags:** Standard. **ABS:** Standard. **Traction control:** Optional. **Head restraints F/R1/R2:** *Windstar 1999:* ★★★/★; *2001–03:* ★★★★/★★★/★★; *Freestar 2004–07:* ★★★★★. **Visibility F/R:** ★★★★★/★★. **Maximum load capacity:** *2001 SE Sport:* 1,360 lb. **Pet transport:** ★★★★★.

SAFETY COMPLAINTS: All models/years: These are the most dangerous minivans on the market. Owners of the 1998 Windstar, for example, have logged over 1,549

safety-related complaints in the NHTSA database, compared to 708 incidents registered against Chrysler's 1998 Caravan, which had more than double the sales. And it gets worse the further back you go. The good news is that the 2004 Freestar, a revamped Windstar, has only generated 70 reports of safety-related failures. *Windstar:* **1999**—The following is a summary of the several hundred complaints in the NHTSA database. Many of these defects have been found in previous model year Windstars too: Airbags fail to deploy. • Stuck accelerator causes unintended acceleration. • Sudden loss of power steering, chronic leakage of fluid, and early replacement of steering components such as the pump and hoses. • Excessive brake fade after successive stops. • ABS module wire burned out. • Complete electrical failure during rainstorm. • Door locks don't stay locked. • Rear defogger isn't operable (lower part of windshield isn't clear) in inclement weather when windshield wipers are activated. • Water pours from dash onto front passenger floor. • Floor cupholder trips passengers. • Continental General tires lose air and crack between the treads. • Unspecified original-equipment tires have sudden tread separation. • Large A-pillar (where windshield attaches to door) seriously impairs forward visibility, hiding pedestrians. • Seat belts aren't as described in owner's manual (supposed to be automatically retractable). • Two incidents where flames shot up out of fuel-tank filler spout when refuelling up. **1999–2000**— While parked, cruising, turning on the ignition, or applying brakes, vehicle suddenly accelerates. • Chronic stalling caused by fuel vapour lock or faulty fuel pump. • Front passenger-side wheel falls off when turning; in one reported incident, dealer found the five lug nuts had broken in half. • Check Engine light constantly comes on because of a faulty gas cap or over-sensitive warning system. • Rear side windows, liftgate window, and windshield explode suddenly. • Windshield wipers fail to clear windshield, are unreliable. • Horn button "sweet spot" is too small and takes too much pressure to activate; one owner says, "Horn doesn't work unless you hit it with a sledgehammer." • Frequent transmission failures, including noisy engagement, won't engage Forward or Reverse, and slips or jerks into gear. In one incident, transmission jumped from Park to Reverse and pinned the driver against a tree. Another popped out of gear while parked and then rolled away, while another jumped out of gear on the highway. This is a common problem affecting Ford vehicles for almost three decades. • Sliding door opens and closes on its own, sticks open or closed, or suddenly slams shut on a downgrade. While underway, the right-side sliding door of one vehicle opened on its own and wouldn't close (see *Sharman* judgment on page 473). Another sliding door released and came crashing down on a child when the vehicle was parked on an incline. **1999–2003**—When brake pedal is depressed, it sinks below the accelerator pedal level, causing the accelerator to be pressed as well—particularly annoying for drivers with large feet. • **2000**—One vehicle caught fire while parked. • Engine shuts down when turning. • Sometimes cruise control won't engage, or engages on its own. • One Ingersoll, Ontario, owner of a 2000 Windstar recounts the following harrowing experience:

> Last week, as my wife was running errands, the support arm that goes from the rear crossmember (not an axle anymore) up under the floor broke in half. The dealer replaced the whole rear end as it is one welded assembly. If she had been on the highway going 80 km/h she would probably have been in a bad accident.

• One driver heard a banging noise and then the Windstar suddenly went into a tailspin; dealer blamed pins that "fell out of spindle." • Many reports of premature transmission replacements. • Emergency brake is inadequate to hold the vehicle. • After several dealer visits, brakes still spongy, pedal goes to floor without braking, and emergency brake has almost no effect. • Dealers acknowledge that brake master cylinders are problematic. • Joints aren't connected under quarter wheel weld; one weld is missing, and three aren't properly connected. • In one incident, the passenger door opened when the vehicle hit a pothole. • Hood suddenly flies up while underway. • Steering in one vehicle failed three times. • Power-steering pump whines and lurches. • Steering wheel is noisy and hard to turn. • When the interior rear-view mirror is set for Night Vision, images become distorted and hard to see. • Second-row driver-side seat belt buckle won't latch. • Original-equipment tire blowouts and sidewall bulging. **2000–01**—Harsh 3–2 shifting when coasting and then accelerating. • Transmission fluid leaks from the main control cover area. • 3.8L engine hum, moan, drone, spark knock, and vibration. • Power-steering grunts or shudders during slow turns; fluid leaks. • Faulty self-activating wipers and door, trunk, and ignition locks. **2000–02**—Transmission lever can be shifted without depressing the brake pedal. **2001**—Airbag may suddenly deploy when the engine is started. • Transmission shudder during 3–4 shifts. • Drifting or pulling while driving. • Rear drum brakes drag or fail to release properly. • Twisted seatback frame. **2001–03**—Interior windows fog up because of inadequate defrosting. **2002**—Back door won't open or close properly. • Both sliding doors won't retract. **2002–03**—Airbags fail to deploy. • Sudden automatic transmission failure. **2003**—Wheel suddenly breaks away. • Sudden, unintended acceleration when braking. • Engine surging. • Chronic stalling from blown fuel-pump fuses. • Coolant leaks from the timing cover gasket. • Advanced tracking system engages on its own, causing vehicle to shake violently. • Steering wheel locks up. • Gas-pedal arm pivot causes the pedal to flip almost horizontally, exaggerating any pedal pressure. • Body seams not sealed; water intrudes into floor seat anchors. • Driver's seat poorly anchored. • Dashboard glare onto the windshield. • Check Tire warning light comes on for no reason. • Tire jack collapses. *Freestar:* **2004**—Sudden loss of steering. • Airbag warning light stays on, may not deploy. • One driver heard a bang and then felt as if the vehicle was running on a flat tire; the A-frame had dropped out of the tie-rod collar. • Front axle suddenly breaks while underway. • One vehicle's left inner brake pad fell apart and locked up brake. Dealer had to change pads and rotor. • Sliding door closes on passenger. • Plastic running board breaks, blocking sliding door operation and locking occupants inside the vehicle. • Headliner-mounted DVD screen blocks rear-view mirror. **2005**—Fuel tank leaks. • Brake failure; brakes feel like sponges. • Brake pad sticks to the rotors. • Vehicle vibrates and shakes when going over bumps, and almost goes out of control. • Excessive force needed to make power-sliding door retract. • Headlight beam pattern is inadequate. • Windshield wiper motor suddenly quits. • Use of a cell phone charger could make the airbags deploy. • Vehicle will not start if the fuel tank is one-quarter full and the van is parked on a steep incline. **2006**—Vehicle can shut down in the rain if the computer module gets wet. • Traction control kicks in at the wrong time:

The anti-slip kicks in when it wants to—I almost got killed twice. They are stating it is a sensor in the steering column that overheats and causes the anti-slip to turn on.

•

The traction control system activates for no reason on perfectly good road conditions. The brakes come on hard, the gas pedal pushes back at you. It happened crossing an intersection one time and I was almost broadsided. The dealer says it is an optical sensor on the steering column, light is somehow hitting it causing this to happen. We were told there is no fix for it right now—just live with it.

• Transmission lever can be shifted from Park into Neutral without depressing the brake pedal. • Frequent power loss while underway. • Factory-issued wiper blades work poorly. • Middle-row seat belt anchor bolt easily pulls out. **2007**—When cruising, vehicle suddenly jumps out of gear.

Secret Warranties/Internal Bulletins/Service Tips

All models/years: Engine intake manifolds: When engine oil mixes with coolant or the engine is losing coolant, this signals the need for revised engine lower intake manifold side gaskets and/or front cover gaskets. The following internal bulletin can go a long way toward getting a repair refund for any Ford model up to 7 years/160,000 km, since it shows that the defect is factory-related, an upgraded part has been devised, and the problem is covered by the much-longer emissions warranty and a U.S. class action settlement:

ENGINE COOLANT LOSS/OIL CONTAMINATION	
BULLETIN NO.: 99-20-7	DATE: OCTOBER 4, 1999

3.8L AND 4.2L ENGINE—LOSS OF COOLANT; ENGINE OIL CONTAMINATED WITH COOLANT
1996–97 THUNDERBIRD
1996–98 MUSTANG, WINDSTAR
1997–98 E-150, E-250, F-150
1996–97 COUGAR
This may be caused by the lower intake manifold side gaskets and/or front cover gaskets allowing coolant to pass into the cylinders and/or the crankcase.
ACTION: Revised lower intake manifold side and front cover gaskets have been released for service.
WARRANTY STATUS: Eligible under the provisions of bumper to bumper warranty coverage and emissions warranty coverage

• An exhaust buzz or rattle may be caused by a loose catalyst or heat shield. • Buzzing noise in speakers caused by fuel pump. • A MIL lit for no reason may simply show that the gas cap is loose. • If the power-sliding door won't close, replace the door controller; if it pops or disengages when fully closed, adjust the door and rear striker to reduce closing resistance. • Bulletin No. 04-2-3, published February 9, 2004, goes into excruciating detail about finding and fixing the sliding door's many failures. • Front wipers that operate when switched off need a revised multi-function switch (service program and recall). *Windstar:* **1999**—Tips for correcting excessive noise, vibration, and harshness while driving; side door wind noise; and windshield water leaks. • Tips on spotting abnormal ABS braking noise, although Ford says some noise is inevitable. • No Reverse engagement may be caused by torn Reverse clutch lip seals. • To improve the defogging of the driver-side door glass, install a revised window de-mister vent. **1999–2000**—A harsh 3–2 downshift/shudder when accelerating or turning may simply mean the transmission is low on fluid. • Diagnostic tips on brake vibration, inspection, and friction material replacement. **1999–2002**—Silencing suspension noise. **1999–2003**—Engines that have been repaired may have an incorrectly installed gear-driven camshaft-position sensor synchronizer assembly. This could cause poor fuel economy, loss of power, and engine surge, hesitation, and rough running. • Tips on troubleshooting automatic transmission faulty torque converters. • Water may enter into the power control module or transaxle vent and cause delayed or harsh shifting, no reverse engagement, an engine misfire, or a rough idle. • Things that go beep in the night:

PARKING ASSIST—FALSE ACTIVATION

BULLETIN NO.: 04-7-1   DATE: APRIL 19, 2004

FALSE ACTIVATION OF WARNING TONE

1999–2003 WINDSTAR	2000–04 NAVIGATOR
1999–2004 EXPLORER	2002–03 BLACKWOOD
2000–04 EXCURSION, EXPEDITION	2003–04 AVIATOR
2001–04 F SUPER DUTY	1999–2004 MOUNTAINEER
2003–05 ESCAPE	2004 MONTEREY
2004 F-150; FREESTAR	

Various 1999–2005 vehicles equipped with the Parking Aid reverse sensing system (RSS) may sound a warning tone when the vehicle is in Reverse, even though there are no objects behind the vehicle. This condition may also occur on vehicles equipped with the forward sensing system (FSS) when vehicle is in Reverse or Drive.

ACTION: The condition MAY NOT be due to proximity sensor(s) malfunction but may be a normal operation characteristic, or due to sensor contamination (sensor being covered with dirt).

• Inoperative rear window defroster. **2001**—Ford admits automatic transmission defects (slippage, delayed shifts) in Special Service Instruction #01T01. **2001–02**—Service tips for reports of premature engine failures. • Vacuum or air leaks in the intake manifold or engine system causing lit warning lights. • Concerns about oil in the cooling system. • Engine cylinder heads that have been repaired may still leak coolant or oil from the gasket area. • Hard starts; rough-running engines. • Shudder while in Reverse or during 3–4 shifts. • Transmission fluid leakage. • Power-steering fluid leaks. • Brake roughness and pulsation. • Rear brake drum drag in cold weather. • Fogging of the front and side windows. • False Low Tire warning. • Repeated heater core failures. • Troubleshooting MIL warning light. **2001–03**—Remedy for a slow-to-fill fuel tank. **2002**—Automatic transmission fluid leaking at the quick connect for the transmission cooler lines. • MIL comes on, vehicle shifts poorly, or vehicle won't start. • Instrument panel beeping. • Buzz, groan, or vibration when gear selector lever is in Park. • Some vehicles may run roughly on the highway or just after stopping. • Defective ignition switch lock cylinders. • Anti-theft system operates on its own. • Battery may go dead after extended parking time. • Sliding doors rattle and squeak. • Steering system whistle/whine. • Loose rear wiper arm. **2003**—Front-end grinding or popping noise when passing over bumps or making turns. • Airbag warning light stays lit. • Faulty rear window defroster. • Inoperative AC; compressor leakage. • Power steering hose leaks. *Freestar:* **2004**—False activation of parking assist. (Remember, I said earlier that this optional safety device would drive you nuts with false warnings.) • Loose rear door trim. **2004–05**—Transmission has no 1–2 upshift (TSB #04-15-12). • Seat belt is slow to retract. • Inoperative power-sliding door and liftgate. • Remedy for front brake squeal or squeak. • Faulty 16-inch Goodyear Integrity tires may be the source of excessive vibration at high speeds. All four tires will be replaced free of charge on a case-by-case basis. **2004–06**—Inoperative AC; compressor leakage. **2004–07**—Power steering hose leaks in cold weather. • Transmission fluid leaks. **2005**—A short circuit may cause the ABS warning light to remain constantly lit. **2005–06**—Tips to silence AC whistling. **2006–07**—A rough-running, knocking, pinging engine may be caused by water entering the PCM. • Engine intake popping noise.

FREESTAR, WINDSTAR PROFILE

	1999	2000	2001	2002	2003	2004	2005	2006	2007
Cost Price ($) (very negotiable)									
Freestar (23%)	—	—	—	—	—	27,295	27,995	22,999	23,299
Windstar (base)	24,295	—	—	—	—	—	—	—	—
Windstar LX	28,195	25,995	26,750	25,995	26,195	—	—	—	—
Windstar SEL	36,195	36,195	33,190	33,685	37,015	—	—	—	—
Used Values ($)									
Freestar ▲	—	—	—	—	—	5,500	7,500	10,500	13,500
Freestar ▼	—	—	—	—	—	4,000	6,000	9,000	12,000
Windstar (base) ▲	2,500	—	—	—	—	—	—	—	—
Windstar (base) ▼	2,000	—	—	—	—	—	—	—	—
Windstar LX ▲	2,500	3,000	3,500	4,000	5,000	—	—	—	—
Windstar LX ▼	2,000	2,500	3,000	3,500	4,000	—	—	—	—
Windstar SEL ▲	3,000	3,500	4,000	4,500	6,000	—	—	—	—
Windstar SEL ▼	2,500	3,000	3,500	3,000	5,000	—	—	—	—
Reliability	1	1	2	2	2	2	2	3	3
Crash Safety (F)	5	5	5	5	5	5	5	5	5
Side	5	4	4	4	4	4	4	4	4
IIHS Side	—	—	—	—	—	—	—	2	2
Offset	3	3	3	3	3	5	5	5	5
Rollover	—	—	4	4	4	4	4	4	4

RATING: Above Average (2008); Average (2004–07); Below Average (1980–2003). **Strong points:** Reasonably well equipped; more-refined powertrain and brakes phased in on the 2004s; good control and instrument layout; adequate interior room; and an acceptable ride. *2008:* Good base warranty, and more reliable than any Detroit front-drive. **Weak points:** Huge and heavy with sloppy handling, similar to the Ram lineup. With earlier vehicles, excessive braking distance and harsh transmission shifting and hunting. Limited second-row legroom and excessive engine, wind, and road noise. Quality control isn't the best, especially with the failure-prone 6.0L diesel engine, the alternators, and the AC compressor. **New for 2008:** Re-engineered and restyled. Improvements include a revised steering system, better front and rear suspensions, and more durable brakes to enhance manoeuvrability and ride. Stability control has been added as a standard safety feature on E-350 passenger wagons, equipped with the 5.4L V8. An engine-only traction control system is used on all other models. 2009 models will return relatively unchanged.

2008 TECHNICAL DATA

POWERTRAIN (REAR-DRIVE)
Engines: 4.6L V8 (225 hp) • 5.4L V8 (255 hp) • 6.8L V10 (305 hp) • 6.0L turbodiesel (325 hp); Transmissions: 4-speed auto. • 5-speed auto.

DIMENSION/CAPACITY
Passengers: 7–15; Wheelbase: 138.0 in.; H: 80.7/L: 211.8/W: 79.3 in.; Headroom N/A; Legroom F/R: 40.0/36.9 in.; Cargo volume: 257.0 cu. ft.; Fuel tank: 132L/ regular/diesel; Tow limit: 3,500–10,000 lb.; Load capacity: 1,995 lb.; GVWR: 10,000–20,000 lb.; Turning circle: 23.4 ft.; Ground clearance: 7.6 in.; Weight: 4,773 lb.

MODEL HISTORY: First launched in 1961 on the Falcon platform, the rear-drive Econoline has long been a fixture in the commercial delivery market, primarily because of its 4,536 kg (10,000 lb.) carrying capacity. Like Chrysler, Ford has made few changes over the last several decades, figuring that a good thing is best left alone. The Ford Club Wagon, which is an Econoline dressed up for passenger duty, offers lots of room with capacity to spare for luggage. Nevertheless, full-sized vans have a very high floor, long panelled windows, and seats that are bolted to the floor, unlike most minivans, which feature powered middle windows and seats that stow into the floor or fold to the side.

Easily found at reasonable prices, Econolines don't possess any glaring virtues or vices. They all perform in a manner similar to that of Chrysler's and GM's large vans, and overall reliability is on par with the companies' comparable full-sized vans.

The 2004 models got a 4.6L V8 base engine; the 7.3L diesel was ditched for a problematic 6.0L turbocharged variant; and a new 5-speed automatic transmission was added (turbo models only) along with rear disc brakes on larger wheels. Much-needed standard electronic stability control was added to the 2006 model lineup, and the 2007s got shorter wheelbase models and standard stability control.

Econolines have had fewer quality-control deficiencies than Chrysler or GM, but they are merely the best of an old-tech bad lot. Admittedly, Ford engine defects are legion. Electrical, fuel, and ignition systems are constantly on the fritz. The 3- and 4-speed automatic transmissions, steering and suspension components (lower steering shaft/tie-rods), and brakes (calipers, pads, rotors, and torn rear caliper boots) have also come under considerable criticism.

Econolines equipped with the 4.9L inline-six engine were offered with a 3- or 4-speed manual, or a 3-speed automatic transmission. All recent V8-equipped vans come with a 4-speed automatic. It would be best to find an earlier Econoline or Club Wagon with the more refined and reliable 4-speed automatic and 5.0L V8 until we see how the base 4.6L handles long-term use. If heavy-duty hauling is your métier, then you'll be interested in getting a used Econoline equipped with the 7.5L V8, capable of moving a gross combined weight rated at 8,392 kg (18,500 lb.).

Body fit and finish are typically below average and have been that way for the past several decades. Still, squeaks and rattles have been notably reduced on more recent models. Premature rusting hasn't been a serious problem since the mid-1980s (except for rusted-out oil pans), but paint delamination and peeling and water leaks through the windshield and doors are quite common.

COST ANALYSIS: The base cost for a 2008 E-Series full-sized van is $29,999—only a few hundred dollars more than last year's model. 2009s are expected to sell for $1,000 less and be discounted by at least $5,000 early in 2009. Stay away from any '05 equipped with the 6.0L diesel powerplant; opt instead for an '04 equipped with a 7.3L diesel engine. The 2006 extended wheelbase models feature standard stability control. **Best alternatives:** Earlier Dodge B-series vans are also worthwhile choices. The GM competition is a warmed-over 1990s design, while Chrysler has embraced the Sprinter, a narrow Mercedes-Benz van with a 152-hp turbodiesel engine, used mainly for commercial deliveries. **Rebates:** $5,000 rebates and discounts on the 2008 and 2009 models. **Delivery/PDI:** $1,200. **Warranty:** Bumper-to-bumper 3 years/60,000 km; rust perforation 5 years/unlimited km. **Supplementary warranty:** An extended warranty is a must. **Options:** Running boards, upgraded sound system, heavy-duty alternator, remote keyless entry, power windows and door locks, and rear air conditioning. Look into a transmission oil cooler for the Overdrive transmission, particularly if you plan to do some trailering. **Depreciation:** Faster than average. **Insurance cost:** Higher than average. **Parts supply/cost:** There's a good supply of cheap parts. **Annual maintenance cost:** Higher than average. **Highway/city fuel economy:** E-150 4.2L: 11.7/16.6 L/100 km; 4.6L: 12.2/17.6 L/100 km; 5.4L: 12.3/17.4 L/100 km.

 QUALITY/RELIABILITY: Mediocre quality control and average reliability. With Ford's constant management reorganizations, the deck chairs get shuffled around, but the ship is still sinking. Many "goodwill" programs cover some of the owner problems listed below. However, this approach is mostly hit or miss, and it's no solution for Ford's poor quality control. **Owner-reported problems:** Poor engine performance characterized by constant stalling; turbocharger, high-pressure pump, and injector malfunctions; automatic transmission breakdowns; and chronic failures of key suspension or steering components, AC compressors, the engine oil pump alternator, and the EGR valve ("coking"):

> "Coking" (un-combustion) deposits form on the EGR valve causing driveability issues such as lack of power, surges, and stalling. This condition is especially dangerous when the bus develops this condition when crossing intersections, railroad tracks, etc., and is transporting passengers both mobile and [disabled]. Drivers have voiced their concern over this condition as they believe it is unsafe for them and their passengers. Ford motor company has replaced EGR valves (approx. 36–40) or recommends a fuel additive to try to take care of the problem.... Previously we had similar Ford vehicles with 7.3L diesel engines operating under identical conditions with no problems. These problems occurred when the 6.0L diesel was introduced.

Additionally, there are frequent electrical glitches, the brakes are noisy and wear out prematurely, and the body is invaded by omnipresent creaks, squeaks, rattles, buzzing, and whining. **Warranty performance:** Quite poor; that's why a getting a used model and taking it to a competent independent mechanic is your best bet.

 SAFETY SUMMARY: Insurance industry statistics show that Ford vans have had a lower-than-average frequency of accident injury claims when compared to all vehicles on North American roads. Many Econolines don't have front-seat head restraints; Club Wagons may have head restraints for the two front seats, depending on the trim level. **Airbags:** There have been reports of airbags failing to deploy. **ABS:** Four-wheel; standard. **Safety belt pretensioners:** Standard. **Head restraints F/R:** 2004: ★. **Visibility F/R:** ★★★★★/★★. **Pet transport:** ★★★★★.

SAFETY COMPLAINTS: All models/years: Airbag malfunctions. • Chronic stalling. • Exhaust fumes enter into the vehicle. • Film covers inside of windshield, causing poor visibility. • Steering tie-rod end failures. • Tire-tread separation. **1999**—Lots of complaints of road wander, vibration, and premature brake rotor warpage and pad wearout, leading to extended stopping distances and front brake lock-up. • Sudden acceleration when idling or when cruise control is activated. • One van rolled away while parked with emergency brake engaged. • Electrical shorts cause fuses to blow and make brakes, turn signals, and transmissions malfunction. • Vehicle tends to pull to one side when cruising. **1999–2002**—Sticking or binding ignition lock cylinder. **2000**—Vehicle is equipped with non-adjustable camber bushings, causing premature outer tire wear in both front tires. • In one incident, a child became trapped between the sofa bed and the captain's chair. **2001**—Flat mirrors create a large blind spot. **2002**—Water enters through the intake, causing engine damage. • Engine surges at idle. • Brake failure caused by brake pads sticking to the rotor. • Vehicle pulls to the right when brakes are hot. • Fuel tank won't fill up completely. • Jammed rear seat belt. **2002–04**—Loss of power steering; steering gearbox failure. **2003**—One vehicle's engine stalled and then exploded. • Transmission slips out of Park into Reverse. • Excessive on-road shake. **2004**—Slow throttle response in 5.4L. • Excessive highway wander; loose steering. • Fuel-pump failure caused by misrouted electrical harness. • Seat belts may be too short. *E-150:* **2005**—When the vehicle stalls going uphill, there are no brakes or steering to maintain control as it backs down. **2006**—Vehicle suddenly shuts down while underway. • Accelerator and brake pedal mounted too close together. *E-250:* **2005**—Passenger-side airbag cannot be disabled when carrying a child. **2006**—Cruise control failure. • Side rear-view mirror is too small. • Allegations that van's interior contains toxic levels of formaldehyde:

> Ford 2005 E-250 has been identified with formaldehyde poison in it at above danger levels to humans, which can cause serious health issues. The van is custom done by a company in Mississippi. The A/C unit in the rear doesn't work and was in for service 3 times and over the 15-day requirement for the lemon law in the state of Florida, where it was sold. After the lemon law is completed I am going to request that a national alert be issued to make sure no one else becomes sick due to toxic fumes.

E-350: **2005**—Assorted electrical wiring and alternator problems affect power-train performance and dash warning lights. • Ambulance firm complained that their diesel-equipped ambulance was constantly stalling when sent out on emergency calls:

> 2005 Ford E-350 ambulance had a total engine failure while driving to a 911 call. The Ford dealership service center diagnosed an oil pump failure as the cause and replaced it under warranty. This is complaint #2 of 6. All of the 2005 Ford ambulances we purchased have suffered total engine failures from either the oil pumps or the wiring harness systems, and several have had AC problems as well. Ford is unwilling to replace these parts on the other units until they fail. They are placing numerous lives in extreme jeopardy and refuse to admit there are major problems with the 6.0L diesel engine in the 2005 series ambulance chassis.

2006—Engine shuts off when braking. • Failure of injectors and internal oil cooler also causes vehicle to shut down. • Faulty hydraulic power assist pumps. • Defective alternators and AC air compressors. • Brake vacuum-pump failure causes loss of brakes. *E-450:* **2005**—Engine surging when foot is taken off the accelerator pedal. • Sticking throttle. • Chronic stalling. • Faulty transmission torque converter. **2007**—Airbags fail to deploy.

Secret Warranties/Internal Bulletins/Service Tips

1999–2000—Paint delamination, peeling, or fading. • A rear axle whine on E-450 Super Duty with a Dana 80 can be silenced by putting in a dampened rear driveshaft. • To prevent the lower rear brake caliper boots from being damaged when driving over gravel roads, Ford will install a brake caliper shield kit. **1999–2001**—Ford admits to faulty 5.4L engines with defective head gaskets. The April 1, 2002, edition of *Automotive News* says the automaker budgeted up to

$4,500 (U.S.) to replace affected engines and $800 (U.S.) to replace the cylinder heads and head gasket. **1999–2003**—7.3L diesel engine turbocharger pedestal may have premature oil pan corrosion or a high-pressure oil pump leak (TSB #04-4-4). **1999–2005**—Troubleshooting broken intake manifold studs. • Tips for correcting a rough idle. **1999–2006**—A driveline clunk may signal that the slip yoke needs lubrication. Check this out first before spending big bucks on more involved tests or repairs. **2000**—Replace the intake manifold gasket if leakage is evident. **2000–03**—Poor engine performance (see bulletin). **2001**—Owner Notification Program says automatic transmission could have internal damage, may lose Second gear, or be unable to engage any gear. • Front shaft seal leakage. • An automatic transmission ticking or clicking may be heard when First gear is engaged. • Water pump shaft seal leakage. **2002**—Repeat heater core leaks. **2003**—Incorrectly machined engine crankshaft. • Exhaust air rush noise, and reduced power. **2003–04**—6.0L diesel engine runs rough, loses power, or has fuel in the oil (Bulletin #04-9-3, published May 11, 2004). **2004–06**—TSB #06-9-7, issued May 15, 2006, gives more diagnostic and repair tips for poorly performing diesel engines. • Reasons why the AC may not cool properly. **2005**—Engine stalls when shifting into Drive or Reverse, or when coming to a stop. **2005–06**—Inadvertent transmission lock-up during 1–2 shifts.

ENGINE CONTROLS—ROUGH IDLE/HESITATION

BULLETIN NO.: 03-9-11   **DATE: MAY 12, 2003**

2000–03 E-350, E-450, EXCURSION, SUPER DUTY F-SERIES

ISSUE: Some F250–F550 Super Duty and Excursion vehicles equipped with a 5.4L or 6.8L engine, and some E350/450 vehicles equipped with a 6.8L engine may exhibit a rough idle and/or hesitation when accelerating. This may occur intermittently within the first 2–3 minutes after start when engine is not warmed up (i.e., conditions other than hot restart). The condition is more likely to occur at ambient temperatures of approximately 60°F (160°C) and higher, and may be aggravated by an unmetered air leak or exhaust leak.

ECONOLINE CARGO VAN, CLUB WAGON PROFILE

	1999	2000	2001	2002	2003	2004	2005	2006	2007
Cost Price ($) (very negotiable)									
Cargo Van (29%)	24,295	26,295	25,970	27,200	28,960	28,480	28,995	29,199	29,799
Club Wagon (24%)	28,195	29,295	28,615	29,000	30,050	31,120	31,375	31,899	32,400
Used Values ($)									
Cargo Van ▲	3,000	3,500	4,500	5,500	7,000	9,000	11,500	14,000	17,000
Cargo Van ▼	2,500	3,000	4,000	5,000	6,000	7,500	10,000	12,500	15,000
Club Wagon ▲	4,000	4,500	5,500	6,000	8,000	11,500	14,500	16,500	20,000
Club Wagon ▼	3,500	4,000	4,500	5,000	7,000	10,000	13,000	15,000	18,500
Reliability	2	3	3	3	3	3	3	3	3
Crash Safety (F)	4	4	4	4	4	4	4	4	—
Rollover	—	—	2	2	2	—	3	3	3

All ratings on a numbered scale where 5 is good and 1 is bad. See page 217 for a more detailed description.

Ford/Nissan

VILLAGER, QUEST ★★★

RATING: *Quest:* Average (2008); Below Average (2004–07). Like driving an aquarium. Factory defects are legion. *Villager and Quest:* Average (1997–2002); Below Average (1995–96); Not Recommended (1993–94). Best used for city commuting rather than for fully loaded, long highway journeys. **Strong points:** Wide side sliding doors; third-row seats fold into the floor; small handgrips easily accessed by children; hefty discounts. *2003 and earlier models:* Impressive highway performance (as long as you're not carrying a full load) and easy, no-surprise, carlike handling. Highway stability is above reproach; occupants get a comfortable ride with lots of seating choices; the 4-speed automatic transmission is particularly smooth and quiet; braking performance is quite good (when the brakes are working properly), and mechanical components have been tested for years on the Maxima. There's plenty of passenger and cargo room—these vans are nearly 30 cm (12 in.) longer and 5 cm (2 in.) wider and higher than Chrysler's short-wheelbase minivans. *Quest:* Carlike handling, lots of interior room, and well appointed. **Weak points:** Unreliable; quirky dash and interior styling. *2003 and earlier models:* These fuel-thirsty minivans are quite heavy, and the 3.0L and 3.3L engines have to go all out to carry the extra weight. Powertrain set-up trails the Odyssey in acceleration and passing. Other minuses: a cheap-looking interior, the control layout can be a bit confusing, suspension is too soft, and rear-seat access can be difficult. Some wind and road noise, and excessive engine noise under heavy throttle. *Quest:* Expensive; suspension bottoms out on rough roads; instrument panel produces windshield glare. **New for 2008:** Nothing much; the Quest will undergo a complete redesign for the 2010 model year.

> ### 2008 QUEST TECHNICAL DATA
>
> **POWERTRAIN (FRONT-DRIVE)**
> Engine: 3.5L V6 (240 hp); Transmission:
> • 5-speed auto.
> **DIMENSION/CAPACITY**
> Passengers: 2/2/3; Wheelbase: 124.0 in.;
> H: 70.0/L: 204.0/W: 78.0 in.; Headroom
> F/R1/R2: 6.5/7.5/3.0 in.; Legroom F/R1/
> R2: 40.0/28.0/32.0 in.; Cargo volume:
> 60.0 cu. ft.; Fuel tank: N/A; Tow limit:
> 3,500 lb.; Load capacity: 1,205 lb.;
> GVWR: 5,732 lb.; Turning circle: 44.0
> ft.; Ground clearance: 4.0 in.; Weight:
> 4,410 lb.

MODEL HISTORY: Smaller and more carlike than most minivans, the pre-2004 Villager and Quest are sized comfortably between the regular and extended Chrysler minivans. These minivans' strongest assets are a 170-hp 3.3L V6 engine that gives them carlike handling, ride, and cornering; modular seating; and reliable mechanical components. Nissan borrowed the powertrain, suspension, and steering assembly from the Maxima, mixed in some creative sheet metal, and then left the job of outfitting the sound system, climate control, dashboard, steering column, and wheels to Ford. This resulted in an attractive, not overly aero-styled minivan.

1999—The Pathfinder's 3.3L V6 replaced the 3.0L V6, giving the Villager and Quest an additional 19 horses. *Villager:* **1999**—A fourth door; more interior room; a revised instrument panel that's easier to reach; restyled front and rear ends; and improved shifting, acceleration, and braking. The suspension was retuned to give a more carlike ride and handling, the old climate control system was ditched for a more sophisticated version with air filtration, and optional ABS was made available with all models. Mercury's top-of-the-line model, the Nautica, was dropped. *Quest:* **1999**—An additional 11.6 cm (4.6 in.) in length and 3.0 cm (1.2 in.) in width, standard ABS brakes, and a driver-side sliding rear door. The second row of seats can be removed, and the third row is set on tracks. Upgraded headlights and rear leaf springs. A cargo shelf added behind the rear seats gives owners an extra 0.28 cubic metres (10 cubic feet) of storage space. **2001–02**—An improved child safety seat anchoring system; performance, suspension, and comfort upgrades; a stabilizer bar on the GLE; freshened exterior styling; and a standard entertainment centre with a large screen. **2004**—Re-engineered and restyled.

2004–09 Quest

A totally different minivan than its predecessor, the Quest is one of the largest minivans on the road. Based on the Altima/Murano platform, it offers a more powerful engine and all the standard high-tech safety, performance, and convenience features one could want. Its long wheelbase allows for the widest opening sliding doors among front-drive minivans, rear seating access is a breeze, and a capacious interior allows for flexible cargo and passenger configurations that can easily accommodate 4′ × 8′ objects with the liftgate closed. Standard fold-flat third-row seats and fold-to-the-floor centre-row seats allow owners to increase storage space without worrying about where to store the extra seats, although third-row headrests must be removed before the seats can be folded away.

Although it feels a bit heavy in the city, the Quest is very carlike when driven on the highway. Ride and handling are enhanced by a new four-wheel independent suspension, along with front and rear stabilizer bars and upgraded anti-lock brakes. Safety features include standard head curtain supplemental airbags for outboard passengers in all three rows, supplemental front-seat side-impact airbags, standard traction control, and ABS brakes with brake assist.

COST ANALYSIS: A 2008 model costs $32,598—only $100 more than a 2007 costs new. In the States, you would pay $26,330 (U.S.). Poor sales will likely keep 2009 model prices low. Unless you require all the newest bells and whistles, you can save yourself thousands by getting a fully loaded 1999–2003 Quest. Stay away from the 2004–07 glitch-ridden models. **Best alternatives:** Other minivans worth considering are Chrysler Caravan, Honda Odyssey, and Toyota Sienna. **Options:** Nothing really worthwhile. **Rebates:** $3,000–$5,000 rebates. **Delivery/PDI:** $1,450. **Depreciation:** Much faster than average due to the huge stockpile of unsold units. **Insurance cost:** Average. **Parts supply/cost:** Good supply and reasonably priced, although the post-2004 models continue to experience long delays for some slow-moving body parts, and they're a bit costly. **Annual maintenance cost:** Average. **Warranty:** Bumper-to-bumper 3 years/80,000 km; powertrain 5 years/100,000 km; rust perforation 5 years/ unlimited km. **Supplementary warranty:** Essential for all model years. **Highway/city fuel economy:** *Villager/Quest: 8.9/13.8 L/100 km; 2004 and later:* 8.2/12.4 L/100 km.

QUALITY/RELIABILITY: Body integrity has always been subpar, with doors opening and closing on their own and poor fit and finish allowing lots of wind noise and water to enter the interior:

> Water has leaked into the car from the area of the sunglass holder on two occasions. The sunglass holder is located in the middle right at the top edge of the windshield. On one occasion it leaked after washing the car. On the second occasion it happened during a heavy rainstorm. The dealer would not fix or investigate the problem further because their glass contractor could not duplicate the problem using a hose.

There have also been some reports of panel and paint defects and premature rusting on the inside sliding door track. **Owner-reported problems:** Most owner-reported problems involve excessive brake noise and premature brake wear, door lock malfunctions, interior noise, and driveline vibrations. There have also been many reports of engine exhaust manifold and crankshaft failures, costing up to $7,000 to repair, and automatic transmission slippage. Other problems include electrical shorts; brake failures caused by vibration, binding, or overheating; premature wear of the front discs, rotors, and pads; chronic stalling, possibly caused by faulty fuel pumps or a shorted electrical system; and loose steering and veering at highway speeds. Owners also complain of film buildup on windshield and interior glass; a sulfur smell from the exhaust system; poor AC performance or compressor failures accompanied by musty, mildew-type AC odours; and a recurring fuel-pump buzzing heard through the radio speakers.

The 2005 and later models have many of the same problems, along with a few new ones, as this owner details:

> Ongoing problems which include: the windows failing to roll up when button is pushed, the gas gauge failing to register gas after filling it up, the gas meter after a half a tank never registers correctly (when light indicates no gas and tank is filled the van will only take 16 gallons [4.2L] and owners manual indicates a 20 gallon [5.3L] tank), the transmission slips, the sliding doors squeak and rattle, rear interior clamps on floor of car are rusting, idiot lights come on intermittently, the gaskets on the doors are coming off, the heated seats haven't worked in high and low, the entertainment system doesn't respond to rear AV, and the air conditioner is not cool enough and it stinks. The automatic slide doors will not stop for small objects but this product was designed for families. These doors will remove a child's finger and the switch to initiate the auto slide is low...one child can push it while another is getting in or has their hand in the way.... I did my own little research test, I got pencils and everywhere I placed a pencil the door closed with the pencil being snapped into many pieces and

crunched up in the door. Then I tried the same thing on my friend's Honda, but the Honda's auto slide doors bounced off every time.

Add these troubles to the above list: The fuel gauge doesn't give accurate readings with a half-full tank; doors rattle and are hard to open or close; the windows won't roll up; and there are water leaks and windshield cracks. **Warranty performance:** Below average.

 SAFETY SUMMARY: The 2008 crashworthiness scores match those of the 2007 and 2006 models. **ABS:** Standard. **Safety belt pretensioners:** Standard. **Head restraints F/R:** *1999–2002:* ★. *Quest 2004–08:* ★. **Visibility F/R:** ★★★★★/★★. **Pet transport:** ★★★★★.

SAFETY COMPLAINTS: 1999—Gas fumes leak into the interior. **1999–2002**—Gas pedal sticks. **1999–2003**—Sudden stalling caused by faulty fuel pump. • Steering wander and excessive vibration. • Chronic ABS failures; brake pads and rotors need replacing every 5,000 km. • Brake failures (extended stopping distance, noisy when applied). • Brake and accelerator pedals are the same height, so driver's foot can easily slip and step on both at the same time. • Cycling or self-activating front door locks; occupants have been trapped in their vehicles. **1999–2004**—Airbags fail to deploy, or deploy inadvertently. • Sudden, unintended acceleration. **2000**— Vehicle tends to lurch forward when the AC is first engaged. • Weak tailgate hydraulic cylinders. • Instrument panel's white face hard to read in daylight hours. **2000–01**—Missing seat belt latch plate stopper button. • Broken shift-lock cable plate causes shift indicator to be misaligned. • A 2-year-old child was able to pull the clasp apart on integrated child safety seat. • Seat belts don't retract properly. • Rear window on liftgate door shatters for unknown reason (replaced under warranty). • Power-steering fluid leakage caused by a split O-ring at rack gear. **2002**—Leaking front and rear struts degrade handling. • Steering wheel is off-centre to the left. • Continental tire-tread separation. **2004**—Sliding door traps occupants; door continually pops open. • Automatic transmission won't downshift. • Dome light fuse blows continually. • Ineffective windshield wipers. **2004–05**—Dashboard reflects onto the windshield, impairing the view forward. **2005**—Vehicle continues to accelerate even though brakes are applied. • Driver's seat belt won't stay latched. • Seat belt clasp gets stuck in the web stitching. • Vehicle rolls backward when stopped on a hill and foot is taken off the brake. • Goodyear tires wear out prematurely ("feathered"). • Seat recall could not go ahead due to a lack of replacement parts. **2005–06**—Sliding door doesn't stop for objects in its path; in one incident, a child's thumb was seriously injured when it was caught in the door. **2006**—Passenger-side airbag disables for no reason. • Transmission hesitates, slips, bucks, and jerks. • Passenger sliding door falls off its tracks. • Driver's seat may suddenly tilt forward. • Sliding door won't open. **2007**—Engine surging.

1999—Tips for correcting windshield water leaks and excessive noise, vibration, and harshness. • An exhaust buzz or rattle may be caused by a loose catalyst or muffler heat shield. 1999–2002—Paint delamination, peeling, or fading. • Repeat heater core failure. • Power door locks that intermittently self-activate are covered in TSB #98-22-5. 1999–2004—Troubleshooting abnormal shifting. • Side windows pop open. 2002–07—Fuel system ticking noise. 2004—No-start, hard start remedies. • Silencing a ticking engine/exhaust noise. • AC blows out warm air from floor vents. • Leaking, overheating cooling system. • Guidelines on troubleshooting brake complaints. 2004–05—Lack of power; automatic transmission sticks in Third gear. • Troubleshooting sliding door rattles and difficult opening/closing. • Water leaks in the cargo area. • Exhaust system rattles when accelerating. • Insufficient AC cooling. • Front power seat won't move. 2004–06—Pop-out window rattling. • "Skyview" roof water leaks.

VILLAGER, QUEST PROFILE

	1999	2000	2001	2002	2004	2005	2006	2007
Cost Price ($) (negotiable)								
Villager GS	24,595	24,595	—	—	—	—	—	—
Villager LS	29,495	29,495	—	—	—	—	—	—
Quest GXE/S (20%)	27,798	30,498	30,498	30,698	32,900	31,698	32,048	32,498
Used Values ($)								
Villager GS ▲	3,500	4,500	—	—	—	—	—	—
Villager GS ▼	2,500	3,500	—	—	—	—	—	—
Villager LS ▲	4,000	5,000	—	—	—	—	—	—
Villager LS ▼	3,500	4,500	—	—	—	—	—	—
Quest GXE/S ▲	4,500	5,000	6,500	8,000	10,500	14,000	16,000	18,000
Quest GXE/S ▼	4,000	4,500	5,500	6,500	9,000	12,500	14,500	16,500
Reliability	3	3	3	3	2	2	3	3
Crash Safety (F)	—	4	5	5	5	5	5	5
Side	—	5	5	5	5	5	5	5
IIHS Side	—	—	—	—	—	—	5	5
Offset	1	1	1	1	5	5	5	5
Rollover	—	—	4	4	4	4	4	4

Note: There was no 2003 model year Villager or Quest. Nissan dropped the 2005 Quest's price to counter slow sales.

General Motors

ASTRO, SAFARI ★ ★ ★

RATING: Average (1996–2005); Below Average (1985–95). Dropped at the end of 2005, these rear-drives are more mini-truck than minivan. Yet they're much more reliable and cheaper to buy and run than the problem-plagued Detroit front-drive minivans and the overpriced Asian competition. Stay away from the unreliable AWD models, though; they're expensive to repair and not very durable. **Strong points:** Good acceleration and trailer-towing capability, lots of passenger room and cargo space, and a well-laid-out instrument panel with easy-to-read gauges. Very low ground clearance enhances this minivan's handling but precludes most off-roading. Good brakes. Rock-bottom used prices, and average reliability and quality control. **Weak points:** Driving position is awkward for many; some drivers will find the pedals too close; obtrusive engine makes for very narrow front footwells that give little room for the driver's left foot to rest. Difficult entry and exit because of the high step-up and the intruding wheelwell. Harsh ride, limited front seatroom, interior noise levels rise sharply at highway speeds, and excessive fuel consumption is made worse by the AWD option.

490

2005 TECHNICAL DATA

POWERTRAIN (REAR-DRIVE)
Engine: 4.3L V6 (190 hp); Transmission: 4-speed auto.
DIMENSION/CAPACITY
Passengers: 2/3/3; Wheelbase: 111.2 in.; H: 74.9/L: 190.0/W: 78.0 in.; Headroom F/R1/R2: N/A; Legroom F/R1/R2: 41.6/36.5/38.5 in.; Cargo volume: 170.4 cu. ft.; Fuel tank: 95L/regular; Tow limit: 5,400 lb.; Load capacity: 1,764 lb.; GVWR: 5,900–6,100 lb.; Turning circle: 40.5 ft.; Ground clearance: 6.8 in.; Weight: 4,321 lb.

MODEL HISTORY: More of a utility truck than a comfortable minivan, these boxy, rear-drive minivans are built on a reworked S-10 pickup chassis. As such, they offer uninspiring handling, average-quality mechanical and body components, and relatively high fuel consumption. Both the Astro and Safari come in a choice of either cargo or passenger van. The cargo van is used either commercially or as an inexpensive starting point for a fully customized vehicle.

1999—A reworked AWD system. **2000**—Only seven- and eight-passenger models available; engine made quieter and smoother, while the automatic transmission was toughened up to shift more efficiently when pulling heavy loads; and a larger fuel tank was installed. **2001**—A tilt steering wheel, cruise control, CD player, remote keyless entry, and power windows, mirrors, and locks. **2002**—A rear heater on cargo models. **2003**—Upgraded four-wheel disc brakes.

The 1985–95 versions suffer from failure-prone automatic transmissions, poor braking systems, malfunctioning AC compressors, and fragile steering components. The early base V6 provides ample power, but it also produces lots of noise, consumes excessive amounts of fuel, and tends to have leaking head gaskets and failure-prone oxygen sensors. These computer-related problems often rob the engine of sufficient power to keep up in traffic. While the 5-speed manual transmission shifts fairly easily, the automatic takes forever to downshift on the highway. Handling isn't particularly agile on these minivans, and the power steering doesn't provide the driver with enough road feel. Unloaded, the Astro provides very poor traction, the ride isn't comfortable on poor road surfaces, and interior noise is rampant. Many drivers find the driving position awkward (there's no left legroom) and the heating/defrosting system inadequate. Many engine components are hidden under the dashboard, making repair or maintenance awkward. Even on more recent models, highway performance and overall reliability aren't impressive. Through the 2005 model year, the 4-speed automatic transmissions are clunky and hard shifting, though they're much more reliable than Ford or Chrysler gearboxes.

Other owners report that the front suspension, steering components, computer modules, and catalytic converter can wear out within as little as 60,000 km. There have also been lots of complaints about electrical, exhaust, cooling, and fuel system bugs; inadequate heating/defrosting; failure-prone wiper motors; and axle seals that wear out every 12 to 18 months.

Body hardware is fragile, and fit and finish is the pits. Water leaks from windows and doors are common yet hard to diagnose. Squeaks and rattles are legion and hard to locate. Sliding-door handles often break off, and the sliding door frequently jams in cold temperatures. The hatch release for the Dutch doors occasionally doesn't work, and the driver-side vinyl seat lining tears apart. Premature paint peeling, delamination, and surface rust are fairly common.

COST ANALYSIS: Get a cheap 2003 for the latest upgrades and best performance. **Best alternatives:** Most front-drive minivans made by Honda, Hyundai, Kia, and Toyota have better handling and are more reliable and economical people-carriers. **Warranty:** Bumper-to-bumper 3 years/60,000 km; rust perforation 6 years/160,000 km. **Supplementary warranty:** A powertrain-only warranty is a wise choice. **Options:** Look for a vehicle with integrated child safety seats and rear AC. Be wary of models that were ordered with AWD; it exacts a high fuel penalty and isn't very dependable. **Depreciation:** Slower than average. **Insurance cost:** Average. **Parts supply/cost:** Good supply of cheap parts. **Annual maintenance cost:** Average. Any garage can repair these rear-drive minivans. **Highway/city fuel economy:** *Rear-drive:* 10.6/14.6 L/100 km; *AWD:* 11.3/15.3 L/100 km.

QUALITY/RELIABILITY: Average; most of Astro's and Safari's defects are easy to diagnose and repair. Early rear axle failures are common. **Owner-reported problems:** Some problems with the automatic transmission, steering, electrical system, and heating and defrosting system as well as rear axle whine, premature brake wear, faulty suspension components, and glitch-prone sliding doors. **Warranty performance:** Average.

 SAFETY SUMMARY: NHTSA has recorded numerous complaints of dashboard fires. Power steering locks up or fails unexpectedly, components wear out quickly, and steering may bind when turning. Seat belt complaints are also common—seat belts tighten up unexpectedly, cannot be adjusted, or have nowhere to latch. **Airbags:** Standard front. Reports of drivers' airbags failing to deploy in a collision. **Anti-lock brakes:** Standard; disc/disc. Reports of ABS failures, brakes hesitating when applied, brakes engaging for no reason, and premature brake wear. **Traction control:** *AWD:* Optional. **Head restraints F/R:** *1999:* ★★; *2001–02:* ★★; *2003–05:* ★. **Visibility F/R:** ★★★★★/★★. **Pet transport:** ★★★★★.

SAFETY COMPLAINTS: 1999—Very few safety-related complaints, compared with most other minivans. Many of the 1999 model problems have also been reported by owners of earlier model years. • Hard shifting between First and Second gear; transmission slippage. • Delayed shifting or stalling when passing from Drive to Reverse. • Vehicle rolls backward on an incline while in Drive. • Leaking axle seals. • Rear cargo door hinge and latch slip off, and door opens 180 degrees. • Floor mat moves under brake and accelerator pedals. • Brake and gas pedals are too close together. • Fuel gauge failure caused by faulty sending unit. **1999–2000**—When brakes are applied, rear wheels tend to lock up. • Vehicle stalls when accelerating or turning. • Extensive damage caused to bumper and undercarriage by driving over gravel roads. **1999–2003**—On a slight incline, sliding door will unlatch and then slam shut, or hinges break. **2001**—Sudden acceleration. • Chronic stalling. • Sudden, total electrical failure, especially when going into Reverse. • Differential in transfer case locks up while driving. • Fuel gauge failure. • Faulty AC vents. • Water can be trapped inside the wheels and freeze, causing the wheels to be out of balance. **2002**—Airbags fail to deploy. • Gas pedal sticks. • Brake pedal goes to floor without braking. • Seat belts in rear are too long; don't fit children or child safety seats. • Driver-side window failures. • Sliding-door window blows out. • Uniroyal spare-tire sidewall cracks. **2003**—Harsh, delayed shifting. • Intermittent windshield wiper failure. **2004**—Rear driver-side window explodes. **2005**—Driver-side airbag fails to fully deploy in an accident.

Secret Warranties/Internal Bulletins/Service Tips

1999–2001—Poor heat distribution in driver's area of vehicle (install new heat ducts). • Exhaust rattle noise. **1999–2003**—Engine noise remedy (see bulletin on following page). **1999–2004**—Booming interior noise at highway speeds. • Silence a boom-type noise heard during engine warm-up by installing an exhaust dampener assembly (TSB #00-06-05-001A). • Automatic transmission malfunctions may be caused by debris in the transmission (Bulletin No.: 01-07-30-038B). **1999–2005**—GM says that a chronic driveline clunk can't be silenced and is a normal characteristic of its vehicles. • Paint delamination, peeling, or fading. **2001**—Harsh automatic transmission shifts. • 2–4 band and 3–4 clutch damage. •

ENGINE RATTLE

BULLETIN NO.: 03-06-01-024B   DATE: MARCH 4, 2004

RATTLE NOISE IN ENGINE (INSTALL TIMING TENSIONER KIT)

1996–2003 Chevrolet Astro, Blazer, Express, S-10, Silverado

1996–2003 GMC Jimmy, Safari, Savana, Sierra, Sonoma

1996–2001 Oldsmobile Bravada with 4.3L V6 Engine

CONDITION: Some customers may comment on a rattle-type noise coming from the engine at approximately 1800 to 2200 RPMs.

CAUSE: The spark, rattle-type noise may be caused by torsional vibration of the balance shaft.

CORRECTION: Install a new tensioner assembly kit.

Steering shudder felt when making low-speed turns. • Excessive brake squeal. • Wet carpet/odour in passenger footwell area (repair evaporator-case drain to cowl seal, or open evaporator-case drain). • Delayed shifts, slips, flares, or extended shifts during cold operation (replace shift solenoid valve assembly). **2002**— Automatic transmission slips, incorrect shifts, and poor engine performance. • Service Engine light comes on, no Third or Fourth gear, and loss of Drive. • Slipping or missing Second, Third, or Fourth gear. • Inadequate heating. • Roof panel has a wavy or rippled appearance. • Water leak in the windshield area. **2002–03**—Engine runs rough, or Check Engine light comes on. • Sliding door difficult to open. **2003**—Hard starts, rough idle, and intermittent misfiring. • Transfer-case shudder. • Right rear door handle breakage. **2003–05**—Vehicle lacks power at high ambient temperatures. **2004**—Silencing a suspension pop.

ASTRO, SAFARI PROFILE

	1999	2000	2001	2002	2003	2004	2005
Cost Price ($) (very negotiable)							
Cargo	23,290	24,015	24,465	—	—	26,390	27,015
CS/base	25,675	25,675	26,440	27,255	27,600	27,615	29,035
Used Values ($)							
Cargo ▲	1,500	1,500	3,000	—	—	8,500	10,000
Cargo ▼	1,000	1,500	1,500	—	—	7,000	8,500
CS/base ▲	3,000	3,500	4,000	5,000	7,000	9,000	10,500
CS/base ▼	2,500	3,000	3,500	4,000	6,000	7,500	9,500
Reliability	3	3	4	4	4	4	4
Crash Safety (F)	3	3	3	3	3	3	3
Side	—	—	—	—	5	5	5
Offset	1	1	1	1	1	1	1
Rollover	—	—	3	3	3	—	—

bad buy

RATING: Not Recommended (1990–2008). These minivans are bad choices for four reasons: They have serious automatic transmission and engine intake manifold gasket defects; quality control has gotten worse over the past fifteen years; GM's warranty is no match for the many factory-related deficiencies; and there's an over-abundance of safety defects that include sliding doors that crush and injure children. These minivans are worse performers than Ford's Windstar/Freestar, and they actually make Chrysler's minivans look good. *Montana SV6, Relay, Terraza, and Uplander:* While Honda, Toyota, and Nissan push the envelope in engineering and styling, these restyled GM minivans join the Ford Freestar as also-ran, pseudo-nouveau entries. **Strong points:** Dual sliding doors, plenty of comfort and convenience features, flexible seating arrangements, good visibility fore and aft, and lots of storage bins and compartments. **Weak points:** Clumsy handling; harsh, noisy ride; average acceleration with a light load; unproven AWD that's no longer available; poorly performing rear drum brakes and excessive brake fading; a high number of safety-related failures and engine exhaust manifold defects; and disappointing fuel economy. Tall drivers will find insufficient headroom, and short drivers may find it hard to see where the front of the vehicle ends. The low rear seats force passengers into an uncomfortable knees-up position, and the narrow cabin makes front-to-rear access a bit difficult. Seat cushions on the centre and rear bench seats are hard, flat, and too short, and the seatbacks lack sufficient lower back support. Cargo may not slide out easily because the rear sill sticks up a few inches. **New for 2008:** Nothing significant.

MODEL HISTORY: These minivans have always had more carlike handling than GM's Astro and Safari, making them competent highway performers, although their engine and transmission are a bit rough. They also provide lots of seating and cargo room. The 2005 model year transformation into the Montana, Relay, Terraza, and Uplander gave these minivans more of an SUV look, along with a bit more length, height, and wheelbase. Seats may accommodate eight and can be folded down flat, creating additional storage space.

2004 MONTANA, SILHOUETTE, VENTURE TECHNICAL DATA

POWERTRAIN (FRONT-DRIVE/AWD)
Engine: 3.4L V6 (185 hp); Transmission: 4-speed auto.

DIMENSION/CAPACITY
Passengers: 2/2/3, 2/3/3; Wheelbase: 120.0 in.; H: 67.4/L: 201.0/W: 72.0 in.; Headroom F/R1/R2: 5.5/4.5/4.0 in.; Legroom F/R1/R2: 41.0/30.0/30.0 in.; Cargo volume: 75.5 cu. ft.; Fuel tank: 94.6L/regular; Tow limit: 3,500 lb.; Load capacity: 1,365 lb.; GVWR: 5,357 lb.; Turning circle: 43.0 ft.; Ground clearance: 4.5 in.; Weight: 3,990 lb.

2008 MONTANA SV6, RELAY, TERRAZA, UPLANDER TECHNICAL DATA

POWERTRAIN (FRONT-DRIVE/AWD)
Engine: 3.9L V6 (240 hp); Transmission: 4-speed auto.

DIMENSION/CAPACITY
Passengers: 2/2/3; Wheelbase: 121.0 in.; H: 68.0/L: 205.0/W: 72.0 in.; Headroom F/R1/R2: 5.0/4.0/3.5 in.; Legroom F/R1/R2: 40.5/26.0/28.0 in.; Cargo volume: 75.5 cu. ft.; Fuel tank: 94.6/regular; Tow limit: 3,500 lb.; Load capacity: 1,290 lb.; GVWR: 5,357 lb.; Turning circle: 43.0 ft.; Ground clearance: 6.0 in.; Weight: 4,380 lb.

The Montana SV6, Relay, Terraza, and Uplander are essentially GM's old minivans dressed up to look new. Powered by 15 more horses than previous versions, there's still ample cargo room thanks to removable second- and third-row seats and flat-folding third-row seats. Early models were equipped with a 201-hp 3.5L V6 engine, an electronically controlled 4-speed automatic transmission, and many standard features such as 17-inch wheels, ABS, strut-type front suspension/non-independent rear suspension, an OnStar security system, and dual-stage driver and passenger front airbags. Important options up through the 2006 model year included AWD (not a good idea), a vehicle stability enhancement system (a good idea), side-impact airbags, and "smart" front airbags. Unfortunately, these new-styled minivans don't have side curtain airbags or flip-and-fold rear seats that merge with the cargo floor.

As with most minivans, be wary of vehicles equipped with a power-assisted passenger-side sliding door. It's both convenient and dangerous—despite an override circuit that should prevent the door from closing when it is blocked, a number of injuries have been reported. Furthermore, the doors frequently open when they shouldn't and can be difficult to close securely.

All model years have had serious reliability problems—notably, engine head gasket and intake manifold defects; electronic module (PROM) and starter failures; premature front brake component wear, brake fluid leakage, and noisy braking; short circuits that burn out alternators, batteries, power door lock activators, and the blower motor; AC evaporator core failures; premature wearout of the inner and outer tie-rods; automatic transmission breakdowns; abysmal fit and finish; chronic sliding door malfunctions; and faulty rear-seat latches. Other problems include a fuel-thirsty and poorly performing 3-speed automatic transmission; a poorly mounted sliding door; side-door glass that pops open; squeaks, rattles, and clunks in the instrument panel cluster area and suspension; and a wind buffeting noise around the front doors.

1999—A 5-hp boost to the base V6 engine (185), de-powered airbags, an upgraded automatic transmission, a rear-window defogger, and heated rear-view mirrors. **2000**—Dual sliding rear side doors. **2001**—Slightly restyled, with a fold-flat third-row seat, driver-side power door, and a six-disc CD player added; cargo version dropped. **2002**—Optional AWD. **2003**—Optional ABS and front side airbags. **2005**—Venture drops the regular length model and AWD in a shortened model year run; Uplander arrives. **2006**—Optional second-row side airbags; introduction of a shorter-length model and an upgraded automatic transmission. *Uplander:* **2007**—A 240-hp 3.9L V6 replaces the 201-hp 3.5L V6; no more optional all-wheel drive or load-levelling suspension.

By the way, don't trust the towing limit listed in GM's owner's manual. Automakers publish tow ratings that are on the optimistic side—and sometimes they even lie. Also, don't be surprised to find that the base 3.1L engine (replaced in 1997) doesn't handle a full load of passengers and cargo, especially when mated to the 3-speed automatic transmission. The ideal powertrain combo would be the 4-speed automatic coupled to the optional "3800" V6 (first used on the 1996 versions). These minivans use a quiet-running V6 powerplant similar to Chrysler's top-of-the-line 3.8L 6-cylinder engine, providing good mid-range and top-end power. The GM engine is hampered by less torque, however, making for less grunt when accelerating and frequent downshifting out of Overdrive when climbing moderate grades. The electronically controlled 4-speed automatic transmission usually shifts smoothly—one advantage over Chrysler and Ford.

The 1997 and later models are less rattle-prone because their body structure is more rigid than that of their predecessors. However, fit and finish quality is still wanting. The front windshield is particularly prone to water leaks from the top portion into the dash instrument cluster (a problem also affecting rear-drive vans and covered by a secret warranty). Owner-reported problems on post-'97s include chronic plastic intake manifold/head gasket failures (covered by a 6-year/100,000 km secret warranty), EGR valve failures, transmission fluid leaks, electrical glitches shorting out dash gauges and causing difficult starting, excessive front brake noise and frequent repairs (rotors and pads), and assorted body deficiencies, including water leaks in the jack well, premature rusting, and extensive paint peeling:

> Our 2002 Venture has a poorly fitted windshield and a misaligned dash and hood, as well as quarter panels, front doors, and the sliding rear door on the passenger side. I have inspected other 2002 and 2003 Chevrolet Ventures and have seen the same windshield fit errors.

> Here are the pics I told you I would send in regards to the 2000 (piece of crap) Montana [see example on page 446]. Some are of the hole in the roof which GM says that a rock could have caused...(my husband's thumb went through it). Also the paint is peeling to the bare metal underneath the wipers and the back hatch. The paint has now cracked on the driver's door coming right up the paneling, and there's a big blister on the hood.

> I asked GM about the service bulletin I had read about the perforated roof and she said that it was covered under warranty up till 160,000 km and since I was hitting almost 200,000 km it was no longer valid to me. So today I called again after getting the *Lemon-Aid* book to again ask about the bulletin and they gave me the same response, so I asked them about the call I made back when it was 140,000 km, and their response was that at that time it was only peeling, flaking, and blistering...no rust had started.

COST ANALYSIS: A 2008 Uplander costs $24,390 in Canada and $22,320 (U.S.) in the States; a Montana SV6 is listed for $25,060 in Canada. Since there is virtually no difference between the 2006 through 2008 models, go for the older, cheaper versions. They should have many of the revamped 2005's bugs worked out (TSB #06-07-030-011 says the automatic transmission got a major upgrade) and sell for much less than their original MSRP. If you need additional engine power, it's better to opt for a 2007 version. Above all, stay away from the 2005 or earlier Venture, Montana, and Silhouette offerings. Yes, they are incredibly cheap, but what you save, you will likely pay out in powertrain repairs. **Best alternatives:** The 1999 or later Honda Odyssey, Hyundai's 2007–08 Entourage, Kia's 2007–08 Sedona, a 1998–2003 Nissan Quest, and the 1998–2003 Toyota Sienna. Full-sized Chrysler (not the Sprinter), GM, and Ford vans are also good choices (except for the 15-passenger versions, which are rolling death traps). **Rebates:** $3,500 rebates and zero percent financing. **Delivery/PDI:** $1,250. **Warranty:** Bumper-to-bumper 3 years/60,000 km; rust perforation 6 years/160,000 km. **Supplementary warranty:** A powertrain-only warranty will do. **Options:** $5,000 (U.S.) Sit-N-Lift electrically powered seats for the physically challenged have performed well. Be wary of the AWD option because it's unreliable. Many of these vans are equipped with Firestone and Bridgestone tires—have them removed by the dealer, or ask for a $400 rebate. Integrated child safety seats are generally a good idea, but make sure they can be easily installed and your child can't slip out or get tangled in the straps. The power-assisted passenger-side sliding door has a reputation as a wrist-breaker and child-crusher. The load-levelling feature is no longer offered, so look for a used model that has it equipped—it's a must-have for front-drive mini-vans. Weight is kept on the front wheels, giving you better steering, traction, and braking. Other options that are worth buying are the extended wheelbase version (provides a smoother ride), traction control, power side windows, a firmer suspension, self-sealing tires, and a rear air conditioner, defroster, and heater. **Depreciation:** Faster than average. **Insurance cost:** Average. **Parts supply/cost:** Powertrain and body parts are generic to GM's other models, so they are reasonably priced and not hard to find. **Annual maintenance cost:** Average during the warranty period, but much higher than average afterwards. Engine, transmission, ABS, and electrical malfunctions will likely cause maintenance costs to rise after the third year of ownership. **Highway/city fuel economy:** 9.3/13.5 L/100 km.

 QUALITY/RELIABILITY: The 1996–2004 models have chronic powertrain problems highlighted by engine manifold, head gasket, and camshaft failures along with frequent automatic transmission breakdowns and clunky shifting (which GM, with a straight face, says is a "normal" condition). **Owner-reported problems:** EGR valve and starter failures; electrical glitches; excessive front brake noise and frequent repairs (rotors and pads); early wheel bearing failures; blurry front windshields; failure-prone AC condensers; and assorted body deficiencies, including chronic windshield chipping, defective power-sliding doors, poor fit and finish, paint peeling and blistering, and roof perforations caused by extensive corrosion (covered by a secret warranty). **Warranty performance:** Very bad. The company still denies it has serious engine problems and often makes payouts only on the courthouse steps. Fed up by GM's stonewalling, Canadians have lodged a $1.2-billion class action that applies to all 1996–2004 models sold in Canada. Settlement talks are underway.

SAFETY SUMMARY: Sudden steering loss occurs in rainy weather or when passing over a puddle (serpentine belt slippage), tie-rod failures may cause loss of control, and the transmission slips from Drive into Neutral during highway driving. ABS brakes fail, the ABS light stays on for no reason, airbags fail to deploy, and fire may ignite around the fuel-filler nozzle or within the ignition switch. Some front-door-mounted seat belts cross uncomfortably at the neck, and there's a nasty blind spot on the driver's side that requires a small stick-on convex mirror to correct. Sliding doors suddenly open, close, come off their tracks, jam shut, stick open, injure children, or rattle; 1997–2001 models were recalled. The 2006 and 2007 minivans all scored a five-star rating for frontal crash protection, four stars for side protection, and three stars for rollover prevention. IIHS rated the 2005 and 2006 Uplander "Good" for offset crash protection. However, the group's side crash rating for the 2006 and 2007 minivans equipped with standard head and torso side airbags was only "Marginal," and their rating dropped to "Poor" on vehicles manufactured after February 2006 that weren't similarly equipped. **Anti-lock brakes:** Standard; disc/drum. **Seat belt pretensioners:** Standard. **Airbags:** Side airbags are standard. **Traction control:** Optional. **Head restraints F/R:** *1999:* ★★★/★; *2001–04:* ★★★; *2005–08:* ★. **Visibility F/R:** ★★★★★. **Maximum load capacity:** *2001 Chevrolet Venture LS and similarly equipped Montana and Silhouette:* 1,365 lb. **Pet transport:** ★★★★★.

SAFETY COMPLAINTS: All models/years: Chronic brake failures, or excessive brake fade. • Airbag malfunctions. • Transmission fails or won't hold gear on a grade. • Power-sliding doors constantly open, close, or jam on their own, plus they may crush anything that gets in their way. **1999**—Headlight assembly collects moisture, burns bulb, or falls out. • Seatback suddenly collapses. • Accelerator and brake pedals are too close together • Fuel slosh or clunk when vehicle stops or accelerates (a new tank is useless). • Self-activating door locks trap occupants outside or inside. • Door handles break inside the door assembly. • Window latch failures. **1999–2001**—Excess padding around horn makes it difficult to depress horn button in an emergency. • Frequent windshield wiper motor failures. **2000–01**—Fire ignites under driver's seat. • One vehicle's windshield suddenly exploded outward while driving with wipers activated. • Firestone tire blowout. • Faulty fuel pump causes chronic stalling, no-starts, surging, and sudden acceleration. • Snapped rear control arm (described by this Montana owner from Kitchener, Ontario):

> In May we were driving our 2002 Pontiac Montana with six adults inside (luckily), on a small two-lane road, doing about 50 or 60 km/h. Suddenly, the right rear control arm snapped and the rear axle rattled and shook.
>
> Our mechanic said in 28 years he had never seen such a thing happen. If we'd been going 120 km/h on a 400 highway we'd be dead.
>
> The dealer we bought it from paid all the costs for a used part to be installed, even though there was no warranty, but our mechanic suggested we photograph the parts he had removed. He was surprised at the thinness of the metal of the control arm. Also

that the control arm is welded to the axle, so it can't be replaced without replacing the entire component. New, they are $2,000!

• Steering idler arm falls off because of missing bolt. • Brakes activate on their own, making it feel as if the van is pulling a load. • Fuel tank is loose because of loose bolts/bracket. • In one incident, fuel tank cracked when passing over a tree branch. • Plastic tube within heating system falls off and wedges behind the accelerator pedal. • Bracket weld pin that secures the rear split seat shears off. • Centre rear lapbelt isn't long enough to secure a rear-facing child safety seat. • Children can slide out of the integrated child safety seat. • Electrical harness failures result in complete electrical shutdown. • Headlights, interior lights, gauges, and instruments fail intermittently (electrical cluster module is the prime suspect). • Weak-sounding horn. • Heater doesn't warm up vehicle sufficiently. • Antifreeze smell intrudes into the interior. • Premature failure of the transmission's Fourth clutch. • Delayed shifts, slips, flares, or extended shifts in cold weather. • Poorly performing rear AC. • Flickering interior and exterior lights. • Airbag warning light stays lit. • Windshield glass distortion. **2002**—One driver's hand was cut when the rear hatch handle broke. • Vehicle jumps out of Park and rolls downhill. • Vehicle suddenly shuts off in traffic. • Windshield water leaks short out dash gauges. **2003**—Rear seat belts fail to release. • Weld holding the lift wheel pin is not adequate to support weight of trailer. **2004**—Engine surging, stalling. • Loss of coolant, engine overheating. • Two incidents where a child's wrist was fractured after elbow and hand were caught between the seat and handle. • Tail lights fail intermittently. • Door opens and closes on its own while vehicle is underway. • Door doesn't lock into position; slides shut and crushes anything in its path:

> We are very concerned that another child, or adult, is going to be injured in this van's automatic sliding door. We were curious just how far the 2004 Venture's door would go before it would bounce back open so we put a stuffed animal in the door and hit the auto door close button. I have to say, the stuffed animal did not fare well. We also put a large carrot and a banana in the door, in an attempt to simulate a small child's arm. The carrot was sliced right in half, and the banana was smashed and oozing out of its peel. I will never purchase a Chevrolet Venture after our experience with the van.

2005–07—Liftgate buzz or rattle. • Front suspension pop, creak. • Power-steering noise. • Inoperative horn. **2006–07**—Engine overheating; no AC or heat. **2007**—Power-sliding door is hard to open. *Uplander:* **2005**—Vehicle will stall if it has only half a tank of fuel and is on a hill. • Excessive swaying and poor handling. • Power-sliding door jams; Door Ajar warning bell sounds constantly. • Power-sliding door opens and closes on its own:

> They may open while going down the road. They will also open when not prompted in the middle of the night, when everyone is asleep. They also will not close on some occasions. They start to close, then give a warning bell and re-open. We bought this vehicle because I have a 24 yr. old son with cerebral palsy. I cannot, in good

conscience, put him in this vehicle...due to the major safety issues. Would you put your child in this vehicle and wonder whether the doors would decide to come open while going 75 [mph] [120 km/h] down the interstate?

• Flickering/dimming headlights and interior lights. • Actuating bar for windshield wipers cuts into wiring harness. • Brakes applied to all four wheels without driver pressing the brake pedal. • Horn is hard to activate (covered by a service bulletin).

Secret Warranties/Internal Bulletins/Service Tips

1999—An inoperative sliding door may have a defective control module. • Upgraded front disc pads will reduce brake squeal. • Diagnostic tips for an automatic transmission that slips, produces a harsh upshift and garage shifts, or causes acceleration shudders. **1999–2000**—GM says that a chronic driveline clunk can't be silenced and is a "normal" characteristic of its vehicles. • Paint delamination, peeling, or fading. • Dealer guidelines for brake servicing under warranty. • Front door windows that are inoperative, slow, or noisy may need the window run channel adjusted or replaced in addition to new weather stripping. • Poor AC performance in humid weather may be caused by an undercharged AC system. • If the engine runs hot, overheats, or loses coolant, try polishing the radiator-filler neck or replacing the radiator cap before considering more expensive repairs. • Before taking on more expensive repairs to correct hard starts or no-starts, check the fuel pump. • An automatic transmission that whines in Park or Neutral, or a Service Engine light that stays on, may signal the need for a new drive sprocket support bearing. **1999–2001**—Poor heat distribution in driver's area of vehicle (install new heat ducts). • Psst! GM minivans may show premature hood corrosion and blistering (no surprise, after seeing readers' comments). A dealer whistle-blower tells me that dealers have been authorized to repair the hoods free of charge (refinish and repaint) up to six years under a GM "goodwill" program. Here's the confidential service bulletin that was given to me:

BLISTERING, BUBBLING PAINT	
BULLETIN NO.: 01-08-51-004	DATE: OCTOBER, 2001

PREMATURE ALUMINUM HOOD CORROSION/BLISTERING (REFINISH)
1997–2001 Trans Sport (export only)
1997–2001 Venture
1997–2001 Silhouette
1997–98 Trans Sport
1999–2001 Pontiac Montana
Some vehicles may have the appearance of blistering or bubbling paint on the top of the hood or under the hood.

1999–2002—Mildew odour; water leaks. • Wind noise at base of windshield. • Transmission noise/no movement:

TRANSMISSION NOISE/NO MOVEMENT IN "D" OR "R"

BULLETIN NO.: 03-07-30-017   DATE: MAY, 2003

GRIND NOISE OR NO VEHICLE MOVEMENT WHEN SHIFTING INTO DRIVE OR REVERSE (INSPECT TRANSAXLE, REPLACE VARIOUS TRANSAXLE COMPONENTS)

1999–2002 Century, LeSabre, Park Avenue

2002 Rendezvous

1999–2002 Monte Carlo, Venture

2000–02 Impala

1999–2002 Intrigue, Silhouette

1999–2002 Bonneville, Grand Prix, Montana

2001–02 Aztek

IMPORTANT: If the vehicle DOES NOT exhibit a grinding condition but DOES exhibit shifting concerns, refer to Corporate Bulletin #00-07-30-002

1999–2003—Incorrect fuel gauge readings caused by a contaminated fuel-tank sensor/sender. If a fuel "cleaner" doesn't work, GM says it will adjust or replace the sensor/sender for free on a case-by-case basis (*Toronto Star*, June 13 and 14, 2003, and December 20, 2003). This failure afflicts GM's entire lineup and could cost up to $800 to repair. **1999–2004**—Engine intake manifold/head gasket failures (GM is in secret settlement talks with class action lawyers). Here is how the problem is described by editor and publisher Andrew Ross in his article "A Fate Sealed: How Factors Conspired to Create GM's Intake Manifold Gasket Troubles," found in the July 2006 edition of *Jobber News*, a Canadian automotive publication:

> First, it should be noted that the construction of the original gasket was a plastic carrier with a silicone sealing bead system.
>
> According to information from engineering sources that wished not to be named for fear of reprisals, at least part of the problem exists with the original material. While plastic carriers aren't bad, the particular plastic chosen was not quite right for life alongside the Organic Acid Technology (OAT) of Dex-Cool. This plastic, part of the nylon family, has a tendency to become hard and crack in an acidic environment.
>
> But that's not the end of it.
>
> In addition, the silicone used as the sealing bead is not quite right for the job, either. Sources say that it is not compatible with the fuel-air mixture or OAT coolant, particularly when that coolant has itself become degraded and more aggressive than the original chemistry might have been.
>
> The cracking that is so prevalent on the failed gaskets is a result of the embrittling of the carrier combined with the swelling of the silicone bead in the presence of the coolant and/or the fuel-air mixture. The swelling puts pressure on the carrier and, because it has been weakened, it fails.

PART FOUR • MINIVANS AND VANS

General Motors can't easily stonewall owners' claims when they come armed with engineering facts like those. Instead, the automaker is settling claims on a case-by-case basis while denying the problem exists:

> I just wanted to let you know that after contacting you back in January regarding our 2001 Chevy Venture head gasket problem, I have just received my judgment through the Canadian Arbitration Program.
>
> I used the sample complaint letter as well as the judgment you have posted in the *Ford Canada vs. Dufour* court case. This combined with an avalanche of similar Chevy Venture complaints that are posted on the Internet helped us to win a $1,700 reimbursement of the $2,200 we were looking for.
>
> The reason for us not receiving the full amount is that the arbitrator stated that GM Canada would have only replaced one head gasket instead of replacing both as we had done, and that a dealer would have supplied us with a car free of charge and therefore did not allow us the car rental expense we incurred.
>
> We are still extremely happy with the results and thank you for your books and website; you have a fan for life.

• Defective catalytic converters that cause a rotten-egg smell in the interior may be replaced free of charge under the emissions warranty. • Second-row seat belt won't release. • Windshield wind noise. **1999–2006**—V6 engine oil leaks at the crankshaft rear main oil seal. **2000–02**—Service Engine light comes on, and automatic transmission is harsh shifting. • Hard start, no-start, stalling, and inoperative fuel gauge. **2000–04**—Tail light/brake light and circuit board burns out from water intrusion. Repair cost covered by a "goodwill" policy (TSB #03-08-42-007A). **2000–06**—Hard starts, stalling, inoperative gauges, and lit warning lights can all be traced to water leaking onto the C305 connector, says TSB #01-08-45-005D. **2001**—Customer Satisfaction Program (read: secret warranty) to correct the rear HVAC control switch. **2001–02**—Poor engine and automatic transmission operation. **2001–03**—Water in jack compartment. **2001–04**—Inability to shift out of Park after installation of Sit-N-Lift device. • Slipping automatic transmission. **2001–06**—Automatic transmission upgrade kit developed to improve durability. This is an excellent "smoking gun" TSB that shows these model year transmissions have quality control problems. **2003**—Shudder, chuggle, hard shifting, and transmission won't downshift. **2003–04**—Power-sliding door binding. • Windshield whistle. **2004–06**—Noisy steering can be silenced by replacing the inner tie-rod boot, says TSB #06-02-32-005. **2005**—Inoperative turn signals and tail lights. • Lumpy seats may require a new cushion. **2005–06**—A defective harmonic balancer may cause severe engine damage. GM will retorque the balancer bolt free of charge. • Hard start, no-start, stalling, and inoperative gauges. • It takes lots of effort to sound horn. • Silencing sliding door rattles. • Inaccurate temperature and fuel readings. • Poor AC performance:

A/C TEMPERATURE WON'T CHANGE/POOR PERFORMANCE

BULLETIN NO.: 06-01-39-004A

DATE: APRIL 25, 2006

2005–06 Montana SV6, Relay, Terraza and Uplander

ATTENTION: THIS IS NOT A RECALL. "GM of Canada" dealers are not authorized to use this bulletin. This bulletin ONLY applies to vehicles in which the customer has commented about this concern AND the EI number shows in GMVIS. All others should disregard this bulletin and proceed with diagnostics found in published service information.

CONDITION: IMPORTANT: If the customer did not bring their vehicle in for this issue, DO NOT proceed with this bulletin.

Some customers may comment that they are unable to change the HVAC mode and/or temperature. Customers may also comment that the A/C may be inoperative or have poor performance.

CORRECTION: GM Engineering is attempting to determine the root cause of this condition. GM has a need to obtain information first hand BEFORE any repairs are made.

WARRANTY INFORMATION:

Labor Operation	Description	Labor Time
D9719*	HVAC — Engineering Investigation	1.0 hr
Add	Recover and Recharge A/C System WITH Rear A/C	0.7 hr
Add	Recover and Recharge A/C System WITHOUT Rear A/C	0.5 hr

*This labor operation is for bulletin use only. It will not be published in the Labor Time Guide.

This is a strange bulletin that excludes Canadians, tells Americans the problem exists but the cause is unknown, and estimates it will take over two hours to investigate. Smart owners will go to the dealer and ask for a fix under warranty. If refused, get an independent repairer to replace the system and then use the above bulletin to get a refund.

MONTANA, MONTANA SV6, RELAY, SILHOUETTE, TERRAZA, TRANS SPORT, UPLANDER, VENTURE PROFILE

	1999	2000	2001	2002	2003	2004	2005	2006	2007
Cost Price ($) (negotiable)									
Montana	25,130	26,625	26,755	27,870	28,520	29,380	32,840	—	—
Montana SV6 (23%)	—	—	—	—	—	—	26,620	23,915	24,550
Silhouette	29,955	30,630	31,105	33,060	35,695	36,290	—	—	—
Relay (22%)	—	—	—	—	—	—	27,995	26,995	27,770
Terraza (23%)	—	—	—	—	—	—	33,745	32,210	33,025
Venture	24,725	24,895	25,230	25,195	25,865	26,680	30,590	—	—
Uplander (22%)	—	—	—	—	—	—	25,405	23,240	23,880
Used Values ($)									
Montana ▲	2,500	3,000	3,500	4,000	4,500	7,500	9,500	—	—
Montana ▼	2,000	2,500	3,000	3,500	4,000	6,000	8,000	—	—
Montana SV6 ▲	—	—	—	—	—	—	8,000	10,500	12,500
Montana SV6 ▼	—	—	—	—	—	—	6,500	9,000	11,000
Silhouette ▲	2,000	3,000	3,500	4,500	6,500	9,000	—	—	—
Silhouette ▼	1,500	2,500	3,000	3,500	5,000	7,500	—	—	—
Relay ▲	—	—	—	—	—	—	9,500	12,500	16,000
Relay ▼	—	—	—	—	—	—	8,000	11,000	14,500

Terraza ▲	—	—	—	—	—	—	10,000	14,000	18,000
Terraza ▼	—	—	—	—	—	—	8,500	12,000	16,500
Venture ▲	2,500	3,000	3,500	4,500	5,000	7,000	9,000	—	—
Venture ▼	2,000	2,500	3,000	4,000	4,500	5,500	8,000	—	—
Uplander ▲	—	—	—	—	—	—	7,500	10,500	12,500
Uplander ▼	—	—	—	—	—	—	6,000	9,000	11,000
Reliability	2	2	2	2	2	2	3	3	3
Crash Safety (F)	4	4	4	4	4	4	4	5	5
Side	5	5	5	5	5	5	5	4	4
IIHS Side	—	—	—	—	—	—	2	1	1
Offset	1	1	1	1	1	1	1	—	—
Montana SV6/Relay/ Terraza/Uplander	—	—	—	—	—	—	5	5	5
Rollover	—	—	3	3	3	—	—	3	3

Note: The higher-priced 2005 Montana is the extended version.

EXPRESS, SAVANA ★★★

RATING: Average (1996–2008). These rear-drive, full-sized vans are about as good as the Ford Econoline, and they're cheaper, more fuel-efficient, and more easily serviced than Chrysler's 2004 and later Sprinter. Nevertheless, the 2003 and earlier Ram Vans have an edge over Ford and GM vans because they are more easily repaired and cost less on the resale market. **Strong points:** A large array of powerful engines; improved ride and transmission and brake upgrades; multiple wheelbase configurations; plenty of interior room; dual side access doors; and more fuel efficient than its rivals, even with the larger engines. **Weak points:** Spartan base model; tacky interior garnishing; difficult to enter and exit; and serious powertrain, brake, and body fit and finish deficiencies. Handling is still ponderous despite improvements. Quite a bit heavier than the typical full-size van. No crashworthiness data. **New for 2008:** Not much, and 2009s are expected to be carryovers. *Express:* Returns relatively unchanged. *Savana:* New front-end styling, a set of side-hinged doors on the driver's side to enhance interior access, and additional storage compartments.

MODEL HISTORY: The product of GM's 1996 redesign of the Chevy Van and GMC Vandura, these full-sized cargo-haulers and people-movers are only a bit better than the vans they replaced. Powered by Vortec engines and a turbocharged diesel, these vans are built on longer wheelbases and use a ladder-type frame, as opposed to the unibody construction of their predecessors. This has improved ride quality somewhat, but overall performance remains unchanged. Both vans are a better choice than the average full-sized van as far as hauling capacity, especially if you often need to carry a lot of cargo or large animals. They also outpull the average full-sized van by a big margin.

All ratings on a numbered scale where 5 is good and 1 is bad. See page 217 for a more detailed description.

These vans are easily found at reasonable prices that are getting even more reasonable as fuel costs chase insurance premiums into the stratosphere. Passenger versions are usually heavily customized and can mean great savings if you don't pay top dollar for accessories you're not likely to use, or if you get a used model.

Overall reliability is average, as owners report serious problems with early 5.7L diesels and V8s as well as with front suspensions, steering components, and cooling, electrical, and braking systems. Interior accommodations are primitive on cargo models. Body assembly quality and paint application are particularly bad, so watch out for premature rust, paint delamination, and peeling. Water/air leaks and rattles are also commonplace.

1999—De-powered airbags, and an upgraded transmission. **2001**—A powerful 8.1L V8 replaced the 7.4L. **2003**—New features include optional all-wheel drive, four-wheel disc brakes, a stiffer box frame, enhanced ride and handling, dual side doors that open outward, and a minor face-lift. Engines and transmissions were revised and the suspension retuned. Although the engine-gasket-challenged 200-hp remained the base engine, GM added the GEN III V8 engines used in full-sized trucks since 1999. **2004**—Standard stability-control on 15-passenger models. **2005**—Upgraded automatic transmission components. **2006**—Addition of a Duramax 6.6L turbodiesel. *Express:* **2007**—An updated interior and a tire pressure monitoring system. Passenger models get side curtain airbags. *Savana:* **2007**—The same upgraded interior and a new steering wheel, switchgear, instrument cluster, and materials.

COST ANALYSIS: A 2008 Express base van sells for $29,590 (*Savana*: $28,930). In the States, the same vehicle costs $23,610 (U.S.). Stay away from the AWD powertrain; it has a high failure rate and is a fuel-waster. **Best alternatives:** The Ford Econoline is an okay second choice, but it also has chronic factory-related defects and doesn't handle as well as the GM vans. Your best Detroit choice is one of the Chrysler 2003 or earlier models equipped with a Cummins diesel and a manual transmission. **Rebates:** Look for $5,000 rebates on the 2008s in the fall and $4,000 rebates on the 2009s early in the new year. **Delivery/PDI:** $1,250. **Warranty:** Bumper-to-bumper 3 years/60,000 km; rust perforation 6 years/160,000 km. **Supplementary warranty:** A toss-up. **Options:** Running boards, rear air conditioning, power windows and door locks, and heavy-duty alternator. You'll find the SLE garnish creates a much cozier interior. Don't go for the base V6 engine; it's not that much more fuel-efficient than the 5.0L offered with earlier models or the 2008's 5.3L V8 (the most engine you will need for everyday driving). If you plan to load up on power-draining optional equipment or do some heavy hauling, choose a model equipped with the 5.7L or 6.0L V8. Be wary of the optional $7,000 6.6L diesel engine; it has yet to prove itself, and next year it will have to deal with reformulated fuel and stricter emissions requirements. **Depreciation:** Higher than average. **Insurance cost:** Much higher than average. **Parts supply/cost:** Average for generic mechanical and body parts. **Annual maintenance cost:** Less than average; any independent garage can repair these vans. **Highway/city fuel economy:** *Express 4.3L with an automatic transmission:* 11.4/16.0 L/100 km; *5.0L and automatic:* 12.5/16.9 L/100 km; *5.7L and automatic:* 11.9/17.3 L/100 km.

QUALITY/RELIABILITY: Quality control and overall reliability have declined since these vehicles were redesigned a decade ago. **Warranty performance:** Average. **Likely failures:** Engine, diesel injectors, turbocharger, and cracked head; automatic transmission 6.5L diesel oil cooler lines and other diesel maladies; electrical system, starter, EMC fuses, fuel pump (black and gray wires fused together inside the fuel tank), and fuel sending unit; catalytic converter, suspension, steering gearbox, and power-steering pump; brake pads and rotors; ABS sensors; AC; tire-tread separation and sidewall splitting; and fit and finish (such as broken door hinges and paint flaking off of mirror, bumpers, and trim). One report of severe rusting around the brake bearing spindles and knock head joints.

SAFETY SUMMARY: Four-wheel ABS was added in 1993 as a standard feature along with variable-ratio power steering. **Airbags:** Standard front and side. **ABS:** Standard; disc/disc. **Visibility F/R:** ★★★★★/★. **Pet transport:** ★★★★★.

SAFETY COMPLAINTS: All models/years: Front wheel flies off. • PCM/VCM computer module shorts from water intrusion. • Vehicle won't decelerate when gas pedal is released. • Power-steering and ABS brake failures. • Premature brake pad/rotor wear • Broken power seat anchor/brackets; seats come off their tracks, costing $900 to repair. • Broken, stiff, or weak side-door hinges. • Fuel gauge failure. • Excessive side-mirror vibration. • Tire-tread separation. **1999**—Airbags deploy for no reason. • Gas pedal sticks when accelerating. • Differential failure. • Loose power-steering line leaks steering fluid. • Nut on steering column falls off, causing loss of steering. • Rear-wheel seal leaks coat rear brakes with oil. • Sticking speedometer needle. • Positive post pulled out of battery. **1999–2001**—Excessive brake fade after successive stops, and pedal will sometimes go to the floor without stopping the vehicle. **2000**—Dashboard fire. • Unnecessary 4–3 downshifts. • Upper ball joint suddenly collapses. • Loose steering wheel. • Braking malfunctions and brake lock-up. • ABS performs erratically. • Rear shoulder belts cross too high on the torso. • Seat belt retractor doesn't lock properly. **2000–01**—Chronic stalling caused by moisture in the distributor. **2001**—Under-hood fire caused by electrical short under dash on passenger side. • Delayed 2–3 transmission shifts. • Windshield tinted strip cuts visibility for tall drivers. • Vehicle wanders all over the road at 100 km/h. • Firestone tread separation. • Faulty tire valve stems leak air. **2002**—Fire ignites at the bottom of driver's door. • Fuel leak. • 5.7L engine loses power when AC is engaged. • Cruise control won't decelerate vehicle when going downhill. • Leaking axle tube seals. • Leaking front grease seals contaminate the front inner disc brake pads, causing loss of braking effectiveness. • Front wheel speed sensor melts. • Tail lights blow when headlights are turned on. • AC Delco battery acid leaks out from broken positive cable post. • Door opens while vehicle is underway. **2003**—Extended stopping distance when brakes are applied; sometimes they fail to hold. • Fire ignites from a short in the right rear door-lock motor. • Tailpipe exhaust leaks where it fits into converter. • Horn and wiper failure. **2005**—Original-equipment Bridgestone tires don't give adequate traction, and they degrade steering and braking performance. • Unsafe vertical mirror design. **2005–06**—Seat belts on 15-passenger vans malfunction, pose a strangulation risk; one passenger had to be cut free. **2006**—Front tires rub against the inside wheelwells. • Seized brake pedal. **2007**—Airbags fail to deploy. • Premature automatic transmission failure.

Secret Warranties/Internal Bulletins/Service Tips

All models/years: GM bulletins say automatic transmission clunks are "normal." • Many diesel engine failures. **1999**—Hard starts on vehicles equipped with a 6.5L diesel engine may signal the need to replace the shutoff solenoid. • Engine bearing knocking on vehicles equipped with a 5.0L or 5.7L V8 may be silenced by using select-fit undersized connecting rod bearings and a special GM countermeasure kit to service the crankshaft. **1999–2000**—Poor starts, no-starts, and backfire on starting all point to the need to replace the crankshaft position sensor. • A rough idle or constantly lit Service Engine light may require that a cleaner be used to unstick and clean the central sequential fuel injection poppet valves. • Stalling or surging can be corrected by installing updated transmission software. • List of procedures to follow in correcting door wind noise. • An inexpensive cure for an overheated engine or coolant loss may be as simple as replacing the radiator cap or polishing the radiator-filler neck. **1999–2001**—Diagnostic procedures to fix AC performance problems and leaks. **1999–2002**—Cargo door binding requires new hinge pins and bushings. **1999–2005**—Paint delamination, peeling, or fading. **2001**—Automatic transmission harsh shifting. • Reports of automatic transmission 2–4 band or 3–4 clutch damage. • Inaccurate fuel gauge. **2002**—Service Engine light comes on, followed by poor engine and automatic transmission performance; transmission feels like it has slipped into Neutral. • Leaking engine oil cooler lines. **2003**—Hard starts, rough idle, and intermittent engine misfiring. • Drive shaft may fracture; a free repair under Customer Satisfaction #03040. • Thumping noise/feel in brake pedal • Voluntary emission recall to replace spark plugs. • Vehicle difficult to fill with fuel. **2003–04**—Suspension clunk and slap. GM will replace the spring insert and insulator for free (see Silverado "Secret Warranties/Internal Bulletins/Service Tips"). **2003–05**—Lack of power when the 4.3L engine is hot. **2003–06**—ABS activation at 3 km/h. • Ignition key cylinder won't turn. **2003–07**—Sliding door malfunctions.

	1999	2000	2001	2002	2003	2004	2005	2006	2007
Cost Price ($) (very negotiable)									
Savana Cargo (21%)	25,330	25,495	24,905	25,025	25,125	26,465	26,835	27,080	27,435
Express (21%)	29,155	29,330	30,885	29,105	29,215	30,000	26,785	27,080	27,670
Used Values ($)									
Savana Cargo ▲	3,000	3,500	4,000	4,500	6,500	9,000	11,500	13,500	16,500
Savana Cargo ▼	2,500	3,000	3,500	4,000	5,500	8,000	10,000	12,000	15,000
Express ▲	3,500	4,000	5,000	6,000	7,000	9,000	11,500	14,000	16,500
Express ▼	3,000	3,500	4,500	5,000	6,000	8,000	10,000	12,500	15,500
Reliability	3	4	4	4	4	4	4	4	4
Crash Safety (F)	—	—	—	—	—	—	5	5	5
Rollover	—	—	—	—	—	—	—	3	3
15-passenger	—	—	—	—	—	3	3	3	3

Note: The 2008 crashworthiness ratings are identical to the 2007 ratings.

Honda

ODYSSEY ★★★★★
best buy

RATING: Recommended (2007–08); Above Average (2003–05); Average (1996–2002; 2006). The upgraded 2005 model passed the Toyota Sienna in safety, performance, and convenience features. Nevertheless, there are some reports of safety- and performance-related failures on year-2005 and earlier Odysseys. Of particular concern are airbag malfunctions, automatic-sliding-door failures, engine failures, transmission breakdowns and erratic shifting, and sudden brake loss. Early Odysseys get only an Average rating because of their small engine and interior—identical shortcomings to those of Mazda's early MPV minivan. **Strong points:**

2005 and later models: More power, room, and safety and convenience features. Additional mid-range torque means less shifting when the engine is under load; uses regular gas (the Sienna can burn regular but needs pricier high-octane to get the advertised horsepower and torque). *Pre-2005 models:* Strong engine performance; carlike ride and handling; easy entry and exit because of low step-up; second driver-side door; quiet interior; lots of passenger and cargo room; and an extensive list of standard equipment. Most controls and displays are easy to reach and read, and Honda is willing to compensate owners for production snafus. **Weak points:** *2005 and later models:* Unlike with the Sienna, all-wheel drive isn't available; middle-row seats don't fold flat like other minivans, so they need to be stowed somewhere else; second-row head restraints block visibility. *Pre-2005 models:* Front-seat passenger legroom is marginal because of the restricted seat travel; you can't slide your legs comfortably under the dash, so some passengers bump their shins on the glove box; the third-row seat is suitable only for children; and the narrow back bench seat provides little legroom unless the middle seats are pushed far forward, inconveniencing others. Radio control access is blocked by the shift lever, and it's difficult to calibrate the radio without taking your eyes off the road. Power-sliding doors are slow to retract; some tire rumble, rattles, and body drumming at highway speeds; premium fuel is required for optimum performance; poor head-restraint crashworthiness rating; and rear-seat head restraints impede side and rear visibility. Poorer quality compared to later models, and a high resale price, making bargains rare. The storage well won't take any tire larger than a "space saver"—meaning you'll carry your flat in the back. **New for 2008:** A slightly restyled exterior (mostly grille and headlights); passenger's seat has 4-way power adjustment (EX-L and above); active front head restraints; improved climate control (EX and above); and a rear-view mirror with rear-view camera display (EX-L and EX-L with RES).

2008 TECHNICAL DATA

POWERTRAIN (FRONT-DRIVE)
Engine: 3.5L V6 (244 hp); Transmission: 5-speed auto.

DIMENSION/CAPACITY
Passengers: 2/3/2; 2/3/3; Wheelbase: 118.1 in.; H: 68.8/L: 202.1/W: 77.1 in.; Headroom F/R1/R2: 4.5/5.5/2.0 in.; Legroom F/R1/R2: 41.5/31.0/28.0 in.; Cargo volume: 66.5 cu. ft.; Fuel tank: 65L/regular; Tow limit: 3,500 lb.; Load capacity: 1,320 lb.; GVWR: 5,567 lb.; Turning circle: 36.7 ft.; Ground clearance: 4.3 in.; Weight: 4,385 lb.

MODEL HISTORY: When it was first launched in 1995, the Odyssey was a sales dud—Canadians and *Lemon-Aid* saw through Honda's attempt to pass off an underpowered, mid-sized, four-door station wagon with a raised roof as a minivan. However, in 1999 and again in 2005, the Odyssey was redesigned, and it's now one of the better minivans on the Canadian market.

1999—A new, more powerful engine and increased size make this second-generation Odyssey a more versatile highway performer; still, steering requires fully extended arms, and power-sliding doors operate slowly. **2001**—User-friendly child safety seat tether anchors, upgraded stereo speakers, and an intermittent rear window wiper. **2002**—A slight restyling, 30 additional horses, disc brakes on all four wheels, standard side airbags, and additional support for front seats. **2005**—

A bigger Odyssey with a torquier 255-hp 3.5L V6, which has 15 more horses than the prior year's version and more horsepower than any other minivan. The new engine uses variable cylinder de-activation to increase fuel economy by up to 10 percent by automatically switching between 6-cylinder and 3-cylinder activation, depending on engine load. Other features are as follows: eight-passenger seating (EX); less road noise; upgraded rear shocks; an upgraded driver's seat; easier access to the back seats; a new power tailgate; more interior volume than the Sienna (interior lengthened by 5 cm/2 in.); second-row middle seats can be folded down to use as an armrest or can be removed completely, much like the middle-row captain's chairs, which can slide fore or aft by 25 cm (10 in.) in unison or separately; second-row power windows; and floor-stowable, 60/40 split third-row seats with more legroom. Safety has been enhanced with a more crashworthy body, vehicle stability assist to prevent rollovers, side curtain airbags with rollover sensors for all rows, and adjustable brake and accelerator pedals. **2008**—The 3.5L engine loses 11 horses.

COST ANALYSIS: The 2008 Odyssey is not much different than last year's version. An LX sells for $33,590 and an EX will fetch $36,990. In the States, these same minivans cost $25,860 and $28,960, respectively. **Best alternatives:** Nissan's 1999–2003 Quest, or any Toyota Sienna except for the 2004 revamped model. If you're looking for lots of towing grunt, the rear-drive GM Astro, Safari, or full-sized vans are best. **Rebates:** Don't expect any substantial incentives before late 2008: $2,000 on the 2008s, and $1,000 on the 2009s. **Delivery/PDI:** $1,540. **Warranty:** Bumper-to-bumper 3 years/60,000 km; powertrain 5 years/100,000 km; rust perforation 5 years/unlimited km. **Supplementary warranty:** Not needed. **Options:** Traction control is a good idea. Remember, if you want the gimmicky video entertainment and DVD navigation system, you also have to spring for the expensive (and not-for-everyone) leather seats. Stay away from the PAX run-flats and ditch the original-equipment Firestone or Bridgestone tires: You don't need the high cost, extra risk, or early wearout. **Depreciation:** Slower than average. **Insurance cost:** Higher than average. **Parts supply/cost:** Moderately priced parts; availability is better than average because the Odyssey uses many generic Accord parts. **Annual maintenance cost:** Average; any garage can repair these minivans. **Highway/city fuel economy:** 2004: 8.5/13.2 L/100 km; 2005: 8.6/12.3 L/100 km. The vehicle burns gas at a horrendous rate if the rear AC is switched on.

QUALITY/RELIABILITY: Reliability is much better than average, but like Toyota, one gets the impression that Honda is coasting on past laurels, at least from the 1999 through the 2005 models. Automatic transmission breakdowns and failure-prone sliding doors continue to bedevil owners. The doors open when they shouldn't, won't close when they should, catch fingers and arms, get stuck open or closed, are noisy, and frequently require expensive servicing. The Check Engine light may stay lit because of a defective fuel-filler neck. There's a fuel sloshing noise when accelerating or coming to a stop, and the transmission clunks or bangs when backing uphill or when shifted into Reverse. There are also reports of rattling and chattering when put into Forward gear. Owners note a loud wind noise and vibration from the left side of the front windshield, along with a constant vibration felt through the steering assembly and front wheels. Passenger doors may also require excessive force to open. And owners have complained of severe static electricity shocks when exiting. Other potential problem areas are frequent and high-cost front-brake maintenance, and trim and accessory items that come loose, break away, or malfunction. **Owner-reported problems:** Faulty engine oil pan seals; engine chirping. Transmission breakdowns—when shifting into Fourth gear, engine almost stalls out and produces a noise like valve clattering; transmission gear whine at 90 km/h or when in Fourth gear (transmission replaced under new "goodwill" warranty). Front-end clunking caused by welding breaks in the front subframe, exhaust rattling or buzzing, severe steering vibrations, and steering pump groaning and screeching while underway, thought to be caused by faulty wheel bearings. Vehicle pulls to the right; premature front brake wear; excessive brake grinding noise; early AC failure and noisy AC blower motor (*www.topix.com/forum/autos/honda-odyssey/TJBOPFUR3SVARKHCJ*); AC condenser is prone to early failure and is easily damaged by road debris:

> Poor design of 2005 Honda Odyssey. I have had to replace air conditioner twice in 18 months due to flying rock punctures. Honda dealership knows of exact repair (chicken wire) but won't do it. Hundreds of people on the Internet are experiencing [the] same problem.

Owners also note frequent electrical glitches; defective remote audio controls; leather seats that split, crack, or discolour; and accessory items that come loose, break away, or won't work. Plastic interior panels have rough edges and are often misaligned; paint peels from the bumpers and chips off the hood; and door weather stripping often falls away, allowing excessive wind and road noise to invade the cabin. Interestingly, 2007 and later redesigned models have been relatively glitch-free. **Warranty performance:** The comprehensive base warranty is usually applied fairly, with lots of wiggle room that the service manager can use to apply "goodwill" adjustments for post-warranty problems. However, after-warranty assistance and dealer servicing have come in for a great deal of criticism from *Lemon-Aid* readers, though the complaints aren't as serious and owners aren't as angry as with problems regarding Toyota Siennas. Owners complain that "goodwill" refunds aren't extended to all model years with the same defect, recall repairs take an eternity to perform, and dealers exhibit an arrogant, uncaring, "take it or leave it" attitude.

 SAFETY SUMMARY: Power-sliding doors are a constant danger. NHTSA front, side, and rollover crash safety scores for the 2006 and 2007 Odyssey mirror the 2005 model ratings. IIHS rates the 2006s "Good" for offset and side crash protection. **Airbags:** Standard side airbags. **ABS:** Standard 4W; disc/disc. **Head restraints F/R:** *1999:* ★★/★; *2001–07:* ★★. *2008 EX:* ★★★★★. **Visibility F/R:** ★★★★★/★. **Pet transport:** ★★★★★.

SAFETY COMPLAINTS: All years: Passenger seatbacks collapsed when one vehicle was rear-ended. • Airbag malfunctions. • Sudden, unintended acceleration when slowing to a stop. • In one incident, when minivan was put in Drive and AC was turned on, vehicle suddenly accelerated, brakes failed, and the vehicle hit a brick wall. • Stuck accelerator. • Automatic transmission failures. • Transmission doesn't hold when stopped on a hill; gas or brakes have to be constantly applied. **1999**—Plastic gas tank cracks, leaks fuel. • Gasoline smell when transmission is put into Reverse. • Side window explodes while underway. • Check Engine light comes on, and vehicle loses all power. • When driving, all the instrument panel lights will suddenly go out (faulty multiplex controller suspected). • When parked on a hill, vehicle may roll backward; transmission doesn't hold vehicle when stopped at a light on a hill and foot is taken off accelerator or brake. • Complete loss of power steering caused by a pinhole in the power-steering return hose. • Poor power-steering performance in cold weather. • Power door locks and unlocks on its own. • Design of the gear shifter interferes with the radio controls. • Seat belt buckle locks up, trapping occupant. • Faulty fuel gauge. • Inconvenient cell phone jack location. **1999–2000**—Fire erupts in the electrical harness or when fuelling. **2000**—Many incidents where driver-side sliding door opens onto fuel hose while fuelling, damaging gas flap hinge and tank. • Catastrophic failure of the right-side suspension, causing wheel to buckle. • Vehicle continually pulls to the right; dealers unable to correct problem. • Excessive steering-wheel vibration at 105 km/h and over. • Electric doors often inoperative. • In one incident, as child slept in safety seat, seat belt tightened progressively to the point where fire department had to be called; other similar incidents. • Chronic automatic transmission problems: won't shift into lower gears, suddenly loses power, torque converter fails, and makes a loud popping sound when put into Reverse. • Two incidents where vehicle was rear-ended because of a transmission malfunction. • Power seatback moves on its own. • Dash lights don't adequately illuminate the dash panel. • Protruding bolts in the door assembly are hazardous. • Seat belt buckle fails to latch. • Driver-side mirror breaks away; mirror glass falls out because of poor design. • Easily broken sliding door handles. **2000–01**—Driver's power seat will suddenly recline on its own, squeezing the rear occupant's legs, even though power switch is off. • On cold days, accelerator pedal is hard to depress. **2001**—In one incident, fuel tank exploded during fuelling. • In a frontal collision, one van caught fire because of a cracked brake fluid reservoir. • Chronic stalling (transmission replaced). • Many reports of sudden transmission and torque converter failure. • When Reverse is engaged, vehicle makes a popping or clunking sound. • Cracked wheel rim. • Check Engine light constantly on (suspect faulty fuel-filler neck). • Entire vehicle shakes excessively at highway speeds and pulls to the right (dealer said bar adjustment was needed). • Passenger-side door window suddenly explodes while underway. • Driver's seatback collapses in rear-end collision. • Rear seat belt tightened up so much that a child had to be cut free. • Too much play in rear lapbelts, which won't tighten adequately, making it difficult to install a child safety seat securely. • Inoperative driver's seat belt buckle. • Faulty speedometer and tachometer. • Remote won't open or lock vehicle. • Placement of the gearshift lever interferes with the radio controls. • Can hear gasoline sloshing in tank while driving. • Frequent static electricity shocks. • Many owners report that the rear head restraints seriously hamper rear and forward visibility and that it's difficult to see vehicles coming from the right side. **2002**— Over 232 complaints registered where normally 50 would be expected. Only 66 complaints recorded against the 2002 Toyota Sienna. • Owners say many engines have faulty timing chains. • Loose strut bolt almost causes wheel to fall off. • Axle bearing wheel failure causes driver-side wheel to fall off. • Left-to-right veering and excessive drivetrain vibration. • Loud popping sound heard when brakes are applied. • Many complaints that the brake pedal goes to floor with no braking capability. • Sticking sliding door. • Head restraints are set too low for tall occupants. • Rear windshield shatters from area where wiper is mounted. • Rear seat belt unlatches during emergency braking. • Brake line freezes up in cold weather. • Abrupt downshift on deceleration. • Driver-side door comes off while using remote control. • Dashboard lights come on and off intermittently. • Passenger window explodes. • Airbag light comes on for no reason. **2003**—Fire ignites in the CD player. • Child injured from a side collision; the second-row seat belt failed to hold her in because of gap caused by door attachment. • Rear seat belts lock for no reason. • Seat belt extenders aren't offered. • Defective speed sensor causes vehicle to suddenly lose power when merging into traffic. • Vehicle suddenly shuts down in traffic. • Hard starts and engine misfiring. • Faulty steering causes wander. • Sudden brake failure. • Driver often shocked when touching door handle. • Fuel spits out when refuelling. • Inaccurate fuel gauge readings. • Sliding door closes on driver's hand; child trapped by the door closing on him. **2004**— Stuck gas pedal. • Fuel smell in the interior. • Front airbags fail to deploy. • Passenger airbag often turns itself off. • Chronic stalling even after recall repairs to the fuel-pump relay to correct the problem. • Automatic transmission slippage:

> At 20,000 miles [32,000 km], the transmission has started to slip. Also, it rolls backwards when it is in Drive in our driveway. Our driveway is not steep. It did not do that when we first got it. The dealer said that was normal. We almost slammed into a car that was parked in front of us on a hill. We were facing downward. I put the van in reverse, then I took my foot off the brake to make some room so I could get around the car parked in front of us. The van rolled forward and I had just enough time to avoid causing major damage. I had to find the owner of the car in front so he could move out of the way so I could get out of there.

• Jammed rear seat belt; passenger had to be cut free. • Problems with automatic doors:

> Problems with door on 2004 Honda Odyssey. The door was ajar 6 inches [15 cm] and would not open nor close all the way. The close button was pressed but nothing happened. The door handle was pulled and the door started to close and crushed the tip of the consumer's finger, fracturing it. The vehicle was inspected but no problems were found.

> •

> One month ago, I opened the passenger side automatic door on my 2004 Honda Odyssey and it pinned a Publix bagger and shopping cart between my vehicle and

another vehicle. The door did not stop and continued to ram itself open. Thankfully, the bagger was not injured.

• Back hatch struts collapse. • Front doors don't have enough tension to stay open; they close on occupants' legs. • Self-locking feature often locks driver out of the van after a delay of about 10 seconds. • Child safety seats are quite difficult to latch securely in the second-row seats. **2005**—Seat belt unlatches on its own, or sometimes won't unlatch. • Hatch struts continue to fail at an alarming rate. • Entire electrical system goes dead. • Faulty VSA control unit disables ABS and braking assist. • Vehicle won't accelerate when foot is on the gas pedal, but it begins to accelerate when the brakes are applied. • Constant steering shimmy. • Driver's seat isn't level; it's lower on the left side. • Windshield leaks; replacements are on back order nationwide. • Painful noise in the cabin when rear windows are opened:

> Very loud pulsating sound when rear windows open. It vibrates and is so loud I thought I had a flat tire. My ears and my children's ears hurt. It occurs when we are driving 35–40 mph [56–64 km/h].

• Power-sliding door opens completely while vehicle is in motion; fails to close and latch. • Automatic sliding door almost crushed child's hand. • Rear windshield wiper self-activates. • Michelin PAX tires wear out prematurely and can be replaced only by authorized dealers at great cost:

> The PAX tire system by Michelin gives marginal tire wear. The tires wore out at 25,000 miles [40,000 km]. The tires can only be changed by PAX authorized dealers making them nearly impossible to find convenient[ly or] inexpensive[ly]. What is meant to make us safer has only made us poorer.

• Poor headlight illumination. **2006**—Cracked transmission casing. • Many AC failures. • Side window suddenly explodes. • Key sticks in the ignition. • Short steering column increases driver fatigue. • Frequent brake failures. • Front brake grinding. • Sliding door slices fingers, and there is no inside over-ride switch. • More PAX tire uneven wear, poor performance complaints:

> Now having problems driving in any snow or ice; narrowly avoided several accidents just driving through town to get home. Price to replace with PAX snow tires is outrageous plus cost to have tires swapped out each winter and spring. Honda and Michelin have both advised that regular tires cannot be put on vehicle as this will void warranty and possibly cause system malfunctions.

2007—Airbags fail to deploy. • Vehicle rolls backward when stopped on an incline. • Poor braking performance ("soft pedal"). • PAX run-flat tires are hard to find.

Secret Warranties/Internal Bulletin/Service Tips

All years: Most of Honda's TSBs allow for special warranty consideration on a "goodwill" basis by the company's District Service Manager or Zone Office, even after the warranty has expired or the vehicle has changed hands. Referring to this euphemism will increase your chances of getting some kind of refund for repairs that are needed to correct obvious factory defects. • There's an incredibly large number of sliding door problems covered by a recall and a plethora of service bulletins too numerous to print here. Ask Honda politely for the bulletins or "goodwill" assistance. If refused, subpoena the documents through small claims court, using NHTSA's summary as your shopping list. • V6 engine oil leaks. **1999–2001**—Extended warranty coverage on Odysseys with defective 4- and 5-speed automatic transmissions to 7 years/160,000 km (100,000 miles) to fix erratic or slow shifting. **1999–2003**—Engine oil leaks will be corrected under a "goodwill" policy. • Deformed windshield moulding. **2000–01**—Third-row seat won't unlatch. • Clunk or bang when engaging Reverse. • Bulletin confirms Honda U.S. is investigating complaints of pulling or drifting (Service Bulletin #99165; Bulletin Sequence #802; 99/09; NHTSA Item #SB608030). • Excessive front brake noise. **2002**—Hesitation when accelerating. • Diagnosing automatic transmission problems. • No-starts; hard starts in cold weather. • Driver's seat heater may not work. • Thump at cold start. • Loose rear wiper arm. • AC can't be turned off while in defog setting. **2002–03**—Free replacement of the engine timing belt auto-tensioner and water pump under both a recall and "product update" campaign:

RECALL—ENGINE TIMING BELT AUTO-TENSIONER AND WATER PUMP

BULLETIN NO.: 03-081   **DATE: OCTOBER 27, 2003**

DEFECT: On certain minivans, sedans, coupes, and sport utility vehicles equipped with V6 engines, a timing belt tensioner pulley on the water pump is misaligned and could cause the timing belt to contact a bolt on the cylinder head. Eventually the belt could be damaged and fail. If the timing belt breaks, the engine will stall, increasing the risk of a crash.

REMEDY: Dealers will inspect the water pump, and if it is one of the defective pumps, the water pump and timing belt will be replaced.

PRODUCT UPDATE

BACKGROUND: The timing belt tensioner is filled with oil to dampen oscillation. Due to a manufacturing problem, the tensioner oil can leak. If enough oil is lost, the timing belt loosens and causes engine noise.

MODELS: 2002–03 Odyssey and 2003 Pilot

CORRECTIVE ACTION: Replace the timing belt auto-tensioner.

2002–04—Free tranny repair or replacement for insufficient lubrication that can lead to heat buildup and broken gears. Transmission noise will signal if there is gear breakage; transmission may also lock up. • Rear brake noise. **2003**—Engine cranks but won't start. • ABS problems. • Power-steering pump noise. • Warning lights blink on and off. • Exhaust rattling. • Remote audio-control troubleshooting. • Leather seat defects. • HomeLink range is too short; hard to program. • Factory security system won't arm. • Faulty charging system; electrical shorts. • Front door howls in strong crosswind. • Squealing from rear quarter windows and motors. • Fuel-tank leak. • Front damper noise. • Steering wheel bent off-centre. • Manual sliding door is difficult to open. **2005**—Free electronic computer module replacement on the EX-L and Touring models. • Excessive steering-wheel vibration. • Windshield cowl noise remedy. • Front and rear AC temperature varies. • Correction for middle-row seat that won't unlatch. **2005–06**—Power seat malfunctions. • Free tire valve stem cap replacement.

ODYSSEY PROFILE

	1999	2000	2001	2002	2003	2004	2005	2006	2007
Cost Price ($) (negotiable)									
LX (18%)	30,600	30,600	30,800	31,900	32,200	32,400	32,700	33,200	33,300
EX (18%)	33,600	33,600	33,800	34,900	35,200	35,400	35,900	36,400	36,900
Used Values ($)									
LX ▲	5,500	7,000	8,500	10,500	11,500	14,000	17,500	20,000	23,000
LX ▼	5,000	6,000	7,500	9,500	10,500	12,500	16,000	18,500	21,500
EX ▲	7,000	8,000	10,000	11,500	13,000	14,500	19,000	22,000	26,000
EX ▼	6,500	7,000	8,500	10,500	11,500	13,000	17,000	20,500	24,500
Reliability	3	3	2	2	2	3	3	3	4
Crash Safety (F)	—	5	5	5	5	5	5	5	5
Side	—	—	—	—	—	—	5	5	5
IIHS Side	—	—	—	5	5	5	5	5	5
Offset	5	5	5	5	5	5	5	5	5
Rollover	—	—	—	4	4	4	—	4	4

Note: The 2008 crashworthiness ratings are identical to the 2007 ratings.

Hyundai/Kia

ENTOURAGE/SEDONA	★★★★★ / ★★★★

RATING: *Entourage:* Recommended (2007–08). *Sedona:* Above Average (2006–08); Average (2002–05). These 2006–08 Kias and Hyundais have all the makings of winners. The 2005 Sedona is a very user-friendly, roomy, practical, versatile, and comfortable mid-sized minivan. It simply lacks refinement and isn't very reliable. **Strong points:** *2006–08:* Reasonably priced and well appointed. Competent engine accelerates well from a stop and merges into traffic reasonably well; transmission shifts smoothly and quietly; and low ground clearance adds to stability and helps access. Low step-in; comfortable ride; convenient "walk-through" space between front seats; well laid-out, user-friendly instruments and controls; lots of storage areas; good visibility; fairly well built; minimal engine and road noise; good braking; and a comprehensive base warranty. Quality control seems to be better than average. *2005 and earlier models:* Quite cheap. **Weak points:** *2006–08:* The Entourage's base price and freight charges are inflated. The automatic transmission has a superfluous manual mode, which seems out of place in a minivan. There's still some road and wind noise (maybe from the mirrors) when cruising. A weak dealer network. *2005 and earlier models:* Engine power is drained by the Sedona's heft; 10–20 percent higher fuel consumption than V6-equipped Dodge Caravan or Toyota Sienna; subpar, vague steering and handling; and excessive engine and wind noise. Quality control is the Sedona's weakest link through the 2005 model. **New for 2008:** Nothing significant. Both Hyundai and Kia put most of their redesign dollars in the last two model years. Next redesign not likely before 2010.

MODEL HISTORY: Forget about previous models—the 2006 and carried-over 2008 and 2009 Sedonas and the 2008 and 2009 Entourage twins are safer, larger, and better performing than previous Sedonas. Almost everything is new or upgraded, like 15 percent more interior room, thanks to a larger wheelbase and a longer, wider platform; a more powerful 3.8L engine; four-wheel ABS; power-adjustable pedals; six airbags (side curtain); optional electronic stability control; an upgraded transmission; larger brakes; four-wheel independent suspension; and fold-flat third-row seats.

The 2005 and earlier models are hardly worth considering, even though they do come with many standard features, including a 195-hp 3.5L V6 engine hooked to an automatic 5-speed transmission, a low step-in height, and a good view of the road. For convenience, there are two sliding side doors (automatic doors aren't available); folding, removable second- and third-row seats; a flip-up hatchback; standard front/rear air conditioning; and a large cargo bay.

Hyundai Entourage

A Kia Sedona clone (don't forget, Hyundai owns Kia and wants a little minivan action of its own), the 2007–08 Entourage is Hyundai's first-ever minivan, so Hyundai is desperate to make it appear more upscale by loading it with oodles of standard features. Auto critics report that the Sedona outpulls the Entourage by a large margin, even though both minivans have the same engine and transmission layout.

COST ANALYSIS: A base Hyundai Entourage L has a Canadian MSRP of $30,995. In the States, a similar model costs $20,695, minus a $500 cash-back rebate. The $725 (U.S.) freight fee is less than half what dealers charge in Canada. 2008 Kia Sedonas range in price from $29,745 (LX) to $32,795 (EX). In the States they sell for $23,595 and $26,195, respectively, minus a $500 cash-back rebate and a cheaper freight fee. The 2005 Sedona isn't as well equipped or as refined as the 2006–08 models; the reworked Sedona has had time to correct the usual first-year glitches that all redesigns engender. Also, a second-series 2006 Sedona will cost thousands of dollars less than a newer version. Test-drive both the Hyundai and Kia and try to choose the dealer who is the most convenient and who doesn't split their inventory among a handful of different automakers. **Best alternatives:** The Honda Odyssey and pre-2004 Toyota Sienna are two other good choices. **Rebates:** Look for $4,000 rebates and low-financing rates on the 2008 Kias in the fall; Entourage's $2,000–$3,000 rebates on the 2008 and 2009 models may not kick in until early 2009. **Delivery/PDI:** *Entourage:* $1,610; *Sedona:* $1,650. **Warranty:** Bumper-to-bumper 5 years/100,000 km; powertrain 5 years/100,000 km; rust perforation 5 years/unlimited km. **Supplementary warranty:** Kia's previous transmission troubles and the likelihood of some first-series factory-related defects afflicting the 2007 Entourage make a powertrain warranty a smart buy. 2008–09 models should be relatively trouble-free. **Options:** Seriously consider the electronic stability control. **Depreciation:** Average. **Insurance cost:** Average. **Parts supply/cost:** Average. **Annual maintenance cost:** Less than average. **Highway/city fuel economy:** 10.9/15.6 L/100 km.

QUALITY/RELIABILITY: Reliability is above average. **Owner-reported problems:** The usual failings seen with most Asian models: seat belts, fuel and electrical systems, prematurely worn brake pads and warped rotors, AC compressors, windows, and fit and finish. **Warranty performance:** Average.

SAFETY SUMMARY: No side airbags on early models. These vehicles come with anti-lock brakes, four-wheel discs, front-seat active head restraints, front-seat side airbags, and side curtain airbags for all three rows. Some owners report that the airbags may fail to deploy. **ABS:** Optional/standard; disc/drum and disc/disc. **Head restraints F/R:** *2002–04:* ★★★★; *2006–08:* ★★★★★. **Visibility F/R:** ★★★★★. **Maximum load capacity:** *Pre-2006 models:* 1,160 lb. **Pet transport:** ★★★★★.

SAFETY COMPLAINTS: All models: 2002—Fuel tank design could cause fuel to spray on hot muffler in a collision. • Oil leaks onto the hot catalytic converter. • Fuel leaks from the bottom of the vehicle. • Loose fuel-line-to-fuel-pump clamp. • Fuel-tank filler hose vulnerable to road debris. • Fuel spits back out when refuelling. • Vehicle continues to accelerate when brakes are applied. • Excessive brake shudder when slowing going downhill. • ABS light comes on randomly. • Power-steering pulley breaks. • Windshield may suddenly shatter for no apparent reason. • Windshields have distortion at eye level. • Second- and third-row seats don't latch as easily as touted. • Sliding doors won't retract if object is in their way. • Stuck rear hatch door. • Child safety seat can't be belted in securely. • Child door safety lock failure. • Inoperative back-seat seat belts. • Seat belt holding child in booster seat tightens progressively, trapping child. • Kumho tire-tread separation. **2002–03**—Brakes fail because of air in the brake lines, pedal simply sinks to the floor. • Electrical shorts cause lights, windows, and door locks to fail. **2002–04**—Chronic stalling. **2003**—Under-hood fire ignites while vehicle is underway. • Airbags fail to deploy. • Sudden, unintended acceleration. • Stuck accelerator pedal. • Fuel odour in cabin. • Broken window regulator. • Following the rear-seat removal instructions can throw your back out. • Tires peel off the rim. • When reclined, passenger seatback releases suddenly and slams occupant forward. • AC condenser vulnerable to puncture from road debris. **2004**—Excessive brake rotor wear. • Parking brake doesn't hold vehicle on an incline. • Windshield has a cloudy haze. **2005**—Sudden acceleration without steering assist. • Delayed recall repairs. • Chronic brake failures. • Gas tank leaks. **2006**—Fuel tank noise.

Secret Warranties/Internal Bulletins/Service Tips

All models: 2002—Correction for engine hesitation after cold starts. • Free replacement of seat belt buckle anchor bolts. **2002–03**—Changes to improve alternator output to prevent hard starts or battery drain. **2004**—Engine head gasket leak. **2005**—Shift flare, harsh engagement, late shifts. **2006**—Free sliding door cable replacement. *Entourage:* **2007**—Engine timing chain noise. • Free inspection and replacement of oil control valve. • Free electronic control module update. • Vehicle won't shift out of Park. • Free rerouting of the stop lamp switch harness. • Free replacement of the rear door power-window switch. • Tips on correcting front suspension strut noise and fuel-pump buzz, hum. • Engine tapping noise with AC on. **2007–08**—Engine misfire, hesitation.

ENTOURAGE, SEDONA PROFILE

	2002	2003	2004	2005	2006	2007
Cost Price ($) (negotiable)						
Entourage GL (26%)	—	—	—	—	—	29,995
Entourage GLS (28%)	—	—	—	—	—	35,695
Sedona LX (24%)	24,595	24,995	25,595	26,995	29,495	29,495
Sedona EX (26%)	27,595	28,295	28,995	29,495	31,895	32,495
Used Values ($)						
Entourage GL ▲	—	—	—	—	—	20,000
Entourage GL ▼	—	—	—	—	—	18,000
Entourage GLS ▲	—	—	—	—	—	22,500
Entourage GLS ▼	—	—	—	—	—	21,000
Sedona LX ▲	5,000	6,000	7,500	10,000	13,500	16,500
Sedona LX ▼	4,000	5,000	6,000	8,500	12,000	15,000
Sedona EX ▲	5,500	6,500	8,000	10,500	14,000	17,500
Sedona EX ▼	4,500	5,500	6,500	9,000	12,500	15,500
Reliability	3	3	3	4	4	4
Crash Safety (F)	5	5	5	5	5	5
Side	5	5	5	5	5	5
IIHS Side	—	—	—	—	—	5
Offset	3	3	3	3	5	5
Rollover	4	4	—	4	4	4

Mazda

MPV ★★

RATING: Below Average (1989–2006). Early models were underpowered, undersized, and overpriced. However, Mazda accomplished an amazing turnaround with the revamped 2002. Subsequent models were smaller, sportier, and more nimble than most of the competition. **Strong points:** Well appointed (lots of gadgets), an adequate engine, smooth-shifting 5-speed automatic transmission, comfortable ride and easy handling, good driver's position, responsive steering, and innovative storage spots. Without a doubt, the MPV manages its limited interior space far better than the competition does. Remarkably few factory-related defects reported at NHTSA or in the service bulletin database. **Weak points:** Smaller than most of the competition. Don't believe for a minute that the MPV will hold seven passengers in comfort—six is more like it. Elbow room is at a premium, and it takes a lithe figure to move down the front- and middle-seat aisle. Excessive engine and road noise, and early door-bottom rusting. Transport and preparation fee is exorbitant. Dealer servicing and head office support have been problematic in the past.

MODEL HISTORY: This small minivan offers a number of innovative features, like theatre seating (the rear passenger seat is slightly higher) and a third seat that pivots rearward to become a rear-facing bench seat or folds into the floor for picnics or tailgate parties. Another feature unique among minivans is Mazda's Side-by-Slide removable second-row seats, which move fore and aft as well as side-to-side while a passenger is seated. Sliding door crank windows are standard on the entry model. Windows are power-assisted on the LS and ES versions.

2006 TECHNICAL DATA

POWERTRAIN (FRONT-DRIVE)
Engine: 3.0L V6 (200 hp); Transmission: 5-speed auto.

DIMENSION/CAPACITY
Passengers: 2/2/3; Wheelbase: 112.0 in.; H: 68.7/L: 188.0/W: 72.0 in.; Headroom F/R1/R2: 6.5/5.0/3.0 in.; Legroom F/R1/R2: 41.0/27.5/27.5 in.; Cargo volume: 56.0 cu. ft.; Fuel tank: 75L/regular; Tow limit: 3,000 lb.; Load capacity: 1,305 lb.; GVWR: 5,229 lb.; Turning circle: 41.0 ft.; Ground clearance: 7.1 in.; Weight: 3,925 lb.

Mazda's only minivan quickly became a bestseller when it first came on the market in 1989, but its popularity fell just as quickly when larger, more powerful competitors arrived. Mazda sales then bounced back as a result of price-cutting and the popularity of the automaker's small cars and pickups. This infusion of cash allowed the company (34 percent of which is owned by Ford) to put additional money into its 2002 redesign. Early MPVs embodied many of the mistakes made by Honda's first Odyssey. Its 170 horses weren't adequate for people-hauling, and it was expensive for what was essentially a smaller van than buyers expected—30 cm (12 in.) shorter than the Ford Windstar and 15 cm (6 in.) shorter than the Toyota Sienna or Nissan Quest.

2000—A new model with front-drive and sliding side doors. 2002—A 200-hp V6 and 5-speed automatic transmission, power-sliding side doors, revised suspension settings, and 17-inch wheels. 2003—More standard features (LX) that include power-sliding rear side doors, 16-inch wheels, a flip-up side table, and a doormat. 2004—Refreshed interior and exterior styling of no real consequence, except additional lumbar support for the driver's seat.

The MPV uses the Taurus 200-hp 3.0L Duratec V6. Some refinements produce a lower torque peak—3000 rpm versus 4400 rpm—giving the Mazda engine better pulling power at a lower speed. Making good use of that power is a smooth-shifting 5-speed automatic transmission, which should cut fuel consumption a bit. One immediate benefit: The 3.0L is able to climb hills without continually down-shifting, and Mazda's "slope control" system automatically shifts to a lower gear when the hills get very steep. Torque is still less than the Odyssey's 3.5L or the 3.8L engine in top-of-the-line Chryslers, though it's comparable with lesser Chrysler products and GM's Venture or Montana. The suspension has been firmed up to decrease body roll, enhancing cornering ability and producing a sportier ride than other minivans. This firmness may be too much for some.

I've been tougher on the MPV than have *Consumer Reports* and others because of Mazda's price-gouging and poor servicing, and the vehicle's small size, underpow-ered drivetrain, and reliability problems (all too common on pre-2000 models). Most of these concerns have been met, although I'm still worried that the 3.0 Duratec may not hold up.

COST ANALYSIS: After the 2006 model year, Mazda dumped the MPV for good. Competent servicing, parts supply, and repair costs will become increasingly problematic the longer these minivans are off the market. Seriously consider the MPV's replacement: the smaller, more fuel-efficient, and sleeker six-passenger Mazda5 wagon/minivan. **Best alternatives:** The MPV is best suited to those owners who don't want the biggest family-hauler on the block, those who prefer sporty handling, and those who don't mind spending less to get less. When compared with Honda's latest Odyssey or the revamped pre-2004 Toyota Sienna, there's not enough savings to make up for the MPV's smaller size and less powerful engine. Other models to consider are GM's Astro or Safari, Nissan's early Quest, and Toyota's pre-2004 Sienna. **Warranty:** Bumper-to-bumper 3 years/80,000 km; powertrain 5 years/100,000 km; rust perforation 5 years/unlimited km. **Supplementary warranty:** An extended warranty is worth having, particularly since powertrain problems have plagued these vehicles after their first three years of use. **Options:** Rear AC and seat height adjustment mechanisms are recommended convenience features. The higher trim levels don't offer much of value except for power windows and door locks and an ignition immobilizer/alarm/keyless entry system. **Depreciation:** Fairly rapid for a Japanese make. **Insurance cost:** Average. **Parts supply/cost:** Often back-ordered and costly; dealers will not add to their MPV parts inventory knowing they're serving a diminishing clientele. **Annual maintenance cost:** Average now, but costs are expected to become quite expensive as service managers turn their attention and parts budget to current models. Any garage can repair these minivans; however, troubleshooting common failures may be time-consuming. Invest $25 (U.S.) in an ALLDATA bulletin printout to quickly get to the source of the problem (see Appendix II). **Highway/city fuel economy:** 7.1/11.0 L/100 km. Owners report fuel consumption may overshoot this estimate by at least 15 percent.

 QUALITY/RELIABILITY: Below-average reliability in early models; a "take it or leave it" attitude when handling warranty claims; mediocre, expensive scheduled maintenance; and high fuel and parts costs make ownership costs higher than normal. Overheating and head gasket failures are commonplace with the 4-banger, and the temperature gauge warns you only when it's too late.

Redesigned 2003 MPVs have improved workmanship, a stronger powertrain, and more rugged construction. Nevertheless, choose a second-series 2003 or later model to avoid the early redesign glitches.

Despite the upgrades, more recent models have their own subset of serious deficiencies; for example, stalling and surging, oil leakage, and valve lifter problems are common. Some cases of chronic engine knocking in cold weather with the 3.0L have been fixed by installing tighter-fitting Teflon-coated pistons. Winter driving is compromised by the MPV's light rear end and mediocre traction, and low ground clearance means that off-road excursions shouldn't be too adventurous.

Owner-reported problems: Owners report that the AC core, radiator, electronic computer module, automatic transmission, upper shock mounts, and front 4×4 drive axles and lash adjusters fail within the first three years:

> Transmission failure in a 2002 Mazda MPV van. There was always erratic shifting especially when engine was cold. After it warmed up it seemed ok but during highway driving if having to suddenly accelerate it would feel like the transmission would, for lack of a better description, "slip" between gear shifts and bog down and then catch again.

Premature brake caliper and rotor wear and excessive vibration/pulsation are chronic problem areas (repairs are needed about every 12,000 km). Cold temperatures tend to fry the automatic window motor, and the power-sliding door is often jammed open or shut. Paint is easily chipped and flakes off early, especially around the hood, tailgate, and front fenders. Apparently this problem afflicts white MPVs the most. Reports of early rusting of the door bottoms (rocker panels) through the 2005 model year. **Warranty performance:** Inadequate base warranty; mediocre servicing that's bound to get worse now that the MPV has been dropped from the lineup.

SAFETY SUMMARY: Airbags: Side airbags are optional on the LX and standard on the ES model. NHTSA has recorded a number of complaints of airbags failing to deploy in a collision. **ABS:** *2W; 4W:* Standard; disc/drum. **Head restraints F/R:** *2000:* ★★★; *2001–03:* ★★/★; *2004–06:* ★. **Visibility F/R:** ★★★★★/★★★. **Pet transport:** ★★★★★.

SAFETY COMPLAINTS: 2000—Fixed seat belt anchors and buckle placement prevent the safe installation of child safety seats. • Vehicle windshield and side glass suddenly shatters while vehicle is parked. • Excessive vibrations while cruising. • Rear hatch door flies open when rear-ended. **2000–01**—Engine valve failure. • Cupholders will spill drinks when making a sharp turn; holders were redesigned in 2002. **2000–03**—Airbags fail to deploy. **2001**—Engine surging. • Malfunctioning #1 spark plug causes chronic engine hesitation. • Tranny lever can be shifted out of Park without key in ignition; sometimes it won't shift out of Park when you want it to. • Brake failure. • Brake caliper bolt falls off, causing vehicle to skid. • Sliding doors don't lock in place. • Rear visibility obstructed by high seatbacks. **2002–03**—Engine oil leakage. • Sudden stalling. • Shifter obscures dash and is easily knocked about. **2003**—Child's neck can get tangled in seat belt. **2004**—Engine seizes when connecting rod fails. • Engine quits due to a faulty electronic computer module. • Transmission failure caused by worn shaft solenoid. • Power-sliding door jams. • Blown tire sidewall. • Tread separation on Dunlop tires. **2005**—Transmission slippage, failure.

Secret Warranties/Internal Bulletins/Service Tips

All years: TSB #006-94 looks into all the causes and remedies for excessive brake vibrations, and TSB #11-14-95 gives an excellent diagnostic flow chart for troubleshooting excessive engine noise. • Serious paint peeling and delamination will be fully covered for up to six years under a Mazda secret warranty, say owners. • Troubleshooting tips for correcting wind noise around doors. • Tips for eliminating a musty, mildew-type AC odour. **2000–01**—Hard starts caused by inadequate fuel system pressure because a fuel pressure regulator is stuck open. • Front brake clunking can be silenced by replacing the eight brake-guide plates under warranty (TSB #04-003/00). • Insufficient airflow at bi-level setting. • Door key difficult to insert or rotate. **2000–03**—Rotten-egg exhaust smell. • A corroded rear heater pipe may leak coolant; Mazda will fix it for free (see TSB #07-004/03). **2000–05**—AC temperature varies between dash vents. **2001**—Rear brake popping, squealing, or clicking. **2002**—Engine tappet noise. **2002–03**—Cargo net hooks detach. **2002–04**—Remedies for shift shock (transmission slams into gear). **2002–05**—Engine camshaft ticking.

	2000	2001	2002	2003	2004	2005	2006
Cost Price ($) (negotiable)							
DX/GX	25,505	25,095	25,975	26,090	26,600	27,595	27,895
LX/GS	29,450	29,450	29,150	29,090	29,995	30,295	30,595
Used Values ($)							
DX/GX ▲	4,000	4,500	6,000	8,500	9,500	11,000	13,500
DX/GX ▼	3,500	4,000	5,000	7,000	8,000	9,500	12,000
LX/GS ▲	4,500	5,000	6,500	9,000	10,500	11,500	14,000
LX/GS ▼	4,000	4,500	5,000	8,000	9,000	10,500	12,500
Reliability	3	3	3	4	4	4	4
Crash Safety (F)	4	4	5	5	5	5	5
Side	5	5	5	5	5	5	5
Offset	3	3	3	3	3	3	3
Rollover	—	3	3	3	—	—	—

Note: The 4×4 models cost about $500 more. There were no 1999 models.

Toyota

SIENNA

RATING: Above Average (2005–08); Average (1998–2004). The Sienna continues to be overrated. Quality control has slipped markedly and there has been a resurgence of safety-related defects reported since the 2004 Sienna was redesigned. Run-flat tires and collapsing liftgate struts, for example, can be killers if you aren't careful. Too bad strong price competition from much-improved feature-laden Hyundai and Kia minivans haven't given Toyota the reality check it sorely needs. **Strong points:** 2005–08: A smooth-running V6 engine and transmission; standard ABS and side airbags (LE, XLE); available AWD; a comfortable, stable ride; a tighter turning circle; plenty of standard safety, performance, and convenience features; a fourth door; easy entry and exit; better-than-average fit and finish and reliability; enhanced seating versatility and storage capacity; and a quieter interior. **Weak points:** Unacceptably high freight and PDI charges; V6 performance compromised by AC and automatic transmission power drain; and it lacks the trailer-towing brawn of rear-drive minivans. Less-efficient rear drum brakes; rear visibility is obstructed by middle roof pillars and rear head restraints; low head-restraint crashworthiness rating; the wide centre pillars make for difficult access to the middle seats; removing middle- and third-row seats is a two-person chore; radio speakers are set too low for acceptable acoustics; and an unusually large number of body rattles and safety-related complaints (158 safety complaints, or three times what is considered normal). Suspect towing capability; mediocre braking; third-

All ratings on a numbered scale where 5 is good and 1 is bad. See page 217 for a more detailed description.

row head restraints are mounted too low; and expensive options. **New for 2008:** Nothing major; the 2009 will likely have additional standard convenience features only, whereas the 2010 models will include a gas-electric hybrid.

MODEL HISTORY: Completely redesigned in 2004, the Sienna provides plenty of interior room to accommodate up to eight passengers, handles fairly well for its size, rides comfortably, and is powered by a competent, fuel-efficient engine. A relatively new 3.5L V6 turns in respectable acceleration times that are almost as good as the Odyssey. Handling is completely carlike, with little vulnerability to wind buffeting and minimal road noise.

The entry-level front-drive is the CE, with either seven- or eight-passenger seating; followed by the LE, in seven- or eight-passenger versions; and the XLE, in a seven-passenger version only, as are the AWD models. Important recommended features such as traction and stability control are standard only on the front-drive XLE and the AWD models. The Sienna's interior and exterior have been gently restyled over the years. Its third-row seats split and fold away (but they're not as user-friendly as Chrysler's Stow 'n Go seating configuration), head restraints don't have to be removed when the seats are stored, and the second-row bucket seats are easily converted to bench seats.

Honda's Odyssey has similar quality and features, except for all-wheel drive. Although GM's extended minivans are slightly longer, there's not as much usable room, and interior trim and amenities look and feel tacky. Ford's Freestar feels cramped inside and doesn't provide comparable performance.

The Sienna is Toyota's Camry-based front-drive minivan. It replaced the Previa for the 1998 model year and abandoned the Previa's futuristic look in favour of a more conservative Chevrolet Venture styling. The base Sienna seats seven and offers dual power-sliding doors with optional remote control. It's built in the same Kentucky assembly plant as the Camry and comes with lots of safety and convenience features, including side airbags, anti-lock brakes, and a low-tire-pressure warning system. Its trailer-towing brawn, however, leaves something to be desired:

> Imagine our surprise when we discovered within the owner's manual a "Caution" stating that one must not exceed 72 km/hr [45 mph] while towing a trailer.... This limit is not stated in the promotional literature we were provided, or on the *Toyota.ca* website, or in any trailer-towing rating guide. This limit was also not mentioned at any time during our purchase negotiations. Alarmingly, Toyota defines a "Caution" as a "warning against anything which may cause injury to people if the warning is ignored." As it turns out, the dealer was not aware of this speed limit.

2008 TECHNICAL DATA

POWERTRAIN (FRONT-DRIVE)
Engine: 3.5L V6 (266 hp); Transmission: 5-speed auto.
DIMENSION/CAPACITY (LE)
Passengers: 2/2/3, 2/3/3; Wheelbase: 119.3 in.; H: 68.9/L: 201.0/W: 77.4 in.; Headroom F/R1/R2: 3.5/4.0/2.5 in.; Legroom F/R1/R2: 40.5/31.5/25.0 in.; Cargo volume: 70.5 cu. ft.; Fuel tank: 79L/regular; Tow limit: 3,500 lb.; Load capacity: 1,325–1,570 lb.; GVWR: 5,690 lb.; Turning circle: 36.8 ft.; Ground clearance: 6.9 in.; Weight: 4,177 lb.

Although the rear seats fold flat to accommodate the width of a 4′ × 8′ board, the tailgate won't close, the heavy seats are difficult to reinstall (a two-person job, and the centre seat barely fits through the door), and the middle roof pillars and rear head restraints obstruct rear visibility. There's also no stability control or traction control for all versions, less-efficient rear drum brakes are used on some versions, the vehicle provides mediocre fuel economy, the low-mounted radio is hard to reach, and third-row seats lack a fore/aft adjustment to increase cargo space.

Reliability is still problematic on 1997–2004 models. Although mechanical and body components are generally reliable except for the sliding doors, there's been a disturbing increase in factory-related powertrain defects reported by owners during the past few years. The most serious reliability problems concern self-destructing, sludge-prone engines on 1997–2002 models and defective automatic transmissions on 1998–2004 Siennas.

Toyota Canada advises owners who notice the telltale signs of engine sludge formation to take their vehicle to their local dealer to have the engine inspected. These signs may include the emission of blue smoke from the tailpipe and excessive oil consumption, which may cause overheating, rough running, or the Check Engine light to come on. Take Toyota's advice, but if the dealer tries to blame the problem on "poor maintenance" or refuses to fix the engine unless you prove the oil was changed regularly, threaten small claims court action.

Other recent model problems reported by owners include a clunk or banging in the driveline; the car jolting or creeping forward when at a stop, forcing you to keep your foot firmly on the brake; premature brake wear and excessive brake noise (mostly screeching); a chronic rotten-egg smell; distracting windshield reflections and distorted windshields; sliding door defects; windows suddenly shattering; and various other body glitches, including water leaks, a hard-to-pull-out rear seat, and excessive creaks and rattles (seat belt, sun visor).

2001—Added a rear defroster, some additional horsepower and torque, and a driver-side sliding door. **2004**—Completely redesigned. **2006**—Standard front and side airbags, and side curtain airbags in all three rows; new bumper, grille, headlights, rear lights, and body side moulding; a standard roof rack for the base CE; new power-folding mirrors with memory; and front and rear wipers clean more windshield area. Top-line model gets a power-folding third-row seat.

COST ANALYSIS: In Canada, a 2008 Sienna CE 7-passenger sells for $29,400 and the equivalent LE goes for $34,880. Stateside, the same vehicles cost $24,340 (U.S.) and $25,865 (U.S.), respectively. The 2008s are essentially warmed-over 2007s. **Best alternatives:** Consider a Honda Odyssey for its peppier engine and rear disc brakes. The small Mazda5 and the pre-2004 Nissan Quest are also acceptable. Bargain hunters take note: Used cargo Siennas (year 2000 or earlier) cost thousands less than the base CE. **Rebates:** $2,000 on the '08s in the fall of 2008. **Delivery/PDI:** $1,390. **Warranty:** Bumper-to-bumper 3 years/60,000 km; powertrain 5 years/100,000 km; rust perforation 5 years/unlimited km.

Supplementary warranty: Not needed. **Options:** Power windows and door locks, rear heater, and AC unit. Be wary of the power-sliding door. As with the Odyssey and GM minivans, these doors can injure children and pose unnecessary risks to other occupants. Go for Michelin or Pirelli original-equipment tires. **Depreciation:** Much slower than average. **Insurance cost:** A bit higher than average. **Parts supply/cost:** Excellent supply of reasonably priced Sienna parts taken from the Camry parts bin. The only exception has been fuel tank components needed for recall repairs. Automatic transmission torque converters are frequently back ordered because of their poor reliability. **Annual maintenance cost:** Like the Camry, much lower than average. **Highway/city fuel economy:** *3.0L V6: 8.8/12.4 L/100 km; 3.3L V6: 8.1/12.2 L/100 km; 3.5L V6: 8.1/11.7 L/100 km; 3.5L V6 and AWD: 9.5/13.3 L/100 km.*

QUALITY/RELIABILITY: Reliability concerns include stalling when the AC engages, electrical shorts, excessive brake squealing noise despite new rear drums and shoes, sliding door defects, and various other body glitches, including excessive creaks and rattles and paint that's easily chipped. **Owner-reported problems:** Tires lose air pressure, rear wiper doesn't work, and blower motor and damper wear out quickly. Premature brake wear and noisy brakes, engine replacement because of sludge buildup, annoying engine hum, automatic transmission failures, fuel-tank leaks, alternator and computer module malfunctions, distracting windshield reflections and distorted windshields, power-sliding door malfunctions, interior squeaks and rattles, and rusting of the AC lines:

> The Sienna's front to back AC lines rust out because they are made of aluminum and are connected to the body frame with another type of metal fastener. This combination causes extensive leakage. Toyota says it will cost $500 to correct this design defect.

Warranty performance: Average, but you have to stand your ground and ignore head office bullcrap to the effect that "goodwill" repair reimbursements apply only if you show maintenance receipts or if repairs were done by the dealer.

SAFETY SUMMARY: Many complaints that the steering wheel locks up when making a turn, won't return to the centre without extreme effort, or simply no longer responds. Owners have also complained that the vehicle pulls sharply to one side or another when driving at moderate speeds. **Airbags:** Reports of airbags failing to deploy in a collision. **ABS:** Standard; disc/drum. Numerous reports of ABS failures, loud grinding or groaning noises when braking, and the brake pedal going to the floor without any braking effect. **Seat belt pretensioners:** Standard. **Head restraints F/R:** *1999: ★; 2001–03: ★★; 2004: ★★★★/★★★; 2005–08: ★:*

> There is no way to properly adjust headrest height for taller people (average male and above) on 2006 Toyota Sienna LE cloth seats first and second row. Even the highest locking position is too low for me and my son. We are approximately 6 ft. tall.

Visibility F/R: ★★★★★/★★. Owners report windshield problems, which have been corrected in the 2007 models:

> The right windshield wiper leaves much water directly in front of me before the left wiper removes it. Every wipe, while the water is in my line of sight, I struggle to see the road. This is definitely a hazard to my family's safety, and should be easily repaired with a simple improvement in the design of the wiper cycle.

•

> The windshield has optical distortion causing eye strain, watery eyes, headaches, nausea, dizziness. Toyota says "all Siennas are like this" so they will not replace the windshield.

Pet transport: ★★★★★.

SAFETY COMPLAINTS: All years: Hesitation and surging when accelerating. • A multiplicity of sliding door defects covered by internal bulletins. • Windshield distortion. • Reflection of the dashboard on the windshield impairs visibility (very bad with black and beige colours). • Faulty tire pressure monitor, especially on 2004–05 models. **1999**—Window explodes while vehicle is stopped. • Rear brake drums may overheat and warp. • Faulty fuel cap causes the Check Engine light to come on. **1999–2000**—Wheel lug nuts break and allow wheel to fall off. **2000**—Driver's seat belt anchor bolt on door pillar unscrews and falls out. • Premature tire blowouts (Dunlop and Firestone). • Right rear passenger window suddenly explodes. **2000–01**—Sudden, unintended acceleration, especially during rainstorm. • Defective transmission torque converter causes chronic transmission failure and the Check Engine light to come on. **2001**—Sudden stalling when the AC is turned on. • Automatic transmission suddenly goes into Neutral while underway. • Vehicle rolls away on a hill with shifter in Park and ignition shut off. • Rear seat belts can't be adjusted. • Centre rear seat belt doesn't tighten sufficiently when children are restrained. • Slope of the windshield makes it hard to gauge where the front end stops. • Rear window explodes as front door is closed. • Sunroof flies off when opened while vehicle is underway. **2002**—Several electrical fires in the engine compartment. • Neither front nor side airbag deploys in a collision. • Defective power steering. • Loss of steering. **2003**—Unsafe transmission Overdrive design. • Child safety seat second-row tethering is poorly designed. • Vehicle jerks to one side when accelerating or stopping. **2004**—Engine surging with minimal pedal pressure. • When proceeding from a rolling stop, acceleration is delayed for about two seconds.

> While parking, accelerating no more than 5 mph [8 km/h] vehicle surged forward. Although I was applying the brake, the car would not stop until it ran into a tree trunk.

• Gearshift lever can be knocked into Drive from Park without the key in the ignition. • Difficulty shifting into a higher gear. • Sluggish transmission downshift; vehicle sometimes seems to slip out of gear when decelerating. • Skid control system lock-up. • Fuel tank leakage after recall repairs; leaking fuel line. • Complete loss of brakes. • Rapid brake degradation (glazed and warped rotors). • Sliding door catches passengers' arms and legs. • Manual door doesn't latch properly, particularly when windows are open. • Door jams, opens when turning, or closes when vehicle is parked on an incline:

> Our two-year-old son pulled on the sliding door handle, and the door began to open (we thought the child locks were on, but this was not the case). He was surprised and was afraid of falling out of the van, so he just held onto the handle. As the door was opening, his head then was dragged between the sliding door and the side of the van. But the van door did not stop opening. It just continued opening, exerting even more force on our son's head. Fortunately we were able to grab the door and forcefully pull it back closed before our son was horribly injured.

• Second-row seat belt locks up; faulty seat belt bracket in rear passenger seat. • Seat belts won't retract. • Battery-saver device doesn't work, particularly if interior lights are left on. • Small brake lights inadequate. • Foot gets stuck between pedals. • Rotten-egg smell. • Daytime running lights blind oncoming drivers (2004 Highlander has the same problem). • Long delay for fuel-tank recall campaign parts. **2004–05**—Automatic interior light shutoff fails intermittently. **2005**—Sudden acceleration when parking or shifting to Reverse. • Many reports that the front and side airbags fail to deploy. • Airbag deploy for no reason while vehicle is underway. • Laser-controlled cruise control jerks back to former speed when the way seems clear; doesn't hold the speed when going downhill. • Automatic transmission shifts erratically. • Gearshift lever can be accidentally knocked from Fourth gear to Reverse. • Brake pedal stiffens intermittently. • Run-flat tires don't signal driver when they are damaged; may catch fire:

> 2005 Toyota Sienna has Bridgestone run flat tires and the back right passenger tire went flat, then smoked and caught fire.

> •

> Catastrophic tire failure on a 2005 Toyota Sienna AWD van with run flat tires. Fortunately, no major injuries or damage this time. The tire pressure monitoring system failed to sense the lack of pressure in one of the tires. Driving on the tire with no air pressure caused catastrophic tire failure.

• Dunlop run-flat tires won't hold more than 25 psi of air, and tire-pressure warning light doesn't illuminate. • When the rear windows are down, the door will not stay open. • Sliding doors fail to latch when they are opened. • Sliding door continues closing even if something is in its way (similar to complaints on previous model year Siennas). • Rear heater core leaks coolant. **2005–07**—Liftgate hydraulic strut failures allow the liftgate to suddenly fall:

I went to put boxes in the rear of my 2005 Toyota Sienna LE and as soon as I lifted the door, it fell on my head. After looking at the door, I noticed what appeared to be oil on my bumper and the ground right below where the struts holding the door were. It worked perfectly fine the previous day, but I am concerned that this really could have injured my children if it were them opening the door. The door will no longer stay up by itself and it is a very heavy door. There was absolutely no indication that there was a problem with the door prior to this. I called the dealership and since I am out of warranty, I will have to pay for the replacement. On top of that, they have replaced the strut so I also will have to pay for new brackets. The 2004 have a TSB on that very part, why not the 2005?

2006—More than average number of complaints registered by NHTSA. • Excess steering vibration, and vehicle veers to the right. • Airbag warning light stays lit. • Driver-side rear window suddenly explodes. • Second-row seats have no armrests. • Door requires excessive force to close, and leaks air and water. • Separation of the door weld requires a new door:

Toyota Sienna '06 with 31,000 miles [50,000 km]. The doors started making noise. I read up on this on some websites and it appears that there is poor welding/bad designs on Toyota Sienna doors.

• Mud and snow builds up on the inside of the wheels. • Sudden brake failure. • Premature brake and tire wear (Dunlop):

Run flats were supposed to be a safety feature on my AWD, instead they have become a safety hazard. One does not carry a spare, and in fact there is no room for one in this Sienna. You would not expect to need 4 new tires at 15,000 miles [24,000 km]!

2007—Toyota has recovered from its redesign glitches; only about a dozen complaints registered. • Tire sensor failures. • Power back door cannot be closed with either the remote or the front dash control. • Loose fuel-line fitting may leak fuel. **2008**—Homelink garage door opener may cause door motor to overheat, risking a house fire.

Secret Warranties/Internal Bulletins/Service Tips

All years: Sliding door hazards, malfunctions, and noise are a veritable plague affecting all model years and generating a ton of service bulletins. • Owner feedback confirms that front brake pads and discs will be replaced under Toyota's "goodwill" policy if they wear out before 2 years/40,000 km. • Loose, poorly fitted trim panels (TSB # BO017-03, revised September 9, 2003). • Rusting at the base of the two front doors will be repaired at no cost, usually with a courtesy car included. According to *www.siennaclub.org*, the proper fix is as follows: Repaint the insides of doors (presumably after removing paint and rust), cover with 3M film, and then replace and coat inside seals with silicone grease. **1999–2000**—An 8-year/160,000 km warranty extension for automatic transmission failure. Owners with Siennas that exceed the limitation should ask for partial compensation. Says Toyota:

> We have recently become aware that a small number of Sienna owners have experienced a mechanical failure in the automatic transaxle, drive pinion bearing. This failure could result in slippage, noise, or a complete lack of movement.
>
> To ensure the continued satisfaction and reliability of your Sienna, Toyota has decided to implement a Special Policy Adjustment affecting certain 1998–2000 Sienna models.... This Special Policy will extend the warranty coverage of the automatic transaxle to 8 years or 160,000 km, whichever occurs first, from the original warranty registration date.

• Power-steering squeaks can be silenced by installing a countermeasure steering-rack end. • Power-steering feel can be improved by replacing the steering-rack guide. **1999–2001**—Tips on fixing power-seat motor cable to prevent a loose seat or inoperative seat adjustment. • Power-sliding door transmitter improvements. • Power-window rattles can be corrected by installing a revised lower window frame mounting bracket. **1999–2002**—Free engine overhaul or replacement because of engine sludge buildup. The program includes 1997 through 2002 Toyota and Lexus vehicles with 3.0L V6 or 2.2L 4-cylinder engines. There is no mileage limitation. Tell Toyota to shove it if they give you a song and dance about proof of oil changes. • Outline of various diagnostic procedures and fixes to correct vehicle pulling to one side. **1999–2003**—A new rear brake drum has been developed to reduce rear brake noise. • An upgraded alternator will improve charging (see TSB #EL013-03). **2000**—Toyota has field fixes to correct washer fluid leakage from the rear washer nozzle. • Correction for an inoperative spare-tire lift. **2000–01**—Speedometer or tachometer troubleshooting. • Troubleshooting interior moisture or odours. **2001**—Entertainment system hum. • Inoperative third-row sliding seat. • Special service campaign to inspect or replace the front subframe assembly on 2001 models. • Water leaking into the trunk area. • Front wheel bearing ticking. **2002–03**—Steering angle sensor calibration. • Loose sun visor remedy. **2003–07**—Windshield ticking. **2004**—Vehicle stability control activates intermittently when it is not needed. • New ECM calibration for a poorly shifting transmission (TSB #TC007-03). • Rear disc brake groan (TSB #BR002-04). • Intermediate steering-shaft noise on turns. • Steering-column pop, squeak, and click. • Front-door area wind noise (TSB #NV009-03). • Charging improvement at idle (TSB #RL013-03). • Seat heaters only operate on high. **2004–05**—No-start in cold temperatures. • Correction for the AWD transmission shifter that may become progressively harder to move. • AC blower motor noise. **2004–06**—Slow-speed front suspension ticking. • Temperature may vary between the front and rear heaters. **2004–07**—A new brake pad kit has been developed to address rapid brake pad wear complaints. • Power back door leaks and shudders.

SIENNA PROFILE

	1999	2000	2001	2002	2003	2004	2005	2006	2007
Cost Price ($) (negotiable)									
Cargo 3d	24,570	24,570	—	—	—	—	—	—	—
CE 4d (25%)	26,940	27,770	29,535	29,335	29,060	30,000	30,000	30,800	32,440
LE 4d (26%)	29,980	30,705	31,900	32,985	31,925	35,000	35,420	36,255	36,860
Used Values ($)									
Cargo 3d ▲	4,500	5,500	—	—	—	—	—	—	—
Cargo 3d ▼	4,000	5,000	—	—	—	—	—	—	—
CE 4d ▲	5,500	6,500	7,000	8,000	10,000	11,500	14,000	19,000	21,000
CE 4d ▼	5,000	6,000	6,500	7,000	8,500	10,000	13,500	17,500	19,500
LE 4d ▲	6,000	7,500	8,500	9,500	11,500	13,000	15,500	21,500	24,000
LE 4d ▼	5,000	6,500	7,500	8,500	10,000	11,500	14,000	20,000	22,500
Reliability	4	4	4	4	4	3	4	4	4
Crash Safety (F)	5	5	5	5	5	5	4	4	4
Side	4	4	4	4	4	5	5	5	5
IIHS Side	—	—	—	—	—	—	5	5	5
Offset	5	5	5	5	5	5	5	5	5
Rollover	—	—	4	4	4	4	4	4	4

Note: The 2008 crashworthiness ratings are identical to the 2007 ratings.

All ratings on a numbered scale where 5 is good and 1 is bad. See page 217 for a more detailed description.

PICKUP TRUCKS

Ford Power Stroke: A Power Joke?

The 6-liter Power Stroke diesel V8, built by a unit of Navistar for Ford, commands nearly half the U.S. market for diesel pickups. But a raft of problems and repeat trips to dealerships for repairs has left some owners upset, threatening Ford's efforts to rebuild a reputation for quality vehicles.

Soon after the new engines went on sale in November in heavy-duty Ford pickups and the Ford Excursion sport-utility vehicle, owners started reporting problems. Among the costliest is diesel fuel seeping into the engine's oil supply in amounts large enough to ruin the engine. Other complaints included engines that ran roughly or stalled, lack of power at low speeds and harsh shifts.

JUSTIN HYDE
REUTERS, AUGUST 20, 2003

Big Trucks: Big Losers

Canadians have always been big fans of large and small pickups, because of their jobs, their geographical locations, or their lifestyles. But then fuel prices broke through $1.50 a litre for regular gasoline last summer and panic set in.

With Canadian gasoline prices galloping toward $1.50 a litre, Ford's gas-guzzling F-150's sales are sinking like a rock. In 2009, Ford will downsize these trucks and offer them as a mini-F-Series, sold under the venerable F-100 brand. The Ranger will be axed.

GM's U.S. sales of trucks were down 39 percent in May, compared with the same month last year. Its overall sales of all vehicles were down 30 percent year-over-year, and auto stock values plummeted. With its back against the wall, GM Canada announced the closure of four SUV and large-truck assembly plants, including its Oshawa facility that turns out Chevrolet Silverados and GMC Sierras. Even GM's Hummer division is expected to be sold to Tata Motors, an Indian conglomerate that recently bought Jaguar and Land Rover from Ford for one-third of what Ford once paid for them.

The collapse of the pickup market couldn't come at a worse time, as Ford and Chrysler prepare to introduce redesigned F-150 and Ram pickups this fall. The predicted downturn of 30 percent fewer trucks sold this year spells disaster for the

Literally going for broke, Chrysler's 2009 Ram extols power and interior comfort over fuel efficiency.

Detroit Big Three, which earn an estimated pre-tax average profit of $8,000–$10,000 per unit sold.

Canadian truck owners are particularly hard hit by the double whammy of fuel that's too expensive to buy and trucks that are too depreciated to sell. In fact, pickups that were bought new three years ago are now worth only a third of what they originally cost. Many pickup owners owe more money on their trucks than the trucks are worth—and resale values continue to drop. For example, last May, 41.2 percent of buyers trading in full-sized pickups owed more than they could get back as a trade-in.

The Detroit Big Three want to keep churning out fuel-wasting, fully loaded large pickups because that's what generates the most profits. Sure, there will be small steps taken to burn less fuel—baby steps—like urging motorists to buy costly hybrids or ethanol-friendly vehicles, knowing that ethanol fuel is unavailable and 30 percent less efficient than gasoline.

Ford is losing money with hybrids, and it has just cut back its ambitious plans to expand hybrids across its model lineup. Instead, the automaker is going after the luxury truck market with the $50,000 (U.S.) 2009 F-150 Platinum. General Motors is adding hybrids to its 2009 Silverado/Sierra lineup, with negligible gas-saving results, and is touting hydrogen- and fuel-cell-powered vehicles for the future—a "future" that has no definite date. Chrysler, stuck with a huge truck inventory, is looking to its revamped 2009 Ram to spark buyer interest. Fat chance.

Gentrified pickups

The traditional "hay hauler" is almost gone. Buyers who can afford the gas want pickups with as much cachet as cargo-hauling capacity, and families are demanding practical features never imagined by the male-dominated trucking crowd. Pickups represent almost half of North America's vehicle production, and they're offering larger interiors and more carlike styling, handling, comfort, and convenience features. Safety features have also been added to give pickups greater stability, better braking, and improved crashworthiness.

In general, entry-level models are cheaper than cars with comparable features, but prices for full-sized pickups can easily top $50,000 for fully equipped versions with extended or crew cabs, 4×4, and a complete list of amenities. Extended cabs have a small rear seat and doors, while crew cabs generally have four full-sized doors, rear windows that roll down, and a full-sized back seat in a large interior that can seat up to six passengers.

This year, more pickups will adopt innovative fuel-saving features like cylinder deactivation, more efficient diesel engines, hybrid electrical/gasoline set-ups, and lightweight aluminum engines. Never mind that aluminum powerplants have encountered serious sealing and durability problems in the past, or that GM's first (and last) 4-6-8-cylinder engine, used in its early '80s Cadillacs, was a fiasco, providing 8-cylinder power in the city and 4-cylinder power just as you were merging onto the highway.

Depreciation

High fuel prices are driving down resale values for full-sized trucks as buyers opt for cheaper-running alternatives. As with cars, imports hold their value better than domestics. For example, a Ford Ranger will be worth less than 30 percent of its initial value after three years, yet a Toyota Tacoma PreRunner Double Cab will retain almost 40 percent of its value during the same period.

Quality decline

Over the past decade, American automakers have churned out millions of new pickups equipped with more complicated and hard-to-service safety, performance, and convenience features. At the same time, they squeeze equipment suppliers to give them more for less, and they constantly change part specifications, confounding suppliers even more.

Industry insiders agree that these actions have contributed largely to a dramatic decline in pickup quality over the past decade—a conclusion also reached by J.D. Power and Associates and *Consumer Reports*. *CR* says their poll results show that American trucks become less reliable as they age and don't match the Asian automakers' trucks for overall quality. They gave top marks to the Toyota Tundra and Nissan Titan (one of *CR*'s few mistakes), and they picked Ford's F-150 as the least reliable pickup. J.D. Power insists that the American automakers are closing the quality gap with their latest models. However, service bulletins and safety defect reports signal that Chrysler, GM, and Mazda are improving, while Ford and Toyota stagnate or decline.

The Dark Side of Diesels

The pickup-truck category is the only vehicle segment that uses diesel engines extensively. In recent years, General Motors and Chrysler have upgraded their diesel lineups to better compete against Ford, the sales leader in diesel-equipped vehicles.

Although diesel engines are promoted by automakers for their dependable, fuel-efficient performance, recent studies and owner complaints indicate that diesels burn more fuel than advertised, are more likely to break down than gasoline-powered engines, and produce emissions that exacerbate the number of emphysema cases and may be responsible for 125,000 cases of pulmonary cancer in the States.

Cancer dangers

Diesel exhaust contains more than 40 chemicals that are listed by the U.S. Environmental Protection Agency as toxic air contaminants, known or probable human carcinogens, or reproductive toxins or endocrine disrupters. In the United States, the national associations of state and local air-quality control officers estimate that almost 120,000 people living in urban areas and about 5,500 in suburban and rural areas will develop cancer after a lifetime of exposure to diesel fumes. There are also hundreds of different chemical compounds in diesel that degrade air quality, contributing to ozone formation, smog, and acid rain.

Unreliable performance

All three Detroit manufacturers have had persistent injector problems with their newer diesel engines. Ford is covering repair costs through a variety of "goodwill" programs, Chrysler is using its 7-year warranty to authorize repair refunds on 2002 through 2004 models, and General Motors has extended fuel injector warranty coverage for owners of all 2001 and 2002 model-year Chevrolet and GMC pickup trucks equipped with Duramax 6600 engines. GM's Special Policy #04039 was set up in June 2004 and gives additional warranty protection for 330,000 km (200,000 mi.) or 7 years from the date the vehicle was placed into service, whichever comes first.

Trucking companies are scouring dealer lots for 2002 and earlier diesel-equipped heavy trucks in an effort to avoid getting cleaner but problem-prone 2003 and later diesels. Mandated by the U.S. Environmental Protection Agency and seconded by Canadian regulators, these newer diesels use new technology to re-circulate exhaust gases through the engine but cost thousands of dollars more than previous versions and are 3–5 percent less fuel efficient. Oil changes are more frequent and repair costs have been much higher than before because few mechanics and dealers have the diagnostic tools and experience to correct factory-related defects that are commonplace with new designs.

For example, J.D. Power's 2004 Vehicle Dependability Study found that the most fuel-efficient vehicles—diesels and gas-electric hybrids—have more engine problems than similar gasoline-powered vehicles, a conclusion backed by automaker service bulletins and complaints sent to NHTSA. The discrepancies are an eye-opener:

- Ford and Chevrolet diesel pickups were worse than similar gas models, while Dodge and GMC trucks were better overall.
- Owners of 2001 Toyota and Honda hybrids reported twice as many engine problems as did owners of gas-engine Toyotas and Hondas.
- Owners of Volkswagen diesels reported up to twice as many engine problems as did owners of gas-burning VWs.

Chrysler

Although Chrysler's Cummins engine is now the most reliable diesel sold by American automakers, it also has a number of serious manufacturing flaws, one of which is the lift pump. Here's how independent mechanic Chuck Arnold (*chuck@thepowershop.com*) describes the problem:

> The Cummins 24-valve injector pumps will not live without an adequate lift pump fuel supply. These pumps are totally fuel-lubricated and cooled. Without excess fuel flow for cooling and lubrication, these injector pumps die if asked to pull heavy loads. Four out of the last ten lift pumps purchased by The PowerShop have been bad. Two brand new pumps would not pump enough to prime the system and start the truck. Two others would not supply enough fuel to maintain pressure under load conditions. Cummins needs to improve quality control on their lift pumps and Dodge should investigate moving the lift pump to inside the fuel tank where cavitation and engine heat can't lead to failure over time. [Unfortunately], the Dodge-recommended lift pump tests do not find marginal performing pumps.

Arnold ends with these comments:

> Low fuel pressure is very dangerous because it is possible for the engine to run very well right up to the moment of failure. There may be no symptom of a problem at all before you are walking. If you notice extended cranking before startup of your Cummins 24-Valve engine you should get your lift pump checked out fast. Addition of fuel lubricant enhancing additives to every tank of fuel may minimize pump damage and extend pump life. Finally, Cummins and Bosch should re-engineer their injector pump to make it less sensitive to low-fuel-pressure-induced failure. Existing safety systems designed to limit performance or signal engine trouble need to be redesigned to work when fuel pressure is inadequate so that very expensive injector pumps are not destroyed without warning.

Incidentally, Chrysler's Customer Satisfaction Notification No. 878 authorizes the replacement of the lift pumps in some 2000 and 2001 Dodge pickups.

Ford

F-Series 2003 and 2004 model-year trucks equipped with the 6.0L Power Stroke diesel engine were so badly flawed that they couldn't be fixed, forcing Ford to buy back over 500 units. Wary customers are snapping up Ford's earlier 7.3L diesels, which are apparently more reliable, though less powerful (275 hp versus 325 hp). Power Strokes have a history of fuel injectors that leak into the crankcase, and on the 7.3L diesel water can leak into the fuel tank, causing the engine to seize. Other glitches affect the turbocharger, the fuel injection control pressure sensor, and the engine control software.

WATER IN THE FUEL TANK BEHIND REAR AXLE—6.0L AND 7.3L DIESEL ENGINE
BULLETIN NO.: 05-11-7

FORD:
1999–2005 F-350, F-450
ISSUE: Some 1999–2005 vehicles equipped with the 6.0L or 7.3L diesel engine and a 40-gallon (151.4L) fuel tank behind the rear axle, may exhibit water in the fuel tank. This is due to snow and ice accumulating around the mushroom vent cap, melting, and being pulled into the tank through the mushroom cap.
ACTION: Replace the mushroom cap with a vent line assembly kit.

One Ford dealer mechanic has seen it all:

> You name it, we've seen it. Oil "blowing" into the cooling system (fortunately, not the other way around), numerous running problems, tubes blowing off the turbos, and oil leaks. We had one truck with 8 miles [13 km] on it that we had to pull the engine on. It was a truck going to Hertz, so it wasn't a big deal to the customer, Ford owned [it] anyway, but still, it was a new truck coming off the autohauler sounding like it had a 5-hp air compressor running under the hood and a dead skip. We're pulling heads off of a 6.0 now with 4,000 miles [6,400 km] on it. All these problems I've mentioned are on trucks with less than 20,000 miles [32,000 km]. My diesel tech constantly wishes that since they had worked all the kinks out of the 7.3, Ford would have kept it. So far, we've had six buybacks. The one we're pulling the heads off of now will be the next. Before this, I only had one buyback in four years.

General Motors

GM's diesel engine failures primarily affect the 6.6L Duramax engine, which has been plagued by persistent oil leaks, excessive oil burning, and defective turbochargers, fuel-injection pumps, and injectors, causing seized engines, chronic stalling, loss of power, hard starts, and excessive gas consumption. To its credit, GM has a Special Policy that extends the warranty to 11 years/193,000 km (120,000 mi.) on injection pumps installed in 1994–2002 models.

Pros and Cons of Pickup Ownership

The pickup has grown in popularity partly by default. The station wagons that used to haul families to the beach and the cottage are practically extinct; minivans don't have the awesome towing capacity and big-engine grunt (torque) that some motorhome owners, boaters, and off-roaders require; and crossovers (tall AWD wagons) aren't as versatile for carrying large objects or heavy loads.

As with sport-utilities, even though it's unlikely you'll need the 4×4 versatility or a brawny V8, it's reassuring to know it's there, just in case. Despite rising fuel costs and a smaller market, pickups will remain popular in Canada because of tradition and necessity.

Pickup advantages

- There are bargains galore, and availability is good south of the border.
- Small pickups have a relatively low base price.
- A large variety of fuel-efficient 4- and 6-cylinder engines are available.
- Gasoline and diesel versions are available.
- The support network for parts and servicing is good.
- Body, engine, and suspension choices are numerous.
- They are available in 4×2, part-time 4×4, or full-time 4×4.
- They're versatile cargo- and RV-haulers.
- It's easy to customize or convert a pickup into a recreational vehicle.
- They are easy to repair, with excellent parts availability at reasonable prices.
- Anti-lock brakes and electronic stability control are standard on many models.
- You get a commanding view of the road.
- Collision repair costs are much lower than average due to the body-on-frame design.

Pickup disadvantages

- Many trucks have dangerous full-strength airbags and may be equipped with dealer-installed, failure-prone Bridgestone, Firestone, Goodyear, or Continental tires.
- Diesel reliability and fuel-economy claims usually aren't true.
- 2007 and later diesel engines will cost more and be less reliable.
- Depreciation on feature-laden medium- and large-sized models is brutal.
- Homeowners' associations may prohibit trucks being parked outside.
- Trucks used commercially are the quickest to lose their value.
- Chassis and box may have rust damage.
- Truck, tools, and cargo are easily stolen.
- Small pickups don't offer much cab room and are often underpowered with a 4-cylinder engine.
- The centre front-seat passenger has little legroom.
- Three adults can't sit comfortably in the rear seat on base models.
- Expect a bone-jarring ride, unless the suspension is modified.

- They can't be driven with rear windows down because of a deafening, painful boom.
- A tire upgrade is usually needed on base models to improve handling.
- Entry and exit may be difficult without running boards or an extra door.
- Some compacts can't haul a 4′ × 8′ sheet of plywood flat on the cargo bed.
- A long box makes in-town parking a problem.
- V6s and V8s are fuel-thirsty.
- Hybrids' fuel economy may be illusory.
- Base models are relatively bare.
- Loading up on options can greatly escalate the base price.
- The rear bench seat usually comes with an uncomfortably upright seatback.
- Rear doors don't always operate independently of the front doors.
- The 4×4 can't always be engaged while running on dry pavement.
- Rear wheels spin on slippery roads.
- Recommended four-wheel ABS isn't always available.
- The rear end tends to swing out when rear-drives corner at highway speeds.
- Heaters may be slow to heat the cabin.
- Taller, narrower trucks can be more prone to rollovers.
- High-mounted headlights can blind other drivers.

Full-sized pickups have changed considerably over the past decade, beginning with Ford's 1996 model redesign, continuing with GM's 1999 and 2004 model revamping, and highlighted by the upgraded 2009 Dodge Ram and Ford F-Series. There's also the innovative Honda Ridgeline, the boldly styled and powerful Nissan Titan, and the quality-challenged Toyota Tundra.

Pickups have been re-engineered to become more carlike, with better handling characteristics and more convenience features (like extra doors, interior space, padding, and carpeting) that enlarge their appeal from trucks for farmers and tradespeople to vehicles for everyday transportation. Still, the half-ton full-sized pickups haven't abandoned their base clientele—they just come in a larger variety of sizes and powertrains to suit more diverse driving needs.

Nevertheless, no matter how carlike these trucks become, you'll be constantly reminded that these are trucks (especially with 2008 and earlier Dodge Rams) whenever you brake, corner, stop for fuel (which will be often), or literally climb on board.

When choosing a pickup, consider cost, reliability, size, and style—in that order. Start small with reliable entry-level Mazda, Honda, or Nissan offerings. If you need more brawn and performance and must buy something Detroit-made, go for Chrysler's Ram series; discounts of $10,000+ are commonplace. And then consider Ford or GM. But be prepared for subpar reliability, high maintenance costs, rapid depreciation, and abysmally poor fit and finish on all Detroit-bred models.

Getting the Best for Less

Full-sized truck prices are plummeting this year because of high fuel costs, a slowing economy, and an unprecedented number of used trucks coming off lease. Over the next few years, the capacity for building light trucks will be far beyond what the market can absorb, leading to much lower MSRPs, more substantial dealer incentives and customer rebates, and fierce price competition for both new and used pickups. In a nutshell, the longer you wait to buy, the more money you will save.

What do you do if all the *Lemon-Aid*-recommended full- or medium-sized pickups are either too expensive or not what you require? Downsize your needs if you can—go down a notch—and buy a cheaper, Japanese-made used compact pickup. Or better yet, wait another year for prices to level out.

PICKUP TRUCK RATINGS

RECOMMENDED
Honda Ridgeline (2007–09)

Nissan Frontier (2006–09)

ABOVE AVERAGE
Ford Ranger/Mazda B-series
   (2003–09)

Honda Ridgeline (2006)
Nissan Frontier (1985–2005)

AVERAGE
Chrysler Dakota/Mitsubishi
   Raider (2005–07)
Chrysler Ram (2002–09)
Ford Ranger/Mazda B-series
   (1984–2002)
General Motors Avalanche (2007–09)

General Motors C/K, Sierra,
   Silverado (2007–09; 1988–98)
General Motors S-10, Sonoma,
   T-10 (2000–04)
Nissan Titan (2008–09)
Toyota Tacoma (1987–2004)

BELOW AVERAGE
Chrysler Dakota/Mitsubishi
   Raider (2008–09; 1987–2004)
Chrysler Ram (1986–2001)
Ford F-Series (1990–2008)
General Motors Avalanche (2002–06)
General Motors C/K, Sierra,
   Silverado (1999–2006)
General Motors Canyon,
   Colorado (2004–09)

General Motors S-10, Sonoma,
   T-10 (1996–99)
Isuzu Space Cab, Hombre
   (1989–2002)
Toyota Tacoma (2005–09)
Toyota Tundra (2001–09)

NOT RECOMMENDED
Ford F-Series (2009)
General Motors S-10, Sonoma,
   T-10 (1986–95)

Nissan Titan (2004–07)

Chrysler

RAM ★★★

RATING: Average (2002–09); Below Average (1986–2001). Rams are mediocre buys; however, when equipped with a manual tranny and a diesel powertrain, they are the best truck buy among the Detroit Big Three automakers. **Strong points:** *2006–09:* Substantial price cuts, cylinder deactivation for better fuel economy, and more power, interior room, and convenience features. The 4.7L V8 is a good alternative to the larger, fuel-thirstier Hemi version. *Pre-2006 models:* Even cheaper to buy. Average quality buttressed by a better-than-average warranty (2002–04), combined with assertive styling, a high-tech engine, full-time 4×4, adequately sized cabs with good stowage utility, one of the longest and roomiest cargo boxes available, and a comfortable and well-designed interior with easily accessed and understood instruments and controls. The 1500-series models have better handling, improved steering, and fewer rattles. Other pluses: powerful Hemi, V8, and V10 engines; a bit more reliable Cummins diesel; good trailering capability; a smooth-shifting automatic transmission (when it's working right); and four-door versatility. **Weak points:** *2006–09:* You won't get the fuel economy, safety features, or manoeuvrability of other full-sized pickups. The ride is jiggly over rough terrain, the steering is vague, the interior is Kmart kitsch, and the climb up to the lofty cab is a chore and is not recommended for anyone in a skirt.

2008 RAM TECHNICAL DATA

POWERTRAIN (4×2/PART-TIME 4×4)
Engines: 3.7L V6 (215 hp) • 4.7L V8 (310 hp) • 5.7L V8 (345 hp) • 6.7L inline-six (350 hp) • 8.3L V10 (500 hp); Transmissions: 6-speed man. • 4-speed auto. OD • 5-speed auto. OD
DIMENSION/CAPACITY (1500 4×2/4×4 REGULAR)
Passengers: 3/3; Wheelbase: 138.7/154.7 in.; H: 70.0/L: 228.0/W: 80.0 in.; Headroom F/R: 6.0/3.5 in.; Legroom F/R: 42.0/27.0 in.; Cargo volume: 121.7 cu. ft.; Fuel tank: 98L/132L regular/diesel; Tow limit: 8,600 lb.; Load capacity: 1,270 lb.; GVWR: 6,010–6,400 lb.; Turning circle: 49.0 ft.; Box length: 5.0/6.5/8.0 ft.; Ground clearance: 9.5 in.; Weight: 5,380 lb.

2008 MEGA CAB TECHNICAL DATA

POWERTRAIN (FULL-TIME 4×4)
Engines: 5.7L Hemi V8 (345 hp) • 8.0L V10 turbo (325 hp); Transmissions: 5-speed man. • 6-speed man. OD • 4-speed auto. OD • 5-speed auto. OD
DIMENSION/CAPACITY (1500 4×2/4×4 REGULAR)
Passengers: 3/3; Wheelbase: 160.5 in.; H: 74.5/L: 247.7/W: 79.5 in.; Legroom F/R: 41.0/44.2 in.; Cargo volume: 7.6 cu. ft.; Fuel tank: 132L; Tow limit: 7,750–15,800 lb.; Load capacity: 2,430 lb.; GVWR: 8,510 lb.; Turning circle: 47.9 in.; Box length: 6.3 ft.; Ground clearance: 7.1 in.; Weight: 6,082 lb.

The Mexican plant where these vehicles are made isn't one of Chrysler's best facilities in terms of quality control, and the jury is still out on the Ram's new cylinder deactivation system. *Pre-2006 models:* The 1500-series engines may be outclassed by Ford and GM powerplants. The Hemi V8 is quite fuel-thirsty and has had a few quality problems during the short time it has been on the road. Considering Chrysler's inability to make reliable and safe ball joints, ABS brakes, and automatic transmissions, the 2005's engine cylinder deactivation feature may become a problem as these trucks reach their critical fifth year of use. The 2500 and 3500 models were left in the Jurassic Age until the 2006 redesigned models came on board. Outdated mechanical components, like an inconvenient transfer case and a solid front axle, make for a jittery ride (on 2500s and 3500s only). The truck sits very high, meaning shorter drivers and passengers will definitely have problems getting into this pickup. Rear entry and exit are problematic (Club Cab); the back seat is tight, hard, and too upright; 4×4 must be disengaged on dry pavement; poor V6 acceleration; slow steering response; bouncy over rough spots; controls aren't easy to calibrate; the 1.8 m (6 ft.) bed looks stubby; and the high hood hides obstacles from view. Very poor fuel economy ties Ford's pickups at a real-world average of about 21.0 L/100 km (11 mpg). As with Ford and GM trucks, Rams also have had a disturbingly large number of safety- and performance-related defects reported to NHTSA. **New for 2008:** *Ram 1500:* This entry-level truck shares the new 4.7L V8, upping horsepower from 235 to 310; a trailer sway-control feature complements the optional electronic stability control program. *Ram 2500/3500:* A slightly restyled trim line; the electric shift transfer is now a standard feature on the 4×4 SLT and Laramie; maximum GCWR is increased to 24,000 lbs (the GCWR is the maximum combined weight of your loaded tow vehicle and the loaded trailer). The 2009s are worth waiting for. They will be heavily discounted and have an interior upgrade, a coil-spring rear suspension, a Ram Box option similar to the Chevy Avalanche's, more storage areas, and a sleeker, more aerodynamic restyling. The 2010 models may get a small diesel engine.

MODEL HISTORY: Not a spectacular performer with its weak standard powertrain hookup, the Dodge Ram is a full-sized pickup that mirrors Ford's and GM's truck lineups, but with a bit more reliability. It's sold in 1500, 2500, and 3500 chassis designations (approximate load capacities: half ton, three-quarter ton, one ton) with Regular Cab, Club Cab, Chassis Cab, and Mega Cab configurations. Drivetrains include 4×2 and part-time 4×4 modes coupled to various engine offerings.

The 2004 and later 1500-series models come with a 3.7L V6 base engine and optional 4.7L and 5.7L V8s. The latter engine is called the Hemi, and it's sold only with a 5-speed automatic transmission. The V6 and 4.7L V8 offer a manual transmission or a 4- or 5-speed automatic, respectively. Automatics include a tow/haul mode for heavy loads.

Chrysler plays the nostalgia card with its 345-hp 5.7L Hemi high-performance engine, last seen as an allegedly 425-hp powerhouse offered from 1965 to 1971. At the time, it was offered as a $500–$1,100 option in Dodge Coronets and Chargers and Plymouth Belvederes and Satellites. Now the Hemi is an optional engine sold with the 1500 series, heavy-duty Ram pickups, and the Dodge 300C/Magnum wagon. Drivers can expect to shave about 3 seconds off the 1500's time of 0–100km/h in 10.5 seconds, all the while praying that the engine doesn't kill the tranny.

2001—Improved steering and an upgraded rear-suspension system. **2002**—Revamped handling and ride comfort. The 1500 models (2500/3500 versions were upgraded in 2003) get more aggressive styling, two new engines, roomier cabs, and optional side airbags. The two-door extended Club Cab is axed, Quad Cabs are given four front-hinged doors, and short-box models gain 7.6 cm (3 in.) of cabin length at the expense of bed length. The 4×4-equipped Rams get an independent front suspension. **2003**—2500 and 3500 series are revised and given the Hemi 345-hp 5.7L V8 and rack-and-pinion steering. The 1500 series gets new wheels. **2004**—An expanded model lineup that includes a Hemi-powered Power Wagon off-roader and the SRT-10 Quad Cab, equipped with the Dodge Viper's 500-hp 8.3L V10 engine. **2005**—More models available with 6-speed manual transmissions (hmmm…word must be spreading that the automatics are "fertilizer"). **2006**—The 1500 Ram gets a stiffer frame, a softer front suspension, reduced-drag brake calipers, high-intensity headlights, an electrically operated front-axle disconnect system, a revised interior and body style (Mega Cab), weather seals, and constrained layer (quiet steel) technology in the dash panel area—improvements that should reduce clunks, rattles, and wind noise. There's also a cylinder cut-off system to boost fuel economy—if it functions properly (feeling lucky?). The Mega Cab option can seat six passengers in comfort, which wasn't possible with earlier models. Comfort is enhanced through reclining rear seats that split, fold down, and move forward. Hauling capacity is more than adequate with the Mega's "mega" engine, a 345-hp 5.7L Hemi V8 mated to a heavy-duty 5-speed automatic transmission. **2007**—A new 350-hp 6.7L inline-six Cummins Turbo Diesel (25 more horses than the 2006 version), and the debut of the Class 3 Chassis Cab, equipped with either a 330-hp 5.7L Hemi V8 or a torquier Cummins Turbo Diesel V8.

COST ANALYSIS: The 2008 rear-drive, entry-level 1500 sells for $17,495; the same truck costs $21,485 (U.S.) in the States. A 4×4 version goes for $21,865 (CDN) or $26,940 (U.S.). These prices make shopping in Canada your best strategy. **Best alternatives:** A second-series Honda Ridgeline or Nissan Frontier. **Rebates:** $2,000–$10,000+ rebates, plus zero percent financing. **Delivery/ PDI:** $1,350. **Warranty:** Bumper-to-bumper 3 years/60,000 km; powertrain 5 years/100,000 km; rust perforation 5 years/160,000 km. **Supplementary warranty:** Buy extended coverage if Chrysler's base warranty has expired, particularly after the fourth year, when quality-control problems multiply. **Options:** Some options worth considering are power windows and locks, a transmission/oil cooler, and running boards. The Hemi engine, bought by about half Ram's shoppers, is a gas-guzzler and hasn't proven itself yet. The 20- and 22-inch wheels degrade ride comfort. **Depreciation:** Slower than average. **Insurance cost:** Higher than average. **Annual maintenance cost:** Average. **Parts supply/cost:** With the exception of some Cummins diesels, parts are easily available and reasonably priced. **Highway/city fuel economy:** *4×2 and 3.9L:* 11.0/15.9 L/100 km; *4×4 and 5.2L:* 13.1/18.9 L/100 km. With the Multi-Displacement System, the Hemi V8 is rated 8.8 L/100 km on the highway and 13.9 L/100 km in the city. The latest V6 engine is estimated at 8.1/12.2 L/100 km. As stated earlier, pre-2006 models' real-world fuel consumption has been reported at 21.0 L/100 km.

QUALITY/RELIABILITY: Below-average quality and reliability. The Ram 2500, 2500 Heavy Duty, SRT10, and Mega Cab are all built in Saltillo, Mexico—not a stellar plant. The factory placed tenth for efficiency among all of Chrysler's full-sized pickup factories, well behind plants in Michigan and Missouri. Fit and finish and powertrain, suspension, steering, brake, electrical, and fuel-system components are still not top quality. Hemi engines have had problems with broken valve springs and rear main seal leaks. The Cummins diesel engine has performed exceptionally well, but some serious problems remain, as confirmed by this Albertan Ram owner:

> I have a 2003 Dodge Ram 2500 4×4 equipped with a Cummins diesel engine. At 7,000 km, I began to experience stalling problems with the engine, specifically at stop signs and lights. The problem came and went until a major failure at 18,500 km. This problem was compounded by poor fuel economy (5–7 mpg [34–47 L/100 km]). The Edmonton dealer took eight days to overhaul the fuel system.
>
> After I left the dealership, my injection pump started leaking fuel (60,500 km). I was told the Toronto "Tech Line" only operated on EST time and I would have to wait until the next day as the mechanics cannot make repairs without consulting the "Tech Line." The next day I was told the injection pump needed to be replaced and I would have to wait another five to eight days for it to arrive from Toronto.
>
> This is my second injection pump, as well as one "transfer" or "lift" pump. The dealer service manager told me, "about two weeks ago we had over eight trucks sitting out there waiting for 'lift' pumps."

There's considerable downtime due to automatic transmission malfunctions and breakdowns. The problem isn't as severe as those of the Dakota, Ford F-Series, or the GM Silverado/Sierra duo, though. **Owner-reported problems:** Owners report chronic automatic transmission, electrical, ignition, engine cooling system, steering, suspension, fuel, brake, and body problems for all years. Cold or wet weather doesn't agree with these trucks, either—generating lots of reports of chronic hard starting and stalling, even when the engine is warm. Chrysler has done little to deal with this basic flaw, which has been a generic Chrysler problem for decades. The ignition system on 1993–96 models earns low reliability marks as well. There have been some reports of misaligned drivelines leading to excessive vibration and prematurely worn clutches. The body is squeak- and rattle-prone, and water and air leaks are common:

The rear window leaks during rainstorms. Mold began to grow in the vehicle because the problem was discovered two months after the incident occurred.

The exhaust system leaks and overheats, and rust tends to start fairly early.

Other owner-reported problems: Electrical fire at the power disbursement box under the hood; sudden transmission and differential failures; and the accelerator pedal jams while backing up. Be wary of front differential damage caused by road debris striking the unprotected housing. Poorly performing brakes must be adjusted at almost every oil change, premature (5,000 km) wearout of the rear brake hubs and front brake pads, and complete ABS brake failure. The weak stabilizer bar is easily bent when passing over potholes; the lack of an anti-sway bar on the rear axle in the trailer towing package means excessive swaying, causing steering instability; and some trailer hitches are cracked. Very loose steering allows the vehicle to wander all over the roadway, and a defective steering pump causes loss of steering control. Constant pulling to the right on the highway; excessive vibration when approaching 100 km/h; excessive shimmy after hitting a bump or pothole; clunk or rattle felt in the steering wheel after running over a rough surface; and faulty steering gearbox. Inadequate cooling because of AC freeze-up, and an odour comes out of the AC ducts. Clunking or rattling noise from the front suspension, ringing noise from the rear of the vehicle, and shudder when pulling away from a stop when near maximum GVWR. The absence of a baffle in the fuel tank allows gas to slam forward and back in the tank, subjecting connections to stress and causing early failure. The ignition fuse link blows intermittently, shutting down the vehicle. Transmission seal leakage and excessive noise through the 2006 models; obstructive rear door latching mechanism prevents easy access to the rear seat; fragile front ball joints; oil-filter adaptor plate and speed-sensor oil seepage; front disc brake noise on the 3500 series; and the lapbelt rides too high on the abdomen, while the shoulder belt lies too close to the neck and jaw. **Warranty performance:** Below average. "Goodwill" payouts have neither rhyme nor reason but track in the 50 percent range. A threat of small claims action can raise the offer to 75 percent just prior to mediation or trial.

 ROAD PERFORMANCE: Acceleration/torque: Owners report the Hemi has trouble getting up to speed, requiring a lot of throttle. Hill climbing is poor until the engine hits the higher rpm at nearly full throttle. Once the Hemi finds its sweet spot, it does well, but towing at high rpm cuts considerably into fuel economy. The Cummins Turbo Diesel won't break any speed records, either, but it will haul just about anything when hooked to the 5-speed manual transmission. The 3.7L V6 is smooth and acceptable for light chores, but the 4.7L V8 gives you the reserve power needed for heavier work. The 5.9L V8 is the engine of choice for hauling or towing anything weighing more than 1,800 kg (4,000 lb.). Shifting into 4×4 is done via a hard-to-reach floor lever; however, the 2002 and later 1500s offer an optional dashboard-mounted switch. **Transmission:** The 4-speed automatic transmission shifts smoothly when it's working right. **Steering:** Vague and slow to respond. Excessive steering wander on Quad Cabs and extended cabs. **Routine handling:** The Ram's performance, ride, and handling are more trucklike than with its Ford or GM rivals. The ride can be especially rough without a full load in back. **Emergency handling:** Although the 2002 and later 1500s ride better, larger Rams are quite jittery on the highway (thanks to an antiquated solid front axle) and ponderous in their handling. They also have a lower ground clearance than their rivals. Rapid cornering isn't advisable because of the excessive rear-end sway. **Braking:** Not impressive, in spite of rear-wheel ABS (100–0 km/h: 45 m). Some fading after repeated application.

SAFETY SUMMARY: The 2008 Rams posted crashworthiness scores identical to the 2007s. A child safety seat can fit in the rear centre seat if an extended belt is used. Most early Dodge trucks won't have head restraints. **Airbags:** Many complaints of airbags failing to deploy or deploying when they shouldn't. **ABS:** Standard 2W; optional 4W; disc/drum. **Head restraints F/R:** *1999:* ★★/★; *2001:* ★; *2003–05 without adjustable lumbar seats:* ★; *2003–05 with adjustable lumbar seats:* ★★★; *2006–08:* ★. **Visibility F/R:** ★★★★★. **Maximum load capacity:** *1999 SLT 5.2L:* 1,265 lb. **Pet transport:** ★★★★★.

SAFETY COMPLAINTS: All years: Sudden acceleration. • Chronic stalling. • Repeated ABS failures; pedal goes to floor without any braking effect. • Severe pull to the side when braking. • Warped rotors and worn-out brake pads. • When parked, vehicle rolls down an incline. • Frequent transmission failures and fluid leaks. • Overdrive engages poorly in cold weather. • Vehicle wanders excessively at highway speeds; loose steering makes for imprecise corrections. Steering wander is especially severe with diesel-equipped vehicles. **1999**—Transmission suddenly jumps into Neutral (transmission shift sensor suspected). • Power-steering binding or lock-up. • Seat belt buckle won't latch. **2000**—The speed control fails to keep an even speed, and the automatic transmission is always gear hunting. • Brakes don't stop the vehicle, requiring constant and expensive maintenance. • Power-steering and rear-wheel brake drum failures. **2001**—Many reports of electrical shorts causing under-hood fires. • Fuse box catches fire because battery cable wasn't properly installed at the factory. • Evaporator canister, power-steering box and hose, and seat belt retractor failures. • Power-steering line blows out. • Brake-pad rivets come loose, and rear brake light fuses keep blowing. • Excessive crankcase oil vapours enter the passenger compartment. • Front suspension bottoms out on speed bumps. • Excessive vibration of side mirrors. • Rear window shatters. • Hood flies up and shatters windshield. **2002**—Front end jumps from side to side when vehicle passes over uneven pavement, or it easily hydroplanes when passing over wet roads. • Bed may damage the cab. • Premature brake master cylinder failure. • Differential and rear axle bearing fail prematurely. • Automatic transmission gets stuck in Reverse. **2003**—Accelerator pedal falls off. • Stalling and hard starting. • Front suspension collapse. • Automatic transmission won't shift into Reverse. • Lowered tailgate falls onto the roadway when vehicle goes over a bump. **2003–04**—Ram 2500 and Ram 3500 pickups with automatic transmissions might roll backward when shifted into the Park position. NHTSA says 42 crashes and three injuries have been linked to the problem. **2004**—Fire ignites in the driver-side rear wheelwell. • Brake lock-up. • Stalling Hemi engine (EGR valve on national back order). • Excessive on-road vibration. • Erratic reading on odometer and speedometer after water gets into the wiring harness. • Wheel bearing failure. • Rear axle breaks. • Horn failure. • Headlight high beams aren't bright enough. **2005**—Electrical fire ignites in the engine compartment. • Vehicle speeds up when going downhill. • Sudden automatic transmission failure. • Transmission slips from Park to Reverse while parked and idling. • Early ball joint failure. • Exhaust pipe leak; catalytic converter shows signs of overheating. • Premature tire wear (scalloping). **2006**—Tie-rod failure. • One vehicle's drive shaft fell off when it was towed. • Gas and brake pedals are mounted too close together. • Rear seat belts tighten up to the point of choking the passenger. **2006–07**—Automatic transmission slips out of Reverse and grinds. • Recall repairs take an inordinate amount of time to carry out. **2007**—Airbags fail to deploy. • Front control arm (suspension/steering) breaks:

> This caused the tire to dislocate from the vehicle. The tire, ball joint, brake system and hoses stayed attached to the rim of the tire. This caused the vehicle to drop and surge to the right, then collide with another vehicle.

• Engine oil sensor failures. • Dashboard cracks may impair airbag deployment. • Wiper arm and blade may fall off. • Michelin tires fail, allegedly due to a factory-related defect.

Secret Warranties/Internal Bulletins/Service Tips

1999—A knocking or tapping noise coming from the engine compartment may be corrected by replacing the duty-cycle purge-valve bracket. • Engine knocking and high oil consumption may be caused by an intake manifold pan gasket oil leak. Stand fast for a refund of repair costs up to 7 years/160,000 km:

ENGINE—SPARK KNOCK/OIL CONSUMPTION			
BULLETIN NO.: 09-05-00			DATE: FEBRUARY 25, 2000
1994–99	(AB)	Ram Van	
1994–99	(AN)	Dakota	
1994–99	(BRIBE)	Ram Truck	
1998–99	(DN)	Durango	
1994–98	(ZJ)	Grand Cherokee	
1996–98	(ZG)	Grand Cherokee	

SUBJECT: Spark Knock and Engine Oil Consumption due to Intake Manifold Pan Gasket Oil Leak

OVERVIEW: This bulletin involves the replacement of the engine intake manifold plenum pan gasket.

• Accelerated front and rear brake lining wear can be controlled by installing countermeasure linings developed to prevent early wearout. **1999–2000**—A rattle from the door area may be corrected by installing a revised window channel. • A squeaking, creaking steering column likely needs a new lock housing and attaching screws. **1999–2001**—If more steering-wheel movement than normal is required to keep the vehicle from wandering (vehicle slow to respond to normal steering-wheel input), have the mechanic perform the Over-Centre Adjustment Repair Procedure. • A squeaking noise coming from the rear leaf springs can be silenced by replacing the spring-tip liners and installing spring-cinch clips and isolators. • Many 4×4 Rams with several years of hard use are developing steering wander because of worn track bars. To check a track bar, start the engine and observe the ends of the track bar while someone saws the steering wheel from side to side. Any movement at either end of the track bar indicates that the track bar is bad. If play is observed, replace the track bar. • Erratic engine operation:

SURGE/LACK OF POWER IN THIRD GEAR/ERRATIC SHIFTS

BULLETIN NO.: 18-006-02 REV. C   DATE: JUNE 3, 2002

OVERVIEW: This bulletin involves selectively erasing and reprogramming the JTEC Powertrain Control Module (PCM) with new software.

MODELS: 1999–2001 (BE/BR) Ram Trucks equipped with a 5.2L, 5.9L, or 8.0L engine.

SYMPTOM/CONDITION: Some vehicles may exhibit one or more of the following performance conditions:

1. Perceived lack of power in Third gear due to converter lock-up in Third gear. This reprogramming eliminates Third gear lock-up.
2. Surge after lock-up (40–45 mph [64–72 km/h]) in Fourth gear. This reprogramming raises torque converter lock-up speed to 52 mph [84 km.h].
3. Transmission does not upshift from Third gear after a 4–3 downshift. (Most often noticed when cruise control is engaged.)

POLICY: Reimbursable within the provisions of the warranty.

1999–2002—A power-steering hissing may only require replacing the power-steering hoses. • Paint delamination, peeling, or fading. **2000–02**—Doors lock and unlock on their own. **2001**—Engine may not crank because of a blown starter-relay circuit fuse. • Engine cranks but won't start, or starts and stalls. • Low fuel output from the transfer pump may be the cause of hard starts or no-starts. • Vehicles used for extended heavy trailering may experience a loss of exhaust manifold bolt torque. • Troubleshooting tips for complaints of poor diesel engine performance. • Low engine power when transmission is in Overdrive. • Harsh transmission engagement when the torque converter clutch is applied. • Remedy for steering wander (1500 series). • Rear may sit too high to attach a fifth wheel. • Spark knock when accelerating. • Tie-rod adjusting sleeve slot may be the source of a high-pitched whistle. • Tapping or knocking during idle. **2001–04**—Water leaks on passenger-side floor (see Dakota "Secret Warranties/Internal Bulletins/

Service Tips"). **2002**—Hard starts and idle speed fluctuation in cold weather. • Inoperative tachometer. • Faulty oil pressure gauge. • Oil pan gasket leaks. • Hood distortion and low spots. • Seat rocking movement when accelerating. **2002–04**—Water leaks at grab handle. **2003**—Low start-up oil pressure with the Hemi engine requires the replacement of the oil pump pick-up tube. • Brake vibration or shudder requires the replacement of many major brake components, says Bulletin #05-008-03, published November 28, 2003. • An erratically shifting automatic transmission may require a re-calibrated PCM or TCM. • Instrument panel whistle. • Poor idle and coasting. • Lack of air from floor vents. • Buzzing, vibration from front of vehicle. **2003–04**—Loose, rattling bug deflector. • Dirt accumulates in door opening area (Chrysler will install an improved secondary door seal). **2003–05**—Steering snaps or ticks. **2004**—Brake kit will be installed to eliminate brake shudder, vibration. • Power-window binding or slow operation. • Torn drip-rail door seam. • Poor sound quality from Infinity speakers.

RAM PROFILE

	1999	2000	2001	2002	2003	2004	2005	2006	2007
Cost Price ($) (negotiable)									
D-150, 1500 (20%)	20,345	20,630	18,750	23,255	23,865	24,910	26,975	26,020	26,395
Quad Cab	—	—	—	27,280	26,900	—	—	—	—
SRT-10	—	—	—	—	—	61,000	58,465	61,555	—
Used Values ($)									
D-150, 1500 ▲	2,000	2,500	4,000	5,000	8,500	10,500	11,500	15,500	17,500
D-150, 1500 ▼	1,500	2,000	3,000	4,000	7,500	9,500	10,000	13,500	16,000
Quad Cab ▲	—	—	—	5,000	11,000	—	—	—	—
Quad Cab ▼	—	—	—	3,500	7,500	—	—	—	—
SRT-10 ▲	—	—	—	—	—	—	29,000	36,000	—
SRT-10 ▼	—	—	—	—	—	—	27,000	34,000	—
Reliability	2	2	2	3	3	3	3	3	3
Crash Safety (F)	—	—	5	4	4	5	5	5	5
Ext. cab	4	4	4	—	—	—	5	5	—
Quad cab	3	3	4	—	—	—	5	5	—
Side	5	5	—	—	—	3	—	—	—
Quad Cab	—	—	—	4	5	3	—	—	—
Offset	1	1	1	5	5	5	5	5	5
Rollover	1	1	3	3	3	—	4	4	4

Chrysler/Mitsubishi

DAKOTA/RAIDER ★★

RATING: Below Average (2008–09; 1987–2004); Average (2005–07). Both vehicles may be dropped after the 2009 model year, compromising parts supply and servicing. However, the real unknown is whether Chrysler's new owner, Chrysler LLC, will keep it's year-old acquisition or sell the different Chrysler divisions piecemeal. If they do the latter, as *Lemon-Aid* predicts, warranties will soon be worthless, servicing costs will soar, and resale values will plummet. At least owners who bought used 2005–07 models will find it easier to get parts and servicing and not get stung too badly from accelerated depreciation. **Strong points:** Brisk acceleration; available 4×4; lots of low-end torque; well-appointed, carlike interior; lots of front headroom and legroom; and attractively styled. It features a competent base V6 that's said to be more fuel-frugal; the 2005–06 V8 also has a bit more power; either engine can be hooked to a new 6-speed manual transmission; and the interior has been upgraded. **Weak points:** Quad Cab uses a shortened 1.6 m (5′3″) bed. *2004 and earlier models:* Poor acceleration with the 4-cylinder engine; underpowered with the entry-level V6; and automatic transmission shifts erratically. Watch out for false tow ratings on the R/T version. Awkward entry and exit from the rear seat (Club Cab); uncomfortable rear seats; and folding rear bench seat is inadequate for three passengers, mainly because of the limited room for legs and knees. Quad truck cannot be driven with rear window down because of a deafening, painful noise created by the vacuum. The steering wheel blocks the driver's view of key instruments and gauges, and sunlight glare off the gauges is distracting. Poor front, rear, and side visibility; inadequate headlight illumination on some versions; interior controls are from the Pleistocene era; lousy fuel economy; poor results in offset crash tests; and an unacceptably large number of performance- and safety-related defects reported to NHTSA and other agencies. **New for 2008:** More V8 power, and revised interior and exterior styling.

MODEL HISTORY: Dakotas come in two body styles: Extended Cab and Quad Cab. Extended Cabs carry a 6.5 ft. cargo bed, rear-hinged back doors, and seating for five. The Quad Crew version has a smaller 5.3 ft. bed, conventional back doors, and seating for six. New for '08 is a 302-hp 4.7L V8 hooked to an automatic transmission (manual is

2008 DAKOTA/RAIDER TECHNICAL DATA

POWERTRAIN (REAR-DRIVE/4×4/AWD)
Engines: 3.7L V6 (210 hp) • 4.7L V8 (302 hp); Transmissions: 6-speed man. • 4-speed auto. OD • 5-speed auto. OD
DIMENSION/CAPACITY
Passengers: 2/3 and 3/3; Wheelbase: 131.3 in.; H: 68.6/L: 218.8/W: 71.7 in.; Headroom F/R: 4.5/3.5 in.; Legroom F/R: 41.5/28.0 in.; Cargo volume: 26.7 cu. ft.; Fuel tank: 57L/68L/regular; Tow limit: 6,500 lb.; Load capacity: 1,710 lb.; GVWR: 6,010 lb.; Turning circle: 44.0 ft.; Box length: 6.5–8.0/6.5 ft.; Ground clearance: 7.9 in.; Weight: 4,296 lb.

not available). It replaces the 230- and 260-hp V8s used previously. The V6 comes with manual or automatic. There are three powertrains: rear-drive, four-wheel drive, and all-wheel drive. The 4×4 system can't be left engaged on dry pavement, but like the AWD system, it does have low-range gearing for off-roading. Safety features include side curtain airbags that cover both seating rows and ABS.

The 2006–07 Dakota and Raider were carryovers from the 2005's much-improved and better-equipped version. Owners still must contend with mediocre handling; a jittery, wandering ride; marginal braking; and subpar quality control.

The 2004 and earlier models are seriously underpowered when equipped with the standard 4- or 6-cylinder engine. With an optional, more powerful engine, the Dakota outclasses the compact competition for sheer towing power.

There are plenty of used, cheap Dakotas around, but plan on spending part of your savings on a $1,500–$2,000 extended powertrain warranty, preferably one sold by Chrysler rather than an independent. You'll need the extended protection because of the many engine, transmission, and electrical glitches and other mechanical and body failings that afflict these trucks.

2000—Four full-sized doors (called the Quad Cab) and a new 4.7L V8; the 2.4 m (8 ft.) bed is gone. **2002**—Arrival of the SXT version, sporting 16-inch wheels and bucket seats. **2003**—Larger tires and an upgraded automatic transmission coupled with the 4.7L V8 and standard four-wheel disc brakes; the puny 4-cylinder engine is dropped. **2004**—Base V6 gets 35 extra horses, while the 4.7L V8 loses 5 horses. R/T model and its 5.9L V8 are gone. **2005**—Redesigned with a more powerful base engine; a roomier, more refined interior; and less noise, vibration, and ride harshness.

COST ANALYSIS: The 2008 Dakota carries an MSRP of $25,695. In the States, a base Dakota is priced at $20,080 (U.S.), and a $2,000 rebate is available in some areas. **Best alternatives:** Considering their many upgrades, the 2005–07 Dakotas are the better buys. Other choices include the Ford Ranger, Honda Ridgeline, Mazda B-series, and Nissan Frontier. **Rebates:** $2,500 rebates and zero percent financing. **Delivery/PDI:** $1,200. **Warranty:** Bumper-to-bumper 3 years/60,000 km; powertrain 5 years/100,000 km; rust perforation 5 years/160,000 km. **Supplementary warranty:** A good idea; try to get a 7-year powertrain warranty thrown in with the deal. **Options:** Although the V6 is adequate for most light-duty chores, invest in the smaller V8 powerplant for best performance and resale value. The remote keyless entry system is also a good idea—it turns on your dome light when pressed, cutting down search time in crowded parking lots. **Depreciation:** A bit slower than average. **Insurance cost:** Above average. **Annual maintenance cost:** Average; easily repaired by independent garages. **Parts supply/cost:** Good parts supply and reasonable costs; easy servicing (Dodge). **Highway/city fuel economy:** *4×2 and 3.9L: 10.4/14.8 L/100 km; 4×4* *and 3.9L: 11.9/16.3 L/100 km; 4×4 and 4.7L: 11.4/16.5 L/100 km; 4×4 and 5.2L: 13.5/18.5 L/100 km.*

QUALITY/RELIABILITY: Very poor quality control. Transmission, axle, ball joint, and fuel system problems are covered by secret warranties; however, they can take the truck out of service for considerable periods of time. Fit and finish is embarrassingly bad. **Owner-reported problems:** Fuel and emissions control systems, transmission, chronic upper ball joint/control arm failures, brakes (premature wear and pulsation), clunks and rattles, and body defects. Other complaints include chronic stalling; excessive engine valve knocking and ticking; a noisy rear end; brake shudder; thunking, erratic-shifting transmission; squeaking ball joints; window fogging; excessive interior noise and a violent cabin shake whenever the rear window is opened; fuel-tank thud when stopping; noisy front CV joint boots; and a thumping noise from the left rear axle. Front wheelwells have a large gap between where the inner fender ends and the frame starts, allowing water and snow to enter the engine compartment. **Warranty performance:** Below average. "Goodwill" after-warranty assistance is spotty at best.

SAFETY SUMMARY: The 2008 models have crashworthiness ratings similar to the 2007 versions. The 1998–99 Dakotas have a towing capacity of only 907 kg (2,000 lb.), despite the fact that Chrysler's sales literature says they can tow over three times as much—2,903 kg (6,400 lb.). Chrysler Canada officials tell me that the higher towing rating was a misprint and that all owners who have complained have been compensated. **Airbags:** Many reports of airbags failing to deploy, or deploying when they shouldn't. **ABS:** Standard 2W; optional 4W. **Traction control:** Optional. **Head restraints F/R:** *1999:* ★★★; *2001–04:* ★★★/★; *2005–08 models without adjustable lumbar seats:* ★★★; *2005–08 with adjustable lumbar seats:* ★. **Visibility F/R:** ★★/★. **Pet transport:** ★★★★★.

SAFETY COMPLAINTS: All years: Vehicle fires. • Airbag failures. • Sudden acceleration with cruise control engaged or because of a sticking accelerator pedal. • Sudden failure and premature wearout of the upper ball joints. • Vehicle wanders all over the road. • Left in Park, vehicle rolls away on an incline. • Frequent transmission failures and noisy operation (grinds and clunks); it sticks in a lower gear. • ABS failures; pedal goes to the floor without stopping the vehicle. • Frequent replacement of front brake pads and rotors. **1999**—Poor brake performance. • Front-brake lock-up on wet roads. **1999–2000**—Intermittent harsh shifting into Reverse. **2000**—One under-hood fire at stoplight believed to be caused by faulty wire. • Another fire, this time started when transmission fluid was pumped out of filler tube onto hot exhaust pipe. • Rear brakes lock up intermittently. • Cruise control fails to disengage. • Chronic stalling. • Transmission fluid leaks onto engine. • Heater core falls off and slips beneath brake pedal. • Exterior mirrors block visibility. • Seatback collapses because weld fails. **2000–01**—Sudden axle failure while vehicle is underway. • Transmission jumps out of gear while cruising. **2001**—Windows fog up because of inadequate heater and defroster. • No outside air flows in through the vents. • Poor braking. • Excessive brake pulsation. • Lug nut failure causes wheel to fly off the vehicle. • Transmission can be shifted without applying brakes. • Brake release handle is easily broken. **2002**—Wheel bearing failures. • Automatic transmission jumps to Reverse when vehicle is put in Park with the engine running. • Shift lever indicator doesn't always show the correct gear. • Without any warning, transmission will shift from Overdrive to Second gear. • Sometimes driver must step on the brakes to get the vehicle to shift. • Vehicle stalls on acceleration. • Excessive steering-wheel play, and steering randomly goes from heavy to light turning assist. • Instrument-cluster light fuse blows repeatedly. **2003**—Gearshift lever can be inadvertently knocked out of gear. **2004**—In one incident, a vehicle rolled over and the driver was suffocated by the airbag and seat belt. • Front wheel falls off because of the lack of an upper ball joint bolt. • Defective upper and lower ball joints replaced at owner's expense. • Steering lock-up. • Hesitates when accelerating, and pops out of gear. **2005**—Vehicle won't go into Reverse on a slight incline; one dealer said all V6-equipped models have the same problem. • Steering-shaft failure causes loss of all steering. • Rear-seat head restraints obscure the view through the rear window. • Seat disassembly is a real knuckle-buster. • Steering wheel blocks the view of the speedometer and other instruments. • Severe rear vibration while underway (vehicle's rear end will hop about); said to be caused by faulty Goodyear Eagle LS tires. • Equally bad vibration when braking. • Excessive stress on the front brake hoses when turning all the way to the left or right. • Right door mirror obstructs front view of traffic.

Secret Warranties/Internal Bulletins/Service Tips

1999—Poor AC performance may require the adjustment of the temperature control cable or the replacement of the evaporator under warranty. **1999–2000**—A squeaking noise coming from the rear leaf springs can be silenced by replacing the spring tip liners and installing spring cinch clips and isolators. **1999–2002**—Paint delamination, peeling, or fading. **1999–2003**—Upper and lower ball joints, control arm, and bushing failures covered by a secret warranty. **2000**—If the central timer module locks up, many of your power-assisted features and lights will malfunction, and the vehicle may not start. **2000–03**—Doors lock and unlock on their own. **2001**—Water leaks around the rear window. • Drivetrain noise or vibration. • Service 4×4 light comes on for no reason. • Vehicle may surge with cruise control engaged. • Steering-column popping noise. **2001–04**—Water leaks on passenger-side floor (see bulletin). **2002**—Automatic transmission filler-tube rattle. **2002–03**—Reprogram the JTEC PCM if the truck won't shift out of Second gear when climbing a grade. **2003**—An erratically shifting automatic transmission may require a re-calibrated PCM or TCM. • Customer satisfaction notification regarding the torque converter drainback valve. • Harsh shifts because of a sticking pressure-sensor transducer. • Transmission shift/speed control improvements. • Transmission may overheat. **2005**—Steering column snaps or ticks. • Chrysler will replace the front glass run channels free of charge to fix windows that operate erratically.

<table>
<tr><td colspan="2">BULLETIN NO.: 23-010-04</td></tr>
</table>

PASSENGER SIDE FLOOR WATER LEAKAGE

BULLETIN NO.: 23-010-04   DATE: APRIL 29, 2004

This bulletin involves sealing the opening for the evaporator hose/drain tube with RTV sealer.
2001–04 Dakota
2000–03 Durango
2001–04 Caravan, Voyager, Town & Country.

DAKOTA/RAIDER PROFILE

	1999	2000	2001	2002	2003	2004	2005	2006	2007
Cost Price ($) (firm)									
4×2 (14%)	17,585	18,380	18,780	21,815	21,960	22,675	24,605	24,925	25,210
4×4	21,490	22,295	22,375	27,915	30,605	—	—	—	—
Used Values ($)									
4×2 ▲	3,000	3,500	4,000	5,000	6,500	8,500	11,500	13,500	15,500
4×2 ▼	2,500	3,000	3,500	4,500	5,500	7,500	10,000	12,000	14,000
4×4 ▲	4,000	4,500	5,000	6,500	11,000	—	—	—	—
4×4 ▼	3,500	4,000	4,500	5,000	9,500	—	—	—	—
Reliability	2	2	2	2	2	2	3	3	3
Crash Safety (F)	—	—	4	4	3	3	5	5	5
Ext. 4×2	—	—	—	3	3	—	5	5	5
Quad 4×2	—	—	—	—	4	—	—	—	—
Side (Ext. 4×2)	5	5	5	5	5	5	5	5	5
Quad 4×2	—	—	—	—	5	—	—	—	—
Offset	1	1	1	1	1	1	3	3	3
Rollover (Ext. 4×2)	—	—	4	4	4	—	4	4	4
Ext. 4×4	3	—	—	—	—	—	—	—	4
Quad 4×2	—	—	—	3	3	—	4	—	—

Ford

F-SERIES   ★

RATING: Not Recommended (2009): Highly glitch-prone during the first six months
of production. Although the 2009s have lots of potential and are much improved
over earlier versions, it is not a smart idea to buy any Ford pickup during the first
six months of a major redesign, especially when prices are spiralling downward.
Below Average (1990–2008). Without question, the F-Series trucks are versatile
and brawny haulers, with much-improved handling, a quieter ride, and a more

2008 F-SERIES TECHNICAL DATA

POWERTRAIN (REAR-DRIVE/4×4)

Engines: F-150: 4.2L V6 (202 hp) •
4.6L V8 (248 hp) • 5.4L V8 (300 hp);
F-250, F-350, etc.: 5.4L V8 (300 hp) •
6.8L V10 (362 hp) • 6.4L V8 diesel (350
hp); Transmissions: 5-speed man. •
6-speed man. • 4-speed auto. OD •
5-speed auto. OD

DIMENSION/CAPACITY (F-150)

Passengers: 3/3; Wheelbase: 138.5/157.1
in.; H: 72.8/L: 220.8/W: 78.4 in.;
Headroom F/R: 5.0/4.0 in.; Legroom F/R:
40.0/32.0 in.; Cargo volume: 55.5/81.3
cu. ft. (bed/interior); Fuel tank: 131L/
regular/diesel; Tow limit: 7,200–24,000
lb.; Load capacity: 1,510 lb.; GVWR:
6,050–10,000 lb.; Turning circle: 47.0 ft.;
Box length: 6.5/8.0 ft.; Ground clearance:
8.0 in.; Weight: 5,690 lb.

comfortable interior incorporated into the 2005 model's redesign. Quality control, however, remains abysmally poor. Over the past decade, I've seen a dramatic increase in owner complaints relating to poor-quality powertrain components and serious safety-related defects that include sudden tie-rod separation, torsion bar failures, unintended acceleration, and the complete loss of braking. Service bulletins reinforce the fact that these trucks aren't well made, and their 2009 model-year redesign has yet to be tested in the real world. **Strong points:** *2009 F-150:* Major improvements everywhere, highlighted by upgraded V8 engines and a Crew Cab that's six inches longer than before, making for a roomier interior for rear-seaters, easier access to the front seats, and better sideways viewing for the driver. *2008 and earlier F-150s:* Easy and predictable handling; pleasant ride on bad roads; well-thought-out ergonomics, instruments, and controls; and fourth-door access. With a few exceptions (like tacky cloth seats), base models are nicely appointed, with lots of handy convenience features and a classy interior. The F-Series offers a commanding view of the road, lots of cab space, and excellent interior ergonomics. The front bench holds three in relative comfort, though there's insufficient footroom for the front centre passenger. One of the quietest pickups available. **Weak points:** *2009 F-150:* A steep price hike in Canada (check U.S. prices, and use them and patience as your main negotiating tools). History tells us the first 6-month production will have many factory-related problems. Engine upgrade creates some reliability and servicing problems. Still needs to lose weight. *2008 and earlier F-150s:* Underpowered base V6 engine and 4.6L V8 don't have sufficient passing power; questionable engine, transmission, suspension/steering, and brake performance and reliability; poor braking performance with four-wheel ABS; and an uncomfortable rear seat. Climate-control system is a bit slow in warming up the cabin. There's no left footrest on some models, and the cramped and upright rear seats can't match GM's for comfort. Cargo flexibility is compromised by the second-row layout. An inordinate number of serious safety-related complaints have been collected by NHTSA, with cruise-control switch fires, tie-rod end and front torsion bar failures, and steering vibration and drivetrain shudder heading the list. Watch out for violent body shaking when passing over a bumpy highway and for severe dash glare onto the front windshield. Warranty payouts have been unacceptably Scrooge-like in the past, and fuel economy is astoundingly poor. **New for 2008:** An XL SuperCrew with a 5.5 or 6.5 ft. Styleside box; an optional rear-view camera and Cargo Management System. *F-250, 350, 450:* Towing capacity increased to 24,000 lb., with a maximum 6,000 lb. payload, an upgraded interior, a stowable bed extender, and power-fold/telescoping exterior mirrors. A slightly restyled Super Duty is planned for the 2011 model year.

There are lots of good reasons to wait on a second-series 2009 F-150, coming out in the spring of 2009, so as to escape many of the start-up factory glitches found with earlier-production models. You will get an entirely new platform and a fully boxed frame made of high-strength steel that's lighter and stronger than the current platform. Ford has added about six inches to the length of the four-door model, making for more rear-seat legroom and a rear floor that is also completely flat. Plus, there's a full array of more refined V8s, inasmuch as the V6 will be dropped in favour of a 4.6L 2-valve V8. The mid-grade engine is a 4.6L 3-valve V8, followed by the 5.4L V8, which gets a small power boost. Other new 2009 features found on the F-150: a tailgate step and a box side step; standard traction and roll stability control, as well as trailer sway control; a capless fuel-filler system; an optional trailer brake controller (TBC); and a Max Trailer Tow Package. The $50,000 (U.S.) luxe-level Platinum makes its debut as a 2009 model.

MODEL HISTORY: In Ford's glory days, it and GM were the only pickup games in town and relations with parts suppliers were cordial. Now, Chrysler, Honda, Nissan, and Toyota are gobbling up Ford's market share, and supplier relations are testy at best. Buyers are clamouring for more versatile and reliable trucks that mix high-tech features with dependability and that are covered by stronger warranties. Unfortunately, Ford's last F-Series revamp in 2005 was too little, too late.

The most obvious changes on the 2005s were a new angular styling, a four-door configuration (a first for entry-level trucks), a deeper bed box, an upgraded interior, and a bigger, quieter cab. Ride comfort was improved by a roomier interior and new rear suspension. SuperCab models gained 15 cm (6 in.) in cab length plus larger rear doors and entry and exit handles. Other nice touches included a power-sliding rear window controlled by a button on the overhead console, power rear side windows, and an easier-to-lift tailgate that houses a built-in torsion-bar-assist mechanism.

The Ford 4.2L V6 is rated better in fuel mileage than the 4.6L V8, but the V8 gets better mileage in the real world. The V6 also was known for oil pump problems, and has been dropped from the reworked F-150. An engine Ford should have dropped, but didn't—the 300-hp 5.4L V8, known for chronic production glitches—was added a few years ago. It features three valves per cylinder, variable-cam timing, and an electronic throttle control that dealer mechanics are still trying to master.

Safety features on the 2005 and later F-150s were augmented to include multi-stage front airbags; a sensor to determine if the front passenger seat is empty; five three-point seat belts, with the front shoulder belts integrated into the seats; and a LATCH (lower anchors and tethers for children) system to facilitate the installation of child safety seats.

2004 and earlier models

The F-150 is Ford's base model, followed by the 250, 250 Heavy Duty, 350, and F-Super Duty. For 2001, the Super Duty F-650 Super CrewZer debuted as Ford's medium-duty pickup, aimed at the horse-trailering crowd. All versions are available with rear-drive or 4×4. A wide variety of wheelbase and box lengths is available.

There's a wide range of engines, making the F-Series a very versatile truck. The standard engine is a 4.2L V6 powerplant, borrowed from the Windstar; two Triton V8s, based on a Lincoln engine; and a 7.3L diesel engine. A 5-speed manual transmission, a 6.8L V10, and a 4-speed electronically controlled automatic transmission are also likely to be found on these carried-over models.

For light-duty use, stick to the F-150 for the best combination of a tolerable ride, decent handling, and good load capacity. Various combinations of extended cabs and longer cargo boxes are available in all years, including the more heavy-duty F-250 and F-350 models. Keep in mind, however, that ride and handling suffer as size and weight increase.

1999—A restyled front end, upgraded front seats, and the arrival of a four-door SuperCab. **2001**—The F-150 Crew Cab debuts with four full-sized doors and a full rear-passenger compartment; the 4.6L V8 gains 20 additional horses; the F-250 and F-350 get a horsepower upgrade for the 7.3L Power Stroke turbodiesel engine; the Trailer Tow package becomes standard on all models, as does four-wheel ABS; and the Lightning gets a slight increase in power and a shorter final drive ratio. **2002**—The mid-year return of the Harley-Davidson Edition; SuperCrew models receive 20-inch wheels and special trim; and the 260-hp 5.4L V8 is joined by a 340-hp supercharged variant. **2003**—Lightning models receive a stiffer rear suspension to support a 635 kg (1,400 lb.) payload. **2004**—The entry-level Heritage debuts. **2005**—Redesigned. **2007**—F-250 and F-350 pickups offer a new 350-hp 6.4L V8 diesel engine to replace the quality-plagued 6.0L diesel used previously.

Hauling capacity, interior comfort, and handling vary greatly depending on the model chosen. Although a bit rough-riding, the half-ton suspension should serve well for most purposes. Early models had poor front/rear brake balance when carrying a light load, so when rear ABS was added in 1987, it was hailed as a much-needed improvement. The euphoria was short-lived, however—owners soon complained that the ABS locked up on wet roads and was failure-prone. These same braking problems have continued through the 2008 models.

COST ANALYSIS: Expect to pay a premium of several thousand dollars to get one of the first reworked 2009 F-150s. Dealers know there is a lot of buyer interest, and they are expecting to get their asking price. They won't, so your best strategy is to wait for the hype to die down by mid-winter and then start looking in earnest for a reasonably priced model in inventory. The debut of the better-designed 2009s will cannibalize 2008 F-series sales, driving down 2008 model prices to levels never seen before. Usually this would be an excellent buying opportunity. However, the 2008s are so inferior in features and performance that they won't be that much of a bargain. Nevertheless, high fuel prices and a contracting economy have already hit F-Series sales particularly hard, forcing Ford to cut production and prices throughout the past year. For example, a 2008 F-150 XL sells for $22,199—about $300 less than last year's model; an upscale 4×4 XL costs $28,699. In the States, the two vehicles go for $17,520 and $23,510 (U.S.), respectively. Here are some other 2008 prices to help you get a cheaper price in Canada. *F-250 XLT 4×4:* $35,999 in Canada and $29,365 in the States; *F-350 XLT 4×4:* $42,899 in Canada and $30,430 in the States; *F-450 XLT 4×4:* $57,699 in Canada and $47,990 in the States. Better yet, dealers across the border routinely beat their own MSRPs by at least 5 percent (ask for the Internet price and give an American zip code like Pompano Beach's 33062); they also charge only about half the Canadian transport fee. **Best alternatives:** Honda, Mazda, and Nissan pickups are a lot safer and more reliable. **Rebates:** Look for the resumption of a "take no prisoners" discount war as GM fights to maintain its pickup gains. Chrysler and Ford will likely counter with their own discounts by mid-winter, once the bloom comes off the upgraded 2009 rose. Look for $3,000 rebates on entry-level models and for zero percent financing. **Delivery/PDI:** $1,300. **Warranty:** Bumper-to-bumper 3 years/60,000 km; rust perforation 5 years/ unlimited km. **Supplementary warranty:** An extended powertrain warranty figured into the base price is a must to counter Ford's poor quality control. **Options:** Get the small V8 engine, or you'll be kicking yourself for getting stuck with the anemic 2008. Short drivers may require the optional power seat with height adjustment and extended pedals to get away from the airbag's explosive deployment. Parking-distance beeper is a waste of money. **Depreciation:** Average. **Insurance cost:** Higher than average. **Parts supply/cost:** With the exception of Power Stroke diesels, parts are generally widely available from independent suppliers and of average cost. **Annual maintenance cost:** Higher than average, but easily repaired by independent garages. **Highway/city fuel economy:** Very poor; average real-world fuel economy hovers around 21.0 L/100 km (11 mpg)—equal to the Dodge Ram. *4×2 and 4.2L:* 11.1/15.1 L/100 km; *4×2 and 4.6L:* 11.3/16.2 L/100 km; *4×2 and 5.4L:* 12.3/17.4 L/100 km; *4×4 and 4.2L:* 12.2/15.9 L/100 km; *4×4 and 4.6L:* 12.9/17.4 L/100 km; *4×4 and 5.4L:* 13.6/18.6 L/100 km.

QUALITY/RELIABILITY: Terrible. It's interesting how Chrysler, Ford, and GM trucks have similar patterns of powertrain, suspension, and brake failures. Could it be because they use the same suppliers and pirate cost-cutting techniques from each other? Interestingly, many owners report that dealer service managers routinely downplay the seriousness of major failures by responding that they're "normal," or that they can't be duplicated or fixed. Apparently, Ford's '97 and '05 redesigns created more bugs than they fixed. In fact, the company's flagship 6.0L diesel engines, introduced in December 2003, were so badly flawed that Ford had to initiate a service program to fix them and buy back over 500 trucks. Their problems included a rough idle, loss of power, stalling, excessive exhaust smoke, leaky fuel injectors, high fuel consumption, and engine seizures. Ford says the engines are fine now, but there are many skeptics. Non-diesel engines aren't very durable, either, and they have severe engine knock through the 2005s. Another serious defect afflicting 1996–2004 models that's likely to gain national attention soon is the collapsing tie-rods/torsion bars in the steering/suspension system that throw the truck out of control when they fail. Ford has sent a letter to owners asking them to *please* have their vehicles inspected and repaired—at their own cost, of course. That's just another example of Ford's crappy customer relations attitude. **Owner-reported problems:** Engine and automatic transmission breakdowns top the list. Owners report failure-prone engine gaskets (covered by a number of special warranty extensions—see "Secret Warranties/Internal Bulletins/Service Tips"), timing belt tensioners, oil pumps, fuel injectors, fuel and ignition systems, and drivelines (principally clutches); poor-quality front and rear brake components that include premature pad and caliper replacement and chronic rotor warping (also covered by a secret warranty—see page 167); faulty powertrain control modules that cause sudden stalling at full throttle; excessive vibration felt throughout the vehicle; a lack of sufficient support in the driver's seat; front suspension and steering problems; and inadequate AC cooling. There are also body defects, including door cracks on 1997–2000 models covered in Ford SSM 12071 (see "Not What It's Cracked Up to Be," *www.F150online.com/articles/cracks.html*). Careful checking of frame rails and underbody panels is a must on older trucks. Both dealers and owners report that late-model Ford trucks and sport-utilities are equipped with defective torsion bars that usually fail while the vehicles are being driven, resulting in loss of vehicle control. Additionally, owner complaints target FX-15 air conditioner compressors, fuel and electrical systems, brakes, premature catalytic converter failure, and poor-quality fit and finish:

> My father purchased a 2003 model F-350 dually last fall for his new ranch truck. This spring when the frost came out of the roads (35 km of gravel) the dirt/mud stuck to the inner plastic fenders and both of them were damaged.... There are a lot of these dually trucks in that area (Fort St. John, B.C.) and the body shop has said many that drive on the dirt roads have this problem.

Other complaints include excessive vibration and shaking at idle and at cruising speed; power steering squeal and suspension thumping; rear-end rattles; exhaust system leaks; loose manifold air intake hoses; transmission rear seal and bushing leaks, squealing, and humming; drive shaft clunks when accelerating or decelerating; excessive brake pedal pulsation when brakes are applied; and front shocks that leak oil. The 2001 models are particularly plagued by engine and rear-end failures. **Warranty performance:** Way below average. While reports of safety- and performance-related defects have soared, Ford's customer relations performance has soured.

SAFETY SUMMARY: The 2004–08 F-150s have all posted identical NHTSA crashworthiness scores. 1997–2000 model-year F-150, F-250, Blackwood pickups, and Expeditions are part of ongoing class actions filed in Canada (see *www.willbarristers.com/soc_ford.htm*) and in the States alleging they have faulty door latches. Ford has settled one lawsuit out of court. Earlier Ford pickups don't have head restraints. **Airbags:** A number of incidents where the airbags deployed without cause. **ABS:** Standard 2W; optional 4W. **Head restraints F/R:** *1999:* ★★/★; *2001:* ★★★/★★; *2002–03:* ★★/★; *2004–08 without integrated seat belts:* ★★; *with integrated seat belts:* ★; *1999 and 2001 F-250:* ★★; *2002–04 F-250:* ★★★/★; *2002–04 F-350:* ★★★. Early production 2001 models lack rear-seat head restraints. **Visibility F/R:** ★★★★★. **Maximum load capacity:** *1999 F-150 XLT 5.4L:* 1,290 lb. **Pet transport:** ★★★★★.

SAFETY COMPLAINTS: All models/years: Tie-rod and front torsion-bar failures send the truck out of control. • Dangerous front-end bounce. • Sudden acceleration and chronic stalling. • Sticking accelerator pedal. • Frequent automatic transmission failures; transmission slippage. • Airbag malfunctions. • Brake failure as pedal goes to the floor. • Wheel lug nut failures. • Firestone and Goodrich tire-tread separation. • Gas and brake pedals are mounted too close together:

> Pulled up to a stop sign. Stepped on brake pedal and accelerator pedal at same time and almost broadsided another vehicle. Backing out of [the] driveway the same thing happened and [the driver] almost hit another vehicle.

2000—A driver's face was burned when airbags deployed and gases caught on fire. • Steering loss because of shearing of the sector shaft. • Loss of brakes caused by prematurely worn calipers and pads. • Transmission torque converter may lock up without warning. • Halogen lights look like high beams to other drivers. • Metal cable breaks, allowing spare tire to fall off while underway. • Left rear tire flies off truck. • Radio heats up to the point where tapes melt. **2000–01**—Truck parked with emergency brake set rolls down incline. **2000–02**—Windows suddenly shatter while vehicle is underway. **2001**—Owners cite most of the aforementioned defects, plus a host of new safety-related failures. • A golf cart bumped one truck while it was parked, and the truck rolled about 4.5 metres. • Suspension is not strong enough for the rated towing capacity. • On early production 2001s, the rear seat doesn't have head restraints, allowing passenger's head to hit the back window. **2001–02**—High seats positioned so that driver stares into the tinted top part of the windshield, and inside rear-view mirror blocks forward visibility. **2001–03**—Driver's seat belt buckle won't fasten. **2002**—Fire ignites under the power-adjusted seat mechanism. • Automatic transmission jerks when vehicle accelerates. • Headlights and dash lights fail intermittently. • Small wheel hubs cause vehicle to vibrate excessively. **2003**—Faulty EGR valve causes throttle to stick wide open and brakes to fail. • Rear axle failure; wheel comes off. • One truck's left front wheel separated, and the truck ran into a wall. • Harley Truck Club (*www.nhtoc.com*) owners report that rubber strips on stainless steel gas pedals peel off, making the pedal too slippery. • Fuel-tank leakage. **2004**—Driving with rear window open makes the cabin vibrate violently. • Painful, high-pitched noise comes from the dash area. • Tire chains cannot be used. • Wiper leaves a 15 cm (6 in.) blind spot near the driver's side pillar. **2004–05**—Tailgate falls off. • Excessive vibration and rear-end shudder at highway speeds:

> 2004 Ford F-150 has extremely high amount of vibration. Vibration is felt throughout the entire operating range in the cab of the vehicle from the floorboard to the roof. The vibration is so bad that it will literally put your feet to sleep after about fifteen minutes and your hands begin to go numb after about thirty minutes.

•

> Excessive frame/tire "wobble" with my 2005 Ford F150 4×4. Vibration at 50–70 mph [80–110 km/h]. Brake pads and rotors overheating, causing warped rotors then increasing vibration with possible "death wobble." Tested three 2005 F150 trucks with service manager who confirmed and later backtracked with: "Ford 2005 F150 trucks wobble, and it's normal..."

2005—Many complaints of sudden, unintended acceleration with complete loss of braking capability. • Airbags continue to fail when needed:

> In auto accident at a high rate of speed, around 45 mph [70 km/h]. Hit truck and the airbags failed to deploy. The impact was so hard I split the other truck in half. I broke my neck in two places.

• When parked, vehicle slips out of gear and goes into Reverse. • Tire jack won't raise truck high enough to allow the mounting of a fully inflated spare. • Faulty ignition keys. **2006**—Many complaints of 5.4L V8 engine hesitating or stalling when accelerating. • Other complaints of unintended acceleration when the brakes are applied. • Reports of faulty fuel pumps leaking fuel onto the exhaust system. • Poorly designed suspension causes the vehicle to jump and shake wildly when passing over a small bump in the road. • Rack-and-pinion steering falls apart. • Sudden brake loss. • Ice accumulates in the wheels. • Many complaints relative to prematurely worn Hankook Dynapro original-equipment tires. **2007**—Unintended acceleration when braking, or when the cruise control is enabled. • Steering failure in rainy conditions. • Fuel gauge shows Empty when the tank is full. • Vision hampered by dash reflection (glare) onto front windshield. *F-250:* **2005**—Faulty diesel engine fuel injectors and exhaust system cause sickening exhaust fumes to enter the cabin:

> Diesel fumes came out of passenger air vents making myself nauseous and sick from CO_2 poisoning. Brought it in to the Ford dealer and service manager smelled the problem, said that there might be a problem with the Y-flange on exhaust manifold. Called back and pulled manifold and didn't see a problem was going to order a new one. Says not an uncommon problem.

• When the diesel engine is turned off for fuelling, it cannot be restarted. • Engine blows because of a faulty camshaft fuse. • Frequent fuel-pump failures. • Truck will not shift down automatically when carrying a load. • On the highway, the truck vibrates excessively and sways uncontrollably. **2006**—Automatic transmission gear slippage and stalling. • Transmission suddenly downshifts into 4×4 mode, abruptly slowing the truck down. • Recessed gauges and windshield glare impair visibility. • Vehicle stalls just as the accelerator pedal is released. **2007**—Truck is easily stolen:

> All it took for a thief to break into my Ford F-250 was, what the police officer determined, a flat-head screwdriver. It is extremely disturbing to think that all a person has to do is jam a screwdriver under the plate, for the door handle/lock plate, pry down and the door pops open.

• Engine goes to idle with no response to the accelerator. • Violent shaking when passing over a bumpy highway. • Severe dash glare onto the front windshield:

> The dashboard's reflection in the windshield is terrible! It is especially bad on a bright, sunny day or when I'm pulling into my garage. The glare makes it so difficult that I must roll down the side window and put my head out to be able to pull into the garage! When I drive it in the dark, the street lights light up the dashboard and that too reflects into the windshield.

F-350: **2007**—Diesel exhaust fumes enter into the cabin, making occupants sick, dizzy, and light-headed. • Long delay when accelerating. • Converter/transmission snap ring and solenoid failures. • Multiple brake failures. • When towing a trailer, the brakes don't work at low speeds (10–15 km/h). • Defective brake booster and engine oil pump. • Weak coil springs won't support a plow.

Secret Warranties/Internal Bulletins/Service Tips

All models: 1999—Countermeasures to correct vibration, noise, and a harsh ride are all listed in TSB #99-11-1. • If you have a hard time removing the key from the ignition, you may have a misaligned shift-column shaft bushing. • A moaning noise coming from the front differential while in 4×2 mode may be fixed by replacing the front differential side and pinion gears with revised gears. • The source of an annoying whistle from the dash may be an air leak at an instrument panel grommet. • If the rear brake drum grabs when cold, install Ford's revised rear brake drum shoe kit. **1999–2000**—Free "goodwill" repairs for door cracks (TSB #01-18-2; Date: September 17, 2001). **1999–2001**—Ford will repair or replace 5.4L engines that have faulty head gaskets. The April 1, 2002, edition of *Automotive News* says that the automaker allocated about $5,300 (U.S.) to replace the engine and cylinder heads/head gasket on each afflicted vehicle. **1999–2002**—High idle speeds; throttle sticks in cold weather. **1999–2004**—Tips for correcting a rough idle. • Paint delamination, peeling, or fading. • Troubleshooting

1997–2005 Expedition, F-150
2002–05 Explorer
1998–2005 Navigator
2003–05 Aviator
2002–05 Mountaineer

ISSUE: Some vehicles may exhibit an axle whine or hum during acceleration, deceleration, and/or cruise.

ACTION: An axle repair kit has been developed, which incorporates most parts required for a comprehensive axle repair. The kit should be used instead of installing a complete axle assembly to repair an axle whine/hum.

broken intake manifold studs. **1999–2005**—Ford will install a special axle kit to stop rear axle noise. Ford's bulletin admission of this defect is actionable in small claims court if the company won't pay for the 6-hour repair (see bulletin). • Water leaks from the roof flange area and accumulates in the headliner, or the leak may occur at the cab floor pan area. • Drivetrain drive-away shudder or vibration. **1999–2006**—A driveline clunk may signal that the slip yoke needs lubrication. Check this out before spending big bucks for more involved tests or repairs. • Vehicle sags to one side. **2000–05**—Seat belts slow to retract. **2001**—Automatic transmission clunk when shifting from Second to First gear. • Erratic 4×4 shifting; vehicle sticks in Fourth gear. • High-speed driveline vibration may damage drivetrain. • No-starts. • Tie-rod end squeaking. **2002**—Throttle may stick in cold weather. • Engine power loss in hot weather. • 4.6L engines may have a higher-than-normal idle speed. • Repaired aluminum engine heads may continue to leak coolant or oil. • Vacuum or air leaks in the intake manifold and engine. • Heater core leaks. • Faulty ignition switch lock cylinder. • Excessive front suspension noise when turning or shifting into Reverse. • A clunk may be heard when parking. **2003–05**—Remedy for false parking-aid warnings. **2003–06**—Inoperative AC; compressor leakage. **2004**—Faulty handle cables could make it impossible to open the doors from the inside. • Steering-wheel vibration at 97 km/h (60 mph) or higher may require replacing the steering gear. **2004–05**—Remedy for warm engine knocking or ticking. • Correction of axle chatter, shudder, or vibration during low-speed turning manoeuvres. • Remedies for steering-wheel and body vibrations. • Upgraded brake rotors will be installed to stop brake shudder and vibration. • Cooling fan noise on trucks equipped with 4.6L and 5.4L engines. • Free butyl bed pad removal to prevent corrosion. **2004–07**—Vibration on hard acceleration. • Aluminum body panel corrosion:

ALUMINUM BODY PANELS—CORROSION—SERVICE TIP

2000–07 Crown Victoria, Taurus; 2005–06 Ford GT; 2005–07 Mustang; 2000–03 Ranger; 2000–07 Expedition; 2002–07 Explorer; 2004–07 F-150

2007 Explorer Sport Trac; 2000–06 Lincoln LS; 2000–07 Town Car, Navigator; 2000–07 Grand Marquis, Sable.

ISSUE: Some vehicles may exhibit a bubbling or blistering under the paint on aluminum body parts. This is due to iron contamination of the aluminum panel.

2004–08—Power steering line fluid seepage in cold weather. • Excessive steering-wheel vibration (80–105 km/h). • High-speed driveline vibration. **2005**—Hard starts or rough running, or engine won't crank. • Cooling system overheats when using a snowplow; an extra-cost clutch fan must be purchased from Ford (offer to pay only half the cost). • Ford will replace faulty transmission snap rings and CD players for free. • Excessive steering-wheel shimmy after passing over bumps. • Steering moan, groan. • Loose roof ditch mouldings. **2005–07**—Power rear sliding window may need a new motor. • Slow power-window upward travel. *Diesels:* **2003–04**—Remedies for 6.0L diesel engines that have fuel in oil, lose power, or run roughly are covered in TSB #03-14-6 and the following bulletin:

DIESEL ENGINE DRIVEABILITY CONCERNS

BULLETIN NO.: 03-20-12   DATE: OCTOBER 13, 2003

2003–04 EXCURSION, F SUPER DUTY

Some vehicles may exhibit various driveability conditions listed below:

- Rough/Rolling Idle When The Engine Is Warm
- Rough/Rolling Idle And White Smoke After Hot Restart
- Lacks Power After Initial Start-Up
- Cold Idle kicker Performance At Warm Ambient Temps
- U0306 Codes After Reprogramming
- P2263 Code Set During Extended Idle
- False P0196 Codes

ACTION: Reprogram the PCM/TCM/FICM modules to the latest calibration level (B27.9) or later. This calibration should only be installed on customer vehicles that exhibit one of the conditions addressed above.

2003–05—Troubleshooting tips for misfire, lack of power, excessive smoke, and excessive cranking to start (see bulletin on the following page). Keep in mind that Ford *must* pay for this troubleshooting and repair under the much longer emissions warranty. Don't take no for an answer. **2003–06**—TSB #06-9-7, issued May 15, 2006, gives more diagnostic and repair tips for poorly performing diesel engines. **2005**—Engine stalls when shifting into Drive or Reverse, or when coming to a stop. **2005–06**—Inadvertent transmission lock-up during 1–2 shifts.

2003–2005 Excursion, F-Super Duty; 2004–2005 E-Series, F-650, F-750

ISSUE: Some 6.0L vehicles may exhibit a misfire, lack of power, buck/jerk, excessive smoke, or crank/no-start. There are several potential causes for these symptoms, including injector concerns.

ACTION: If normal diagnostics lead to an injector concern, use the following diagnostics to confirm the cause of injector failure and/or to rule out other conditions which may cause the same symptoms as a failed injector.

LOW OR NEGATIVE FUEL PRESSURE

Internal injector damage can be caused by lack of fuel system supply pressure. Restricted fuel filters and/or fuel line(s), or an inoperative fuel pump can create a low or negative fuel supply pressure. Low or negative pressures may hinder the return stroke of the injector intensifier plunger to its rest position, leading to internal injector damage. To diagnose for low or negative fuel pressure and to confirm if any injectors have been damaged:

1. Perform standard diagnostic procedures, including verification of supply fuel pressure while the symptom is evident.
2. Repair causes for low pressure on the supply side of the fuel system.
3. Diagnose for failed injector(s) only after rectifying fuel supply pressure.

COMBUSTION GAS ENTERING THE FUEL SYSTEM

1. Remove outlet fuel lines from the fuel filter housing on top of engine.
2. Install a balloon over each fuel line with a zip tie.
3. Disable the fuel pump and FICM relays.
4. Crank engine and watch for compression pulses in the balloon.
5. For each line where compression pulses are evident, remove all but one of the glow plugs from the affected cylinder head(s).
6. Crank engine and watch again for compression pulses.
7. Remove the glow plug and transfer it to the next cylinder in the head and repeat Step 6.
8. For each cylinder where compression pulses are evident remove injector(s) and inspect copper gasket and lower O-ring, replace if necessary. If gasket(s) and O-ring(s) are OK, replace injector(s). Retest to confirm repair.

ERRATIC HIGH PRESSURE OIL SUPPLY

Erratic supply of high pressure oil to injectors may cause a rough running engine. High pressure oil flow can be disrupted by faulty check valve(s) or a faulty IPR valve.

To diagnose, first perform a slow neutral run up in park/neutral. If the engine runs rough between 1200 and 1900 RPM proceed to Check Valve Diagnosis; if the engine runs rough between 3000 and 4000 RPM replace the IPR valve.

CHECK VALVE DIAGNOSIS

1. To isolate the bank with the faulty check valve, disconnect all of the injector electrical connectors on one bank.
2. Perform a Power Balance test. Engine misfires should be constant on the four disconnected cylinders and the operational cylinders should be contributing evenly.
3. Repeat steps 1 and 2 on the opposite bank.
4. If the operating contribution is erratic on one bank, replace the check valve on that bank.

WARRANTY STATUS: Eligible under provisions of New Vehicle Limited Warranty Coverage and Emissions Warranty Coverage

F-SERIES PROFILE

	1999	2000	2001	2002	2003	2004	2005	2006	2007
Cost Price ($) (negotiable)									
XL (20%)	22,995	22,295	22,710	23,310	23,380	22,850	23,840	22,499	22,499
Used Values ($)									
XL ▲	4,500	5,000	5,500	6,500	8,500	10,500	12,500	14,500	16,500
XL ▼	4,000	4,500	5,000	5,500	7,500	9,500	11,500	13,500	15,000
Reliability	2	2	2	2	2	2	2	2	2
Crash Safety (F)	4	4	5	5	—	5	5	5	5
Side	5	5	5	5	5	—	—	—	—
Ext. cab	—	—	4	4	4	—	—	—	—
IIHS Side	—	5	5	5	5	—	—	—	—
SuperCrew	—	—	—	5	5	—	—	—	—
Offset	1	1	1	1	1	5	5	5	5
Rollover	—	—	—	—	3	4	4	4	4
4×4	—	—	—	—	2	4	4	4	4

Ford/Mazda

RANGER/B-SERIES   ★★★★

RATING: Above Average (2003–09); Average (1984–2002). Mazda pickups are generally the least expensive of the "gang of three" small Japanese pickups (Mazda, Nissan, and Toyota). Actually, from the 1994 model onward, your Mazda is really a Ford Ranger. Overall, they're acceptable, but performance-wise they are only mediocre. Powertrain defects are worrisome. **Strong points:** Good engine performance (4.0L V6), well-designed interior, comfortable seating, classy interior trim, user-friendly control layout, four-door extended cab, good off-road handling, and good resale value. **Weak points:** Weak 4-cylinder engine (carried over into early 2001), barely adequate 3.0L V6, harsh ride, excessive braking distance, 4×4's extra height hinders easy entry and exit, rear doors are hinged at the back and won't open independently of the front doors, spare tire is difficult to remove, and many safety-related complaints reported to NHTSA. **New for 2008:** A tire-pressure monitoring system; larger foglights; an improved Off-Road model.

MODEL HISTORY: Base Rangers come with a SuperCab option, they have 4×2 and part-time 4×4 versatility, and flare-side models are available with XL and XLT models. Mazdas follow the same program, shared among three badges: the B2500, B3000, and B4000.

2008 RANGER/B-SERIES TECHNICAL DATA

POWERTRAIN (4×2/PART-TIME 4×4)
Engines: 2.3L 4-cyl. (143 hp) • 3.0L V6 (154 hp) • 4.0L V6 (207 hp); Transmissions: 5-speed man. • 5-speed auto. OD

DIMENSION/CAPACITY (REG. CAB 4×2/4×4)
Passengers: 3/2; Wheelbase: 126.0 in.; H: 64.1/L: 202.0/W: 70.0 in.; Legroom F/R: 42.4/35.1 in.; Cargo volume: 37.3 cu. ft.; Fuel tank: 64L/79L/regular; Tow limit: 3,180–6,070 lb.; Load capacity: 1,250–1,650 lb.; GVWR: 4,700/5,100 lb.; Turning circle: 45.0 ft.; Box length: 6.0/7.0 ft.; Ground clearance: 6.1/7.2 in.; Weight: 3,870 lb.

Properly equipped, these vehicles almost match the versatility of a full-sized pickup. Since the 4-cylinder engine is unsuitable for anything but the lightest chores, the larger V6 is the preferred engine choice. Its additional torque can better handle serious towing and off-roading, and fuel economy is practically the same as with the smaller V6. An electric shift transfer case and shift-on-the-fly controls are standard on 4×4 models. The upscale trim level should appeal to buyers who want to combine reliability with a more sedan-like interior.

1999—Ranger and B-series return unchanged from 1998's extensive redesign, except for the SuperCab's fourth door, while the following year's models get torsion bar suspension and a larger wheel/tire package for the 4×2. **2001**—Models get the Explorer's 207-hp 4.0L SOHC V6. The flexible-fuel feature on the 3.0L V6 is dropped; and a new base 2.3L 4-cylinder replaces the 2.5L. ABS becomes a standard feature. **2002**—Models are joined by an XLT FX4 off-road 4×4 model, heavy-duty suspension, 31-inch tires, a heftier skid plate, and tow hooks. **2003**—The extension of Quadrasteer to other models, and an improved electrical system and passenger-side airbag sensors.

COST ANALYSIS: The base 2008 Ranger XL sells for $15,399; a 4×4 XL goes for $19,499. Similar Mazda trucks cost $14,995 and $22,375 (equipped with a 4.0L engine), respectively. Buying your Ranger in the States won't save you much money; however, the base XL is priced at $14,220 (U.S.), the 4×4 at $18,065 (U.S.). On the Mazda side, the base truck sold in the States carries a $15,535 (U.S.) price tag; the 4×4, $22,045 (U.S.). Remember, Ranger may be dropped next year. **Best alternatives:** The Honda Ridgeline and Nissan Frontier. **Options:** The 4.0L V6, four-wheel ABS, running boards, transmission/oil cooler, remote keyless entry/ anti-theft system, upgraded sound system, and power windows and door locks. Dealers are using Firestone space-saver tires as spares; ask for regular-sized tires from a different manufacturer. Stay away from the weak 2.5L 4-cylinder engine. **Rebates:** $2,000 rebates and low financing rates on all model years. **Delivery/ PDI:** *Ford:* $1,200; *Mazda:* $1,390. **Depreciation:** Much slower than average. **Insurance cost:** Average. **Annual maintenance cost:** Below average. **Parts supply/cost:** Excellent supply, and relatively inexpensive from independent suppliers. **Warranty:** Bumper-to-bumper 3 years/60,000 km; rust perforation 5 years/unlimited km. **Supplementary warranty:** A good idea, judging by recent owner complaints. **Highway/city fuel economy:** *4×2 and 2.5L:* 8.8/11.7 L/100 km; *4×2 and 3.0L:* 9.4/14.0 L/100 km; *4×2 and 4.0L:* 9.7/13.9 L/100 km; *4×4 and 3.0L:* 10.6/14.8 L/100 km; *4×4 and 4.0L:* 10.9/14.7 L/100 km. Owners report fuel consumption is often way higher than these averages.

QUALITY/RELIABILITY: Assembly and component quality are below average. Reliability isn't impressive. Owners note serious engine problems (poor idle, surge, and stalling), erratic transmission performance and failure, brake and fuel system issues, and breakdowns. **Warranty performance:** Below average with Ford; average with Mazda staffers. **Owner-reported problems:** The 3.0L engines may have a spark knock (ping) under acceleration; the camshaft may have been incorrectly heat-treated; Flex-Fuel engines may experience a hard start or no-start; and 4.0L engines may have excessive oil consumption and surging, clogged, or plugged fuel injectors. Extremely poor gas mileage; transmission fluid leak from the transmission extension housing; oil leak from the rear seal of the transmission extension housing; no 4×4 Low range, or gets stuck in Low range; and oil leak from the front-axle pinion oil seal area. Manual transmission clutch squawks on takeoff, or makes buzzing, grinding noise during 2–3 upshift; manual-transmission-equipped 3.0L vehicles may maintain a too-high engine idle when decelerating; automatic transmission fluid leaks at radiator. Steering vibration at idle or at low speeds; wind noise from the windshield cowl, top-of-door glass seal, or the weather stripping moulding area; side mirrors flutter or shake at highway speeds; chucking, squeaking noise from rear doors; poor AC performance; faulty dome and Door Ajar lights; rear-end sag; and premature paint peeling and delamination. Water leaks through the rear window are likely caused by the seat pushing up against the glass. Front wipers operate even when switch is set to Off.

SAFETY SUMMARY: The 2008 Ranger and B-series' crashworthiness ratings are identical to the 2007 models'. ABS is standard on rear wheels only, making for less-than-impressive braking with the 1997 version. **Airbags:** There have been reports of airbags failing to deploy, or deploying when they shouldn't, resulting in severe injuries. **ABS:** Standard 2W; disc/drum. **Safety belt pretensioners:** Standard. **Head restraints F/R:** *Ranger 1999:* ★★; *2001–03:* ★★/★; *2004–05:* ★★★★★; *2006–08:* ★. *B-series 1999–2003:* ★; *2004–05:* ★★★★★; *2006:* ★. **Visibility F/R:** *2004–05:* ★★★★★/★. **Pet transport:** ★★★★★.

SAFETY COMPLAINTS: All models/years: Passengers slam their heads into the back glass during sudden stops or in rear-end collisions. • Steering-wheel lock-up. • Excessive shaking when cruising. • Malfunctioning airbags, and burns caused by airbag deployment. • Defective tie-rod. • When parked on an incline with shifter lever in Park, vehicle jumps into Neutral and rolls away. • Transmission failures:

> I suffered a complete transmission failure and was forced to limp into a local Ford truck sales place. The failure occurred without any advance warning and left me limping along at 35–40 mph [55–65 km/h] on the I-90 thruway during rush hour, with heavy traffic travelling 65–70 mph [105–115 km/h]. I had totally lost Reverse gear and had substantial slippage occurring in forward gears.
>
> Ford tech consultants revealed that this is happening to many Ford Rangers, but no recall has been issued. Apparently, the torque on the transmission was increased

without redesigning the transmission or seals to be able to withstand the higher torque.

• Drive shaft shears off while driving at high speed. • Fuel leaks (tank and fuel lines). • Sudden acceleration, often when braking. • A faulty idle air control valve may be responsible for the vehicle not decelerating properly. • Stalling. • Complete loss of ABS. • Gas and brake pedals are too close together. • Brakes don't work properly, with stuck brake calipers, overheating, and excessive pad and rotor wear. • Windshield wiper comes on by itself, or won't come on at all. • Tire-tread separation. *Ranger:* **1999**—Jerks to the side when braking or accelerating. • Chronic window fogging. **2000**—Left front wheel flies off vehicle. **2001**—Excessive wander on the highway, especially bad when passing over uneven terrain or after hitting potholes. • Inaccurate fuel-tank level indicator and fuel gauge. • Fuel tank overflows when refuelling. • Faulty engine computer causes hard starts. • Brake line abraded by rubbing against leaf spring. • Excessive vibration called "harmonic imbalance" by dealer. • Passenger-side seat belt unbuckles at random. **2002**—A large number of serious safety-related incidents have been reported. • Sudden acceleration after vehicle jumps from Park into gear. • Premature replacement of clutch slave cylinder. • Complete brake failure because of a defective idle control, among other causes. • Rear shock absorbers quickly wear out. • Front tire falls off because of defective carter pin. • Interior and exterior lights go out intermittently. **2003**—Throttle sticks as pedal sinks to the floor. • Misaligned driver-side door allows wind and water entry. **2004**—Chronic stalling, loss of power. • Stuck accelerator. • One vehicle left in Park with the engine idling shifted into Reverse. • Transmission slippage; slams into gear. • Frequent brake lock-up when brakes are applied. • Premature front tire wear, and tread separation on front and rear tires. • Rear window pops out when seat pushed back. • Odometer can't be seen in daylight. **2004–05**—High rear head restraints block side and rear visibility. **2004–07**—Airbags fail to deploy. **2005**—Vehicle stalls on the highway repeatedly because of a defective inertia switch. • Ford assembly-line worker says the Ranger rear axle sway bar is mounted incorrectly and designed poorly. **2006**—Vehicle rolls backward when stopped on an incline. • Steering-wheel gap catches clothing. **2007**—Fire originates near the passenger-side airbag. • A violent shaking occurs at 100 km/h because ice builds up within the wheel. • Outside mirrors are too small and cowling/trim is too restrictive for reasonable visibility.

Secret Warranties/Internal Bulletins/Service Tips

All models/years: Keep in mind that Ford service bulletins will likely also apply to Mazda. *Ranger:* **1999–2000**—Excessive clutch noise on vehicles equipped with manual transmissions may require a new clutch disc and revised pressure plate assembly. **1999–2002**—Paint delamination, peeling, or fading. • Loud AC clutch cycling. • Automatic transmission slips or has a delayed engagement. **2007**—Difficulty shifting out of Park. *B-series:* **1999–2003**—Seat track rattling. **1999–2005**—Driveline clunk remedy. • Front axle leaks:

1995–2001 EXPLORER
1997–2003 RANGER
2001–03 EXPLORER SPORT TRAC; EXPLORER SPORT
1997–2001 MOUNTAINEER

Article 02-4-2 is being republished in its entirety to update the model year applications.

ISSUE: Fluid may leak out of the front axle vent tube after being thrown toward the axle vent by the gears during vehicle operation.

ACTION: Replace the axle cover and install the Axle Cover kit (F6TZ-4033-BA).

1999–2007—Excessive wind noise around the doors. **2001**—Unable to reach wide open throttle; lack of power. • 3.0L engine leaks oil at the oil filter mounting surface. • Vacuum or air leaks in the intake manifold. • 4.0L engine may lose power or have a low idle when first started. • Clutch may be hard to disengage. • Front axle squeal or whistle. • 4×4 SuperCab models may have a drive shaft thump and vibration when accelerating or stopping. • Inaccurate fuel gauge. • Front end may produce a squeal or whistle. • Delayed Reverse engagement. **2001–03**—Transmission whine on vehicles with the 4.0L engine. **2002**—Check Engine light troubleshooting. • 4.0L engine may produce a spark knock or fluttering noise, or may leak oil. • 2.3L engine may idle poorly and surge or hesitate when accelerating. • Automatic transmission fluid leaks. • Manual-transmission-equipped vehicles may lose power when decelerating. • Damaged fuel-return line. • Fluid leaks from the front axle vent tube. • Heater core leaks. • Air leaks or vacuum in the intake manifold or engine. • Faulty ignition switch lock cylinder. • Inaccurate temperature gauge. **2002–03**—Noisy manual transfer-case shifter. **2002–05**—Rear brake "grabbing." **2003–06**—Inoperative AC; compressor leakage. **2004–05**—No Third gear. • Wrong transmission fluid put in originally by Ford may cause harsh, delayed shifts. **2005–07**—2.3L engine may have starting problems, lose timing, or be seriously damaged.

RANGER/B-SERIES PROFILE

	1999	2000	2001	2002	2003	2004	2005	2006	2007
Cost Price ($) (negotiable)									
Base/XL 4×2 (20%)	15,995	16,395	16,995	18,595	17,395	16,775	17,810	18,299	18,299
Base/XL 4×4	20,295	21,395	24,675	23,715	24,495	—	—	—	—
Used Values ($)									
Base/XL 4×2 ▲	2,000	2,500	3,000	3,500	5,000	6,500	8,000	9,500	11,000
Base/XL 4×2 ▼	1,500	2,000	2,500	3,000	4,000	5,000	6,500	8,000	9,500
Base/XL 4×4 ▲	3,500	4,000	4,500	5,500	7,000	—	—	—	—
Base/XL 4×4 ▼	3,000	3,500	4,000	4,500	5,500	—	—	—	—

Reliability	3	3	3	3	3	3	4	4	4
Crash Safety (F)	4	4	—	4	4	4	4	4	5
Ext. cab	—	4	4	4	4	4	4	4	5
Side	5	5	5	5	5	5	5	5	5
Ext. cab	—	4	4	4	4	4	4	4	4
Offset	3	3	3	3	3	3	3	3	3
Rollover (4×2)	—	—	—	—	3	—	3	3	3
4×4	—	—	—	—	2	—	2	2	2
Ext. cab (4×2)	—	—	—	—	3	—	3	3	3
Ext. cab (4×4)	—	—	—	—	3	—	2	2	2

General Motors

AVALANCHE ★★★

RATING: Average (2007–09); Below Average (2002–06). **Strong points:** A cheap used Suburban clone; drives much like the similarly equipped Suburban and Silverado/Sierra; plenty of passenger and cargo room; a relatively high towing limit achieved through a variety of V8 engines; a smooth powertrain (with some exceptions); and plenty of standard amenities. The 2004 and later models' hydroboost brake feature enhances brake feel, but no word as to whether the poor durability problem has been addressed. Four doors provide easy access for six occupants who are given plenty of headroom and legroom. "Midgate" panel adds to the pickup's practicality. Angular styling similar to the Cadillac Escalade and Pontiac Aztek gives the Avalanche an aggressive stance. Other positives are a high ground clearance and a comfortable, quiet ride. **Weak points:** Loses value quickly. Excess weight cripples performance and fuel economy; premature brake wear; suspension and steering vibrations; numb steering even after the 2007 redesign; and powertrain deficiencies similar to those afflicting the Suburban and Silverado. The cabin, although improved this year, still has thinly padded armrests and an abundance of hard plastic interior trim. Front and rear visibility is not reassuring for parking or merging with traffic. The 4-speed automatic transmission is inadequate; it kicks in as early as 70 km/h, and you have to stomp on the accelerator to get it to kick down when passing other vehicles. Noisy Bridgestone tires. **New for 2008:** Head-

2008 AVALANCHE TECHNICAL DATA

POWERTRAIN (4×2/4×4)
Engines: 5.3L V8 (320 hp) • 6.0L V8 (366 hp); Transmission: 4-speed auto.

DIMENSION/CAPACITY
Passengers: 3/3; Wheelbase: 130.0 in.; H: 77.0/L: 221.0/W: 79.0 in.; Headroom F/R: 4.0/4.0 in.; Legroom F/R: 41.5/29.0 in.; Cargo volume: 53.9 cu. ft.; Fuel tank: 117L–142L/regular; Tow limit: 7,800–8,000 lb.; Load capacity: 1,408 lb.; GVWR: 6,800–8,600 lb.; Turning circle: 43.0 ft.; Box length: 5.3–8.1 ft.; Ground clearance: 9.1 in.; Weight: 5,478 lb.

protecting side-impact airbags. There is no reason to pay more for an identical 2009 model. GM plans to slightly restyle the 2010 version; however, no major engineering refinements are scheduled until 2012.

MODEL HISTORY: Sharing 85 percent of its parts with the Suburban, the Avalanche is a full-sized crew-cab pickup with a unique bed and cab design, and performance features that make it one of the most versatile and powerful sport-utility/truck crossovers you can find. But it looks like a gimmicky "What's that?" kind of vehicle not seen since the El Camino sedan-*cum*-pickup, or the weirdly styled Aztek. Carrying a base 5.3L V8 engine mated to a rear-drive/4×4 4-speed automatic powertrain, the Avalanche nevertheless comes loaded with potential. For example, its Convert-a-Cab feature allows you to fold the rear passenger seat/midgate and extend the standard bed by about 86 cm (34 in.), giving the bed an impressive 2.5 m (8′1″) length. Or you can remove the rear window, fold the midgate, and get an open-air feel. The Avalanche won't win any fuel economy or retained-value prizes, and its price and factory-related deficiencies will discourage all but the most daring. Best advice: Don't look for a Swiss-Army-knife SUV; determine your most basic requirements and buy a simpler, less costly, and less gimmicky pickup. **2003**—A redesigned dash; optional power-adjustable brake and accelerator pedals; and standard front side airbags become optional. **2004**—Optional anti-skid control. **2007**—A longer bed and an all-new platform, interior, and look, also found on GM's 2007 Tahoe and Suburban. The fuel-saving Active Fuel Management feature is standard, and an improved 6.0L V8 joins the lineup. GM's stability control system is also standard, while head-protecting side curtain airbags remain optional.

COST ANALYSIS: The 2008 model is way overpriced at $38,985. A better choice would be a used 2007 version with optional head-protecting side airbags for $25,000–$27,000. However, prices are very soft for both model years. There is a $4,500 difference if you buy your new Avalanche in the States ($34,335). **Best alternatives:** The Dodge Ram Quad Cab, Honda Ridgeline, and Nissan Frontier. **Options:** Consider electric adjustable pedals, AC, and an engine block heater. Ditch the Bridgestone AL2 all-season tires—they lack sufficient grip and are noisy. **Rebates:** $5,000–$7,000 rebates and low financing rates on all model years. **Delivery/PDI:** $1,300. **Depreciation:** Faster than average. **Insurance cost:** Higher than average. **Annual maintenance cost:** Average. **Parts supply/cost:** Excellent supply, and relatively inexpensive from independent suppliers. **Warranty:** Bumper-to-bumper 3 years/60,000 km; powertrain 5 years/160,000 km; rust perforation 5 years/unlimited km. **Supplementary warranty:** A good idea, judging by owner complaints relative to powertrain failures. **Highway/city fuel economy:** 12.0/16.2 L/100 km. Owners say they get much worse fuel economy than what the government's and automaker's figures predict.

 QUALITY/RELIABILITY: Poor-quality mechanical and body components impair the Avalanche's overall reliability. Major problem areas are engine malfunctions, automatic transmission failures and subpar performance, and brake/fuel system breakdowns. **Owner-reported problems:** Faulty engine, steering, seat belts, airbags, and transmission (clunky, grinding noise when accelerating, and glitch-prone). Early brake pad and rotor replacement, constant AC humming and vibration, premature paint peeling and delamination, and the steering assembly produces a "popping" noise when turning. Water leaks into the bed area and through the midgate and doors:

> Water enters the cab through the mid gate, causing the carpet and matting to become soaked with water to the point that water pools on top of the carpet. This more than likely will result in the immediate rusting of the floor and possible growing of mold in the constantly wet carpet and matting.... Dealership has replaced...seals on several location[s as] well as added additional silicone, although no attempt at repair[s] have been successful in slowing down or stopping the water leak.

•

> The linear positions of doors are irregular. The front fender is beyond specs. The plastic structure of the back is not in alignment with the body. The rear-view mirror vibrates, which is a hazard at night...since the doors are not properly aligned the wind, dirt and water bypass the weatherstrip. Repairs to the fuel pump, distortion of the windshield, body defects, loud squealing brakes, and door handles/steering wheel inner face have peeled.

Owners also mention that pad and rotor problems cause excessive vibration when braking and that components frequently overheat. Extremely poor real-world fuel economy. **Warranty performance:** Unsatisfactory.

 SAFETY SUMMARY: The 2008 model's safety ratings are similar to the 2007's. **Airbags:** Standard front airbags; optional side curtain airbags. **ABS:** Standard 4W; disc/disc. The redesigned 2007 ABS brakes work flawlessly. **Safety belt pretensioners:** Standard. **Head restraints F/R:** Rear head restraints appear to be useless; no restraint for the rear middle seat. **Visibility F/R:** ★★/★. **Maximum load capacity:** 1,230 lb. **Pet transport:** ★★★★★.

SAFETY COMPLAINTS: 2002–06—Braking is dangerously poor on wet pavement. **2004**—Chronic warm-weather stalling. • Exterior light lenses have excessive condensation, which reduces their effectiveness. • Electrical charge passing through cabin may be a health hazard:

> The electricity from the automatic control monitor that controls the air conditioning and temperature control on the roof of the truck was causing the consumer to experience severe headaches and she was no longer able to drive the vehicle with the heat or air on. She had to pull the fuse that controlled the monitor because [after] turning it off the wave of electricity was still flowing. The gauss meter that checked the wave of electricity was flashing red when she held it up to her head. It was not supposed

to be like that. The symptoms were: her scalp was [really] tender and swollen, her left side of shoulder and neck was hurting a lot, and she had to use contacts in her left eye because of vision problems. All of these symptoms were from the automatic control monitor. She has never had any of these symptoms prior to this. Since she unplugged the fuse these symptoms disappeared, and she felt better. Her concern was that other people driving this vehicle may never be able to figure out what caused these problems.

• Too much tire side wall flex and an under-sprung suspension cause the back end to kick out dangerously when passing over bumps or expansion joints. • Brakes come on by themselves. • Clunks when turning; GM bought one vehicle back after many repairs proved futile. • Tailgate falls down when truck accelerates. • Cracked wheel rims. **2005**—Airbags don't deploy when needed. • Fuel spews out when refuelling. • Truck stalls when turning. • Automatic transmission fails. • Vehicle wanders into oncoming traffic. • Instrument panel "blows out" and shuts down; cost: $600+. • Headlight falls out. • Tires rub on the front fenders. • The GM Passlock anti-theft system can be easily bypassed through a pin hole in the driver-side key tumbler; an aftermarket anti-theft system must be added. • Sudden blowout of Firestone Wilderness tires. **2006**—Brake and steering failures. • Flex/gas lines connected to the fuel regulators rub against each other and leak fuel. • Trailer-hitch-receiver weld failure. **2007**—Faulty rear axle pinion seal causes fire. • Fire ignites in the dash area. • Sun gear/sprag gear transmission failure. • Transmission suddenly downshifts at the wrong time. • Chronic electrical short-circuits. • Speedometer malfunctions. • Rear head restraints do not extend high enough and do not lock into place when fully extended. • Centre front-seat passenger must sit with knees positioned toward the right side of the vehicle. • GM suggests 30 psi tire pressure; tiremaker advises 44 psi. Handling is far better with the higher pressure.

Secret Warranties/Internal Bulletins/Service Tips

2002–04—Suspension clunk, slap. GM will replace the spring insert and insulator for free (see Silverado "Secret Warranties/Internal Bulletins/Service Tips"). **2002–06**—Discoloured cargo covers or body cladding (seen as a chalky colour) will be corrected under a secret warranty. **2003–04**—Remedies for an inoperative front power window and a steering-wheel clunk. **2004–06**—Automatic transmission shudder due to water intrusion (see Tahoe section). **2006–07**—V8 engine oil leaks (see bulletin on following page). • AC doesn't cool; compressor is noisy. **2007**—Inoperative 4×4. • Steering fluid leaks. • Instrument panel buzz, rattle. • Driver-seat squeak, creak. • Upper door squeak, scratching noise. • Front bumper paint peeling. **2007–08**—It takes a lot of effort to close the hood. • Steering whistle. • Front right fender buzz, rattle.

V8 ENGINE OIL LEAKS/LOW OIL LAMP ON

BULLETIN NO.: 07-06-01-004   DATE: MARCH 16, 2007

LOW OIL LEVEL INDICATOR LAMP ON AND/OR ENGINE OIL LEAK (RESEAL OIL PRESSURE SENSOR)

2006–07 Buick Rainier; Cadillac Escalade, CTS-V; Chevrolet Corvette Z06, Impala SS, Monte Carlo SS; Chevrolet Avalanche, Silverado, Silverado HD, Suburban, Tahoe, TrailBlazer, TrailBlazer SS; 2006–07 GMC Envoy, Envoy Denali, Sierra, Sierra HD, Sierra Denali, Yukon, XL, Yukon Denali XL; Pontiac Grand Prix GXP; Saab 9-7X V8

CONDITION: Some customers may comment on a low oil level indicator lamp on and/or engine oil leak. Upon further investigation, the technician may find that the oil leak is at the oil pressure sensor that is threaded into the valve lifter oil manifold (VLOM) assembly and/or engine valley cover.

CORRECTION: If the engine oil leak was found to be at the engine oil pressure sensor, then remove the oil pressure sensor and reseal with a pipe sealant with Teflon or equivalent, P/N 12346004 (in Canada, P/N 10953480). Refer to Engine Oil Pressure Sensor and/or Switch Replacement in SI.

AVALANCHE PROFILE

	2002	2003	2004	2005	2006	2007
Cost Price ($) (negotiable)						
Avalanche (21%)	37,372	38,135	39,155	39,910	40,400	38,985
Used Values ($)						
Avalanche ▲	10,500	13,000	16,500	18,000	23,000	27,000
Avalanche ▼	9,000	11,000	14,500	17,000	21,000	25,000
Reliability	3	3	3	3	3	3
Crash Safety (F)	3	3	3	3	3	5
Side	—	—	—	—	—	5
Rollover	2	2	—	3	3	3

C/K, SIERRA, SILVERADO ★★★

RATING: Average (2007–09; 1988–98); Below Average (1999–2006). Both models are living on borrowed time. GM's last redesign of its 2007 models produced mediocre trucks with only marginally improved performance and reliability. The new diesel engines are expected to have serious performance and quality failings during their first few years on the market, judging by the Duramax's prior performance. **Strong points:** *2007 and later models:* A cylinder deactivation feature that *may* actually cut fuel usage; a more stylish interior. *All models:* A well-appointed vehicle with a large choice of powertrains that can tow and haul almost anything. User-friendly controls for the full-time 4×4 system; well laid-out instruments and controls; seats are roomy and supportive; lots of leg clearance; a contoured cushion and a reclined seatback to further enhance comfort; doors open wide and feature useful pull-lever handles; a large cabin; a high ground clearance; good noise insulation; and a rattle-resistant body. **Weak points:** Production cutbacks will slash resale values and complicate parts availability (especially hybrids'). *2007 and later models:* Hybrid systems and cylinder deactivation haven't produced promised fuel savings when used on the 2007 Avalanche and Tahoe. A mediocre ride, problems with brakes and steering, and serious handling problems—lots of body roll and understeer when cornering, and serious chassis shake when going over potholed roads. Poor quality control. *2006 and earlier models:* The 6.0L Duramax diesel has serious reliability and performance problems. The base 4.3L V6 needs more grunt, the transmission hunts for the right gear and produces an incessant whine, the base suspension provides a too-compliant ride, and there's insufficient room for the driver to reach between the door panel and seat to access the seat-adjusting mechanism. Serious reliability problems. An incredibly high number of performance- and safety-related complaints have been reported to NHTSA and confirmed through confidential bulletins and whistle-blowers.

New for 2008: Upgraded gauges and seats. Gas-electric hybrids will be offered on the 2009s. The GM–Daimler joint-venture two-mode hybrid uses motors in the transmission to power the electric motor/generators when the vehicle is running at low road speeds.

MODEL HISTORY: Similar to Detroit's other pickups, these models are classed as 1500 half-ton, 2500 three-quarter-ton, and 3500 one-ton models. They come with a wide range of engine options, body styles, and bed sizes. The "C" designation refers to 4×2, and the "K" designation to 4×4. The 3500 series offers a four-door cab with a full rear seat. The variety of cab and cargo bed combinations, along with a choice of suspensions, makes these pickups adaptable to just about any use. Standard features include one of the biggest cabs among pickups, a fourth door, a three-piece modular truck frame, rack-and-pinion steering, and four-wheel disc brakes with larger pads and rotors.

An AutoTrac AWD drivetrain allows the driver to select an automatic mode that delivers full-time 4×4 (particularly useful if you live in a snowbelt area), while a 4-speed automatic features an innovative tow/haul mode that stretches out the upshifts to tap the engine's power at its maximum. There's also a potent family of four Vortec V8s in addition to a 6.6L turbodiesel (360 hp), 16-inch tires and wheels, and the highest minimum ground clearance among the Big Three pickups.

2008 TECHNICAL DATA

POWERTRAIN (REAR-DRIVE/4×4)
Engines: 4.3L V6 (195 hp) • 4.8L V8 (295 hp) • 5.3L V8 (295 hp) • 5.3L V8 (315 hp) • 6.0L V8 (300 hp) • 6.0L V8 (367 hp) • 6.4L V8 turbodiesel (320 hp) • 6.6L V8 turbodiesel (360 hp); Transmissions: 5-speed man. • 6-speed man. • 4-speed auto. OD • 5-speed auto. OD • 6-speed auto.

DIMENSION/CAPACITY (1500/2500)
Passengers: 3/3; Wheelbase: 144.0 in.; H: 68.0/L: 230.7/W: 79.0 in.; Headroom F/R: 6.5/4.5 in.; Legroom F/R: 42.0/30.0 in.; Cargo volume: 60.7 cu. ft.; Fuel tank: 95L–129L/regular/ diesel; Tow limit: 7,500–15,900 lb.; Load capacity: 1,655–1,965 lb./2,614–3,334 lb.; GVWR: 6,200/9,200 lb.; Box length: 6.5/8.0 ft.; Ground clearance: 9.0 in.; Weight: 4,453–5,164 lb. (4x2), 4,678–5,379 lb.(4x4)

Chevy and GMC full-sized pickups are good domestic workhorses—when they're running. Of course, that's the problem—they're not dependable. On the one hand, they have a large, quiet cabin and give relatively easy access to the interior. On the other hand, their size and heft make for lousy fuel economy, a mediocre ride, and subpar handling and braking. Resale value? Don't ask.

Early full-sized GM trucks may look like bargains, but they have as many serious factory-related deficiencies as their smaller S-10 cousins, if not more. Consequently, be sure to get extended warranty coverage. Keep in mind that engine and automatic transmission failures are quite common, and together they can give you a $7,000 headache. Also, try to find a pickup with running boards already installed. You'll save a few hundred dollars and make entry and exit a lot easier. Check out towing claims carefully as well. One owner reports that his truck was advertised as able to pull 3,856 kg (8,500 lb.), but the owner's manual says the towing limit is 3,402 kg (7,500 lb.).

Earlier versions will have a 4-speed manual or 3-speed automatic transmission; later ones come with 5- or 6-speed manuals, or 4-, 5-, or 6-speed automatics. Three-quarter-ton pickups offer more cargo capacity, but their harder suspension makes for an uncomfortable ride when lightly loaded, and also affects handling. The 1999–2006 models got many new features that make them more powerful, versatile, and accommodating, and they're safer than previous models. However, these changes also make them less reliable than the pickups they replaced. Major powertrain, brake, suspension, electrical system, and body deficiencies have turned these "dream machines" into motoring nightmares.

For over a decade, Sierras and Silverados have been plagued with severe vibrations that GM has routinely ignored. Owners have nicknamed their trucks "Shakerados," and they say that the new frame braces added to the 2001s to stop the shakes haven't worked (see *agmlemon.freeservers.com/index.html*).

2000—The 2000 Sierra and Silverado come with an optional fourth door on extended-cab models, and a small power boost for the Vortec 4800 and 5300 V8 engines. **2001**—Debut of three-quarter-ton and one-ton versions of the Silverado. They offer two engines: the 6.6L Isuzu-built Duramax V8 diesel and GM's home-grown 8.1L Vortec V8. A traction-assist feature becomes available on rear-drive V8 automatics. The Sierra C3 luxury truck offers a number of new features, including a 325-hp 6.0L Vortec V8; full-time all-wheel drive (no two-speed transfer case for serious off-roading, though); upgraded four-wheel disc anti-lock brakes; an increased-capacity suspension system; and a luxuriously appointed interior. The Sierra HD truck lineup comes with stronger frames; beefed-up suspensions, axles, brakes, and cooling systems; new sheet metal; bigger interiors; and three new V8s: a 6.6L Duramax turbodiesel and two gas engines, a hefty 8.1L and an improved 6.0L. One of the four transmissions, a new Allison 5-speed automatic, is designed especially for towing and hauling with GM's tow/haul mode and a new grade-braking feature. **2003**—Quadrasteer expanded to other models, improved electrical system and passenger-side airbag sensor, a new centre console, and dual-zone temperature and steering-wheel controls. **2004**—Standard cruise control, power door locks, and a CD player. **2006**—A new 360-hp 6.6L V8 turbodiesel engine late in the model year; Quadrasteer option dropped. **2007**—Active Fuel Management cylinder deactivation with the 5.3L V8; more powerful engines (the 4.8L V8 gets 10 more horses, the 5.3L has five more, and the 6.0L is given 22 more); a 980 kg (2,160 lb.) payload rating; and towing capability boosted to 4,763 kg (10,500 lb.). Other improvements: a reinforced chassis, upgraded suspension and steering systems, a larger cabin and bed, and new exterior and interior styling. Standard stability control on Crew Cabs.

COST ANALYSIS: Buy an upgraded, nearly identical second-series 2007 for $15,000 if you really want to save money. Otherwise, expect to pay $23,520 for a 2008 rear-drive Silverado 1500 Regular Cab base model, or $27,120 for the 4×4 variant. In the States, these vehicles go for $18,425 (U.S.) and $21,860 (U.S.), respectively. Enough of a difference to make it worthwhile shopping across the border. Remember, anything but a bare-bones version will be quite expensive at first, before hard bargaining. **Best alternatives:** A used Dodge Ram (mainly for the warranty and the less troublesome, but not perfect, Cummins diesel), a Honda Ridgeline, a Mazda B-series, or a Nissan Frontier V6. **Rebates:** Up to $11,000 rebates on fully loaded models. **Delivery/PDI:** $1,300. **Warranty:** Bumper-to-bumper 3 years/60,000 km; power train 5 years/160,000 km; rust perforation 6 years/160,000 km. **Supplementary warranty:** A good idea for the powertrain, judging by consumer complaints and the high incidence of diesel engine deficiencies. **Options:** This is where GM really sticks it to you. Consider the remote keyless entry, upgraded sound system, heavy-duty battery, and transmission fluid and oil coolers. **Depreciation:** Faster than average. **Parts supply/cost:** Mechanical parts are widely available and reasonably priced due to the proliferation of independent suppliers. The 2007 model's body parts may be costly and in short supply. **Insurance cost:** Higher than average. **Annual maintenance cost:** Upkeep costs for these trucks are high; use independent garages to keep costs down. **Highway/city fuel economy:** *4.3L V6 and manual: 9.5/14.1 L/100 km; 4.3L V6 and automatic: 10.6/14.6 L/100 km; 4.8L V8 and automatic: 10.5/14.6 L/100 km; 5.3L V8 and automatic: 12.0/16.2 L/100 km; 5.3L V8 hybrid and automatic: 13.2/10.4 L/100 km.*

QUALITY/RELIABILITY: Below average. Powertrain and brake repairs and trouble-shooting complaints of excessive vibration often sideline the vehicle for days at a time, and repair suggestions don't make any sense:

> Then after the shimmy vibration continued, GM Technical Assistance to the dealership stated that all the 2004 Chevrolet Silverado 1500 Series have this vibration and it is classified as "beam shake." Their solution was to put 200 pounds [90 kg] of weight over the axle in the bed of the truck, stating, "It will ride like a Cadillac." The weight did not change the vibration and now they have a GM field engineer coming to look at the truck.

GM plant workers claim that the porous frame on both Sierras and Silverados cracks behind the cabin and near the tow hook. Original-equipment springs are also failing en masse:

> The front springs on 2003 Chevrolet 1500 [Silverado] Quad Cab trucks are collapsing and GMC/Chevrolet knows about problem and says...the owners [are] responsible to fix their mistake in designing and engineering the truck. They sent out a technical service bulletin to all dealers about [the] problem and [it] says...the owners need to pay $18.00...for rubber bushing to push up spring and $380.00 in labor. It's not the company's fault. I think they need a recall and [need to] replace the springs with heavy duty springs at their cost not the owner's cost.

Owner-reported problems: Vehicle lacks power at high ambient temperatures. Excessive engine knock (faulty engine-connecting rod bolts, confirmed by internal bulletins) and exhaust system noise; diesel engine ticking noise; rough idle; and excessive oil consumption. Check Engine light often comes on and requires replacement of many emissions components before it goes out. Many complaints of rear differential pinion seal oil leaks; transmission failures; shifts for no reason from 4×4 to 4×2 or from 4×2 to 4×4 Low; delayed transmission shifting; failure to upshift; slipping in Overdrive; and shuddering in Drive or Reverse. Other problems include AC blower motor failure and wipers that don't shut off unless you replace the motor cover and controller module for $100+:

> While driving home during a rain storm my windshield wipers started to malfunction. I had them on an intermittent speed and they all of a sudden went to high. Once I was home, I attempted to turn my wipers off and they only went to low. I am unable to turn my wipers off. I had to remove the fuse. If I need my wipers I must put the fuse back in. I am working now to determine if it is the multiple function switch that has gone bad. Upon looking up data about my vehicle online I found trucks dating back to the mid 90s with the same issue.

There are also excessive steering gearbox failures; front-end vibrations felt throughout the chassis, steering, and floorboards at 100 km/h (dealers blame vibrations on Goodyear tires, but the problem persists after tires are replaced); defective lower control arm and steering bushings, suspected as the cause of excessive vibrations; premature wheel bearing wear on 2003 through 2006 models; and frequent and costly brake repairs involving rotor and pad replacement for all model years:

> I recently took the vehicle in for servicing. GM advised that it is "normal" for pads to be replaced every 15–20,000 km. I said I disagreed very strongly with this estimate, and that pads alone should last at least 25,000 km under any conditions. The GM rep also said brake rotors on these vehicles cannot be reconditioned (turning) as they are "too thin," and generally require replacement in the 50–60,000 km range. I asked if there were "known problems" with the brake system on these vehicles that contribute to these early failures. The representative said there were no known problems, just normal wear.

After taking the vehicle to a third party for inspection, I was told that the pads are finished and that all four rotors must be replaced as they are rusted through. I inspected the vehicle myself in the shop and found that the third party was completely correct in this. The net cost for this work is expected to be in the $1,600–$2,000 range. I find the thought of a $2,000 bill every three years for replacement brakes unacceptable.

And there are even more complaints that include excessive brake rumble and screech, steering-column and pump noises, an inadequate front defroster, a front-end popping noise, hubcaps that often fly off the vehicle, tires that won't stay balanced, front seats that are insufficiently padded, and poorly fitted trim and body panels. **Warranty performance:** Average. Hybrid models have not shown any serious defects so far. GM has a number of extended warranties in place to compensate owners for defects on all its vehicles, but getting information on which "secret" warranties apply and obtaining compensation isn't easy.

 SAFETY SUMMARY: Very few early versions were sold with front-seat head restraints, and the driver's head is way too close to the rear window on regular-cab versions. **Airbags:** Reports of airbags failing to deploy. **ABS:** Standard 4W; disc/drum. **Traction control:** Optional. **Head restraints F/R:** *Silverado 1500 1999:* ★; *2001–06:* ★. **Visibility F/R:** ★★★★★. **Maximum load capacity:** 1,655 lb. **Pet transport:** ★★★★★.

SAFETY COMPLAINTS: All models/years: Sudden, unintended acceleration. • Airbag fails to deploy. • Intermittent loss of power steering. • Brake failures (pedal goes to the metal with no braking effect) with ABS light lit constantly. • Brake pad failure and warped rotor. • Parking brake doesn't hold. • ABS doesn't engage; results in extended stopping distances and wheel lock-up. • Chronic stalling. • 1500 regular-cab model vibrates excessively at highway speeds ("beam shake"), rendering mirrors useless:

> The vehicle shimmied in the front and rear at 40–60 mph [64–96 km/h]. The contact was unable to see out of the rear view and passenger side mirrors due to the severe vibration. The dealership informed the contact there was a problem with the frame on the 1999–2006 model years.

1999—Inability to shut off headlights without shutting down vehicle. • Delayed transmission shifting in cold weather. • Broken spare-tire cable allows spare to fly off. **2000**—A very common problem appears to be that the rear frame breaks from the bottom up to about 5 cm (2 in.) in front of the tow hook attachment. • Transmission jumps from Park into Reverse. • Fuel line leakage. • Several cases relating to a broken power-steering pump shaft. • Rear left emergency brake shoe and drum allow salt and debris to get into drum and drum elbow. **2001**—Loose lug nuts cause left rear wheel to fall off. • Spongy brakes lead to extended stopping distances. • After driving in snow and parking vehicle, brakes won't work. • When accelerating from a stop, vehicle momentarily goes into Neutral. • Sometimes, transmission suddenly shifts from Fifth down to Third or Second gear while cruising on the highway. • Defective transmission valve body results in transmission jumping out of gear. • Truck drifts all over the highway. • Driver's seat belt causes pain in the shoulder. • Upper ball joint and right sway bar ends may be missing nuts and cotter keys. • Fuel line leak allows fuel to spray out rear. **2002**— Fire ignites in the dash. • Throttle sticks. • Chronic engine surging when braking. • Automatic transmission suddenly downshifts when accelerating, as engine surges then clunks into gear. • Passenger-side front end suddenly collapses (replaced outer tie-rod end). • Steel wheel collects water that freezes and throws wheel out of balance. • Steering-column bolt comes apart. • Interior rear-view mirror distortion. • Dimmer switch overheats. • Driver's seatback will suddenly fall backwards. • Head restraint blocks vision to right side of vehicle. **2002–04**— Steering wheel locks up while driving. **2003**—Fire ignites in the engine compartment. • Cracked transmission transfer case. • Automatic transmission slips when shifting from First to Second gear. • 4×4 shifts erratically, causing serious highway instability. • Seat belts lock up. • Tailgate pops open. **2004**— Front axle assembly collapses. • Sway bar mounting bracket breaks, causing the frame and mounting bar to come off. • Brakes fail when coasting downhill or when decelerating. • Brakes are too soft and set too close to the accelerator pedal. • Cruise control surges when going downhill. • Transmission suddenly jumps from Second gear to Reverse. • Tailgate falls apart. • Doors won't unlock in cold weather. • Driver's door window shatters for no reason. • Hood coil spring fails. • Jack slips off the vehicle. • Side mirrors constantly vibrate and are easily scratched when wiped clean. **2005**—Airbag warning light comes on, even when seat is occupied by an adult. • Sudden acceleration and chronic stalling:

> Diesel system has a problem transferring fuel into the truck for use. It runs out while the front fuel tank is still full of fuel. The fuel tank never reads over half full.

• Transmission slips when accelerating, making the truck an easy target when turning into an intersection. • Sudden drive shaft failure:

> GMC Sierra 1500 Crew Cab; while driving at interstate speed, the drive shaft fell off the vehicle and shattered. There was substantial damage to the underside of the vehicle, including muffler, yoke, heat shield, and drive shaft.

• The 4.3L engine and 4-speed automatic transmission work poorly together, constantly downshifting and gear hunting when going up an incline. • On diesels, fuel gauge and transfer pump fail repeatedly. • Rear diesel tank sprays fuel on the highway. • Vehicle is hard to move from a stopped position; feels like the rear brakes are locked up (master cylinder was changed). • Front brakes seem to stick, then overheat and catch fire. • Leaf springs aren't very durable. • Wheel hubcap nuts overheat and the hubcaps fly off. • Interior door handles easily snag clothes or purse straps when opening the door. • Front doors won't close properly. •

Inoperative power-seat keyless fob. • Outside rear-view mirrors don't show the rear bumper area when backing up and are useless when hauling a trailer. • Jack bends under weight of vehicle and collapses. • Tire-tread separation. **2006**— Erratic cruise control performance:

> When you are driving using the cruise control and start up a hill the truck slows down at least 10 miles an hour [16 km/h] then suddenly without warning the cruise control system jolts the truck forward trying to compensate for the loss of speed. This is startling to say the least. It has happened to us going up hills and around hilly curves. If I did not keep both hands on the wheel I very well could have lost control and crashed. I have met one other person who owns a Chevrolet SUV and he told me he has the same problem. He simply stated that he "just doesn't use the cruise control."

• Rear drum brakes perform poorly. • Loose steering:

> The intermediate shaft on the steering wheel column is loose. The dealer and manufacturer have told me that they are aware of this problem, but there is no fix for it. The front end on the vehicle will feel loose and bounce while driving over uneven pavement and bumps and more so while driving on freeways.

• Out-of-round General tires; Goodyear Wrangler tire-tread separation. • Front tires rub against the suspension when the steering wheel is turned. • Automatic door lock cannot be overridden. • Headliner falls down. **2006–07**—Hard-shifting manual transmission. **2007**—Passenger-side airbag is disabled even though an adult is seated. • The 5.3L V8 with Active Fuel Management will not idle properly or slow down in a timely manner. • Steering, brake lock-up. • Dash gauges are hard to read in daylight (especially the speedometer). • Truck bounces all over the road. • Failed welds under the front seat. • Windshield distortion. • Windshield wiper and washer fluid come on for no reason. • Prematurely worn Bridgestone Dueler tires. • Inoperative tire-pressure monitor system. • Cracked tow hitch receiver.

Secret Warranties/Internal Bulletins/Service Tips

All models: 1999—If the 4×4 won't engage, you may need to install a new transfer-case actuator and shift detent plunger. • Before you spend big bucks overhauling the transfer case, remember that a bump or clunk heard on acceleration may be silenced by simply changing the transfer-case fluid. • If the front wheels slip while in 4×4, consider replacing the transfer-case clutch plates and front-drive axle lubricant. • A steering-column squeak may be silenced by replacing the steering-wheel SIR module coil assembly. **1999–2000**—Wind noise coming from the side may be silenced by replacing the quarter window assembly under warranty. **1999–2003**—An exhaust moan or vibration can be corrected by installing an exhaust-system flex pipe kit. **1999–2004**—Chronic engine knock or pist on slap. • Prematurely worn and noisy brake rotors and pads may be replaced with higher-quality aftermarket parts for about half the price. • GM says in TSB

#00-05-23-005B that owners should invest in a GM mud flap kit (#15765007) to make their rear brakes last longer. Again, save money by shopping at independent retailers. • Inoperative power windows. • Remedy for steering-wheel clunk. • Suspension clunk, slap. GM will do this repair for free as "goodwill" up to 3 years/60,000 km and will offer a 50 percent refund thereafter:

SUSPENSION—REAR LEAF SPRING SLAP OR CLUNK NOISE

BULLETIN NO.: 03-03-09-002A   DATE: APRIL 29, 2004

REAR LEAF SPRING SLAP OR CLUNK NOISE (REPLACE SPRING INSERT AND INSULATOR)

1999–2004 Chevrolet Silverado 1500/2500 Series Pickups

2000–04 Chevrolet Suburban 2500 Series

2002–04 Chevrolet Avalanche 2500 Series

2003–04 Chevrolet Express 2500/3500 Vans with 8500 GVWR (RPO C5F), 8600 GVWR (RPO C6P) or 9600 GVWR (RPO C6Y)

1999–2004 GMC Sierra 1500/2500 Series Pickups

2000–04 GMC Yukon XL 2500 Series

2003–04 GMC Savana 2500/3500 Vans with 8500 GVWR (RPO C5F), 8600 GVWR (RPO C6P) or 9600 GVWR (RPO C6Y)

Some customers may comment on a rear leaf spring slap or clunk noise. This noise is most apparent when the vehicle is operated over irregular road surfaces.

1999–2005—Install an exhaust system flex pipe kit to stop an exhaust moan, vibration. **1999–2007**—Engine misfire may be due to an ECM ground terminal that has corroded with rust over time. Inspect the main engine wiring harness ground terminal (G103) for this condition. **1999–2008**—Silencing rear leaf spring noise. **2000–04**—Troubleshooting delayed gear engagement. **2000–05**—Rattle, squeak from front of vehicle. **2001**—Loose engine connecting-rod bolts may cause engine knock and complete engine failure. • Loss of turbo boost accompanied by thick black smoke. • No-starts or hard starts. • Harsh shift remedies. • When in 4×4 and in Reverse gear, engine won't go over 1000–1300 rpm. • Transmission slips when placed in 4×4. • 6-speed manual transmission clutch fluid may be contaminated by water entering through the reservoir cap. • Automatic transmission 2–4 band or 3–4 clutch damage. • Inoperative wiper motor; fuse blows repeatedly. • Windows are slow to defrost. • Steering-column lock shaft doesn't lock. **2001–02**—Troubleshooting tips to correct slow or no automatic transmission engagement, no-starts, or a blank PRNDL. **2001–03**—The torque converter relief spring and lube regulator spring may need to be changed to correct automatic transmission delayed shifts or loss of power. GM service bulletins TSB #01-07-30-043 and 03-07-30-031 explain why the automatic transmission may slip or leak. **2001–05**—Fuel gauge reads empty on trucks with a spare tank. **2002**—Check Engine light comes on as automatic transmission begins shifting erratically. • 1–2 shift shudder. • Diagnostic tips for a slipping automatic transmission. • Clunk noise from under the hood. • Clunk, bump, or squawk heard when accelerating or coming to a stop. • Shudder or vibration when accelerating from a stop. • Driveline growl or prop shaft ring noise. • Steering shaft clunk. • Noisy brakes. • Water leak at the roof centre clearance light. • Inability to control temperature setting. • Intermittent failing of the tail lights, backup lights, or trailer harness. **2003**—Harsh automatic transmission 1–2 shifting; slipping caused by a faulty pressure control solenoid (Bulletin #03-07-30-020, May 2003). **2003–04**—Remedies for buzz noise or vibration felt in floor or throttle pedal. • Inoperative front power window. **2003–05**—AC blower motor won't shut off. **2004–05**—Front end pop or snap. **2004**—Cold engine rattling. **2004–06**—Automatic transmission shudder due to water intrusion (see Tahoe section). **2005**—Poor automatic transmission performance troubleshooting tips (2005 and earlier models). • Free replacement of the powertrain/engine control module; courtesy transportation available. • Loose, rattling hubcaps. **2005–06**—Troubleshooting a steering-column shaft clunk. **2006–07**—AC doesn't cool; noisy compressor. • V8 engine oil leaks. **2007**—No-starts; loss of power. • Power-steering leaks. • Water leaks into the rear footwell area. • Steering whistle. • Exhaust system noise. • Turn signals get an increased flash rate. • Vertical lines show up on the rear door outer panel (extended-cab rear door). • Some 2007 model year 1500 Series, 4×4, regular-cab, long-box Chevrolet Silverado and GMC Sierra vehicles have an incorrect GVWR on the Certification Label, and an incorrect capacity shown on the Tire and Loading Information Label. Both of these numbers should be increased by 181 kg (400 lb). **2007–08**—Front fender buzz, rattle. *Diesel engines:* **1999–2002**—Special policy covers fuel injection pump failure up to 11 years/193,000 km. **2001**—Excessive vibration and surging. **2001–02**—"Goodwill" warranty will pay for faulty fuel injectors:

SPECIAL POLICY ADJUSTMENT (REPLACE INJECTOR)

BULLETIN NO.: 04039   **DATE: JUNE 2004**

2001–02 Silverado/Sierra (6.6L Duramax Diesel)

CONDITION: Some customers of 2001–02 model year Chevrolet Silverado and GMC Sierra vehicles, equipped with a 6.6L Duramax Diesel (RPO LB7 – VIN Code 1) engine, may experience vehicle service engine soon (SES) light illumination, low engine power, hard start, and/or fuel in crankcase, requiring injector replacement, as a result of high fuel return rates due to fuel injector body cracks or ball seat erosion.

SPECIAL POLICY ADJUSTMENT: This special policy covers the condition described above for a period of 7 years or 200,000 miles (320,000 km), whichever occurs first, from the date the vehicle was originally placed in service, regardless of ownership. The repairs will be made at no charge to the customer.

2001–04—Free O-ring replacement (see bulletin on following page). **2001–06**—Troubleshooting a turbocharger failure. **2004–07**—Noisy engine drivebelt.

DIESEL ENGINE OIL LEAK

BULLETIN NO.: 02-06-01-023C   DATE: JULY 20, 2004

OIL LEAK AT OIL COOLER TO 6.6L DIESEL ENGINE BLOCK MATING SURFACE (REPLACE O-RINGS, APPLY SEALANT)

2001–04 Chevrolet Silverado 2500/3500

2001–04 GMC Sierra 2500/3500

2003–04 Chevrolet Kodiak C4500/5500

2003–04 GMC Topkick C4500/5500

CAUSE: Minor imperfections in the engine block machined surfaces at the oil cooler interface may allow oil seepage past the oil cooler O-rings.

C/K, SIERRA, SILVERADO PROFILE

	1999	2000	2001	2002	2003	2004	2005	2006	2007
Cost Price ($) (very negotiable)									
C/K	21,735	—	—	—	—	—	—	—	—
Sierra, Silverado (25%)	21,895	22,100	22,060	22,410	23,240	24,070	24,925	24,900	24,900
Hybrid (28%)	—							—	33,025
Used Values ($)									
C/K ▲	2,000	—	—	—	—	—	—	—	—
C/K ▼	1,500	—	—	—	—	—	—	—	—
Sierra, Silverado ▲	3,500	4,000	5,000	6,500	8,500	10,000	12,500	14,000	16,000
Sierra, Silverado ▼	3,000	3,500	4,500	5,500	7,500	9,000	11,000	12,500	14,500
Hybrid ▲	—	—	—	—	—	—	—	—	25,000
Hybrid ▼	—	—	—	—	—	—	—	—	24,000
Reliability	2	2	2	2	2	3	3	3	3
Crash Safety (F)	—	—	—	—	—	4	4	4	5
Ext. cab	—	3	3	3	4	4	4	—	5
Side	—	—	—	—	—	4	4	4	5
Offset	2	2	2	2	2	2	2	2	—
Rollover	—	—	—	—	—	4	4	4	4
Ext. cab	—	3	3	3	4	4	4	4	4
Ext. cab 4×4	—	3	3	3	3	4	4	4	4

General Motors/Isuzu

CANYON, COLORADO, S-10, SONOMA, T-10/HOMBRE ★★

RATING: *Canyon, Colorado:* Below Average (2004–09). GM's 2009 model redesign isn't likely to improve overall performance or reliability much. Furthermore, Isuzu's withdrawal from North America this year will depress resale prices and complicate servicing. *S-10, Sonoma, T-10:* Average (2000–04); Below Average (1996–99); Not Recommended (1986–95). These pickups are no match for the Japanese competition in almost every category. Like GM's full-sized pickups, the Sonoma hasn't shown much improvement during its 15-year run. *Space Cab, Hombre:* Below Average (1989–2002). The Space Cab was re-designated the Hombre for the 1997 model year. **Strong points:** A well-appointed pickup, good V6 acceleration, reliable and smooth-shifting automatic transmission, and user-friendly controls and instruments. Extended cab offers a spacious interior and storage space, airbag cut-off switch, easy loading and unloading, and one of the quietest interiors you'll find. **Weak points:** Wimpy 4-cylinder engine, harsh ride, poor handling, difficult entry and exit on the 4×4 version, limited rear-seat room, and an extraordinary number of safety-related defects reported to NHTSA. Plastic door panels make for a tacky-looking cabin, awkward rear access almost makes the optional third door a necessity, and jump seats in the extended cab are tiny and uncomfortable. Resale value is low, and Isuzu servicing will soon dry up. *Colorado:* No outside key door lock. **New for 2008:** *Canyon, Colorado:* Standard halogen foglamps; a redesign is planned for the 2009 model year.

> ### 2008 CANYON, COLORADO TECHNICAL DATA
>
> **POWERTRAIN (4×2/PART-TIME 4×4)**
> Engines: 2.9L 4-cyl. (185 hp) • 3.7L 5-cyl. (242 hp); Transmissions: 5-speed man. • 4-speed auto.
> **DIMENSION/CAPACITY (REGULAR CAB/ EXTENDED CAB)**
> Passengers: 3/3; Wheelbase: 126.0 in.; H: 62.0/L: 207.0/W: 69.0 in.; Headroom F/R: 5.0/3.0 in.; Legroom F/R: 42.0/26.0 in.; Cargo volume: 26.8 cu. ft.; Fuel tank: 74L/regular; Tow limit: 4,000 lb.; Load capacity: 1,125 lb.; GVWR: 4,700–5,300 lb.; Turning circle: 48.0 ft.; Box length: 6.0/7.5 ft.; Ground clearance: 8.0 in.; Weight: 4,270 lb.

MODEL HISTORY: These mostly identical pickups (they vary somewhat in trim and equipment) are compact, light-duty vehicles that are available in regular and extended-cab versions. For easier entry and exit, a driver-side third door is available on the extended-cab pickups.

S-10, Sonoma, T-10

The attractively styled S-series pickups do have some good points, like a cheap price and user-friendly controls. But the advantages have to be weighed against some rather serious shortcomings: a wimpy 4-cylinder engine (also a Canyon and Colorado problem), a clunky and quirky automatic transmission, difficult entry and exit, a harsh ride, and excessive gas consumption. S-10s don't offer any space or load capacity advantages over their Japanese counterparts.

1999—Extreme Sport package replaces the SS, more automatic transmission enhancements are carried out to improve sealing and durability, and a new AutoTrac electronic push-button transfer case is added. The following year, GM feels compelled to upgrade the engine (same horsepower, though), manual transmission, ABS, and exhaust system again. **2000**—Trucks carrying the ZR2 package are given a new axle ratio for better acceleration. **2001**—A new four-door crew-cab 4×4 version is offered, with enough room for five (small) passengers, plus an InstaTrac 4×4 system and SLS trim. Powertrain upgrades include an advanced control module for the V6 and Flex-Fuel capability for the 4-cylinder. There are also new aluminum wheels with the sport suspension, and programmable power door locks. **2002**—Standard air conditioning and a long cargo bed option (initially dropped, then reinstated). **2003**—A new fuel injection system and a minor face-lift. **2004**—Canyon and Colorado arrive.

Hombre

This Isuzu-built pickup, once sold through GM's short-lived Passport division, is barely acceptable basic transportation in small-truck guise. Its main drawbacks are underperforming engines, weak brakes, spotty reliability, and hard-to-find parts.

The standard engines are weak 2.2L and 2.3L 4-cylinders; if you intend to do hauling or light towing, look for a version equipped with the optional 2.6L 4-banger mated to a 5-speed manual or 4-speed automatic transmission. For off-roading, the 4×4 is the best choice, with its GM-built V6 coupled to a 5-speed manual gearbox.

The 1997–2000 Hombre is essentially a Chevrolet S pickup with Isuzu sheet metal; quality control is only marginally better than what you'd find with GM's homegrown counterpart. Initially, the only engine choice was GM's anemic 4-banger. The 1999–2000 model years saw few changes from the two previous years, as these vehicles remained near mirror images of GM's S-10, lacking some configurations such as V6-equipped regular cabs and manual-transmission-equipped 4×2 V6 extended cabs.

Canyon, Colorado

Replacing the S-10, these small light-duty pickups sacrifice hauling capacity for good fuel economy and a softer, quieter ride. They are slightly larger than the S-10, and come with 4×2 or 4×4 and in regular-cab, extended-cab, and crew-cab configurations. Three suspension packages are available: standard, sport, and off-road.

The 3.7L inline 5-cylinder is derived from GM's 4.2L inline-six, first used in the 2002 Chevrolet TrailBlazer. Dual balance shafts within each engine help eliminate vibrations, while variable valve timing improves idle smoothness, reduces emissions, and increases gas mileage. Other features include a shift-on-the-fly 4×4 system, an optional locking differential, and traction control. Both mid-sized pickups include federally mandated child seat anchors, four-door child locks, front-seat airbag Off switches for regular cab models, and the same three-point safety belts found in automobiles. On the minus side, no V6 is available, towing capacity is limited, and the 5-cylinder engine is unproven.

COST ANALYSIS: The base 2008 Colorado costs $21,135, versus $15,850 (U.S.) for the same truck bought in the States. A stripped-down commercial variant costs a couple thousand dollars less, but it's hard to find because dealers often load these pickups with thousands of dollars' worth of non-essential options. A 4×4 costs almost $4,000 more. **Best alternatives:** Remember, there are many overlapping features between GMC, Chevrolet, and Isuzu pickups. Also, consider the Mazda B-series, Nissan Frontier, and Toyota Tacoma. **Rebates:** Up to $5,000 discounts and low-cost financing on the 2008s; 2009s will be carried over without a price increase and subject to similar discounts and financing terms by the summer of 2009. **Delivery/PDI:** $1,200. **Warranty:** Bumper-to-bumper 3 years/ 60,000 km; powertrain 5 years/160,000 km; rust perforation 6 years/160,000 km. **Supplementary warranty:** An extended powertrain warranty would be a good idea. **Options:** The V6 is a prerequisite if the vehicle is equipped with an automatic transmission—a choice not available with the Canyon and Colorado. **Depreciation:** Faster than average. **Insurance cost:** Average. **Annual maintenance cost:** Average. **Parts supply/cost:** Japanese-sourced parts can be hard to find and are fairly costly. **Highway/city fuel economy:** *4×2 and 2.2L:* 8.5/12.4 L/100 km; *4×2 and 4.3L:* 10.1/14.2 L/100 km; *4×4 and 4.3L:* 10.6/14.7 L/100 km. There are many complaints that actual fuel consumption on the Canyon and Colorado is far more than the above figures show.

 QUALITY/RELIABILITY: Average. *Canyon, Colorado:* General Tire sidewall blowouts, water leaks, and a bad odour from the AC. On 2003 and earlier models, owners complain of engine knock, automatic transmission malfunctions, wire harness melting, expensive oxygen sensor replacements, electrical shorts, upper control-arm bushings that rapidly wear out, worn brake rotors and pads, power-window failures, and inaccurate fuel gauges. Fit and finish isn't as good as with most other pickups; there's excessive wind noise, especially with the Colorado; and the thickness of the paint coat varies considerably, and paint will chip easily (the worst is Midnight Blue). Watch out for Colorado and Canyon engine failures, writes one *Lemon-Aid* reader from North Bay, Ontario:

> I purchased a 2004 GMC Canyon SLE Crew Cab on August 14, 2004. In October, I noticed the engine light come on flashing, indicating an engine misfire. After hooking a recorder to it, the dealer was able to see what was happening. GM advised them to replace the valve springs. This took one month to complete between Dec. 15 and Jan. 15.

Problem was not solved and it took a replaced O$_2$ sensor and a new intake manifold. Still the light came on. This time I called the customer care at GM, it helped in that the next solution was "reprogramming the computer," since I complained that I was tired of seeing the engine taken apart and [the repairs] not solving anything.

This repair lasted a month, and then the light came back with conviction. I turned the truck over on May 28 to have a new cylinder head installed, and also all new valves.

Colorado: Fuel lines are easily cracked; excessive vibration when underway; side-door water leaks; the lumbar support may be too high for some people; lots of squeaks and rattles; and body panels are very thin. **Warranty performance:** Below average.

 SAFETY SUMMARY: The 2008 crashworthiness ratings are identical to the 2007 scores. The lack of head restraints on early models is a safety hazard. The most frequent failures are sudden, unintended acceleration; head restraints that can't be adjusted and are too low to be effective; airbags that fail to deploy; blown engine head gaskets; an ABS that doesn't brake but does break; intermittent windshield wiper failures (they also often stop in the middle of the windshield); tires that rub the front wheelwell when turning; and spare tires that fall off on the highway. Most 2007 models earned four-star crashworthiness scores in front, side, and rollover crash tests; however, the 2007 four-door Canyon and Colorado earned five stars for occupant protection in a frontal collision. **Airbags:** The airbag cut-off switch permits the use of a child safety seat up front. **ABS:** Standard 4W; disc/drum. **Safety belt pretensioners:** Front. **Head restraints F/R:** *S10 1999:* ★★★★; *2001–03:* ★★★★/★; *2004–08:* ★★. **Visibility F/R: ★★★★★/★★. Maximum load capacity:** *2001 S-10 LS V6:* 1,000 lb.; *2007 Canyon/Colorado V6:* 1,125 lb. **Pet transport: ★★★★★.**

SAFETY COMPLAINTS: All models/years: No airbag deployment. • Chronic stalling. • Transmission and differential failures. • ABS failures. • Premature front pad wear and rotor warping. • Frequent rear brake failures. • Plastic gas tank is easily punctured. • Driver's seat slides back and forth while driving. *S-10, Sonoma, T-10:* **1999**—Transmission lock-up, poor braking performance, and headlight failures. *Canyon, Colorado:* **2004**—Engine surging. • Brake pedal goes to floor without effect. • Tailgate falls down while vehicle is underway. • Transmission failures. • Excessive on-road vibration. **2006**—Passenger side airbag is disabled even though an average-sized passenger is seated. *Canyon:* **2005**—Front wheels suddenly lock up while vehicle is driving at highway speeds. • Excessive vehicle shaking while underway. • Windshield cracks easily. **2006**—One vehicle's 5-cylinder engine had to be replaced after only 80,000 km. • Gas and brake pedals are mounted too close together. • Frequent electrical malfunctions affecting turn signals and interior lights. *Colorado:* **2005**—Complete brake failure. • Rear drum brakes fail at 10,000 km; pistons blow out of cylinders. • Rear drive shaft breaks off at universal joint while vehicle is underway. • Many rear main seal leaks. • ABS doesn't work properly. • Poor headlight illumination. **2006**—Chronic engine misfire. • Cruise control does not hold the set speed when going downhill. • 5-cylinder engine suddenly shuts down. • Column shifter won't go into the Park position. • Brake failures. • Passenger-side door does not have a keyed lock:

> The contact stated the only way to unlock the passenger side door of the vehicle is to crawl in on the driver's side. There is not a lock cylinder on the vehicle and it is not equipped with keyless entry. This was not explained when the vehicle was purchased.

• Left rear leaf assembly (suspension) fractures, sending vehicle out of control. • Premature wear of the General Ameri GS60 tire tread. • Rear head restraints obstruct vision. **2007**—Accelerator pedal sticks. • With cruise control engaged, the truck will suddenly lose power and stall. • Transmission is hard to shift into Reverse. • Dash reflection onto the windshield and high head restraints obstruct vision. • Parking brake release handle falls off. • Headlight separates from its mounting.

Secret Warranties/Internal Bulletins/Service Tips

S-10, Sonoma, T-10: **1999**—Cure AC odours by installing GM's cooling coil coating kit. • Incorrect fuel gauge readings can be corrected by reprogramming the VCM module. **1999–2001**—Hood hinge rattling. • Transmission stuck in Third gear, MIL comes on, and instrument cluster is inoperative. **1999–2002**—Paint delamination, peeling, or fading. • A rough idle or lit Check Engine light may only signal the need to clean the fuel injection system. • AWD malfunctions. **1999–2004**—Vehicle stalls and won't restart. • Vehicle appears to be out of fuel, but the fuel gauge reads above Empty. **2000–03**—Hard starts, poor idle, and misfires. **2001**—Engine-oil cooler hose is incorrectly oriented. • Harsh shifts. • Automatic transmission 2–4 band or 3–4 clutch damage. • Security light flashes. • Engine stalls or won't start. • Rear suspension popping noise when going over a bump or when turning. • Lights flicker while driving at night. *Hombre:* **All years:** Replace the distributor seal to stop engine oil from leaking into the distributor. • Knocking from the steering column when the wheel is turned from side to side can be fixed with a steering shaft repair kit (TSB #8-97077-575-0) and rubber boot (TSB #8-97079-655-0). • TSB #SB96-11-L002 suggests the front fender inner liners be replaced to prevent ice buildup around the lower door-to-fender area, which can damage the door and fender. *Canyon, Colorado:* **2004**—Automatic transmission slipping. **2004–05**—Popping, snapping noise coming from the exhaust system. • AC hum, whistle, hiss. • Premature front tire wear. **2004–07**—GM says it's "normal" to hear a shift clunk. (Sigh...) **2005**—Harsh 1–2 upshifts. **2005–07**—Excessive rear brake grab, lock-up. • Sunroof water leaks. **2007**—Driver-seat/floor creak, squeak.

CANYON, COLORADO, S-10, SONOMA, T-10, HOMBRE PROFILE

	1999	2000	2001	2002	2003	2004	2005	2006	2007
Cost Price ($) (negotiable)									
S-10	16,410	16,495	18,217	17,060	17,870	—	—	—	—
T-10 4×4	21,370	21,170	26,097	—	—	—	—	—	—
Sonoma	16,410	16,495	17,025	17,060	17,870	—	—	—	—
Hombre	13,995	14,095	—	—	—	—	—	—	—
Hombre 4×4	22,961	26,995	—	—	—	—	—	—	—
Canyon/Colorado (20%)	—	—	—	—	—	16,995	17,195	17,195	20,995
Used Values ($)									
S-10 ▲	1,500	2,500	3,000	3,500	5,000	—	—	—	—
S-10 ▼	1,000	2,000	2,500	3,000	3,500	—	—	—	—
T-10 4×4 ▲	2,500	4,000	5,000	—	—	—	—	—	—
T-10 4×4 ▼	2,000	3,500	4,000	—	—	—	—	—	—
Sonoma ▲	2,500	3,000	3,500	4,000	5,000	—	—	—	—
Sonoma ▼	2,000	2,500	3,000	3,500	4,000	—	—	—	—
Hombre ▲	1,500	2,500	—	—	—	—	—	—	—
Hombre ▼	1,000	2,000	—	—	—	—	—	—	—
Hombre 4×4 ▲	2,000	2,500	—	—	—	—	—	—	—
Hombre 4×4 ▼	1,500	2,000	—	—	—	—	—	—	—
Canyon/Colorado ▲	—	—	—	—	—	6,000	8,000	9,500	14,000
Canyon/Colorado ▼	—	—	—	—	—	5,000	6,500	8,500	12,000
Reliability									
S-10, Sonoma, T-10	1	1	2	2	2	—	—	—	—
Hombre	4	4	4	4	4	—	—	—	—
Canyon/Colorado	—	—	—	—	—	3	3	3	3
Crash Safety (F)									
S-10 4×2	—	3	3	3	3	—	—	—	—
S-10 Ext.	2	2	2	2	2	—	—	—	—
S-10 4×4	—	—	2	—	—	—	—	—	—
Sonoma	2	3	3	—	—	—	—	—	—
Sonoma Ext.	—	2	2	—	—	—	—	—	—
Hombre	—	3	—	—	—	—	—	—	—
Canyon/Colorado	—	—	—	—	—	4	4	5	5
Side									
S-10 4×2	—	4	4	4	4	—	—	—	—
S-10 Ext.	3	3	3	3	3	—	—	—	—
S-10 4×4	—	—	3	—	—	—	—	—	—
Sonoma	—	4	—	—	—	—	—	—	—
Sonoma Ext.	—	3	—	—	—	—	—	—	—
Hombre	—	4	—	—	—	—	—	—	—
Canyon/Colorado	—	—	—	—	—	4	5	5	5
Offset	2	2	2	2	2	5	5	5	5
Rollover	—	—	3	3	3	4	4	4	

Note: The 2007 Canyon/Colorado price jump reflects the absence of a Commercial version.

All ratings on a numbered scale where 5 is good and 1 is bad. See page 217 for a more detailed description.

Honda

RIDGELINE ★★★★★

best buy

RATING: Recommended (2007–09); Above Average (2006). Honda's first-year vehicles and redesigns haven't been as glitch-prone as Detroit's new products, Toyota's redesigned 2004 Sienna, or Nissan's revamped Quest. **Strong points:** Soft prices due to slumping sales. Very smooth engine performance with exceptionally quick, carlike throttle response; agile handling and enhanced ride comfort, thanks to a front and rear independent suspension; good braking. Uses a smooth and reliable 5-speed automatic transmission borrowed from the Pilot; extra traction can be obtained by using a dash-mounted button to lock in power to the rear wheels. Well appointed, with plenty of innovative and easily accessed cabin storage compartments; large, user-friendly cabin instruments and controls; plenty of rear legroom; rear seats can be stowed vertically, creating extra storage space. The versatile box has a trunk built into the floor, accessed through a tailgate that swings out as well as down; the bed surface has a strong plastic protective layer with tie-down hooks and tire indents to carry motorcycles or an ATV; and there's no rear wheelwell intrusion into the bed area. A five-star safety rating for both front- and side-impact occupant protection, and a four-star score for rollover protection. Excellent fit and finish; unibody construction reduces body flexing and creaking, keeping road noise to a

2008 RIDGELINE TECHNICAL DATA

POWERTRAIN (4×2/PART-TIME 4×4)
Engine: 3.5L V6 (247 hp); Transmission: 5-speed auto.

DIMENSION/CAPACITY
Passengers: 2/3; Wheelbase: 122.0 in.; H: 70.3/L: 207.0/W: 77.8 in.; Headroom F/R: 6.5/4.5 in.; Legroom F/R: 42.0/28.0 in.; Cargo volume: 26.2 cu. ft.; Fuel tank: 83L/regular; Tow limit: 5,000 lb.; Load capacity: 1,549 lb.; GVWR: 6,050 lb.; Turning circle: 42.6 ft.; Box length: 5.0 ft.; Ground clearance: 8.2 in.; Weight: 4,550 lb.

minimum. Good quality control. **Weak points:** Overpriced for a compact truck. Acceleration is a bit slower than with competitive V6-equipped pickups; lacks low-range gearing; low-speed steering is a bit slow; not built for heavy-duty hauling or serious off-roading; excessive body lean when cornering. Rear visibility is hampered by the sloping sides and small rear window, rear-seat padding is thin and seatback is too upright, and door openings are a bit narrow. **New for 2008:** Nothing important. Although a hybrid may be offered for the 2009 model year, there aren't any major changes planned until 2011.

MODEL HISTORY: The Ridgeline, built in Alliston, Ontario, is Honda's first truck—a crew cab cloned from the company's Pilot sport-utility. It's about as long as the Explorer Sport Trac and comes with lots of standard features like all-wheel drive, a 5-speed automatic, Vehicle Stability Assist (electronic stability control) with traction control, ABS brakes, front side airbags and full-length side curtain airbags with rollover sensor, and power locks, windows, and mirrors.

COST ANALYSIS: $35,820 for an LX 4×2 in Canada; $28,000 (U.S.) for a 4×2 in the States. Poor sales mean lower prices by the winter of 2008. **Best alternatives:** Consider the Mazda B-series or Nissan Frontier. **Rebates:** $3,000–$5,000 discounts, $1,500 rebates, plus zero percent financing. **Delivery/ PDI:** $1,540. **Warranty:** Bumper-to-bumper 3 years/60,000 km; powertrain 5 years/100,000 km, and rust perforation 3 years/unlimited km. **Supplementary warranty:** Not needed. **Options:** This well-appointed truck doesn't require anything extra. Honda's extra-cost bed extender needs to be flipped out whenever the trunk lid is opened. The Music Link iPod adaptor may be a waste of money and unduly distracting:

> The Honda Music Link iPod adapter was a waste of $475.00. The Honda Music Link is almost impossible to use and is actually a hazard to safe driving. The software requires significant user intervention and distracts the driver's attention from safely operating the vehicle. These sentiments are well documented at *www.nuxx.net/hondamusiclink. html* and *digg.com/apple/honda_music_link_ipod_adapter_review.*

Depreciation: Higher than average because of the Ridgeline's high MSRP. **Insurance cost:** Fairly expensive to insure. **Annual maintenance cost:** Average. **Parts supply/cost:** Parts are in short supply, but parts costs are reasonable. **Highway/city fuel economy:** 10.1/14.4 L/100 km.

 QUALITY/RELIABILITY: Better-than-average assembly and component quality. Getting "goodwill" free repairs is like pulling teeth, however. **Owner-reported problems:** Hesitation when accelerating. Fuel pump, tie-rod, and suspension strut failures. Many complaints of water leaking into the cabin. Windshield stress cracks; windshield wipers cannot handle heavy snow. Odometer registers more mileage than actually travelled. Truck bed is easily scratched, contrary to advertising. Early Ridgelines don't support trailers with surge brakes; the trailer cannot be backed up. When pulling a trailer, the rear axle can collapse. Cracked wheel rims. Driver's power seat "rocks"; it costs $1,200 to replace the seat and mechanism.

SAFETY SUMMARY: The 2008 models' crashworthiness ratings are identical to the 2007s' scores. **Airbags:** There have been reports of airbags failing to deploy. **ABS:** Standard 2W, 4W. **Safety belt pretensioners:** Standard. **Traction control:** Optional. **Visibility F/R:** ★★★★. **Pet transport:** ★★★★★.

SAFETY COMPLAINTS: 2006—Fire originating in the AC. • Airbags fail to deploy, and seat belt malfunctions in a collision. • Some child safety seats cannot be installed. • Accelerator surging. • Engine shuts down suddenly; must be replaced. • Fuel tank is easily punctured by road debris. • Parking lights will not stay lit. • Tire jack will not raise vehicle high enough to change a tire. **2007**—Complete separation of side wall tread from Michelin tires. • Child safety seat tether strap fails to lock. • Gas and brake pedals mounted too close together.

Secret Warranties/Internal Bulletins/Service Tips

2006–07—Automatic transmission is hard to shift into Fourth gear. • Vehicle pulls, drifts to one side. • Drivetrain ping, squeal, or rattle upon light acceleration. • Rear differential noise, judder on turns. • Steering wheel, interior squeaking noise.

RIDGELINE PROFILE

	2006	2007
Cost Price ($) (negotiable)		
LX (25%)	35,200	35,600
EX-L (28%)	39,700	40,300
Used Values ($)		
LX ▲	22,000	25,000
LX ▼	20,000	23,000
EX-L ▲	25,000	29,000
EX-L ▼	23,000	27,000
Reliability	4	5
Crash Safety (F)	5	5
Side	5	5
Rollover	4	4

Nissan

★ best buy ★ **FRONTIER** ★★★★★

RATING: Recommended (2006–09); Above Average (1985–2005). Nissan has hit a home run with its Frontier. Year after year, this "Baby Titan" pickup performs well without any major complications, bypassing the serious design glitches found with earlier Titans. It's as good as the Mazda and Toyota competition, and better than Chrysler's over-hyped and fuel-guzzling semi-Hemi, Ford's quality-challenged Ranger, and GM's puny, Isuzu-bred Canyon/Colorado munchkins and Silverado/Sierra hulks. Let's face it, the pre-2005 models are mediocre performers; nevertheless, they are reliable, relatively inexpensive, competent for light chores, easy to maintain, and fun to drive. **Strong points:** *2005–08:* Better-performing, more powerful engines (especially with the V6 and vehicles equipped with a manual transmission); the new 5-speed automatic transmission shifts more smoothly than the previous 4-speed, and it conserves fuel; nice handling; very comfortable ride up front; fairly reliable; and a high resale value. *2004 and earlier models:* Standard four-wheel ABS on some models; a user-friendly interior layout; extremely reliable; an acceptable ride over smooth roads; and reasonably good handling. **Weak points:** The 4.0L will run on regular fuel (wink, wink; nudge, nudge), but 91-octane is recommended. Test-drive your choice for engine performance—Nissan has been notorious for overrating their engines.

2008 FRONTIER TECHNICAL DATA

POWERTRAIN (REAR-DRIVE/PART-TIME 4×4)

Engines: 2.5L 4-cyl. (152 hp) • 4.0L V6 (265 hp); Transmissions: 5-speed man. • 6-speed man. • 5-speed auto. OD

DIMENSION/CAPACITY

Passengers: 2/3; Wheelbase: 126.0 in.; H: 68.0/L: 206.0/W: 73.0 in.; Headroom F/R: 3.0/3.5 in.; Legroom F/R: 40.0/27.0 in.; Cargo volume: 27.0 cu. ft.; Fuel tank: 60L/regular; Tow limit: 6,100 lb.; Load capacity: 1,160 lb.; GVWR: 4,701–5,202 lb.; Turning circle: 46.0 ft.; Box length: 4.6/6.2 ft.; Ground clearance: 8.5 in.; Weight: 4,650 lb.

2005–08: Powertrain glitches, poor steering feedback, a cheap-looking interior, and limited rear seating on base models. *2004 and earlier models:* Poor acceleration (4-cylinder); lots of body lean when cornering; mediocre braking; small cargo bed on the Crew Cab; few standard features; drive shaft carrier bearing failures on earlier models; and lots of engine, wind, and tire noise. Automatic transmission shifter obstructs view of the climate controls and blocks access to the wiper switch; choppy ride over uneven terrain ("rear-end hop") is accentuated with an empty load; slow, vague steering offers little feedback. Difficult rear entry and exit (King Cab); limited rear legroom on the hard rear bench seat; low seats make the height-adjustment feature essential for many drivers; and the King Cab's rear jump seat is laughably small. The cabin looks like plastic central, and many gauges are too recessed to be easily read. Mediocre fuel economy on 2001–04 models. Triple-whammy safety complaints: sudden acceleration, brake failures, and Firestone tire defects. **New for 2008:** Nothing of importance; a redesign is scheduled for the 2010 models.

MODEL HISTORY: The 2006–09 Frontier is a significantly improved pickup that's larger, more powerful, easier to handle, and safer than previous models. Did somebody mention power? The entry-level King Cab carries a 152-hp 2.5L 4-cylinder engine, while most other Frontiers use a 265-hp 4.0L V6. A 5-speed automatic replaced the 4-speed. A new dual-range 4×4 set-up with shift-on-the-fly electronic control, rack-and-pinion steering, and a slew of handling improvements was also carried over this year. Occupant crash protection is improved on the 2005–07 models through the use of new front side airbags and optional side curtain airbags triggered by rollover sensors.

Frontier pickups have always been reliable and versatile haulers. Most models initially used a lethargic 143-hp 2.4L 4-cylinder, supplemented by a better-performing 180-hp 3.3L V6 and a barely-worth-the-trouble, premium-fuelled, and temperamental supercharged 210-hp V6 variant. The King Cab V6 addition gave these pickups the power boost they lacked in the past. ABS is standard on the rear wheels and optional on all four wheels. It's standard, however, on all recent 4×4s and Crew Cabs and on the Desert Runner.

Introduced in 1985, these pickups perform better, are more comfortable, and aren't as rust-prone as their Datsun predecessors. The different 4-cylinder engines offered through the years have all provided adequate power and reasonable reliability. Although the powerful 6-cylinder is more fuel-thirsty, it's the engine of choice for maximum hauling and off-roading versatility.

You won't have to look far to find a reasonably priced used Nissan pickup. These small pickups, like Mazda's trucks, didn't cost much when they were new, and their used prices have drifted downward accordingly. On newer models, though, you'll find prices have firmed up considerably because of the general popularity of 2- and 3-year-old crew-cab pickups and downsized sport-utilities. Depending on the year, you'll find a standard 4- or 5-speed manual or an optional 3- or 4-speed automatic. Later 4-speed automatics have a fuel-saving lock-up torque converter, but a manual transmission will get the most power and economy out of these motors. The 4×4 option is available with either manual or automatic hubs. The manual version is a pain because you have to stop and turn the hubs. The automatic isn't much better because it can't be engaged above 50 km/h, and to disengage it you have to stop and back up a metre or two. These pickups handle impressively well and have firm but reasonably comfortable rides, although some owners say the bucket seats fit only bucket bottoms. The King Cab is a must for tall drivers or those who require extra interior storage space.

1999—King Cabs get more powerful V6 engines and a host of other standard and optional features. **2000**—A Crew Cab model is given a full-sized forward-hinged fourth door and a short bed. **2001**—A supercharged 210-hp V6 on SE King Cabs and Crew Cabs along with a slight restyling and standard 17-inch wheels. Other additions: a new instrument cluster, interior upgrades, and a security system. **2002**—The regular-cab model is dropped, Crew Cabs are offered with a long bed, and all pickups get a restyled interior. **2003**—6-cylinder engines for the 4×4s, Crew Cabs get 10 more horses, and more options are added, like a tire-pressure monitor and anti-skid/traction control. **2006**—Redesigned.

COST ANALYSIS: The price for the base 2008 front-drive XE King Cab is $24,448, and $29,748 will get you the SE 4×4. Prices are soft, and all models will be discounted by about 20 percent as winter 2008 approaches and truck sales continue to sour. In the States, expect to pay $16,250 and $21,000, respectively. Don't waste money on a warmed-over 2009 model. A good used choice would be the much-improved second-series 2006 version ($13,000–$14,000). **Best alternatives:** Some other small pickups you might want to consider are the Mazda B-series and Toyota Tacoma. **Rebates:** $2,500 discounts or rebates plus zero percent financing. **Delivery/PDI:** $1,350. **Warranty:** Bumper-to-bumper 3 years/60,000 km; powertrain 5 years/100,000 km; rust perforation 5 years/unlimited km. **Supplementary warranty:** An extended warranty isn't needed. **Options:** Consider a limited slip differential, four-wheel ABS, and running boards. Don't go for the Off-Road Package unless you crave a bouncier ride. **Depreciation:** Slower than average. **Insurance cost:** Average. **Parts supply/cost:** These trucks have been around for decades with few design changes, so parts are widely available and relatively inexpensive. **Annual maintenance cost:** Below-average maintenance costs; the simple design makes for easy servicing by any independent garage. **Highway/city fuel economy:** *2.4L and auto.: 9.1/12.0 L/100 km; 3.3L V6 and 4×4: 11.5/15.3 L/100 km.*

QUALITY/RELIABILITY: Assembly and component quality are above average. Fortunately, Nissan products are generally so well made that they don't need lots of warranty work. But when they do, owners report that the company's customer relations staff in Canada isn't all that sensitive to their needs. For example, in several instances, Nissan Canada and its Infiniti spin-off have refused to recognize "goodwill" programs detailed in the company's U.S. service bulletins. Their reasoning? Apparently, Nissan Canada isn't obligated to give the same treatment to Canadian owners. Hmmm…let's see Nissan put that in their TV ads! **Owner-reported problems:** Engine exhaust intake manifold failures have been common; drive shaft and ball joint defects cause excessive vibration; minor trim and accessory defects; premature front-brake wear; and electrical short circuits.

ROAD PERFORMANCE: Acceleration/torque: The fuel-sipping 4-cylinder engine is adequate for light-duty use. However, add an automatic transmission, and you'll wish you had the V6. The supercharged V6 is an impressive performer that's less noisy than the 4-banger. **Transmission:** Easy-shifting manual transmission, and the electronically controlled automatic transaxle is both smooth and predictable. **Steering:** Acceptable, but not very responsive or precise; the 2005 model corrects this problem. **Routine handling:** Average for a truck; improved with the upgraded suspension added in 1998 and steering/suspension enhancements found on the 2005s. Firmer ride with long wheelbase and supercharged models. **Emergency handling:** Better than average, in spite of the pickup's heft and size. **Braking:** Mediocre (100–0 km/h: 44 m).

SAFETY SUMMARY: The 2008 models' crashworthiness scores were identical to the 2007s' scores. **Airbags:** There have been reports of airbags failing to deploy, or deploying when they shouldn't, resulting in severe injuries. **ABS:** Standard 2W, 4W. **Safety belt pretensioners:** Standard. **Traction control:** Optional. **Head restraints F/R:** *1999:* ★★★; *2001:* ★★★; *2002–04:* ★★; *2005–08:* ★. **Visibility F/R:** ★★★★★. **Pet transport:** ★★★★★.

SAFETY COMPLAINTS: 1999—Rattles inside steering column. • Exhaust leak under driver's seat. • Drive shaft failure. • Tires lose traction on wet roads. **1999–2000**—Brake pedal goes to floor without braking. • Stalling at full throttle. • Severe vibration during acceleration or while pulling a load. **2000**—Under-hood fire. • Sudden acceleration. • Sheared front-end bushing bolt. • Brake master cylinder failure. • Faulty drive shaft carrier bearing; Nissan's "fix" is inadequate. • When parked on an incline, emergency brake fails and truck rolls away. • Too-soft suspension causes serious swaying. **2001**—Front passenger seat belt can't be pulled out for usage (on national back order). • High idle at low speeds with clutch depressed. • Fuel overflows from filler neck. • Brakes lack sufficient hydraulic pressure to stop vehicle. • Blocked cowl vent restricts fresh air flow. **2001–02**—Airbags fail to deploy. **2002**—Automatic transmission jumps out of Park into Reverse. • Leaking fuel tank. • Brake failure. • ABS light comes on for no reason. • Sudden loss of power caused by defective oxygen sensor or Nissan speed limiter kicking in. • Controller fuse blows repeatedly, shutting vehicle down. • Gas and brake pedal set too close together. • Tail light fills with water. • Defective side walls on General Grabber tires. **2003**—Sudden, unintended acceleration when brakes are applied. • Engine has to be shut down to turn off AC if defroster is engaged. **2004**—Truck slips out of Park and rolls downhill. • Excessive vibration caused by corroded upper and lower ball joints. **2005**—Truck won't start because of a corroded fuel-sending unit. • Power-assisted driver-side mirror can't be adjusted to eliminate a blind spot. • Original-equipment tires wear out prematurely (tread peels away). • Tailgate falls off due to its poor design. • Tailgate gap allows sand or other fine material to spew out. • Water leaking into the tail light can cause the truck to shut down. **2006**—Rollover airbags deploy for no reason:

> As a result of Nissan's design, a side air bag sensor, 2 rollover air bag assemblies, 2 seat belt assemblies, a headliner and plastic trim items were replaced. The old parts, exclusive of the headliner, are available. On the rear quarter panel, the vehicle is labeled "off road" and is clearly intended for that use according to Nissan's advertising. Nissan's own statement proves that their control system for rollover airbags is defective in that their rollover air bags may deploy because the "signal which is sent to the sensor in some underbody impacts is very similar to the signal sent to the sensor in rollover situations."

• Powertrain transfer case sticks in 4×4. • Gas and brake pedals are mounted too close together. • Right front wheel falls off due to the shearing of the wheel lug nuts. • Rear brake assembly bolts fall out, and the disc caliper flies off. • Transmission doesn't hold a vehicle stopped on an incline. • Many complaints of loss of steering due to defective steering-column bearing. **2007**—Engine surges when brakes are applied. • Poor braking causes excessive stopping distance. • Steering pulls suddenly to the right; steering doesn't return to centre. • Electronic computer module failure causes the vehicle to suddenly shut down.

Secret Warranties/Internal Bulletins/Service Tips

1999—An easy fuel gauge fix is outlined in TSB #NTB99-064. **1999–2000**—A pop or clunking noise is addressed in TSB #NTB00-075. **1999–2001**—Repair tips for a cracked exhaust manifold. **1999–2002**—Troubleshooting tips for noisy, hard transfer-case shifting. • Loss of supercharged engine power. • Surging, no automatic transmission upshifts. • Steering pull during braking. • MIL may malfunction. • Silencing bearing noise from the transfer-case area. • Knocking noise above idle. **1999–2004**—A faulty radiator cap may be the cause of coolant loss or engine overheating. **2000**—Idle fluctuation when coasting to a stop with the clutch depressed. • Remedy for excessive body vibration at 100 km/h. • Water may enter the distributor assembly. • Rough idle or excessive engine vibration at idle. • Clunk or rattle heard when turning the steering wheel. • Front bumper rattling. • Troubleshooting squeaks and rattles. **2000–03**—ABS warning light stays lit. **2001**—Cloudy, hazy appearance of plastic headlight. • Warm air from fresh air vents. • Speedometer may not work. **2003**—Remedy for AC that won't turn off. **2003–04**—Cold engine start-up rattle. **2004–05**—Troubleshooting spray-in bed liner defects. **2005**—More engine rattles. • Free body control module sub-harness to improve electrical connection for trailering. **2005–06**—Rear leaf spring squeaks • Right front seatback rattles and moves sideways. **2005–07**—Buzzing, whining engine timing chain. • Engine chirping, squealing.

FRONTIER PROFILE

	1999	2000	2001	2002	2003	2004	2005	2006	2007
Cost Price ($) (negotiable)									
4×2 (15%)	14,498	14,498	20,998	22,890	23,498	23,450	22,998	24,298	24,448
4×4 (16%)	21,498	21,498	26,498	27,553	27,398	27,400	28,998	29,598	29,748
Used Values ($)									
4×2 ▲	3,000	3,500	4,000	5,000	7,000	9,000	12,000	14,000	16,000
4×2 ▼	2,500	3,000	3,500	4,500	5,500	7,500	10,500	13,000	14,500
4×4 ▲	4,000	4,500	5,500	7,000	9,500	11,500	14,500	18,000	21,000
4×4 ▼	3,500	4,000	5,000	5,500	8,000	10,000	13,000	16,000	19,000
Reliability	4	4	5	5	5	5	5	5	5
Crash Safety (F)	3	3	—	4	4	4	4	4	4
Ext.	—	—	—	—	—	—	—	3	3
Side	—	4	4	5	5	4	5	5	5
Offset	2	2	2	2	2	2	5	5	5
Rollover	—	—	3	3	3	—	—	3	3

TITAN ★★★

RATING: Average (2008–09); Not Recommended (2004–07). Early models are risky buys from a safety and pocketbook perspective. *Lemon-Aid* has downgraded the Titan's rating as evidence of its performance and factory-related faults has come in from government agencies, owner forums, and owner emails. Owner complaints will likely intensify as the base warranty expires. Safety-related defects are legion, and Nissan's customer relations staff has been totally incapable of providing fair and adequate warranty support:

> Rear end in my new (2,500 miles [4,000 km]) Nissan Titan was on its way out (humming). Complained to dealer; they said that the hum and metal shavings in the differential were normal. Had to threaten to park truck in their showroom through the window to get them to even look at it. When they did they kept the truck for 5 days to replace rear end that was "normal" according to their tech.

Strong points: Poor sales mean major discounting. The powerful V8 engine has slightly more torque than does the Chrysler Hemi and notably more than the Ford, Chevrolet, or GMC V8s in standard-duty trucks. Good off-road performance; a roomy interior; the King Cab's rear doors swing back almost flat against the side of the cargo box; high utility-bed option is a hauler's dream; a security system with an

2008 TITAN TECHNICAL DATA

POWERTRAIN (4×2/PART-TIME 4×4)
Engine: 5.6L V8 (317 hp); Transmission: 5-speed auto.
DIMENSION/CAPACITY
Passengers: 3/3; Wheelbase: 140.0 in.; H: 70.0/L: 224.0/W: 79.0 in.; Headroom F/R: 5.5/5.0 in.; Legroom F/R: 41.5/32.0 in.; Fuel tank: 76L/regular; Tow limit: 9,400 lb.; Load capacity: 1,650–2013 lb.; GVWR: 16,200 lb.; Turning circle: 49.0 ft.; Box length: 6.7 ft.; Ground clearance: 10.0 in.; Weight: 5,380 lb.

immobilizer is standard; high-quality, factory-applied spray-on bed liner; optional adjustable pedals. **Weak points:** Brutal depreciation; a plethora of factory-related deficiencies; insensitive Nissan staffers; the only engine available is a fuel-thirsty 5.6L gasoline V8; a jumpy throttle causes jerky acceleration; one wheelbase must fit all; no standard regular-cab or heavy-duty versions; excessive on-road vibration and a hopping ride; nonstop exhaust roar; premature brake wear, and a plastic-laden interior. Part-time 4×4 must be shifted out of 4×4 on dry or hard surfaces, while Chevy and GMC trucks have a full-time system. **New for 2008:** Improved brakes; increased payload capacity; a slightly restyled front end; two long-wheelbase versions of the crew cab and extended cab with 7-foot and 8-foot beds; and improved seats, centre stack and gauge cluster. An unproven diesel option may be offered with the 2009 lineup; the next redesign is scheduled for the 2011 model year.

MODEL HISTORY: Introduced as a 2004 model, the Titan's bold, rugged look harkens back to the macho, in-your-face styling of the Dodge Ram when it starred in the movie *Twister*. This large pickup has lots of engine torque, headroom, rear-seat legroom, and 4×4 ground clearance—and horrendous problems. The Titan also offers a lighted tailgate, a cargo access area in the rear quarter panel, King Cab rear doors that swing open 168 degrees, and an optional locking rear differential (historically, a major problem area).

COST ANALYSIS: Recent owner complaints reinforced by service bulletins confirm the Titan's status as a very risky buy through the 2007 model year. If you must buy a Titan, get the discounted 2008 version and hope that some of the ongoing safety- and performance-related defects have been corrected. The base price for a 2008 4×2 is $32,998 ($39,998 for the 4×4 version). Both models cost much less in the States: $25,330 and $28,180, respectively. Don't wait for the 2009 model; it will be carried over substantially unchanged. Used models are cheap but lemony. **Best alternatives:** Honda's Ridgeline and Chrysler pickups equipped with a manual transmission. The Chevrolet Silverado/GMC Sierra are good second choices, while Toyota's Tacoma and Tundra are smaller and more problem-prone. **Rebates:** Poor sales have led to fairly generous discounts in the $5,000–$7,000 range, along with some financing incentives likely to be offered throughout 2008. **Delivery/PDI:** $1,385. **Warranty:** Bumper-to-bumper 3 years/60,000 km; powertrain 5 years/100,000 km; rust perforation 5 years/unlimited km. **Supplementary warranty:** An extended warranty for the powertrain. **Options:** Nothing significant; these cars come loaded with standard features. **Depreciation:** Average. **Insurance cost:** Higher than average. **Parts supply/cost:** Average availability, but parts can be expensive. **Annual maintenance cost:** High maintenance costs; the new design requires dealer servicing. **Highway/city fuel economy:** 4×2: 11.5/17.1 L/100 km; 4×4: 12.2/18.0 L/100 km.

QUALITY/RELIABILITY: Below-average quality control makes the early models both dangerous and unreliable. Their noisy, failure-prone powertrains have been used in Jeeps for years. It's not surprising that early rear axle seal failures are showing up in alarming numbers on 2004 through 2006 model year Titans:

The rear axle seals on the Nissan Titan years 2004–current have a severe and persistent problem with leaking. I have had my 2006 Nissan Titan in the shop once to replace the right rear axle seal at 18,000 miles [28,880 km] and now at 20,000 miles [32,000 km] it is leaking again. The location of the leak is what worries me. When the axle seal fails, it sprays gear oil on the brake components (rotors, calipers, pads) and I am worried that the pads will become contaminated and not work.

Owners report brake rotors warping within a few months and pads wearing out early; power-window and driver's power-seat malfunctions; a driver's seat that may be crooked; rear axle leakage; dash rattles and steering-wheel clicks; easily chipped paint; and water leaks from the AC evaporator drain tube and between the headliner and rear window:

Water leaks inside of truck through the fire wall. A/C drain hose fix was done but it still leaks water. Dealership is unable to repair. Water inside of truck caused mold to grow in the carpet and spores into the HVAC system. This caused two people to have to go to the doctor for difficulty breathing. This is an ongoing problem for 1 1/2 years.

Radio reception is terrible, and it fades out of stereo and FM mode. Plus, the $1,800 premium Fosgate radio uses cheap Clarion components.

SAFETY SUMMARY: The 2008 models posted crashworthiness scores identical to the 2007 versions. The much-needed electronic stability control is an optional feature, whereas the competition offers it as a standard item. **Airbags:** Side curtain airbags are optional. Some reports of airbags failing to deploy, or deploying when they shouldn't, resulting in severe injuries. **ABS:** Standard 4W. **Safety belt pretensioners:** Standard. **Traction control:** Optional. **Head restraints F/R:** 2005–08: ★★★. **Visibility F/R:** ★★★★★. **Pet transport:** ★★★★★.

SAFETY COMPLAINTS: All years: Serious design and manufacturing deficiencies jeopardize both your life and your wallet. **2004**—Over 331 safety-related defects recorded by NHTSA; 50 or so would be normal. • Rear axle seal blowouts are legion. • Fuel spews out when refuelling. • Transmission overheats towing 3,630 kg (8,000 lbs.), despite rating of 4,345 kg (9,600 lbs). • Vehicle jumps out of Park into Reverse. • Complete steering loss. • Airbag is disabled even though a 170-pound passenger is seated. • Headlight switch easily bumped to On or Off—not enough resistance to rotation. • Brake rotors are too small, warp easily:

The vehicle is now in the shop with 12,113 miles [19,500 km], having the rotor replaced again. I believe that there is a defective part manufactured for this vehicle. My driving habits are not such that they would cause this much excessive brake rotor warping. These brakes are not cheap to replace, I think it is unrealistic to advertise [that] a vehicle can tow 9,400 lbs [4,264 kg] and cannot even stop with its own body weight, [let alone do] any towing. The brake system in my opinion is undersized or there is a manufacture spec that is not being met. God forbid I actually used this vehicle to tow, as advertised.

• Defective Bridgestone Dueler A/T 110S tires. • Faulty seat belt retractors. **2005**—A much higher-than-average number of safety-related failures recorded to NHTSA; many relate to rear axle seals. • Right front wheel spindle fractures. • Vehicle shakes violently when brakes are applied because of warped rotors and worn-out pads. • Brake failures caused by faulty ABS sensors. • Many of the brake components and an upgraded brake kit are on nationwide back order. • Transmission failures. Writes one Kamloops, B.C., 2005 Titan owner:

> The complete wiring harness in the engine compartment has to be replaced due to corrosion issues. There was only one available in Canada, and it was flown in. While it was being installed, something else went wrong, and the last one left in North America was flown in.
>
> I finally I got a phone call: They're still having electrical issues with my truck. Prognosis unknown. It's now into week 3.
>
> The initial diagnosis into the corrosion issue was made because of a factory bulletin detailing the same problem on 2004 models of the Titan and since my Titan was built in Aug. 2004 (a 2005 model) the mechanic had a hint of where to look. I spoke to a Nissan rep in Mississauga about getting the warranty extended to cover wiring issues, and was stonewalled.

• One vehicle's seat belt would not release; child had to be cut free. **2006**—Airbags fail to deploy in a rollover. • Frequent rear differential failures preceded by excessive vibration, a humming noise, and metal shavings in the transmission fluid:

> The differential failed when turning right onto a busy street. There was a loud bang then a grinding sound. The truck would not drive after that. Every time I tried to accelerate the truck would just grind and not move.

• Excessive steering shudder when braking. • Driver's window rolls up only halfway. • Fuel gauge doesn't work after refuelling. • Broken rear door latch. • Poorly performing Goodyear Wrangler tires. **2007**—Defective cruise control causes sudden, unintended acceleration. • Differential/axle failures. • Poor-quality wheel rims. • Early wearout of tires and brakes. • Door latches won't open in cold weather.

Secret Warranties/Internal Bulletins/Service Tips

2004—Warranty payout guidelines and troubleshooting tips for brake shudder and vibration are detailed in TSB #BR00-004a and NTB00-033a, dated June 11, 2003. • Slow tire leak. • Inoperative DVD. • Coolant leaks and engine overheating blamed on faulty radiator cap. **2004–05**—No-start; engine doesn't crank. • Idle speed too high. • Transmission fluid leaks from the air cooler line. • Tips for correcting brake vibration. • Water leaks from the rear sliding window track. • Poor

AC cooling in hot weather. • AC condenser fan rattling. • Discolouration of sprayed-on bed liner. • Free body control module sub-harness to improve electrical connection for trailering. • Fuel gauge stays on Full. • Front door creaking or ticking. • Back-glass water leaks. **2004–06**—Right front seatback rattles and moves sideways. • Tips on troubleshooting spray-in bed liner defects. **2004–08**—Loss of power when accelerating. **2007**—Engine overheating; inoperative condenser fan. • Low-speed wheel noise. • Faulty tire-pressure monitoring system.

TITAN PROFILE

	2004	2005	2006	2007
Cost Price ($) (negotiable)				
4×2 (22%)	31,900	31,900	32,398	32,798
4×4 (23%)	38,200	38,500	38,998	39,398
Used Values ($)				
4×2 ▲	15,000	18,000	21,000	24,000
4×2 ▼	13,500	16,000	19,000	22,000
4×4 ▲	18,500	23,000	27,000	30,000
4×4 ▼	17,000	21,000	25,000	28,000
Reliability	2	2	3	3
Crash Safety (F)	4	5	5	5
Offset	5	5	5	5
Rollover	—	4	4	4
4×4	—	3	3	3

Toyota

TACOMA ★★

RATING: Below Average (2005–09); Average (1987–2004). This is a low-tech, unadorned pickup that was more reliable during its early years. The 2005 improvements make Tacoma a big pickup player, albeit with a dangerously defective powertrain. **Strong points:** *2005–08:* Incredibly powerful 4- and 6-cylinder engines give smooth performance without guzzling fuel; ride and handling are improved with firmer, shorter springs, gas shocks, a limited slip differential, and larger tires; towing capability increased by 680 kg (1,500 lb.); additional interior room makes back seats acceptable for adult passengers. Upgraded interior and a new composite cargo bed with extra storage compartments and adjustable tie-down anchors. Additional safety features like side curtain airbags. *2004 and earlier models:* Competent V6 engine performance; rugged, impressive off-road capability; good braking; roomy interior; and good build

2008 TACOMA TECHNICAL DATA

POWERTRAIN (4×2 OR 4×4/PART-TIME 4×4)

Engines: 2.7L 4-cyl. (159 hp) • 4.0L V6 (236 hp); Transmissions: 5-speed man. • 6-speed man. • 4-speed auto. • 5-speed auto.

DIMENSION/CAPACITY

Passengers: 2/3; Wheelbase: 128.0 in.; H: 64.0/L: 208.0/W: 75.0 in.; Headroom F/R: 4.0/3.0 in.; Legroom F/R: 42.5/28.0 in.; Cargo volume: 25.9 cu. ft.; Fuel tank: 57L/regular; Tow limit: 6,500 lb. (4×4); Load capacity: 910–1,685 lb.; GVWR: 4,244–5,104 lb. Turning circle: 43.0 ft.; Box length: 6.2 ft.; Ground clearance: 8.5 in.; Weight: 4.115 lb.

quality. The high resale value, above-average reliability, slow depreciation, and good fuel economy somewhat offset the stiff purchase price. **Weak points:** Handling can be extremely dangerous due to hazardous cruise control malfunctions and engine surging when braking. Overall handling is still somewhat trucklike; 6-speed manual transmission is a bit clunky; rear drum brakes (Toyota says they perform better in wet conditions); and a small 1.5 m (5 ft.) bed. *2004 and earlier:* Mediocre ride and wet-weather handling, and lots of engine and road noise. It has less towing capability than domestic competitors, and it may not achieve stated towing capacity (be very wary). Bereft of many standard features offered by competitors; the front seat is set too low and far back; cushions are too small in the rear seat, where legroom is limited; climate controls are obstructed by the cupholders; difficult entry and exit require a higher step-up than with other 4×4 pickups. Smaller bed than many competitors, and the StepSide bed is quite narrow. **New for 2008:** Nothing significant. Wait for the 2009 model, which is scheduled for a slight revamping.

MODEL HISTORY: Redesigned for the first time in 10 years, the 2005 Tacoma targeted the Dodge Dakota crowd with a powerful V6 and a 6-speed manual/5-speed automatic transmission to counter Dodge's less sophisticated powertrain set-up at the time. Set on the same platform as the 4Runner and Lexus GX 470, recent Tacomas are about 15 cm (6 in.) longer, 10 cm (4 in.) wider, and 5 cm (2 in.) taller than 2004 and earlier versions.

This compact pickup is available as a Regular Cab, Xtracab, or Double Cab (a four-door crew cab) in 4×2 or 4×4. There's no denying the added convenience of four doors, but the Double Cab also provides a 60/40 folding rear bench seat for more versatility. The 236-hp V6 beats Dodge's 215-hp 3.7L V6, Ford's 202-hp 4.2L V6, and GM's 200-hp 4.3L V6. Available engines on 2004 and earlier models are a 2.4L and 2.7L 4-cylinder and a 3.4L V6. A dealer-installed supercharger package will give the V6 59 additional horses. The shift-on-the-fly 4×4 system is optional on 4×4 trucks and standard on the 4×4 SR5 V6.

Toyota has been building good cars for quite a while, but its pickups have always missed the quality and performance mark because they were undersized, under-powered, and glitch-prone. Their mechanical reliability is no longer any better than that of American pickups, which is shameful. Tacomas don't offer a lot of razzle-dazzle or carlike handling, and their powertrain deficiencies can be dangerous to life, limb, and your pocketbook.

1999—Seat belt pretensioners and force limiters added. **2000**—Improved gearing on 4×4. **2001**—Debut of the Double Cab and a new StepSide version, revised front styling and new alloy wheels, a differential locking system, 31-inch tires on alloy wheels, and a tachometer. **2003**—Standard ABS and upgraded child restraint anchors. **2005**—Larger, more powerful, and equipped for the first time with side curtain airbags.

COST ANALYSIS: Tacoma has been coasting since its 2005 model redesign, so neither the 2007 nor the 2008 models give you much more for the extra money. If you get a new Tacoma, understand that it will cost you at least $22,760; an AWD version costs about $7,000 more and really isn't worth the extra money. In the States, the base model sells for $15,015 and an AWD goes for $21,555. In 2002–04 models, the 2,250 kg (5,000 lb.) towing capability may not be possible. **Best alternatives:** The Mazda B-series and Nissan Frontier are credible alternatives. Watch out: As with Mazda's B-series, you'll pay way over the base price for a loaded Tacoma. It's interesting that the new 4×4 sells for about $7,000 more than the 4×2 and then depreciates almost to the 4×2's level after five years. **Rebates:** Look for $2,000–$3,000 rebates and zero percent financing. **Delivery/ PDI:** $1,390. **Warranty:** Bumper-to-bumper 3 years/60,000 km; powertrain 5 years/100,000 km; rust perforation 5 years/unlimited km. **Supplementary warranty:** An extended powertrain warranty would be a wise buy. **Options:** Try to get a model equipped with electronic stability control. Ditch the Firestone and Bridgestone tires. **Depreciation:** Slower than average. **Insurance cost:** Average. **Parts supply/cost:** Parts are easily found at dealerships and independent suppliers, and costs are very reasonable. **Annual maintenance cost:** Far below average when compared with the American competition and most other Japanese automakers. Good dealer network and service. **Highway/city fuel economy:** *4×2, 2.4L, and automatic:* 8.8/11.1 L/100 km; *4×4 and 2.7L:* 10.4/13.1 L/100 km; *4×4 and 3.4L:* 10.9/13.6 L/100 km; *4×4 and 4.0L:* 10.9/15.0 L/100 km.

QUALITY/RELIABILITY: Worse than average. Reliability has been compromised during the past several decades by lapses in quality control, leading to expensive V6 engine head gasket failures through 2004. Automatic transmission and brake problems have carried over to the latest models.

The 2005's changes have brought their own set of problems to subsequent model years, including chronic cruise control and transmission breakdowns; oil leaks between the transmission and crankshaft; assorted short circuits; water leaks onto the floorboard from the A-pillar; easily chipped paint (rocker panels, lower doors, and front of the bed sides); tailgates that fail while vehicles are underway; and acid sprayed around the engine compartment by the Delphi battery. Cabin mount bolts and bushings contract and loosen in cold weather, resulting in a loud banging noise in the cabin area. **Owner-reported problems:** Transmission, cruise control breakdowns causing transmission to slam into gear and engine to surge; electrical, suspension, and brake failures; noise. *2004 and earlier models:*

Powertrain, brake (especially 2000–03 models), and AC failures; electrical shorts; premature front brake wear; and subpar fit and finish (excessive paint chipping). Some reports that the engine seizes after ingesting water when the vehicle passes through a puddle, the truck is hard to start, and the driver's seat's inadequate lumbar support is painful on long drives. **Warranty performance:** Average. Owners allege that speedometer readings are inflated by 8 percent, robbing owners of the same percentage of warranty coverage:

> My 2005 Tacoma's speedometer has been reading approximately 7 miles per hour [11 km/h] faster than actual. I couldn't figure out why so many cars were passing me on the highway when I was doing around 65 [105 km/h]! I checked it by following my wife in her car and also compared against mile markers. I took [the vehicle] to the dealer and they hooked it up to the diagnostic computer and found nothing wrong.

 SAFETY SUMMARY: The crashworthiness scores on the 2006–08 models are identical and will likely be applicable to the 2009 Tacoma. Xtracab's right rear seat will accommodate a child safety seat. Owners report that the truck's suspension can barely handle a 227 kg (500 lb.) payload, despite Toyota's assertion that it has a 544 kg (1,200 lb.) rating. **Airbags:** Front. There have been reports of airbags failing to deploy. **ABS:** Optional 2W and 4W. **Safety belt pretensioners:** Standard. **Head restraints F/R:** *1999:* ★; *2001–04:* ★; *2005–08 with bucket seats:* ★★; *2007–08 with standard seats:* ★★★★★; *1999 Extended Cab:* ★★. **Visibility F/R:** ★★★★★. **Pet transport:** ★★★★★.

SAFETY COMPLAINTS: All years: Airbag malfunctions. • Sudden acceleration. • Brake failures, overheating, extended stopping distance, and prematurely worn calipers and rotors. • Vehicle wanders all over the road after hitting a bump. • Firestone, Goodyear, and Dunlop tire-tread separation. • Loose or poorly fitted trip panels. **1999**—Stuck accelerator. • When one vehicle's airbag deployed, it melted a hole in the dash. • ABS brakes lock up. • Truck accelerates when heater motor comes on. • Shift lever jumps from First to Second gear. • Transfer-case seizure. • Left front axle assembly failure caused by defective front ball joint nut. • Rear differential fails. • Check Engine and Airbag warning lights stay on constantly. • Rear leaf spring and overload spring break easily when passing over rough terrain. **1999–2000**—Under-hood fires. • Excessive vibration when underway. • Turn signals don't work. **2000**—Parking brake fails. • Side mirror is hard to focus. • Nothing in place to prevent rear-seat passengers' heads from striking the rear window in a collision. **2001**—Incorrectly installed ABS sensor leads to brake failure. • Vehicle is prone to hydroplaning over wet roads at relatively slow speeds. • Intermittently, alarm system fails to unlock vehicle. • Loose front drive shaft bolts. • Rear wheel falls off. **2002**—Brake and gas pedal mounted too closely together. • Brake master cylinder leaks. • Automatic transmission shudders, clunks, surges, shifts erratically, and jumps from gear to gear. • Transmission line blows out. • Defective front and rear shock absorbers. • Water enters the cabin through the driver-side support handle. • Defective wheel rims and tires. •

Poorly designed jack handle makes for risky tire-changing. **2003**—Sudden roll-over. • Sudden engine surging caused by a defective throttle actuator control. • Loss of power caused by a faulty throttle body sensor:

> You can only open the throttle body butterfly the first 25% with the pedal, then the computer opens it the rest of the way. These throttle by wire [or highly-responsive accelerators] are crapping out left and right and Toyota is...claiming [they are covered under the less-generous 3 year/60,000 km bumper-to-bumper warranty and not the 5 year/100,000 km powertrain warranty].

• Truck sways and pitches excessively. • Shifter can be accidentally bumped and will shift into Neutral. • Front seats rock back and forth. • Water leaks onto the driver-side floor and through the passenger door. • Doors don't close fully or lock. • Broken wheel lug nuts:

> While the inspector was placing the tires back onto the truck, two of the wheel studs broke on the front hub. He stated that this happens on almost every 2000–2003 Toyota pickup they work on. He even showed me that the stud wasn't cross-threaded and removed the stud from the lug nut using a pair of pliers. The stud came right out with little pressure.

• Defective Firestone and Goodyear Wrangler tires. **2004**—Several incidents of fires igniting while vehicles are being driven. • Front airbags don't deploy as required. • Transmission jerks when going into gear. • Both rear springs fail when cornering. • Side mirrors fog up badly. • Goodyear Wrangler sidewall blowout. • Loss of braking ability in inclement weather. • Parking brake hits driver's knee. • Seat lumbar supports cause lower back pain. **2005**—6-speed manual transmission has serious judder and shifts only with considerable difficulty:

> The judder problem was particularly bad and was evident with every start in First gear and sometimes in Second gear. It became more violent with each start and at one point, after the clutch pedal was fully released, there was a sudden slip of the clutch disc followed by sudden friction. This resulted in loss of traction of the drive wheels and subsequent total loss of control of the vehicle. Control was regained relatively quickly by depressing the clutch pedal to remove drive power from the wheels and a catastrophic event was narrowly avoided.

• Skid plate catches air and causes the vehicle to shake violently at highway speeds. • Exhaust crossover pipe hangs below the transfer-case mount and can be easily crushed when off-roading. This would allow carbon monoxide to enter into the cabin. • Left turn signal quits intermittently. • Right side mirror vibrates excessively (especially on windy days) and also creates a large blind spot in the right front quarter of the vehicle. • Defective Firestone and Bridgestone Potenza RE050A tires crack and split. • Tailgate is dangerously weak, unable to support normal weight without bending out of shape. **2006**—Over a 100 reports of life-threatening, factory-related component failures. • Surging when braking, particularly on vehicles equipped with cruise control. • Throttle sticks. • Erratic cruise control/transmission operation causing violent gear shifts into the wrong gear. • Transmission pressure plate failure. • Sun visor drops down when pushed forward. • Firestone tire blowouts; cuts in the bead (tread). • Water leaks through the firewall. **2007**—More than the average number of safety-related complaints for Toyota vehicles, including many hair-raising incidents where the vehicle suddenly accelerates during braking:

> Over a period of several months after purchasing a new 2007 Toyota Tacoma, I experienced five incidents of brake/acceleration problems finally resulting in a crash. First incident: Stopped at a traffic light with my foot on the brake, the truck lunged forward a few feet. The dealership told me they could not find any problem. A month later, stopped in a gas station drive with my foot on the brake waiting to exit, the rear wheels began spinning out of control. I pressed on the brake as hard as I possibly could to keep from entering traffic. Three weeks later, approaching the bottom of a hilly sharp turn, I tapped the brakes to slow down. Again the rear wheels accelerated to a high rate of speed. I could not stop the truck to keep from striking a van in front of me so I crossed over a double yellow line to avoid a collision. It took about a thousand yards to gain control.

• Many complaints that the cruise control suddenly goes into Overdrive. • Extremely fast idle and engine surge after a cold start.

Secret Warranties/Internal Bulletins/Service Tips

All years: If there is a delay when shifting from Park or Neutral to Reverse, Toyota will install an upgraded B3 return spring, B3 Brake piston O-rings, and a low-coast modulator spring to correct the problem. Toyota doesn't say if the repair will be covered by its base warranty or "goodwill"; however, a good rule of thumb is that any transmission malfunction, like a delay in this case, would be the automaker's responsibility for at least the first 7 years/160,000 km. • To minimize noise when shifting 4×4 automatic transmissions, Toyota will change various transmission components under the base warranty. A Toyota insider tells me that the work will also be done for free up to 5 years/80,000 km under a "goodwill" special policy. • Consult TSB #AC002-97, issued May 9, 1997, to eliminate musty odours emanating from the AC. Usually, the problem is caused by a blocked evaporator-housing drain pipe. • Countermeasures for rotten-egg smell from exhaust. • TSB #BR95-003 says Toyota has a new brake pad kit that reduces brake noise and increases brake durability. • Consult TSB #BR94-002 and #BR95-001, where the company outlines all the possible ways brake pulsation/vibration can be further reduced. Incidentally, this problem has affected almost all of Toyota's cars and trucks over the past decade. • Toyota has also developed a new grease to prevent brake pad clicking. **1999**—Install an upgraded clutch pedal kit to silence pedal squeaking. **1999–2000**—That undercarriage noise you hear may be caused by a loose exhaust manifold heat shield. **1999–2004**—Tips on plugging body water leaks.

2000—Fix to prevent paint chipping on the rear quarter panels. • Dirt builds up on shoulder belt. • Squeak and rattle noises from the idler pulley. 2001—Faulty power door locks. 2001–02—Tube step knocking, squeaking, and rattling fix. • Dash pad rattles. • Loose fender flare pad. • Tearing of the seat material on Double Cabs. 2001–03—Special Service Campaign relative to the fuel inlet protector. 2001–04—Dash pad rattle repair tips. 2002—Off-centre steering wheel. • MIL stays lit. 2002–06—Correction for vehicles that pull to the side. 2003–07—Tips for silencing an upper or lower windshield ticking noise. 2005—No-start in cold temperatures. • Front cowl water leaks. • Suspension slap, squeak noise. 2005–06—Deformed window runs. 2005–07—Intermittent no-start condition. • Front brake noise when brakes applied while backing up. • Harsh rear spring ride. • Windshield wind noise. • Bent rear tailgate.

TACOMA PROFILE

	1999	2000	2001	2002	2003	2004	2005	2006	2007
Cost Price ($) (negotiable)									
Base (15%)	16,390	16,765	21,630	21,920	22,370	22,570	22,125	22,535	22,635
4×4 (17%)	25,705	26,150	27,045	27,335	28,065	29,400	29,240	29,560	29,660
Used Values ($)									
Base ▲	3,500	4,000	4,500	6,000	7,500	9,000	11,000	13,500	16,000
Base ▼	3,000	3,500	4,000	5,000	6,000	7,500	9,000	12,500	14,000
4×4 ▲	4,500	5,000	6,500	7,000	9,000	11,000	15,000	18,000	21,000
4×4 ▼	4,000	4,500	5,500	6,500	7,500	9,500	13,500	16,000	19,000
Reliability	4	4	4	4	3	3	4	4	4
Crash Safety (F)									
4×2	—	—	—	4	—	—	5	5	5
Ext. Cab	—	3	3	3	3	3	5	5	5
Double	—	—	—	—	4	4	—	—	—
Side									
4×2	—	—	—	5	—	—	5	5	5
Ext. Cab	1	3	3	3	3	3	5	5	5
Double	—	—	—	—	5	5	—	—	—
Offset	3	3	3	3	3	3	5	5	5
Rollover	—	2	2	2	4	4	—	4	4
Ext. Cab	—	—	—	—	2	—	—	4	4

RATING: Below Average (2001–09). The rating has been downgraded because the competition has better-performing models, higher levels of quality control, and cheaper prices. The many brake and transmission failure complaints and severe "bed bounce" are other negative factors. **Strong points:** Plenty of power and a nice selection of standard safety and convenience features. Soft retail prices. *2006 and earlier:* Twin-cam V8 acceleration; low-range gearing for off-roading; smooth, quiet ride; a roomier Double Cab (2004); passenger-side airbag can be switched off with a key; well appointed; easy front access; good fit and finish; standard transmission and engine oil coolers; slow depreciation; better-than-average predicted reliability. **Weak points:** Believe it or not, these trucks exhibit extremely poor quality control. Steering and suspension design is so bad that the truck can easily go out of control when passing over slightly irregular roadways. Electronics and brakes continue to be seriously weak areas. *2006 and earlier:* Less engine torque than the competition; difficult rear exit and entry; 4×4 can't be used on dry pavement (unlike the GM Silverado and Sierra); excessive body sway, and tends to be a bit bouncy; poorly performing rear brake drums; rear-hinged back doors on the Access Cab don't open independently of the front doors; no four-door Crew Cab model available; and the V8 requires premium fuel. The 2003 and earlier models aren't as roomy in the rear half of the extended cab as other extended full-sized trucks—you feel like you're entering a Dodge Dakota or Ford Ranger. Paint is not up to Toyota standards. Dash LCDs are unreadable with sunglasses. Weak door indents; bland styling; and incredibly high rate of safety-related defects involving brake, airbag, and seat belt failures. **New for 2008:** Nothing major. Next redesign is scheduled for 2012, so there is no reason to pay more money for a 2009 or later version.

2008 TUNDRA TECHNICAL DATA

POWERTRAIN (4×2/4×4)
Engines: 4.0L V6 (236 hp) • 4.7L V8 (276 hp) • 5.7L V8 (381 hp); Transmissions: 6-speed man. • 5-speed auto.

DIMENSION/CAPACITY
Passengers: 3/6; Wheelbase: 145.6 in.; H: 75.7/L: 228.7/W: 79.9 in.; Headroom F/R: 5.5/3.5 in.; Legroom F/R: 42.5/28.5 in.; Cargo volume: N/A; Fuel tank: 100L/ regular; Tow limit: 8,400–10,300 lb.; Load capacity: 1,580 lb.; GVWR: 6,800 lb.; Turning circle: 44.0 ft.; Box length: 78.7–97.6 in.; Ground clearance: 10.4 ft.; Weight: 4,990–5,235 lb.

MODEL HISTORY: Larger, stronger, safer, and roomier than its T100 predecessor, the 2001 Tundra was Toyota's first serious foray into the lucrative, though crowded, full-sized pickup market. Unfortunately, Toyota's new truck wasn't quite full-sized, and sales suffered.

Toyota corrected that shortcoming with its 2004 models by stretching the Dana-built frame to make the Tundra more competitive with Detroit's Big Three pickups. This improvement was accompanied by a slight decline in quality, which was addressed in subsequent years. Two engines, a 190-hp 3.4L V6 and a 240-hp 4.7L V8, are offered up to the 2005 model year, when the 4.0L came on board.

2002—The Limited gets a standard in-dash CD changer, anti-lock braking, and keyless remote entry. **2003**—A new V8-equipped Access CAB StepSide model; ABS, grille, bumper, power-sliding rear window (Limited), 17-inch wheels (optional on the SR5), new centre console, and vinyl flooring. **2004**—A more powerful, brawnier Double Cab that gains 30 cm (12 in.) in wheelbase and length and 7 cm (3 in.) in width. **2005**—More power, new transmissions, and optional side curtain airbags; a 245-hp 4.0L V6 replaces the 190-hp 3.4L; a 6-speed manual transmission replaces the 5-speed, and a 5-speed automatic replaces the 4-speed; the 4.7L V8 gets 42 more horses. **2007**—The redesigned Tundra is larger, more powerful, and better appointed, and it provides many new body and engine configurations. Other new features: a lockable tailgate with safety hinges, extra-large side mirrors, a centre console big enough to hold a file folder, and a trailer hitch integrated into the frame. In a bid to attract more commercial users, the new cabin has large door handles and controls that can be operated with gloves on, and headroom has been increased to accommodate occupants wearing hardhats. Braking is improved via heavy-duty front disc brakes with four-piston calipers and vented rotors increased by nearly 4 cm (1.5 in.) as well as standard rear disc brakes. High capacity cooling and electrical systems have been added to enhance towing capability.

COST ANALYSIS: A 2008 entry-level Tundra 4×4 DLX sells for $27,540 in Canada; Americans pay about $1,000 less. This makes it hardly worthwhile to shop in the States for the cheaper models. On the other hand, a top-of-the-line 4×4 5.7L V8 Limited costs $46,000 in Canada and about $6,000 less in the States. **Best alternatives:** Consider the Honda Ridgeline, Mazda B-series, and Nissan Frontier. **Rebates:** Look for $6,000 rebates and low financing on the fully loaded 2008 models; 2009 prices are expected to stay soft. **Delivery/PDI:** $1,390. **Options:** Choose optional equipment judiciously—you could easily pay almost $40,000 for a loaded version. Recommended are running boards and the All Weather Guard package that includes a heavy-duty starter and heater. **Depreciation:** Much slower than average. **Insurance cost:** Higher than average. **Parts supply/cost:** Most parts are widely available and of average cost. Some drivers wait as long as two months for powertrain components, though. **Annual maintenance cost:** Maintenance and repair costs have been much less than average; however, the 2007 Tundra could turn out to be more difficult to service and, hence, more costly to maintain. The service bays at many Toyota dealerships cannot handle these behemoths, so they'll have to be retrofitted to accommodate the new Tundra. The bays are too small and too close together, lifts can't raise the truck high enough to work on, and the alignment racks are too short. **Warranty:** Bumper-to-bumper 3 years/60,000 km; powertrain 5 years/100,000 km; rust perforation 5 years/unlimited km. **Supplementary warranty:** An extended warranty is a waste of money. **Highway/city fuel economy:** *4×2, 3.4L, and man.:* 11.1/14.3 L/100 km; *4×2, 3.4L, and auto.:* 10.9/14.1 L/100 km; *4×4, 3.4L, and man.:* 12.1/15.4 L/100 km; *4×4, 3.4L, and auto.:* 12.3/14.4 L/100 km; *4×2, 4.0L, and auto.:*

9.7/12.7 L/100 km; *4×2, 4.7L, and auto.:* 11.9/15.6 L/100 km; a nd *4×4, 4.7L, and auto.:* 12.6/15.4 L/100 km.

QUALITY/RELIABILITY: Below average. Quality declined even more with the revamped 2007–08 models. Early defects relate to brake failures, excessive brake caliper and rotor wear, premature transmission replacements, engine manifold rust-outs, paint peeling, and poor-quality original-equipment tires. The 2007 and 2008 models have mostly been plagued by faulty camshafts and torque converters and cracking tailgates. **Owner-reported problems:** Excessive front-brake vibration or pulsation makes the truck almost uncontrollable and causes the Tundra to shake violently when brakes are applied. Brake drums and rotors warp within 7,000 km; steel wheels rust prematurely; ABS brakes make a loud banging sound upon engagement; 4×4 system grinds and pops out of gear; chronic rear axle noise and suspension knocking; V8 engine knocking when started in cold weather; excessive drivetrain vibration at 100 km/h; automatic transmission binding; poor transmission performance:

> I have a 2005 Toyota Tundra. At times, it doesn't shift up properly and the engine revs up very high, but the truck doesn't accelerate. At times, when I am coasting down a hill, it will shift down, causing the truck to slow down. I took it to the dealer and was told that the transmission is completely electronic and that happens sometimes. I feel that this is a factory defect. Last week, I was trying to make a left turn at an intersection. I pressed the pedal but the truck didn't accelerate. I could have been hit by an oncoming car.

Paint is easily chipped; oil dipstick is incorrectly calibrated or too short, leading to incorrect readings; loose windows rattle constantly; exhaust smells like rotten eggs. **Warranty performance:** Average, but Toyota must stop blaming its customers for its own manufacturing errors and stonewalling legitimate claims.

SAFETY SUMMARY: The 2008 models have crash protection ratings identical to the 2007s. **Airbags:** Front and side curtain; there have been reports of airbags failing to deploy. **ABS:** 4W standard; disc/disc. **Safety belt pretensioners:** Front; seat belt failures are also common. **Head restraints:** *2001–02:* ★★★★; *2003–04:* ★★★★/★★★; *2005–06 models with adjustable lumbar seats:* ★★; *2005–06 models without adjustable lumbar seats:* ★★★; *2005–08 models with bucket seats:* ★★; *2007–08 models with standard seats:* ★★★★★. **Visibility F/R:** ★★★★★. **Maximum load capacity:** *2000 SR5 4.7L:* 1,340 lb. **Pet transport:** ★★★★★.

SAFETY COMPLAINTS: All years: Airbags fail to deploy. • Seat belt/retractor failures. • Vehicle rolls away after it is put in Park and the emergency brake is applied. • An incredibly high number of brake complaints relative to brake failures, rotor and drum warping, and excessive vibration/shudder. • Brakes overheat and fade after successive application; extended braking distance. • Loose, poorly fitted trim panels. • Ball joint failure causes wheel to separate:

While I was driving 55 mph [88.5 km/h] on a two lane highway, my 2005 Toyota Tundra 4WD driver side front wheel detached, folding under the front left side frame behind the wheel well with the truck landing on the flat side of the wheel. I was then in a controlled skid on a straight part of the highway and held the steering wheel in that position. I did not apply the brakes as I did not want to alter the direction of the skid. The vehicle drifted slightly to the right after about a 150 foot [45 metre] skid. The wheel hub had separated from the upper and lower control arm, the ball joint had detached from the A-frame.... I contacted my Toyota dealer who didn't seem too interested since there were no injuries. This incident occurred with 72,000 miles [115,900 km] on the truck meaning that the 36 month, 36,000 mile [57,940 km] warranty would not cover the damage. In researching the ball joint complaint I found that there was a recall on the 2004 Tundra.

2001—Sudden, unintended acceleration caused by faulty oxygen sensors, which are frequently back ordered. • Exhaust manifold cracking. • With a full fuel tank and when riding uphill, gas fumes enter the cabin. • Gear selector fails to engage the proper gear. • When applying lube to the drive shaft bearings, the grease just squirts around the fitting, not in. • Broken weld in tow hitch. 2002—Cab separates from chassis. • Automatic transmission goes into the wrong gear or slams into gear. • Sudden brake lock-up. • Lug nuts are easily broken when tightened. • Bent wheel rims. • Bridgestone tread cracking. • Tires hydroplane easily. 2003—Vehicle stalls out. • Engine oil leaks. • Sudden tie-rod failure can cause Tundra to flip. • Transfer-case malfunction leads to reduced power and excessive vibration. • Faulty transmission Overdrive causes engine surge. 2004— Sudden, unintended acceleration. • Many reports of the ball joint or lower control arm suddenly failing on vehicles not included in the recall to fix the problem. • Broken wheel lug nuts. • Defroster brings in carbon monoxide. • Goodrich Rugged Trail tire cracks. • Rear window pops out, and sunroof explodes. 2005—Automatic transmission failure (won't go into gear, or jumps out of Drive into Neutral). • Cruise control downshifts two gears on slight upgrades. • Extreme pulling to the left and right. • Driver's captain chair rocks back and forth. • Faulty tire-pressure monitoring system. 2006—Vehicle suddenly shuts down. • Malfunctioning cruise control. • Sudden brake loss. • Excessive Bridgestone tire wear. • When fuelling, the filler nozzle will eject from the vehicle. 2007—Floor mats slide forward, causing sudden acceleration. • Instruments cannot be seen in daylight. • Headlights are difficult to aim properly. • Heat duct falls and blocks access to the brake pedal. • Bad Bridgestone Dueler tires. • Truck is bouncy on the highway; described by one owner as producing excessive cab shake, wobble, and jerkiness:

The vehicle bounces horribly at speeds of 60–80 mph [96–129 km/h] on concrete freeways. As per dealer I have added 200 lb. of weight to the rear...the problem still occurred. The bouncing is very noticeable in the rear seats, so much so that I am not comfortable having my 2 year old daughter as a passenger. I feel the vehicle is unsafe and could very easily become unstable.

Secret Warranties/Internal Bulletins/Service Tips

2000–02—Hard starts/no-starts. **2000–04**—If the AC doesn't sufficiently cool the cabin, TSB #AC004-04 says the water control valve is the likely culprit. **2000–05**—Troubleshooting front and rear brake vibrations. • Engine squealing noise on cold start-up. • Front-door window rattles. **2001**—New parking struts developed to reduce rear brake vibration. • Inaccurate temperature gauge. • Inadequate application of seam sealer in driver's footwell area. **2001–03**—Oil pressure gauge reads abnormally low. • Front brake repair tips. **2002–06**—Remedy for vehicle pulling hard to the left or right. **2003–07**—Tips for silencing an upper or lower windshield ticking noise. **2004–05**—Rear shock squeaking. • No-start in cold temperatures. • AC blower noise. **2004–06**—Ticking noise from lower A-pillar when passing over rough terrain. **2007**—Automatic transmission shifter slide binding. • Rear brake squeak. • Tailgate latch won't open.

TUNDRA PROFILE

	2000	2001	2002	2003	2004	2005	2006	2007
Cost Price ($) (negotiable)								
Base (18%)	23,915	23,110	23,520	23,520	24,565	25,580	26,100	25,255
4×4 V6/V8 (20%)	28,380	28,600	29,270	29,270	30,320	30,650	31,080	29,320
Used Values ($)								
Base ▲	4,000	5,000	6,500	8,000	11,000	13,000	15,000	17,000
Base ▼	3,500	4,500	5,500	7,000	8,500	10,500	13,500	15,000
4×4 V6/V8 ▲	6,000	7,500	8,000	9,000	12,000	14,000	17,500	19,000
4×4 V6/V8 ▼	5,000	7,000	6,500	8,000	9,500	12,500	16,000	18,000
Reliability	2	2	2	2	2	2	2	2
Crash Safety (F)	4	3	4	4	4	4	4	4
Side	—	—	—	5	5	5	5	—
Offset	5	5	5	5	5	5	5	5
Rollover	—	—	—	—	—	—	3	3
Ext.	—	3	3	—	—	—	3	3

OLD BARGAINS AND NEW PRODUCTS

High fuel prices have caused large vehicle prices to fall as much as 30 to 50 percent during the past year, making for lots of cheap used SUVs, vans, and trucks that perform well, come fully loaded, and are fairly reliable. On the other hand, 2009 will see a number of new crossover models that will cost you more simply because they are more fuel-efficient and stylish. The trick is to pick substance over gadgetry and buy that which can be easily fixed by an automaker that will likely stay in business. Be especially wary of vehicles sold by Chrysler, Isuzu, Jaguar, Land Rover, and Volvo. These companies are far from stable and will likely be sold piecemeal to equity investors over the next few years or so.

To get the best for less, consider the following 10 rules:

The Buick Enclave, GMC Acadia, and Saturn Outlook (above) join Ford's Edge and Flex as new SUVs with lots of potential.

1. Looks don't matter. GM's Astro and Safari minivans are boxy and bland, fairly reliable, cheap, and easy to find.
2. Used is always a better buy than new. There's less depreciation and no bogus administrative or freight charges.
3. American front-drives are usually poor buys. They are less reliable than rear-drives and cost more to repair.
4. Be wary of "orphans" like the Ford Windstar, Jeep Cherokee, and Toyota Previa. Their parts will be hard to find, and no one will want to service them.
5. Stay away from European luxury lemon SUVs like the Mercedes M-Class and the BMW X3 or X5. They are way overrated and overpriced. Depreciation is relentless. Parts availability and servicing can be a problem, and quality control is declining. Heck, recent polls show that Europeans don't trust their own automakers and tend to prefer Japanese makes. *Mais oui!*
6. Look for 5-year-old Asian vehicles—unless they're Kias or Isuzus.
7. Buy small, entry-level Japanese pickups from Mazda, Nissan, or Toyota. Don't worry about paying too much; you'll get the extra dollars back when you sell.
8. Shop for rear-drive, full-sized vans instead of front-drive American minivans. High gas prices have sent vans' resale values somewhere south of Patagonia; a few thousand dollars more off the selling price will buy lots of fuel.

9. Don't buy for fuel economy alone. A 4-cylinder minivan or SUV is cheap to run, but highway merging will scare the heck out of you. Nor should you believe the hybrid- and diesel-savings hype; your hybrid fuel economy may be 40 percent *less* than what is advertised, and Chrysler, Ford, and GM diesels have become as temperamental and failure-prone as gasoline-fed engines.

10. Finally, if a vehicle's alphanumeric name doesn't make sense or can't be pronounced, get something else—forget the Cadillac SRX, Lincoln MKS/MKX/MKZ, Saab 9-7X, and VW Touareg.

Decade-Old Models?

It's getting pretty hard to find a 10-year-old vehicle that's safe and reliable. Personally, I'd be reluctant to buy any decade-old vehicle from someone I didn't know, or that has been brought in from another province. All of that accumulated salt is a real body killer, and it's just too easy to fall prey to scam artists who cover up major mechanical or body problems resulting from accidents or environmental damage.

Nevertheless, if you know the seller and an independent mechanic gives you the green light, you might seriously consider a 10-year-old, beat-up-looking pickup or van. Look for one of those listed in this appendix, or if you have a bit more money to spend and want to take less of a risk, look up the 1999 and later Recommended or Above Average models found in Part Four.

It's hard to go wrong with a 10-year-old Japanese small pickup, like this Mazda B-series.

Model Choices

The following new and used choices will help you hunker down and choose reliable, safe, fuel-efficient, and inexpensive wheels that will tide you over until you can get that more expensive dream machine you've always wanted.

Warning: No matter what you buy or how much you spend later on, you will remember your first "beater" as one of the best cars you ever owned. Furthermore, you'll quickly learn to drive with the windows and sunroof closed to avoid the painful, deafening boom so common to most SUVs, vans, and trucks.

Sport-Utilities

Anyone buying a sport-utility that's a decade old or more is asking for trouble, because many SUVs are worked hard off-road. The danger of rollovers for vehicles not equipped with electronic stability control is also quite high, particularly with Ford, Isuzu, and Suzuki versions; safety features are rudimentary, dangerous, and unreliable (especially airbags and ABS); overall quality control is very poor; and performance and handling cannot match today's models.

It's no wonder that many buyers are opting for new or almost-new SUVs manufactured during the past three years. During that time, prices have come down considerably because more products are in the supply line, electronic stability control and full-torso side airbags are more widely available as standard features, and crashworthiness scores have climbed higher.

Nevertheless, new models need at least a year to prove their overall reliability, real-world performance, and degree of factory and dealer support. For these reasons, many of the following recommendations counsel buyers to either put off their purchases until the aforementioned data can be studied or choose one of *Lemon-Aid*'s suggested alternatives.

An Above Average buy, the **Acura RDX** is marketed as the SUV version of Acura's sporty TSX. This $41,400 ($33,195 in the States) luxury crossover combines an innovative powertrain (turbocharger, etc.), lots of safety gear and high-tech standard features, a sporty platform, and a versatile, plush interior. It was launched as a 2007 model, and returns in 2009 relatively unchanged, except for an engine upgrade (likely trading the turbocharged 4-banger for a V6) and a $1,775 freight fee. Until then, the Mazda CX-7 represents a better buy as a much cheaper alternative with similar horsepower, torque, drivetrain, and body styling. Both the 2007 and 2008 RDX have earned five-star ratings for front and side crashworthiness and four stars for rollover resistance. IIHS safety ratings are "Good" for offset/side occupant protection and head-restraint effectiveness. A 2007 version can be found for about $30,000, or about $11,000 less than its original selling price.

Road noise is omnipresent, and the ride is stiff. You get the impression that the RDX is trying too hard to target the BMW "sporty" SUV market, especially since the 42 buttons and knobs mounted in the centre console area seem to be copying BMW's confusing iDrive cockpit controls.

Ever hear of **American Motors**? Well, back in 1981, this automaker brought out the first 4×4 passenger car/sport-utility—which was basically a Concord 4×4—called the **Eagle** (although others called it the Turkey). Not Recommended today, the Eagle was a sales flop due to its failure-prone powertrain, poor parts distribution, and problematic servicing. It now sells for less than $500. Be wary of its unreliable engine, transmission, and electrical system; clutch seal leaks; master slave cylinder leaks; low rust resistance; and marginal crash protection. But at least it doesn't easily tip over, something that can't be said of Ford's Bronco.

Chrysler's **Aspen** is a Not Recommended model that's essentially a $49,995 ($32,805 in the States) Dodge Durango with a different front grille. Chrysler says the 2009 Aspen lineup may include a hybrid model. *Lemon-Aid* says the vehicle may not be around that long.

The **Dodge Journey** is a $19,995 ($19,985 in the States—hardly worth a trip across the border) car-based SUV that uses the Chrysler Sebring/Dodge Avenger platform to create a small five-passenger SUV. A tiny third-row seat will accommodate two

The Dodge Journey is nicely styled, but its jerky automatic transmission and wimpy 4-banger relegate it to light-duty chores.

additional passengers in a pinch (literally). It is easy not to recommend a vehicle during its first year on the market due to a lack of data from owner and service bulletin feedback. However, the preliminary data we do have on the Journey already reinforces our Not Recommended rating. The 173-hp 2.4L 4-cylinder engine hooked to a 4-speed automatic transmission lacks sufficient torque to handle a full load of passengers and cargo; smart buyers will choose the optional 235-hp 3.5L V6. However, no matter which engine you choose, the automatic transmission's gear changes are often annoyingly abrupt, and steering, handling, and braking are acceptable but not reassuring. Six-footers will find headroom inadequate, the thick steering wheel blocks the view to some gauges, and the audio controls are mounted too low for easy access. Interior garnishing relies too much on cheap-looking hard plastics. On the other hand, there are a surprising number of innovative and easily accessed storage areas, and the front passenger seat folds flat to increase carrying capacity. NHTSA crashworthiness ratings are surprisingly good for an SUV this small: five-star front- and side-impact occupant protection and four-star rollover resistance.

Ford's **Bronco** is another SUV that's Not Recommended, particularly the 1981–90 models, even though their $500–$1,000 price may seem like a bargain. Broncos are unreliable, rollover-prone, rust-attracting 4×4s that are forever finding new ways to strand you. You can cut repair costs by using independent garages, but parts can be quite expensive (especially TFI ignition components and computer modules). Between 1985 and 1989, the Bronco II was the undisputed leader in rollover deaths in the U.S. According to internal memoranda, Ford released the Bronco II in 1981 with full knowledge of the stability dangers inherent in the design. Critics contend that the present-day Explorer's rollover problems can be traced back to its Bronco heritage.

This sport-utility suffers from worse-than-average reliability. The 4-speed automatic transmission has been the worst contributor to owners' woes. The complicated electronic fuel-injection system is a headache to diagnose and has a bad repair history. Brakes and 4×4 components are also often included on the list of potential problems. Overall, body assembly and paint quality are mediocre.

The Ford **Edge** and **Lincoln MKX** are Not Recommended buys selling for $34,349 and $43,299 in Canada (an AWD version carries a $2,000 premium). In the States, you will pay $25,735 and $35,840, respectively. These practically identical small, car-based SUVs use the Mazda6 platform, share Volvo CX-7 parts, and take their styling cues from the Ford **Fusion**. In the past, an infusion of Mazda parts has always helped bring up the quality of Ford's cars and trucks, including the Escort/Tracer, Probe/MX6, and Escape/Tribute. However, mixing in Volvo components as well presents added risks. Prudent buyers may wish to wait another year to get a better fix on quality and servicing. The 3.5L V6 (265 hp), mated to a 6-speed automatic transmission, makes both vehicles better-than-average performers. Big minuses, though, are the absence of third-row seating, unlike the Taurus X, and mediocre fit and finish. Crash test scores are excellent, however. Competitors worth considering: the Honda CR-V, Hyundai Tucson or Santa Fe, Nissan Murano, and Toyota RAV4.

The Ford **Taurus X** is no more than a renamed Ford Freestyle. It is rated an Above Average buy and sells for $33,999 for the **SEL** and $41,999 for the **AWD Limited**. In the States, you will pay $27,030 and $32,600, respectively. With the Taurus X, you get all of the attributes of a minivan, an SUV, and a station wagon, but few of the disadvantages inherent in each category. There is plenty of interior room for passengers and pets, and the third-row seat can actually accommodate adults. Ride and handling are first class, and the inclusion of electronic stability control as a standard feature has eliminated the fishtailing instability sometimes felt with the Freestyle. Although real-world fuel economy is about 10 percent less than advertised, the 3.5L V6 has plenty of power for most driving activities. NHTSA crashworthiness scores are also quite good: five stars for front- and side-impact occupant protection, and four-star rollover resistance.

The Taurus X looks like a winner for those buyers who want the features of an SUV, a station wagon, and a minivan all in one vehicle.

Although it's a Not Recommended buy during its first year on the market, the Flex has lots of potential and may be a viable alternative to GM's Acadia, Enclave, or Outlook.

For 2009, Ford will offer a spin-off of the Taurus X called the **Flex**, a replacement for the Windstar/Freestar, priced at $25,523 U.S. (see the following page for a U.S. price chart; Canadian prices aren't yet available). Like the Taurus X, it also uses a raised wagon platform, carries a 260-hp 3.5L V6 hooked to a 6-speed automatic transmission, and provides plenty of interior room in a layout similar to a traditional minivan. Although the Flex will seat seven passengers, higher-end versions will seat only six due to the space taken up by the second-row captain's chairs.

Competitors to the Taurus X worth considering: the Honda CR-V, Hyundai Tucson or Santa Fe, Mazda CX-7 or CX-9, Nissan Murano, and Toyota RAV4. Flex competitors are the Buick Enclave, GMC Acadia, and Saturn Outlook.

2009 FORD FLEX
PRICE LIST
(PRICE LEVEL CODE 915)

MODEL	SERIES CODE	BASE VEHICLE PRICE	DEALER PRICE	DEALER INVOICE W/HOLDBACK	SUGGESTED RETAIL
SE	K51	SE FWD --(110A)	$ 25,523	$ 26,707	$ 28,295
SEL	K52	SEL FWD -- (120A)	28,562	29,859	32,070
Limited	K53	Limited FWD -- (130A)	30,880	32,256	34,705
SEL	K62	SEL AWD -- (220A)	30,190	31,543	33,920
Limited	K63	Limited AWD -- (230A)	32,508	33,940	36,555
ALL MODELS		Destination and Delivery	700	700	700

	OPTION CODE	POWERTRAINS	DEALER PRICE	DEALER INVOICE W/HOLDBACK	SUGGESTED RETAIL
ENGINE	99C	3.5L V6 Duratec 35	Std	Std	Std
TRANSMISSION	44J	6 Speed Auto Transmission	Std	Std	Std

MODEL	OPTION CODE	TIRES	DEALER PRICE	DEALER INVOICE W/HOLDBACK	SUGGESTED RETAIL
SE	64F	17 in. Aluminum Wheel w/ P235/60R17 BSW (SE)	N/C	N/C	N/C
	64R	18 in. Painted Aluminum Wheel w/ P235/60R18 BSW (SE)	Std	Std	Std
SEL	64T	18 in. Machined Aluminum Wheel w/ P235/60R18 BSW (SEL)	Std	Std	Std
Limited	64V	19 in. Polished Aluminum Wheel w/ P235/55R19 BSW (Limited)	Std	Std	Std

	OPTION CODE	OTHER OPTIONS	DEALER PRICE	DEALER INVOICE W/HOLDBACK	SUGGESTED RETAIL
AVAILABLE ON ALL MODELS UNLESS OTHERWISE NOTED	65L	Convenience Package (SEL)	$ 808	$ 838	$ 985
		Convenience Package (Limited)	Std	Std	Std
	86L	Lighting Package (SEL)	734	761	895
	53G	Trailer Towing Prep Package - Class III	467	484	570
	21D	2nd Row 40/40 Reclining Seats (SE & SEL)	631	654	770
		2nd Row 40/40 Heated Reclining Seats (Limited)	713	739	870
	51C	2nd Row Floor Console (SEL & Limited)	82	85	100
	62R	Rear Console Refrigeration System (SEL & Limited)	623	646	760
	16W	All Weather Floor Mats	45	47	55
	901	DVD Rear Entertainment Center (SEL & Limited)	836	867	1,020
	43P	Vista Roof (SEL & Limited)	1,226	1,271	1,495
	87W	Two-Tone Roof - White Suede	324	336	395
	87G	Two-Tone Roof - Brilliant Silver	324	336	395
	PUG	Tricoat Paint (SEL & Limited)	324	336	395
	66B	SYNC (SE & SEL)	324	336	395
	68B	Roof Rack Side Rails - Black (SE)	82	85	100
	68C	Roof Rack Side Rails - Chrome (SEL & Limited)	82	85	100
		AUDIO			
		Single CD (SE)	Std	Std	Std
	581	CDX6 w/ Satellite Radio (SE)	353	366	430
		CDX6 w/ Satellite Radio (SEL & Limited)	Std	Std	Std
	85N	Navigation System w/ Rear Back Up Camera (Limited)	1,948	2,019	2,375

	OPTION CODE	LIMITED PRODUCTION OPTIONS	DEALER PRICE	DEALER INVOICE W/HOLDBACK	SUGGESTED RETAIL
AVAILABLE ON ALL MODELS UNLESS OTHERWISE NOTED	41H	Engine Block Heater	$ 29	$ 30	$ 35
	67R	PowerCode Remote Start	242	251	295
		Fleet Marketing Credit (no code required; automatic w/ valid FIN)	(340)	(340)	0

This confidential U.S. price list for the 2009 Ford Flex and its options can be a helpful resource for negotiating a fair Canadian price for almost any Ford model and its accessories.

GM Acadia, **Enclave**, and **Outlook**—In Canada, these Above Average, practically identical mid-sized models sell for $36,495, 40,895, and $34,535, respectively. Stateside, you would pay $39,470, $33,505, and $28,995. They all offer front-drive/all-wheel-drive powertrains and use a car-based platform that incorporates a third-row seat, which allows for a maximum of eight passengers. Power is provided by a 3.6L V6 mated to a newly designed 6-speed automatic transmission. GM says the upgraded powertrain set-up gives 8 percent improved performance and up to 4 percent improved fuel economy when compared with current front-drive 4-speed automatics. Competing models worth considering are the Chrysler Pacifica, Honda Pilot, Nissan Murano, Mazda CX-9, and Toyota Highlander.

Saturn's Outlook, the first model released, replaced the Relay minivan for the 2008 model year. It rides on a unibody platform, which cuts weight by eliminating the usual hefty trucklike frame and other heavy-duty chassis components. The user-friendly interior resembles GM's Yukon and Tahoe cabins, with roomy and easily accessed seating. Furthermore, an innovative second-row seat can be pushed forward and folded against the front row, thereby enlarging the pathway to the third-row seating area. Entry and exit height is low, and the rear tail light design isn't to everyone's taste.

The Saturn Outlook.

As with most of GM's recent SUVs, standard safety features abound. For example, there's electronic stability control with rollover mitigation, front and side airbags plus two head-protecting side curtain airbags for all three rows, and four-wheel anti-lock brakes. A wide stance and low centre of gravity reduce the threat of a rollover. NHTSA crashworthiness scores are quite good: five stars for front- and side-impact occupant protection and four stars for rollover resistance.

Some of the minuses inherent in GM's new crossover trio: Outlook prices will be unacceptably high until the third quarter of 2008, when they should drop by about 15 percent as the new Acadia and Enclave cannibalize the market. Third-row seating is a bit cramped, the new 6-speed tranny has yet to prove itself, and the V6 powerplant is a mixed-breed design from Australia, Germany, Sweden, and North America that was first introduced on Cadillac's CTS sedan and SRX SUV crossover. SRX and CTS complaints logged by NHTSA and others frequently mention engine and transmission/differential failures. Furthermore, GM's touted fuel economy savings associated with its new powertrain (*front-drive:* 9.4/13.8 L/100 km; *AWD:* 9.8/14.7 L/100 km) may be illusory when compared to real driving reports. Finally, mechanics will need at least another year to figure out how to troubleshoot these new designs.

The **Cadillac SRX**, a Below Average buy, is a mid-sized rear-drive or all-wheel-drive luxury crossover. It has been on the Canadian market since 2004, when the car originally sold for $52,250 as a front-drive SUV, $54,875 with AWD, and $63,965 for a V8 AWD. Today, the same vehicles are worth $17,500, $19,000, and $21,500, respectively. The 2008 SRXs have also been hit especially hard by cheaper competitors. In Canada, they are now listed at $46,695, $49,320, and $62,925—less than the original selling prices of new models three years ago. In the States, you can pick them up for $38,390, $39,515, and $46,515—well worth a trip across the border.

SRX owners report frequent transmission and differential breakdowns in addition to brake and electrical failures and fit and finish deficiencies. The 2004–07 models earned four stars for front crashworthiness and five stars for side-impact protection. The 2008 models got similar ratings, but they also scored three stars for front-drive rollover resistance and four stars for AWD rollover protection.

First launched as a 2003 model, the 2003–08 GM **Hummer H2 SUV** and **SUT** (SUT is the pickup version launched as a 2005 model) are Not Recommended due to their overall poor reliability, mediocre highway performance, and mind-spinning depreciation. A 2003 H2 SUV that originally sold for $71,000 is now barely worth $20,000; a 2007 SUV or SUT that sold for $67,700 new has already lost $25,000 of its trade-in value. Outward visibility is severely compromised by the small windshield and wide roof pillars, and NHTSA hasn't crash-tested the H2 yet. Still, the H2 is a good off-road performer (it uses the Tahoe's previous generation platform) and appeals to those who like ultra-macho styling. The 2008 models get a new, classier-looking interior. GM may drop the Hummer line in 2009.

The more moderately priced 2006–08 **Hummer H3** is also Not Recommended, mainly because its mechanicals are derivative of the poor-quality GM Canyon/Colorado, and it has been on the market only a few years. Depreciation is unusually rapid; a $40,000 2006 H3 now fetches $23,000. Like its big brother, the H3 is a good off-roader, but for this attribute you must sacrifice access, visibility, a quiet interior, and a comfortable ride. The base engine is noisy, has little grunt, and is a gas-guzzler. It was replaced by a 3.7L engine in late 2007. A 300-hp 5.3L V8 powers the new 2008 H3 Alpha variant. NHTSA has given the H3 its top five-star rating for frontal and side crashworthiness beginning with the 2006 model, although passenger protection is rated only four stars in side impacts.

Isuzu's 1993–2004 **Ascender**, **Axiom**, **Rodeo**, **Rodeo Sport**, and **Trooper** are competent SUVs for light city commuting. However, Isuzu's decision to abandon the North American truck market in 2009 means all of the automaker's vehicles are destined to become automotive orphans, and for this reason are Not Recommended buys. Although they look tacky and feel outdated, Isuzus are good performers with powerful V6s, shift-on-the-fly capabilities, versatile transmissions, predictable rear-drive handling, spacious interiors, and very few complaints of safety-related defects. Less attractive characteristics are a wimpy 4-cylinder engine, part-time 4×4 that can't be used on dry pavement, a harsh ride over bumpy terrain, excessive body lean when cornering, obstructed rear visibility, narrow rear doors, excessive road and engine noise, and poor fuel economy. Some of the safety-related failures tabulated by NHTSA include brake loss, automatic transmission failures, and sudden, unintended acceleration.

Older **Jeeps** are Not Recommended, despite the fact that they and Chrysler's minivans are the best of a bad lot. To be fair, the Jeep's tendency to roll over isn't as high as that of other small sport-utilities; parts are not yet hard to find; and servicing, if not given with a smile, at least isn't accompanied by a snarl or head-scratching. Nevertheless, Chrysler's string of money-losing years and its penny-pinching new owners make the Jeep division a prime candidate for the auction block in 2009. And if the company is sold, there will be fewer dealers, warranties will be worthless, parts will be hard to find, and resale values will plummet. Early Cherokees, CJs, and Wagoneers have been known for their rattle-prone bodies, air and water leaks, electrical glitches, and high-cost brake maintenance. Expect to spend $1,500 tops for a decade-old entry-level CJ, and a thousand more for an even older Wagoneer.

The **Kia Borrego** is a new seven-seat mid-sized SUV that will be sold as a 2009 model for $27,000–$30,000. The car is Not Recommended due to its unproven record in Canada.

Kia's quality control has dramatically improved over the past three years, since Hyundai bought a 39 percent controlling interest in the automaker.

Based on a stretched body-on-frame Sorento platform, the Borrego will be powered by a standard 3.8L V6 or an all-new 4.6L V8. Both models will be offered with either rear-drive or four-wheel drive. The V8 will be hooked to a 6-speed automatic transmission, another first for Kia, and towing capacity is a very respectable 5,000 lb. with the V6 and 7,500 lb. with the V8 engine.

Borrego's 114-inch wheelbase, overall length of 192.1 inches, and overall width of 75.4 inches puts it into direct competition with the Ford Explorer, Chevrolet TrailBlazer, Nissan Pathfinder, and Toyota 4Runner.

Ride quality and off-road stability are enhanced by the new platform's four-wheel independent suspension, with coil-over springs front and back. Full-torso side curtain airbags cover all three rows of seats, and there's a long list of standard safety features like ABS, electronic stability control, downhill assist control (DAC), and hill assist control (HAC), which help maintain stability on steep slopes.

Don't assume that European luxury SUVs are as reliable as Asian makes. They aren't. In fact, some of the European makes with the most snob appeal have the worst reliability records. BMW, Land Rover, Porsche, and Mercedes-Benz SUVs have all garnered a reputation for building poor-quality vehicles with head-spinning depreciation.

As predicted last year by *Lemon-Aid,* **Land Rover** was sold on March 26, 2008, to Tata Motors, an Indian conglomerate that also picked up Jaguar for about $2.3 billion (U.S.). News of the deal sent Tata shares down when it was learned that the purchase was financed by a $3-billion, 15-month loan.

This sale means Tata will have the unenviable position of paying the annual $2-billion losses these two companies are expected to incur, judging by past performance. Our prediction: Ta-ta, Land Rover; ta-ta, Jaguar.

LAND ROVER QUALITY IS NOT "JOB 1"

Problems per 100 vehicles, compared with industry average

YEAR	LAND ROVER	INDUSTRY
2006	204	124
2005	149	118
2004	148	119
2003	190	133

Source: J.D. Power and Associates 2006 Initial Quality Study.

Land Rover's **Discovery** was replaced by the 2005 and 2006 **LR3 SE/HSE** ($61,900/$67,900), a much more refined vehicle that was completely re-engineered by Ford and given a Jaguar-sourced 300-hp 4.4L V8 along with decent disc/disc brakes. It is now worth between $24,000 and $26,000. A new 2008 LR3 will run about $57,990. A 2008 $44,900 **LR2** came on the scene as the Freelander's replacement. It shares most of its powertrain and other major components with Volvo's S80 and S40, including the S80's 230-hp 6-cylinder engine.

All of the above prices can be easily beaten by shopping for your Land Rover in the States. For example, both the 2008 LR2 and the LR3 cost about $9,000 less there ($36,150 and $39,300, respectively).

According to J.D. Power's 2006 Initial Quality Study (IQS), Land Rover anchored the bottom of the quality heap with 204 problems per 100 vehicles—more than two problems per vehicle, and a far cry from the industry average of 124 problems. Nevertheless, the poor showing is no surprise for the British automaker now owned by Tata Motors. It has been a perennial bottom-feeder in quality surveys for the past several decades. Industry watchers say the company's dead-last IQS finish was the result of electronic glitches that followed the replacement of Land Rover's BMW-sourced engines with Jaguar engines during the 2006 model year. For example, the 2006 Range Rover adopted the Jaguar engine but retained the original BMW electrical architecture—a sure-fire recipe for trouble and a constantly lit Check Engine light.

Land Rover also tied for last with Hummer and Porsche in *Consumer Reports'* 2006 car reliability survey, and it was only one of six makes that did not have a model whose reliability was "Good" or above, a "distinction" shared with Mercedes-Benz, Volkswagen, and Jaguar.

The following year, Land Rover placed second-to-last in the same *Consumer Reports* reliability survey. (Mercedes-Benz took the bottom spot.) The V8-equipped LR3/ Discovery was ranked the second-least reliable mid-sized SUV. (The Mercedes-Benz M-Class SUV took last place.)

Range Rover launched a sportier-looking $77,800–$93,800 **Sport** for the 2006 model year. Equipped with the LR3's V8 engine (an optional supercharger adds 25 horses) and loaded with performance features, the Sport targets the FX45 and Porsche Cayenne crowd. However, Sport sales have been underwhelming, and

2006s models have lost so much of their original value that they sell for as little as $40,000 and $47,000.

Rapid depreciation has spared none of the Land Rover lineup over the past few decades. Range Rover and Discovery versions have been particularly hard hit. A 1996 $42,000 Discovery is now worth about $6,000, and the same-year Range Rover, originally priced at $80,000, *may* fetch $9,000 on a good day.

The cheapest of the three is the **Freelander**, launched in 2002 with an entry-level price of $34,800 and a resale value now of about $7,000. It survived only four model years. The 2005 versions included the **SE** and **SE3** ($25,000/$27,000). They carry a wimpy 174-hp 2.5L V6 engine, feature a removable hardtop that takes a two-man crew to install, and use antediluvian disc/drum brakes.

More softly styled than its larger, squared-off Discovery brother, the Freelander is a small, underpowered, cramped truck with luxury SUV pretensions. Headroom is at a premium for tall drivers (don't look for the seat height-adjustment control—there isn't one), and storage space behind the back seats is clearly inadequate. Ground clearance is also quite low when compared with the competition. When pushed, the 174-hp V6 engine whines and struggles to hold its own. A stick shift isn't available, so there's no way to improve the mediocre 15.0 L/100 km average fuel economy.

On paper, the latest rendition of these models looks impressive indeed, with a long list of standard safety, performance, and convenience features. But, as with other Land Rovers, when you buy one of these entry-level British imports, you are buying into a make that's unreliable, outclassed by most other automakers, and served by a limited, chaotic dealer network that was poorly administered by Ford and is now Tata Motors' headache.

Mazda's **CX-7** and **CX-9** are Above Average buys that sell in Canada for $32,095 and $39,995, respectively (an AWD version costs about $2,000 more). In the States, these two Mazdas sell for $23,750 and $30,035—again, reason enough to buy from an American dealer. AWD will add a couple thousand dollars to the base price. The sporty five-passenger CX-7 is a promising new unibody, four-door crossover SUV based on the Mazda5 and Mazda6. It's not suitable for off-roading, though, even though it looks like it could go anywhere. The turbocharged 4-cylinder engine is taken from the MazdaSpeed6 and hasn't accumulated enough road time to determine its long-term durability. Electronic stability control is a standard feature. A longer version, the CX-9, is equipped with a V6 and a third-row seat. Both models have earned high crashworthiness rankings for the 2007–08 models: five-star occupant protection in front and side impacts, and four stars for rollover resistance.

Next, we come to **Mercedes-Benz** and its problem-racked foray into luxury sport-utilities, first launched in 1997. Known collectively as the **M-Class**, these SUVs are Not Recommended buys from 1998 to 2009. **ML320, ML350, ML430,** and **ML500** models are a far cry from being cheap wheels, even though they depreciate about 50 percent after five years (a $48,600 2001 ML320 is now worth about $10,500). The main drawbacks of these luxury lemons are poor quality control; unreliable, limited servicing; and so-so parts availability. Owners report automatic transmission failures, frequent engine oil leaks and engine oil sludge, and electrical system shorts. Other problems afflict brake pads, rotors, master cylinders, fuel pumps, oxygen sensors, mass airflow sensors, and fit and finish.

Mercedes-Benz redesigned the 2006 M-Class to make it longer, lower, and wider. It handles and rides in a more carlike fashion because of the retuned suspension and the removal of its truck frame. Power is supplied by a 268-hp 3.5L V6 or by a 302-hp 5.0L V8. Off-roaders can order a 2-speed 4×4 transfer case. The ML350 was launched as a 2003 model and sold for $50,600; it's now worth about $17,000. A 2005 ML500 that originally sold for $68,690 is now worth approximately $29,000.

Is the redesigned 2006 and later M-Class more reliable and glitch-free?

No, nothing indicates that this is the case. In fact, consumer complaints are still highlighting electronic, brake, and powertrain problems as the car's more common failings.

The same caveat applies to Mercedes' **R-Class**, launched in 2006. It fills the gap between a wagon and the M-Class with a six-passenger crossover reminiscent of the Chrysler Pacifica. It's available with a 268-hp 3.5L V6, a 302-hp 5.0L V8, and an incredibly powerful and totally inappropriate 360-hp 5.5L V8 AMG engine. On- and off-road driving is aided by the electronically controlled 4ETS four-wheel-drive system used in the M-Class and G-Class, an Airmatic air suspension system, and a high-pressure brake system. A 2006 **R350** sold for $64,400 and can be bought used for $37,000. A used 2006 **R500** takes a harder hit: Sold originally for $75,950, it is now worth about $45,000.

All of these Mercedes models can be bought in the States for tens of thousands of dollars less than what Canadian dealers charge. And, theoretically, you could buy your Benz in the States while on vacation, drive it in Canada for three years, and then sell it in Canada for as much as you paid originally, or even more.

But do you want the headache of constant repairs and adjustments, and to see your service manager more than your spouse? Again, no matter how low their prices, these SUVs, like Mercedes' other vehicles, are mainly for buyers with more money than common sense.

If you want to make a killing buying a luxury vehicle in the States, stick with Acura, Porsche, or Lexus.

The $24,998 **Nissan Rogue** is too new to recommend, although it has lots of potential. Priced at $19,250 in the States, it looks like a downsized Murano, and it uses the Sentra's 170-hp 2.5L 4-cylinder engine hooked to a fuel-efficient standard continuously variable transmission that includes a locking centre differential for more difficult off-road terrain.

Like the Murano, the Rogue favours curvy looks over boxy utility. This limits visibility somewhat (though not as badly as in the Murano). We were impressed, however, with the wide, flat cargo area, with no intruding strut towers—made possible by the independent rear suspension—that's ideal for carrying small animal crates. The front passenger seat also folds flat to accommodate longer cargo.

The 2009 Nissan Rogue: $24,998 in Canada; $19,250 in the States.

On the road, the Rogue's small engine handles most driving tasks quite easily, though it is a bit noisy when pushed. Handling is above average, the ride is comfortable and well controlled, and braking is better than average.

For a small SUV, the Rogue offers a full complement of standard safety features, including electronic stability control, traction control, curtain airbags, and ABS. It also has a surprising array of upscale options like a Bluetooth-compatible Bose stereo with XM satellite radio, Xenon HID headlights, and heated leather seats.

The Rogue's long-term reliability and repairability should be quite good, thanks to its use of good-quality, easily found Sentra components and to its simple design. NHTSA crash tests offer up more good news: a five-star rating for front- and side-collision occupant protection, and four stars awarded for rollover resistance.

First launched as a 2003 model, the **Volvo XC90** mid-sized SUV is another poor performer from Europe that's Not Recommended. Available with either a 6-cylinder or a Yamaha-sourced V8 engine, this $50,995 four-door has a well-appointed, roomy, and versatile interior that provides lots of space for animal crates and gear, as well as tons of standard safety and convenience features.

NHTSA crashworthiness rankings for the 2004–08 models have been quite good: five stars for front- and side-collision occupant protection, and four-star rollover resistance. The 2003 models earned four stars for front and side occupant protection but were not tested for rollover protection.

The three factors that make the purchase of any Volvo a risky deal are an unjustifiably high price (in the States, you can pick up an entry-level XC90 for only $36,210), a rapid decline in Volvo quality since Ford bought the company in 1999 for $6.4 billion (U.S.), and a small, dispirited dealer network that fears Ford will close them down or sell Volvo to an independent, upstart automaker like India's Tata Motors. Resale values, long a Volvo strength, are no longer impressive. For example, a 2003 XC90 that originally sold for $54,995 is now worth about $16,000.

Other failings: mediocre acceleration with the 6-cylinder powerplant, excessive fuel consumption with the must-have V8, and a history of automatic transmission, electrical system, suspension, brake, AC, and body fit and finish deficiencies. Last time Yamaha built engines for Ford, thousands of Ford Taurus owners sued the company for selling them self-destructing engines that cost up to $10,000 to repair before failing again.

Porsche Cayennes don't hold their values as well as most Japanese luxury cars. For example, a $78,250 2003 Cayenne is now worth barely $30,000.

Porsche's **Cayenne** is a Below Average buy mainly due to its limited servicing network, mediocre performance, and outrageously high retail price reserved for Canadians who are too naive to know they are being scammed. In fact, we are paying a retail price that is still way too high even after having been cut by more than $10,000 following *Lemon-Aid*'s criticism of Porsche's greed in late 2007. For example, Canadian dealers want $55,200, $72,200, and $115,300 (for the V6, V8, and AWD V8 Turbo, respectively) for this luxury SUV that sells for $43,400/$57,900/$93,700 in the States. Who in their right mind would pay a Canadian dealer $12,000 more for the same entry-level vehicle, or throw away almost $22,000 for a top-of-the-line Cayenne bought in Canada?

First launched as a 2003 model, the Cayenne skipped the 2007 model year and has returned as a 2008 model. A mid-sized unibody SUV, the Cayenne shares many of the VW Touareg's parts (remember, VW, Audi, and Porsche are all under the same corporate umbrella); hence, reliability has been subpar. Cayenne does have some limited off-road capability, thanks to its low gearing, sophisticated electronics, and Touareg-sourced V6 engine, plus Porsche V8 and twin-turbo variants—a 3.2L V6 (247 hp), 4.5L V8 (340 hp), 4.5L Twin-Turbo V8 (450 hp), and another, more powerful 4.5L Twin-Turbo V8 (520 hp). Transmissions consist of a 6-speed manual and a 6-speed automatic. On-road capability is a big disappointment, however, since the vehicle lacks Porsche's handling prowess. Furthermore, many of the cabin controls are needlessly complex and confusing. Crashworthiness has not yet been rated.

The 2003–06 **Subaru Baja** is an Average all-wheel-drive crossover that provides the handling and passenger-carrying characteristics of a car with its open-bed versatility and, to a lesser degree, the load capacity of a pickup truck (think of a small 1959–60 Chevrolet El Camino, or a mini GM Avalanche). Baja's unibody platform borrows heavily from Subaru's Legacy and Outback.

The car is too small to offer much that is useful or fun. Still, poor sales mean deeply discounted used prices. For example, a 2006 version that sold new for almost $30,000 is now available for about $17,000. In the States, used prices are cut another 15 percent. Some of the Baja's minuses: uncomfortably upright rear seating; the bed is too short to carry a bike without extending the tailgate into part of the bed; there's no 5-speed automatic transmission; and the absence of a folding midgate means the flip-and-fold versatility isn't as practical as Subaru pretends. Head restraints are ranked "Marginal" by IIHS, and no crashworthiness tests were carried out by NHTSA, although the Legacy Outback was awarded five stars for front- and side-impact occupant protection and four stars for rollover resistance.

The Baja is basically a Legacy Outback with its rear roof chopped off and 15 cm (6 in.) added to the rear floor to make a mini pickup bed. It uses a switchback door similar to the trunk pass-through door in a sedan, creating a 2.5 m (7.6 ft.) cargo bed. The car/truck comes with standard four-wheel disc ABS, AC, a sunroof, an anti-theft device, a front passenger-side airbag, a 5-speed manual or 4-speed automatic transmission, and upgraded child restraint anchors.

Baja projects a rugged, utilitarian look with its large fender flares, 16-inch alloy wheels, and sport bars, but its 165-hp flat-four engine fails to deliver the driving performance its styling promises. A turbocharged variant of the same 4-banger provides more power, but it exacts a 10 percent fuel penalty. Nevertheless, if you aren't in a hurry to go anywhere and you value fuel economy (7.6/10.3 L/100 km) over driving thrills, the all-wheel-drive Baja equipped with the non-turbo engine will fill the bill.

The 1987–94 **Suzuki Samurai** is an orphan you shouldn't buy, despite its low cost ($500–$750). Parts are almost impossible to find and are quite expensive. Crash test results for the 1986 model, which can be extrapolated to later versions, concluded that the driver and passenger would have sustained severe leg trauma. Unsteady road manners, coupled with a high centre of gravity, make the Samurai susceptible to sudden rollovers if the vehicle is not driven carefully, especially on rough terrain. This is particularly true of the 1987–88 models, where NHTSA records show the largest grouping of owner complaints and accident injury reports.

The **Toyota FJ Cruiser** takes its inspiration from the Toyota FJ40 Land Cruiser, built between 1956 and 1983, and sells for $30,725 ($22,545 in the States). It's an Average buy that competes especially well off-road against the Ford Escape, Honda Element, Jeep Liberty or Wrangler, and Nissan Xterra. It is powered by a competent 239-hp 4.0L V6 that can be used for either two- or four-wheel drive. A 5-speed automatic transmission comes with both versions, and a 6-speed manual gearbox is available with the all-wheel drive. Although the FJ's turning circle is about 1.5 m (5 ft.) larger than those of similar-sized SUVs, off-roading should be a breeze if done carefully, thanks to standard electronic stability control, short overhangs, and better-than-average ground clearance.

Interestingly, NHTSA crashworthiness scores for front and side impacts have been five stars; however, the rollover rating was only three stars, an "Average" rating. This is disappointing, and it's almost never seen with vehicles that are equipped with electronic stability control.

The rear side doors are taken from the Honda Element, which means rear and side visibility is severely limited. There is also some side-wind vulnerability, and annoying wind noises are generated by the large side mirrors. Although touted as a five-passenger conveyance, a normal-sized fifth passenger in the back seat won't be comfortable. Plus the rear seats are hard to access, forcing front occupants to unbuckle every time a rear occupant gets in or out. Front-seat headrests may be uncomfortably positioned for short occupants. Another minus is that premium fuel must be used.

Of course, if you don't mind driving a really old Toyota, there's nothing wrong with a 1987–89 Toyota **Land Cruiser**, which sells for about $3,000. Just be sure to pull the wheels off to examine the brakes, to check for undercarriage corrosion, and to make sure the engine head gasket is okay.

If you have $53,000 (U.S.) to spend, this summer's 2009 **BMW X6** will give you all-wheel drive, a high seating position, large wheels and tires, and all the major components found in BMW's other two crossovers, the X3 and X5. Built on the same South Carolina assembly line as the other BMWs, the X6 uses a fastback body, is slightly longer and wider than the X5, though significantly lower, and provides only four full seats. Second-row seating is tight, though fairly accessible; exiting takes some acrobatics, however.

It will have two engine variants: The xDrive35i ($53,275, including shipping), equipped with a 3.0L 306-hp inline twin-turbo 6-cylinder engine, and a more powerful xDrive50i ($63,775, including shipping), equipped with a new 4.4L 407-hp V8 twin-turbo engine. A 6-cylinder (235–286-hp) diesel variant is scheduled for early 2009.

BMW is marketing the X6 to appeal to owners of the Porsche Cayenne, Infiniti FX, and Land Rover Range Rover Sport SUVs. The X6 is a Not Recommended buy due to its high price tag, limited seating, short time on the market, and limited dealer support.

VW's **Touareg** is a Not Recommended buy that is living on borrowed time due to poor sales and quality-control deficiencies. Restyled in 2007, it's now cleaner-burning and more fuel-efficient. But the Touareg has already earned a bad reputation for poor reliability and expensive servicing ever since it was first launched as a 2005 luxury SUV listed at $55,010 (now worth $22,000). A new 2006 sold for almost 10 percent less at $50,790, and the 2008 retails for $49,975. The 2004 is now worth about $18,000, and a 2005 will fetch about $4,000 more. Prices in the States are easily 20 percent less.

Despite its sharing of some parts with the Porsche Cayenne, all you get as a trade-off are befuddled mechanics; long waits for parts; complicated controls; a modest cargo area; myriad electrical, powertrain, and brake problems; premature tire wear; and performance and handling that's abysmal. A 276-hp 3.6L V6 became the standard engine in the summer of 2006; however, it is just as thirsty and only slightly less lethargic than the earlier 3.2L V6. An optional 4.2L V8 offers a bit better performance, but only the turbocharged V10 diesel is adequate to give this beast the grunt it requires, especially when used for off-roading.

Crashworthiness ratings are fairly impressive. The 2005 and 2006 models scored four stars for frontal collision occupant protection and five stars in side-impact tests. The 2007 and 2008 models were judged to give five-star protection in both tests. Rollover resistance was rated four stars.

Minivans and Wagons

Assuming that you can't afford to spare the big bucks for a Honda Odyssey or Toyota Sienna, you have a number of cheaper old minivans to choose from: Chrysler's Colt/Summit/Vista wagons; Ford's Aerostar; GM's Astro and Safari; and Nissan's Axxess. The 2006 and 2007 Mazda5 mini-minivans also show a lot of promise.

Chrysler's **Colt**, **Summit**, and **Vista** are Average small minivans with five- to seven-passenger seating. They have excellent crash ratings and are more reasonably priced, practical, and fuel efficient than many other small wagons. The five-passenger Colt wagon, like the Summit and Nissan Axxess, offers the extra versatility of a third seat in the back and a tall body. The wagon series is available in 4×4 (not recommended) and uses practically the same mechanical components as the other Colt models.

Priced from about $500 for an '88 version to about $1,000 for a '95, these are three fairly reliable, easy-to-repair, and fuel-efficient Mitsubishi imports. The only exceptions are the older 1985–88 models, which were quite troublesome. On post-1990 Colts and Summits, the 2.4L head gasket is known to fail frequently. Shocks aren't very durable, braking isn't impressive, and the front brakes have a short lifespan. Be especially wary of the troublesome 4×4 powertrain on 1989–91 wagons and the 16-valve turbo, dropped in 1990.

The 1995–97 **Ford Aerostar** is a Below Average buy, with 1986–94 models representing the poorest choices. A 1992 XL would cost about $1,500, while a fully equipped 1997 version (1997 was the Aerostar's last year) should cost between $2,500 and $3,000. These primitive rear-drives are brawnier and more reliable than Chrysler, Ford, and GM front-drive minivans, and they've posted impressive crashworthiness scores since 1992. Check for cracked coil springs, a common failing.

Nissan's 1991–95 **Axxess** small minivan is an Above Average choice. It is fairly reliable, easily serviced, and has posted respectable crash protection ratings. Expect to pay from $1,500 to $2,500 for the top-of-the-line SE. You may have trouble finding one; word has gotten out that they are "beater" bargains.

The 2006–09 **Mazda5** is an Above Average buy that's a modern version of the Nissan Axxess and Colt/Eagle/Summit, which were dropped more than a decade ago. It is basically a compact MPV that's based broadly on the Mazda3 and carries six passengers in three rows of seats. Suited mostly for urban errands and light commuting, the "5" shares with the Mazda3 its peppy, fuel-frugal 157-hp 2.3L 4-cylinder engine hooked to a standard 5-speed manual transmission or a 4-speed automatic (a 5-speed automatic came online with the 2008 model). The engine's biggest downside is its lack of power when fully loaded or when passing over hilly terrain. Few powertrain problems have surfaced during the four years the Mazda5 has been sold in Canada.

The Mazda5 combines minivan seating with better-than-average fuel economy.

This is a relatively tall and narrow car with a thick, obtrusive front A-pillar. Nevertheless, it is very fuel-frugal, and it handles well, despite steering that's a bit vague and some body roll. Drivers will find it a breeze to park, easy to manoeuvre, and fairly spacious inside. Two wide-opening sliding doors make for easy entry and exit; however, the lower door hinge can trap little feet. Headroom is adequate, legroom is limited, and the rear seat is for children only. Seats can't be removed, but they do fold forward to make a flat cargo floor.

Available in European and Asian markets since 1999, these small vans have had some first-year production bugs that cause automatic transmission gear-hunting, rapid brake wear, and electrical system shorts. Nevertheless, their overall popularity means that most dealers will be selling them close to the listed MSRP. Still, buyers will score a decent small minivan for much less than the larger minivans sold by the competition. The GS retails for $19,995, and the upscale GT for $22,895—thousands of dollars less than the self-destructing Chevrolet Uplander and other poor-quality GM and Ford front-drive minivans, and about $10,000 below the more reliable Honda Odyssey and Toyota Sienna. Used Mazda5s depreciate about $2,000 a year.

Stay away from bargain-priced old minivans that have always needed frequent and costly repairs. Chief among these are $1,000–$4,000 **Chrysler minivans** (1984–2001) and $1,500–$2,000 **Mercury Villager/Nissan Quest** models (1993–96). Chrysler minivans have a history of engine, drivetrain, suspension, electrical and fuel-system, AC, brake, and body deficiencies galore. Villagers and Quests have similar component failings. In fact, Quests built since 2005 are known to be particularly troublesome. **VW Campers** are a good idea that's poorly executed. They are nicely laid out, but they aren't reliable, and servicing is practically non-existent. Expect to pay $2,000–$2,500 for a 1985–89 model.

Pickups

As a general rule, old trucks aren't very col-
lectible, unless they're trucks that were used
for a specific purpose, like fire trucks, army
vehicles, or commercial vehicles (milk trucks,
etc.). For most decade-old small trucks made
by the Detroit Big Three, you can expect to
pay $2,000–$3,000 for a fuel-thirsty, poor-
quality truck that can be repaired almost
anywhere. Asian imports may cost a few
thousand more because of their reputation
for being better made and more reliable. If
you're looking for a larger pickup, the price
may vary from $3,000 to $5,000, with no real
Asian competition in sight until the 2004 model year.

Your best pickup choice for the past decade or so is a Dodge truck equipped with a manual transmission and a Cummins diesel engine.

Old trucks are bought for function, not appearance. Full-sized Chrysler, Ford, and GM pickups from the first half of the '70s are all practically equal in performance and reliability (although Ford vehicles were extremely rust-prone). After 1976, strin-gent emissions regulations mandated the use of failure-prone fuel injectors, computer modules, and catalytic converters. As leaded fuel was phased out, vehicles became much more complicated to troubleshoot, more expensive to repair, and less reliable.

Post-'76 **GM trucks** are afflicted with poor-quality computer modules that make for hard starts and poor engine performance, early catalytic converter failures, unre-liable diesel engines (mostly injectors), and poorly engineered braking systems, with rear brakes that are vulnerable to premature backing-plate corrosion. GM's use of the "side-saddle" gas tank design also increased the risk of fire in a collision. From late 1998 to the present, GM's truck quality hasn't improved much. Engines, trans-missions, brakes, and fit and finish continue to be major trouble spots.

From the late '70s to the present, **Ford**'s **trucks** have been gas hogs; their fuel and ignition systems often fail, causing fires and full-throttle stalling; and fuel pumps, AC, and electrical systems can be chronically dysfunctional. Automatic transmis-sions have become "bump and jump" affairs, and collapsed coil springs and steering/suspension tie-rod failures bring new meaning to the term "off-roading."

Chrysler's **trucks** are no better, except for their fairly reliable Cummins diesel powerplants. And even these engines can get nasty with fuel injection problems. Chrysler's trucks have always been plagued by persistent brake, computer module, suspension, and automatic transmission failures. They have a tendency to wander all over the road and are often hard to troubleshoot.

Recommendations? Stick with the smallest, most recently made Japanese truck you can find that will do the job. This means choosing a small pickup like the **Mazda B-series**, the **Nissan King Cab**, or **Toyota**'s **Pickup, Tacoma**, or **T100**.

Appendix II
INTERNET SECRETS

Ford's F-Series trucks can be overpriced by more than $10,000. Your best strategy? Find out the U.S. price, buy off-season, and get the dealer to "bid" for your business.

Recent surveys show that close to 80 percent of car buyers get reliability and pricing information from the Internet before visiting a dealer or private seller. This trend has resulted in easier access to confidential price margins and secret warranties—if you know where to look.

Here's what to do: First, compare a new vehicle's "discounted" MSRP prices published on different automakers' websites with invoices downloaded from sites such as *CarCostCanada.com*, *OnTheHoist.com*, the Automobile Protection Association (*www.apa.ca*), the Canadian Automobile Association (CAA, *www.caa.ca*), and a host of other agencies. Second, check the prices you find against the ones listed in this book. Pay particular attention to the prices charged in the States. There is no reason why you should pay more in Canada. And this includes freight and pre-delivery inspection fees.

Unearthing reliability information from independent sources on the Net takes a bit more patience. You should first wade through the thousands of consumer complaints logged in the NHTSA database. Next, use the NHTSA and ALLDATA service bulletin databases to confirm a specific problem's existence, to find out if it's caused by a manufacturing defect, and to learn how to correct it. Augment this information with tips found on car forums and protest/information sites. *Lemon-Aid* does this for you in its guides, but you can stay current about your vehicle's problems or research a particular failure in greater depth on your own by using the above search methods.

Automobile companies have helpful—though self-serving—websites, most of which feature detailed sections on their vehicles' histories and research and development, as well as all sorts of information of interest to auto enthusiasts. Manufacturers can easily be accessed through a search engine like Google or by typing the automaker's name into your Internet browser's address bar followed by ".com" or ".ca". Or for extra fun and a more balanced presentation, type in the vehicle model or manufacturer's name into a search engine, followed by "lemon."

Auto Safety, Costs, Servicing, and Reviews

Alberta Vehicle Cost Calculator *(www1.agric.gov.ab.ca/app24/costcalculators/ vehicle/getvechimpls.jsp)*

Estimate and compare the ownership and operating costs of vehicles with variations in purchase price, options, fuel type, interest rates, or length of ownership.

ALLDATA Service Bulletins *(www.alldatadiy.com/recalls)*

Free summaries of automotive recalls and technical service bulletins. Detailed summaries will cost only $25 (U.S.) for hundreds of bulletins applicable to your vehicle, dating back over 30 years.

Automobile Protection Association *(www.apa.ca)*

APA is a membership-based, non-profit, national association dedicated to promoting consumer interests in the marketplace. It is the oldest and toughest of Canada's Nader-associated consumer groups. In 2008, the APA launched a cross-border buying service, helping Canadian shoppers save over $10,000 by buying through the Association. Says APA President, George Iny:

> There are still a few models where importing the U.S. equivalent makes sense, even with warranty issues. We are working exclusively with brokers. All-in with their markup and transport to Canada, it adds about $2,500 to $3,000 to the U.S. price.

BBA-reman.com *(www.bba-reman.com)*

BBA-reman specializes in automotive remanufacturing, providing a quality alternative to buying expensive new parts. All of their remanufactured products are covered by a 2-year warranty. The website also catalogues automakers' parts with high failure rates and identifies the symptoms pointing to each part's failure.

BBC TV's *Top Gear* Car Reviews *(www.topgear.com)*

Hated by European automakers, *Top Gear* gives raw, independent reviews of the best and worst European-sold vehicles, auto products, and industry practices. When they tested South Korean cars, the hosts put paper bags over their heads.

Canadian Automobile Association *(www.caa.ca)*

The CAA provides good general-interest automobile articles, despite its fear of riling automakers. There's a nice checklist for "Keeping Track of Your Own Vehicle Costs" in their *Driving Costs* pamphlet, available at *www.caasco.com/automotive/ driving-costs-broch-08.pdf.*

CanadianDriver *(www.canadiandriver.com)*

A homegrown, exceptionally well-structured, and current website for new- and used-vehicle reviews, MSRPs, and consumer reports. Other auto magazines' websites you should take a look at are as follows:

- *Automotive News (www.autonews.com)*—engine "sludge," GM "piston slap," etc.
- *Car and Driver (www.caranddriver.com)*—good hybrid reports

- *Motor Trend* (*www.motortrend.com*)
- *Road & Track* (*www.roadandtrack.com*)
- *Trailer Life* (*www.trailerlife.com*)—check out the trailering forum

CarProof (*www.carproof.com*)
Operating out of London, Ontario, this service starts at $34.95 plus GST per report. It lists liens, the past history of the vehicle and its owners, accident claims, and much more (Tel: 519-675-1415). Information requests can be processed online. In most provinces, you can do a lien and registration search yourself, but it's hardly worth the effort, considering the low cost of this service.

CBC TV's *Marketplace* (*www.cbc.ca/consumers/market/files/cars/index.html*)
An impressive array of auto consumer info gathered from investigative reports and other sources.

Center for Auto Safety (*www.autosafety.org*)
A Ralph Nader–founded agency that provides free online info on safety- and performance-related defects on each vehicle model. Free vehicle reports based on owner complaints and service bulletins are sometimes dated, but it's a good site nonetheless.

Chrysler Products' Problem Web Page (*www.wam.umd.edu/~gluckman/Chrysler*)
This is a great site for finding technical info and tips on getting action from Chrysler.

Consumer Reports and Consumers Union (*www.consumerreports.org*)
It costs $5.95 (U.S.) monthly or $26.00 (U.S.) annually to subscribe online, but *CR*'s database is chock full of comparison tests and in-depth stories on products and services. Pay the monthly rate once and then download all the info you need during the first month of your subscription.

Crashtest.com (*www.crashtest.com/netindex.htm*)
A website where crash tests from around the world can be analyzed and compared.

Edmunds and *Kelley Blue Book* (*www.edmunds.com*, *www.kbb.com*)
In-depth reviews and owner critiques of almost every vehicle sold in North America, plus an informative readers' forum. Ignore the zip code request.

Ford insider info (*www.blueovalnews.com*)
This website is the place to go for all the latest insider info on Ford's quality problems and future models.

Fuel prices (*www.gastips.com* and *www.gasbuddy.com*)
Hourly listings of the cheapest gas stations in most major North American cities.

Lemon-Aid (*www.lemonaidcars.com*)
The official website of the *Lemon-Aid* annual consumer car guides. It is frequently updated with follow-up stories and comments from regional correspondents. And, like Tim Hortons doughnuts and Buckley's Mixture, it's made for Canadians but good for Americans too.

Metric conversions online (*www.sciencemadesimple.net/conversions.html*)
A great place to instantly convert gallons to litres, miles to kilometres, etc. Also, an excellent website for converting fuel economy figures is *www.pege.org/fuel/convert. htm* (Planetary Engineering Group). When considering fuel economy, keep in mind that North American figures are generally quoted in miles per U.S. gallon (mpg), which measures about five-sixths of the larger British gallon.

National Highway Traffic Safety Administration (*www.nhtsa.dot.gov/cars/ problems*)
This American site has a comprehensive, free database covering owner complaints, recall campaigns, crashworthiness and rollover ratings, defect investigations, service bulletin summaries, and safety research papers.

OnTheHoist.com (*www.onthehoist.com*)
Kurt Binnie is a freelance auto expert who hails from Toronto. His site is both comprehensive and current, and he doesn't play any favourites. If he doesn't know the answer, he knows who does.

Finally, here are a number of other websites that may be helpful:

General Auto Sites:

forum.freeadvice.com
www.all-lemons.com
www.autoblog.com
www.auto123.com/en
www.autowarrantyreviews.org
www.baileycar.com
www.canadianwarrantycorp.com/news_tips.htm
www.carcostcanada.com
www.carforums.com/forums
www.everythingfordrivers.com/carforums.html
www.mycarsucks.com
www.samarins.com
www.straight-six.com
www.which.co.uk and *www.60millions-mag.com/page/common.accueil* (British and French car ratings)

Automakers

AUDI: *www.audiworld.com*

BMW: *www.bmwboard.com*
www.mwerks.com

CHRYSLER: *dodgestories.blogspot.com*
www.angelfire.com/pa5/mspaul/autohome.html
www.cs.cornell.edu/Info/People/kreitz/Jeep/main.html
www.daimlerchryslervehicleproblems.com
www.datatown.com/chrysler
www.donotbuydodge.ca
www.dontbuyone.org
www.flinksnorph.com/chrysler.html
www.minerich.com/dodge_ram.htm

FORD: *www.consumeraffairs.com/automotive/ford_spark.html* (Ford cars and trucks
spitting out spark plugs)
www.consumeraffairs.com/automotive/ford_transmissions.htm (Ford's faulty
transmissions)
www.ford-trucks.com/forums
www.v8sho.com/SHO/autoweek_online_cam_story.htm
www.v8sho.com/SHO/BlueOvalNewsCoverageofCamSprocketLawsuit.htm
www.v8sho.com/SHO/CamFailureClassActionSuitFiled.htm

GM: *agmlemon.freeservers.com/index.html*
experts.about.com/q/GM-GMC-781/6-5-lt-diesel.htm (Lots of diesel dirt)
forums.gminsidenews.com
www.mygmlink.com

LEXUS: *www.lexusownersclub.com*

MAZDA: *www.finishlineperformance.com* (Service bulletins for all Mazdas)

MERCEDES-BENZ: *www.benzworld.org*
www.mercedesproblems.com
www.nagele.co.uk/ml320.htm
www.troublebenz.com/my_opinion/actions/links.htm

MITSUBISHI: *www.mitsubishisucks.com*

SAAB: *www.saabclub.co.uk*

TOYOTA: *www.siennaclub.org*

VW: *www.myvwlemon.com*
www.tdiclub.com
www.thesamba.com/vw
www.vwvortex.com

Help for Consumers

ARTICLES AND CONSUMER INFO: *www.autosafety.org/article.php?did=312&scid=93* (Why regional recalls are a scam)
www.consumersearch.com/www/automotive/tires (Lots about tires)
www.dieseldoctor.com/messageboard/data/31.html (Can you handle the truth?)
www.driveandstayalive.com/info%20section/research/road%20safety%20research%20papers%20and%20publications%20--%20index.htm (Highway safety research papers from around the world; impress and worry your friends)

GOVERNMENT AND NON-GOVERNMENT ASSOCIATIONS: *www.carhelpcanada.com*
www.consumeraffairs.com
www.epa.gov/otaq/consumer/warr95fs.txt

INSURANCE: *www.autoinsurancetips.com*
www.insurance-canada.ca/consquotes/onlineauto.php
www.insurancehotline.com

JUDGMENTS AND CAMPAIGNS: *www.bettersuv.org*
www.ontariocourts.on.ca/decisions/2004/june/barrickC39837.htm (A cautionary tale—your freedom to speak out against a corporation in public or on the Internet is not limitless if your statements are deemed to be defamatory or libelous)
www.stuevesiegel.com
www.law.fsu.edu/journals/lawreview/downloads/282/Rearden.pdf (The replacement part rip-off—why pay $101,000 for a $23,000 Camry?)
www.law-lib.utoronto.ca/resguide/chapt4a.htm (A good place to look for supporting court decisions)
www.vehicle-injuries.com/suv-safety-news.htm

LEMON-PROOFING BEFORE YOU BUY

Buyers' Rights

This section shows you how to check out what's offered without a lot of hassle. But if you are deceived by a seller despite your best efforts, don't despair. As discussed in Part Three, Canadian federal and provincial laws dish out harsh penalties to new- and used-car dealers who hide or embellish important facts. Ontario's *Consumer Protection Act* (*www.e-laws.gov.on.ca/html/statutes/english/elaws_statutes_02c30_e.htm*), for example, lets consumers cancel a contract within one year of entering into an agreement if a seller makes a false, misleading, deceptive, or unconscionable representation. This includes using exaggeration, innuendo, or ambiguity about a material fact, or failing to state a material fact, if such use or failure deceives or tends to deceive.

Just keep in mind the following points:

- Dealers are *presumed* to know the history, quality, and true performance of what they sell.
- Even details like a vehicle's fuel economy can lead to a contract's cancellation if the dealer gave a higher-than-accurate figure. In *Sidney v. 1011067 Ontario Inc. (c.o.b. Southside Motors) 15,* the plaintiff was awarded $11,424.51 plus pre-judgment interest. The plaintiff claimed the defendant advised him that the vehicle had a fuel efficiency of 800–900 km per tank of fuel, when in fact, the maximum efficiency was only 500 km per tank.

A Check-Up Checklist

Now, let's assume you are dealing with an honest seller and that you've chosen a vehicle that's priced right and seems to meet your needs. Take some time to assess its interior, its exterior, and its highway performance with the checklist below. If you're buying from a dealer, ask to take the vehicle home overnight in order to drive it over the same roads you use in your daily activities. Of course, if you're buying privately, it's doubtful that you'll get the vehicle for an overnight test—you may have to rent a similar one from a dealer or rental agency.

Safety Check
1. Is the vehicle equipped with electronic stability control and full-torso side airbags, and has it earned a high crashworthiness ranking?
2. Is outward visibility good in all directions?
3. Are there large blind spots impeding vision, such as side pillars?

4. Are the mirrors large enough for good side and rear views? Do they block your view?
5. Are all instrument displays clearly visible (not washed out in sunlight)? Is there daytime or nighttime dash glare upon the windshield? Are the controls easy to reach?
6. Are the handbrake and hood release easy to reach and use?
7. Does the front seat have sufficient rearward travel to put you at a safe distance from the airbag's deployment (about 30 cm/12 in.) and still allow you to reach the brake and accelerator pedals? Are the brake and accelerator pedals adjustable and spaced far enough apart?
8. Are the head restraints adjustable or non-adjustable? (The latter is better if you often forget to set them.)
9. Are the head restraints designed to permit rear visibility? (Some are annoyingly obtrusive.)
10. Are there rear three-point shoulder belts similar to those on the front seats?
11. Is the seat belt latch plate easy to find and reach?
12. Does the seat belt fit comfortably across your chest, release easily, retract smoothly, and use pretensioners for maximum effectiveness?
13. Are there user-friendly child-seat anchor locations?
14. Are there automatic door locks controlled by the driver, or childproof rear door locks? Does the automatic side sliding door latch securely, and does it immediately stop when encountering an object as it opens or closes?
15. Do the rear windows roll only halfway down? When they are down, are your ears assailed by a booming wind noise, or does the vehicle vibrate excessively?

Exterior Check

Rust

A serious problem with the roofs of GM vans and the undercarriages of Toyota Tacomas for more than two decades, rust is a four-letter word that means trouble. Don't buy any used vehicle with extensive corrosion around the roof rails, rear hatch, wheelwells, door bottoms, or rocker panels.

Cosmetic rusting (rear hatch, exhaust system, front hood) is acceptable and can even help push the price way down, as long as the chassis and other major structural members aren't affected. Premature corrosion or repairs resulting from an accident may cause bumps, bubbles, or ripples under the paint. Don't dismiss this as a mere cosmetic problem—the entire vehicle will have to be stripped down, re-primed, and repainted. GM has a secret warranty covering these hood repairs that can be extrapolated to other models and different body panels (see GM Montana/Venture minivans in Part Four).

Knock gently on the front fenders, door bottoms, rear wheelwells, and rear doors—places where rust usually occurs first. Even if these areas have been repaired with plastic, lead, metal plates, or fibreglass, once rusting starts, it's difficult to stop. Use a small magnet to check which body panels have been repaired with non-metallic body fillers.

Use a flashlight to check for exhaust system and suspension component rust-out. Make sure the catalytic converter is present. In the past, many drivers removed this pollution-control device in the mistaken belief that it would improve fuel economy. The police can fine you for not having the converter, and you'll be forced to buy one ($400+) in order to certify your vehicle.

Tires

Be wary of tire brands that have poor durability records. Stay away from Firestone/ Bridgestone. Don't be concerned if the tires are worn, since retreads are inexpensive and easy to find. Look at tire wear for clues that the vehicle is out of alignment, needs suspension repairs, or has serious chassis problems. Getting an alignment and new shocks and springs is part of routine maintenance, and it's relatively inexpensive to do with aftermarket parts. However, if your vehicle is a 4×4 or the MacPherson struts have to be replaced, you're looking at a $1,000 repair bill.

Accident damage

Accident repairs require a further inspection by an independent body shop in order to determine if the frame is aligned and the vehicle is tracking correctly. Frameless minivans need extensive and expensive work to straighten them out, and proper frame and body repairs can often cost more than the vehicle is worth. In British Columbia, all accidents involving more than $2,000 in repairs must be reported to subsequent buyers.

Here are some tips on what you can do to avoid buying a damaged vehicle. First, ask the following questions about the vehicle's accident history:

- Has it ever been in an accident?
- If so, what was the damage and who fixed it?
- Is the auto body shop that repaired the vehicle registered with the provincial government? Is there any warranty outstanding? Can I have a copy of the work order?
- Has the vehicle's certificate of title been labelled "salvage"? ("Salvage" means that an expert has determined that the cost to properly repair the vehicle is more than its value. This usually happens after the vehicle has been in a serious accident.)

If the vehicle has been in an accident, you should either walk away from the sale or have the vehicle checked by a qualified auto body expert. Remember, not all salvage vehicles are bad—properly repaired ones can be a safe and sound investment if the price is low enough.

What to look for

1. If the vehicle has been repainted recently, check the quality of the job by inspecting the engine and trunk compartments and the inside door panels. Do it on a clear day so that you'll see any waves in the paint.
2. Check the paint—do all of the vehicle's panels match?
3. Inspect the paint for tiny bubbles. They may identify a poor priming job or premature rust.
4. Is there paint overspray or primer in the door jambs, wheelwells, or engine compartment? These are signs that the vehicle has had body repairs.
5. Check the gaps between body panels—are they equal? Unequal gaps may indicate improper panel alignment or a bent frame.
6. Do the doors, hood, and rear hatch open and shut properly?
7. Have the bumpers been damaged or recently repaired? Check the bumper support struts for corrosion damage.
8. Test the shock absorbers by pushing hard on a corner of the vehicle. If it bounces around like a ship at sea, the shocks need replacing.
9. Look for signs of premature rust or displacement from a collision on the muffler and exhaust pipe.
10. Make sure there's a readily accessible spare tire as well as a jack and tools for changing a flat. Also look for premature rusting in the side wheelwells, and for water in the rear hatch channel.
11. Look at how the vehicle sits. If one side or end is higher than the other, it could mean that the suspension is defective.
12. Ask the seller to turn on the headlights (low and high beams), turn signals, parking lights, and emergency blinking lights, and to blow the horn. From the rear, check that the brake lights, backup lights, turn indicators, tail lights, and licence plate light all work.

Interior Check

The number of kilometres on the odometer isn't as important as how well the vehicle was driven and maintained. Still, high-mileage vehicles depreciate rapidly because most people consider them to be risky buys. Calculate 20,000 kilometres per year as average and then subtract about $200 for each additional 10,000 kilometres above this average from your offer. Be suspicious of the odometer reading. Confirm it by checking the vehicle's maintenance records.

The condition of the interior will often give you an idea of how the vehicle was used and maintained. For example, sagging rear seats plus a front passenger seat in pristine condition indicate that your minivan may have been used as a minibus. Delivery vans will have the paint on the driver's doorsill rubbed down to the metal, while the passenger doorsill will look like new.

What to look for

1. Watch for excessive wear of the seats, dash, accelerator, brake pedal, armrests, and roof lining.

2. Check the dash and roof lining for radio or cellular phone mounting holes (as used in police cruisers, taxis, and delivery vans). Is the radio tuned to local stations?
3. Turn the steering wheel: Listen for unusual noises and watch for excessive play (more than 2.5 cm/1 in.).
4. Test the emergency brake with the vehicle parked on a hill.
5. Inspect the seat belts. Is the webbing in good condition? Do the belts retract easily?
6. Make sure that door latches and locks are in good working order. If rear doors have no handles or locks, or if they've just been installed, your minivan may have been used to transport prisoners.
7. Can the seats be moved into all the positions intended by the manufacturer? Look under them to make sure that the runners are functioning as they should.
8. Can headrests be adjusted easily?
9. Peel back the rugs and check the metal floor for signs of rust or dampness.

Road Test

1. Start the vehicle and listen for unusual noises. Shift automatics into Park and manuals into Neutral with the handbrake engaged. Open the hood to check for fluid leaks. Do this test with the engine running and then repeat it 10 minutes after the engine has been shut down following the completion of the test-drive.
2. With the motor running, check out all dashboard controls: windshield wipers, heater and defroster, and radio.
3. If the engine stalls or races at idle, a simple adjustment may fix the trouble. But loud clanks or low oil pressure could mean potentially expensive repairs.
4. Check all ventilation systems. Do the rear side windows roll down? Are there excessive air leaks around the door handles?
5. While in Neutral, push down on the accelerator abruptly. Black exhaust smoke may require only a minor engine adjustment; blue smoke may signal major engine repairs.
6. Shift an automatic into Drive with the motor still idling. The vehicle should creep forward slowly without stalling or speeding. Listen for unusual noises when the transmission is engaged. Manual transmissions should engage as soon as the clutch is released. Slipping or stalling could require a new clutch. While driving, make absolutely sure that a four-wheel drive can be engaged without unusual noises or hesitation.
7. Shift an automatic transmission into Drive. While the motor is idling, apply the emergency brake. If the motor isn't racing and the brake is in good condition, the vehicle should stop.
8. Accelerate to 50 km/h while slowly moving through all the gears. Listen for transmission noises. Step lightly on the brakes. The response should be immediate and equal for all wheels.
9. In a deserted parking lot, test the vehicle's steering and suspension by driving in figure eights at low speeds.